Fodor's

Road Guide USA

Oregon
Washington

First Edition

Fodor's Travel Publications
New York Toronto London Sydney Auckland
www.fodors.com

Fodor's Road Guide USA: Oregon, Washington

Fodor's Travel Publications
President: Bonnie Ammer
Publisher: Kris Kliemann
Executive Managing Editor: Denise DeGennaro
Editorial Director: Karen Cure
Director of Marketing Development: Jeanne Kramer
Associate Managing Editor: Linda Schmidt
Senior Editor: Constance Jones
Director of Production and Manufacturing: Chuck Bloodgood
Creative Director: Fabrizio La Rocca

Contributors
Editor: Kathryn Green
Editorial Production: Kristin Milavec
Additional Editing: Karen Licurse
Writing: Jeffrey Boswell (Oregon attractions, restaurants, and lodgings), John Doerper (Washington), and Dianna Schmid (Oregon lodgings), with Eric Reymond, Alan Ryan, and Kirsten Weisenberger
Research: Nathan Semler and Lindsey Sharp
Black-and-White Maps: Rebecca Baer, Robert Blake, David Lindroth, Todd Pasini
Production/Manufacturing: Bob Shields
Cover: Scott Barrow (background photo), Bart Nagel (photo, illustration)
Interior Photos: Corbis (Oregon), Photodisc (Washington)

First Edition
ISBN 0-679-00513-7
ISSN 1528-1558

Special Sales
Fodor's Travel Publications are available at special discounts for bulk purchases for sales promotions or premiums. Special editions, including personalized covers, excerpts of existing guides, and corporate imprints, can be created in large quantities for special needs. For more information, contact your local bookseller or write to Special Markets, Fodor's Travel Publications, 280 Park Avenue, New York, NY 10017. Inquiries from Canada should be directed to your local Canadian bookseller or sent to Random House of Canada, Ltd., Marketing Department, 2775 Matheson Boulevard East, Mississauga, Ontario L4W 4P7. Inquiries from the United Kingdom should be sent to Fodor's Travel Publications, 20 Vauxhall Bridge Road, London SW1V 2SA, England.

PRINTED IN THE UNITED STATES OF AMERICA
10 9 8 7 6 5 4 3 2 1

CONTENTS

v **GREAT ROAD TRIPS**

vi **HOW TO USE THIS BOOK**

3 **OREGON**

Boxes Your Car's First-Aid Kit...36
Oregon's Covered Bridges...52
Kodak's Tips for Taking Great Pictures...57
Kodak's Tips for Night Photography...59
Oregon: Lighthouse Lore...68
Packing Ideas for Hot Weather...72
Oregon Trail, 1853...97
Vacation Countdown: Your Checklist for a Perfect Journey...117
Kodak's Tips for Photographing the City...130
Microbrews of the Pacific Northwest...133
Kodak's Tips for Photographing Weather...177
Top Tips for Travelers...181

Maps Oregon Regions...6
The Oregon Coast Driving Tour...15
The Columbia River Gorge, the High Desert, and Mt. Hood Driving Tour...18
Crater Lake National Park...54

185 **WASHINGTON**

Boxes Kodak's Tips for Using Lighting...211
The Return of the Mosquito Fleet...227
Useful Extras You May Want to Pack...242
Bald Eagles...264
What to Pack in the Toy Tote for Kids...273
Sea Kayaking...278
Mt. St. Helens...290
Your First-Aid Travel Kit...305
Where the Cowboys Were Indians...311
Packing Ideas for Cold Weather...330
Pig War...339
Kodak's Tips for Photographing People...343
Car Rental Tips...368
The Tarheels...372
Kodak's Tips for Photographing Landscapes and Scenery...393
Ferries and Other Scenic Obstacles...397

Maps Washington Regions...189
A Volcano and Wine Tour...200–201
The Washington Waterfront Driving Tour...204
Mt. Rainier National Park...286–287
Olympic National Park...306–307

417 **INDEX**

COLOR ATLAS

Great Road Trips

Of all the things that went wrong with Clark Griswold's vacation, one stands out: The theme park he had driven across the country to visit was closed when he got there. Clark, the suburban bumbler played by Chevy Chase in 1983's hilarious *National Lampoon's Vacation,* is fictional, of course. But his story is poignantly true. Although most Americans get only two precious weeks of vacation a year, many set off on their journeys with surprisingly little guidance. Many travelers find out about their destination from friends and family or wait to get travel information until they arrive in their hotel, where racks of brochures dispense the "facts," along with free city magazines. But it's hard to distinguish the truth from hype in these sources. And it makes no sense to spend priceless vacation time in a hotel room reading about a place when you could be out seeing it up close and personal.

Congratulate yourself on picking up this guide. Studying it—before you leave home—is the best possible first step toward making sure your vacation fulfills your every dream.

Inside you'll find all the tools you need to plan a perfect road trip. In the hundreds of towns we describe, you'll find thousands of places to explore. So you'll always know what's around the next bend. And with the practical information we provide, you can easily call to confirm the details that matter and study up on what you'll want to see and do, before you leave home.

By all means, when you plan your trip, allow yourself time to make a few detours. Because as wonderful as it is to visit sights you've read about, it's the serendipitous experiences that often prove the most memorable: the hole-in-the-wall diner that serves a transcendent tomato soup, the historical society gallery stuffed with dusty local curiosities of days gone by. As you whiz down the highway, use the book to find out more about the towns announced by roadside signs. Consider turning off at the next exit. And always remember: In this great country of ours, there's an adventure around every corner.

HOW TO USE THIS BOOK

Alphabetical organization should make it a snap to navigate through this book. Still, in putting it together, we've made certain decisions and used certain terms you need to know about.

LOCATIONS AND CATEGORIZATIONS

Color map coordinates are given for every town in the guide.

Attractions, restaurants, and lodging places are listed under the nearest town covered in the guide.

Parks and forests are sometimes listed under the main access point.

Exact street addresses are provided whenever possible; when they were not available or applicable, directions and/or cross-streets are indicated.

CITIES

For state capitals and larger cities, attractions are alphabetized by category. Shopping sections focus on good shopping areas where you'll find a concentration of interesting shops. We include malls only if they're unusual in some way and individual stores only when they're community institutions. Restaurants and hotels are grouped by price category then arranged alphabetically.

RESTAURANTS

All are air-conditioned unless otherwise noted, and all permit smoking unless they're identified as "no-smoking."

Dress: Assume that no jackets or ties are required for men unless otherwise noted.

Family-style service: Restaurants characterized this way serve food communally, out of serving dishes as you might at home.

Meals and hours: Assume that restaurants are open for lunch and dinner unless otherwise noted. We always specify days closed and meals not available.

Prices: The price ranges listed are for dinner entrées (or lunch entrées if no dinner is served).

Reservations: They are always a good idea. We don't mention them unless they're essential or are not accepted.

Fodor's Choice: Stars denote restaurants that are Fodor's Choices—our editors' picks of the state's very best in a given price category.

LODGINGS

All are air-conditioned unless otherwise noted, and all permit smoking unless they're identified as "no-smoking."

AP: This designation means that a hostelry operates on the American Plan (AP)—-that is, rates include all meals. AP may be an option or it may be the only meal plan available; be sure to find out.

Baths: You'll find private bathrooms with bathtubs unless noted otherwise.

Business services: If we tell you they're there, you can expect a variety on the premises.

Exercising: We note if there's "exercise equipment" even when there's no designated area; if you want a dedicated facility, look for "gym."

Facilities: We list what's available but don't note charges to use them. When pricing accommodations, always ask what's included.

Hot tub: This term denotes hot tubs, Jacuzzis, and whirlpools.

MAP: Rates at these properties include two meals.

No smoking: Properties with this designation prohibit smoking.

Opening and closing: Assume that hostelries are open year-round unless otherwise noted.
Pets: We note whether or not they're welcome and whether there's a charge.
Pools: Assume they're outdoors with fresh water; indoor pools are noted.
Prices: The price ranges listed are for a high-season double room for two, excluding tax and service charge.
Telephone and TV: Assume that you'll find them unless otherwise noted.
Fodor's Choice: Stars denote hostelries that are Fodor's Choices—our editors' picks of the state's very best in a given price category.

NATIONAL PARKS

National parks protect and preserve the treasures of America's heritage, and they're always worth visiting whenever you're in the area. Many are worth a long detour. If you will travel to many national parks, consider purchasing the National Parks Pass ($50), which gets you and your companions free admission to all parks for one year. (Camping and parking are extra.) A percentage of the proceeds from sales of the pass helps to fund important projects in the parks. Both the Golden Age Passport ($10), for those 62 and older, and the Golden Access Passport (free), for travelers with disabilities, entitle holders to free entry to all national parks, plus 50% off fees for the use of many park facilities and services. You must show proof of age and of U.S. citizenship or permanent residency (such as a U.S. passport, driver's license, or birth certificate) and, if requesting Golden Access, proof of your disability. You must get your Golden Access or Golden Age passport in person; the former is available at all federal recreation areas, the latter at federal recreation areas that charge fees. You may purchase the National Parks Pass by mail or through the Internet. For information, contact the National Park Service (Department of the Interior, 1849 C St. NW, Washington, DC 20240-0001, 202/208—4747, *www.nps.gov*). To buy the National Parks Pass, write to 27540 Ave. Mentry, Valencia, CA 91355, call 888/GO—PARKS, or visit www.nationalparks.org.

IMPORTANT TIP

Although all prices, opening times, and other details in this book are based on information supplied to us at press time, changes occur all the time in the travel world, and Fodor's cannot accept responsibility for facts that become outdated or for inadvertent errors or omissions. So always confirm information when it matters, especially if you're making a detour to visit a specific place.

Let Us Hear from You

Keeping a travel guide fresh and up-to-date is a big job, and we welcome any and all comments. We'd love to have your thoughts on places we've listed, and we're interested in hearing about your own special finds, even the ones in your own back yard. Our guides are thoroughly updated for each new edition, and we're always adding new information, so your feedback is vital. Contact us via e-mail in care of roadnotes@fodors.com (specifying the name of the book on the subject line) or via snail mail in care of Road Guides at Fodor's, 280 Park Avenue, New York, NY 10017. We look forward to hearing from you. And in the meantime, have a wonderful road trip.

THE EDITORS

Important Numbers and On-Line Info

LODGINGS

Adam's Mark	800/444—2326	www.adamsmark.com
Baymont Inns	800/428—3438	www.baymontinns.com
Best Western	800/528—1234	www.bestwestern.com
	TDD 800/528—2222	
Budget Host	800/283—4678	www.budgethost.com
Clarion	800/252—7466	www.clarioninn.com
Comfort	800/228—5150	www.comfortinn.com
Courtyard by Marriott	800/321—2211	www.courtyard.com
Days Inn	800/325—2525	www.daysinn.com
Doubletree	800/222—8733	www.doubletreehotels.com
Drury Inns	800/325—8300	www.druryinn.com
Econo Lodge	800/555—2666	www.hotelchoice.com
Embassy Suites	800/362—2779	www.embassysuites.com
Exel Inns of America	800/356—8013	www.exelinns.com
Fairfield Inn by Marriott	800/228—2800	www.fairfieldinn.com
Fairmont Hotels	800/527—4727	www.fairmont.com
Forte	800/225—5843	www.forte-hotels.com
Four Seasons	800/332—3442	www.fourseasons.com
Friendship Inns	800/453—4511	www.hotelchoice.com
Hampton Inn	800/426—7866	www.hampton-inn.com
Hilton	800/445—8667	www.hilton.com
	TDD 800/368—1133	
Holiday Inn	800/465—4329	www.holiday-inn.com
	TDD 800/238—5544	
Howard Johnson	800/446—4656	www.hojo.com
	TDD 800/654—8442	
Hyatt & Resorts	800/233—1234	www.hyatt.com
Inns of America	800/826—0778	www.innsofamerica.com
Inter-Continental	800/327—0200	www.interconti.com
La Quinta	800/531—5900	www.laquinta.com
	TDD 800/426—3101	
Loews	800/235—6397	www.loewshotels.com
Marriott	800/228—9290	www.marriott.com
Master Hosts Inns	800/251—1962	www.reservahost.com
Le Meridien	800/225—5843	www.lemeridien.com
Motel 6	800/466—8356	www.motel6.com
Omni	800/843—6664	www.omnihotels.com
Quality Inn	800/228—5151	www.qualityinn.com
Radisson	800/333—3333	www.radisson.com
Ramada	800/228—2828	www.ramada.com
	TDD 800/533—6634	
Red Carpet/Scottish Inns	800/251—1962	www.reservahost.com
Red Lion	800/547—8010	www.redlion.com
Red Roof Inn	800/843—7663	www.redroof.com
Renaissance	800/468—3571	www.renaissancehotels.com
Residence Inn by Marriott	800/331—3131	www.residenceinn.com
Ritz-Carlton	800/241—3333	www.ritzcarlton.com
Rodeway	800/228—2000	www.rodeway.com

Sheraton	800/325—3535	www.sheraton.com
Shilo Inn	800/222—2244	www.shiloinns.com
Signature Inns	800/822—5252	www.signature-inns.com
Sleep Inn	800/221—2222	www.sleepinn.com
Super 8	800/848—8888	www.super8.com
Susse Chalet	800/258—1980	www.sussechalet.com
Travelodge/Viscount	800/255—3050	www.travelodge.com
Vagabond	800/522—1555	www.vagabondinns.com
Westin Hotels & Resorts	800/937—8461	www.westin.com
Wyndham Hotels & Resorts	800/996—3426	www.wyndham.com

AIRLINES

Air Canada	888/247—2262	www.aircanada.ca
Alaska	800/426—0333	www.alaska-air.com
American	800/433—7300	www.aa.com
America West	800/235—9292	www.americawest.com
British Airways	800/247—9297	www.british-airways.com
Canadian	800/426—7000	www.cdnair.ca
Continental Airlines	800/525—0280	www.continental.com
Delta	800/221—1212	www.delta.com
Midway Airlines	800/446—4392	www.midwayair.com
Northwest	800/225—2525	www.nwa.com
SkyWest	800/453—9417	www.delta.com
Southwest	800/435—9792	www.southwest.com
TWA	800/221—2000	www.twa.com
United	800/241—6522	www.ual.com
USAir	800/428—4322	www.usair.com

BUSES AND TRAINS

Amtrak	800/872—7245	www.amtrak.com
Greyhound	800/231—2222	www.greyhound.com
Trailways	800/343—9999	www.trailways.com

CAR RENTALS

Advantage	800/777—5500	www.arac.com
Alamo	800/327—9633	www.goalamo.com
Allstate	800/634—6186	www.bnm.com/as.htm
Avis	800/331—1212	www.avis.com
Budget	800/527—0700	www.budget.com
Dollar	800/800—4000	www.dollar.com
Enterprise	800/325—8007	www.pickenterprise.com
Hertz	800/654—3131	www.hertz.com
National	800/328—4567	www.nationalcar.com
Payless	800/237—2804	www.paylesscarrental.com
Rent-A-Wreck	800/535—1391	www.rent-a-wreck.com
Thrifty	800/367—2277	www.thrifty.com

Note: Area codes are changing all over the United States as this book goes to press. For the latest updates, check www.areacode-info.com.

Fodor's Road Guide USA

Oregon
Washington

Oregon

Oregonians tend to identify with the state tourism department's slogan "Things Look Different Here." Whether it is the abundance of natural resources, the variety of topographies and climates, or the unusual, sometimes trendsetting perspective of its diverse residents, Oregon's distinctiveness is not only in the view, but also in the viewing.

Oregon's vast forests and fertile farmlands have long provided the foundation for the state's economy. Nearly half of the state's 61-plus million acres of land is forested. Oregon is among the nation's leading timber producers and until recently most of the state's jobs were related to wood products. Although logging and lumber mills now account for a declining percentage of the state's workforce, the forests continue to make up a major component of the state's economy. Reforestation is required after timber harvests, and about 100 million seedlings are planted each year. Recreation has now become the top priority as managers develop and integrate non-timber uses for forests across the state.

Almost one-fifth of the state's economy is related to agriculture. Notable among Oregon crops are Christmas trees, grass seed, hazelnuts, peppermint, raspberries and other cane berries, hops, strawberries, prunes and plums, nursery products, pears, onions, and cauliflower. Oregon exports commodities such as hay, cattle, processed vegetables, and wheat to countries throughout the Pacific Rim and the Middle East.

In the past few years, Oregon's economy and culture have shifted toward technology and tourism, with only slight growth in forest products and agriculture-related jobs. Farmlands are giving way to urban and suburban applications. The natural resources of the mountains, meadows, rivers, deserts, and ocean are promoted to visitors from around the country and the world for their recreational appeal, rather than their value solely as a harvest. At the same time, the number of employees in high-technology

CAPITAL: SALEM	POPULATION: 3,082,000	AREA: 97,060 SQUARE MI
BORDERS: CA, NV, ID, WA, PACIFIC OCEAN	TIME ZONE: PACIFIC, MOUNTAIN	POSTAL ABBREVIATION: OR
WEB SITE: WWW.STATE.OR.US		

and service sectors is dramatically on the rise. Oregon's technology products include software, semiconductors, computers, instruments and other capital equipment that is the purvey of major employers such as Intel, Tektronix, Hewlett-Packard, and Sony. While the largest concentration of high-tech employers is in the "Silicon Forest" of Washington County (west of Portland), the Willamette Valley areas of Wilsonville, Corvallis, and Eugene, as well as communities in southern and central Oregon, have also reaped benefits in the transition from farm and forest to technology and tourism.

This economic and cultural shift has been coupled with a rapid population growth from people moving into the state. Ignoring the pleas of the late Governor Tom McCall, who, during his tenure from 1967–1975, urged non-Oregonians to visit but not to stay, many newcomers point to the clean air and water, outdoor recreation, and open space as reasons for their relocation. Ironically, the population growth now threatens the very qualities for which new residents were searching. Congested roadways, an overburdened infrastructure, shrinking farm and forest spaces, the buzzing of bulldozers and all-terrain vehicles, as well as air and water pollutants challenge the public and private interests of new and longtime Oregonians alike.

Oregonians' ability to look at things differently may best serve the state in addressing these challenges. It would not be the first time. At the beginning of the 20th century, Oregonians assured the citizen's voice would be heard by creating the "Oregon System" of direct legislation, the initiative and referendum, followed soon thereafter by the direct primary and the recall of public officials. The use of initiative and referendum put Oregon on the map nationally for its progressive approach to citizen participation in government. That spirit continued in the second half of the century as Oregon held the first statewide vote-by-mail election, as well as the first mail contest for a federal office. It extended to environmental legislation with such citizen-supported measures as the Scenic Rivers Act; land planning to conserve forests and farmlands while directing growth to appropriate places; public ownership of ocean beaches, which to this day keeps the beaches accessible to everyone and more than 50 percent of the ocean front in public hands; and the nation's first "bottle bill."

Historian Terence O'Donnell has suggested that the state's first settlers believed Oregon to be a kind of Eden and that their descendants appear determined to see that it remains so. Perhaps that aspiration is best served by appreciating how "Things Look Different Here."

History

The first Oregonians were tens of thousands of Native Americans, organized in hundreds of bands and tribes. The earliest residents are thought to have arrived from Asia more than 10,000 years ago. Some lived along the Pacific Coast, others near the Columbia and Willamette Rivers, and still others near Klamath Lakes to the south, in the Great Basin to the east, and in the northeast from the Columbia to the Wallowas. Their languages and lifestyles were as different as the regions of Oregon in which they lived.

OR Timeline

1543
A Spanish expedition led by Cabrilho sails from Acapulco and reaches the Rogue River.

1603
Martin d'Aguilar sails along the Oregon coast and sights what is later named the Columbia River.

1765
"Ouragon," first approximation of state's name, is written by Major Robert Rogers.

1788
Robert Gray becomes the first American and Markus Lopius first black American to set foot on Oregon soil.

In the mid-1500s, explorers apparently seeking a shortcut to the Atlantic Ocean happened upon Oregon's shores. The Portuguese explorer João Rodrigues Cabrilho is thought to have been the first of many European mariners, buccaneers, and traders to set foot in Oregon. Others were Sir Francis Drake, Bruno Heceta, Captain James Cook, George Vancouver, and Robert Gray. It was not until almost 300 years after the first navigators arrived that Oregon's most famous land travelers made their appearance. Meriwether Lewis and William Clark reached the mouth of the Columbia River in late 1805, after an unparalleled 19-month cross-continent expedition that opened the vast West to eventual U.S. claims and settlement. About the same time, the mouth of the Columbia became the business focus for John Jacob Astor, a German immigrant trader who founded Astoria, the oldest U.S. city on the West Coast. Astoria began as an American fur-trading post, but became an outpost of a British company for the few decades during which the British dominated the region.

Among British authorities empowered to manage the Pacific Northwest through the early 1800s was the man known as "The Father of Oregon," Dr. John McLoughlin. He is credited with numerous firsts in Oregon, among them encouraging the first settlements, despite his orders to discourage settlers. In fact, more than 50,000 immigrants traveled the Oregon Trail between 1840 and 1860 to settle in the Willamette Valley and begin farming. By the late 1860s, the wealth of eastern Oregon was realized through the discovery of gold as well as the development of livestock and grain cultivation. The coastal communities of the state were some of the last to take footing, except for Astoria, where the first salmon-canning factory was built in 1864, and Seaside, which shortly thereafter became a resort destination. The final years of the 19th century saw the growth of a dairy and cheese-making industry in the Tillamook area, the discovery of a treasure chest of oysters in Yaquina Bay, near Newport, and the marriage of a heavily timbered area with the natural port at Coos Bay. At the same time, nine now-famed lighthouses came to distinguish the Oregon coast.

Also at the end of the 1800s, the state became more economically and socially unified, thanks to the railroads that linked Oregon to the East Coast and to San Francisco as well as to the coastal, interior, and valley communities of the state. At the hub was Portland, which entered the 20th century with a population of about 90,000 people. By 1910 the population had almost tripled, thereby achieving one of the goals for the 1905 Lewis and Clark Centennial and American Pacific Exposition and Oriental Fair, which drew nearly 3 million visitors to the Rose City. It was also the finish line for the first transcontinental car race and the beginning of the urbanization of the state.

The first decades of the 20th century were relatively comfortable for Oregonians. Despite social polarization during World War I, the state's economy was bolstered by shipyards' need for timber and increased demands for food production and processing. Even the Depression did not have as severe an impact on Oregon as it did on other states. One reason was the construction of Bonneville Dam, hailed at the time as a cheap and abundant source of power, a fortune that would be reversed decades later

1792
Gray discovers and names the Columbia River after his ship.

1805
Lewis and Clark arrive at the mouth of the Columbia River.

1811
John Jacob Astor's fur traders establish a trading post at what would become Astoria.

1814
Jane Barnes becomes the first white woman to land in the Pacific Northwest.

1827
Dr. John McLoughlin builds the first sawmill in the Northwest.

because of environmental damage wreaked by damming the Columbia. By the time of World War II, aluminum brought yet another timely stimulus to Oregon's economy and buffered the state financially from some of the nation's wartime stresses.

All the while, the first Oregonians have reaped the fewest benefits of the state's bounty during the past couple of hundred years. While the entire state once was home to dozens of tribes, only nine tribes and six reservations survive in Oregon today. Now recognized as sovereign entities, the tribes include Warm Springs, Umatilla, Burns Paiute, Siletz, Grande Ronde, Cow Creek, Klamath, Coquille, and the Confederated Tribes of Coos, Lower Umpqua, and Siuslaw. The reservations are Warm Springs, Umatilla, Burns Paiute, Siletz, Coquille, and Grande Ronde.

Regions

1. OREGON COAST

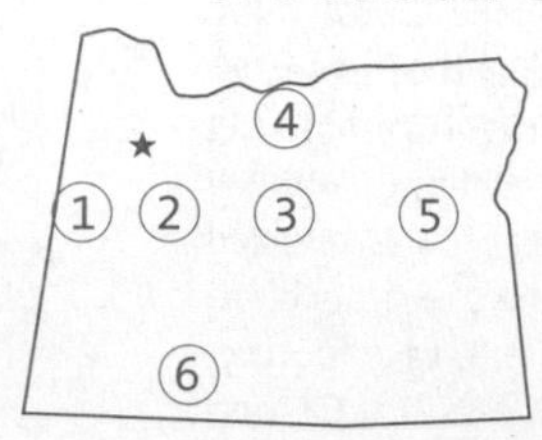

One Clatsop Indian legend has it that the rough-hewn Oregon coastline was created by Coyote, the trickster god who stood at the top of Neahkahnie Mountain on the north coast and hurled chunks of molten rock into the water below. Waters continue to boil at Devil's Punch Bowl, Cape Perpetua, Cape Foulweather, and Deception Bay. More than 200 shipwrecks near the mouth of the Columbia River between 1725 and 1961 are testament to the churning waters, although there are ample shelters on the Oregon coast as well. Along the 296 mi of coastline that stretch from California to Washington are 14 major bays with direct access to the Pacific Ocean. Among them on the north coast is Depoe Bay, which boasts the world's smallest harbor, only 50 ft wide at its mouth.

Oregon's coastal region, flanked to the east by the Coast Range and dotted by 9 lighthouses from north to south, is characterized by pristine beaches, fishing villages, and arts communities. In 1913 Oregon's governor declared the beaches public property, assuring public access to every mile of coastline. And while some locales along the coast receive as much as 80 inches of rain per year, even the dampest winter months can be popular with tourists, owing in part to the gray whales that migrate along Oregon's shores from December through April. Whale watching is the most popular winter sport on the coast, and there are dozens of whale-watching viewpoints as well as tours by charter boats.

Towns listed: Astoria, Bandon, Brookings, Cannon Beach, Coos Bay, Depoe Bay, Florence, Gleneden Beach, Gold Beach, Lincoln City, Manzanita, Newport, North Bend, Pacific City, Port Orford, Reedsport, Rockaway Beach, Seaside, Tillamook, Yachats

2. WILLAMETTE VALLEY

The Willamette Valley extends more than 100 mi in length, from south of Eugene north to the Portland area, and in width about 20 to 30 mi, from the Coast Range to the

1829
Oregon City, first incorporated town in the West, founded.

1833
The first timber to be shipped from Oregon heads for China.

1842
Willamette, the first university west of the Mississippi, founded in Salem.

1848
The Oregon Territory is established.

1851
Portland is incorporated.

Cascades. It is essentially a flat green prairie, the watershed of the circuitous, 187-mi north-flowing Willamette River; buttes, rolling hills, lush vegetation, streams, waterfalls, and springs give dimension to the area. Sometimes called the "breadbasket of the West," the valley produces much of the nation's food as well as grass seed and sod, Christmas trees, and flower bulbs. Driving along Interstate 5 or many of the meandering side routes, one finds fields of irises, dahlias, tulips and daffodils that give way to acres of mint, corn, hops, vegetables, berries, wheat, hazelnut groves, orchards, and nurseries. A temperate climate, a long growing season, and clay-based soil have also given birth to the state's burgeoning wine industry. Within minutes of I–5 are at least 35 wineries that grow numerous varieties of grapes, but have become internationally known for their superior Pinot Gris and Pinot Noir.

The majority of the state's residents live in the Willamette Valley, most of them in or near the three largest cities: Portland, Eugene, and Salem. Within the cities and throughout the countryside, hundreds of miles of bicycle paths provide an alternative avenue for combining sightseeing and recreation. Oregon sets aside 1% of all highway taxes to preserve and construct bike paths. Among the most compelling of the out-of-the-way destinations are Oregon's 53 covered bridges, most of which are in the valley. Originally built to keep ice from forming on the wooden roadways that cross rivers and streams, Oregon's collection is the largest west of the Mississippi. Each has its own architectural style, from Gothic shingle roofs to exposed trusses.

Towns listed: Albany, Beaverton, Corvallis, Cottage Grove, Drain, Eugene, Forest Grove, Hillsboro, Lake Oswego, McKenzie Bridge, McMinnville, Newberg, Oregon City, Portland, Salem, Silverton, Sweet Home

3. CENTRAL OREGON

East of the Cascade Mountains, central Oregon can be seen as a spine extending through the middle of the state, from the Columbia River Gorge in the north, along Highway 97, through Bend, and south through the Klamath Basin. The landscape is an awesome monument to the volcanoes that began erupting more than 45 million years ago. Enlivened by rivers, forests, lava beds and caves, volcanic peaks, and other mountain slopes, it's one of the Northwest's most popular recreational playgrounds. Twenty golf courses; one of the nation's top 10 ski areas for downhill, cross-country, and snowboarding; rivers and streams that offer world-class fly-fishing; trails for the most ambitious mountain bikers; and numerous venues for hiking, rock climbing, kayaking, rafting, and canoeing all draw outdoor enthusiasts from around the globe.

Central Oregon is home to two groups of original Oregonians: The Klamath Indian tribe is based near the southern reach of the region, while the Warm Springs reservation occupies more than 640,000 acres toward the northern section. Bend, near the center of the state, is the population and market hub of central Oregon. Defying Oregon's reputation for perpetual precipitation, Bend counts about 250 days of

1859
Oregon becomes the 33rd state.

1872
The Modoc Indian War takes place.

1876
The University of Oregon opens in Eugene.

1877
The Nez Perce War begins.

1878
The Bannock Indian War takes place.

sunshine every year, and most of central Oregon receives only about one-fourth of the precipitation that falls on the Willamette Valley.

Towns listed: Bend, Crater Lake National Park, Madras, Prineville, Redmond, Sisters, Warm Springs

4. COLUMBIA RIVER GORGE AND MOUNT HOOD

The Columbia River Gorge National Scenic Area stretches for 60 mi between Portland and Biggs. Carved out by the Columbia River as it passes through the Cascade Mountain Range, the gorge was born of volcanoes, lava flows, and Ice Age floodwaters and glaciers. Basaltic cliffs rise 1,500 to 3,000 ft above the river while 77 waterfalls tumble from the glaciers and snowfields of Mount Hood, including the 620-foot Multnomah Falls, the fourth highest in the United States. The Columbia River is the natural border between Oregon and Washington and Native Americans have hunted and fished along the river for thousands of years. Local tribes still have exclusive fishing rights on many areas of the river. An especially scenic alternative to the trip through the gorge on I–84 is accessible on the historic Columbia River Highway.

Majestically towering 11,235 ft above the gorge, Mount Hood is what remains of the original north wall and rim of a volatile crater. Although the peak no longer spews ash or spits fire, active steam vents can be spotted high on the mountain. Native Americans in the area believed the mountain itself to be a spirit and called it Wy'east. Mount Hood offers the only year-round skiing in North America, with three major ski areas and 26 lifts, as well as extensive areas for cross-country skiing and snowboarding. Many of the ski runs turn into mountain bike trails during the summer. The mountain is also popular with climbers and hikers. In fact, some hikes follow parts of the Oregon Trail, and signs of the pioneers' passing are still evident.

Towns listed: Gresham, Hood River, Maupin, Mt. Hood National Forest, The Dalles, Troutdale

5. EASTERN OREGON

Eastern Oregon, which borders Washington, Idaho, and Nevada, is at once the largest and the least populated expanse of Oregon. It ranges from the Columbia River before it winds northward to the Wallowa Mountains and the towns of Pendleton and La Grande in the north, then over to the Crooked Creek Range and the towns of Lakeview and Frenchglen in the south. In the northeast corner, Hells Canyon National Recreation Area is North America's deepest gorge, forged by the Snake River. Nearby, in the Blue Mountains or the Eagle Cap Wilderness, rugged adventures can be had in the form of fishing, hiking, river rafting, mountain biking, and llama trekking.

While wildlife preserves in the southern section and abundant recreation in both the north and south provide the region's most notable draws today, eastern Oregon's fame in previous times may have had more historical significance. Oregon Trail

1902
Oregon becomes the first state to adopt a citizen-driven initiative and referendum.

1912
Women's suffrage is adopted in Oregon.

1922
Compulsory education becomes law.

1935
Oregon Shakespeare Festival, one of nation's largest regional theater companies, is established.

1937
Timberline Lodge is built as part of Works Progress Administration, and the largest U.S. producer of hydroelectric power, Bonneville Dam, is completed.

emigrants first set foot in the state near Ontario and Nyssa, while Baker City, through which the Oregon Trail also winds, was the site of a gold rush in the 1860s. Signs of even earlier times survive, from the John Day Fossil Beds with its fragments of saber-toothed tigers, giant pigs, and three-toed horses to Native American writings and artifacts hidden within canyon walls in Malheur County's Leslie Gulch.

Towns listed: Baker City, Burns, Enterprise, Frenchglen, Hermiston, La Grande, John Day, Joseph, Lakeview, Ontario, Pendleton, Umatilla

6. SOUTHERN OREGON

Southern Oregon extends south from the Willamette Valley in western Oregon to the California border, with such well-known communities along I-5 as Roseburg, Grants Pass, Medford, and Ashland. The valleys of the Umpqua River, with its north and south branches, mark the northern area of the region, while the Rogue River Valley stretches across the southernmost part of southern Oregon. Both are known for the white water of the rivers, encouraging rafting, kayaking, fishing, skiing, and jet boating. Hiking, camping, and biking, as well as the less exuberant sightseeing, are also popular.

In addition to the hot springs and waterfalls of the Umpqua area, there are also six bridges and six wineries in the area. Cultural attractions include the Oregon Shakespeare Festival in Ashland and the Peter Britt Music Festival in Jacksonville, both of which draw art aficionados from around the world.

The centerpiece of the region is actually at its eastern edge: Created by the violent eruption of Mount Mazama, at 1,932 ft Crater Lake is the deepest lake in the United States. Its dark blue clarity is mesmerizing on sunny days but equally stunning in winter, when its rim is snow-covered.

Towns listed: Ashland, Cave Junction, Grants Pass, Jacksonville, Klamath Falls, Medford, Roseburg

When to Visit

When to visit Oregon depends on your recreational interests and weather preferences. Western Oregon receives an abundance of rain, not unusually six inches per month from November through March, and moderate temperatures, ranging from the mid-30s to 50s in winter to the 80s in summer. Central Oregon, wedged between the Cascade Mountains and the high desert, receives less rain than Los Angeles and in winter there is an accumulation of a couple of feet of snow at the base of the mountains, while temperatures range from the 20s in winter to the 80s in summer. The desert and mountains of eastern Oregon vary the most, with several feet of snow and temperatures in the teens during winter, to frequent mercury readings in the 90s in summer.

1948
Vanport Flood destroys 17,500 residences in an area built to house wartime workers.

1971
First bottle bill in the nation is approved.

1980
Mount St. Helens erupts just across the Columbia in Washington and temporarily closes the river to ship traffic.

1991
Barbara Roberts becomes the first woman governor.

1993
Oregon holds the first vote-by-mail election.

There are 10 climate zones worldwide and 7 of them appear in Oregon. Flexibility and layered clothing year-round are the best approaches for tourists. From fall through spring in particular, an umbrella and waterproof jacket are standard issue. Oregonians are relatively weather-resistant and plan outdoor festivals even in spring and well into fall, but summertime events might prove more appealing to those who prefer fair weather. The most vibrant colors in fields of irises, tulips, and dahlias bloom during springtime in the Willamette Valley and with the autumn leaves in the Columbia Gorge. Winters bring snow to the Cascades and points east, and in smaller amounts to the Coast Range, so drivers should be prepared with traction devices. Sports enthusiasts thrive in every season in every region. Throughout winter, they make their way to the Cascades and other mountains for skiing, snowboarding, snowmobiling, and ice fishing. In spring, summer, and fall, the tempo extends to the water as well, with plentiful options around the state for boating, surfing, sailing, sailboarding, waterskiing, fishing, and swimming, in addition to hiking, climbing, and biking.

CLIMATE CHART

Average High/Low Temperatures (°F) and Monthly Precipitation (in inches)

	JAN.	FEB.	MAR.	APR.	MAY	JUNE
ASTORIA	48/36	51/38	53/38	56/40	60/45	64/50
	10.3	6.8	6.3	4.6	2.8	2.4
	JULY	AUG.	SEPT.	OCT.	NOV.	DEC.
	68/53	69/53	68/41	61/44	54/40	48/37
	1.0	1.6	2.1	5.2	8.9	10.6

	JAN.	FEB.	MAR.	APR.	MAY	JUNE
BEND	42/22	42/22	46/25	51/26	58/29	65/35
	1.8	1.99	.97	.92	.6	.77
	JULY	AUG.	SEPT.	OCT.	NOV.	DEC.
	74/41	82/45	81/45	73/38	63/31	49/27
	.86	.49	.58	.47	.65	1.57

	JAN.	FEB.	MAR.	APR.	MAY	JUNE
LAGRANDE	40/28	49/32	55/38	65/42	75/50	80/55
	1.47	1.48	1.42	1.61	1.43	.63
	JULY	AUG.	SEPT.	OCT.	NOV.	DEC.
	90/59	88/55	80/55	70/45	55/35	45/31
	.92	.97	1.24	3.32	2.69	3.23

	JAN.	FEB.	MAR.	APR.	MAY	JUNE
MEDFORD	45/30	55/33	60/35	68/46	76/47	80/50
	5.35	1.93	1.82	1.16	1.0	.58
	JULY	AUG.	SEPT.	OCT.	NOV.	DEC.
	90/54	91/55	83/45	70/42	60/35	49/30
	.26	.52	.86	2.67	3.56	3.85

	JAN.	FEB.	MAR.	APR.	MAY	JUNE
PORTLAND	45/34	51/36	56/39	61/41	67/47	74/53
	5.35	3.85	3.56	2.39	2.06	1.48
	JULY	AUG.	SEPT.	OCT.	NOV.	DEC.
	80/57	80/57	75/52	64/45	53/40	46/35
	0.63	1.09	1.75	2.67	5.34	6.13

FESTIVALS AND SEASONAL EVENTS

INTRODUCTION
HISTORY
REGIONS
WHEN TO VISIT
STATE'S GREATS
RULES OF THE ROAD
DRIVING TOURS

WINTER

Feb.–Nov. **Oregon Shakespeare Festival.** More than 100,000 Bard-loving fanatics descend on Ashland for this well-known event. Its accomplished repertory company mounts some of the finest Shakespearean productions you're likely to see this side of Stratford-upon-Avon—plus works by Ibsen, Williams, and contemporary playwrights. | 541/482–4331.

SPRING

Apr. **Hood River Valley Blossom Festival.** Celebrate the springtime floral spectacle in apple and pear orchards, which can be viewed from a train run by the Mt. Hood Scenic Railroad. | 541/386–2000 or 800/366–3530.

May **Azalea Festival.** The popular flower is celebrated at the Azalea City Park in Brookings on Memorial Day weekend. | 541/469–3181.

May–June **Portland Rose Festival.** One of the largest events on the West Coast, this extravaganza on the Portland waterfront packs diverse events—an air show, three parades, auto racing, and a riverside carnival among them—into one month. | 503/227–2681.

June **Sandcastle Contest.** One of the largest sand building contests on the West Coast, this event transforms Cannon Beach into a sculptured fantasyland. | 503/436–2623.

SUMMER

June–July **Oregon Bach Festival.** Concerts, chamber music, and social events—held mainly in Eugene at Hult Center and the University of Oregon School of Music, but also in Corvallis and Florence—celebrate this beloved composer. | 541/682–5000 or 541/346–5666, 800/457–1486.

July **Oregon Coast Music Festival.** Classical, bluegrass, and jazz concerts are featured at this popular festival which takes place at various locations in Coos Bay, North Bend, Charleston, Bandon, and Reedsport. | 541/269–2720 or 800/676–7563.

July **Salem Art Fair and Festival.** Oregon's biggest art fair at Bush's Pasture Park has exhibits, food, live performances, and tours of historic mansions. | 503/581–2228.

Aug. **Mt. Hood Jazz Festival.** Since 1982 this three-day musical event has brought nationally acclaimed jazz musicians to suburban Gresham for performances in an outdoor setting. | 503/219–9833.

Aug.–Sept. **Oregon State Fair.** This 12-day fair in Salem on the Oregon State Fairgrounds features livestock competitions and a horse show, as well as a carnival, performances by big-name musicians, and arts exhibits. | 503/378–3247.

State's Greats

Oregon is a state of many contrasts—geological, biological, and social. The coast has gigantic rocks and steep cliffs offering panoramic views of the very blue but very cold Pacific Ocean. The Cascade Mountain range is still covered with an almost endless forest filled with fir and pine trees. Its many volcanic, snow-capped mountains are some of the most spectacular in North America. The cliffs of the Columbia River Gorge are lined with breathtaking waterfalls.

The Willamette Valley is lush and green and filled with flora that bloom year-round. It's one of the nation's leading flower- and tree-producing regions. Meanwhile, Eastern Oregon seems almost barren, the high desert only sparsely dotted with vegetation.

Portland is fast-paced, liberal, and cosmopolitan, with a rapidly growing, diverse population, making it a true player among Pacific Rim cities. It is a key center of high-tech industry and chockablock with culture. On the other hand, towns in Eastern Oregon such as Pendleton are slow-paced, cowboy-oriented, and politically conservative.

Beaches, Forests, Parks

Oregon is an outdoor paradise. Its beaches are among the most dramatic and rugged of any in North America. Forests are everywhere, even in urban areas. Several rivers have been designated as "Wild and Scenic," a designation that limits development. And there are more than 100 state parks offering upwards of 5,500 campsites.

Whale watching is popular all along the coast during the December–March migration of thousands of California gray whales. A resident group of whales can be seen in Depoe Bay, just south of Lincoln City.

The Oregon coast has nine historic lighthouses, from Cape Meares near Tillamook in the north to Cape Blanco near Port Orford in the south. Many have parks with views of the ocean, and some are open for public tours.

One of the state's most popular coastal towns is **Cannon Beach,** with its famous Haystack Rock. South of Cannon Beach is the **Oregon Coast Aquarium** in Newport, former home of Keiko the killer whale. South of Newport are **Sea Lion Caves,** where you can see sea lions, auklets, and cormorants in their native environment, and the **Oregon Dunes National Recreation Area,** a 41-mi stretch of natural sand-dune beachfront.

Portland's **Forest Park** is the largest urban park in the U.S. Nearby **Washington Park** offers (on clear days) a panoramic view of the Portland skyline and Mount Hood. Also here are the Oregon Zoo, the peaceful Japanese Garden, and the renowned International Rose Test Garden.

Crater Lake National Park is one of the most spectacular natural wonders in the world. The lake, created 7,600 years ago with the eruption of Mount Mazama, is the clearest and deepest in the United States.

The **Columbia River Gorge,** which divides Washington from Oregon, is highlighted by steep cliff walls and waterfalls, including Multnomah Falls, about 30 mi east of Portland. Bonneville Dam, one of the nation's largest hydroelectric producers, is also here.

The **Deschutes National Forest** is home to several snow-capped mountains including Mt. Bachelor, Mt. Jefferson, Mt. Washington, and Three Sisters.

Mount Hood, just east of and visible from downtown Portland, is the state's tallest peak. The forest lands and many lakes around the mountain provide excellent skiing, hiking, and swimming.

Hells Canyon National Recreation Area on the Snake River is a rugged wilderness with a canyon deeper than the Grand Canyon.

Culture, History, Arts

Portland may be the cultural and arts center of the state, but history can be found in most cities and small towns. There are dozens of museums exhibiting artifacts and memorabilia of the pioneers' trek westward along the Oregon Trail in the 1800s. The **End of the Oregon Trail Interpretive Center** in Oregon City provides an informative display.

The **Museum of Natural History** on the campus of the University of Oregon shows Oregon's geologic past and artifacts of early Native Americans. The state also has more than 50 historic wooden **covered bridges,** many dating from the early part of the 20th century.

Portland's performing arts venues include the **Arlene Schnitzer Concert Hall,** home of the Portland Symphony, and the **Civic Auditorium,** where the Portland Opera and Portland Ballet perform. Eugene's **Hult Center** hosts the Oregon Bach Festival in June and July as well as the Eugene Opera, Eugene Ballet, and Eugene Symphony.

Artsy Ashland near the California stateline draws hundreds of thousands of theater lovers every year to its **Oregon Shakespeare Festival.** Performances run from February to November.

The **Portland Art Museum** houses collections of Native American and Asian art, masterpieces by European greats, and traveling exhibits. The University of Oregon's **Museum of Art** includes exhibits of Chinese imperial tomb figures.

Sports

Oregon has few spectator sporting options, but abounds in participant sports. Although Portland is now the 22nd-largest metropolitan area in the United States, it still is home to only one major sports franchise—the National Basketball Association **Trail Blazers,** who play in the 20,000-seat Rose Garden arena.

Baseball and football fans turn their attention to Seattle and San Francisco teams, whose games are carried on local television. But plans are under way to renovate and expand the existing Civic Stadium to attract a major league baseball team. And ice aficionados are plotting to attract a National Hockey League team to the Memorial Coliseum.

Participant sports options are plentiful. The slopes on the many snow-capped peaks permit skiing well into summer. The Columbia River Gorge near Hood River provides some of the best windsurfing in the nation. The waves off the Oregon coast are ideal for surfing. Scenic golf courses are found in every region of the state. And the rapids of the **Deschutes and Rogue Rivers** are perfect for white-water rafting. The Deschutes is a day trip from Portland.

Other Points of Interest

West of Portland and continuing south along the Coast Range is Oregon's **wine country** where you'll find dozens of vineyards producing excellent Cabernet, Chardonnay, and Riesling varieties. And in Portland dozens of **microbreweries** turn out world-class beers. Most wineries and breweries offer tours and tastings.

Oregon has several casinos operated by Native American tribes. **Chinook Winds** in Lincoln City and **Spirit Mountain** in Grand Ronde, about an hour's drive from Portland, are the biggest. Both offer slots and table gaming and attract big-name entertainers.

Rules of the Road

License Requirements: To drive in Oregon, you must be at least 16 years old and hold a valid driver's license or 15 years old with an instruction permit and accompanied by a licensed driver at least 21 years old. Residents of other states and countries may drive as long as they hold valid licenses from their home states or countries.

Speed Limit: The maximum speed limit in any city and on urban interstates and highways is 55 mph, while on rural interstate highways it is 65 mph. The maximum for trucks and passenger transport vehicles is 55 mph on all roads. The maximum speed allowed in residential districts and public parks is 25 mph. In school districts, fines for exceeding the limit of 20 mph can be doubled.

Right Turn on Red: A right turn may be made onto a two-way street after stopping at a red light and yielding as necessary, unless otherwise prohibited by a sign or police officer. When entering a one-way street, you may turn right or left with the movement of the traffic after stopping for the red light and yielding as necessary.

Seatbelt and Helmet Laws: Safety belt use is mandatory for all drivers and passengers in all available seating positions when the vehicle is in motion. Children under 4 who weigh 40 pounds or less are required to be in an approved child safety seat. Anyone under 16 riding a bicycle or being carried on a bicycle is required to wear approved protective headgear. All motorcycle operators and passengers and moped operators are required to wear motorcycle helmets at all times when operating motorcycles or mopeds on public streets.

For More Information: Contact Oregon Driver and Motor Vehicles Services at | 503/945–5000.

The Oregon Coast Driving Tour

FROM ASTORIA TO BROOKINGS

Distance: Approximately 306 miles (without scenic byway detours) Time: 3–4 days
Breaks: Cannon Beach, on the north coast, is a lively tourist mecca with restaurants, seaside motels, and shopping. In Newport, on the central coast, stop and visit the famed Oregon Coast Aquarium and have lunch or dinner along the Bayfront. Cape Perpetua Caves is also worth a visit. You'll find B&B's, surfside motels, and places to dine in nearly every town along the coast.

When it comes to scenic drives, Oregon offers a veritable smorgasbord of possibilities. The Oregon coast is perhaps the most dazzlingly dramatic of all. U.S. 101 runs the entire length of this ever-changing and always fascinating coastline. Passing through small beach towns, fishing villages, and maritime resorts, the highway dips, climbs, and curves through stretches of forest and along rocky headlands, windswept cliffs, and pristine white-sand beaches. Numerous state parks, overlooks, and scenic byways provide access to breathtaking ocean vistas, historic lighthouses, and marine wildlife sanctuaries. Best of all, every amazing inch of the Oregon coast is accessible to the public.

The weather along the coast is generally mild, especially south of Gold Beach, but it is unpredictable. Pack a raincoat as well as a swimsuit.

❶ **Astoria** is located where the mighty Columbia River empties into the Pacific, 96 mi west of Portland on Route 30. Maritime history buffs should stop in at the **Columbia River Maritime Museum** to see memorabilia salvaged from the almost 2,000 ships that have foundered in the treacherous waters; you can also explore a fully operational U.S. Coast Guard ship. Tour **Flavel House,** to see inside a restored mansion from the 1880s. The observation platform atop the 125-ft **Astoria Column** offers a breathtaking view over Astoria, the Columbia River, and the Coast Range.

❷ Having finally reached the Pacific Ocean, the explorers Lewis and Clark spent the rainy winter of 1806 in a small wooden fort that has been faithfully replicated at **Fort Clatsop National Memorial,** 5 mi south of Astoria on Alt. U.S. 101.

PACIFIC OCEAN
WASHINGTON
CALIFORNIA
Astoria
Fort Clatsop National Memorial
Seaside
Tillamook Head
ECOLA STATE PARK
Cannon Beach
OSWALD WEST STATE PARK
Nehalem Bay
TILLAMOOK STATE FOREST
Tillamook Bay
Garibaldi
CAPE MEARES STATE PARK
Tillamook
CAPE LOOKOUT STATE PARK
Three Capes Loop
CAPE KIWANDA STATE NATURAL AREA
Pacific City
Lincoln City
Depoe Bay
Otter Crest Loop
Yaquina Head
Newport
Waldport
Yachats
Cape Perpetua
SIUSLAW NATIONAL FOREST
Sea Lion Caves
Florence
HONEYMAN MEMORIAL STATE PARK
OREGON DUNES NAT'L. REC. AREA
Reedsport
Winchester Bay
Umpqua Lighthouse Park
Charleston
North Bend
Coos Bay
SHORE ACRES STATE PARK
CAPE ARAGO STATE PARK
Bandon
Myrtle Point
CAPE BLANCO STATE PARK
Port Orford
Rogue R.
Agness
Gold Beach
SISKIYOU NATIONAL FOREST
Pistol River
Chetco R.
SAMUEL H. BOARDMAN STATE PARK
LOEB STATE PARK
Brookings
Harbor
Columbia River
Forest Grove
Portland
Yamhill
Newberg
Dundee
McMinnville
Aurora
Salem
Sublimity
Albany
Corvallis
Brownsville
Eugene
Springfield
Cottage Grove
Oakridge
Oakland
Steamboat
UMPQUA NATIONAL FOREST
Roseburg
Winston
UMPQUA VALLEY
Canyonville
Prospect
Grants Pass
Medford
Jacksonville
Cave Junction
Ashland
Mt. Ashland
N
0 30 miles
0 45 km

3. **Seaside** (12 mi south of Astoria on U.S. 101), one of the most tourist-oriented towns on the Oregon coast, has a long, sandy beach with a 2-mi boardwalk surrounded by hotels and restaurants.

4. **Cannon Beach** (10 mi south of Seaside on U.S. 101), another popular tourist mecca, is named for a cannon that washed ashore from a schooner in 1846. There are plenty of shopping opportunities in this hamlet—one of the more upscale resort towns on the Oregon coast—but the real glory of the place is its broad, sand beach, great for walking and kite flying, and presided over by a formidable offshore monolith known as **Haystack Rock.**

5. **Tillamook** (40 mi south of Cannon Beach on U.S. 101), surrounded by lush green fields, has long been known for its dairy industry. Stop in at the **Tillamook County Creamery** to sample the cheese and ice cream that have made this town famous.

6. From Tillamook, take the **Three Capes Loop** (marked turnoff in town), a 35-mi scenic byway that passes three magnificent headlands—**Cape Meares, Cape Lookout,** and **Cape Kiwanda**—as it winds along the coast, rejoining U.S. 101 just south of Pacific City.

7. What **Lincoln City** (16 mi south of Pacific City on U.S. 101) lacks in charm it more than makes up for in tourist amenities. The most popular destination on the Oregon coast sprawls along the Coast Highway and offers some good restaurants, a full range of motels, and lots of shops and galleries.

8. From the tiny harbor at **Depoe Bay** (12 mi south of Lincoln City on U.S. 101), excursion boats run by **Tradewinds** head out, when conditions permit, on whale-watching cruises. Some of the gigantic gray whales that annually migrate along the Oregon coast break away from the pod to linger year-round in Depoe Bay.

9. The **Otter Crest Loop** (5 mi south of Depoe Bay, off U.S. 101) scenic byway winds along the cliff tops to **Cape Foulweather,** a 500-ft headland, and down to a fascinating sea cave known as the **Devil's Punchbowl** before rejoining U.S. 101 north of Newport. Once you are back on U.S. 101, take the well-marked turnoff to **Yaquina Head,** where the gleaming white **Yaquina Bay Lighthouse,** activated in 1873, acts as the focal point for what has been designated an Outstanding Natural Area. On the rocky offshore islands you can often see harbor seals, sea lions, cormorants, murres, puffins, and guillemots.

10. **Newport** (12 mi south of Depoe Bay on U.S. 101) has an old **Bayfront** area where you'll find galleries, stores selling fresh crab and fish, and good seafood restaurants. A colorful fleet of fishing boats is docked in Yaquina Bay. As you leave Newport, signs on the south side of Yaquina Bay Bridge will direct you to the famous **Oregon Coast Aquarium,** a 4½-acre complex that provides a wonderful introduction to the various marine habitats found along the Oregon coast.

11. **Yachats** (pronounced YA-hots and located 23 mi south of Newport on U.S. 101) is a small, attractive coastal hamlet with B&Bs, restaurants, and a rocky, surf-pounded beach with tidepools.

12. Towering 800 ft above the Pacific, **Cape Perpetua** (9 mi south of Yachats on U.S. 101) is the highest lookout point on the Oregon coast. For more information on this 2,700-acre scenic area, popular with hikers, naturalists, campers, and beachcombers, stop in

at the **Cape Perpetua Visitors Center.** A well-marked auto tour winds through Siuslaw National Forest to the ¼-mi **Whispering Spruce Trail,** where the views extend some 150 mi north and south and 37 mi out to sea.

⓭ On U.S. 101, 11 mi south of Cape Perpetua stop for the **Sea Lion Caves,** one of the Oregon Coast's premier attractions.

⓮ From there the restored waterfront Old Town in **Florence** is just 13 mi south. This is another good place to find restaurants serving fresh seafood, or to stay the night. The town serves as the jumping-off point for the **Oregon Dunes National Recreation Area** (Visitor Center south side of Umpqua River Bridge), an awesome 41-mi-long stretch of dunes with forests, lakes, and camping facilities.

⓯ In **Reedsport** (20 mi south of Florence on U.S. 101) you may want to stop at the **Umpqua Discovery Center,** where the chief attraction is the *Hero,* the laboratory ship used by Admiral Byrd on his expeditions to the Antarctic.

⓰ Some of the highest sand dunes in the country are found in **Umpqua Lighthouse Park** (turnoff 6 mi south of Reedsport on U.S. 101). The **Umpqua River Lighthouse,** built in 1861, flashes its warning beacon from a bluff overlooking the south side of Winchester Bay.

⓱ **Coos Bay** (27 mi south of Reedsport on U.S. 101), a former lumber town, lies on the largest natural harbor between San Francisco and Seattle's Puget Sound. The town itself is not particularly attractive, but west of it there are three beautiful oceanfront parks.

⓲ Head first to Charleston (7 mi west of Coos Bay on Newmark Ave.), a small fishing village; the road becomes Cape Arago Highway as it loops into town. **Sunset Bay State Park** (2 mi south of Charleston off Cape Arago Highway) features a protected lagoon where you can actually swim (if you're brave enough for the cold waters) without worrying about currents and undertows. **Shore Acres State Park** (1 mi south of Sunset Bay State Park) is the setting for a beautifully landscaped garden—part of a former seaside estate—that incorporates formal English and Japanese design elements. **Cape Arago State Park** (1 mi south of Shore Acres State Park) overlooks the **Oregon Islands National Wildlife Refuge,** where offshore rocks, beaches, islands, and reefs provide breeding grounds for seabirds and marine mammals. From Cape Arago State Park you'll have to backtrack to Coos Bay to regain U.S. 101.

⓳ At **Gold Beach** (35 mi south of Cape Blanco on U.S. 101), the fabled **Rogue River,** one of the few U.S. rivers to merit Wild and Scenic status from the federal government, pours into the Pacific. The town's seasonal tourist industry is based largely on fishing and jet-boat trips up the Rogue. For more information, contact **Jerry's Rogue Boats** or **Rogue River Mail Boat Trips.**

⓴ Nearly 90 percent of the nation's potted Easter lilies are cultivated in **Brookings** (27 mi south of Gold Beach on U.S. 101). With its mild year-round climate, this southern part of the Oregon coast is sometimes referred to as Oregon's Banana Belt. The town, located at the mouth of the Chetco River is equally renowned as a commercial and sport-fishing port.

The Columbia River Gorge, the High Desert, and Mt. Hood Driving Tour

INTO CENTRAL OREGON AND BACK TO PORTLAND

Distance: Approximately 624 miles Time: 3–4 days
Breaks: On the first day, stop for lunch at Multnomah Falls Lodge or in Hood River before heading on to the Maryhill Museum. Hood River is a good place to stay overnight before heading into the high desert. Plan to spend most of the second day exploring the John Day Fossil Beds. Depending on your schedule and interests, you can stay overnight in Dayville, Mitchell, or Shaniko. Timberline Lodge is a wonderful place to have lunch or dinner or to spend the third night.

This drive highlights the exceptional variety of Oregon's topography and focuses on three areas of scenic grandeur: the Columbia River Gorge, the high desert country in central Oregon, and Mt. Hood.

The journey enters some semi-remote areas; all roads are paved and marked, but a good Oregon road map is essential. Late spring to early autumn are the best times to make this trip. Winter snows on Mt. Hood can last until April; summer daytime temperatures east of the mountains can be sizzling, although the nights cool off considerably.

1. The town of **Troutdale** (13 mi east of Portland on I-84) marks the beginning of the **Columbia River Gorge National Scenic Area.**

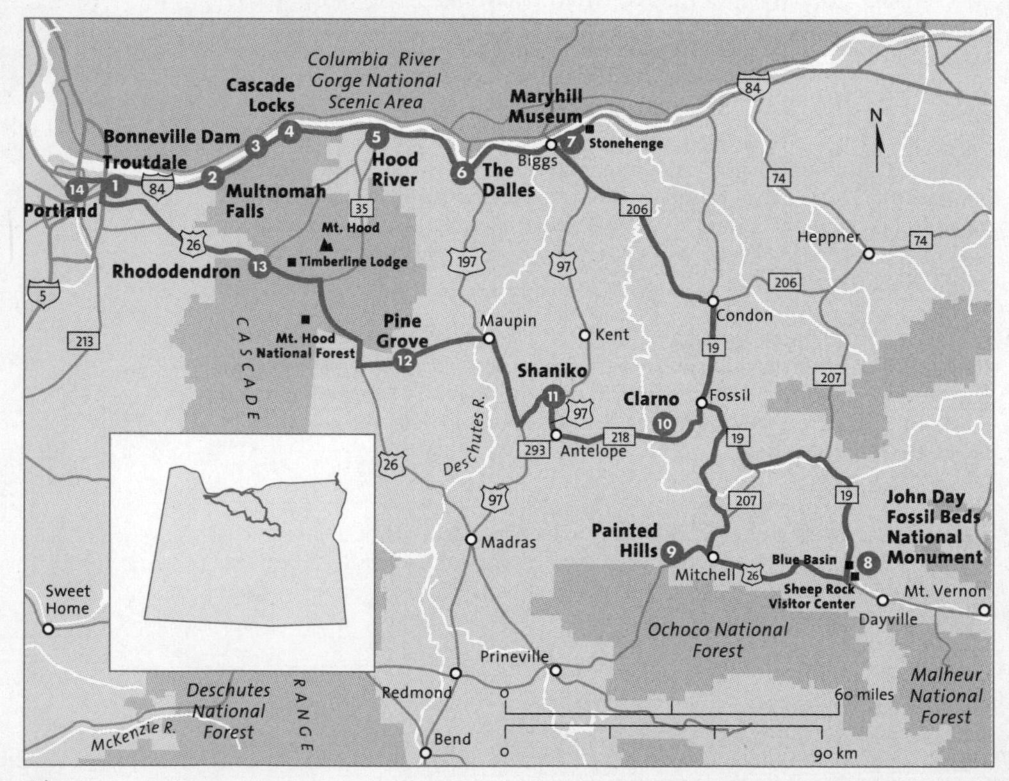

2. From here **Multnomah Falls** (20 mi east of Troutdale on I-84), the nation's fifth highest waterfall, pours down some 620 ft in a double-decker torrent. Paved walking paths climb up the hillside to a bridge overlooking the cataract, one of the state's most popular attractions.

3. Dedicated in 1937 by President Franklin D. Roosevelt, **Bonneville Dam** (5 mi east of Multnomah Falls on I-84) was the first federal dam to span the Columbia. If you want to tour this historic hydroelectric behemoth, there is a **Visitors Center** (Exit 40 from I-84) on Bradford Island.

4. The locks that gave the town of **Cascade Locks** (4 mi east of Bonneville Dam on I-84) its name were built in 1896 to tame the rapids that bedeviled early pioneers heading west toward the Willamette Valley on rafts. Between mid-June and late September you can view the awesome Gorge scenery aboard the sternwheeler ***Columbia Gorge*** (2-hr cruises leave from Marine Park in Cascade Locks).

5. In the past decade, thanks to the strong, ever-present winds blowing down the Columbia Gorge, **Hood River** (17 mi east of Cascade Locks on I-84) has become the self-proclaimed windsurfing capital of the world. Chances are you'll see dozens of windsurfers racing back and forth across the river. The Columbia widens at this point (you're now east of the Cascades), and the climate is noticeably drier. Hood River, located in one of Oregon's prime fruit-growing regions, offers a full array of restaurants and accommodations.

6. In pioneer days, **The Dalles** (20 mi east of Hood River on I-84) marked the end of the Oregon Trail. From here, would-be settlers had to decide whether to continue west via rafts, braving the treacherous rapids of the Columbia River, or trek overland across Mt. Hood. For a glimpse into the town's 19th-century pioneer and military past, visit the **Ford Dalles Museum.**

7. Without a doubt, the most unusual cultural attraction in the Columbia Gorge is **Maryhill Museum** (20 mi east of the Dalles on I-84, 2 mi north of Biggs on U.S. 97, 1 mi east of Rte. 14), on the Washington side of the river. An even stranger landmark in this unpopulated desert country is the replica of **Stonehenge** (3 mi east of the museum off Rte. 14), also part of Maryhill Museum.

8. Formed by explosive volcanic activity during the Cenozoic era, 5 to 50 million years ago, the geological formations that make up the **John Day Fossil Beds National Monument** cover hundreds of square miles but are divided into three "units." Driving south through the dry, shimmering heat of central Oregon, it may be difficult to imagine this area as a humid, subtropical forest filled with 50-ton brontosauruses and 50-ft-long crocodiles. The eroded hills and sharp, barren-looking ridges contain the richest concentration of prehistoric plant and animal fossils in the world.

   Head first to the **Sheep Rock Visitor Center** (Rte. 19; approximately 155 mi southeast of Biggs; 84 mi south and east to Ruggs on Rte. 206, 41 mi south on Rte. 207, 30 mi south on Rte. 19), where exhibits, a video, and handouts outline the significance of the John Day Fossil Beds. Winding through the impressive **Blue Basin** (2 mi north of the Visitor Center on Rte. 19), a badlands canyon with sinuous blue-green rock spires, is the **Island in Time Trail,** where trailside exhibits explain the area's 28-million-year-old fossils.

9. The fossils at **Painted Hills** (37 mi west of Sheep Rock on U.S. 26), the second unit of the John Day Fossil Beds, date back about 33 million years and reveal a climate that

had become noticeably drier than that of the Sheep Rock area. Take the ¾-mi **Carroll Rim Trail** for a commanding view of the hills, or enjoy the view from the parking lot at the trailhead, about 2 mi beyond the picnic area.

⑩ The 48-million-year-old fossil beds at **Clarno** (64 mi north of Painted Hills on Rte. 19) have yielded the oldest fossils in the national monument. Another trail climbs ¼-mi from the second parking lot to the base of the **Palisades,** a series of abrupt, irregular cliffs created by ancient volcanic mud flows.

⑪ **Shaniko** (23 mi northwest of Clarno on Rte. 218) is the closest thing to a ghost town in central Oregon. But there is life here, though the days when the dusty boardwalked hamlet was a gathering spot for ranchers and Basque sheepherders are long gone.

⑫ If the high desert has made your eyes hungry for green and your skin eager for some moisture, relax: Just west of **Pine Grove** (52 mi northwest of Shaniko; 12 SW on U.S. 97, 25 mi north on Rte. 197, 13 mi west on Rte. 216) the drive begins to climb north through the 1.1-million-acre **Mt. Hood National Forest.** A panorama of densely forested Cascade peaks and valleys unfolds as you ascend the southern slope of 11,325-ft **Mt. Hood,** the highest mountain in Oregon.

⑬ Near **Rhododendron** (39 mi north of Pine Grove on U.S. 26; 14 mi west on Rte. 216, 25 mi north on U.S. 26), you are approaching the summit of Mt. Hood. Take the well-marked turnoff from U.S. 26 for the final ascent to **Timberline Lodge** (Timberline Rd.), the highest spot in Oregon accessible by car. Breathtaking views of forested mountain peaks cupping jewel-like alpine lakes open up along the winding road.

⑭ Oregon's largest city, **Portland** (54 mi west of Rhododendron on U.S. 86 and I-84) marks the end point of the tour. After the vast open spaces you've seen on this trip, it's time to enjoy the comforts of civilization. Call or stop in at the **Portland/Oregon Visitors Association** (2 World Trade Center, 26 S.W. Salmon) for more information on what the Rose City has to offer.

ALBANY

MAP 3, D4

(Nearby towns also listed: Corvallis, Salem, Sweet Home)

Named by Thomas and Walter Monteith after their hometown in New York State, Albany is believed to be home to one of the largest and most varied collections of historic buildings in Oregon. An 80 square block area is listed on the National Register of Historical Places, and visitors are invited to tour some of the Victorian-era residences in late July and again before Christmas. Almost 40,000 people live in this town in the heart of the Willamette Valley. The area is so rich with agricultural crops that it is known as the "grass seed capital of the world."

Information: Albany Area Chamber of Commerce | 435 1st Ave. W, Albany 97321 | 541/926–5617 or 800/526–2256 | info@albanyvisitors.com | www.albanyvisitors.com.

Attractions

Monteith House Museum. The first frame house in Albany was Monteith House, which was built in 1849. Now restored and filled with period furnishings and historic photos, it is widely thought to be the most authentic restoration of a Pacific Northwest pioneer–era home. | 518 2nd Ave. SW | 800/526–2256 | fax 541/926–1500 | www.albanyvisitors.com | Donation | Mid-June–mid-Sept., Wed.–Sat. noon–4; mid-Sept.–mid-June, by appointment.

ON THE CALENDAR

JULY: ***Historic Interior Homes Tours.*** Local homes which have been carefully restored are open to the public for tours. The ticket price includes live entertainment, horse-drawn wagon rides, and refreshments. | Tickets are available at 250 Broadalban St., Suite 110 | 541/928–0911 or 800/526–2256.

JULY: ***Wah Chang Northwest Art and Air Festival.*** Albany itself nearly flies when this air festival takes off on the last weekend in July. There's entertainment, food, activities for the kids, model airplanes, a parachute jump, hot-air balloons, an artshow in Timber Linn Park, and a free air show at Albany airport. | 800/526–2256.

JULY: ***World Championship Timber Carnival.*** This is the world's largest logging event. It's been held since 1941 at 90-acre Timber Linn Park on July 4th weekend. Competitive events include log chopping, high climbing, jousting, log rolling, and axe throwing. Contestants compete for prize money and trophies. A parade is held downtown on opening day. There's also a fireworks display. | 541/928–0911 or 800/526–2256.

NOV.: ***Veterans Day Parade.*** America's servicemen are remembered in this brief downtown event which begins on Lion St. | 541/451–5799.

Dining

Buzz Saw. Contemporary. Fresh seafood and prime ribs are the most popular items at this riverside restaurant, along with steaks and pasta dishes. Window tables and raised booths all have a view of the river. The hottest club in town, with the same name, is right next door where a DJ keeps things moving five nights a week. There are pool tables, too. | 421 Water St. | 541/928–0642 | fax 541/928–0644 | No lunch | $6.95–$25.95 | AE, DC, MC, V.

Capriccio. Italian. Capriccio is *the* place for pasta in Albany. The house specialty is spinach ravioli in a cream sauce, but you might also choose from osso bucco Orvieto, lemon chicken, or New York strip steak, and there's fresh fish every day. | 442 W. 1st St. | 541/924–9932 | fax 541/967–9454 | Closed Sun.–Mon. No lunch | $13.50–$19.75 | AE, D, DC, MC, V.

Novak's Hungarian Paprikas. Hungarian. The owners of this unpretentious restaurant turn out native dishes such as *kolbasz* (homemade sausages with sweet-and-sour cabbage) and beef *szelet* (crispy batter-fried cutlets). | 2835 Santiam Hwy. SE | 541/967–9488 | Closed Sun. No lunch Sat. | $20 | MC, V.

Lodging

Best Western Pony Soldier Motor Inn. Rooms at this basic motel face an attractive courtyard with a pool. It's close to golf, tennis, shopping, and restaurants. | 72 rooms. Complimentary Continental breakfast, in-room data ports, microwaves, refrigerators, cable TV, pool, hot tub, exercise equipment, pets allowed. | 315 Airport Rd. SE | 541/928–6322 or 800/634–7669 | fax 541/928–8124 | $74–$90 | AE, D, DC, MC, V.

Brier Rose Inn. This 1886 Queen Anne is in a neighborhood filled with Victorian homes and within walking distance of the 1st Avenue antiques shops and several fine restaurants. It's two blocks from the Amtrak station. The Parlor Room is furnished entirely with antiques, the Garden Suite has a balcony and a sitting room, and the Jacuzzi Room has, yes, a hot tub. | 5 rooms (2 share bath). Complimentary breakfast, TV in common area, no smoking. | 206 7th Ave. SW | 541/926–0345 | fax 541/926–6861 | brierroseinn@email.com | www.cmug.com/~brierroseinn | $89–$125 | AE, D, MC, V.

Budget Inn. There's nothing fancy here, but it's a good choice if you prefer an inexpensive alternative. | 48 rooms. Cable TV, laundry facilities, pets allowed. | 2727 Pacific Blvd. SE | 541/926–4246 | fax 541/926–5208 | $40–$45. | AE, D, DC, MC, V.

Comfort Suites. This predictable all-suite chain hotel is less than ½ mi from Hwy. 5 and next to the Albany Municipal Airport. | 86 suites. Continental breakfast, indoor pool, hot tub, microwaves, refrigerators, exercise equipment, business services, laundry facilities, air-conditioning, cable TV. | 100 Opal Ct. NE, | 800/517–4000, 541/928–2053 | fax 541/928–2592 | $79–$119 | AE, D, DC, MC.

Hawthorne Inn and Suites. A fireplace and antiques in the lobby welcome you to the rustic interior of the Hawthorne Inn. Quite a variety of amenities are available and it's near both the airport and the fairgrounds. | 50 rooms. Complimentary buffet breakfast, cable TV, indoor pool, hot tub, exercise equipment, laundry facilities, business services, pets allowed. | 251 Airport Rd. SE | 541/928–0921 | fax 541/928–8055 | $69–$139 | AE, D, DC, MC, V.

ASHLAND

MAP 3, D8

(Nearby towns also listed: Jacksonville, Klamath Falls, Medford)

Home of the world-renowned, Tony award–winning Oregon Shakespeare Festival, Ashland has become a haven for contemporary theater as well as for music and dance. The small, arts-oriented community with a population of just under 20,000 is perfect for walking, bike riding, and running. At its heart is Lithia Park, a 100-acre refuge of footpaths, lawns, playgrounds, and picnic areas, with a Japanese garden and a formal rose garden.

Information: Ashland Chamber of Commerce | 110 E. Main St., Ashland, 97520 | 541/482–3486 | www.ashlandchamber.com.

Attractions

Exhibit Center. At the Exhibit Center in the Oregon Shakespeare Festival complex, you can try on costumes and see displays that outline the festival's history. On the guided backstage tour, see production shops, the Angus Bowmer Theatre and go up to the "heavens" above the Elizabethan stage. | 15 S. Pioneer St. | 541/482–4331 | fax 541/482–8045 | www.osfashland.org | Exhibit center $3. Backstage tour $12 (early June–early Oct.), $9 (Feb.–early June). Under 5 not admitted | June–Oct., Tues.–Sun. 10–4; Oct.–June 10:30–1:30.

Lithia Park. A flour mill originally occupied this site next to City Plaza before the park was established in 1892. A domed building here is home to the Elizabethan Theatre while the 1-mi-long Woodland Trail winds through native, ornamental, and exotic plants and trees. | Between Granite and Pioneer Sts. | 541/488–5340 | Free | Weekdays 8–5.

Mt. Ashland Ski Area. This winter sports playground in the Siskiyou Mountains is halfway between San Francisco and Portland. The ski runs get more than 300 inches of snow each year. There are 23 trails in addition to chute skiing in a glacial cirque called the bowl. The 6,350-ft mountain has a vertical drop of 1,150 ft. | Exit 6 off I-5. Access road to top | 541/482–2754 (snow conditions) or 541/482–2897 | mtashland.ashland.or.us | Nov.–Apr., 9–4.

ON THE CALENDAR

JUNE: *Feast of Will.* The Feast of Will in Lithia Park celebrates the opening of the Oregon Shakespeare Festival. It's brief, taking place from 6–7 PM between the matinee and evening performances at the adjoining theatre, but it's colorful and fun with music, dancing, bagpipes, and food. Tickets are available from the festival box office. | 541/482–4331.

★ **FEB.–NOV.: *Oregon Shakespeare Festival.*** From February through November this small community and its accomplished repertory company stage eleven rotating plays in three theaters. Between June and October, plays are staged in the 1,200-seat outdoor Elizabethan Theatre, an atmospheric re-creation of the Fortune Theatre in London. The festival operates close to capacity, so book ahead. | 541/482–4331.

Dining

Arbor House. Eclectic. The Arbor Housein the nearby town of Talent has a varied international menu that includes jambalaya, curries, braised lamb, and charbroiled steaks. Local people in the know come here most often for the seafood and the personal service. | 103 W. Wagner St., Talent | 541/535–6817 | Closed Sun.–Mon. No lunch | $10.95–$17.95 | No credit cards.

Ashland Bakery and Café. Vegetarian. This popular café is famous for its vegetarian fare. The bakery turns out artisan breads, pastries, cakes, and gourmet box lunches. It's on the Plaza around the block from Lithia Park and the Shakespeare Festival. No smoking. | 38 E. Main St. | 541/482–2117 | Breakfast also available. Closed Tues. No supper Mon. | $12–$20 | MC, V.

Chata. Eastern European. This restaurant in a cozy roadside cottage serves up excellent Polish dishes. There are six tables in the flower-filled grapevined arbor patio. Try the cabbage rolls. | 1212 S. Pacific Hwy. | 541/535–8949 | $20–$25 | MC, V.

Chateaulin. French. Inside this ivy-covered storefront, a block from the Oregon Shakespeare Festival, is one of southern Oregon's most romantic restaurants. The service is impeccable. Try the pan-roasted rack of lamb with a white-wine demi-glace sauce of roasted garlic, fresh basil, black olives, and sun-dried tomatoes. Kids' menu. No smoking. | 50 E. Main St. | 541/482–2264 | No lunch | $35–$40 | AE, D, MC, V.

Gepetto's. American/Casual. Gepetto's is fast, friendly, and unpretentious at breakfast, lunch, and dinner, serving up soups, salads, and unusual sandwiches such as grilled marinated turkey on crispy cheese bread. | 345 E. Main St. | 541/482–1138 | $12–$21.50 | D, MC, V.

Il Giardino. Italian. An orange Vespa parked in the front entrance marks the place where pasta dishes that use local ingredients in traditional recipes are served nightly. There are meat and fish dishes, as well. | 5 Granite St. | 541/488–0816 | Reservations essential | No lunch | $8.75–$22 | MC, V.

Macaroni's. Italian. This downtown Ashland restaurant is known for its Caesar salad, as well as good pizzas, pastas, and salads. | 58 E. Main St. | 541/488–3359 | No lunch | $11–$17 | D, MC, V.

Peerless Restaurant. Contemporary. Chef Stu Stein came here from San Francisco and specializes in seasonal Northwest Pacific entrees, using produce from local farms and offering pheasant, rabbit, venison, and other game dishes, along with a good wine list. Local people come for the double-cut veal chop. You can choose the dining room, which also offers garden seating, or the more casual bistro. This is a separate building from the Peerless Hotel. | 265 4th St. | 541/488–6067 | fax 541/488–5508 | No lunch Sept.–June, Sun.–Mon. | $13.95–$29.95 | AE, MC, V.

Thai Pepper. Thai. Coconut prawns and Thai beef salad for appetizers, and spicy curries and stir-fries for dinner are the specialties here. The restaurant is filled with local art and rattan furniture, and there are upper and lower patios overlooking Ashland Creek. | 84 N. Main St. | 541/482–8058 | No lunch Sun.–Mon. | $11.95–$17.50 | AE, DC, MC, V.

Winchester Country Inn. Continental. The menu is small, but imaginative at the restaurant inside this inn built in 1886. The high-windowed dining rooms are set among manicured gardens. The menu items are seasonal but sometimes include an ambrosial roast duck. Open-air dining includes seating on the patio and front porch. Sun. brunch. | 35 S. Second St. | 541/488–1115 | Closed Mon. No lunch | $25–$40 | AE, D, MC, V.

Lodging

Arden Forest Inn. This early-20th-century cross-gabled farmhouse is on a quiet street only 5 blocks from the Oregon Shakespeare Festival theaters. Bold colors, light pine furnishings, a collection of fantasy art, a library of current novels, plus a garden, lawn, and shade trees all make it casual and comfortable. Two rooms and the common areas are wheelchair-accessible. | 4 doubles with bath, 1 2-bedroom suite. Complimentary breakfast, in-room data ports, room phones, pool, no kids under 10, no smoking. | 261 W. Hersey St. | 541/488–1496 or 800/460–3912 | aforest@afinn.com | www.afinn.com | $110–$155 | MC, V.

Ashland Main Street Inn. Every room in this 1883 Victorian home 1½ blocks from the city plaza is filled with antiques and has access to a balcony. | 3 rooms. Continental breakfast. No in-room phones. Air-conditioning, refrigerators. | 142 N. Main St. | 541/488–0969 | $85.

Bayberry Inn Bed and Breakfast. This white-trimmed gray clapboard 1925 Craftsman house is quiet despite its Main Street location only five short blocks from the theaters. The interior is primarily English country, with floral prints and lace draperies. There's a sunny deck in back for morning coffee. | 6 rooms (all with private bath). Complimentary breakfast, TV in common area, laundry facilities, no kids under 12, no smoking. | 438 N. Main St. | 541/488–1252 or 800/795–1252 | harriet@bayberryinn.com | www.bayberryinn.com | $110 | Closed Nov. | MC, V.

Best Western Bard's Inn. This Best Western, in a beautiful rose garden setting, is only one block from downtown. Rooms have views of the surrounding mountains. | 92 rooms, 7 suites. Refrigerators, some in-room hot tubs, cable TV, pool, hot tub, cross-country and downhill skiing, business services, airport shuttle, pets allowed (fee). | 132 N. Main St. | 541/482–0049 | fax 541/488–3259 | $98–$134, $138–$175 suites | AE, D, DC, MC, V.

Black Sheep. English. An authentic red British phone booth, tiny gold stars painted on the ceiling, and tall picture windows with sunset views set the scene for traditional fish and chips as well as creative dishes like venison with gin and juniper berry sauce. This restaurant and pub is in an 1879 downtown building that once housed the International Order of Oddfellows. | 51 N. Main St. | 541/482–6414 | $10–$22 | MC, V.

Cedarwood Inn. All the rooms at this motel in a residential area 2 mi from downtown have queen- or king-size beds. Courtyard rooms have semi-private patios or decks. | 64 rooms (14 with shower only). Picnic area, some kitchenettes, cable TV, 2 pools (1 indoor), cross-country and downhill skiing, business services, some pets allowed during winter months. | 1801 Siskiyou Blvd. | 541/488–2000 or 800/547–4141 (for reservations) | fax 541/482–2000 | $68–$134 | AE, D, DC, MC, V.

Chanticleer Inn. Some rooms at this quaint country French inn four blocks from the theaters overlook the Bear Creek Valley and Cascade foothills; others open onto a peaceful garden patio. The bright rooms are furnished with antiques and have fluffy comforters and fresh flowers. | 6 rooms. Complimentary breakfast, hot tub, airport shuttle. | 120 Gresham St. | 541/482–1919 or 800/898–1950 | www.ashlandbnb.com | $150–$250 | AE, MC, V.

Country Willows Bed and Breakfast Inn. This country inn, built in 1896, is set against a rolling hillside on 5 acres of farmland, surrounded by the Siskiyou and Cascade Mountains. It is 2 mi from downtown Ashland. | 9 rooms (3 with shower only), 4 suites. Complimentary 2-course breakfast, in-room data ports, microwaves, some refrigerators, no TV in some rooms, cable TV in common area, pool, hot tub, business services, no kids under 12, no smoking. | 1313 Clay St. | 541/488–1590 or 800/945–5697 | fax 541/488–1611 | willows@willowsinn.com | www.willowsinn.com | $95–$195 | AE, D, MC, V.

Hillside Inn. This modern inn is conveniently located within walking distance of the university. | 31 rooms. Kitchenettes, cable TV, pool. | 1520 Siskiyou Blvd. | 541/482–2626 or 800/326–9903 | fax 541/482–1472 | ljjansen@teleport.net | www.hotel.worldres.com | $79 | AE, D, MC, V.

Knights Inn. You'll find clean, comfortable rooms with king- or queen-size beds at this chain property located 2 mi from downtown. | 40 rooms. Restaurant, bar, cable TV, pool, hot tub, some pets allowed (fee). | 2359 Hwy. 66 | 541/482–5111 or 800/547–4566 (for reservations) | $53–$74 | AE, D, DC, MC, V.

Lithia Springs Inn. A hot spring on the 8-acre property supplies water for the whirlpool baths in all but two of the rooms in this sprawling 1993 Cape Cod–style inn. Gardens, ponds, and meandering paths surround the inn. Amusing trompe l'oeil touches enliven the interior. | 4 rooms, 6 suites, 8 cottages. Complimentary breakfast. Some refrigerators, some minibars, no room phones, TV in common area, no kids under 12, no smoking. | 2165 W. Jackson

Rd. | 541/482–7128 or 800/482–7128 | fax 541/488–1645 | lithia@ashland.net | www.ashlandinn.com | $105–$225 (3-night minimum on summer weekends) | AE, D, MC, V.

McCall House. A National Historic Landmark, this small inn is a former residence of a Civil War veteran and mayor of Ashland. It's 1 block from the theaters. | 9 rooms. Complimentary breakfast, no kids under 12, no smoking. | 153 Oak St. | 541/482–9296 or 800/808–9749 | fax 541/482–2125 | mccall@mccallhouse.com | www.mccallhouse.com | $130–$180 | MC, V.

Morical House. Fine woodwork and stained-glass windows highlight this restored farmhouse that was built in 1882. All the rooms here, 1 mi north of downtown, have period antiques. The parlor has a baby grand piano and cozy fireplace. | 7 rooms. Picnic area, complimentary breakfast, in-room data ports, microwaves, refrigerators, some in-room hot tubs, business services, no kids under 12, no smoking. | 668 N. Main St. | 541/482–2254 or 800/208–0960 | fax 541/482–1775 | moricahse@aol.com | www.garden-inn.com | $110–$160 | AE, D, MC, V.

★ **Mt. Ashland Inn.** This intimate two-story lodge, hand built of cedar logs, has magnificent views of Mount Shasta and the rest of the Siskiyous. A large stone fireplace, antiques, hand-stitched quilts, and natural wood provide welcoming warmth. | 5 rooms, 3 suites. Complimentary breakfast, some microwaves, no room phones, hot tub, sauna, business services, no kids under 10, no smoking. | 550 Mt. Ashland Ski Rd. | 541/482–8707 or 800/830–8707 (for reservations) | fax 541/482–8707 | www.mtashlandinn.com | $99–$120 | D, MC, V.

Oak Hill Country Bed and Breakfast. Rooms in this remodeled 1910 farmhouse are bright and spacious and decorated in flower motifs. All have queen-size beds. | 6 rooms. Complimentary breakfast, no room phones, bicycles, no kids under 12, no smoking. | 2190 Siskiyou Blvd. | 541/482–1554 or 800/888–7434 | fax 541/482–1378 | oakhill@mind.net | www.oakhillbb.com | $105 | MC, V.

Pedigrift House. Built in 1888, this restored Queen Anne Victorian, 6 blocks from downtown, is on the National Historic Register. All rooms have queen-size beds. | 4 rooms. Picnic area, complimentary breakfast, cross-country and downhill skiing, no kids under 12, no smoking. | 407 Scenic Dr. | 541/482–1888 or 800/262–4073 | fax 541/482–8867 | www.opendoor.com/pedigrift | $120 | MC, V.

Peerless Hotel. A boarding house for railroad workers around 1900, this brick building was abandoned, then restored in the early 1990s, and is now on the National Register of Historic Places. The rooms are filled with antiques, hand-painted murals, and Oriental rugs, while one has West Indies–style furniture. Breakfast is served next door in the Peerless Restaurant. Guests have access to a health club. | 4 doubles with bath, 2 suites. Complimentary breakfast, refrigerators, some in-room hot tubs, TV in common area, no kids under 14, no smoking. | 243 4th St. | 541/488–1082 or 800/460–8758 | fax 541/488–5508 | www.peerlesshotel.com | $105–$195 | AE, D, MC, V.

Rodeway Inn. This modern hotel is across from Southern Oregon State College. | 64 rooms. Cable TV, pool, cross-country and downhill skiing, business services, some pets allowed (fee). | 1193 Siskiyou Blvd. | 541/482–2641 | fax 541/488–1656 | $72–$82 | AE, D, DC, MC, V.

Romeo Inn. Set amid pine trees and gardens in a quiet residential neighborhood, the rooms in this Cape Cod–style house have fireplaces and king-size beds with hand-stitched Amish quilts. Each room is decorated with a blend of antique and traditional furnishings. | 6 rooms. Complimentary breakfast, pool, hot tub, cross-country and downhill skiing, no kids under 12, no smoking. | 295 Idaho St. | 541/488–0884 or 800/915–8899 | fax 541/488–0817 | $130–$180 | MC, V.

Stratford Inn. This property is only 5 blocks from the Shakespearean theaters. | 55 rooms, 6 suites. Complimentary Continental breakfast, some kitchenettes, some microwaves, refrigerators, cable TV, indoor pool, hot tub, cross-country and downhill skiing, no smoking. | 555 Siskiyou Blvd. | 541/488–2151 or 800/547–4741 | fax 541/482–0479 | $60–$125, $130–$150 suites | AE, D, DC, MC, V.

Timbers Motel. Next to Southern Oregon University and 1 mi from downtown, this small motel offers clean, basic rooms with few frills. | 29 rooms. Cable TV, pool. | 1450 Ashland St. | 541/482–4242 | fax 541/482–8723 | $55–$80 | AE, D, MC, V.

Winchester Inn. The restored Victorian main house, built in 1886 and on the National Historic Register, once served as the area's first hospital. The individually decorated rooms have period furnishings. A gazebo highlights the surrounding tiered English tea garden. The inn is 2 blocks south of the Oregon Shakespeare Festival theaters. | 18 rooms, 2 suites in carriage house, 2 suites in cottage. Restaurant, complimentary breakfast, some in-room hot tubs, no TV in some rooms, cross-country and downhill skiing, no smoking. | 35 S. 2nd St. | 541/488–1113 or 800/972–4991 | fax 541/488–4604 | ashlandinn@aol.com | www.winchesterinn.com | $155–$200, $203–$210 suites | AE, D, MC, V.

Windmill Inn of Ashland. The Oregon Shakespeare Festival box office is 3 mi from this hotel where the rooms are plush and comfortable. | 159 rooms, 72 suites. Complimentary Continental breakfast, microwaves (in suites), refrigerators (in suites), pool, beauty salon, hot tub, tennis, cross-country and downhill skiing, exercise equipment, laundry facilities, airport shuttle, pets allowed. | 2525 Ashland St. | 541/482–8310 or 800/547–4747 | fax 541/488–1783 | info@windmillinns.com | www.windmillinns.com/ | $99–$109, $119 suites | AE, D, DC, MC, V.

Woods House. The rooms in this Craftsman-style house, built in 1908, are beautifully furnished with antiques, highlighted with fresh flowers, and come with soft robes. The B&B, surrounded by terraced gardens, is four blocks from downtown. | 6 rooms. Complimentary breakfast, no room phones, cross-country and downhill skiing, airport shuttle, no kids under 7, no smoking. | 333 N. Main St. | 541/488–1598 or 800/435–8260 | fax 541/482–8027 | woodshse@mind.net | www.mind.net/woodshouse | $110–$120 | MC, V.

ASTORIA

MAP 3, C1

(Nearby towns also listed: Cannon Beach, Seaside)

Astoria is the oldest city west of the Rockies. It was the arrival point for its founder, John Jacob Astor, and his trading company in 1811. Since that time, it has been a seaport, a cannery town, and a logging and fishing community. Many of the 10,000 residents can trace their roots to a Scandinavian heritage, which is evidenced in the town's shops and festivals. The scores of Victorian houses perched on the hillsides flanking the downtown area are especially picturesque.

Information: Astoria-Warrenton Area Chamber of Commerce | 111 W. Marine Dr., Astoria, 97103-0176 | 503/325–6311.

Attractions

Astoria Column. Follow scenic drive signs to Coxcomb Hill to see this 125-ft monument, which is listed in the National Register of Historic Places. It was erected in 1926 on the site of the first permanent U.S. settlement west of the Rockies. A spiral staircase leads to a viewing platform at the top where you get a panoramic view of the Astoria Bridge, the Pacific Ocean, and the mouth of the Columbia River. | Free | Daily.

★ **Columbia River Maritime Museum.** The highlight at this downtown waterfront museum is the U.S. Coast Guard lightship *Columbia*. There are also exhibits and artifacts relating to lighthouses, shipwrecks, navigation, fishing, and naval history. | 1792 Marine Dr. | 503/325–2323 | www.crmm.org | $5 | Daily 9:30–5.

Flavel House. This 1885 Queen Anne Victorian home has six fireplaces with hand-carved mantels and tiles imported from Italy, Holland, Belgium, and Algeria. It was built by Captain George Flavel, a Columbia River bar pilot. | 441 8th St. | 503/325–2203 | $5 | May–Sept., daily 10–5; Oct.–Apr., daily 11–4.

★ **Fort Clatsop National Memorial.** Capts. Meriwether Lewis and William Clark camped here during the winter of 1805–06. A replica of their fort is the highlight of the 125-acre park which is 5 mi southeast of Astoria. Demonstrations on making candles and clothing, smoking meat, building canoes, and firing flintlocks add life to the expedition displays. | 92343 Ft. Clatsop Rd., | 503/861–2471 | www.nps.gov/focl | $2; $4 per car | Oct.–May 8–5; June–Sept. 8–6.

Fort Stevens State Park. Fort Stevens is the only military installation in the continental U.S. to have been fired upon since the War of 1812. The park, 6 mi southwest of Astoria, has a museum of U.S. military history, a blacksmith shop, guided tours, and daily Civil War era cannon and rifle demonstrations. On Labor Day weekend a Civil War re-enactment is staged. | Warrenton Hammond Rd. | 503/861–1671 or 800/551–6949 | www.prd.state.or.us | $3 per car | May–Oct., daily 10–6; Nov.–Apr., daily 10–4.

Josephson's. This is one of the Oregon coast's oldest commercial smokehouses, using alderwood for all processing and specializing in Pacific Northwest chinook and coho salmon. You can also buy smoked sturgeon, tuna, oysters, mussels, scallops, and prawns by the pound or in sealed gift packs. An exhibit of photos and magazine articles provides a history of the smokehouse. | 106 Marine Dr. | 503/325–2190 | fax 503/325–4075 | www.josephsons.com | Free | Weekdays 8–5:30; weekends 10–5:30.

ON THE CALENDAR

APR.: ***Astoria-Warrenton Crab and Seafood Festival.*** Pacific Northwest seafood is the highlight of this three-day event held at Hammond Mooring Basin the last weekend in April. Fine wines, arts and crafts, gifts, and live music are also featured. | 503/325–6311 or 800/875–6807.

AUG.: ***Astoria Regatta Festival.*** This festival, on the second weekend in August, began in 1894 and is the oldest of its kind in the Northwest. It begins with the coronation of the regatta queen on Wednesday night followed by a concert on Thursday, plus a parade, salmon barbecue, kids' activities, fireworks on Saturday night, and the "Shanghaied in Astoria" melodrama. Viewing of the regatta is in the waterside park. | 503/325–6311.

Dining

Columbian Café. Contemporary. The unpretentious south-of-the-border appeal of this diner keeps the locals coming back for more. The food is fresh and simple while the portions are huge. Try the crêpes with broccoli, cheese, and homemade salsa for lunch or the grilled salmon and pasta with a lemon-cream sauce for supper. | 1114 Marine Dr. | 503/325–2233 | No supper Sun.–Tues. | $25–$35 | No credit cards.

Gunderson's Cannery Cafe. Seafood. Overlooking the Columbia River on Pier 6 in a century-old cannery, Gunderson's in-season seafood is prepared fresh and never fried. The lime prawns, halibut burger, or crab and shrimp cakes are a good choice. Homemade soups, focaccia pizza, breads, and desserts are also served. | One 6th St. | 503/325–8642 | No supper Sun.–Mon. | $12–$25 | D, DC, MC, V.

Home Spirit Bakery Café. Contemporary. This unique restaurant is in an 1891 Queen Anne house with a river view and it's filled with artifacts from the 1902–1912 Arts and Crafts period. It's known locally for its baked goods. The owners serve lunch five days a week. On Thurs.–Sat. a prix-fixe dinner is served with a choice of four entrées: seafood, chicken, red meat, and vegetarian. The price of the meal depends on the night; Saturday is highest. | 1585 Exchange St. | 503/325–6846 | Closed Sun.–Mon. No dinner Tues.–Wed. | $9.95–$21 | No credit cards.

Pier 11 Feed Store Restaurant. Seafood. This restaurant has an old fashioned rustic feel and overlooks the Columbia River. There is an assortment of seafood entrées as well as steak and chicken dishes. | 77 11th St. | 503/325–0279 | Breakfast available Fri.–Sun. | $15–$35 | D, MC, V.

Ship Inn. Seafood. The Ship Inn is well known among locals and savvy tourists for its casual style and famous fish (halibut is used) and chips. But don't overlook the wide array of other seafood prepared with a Pacific Northwest flair. | 1 2nd St. | 503/325–0033 | Closed major holidays | $6.50–$21.95 | AE, D, MC, V.

Lodging

Astoria Dunes. Many of the clean, plain rooms in this motel, located under the Astoria Bridge right on the Columbia, have a view of the river. | 58 rooms. No air-conditioning in some rooms, cable TV, indoor pool, hot tub, laundry facilities, business services. | 288 W. Marine Dr. | 503/325–7111 or 800/441–3319 | fax 503/325–0804 | $68–$75 | AE, D, DC, MC, V.

Astoria Inn. This Queen Anne farmhouse with gingerbread trim sits atop a hill in a quiet residential area high above the Columbia River. The views are inspiring, especially from the appropriately named Cape Lookout guest room. The rooms and a library are filled with antiques and wingback chairs. Guests here report that they love the breakfast. | 4 doubles with bath. Complimentary breakfast, TV in common area, no smoking. | 3391 Irving Ave. | 503/325–8153 or 800/718–8153 | www.moriah.com/astoriainn | $70–$85 | D, MC, V.

Bayshore Motor Inn. The rooms in this motel are housed either in a two-story or newer four-story building. Set on the riverbank, it is close to Astoria's historic district. | 76 rooms. Complimentary Continental breakfast, no air-conditioning in some rooms, cable TV, indoor pool, hot tub, laundry facilities, business services, some pets allowed (fee). | 555 Hamburg Ave. | 503/325–2205 or 800/621–0641 | fax 503/325–5550 | $64–$128 | AE, D, DC, MC, V.

Benjamin Young Inn. This handsome 5,500-square-ft Queen Anne inn is surrounded by century-old gardens. Known until 1994 as K. C.'s Mansion by the Sea, it is now on the National Register of Historic Places. Among the ornate original details are faux graining on frames and molding, shutter-blinds in windows, and Povey stained glass. The spacious guest rooms mix antiques with contemporary pieces, and have views of the Columbia River from their tall windows. City tennis courts are right next door. | 4 doubles with bath, 1 2-bedroom suite. Complimentary breakfast, no air-conditioning, some in-room hot tubs, no TV in some rooms, no smoking. | 3652 Duane St. | 503/325–6172 or 800/201–1286 | fax 503/325–6172 | benjamin@benjaminyounginn.com | www.benjaminyounginn.com | $80–$135 (2 night minimum on holiday weekends and July–Aug. weekends) | AE, D, MC, V.

Columbia River Inn Bed and Breakfast. Some of the tastefully decorated rooms in this 1870 Victorian have views of the river. The inn is filled with antiques. It's a short walk to the Columbia River Maritime Museum and downtown shopping. | 4 rooms. Complimentary breakfast, refrigerators, some in-room hot tubs, no room phones, airport shuttle, no kids under 12. | 1681 Franklin Ave. | 503/325–5044 or 800/953–5044 | $75–$125 | AE, D, MC, V.

Crest Motel. This is an older, no-frills motel on 2½ acres overlooking the mouth of the Columbia River. There is a large backyard where you can watch the river traffic. | 40 rooms. Free Continental breakfast, no air-conditioning, some refrigerators, cable TV, hot tub, laundry facilities, business services, pets allowed. | 5366 Leif Erickson Dr. | 503/325–3141 or 800/421–3141 | $52–$89 | AE, D, DC, MC, V.

Franklin Street Station Bed and Breakfast. On the slope above downtown Astoria, this cream-colored 1900 Victorian displays handsome detail in its interior moldings and built-ins, and there's a fine old greenstone fireplace in the dining area. The rooms variously have iron and brass beds, arched windows, and a deck. The Starlight Suite has a fireplace and a telescope, hence the name. | 5 rooms, 1 suite. Complimentary breakfast, in-room data ports, some in-room safes, some kitchenettes, some minibars, some microwaves, some refrigerators, no TV in some rooms, no smoking. | 1140 Franklin St. | 503/325–4314 or 800/448–1098 | fax 801/681–5641 | franklinststationbb@yahoo.com | www.franklin-st-station-bb.com | $68–$120 | MC, V.

Grandview Bed and Breakfast. The outside of this part-shingled, part-vinyl 1896 house isn't impressive, but its setting on a steep hillside street provides spectacular views of the Columbia River and the Coast Range. You can walk to restaurants, including the Home Spirit Bakery Café. One suite has a separate entrance. No alcohol is allowed. | 3 rooms, 1 suites. Complimentary breakfast, no air-conditioning, no room phones, no smoking. | 1574 Grand Ave. | 503/325–5555 or 800/488–3250 | grandviewbedandbreakfast@go.com | www.go.to/grandviewbedandbreakfast | $61–$100 | D, MC, V.

Red Lion Inn. Many of the rooms, decorated in earth tones, have views of the Columbia River, the marina, and Astoria Bridge. This dependable chain's Astoria property is on the river bank and 8 blocks from the City Center. | 124 rooms. Restaurant, bar with entertainment, room service, cable TV, business services, airport shuttle, some pets allowed (fee). | 400 Industry St. | 503/325–7373 | fax 503/325–5786 | $124 | AE, D, DC, MC, V.

Rosebriar Hotel. Built in 1902, this building was once used as a convent. Some rooms have fireplaces and views of the Columbia River and downtown. All of the rooms are decorated with antiques. | 11 rooms. Complimentary full breakfast, no air-conditioning, some in-room hot tubs, business services. | 636 14th St. | 503/325–7427 or 800/487–0224 | fax 503/325–6937 | $75–$149 | MC, V.

Shilo Inn. This Shilo property is 1 mi south of town near the Pacific. | 63 rooms. Restaurant, bar, complimentary breakfast, some kitchenettes, microwaves, refrigerators, room service, cable TV, indoor pool, hot tub, exercise equipment, laundry facilities, business services, airport shuttle, pets allowed (fee). | 1609 E. Harbor Dr., Warrenton | 503/861–2181 | fax 503/861–2980 | $79–$119 | AE, D, DC, MC, V.

BAKER CITY

MAP 3, J4

(Nearby town also listed: La Grande)

Oregon Trail pioneers first glimpsed the Oregon Territory from the Baker Valley. History buffs will be particularly interested in Baker City, originally a mining town and now the location for the National Historic Oregon Trail Interpretive Center. At the same time, outdoor enthusiasts will appreciate the nearby recreational opportunities for fishing, hunting, waterskiing, canoeing, hiking, cycling, and skiing. Baker City has received national recognition for its historic restoration efforts and success in attracting visitors to its out-of-the-mainstream location near the Eagle Cap and Wallowa Mountains.

Information: Baker County Chamber of Commerce | 490 Campbell St., Baker City, 97814 | 541/523–5855 | bakerchamber@bakercity.com.

Attractions

Anthony Lakes Ski Area. This ski area in the Wallowa-Whitman National Forest has a vertical drop of 900 ft and a top elevation of 8,000 ft. There are 22 trails and a 13-km cross-country route. Snowboards are permitted. | Exit 285 off I–84 to Anthony Lakes Rd. | 800/523–1235 | Nov.–Apr., Thurs.–Sun. 9–4.

Eastern Oregon Museum. The museum has 10,000 household, farming, mining, and pioneer artifacts. On the grounds is the old Union Pacific depot, built in the 1880s and given to the museum when the railroad discontinued stops at Haines in 1962. | 610 3rd St., Haines | 541/856–3233 | Donations accepted | mid-April.–mid-Oct., daily 9–5.

Elkhorn Drive. The scenic 106-mi loop of Elkhorn Drive winds from Baker City through the Elkhorn Range of the Blue Mountains. Only white-bark pine can survive on the range's sharp ridges and peaks, which top 8,000 ft; spruce, larch, Douglas fir, and ponderosa pine thrive on the lower slopes. The route is well marked; start on Hwy. 7 west of Baker City, turn onto County Rd. 24 toward Sumpter, pass Granite on Forest Service Rd. 73, and then return to Baker City along U.S. 30.

National Historic Oregon Trail Interpretive Center. The history of westward migration is the main focus here. Replicas of wagons, scenes of pioneer life, and various artifacts allow you to experience a typical trip along the Oregon Trail and the toll it took on its participants. | Flagstaff Hill | 800/523–1235 | www.or.blm.gov/nhotic | $5 | Apr.–Oct., daily 9–6; Nov.–Mar. 9–4.

Oregon Trail Regional Museum. Regional history, an outstanding rock collection, an impressive butterfly collection, and period clothing are featured. | 2490 Grove St. | 800/523–1235 | $2.50 | Mar.–Oct., daily 9–5.

Sumpter Valley Railroad. The original track of the Sumpter Valley Railway was scrapped in 1947. With an all-volunteer work force, the railroad has rebuilt more than 7 mi of track on the original right-of-way. Today it operates along a 5.1-mi route in Sumpter, about 25 mi from Baker City. | On Hwy. 7 | 800/523–1235 | www.svry.com | $9 | Memorial Day–Sept., weekends.

Unity Lake State Park. The smell of juniper fills the air at this high desert park which is 26 mi from town. The Burnt River runs through the park where Unity Dam created the small lake. There are a boat ramp, 21 electrical camp sites, and 2 tepees. | Rte. 245 at U.S. 26 | 541/932–4453 or 800/551–6949 | www.prd.state.or.us | Free | Apr.–Oct., daily.

U. S. Bank. The display of gold here takes on many forms: gold coins, gold leaf, pea gold, crystallized gold, gold nuggets, and more. The highlight is the 6¾-pound Armstrong Nugget, found on June 19, 1913 in Oregon's Grant County. | 2000 Main St. | 541//523–7791 or 800/872–2657 | www.usbank.com | Free | Mon.–Thurs. 10–5; Fri. 10–6.

Wallowa-Whitman National Forest. The 2.3-million-acre forest ranges in elevation from 875 ft in the Hells Canyon Wilderness to 9,845 ft in the Eagle Cap Wilderness. There are two other wilderness areas: Monument Rock and North Fork John Day. | Exits 302, 304 off I–84 | 541/523–6391 | www.fs.fed.us/r6/w-w/index.htm | Free | Daily.

ON THE CALENDAR

JULY: *Pioneer Heritage Festival.* On the last Saturday in July, the Oregon Trail Interpretive Center presents a day-long festival of living history with food prepared from authentic pioneer recipes; trappers, goldsmiths, and other artisans demonstrating their crafts in period costume; old-time games for the kids; and other activities. | 541/523–1843.

Dining

Baker City Cafe–Pizza à Fetta. Pizza. The inventive pizzas here are made from hand-thrown dough. The pesto and three-tomato pies are standouts. Pastas, salads, Italian sodas, and espresso are also served. | 1915 Washington Ave. | 541/523–6099 | Closed Sun. No dinner Sat. | $6.95–$22 | MC, V.

Geiser Grand Hotel. Steak. The Palm Court dining room in the Geiser Grand Hotel is Baker City's finest restaurant, serving prime ribs that are hickory-smoked in the house, plus steaks, fresh fish, and pasta dishes. Breakfast and lunch are also served. The Geiser Grand itself is a quadrangle and the spacious Palm Court, covered by a stained-glass ceiling, fills the central area. | 1996 Main St. | 541/523–1889 or 888/434–7374 | fax 541/523–1800 | $9.95–$19.95 | AE, DC, MC, V.

Gold Skillet Diner. American. You don't have to be a train enthusiast to enjoy breakfast or lunch in this authentic 1932 Union Pacific railroad car. The classic American diner menu has been raised to a new level with everything from huckleberry pancakes to homemade gravies, all served with a warm welcome. | 781 Campbell St. | 541/523–4657 | Closed Mon. No dinner | No credit cards.

Phone Company. Contemporary. This suitably named restaurant is in an old Bell Telephone building in the Victorian historic district. The staples here are steak, chicken, salads, pastas, and seafood, especially salmon. The real specialty, though, is chicken *mamou*, a New Orleans pasta dish you can order in a mild, medium, hot, or nuclear version! | 1926 First St. | 541/523–7997 | Closed Sun.–Mon. No lunch Sat. | $8–$19.95 | MC, V.

Lodging

Always Welcome Inn. The owners of this hillside inn overlooking the Elkhorn Mountains pride themselves on keeping the large, soundproofed rooms spotlessly clean. And if you stay in one day and need a refrigerator or microwave, they'll happily bring one to your room. | 24 rooms. Complimentary Continental breakfast, in-room data ports, cable TV, no smoking. | 175 Campbell St. | 541/523–3431 or 800/307–5206 | welcome@eoni.com | www.easyfinder.com/exit/or/welcomeinn.htm | $65 | D, MC, V.

Best Western Sunridge Inn. The rooms at this five-building inn are large and surround a swimming pool; poolside rooms are preferable because the mountain-view rooms also overlook the parking lot. | 156 rooms. Restaurant, in-room data ports, cable TV, pool, hot tub, business services, airport shuttle. | 1 Sunridge Lane | 541/523–6444 or 800/233–2368 | fax 541/523–6446 | $63–$170 | AE, D, DC, MC, V.

Bridge Street Inn. The rooms at this downtown motel are clean and good value. | 40 rooms. Complimentary Continental breakfast, some microwaves, refrigerators, cable TV, pets allowed. | 134 Bridge St. | 541/523–6571 or 800/932–9220 | fax 541/523–9424 | reservations@bridgestreetinn.com | www.bridgestreetinn.com | $31–$50 | AE, D, MC, V.

Eldorado Inn. This small motel has clean rooms and low rates. | 56 rooms. Restaurant, cable TV, indoor pool, hot tub, business services, pets allowed (fee). | 695 E. Campbell St. | 541/523–6494 or 800/537–5756 | fax 541/523–6494 | $45–$54 | AE, D, DC, MC, V.

Geiser Grand Hotel. The Italian Renaissance Revival three-story building was built in 1889 during the height of the gold rush. The rooms, filled with period furnishings and every modern amenity, have 18-ft ceilings, enormous windows (many overlooking the nearby mountains), and large baths. | 30 rooms. Restaurant, bar, no smoking floors, room service, cable TV. | 1996 Main St. | 541/523–1889 or 888/434–7374 | fax 541/523–1800 | $75–$170 | AE, D, MC, V.

Oregon Trail Motel & Restaurant. The Oregon Trail is two blocks from Main Street, near shops, restaurants, and the Oregon Trail Interpretive Center. The restaurant here serves breakfast, lunch, and dinner. | 54 rooms. Restaurant, in-room data ports, microwaves, refrigerators, cable TV, pool, sauna. | 211 Bridge St. | 541/523–5844 or 800/628–3982 | otm@triax.com | $54 | AE, D, DC, MC, V.

Quality Inn. The rooms here are basic but clean. | 54 rooms. Complimentary Continental breakfast, some refrigerators, cable TV, pets allowed (fee). | 810 Campbell St. | 541/523–2242 | fax 541/523–2242, ext. 400 | $42–$62 | AE, D, DC, MC, V.

Super 8. Standard rooms are bright and have queen- or king-size beds. | 68 rooms, 4 suites. Some kitchenettes, some microwaves, refrigerators, cable TV, in-room hot tubs (in suites), indoor pool, laundry facilities, business services. | 250 Campbell St. | 541/523–8282 | fax 541/523–9137 | $42–$62, $121 suites | AE, D, DC, MC, V.

Western Motel. If you're running low on funds, this small and simple in-town motel offers an inexpensive alternative. | 14 rooms | 3055 10th St. | 541/523–3700 or 800/481–3701 | $28–$38 | MC, V.

BANDON

MAP 3, B7

(Nearby towns also listed: Coos Bay, North Bend, Port Orford)

Referred to by some who cherish its romantic lure as "Bandon-by-the-Sea," Bandon is both a harbor town and a popular vacation spot. Bandon is famous for its cranberry products and its cheese factory, as well as its artists' colony, complete with galleries and shops. Two National Wildlife Refuges, Oregon Islands, and Bandon Marsh are located within the city limits. Newly developed on natural rolling dune land along the Pacific Ocean, the Bandon Dunes links-style course is attracting interest from golfers worldwide.

Information: **Bandon Chamber of Commerce** | 300 S. 2nd St., Bandon, 97411 | 541/347–9616 | bandoncc@harborside.com | www.harborside.com/bandon.

Attractions

Bandon Beach State Park. This small park, located along the Beach Loop Road 5 mi south of Bandon has access to beaches, fishing, and hiking trails. | Bradley Lake Rd. | 541/347–3501 or 800/551–6949 | www.prd.state.or.us | Free | Daily.

Bullards Beach State Park. The campground is sheltered in a grove of shore pine trees at this park, which is 2 mi north of Bandon. Across the Coquille River is the Bandon Marsh National Wildlife Refuge. The Coquille River Lighthouse is at the end of a road that wanders through the park. There are 90 full hookups, 95 electrical, and 13 yurts. | U.S. 101 | 541/347–3501 or 800/551–6949 | www.prd.state.or.us | Free | Daily.

Coquille River Museum. The museum, in the old City Hall building, documents Bandon's past with displays of pioneer furniture, glassware, and clothing, plus exhibits on the Bandon fire of 1936 and the local lumber, cranberry, creamery, and maritime industries. | 270 Fillmore St. | 541/347–2164 | $2 | Mon.–Sat. 10–4; plus Memorial Day–Sept., Sun. noon–3.

Cranberry Sweets and More. This shop is the source for delicious handmade candies, including cranberry-nut jellies, "lemon pies" (white chocolate around a lemon jelly center), and other goodies. | 1005 Newmark Ave. | 541/347–9475 or 800/527–5748 | fax 541/888–2824 | www.cranberrysweetsandmore.com | Daily 9–6.

Face Rock Wayside. The stone sculptures at the shore here, formed only by wind and rain, have names such as Elephant Rock, Table Rock, and Face Rock. To reach them follow signs from Bandon south along Beach Loop Road, then walk down a stairway to the sand. | Free | Daily.

West Coast Game Park. The "walk-through safari" on 21 acres has free-roaming wildlife: 450 animals and 75 species including lions, tigers, snow leopards, bears, chimps, cougars, and camels, making it one of the largest wild animal petting parks in the United States. The big attractions here are the young animals: bear cubs, tiger cubs, whatever is suitable for actual handling. It is 7 mi south of Bandon on U.S. 101. | U.S. 101 | 541/347–3106 | www.gameparksafari.com | $9.00 | Mar.–Nov., daily 9–sunset; Dec.–Feb., call for hours.

ON THE CALENDAR

MAY: ***Seafood and Wine Festival.*** This benefit for the Bandon Historical Society is held at the Community Center on Memorial Day weekend and includes wine tasting, food booths, and live entertainment. | 541/347–7006.

SEPT.–OCT.: ***Cranberry Festival.*** In late September or early October, Bandon celebrates the harvest and its status as the Cranberry Capital of Oregon with a three-day festival. | 541/347–9616.

Dining

Bandon Bill's Steak and Seafood. Contemporary. The selection of steaks and fresh seafood here is expanded with such specials as Kahlua honey-smoked game hen and New Orleans–style Bayou steamers, prepared in a gumbo broth. You can enjoy your meal with a view on the outside deck. | 3225 Beach Loop Rd. | 541/347–9441 or 800/638–3092 | fax 541/347–2532 | $7.75–$25 | AE, D, DC, MC, V.

Bandon Boatworks. Seafood. A local favorite, this romantic jetty-side eatery serves up its seafood, steaks, and prime rib with a view of the Coquille River harbor and lighthouse. Try the panfried oysters flamed with brandy and anisette or the quick-sautéed seafood combination that's heavy on scampi and scallops. There is a salad bar and kids' menu. No smoking. | 275 Lincoln Ave. SW | 541/347–2111 | $12–$17 | AE, D, MC, V.

Lord Bennett's. Seafood. This bright restaurant overlooking the Pacific serves fresh regional or imported seafood and pasta. Other options include steak, chicken, lamb, and pork loin. Try the fettucine with scallops and prawns in Alfredo sauce. Kids' menu. Sun. brunch. | 1695 Beach Loop Dr. | 541/347–3663 | $21–$28 | AE, D, MC, V.

Wheelhouse. Seafood. Enjoy a view of the harbor and fishing boats while dining on seafood in this restored fish warehouse. | 125 Chicago Ave. | 541/347–9331 | $20–$30 | AE, MC, V.

Lodging

Harbor View Motel. Rooms at this motel on the Coquille River have ocean views. It's close to Old Town shopping and restaurants. | 59 rooms. Complimentary Continental breakfast, refrigerators, cable TV. | 355 U.S. 101 | 541/347–4417 or 800/526–0209 | fax 541/347–3616 | $80–$95 | AE, D, DC, MC, V.

Inn at Face Rock. This modern resort hotel, beautifully landscaped with flowers and greenery, is across the road from Bandon's great walking beach. The rooms are spacious and each suite has a fireplace and an ocean view. Seven of the suites also have large hot tubs. The restaurant on the premises is Bandon Bill's Steak and Seafood, and there's a 9-hole golf course right next door. | 54 rooms, 20 suites. Restaurant, bar, no air-conditioning, some kitchenettes, some microwaves, some refrigerators, some in-room hot tubs, cable TV, room phones, pool, hot tub, sauna, gym, laundry facilities, laundry service, business services. | 3225 Beach Loop Rd. | 541/347–9441 or 800/638–3092 | fax 541/347–2532 | facerock@facerock.net | www.facerock.net | $105 | AE, D, DC, MC, V.

The Lighthouse. Wide windows and a porch off the dining room of this 1980 cedar home on Bandon's waterfront, within walking distance of Old Town and restaurants, provide great views of the Coquille River Lighthouse across the estuary. The simple furnishings include antiques and plants. Three guest rooms have dramatic ocean and sunset views and guests say the Gray Whale Room has the best view on the Oregon coast, right from the room's hot tub. | 5 doubles with bath. Complimentary breakfast, some in-room hot tubs, no TV in some rooms, TV in common area, no smoking. | 650 Jetty Rd. | 541/347–9316 | www.lighthouselodging.com | $105–$175 | Closed July 4 | MC, V.

Sunset Motel. Many rooms at this rustic property have decks with ocean views; some are oceanfronts, some have fireplaces. Beach houses are also available. | 58 rooms; 5 beach houses. Restaurant, some kitchenettes, cable TV, hot tub, laundry facilities, business services, airport shuttle, some pets allowed (fee). | 1755 Beach Loop Rd. | 541/347–2453 or 800/842–2407 | fax 541/347–3636 | sunset@harborside.com | www.sunsetmotel.com | $52–$110, $155–$165 beach houses | AE, D, DC, MC, V.

BEAVERTON

MAP 3, B3

(Nearby towns also listed: Forest Grove, Hillsboro, Oregon City, Portland)

Named for its location in the midst of a large network of beaver dams, Beaverton has itself become a network of residential neighborhoods, shopping areas, and business parks spanning 15 square miles. Once a small town surrounded by thriving Washington County farm fields, today Beaverton is home to well over 60,000 residents. At 7 mi from Portland it is considered Portland's long-expanding, affluent suburb to the west.

The roots of Oregon's Silicon Forest are in Beaverton, with some of the state's largest high-tech employers contributing to the town's popularity. Among Beaverton's other high-profile employers are Adidas and Nike, whose famous world headquarters campus is regularly visited by celebrities.

Beaverton can boast of more than 100 parks spread over 1,000 acres. There is an extensive system of hiking trails and bike paths, as well as many numerous public and private golf courses and tennis courts.

Information: Beaverton Area Chamber of Commerce | 4800 S.W. Griffith Dr., #100, Beaverton, 97005 | 503/644–0123 | www.beaverton.org.

Attractions

Tualatin Hills Nature Park. Right in the heart of the Silicon Forest is a real forest with creeks, ponds, fir trees, and red cedars. The 195-acre urban wilderness is home to beavers, great blue herons, and dozens of other bird species. There are several trails, some have boardwalks. Take the MAX light rail to the Merlo Road Station. No dogs allowed. | 15655 S.W. Millikan Blvd. | 503/644–5595 | www.thprd.com/facilities/nature | Free | Daily dawn to dusk.

ON THE CALENDAR

JULY: *A Taste of Beaverton.* This event held the second weekend in July in Beaverton's Griffith Park attracts big-name entertainers to a three-day bash. A food pavilion presents Pacific Northwest specialties while the bands play on. | 503/644–0123.

Dining

Koji Osakaya. Japanese. Sushi, sashimi, and creative rolls are the draw here, but udon noodles are offered as well. Eel, yellowfin tuna, and salmon are good sashimi choices. There are four other locations in the Portland metro area including downtown at 606 S.W. Broadway. Try the California, Philadelphia, and Oregon rolls, which use ingredients from their respective areas. | 11995 S.W. Beaverton-Hillsdale Hwy. | 503/646–5697 | $12–$20 | AE, MC, V.

McCormick's Fish House & Bar. Seafood. The neighborhood feeling of this restaurant belies its association with the national chain. Try creative seasonal preparations like macadamia nut–crusted Alaskan halibut with mango–beurre blanc sauce, or salmon baked on a cedar plank. Mounted fish are displayed on the ceiling of the rusty-brown main dining room. The restaurant is popular with local families. | 9945 S.W. Beaverton-Hillsdale Hwy. | 503/643–1322 | No lunch Sun. | $8–$24 | AE, D, DC, MC, V.

Pavillion Trattoria. Contemporary. Seasonal Pacific Northwest cuisine is presented in a garden setting at this suburban Portland restaurant. Try the grilled salmon served on a warm beet salad with roasted shallot vinaigrette or the applewood-smoked prime rib served with sweet onion rings. Entertainment Fri.–Sat. Kids' menu, early-bird suppers. Sun. brunch. | 10700 S.W. Allen Blvd. | 503/626–4550 | Breakfast also available | $17–$31 | AE, DC, MC, V.

Sayler's Old Country Kitchen. Steak. Home of the massive 72-ounce steak, this downtown Beaverton restaurant also serves chicken and fish in a casual setting. Kids' menu. | 4655 S.W. Griffith Dr. | 503/644–1492 | $13–$17 | AE, D, MC, V.

Lodging

Courtyard by Marriott. This contemporary three-story building has a courtyard with a gazebo. It is 3 mi from downtown. | 149 rooms, 12 suites. Restaurant, bar, in-room data ports, refrigerators (in suites), cable TV, indoor pool, hot tub, exercise equipment, laundry facilities, business services. | 8500 S.W. Nimbus Dr. | 503/641–3200 | fax 503/641–1287 | $89–$104, $114 suites | AE, D, DC, MC, V.

Greenwood Inn. This suburban hotel, built in 1974, is in a quiet residential area, 1 mi from downtown. The grounds of this contemporary two-story building are beautifully landscaped with lots of flowers and trees. | 250 rooms. Restaurant, bar with entertainment, in-room data ports, some kitchenettes, some refrigerators, room service, cable TV, 2 pools, hot tub, laundry facilities, business services, pets allowed (fee). | 10700 S.W. Allen Blvd. | 503/643–7444 or 800/289–1300 | fax 503/626–4553 | www.greenwoodinn.com | $79–$99 | AE, D, DC, MC, V.

Hilton Garden Inn. This tastefully appointed Hilton, just off U.S. 26, is in a pleasant suburban setting. | 150 rooms. In-room data ports, microwaves, refrigerators, indoor pool, hot tub, business services. | 15520 N.W. Gateway Court | 503/439–1717 or 800/445–8667 | fax 503/439–1818 | $150–$250 | AE, D, DC, MC, V.

Lamplighter Inn. Embankments muffle the noise from the nearby highway at this inexpensive option. Rooms are decorated in blues and mauves. There's a small shopping mall across the street with a supermarket, a lounge, and other stores, and restaurants are within walking distance. | 54 rooms, 2 suites. In-room safes, some kitchenettes, microwaves, refrigerators, cable TV, room phones. | 10207 S.W. Parkway Ave. | 503/297–2211 | fax 503/297–0915 | $55 | AE, D, DC, MC, V.

Pepper Tree Motor Inn. At this motel-style inn, built in 1979, you can drive right up to your room. It's just on the edge of Beaverton in a quiet residential area about 1 mi from downtown. | 73 rooms. Complimentary Continental breakfast, microwaves, refrigerators, cable TV, in-room VCRs, pool, hot tub, exercise equipment, laundry facilities, business services. | 10720 S.W. Allen Blvd. | 503/641–7477 or 800/453–6219 | fax 503/641–7477 | www.peppertreeinn.com | $70–$80 | AE, D, DC, MC, V.

Phoenix Inn. This four-story hotel off U.S. Highway 26 was built in 1997 and has bright, clean rooms. | 98 rooms. Indoor pool, hot tub, microwaves, refrigerators, air-conditioning, cable TV, exercise equipment. | 15402 N.W. Cornell Rd. | 503/514–8100, 888/944–8100 | $79–$89 | AE, D, DC, MC, V.

Ramada Inn. This Ramada is right off Main Street in downtown Beaverton. Near Nike headquarters, it has comfortable and contemporary rooms. | 142 rooms. Complimentary Continental breakfast, some kitchenettes, cable TV, pool, exercise equipment, business services. | 13455 S.W. Canyon Rd. | 503/643–9100 | fax 503/643–0514 | $90–$140 | AE, D, DC, MC, V.

BEND

MAP 3, F5

(Nearby towns also listed: Prineville, Redmond)

Bend is Oregon's largest city east of the Cascades. It has a population of about 35,000 and was named for the last viewpoint on the Deschutes River, Farewell Bend. The city is situated at the base of the Cascades and along the Deschutes and is famous for the recreational opportunities its location allows. Skiing, snowboarding, and other winter sports attract visitors to Bend before and after snow graces more western locales, while outdoor enthusiasts find plentiful opportunities for hiking, rafting, kayaking, fishing, golfing, and riding during the rest of the year.

Although once a timber-oriented mill town, Bend is now a popular year-round vacation destination. Shops, galleries, and restaurants abound in the downtown area, bordered by Drake Park and the river. Music festivals, arts and crafts shows, and markets keep visitors outdoors during summer months.

Information: Bend Chamber/Visitor & Convention Bureau | 63085 N. Hwy. 97, Bend, 97701 | 541/382–3221 | cityofbend@bend-or.com | www.bend-or.com/-cityofbend.

Attractions

Century Drive. For 100 mi, this forest-highway loop beginning and ending in Bend meanders among dozens of high mountain lakes offering fishing, hiking, waterskiing, and camping. To find it take Highway 46 for the first two-thirds of the trip, then take Highway 97 at LaPine to return to Bend. | Free.

Deschutes Historical Museum. Among the displays here are Indian artifacts, historical photos of the region, and a pioneer schoolroom. | 129 N.W. Idaho | 541/389–1813 | Free | Tues.–Sat. 10–4:30.

Deschutes National Forest. This 1.6-million-acre forest has 20 peaks higher than 7,000 ft, including three of Oregon's five highest mountains, more than 150 lakes, and 500 mi of streams. The Deschutes National Forest is part of the Regional Trail Park fee demonstration project. A pass is required for all day and overnight use of the trailhead facilities in 13 national forests in Oregon and Washington. | Cascades Lakes Hwy. | 541/388–2715 | fax 541/383–5531 | www.fs.fed.us/r6/deschutes | Park pass required | Daily.

High Desert Museum. The museum is on 150 acres, just next to Deschutes National Forest. There are both indoor and outdoor exhibits that focus on Western history, Native American culture, art, and wildlife. You can see live animals like raptors, river otters, porcupines, and lizards. | 59800 S. U.S. 97 | 541/382–4754 | www.highdesert.org | $7.75 | Daily 9–5.

Lava Butte and Lava River Cave. Lava River Cave is a 1-mi-long lava tube, 10 mi south of Bend. The Lava Butte area contains several large basalt lava flows as well as the 500-ft Lava Butte cinder cone. You can enter by the visitors center. | 58201 S. U.S. 97 | 541/593–2421 | $5 | May–Sept., daily 9–5.

YOUR CAR'S FIRST-AID KIT

- ❑ Bungee cords or rope to tie down trunk if necessary
- ❑ Club soda to remove stains from upholstery
- ❑ Cooler with bottled water
- ❑ Extra coolant
- ❑ Extra windshield-washer fluid
- ❑ Flares and/or reflectors
- ❑ Flashlight and extra batteries
- ❑ Hand wipes to clean hands after roadside repair
- ❑ Hose tape
- ❑ Jack and fully inflated spare
- ❑ Jumper cables
- ❑ Lug wrench
- ❑ Owner's manual
- ❑ Plastic poncho—in case you need to do roadside repairs in the rain
- ❑ Quart of oil and quart of transmission fluid
- ❑ Spare fan belts
- ❑ Spare fuses
- ❑ Tire-pressure gauge

*Excerpted from *Fodor's: How to Pack: Experts Share Their Secrets*

Mt. Bachelor Ski Area. There are five ski lodges with restaurants and bars at this ski resort 22 mi from Bend. The 9,000-ft mountain has a base at about 5,600 ft and a vertical drop of about 3,365 ft. There are lots of cross-country trails and 70 downhill runs. | Cascade Lakes Hwy | 541/382–2607 or 800/829–2442 | www.mtbachelor.com | Nov.–July, daily 8–4.

Newberry National Volcanic Monument. As you drive through this central Oregon area 10 mi south of Bend, keep in mind that you are within the caldera of a 500-square-mi volcano, one that remains very active. The monument contains 50,000 acres of lakes, lava flows, and geologic features. At its summit is Paulina Peak. | Visitor Center, 58201 S. U.S. 97 | 541/388–2715 | $3 | May–Oct., daily.

Pine Mountain Observatory. Three reflecting telescopes, with 15"-, 24"-, and 32"-diameter mirrors, each in its own domed building, monitor the universe from atop 6,500-ft Pine Mountain. Take a peek, 26 mi east of Bend. | U.S. 20, near Millican | 541/382–8331 | www.pmo-sun.uoregon.edu | $2 | Call for hours.

La Pine. This campground 27 mi south of Bend is located in a subalpine forest on a small river. It has 95 full hookups, 50 electrical sites, 5 cabins, and 3 yurts. | 5 mi off U.S. 97 | 541/388–6055 | Free; camping fee | Daily.

Pilot Butte. Three trails lead to the summit of an old cinder cone, which offers a panoramic view of Three Sisters, Mt. Jefferson, Black Butte, and Mt. Hood. | U.S 20 | 541/388–6055 | Free | Daily.

Tumalo. This campground, 5 mi northwest of Bend on U.S. 20 on the Deschutes River, has 22 full hookups, 65 tent sites, 2 tepees, and 4 yurts. There are miles of hiking and biking trails. Other recreational activities include swimming and fishing. | Off U.S. 20 | 541/382–3586 or 541/388–6055 | $3 day-use fee | Daily dawn–dusk.

Tumalo Falls. Water plunges 97 ft down the side of a mountain in a pine forest 10 mi out of town. | Franklin Ave. to Galveston Ave. | 541–388 5664 | Free | Daily.

Whitewater Rafting—Sun Country Tours. The most popular trip is the Big Eddie Thriller, which is a 3-mi trip that will take you through some class-4 rapids. Six departure times are offered daily from Bend and the Sunriver Marina. | 531 S.W. 13th St. | 541/382–6277 | www.sunriverinfo.com/recreation/rafting/suncountry | Call for prices | May–Sept., daily 7:30–7.

ON THE CALENDAR

MAY: *Pole Pedal Paddle Race.* This athletic event takes place on a weekend in mid-May. At 8 AM, contestants set out from Mt. Bachelor, 35 mi away, via alpine and cross-country skiing, bike, running, canoe, kayak, and a sprint to the finish line at Drake Park in Bend. On Sunday, there's a mini-pole-pedal-paddle race for the kids. | 541/388–0002.

Dining

Coho Grill. Contemporary. This respected restaurant serves American classics such as salmon, pot roast, and lamb. Expect seasonal Pacific Northwest dishes, too, such as fresh fish and Cascade morels in the spring, and Oregon crab in the fall. | 61535 Fargo La. | 541/388–3909 | fax 541/385–8347 | Closed Sun., Nov.–Apr. | $14–$25 | D, MC, V.

Deschutes Brewery & Public House. Contemporary. This upscale brew pub serves Black Butte Porter and Mirror Pond Pale Ale, along with burgers and sandwiches, such as smoked salmon and brewery-cured pastrami, plus chicken enchiladas, a smoked vegetable sandwich, and vegetarian black bean chili. Daily blackboard dinner specials might include smoked prime rib or grilled marlin. Portions are large. The most popular lunch items are stir fry and fish and chips, and prices are reduced on Monday nights. | 1044 N.W. Bond St. | 541/382–9242 | Reservations not accepted | $6–$25 | MC, V.

Ernesto's Italian Restaurant. Italian. Authentic Italian cuisine is served in a former church building. Choose from pizzas, calzones, or a selection of pasta dishes. Kids' menu. | 1203 N.E. 3rd St. | 541/389–7274 | No lunch | $12–$22 | V.

Giuseppe's Ristorante. Italian. This award-winning downtown restaurant serves authentic Italian dishes: homemade pastas, chicken, seafood, steak, vegetarian dishes, and a very popular veal piccata. | 932 N.W. Bond St. | 541/389–8899 | Closed Mon. No lunch | $10.95–$18.95 | AE, DC, MC, V.

Meadows. Contemporary. This dining room with a view of the Sunriver Resort and surrounding mountains features Pacific Northwest cuisine. Entrées include fresh pastas and regional fish. No smoking. | 1 Center Dr. | 541/593–3740 | $22–$40 | AE, D, DC, MC, V.

Pine Tavern. Contemporary. Opened in 1936, this is Bend's oldest restaurant. The 200-year-old, 100-ft-tall Ponderosa pines growing inside are the centerpiece of the dining room that overlooks the Deschutes River. Known for seafood and steak, all the produce is locally grown. There is seating on the patio which looks onto a pond and beautifully landscaped area. Salad bar. Kids' menu. No smoking. | 967 N.W. Brooks | 541/382–5581 | No lunch Sun. | $20–$30 | AE, D, DC, MC, V.

Roszak's Fish House. Seafood. This fish house, which opened in 1981, serves more than just fish—the menu includes other seafood entrées, plus prime rib, salads, and pasta dishes. Kids' menu. No smoking. | 1230 N.E. 3rd St. | 541/382–3173 | No lunch weekends | $12–$23 | MC, V.

Tony's. Italian. Set in an early American building, this restaurant serves up good pizza and sandwiches. The fireplace is a warm friend on a cold Bend night. Kids' menu. | 415 N.E. 3rd St. | 541/389–5858 | Breakfast also available | $8–$16 | D, MC, V.

Westside Bakery and Café. American. Breakfast selections and baked goods are the draws at this kid-friendly café. The three dining rooms are chock-full of antiques and toys. Kids' menu. | 1005 N.W. Galveston Ave. | 541/382–3426 | Breakfast also available. No supper | $5–$10 | D, MC, V.

Lodging

Bend Riverside Motel. Comfort and efficiency are the bywords at this nicely landscaped property only four blocks from downtown and within walking distance of shops and restaurants, including Deschutes Brewery & Public House. Every room has a balcony overlooking Pioneer Park along the river. | 68 rooms. Some kitchenettes, some microwaves, some refrigerators, cable TV, indoor-outdoor pool, outdoor hot tub, 1 tennis court, laundry facilities, laundry service, business services. | 1565 N.W. Hill St. | 541/388–4000 or 800/228–4019 | fax 541/388–4000 or 800/228–4019 | bendrive@teleport.com | $58–$89 | AE, D, DC, MC, V.

Best Inn & Suites. You can walk from here to a pub next door, restaurants, and all the bargains at Prime Outlets, and it's only five minutes to the High Desert Museum. There's a fireplace and complimentary coffee in the lobby at this friendly place, and the sauna is open 24 hours. The mural of a lake scene in the pool area was painted by a local artist. | 59 rooms, 6 suites. Complimentary breakfast, in-room data ports, some kitchenettes, some microwaves, some refrigerators, some in-room hot tubs, cable TV, indoor pool, hot tub, sauna, gym, laundry facilities, laundry service, business services. | 61200 S. Hwy. 97 | 541/388–2227 or 800/237–8466 | fax 541/388–8820 | $50–$59 | AE, D, DC, MC, V.

Best Western Entrada Lodge. Next to the Deschutes National Forest and 1 mi from the Deschutes River, this Best Western property in southwest Bend is surrounded by pine trees. | 79 rooms. Complimentary Continental breakfast, in-room data ports, cable TV, pool, hot tub, cross-country and downhill skiing, business services, pets allowed (fee). | 19221 Century Dr. | 541/382–4080 | $59–$99 | AE, D, DC, MC, V.

Black Butte Ranch. This resort is near the town of Sisters on 1,830 wooded acres. All condo units and homes have wood-burning fireplaces. Many rooms look onto a golf course. | 120 rooms. Bar, dining room, snack bar, some kitchenettes, some microwaves, in-room VCRs, 4 pools, wading pool, driving range, 18-hole golf courses, putting green, tennis, exercise equipment, bicycles, cross-country and downhill skiing, video games, Ping-Pong, air hockey, children's programs (ages 3–12), playground, business services. | 13653 Hawkes Bared | 541/595–6211 or 800/452–7455 | fax 541/595–2077 | www.blackbutte.com | $85–$178 apartments (7–day minimum in July, Aug.); $130–$315 houses (7–day minimum in July, Aug.) | AE, D, DC, MC, V.

Cimarron Motor Inn—North. This late 1970s motel in central Bend has comfortable rooms with king-size beds. It is close to the downtown commercial area. | 60 rooms. Complimentary Continental breakfast, some microwaves, cable TV, pool, cross-country and downhill skiing, business services, some pets allowed (fee). | 201 N.E. Third St. | 541/382–8282 or 800/304–4050 | fax 541/388–6833 | $45–$74 | AE, D, DC, MC, V.

Hampton Inn. You'll find contemporary rooms at this property set on three landscaped acres close to downtown Bend. | 99 rooms. Complimentary Continental breakfast, in-room data ports, cable TV, pool, hot tub, business services, pets allowed. | 15 N.E. Butler Market Rd. | 541/388–4114 | fax 541/389–3261 | www.hamptoninn.com | $74–$89 | AE, D, DC, MC, V.

Inn of the Seventh Mountain. Nestled in ponderosa pines, 7 mi west of Bend in the Deschutes National Forest, the Inn has been offering year-round outdoor activities and relaxation for 25 years. In summer, white-water rafting and fishing are right out your door. Five golf courses are within 15 minutes, and Mt. Bachelor is 14 mi away. Canoe and rafting trips can be organized. | 220 studios and apartments. Bar, dining rooms, picnic area, some kitchenettes, microwaves, some refrigerators, cable TV, 2 pools, wading pool, hot tubs, tennis, boating, fishing, bicycles, ice-skating, cross-country and downhill skiing, sleigh rides, snowmobiling, children's programs (ages 4–11), playgrounds, laundry facilities, business services. | 18575 S.W. Century Dr. | 541/382–8711 | fax 541/382–3517 | reservations@7thmtn.com | www.7thmtn.com | $64–$130 studios, $260–$302 apartments | AE, D, DC, MC, V.

Lara House Bed and Breakfast Inn. This cross-gabled 1910 Craftsman house stands on a sloping street above Drake Park and Mirror Pond, a five-minute walk from downtown. It has original woodwork, an alderwood-coffered ceiling in the living room, a lodge-size fireplace, and a huge sunroom overlooking the park. All the guest rooms have seating areas, and breakfast can be taken in the dining room or sunroom or on the terraced redwood deck. | 6 rooms. Complimentary breakfast, some microwaves, some refrigerators, some in-room hot tubs, no TV in some rooms, TV in common area, outdoor hot tub, no smoking. | 640 N.W. Congress St. | 541/388–4064 or 800/766–4064 | fax 541/388–4064 or 800/766–4064 | www.moriah.com/larahouse | $125 | AE, D, MC, V.

Mt. Bachelor Village Resort. River Ridge units have river views and gas fireplaces. The resort is in a woodland setting along the Deschutes River. Ski house condos are also available. | 130 apartments. Restaurant, picnic area, some microwaves, refrigerators, in-room hot tubs, pool, 6 tennis courts, cross-country and downhill skiing, laundry facilities, business services. | 19717 Mt. Bachelor Dr. | 541/389–5900 or 800/452–9846 | fax 541/388–7820 | mbvr@enpnet.com | www.mtbachelorvillage.com | $105–$335 | AE, MC, V.

Red Lion Inn—North. This is a small two-story building with limited services, just 5 minutes walk from downtown. Red Lion's rooms are comfortable in a quiet area that caters to both families and businesspeople. | 75 rooms. Restaurant, in-room data ports, cable TV, pool, hot tub, business services, pets allowed. | 1415 N.E. Third St. | 541/382–7011 | fax 541/382–7934 | $54–$79 | AE, D, DC, MC, V.

Riverhouse Motor Inn. Rooms at this motel on the Deschutes River are spacious with contemporary oak furniture. Some of the rooms have fireplaces while many have river views. It is a cut or two above what you'd expect given its very reasonable rates. | 220 rooms, 29 suites. Restaurant, in-room data ports, some kitchenettes, some microwaves, room service, cable TV, in-room VCRs (movies), 2 pools (1 indoor), driving range, 18-hole golf course, putting green, exercise equipment, laundry facilities, business services, pets allowed. | 3075 N. U.S. 97 | 541/389–3111 or 800/547–3928 | fax 541/389–0870 | $77–$209, $114–$209 suites | AE, D, DC, MC, V.

Rock Springs. Horseback riding is the focus at this guest ranch set amid ponderosa pines in the Cascade foothills—there are 65 horses and access to 12,000 acres of high desert. | 26 cottages. Dining room, picnic area, refrigerators, no TV in cottages, TV in common area, pool, pond, hot tub, tennis, exercise equipment, horseback riding, cross-country and downhill skiing, game room with video games and Ping-Pong, children's programs (ages 3–16), laundry facilities, business services, airport shuttle. | 64201 Tyler Rd. | 541/382–1957 or 800/225–3833 | fax 541/382–7774 | info@rocksprings.com | www.rocksprings.com | $675–$1000/week (7–day minimum stay in summer) | Closed Sept.–mid-June | AE, D, DC, MC, V.

Sather House Bed and Breakfast. Three blocks from Drake Park on the river and within walking distance of downtown, this 1911 house, on the National Register of Historic Places, combines Colonial Revival and Craftsman styles. Period furnishings complement the original Douglas fir woodwork. Guest rooms are light and airy; the Garden Room has four windows; and the house has a wraparound porch with wicker furniture. Breakfast is served in the formal dining room and afternoon tea is served. | 4 rooms with bath. Complimentary breakfast, no air-conditioning, cable TV, no room phones, no kids under 6, no smoking. | 7 N.W. Tumalo Ave. | 541/388–1065 or 888/388–1065 | fax 541/330–0591 | www.moriah.com/sather | $80–$115 | AE, D, MC, V.

Shilo Inn Suites Hotel. On the Deschutes River and across from the Bend River Mall, this Shilo was recently remodeled. | 151 rooms. Bar, complimentary breakfast buffet, some kitchenettes, microwaves, refrigerators, cable TV, 2 pools (1 indoor), exercise equipment, cross-country and downhill skiing, laundry facilities, business services, airport shuttle, pets allowed (fee). | 3105 O.B. Riley Rd. | 541/389–9600 | fax 541/382–4310 | $99–$139 | AE, D, DC, MC, V.

Sunriver Resort. The Deschutes River flows through Sunriver, one of Oregon's premier outdoor resort destinations. It's convenient to skiing at Mt. Bachelor as well as white-water rafting, canoeing, high-desert hiking and mountain biking. A former army base, the self-contained community has stores, a nature center, entertainment, and even a private airstrip—all in a pine-scented desert landscape. | 260 apartments and houses. 3 restaurants, pub, picnic area, some kitchenettes, cable TV, 3 pools, 3 wading pools, barbershop, beauty salon, hot tubs, driving range, 18-hole golf courses, putting green, 28 tennis courts, horseback riding, racquetball, marina, water sports, boating, fishing, bicycles, ice-skating, cross-country and downhill skiing, children's programs (ages 3–14), playground, laundry facilities, business services, airport shuttle. | 1 Center Dr., Sunriver | 541/593–1000 or 800/547–3922 | fax 541/593–5458 | www.sunriver-resort.com | $209 apartments; $200–$550 houses | AE, D, DC, MC, V.

BROOKINGS

MAP 3, B8

(Nearby towns also listed: Coos Bay, Gold Beach)

The little town of Brookings, on the southern Oregon Coast just north of the California border, calls itself Oregon's "banana belt" and, in fact, is often noted for having the highest temperatures in the state. As a result, Brookings also bills itself as the home of winter flowers. The area supplies the majority of lilies in the United States. A botanical garden and an azalea park are among the town's prized assets.

Information: Brookings-Harbor Chamber of Commerce | 16330 Lower Harbor Rd., Brookings 97415 | 541/469–3181 | 541/469–4094 | chamber@wave.net | www.brookingsor.com.

Attractions

Alfred A. Loeb State Park. This park, which is set in a fragrant myrtle forest on the Chetco River 10 mi from Brookings, offers some of the best salmon and steelhead fishing in southern Oregon. | Off U.S. 101 | 541/469–2021 or 800/551–6949 | www.prd.state.or.us | Free | Daily.

Azalea City Park. Five varieties of the flower bloom at this park on the edge of town, which also includes a playground filled with imaginatively designed wooden equipment. | Off North Bank Chetco River Road | 541/469–2163 | Free | Daily.

Chetco Valley Historical Museum. This museum, 2 mi south of Brookings, is inside a mid-19th-century stagecoach stop and trading post. An iron casting with a likeness of Queen Elizabeth I has led to speculation that it was left during a landing by Sir Francis Drake. On a nearby hill stands the World Champion Cypress Tree, 99 ft tall with a 27-ft circumference. | 5461 Museum Rd. | 541/469–6651 | Donation | Memorial Day–Labor Day, Wed.–Sun. noon–5; Labor Day–Memorial Day, Fri.–Sun. noon–5.

Harris Beach State Park. There is plenty to see and do at this park where you can watch the gray whales migrate in spring and winter. Bird Island, also called Goat Island, is a National Wildlife Sanctuary and a breeding site for rare birds. There is a campground with 34 full hookups, 52 electrical and 66 tent sites, and 4 yurts. | U.S. 101 | 541/469–2021 or 800/551–6949 | www.prd.state.or.us | Free | Daily.

Samuel H. Boardman State Park. This 12-mi-long linear park, 4 mi north of Brookings, runs along the rugged, steep coast. Highlights include a view of Arch Rock and Natural Bridges, as well as a 27-mi-long Oregon Coast Trail which can be walked. | U.S. 101 | 541/469–2021 or 800/551–6949 | www.prd.state.or.us | Free | Daily.

ON THE CALENDAR

MAY: *Azalea Festival.* The popular flower is celebrated at this event held annually at Azalea City Park every Memorial Day weekend. There is an Azalea Festival Parade as well as a street fair. | 541/469–3181.

JULY: *Southern Oregon Kite Festival.* On the third weekend in July, this festival at the Port of Brookings Harbor attracts both amateur and world-class kite fliers and teams for demonstrations, crafts shows, and kids' activities. | 541/469–2218.

Dining

City Grill. American. This downtown, Victorian-style place done in mauve and burgundy is in the 1915 Historic Central Building, formerly the California & Oregon Lumber Company. Try Uncle Hootie's special—prawns in Alfredo sauce over linguine with steak on the side—or if you're in the mood for something lighter, order fish and chips. | 703 Chetco Ave. | 541/412–0375 | Closed Mon. | $10–$20 | AE, D, DC, MC, V.

Smuggler's Cove. Seafood. Fishing vessels docked in the next boat basin and picture windows looking out to sea lend a salty ambience to this low-key restaurant. The daily seafood specials—usually halibut and salmon—are the best bets. Try the fish and chips or the crab melt for lunch. | 16011 Boat Basin Rd. | 541/469–6006 | $12–$25 | MC, V.

Lodging

Best Western Beachfront Inn. The ocean is right outside your window at this hotel. All rooms have balconies facing the ocean, no more than 50–300 ft away so you will be closer to the water than at any other hotel in southern Oregon. | 99 rooms, 3 suites. No air-conditioning, in-room data ports, some kitchenettes, microwaves, refrigerators, some in-room hot tubs, cable TV, outdoor pool, outdoor hot tub, laundry facilities, business services. | 16008 Boat Basin Rd. | 541/469–7779 or 800/468–4081 | fax 541/469–0283 | www.bestwestern.com | $79 | AE, D, DC, MC, V.

Best Western Brookings Inn. Built 30 years ago, this small hotel is right on U.S. 101, ½ mile from downtown Brookings and minutes from the Pacific. The rooms are comfortable and the pool is glass enclosed. | 68 rooms. Restaurant, cable TV, some in-room hot tubs, indoor pool, hot tub. | 1143 Chetco Ave. U.S. 101 | 541/469–2173 or 800/822–9087 | fax 541/469–2996 | www.bestwestern.com | $70–$92 | AE, D, DC, MC, V.

★ **Chetco River Inn.** Forty acres of private forest surround this remote inn 17 mi from Brookings up the North Bank Road along the Chetco River. The house stands only 100 ft from one of the cleanest rivers in the country, so you can swim in summer and fish in fall and winter. Guests also come here to hike, hunt wild mushrooms, and relax in the library or in front of the fireplace. There's a lavender and herb garden, as well. Rooms have panoramic river and forest views. | 5 rooms, 1 cottage. Picnic area, complimentary breakfast, no air-conditioning, some in-room hot tubs, no room phones, boating, fishing, library, laundry facilities, no smoking. | 21202 High Prairie Rd. | 541/670–1645 or 800/327–2688 | fax 541/469–4341 | www.chetcoriverinn.com | $125 | MC, V.

Spindrift Motor Inn. This motel is on top of a cliff overlooking the ocean. All the rooms have balconies and good views. | 35 rooms. Refrigerators, cable TV, business services. | 1215 Chetco Ave. | 541/469–5345 or 800/292–1171 | fax 541/469–5213 | $49–$65 | AE, D, DC, MC, V.

BURNS

MAP 3, I6

(Nearby town also listed: Frenchglen)

Named after poet Robert Burns, this town was the unofficial capital of the 19th-century cattle empires that staked claims to these southeastern Oregon high-plateau grasslands. Today, Burns is a small cowboy town with only about 3,000 residents, surrounded by the wide-open range lands of Harney County, the ninth largest county in the United States. Outdoor recreation options at this gateway to the Steens Mountains include fishing, backpacking, camping, boating, and hiking. The Malheur National Wildlife Refuge, just 30 miles to the south, offers unrivaled bird-watching opportunities.

Information: **Harney County Chamber of Commerce** | 76 E. Washington St., Burns 97720 | 541/573–2636 | www.harneycounty.com.

Attractions

Harney County Historical Museum. This small museum is located on the site of a former brewery. A photo collection documents the area's history. There's also a display of handmade quilts and a turn-of-the-20th-century kitchen exhibit. | 18 W. D St. | 541/573–5618 | Free | May–Oct., Tues.–Sat. 9–5.

Malheur National Wildlife Refuge. More than 320 species of birds can be seen at this 185,765-acre refuge which is 32 mi southeast of Burns. At least 250 species also use the area as a feeding stop during migration. It is also home to as many as 58 mammal species. | Hwy. 205 | 541/493–2612 | www.rl.fws.gov/malheur | Free | Daily.

Rockhounding. Rock hounds love Harney County for its fossils, jasper, obsidian, oolite, agates, and thunder eggs. In the Stinkingwater Mountains, 30 mi east of Burns, you can find petrified wood and gemstones. Warm Spring Reservoir has agates. At Charlie Creek, west of Burns, and at Radar, to the north, you can find obsidians. Remember these are public lands and it's illegal to remove arrowheads and other artifacts. The Harney County Chamber of Commerce can give you more information. | 541/573–2636 | www.harneycounty.com.

ON THE CALENDAR

APR.: ***John Scharff Migratory Bird Festival.*** Thousands of migratory birds rest and feed in the high desert surrounding Burns. Tours, workshops, and a wildlife art show and auction are featured. Tours leave from Burns High School. The dinner is held at the Elks Lodge or the Old Camp Casino. | 541/573–2636.

JUNE: ***Intertribal Pow Wow.*** The second weekend of the month you can view traditional tribal dances and browse the wares of Native American vendors at the Harney County Fairgrounds. | 541/573–2088.

SEPT.: ***Harney County Rodeo & Fair.*** This local fair with carnival rides, livestock, and craft displays also has a rodeo with bucking broncos. The event draws up to 5,000 people each day to the Harney County Fairgrounds for five days, beginning right after Labor Day. | 541/573–6852.

Dining

El Toreo. Mexican. Here you can get large portions of Mexican staples: enchiladas, tacos, tostadas, tamales, chili rellenos, and chimichangas. But most folks still come here for fajitas. | 293 N. Broadway | 541/573–1829 | $7.50–$14 | MC, V.

Hilander Restaurant. Eclectic. The wood-paneled Hilander caters to tradition with such popular American dishes as pork chops with apple sauce and roast beef with brown gravy, but the Chinese menu is the main thing here, with spicy Szechuan chicken, curried beef, foo yung, and chow mein dishes. | 195 N. Broadway | 541/573–2111 | Closed Mon. | $7–$10 | MC, V.

Pine Room Cafe. Steak. Paintings of Harney County scenery cover the walls of this restaurant, which features steaks and seafood. Try the chicken liver Bordelaise or the stuffed prawns. Kids' menu. | 543 W. Monroe St. | 541/573–6631 | Closed Sun.–Mon. No lunch | $12–$28 | MC, V.

Lodging

Bontemps Hotel. With its mixture of old and new furnishings, old-fashioned tile showers, and mirrored alcoves, the Bontemps has a 1930s charm recalling the days when motels were cozy and had distinct personalities. The whole town of Burns is within walking distance. | 12 rooms, 3 suites. Some kitchenettes, some microwaves, some refrigerators, cable TV. | 74 W. Monroe St. | 541/573–2037 or 800/229–1394 | fax 541/573–2577 | $36.95 | MC, V.

Days Inn. This is the closest hotel to the downtown area. The two-story stucco building was built in 1959 and has a courtyard filled with trees and plants. | 52 rooms. Cable TV, pool, gym, business services, pets allowed. | 577 W. Monroe | 541/573–2047 | fax 541/573–3828 | www.daysinn.com | $41–$85 | AE, D, DC, MC, V.

Silver Spur. Thirty-five mi from the Malheur National Wildlife Refuge and near two national forests, this hotel is known for its down-to-earth, home-style coziness. | 26 rooms. Complimentary Continental breakfast, cable TV, airport shuttle. | 789 N. Broadway | 541/573–2077 | fax 541/573–3921 | $38–$50 | AE, D, DC, MC, V.

CANNON BEACH

MAP 3, C2

(Nearby towns also listed: Astoria, Manzamith, Rockaway Beach, Seaside, Tillamook)

Marked by the monolithic Haystack Rock just offshore, Cannon Beach is considered by many to be Oregon's premier artsy haven on the Pacific Coast. On any given day, a visitor might be entertained by a sky filled with colorful kites or groups of enthusiastic sand-castle builders along the miles of wide beach. But just as enticing are the dozens of galleries, shops, and bistros that beckon beachgoers. Strict planning regulations have helped Cannon Beach maintain its avant-garde, upscale air, replete with bookstores, but minus arcades.

Information: Cannon Beach Chamber of Commerce | Box 64, Cannon Beach 97110 | 503/436–2623.

Attractions

Ecola State Park. A winding road along Tillamook Head will lead you to an extraordinary view of the Pacific Ocean. At this park, 2 mi north of Cannon Beach, you might see elk and deer as you drive through the forest. | U.S. 101 | 503/436–2844 or 800/551–6949 | www.prd.state.or.us | $3 | Daily.

Neahkahnie Mountain. The road takes hair-raising curves as it climbs to 700 ft above the Pacific around the flank of this 1,661-ft mountain south of Cannon Beach. The views are dramatic. Carvings on nearby beach rocks and old Native American legends gave rise to a tale that a fortune in gold doubloons from a sunken Spanish galleon is buried somewhere on the mountainside. | U.S. 101.

Oswald West State Park. Several different trails wind through the park, taking you to the beach and the Cape Falcon overlook. | Ecola Park Road | 503/436–2623 or 800/551–6949 | www.prd.state.or.us | Free | Mar.–Nov., daily.

ON THE CALENDAR

JUNE: *Sandcastle Contest.* One of the largest sand building contests on the West Coast, this two-day event features hundreds of sand sculptures, castles, and drawings built on downtown Cannon Beach. | 503/436–2623.

NOV.: *Stormy Weather Arts Festival.* On the first weekend in November, six to eight local artists are honored with a special exhibition and auction in the Chamber of Commerce hall. A reception to meet the artists is open to visitors. | 503/436–2623.

Dining

★ **The Bistro.** Contemporary. This 12-table restaurant enhances the three-course prix-fixe dinners with flowers, candlelight, and classical music. The menu includes imaginative Continental-influenced renditions of fresh local seafood and specials such as lamb, prawns, oysters, and a Pacific seafood stew. | 263 N. Hemlock St. | 503/436–2661 | Reservations essential | Closed Tues., Nov.–Jan. No lunch | $13.75–$22 | MC, V.

Dooger's. Seafood. Like the original Dooger's in Seaside, the Cannon Beach branch serves superb seafood and steaks in a casual, contemporary setting. Don't pass up the clam chowder. No smoking. Kids' menu. | 1371 S. Hemlock St. | 503/436–2225 | Closed 2 wks in Jan. | $20–$30 | AE, MC, V.

Lazy Susan Café. Café. This laid-back spot, a favorite for breakfast in Cannon Beach, welcomes you with quiche, omelets, hot cereal, waffles, home fries, and fresh-baked scones. | Coaster Square, 126 N. Hemlock St. | 503/436–2816 | Reservations not accepted | Closed Tues. No dinner Sun.–Mon., Wed.–Thurs. | $7.95–$10.95 | No credit cards.

Stephanie Inn. Contemporary. The dining room of this handsome oceanfront hotel 1¼ mi south of town has a river-rock fireplace, an open kitchen, and views of mountain scenery. There are two seatings for the four-course prix-fixe meal, which offers a choice of seafood or non-seafood entrées (such as shrimp-stuffed halibut and NY strip steak), but vegetarian and other requests can be honored. | 2740 S. Pacific | 503/436–2221 or 800/633–3466 | fax 503/436–9711 | Reservations essential | $36.95 | AE, D, DC, MC, V.

Lodging

Cannon Beach Hotel. Walk to the beach and downtown shopping from this restored, turn-of-the-20th-century, European-style inn located at the entrance to Haystack Rock. There's a cozy fireplace in the lobby. Some rooms have a fireplace. | 9 rooms. Restaurant, complimentary Continental breakfast, no air-conditioning, some in-room hot tubs, cable TV, hot tub, business services, no smoking. | 1116 S. Hemlock | 503/436–1392 | fax 503/436–2101 | $73–$157 | AE, D, DC, MC, V.

Grey Whale Inn. This small charming inn dates from 1948. It is in a very quiet residential neighborhood, just a 5-minute walk to the beach or a 20-minute walk to Haystack Rock. All the rooms are individually decorated with original artwork, done either by the family or local artists. | 5 rooms (with shower only). No air conditioning, some kitchenettes, cable TV, in-room VCRs, no smoking. | 164 Kenai St. | 503/436–2848 | $64–$84 | MC, V.

Hallmark Resort. Large suites with fireplaces and great views make this triple-decker oceanfront resort a good choice for families or couples looking for a romantic splurge. The rooms, all with oak-tile baths, have soothing color schemes. The least expensive units do not have views. | 131 rooms, 63 suites; 4 cottages. Some kitchenettes, refrigerators, cable TV, some in-room hot tubs, indoor pool, wading pool, hot tub, exercise equipment, laundry facilities, business services, airport shuttle, pets allowed (fee). | 1400 S. Hemlock | 503/436–1566 or 800 888/448–4449 | fax 503/436–0324 | $174–$269 | AE, D, DC, MC, V.

Stephanie Inn. This three-story inn is the premier oceanfront hotel in town, right on the beach and boasting superior service and luxurious rooms with country-style furnishings, fireplaces, large bathrooms with hot tubs, and balconies with an outstanding view of Haystack Rock. It even has a library, where guests are served complimentary wine in the afternoon. | 50 rooms. Restaurant, complimentary breakfast, room service, refrigerators, in-room hot tubs, cable TV, room phones, massage, library, business services, no kids under 12, no smoking. | 2740 S. Pacific | 503/436–2221 or 800/633–3466 | fax 503/436–9711 | smajor@stephanie-inn.com | www.stephanie-inn.com | $249–$379 | AE, D, DC, MC, V.

Surfsand Resort. Many of the bright, modern rooms at this resort, within walking distance of downtown, have views of Haystack Rock and the Pacific Ocean; some are oceanfront. Many rooms have fireplaces. | 86 rooms; 5 cottages. Restaurant, bar, no air-conditioning, some kitchenettes, refrigerators, some in-room hot tubs, cable TV, in-room VCRs (movies), indoor pool, hot tub, beach, laundry facilities, airport shuttle, pets allowed (fee). | Ocean and Gower St. | 503/436–2274 or 800/547–6100 | fax 503/436–9116 | www.surfsand.com | $129–$309, $285–$375 cottages | AE, D, DC, MC, V.

Webb's Scenic Surf. This small hotel right on the beach is now run by the third generation of Webbs and suggests simpler times in Cannon Beach. One of the best deals in town, it's lovingly tended with lots of special touches: pillow shams, duvets, candles, and fresh flowers in attractive pottery. There's a nice view of Tillamook Lighthouse and you can walk to shops and galleries. | 7 rooms, 7 suites. No air-conditioning, some in-room data ports, some kitchenettes, microwaves, refrigerators, cable TV, room phones, baby-sitting, laundry facilities, no smoking. | 255 N. Larch St. | 503/436–2706 or 800/374–9322 | fax 503/436–1229 | www.at-e.com/webbsurf | $134.50 | AE, D, MC, V.

CAVE JUNCTION

MAP 3, C8

(Nearby town also listed: Grants Pass)

Once known for its nearby gold fields, the Illinois River valley of southern Oregon now is becoming better known for its vineyards and wineries, which offer tours and tastings to visitors. Cave Junction, in the heart of the valley, is a primary access point to Oregon's first national monument, the Oregon Caves, just 19 miles along the Caves Highway in the Siskiyou Mountains.

Information: Illinois Valley Chamber of Commerce | 201 Caves Hwy., Cave Junction 97523 | 541/592–3326 | www.cavejunction.com.

Attractions

Kerbyville Museum. This museum documenting area Native American and pioneer history is centered in an 1871 home on the National Registry of Historic Places. You can investigate your pioneer and mining ancestors in the research library and see exhibits of taxidermy and antique dolls, as well as local Native American artifacts. | 24195 Redwood Hwy. | 541/592–5252 | $3 | May 15–Sept. 15, Mon.–Sat. 10–5, Sun. noon–5; Sept.–May, by appointment only.

Oregon Caves National Monument. The monument is 483 acres. Above ground is what's left of an old-growth forest, which is home to a Douglas fir with the widest known base in Oregon. Three hiking trails access this forest. Below ground is an active marble cave. You can stay in the monument's Oregon Caves Lodge or dine in its restaurant, open from March through December. | Oregon Caves Rd. | 541/592–3400 | fax 541/592–6654 | www.oregoncaves.com | $7.50 | Mar.–Nov., daily 10–4.

ON THE CALENDAR

AUG.: *Wild Blackberry Festival.* The popular fruit that grows in abundance throughout Oregon is celebrated at a street fair in this small town near Oregon Caves National Monument. Food booths. | 541/592–3326.

SEPT.: *Labor Day Celebration.* The local Lion's Club puts on a three-day family extravaganza with train rides and food stands. Kids can climb poles in obstacle courses and search for money in haystacks. The celebration culminates in a parade. | 541/592–3326.

Dining

Wild River Pizza Company & Brewery. Pizza. You sit at communal redwood picnic tables in this pizza parlor on the north end of town. If you aren't in the mood for pizza, choose from fish and chips, chicken dishes, and sandwiches. There is an all-you-can eat buffet, and the restaurant's own seasonal brews are on tap. | 249 N. Redwood Hwy. | 541/592–3556 | $5–$9 | D, MC, V.

Lodging

Country Hills Resort. A motel, cabins, camping in tents, and RV parking are all available at this resort 12 mi from the Oregon Caves. A golf course is nearby. | 11 rooms. Complimentary Continental breakfast, some kitchenettes, laundry facilities, pets allowed. | 7901 Caves Hwy. | 541/592–3406 or 800/99–RVING | mike@crater-lake.com | $42–$59 | AE, D, MC, V.

Oregon Caves Lodge. This chateau hotel is located in the Oregon Caves National Monument, 20 mi east of Cave Junction. Built in 1934, the original 1930s furnishings have been retained, giving all the rooms a cozy rustic feeling. There is a beautiful fireplace in the lounge. | 22 rooms, 3 suites. Restaurants, no air-conditioning, room service, no room phones, business services, picnic area, no smoking. | 2000 Caves Hwy. | 541/592–3400 | fax 541/592–6654 | www.crater-lake.com/caves/ | $90–$125 | Closed Nov.–Apr. | MC, V.

Out N' About. You sleep among the leaves in the treehouses of this extraordinary resort—the tallest is 37 ft. One has an antique, claw-foot bath, another has separate kids' quarters connected to the main room by a swinging bridge. There is also an earthbound cabin with a view of the old-growth forest. There is a two-night minimum stay Memorial Day–Labor Day. | 7 suites. Continental breakfast. No phones, no TV, no air-conditioning. Some kitchenettes, horseback riding. | 300 Page Creek Rd. | 541/592–2208, 800/200–5484 | www.treehouses.com | $85–$150 | No credit cards.

COOS BAY

MAP 3, C6

(Nearby towns also listed: Bandon, Brookings, North Bend, Reedsport)

Coos Bay's heritage as a timber town is evident at first glance. Stands of Sitka spruce, western hemlock, and mixed evergreens surround the town; wood-chip piles for paper production and once productive lumber mills linger from its days as the largest timber-shipping port in the world. Additionally, Coos Bay has the largest natural harbor between Puget Sound and San Francisco and remains a major shipping center as well as a busy sports- and commercial-fishing port.

Coos Bay is known not only for the usual coastal attractions and activities, but also for its myrtlewood factory and three nearby state parks, including magnificent horticulture on display year-round at Shore Acres State Park and Botanical Gardens.

Information: Bay Area Chamber of Commerce | 50 E. Central, Coos Bay 97420 | 800/824–8486 | bacc@ucinet.com | www.ucinet.com/~bacc.

Attractions

Cape Arago Lighthouse. Cape Arago Lighthouse stands on a rock island just 12 mi offshore south of Coos Bay. The first lighthouse was built here in 1866, but it was destroyed by storms and erosion. A second, built in 1908, suffered the same fate. The current white tower, built in 1934, is 44 ft tall and towers 100 ft above the ocean. If you're here on a foggy day, listen for its unique foghorn. The lighthouse is connected to the mainland by a bridge. Neither are open to the public, but there's an excellent spot to view this lonely guardian and much of the coastline. From Hwy. 101, take Cape Arago Hwy. to Gregory Point, where it ends at a turnaround, and follow the short trail.

Cape Arago State Park. This park, 14 mi southwest of Coos Bay, juts out into the Pacific Ocean. It's a good place to watch for whales while seals and sea lions can be seen from the north cove trail. | Cape Arago Hwy., off U.S. 101, | 541/888–8867. | Free | Daily.

Charleston Marina Complex. The marina includes a launch ramp, a store where you can buy tackle and marine supplies, a 110-space RV park, a motel, restaurants, and gift shops. Fishing charters also set out from here. | 4535 Kingfisher Drive, Charleston | 541/888–2548 | www.charlestonmarina.com | Free | Daily.

Golden and Silver Falls State Park. Twenty-four mi north of Coos Bay on Hwy. 101, this park's old-growth forest, sprinkled with maidenhair ferns, hides two natural wonders. Silver Falls pours over a 200-ft-high semicircular rock ledge. One-quarter mi to the northwest, thundering Golden Falls is even more impressive, especially in the spring. | No phone | Free | Daily dawn–dusk.

The Oregon Connection. The gift shop sells more than 200 myrtlewood items made at the on-site factory, plus Oregon foods and wines, jewelry, homemade fudge, and Pendleton woolen clothes. You can take a free tour of the factory. | 1125 S. 1st St. | 541/267–7804 or 800/255–5318 | Free | Daily 9–5.

Shore Acres State Park and Botanical Gardens. Once the grand estate of a pioneer timber baron, Shore Acres, set on rugged sandstone cliffs high above the ocean, off U.S. 101, features lushly planted gardens with plants and flowers from around the world. | Cape Arago Hwy. | 541/888–3732 or 541/888–8867 | $3 | Daily 8–dusk.

South Slough National Estuarine Research Reserve. This 4,700-acre natural area, 5 mi southwest of Coos Bay, covers 600 acres of tidal marshes, mudflats, and open water channels. Some of the species represented include the great blue heron, elks, and ghost shrimp. | Seven Devils Rd., Charleston | 541/888–5558 | www.southsloughestuary.com | Free | Visitors Center: June–Aug., daily 8:30–4:30; Sept.–May, weekdays 8:30–4:30; trails open daily dawn to dusk.

Sunset Bay State Park. This park, 2 mi south of Charleston, includes cliffs and beaches, and a campground with 29 full hookups, 34 electrical and 72 tent sites, and 4 yurts. Its lagoon is protected from the sea, making it one of the few places on the Oregon coast where you can swim without worrying about the undertow or currents. You can also hike to Shore

Acres and Cape Arago state parks from here. | Cape Arago Hwy., off U.S. 101 | 541/888–4902 or 800/551–6949 | www.prd.state.or.us | Free | Daily.

ON THE CALENDAR

JULY: *Oregon Coast Music Festival.* What began as a three-day celebration of the music of Haydn has grown into a two-week bonanza of music including classical, jazz, folk, dance, choral, concert band, blues, chamber, and eclectic offerings held at various locations in Coos Bay, North Bend, Charleston, Bandon, and Reedsport. The centerpiece of this summer event is the Festival Orchestra. An internationally recognized soloist performs as special guest. | 541/267–0938.

AUG.: *Blackberry Arts Festival.* Since 1987, the Blackberry Arts Festival takes place each year on the last weekend of August. For two days, three or four blocks of Central St. are lined by booths of vendors selling arts and crafts and, of course, goodies made with blackberries: pies, cobblers, ice cream, jams and jellies, and more. There are music and entertainment, too. | 541/751–9663.

Dining

★ **Blue Heron Bistro.** American. Subtle preparations of local seafood, chicken, and pasta are served up at this busy bistro. The innovative soups and desserts are excellent. The skylit tile-floor dining room is decorated with natural wood and blue linen and there is dining outside on the patio. | 100 W. Commercial St. | 541/267–3933 | Closed Oct. and Sundays | $12–$16 | AE, D, MC, V.

Kum-Yon's. Pan-Asian. This small place on the main drag may seem simple, but the Korean and Japanese dishes, including sushi, sashimi, and kung-pao shrimp, are satisfying and cheap. | 835 S. Broadway | 541/269–2662 | fax 541/267–3821 | Closed Mon. | $9–$20 | AE, D, MC, V.

Portside. Seafood. You will be eating fish caught that day at this nautical-theme restaurant that overlooks the Charleston boat basin off of U.S. 101. The view of the harbor through the restaurant's picture windows is pretty and peaceful. When the weather cooperates, there is dining on the patio. Friday nights there is an all-you-can-eat seafood buffet. Try the steamed Dungeness crab with drawn butter, bouillabaisse, or fresh salmon. Entertainment Wed.–Sun. Kids' menu. | 8001 Kingfisher Rd., Charleston | 541/888–5544 | $13–$26 | AE, DC, MC, V.

Lodging

Best Western Holiday. You can walk to the beach from this chain motel; the boardwalk is two blocks away. The motel is surrounded by a large lawn set with tables and benches. | 77 rooms, 6 suites. Complimentary Continental breakfast, refrigerators, in-room hot tubs (in suites), cable TV, exercise equipment, indoor pool, hot tub, laundry facilities. | 411 N. Bayshore Dr. | 541/269–5111 or 800/228–8655 | www.bestwestern.com | $81–$91, $88–$115 | AE, D, DC, MC, V.

Coos Bay Manor. This 1912 Colonial Revival home is on the National Register of Historic Places. There are detailed woodwork, high ceilings, antiques and period reproductions, and an unusual interior balcony on the second floor that leads to the large rooms. Breakfast is served in the wainscotted dining room or on the balcony. | 5 rooms. Complimentary breakfast, no air-conditioning, some in-room data ports, cable TV, laundry facilities, no kids under 4, no smoking. | 955 S. 5th St. | 541/269–1224 or 800/269–1224 | fax 541/269–1224 | cbmanor@gte.net | $79–$100 | AE, D, MC, V.

Red Lion Inn. This motel is on the bay, six blocks north of the city center and boardwalk. There is a putting green on the grounds. | 143 rooms. Restaurant, bar with entertainment, in-room data ports, room service, cable TV, pool, business services, some pets allowed. | 1313 N. Bayshore Dr. | 541/267–4141 | fax 541/267–2884 | $65–$99 | AE, D, DC, MC, V.

CORVALLIS

MAP 3, D4

(Nearby towns also listed: Albany, Eugene, Salem)

The town of Corvallis is situated in the lush Willamette Valley with the Willamette River nearby. Its name derives from the Latin expression meaning "heart of the valley." Corvallis is familiar to most people as the location of Oregon State University; however, its 50,000 residents are involved in more than academic pursuits. Driving the area's economy is a growing engineering and high-tech industry, including longtime Corvallis employer Hewlett Packard, a burgeoning wine industry, and more traditional local agricultural crops, such as grass and legume seeds.

Corvallis offers plenty of outdoor activities as well as scenic attractions, from covered bridges to local wineries and gardens.

Information: Corvallis Convention and Visitor's Bureau | 420 N.W. 2nd, Corvallis 97330 | 541/757–1544 | ccvb@visitcorvallis.com | www.visitcorvallis.com.

OR

Attractions

Avery Park. This 75-acre park includes rose and rhododendron gardens, jogging trails, and picnic shelters. | South 15th St. and U.S. 20 | 541/757–6918 | Free | Weekdays.

Benton County Historical Museum. There are more than 20,000 pioneer and Native American artifacts on display. There is also a cut glass and porcelain collection, the reconstruction of a Victorian parlor, and a costume exhibit. | 1101 Main St., Philomath | 541/929–6230 | Free | Tues.–Sat. 10–4, Sun. 1–5.

Finley National Wildlife Refuge. This refuge is a bird watcher's paradise, with large fields of grasses and grains and a wetland area that attract Canada geese, grouse, pheasants, quail, wood ducks, and other varieties of birds, as well as numerous deer. A herd of large Roosevelt elk also calls this area home. | 26208 Finley Refuge Rd. | 541/757–7236 | fax 541/757–4450 | www.fwf.gov | Free | Dawn to dusk.

Oregon State University. Oregon's second largest university, set on a 500-acre campus, is home to 15,000 students. The academic focus is on agricultural sciences and engineering. The Horner Museum (Gill Coliseum, 26th and Washington Sts.) has displays of Oregon's animal, mineral, and human history. | 15th and Jefferson Sts. | 541/737–0123 or 541/737–1000 | www.oregonstate.edu | Free | Daily.

Siuslaw National Forests. The highest point in the Coast Range at 4,097 ft, Mary's Peak offers panoramic views of the Cascades, Willamette Valley, and the rest of the Coast Range. On a clear day you can see as far as the Pacific Ocean. There are several picnicking areas, more than 10 mi of hiking trails, and a small campground. There are stands of noble fir and alpine meadows. The forest, which is 2 mi from Corvallis, includes the Oregon Dunes National Recreation Area, and the Cape Perpetua Interpretive Center. | Rte. 34 Hwy. 3024 | 541/750–7000 | www.fs.fed.us/r6/siuslaw | Free | Daily.

Tyee Wine Cellars. This winery makes Pinot Noir, Pinot Gris, Pinot Blanc, Chardonnay, and Gewürztraminer. | 26335 Greenberry Rd. | www.winepressnw.com/wineries/corvallis/tyee.html | 541/753–8754 | Free | July–Aug., Fri.–Mon. noon–5; May–Dec., weekends noon–5; Jan.–Mar. by appointment.

ON THE CALENDAR

JULY: *Da Vinci Days.* Educational, artistic, scientific, and technological assets of the region are showcased at this three-day event held on the Oregon State University campus the third weekend in July. Music is performed on several stages. There are also races, street performers, food booths, and a children's village. | 541/757–6363.

AUG.: ***Benton County Fair and Rodeo.*** Festivities include animal exhibits and events, quilting and sewing, and a farmers market. Well-known musical entertainers perform on the main stage. | 110 S.W. 53rd St. | 541/757–1521.

SEPT.: ***Corvallis Fall Festival.*** An arts and crafts fair includes more than 180 booths featuring textiles, wearable art, hand-crafted ceramics, decorative and functional wood, pottery, jewelry, leather, and photography. There is also a street dance and live entertainment held in Central Park. | 541/752–9655.

Dining

Big River. Contemporary. This popular Corvallis restaurant is in the former Greyhound bus depot. The menu emphasizes foods from Oregon such as pan-seared salmon, as well as grilled chicken and roasted lamb shank. There's live jazz and blues on Friday and Saturday night. | 101 N.W. Jackson St. | 541/757–0694 | fax 541/757–0698 | Closed Sun. No lunch Sat. | $12–$20 | AE, MC, V.

The Gables. Continental. The most romantic restaurant in Corvallis has dark wood paneling and a straightforward menu of steaks, seafood, local lamb, and prime ribs. The portions are huge and satisfying. Kids' menu, early-bird suppers (weekdays). | 1121 N.W. 9th St. | 541/752–3364 | No lunch | $18–$30 | AE, D, DC, MC, V.

Michael's Landing. Contemporary. Located in a former railroad depot overlooking the Willamette River, this restaurant is known for its large menu of steak, seafood, chicken, and pasta dishes. Try the Northwest salmon baked in a wine and butter sauce. Kids' menu. | 603 N.W. 2nd St. | 541/754–6141 | Breakfast also available | $20–$25 | AE, D, DC, MC, V.

Lodging

Best Western Grand Manor Inn. This comfortable chain motel is conveniently located 1½ mi from Oregon State University. The three-story building is in a business district and within walking distance of a movie theatre. The high-ceiling lobby has a fireplace. | 55 rooms. Complimentary Continental breakfast, in-room data ports, microwaves, refrigerators, cable TV, pool, exercise equipment, business services. | 925 N.W. Garfield | 541/758–8571 | fax 541/758–0834 | www.bestwestern.com | $69–$150 | AE, D, DC, MC, V.

Hanson Country Inn. This huge 7,100-square-ft 1928 Dutch Colonial on a high knoll overlooking the Willamette Valley was once headquarters of a poultry-breeding business. Restored, it now boasts a massive fireplace in the living room, many sitting areas, tall windows, and a sunporch with stained-glass windows and rattan furniture. Rooms have views of either the English garden or the valley, and the largest has broad views from windows on three sides. The cottage is at the edge of the woods and has two bedrooms, a front porch, and a rear deck. | 3 suites, 1 cottage. Picnic area, complimentary breakfast, in-room data ports, cable TV, room phones, laundry service, no kids under 13, no smoking. | 795 S.W. Hanson St. | 541/752–2919 | heibb@aol.com | $95–$135 | AE, D, DC, MC, V.

Harrison House Bed and Breakfast. Built in 1939 in the Colonial Williamsburg–era style, the inn has bright, cozy, comfortable rooms with antique furnishings. It's three blocks from the Oregon State University campus. Afternoon refreshments are served in the sun room or you can relax in the English cottage garden. | 4 rooms. Complimentary breakfast and afternoon refreshments, no air-conditioning in some rooms, in-room data ports, room service, no TV in some rooms, cross-country skiing, business services, no smoking. | 2310 N.W. Harrison Blvd. | 541/752–6248 or 800/233–6248 (for reservations) | fax 541/754–1353 | harrisonhouse@proaxis.com | www.proaxis.com/~harrisonhouse | $70–$80 | AE, D, MC, V.

Ramada Inn. This full-service motel near Oregon State University has a lobby filled with the flags of PAC 10 football teams. | 100 rooms, 20 suites. Restaurant, bar, room service, in-room data ports, in-room safes, some kitchenettes, some refrigerators, cable TV, room phones, pool, laundry facilities, laundry service. | 1550 N.W. 9th St. | 541/753–9151 or 800/272–6232 | fax 541/758–7089 | www.ramada.com | $109 | AE, D, DC, MC, V.

Shanico Inn. This three-story quiet motel is 1 mi from downtown and close to the Oregon University campus. It's set on 1 acre of property with a picnic area and plenty of benches to sit on. The rooms are basic, but functional. | 76 rooms. Complimentary Continental breakfast, pool, some pets allowed. | 1113 N.W. 9th St. | 541/754–7474 or 800/432–1233 | fax 541/754–2437 | shanicoinn@aol.com | $53–$60 | AE, D, DC, MC, V.

COTTAGE GROVE

MAP 3, D5

(Nearby town also listed: Eugene)

With more than a half dozen historic "creek covers" close by, Cottage Grove's self-proclaimed title as "the covered bridge capital of Oregon" is well deserved. Of particular note is the Chambers Railroad Bridge, the only one of its kind west of the Mississippi River, built in 1925 to carry logs to mill. Cottage Grove's picturesque and historic downtown, through which the Willamette River flows, has attracted moviemakers and light industrial developers alike.

Information: Cottage Grove Chamber of Commerce | 330 Hwy. 99 S, Suite B, Cottage Grove 97424 | 541/942–2411 | cgchamber@oip.net | www.cottagegrove.org.

Attractions

Chateau Lorane Winery. This winery, 1 mi outside Cottage Grove, in the Coast Range foothills bottles Pinot Noir, Riesling, Chardonnay, Sauvignon Blanc, Gewürztraminer, and Cabernet Sauvignon. The tasting room overlooks the Chateau's private 24-acre lake. | 27415 Siuslaw River Rd., Lorane | 541/942–8028 | fax 541/942–5830 | Free | June–Oct., weekdays noon–5; Nov., Dec., Mar.–May, weekends noon–5; also by appointment.

Cottage Grove Museum. Industrial, farm, mining, and household tools are on display here. The museum features a 19th-century octagonal church with its original stained-glass windows. | 147 H St. | 541/942–3963 | Free | Mid-June–Labor Day, Wed.–Sun. 1–4; Labor Day–mid-June, weekends 1–4.

Covered Bridges. Oregon has the largest collection of covered bridges in the western United States. The Willamette Valley has more than 34 of the wooden structures. There are six bridges on a loop drive just outside Cottage Grove; driving directions can be obtained through the website. The widest bridge in the state is off Highway 58 near Lowell. Four others are nearby. | 503/986–3514 | www.odot.state.or.us/eshtm/br.htm | Free | Daily.

Dorena Lake. Three parks at this reservoir built in the 1940s offer boating, swimming, sailing, fishing, and water skiing. Schwartz Park, located downstream from the dam, and Baker Bay Park, on the south side of the lake, have campgrounds. | Row River Rd., at exit 174 off I–5 | 541/942–1418 | Free | Daily.

Row River Trail. You can access this 15.6 mi scenic, flat, hiking and biking trail, which used to be a railroad track, by following the Row River 3 mi east of town at the Mosby Bridge. | 541/942–2411.

ON THE CALENDAR

JULY: *Bohemia Mining Days Celebration.* This celebration kicks off with a Grand Miner's Parade which travels down Main Street; the only road in the world paved in gold. There is also a Gold Panning Championship and the largest mining manufacturer expo on the West Coast. A simulated shoot-out on Main Street and a Native American Powwow hosted by the Confederated Tribes Rogue Table and Associated Tribes of Medford take place as well in downtown Cottage Grove. | 541/942–7134.

AUG.: ***Western Oregon Exposition Fair.*** Musical performances and livestock showings highlight this small, locally popular, annual, weekend-long event held at the fairgrounds of the same name. | 541/942–2411.

Dining

Cottage. Contemporary. Wood heat from a single wood-burning stove and heat gain from the sun are the only sources of heating at this environmentally friendly restaurant, which features healthy cooking. Entrées include seafood, steak, and chicken. There's also a wide selection of sandwiches, soups, salads, and burgers. Kids' menu. | 2915 Row River Rd. | 541/942–3091 | Closed Sun. | $8–$25 | MC, V.

© Corbis

OREGON'S COVERED BRIDGES

Oregon has the largest collection of covered bridges in the western United States. At its peak, the state had more than 400 covered bridges. Most fell victim to fire, flood, or general neglect. Today, 51 bridges remain with the heaviest concentration being in the southern Willamette Valley, in the vicinity of Eugene. Lane County with 19 has the most. Other counties with bridges include Benton, Coos, Deschutes, Douglas, Jackson, Josephine, Lincoln, Linn, Marion, Multnomah, and Polk. Linn County has nine bridges.

The covered bridges, which use truss designs to distribute the weight loads, were built from around 1916 to 1987, mostly in rural areas over creeks and narrow rivers. Wooden construction was chosen because of a lack of steel during World Wars I and II and the wide availability of timber in the state. The bridges were covered to help protect the trusses from the region's heavy rains. Covered bridges had a lifespan of about 80 years versus less than 10 years for uncovered varieties. Most of Oregon's bridges are a single lane wide, and today about half are open only to pedestrian traffic.

With six covered bridges, Cottage Grove in Lane County has the distinction of being known as the "Covered Bridge Capital of Oregon." Centennial Bridge is located in downtown Cottage Grove next to City Hall. It was built in 1987 with recycled timber from a dismantled bridge. Also in Cottage Grove is the privately owned Chambers Railroad Bridge, the only covered railroad bridge in the state. Trains used the bridge to carry logs to a nearby lumber mill until 1943.

At 165 ft, Goodpasture Bridge over the McKenzie River in Lane County is the longest wooden span in Oregon. With its Gothic-louvered windows, it is the state's most photographed bridge. Neal Lane Bridge in Douglas County and North Fork Yachats Bridge in coastal Lincoln County are the state's shortest at 42 ft. All three of these bridges are open to auto traffic.

The only covered bridge near Portland is the Cedar Crossing Bridge. However, it is not an authentic covered bridge—it is not a truss-support structure and it has a concrete span. To see this bridge, built in 1982, take Foster Road east from I–205 to 134th Avenue; turn right and continue ½ mi south. South of metropolitan Portland northeast of Salem is Gallon House. Built in 1916, this span over Abiqua Creek is Oregon's oldest covered bridge.

For more information on Oregon's covered bridges contact the Covered Bridge Society of Oregon (2495 SW Neill Road, Sherwood 97120, 503/628–1906).

—By Jeff Boswell

Stacy's Covered Bridge Restaurant. Contemporary. This white-linen restaurant, in a 1906 bank building, is across the street from the covered bridge and City Hall. The specialty here is Chicken Taylor (breast of chicken with sautéed prawns and a peanut-pepper sauce), but you can also choose chicken Cordon Bleu, fresh seafood, pastas, steaks, and, on the weekend, prime rib. The menu changes according to the availability of fresh ingredients. There's a nice selection of Oregon and California wines, too. | 401 E. Main St. | 541/767–0320 | fax 541/767–0291 | $9.95–$17.95 | AE, D, DC, MC, V.

Lodging

Apple Inn Bed and Breakfast. This modern country home just outside Cottage Grove has open-beam ceilings and large windows with a view of 190 acres of surrounding forest. The interior runs to country kitsch but the guest rooms have handmade quilts, antiques, and country-style furnishings, and one has a private entrance. The hosts provide a hearty breakfast and evening snacks. | 2 doubles with bath. Complimentary breakfast, no air-conditioning, cable TV, room phones, outdoor hot tub, no smoking. | 30697 Kenady La. | 541/942–2393 or 800/942–2393 | fax 541/767–0402 | appleinn@moriah.com | www.moriah.com/appleinn | $75–$95 | D, MC, V.

Best Western Village Green. This chain hotel was originally built in the 1950s as a resort on 16 acres of property. Situated in a business area of Cottage Grove, it's a five-minute drive to downtown. It's close to the covered bridges and about 20 mi from Eugene. The rooms are clean and comfortable. | 96 rooms. Restaurant, bar, some refrigerators, cable TV, pool, hot tub, tennis, playground, laundry facilities, business services, pets allowed. | 725 Row River Rd. | 541/942–2491 | fax 541/942–2386 | www.bestwestern.com | $69–$79 | AE, D, DC, MC, V.

Holiday Inn Express. Contemporary accommodations are available at this hotel just off the freeway. Built in 1993, it is right next door to a golf course. | 41 rooms. Pool, hot tub, coin laundry, tennis courts, laundry/valet, business services, pets allowed (fee). | 1601 Gateway Blvd., | 541/942–1000 or 800/465–4329 | www.holidayinn.com | $68–$110 | AE, D, DC, MC, V.

CRATER LAKE NATIONAL PARK

MAP 3, E7

(Nearby town also listed: Klamath Falls)

Oregon's only national park and certainly one of its most famous tourist attractions, Crater Lake owes its existence to Mount Mazama, which erupted some 7,700 years ago. Rain and melted snow eventually filled the caldera, creating a sapphire-blue lake so clear that sunlight can penetrate 400 ft beneath the surface.

The 286-square-mi area was designated a national park in 1902. The lake itself has an area of 21 square mi and a depth of 1,932 ft. Heavy snows keep the park closed most of the year, but the north and south entrance roads are generally clear by early June. Peak visiting times are July and August.

Information: Superintendent, Crater Lake National Park | Box 7, Crater Lake 97604 | 541/594–2211 ext. 402.

Attractions

★ **Crater Lake Volcano Cruises.** Crater Lake, the deepest lake in the U.S. and the fifth deepest in the world, was formed by the explosion and collapse of 12,000-ft Mt. Mazama some 7,700 years ago. Take a boat tour around the caldera on the pristine blue waters and view the major formations such as Llao Rock, Phantom Ship, and Wizard Island. You can get off on Wizard Island and take the next boat back. Tours depart from Cleetwood Cove several times each day and last about 2 hrs. The park has a lodge with refurbished suites and elegant guest rooms with spectacular views and restaurants. | 541/830–8700 | www.craterlake.com | Free, parking $10 | Closed mid-Oct.–mid-May, daily, call for schedule.

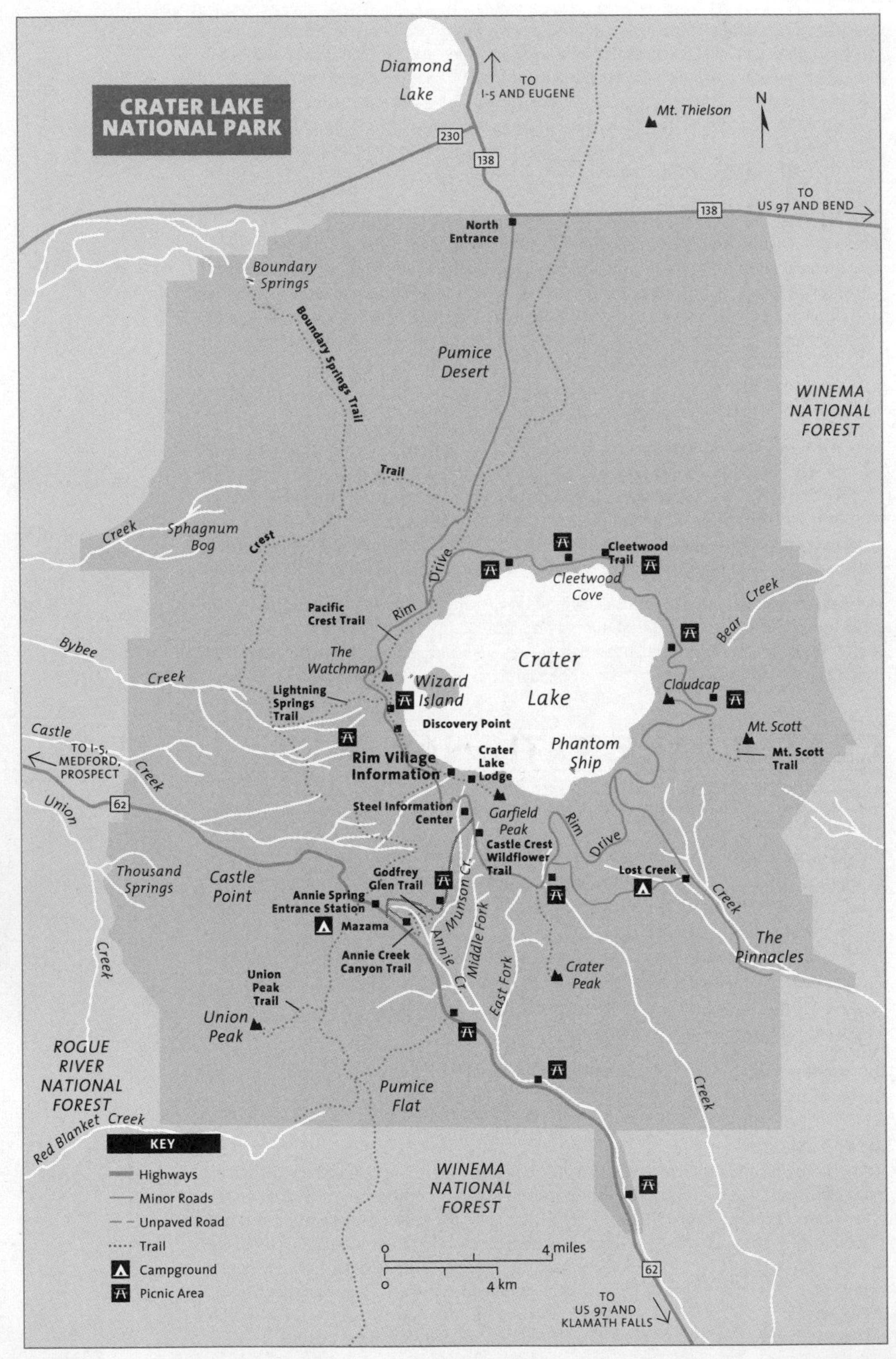
CRATER LAKE NATIONAL PARK
Diamond Lake
TO I-5 AND EUGENE
Mt. Thielson
N
230
138
TO US 97 AND BEND
138
North Entrance
Boundary Springs
Boundary Springs Trail
Pumice Desert
WINEMA NATIONAL FOREST
Trail
Creek
Sphagnum Bog
Crest
Cleetwood Trail
Rim Drive
Cleetwood Cove
Pacific Crest Trail
Bear Creek
Bybee
The Watchman
Crater Lake
Creek
Wizard Island
Cloudcap
Lightning Springs Trail
Castle
Discovery Point
Mt. Scott
TO I-5, MEDFORD, PROSPECT
Crater Lake Lodge
Phantom Ship
Mt. Scott Trail
Rim Village Information
Creek
Union
62
Steel Information Center
Garfield Peak
Rim Drive
Castle Crest Wildflower Trail
Thousand Springs
Castle Point
Godfrey Glen Trail
Lost Creek
Annie Spring Entrance Station
Munson Cr.
Creek
Mazama
Middle Fork
The Pinnacles
Annie Cr.
Creek
Annie Creek Canyon Trail
Crater Peak
East Fork
Union Peak Trail
Union Peak
ROGUE RIVER NATIONAL FOREST
Pumice Flat
Creek
Red Blanket Creek
KEY
Highways
Minor Roads
Unpaved Road
Trail
Campground
Picnic Area
WINEMA NATIONAL FOREST
0
4 miles
0
4 km
62
TO US 97 AND KLAMATH FALLS

Dining

Dining Room at Crater Lake Lodge. Contemporary. This restaurant serves ambitious fare in upscale surroundings. The room itself is magnificent, with a large stone fireplace and views out over the clear blue waters of Crater Lake. The supper menu includes fresh Pacific Northwest seafood, a pasta dish, pork medallions, and steak Oscar. The wines are from Oregon and Washington. | Crater Lake Lodge, Rim Village | 541/594–2255 | Reservations essential (for supper) | Closed mid-Oct.–mid-May | $14–$28 | MC, V.

Watchman Restaurant. American. This is the casual dining alternative at Crater Lake Lodge. There is no menu—an all-you-can-eat buffet includes salads, soups, potato bar, taco bar, and entrées like salmon, salisbury steak, and chicken. The dining room has a view of the lake. | Crater Lake Lodge, Rim Village | 541/594–2255 | No lunch | Closed mid-Sept.–mid-May | $12 | MC, V.

Lodging

Crater Lake Lodge. This historic 1915 lodge is on the rim of the caldera and has views of the lake. Lodgepole pine columns, gleaming wood floors, and stone fireplaces grace the common areas, and the contemporary furnishings blend in perfectly. The lodge has only two telephones, which are in the lobby area. There are no electronic diversions of any kind. | 71 rooms. Restaurant, picnic area, no air-conditioning, no room phones, no TV in rooms, no smoking. | 565 Rim Village Dr., Crater Lake | 541/594–2255 or 541/830–8700 (for reservations) | fax 541/594–2622 | www.craterlakelodge.com | $119–$162 | Closed mid-Oct.–mid-May | MC, V.

Mazama Village Motor Inn. This Forest Service complex, reached from Hwy. 62, is in a wooded area 7 mi south of the lake. It has minimal but adequate accommodations and all the rooms have a private bath. There's also a campground with 210 sites. | 40 rooms in 10 A-frame buildings. No room phones, no TV. | Mazama Village Rd. | 541/594–2255 x3704 | fax 541/594–2622 | $89 | Closed mid-Oct.–May | MC, V.

DEPOE BAY

MAP 3, C4

(Nearby towns also listed: Lincoln City, Newport)

The small town of Depoe Bay was founded in the 1920s and named in honor of Charles DePot, of the Siletz tribe whose name was taken from his employment at a U.S. Army depot in the late 1800s.

Today Depoe Bay is best known for its whale-watching opportunities. A pod of gray whales makes its home for about 10 months of the year in the "world's smallest navigable harbor," which is just 6 square acres. Along the sea wall north of the harbor, natural rock tubes are flooded by incoming tides often spouting geyserlike sprays which tend to douse visitors and vehicles along nearby Highway 101.

Information: Depoe Bay Chamber of Commerce | 630 Hwy. 101, Depoe Bay 97341 | 541/765–2889 | dbchamber@netportnet.com | www.depoebaychamber.org.

Attractions

Depoe Bay Park. This park runs along the beach in front of the town's retail district. With a narrow channel and deep water the tiny harbor is also one of the most protected on the coast. It supports a thriving fleet of commercial- and charter-fishing boats. The Spouting Horn, a natural cleft in the basalt cliffs on the waterfront, blasts seawater skyward during heavy weather. | South on U.S. 101 | 541/765–2889 | www.stateoforegon.com/depoe_bay/chamber/ | Free | Daily.

Fogarty Creek State Park. Bird-watching and viewing the tidepools are the key draws here, but hiking and picnicking are popular, at this park 4 mi north of Depoe Bay on U.S. 101. Wooden footbridges arch through the forest. The beach is rimmed with cliffs. | U.S. 101 | 541/265–9278 or 800/551–6949 | www.prd.state.or.us | $3 per vehicle day-use fee | Daily.

Attractions

Tradewinds. Every year a few of the gigantic gray whales migrating along the coast decide to linger in Depoe Bay and, for more than six decades, Tradewinds has operated whale-watching cruises. The skippers are all marine naturalists who give a running commentary, and the boats can accommodate from 6–40 passengers. Daylight hours only. The ticket office is on Highway 101 at the north end of Depoe Bay Bridge. | Hwy. 101 | 541/765–2345 or 800/445–8730 | fax 541/765–2282 | www.tradewindscharters.com | $13 (1 hr), $19 (2 hrs) | Closed Christmas.

ON THE CALENDAR

APR.: ***Classic Wooden Boat Show and Crab Feed.*** Boats are displayed and Pacific Northwest seafood is consumed in large quantities at this annual event, held at the Depoe Bay Marina the last weekend in April. | 541/765–2889.

MAY: ***Fleet of Flowers Ceremony.*** Held on Memorial Day each year since 1945, this event in Depoe Bay Harbor is a tribute to those who have lost their lives at sea. | 541/765–2889.

JULY: ***Fireworks in Boiler Bay.*** Little Depoe Bay gets a day's jump on other towns by staging its Fourth of July fireworks on the third. The fun is in Boiler Bay State Park and there are lots of food vendors on hand. | 541/765–2889.

SEPT.: ***Salmon Bake.*** Salmon is cooked Native American–style on alder stakes over an open fire and sold at this event in Depoe Bay City Park the third Saturday in September. There's also live entertainment. | 541/765–2889.

Dining

Sea Hag. Seafood. This friendly publike restaurant, famous for its clam chowder, has been serving up fresh seafood for more than 30 years. Come for the Friday night seafood buffet or the prime rib with Yorkshire pudding on Saturday. On a cold winter evening you can dine at a counter surrounding the fireplace. | 53 U.S. 101 | 541/765–2734 | $15–$40 | AE, D, DC, MC, V.

Tidal Rave. Seafood. Every table at this locally popular seafood grill has an ocean view. There are fresh fish specials everyday. Try crab casserole, Thai barbeque prawns, or breaded halibut. | 279 N.W. Hwy. 101 | 541/765–2995 | Reservations essential | $12–$19 | MC, V.

Lodging

Channel House Inn. This modern oceanfront inn is built on a cliffside overlooking Depoe Bay channel. Most of the rooms have fireplaces. Each of the rooms has a different theme with contemporary furnishings. | 5 rooms, 9 suites. Complimentary buffet breakfast, some kitchenettes, some in-room hot tubs, cable TV, business services, no kids under 12, no smoking. | 35 Ellingson St. | 541/765–2140 or 800/447–2140 | fax 541/765–2191 | cfinseth@newportnet.com | www.channelhouse.com | $85–$175, $180–$235 | AE, D, MC, V.

Crown Pacific Inn. This 1999 cedar-shingle inn is set on a hillside across the highway from the ocean. Every room has a balcony with an ocean view, and some rooms have fireplaces. You're welcome to use the barbecue and picnic tables on the grounds. | 31 rooms. Complimentary Continental breakfast, no air-conditioning, microwaves, refrigerators, some in-room hot tubs, cable TV, hot tub. | Hwy. 101 and Bechill St. | 541/765–7773 or 888/845–5131 | fax 541/765–7740 | crownpac@teleport.com | www.crownpacificinn.com | $85–$105 | AE, MC, V.

Inn at Arch Rock. This 1930s inn, white with black trim, stands on the cliffs above the ocean, between two coves, but it's still within walking distance of town. Some of the warmly decorated rooms have fireplaces. The penthouse suite has two bedrooms, a fireplace, a mas-

KODAK'S TIPS FOR TAKING GREAT PICTURES

Get Closer
- Fill the frame tightly for maximum impact
- Move closer physically or use a long lens
- Continually check the viewfinder for wasted space

Choosing a Format
- Add variety by mixing horizontal and vertical shots
- Choose the format that gives the subject greatest drama

The Rule of Thirds
- Mentally divide the frame into vertical and horizontal thirds
- Place important subjects at thirds' intersections
- Use thirds' divisions to place the horizon

Lines
- Take time to notice lines
- Let lines lead the eye to a main subject
- Use the shape of lines to establish mood

Taking Pictures Through Frames
- Use foreground frames to draw attention to a subject
- Look for frames that complement the subject
- Expose for the subject, and let the frame go dark

Patterns
- Find patterns in repeated shapes, colors, and lines
- Try close-ups or overviews
- Isolate patterns for maximum impact (use a telephoto lens)

Textures that Touch the Eyes
- Exploit the tangible qualities of subjects
- Use oblique lighting to heighten surface textures
- Compare a variety of textures within a shot

Dramatic Angles
- Try dramatic angles to make ordinary subjects exciting
- Use high angles to help organize chaos and uncover patterns, and low angles to exaggerate height

Silhouettes
- Silhouette bold shapes against bright backgrounds
- Meter and expose for the background illumination
- Don't let conflicting shapes converge

Abstract Composition
- Don't restrict yourself to realistic renderings
- Look for ideas in reflections, shapes, and colors
- Keep designs simple

Establishing Size
- Include objects of known size
- Use people for scale, where possible
- Experiment with false or misleading scale

Color
- Accentuate mood through color
- Highlight subjects or create designs through color contrasts
- Study the effects of weather and lighting

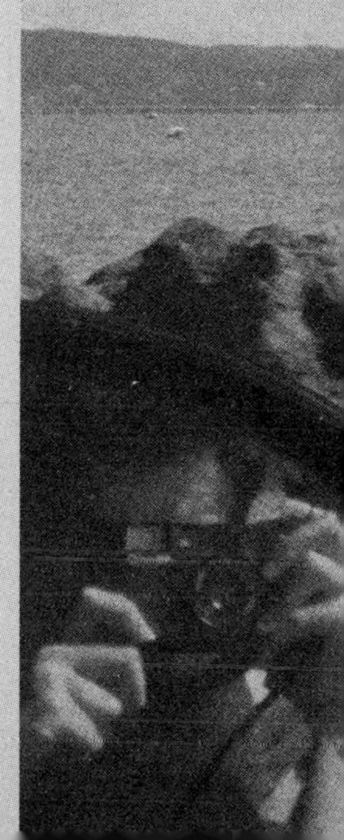

sive hot tub, and two private decks. All but one of the rooms have views of the ocean, the town, and some dramatic spouting horns. | 10 rooms, 3 suites. Picnic area, complimentary Continental breakfast, no air-conditioning, some kitchenettes, refrigerators, some in-room hot tubs, cable TV, room phones. | 70 N.W. Sunset St. | 541/765–2560 or 800/767–1835 | fax 541/765–3036 | archrock@wcn.net | www.innatarchrock.com | $99–$149 | AE, D, MC, V.

Inn at Otter Crest. Surrounded by thousands of rhododendrons and 35 acres of forest, this inn 5 mi south of Depoe Bay is a great spot for a getaway. The beach and tide pools are right out the door while the contemporary furnished rooms are spacious and bright. | 120 rooms, 40 suites. Restaurant, bar, some microwaves, refrigerators, cable TV, pool, hot tub, tennis, laundry facilities, business services. | 301 Otter Crest Loop, Otter Rock | 541/765–2111 or 800/452–2101 | fax 541/765–2047 | ottercrest@newportnet.com | www.ottercrest.com | $129, $179–$199 suites | AE, D, DC, MC, V.

Surfrider Oceanfront Resort. There are six buildings on five landscaped acres, 2 mi from the center of Depoe Bay. Every room has an oceanfront deck and direct access to the beach. The resort is close to whale watching and you can enjoy bald eagles nesting within view of the lodging. | 50 rooms. Restaurant, bar, no air-conditioning, some kitchenettes, some in-room hot tubs, cable TV, indoor pool, hot tub, airport shuttle, pets allowed. | 3115 N.W. Highway 101 | 541/764–2311 or 800/662–2378 | fax 541/764–2634 | stay@surfriderresort.com | www.surfriderresort.com | $80–$137 | AE, D, DC, MC, V.

DRAIN

MAP 3, D6

(Nearby towns also listed: Cottage Grove, Elkton)

Famous for its castle and covered bridge, this small timber town between Roseburg and Eugene also has several other Victorians and some good antiques shops worth checking out. Other nearby attractions in Douglas County include Wildlife Safari and Crater Lake National Park. Drain is about 30 mi south of Eugene at the junction of Highway 99 and Hwy. 38.

Information: **Drain Chamber of Commerce** | Box 885, 129 W. Sea Ave., Drain, 97435 | 541/836–2417.

Attractions

Cottage Grove Lake. Located on the Coast Fork of the Willamette River, this reservoir built in the 1940s is 3-mi long. There are two parks and two campgrounds. Recreational activities include boating, swimming, waterskiing, fishing, and picnicking. The area is home to many birds (including bald eagles), and blacktail deer. | 75166 Cottage Grove Lake Rd. | 541/942–8657 or 541/942–5631.

Drain Castle. Residents Charles and Anna Drain donated 60 acres of land to found the town of Drain. This Victorian, which was built in 1895 and is on the National Register of Historic Places, today serves as a school district administration office. | 500 S. Main | 541/836–2223.

Pass Creek Covered Bridge. This is the only Oregon covered bridge within a city limits. Built in the 1870s and rebuilt in 1925, Pass Creek bridge was moved to Drain City Park in the late 1980s. The 61-ft-long span carried cars until 1981. Today only pedestrians are welcome. | Behind 205 W. A St. | 541/836–2417.

ON THE CALENDAR

JULY: ***North Douglas County Fair.*** A cousin to the main county fair in Roseburg, this version held at the Drain Civic Center features music, dancing, and food and crafts booths. | 541/836–2417.

Dining

Fat Cat Diner. American/ Casual. This diner features burgers, sandwiches, and salads. | 116 E. B St. | 541/836–7184 | Closed Mon. | $5–$12 | No credit cards.

Peggy's Restaurant. American/ Casual. Breakfast is served all day at this friendly diner. Entrées include chicken, steaks, seafood, and pasta. | Exit 148 on I–5 at Rice Hill | 541/849–2841 | $5–$12. | MC, V.

Road Kill Grill. American. People are driving from nearby cities for the home cooking at this popular barbecue restaurant that looks like a 1950s throwback. There are hubcaps as light fixtures and tire marks on the floor with tinsel road kill. They don't serve skunk, but they do dish up great barbecued chicken, steaks, and—their specialty—ribs. | 306 Hwy. 38 | 541/836–2156 | No lunch. Closed Mon. | $6–$14 | No credit cards.

Lodging

Big K Guest Ranch. A 12,000-square-ft log lodge, 4 mi south of Highway 38 and 20 mi from Drain, anchors this working ranch secluded in a wooded setting on the Umpqua River. Fly-fishing is a staple here. | 20 cabins. Restaurant, conference room, rafting, hiking, fishing, swimming, horseback riding. | 20029 Hwy. 138W, Elkton, | 541/584–2295 or 800/390–2445 | fax 541/584–2395 | www.big-k.com | $195–$225 | AE, D, DC, MC, V.

Tuckaway Farm Inn. This small bed and breakfast in a restored 1920s farmhouse is in a quiet valley a few miles east of Drain. The rooms have private baths and are decorated with antiques. | 3 rooms. Hot tub, fishing, hiking, no smoking. | 7179 Scotts Valley Road, Yoncalla | 541/849–3144 | www.moriah.com/tuckaway | $75–$85 | Full breakfast | MC, V.

ENTERPRISE

MAP 3, K3

(Nearby town also listed: Joseph)

The seat of Oregon's northeasternmost county, Enterprise is surrounded by some of the region's most rugged natural beauty. There are numerous opportunities for equally

KODAK'S TIPS FOR NIGHT PHOTOGRAPHY

Lights at Night
- Move in close on neon signs
- Capture lights from unusual vantage points

Fireworks
- Shoot individual bursts using a handheld camera
- Capture several explosions with a time exposure
- Include an interesting foreground

Fill-In Flash
- Set the fill-in light a stop darker than the ambient light

Around the Campfire
- Keep flames out of the frame when reading the meter
- For portraits, take spot readings of faces
- Use a tripod, or rest your camera on something solid

Using Flash
- Stay within the recommended distance range
- Buy a flash with the red-eye reduction mode

From *Kodak Guide to Shooting Great Travel Pictures* © 2000 by Fodor's Travel Publications

rugged outdoor recreation adventures, both winter and summer. To the west lie the Eagle Cap Wilderness, the alpine Wallowa Mountains and pristine Wallowa Lake, and to the east is the Hells Canyon National Recreation Area.

Information: Wallowa County Chamber of Commerce | 107 S.W. 1st, Enterprise 97828 | 541/426–4622 | wallowa@eoni.com | www.eoni.com/~wallowa/.

Attractions

Wallowa Outdoors. This shop is the place for fishing gear and backpacking and camping supplies. They'll give you information on fishing and river conditions, too. | 110 S. River St. | 541/426–3493 | fax 541/426–3616 | www.wallowaoutdoors.com | Weekdays 8–6, Sat. 9–4.

ON THE CALENDAR

AUG.: *Wallowa County Fair.* Lasting for a week in early August, this fair (no midway) held at the Wallowa County Fairgrounds puts the emphasis on old-fashioned fun. The local grange shows livestock and there's a 4-H horse show; there are old-time fiddle music and homemade pies; exhibits of knitting, crafts, baked goods, flowers, and vegetables; and lots of kids' activities and events, including the popular "pig-and-lamb scramble." | 541/426–3143.

Dining

House Cafe. American. Sink your teeth into an Angus beef burger or try the popular Chinese chicken salad at this local favorite. The owner's model car collection decorates the dining room. | 307 W. North | 541/426–9055 | No dinner | $5–$8.

Lodging

Wilderness Inn. Despite its name, the Wilderness Inn is in the center of town, within walking distance of restaurants and the courthouse. Even so, some of the rooms have a view of the Wallowa Mountains. | 28 rooms, 1 suite. Some kitchenettes, some refrigerators, cable TV, room phones, sauna. | 301 W. North St., | 541/426–4535 or 800/965–1205 | fax 541/426–0128 | $64 | AE, D, DC, MC, V.

EUGENE

MAP 3, D5

(Nearby towns also listed: Corvallis, Cottage Grove, McKenzie Bridge)

Home to about 130,000 people within its city limits and more than 200,000 people in its metro area, Eugene is Oregon's second-largest city. Eugene itself is a community of contrasts, with a high percentage of professionals, a sizeable subculture of alternative life-styles, and a legacy as a timber town. Students also have a significant presence in the Eugene area, which is home to the University of Oregon as well as three smaller colleges.

The Willamette River flows on a diagonal course through the center of the city and meets up with the McKenzie River north of town. Internationally famous for its rhododendron gardens, Hendricks Park is nestled into southeastern Eugene, amid a rich forest of Douglas fir trees and thousands of ornamental plants.

Recreation and the arts both flourish in Eugene. Miles and miles of biking, walking, and running paths wind along the river and through parks, contributing to Eugene's reputation as one of the top cycling cities in the country. Water sports abound on the rivers as well as on nearby lakes. At the same time, the performing arts flourish in Eugene, with concert halls at both the University of Oregon and the Hult Center, which, in addition to ballet, symphonies, and opera, also hosts the internationally acclaimed Oregon Bach Festival.

DRIVING AROUND EUGENE

Parking at meters costs $.25 for 20 minutes or $.75 per hour. Meters are running from 7 AM–6 PM, Monday through Saturday. Parking is free on Sunday and some selected holidays. Time limits on meters vary depending on the area, usually from 30 min. to 10 hrs. Meters in business districts have time limits from 30 min. to 2 hrs.

On the University of Oregon campus, temporary visitor parking permits are available at the kiosk at 13th and Agate Streets. Permits are good from one day to up to 3 weeks.

Information: Convention & Visitors Association of Lane County | 115 West 8th St., Eugene | 800/547–5445 | cvalco@cvalco.org | www.cvalco.org.

Attractions

BEACHES, PARKS, AND NATURAL SIGHTS

Alton Baker Park. On Centennial Boulevard, east of the Ferry St. Bridge, Alton Baker Park is larger than Gateway and Skinner Butte Parks, which adjoin it along the Willamette River. It has good hiking, biking, and a riverside footpath. | Centennial Blvd. | 541/682–4800 | www.cieugene.or.us | Free | Daily 10–10.

Armitage County Park. Fishing and picnicking are popular activities at this 57 acre park on the McKenzie River off I–5. | Coburg Rd. | 541/682–2000 | Free, parking $3 | Daily.

Eugene Saturday Market. Every Saturday between April and Christmas, local craftspeople, farmers, and chefs provide cheap eats and nifty arts and crafts at this outdoor market. | 8th and Oak Sts. | 541/686–8885 | Free | Sat. 10–5.

Euphoria Chocolate Company. This little company a few blocks south of the heart of downtown Eugene makes some of the best-loved chocolate in Oregon. You can get chocolate-covered cookies, and both the caramels and the extra-rich truffles are made with heavy cream. | 6 W. 17th Ave. | 541/343–9223 | fax 541/343–6866 | www.euphoriachocolate.com | Free | Weekdays 10–6, weekends 11–5; July–Aug., closed Sun.

5th Street Public Market. A former chicken-processing plant (a three-story open square with a central fountain) in the Historic District houses this combination mall and food court. You can eat at sit-down restaurants and bakeries filled with goodies, or choose from an array of international foods, including Thai, Greek, French, and Chinese, on the second-floor esplanade. The Nike Heritage Store here was the first Nike store in the world. Other stores range from a video arcade to galleries featuring the work of local artisans. | 296 E. 5th Ave. | 541/484–0383 | www.5stmarket.com | Free | Shops: Daily 10–6. Restaurants: Weekdays 7 AM–9 PM, weekends 7 AM–10 PM.

Hendricks Park Rhododendron Garden. This park east of the University of Oregon is best visited in May when its rhododendrons and azaleas explode in pinks, yellows, reds, and purples. | Summit and Skyline Drs. | 541/682–5324 | www.darkwing.uoregon.edu/ | Free | Daily.

Lookout Point and Dexter Reservoirs. These two reservoirs on the Willamette River are joined and stretch for 17 mi. Fishing, waterskiing, and sailing are popular. The area, 15 mi from I–5, is home to many bird species, elk, and deer. | Rte. 58 | 541/937–2131 | Free | May–Oct., daily.

Maude Kerns Art Center. This 1896 church, the oldest in Eugene, two blocks east of the university, houses an arts facility that exhibits contemporary fine arts and crafts. The large exhibit space is filled with paintings and sculpture, most by Oregon artists. | 1910 E. 15th Ave. | 541/345–1571 | fax 541/345–6248 | www.mkartcenter.org | Donation, $2 suggested | Weekdays 10–5:30; for special exhibitions, also Sat. noon–4.

Owen Municipal Rose Garden. More than 4,500 roses bloom from June to September at this 9-acre garden west of Skinner Butte Park, along the Willamette River. Magnolia, cherry, and oak trees dot the grounds. | 300 N. Jefferson St. | 541/682–4824 | Free | Daily.

Skinner Butte Park. Founding father Eugene Skinner staked the claim here that first put Eugene on the map. A strenuous hike on two trails will take you to the top of Skinner Butte across sometimes difficult terrain through a mixed-conifer forest, but you can also drive up on an access road. The park also has a playground, picnic area, and baseball diamond. | 2nd Ave. and High St. | 541/682–4800 | www.cieugene.or.us | Free | Daily 10–10.

Waldo Lake. Hidden in old-growth forest at 5,400 ft, Waldo Lake is 420 ft deep and is renowned for the clarity and purity of its water. There's a 22-mi trail around the lake for hiking or biking, and there are three campgrounds. Take Highway 58 from Eugene and follow signs. When you're on Forest Road #5897, it's about 7 mi to the lake. | Waldo Lake Wilderness Area | 541/782–2283 | fax 541/782–5306 | www.fs.fed.us/rb/willamette | Free | July–Oct.

Willamette National Forest. This 1.6-million-acre forest is about the size of New Jersey and stretches for 110 mi along the western slopes of the Cascades. The glaciated landscape includes mountains, volcanoes, and cinder cones. There are eight wilderness areas totaling 380,805 acres and more than 80 campgrounds and picnic sites are in the forest where cougars and black bears are among the wildlife. | Rte. 58 | 541/465–6521 | Free, parking $3 | Daily.

CULTURE, EDUCATION, AND HISTORY

Hult Center for the Performing Arts. This is the locus of Eugene's cultural life. Renowned for the quality of its acoustics, the center houses two theaters that are home to Eugene's symphony and opera. | One Eugene Center at 7th Ave. and Willamette St. | 541/682–5087 or 541/682–5000 (tickets) or 541/682–5746 (24-hr event recording) | Call for hours.

Knight Library. On the west side of the campus, this is the main building in the university's library system, which has more than 2 million volumes. | Kincaid St. and E. 15th Ave. | 541/346–3054 | Free | Daily.

University of Oregon. Several fine old buildings can be seen on the 280-acre campus; Deady Hall, built in 1876, is the oldest. More than 400 varieties of trees grace the grounds, along with many outdoor sculptures. The state's largest university has an enrollment of 17,000 students and is home to the Fighting Ducks of the PAC-10 Conference. | Bordered by Franklin Blvd. and 18th Ave., Alder and Moss Sts. | 541/346–3014 | www.uoregon.edu | Free | Weekdays.

University of Oregon Museum of Art. More than 12,500 works are housed in Oregon's second largest museum. The collection of Asian art includes examples of Chinese imperial tomb figures, textiles, and furniture. There's also a Pacific Northwest collection. | 1430 Johnson La. | 541/346–3027 | $2 (suggested) | Wed.–Sun. noon–5.

University of Oregon Museum of Natural History. Devoted to Pacific Northwest anthropology and the natural sciences, the museum's highlights include a collection of fossils found in Oregon. | 1680 E. 15th Ave., | 541/346–3024 | $2 (suggested) | Tues.–Sun. noon–5, closed Mon.

Willamette Science and Technology Center (WISTEC). This hands-on learning facility assembles rotating exhibits designed especially for the young and curious. The adjacent planetarium, one of the largest in the Pacific Northwest, presents star shows and entertainment events. | 2300 Leo Harris Pkwy. | 541/682–7888 or 541/687–STAR | $4 | Wed.–Fri. noon–5, weekends 11–5.

MUSEUMS

Lane County Historical Museum. Collections dating from the 1840s to the present are housed in a 14,000-square-ft building. Exhibits include period rooms, vehicles, early trades, Oregon Trail and early settlement, historic photographs, and memorabilia from the 1920s and 1930s. | 740 W. 13th Ave. | 541/682–4242 | $2 | Wed.–Fri. 10–4, Sat. noon–4.

SPORTS AND RECREATION

Fall Creek Trail. Fall Creek parallels this 14-mi trail that is 2 mi north of Fall Creek Lake in the Willamette National Forest. | Rte. 58 to Lowell, follow signs to Fall Creek Dam | 541/937–2129 | Free | May–Sept. daily.

Willamette Pass. This ski area southeast of Eugene has a vertical rise of 1,563 ft and gets about 300 inches of snow a year. The summit is 6,683 ft. | Rte. 58 at milepost 62 | 541/687–8557 | www.willamettepass.com | $29 | Nov.–Apr., daily 9–9.

ON THE CALENDAR

JUNE–JULY: *Oregon Bach Festival.* Concerts, chamber music, and social events—held mainly in Eugene at the Hult Center and the University of Oregon School of Music, but also in Corvallis and Florence—are part of this internationally known 17-day event. | 541/682–5000 or 541/346–5666, 800/457–1486.

AUG.: *Oregon Festival of American Music.* The first two weeks in August come alive with music during this inventive and adventurous festival with concerts at the Hult Center and as many as eight other venues around town, both indoors and out. Past themes have included Le Jazz Hot: Louisiana Gumbo and How Sweet the Sound: From Gospel to Swing. The festival has featured such rarities as the music of Louis Moreau Gottschalk and the world premiere of a "lost" ballet score by jazz legend Sidney Bechet. Another festival in January focuses on American classical composers. | 541/687–6526 or 800/248–1615.

AUG.: *Lane County Fair.* The latest developments in technology, especially in Lane County, are highlighted at this six-day event, at the Hall of Technology on the Lane County Fairgrounds. Gardening and livestock exhibits, food booths, and live entertainment are also featured. | 541/682–4292.

EUGENE WALKING TOUR

Downtown Eugene is home primarily to retail establishments and restaurants but there are areas nearby, particularly picturesque parks along the Willamette River, that can be reached on foot. Begin your tour at the **University of Oregon** (Agate St. and Franklin Blvd.). The shady UO campus has more than 400 varieties of trees. Notable attractions include the **Museum of Art.**

From the **Museum of Natural History** walk north up Agate Street and turn left on Franklin Boulevard. Follow Franklin to the path that leads to the Autzen Footbridge, which crosses the Willamette River to the **Alton Baker Park,** site of the university's football stadium. The park has trails for hiking and biking.

On the north side of the park is **Wistec,** the Willamette Science and Technology Center. Wistec features rotating exhibits geared to young people and a planetarium, one of the largest in the Pacific Northwest.

Head west on Centennial Boulevard and you'll reach the Ferry Street Bridge. Cross back over the river into **Gateway Park** and adjacent **Skinner Butte Park.** These parks lie north of the downtown district along the south banks of the Willamette River. Skinner Butte includes a hill of the same name. A road leads to the top of the butte where outstanding views of the Eugene metropolitan area can be seen. Also here is the **George E. Owen Memorial Rose Garden,** which has more than 4,500 roses and ornamental plants.

End your tour south of Skinner Butte Park at **5th Street Public Market** (5th Avenue and High Street), a shopping mall and food court.

Dining

INEXPENSIVE

Ambrosia. Italian. Northern Italian dishes and specialty pizzas are cooked in a wood-fired oven at this popular casual downtown restaurant. Seafood and vegetarian dishes are on the menu and there are sidewalk tables for open-air dining. | 174 E. Broadway | 541/342–4141 | No lunch Sun. | $12–$20 | D, MC, V.

Mekala's. Thai. Mekala's first opened in Thailand in 1960 and came here to the 5th Street Public Market in 1988. The owners grow their own mint and lime leaves as well as other ingredients for the traditional Thai recipes, including such popular staples as pad thai and curries. They've decorated the restaurant with family photos and wall hangings from Thailand. | 296 E. 5th Ave. | 541/342–4872 | $8.95–$14.95 | AE, D, MC, V.

Poppi's Anatolia. Greek. This genuinely home-style Greek restaurant attracts diners with moussaka and *kalamarakia* (fried squid), and, of course, retsina. You can also choose Indian specialties, like the hot curry vindaloo, but on Sunday nights the chef prepares only Greek dishes. Wooden beams, an open kitchen, and (Asian) Indian bedspreads on the walls make the place friendly and casual. | 992 Willamette St. | 541/343–9661 | No lunch Sun. | $7.25–$11.95 | MC, V.

MODERATE

Cafe Navarro. Caribbean. Choose from seafood, meat, or vegetarian entrées with an island flair at this restaurant, which is one block from the Hult Center for the Performing Arts and the Eugene Hilton. Weekend brunch. No smoking. | 454 Willamette St. | 541/344–0943 | Closed Mon. | $18–$25 | D, MC, V.

Cafe Zenon. Eclectic. You never know what you'll find on the menu here—Thai, Indian, Italian, South American, or down-home barbecue—but it's sure to be memorable and expertly prepared. Two full-time bakers produce 20 to 30 desserts daily. There is open-air dining on tree-lined Broadway. Sun. brunch. No smoking. | 898 Pearl St. | 541/343–3005 | Breakfast also available | $20–$30 | MC, V.

Chanterelle. Continental. Casual, intimate dining. Some diners might find the European cuisine at this romantic 14-table restaurant old-fashioned. The region's beef, lamb, seafood, and wild game are prepared in a traditional Old World manner. Crystal and fresh flowers fill the restaurant which is in an old warehouse. No smoking. | 207 E. Fifth Ave. | 541/484–4065 | Closed Sun.–Mon. No lunch | $15–$26 | AE, DC, MC, V.

Excelsior Cafe. Continental. The delicious food served here only enhances the appealing European elegance of this intimate, informal restaurant, bar, and bistro-style café across from the University of Oregon. The menu changes according to the season, but the staples, which take advantage of local produce, include delicious salads and soups, gnocchi, grilled chicken, broiled salmon, and sandwiches. There is a landscaped garden with a courtyard for dining out of doors and a private patio is also available. Kids' menu. Sun. brunch. No smoking. | 754 E. 13th St. | 541/342–6963 | Breakfast also available | $22–$35 | AE, D, DC, MC, V.

North Bank. Contemporary. This restaurant has a great view of the scenic Willamette River. In addition to the many seafood entrées, which include scallops, oysters, crab, shrimp, and fish, there are chicken dishes, vegetarian lasagna, steaks, prime rib, and combination suppers. Outside is a 21-and-over lounge with about 15 tables. | 22 Club Rd. | 541/343–5622 | No lunch | $21–$37 | AE, D, DC, MC, V.

Oregon Electric Station. Contemporary. The menu at this busy eatery in a renovated 1912 railroad depot, a National Historic Building, features steaks, prime rib, and seafood. You can also dine in an antique train dining car or on the deck in the garden. Kids' menu. | 27 E. Fifth St. | 541/485–4444 | No lunch weekends | $20–$25 | AE, D, MC, V.

Sweetwaters. Contemporary. The dining room at the Valley River Inn, which overlooks the Willamette at water level, features Pacific Northwest cuisine. Try the salmon with Szechuan peppercorn crust and cranberry vinaigrette or the grilled beef fillet with Oregon blue cheese crust. There is a bar area outside as well as a deck for open-air dining. Kids' menu. Sun. brunch. | 1000 Valley River Way | 541/687–0123 | $25–$40 | AE, D, DC, MC, V.

Lodging

INEXPENSIVE

Pacific 9 Motor Inn. This three-story motel is in a business area, surrounded by restaurants and shopping. There are several parks nearby and it is 5 mi to the University of Oregon. | 119 rooms. No-smoking rooms, cable TV, pool. | 3550 Gateway St., Springfield | 541/726–9266 or 800/722–9462 | fax 541/744–2643 | $38–$44 | AE, D, DC, MC, V.

MODERATE

Best Western Grand Manor Inn. Built in the 1990s, this chain hotel is near the University of Oregon, Hult Center, and Autzen Stadium. Some of the rooms have balconies. | 65 rooms. Complimentary Continental breakfast, in-room data ports, refrigerators, cable TV, indoor pool, exercise equipment, laundry facilities, business services. | 971 Kruse Way, Springfield | 541/726–4769 | fax 541/744–0745 | $70–$80 | AE, D, DC, MC, V.

Best Western New Oregon. The plush furnishings and comprehensive amenities at this midsize motel near the University of Oregon come as a bit of a surprise, given the property's price range. Some rooms overlook a creek. | 129 rooms. In-room data ports, refrigerators, cable TV, indoor pool, hot tub, exercise equipment, laundry facilities, business services, some pets allowed (fee). | 1655 Franklin Blvd., | 541/683–3669 | fax 541/484–5556 | neworegon@aol.com | $65–$125 | AE, D, DC, MC, V.

Campus Inn. Walk to shopping and Autzen Stadium from this hotel which is in the heart of downtown Eugene. The rooms are bright and clean. | 58 rooms. Complimentary Continental breakfast, in-room data ports, cable TV, pets allowed (fee). | 390 E. Broadway | 541/343–3376 or 800/888–6313 | eugene@campus-inn.com | www.campus-inn.com | $62–$96 | AE, D, DC, MC, V.

Country Inn Bed & Breakfast. This 1874 homestead 4 mi north of town is truly a country inn, down to the cast-iron pot used by the inn's founders, which still hangs in the fireplace. The inn is set on 10 acres of gardens that contain more than 500 rosebushes and a pond with two resident swans and a gazebo. The Victorian-style rooms have four-poster beds and floral comforters. | 2 rooms. Complimentary breakfast. | 4100 County Farm Rd. | 541/345–7344, 877/816–8757 | fax 541/345–0172 | www.cibab.com | $85–$95 | AE, MC, V.

Enchanted Country Inn Bed & Breakfast. You are welcomed to this B&B, nestled in a forest of Douglas firs, cedars, and redwoods, with the innkeeper's homemade wines and fresh flowers in your room. Wicker furniture and hardwood floors and floral prints accent the interior of this, the closest inn to the Eugene Airport. The inn is also only 2 mi from town. The cottage has a full kitchen. | 3 rooms, 1 cottage. Complimentary breakfast. No in-room phones. TV in common area. No air-conditioning. No smoking. No pets. | 29195 Gimpl Hill Rd. | 541/465–1869 | fax 541/465–1507 | $75–$100, cottage $125 | AE, MC, V.

Eugene Travelodge. This chain property is within walking distance of the University of Oregon campus and within 1 mi of Hult Center and downtown Eugene. | 60 rooms, 4 suites. Complimentary Continental breakfast, in-room data ports, refrigerators (in suites), cable TV, hot tub, sauna, business services, some pets allowed. | 1859 Franklin Blvd. | 541/342–6383 | $51, $75 suites | AE, D, DC, MC, V.

Excelsior Inn. This small hotel in a former frat house manifests a quiet sophistication more commonly found in Europe than in America. Crisply detailed, with cherry-wood doors and moldings, it has rooms furnished in a refreshingly understated manner, each with a marble-and-tile bath. The ground-level Excelsior Café is one of Eugene's best restaurants. | 14 rooms. Restaurant, bar, complimentary breakfast, in-room data ports, no smoking rooms, in-room VCRs. | 754 E. 13th Ave. | 541/342–6963 or 800/321–6963 | fax 541/342–1417 | $69–$180 | AE, D, DC, MC, V.

Holiday Inn. Rooms at this chain motel 3 mi from downtown Eugene are plain but comfortable. | 58 rooms. Complimentary Continental breakfast, in-room data ports, cable TV, indoor pool, exercise equipment, laundry facilities, business services, pets allowed (fee). | 3480 Hutton St., Springfield | 541/746–8471 | fax 541/747–1541 | $70–$76 | AE, D, DC, MC, V.

Kjaer's House in the Woods. This 1910 Craftsman B&B on the outskirts of town is a member of the Green Hotels Association (for ecologically conscious accommodations) and is 2½ mi from the University of Oregon campus. Both guest rooms have bright white bed spreads, one over an iron bedstead and one over a solid wood frame. A rosewood square grand piano, Danish plate collection, and other antiques fill the common areas. Complimentary breakfast. No air-conditioning. No TV. No in-room phones. No pets. | 814 Lorane Hwy. | 541/343–3234, 800/437–4501 | 2 rooms | $70–$85.

Red Lion Inn. You'll find larger than standard rooms at this hotel, which is 3 mi from the Lane County Fairgrounds and across the street from a shopping center. | 137 rooms. Restaurant, bar with entertainment, in-room data ports, room service, cable TV, pool, hot tub, exercise equipment, business services, airport shuttle, some pets allowed. | 205 Coburg Rd. | 541/342–5201 | fax 541/485–2314 | $59–$110 | AE, D, DC, MC, V.

EXPENSIVE

Campbell House. Built in 1892, Campbell House is one of the oldest structures in Eugene and is surrounded by an acre of landscaped grounds. The parlor, library, and dining rooms have their original hardwood floors and curved-glass windows. Differing architectural details, building angles, and furnishings (a mixture of century-old antiques and reproductions) lend each of the rooms a distinctive personality. There are 10 mi of jogging and biking paths and the inn is walking distance from downtown. | 12 rooms. Complimentary breakfast, dining rooms, in-room data ports, some microwaves, refrigerators, some in-room hot tubs, cable TV, library, business services, no smoking. | 252 Pearl St. | 541/343–1119 or 800/264–2519 | fax 541/343–2258 | $86–$289 | AE, D, MC, V.

Campus Cottage Bed & Breakfast. All rooms have plush comforters and overlook the sculpted European garden with its trickling fountain at the town's first B&B, only two blocks from the University of Oregon campus. | 3 rooms. Complimentary breakfast, refrigerators, in-room phones, cable TV. No air-conditioning. No kids under 12. No smoking. No pets. | 1136 E. 19th Ave. | 541/342–5346, 877/700–5346 | fax 541/241–0535 | www.campuscottage.com | $100–$130 | AE, D, DC, MC, V.

Oval Door Bed and Breakfast Inn. The wraparound porch on this 1990 house is in keeping with the 1920s neighborhood. It is near the university, the Hult Center, the Saturday Market, and restaurants. Guest rooms are named for Oregon wildflowers with decorative touches to match. A mixture of antiques, reproductions, floral prints, and an outdoor swing assure comfort. Both owners are chefs and showcase their talent at breakfast. And, yes, the house does have an oval door. | 4 doubles with bath. Complimentary breakfast, in-room data ports, cable TV, hot tub, no smoking. | 988 Lawrence St. | 541/683–3160 or 800/882–3160 | fax 541/485–0260 | ovaldoor@ovaldoor.com | www.ovaldoor.com | $125 | AE, MC, V.

Phoenix Inn. This all-suites hotel caters to a corporate clientele. It's 5 blocks from downtown Eugene and within walking distance of Autzen Stadium. | 97 rooms. Complimentary Continental breakfast, in-room data ports, microwaves, refrigerators, cable TV, indoor pool, hot tub, exercise equipment, laundry facilities, business services. | 850 Franklin Blvd. | 541/344–0001 or 800/344–0131 (for reservations) | fax 541/686–1288 | $76–$135 | AE, D, DC, MC, V.

Shilo Inn. You'll find Shilo's consistently dependable, comfortable, cozy rooms at this location 3½ mi northeast of Eugene. It is right next to 3 golf courses and 3½ blocks from Gateway Mall. | 140 rooms. Restaurant, bar, complimentary Continental breakfast, some kitchenettes, some microwaves, room service, cable TV, pool, laundry facilities, business services, airport shuttle, some pets allowed (fee). | 3350 Gateway St., Springfield | 541/747–0332 | fax 541/726–0587 | $89–$109 | AE, D, DC, MC, V.

VERY EXPENSIVE

Eugene Hilton. Location, amenities, and service make this downtown hotel Eugene's most convenient and comfortable. Sliding glass doors in each of the rooms open out to the city. The Hilton and its extensive convention facilities adjoin Eugene's Hult Center for the Performing Arts. Downtown shopping, the Willamette River, and more than 30 restaurants are within easy walking distance. | 272 rooms. Restaurant, bar with entertainment, some refrigerators, cable TV, indoor pool, hot tub, exercise equipment, business services, airport shuttle, some pets allowed (fee). | 66 E. Sixth Ave. | 541/342–2000 | fax 541/302–6660 | $100–$175 | AE, D, DC, MC, V.

★ **Valley River Inn.** Eugene's only four-star hotel, and one of only a few in the state of Oregon, is set on the picturesque bank of the Willamette River. Rooms have an outdoor patio or balcony, some have river or pool views. Concierge rooms on the third floor have access to a private lounge that serves a complimentary happy hour buffet with open bar. The Valley River Center, the largest shopping center between Portland and San Francisco, is across the parking lot. | 257 rooms. Restaurant, bar with entertainment, in-room data ports, room service, cable TV, pool, wading pool, hot tub, gym, business services, airport shuttle, free parking, some pets allowed. | 1000 Valley River Way | 541/687–0123 or 800/543–8266 | fax 541/683–5121 | reserve@valleyriverinn.com | www.valleyriverinn.com | $150–$180 | AE, D, DC, MC, V.

FLORENCE

MAP 3, C5

(Nearby towns also listed: Reedsport, Yachats)

Seventy-five creeks and rivers empty into the Pacific Ocean in and around Florence, and the Siuslaw River flows right through town. When the numerous nearby lakes are added to the mix, it makes for one of the richest fishing areas in Oregon. Salmon, rainbow trout, bass, perch, crabs, and clams are among the water's treasures. Fishing boats and pleasure craft moor in Florence's harbor, forming a picturesque backdrop for the town's restored buildings that now house galleries, restaurants, and shops. South of town, miles of white sand dunes lend themselves to everything from solitary hikes to rides aboard all-terrain vehicles.

Information: Florence Area Chamber of Commerce | 270 Hwy. 101, Florence 97439 | 541/997–3128 | www.florencechamber.com.

Attractions

C and M Stables. You can choose a 10-minute corral ride or take a horse out for the day to explore the beach or dunes. Children must be at least 8 yrs old for the beach ride or 6 yrs old for the dune trail rides. There are also 6 overnight RV spaces. | 90241 Hwy. 101 N | 541/997–7540 | www.touroregon.com/horses/index.html | $25–$40/hr | Daily 10–dusk.

Darlingtonia. This park is the only place in Oregon that has been set aside solely for plants. The carnivorous plants are visible from the boardwalk trail, 5 mi north of Florence. No pets allowed. | U.S. 101 | 800/551–6949 | www.prd.state.or.us | Free | Daily.

Devil's Elbow State Park. Heceta Head Lighthouse is in this park, 13 mi north of Florence, set in a cove at the mouth of Cape Creek, which has natural caves and tidepools. | U.S. 101 | 800/551–6949 or 541/997–3851 | www.prd.state.or.us | $3 per vehicle | Daily.

The beacon that shines from **Heceta Head Lighthouse** in Devil's Elbow State Park, visible for more than 21 mi, is the most powerful on the Oregon coast. A trail leads from the lighthouse to Heceta House, a pristine white structure said to be haunted by the wife of a lighthouse keeper whose child fell to her death from the cliffs shortly after the beacon was lit in 1894. The house, which was once the light keeper's residence, is now one of Oregon's most remarkable bed and breakfasts. The lighthouse is accessed via a half-mi-long trail from the parking lot in Devil's Elbow State Park. | U.S. 101 | 541/997–3851 | www.hecetalighthouse.com | $3 per vehicle | Memorial Day–Labor Day, tours daily by appointment.

Jessie M. Honeyman Memorial. Two mi of sand dunes lie between the park and the ocean. Two natural freshwater lakes are within the 522-acre park, 3 mi south of Florence, which has the second-largest campground in the state. There are 50 full hookups, 91 electrical and 237 tent sites, and 10 yurts. | U.S. 101 | 541/997–3851 | www.prd.state.or.us | Free, $3 per vehicle | Daily.

Incredible and Edible Oregon. This store in Florence's Old Town is devoted to Oregon's own products: wine, fruit preserves, books, and gift items. Especially popular are Pendleton blankets and items made from Oregon's unique myrtlewood. | 1350 Bay St. | 541/997–7018 | www.incredibleedible.com | June–Aug., daily 10–7; Sept.–May, daily 10–5.

Sandland Adventures. Just 1 mi south of town, Sandland rents ATVs and single-person dune buggies. There's an 8 mi stretch of sand dunes to explore right here. Sandland also has miniature golf and a go-kart track. | 85366 Hwy. 101 | 541/997–8087 | www.sandland.com | June–Sept., daily 9–6; Sept.–June, daily 9–3.

OREGON: LIGHTHOUSE LORE

Ten lighthouses stand on the 360 miles of Oregon's rocky, rugged coastline. But it's a wonder that they're standing at all. It's in the nature of lighthouses to take the brunt of storms, but Oregon's sentinels have occasionally crumbled before the winter onslaughts of rain and wind.

The Cape Arago Lighthouse at Coos Bay was first built in 1866. It had to be replaced with a new structure in 1908, and then again in 1934. (There's a good view of the current lighthouse from Shore Acres Botanical Gardens.) But Reedsport's Umpqua River Lighthouse fared even less well than that. Built in 1857, it quickly succumbed to the slings and arrows of outrageous winter storms and came crashing down only four years later. It was replaced in 1894.

The Cape Blanco Lighthouse qualifies for several titles. Not only is it Oregon's most southerly lighthouse, it's also the most westerly, the longest in continuous service (since 1870) and, at 245 ft, it towers highest above sea level. The light's first keeper, James Langlois, served here for 42 years; his name is preserved in the village of Langlois, just north of Cape Blanco on Highway 101. Another title goes to Cleft of the Rock Lighthouse in Yachats. It's the only Oregon light that is privately owned and operated. Maritime writer and former lighthouse keeper Jim Gibbs now has one of his very own.

Most interesting is Tillamook Rock at Cannon Beach. "Terrible Tilly," as local people know it, stands on a small rock island a mile and a half offshore, and Tilly's dark history began early. During construction in 1880, the land surveyor on the job drowned at the base of the rock. A century later, after the light was decommissioned, a private party bought the lighthouse and turned it into the Eternity at Sea Columbarium, its interior lined with shelves of urns containing the ashes of departed souls who wanted to be buried at sea . . . but not quite. The management's literature invites you to "be part of a preservation." Literally!

From south to north, Oregon's ten lighthouses are Cape Blanco (Port Orford), Coquille River (Bandon), Cape Arago (Coos Bay), Umpqua River (Reedsport), Heceta Head (Florence), Cleft of the Rock (Yachats), Yaquina Bay and Yaquina Head (Newport), Cape Meares (Tillamook), and Tillamook Rock (Cannon Beach).

—By Alan Ryan

Sea Lion Caves. An elevator near the ticket office at the cliff top, 11 mi north of Florence on U.S. 101, descends to the floor of the cavern, near sea level, where Stellar and California sea lions and their fuzzy pups can be viewed from behind a wire fence. In spring and summer the sea lions are on the rocky ledges outside the cave; during fall and winter they are usually inside the cave. You'll also see several species of sea birds here, including migratory pigeons, guillemots, cormorants, and three varieties of gulls. Gray whales are visible during their northern and southern migrations, from October to December and from March to May. | U.S. 101 | 541/547–3111 | www.sealioncaves.com | $6.50 | Daily 9–sunset.

Siuslaw Pioneer Museum. Formerly a Lutheran Church, the focus at this museum is on pioneer and Native American history. | 85294 U.S. 101 S | 541/997–7884 | $1 (suggested) | Jan.–Nov., Tues.–Sun. 10–4.

Carl G. Washburne Memorial. A trail from this park connects you to the newly completed Heceta Head trail, which you can use to reach the Heceta Head lighthouse. The campground has 58 full hookups, 2 tent sites, and 2 yurts. | 93111 Hwy. 101 N | 541/547–3416 | www.prd.state.or.us | Free, $3 per vehicle | Daily.

***Westward Ho!* Sternwheeler.** This Victorian riverboat leaves from the Old Town Docks and cruises the Siuslaw River past forests and the Oregon Dunes National Recreation Area. | Bay and Maple Sts. | 541/997–9691 | www.westward-ho.com | $12 adults | Apr.–Oct., daily; call for schedules.

ON THE CALENDAR

MAY: *Rhododendron Festival.* In spring thousands of rhododendrons bloom around Florence, and this annual rite is celebrated downtown with a carnival, a parade, a barbecue, an arts and crafts show, and a dance. | 541/997–3128.

SEPT.: *Chowder Blues and Brews Festival.* The fourth weekend in September brings live bands playing blues and jazz; a chowder cook-off by restaurants from Seaside to Bandon; local breweries offering tastings; a carnival; and fun for the kids, all of it at the Florence Event Center. | 541/997–3128.

Dining

Bridgewater Seafood Restaurant. Seafood. Freshly caught seafood—25 to 30 choices nightly—is the mainstay of this creaky-floored Victorian-era restaurant in Florence's Old Town. The cooking is plain and not exactly inspired, but the locals seem to like it that way. | 1297 Bay St. | 541/997–9405 | $14–$30 | MC, V.

Mo's. American. Mo's chain of family-style restaurants has been an institution on the Oregon coast for more than four decades. At this location, built right out over the water, bayfront views combine with fresh seafood, creamy clam chowder, and down-home service to keep it busy. | 1436 Bay St. | 541/997–2185 | fax 541/997–3504 | $6.95–$10.95 | D, MC, V.

Windward Inn. Seafood. One of the south coast's most elegant eateries, this tightly run ship prides itself on its vast menu, which includes fresh seafood and home-baked breads and desserts. Steak is also on the menu, but try the Chinook salmon fillets poached in Riesling or the shrimp and scallops sautéed in white wine. A pianist plays on weekends. Kids' menu. | 3757 U.S. 101 N | 541/997–8243 | Breakfast also available | $9–$21 | AE, D, MC, V.

Lodging

Best Western Pier Point Inn. This motel is built on a cliff overlooking the Siuslaw River. Most of the rooms have views of the waterfront and Old Town. It's 3 mi to the beach and ½ mi from downtown Florence. | 55 rooms. Complimentary Continental breakfast, cable TV, indoor pool, hot tub. | 85625 U.S. 101 S | 541/997–7191 | fax 541/997–3828 | $80–$130 | AE, D, DC, MC, V.

Driftwood Shores Resort. The chief amenity of this resort is its location directly above Heceta Beach, one of the longest sand beaches on the south coast. The simple rooms have ocean views while the three-bedroom suites have fireplaces. | 107 rooms, 21 suites. Kitchenettes. | 88416 1st Ave. | 541/997–8263 or 800/422–5091 | fax 541/997–5857 | $86–$130, $198–$265 suites | AE, D, DC, MC, V.

Holiday Inn Express. Just 3 mi from the beach and close to restaurants and shopping, this Holiday Inn Express combines convenience and comfort. | 51 rooms. Complimentary Continental breakfast, in-room data ports, cable TV, hot tub, exercise equipment. | 2475 U.S. 101 | 541/997–7797 | fax 541/997–7895 | $90 | AE, D, DC, MC, V.

Johnson House. The guest rooms in this 1892 Italianate Victorian in Old Town have lace curtains, crocheted doilies, and goose-down comforters, but best is the tiny cottage surrounded by gardens that supply the house with fruits, herbs, and edible flowers. The house is preserved with careful attention to detail and the period and antique furnishings are genuine. You can drive to the beach in 10 minutes, and it's a short walk to the antiques shops, crafts boutiques, and eateries on the bay dock. | 3 rooms, 1 suite, 1 cottage. Complimentary breakfast, no air-conditioning, no kids under 12, no smoking. | 216 Maple St. | 541/997–8000 or 800/768–9488 | fax 541/997–2364 | fraese@presys.com | www.tourore-gon.com/thejohnsonhouse | $95–$125 | D, MC, V.

Landmark Inn. The new Landmark, on a hilltop above the Siuslaw River, is surrounded by rhododendrons. It's near Dunes National Park, you can walk to Old Town, and the grounds offer a great view of the Fourth of July fireworks. The rooms have vaulted ceilings and the owners pride themselves on their clean and quiet home. | 4 rooms, 6 suites. Complimentary Continental breakfast, no air-conditioning, in-room data ports, some kitchenettes, some microwaves, some refrigerators, some in-room hot tubs, cable TV, spa, no smoking. | 1551 4th St. | 541/997–9030 or 800/822–7811 | landmarkinn@presys.com | www.presys.com/~land-markinn/ | $60–$95.

Money Saver. This two-story motel is 2 mi from the beach in a commercial neighborhood. | 40 rooms. No air-conditioning, cable TV, some pets allowed (fee). | 170 U.S. 101 | 541/997–7131 | $60–$80 | AE, D, MC, V.

Riverhouse. This motel on the river is within walking distance of restaurants and local shopping. Some of the rooms have waterfront views. | 40 rooms. No air-conditioning, some in-room hot tubs, cable TV, laundry facilities. | 1202 Bay St. | 541/997–3933 | fax 541/997–6263 | $70–$81 | AE, D, MC, V.

FOREST GROVE

MAP 3, D3

(Nearby towns also listed: Beaverton, Hillsboro, Portland)

Though it is named for a large grove of Oregon white oak trees situated on a knoll above the Tualatin Plains, Forest Grove is also surrounded by stands of Douglas firs and giant sequoia, including the largest giant sequoia in the state. Forest Grove, with a population 16,000, is home to Pacific University and the Pacific Northwest's only sake brewery, Momokawa Sake.

Information: Forest Grove Chamber of Commerce | 2417 Pacific Ave., Forest Grove 97116 | 503/357–3006 | www.grovenet.org/forestgrove/chamber/index.html.

Attractions

Montinore Vineyards. Sample local wines for free in the tasting room of this vineyard, or explore acres of perennial gardens with vine views. The gardens are a favorite picnic spot. | 3663 S.W. Dilley Rd. | 503/359–5012 | Apr.–Dec., daily 11–5; Jan.–Mar., weekends 11–5.

Pacific University. This small university with 1,800 students is located on a shady campus. Concerts and special events are held in McCready Hall in the Taylor-Meade Performing Arts

Center. The university is also home to the College of Optometry. | 2043 College Way | 503/357–6151 | www.pacificu.edu | Free | Daily.

Scoggin Valley Park and Hagg Lake. A beautiful area in the Coast Range foothills, this park has a 15-mi-long hiking trail that surrounds the lake. Bird-watching is best in spring. Recreational activities include fishing, boating, waterskiing, and picnicking. | Scoggin Valley Rd. | 503/846–3692 or 503/693–4890 | $3 | Daily dawn to dusk; facilities: Apr.–Oct.

ON THE CALENDAR

MAR.: ***All-Northwest Barbershop Ballad Contest.*** Quartets compete for prize money at this annual musical event held at the Pacific University's Field House. | 503/292–5673.

APR.: ***Hawaiian Luau.*** Pacific University's student body is 10 percent Hawaiian. This nighttime event held on the University Commons celebrates Hawaiian culture and features dining, Polynesian dancing, and colorful costumes. | 503/359–2107.

JULY: ***Concours d'Elegance.*** The Rotary Club hosts this event that features restored antique, classic, sport, and collector automobiles. There is also food and live entertainment offered on the tree-shaded campus of Pacific University on the third Sunday in July. | 503/357–2300.

AUG.: ***Elephant Garlic Festival.*** On the third weekend in August, the local motto becomes "Fun Stinks" when farmers from the surrounding Coast Range foothills bring their crop of the giant garlic to rural North Plains. This annual three-day festival takes place at the Jessie Mays Community Center, 8 mi from Forest Grove. You'll find a parade, arts and crafts booths, kids' activities, and music, and every food vendor must offer at least one garlic-flavored item. You might even find garlic beer and garlic ice cream. | 503/647–2207.

SEPT.: ***Founders Day and Corn Roast.*** A dinner with live entertainment is the highlight of this fall harvest event held at the Pacific University Center, the third weekend in September. | 503/357–3006.

Dining

Pub at McMenamin's. American. This open, airy pub in McMenamin's Lodge serves beef stew, burgers, gumbo, and a highly popular chicken pot pie to diners at booths and tables. | 3403 Pacific Ave. | 503/922–9533 | Breakfast also served | $8–$14 | MC, AE, V.

Lodging

McMenamin's Grand Lodge. The cornerstone of this former Masonic retirement home was laid in 1920. Now the building is full of plain guest rooms with borders hand-painted by local artisans and friendly common spaces with fireplaces, sofas, and a pool table. Each room has a sink and mirror, but the bathrooms are communal. Live music weekly. | 76 rooms, 1 suite. Complimentary breakfast. 2 restaurants, bar, outdoor pool, spa, in-room phones. No TV. No air-conditioning. | 3505 Pacific Ave. | 503/922–9533 | $45–$90, suite $200 | AE, D, MC, V.

Travelodge Suites. This chain property near Pacific University has rooms with expanded living and working space. | 41 rooms. Bar, complimentary Continental breakfast, in-room data ports, refrigerators, cable TV, indoor pool, hot tub, exercise equipment, laundry facilities, business services. | 3306 Pacific Ave. | 503/357–9000 | $63–$93 | AE, D, DC, MC, V.

FRENCHGLEN

MAP 3, I7

(Nearby town also listed: Burns)

The small town of Frenchglen is right at the base of Steens Mountain. While the mountain itself has almost no trees, it does have gorgeous wildflowers which begin appearing in June. Mainly meadow hay is grown in the area as the climate is usually mild year-round with temperatures seldom getting below zero. The entire Frenchglen Valley (all 150,000 acres) was originally owned by Pete French who established a ranch and a livestock company. Today the town is mainly known for its two bed and breakfasts and as a neighbor to the town of Burns 59 miles away.

Information: **Harney County Chamber of Commerce** | 76 E. Washington St., Burns, 97720 | 541/573–2636 | l.johnso@oregonvos.net.

Attractions

East Rim Viewpoint At 5,000 ft above the valley floor, on a clear day you can see as far as Alvord Desert, which stretches into Idaho and Nevada. You can reach it from the south end of Frenchglen. | Hwy. 205 | 541/573–2636 | Free | mid-July–Oct.

Steens Loop Road. This 52-mi road will take you around Steens Mountain and over to Kiger Gorge. The gorge has a U-shape path which was carved out by a glacier. The views are incredible and you might pass some bighorn sheep or golden eagles on the way. Pick up the loop road from Hwy. 205 and return to the highway about 9 mi south of Frenchglen. | Off Hwy. 205 | 541/573–2636 | Free | Mid-July–Oct.

ON THE CALENDAR

AUG.: *Steens Mountain Rim Run and Walk.* This annual Frenchglen event, held on the first Saturday in August, features a 10k-course: starting at an elevation of 7,835 ft, following the east rim of the mountain, and finishing at a viewpoint at an elevation of 9,700 ft. | 541/573–6341.

Dining

Buckaroo Room. American. This small restaurant adjoins Frenchglen's only store–the Frenchglen Mercantile. Now serving three meals a day, people come from miles around for the filet mignon. | Hwy. 205 | 541/493–2738 | fax 541/493–2835 | Reservations essential for dinner | Closed mid-Nov.–mid-March | $20–$23 | AE, D, MC, V.

Lodging

Frenchglen Hotel. This two-story wood-frame home is owned by the Oregon State Parks Department. The rooms are basic, but charming. The Malheur National Wildlife Refuge is across the street, making this a good spot for bird watchers to stay. A family-style dinner is served each evening at 6:30 sharp. | 8 rooms, 2 share bath. Breakfast, lunch and dinner served, no room phones, no TV. | Hwy. 205 | 541/493–2825 | fax 541/493–2828 | $58; 1 room with double bed and single, $62 | Closed Nov. 15–March 15 | Reservations for dinner essential | D, MC, V.

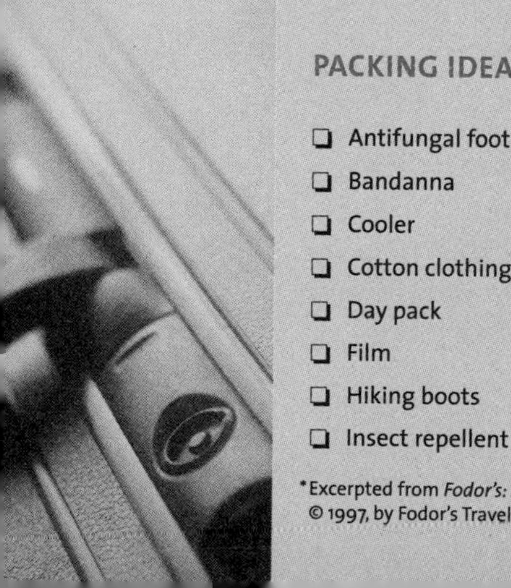

PACKING IDEAS FOR HOT WEATHER

- ❑ Antifungal foot powder
- ❑ Bandanna
- ❑ Cooler
- ❑ Cotton clothing
- ❑ Day pack
- ❑ Film
- ❑ Hiking boots
- ❑ Insect repellent
- ❑ Rain jacket
- ❑ Sport sandals
- ❑ Sun hat
- ❑ Sunblock
- ❑ Synthetic ice
- ❑ Umbrella
- ❑ Water bottle

*Excerpted from *Fodor's: How to Pack: Experts Share Their Secrets*

Steens Mountain Inn. Both bedrooms at this small inn have decks that look out over the Steens Mountain and the Malheur National Wildlife Refuge. Decorated with a western flair, the inn deftly combines Western art with antiques. | 2 rooms. Restaurant, no room phones, no TV. | Hwy. 205 | 541/493–2738 | fax 541/493–2835 | $65 | Closed mid-Nov.–mid Mar. | AE, D, MC, V.

GLENEDEN BEACH

MAP 3, C4

(Nearby town also listed: Lincoln City)

South of Lincoln City, the unincorporated community of Gleneden Beach is primarily known as the site of Salishan Lodge, the most famous resort on the Oregon coast. The ritzy collection of guest rooms, condos, vacation homes, restaurants, tennis courts, and an acclaimed 18-hole golf course are nestled in a forest preserve. State waysides and parks in the Gleneden Beach area also provide good beach access.

Information: Lincoln City Chamber of Commerce | 4039 N.W. Logan Road, Lincoln City 97367 | 541/994–3070 | fax 541/994–83339 | www.lcchamber.com.

Attractions

Gallery at Salishan. This long-established gallery has a well-informed staff that will guide you through the collections of work by Northwest artists, including paintings (pastels, oils, and watercolors), glassworks, bronze and metal, furniture, and ceramics and porcelain. | 7755 N. Hwy. 101 | 541/764–2318 or 800/764–2318 | fax 541/764–3531 | www.salishan.com/gallery | Memorial Day–Labor Day, Mon.–Sat. 10–6, Sun. 10–5; Labor Day–Memorial Day, daily 10–5.

ON THE CALENDAR

JULY: *Fourth of July Parade.* The entire town comes out for this annual event, which has its own planning committee. An old-timer's washtub group, local dogs, and floats from area businesses march through the center of town. | 541/994–3070.

Dining

★ **Chez Jeannette.** French. The dining room in this country-French cottage is quiet, with a fireplace, antiques, and tables set with linen and crystal. The menu puts a Parisian spin on locally grown food. The restaurant is known for its skillfully prepared seafood, rack of lamb, and game. Try the carpetbagger steak, a thick fillet stuffed with tiny local oysters, wrapped in bacon, in a sauce of crème fraîche, scallions, spinach, and bacon. Kids' menu. | 7150 Old U.S. 101 | 541/764–3434 | No lunch | $21–$30 | AE, D, MC, V.

Dining Room at Salishan. Contemporary. The Salishan resort's multilevel main dining room features artfully prepared Pacific Northwest cuisine. The wine list is extensive with more than 10,000 bottles in the wine cellar. Kids' menu. Sun. brunch. | 7760 U.S. 101 | 541/764–2371 | Breakfast also available | $35–$50 | AE, D, DC, MC, V.

Sidedoor Cafe. Contemporary. This dining room with a high ceiling, exposed beams, a fireplace, and many windows just under the eaves shares a former tile factory with the Eden Hall performance space. The menu changes constantly—fresh preparations have included mushroom-crusted rack of lamb and broiled swordfish with citrus-raspberry vinaigrette over coconut-ginger basmati rice. | 6675 Gleneden Beach Loop Rd. | 541/764–3825 | Closed Tues. | $17–$25 | MC, V.

Lodging

Beachcombers Haven. The comfortable condo units at this small inn right on the beach have roomy living rooms and wood stoves or fireplaces. The decor is contemporary. Choose from 1-, 2-, or 3-bedroom units. | 7 rooms. Kitchenettes, some in-room hot tubs, in-room VCRs, laundry facilities. | 7045 N.W. Glen Ave. | 541/764–2252 or 800/428–5533 | fax 541/764–4094 | $125–$165 | D, MC, V.

Cavalier Beachfront Condominiums. Every condo in this three-story building has two bedrooms, a private deck, and an ocean view. There is little traffic noise at this place at the end of the road: you hear only the waves. | 30 condos. Indoor pool, cable TV, in-room phones, beach, game room, library. | 325 N.W. Lancer St. | 888/454–0880 | $185 | MC, V.

Salishan. Nestled on a 700-acre hillside forest preserve on the Oregon coast, Salishan comprises multiple buildings connected by bridges and walkways. Views of the ocean, forest, and golf course are available and there is a self-guided nature trail. The rooms feature gas fireplaces and art work by Oregon artists. | 205 rooms. Restaurant (*see* The Dining Room at Salishan), bar with entertainment, refrigerators, room service, cable TV, indoor pool, hot tub, driving range, 18-hole golf course, putting green, tennis, gym, shops, library, business services, some pets allowed (fee). | 7760 U.S. 101 | 541/764–2371 or 800/452–2300 | fax 541/764–3681 | www.salishan.com | $249–$349 | AE, D, DC, MC, V.

GOLD BEACH

MAP 3, B8

(Nearby towns also listed: Brookings, Port Orford)

Situated on the shores of the Rogue River and the Pacific Ocean just 37 miles north of California, Gold Beach was christened for the gold found in its sands. Today the treasures of Gold Beach are mostly to be found in its waters. The area is a year-round deep sea and freshwater angler's paradise, rich with salmon, steelhead, and cutthroat trout, among others. At the same time, numerous operators offer short and long excursion and jet boat tours of the Rogue, one of America's original wild and scenic rivers.

Information: Gold Beach Chamber of Commerce | 29279 Ellensburg Ave., #3, Gold Beach 97444 | 541/247–7526 or 800/525–2334 | goldbeach@harborside.com | www.harborside.com/gb.

Attractions

Cape Sebastian State Park. The parking lots here are more than 200 ft above sea level. At the south parking vista you can see up to 43 mi north to Humbug Mountain. Looking south you can see nearly 50 mi toward Crescent City, California, and the Point Saint George Lighthouse. A deep forest of Sitka spruce covers most of the park. There's a 1.5-mi walking trail. | U.S. 101 | 541/469–2021 or 800/551–6949 | www.prd.state.or.us | Free | Daily.

Cedar Bend Golf Course. Two tees at each hole of this 9-hole course 10 mi north of town allow you to golf 18 holes among the deer, elk, hawk, eagles, and other wildlife that inhabit the valley around Cedar Fork Creek. | 34391 Squaw Valley Rd. | 541/247–6911 | 9 holes $15, 18 holes $20.

Curry County Historical Museum. Area Native American baskets, historic photos, and documents are featured at this small museum on the Curry County Fairgrounds | 920 S. Ellensburg | 541/247–6113 | Free | June–Sept., Tues.–Sat. noon–4; Oct.–May, Sat. 10–4.

Jerry's Rogue River Jet Boat Trips. Take a 64-, 80-, or 104-mi round trip up the Wild and Scenic–designated section of the Rogue River. The trips last from 6–8 hours and leave from the Rogue River Bridge at the port of Gold Beach Boat Basin. | 541/247–4571 or 800/451–3645 | fax 541/247–7601 | www.roguejets.com | $30–$75 | May–Oct., daily; call for hours.

Official Rogue River Mail Boat Hydro-Jet Trips. This company located slightly upstream from the north end of Rogue River Bridge in Wedderburn has provided over 100 years of continuous postal service and you can ride along on its 64-, 80-, or 104-mi trips along the

Rogue River. Bring along a picnic lunch, although reasonably priced meals are available at one of three lodges in Agness. Keep an eye out for bears. | Mail Boat Dock | 541/247–7033 or 800/458–3511 | www.mailboat.com | May–Oct., daily; call for hours.

Prehistoric Gardens. These colorful life-size replicas of dinosaurs are the artistic interpretations of the late sculptor E. V. Nelson. The "Dinopark" is 15 mi from Gold Beach in a rain forest filled with giant ferns. | U.S. 101, in Oregon's rain forest | 541/332–4463 | $6 | Daily, 8–dusk; call for hours in winter.

ON THE CALENDAR

JAN.: ***Whale of a Wine Festival.*** Area restaurants and caterers present food selections and cooking demonstrations at this three-day winter event held on the Curry County Fairgrounds. Wine tasting from 10 to 12 select wineries, and a large selection of work by area artists is also featured. Musical entertainment, crafts booths, and a wine and art auction round out the festivities. | 541/247–7526.

MAY: ***Clam Chowder Festival, Flower and Art Show.*** This two-day spring festival at the Curry County Fairgrounds has booths for clam-chowder tasting and a floral show. | 541/247–4541 or 800/525–2334.

JUNE: ***Rogue River Jet Boat Marathon.*** You can watch power-boat racers from all corners of the continent speed up to 100 mi per hour at this annual two-day festival. There is also a dinner, a boat show, and live music. | 541/247–2232.

JULY: ***Curry County Fair.*** This coastal community presents its annual county fair and rodeo on grounds right on the oceanfront, the last weekend in July. | 541/247–4541.

Dining

Captain's Table. American. This restaurant has been housed in a early-20th-century Craftsman bungalow since 1965. It's the good steaks and fresh seafood that matter here, along with a nice view of the ocean. Local people come for the sautéed mushrooms, steamed clams, and such special dishes as salmon teriyaki. | 29251 Ellensburg Rd. (Hwy. 101) | 541/247–6308 | Reservations not accepted | No lunch | $12–$20 | MC, V.

Nor'wester Seafood. Continental. This restaurant overlooking the boat harbor and the Rogue River serves good seafood, steaks, and pasta. Kids' menu. | 29971 Harbor Way | 541/247–2333 | Closed Dec.–Jan. No lunch | $15–$23 | AE, MC, V.

Tu Tu' Tun Lodge. Contemporary. Dinner in the Lodge's restaurant, 7 mi upriver from Gold Beach, is open to non-guests and consists of a five-course prix-fixe meal that changes nightly. Portions are memorably large. | 96550 N. Bank Rogue | 541/247–6664 or 800/864–6357 | fax 541/247–0672 | Reservations essential | Closed Nov.–Apr. | $35.50–$41.50 | D, MC, V.

Lodging

Best Western Inn of the Beachcomber. As the name suggests, this is a great place for beachcombing and hunting for beach agates, sand dollars, and other treasures. The hotel is no more than 300 ft from the water and most rooms have a view of the ocean. You can walk to restaurants and the county fairgrounds. The Visitors Center is across the street. | 44 rooms, 5 suites | 29266 Ellensburg Rd. (Hwy. 101) | 541/247–6691 or 888/690–2378 | fax 541/247–7981 | www.bestwestern.com | $87–$94 | AE, D, MC, V.

Inn at Nesika Beach. The beautifully decorated rooms at this intimate Victorian-style B&B, 6 mi north of Gold Beach, have hardwood floors and ocean views. | 4 rooms. Complimentary breakfast, in-room hot tubs, no room phones, no smoking. | 33026 Nesika Rd. | 541/247–6434 | www.moriah.com/nesika | $100–$130 | No credit cards.

Ireland's Rustic Lodges. You can see the ocean from most of the rustic-seeming rooms in the main building here, which sits on oceanfront property amid landscaped gardens. The older cabins have a rough-hewn charm, some have decks overlooking the ocean, and most have fireplaces. | 40 rooms, 9 cabins. Some kitchenettes, some microwaves, some refrigerators, cable TV, no room phones, playground, laundry facilities. | 29330 Ellensburg Rd. (Hwy. 101) | 541/247–7718 | fax 541/247–0225 | www.tsun.net/shorecliffinn | $50–$70 | AE, D, MC, V.

Shore Cliff Inn. The rooms are bright, but the decor is a bit dated. The inn is right on the beach and most rooms have oceanfront views. | 40 rooms. Some kitchenettes, cable TV, pets allowed. | 29346 Ellensburg Ave. (U.S. 101) | 541/247–7091 | $50–$70 | AE, MC, V.

★ **Tu Tu' Tun Lodge.** All the units in this small fishing resort on the Rogue River, 7 mi upriver from Gold Beach, are cozy and warm, mimicking its rustic setting. Private decks overlook the river and old-growth trees. The restaurant which is closed from November through April serves breakfast, lunch, and dinner. Dinner is open to nonguests, although reservations are hard to come by. The lodge also offers white-water boat trips. | 16 rooms, 2 suites, 1 garden house. Restaurant, bar, complimentary hors d'oeuvres, in-room data ports, some in-room hot tubs, pool, dock, boating, business services, airport shuttle. | 96550 N. Bank Rogue | 541/247–6664 or 800/864–6357 (for reservations) | fax 541/247–0672 | www.tututun.com | $85–$125, $125 suites, $125 garden house | D, MC, V.

GRANTS PASS

MAP 3, D8

(Nearby towns also listed: Cave Junction, Jacksonville, Medford)

The seat of Josephine County, Grants Pass distinguishes itself as the "white-water capital of Oregon." The Rogue River, preserved by Congress in 1968 as a National Wild and Scenic River, runs right through town. Several opportunities are available for exploring the Rogue, from jet boat to raft or fishing boat. The downtown area attracts attention with its National Historic District, antique shops, and bed-and-breakfasts. But it's the white waters and Hellgate Canyon, with sheer rock walls rising 250 ft, that moviemakers and visitors alike find the most compelling.

Information: Grants Pass/Josephine County Chamber of Commerce | 1995 N.W. Vine St., Grants Pass 97526 | 541/476–7717 | gpcoc@grantspass.com | www.grantspass.com/chamber.

Attractions

Grants Pass Museum of Art. This city museum in Riverside Park displays classic and contemporary art including the works of local artists. | 229 S.W. G St. | 541/479–3290 | Free | Tues.–Sat. noon–4.

Hellgate Jetboat Excursions. You'll see some of Oregon's most magnificent scenery on a tour to Hellgate Canyon which departs from Riverside Inn. The 36-mi round trip from Grants Pass through Hellgate Canyon takes 2 hours. There is also a 5½-hr, 75-mi round trip from Grants Pass to Grave Creek with a stop for a meal on an open-air deck (cost of meal not included). | 966 S.W. 6th | 541/479–7204 or 800/648–4874 | www.hellgate.com | 2-hr trip $25; 5½-hr trip $45; brunch cruises $36; supper cruises $41; special rates for children | May–Sept., daily; brunch cruises May–Sept., weekends 9:15; supper cruises May–Sept., weekends 4:15 (3:15 in Sept.).

Siskiyou National Forest. Located in the Klamath Mountains and the Coast Ranges of southwestern Oregon, this 1.1-million-acre forest is home to the 35-mi-long Wild and Scenic section of the Rogue River, which races through the Wild Rogue Wilderness Area, and the Illinois and Chetco Wild and Scenic Rivers, which runs through the 180,000-acre Kalmiopsis Wilderness Area. Activities include white-water rafting, camping, and hiking, but many hiking areas require trail-park passes. There are 25 campgrounds. | Off U.S. 199 | 541/471–6516 | www.fs.fed.us/r6/siskiyou | Park pass required | Daily.

Valley of the Rogue State Park. This park has a 1¼-mi hiking trail that follows the Rogue River bank. A campground along 3 mi of shoreline has 97 full hookups, 49 electrical and

21 tent sites, and 6 yurts. There are picnic tables, walking trails, playgrounds, and rest rooms. | Exit 45B off I–5 | 541/582–1118 or 800/551–6949 | www.prd.state.or.us | Free; $3 per vehicle | Daily.

ON THE CALENDAR

MAY: *Boatnik Festival.* The main event at this four-day festival, which takes place at Riverside Park on Memorial Day weekend, is a hydroboat race, but there are also a parade, rafting, and contests. | 541/476–5510.

MAY–JULY: *Parimutuel Horse Racing.* You can wager on local ponies at the fairgrounds from the end of May through July 4. | 541/476–3215.

JULY: *Back to the 50s Summer Celebration.* Even before the last weekend in July, Grants Pass steps back into the '50s with a rock 'n' roll concert on Tuesday evening. On Friday evening, there's a Classic Car Cruise on 6th and 7th Streets, with more than 500 cars, and there's a big free outdoor rock 'n' roll dance that lasts until the wee hours. On Saturday, you can see the cars close up and talk to their owners at Riverside Park, and from 4–6 there's a Wine Stroll where local wineries provide tastings. There's a charge for some activities but prices are modest. | 541/476–5773.

AUG.: *Josephine County Fair.* This old-fashioned summer county fair has baking, crafts, and hobby contests, livestock auctions, entertainment, carnival rides, a four-wheel-drive pull, and even pig races. | 1451 Fairgrounds Rd. | 541/476–3215.

SEPT.: *Jedediah Smith Mountain Man Rendezvous and Buffalo Barbecue.* Flash back to the 1800s at this festival that lasts for several days at Sportsman Park over Labor Day weekend. Muzzle loaders and authentic clothing turn the park into a pioneer settlement. | 541/476–7717 or 541/476–5510.

Dining

Big Daddy's. American/Casual. Cherry-red bar stools, Formica tables, and a black-and-white-check floor welcome you to this back-to-the-50s diner that prides itself on shakes and burgers. | 956 Rogue River Hwy. | 541/479–8667 | $3–$5.

The Brewery. Seafood. No beer has been brewed in this 1886 building since Prohibition, but the name sounds good anyway. You can order Australian lobster tails, steak, Caribbean jerk catfish, and other surf-and-turf dishes from the extensive menu. Dine under exposed beams between the original brick walls, which surround three dining rooms filled with booths and oak tables. Sun. brunch. | 509 S.W. G St. | 541/479–9850 | No lunch Mon. and Sat. | $8–$40 | AE, D, DC, MC, V.

Hamilton River House. Contemporary. Familiar dishes prepared with special care are the draw here: brick-oven pizza, salmon ravioli, baby back ribs, rotisserie chicken, Caesar salad with blackened salmon, seafood fettucini, and steaks and fresh seafood. A deck overlooks the river and all tables, some elevated, have a river view. There are jazz and blues on weekends and a popular live jam on Wednesday night. | 1936 Rogue River Hwy. | 541/479–3938 | $7.50–$16.95 | AE, D, MC, V.

Legrand's. Continental. In a converted 1930s house on one of the town's main streets, the French chef-owner prepares such dishes as duck in orange sauce, rack of lamb, pork with ginger and apple, and of course escargots, and there's a very special chocolate mousse cake for dessert. He also bakes his own breads and pastries and makes his own pasta. The small restaurant is decorated with paintings by the talented staff, all of which are for sale. | 323 N.E. E St. | 541/471–1554 | Closed major holidays | $10.75–$19.95 | D, MC, V.

Matsukaze. Japanese. Matsukaze means "breeze through the pines" in Japanese and the setting is enhanced with woodwork, rice-paper lanterns, and wood-slat lamps. Chicken teriyaki, tempura, and beef cooked on a grill at the table are the most popular items, but you can also have sushi, sukiyaki, mahi mahi, and the special spicy barbecued chicken. There are some Korean dishes, too, and, because of the owners' background, the menu has a somewhat Hawaiian flair. | 1675 N.E. 7th St. | 541/479–2961 | fax 541/479–2961 | Closed Sun. | $7.95–$16.95 | D, MC, V.

Morrison's Rogue River Lodge. Contemporary. This rafting and fishing resort on the Rogue River serves country-style cuisine. Priority seating is given to guests staying at the lodge. Supper is an all-inclusive four-course meal. | 8500 Galice Rd., Merlin | 541/476–3825 | Reservations essential | Closed Nov.–Apr. No lunch | $22–$35 | D, MC, V.

Royal Barge Thai Cuisine. Thai. As you enter the Royal Barge, you're greeted by a life-size statue of a Thai girl in traditional costume, a fixture in many restaurants in Thailand. Pictures of the country enhance the mood. Many dinners are served family-style, and there are curries, vegetarian dishes with brown rice, and barbecued chicken with Thai spices and seasonings. End your meal, as most diners do, with the homemade coconut ice cream. | 120 S.W. H St. | 541/474–6942 | Closed major holidays | $7.95–$9.95 | AE, D, DC, MC, V.

Sunshine Natural Foods. Organic. In the downtown business district, conveniently located near parks, shops, and galleries, this very popular lunch spot offers an impressive buffet plus sandwiches. Those in the know come for the curry bowtie pasta. | 128 S.W. H St. | 541/474–5044 | Reservations not accepted | No dinner | MC, V.

Yankee Pot Roast. American. The restaurant in this restored 1905 house is famous for—what else—biscuits, as well as pot roast. But they also serve fresh halibut, salmon, meat loaf, roast chicken, and steak. | 720 N.W. Sixth St. | 541/476–0551 | Closed Tues. No lunch | $13–$22 | MC, V.

Lodging

Best Western Grants Pass Inn. This motel is located right off the interstate, 1 mi from Rogue River. | 84 rooms, 6 suites. Restaurant, bar, in-room data ports, some refrigerators, some in-room hot tubs, cable TV, pool, hot tub, laundry facilities, business services. | 111 N.E. Agness Ave. | 541/476–1117 | fax 541/479–4315 | www.bestwestern.com | $73–$83, $110–130 suites | AE, D, DC, MC, V.

Best Western Inn at the Rogue. Best Western's newer Grants Pass property is across from the Rogue River and has the relaxed feeling of a lodge. Fishing and white-water rafting are minutes away. Some rooms have river views. | 54 rooms. Bar, complimentary Continental breakfast, minibars, microwaves, some refrigerators, some in-room hot tubs, cable TV, pool, hot tub, exercise equipment, laundry facilities, business services, some pets allowed (fee). | 8959 Rogue River Hwy. | 541/582–2200 | fax 541/582–1415 | www.bestwestern.com | $85–$95 | AE, D, DC, MC, V.

Comfort Inn. It's only 1 mi to Rogue River. | 59 rooms. Complimentary Continental breakfast, some refrigerators, cable TV, pool, pets allowed. | 1889 N.E. Sixth St. | 541/479–8301 | fax 541/955–9721 | www.comfortinn.com | $40–$55 | AE, D, DC, MC, V.

Crest Motel. This tiny roadside motor lodge with standard rooms is across from a store where everything is a dollar. This might just be the best deal in town. | 10 rooms. Cable TV, air-conditioning. | 1203 N.E. 6th St. | 541/479–0720 | $30–$35 | AE, MC, V.

Doubletree Ranch. The four cabins on this 160-acre 1891 homestead with almost a mile of private Rogue River frontage are filled with furniture that has been on the ranch for four generations. You can enjoy the peace and quiet and mountain or river view from the deck of your cabin 11 mi northwest of town. | 4 cabins. Hiking, fishing, kitchenettes, air-conditioning. No in-room TV. TV available. No in-room phones. | 6000 Abegg Rd., Merlin | 541/476–0120 | $75–$125 | Closed Oct.–May.

Flery Manor. Situated on seven acres of mountainside, this secluded inn has cozy, elegant rooms filled with antique furniture and fresh flowers. Some of the rooms have fireplaces. Robes are provided. Coffee or tea is delivered to your door before breakfast. | 4 rooms. Picnic area, complimentary breakfast, no TV in rooms, TV in common area, business services, no kids under 10, no smoking. | 2000 Jumpoff Joe Creek Rd. | 541/476–3591 | fax 541/471–2303 | flery@flerymanor.com | www.flerymanor.com | $75–$125 | MC, V.

Hawthorne Inn & Suites. This three-story hotel has some standard rooms and some with country-style quilts, light bed frames, and night stands. | 28 rooms, 31 suites. Complimentary breakfast, cable TV, some kitchenettes, indoor pool, some hot tubs, sauna, air-conditioning. Pets allowed. | 243 N.E. Morgan La. | 541/472–1808 | $62–$78 | AE, D, DC, MC, V.

Holiday Inn Express. This four-story hotel is in a quiet neighborhood. It is very close to the Rogue River and within walking distance of restaurants and movie theaters. | 80 rooms. Complimentary Continental breakfast, in-room data ports, cable TV, pool, hot tub, laundry facilities, business services, some pets allowed (fee). | 105 N.E. Agness Ave. | 541/471–6144 | fax 541/471–9248 | www.holiday-inn.com | $81–$91 | AE, D, DC, MC, V.

Ivy House. This 1908 English Arts and Crafts brick home in the Historic District was originally a restaurant and tea room. The restored interior is unfussy, but the guest rooms have eiderdown quilts and antiques and there are two sitting rooms for guests. From the porch, you can enjoy the rose bushes which were planted in 1908. Restaurants, theatres, galleries, and the river are all within walking distance. The charming English owner observes a fine old tradition: you can have morning tea and biscuits in bed before your full English breakfast. | 5 rooms. Complimentary breakfast, TV in common area, no smoking. | 139 S.W. St. | 541/474–7363 | fax 541/474–7363 | ivyhousebbemail@msn.com | $60–$75 | D, MC, V.

Morrison's Rogue River Lodge. Twelve mi west of Grants Pass on a peaceful bend in the Rogue River, guests of Morrison's tend to favor the nearby rafting and fishing. The rooms have fireplaces, private decks, and covered parking. | 4 rooms in lodge, 9 cottages. Restaurant, picnic area, refrigerators, in-room VCRs, pool, tennis, business services. | 8500 Galice Rd., Merlin | 541/476–3825 or 800/826–1963 | fax 541/476–4953 | info@morrisonslodge.com | www.morrisonslodge.com | $100–$150/person | Closed mid-Nov.–Apr. | D, MC, V.

Motel Del Rogue. This motel is right on the Rogue River where the steelhead and salmon are plentiful. Three mi from the center of town, the rooms at this small motel have private decks, many overlooking the landscaped lawn. Fishing guides are nearby. | 14 rooms. Picnic area, many kitchenettes, some microwaves, cable TV, laundry facilities. | 2600 Rogue River Hwy. | 541/479–2111 | $45–$55 | MC, V.

Pine Meadow. This inn is a Midwestern-style farm house furnished with turn-of-the-20th-century antiques on nine acres of meadow and woods. | 4 rooms. Complimentary breakfast, outdoor hot tub, no smoking. | 1000 Crow Rd., Merlin | 541/471–6277 or 800/554–0806 | pmi@pinemeadowinn.com | www.pinemeadowinn.com | $80–$110 | D, MC, V.

Ponderosa Pine Inn. This white home built in 2000 sits on 5 acres 8 mi south of town and has a wide wraparound veranda and 2 country guest rooms, one with a rattan sofa, the other with wicker furnishings and a quilt. You can hike through the woods to the old logging trail behind the house. | 2 rooms. Complimentary breakfast, TV in common area, air-conditioning. No in-room phones. | 907 Stringer Gap | 541/474–4933 | $90–$95 | MC, V.

Redwood Motel. This motel is in a park-like setting that is filled with a wide variety of flora, which are all identified with markers. The rooms are bright and comfortable. | 28 rooms. Picnic area, complimentary Continental breakfast, some kitchenettes, some microwaves, some refrigerators, some in-room hot tubs, cable TV, pool, playground, laundry facilities, some pets allowed (fee). | 815 N.E. Sixth St. | 541/476–0878 | fax 541/476–1032 | info@redwoodmotel.com | www.redwoodmotel.com | $66–$97 | AE, D, DC, MC, V.

Riverside Inn Resort and Conference Center. This large resort on the Rogue River covers three city blocks. The rooms are cozy and decorated with fabrics highlighting Pacific Northwest themes. Almost all rooms overlook the river. Hellgate Jetboat Excursions depart from a nearby dock May–Sept. | 174 rooms. Restaurant, bar, some in-room hot tubs, cable TV in-room, 2 pools, hot tubs, business services, some pets allowed (fee). | 971 S.E. Sixth St. | 541/476–6873 or 800/334–4567 | fax 541/474–9848 | riverinn@budget.net | www.riverside-inn.com | $88–$98 | AE, D, DC, MC, V.

Royal Vue. Every room in this hotel, which is close to I–5, has a patio or a balcony. Restaurants and shopping are nearby. | 60 rooms. Restaurant, bar with entertainment, refrigerator, room service, cable TV, pool, hot tub, laundry facilities, pets allowed. | 110 N.E. Morgan Lane | 541/479–5381 or 800/547–7555 (outside Oregon), 800/452–1452 | $48–$53 | AE, D, DC, MC, V.

Shilo Inn. This modern motel in a residential neighborhood, 2 mi from the city center and 3 mi from the Rogue River, provides comfortable convenient lodging. | 70 rooms. Continental breakfast, cable TV, pool, pets allowed (fee). | 1880 N.W. Sixth St. | 541/479–8391 | fax 541/474–7344 | grantspass@shiloinns.com | $84–$105 | AE, D, DC, MC, V.

Weasku. Set among tall pine trees in the heart of the Rogue Wilderness, this rustic inn built in 1924 has nine suites with fireplaces and private decks overlooking the Rogue River. There is also an A-frame cabin and two spacious suites with dining areas, fireplaces, and private decks. The lodge, which is filled with antiques, also has five second-floor standard rooms. | 5 rooms, 11 suites in lodge, 1 cabin. Picnic area, complimentary Continental breakfast, some in-room hot tubs, cable TV, business services, no kids under 12, no smoking. | 5560 Rogue River Hwy. | 541/471–8000 or 800/493–2758 (for reservations) | fax 541/471–7038 | www.weasku.com | $85–$250, $225–$295 suites, $125–$195 cabin | AE, D, DC, MC, V.

GRESHAM

MAP 3, E3

(Nearby towns also listed: Lake Oswego, Portland, Troutdale)

Gresham was founded in the mid-1800s by westward-bound pioneers who cut a trail in the wilderness as they descended Mount Hood. Today, it remains a well-traveled passageway between the Columbia River Gorge and the Mount Hood recreation areas.

With a population of about 80,000 people, Gresham is Oregon's fourth-largest city and is recognized as Portland's largest suburb to the east, with light manufacturing, technology, and agriculture forming its employment infrastructure. Gresham calls itself the "city of music" for the festivals that have flourished in its midst. The first and most notable is the annual Mount Hood Jazz Festival, hosted by Gresham and Mount Hood Community College in early August.

Information: Gresham Area Chamber of Commerce | 150 W. Powell, Gresham | 503/665–1131.

Attractions

Gresham Farmers' Market. Every Saturday in summer, rain or shine, you can buy fresh produce and flowers from local growers at this outdoor market on Roberts Avenue between 2nd and 5th Streets. Other vendors sell honey, baked goods, food, and gourmet coffee, and there's entertainment, too. | Roberts St. between 2nd and 5th Aves., 97030 | 503/727–9828 | Free | Mother's Day–Oct., Sat. 8:30 AM–2 PM.

ON THE CALENDAR

AUG.: ***Mt. Hood Jazz Festival.*** This three-day jazz festival, one of the best in the country, began in 1982 and features jazz and blues artists on two stages at Mt. Hood Community College. Get information on performers, schedules, and tickets at www.mthoodjazz.com. | For information: 503/219–9833. For tickets: 503/224–8499 or 800/992–8499.

Dining

Persimmon Grille. Contemporary. The Grille is at the Persimmon Country Club, tucked away in the hills 5 mi from Gresham. On the lower level of the hillside clubhouse, this light and airy room overlooks the golf course with a view of Mt. Hood in the background. Northwest touches accent the menu of Black Angus prime rib, charbroiled salmon, baked halibut, Dungeness crab and shrimp salad, as well as a very special local dessert, marion-berry cobbler. | 500 S.E. Butler Rd. | 503/666–4797 | fax 503/667–3885 | Closed Oct.–March; closed Mon. | $13–$23 | AE, D, MC, V.

Lodging

Sleep Inn. This Sleep Inn, within sight of Exit 13 from I–84, offers economy and convenience. It's 13 mi from downtown Portland and only 5 mi from the Columbia River Gorge. It's also within walking distance of restaurants, and half a block away you can visit the Candy Basket Factory Outlet with its chocolate waterfall. The hotel has a two-story atrium. | 76 rooms. Complimentary Continental breakfast, in-room data ports, some microwaves, some in-room hot tubs, cable TV, room phones, pool, laundry facilities, laundry service, business services, free parking. | 2261 N.E. 181st Ave. | 503/618–8400 or 800/753–3746 | fax 503/618–9711 | www.sleepinn-portland.com. | $69 | AE, D, DC, MC, V.

HERMISTON

MAP 3, I2

(Nearby towns also listed: Pendleton, Umatilla)

Although its population is just over 10,000 residents, Hermiston is the urban service center for nearly three times that many people in the expansive and productive agricultural industry that surrounds it. Irrigated farmlands and ranch lands produce a variety of livestock and crops, including alfalfa, potatoes, corn, wheat, and the watermelons for which Hermiston is best known. The town was named for Robert Louis Stevenson's unfinished novel, *The Weir of Hermiston*. Hermiston contains more than 75 acres of city parks, with the Columbia River just 6 mi to the north and the Umatilla River and Blue Mountains nearby.

Information: Greater Hermiston Chamber of Commerce | 415 S. Hwy. 395, Hermiston 97838 | 541/567–6151.

Attractions

Maxwell Siding Railroad Display. The railroad came to Hermiston in 1883 and some of the original tracks are still here at this outdoor display of railroad cars and memorabilia. There is a 1910 rotary snowplow, a 1913 diner from the Oregon Short Line, a 1912 passenger car, a 1949 steam-powered snowplow (the last of its kind used in the U.S.), and two cabooses. If you like, you can arrange to get married in one of them. There are some unusual automobiles too, including a rare 1922 Buda. | 200 W. Highland Ave. | 541/567–8532 or 541/567–3759 | Donation | Open Sat. and by appointment.

Dining

Fontaine's Restaurant. Contemporary. With its comfortable booths and candlelight, Fontaine's is a sophisticated choice for dinner. The menu offers high-quality basics such as fresh seafood, prime rib, and steaks. Fontaine's has a good wine list and there's a lounge that is perfect for an after-dinner drink. | 845 N. 1st St. (Hwy. 395) | 541/567–9544 | Closed Sun. and major holidays | $10–$17.95 | AE, D, MC, V.

Lodging

Economy Inn of Hermiston. You'll find roses out front, a family atmosphere, and rooms that are larger than usual at this inexpensive and centrally located older inn. There are four restaurants within walking distance. | 35 rooms, 4 suites. Restaurant, complimentary Continental breakfast, in-room data ports, some kitchenettes, microwaves, refrigerators, cable TV, room phones, pool. | 835 N. 1st St. (Hwy. 395) | 541/567–5516 or 888/567–9521 | fax 541/567–5516 | $40–$75 | AE, D, DC, MC, V.

Oxford Inn. Right in the center of town, this hotel is close to area restaurants and shops. The rooms are clean, basic, and inexpensive. | 90 rooms. Restaurant, complimentary Continental breakfast, some kitchenettes, pool, pets allowed. | 655 N First | 541/567–7777 | fax 541/567–3085 | $42 | AE, D, DC, MC, V.

HILLSBORO

MAP 3, D2

(Nearby towns also listed: Beaverton, Forest Grove, Oregon City, Portland)

Over the past twenty years Hillsboro has experienced rapid growth associated with the Silicon Forest. Its population has grown to 60,000 residents. Several of Intel's industrial campuses are located in Hillsboro, as are the facilities of other leading electronics manufacturers.

Businesses related to its original agricultural roots remain a significant part of Hillsboro's culture and economy. Alpaca ranches, nurseries, berry farms, nut and fruit orchards, and numerous wineries are among the area's most active agricultural businesses.

Information: Greater Hillsboro Chamber of Commerce | 334 S.E. 5th Ave., Hillsboro 97123 | 503/648–1102 | sueleblanc@hilchamber.org | www.hilchamber.org.

Attractions

Rice Northwest Museum of Rocks and Minerals. In 1938, Richard and Helen Rice began collecting beach agates. Over the years, they developed one of the largest private mineral collections in the U.S. The most popular item here is the Alma Rose Rhodochrosite, a 4" red crystal. The museum (housed in a ranch-style home) also has a collection of petrified wood from all over the world and a gallery of Northwest minerals, including specimens of rare crystallized gold. | 26385 N.W. Groveland Dr. | 503/647–2418 | fax 503/647–5207 | www.ricenwmuseum.org | $2 | Closed major holidays | Open Wed.–Sun. 1–5.

ON THE CALENDAR

JUNE: *Rose Festival Airshow.* This is one of the nation's best airshows and it is part of the Portland Rose Festival. Every year it draws huge crowds to the Hillsboro Airport. Dozens of aircraft, from biplanes to fighter jets, buzz the west side of town during the three-day event. The Air Force's Thunderbirds have appeared in past shows. | 503/227–2681.

Dining

Eddie Rickenbacker's. Italian. This restaurant is on the second floor of the terminal building at small but busy Hillsboro airport, which is home to the Nike corporate jet. A 90-ft stretch of windows looks out on the planes and airport activity. A fourth-generation Italian chef prepares such delights as a 16-ounce Argentine rib-eye, *gamberetti imbriagi* (drunken prawns), and angel hair pasta in a fresh pomodoro sauce, but try to save room for Death by Chocolate cake for dessert. Serving both travelers and locals, the restaurant stays open until midnight every night and until 2 AM on Friday and Saturday. | 3355 N.E. Cornell Rd. | 503/640–9601 | fax 503/648–3355 | $8–$24 | AE, D, MC, V.

Miller's Homestead Restaurant. American. This family-style restaurant, right around the corner from the Hillsboro Travelodge, serves three meals and you can get breakfast all day. Try the meat loaf, pork chops, chicken-fried steak, and (on Friday and Saturday) prime ribs, but there's also fettucini. Pasta primavera is the local favorite. | 640 S.E. 10th Ave. | 503/640–4730 | fax 503/640–5108 | $10.95–$16.95 | AE, D, MC, V.

Lodging

Best Western Cavanaughs Hillsboro Hotel. This motel is located across from the Hillsboro Airport in the middle of the Silicon Forest. Spa rooms and suites are available. | 123 rooms. Restaurant, bar, in-room data ports, some in room hot tubs, cable TV, pool, hot tub, exercise equipment, laundry facilities, business services. | 3500 N.E. Cornell Rd. | 503/648–3500 | fax 503/640–2789 | $85–$114 | AE, D, DC, MC, V.

Hillsboro Travelodge. This modest hotel, just 1 mi from Hillsboro, offers considerable convenience. You can walk to restaurants, a park, and picnic area. Right across the street is the Hillsboro Aquatic Center with an indoor-outdoor pool, exercise room, and tennis courts. Pumpkin Ridge golf course is 7 mi away. | 58 rooms. Complimentary Continental breakfast. Refrigerators, cable TV, room phones, laundry facilities. | 622 S.E. 10th Ave. | 503/640–4791 or 800/548–0163 | fax 503/640–8127 | $65–$95 | AE, D, MC, V.

Park Dunes. You will be in the center of Hillsboro, close to the Intel campus at this standard motel. | 58 rooms. Microwaves, refrigerators, cable TV, laundry facilities, business services. | 622 S.E. 10th | 503/640–4791 or 800/548–0163 | fax 503/640–8127 | $43–$52 | AE, D, MC, V.

Residence Inn by Marriott. Located in the heart of the Silicon Forest, this all-suites inn is popular with people relocating to Portland. It's within walking distance of several restaurants, a shopping center, and a multiplex theater. A Courtyard by Marriott, which has a restaurant, is right next door. | 122 suites. Complimentary Continental breakfast, in-room data ports, kitchenettes, no smoking rooms, pool, hot tub, tennis, gym, laundry facilities, business services. | 18855 N.W. Tanasbourne Dr. | 503/531–3200 or 800/331–3131 | fax 503/645–1581 | $119 | AE, D, DC, MC, V.

Stonebrook Suites. Stonebrook opened this property in 1999. Standing amid high-tech Silicon Forest companies, its nicely landscaped grounds and nine buildings have a residential look and feel. The fireplace in the lobby suggests a living room. Stonebrook prides itself on its comfortable suite accommodations with oversize bathrooms. | 136 suites. Complimentary Continental breakfast, in-room data ports, kitchenettes, microwaves, refrigerators, cable TV, room phones, pool, outdoor hot tub, basketball, gym, laundry facilities, laundry service. | 6550 N.E. Brighton Dr. | 503/268–6000 or 800/877–0807 | fax 503/268–6050 | hillsboro@stonebrooksuites.com | www.stonebrooksuites.com | $95 | AE, D, DC, MC, V.

HOOD RIVER

MAP 3, F2

(Nearby town also listed: The Dalles)

Hood River, central to the Columbia River Gorge National Scenic Area, has achieved worldwide prominence among windsurfing aficionados. Sailboarders know that the wind in the gorge and the current of the river combine to produce optimum conditions for their sport. In winter, many of these same athletes stay in town but turn south to ski on mountain slopes that are only a short drive away. Other outdoor enthusiasts find the area's fishing, boating, swimming, and hiking venues the best in the region. For the less athletically inclined there are plenty of attractions to keep you busy.

Vast orchards surround Hood River with bounteous supplies of apples, pears, cherries, and peaches. Equally abundant are legends of Big Foot, also known as the Abominable Snowman and Sasquatch, a half-man, half-ape who is said to have roamed the gorge for ages and who is celebrated in regional Native American ritual and art.

Information: Hood River County Chamber of Commerce | 405 Portway Ave., Hood River 97031 | 541/386–2000 or 800/366–3530 | www.gorge.net/hrccc.

Attractions

Bonneville Lock and Dam. Columbia River water passing through this structure's power generation station produces 1 million kilowatts of hydroelectricity, which is enough to supply more than 200,000 single-family homes. The dam's fish hatchery teems with fingerling salmon, fat rainbow trout, and 6-ft-long sturgeon. Tour the fish ladders and power generation station yourself, or take a 30- to 60-minute interpretive tour. | Exit 40 off I–84 | 541/374–8820 | www.nwp.usace.army.mil/op/b | Free | Visitors center and tours: daily 9–5.

Columbia Gorge Sailpark. This downtown park area on the Columbia River has a boat basin, a swimming beach, jogging trails, picnic tables, and rest rooms. It's fun for families, and it's a great place for serious windsurfers and kiteboarders. | 720 E. Port Marina Dr. | 541/386–1645 | Parking $3 | Daily, dawn to dusk.

Lost Lake. This tiny secluded lake has a campground with 125 sites on the northwest side of Mt. Hood, where there is fishing and hiking. | Dee Secondary Hwy. in Mt. Hood National Forest | 541/386–6366 | $5 | mid-May–mid-Oct., daily.

Mt. Hood Scenic Railroad and Dinner Train. This is a great way to see Mount Hood and the Hood River Valley—especially during spring and fall. The Excursion Train offers light concessions on-board. The Dinner Train provides a full range of beverages in the lounge car. Entrees include prime rib, chicken, salmon, and a vegetarian selection. There's also a Murder Mystery Dinner Train. | 110 Railroad Ave. | 541/386–3556 | www.mthoodrr.com | Excursion: $22.95; brunch: $56; dinner: $68.50 | Apr.–Dec., call for schedule.

Sternwheeler *Columbia Gorge*. This 600-passenger commodious ship churns its way upriver, then back again, on two-hour narrated excursions through some of the Gorge's best scenery. | Port of Cascade Locks | 541/374–8427 | www.sternwheeler.com | 2-hr cruises (no meal) $12.95; brunch and dinner cruises $26–$38 | Mid-June–early Oct., call for schedules.

Winery Tours. Flerchinger Vineyards. This winery, one of Oregon's newest, in the scenic Hood River Valley has a 6-acre vineyard nearby where Riesling and Chardonnay grapes are grown. | 4200 Post Canyon Dr. | 541/386–2882 or 800/516–8710 | www.flerchinger.com | Free | Daily 11–5.

Hood River Vineyards. Chardonnay, Sauvignon Blanc, Pinot Noir, Cabernet Sauvignon, and Merlot are among the varieties produced at this family-owned winery overlooking the Columbia River Gorge and Hood River Valley. | 4693 Westwood Dr. | 541/386–3772 | Free | Mar.–Dec., daily 11–5.

ON THE CALENDAR

APR.: ***Hood River Valley Blossom Festival.*** The orchards are in bloom during this arts and crafts fair that is centered around the towns of Odell and Parkdale. It coincides with the opening of the Mt. Hood Scenic Railroad, which offers trips through the apple and pear orchards in the area. There are also food booths. | 541/386–2000 or 800/366–3530.

JUNE: ***Return of the Sternwheeler Days.*** When the sternwheeler *Columbia Gorge* returns to its summer port, the town celebrates in Marine Park with a parade, bingo, an arts and crafts fair, live music in the park, and a salmon dinner. | 541/374–8427.

JULY: ***Hood River County Fair.*** The Hood River County Fairgrounds, 19 acres of green grass, are 7 mi from Hood River in Odell. The fair starts on the last Wednesday in July and features a 4-H livestock competition, a carnival and midway, and music and entertainment each evening through the weekend. | 541/354–2865.

SEPT.: ***Cross Channel Swim.*** Every Labor Day, 550 participants take this 1-mi swim across the Columbia River. The event has been held for over 55 years. The starting point is the Chamber of Commerce, 405 Portway Avenue in Hood River. | 800/366–3530.

OCT.: ***Hood River Valley Harvest Fest.*** At this fair which is held the 1st weekend in October, booths with food, farmers' produce, and arts and crafts are featured along with wine tastings, live music, and pumpkin carvings. | 541/386–2000.

Dining

Columbia River Court Dining Room. Continental. Enjoy a dramatic view of the Columbia River Gorge from your table at this dining room that serves Pacific Northwest cuisine. Try the wilted spinach salad with apple-smoked duck and fresh salmon. The Hood River apple tart is made with local apples. The restaurant also serves a farm breakfast. There is a pianist in the evening. No smoking. | 4000 Westcliff Dr. | 541/386–5566 | Reservations essential (holidays) | Breakfast also available | $20–$30 | AE, D, DC, MC, V.

Full Sail Tasting Room and Pub. American/Casual. In the former Diamond cannery building, this glass-walled microbrewery with a windswept deck overlooking the Columbia River won major awards at the Great American Beer Festival. Nachos, beer sausage, and other snack foods complement the fresh ales. During the summer months only, there's a grill menu offering chicken, veggie burgers, salmon burgers. Wheelchair accessible. | 506 Columbia St. | 541/386–2281 or 888/244–2337 | fax 541/386–7316 | $6–$10 | MC, V.

6th Street Bistro and Loft. Contemporary. The daily menus here concentrate on Pacific Northwest flavors in fresh seafood, grilled salmon, rib-eye organic steaks, and other dishes, all using local meats and produce. The popular dessert is the homemade apple pie. The Bistro is downstairs. The upstairs Loft is more casual but serves the full menu. | 509 Cascade St. | 541/386–5737 | $10–$20 | MC, V.

Stonehedge Gardens. Contemporary. Outside this early-20th-century house are 6½ acres of gardens and a wooded area. The menu is a perhaps uneasy mix of Northwest and Continental dishes, ranging from shrimp Pernod to smoked salmon lasagna, but the setting is certainly attractive. Wheelchair accessible. | 3405 Cascade St. | 541/386–3940 | Reservations essential | Closed Mon.–Tues. No lunch | $12.95–$25.95 | AE, MC, V.

Lodging

Beryl House. This 1910 Craftsman farmhouse stands amid apple and pear trees 4 mi from Hood River and 3 mi from the Columbia River Gorge. Upstairs, braided rugs, Mission-style furnishings, and the original fir floors, plus robes and slippers for guests, make the rooms comfortable. There's a wraparound porch and breakfast may be served on a sundeck overlooking the pear trees. | 4 rooms. Complimentary breakfast. No room phones, TV in common area, no smoking. | 4079 Barrett Dr. | 541/386–5567 | berylhouse@aol.com | www.moriah.com/beryl | $80 | MC, V.

Best Western Hood River Inn. This chain property is on the Columbia River, next to the marina and a park popular with windsurfers. | 149 rooms. Restaurant, bar with entertainment, in-room data ports, room service, cable TV, pool, hot tub, water sports, laundry facilities, business services, airport shuttle. | 1108 E. Marina Way | 541/386–2200 | fax 541/386–8905 | $84–$109 | AE, D, DC, MC, V.

Columbia Gorge Hotel. Situated next to the top of a waterfall overlooking the Columbia River gorge, this small hotel in a restored 1920s building has a "jazz age" atmosphere and formal manicured gardens. There is windsurfing nearby. | 40 rooms. Restaurant, bar, complimentary Continental breakfast, no air-conditioning, cable TV, business services, pets allowed. | 4000 Westcliff Dr. | 541/386–5566 or 800/345–1921 | fax 541/387–5414 | cghotel@gorge.net | www.columbiagorgehotel.com | $179–$279 | AE, D, DC, MC, V.

Hood River Hotel. The interior of this 1913 landmark, originally a hotel for railroad workers and now on the National Register of Historic Places, is rich with beveled glass, warm woods, and jade and cream fabrics. The guest rooms have fir floors, Oriental carpets, and four-poster beds, and nine of them have skylights. The suites can sleep five. The bar in the lobby is lively and Pasquale's Restaurant is here, as well. Breakfast is included for guests paying non-discounted room rates. | 33 rooms, 9 suites. Restaurant, bar, complimentary breakfast, some in-room data ports, some kitchenettes, some microwaves, some refrigerators, cable TV, room phones, hot tub, sauna, gym. | 102 Oak St. | 541/386–1900 or 800/386–1859 | fax 541/386–6090 | hrhotel@gorgenet.com | www.hoodriverhotel.com | $75–$119 | AE, D, DC, MC, V.

Inn of the White Salmon. This quiet, cozy, European-style two-story brick inn was built in 1937. It is filled with antiques and original art. | 16 rooms, 5 suites. Complimentary breakfast, hot tub, pets allowed. | 172 W. Jewett, White Salmon, WA | 509/493–2335 or 800/972–5226 | innkeeper@gorge.net | www.innofthewhitesalmon.com | $99, $109–$129 suites | AE, D, DC, MC, V.

Vagabond Lodge. This motel is on five acres of quiet, wooded grounds at the edge of the Columbia River Gorge cliffs. The decor is simple. Most rooms have views of the river, some have fireplaces. Ponderosa pines tower 110 ft over the courtyard. | 42 rooms, 7 suites in 5 buildings. Picnic area, some kitchenettes, some in-room hot tubs, cable TV, playground, pets allowed. | 4070 Westcliff Dr. | 541/386–2992 | fax 541/386–3317 | $52–$72, $85 suites | AE, DC, MC, V.

JACKSONVILLE

MAP 3, D8

(Nearby towns also listed: Ashland, Grants Pass, Medford)

Historic Jacksonville was founded amid the frenzy of the 1851 gold rush, and its main street still appears to have emerged from a Western movie. (It's been in a few.) A highlight of this National Historic Landmark town's buildings and museums are living-history exhibits that offer visitors a personal glimpse of pioneer life. Summer is particularly eventful in Jacksonville, with horse-drawn carriage rides and cable car tours, as well as the renowned Peter Britt Music Festival. The festival takes place among ponderosa pines and native madrones, at the estate of the pioneer photographer for whom it was named. Throughout the summer, a variety of world-class musicians and other artists perform in the natural, open-air amphitheater.

Information: **Jacksonville Chamber of Commerce** | 185 N. Oregon St., Jacksonville 97530 | 541/899–8118 | jvillechamber@wave.net | www.jacksonvilleoregon.org.

Attractions

Beekman House. History comes alive as actors dressed in costumes of the period portray the Beekman family at this 1875 house that contains original furnishings. The Beekman Bank, established in 1863, is also open to the public. | 352 E. California St. | $2 | Memorial Day–Labor Day, daily 1–5.

Children's Museum. This museum in the 1920 Jackson County Jail has hands-on exhibits of pioneer life and a collection of antique toys. There's an Indian tepee and an old-fashioned store to play in. A special display highlights local resident Pinto Colvig, who was the original Bozo the Clown, co-composed "Who's Afraid of the Big Bad Wolf," and was the voice of a Munchkin, Goofy, both Sleepy and Grumpy, and many other animated film characters. | 206 N. 5th St. | 541/773–6536 | fax 541/776–7994 | www.sohs.org | $3 | Wed.–Sat. 10–5, Sun. noon–5.

Jacksonville Museum. Artifacts from the gold rush-era are on display in the restored 1883 former Jackson County Courthouse. "Jacksonville! Boomtown to Hometown" sets out the area's history from mining camp to National Historic Landmark City. | 206 N. 5th St. | 541/773–6536 | fax 541/776–7994 | www.sohs.org | $2 | Memorial Day–Labor Day, daily 10–5; Labor Day–Memorial Day, Wed.–Sat. 10–5, Sun. noon–5.

Oregon Vortex Location of the House of Mystery. Native Americans avoided this area, referring to it as "forbidden ground." Birds and other wildlife appear to avoid it as well. In fact, tennis balls really do seem to roll uphill here and brooms do stand on end in this 1-acre spherical area. It opened as a tourist attraction around 1930. | 4303 Sardine Creek Rd., Gold Hill | 541/855–1543 | www.oregonvortex.com | $6.50 | Mar., April, May, Sept. and Oct. daily 9–5; last tour at 4:15; June–Aug., daily 9–6; last tour at 5:30.

ON THE CALENDAR

JUNE–SEPT.: *Peter Britt Music Festival.* Every summer some of the finest musicians in the world gather here for outdoor concerts and theater presentations. Contemporary and classical performances are staged in an outdoor amphitheater on the estate of 19th-century photographer and painter Peter Britt. | 541/779–0847 or 800/882–7488.

JULY: *Children's Festival.* A three-day festival for children has been held since 1967 on the third weekend of July at Jacksonville County Britt Park. There's Mother Goose Land with petting animals, plus a science booth, candlemaking and pottery, and panning for gold, plus performances by children's dance groups and bands. Fast food is available. | 541/774–8678.

Dining

Bella Union. Contemporary. A sophisticated menu in an unpretentious restaurant makes this 1870s saloon popular. Fresh fish, including such exotic items as Hawaiian opah and mako shark, are flown in daily, and the pastas are homemade. It's downtown near the Britt Festival, and there's a deck and a patio covered by an old wisteria tree. Local folks come for the pizza. | 170 W. California St. | 541/899–1770 | $9.95–$19.95 | AE, D, MC, V.

Gogi's Restaurant. Eclectic. Locally famous Chef William Prahl's philosophy that the continents can be united through our taste buds is manifest in the international menu of seasonally varied dishes, including traditionally prepared rack of lamb, Asian hoisin-glazed prawns, and hazelnut salmon croquettes. The dining room, at the foot of the Britt Gardens, has white table cloths, warm yellow walls, and rich, dark-wood tables and bar. | 235 W. Main St. | 541/899–8699 | No lunch. Closed Mon. | $16–$20 | D, MC, V.

Jacksonville Inn. Continental. The Continental fare and 600-label wine cellar at this dining room in a gold-rush-era bed and breakfast are among the best in southern Oregon. Book well in advance, particularly between late June and August, during the Britt Festival. Try the fresh razor clams and veal dishes. There are tables on the patio for dining al fresco. Sun. brunch. No smoking. | 175 E. California St. | 541/899–1900 | Reservations essential | Breakfast also available. No lunch Mon. | $15–$30 | AE, D, DC, MC, V.

McCully House. Contemporary. The charming dining room at this small bed and breakfast, in one of the first houses built in Jacksonville, features seafood, steak, lamb, and chicken entrées, which include clam chowder or salad, potato or rice, and fresh vegetables. Try the dijon-crusted fresh Atlantic salmon filet topped with béarnaise sauce. There are tables in the rose garden which also has a gazebo and a waterfall. Sun. brunch. No smoking. | 240 E. California St. | 541/899–1942 | www.mccullyhouseinn.com | Reservations essential | No lunch | $30 | AE, MC, V.

Mediterranean Restaurant. Mediterranean. Greek, French, Italian, and Lebanese dishes are on the menu here. Everything from the spanakopita and moussaka to the breaded pork loin is fresh and authentic. The room is bright and airy and there's handmade paper under the glass tabletops. You can eat out on the patio, too. The mural of a Greek scene at the entrance was painted by one of the waiters. | 210 E. California St. | 541/899–3995 | $9.95–$17.95 | AE, D, MC, V.

Lodging

Applegate River Lodge. Each room is different in this lodge 15 mi east of town. One has century-old barn wood and gold-mining tools and one has an old wagon wheel, saddle, and chaps. Every room has a deck overlooking the Applegate River and Pioneer Bridge. | 7 rooms. Continental breakfast, restaurant, air-conditioning, no TV, no in-room phones. | 15100 Hwy. 238 | 541/846–6690 | $125–$145 | MC, V.

Combest House. This downtown home just a block from Main Street and a short walk to the Britt Festival grounds was first built by homesteaders in 1862 and named for its one-time owner Valentine Combest, who mined on the property. There are two guest suites, one with two bedrooms and a shared bathroom, the other with one bedroom and a kitchenette. | 2 suites. Cable TV, air-conditioning, in-room phones. | 160 W. C St. | 541/899–7537 | $95–$105 | MC, V.

Hannah House. You can hear the Britt Music Festival concerts from the front porch of this 1868 house across from the festival grounds. One suite has its own wine cellar, one has a screened balcony, and every suite is filled with antiques and has a full kitchen. | 4 suites. Air-conditioning, in-room phones. | 285 S. 1st St. | 800/373–9775 | $165 | D, MC, V.

Historic Orth House B&B. This 1880 Italianesque brick villa, on the National Register of Historic Places, is on a corner and bordered by a white picket fence. Although it's in town and close to restaurants and the music festival, it's quiet and the swing and the porch with wicker furniture add to the calm. Guest rooms and the interior are filled with Victorian antiques and a collection of teddy bears. The suite has two bedrooms, a deck, and a balcony. | 2 rooms, 1 suite. Complimentary breakfast, TV in common area, no smoking. | 105 W. Main St. | 541/899–8665 or 800/700–7301 | fax 541/899–9146 | orthbnb@historicorthhousebnb.com | www.historicorthhousebnb.com | $120–$135 | MC, V.

Jacksonville Inn. This small 1863 vintage inn is filled with period antiques. A block away are three larger and more luxurious cottages with fireplaces. | 8 rooms; 3 cottages. Restaurant, bar, complimentary breakfast, in-room data ports, microwaves, refrigerators, some in-room hot tubs, cable TV, shops, business services, airport shuttle. | 175 E. California St. | 541/899–1900 or 800/321–9344 (for reservations) | fax 541/899–1373 | www.jacksonvilleinn.com | $115–$150, $210–$245 cottages | AE, D, DC, MC, V.

Laurelwood Manor. This antebellum Victorian inn two blocks from downtown is on the National Register of Historic Places. You can relax in the perennial flower garden, on the wide front porch, or in your antique-filled room. | 6 rooms. Complimentary breakfast, TV in common room, air-conditioning. No in-room phones. | 540 E. California St. | 541/899–2848, 800/846–8422 | $95–$125 | AE, MC, V.

McCully House Inn. One of Jacksonville's six original homes, this white 1860 Gothic Revival mansion is surrounded by a rose garden. The guest rooms are filled with antiques and one has a fireplace. There's a restaurant downstairs. | 3 rooms. Restaurant, bar, complimentary breakfast, room phones, no TV, no smoking. | 240 E. California St. | 541/899–1942 or 800/367–1942 | fax 541/899–1560 | www.mccullyhouseinn.com | $125 | AE, MC, V.

Potting Shed. This downtown cottage one block from the Britt Festival grounds is affiliated with the Llamas and Llambs shop, which specializes in local woolens. The suite has vaulted ceilings with fans, several windows, a full kitchen, and a cedar deck. Two-night minimum stay. | 1 suite. In-room phone, kitchen, TV, VCR. | 180 N. Oregon St. | 541/899–9141 | $115 | MC, V.

Stage Lodge. In the heart of historic Jacksonville and close to the Britt Festival, this bed and breakfast is plush and modern with fireplaces in the rooms. | 27 rooms, 2 suites. Complimentary Continental breakfast, microwaves, some refrigerators, cable TV, some pets allowed (fee). | 830 N. 5th St. | 541/899–3953 or 800/253–8254 | www.stagelodge.com | $65–$140, $125–$145 suites | AE, D, DC, MC, V.

Touvelle House. This intimate bed and breakfast in a restored 1916 Craftsman is filled with antiques. It is only two blocks from the center of Jacksonville and four blocks from the site of the Britt Music Festival. | 3 rooms, 2 suites. Picnic area, complimentary breakfast, in-room data ports, TV in common area, pool, hot tub, business services, no kids under 12. | 455 N. Oregon St. | 541/899–8938 or 800/846–8422 (for reservations) | fax 541/899–3992 | touvelle@wave.net | www.wave.net/upg/touvelle | $115–$135 | AE, D, DC, MC, V.

JOHN DAY

MAP 3, I4

(Nearby town also listed: Burns)

More than $26 million in gold was mined in the John Day area. The town was founded shortly after gold was discovered there in 1862. Yet John Day is better known to contemporaries for the plentiful outdoor recreation it offers and for the nearby John Day Fossil Beds, a 14,000-acre site with records of ancient life preserved in volcanic ash. The beds, which were designated a National Monument in 1974, contain bones, leaves, wood, nuts, and seeds from the Age of Mammals, between the time when the dinosaurs become extinct and the beginning of the Ice Age.

Information: Grant County Chamber of Commerce | 281 W. Main, John Day 97845 | 541/575–0547 | grantccc@eoni.com.

Attractions

Grant County Historical Museum. Memorabilia from the Gold Rush is on display at this museum along with Native American artifacts, and antique musical instruments. | 101 S. Canyon City Blvd., Canyon City | 541/575–0362 or 541/575–1993 | $2 | End June–Sept., Mon.–Sat. 9–4:30, Sun. 1–5.

★ **John Day Fossil Beds National Monument.** The geological formations that make up the monument cover hundreds of square miles but are divided into three "units"—Sheep Rock, Painted Hills, and Clarno. Located 40 mi west of John Day, they were formed as a result of volcanic activity during the Cenozoic era 5 million to 50 million years ago. | U.S. 26 at Rte. 19 | 541/987–2333 | Free | Daily.

The 48-million-year-old beds in the **Clarno Unit** have yielded the oldest fossils in the national monument. The drive to the beds traverses forests of ponderosa pines and sparsely populated valleys along the John Day River before turning through a landscape filled with spires and outcroppings that attest to the region's volcanic past. A short trail that runs between the two parking lots contains fossilized evidence of an ancient subtropical forest. Another trail climbs ¼ mi from the second parking lot to the base of the Palisades, a series of abrupt, irregular cliffs created by ancient volcanic mud flows. | Rte. 218 | 541/575–0547 | Free | Daily.

The fossils at **Painted Hills** date back about 33 million years and prove that the climate had been noticeably drier than during Sheep Rock's era. The eroded buff-color hills reveal striking red and green striations that were created by minerals in the clay. Come at dusk or just after it rains, when the colors are most vivid. | Off U.S. 26 | 541/575–0547 | Free | Daily.

You will find exhibits, a video, and handouts at the visitors center at the **Sheep Rock Unit** that will outline the significance of the John Day Fossil Beds. Two mi north of the visitors center on Highway 19 lies the impressive Blue Basin, a badlands canyon with sinuous blue-green spires. Winding through this basin is the ½-mi Island in Time Trail, where trailside exhibits explain the area's 28-million-year-old fossils. The 3-mi Blue Basin Overlook Trail loops around the rim of the canyon, yielding some splendid views. | U.S. 26 to Rte. 19 | 541/987–2333 | Free | Labor Day–Memorial Day, daily; Memorial Day–Labor Day, weekdays 9–4.

The **Kam Wah Chung and Co Museum** is housed in a small building that was a trading post on The Dalles Military Road in 1866 and 1867. Later, this same building was a Chinese doctor's shop, an opium den, and a general store. It contains a completely stocked Chinese pharmacy, items that would have been sold at the general store, and re-created living quarters. Next to the City Park, the museum offers a unique glimpse into the early Chinese community in Oregon. | 250 N.W. Canton St. | 541/575–0028 | $3 | Mon.–Thurs., 9–noon and 1–5; weekends 1–5.

Malheur National Forest. You can cut through this 1.4-million-acre forest in the Blue Mountains as you drive from John Day to Burns on U.S. 395. It contains alpine lakes, meadows, creeks, and grasslands, while the area wildlife include mule deer, bighorn sheep, antelope, elk, bobcats, and mountain lions. There are 100 mi of trails and within its boundaries is the Strawberry Mountain Wilderness Area. | At the intersection of U.S. 395 and U.S. 26 | 541/575–3000 | Free | Daily.

ON THE CALENDAR

JUNE: *'62 Days Celebration.* The discovery of gold in nearby Canyon Creek in 1862 is celebrated at this annual event held in Canyon City on the 2nd weekend in June. | 541/575–0329.

JULY: *Sol-rest Renewable Energy Fair.* You can explore every facet of solar and other renewable energy resources at this annual event the last weekend of the month. There are over 25 how-to workshops in topics like installing solar panels and solar water heating. Don't miss the electric car race with contestants from all over the northwest. | 541/575–3733.

AUG.: *Grant County Fair and Rodeo.* A traditional rural event held on the Grant County Fairgrounds that features livestock and agricultural exhibits and competitions, food, and entertainment. | 541/575–1900.

Dining

Stagecoach Steakhouse. American. The Stagecoach, located at the John Day Sunset Inn, has wood paneling and western pictures on the walls. Hearty fare in the form of steaks and lobster is served. | 390 W. Main St. | 541/575–3634 | Closed Mon. | $8.50–$16 | AE, D, DC, MC, V.

Lodging

Dreamers Lodge. This hotel in the center of town has the closest access to the John Day Fossil Beds. The rooms are homey, comfortable, and spacious. There is fishing and golf nearby. | 25 rooms. Refrigerators, cable TV, cross-country skiing, business services, airport shuttle, pets allowed. | 144 N. Canyon Blvd. | 541/575–0526 or 800/654–2849 | fax 541/575–2733 | $46–$54 | AE, D, DC, MC, V.

John Day Sunset Inn. The modest and inexpensive Sunset Inn is near the center of town and you can walk to a city park and swimming pool. The Stagecoach Steakhouse is the resident restaurant. | 43 rooms. Restaurant, bar, picnic area, some microwaves, refrigerators, cable TV, room phones, pool, hot tub. | 390 W. Main St. | 541/575–1462 or 800/452–4899 | fax 541/575–1471 | $48–$53.50 | AE, D, DC, MC, V.

JOSEPH

MAP 3, K3

(Nearby town also listed: Enterprise)

The town is named for Chief Joseph, leader of the Nez Percé tribe, who lived in the Wallowa Lake area during the summer months. The story of the tribe and their eventual exile to Idaho is highlighted in area museums.

The Wallowa Mountains, which loom 5,000 ft above the town and lake, provide a scenic backdrop for most of the area's readily available and accessible attractions.

Information: **Wallowa County Chamber of Commerce** | Box 427, Enterprise 97828 | 541/426–4622 | wallowa@eoni.com | www.eoni.com/~wallowa/.

Attractions

David and Lee Manuel Museum. If you've seen the bronze statue of a U.S. marshall in front of the Justice Department building in Washington, D.C., you know the work of artist David Manuel. His foundry is here and, in a separate building, a museum with a superb collection of Nez Percé clothing and artifacts, including a tepee, as well as pioneer wagons, a children's museum with old dolls and toys, and an exhibit of the artist's work in bronze. | 400 N. Main St. | 541/432–7235 | fax 541/432–9002 | www.davidmanuel.com | $6 | June–Oct., Mon.–Sat. 8–8; Nov.–May, Mon.–Sat. 10–4.

Hells Canyon National Recreation Area. You can spot over 422 different species of animals including one of the largest elk herds in the U.S. at this remote place along the Snake River. The canyon, 30 mi northeast of Joseph, is 7800 ft deep, making it the world's deepest river gorge. You can see it from the overlook on the Wallowa Mountain Loop (see below). For a wilder ride, adventurers can take the 60-mi round-trip route that winds along the edge of Hells Canyon Reservoir. Following Highway 86 north from Copperfield, you will cross the Snake River and continue on to the 700,000-acre Hells Canyon National Recreation Area. About 67 mi of the Snake River is part of the National Wild and Scenic Rivers System. | Rte. 350 in the Wallowa-Whitman National Forest | 509/758–1957 or 541/426–4978 | www.fs.fed.us/r6/w-w | Free | Daily.

Valley Bronze of Oregon. Fine art bronze sculpture castings are produced, displayed, and sold here. Tours of the foundry, ¼ mi away, leave from the showroom. | 018 S. Main | 541/432–7551 | www.valleybronze.com | $5 | May–Nov., daily; Dec.–Apr. by appointment.

Wallowa County Museum. The museum has a small but moving collection of artifacts and photos chronicling the 1870s Nez Percé Wars. The 1888 building, originally a bank, was robbed in 1896, an event reenacted with music, dance-hall girls, and gunshots at 1 PM every Wednesday in summer. | 110 S. Main St. | 541/432–6095 | Free | Memorial Day–Sept., daily 10–5.

Wallowa Lake State Recreation Park. This campground is 6 mi south of Joseph and surrounded on three sides by 9,000-ft-tall snow-capped mountains and is a gateway to Hells Canyon. It has 121 full hookups, 89 tent sites, and 2 yurts. Popular activities include fishing and boating as well as hiking on wilderness trails, horseback riding, bumper boats, canoeing, and miniature golf. You can ride a tramway to the top of one of the mountains (see below). | Rte. 82 | 541/432–4185 or 800/551–6949 | www.prd.state.or.us | $3/vehicle for day use | Daily.

Wallowa Lake Tramway. The steepest gondola in North America rises to the top of 8,150-ft Mount Howard in 15 minutes for an incredible view of mountain peaks, the forest, and Wallowa Lake far below. It is 6 mi north of Joseph. | Rte. 82 | 541/432–5331 | $14.95 | May–Sept., 10–4 till June, then 9–5.

Wallowa Mountain Loop. This trip will take about 3½ hours as you go through the national forest from Joseph and end up in Baker City. Leaving Joseph, take Little Sheep Creek Highway east for 8 mi, then turn south onto Forest Service Road 39, and continue until it meets Highway 86. Be particularly careful in winter and always check with the local Chamber of Commerce about the driving conditions.

ON THE CALENDAR

JULY: *Chief Joseph Days.* This event, which began in 1945 in honor of Nez Percé Chief Joseph, includes rodeo performances, a parade, a bucking horse stampede down Main Street, a carnival, a golf tournament, and a Nez Percé Tribe Powwow. It's held the last full weekend in July. 541/432–1015

AUG.: *Bronze, Blues & Brews.* The town of Joseph is all about bronze but, for this annual August Saturday event, it's also about beer and music. For a modest fee, you can sample the wares of local microbreweries (there are food booths, too) and enjoy the music of several bands all afternoon and into the evening at Joseph City Park. For the day, Joseph's bronze foundries display their work in the park and also on Main St. 541/426–4622

Dining

Magnoni's Market Place. Italian. Upstairs at Magnoni's, you can enjoy an array of pastas, salads, and homemade breads, or do as local people do and come for the lasagna and seafood fettucini. The restaurant is open on three sides and tables have bright umbrellas under the roof. Downstairs there's a gift shop and an even more casual café serving espresso, lattes, and such, as well as the full menu from upstairs. Magnoni's is right across the street from the David and Lee Manuel Museum. | 403 N. Main St. | 541/432–3663 | fax 541/432–3663 | Dinner $10, lunch $7 | AE, D, MC, V.

Summit Grill and Alpine Patio. American/Casual. At an altitude of 8,200 ft on Mt. Howard, this is the Northwest's highest restaurant, reached by a 15-minute ride on the Wallowa Lake Tramway. The menu is limited to burgers, sandwiches, burritos, salads, chili, soups, and Oregon beers and wines, but the view of four bordering states is striking. There are 2½ mi of hiking trails. | 59919 Wallowa Lake Hwy. | 541/432–5331 | fax 541/432–1300 | Open Memorial Day–Labor Day, daily 10–4 | $4–$7 | No credit cards.

Wallowa Lake Lodge. American. The restaurant in this rustic wood-paneled lodge serves such popular fare as seafood (with salmon at the head of the list), pastas, and lemon-herb chicken. Both the dining room and the outside deck have views of either the lake or the mountains. | 60060 Wallowa Lake Hwy. | 541/432–9821 | fax 541/432–4885 | Open Memorial Day–Labor Day, daily. No lunch | $12.50–$21.50 | D, MC, V.

Lodging

Chandler's Bed, Bread and Trail. This lodgelike modern house is located between Joseph and Wallowa Lake. The rooms have high, sloping, beamed ceilings and are eclectically furnished. The "bread" in the inn's name refers to owner Ethel Chandler's homemade loaves, a staple of the breakfasts (included in the room rates) she prepares daily. As for the "trail" part, Ethel and her husband, Jim, will advise you on the best places to hike or backpack and provide a shuttle service to nearby trailheads. | 5 rooms (2 with shared bath). Picnic area, complimentary breakfast, no air-conditioning, hiking, cross-country and downhill skiing, no kids under 11, no smoking. | 700 S. Main St. | 541/432–9765 or 800/452–3781 | fax 541/432–4303 | $60–$80 | MC, V.

Collett's Cabins and Fine Arts. Collett's cabins are 6 mi from Joseph via Hwy. 82, a ten-minute walk from Wallowa Lake, and a short rural stroll to the Wallowa Lake Lodge and the Wallowa Lake Tramway. Surrounded by ponderosa, firs, spruce, and lots of deer, the cabins range from studios to two-bedroom units, some with gas fireplaces. The owners are artists and the cabins are filled with original artwork. A small gallery and shop displays more of their work in paint, pastel, and charcoal, as well as glass, pottery, and wood by mainly Northwest artists. | 2 suites, 8 cabins. Picnic area, no air-conditioning, kitchenettes, microwaves, cable TV, no room phones, no smoking. | 84681 Ponderosa La. | 541/432–2391 | fax 541/432–2391 | smcollet@eoni.com | www.eoni.com/~smcollet | $65–$120 | D, MC, V.

Eagle Cap Chalets. The standard rooms here are as efficient as any motel-style rooms, while the log cabins vary from studios to two-bedroom apartments. They all stand on landscaped grounds in this wooded wilderness area at the mouth of Wallowa Lake. There are also 48 RV sites, and you can walk to some restaurants. | 22 rooms in 1 building, 12 cabins. Picnic area, no air-conditioning, in-room data ports, some kitchenettes, some microwaves, refrigerators, some in-room hot tubs, cable TV, room phones, pool, hot tub, miniature golf. | 59879 Wallowa Lake Hwy. | 541/432–4704 | fax 541/432–3010 | eaglecc@oregontrail.net | www.neoregon.net/eaglecapchalets | $55–$60 | AE, D, MC, V.

Flying Arrow Resort. One- to four-bedroom fully equipped cabins with sundecks are available at this resort ½ mi south of Wallowa Lake. Walking trails are right on the property which is 5 mi outside of Joseph. | 20 rooms. Picnic area, refrigerators, cable TV, pool, hot tub. | 59782 Wallowa Lake Hwy. | 541/432–2951 | www.flyingarrowresort.net | $60–$130 | D, MC, V.

Indian Lodge. A lake is 1 mi away from this small motel, which belonged to actor Walter Brennan in the 1950s. The rooms are cozy and comfortable and modern. | 16 rooms. Cable TV. | 201 S. Main St. | 541/432–2651 | fax 541/432–4949 | $37–$63 | D, MC, V.

Wallowa Lake Lodge. The rustic atmosphere at this friendly 1920s lodge on the lake is tasteful and true to the period. Handmade replicas of the structure's original furniture fill a large common area that contains a massive fireplace. The cabins, all with fireplaces and some with lake views, are small, old-fashioned havens of knotty pine. An on-site restaurant serves standard American fare for breakfast, lunch, and dinner. | 22 rooms, 2 suites, 8 cabins. Restaurant, no air-conditioning, kitchenettes (in cabins), room phones. Downhill skiing, no smoking. | 60060 Wallawa Lake Hwy. | 541/432–9821 | fax 541/432–4885 | $78–$88, $110–$135 suites, $145–$175 cabins | D, MC, V.

KLAMATH FALLS

MAP 3, F8

(Nearby towns also listed: Ashland, Jacksonville, Medford)

Klamath Lake is the largest freshwater lake in Oregon and is anchored at its south end by the city of Klamath Falls. This city, which has year-round sunshine, is home to acres of parks and marinas from which to enjoy watersports and bird watching. There are more than 82 lakes and streams in Klamath County, including upper Klamath Lake, which covers 133 square mi. Seven bird sanctuaries are located in the Klamath Basin, and hundreds of species of migratory birds stop over at the lake each year. There are also reminders of the city's pioneer past represented in local museums and commemorative parks.

Information: Klamath County Chamber of Commerce | 701 Plum Ave., Klamath Falls 97603 | 541/884–5193 | klamcham@cdsnet.net | www.klamath.org.

Attractions

Collier Memorial State Park and Logging Museum. The museum, 30 mi north of Klamath Falls, sits on land given to the state of Oregon by the locally born Collier brothers in honor of their parents. An historic log cabin exhibit and a display of antique logging equipment dating to the 1880s are among the features. The park also has picnic areas and a campground. | 46000 Hwy. 97, Chiloquin | 541/783–2471 | www.collierloggingmuseum.org/ | Free | May–Oct., daily 8–8; Nov.–Apr., daily 8–4.

Favell Museum of Western Art and Native American Artifacts. More than 100,000 Native American artifacts, the works of 300 major contemporary Western artists, and the largest miniature gun collection in the world are on display in a building made from local volcanic rock. | 125 W. Main St. | 541/882–9996 | $4 | Mon.–Sat. 9:30–5:30.

Ft. Klamath Museum and Park. A frontier military post was established in 1863 at this site south of Fort Klamath to fend off Indian attacks. Eight acres of the original post, including the original buildings, were dedicated as Klamath County Park in 1973. | Hwy. 62 | 541/883–4208 or 541/381–2230 | www.kchs.org | Suggested donation $1 | June–Labor Day, Wed.–Sun. 10–6.

Jackson F. Kimball State Park. This park, 3 mi north of Fort Klamath, is at the headwaters of the Wood River, which offers good fishing. A campground with 10 primitive sites is next to a spring-fed lagoon. | U.S. 97 | 541/783–2471 or 800/551–6949 | www.prd.state.or.us | $3/vehicle for day use | Mid-Apr.–Oct., daily.

Klamath Basin National Wildlife Refuge Complex. This area sometimes hosts as many as 1,000 birds, making it the largest wintering concentration of bald eagles in the contiguous United States. Many species of migratory birds also congregate in the Klamath Basin, 24 mi south of Klamath Falls on the California–Oregon border, including the largest concentration of migratory waterfowl on the continent. The Nature Conservancy has called the basin "a western Everglades" because it is the largest wetland area west of the Mississippi. | Route 1, Box 74, Tulelake, CA | 530/667–2231 | Free (fee for tours) | Daily.

Klamath County Museum. This museum features the anthropology, history, geology, and wildlife indigenous to the Klamath Basin. | 1451 Main St. | 541/883–4208 | www.kchs.org | $2 | June–Sept., Mon.–Sat. 8:30–5:30; Oct.–May, Mon.–Sat. 8–5.

Kla-Mo-Ya Casino. On nine acres along the Williamson River, 22 mi north of Klamath Falls, the casino—owned by the Klamath, Modoc, and Yahooskin tribes—has 300 slot machines, poker, blackjack, a deli, and a buffet restaurant. | 34333 Hwy. 97 N., Chiloquin | 541/783–7529 or 888/552–6692 | fax 541/783–7543 | Free | May–Oct., Sun.–Thurs. 9 AM–1 AM, Fri.–Sat. 24 hrs; Nov.–Apr., daily 9 AM–midnight.

Ross Ragland Theater. This 800-seat theater hosts the 30-year-old Linkville Players theater group, as well as traveling and local plays and musical performances. | 218 N. 7th St. | 541/884–0651.

Senator George Baldwin Hotel Museum. The history of the region is the focus of a guided tour and exhibits here. Some of the photographs on display were part of Senator Baldwin's daughter Maud's own collection. In summer you can take a replica street trolley from here to the Klamath County Museum. | 31 Main St. | 541/883–4207 or 541/883–4208 | www.kchs.org | $4 | June–Sept., Tues.–Sat. 9–4.

Winema National Forest. This forest, 12 mi north of Klamath Falls, covers 1.1 million acres on the eastern slopes of the Cascades. It borders Crater Lake National Park. Hiking, camping, fishing, and boating are popular. In winter snowmobiling and cross-country skiing are available. | U.S. 97 | 541/883–6714 | www.fs.fed.us/r6/winema | $3/vehicle for day use | Daily; campgrounds, picnic areas: Memorial Day–Labor Day.

ON THE CALENDAR

FEB.: ***Klamath Basin Bald Eagle Conference.*** Nature enthusiasts from around the world flock to the Oregon Institute of Technology in Klamath Falls each February for the nation's oldest birding festival. | 541/884–5193 or 800/445–6728.

AUG.: ***Klamath County Fair and Jefferson Stampede Rodeo.*** A traditional event that features livestock and agricultural exhibits and competitions, food, and entertainment, plus the Jefferson Stampede Rodeo. | 541/883–3796.

DEC.: ***Snowflake Festival.*** Every winter a week of holiday season-inspired activities—from a gingerbread house contest, to a bazaar—culminates in a fully lighted night parade including floats and regional bands drawing 40,000 people downtown. | 541/884–5193.

Dining

Chez Nous. French. The dark wood dining room in this 1920 house suggests more formal pleasures but encourages dining in a relaxed mood. A thoughtful French chef prepares duck in orange sauce, Chateaubriand, veal dishes, and the house specialty, rack of lamb. Fresh strawberry shortcake often appears on the menu and there's a good wine list. | 3927 S. 6th St. | 541/883–8719 | fax 541/883–3996 | Closed Sun.–Mon. No lunch | $15–$26 | AE, MC, V.

Fiorella's. Italian. This restaurant serves classic northern Italian cuisine in a formal dining experience. Try the pastisio, ravioli, gnocchi, or filet mignon. Kids' menu. | 6139 Simmers Ave. | 541/882–1878 | Closed Sun.–Mon. No lunch | $15–$30 | AE, D, MC, V.

Mia & Pia's Pizzaria and Brewhouse. American/Casual. You can sit on the garden patio among the fountains or in the huge 200-seat dining room and sample the house brews from the off-site brewery—the only microbrewery in the county. The large menu features pizza but also includes burgers, soups, salads, and chicken dishes. | 13788 Matney Rd. | 541/884–4880 | $5–$10 | MC, V, D.

Satellite Restaurant. American/Casual. This airport restaurant gets most of its business not from travelers but from neighborhood residents. Tuck into prime rib, a char-broiled burger, or a plate of pasta as you watch planes take off from the runway. | 3000 Airport Way, Ste. 200 | 541/882–5509 | $9–$30 | D, MC, V.

Schatzie's on the Green. German. The 13-table dining room with its white linens, crystal, and local western artwork overlooks Payne Canyon and the first hole of the Running Y Resort golf course. In summer you can eat outside on the patio. Traditional German specialties like *Kasslerschnitchen* (pork loin) and a variety of schnitzels are the fare. | 5391 Running Y Rd. | 541/850–5777 | Closed Mon. and Tues., Nov. 15–Apr. 15 | $14–$23 | AE, D, MC, V.

Lodging

Best Western Klamath Inn. You will be staying right on Klamath Lake at this property, which is within 1 mi of the Jefferson Square Mall and only 1/4 mi from the fairgrounds. The back of the inn has tables and chairs for outdoor relaxing. | 52 rooms. Complimentary Continental breakfast, in-room data ports, microwaves, refrigerators, some in-room hot tubs, cable TV, indoor pool, some pets allowed. | 4061 S. Sixth St. | 541/882–1200 | fax 541/882–2729 | www.bestwestern.com | $63–$68 | AE, D, DC, MC, V.

Best Western Olympic Inn. Here the rooms are clean and basic. You will be down the block from the Jefferson Square Mall and only 2 mi from downtown Klamath Falls. | 71 rooms. Complimentary Continental breakfast, in-room data ports, microwaves, refrigerators, cable TV, pool, hot tub, gym, business services. | 2627 S. Sixth St. | 541/882–9665 | fax 541/884–3214 | www.bestwestern.com | $77–$89 | AE, D, DC, MC, V.

Cimarron Motor Inn. This is the largest lodging facility in Klamath Falls. It's near restaurants and shopping. | 163 rooms. Complimentary Continental breakfast, microwaves, refrigerators, cable TV, pool, business services, pets allowed (fee). | 3060 S. Sixth St. | 541/882–4601 or 800/742–2648 | fax 541/882–6690 | $54–$64 | AE, D, DC, MC, V.

Holiday Inn Express Hotel and Suites. Only 3/4 mi from downtown Klamath Falls, this chain hotel has comfortable, spacious rooms. | 57 rooms, 10 suites. Complimentary Continental breakfast, microwaves, cable TV, indoor pool, hot tub, exercise equipment, laundry facilities, business services. | 2500 S. Sixth St. | 541/884–9999 | fax 541/882–4020 | www.holiday-inn.com | $73, $130 suites | AE, D, DC, MC, V.

Maverick Motel. This friendly, quiet, clean, and inexpensive motel, built in 1964, is a good value. It's downtown and you can walk to restaurants and antiques shops. | 49 rooms. Complimentary Continental breakfast, cable TV, room phones, pool. | 1220 Main St. | 541/882–6688 or 800/404–6690 | fax 541/885–4095 | $39 | AE, D, DC, MC, V.

Quality Inn. This chain hotel is in city center and within walking distance to many area attractions. | 80 rooms, 4 suites. Complimentary Continental breakfast, in-room data ports, microwaves, some in-room hot tubs, cable TV, pool, laundry facilities, business services, some pets allowed. | 100 Main St. | 541/882–4666 or 800/732–2025 | fax 541/883–8795 | $59–$60, $63–$79 suites | AE, D, DC, MC, V.

Red Lion Inn. The rooms in this chain hotel are bright and comfortable. It is across the street from the Klamath County Event Center and near a good French restaurant, Chez Nous. | 100 rooms, 8 suites. Restaurant, bar, complimentary Continental breakfast, in-room data ports, some microwaves, some refrigerators, some in-room hot tubs, cable TV, room phones, pool, outdoor hot tub, laundry facilities, laundry service. | 3612 S. 6th St. | 541/882–8864 | fax 541/884–2046 | www.redlion.com | $79–$89 | AE, D, DC, MC, V.

Running Y Ranch Resort. This 3,600-acre ranch on the Caledonia Marsh 7 mi west of town is on the Pacific Flyway and sees flocks of swan, geese, and ducks each spring and fall. The vaulted ceilings, stone floors, and stone fireplace with a tall chimney in the lobby complement the stained-wood exterior of the lodge. Rooms have either forested or golf-course views. The 18-hole golf course was *Golf Digest*'s #1 public course in 1998. | 73 rooms, 6 suites, 13 town homes. Restaurant, hiking, biking, horseback riding, boating, indoor pool, hot tub, exercise equipment, basketball, tennis, spa, golf, some kitchenettes. | 5391 Running Y Rd. | 541/850–5500, 888/850–0275 | fax 541/885–3194 | rooms $115, suites $229, town homes $199–$249 | AE, D, MC, V.

Shilo Inn Suites. This all-suites hotel overlooks the Cascades and Upper Klamath Lake. Most of the rooms have a view of the lake. It's 2 mi to the center of town. | 143 suites. Restaurant, bar, complimentary Continental breakfast, in-room data ports, room service, microwaves, refrigerators, cable TV, in-room VCRs (movies), indoor pool, hot tub, gym, laundry facilities, business services, airport shuttle, some pets allowed (fee). | 2500 Almond St. | 541/885–7980 | fax 541/885–7959 | $99–$125 suites | AE, D, DC, MC, V.

Super 8. This lodging is close to local restaurants. | 61 rooms. In-room data ports, cable TV, hot tub, laundry facilities, pets allowed. | 3805 U.S. 97 N | 541/884–8880 | fax 541/884–0235 | $50–$67 | AE, D, DC, MC, V.

LA GRANDE

MAP 3, J3

(Nearby towns also listed: Baker City, Pendleton)

The tracks of the Oregon Trail are evident in La Grande, and if you go to the Oregon Trail Interpretive Park at Blue Mountain Crossing you can walk along the actual ruts made by the wheels of those long ago pioneer wagons. Situated in the midst of cattle country, La Grande is the seat to Union County and is flanked on one side by the Wallowa Mountains and the other by the Blue Mountains, both attractive venues for hikers, skiers, riders, anglers, hunters, and rock climbers.

Information: **La Grande–Union County Chamber of Commerce** | 1912 4th St., #200, La Grande 97850 | 541/963–8588 or 800/848–9969.

Attractions

Catherine Creek State Park. Set in a canyon created by the creek, the peaceful park encourages fishing, hiking, picnicking, and camping. A campground has 18 primitive sites. | Hwy. 203, Meacham | 800/551–6949 | www.prd.state.or.us | Free | Mid-Apr.–Oct.

Eastern Oregon University. This public university's claim to fame is the fact that all undergraduate students, regardless of their state of residence, pay the same tuition. The Grande Ronde Symphony Orchestra performs on campus. | 1410 L Ave. | 541/962–3672 | www.eou.edu | Free | Daily.

Hilgard Junction State Recreation Area. The Grande Ronde River, which flows through this forest of cottonwood and ponderosa pine, is popular with anglers, rafters, and swimmers. A campground has 18 primitive sites. It's 8 mi west of La Grande at the intersection of Hwy. 244 | Off I–84 | 541/983–2277 or 800/551–6949 | www.prd.state.or.us | Free | Mid-Apr.–Oct., daily.

ON THE CALENDAR

AUG.: ***Union County Fair.*** This traditional summer event is held at the Union County Fairgrounds and features livestock and agricultural exhibits and competitions, food, and entertainment. | 541/963–8588.

AUG.: ***Oregon Trail Days.*** The town celebrates its pioneer heritage during this annual event with a pioneer encampment, arts and crafts fair, live entertainment, a buffalo barbecue, an old-time fiddlers contest, and a Dutch-oven cook off. | Riverside Park information booth, N. Spruce St. | 541/963–8588 or visitors information 800/848–9969.

Dining

Mamacita's. Mexican. Daily specials include fajitas, enchiladas, tacos, tostadas, burritos, and salads. The food here is considered by many to be the best in town. | 110 Depot St. | 541/963–6223 | Closed Mon. No lunch weekends | $6.50–$11.95 | No credit cards.

Smokehouse. American. This family-style restaurant, popular with local people, serves steaks, seafood, and sandwiches, and there's a salad bar, too. You can get breakfast all day. | 2208 E. Adams Ave. | 541/963–9692 | $5.95–$11.95 | D, MC, V.

OREGON TRAIL, 1853

Wednesday, June 1st. It has been raining all day long and we have been traveling in it so as to be able to keep ahead of the large droves. The men and boys are all soaking wet and look sad and comfortless. (The little ones and myself are shut up in the wagons from the rain. Still it will find its way in and many things are wet; and take us all together we are a poor looking set, and all this for Oregon. I am thinking while I write, "Oh, Oregon, you must be a wonderful country." Came 18 miles today.)

Wednesday, June 15th. passed Independence Rock this afternoon, and crossed Sweetwater River on a bridge. Paid 3 dollars a wagon and swam the stock across. The river is very high and swift.

Wednesday, July 27th. Another fine cow died this afternoon. Came 15 miles today, and have camped at the boiling springs, a great curiosity. They bubble up out of the earth boiling hot. I have only to pour water on to my tea and it is made.

Monday, August 1st. This evening another of our best milk cows died. Cattle are dying off very fast all along this road. We are hardly ever out of sight of dead cattle on this side of the Snake River. This cow was well and fat an hour before she died. Cut the second cheese today.

Monday, August 8th. We have to make a drive of 22 miles, without water today. Have our cans filled to drink. Here we left unknowingly our Lucy behind, not a soul had missed her until we had gone some miles, when we stopped a while to rest the cattle; just then another train drove up behind us with Lucy. She was terribly frightened and so were some more of us when we found out what a narrow escape she had run. The little ones have curled down and gone to sleep without supper. Wind high, and it is cold enough for a great coat and mittens.

Friday, August 19th. Quite cold this morning, water frozen in the buckets. Traveled 13 miles over very bad roads without water. After looking in vain for water, we were about to give up as it was near night, when husband came across a company of friendly Cayuse Indians about to camp, who showed him where to find water. The men and boys have driven the cattle down to water and I am waiting for water to get supper. This forenoon we bought a few potatoes from an Indian, which will be a treat for our supper.

Thursday, September 1st. we have encamped not far from the Columbia River. Made a nice dinner of fried salmon. Quite a number of Indians were camped around us, for the purpose of selling salmon to the emigrants.

Thursday, September 8th. There is very little chance to turn out of this road, on account of timber and fallen trees, for these mountains are a dense forest of pines, fir, white cedar or redwood (the handsomest timber in the world must be here in these Cascade Mountains). Many of the trees are 300 feet high and so dense to almost exclude the light of heaven. We have camped on a little stream called Sandy.

Tuesday, September 13th. here we are in Oregon making our camp in an ugly bottom, with no home, except our wagons and tent. It is drizzling and the weather looks dark and gloomy.

Friday, September 17th. In camp yet. Still raining. Noon—It has cleared off and we are all ready for a start again, for some place we don't know where.

A few days later my eighth child was born. After this we picked up and ferried across the Columbia River, utilizing skiff, canoes and flatboat to get across, taking three days to complete. Here husband traded two hoke of oxen for half section of land with one-half acre planted to potatoes and a small log cabin and lean-to with no windows. This is the journey's end.

—*Diary of Amelia Knight, 1853*

Lodging

Best Western Rama Inn and Suites. This Best Western is 2 mi from Exit 261 on I–84, on the way to Wallowa Lake or Joseph, and halfway between Portland and Boise. The large Grande Ronde shopping center is a block away. | 47 rooms, 18 suites. Complimentary Continental breakfast, in-room data ports, microwaves, refrigerators, some in-room hot tubs, cable TV, room phones, pool, hot tub, sauna, gym, laundry facilities, business services. | 1711 21st St. | 541/963–3100 or 888/726–2466 | fax 541/963–8621 | www.bestwestern.com | $79 | AE, D, DC, MC, V.

La Grande Howard Johnson. This hotel, 1 mi from downtown, is close to the university and area restaurants. It is also within a one-hour drive of all area parks and recreation facilities. | 146 rooms. Refrigerators, complimentary Continental breakfast, in-room data ports, cable TV, pool, hot tub, gym, laundry facilities, business services, pets allowed. | 2612 Island Ave. | 541/963–7195 | fax 541/963–4498 | $67–$77 | AE, D, DC, MC, V.

Royal Motor Inn. This well-kept motor inn is right downtown and within walking distance of area restaurants. | 43 rooms. Complimentary Continental breakfast, cable TV. | 1510 Adams Ave. | 541/963–4154 | fax 541/963–3588 | $30–$39 | AE, D, DC, MC, V.

Stang Manor Bed and Breakfast. This 10,000-square-ft Georgian Revival mansion has remained almost unchanged since it was built by a timber baron in 1926. A large stone fireplace, French doors, Italian tiles, white rattan furniture, a patio, and rose garden keep the Jay Gatsby era alive. The lavish breakfast is served in the formal dining room under a pewter and crystal chandelier. This is in a residential area, within walking distance of restaurants. | 3 rooms, 1 suite. Complimentary breakfast, no air-conditioning, in-room data ports, cable TV, no TV in some rooms, TV in common area, no kids under 10, no smoking. | 1612 Walnut St. | 541/963–2400 or 888/286–9463 | fax 541/963–2400 | pmcclure@stangmanor.com | www.stangmanor.com | $85–$98 | MC, V.

Super 8. This clean chain is 1 mi from the university and ½ mi from downtown. | 64 rooms, 8 suites. Refrigerators, some in-room hot tubs, cable TV, indoor pool, hot tub, exercise equipment, laundry facilities. | 2407 East R Ave. | 541/963–8080 | fax 541/963–2925 | www.super8.com | $60, $78–$88 suites | AE, D, DC, MC, V.

LAKE OSWEGO

MAP 3, E3

(Nearby towns also listed: Beaverton, Gresham, Portland)

Contrary to the intentions of its early founders, who built iron smelters in an effort to turn the area into "the Pittsburgh of the West," Lake Oswego is an affluent residential community immediately to the south of Portland. Its 33,000 residents enjoy nearly twice the average household income of other Portland suburbs. In the older neighborhoods many of the homes have a distinctly English feel because they were designed between 1920 and 1940 by the architect Richard Sundeleaf.

Lake Oswego is situated between the Willamette and Tualatin Rivers. The Willamette Shore Trolley, operated by the Oregon Electric Railway Historical Society, carries passengers along the Willamette between downtown Lake Oswego and the Riverplace area at the south end of Portland's downtown.

Information: Lake Oswego Chamber of Commerce | 242 B Ave., Lake Oswego 97034 | 503/636–3634 | lakeoswego@lake-oswego.com | www.lake-oswego.com.

Attractions

Willamette Shore Trolley. This railroad line was originally built in 1887. Since 1987, one standard and one double-decker trolley, both of museum quality, have carried passengers on the 45-minute ride to Portland. The scenic 7-mi route provides views of Mt. Hood and the wooded banks of the Willamette River. In summer, there are four departures daily from Lake Oswego. Reservations are recommended. In December, there are special Lights Along the River excursions. | 311 N. State St. | 503/222–2226 | fax 503/222–2226 | www.trainweb.org/oerhs/wst.htm | $7 round-trip | Memorial Day–Labor Day, Thurs.–Sun.; Sept., Fri.–Sun.

ON THE CALENDAR

JUNE–AUG.: ***Sound of Summer Concert Series.*** Throughout the summer, Lake Oswego sponsors a series of concerts at 6 PM on Wednesday and Sunday evenings and noon on Friday, all in three different parks in this small town. | 503/636–9673.

Dining

Riccardo's Ristorante. Northern Italian. You can dine outside in the Italian courtyard or in the softly lit dining room among the realtors who frequent this place, charming their clients with the residential neighborhood. All the ingredients are organic and hormone-free. Try the eight-layer lasagna smoothered in béchamel sauce. | 16035 S.W. Boones Ferry | 503/636–4104 | Closed Sun. | $15–$24 | AE, DC, MC, V.

Lodging

Crowne Plaza. Rooms are modern with all the amenities. There is a complimentary van service within a 5-mi radius. | 161 rooms. Restaurant, bar, room service. Indoor-outdoor pool, hot tub, exercise equipment, business services, free parking, pets allowed. | 14811 S.W. Kruse Oaks Blvd. | 503/624–8400 | fax 503/684–8324 | thecrowne@aol.com | www.crowne-plaza.com | $154–$280 | AE, D, DC, MC, V.

Phoenix Inn—Lake Oswego. This all-minisuites motel has a patio for relaxing. It's 3 mi from the Washington Sq. Mall. Rooms overlook picturesque Lake Oswego | 62 suites. Complimentary Continental breakfast, in-room data ports, minibars, microwaves, refrigerators, cable TV, indoor pool, hot tub, exercise equipment, laundry facilities, business services. | 14905 S.W. Bangy Rd. | 503/624–7400 or 800/824–9992 | fax 503/624–7405. | $84–$99 suites | AE, D, DC, MC, V.

Residence Inn by Marriott—South. This all-suites property is within walking distance of neighborhood restaurants. The units all have fireplaces and full kitchens. | 112 suites. Picnic area, complimentary Continental breakfast, cable TV, pool, hot tub, laundry facilities, business services, pets allowed (fee). | 15200 S.W. Bangy Rd., Lake Oswego | 503/684–2603 | fax 503/620–6712 | $120–$175 suites | AE, D, DC, MC, V.

LAKEVIEW

MAP 3, H8

(Nearby town also listed: Klamath Falls)

At 4,800 ft of elevation, Lakeview is the highest town in Oregon. It is surrounded by such natural wonders as Old Perpetual Geyser (in Hunter's Hot Springs), which erupts every 90 seconds, consistently shooting 60 ft in the air. There's also Abert Rim, about 20 mi to the north of town, the best known of the numerous earthquake and volcano remnants. This earth fault is more than 2,000 ft deep and 30 mi long. The Lakeview area is considered one of the state's best for hang gliding, rockhounding, fishing, and winter sports.

Information: Lake County Chamber of Commerce | 126 N. E St., Lakeview 97630 | 541/947–6040 | lakeview@triax.com | www.lakecountychamber.org.

Attractions

Drews Reservoir. It is possible to camp, picnic, boat, ski, or swim at this lake in the high desert of the Fremont National Forest. | 1300 S. G St. | 541/947–2151 | www.fs.fed.us/r6/fremont/ | Free | Daily.

Fremont National Forest. This 1.2-million-acre forest is 2 mi north of Lakeview and supports small populations of cougars, bobcats, and black bears, as well as the bald eagle and the peregrine falcon. There are 600 mi of streams and many lakes and reservoirs scattered throughout the forest. Anglers will find that the largemouth bass, yellow perch, black and white crappie, bullhead, and trout are plentiful. The winter recreation season, which runs from December through March, provides downhill and cross-country skiing, snowmobiling, snowshoeing, and ice fishing. In summer there's backpacking and camping. | Rte. 140 | 541/947–2151 | www.fs.fed.us/r6/fremont/ | Free | Daily.

Hunter's Hot Springs. The Old Perpetual Geyser spouts every 30 seconds here. Hang gliding is also popular at the site just on the edge of town. | U.S. 395 | 541/947–6040 | Free | Daily.

Old Perpetual. One mi north of Lakeview, on the grounds of Hunter's Hot Springs Resort and next to the Interstate 8 Motel, Old Perpetual is the only active geyser in the Far West. | Hwy. 395 .

Paisley. Prehistoric people lived here as many as 10,000 years ago. Evidence of their existence has been found in caves and rock paintings in the area which is 48 mi from Lakeview. Eventually the Northern Paiute, Modac, and Klamath Indians settled here. Recreational activities include fishing, bird watching, rock hounding, hiking, and camping. | Rte. 31 | 541/947–6040 | Free | Daily.

Schminck Memorial Museum. This museum, run by the Oregon chapter of the Daughters of the American Revolution, is home to glassware, china, books, tools, toys, and dolls from pioneer Lake County families. | 128 S. E St. | 541/947–3134 | $2 | Feb.–Nov., Tues.–Sat. 1–5; also by appointment.

ON THE CALENDAR

JUNE: ***Junior Rodeo.*** A rodeo competition for young people 18 and under is held at the Lake County Fairgrounds. | 541/947–6040.

JULY: ***World-Class Hang-Gliding Festival.*** "The Hang Gliding Capital of the West" rolls out the red carpet every year for this event. | 541/947–6040.

AUG.: ***Lake County Hangar Hop and Classic Car Cruise.*** On Saturday of the third weekend in August, Lakeview owners cruise about 100 classic cars along E Street and there are hot-wheels races for kids, creeper races, and a poker run. On Sunday, there are drag races, open to any kind of car, at the Lake County Sports Park on Hwy. 140, next to the airport about 5 mi from town. | Hwy. 140 | 541/947–4458.

SEPT.: ***Lake County Fair and Roundup.*** This Labor Day event has a rodeo, destruction derby, country and western music, plus a midway of fun. | 1900 N. 4th St. | 541/947–6040.

Dining

Heryford Inn. Continental. This small place with heavy, dark tables, white tablecloths, and candles serves dinner family-style, with only one choice of meal per night. Everyone has the same prix-fixe menu, with salad, soup, and dessert included in the price. Entrées may include steak with blue-cheese sauce, or shrimp scampi. Lunch is served from a small menu. | 108 S. F St. | 541/947–2380 | $17–$20 | No lunch Sat. No dinner Wed. Closed Sun.–Tues. | $17–$19.

Indian Village. American. Arrowheads and Native American artifacts line the walls of this booth-filled downtown local favorite, where a petroglyph—-a painting on stone—dominates the facade. Biscuits and gravy, and Indian fry bread with cinnamon are popular breakfast choices, as are the chicken-fried steak and steak sandwiches at dinner. There is also a salad bar. | 508 N. 1st St. | 541/947–2833 | $5–$15 | D, MC, V.

Lodging

Best Western Skyline Motor Lodge. This motel is a good choice for anglers because it's 2 mi from a popular fishing area. For everyone else, it's in the center of town. | 38 rooms.

Complimentary Continental breakfast, in-room data ports, cable TV, indoor pool, hot tub, laundry facilities, cross-country and downhill skiing, business services. | 414 North G St. | 541/947–2194 | fax 541/947–3100 | www.bestwestern.com | $55–$62 | AE, D, DC, MC, V.

Interstate 8 Motel. This inexpensive motel 1 mi north of town is right next to the Old Perpetual geyser and just two blocks from the junction of I–395 and Highway 140 W. | 32 rooms. Complimentary Continental breakfast, some microwaves, some refrigerators, cable TV, room phones. | 354 N. K St. | 541/947–3341 | fax 541/947–4288 | $38–$48 | AE, D, DC, MC, V.

Lakeview Lodge Motel. Basic accommodations are to be found in this secluded area surrounded by hills and mountains. The rooms have beautiful views of the mountains. | 40 rooms. Cable TV, hot tub, exercise equipment, cross-country and downhill skiing, pets allowed. | 301 North G St. | 541/947–2181 | fax 541/947–2572 | bobkings@triax.com | $44–$50 | AE, D, DC, MC, V.

LINCOLN CITY

MAP 3, C5

(Nearby towns also listed: Depoe Bay, Newport, Tillamook)

Lincoln City was formed about 30 years ago by consolidating five smaller towns that were growing into each other. Now an oceanside continuum of restaurants, grocery stores, motels, galleries, and factory outlets, this central coast community of nearly 7,000 permanent residents offers a variety of tourist accommodations. Two state parks, two state waysides with beach access, and 10 city parks all lie within the city. Surfing, seal watching, fishing, kite flying, and beachcombing all are popular pastimes.

Information: **Lincoln City Chamber of Commerce** | 4039 N.W. Logan Rd., Lincoln City 97367 | 541/994–3070.

Attractions

Alder House II. The imaginative craftspeople at this studio turn molten glass into vases and bowls, which are available for sale. It is the oldest glass-blowing studio in the state. | 611 Immonen Rd. | 541/996–2483 | www.alderhouse.com | Free | Mid-Mar.–Nov., daily 10–5.

Chinook Winds. The only casino located directly on the beach in Oregon has slot machines, blackjack, poker, keno, and off-track betting. There's no hotel, but the Shilo Inn is located right next door. The entry atrium is accented with a two-story waterfall and natural rocks, trees, and plants to replicate the fishing ground of the Confederated Tribes of the Siletz, who own the casino. The Siletz Room offers fine dining, and there is an all-you-can-eat buffet, a snack bar, and a lounge. An arcade will keep the kids busy while you are on the gambling floor. Big-name entertainers perform in the showroom. | 1777 N.W. 44th St. | 541/996–5825 or 888/244–6665 | Free | Daily.

Devil's Lake State Park. Canoeing and kayaking are popular on this small lake that is home to coots, loons, ducks, cormorants, bald eagles, and grebes. It's the only Oregon coast campground located in a city. There are 32 full hookups, 55 tent sites, and 10 yurts. | 1452 N.E. 6th St. | 541/994–2002 or 800/551–6949 | Free | Daily.

Theatre West. This community performing arts center showcases local talent in a variety of shows. | 3536 S.E. U.S. 101 | 541/994–5663 | Thurs.–Sat., call for hours.

ON THE CALENDAR

SEPT.: ***Annual Fall International Kite Festival.*** Kite-flying and kite-building contests are free and open to anyone who registers on the day of the festival at the River wayside, S.W. First Street and Highway 101. | 800/452–2151.

Dining

Bay House. Seafood. This restaurant inside a charming bungalow overlooks sunset-gilded Siletz Bay. The seasonal Northwest cuisine includes Dungeness crab cakes with roasted-chili chutney, fresh halibut Parmesan, and roast duckling with cranberry compote. The service is impeccable. | 5911 S.W. U.S. 101 | 541/996–3222 | Closed Mon.–Tues., Nov.–Apr. No lunch | $23–$35 | AE, D, MC, V.

Dory Cove. Seafood. This seafood restaurant has been offering an extensive menu of seafood and steak for more than 25 years. The clam chowder is legendary. They have a large selection of low-cholesterol dishes, no smoking. | 5819 Logan Rd. | 541/994–5180 | $12–$20 | AE, D, MC, V.

Fathoms Restaurant and Bar. Contemporary. This restaurant on the tenth floor of the Inn at Spanish Head provides a fine view of the ocean along with seafood, steaks, and an oyster bar. There are monthly specials, and a popular favorite here is fish and chips. Breakfast, lunch, dinner, and Sunday brunch are served in a bright, airy, contemporary setting. | 4009 S.W. Hwy. 101 | 541/996–2161 or 800/452–8127 | fax 541/996–4089 | $8.95–$15.95 | AE, D, DC, MC, V.

Kyllo's. Seafood. Light-filled Kyllo's rests on stilts beside the D River, which is proudly hailed as the world's shortest river. It's one of the best places in Lincoln City to enjoy casual but well-prepared seafood, pasta, and meat dishes. There's a second location at 1441 N.E. 11th St. | 1110 N.W. 1st Court | 541/994–3179 | $10–$25 | AE, D, MC, V.

McMenamin's Lighthouse Brew Pub. American/Casual. This westernmost outpost of the Portland-based microbrewery chain has fresh local ales and straightforward sandwiches, burgers, and salads. It also has psychedelic art by Pacific Northwest painters. This is a family place and a good one for fish and chips. | 4157 N. Hwy. 101 | 541/994–7238 | fax 541/994–9401 | Reservations not accepted | $4.25–$9.75 | AE, D, MC, V.

Rogue River Room. Contemporary. This restaurant on the upper floor of the Chinook Winds Casino overlooks the Pacific and every candlelit table has an ocean view. Local people come regularly for the salmon and prime rib, but you can choose steaks, Dungeness crab, seafood Louis, fettucini, scampi, lobster, and many other selections. | 1777 N.W. 44th St. | 541/996–5825 or 888/244–6665 | fax 541/996–5852 | $10.95–$17.95 | AE, D, MC, V.

Yuzen Japanese Cuisine. Japanese. Japanese posters, an open kitchen, and even a drive-thru window add to the casual air here in the center of town near gift and antique shops. You can get familiar tempura dishes and some sushi and sashimi, but you can also have yaki soba, lobster roll, papaya roll, and katsudon (deep fried white-meat chicken with a special sauce and rice). | 828 N.E. Hwy. 101 | 541/557–6000 | Closed Mon. | $7–$18 | MC, V.

Lodging

Ashley Inn. The rooms here are comfortable and homey and the inn is set within a garden filled with flowers. Six blocks from the ocean, seven from the Chinook Winds Casino (and there's a shuttle bus, too), close to restaurants, and only 2 mi from the Factory Stores makes it convenient, as well. | 65 rooms, 10 suites. Complimentary Continental breakfast, in-room data ports, some kitchenettes, microwaves, refrigerators, some in-room hot tubs, cable TV, room phones, pool, hot tub, sauna, gym, laundry service. | 3430 N.E. Hwy. 101 | 541/996–7500 or 888/427–4539 | fax 541/996–7765 | ashleyinn@harborside.com | www.ashley-inn.com | $99–$109 | AE, D, DC, MC, V.

Best Western Lincoln Sands Inn. This inn is right on the beach so all the rooms have a private balcony or patio with ocean view. | 33 suites. Complimentary Continental breakfast, in-room data ports, kitchenettes, microwaves, some in-room hot tubs, cable TV, in-room VCRs, pool, hot tub, sauna, no pets. | 535 N.W. Inlet Ave. | 541/994–4227 | fax 541/994–2232 | www.bestwestern.com | $99–$349 suites | AE, D, DC, MC, V.

Coho Inn. Close to the center of the city, in a residential neighborhood, all the rooms overlook the ocean. | 50 rooms. No air-conditioning, some kitchenettes, cable TV, hot tub, business services, some pets allowed (fee). | 1635 N.W. Harbor Ave. | 541/994–3684 or 800/848–7006 | fax 541/994–6244 | $107–$177 | AE, D, MC, V.

Cozy Cove Beach Front Resort. Some rooms at this comfortable inn on the beach have fireplaces, while half the rooms have ocean views and balconies. The casino is less than 2 mi away. | 70 rooms. Picnic area, some kitchenettes, some in-room hot tubs, cable TV, pool, hot tub, business services. | 515 N.W. Inlet Ave. | 541/994–2950 or 800/553–2683 | fax 541/996–4332 | $95–$100 | D, DC, MC, V.

"D" Sands. Suites and mini-suites at this beachfront condominium have ocean views. There is a free shuttle to Chinook Winds casino, which is 2 mi from here. | 63 suites. Kitchenettes, cable TV, indoor pool, hot tub, business services. | 171 SW U.S. 101 | 541/994–5244 or 800/527–3925 | fax 541/994–7484 | $124–$149 suites | AE, D, MC, V.

Dock of the Bay. The spacious condominium units at this small property have fireplaces. A shuttle bus leaves for the Chinook Winds casino every hour. All the rooms have furnished patios overlooking Siletz Bay. | 20 suites. Hot tub. | 1116 S.W. 51st St. | 541/996–3549 or 800/362–5229 | fax 541/996–4759 | $119–$139 1–bedroom suites, $139–$179 2–bedroom suites | MC, V.

Ester Lee Motel. This long-established small motel on a 100-ft bluff overlooking the Pacific gets lots of repeat business, not least for its panoramic views of the ocean and coast. Separate entrances to many of the rooms give them the feeling of a cottage. Many rooms have an ocean view, knotty pine paneling, fireplace, and bay windows. From here, it's only 1 mi north to the Factory Stores and 5 to the Chinook Winds Casino. | 18 rooms, 35 suites. No air-conditioning, in-room data ports, some kitchenettes, refrigerators, cable TV, room phones. | 3803 S.W. Hwy. 101 | 541/996–3606 or 888/996–3606 | fax 541/996–6743 | esterlee@harborside.com | www.esterlee.com | D, MC, V.

Inn at Spanish Head. You'll find tidal pools right outside your door at this condominium resort set on a bluff. All of the bright, contemporary units have ocean views and each is decorated in a different style. Choose from one-bedroom suites, deluxe studios, or deluxe rooms. | 120 rooms, 25 suites. Restaurant, bar, room service, cable TV, pool, hot tub, exercise equipment, game room with a pool table and Ping-Pong, business services. | 4009 S. Hwy 101 | 541/996–2161 or 800/452–8127 | fax 541/996–4089 | spanishhead@newportnet.com | www.spanishhead.com | $145, $165–$229 suites | AE, D, DC, MC, V.

Liberty Inn. The big Liberty Inn still manages to look like a large private home in this quiet and prosperous residential area on the north side of town. Ivory with green trim, and surrounded by trees, flowers, and shrubbery, this inn blends smoothly into the scenery. The modern rooms are spacious, done in dark green and burgundy with cherrywood furnishings. You can walk to both the Chinook Winds Casino and McMenamin's Brew Pub. | 76 rooms. Complimentary Continental breakfast, in-room data ports, microwaves, refrigerators, some in-room hot tubs, cable TV, room phones, pool, hot tub, laundry facilities. | 4990 N. Logan Rd. | 541/994–1777 or 877/994–1777 | fax 541/994–1888 | www.libertyinn.com | $69–$149 | AE, D, DC, MC, V.

Lincoln Shores. This motel, which overlooks Devil's Lake and the D River, has an alpine-style exterior. | 30 rooms. Some kitchenettes, cable TV, business services. | 136 N.E. U.S. 101 | 541/994–8155 or 800/423–6240 | fax 541/994–5581 | $79–$199 | AE, D, DC, MC, V.

Nordic. The beach is close to this hotel, which is in a quiet neighborhood, near to area attractions. | 52 rooms. Complimentary Continental breakfast, some kitchenettes, cable TV, in-room VCRs, indoor pool, hot tub, game room, business services. | 2133 N.W. Inlet Ave. | 541/994–8145 or 800/452–3558 (western U.S.), 800/243–3558 (Canada) | fax 541/994–2329 | $79–$110 | D, DC, MC, V.

Pelican Shores Inn. This inn on the beach is furnished in a contemporary manner. All the rooms have oceanfront views. | 32 rooms, 19 suites. Some kitchenettes, cable TV, indoor pool, laundry facilities, business services. | 2645 N.W. Inlet Ave. | 541/994–2134 or 800/705–5505

| fax 541/994–4963 | stay@pelicanshores.com | www.pelicanshores.com | $89–$99, $109–$119 suites | AE, D, DC, MC, V.

Rodeway Inn on the Bay. This Rodeway is at the south end of town. The bay beach is across the road and the Pacific beach is only a mile away. You can eat at the local branch of Mo's, which is opposite the entrance. This is a cozy, older inn, and some rooms have heart-shaped hot tubs along with gas fireplaces, balconies, and bay views. | 29 rooms, 11 suites. Complimentary Continental breakfast, no air-conditioning, in-room data ports, some kitchenettes, some microwaves, some refrigerators, some in-room hot tubs, cable TV, room phones. | 861 S.W. 51st St. | 541/996–3996 or 800/843–4940 | fax 541/994–7554 | rodewayinn@harborside.com | www.hotels-west.com | $39–$99 | AE, D, DC, MC, V.

Shilo Inn—Oceanfront Resort. This beachfront motel is very popular because of its convenient location next door to the Chinook Winds Casino. The room are furnished simply, but the newer building has suites with fireplaces and ocean views. | 247 rooms. Bar, picnic area, some kitchenettes, some microwaves, some refrigerators, room service, cable TV, indoor pool, hot tub, exercise equipment, laundry facilities, business services, airport shuttle, some pets allowed (fee). | 1501 N.W. 40th Place | 541/994–3655 | fax 541/994–2199 | $125–$169 | AE, D, DC, MC, V.

MADRAS

MAP 3, G4

(Nearby towns also listed: Prineville, Redmond, Warm Springs)

Madras is the seat of Jefferson County at the junctions of Highways 26 and 97. It is the northern gateway to the popular year-round recreational region of central Oregon. The town is less than 15 miles from the Warm Springs Indian Reservation and comprises one of the most ethnically diverse communities in Oregon as more than 20 percent of its 5,000 residents are Native Americans or Hispanic.

High desert sage, juniper, and wild grass color the landscape, flanked to the west by the Cascade foothills. Geologic delights, including agates and the world's richest deposit of thunder eggs, attract rock hounds, while fly and lure fishing and white-water rafting draw visitors to the nearby Deschutes River. The Deschutes meets up with the Crooked and Metolius rivers in a spectacular canyon to form Lake Billy Chinook, where Cove Palisades State Park hosts more than 500,000 people each year for water sports and camping.

Information: Madras–Jefferson County Chamber of Commerce | 274 S.W. 4th St., Madras 97741 | 541/475–2350 or 800/976–3564.

Attractions

Jefferson County Museum. Located in the former city hall built in 1917, this small museum displays pioneer artifacts. | 34 S.E. D St. | 541/475–3808 | Free | June–Sept., Tues.–Fri. 1–5.

Lake Simtustus RV Park. You can rent boats and fish on the lake, swim, picnic, and camp at this park, which is quieter and less trafficked than Cove Palisades State Park. | 2750 N.W. Pelton Dam Rd. | 541/475–1085 | Mid-Apr.–Oct.

Richardson's Recreational Ranch. This site, 15 mi north of Madras, has the largest concentration of thunder eggs in North America. You can also hunt for agates here. | Off US 97 N | 541/475–2680 | Free | Store: daily 7–5; diggings dependent on weather, call for information.

The Cove Palisades State Park. Located in the high desert, 14 mi west of Madras, this park's towering cliffs surround Lake Billy Chinook. There are 10 mi of hiking trails. A store, a restaurant, a marina, and rental services are within the park. A full-service campground has 87 full hookups, 91 electrical and 94 tent sites, houseboats, and cabins. | Old Culver Hwy. | 541/546–3412 or 800/551–6949 | www.prd.state.or.us | $3/vehicle day-use fee | Daily.

ON THE CALENDAR

JULY: *Jefferson County Fair.* The Jefferson County Fairgrounds, 1 mi from Madras, is the site of a four-day fair beginning on the Wednesday before the third weekend of July. You can see livestock displays and competitions, a show of 90–100 quilts, a large Native American exhibition of bead- and leatherwork, a display of demo gardens, nonstop entertainment, and a two-day rodeo. There's fun for the kids, too, and on Saturday night there's a big Western dance. | 541/475–4460.

Dining

Grandma Hoffy's Restaurant. American. Once inside, a 6-ft wooden chain-saw sculpture of a cowboy greets you at the door while the walls are hung with painted saws. A second-generation Grandma presides over breakfast, lunch, and dinner. The straightforward family-style home cooking is on the order of soups, burgers, fish and chips made with halibut, and a salad bar. | 590 N. Hwy. 26 | 541/475–7369 | $4–$13 | AE, D, DC, MC, V.

Lodging

Hoffy's Motel. Hoffy's rooms are in five buildings on landscaped lawns, on the road between Portland and Madras. If you want, you can rent the tepee outside; it sleeps up to six, but you'll need camping gear. Grandma Hoffy's Restaurant is next door. | 90 rooms, 8 suites. In-room data ports, some microwaves, some refrigerators, some in-room hot tubs, cable TV, room phones, pool, putting green, basketball, laundry facilities. | 600 N. Hwy. 26 | 541/475–4633 or 800/227–6865 | fax 541/475–7872 | $40 | AE, D, DC, MC, V.

Sonny's. This medium-size motel has basic accommodations. It is on the highway, about 12 mi from the lake and water ski resort areas. | 44 rooms, 2 suites. Restaurant, bar, complimentary Continental breakfast, some microwaves, some in-room hot tubs, pool, hot tub, laundry facilities, business services, pets allowed (fee). | 1539 S.W. U.S. 97 | 541/475–7217 or 800/624–6137 | fax 541/475–6547 | www.sonnysmotel.com | $55–$58, $90–$110 suites | AE, D, DC, MC, V.

MAUPIN

MAP 3,G3

(Nearby town also listed: The Dalles)

Maupin is east of the Cascade Range on the banks of the Deschutes, a popular white-water rafting river that begins in the Cascades south of Three Sisters and flows swiftly through Maupin to Celio where it meets the Columbia. On summer weekend days the small tourist town is jam-packed with rafting aficionados and sun worshippers. Don't expect anything fancy here, just basic rooms and eats. Maupin is 40 mi south of The Dalles on U.S. 197, about 2 hours from Portland.

Information: **Deschutes River Information Center** | West end of bridge on Hwy. 197, Maupin, 97037 | 541/395–2270 | www.nps.gov/rivers/deschutes.html.

Attractions

Maupin City Park/Deschutes River. Launch your raft or park your RV in Maupin's city park on the banks of the Deschutes River. There are 20 RV spaces ($3 day use, $16 overnight with hookups). CJ Lodge, with its restaurant and store, is next door. Popular spots on the river just north of town on Deschutes River Road are Sherars Falls and Trestle Hole. | 206 Bakeoven Road | 541/395–2252 | Free | Daily.

White River Falls State Park. This waterfall looks out of place in the middle of Tygh Valley farm fields. It's in a canyon 4 mi east of Highway 197 cut through the White River. The dramatic 90-ft plunge is surrounded by scenic mesa formations. Hike down a quarter-mi trail to the remains of an old river powerhouse that supplied power to the area from 1910 to

1960. The river flows into the Deschutes a few miles to the east. The small park above has picnic tables and rest rooms. | Hwy. 216 | 800/551–6949 | www.prd.state.or.us | Free | Early spring–late fall dawn to dusk.

ON THE CALENDAR

AUG: *Wasco County Fair.* All the usual rural fare at this county fair in Tygh Valley: agricultural exhibits, food and crafts booths, and entertainment at 81849 Fairgrounds Road. | 541/483–2288.

Dining

Deschutes River Inn. American/Casual. Down-home cooking rules the day at this popular spot which features barbecued meat as well as seafood, salads, beer, and wine. | 509 Deschutes Ave. | 541/395–2468 | $8–$18 | MC, V.

Juniper Room. American. The CJ Lodge's cozy dining room is Maupin's nicest restaurant. The menu changes frequently but usually features barbecued ribs and chicken and always includes fish and vegetarian options. Organic vegetables and herbs are used in season. Dine outdoors in nice weather. | 304 Bakeoven Road | 541/395–2404 | $8–$20 | AE, D, MC, V.

Ole Country Kitchen. American. This downtown eatery serves food—breakfast, lunch, and dinner seven days a week. Chicken-fried steak, halibut, oysters, and shrimp are favorites. They also make pizzas. | 505 Deschutes Ave. | 541/395–2708 | $6–$18.

Lodging

CJ Lodge. All the rooms at this inn on the banks of the Deschutes River have private baths. Some have river views and whirlpool tubs. The lodge operates white-water rafting excursions ($75 day trip) from April to October. | 11 rooms. Restaurant, rafting, boat rental, fishing, swimming. | 304 Bakeover Road | 541/395–2494 or 800/395–3903 | fax 541/395–2494 | www.deschutesriver.com | $70–$110 | Full breakfast | AE, D, MC, V.

Deschutes Motel. Looking like something you might have seen along Route 66 in the 1950s, this rural motel has plain rooms, nothing more. | 12 rooms. No pets. | 616 Mill St. | 541/395–2626 | $45–$55 | MC, V.

Oasis Resort. The small cabins are very basic at this property on the south side of the river. They also operate rafting excursions and a river shuttle. | 11 cabins. Restaurant, rafting, swimming, fishing, pets allowed. | 609 Hwy. 197 | 541/395–2611 | www.deschutesriveroasis.com | $35–69 | MC, V.

MANZANITA

MAP 3, C2

(Nearby towns also listed: Cannon Beach, Rockaway Beach, Seaside, Tillamook)

Manzanita is a secluded seaside community with only 500 full-time residents. It is situated on a sandy peninsula peppered with tufts of grass on the northwestern side of Nehalem Bay. It is a tranquil small town, but its restaurants, galleries, and 18-hole golf course have increased its appeal to tourists. Manzanita and Nehalem Bay both have become popular windsurfing destinations.

Information: **Nehalem Bay Area Chamber of Commerce** | 13015 Hwy. 101, Nehalem 97131 | 503/368–5100.

Attractions

Nehalem Bay Winery. Established in 1974 and the sixth-oldest winery in Oregon, Nehalem Bay is known for its Pinot Chardonnay and blackberry and plum fruit wines. You can taste them here, in a building that was once the Mohler Cheese Factory, and enjoy the picnic area. The winery also has a busy schedule of events with concerts, barbecues, an occasional pig roast, children's activities, performances at the Theatre Au Vin, and a bluegrass festival in the third week of August. | 34965 Hwy. 53, Nehalem | 503/368–9463 or 888/368–9463 | fax 503/368–5300 | www.nehalembaywinery.com | Daily 9–6.

ON THE CALENDAR

JULY: *Pancake Breakfast and Parade.* The traditional 4th of July pancake breakfast begins at 8:30 in the Pine Grove Community Center. The parade begins at 1:30, winds through the center of this small town and along Ocean Street next to the beach, and features floats, children, horses, and perhaps an Elvis impersonator. Watch the fireworks from the beach. | 225 Laneda Avenue | 503/368–5100.

Dining

Blue Sky Cafe. Eclectic. Stained glass, a jungle of plants, and tables covered in butcher's paper lend a quirky air to this casual hole-in-the-wall café in nearby Manzanita, 13 mi south of Cannon Beach. Try the crab and rock shrimp baked in parchment, the Thai coconut-curry soup, and the memorably rich desserts. | 154 Laneda St., Manzanita | 503/368–5712 | Closed Mon.–Tues. during Oct.–June. No lunch | $25–$30 | No credit cards.

Lodging

Inn at Manzanita. This 1987 Scandinavian structure, filled with light-colored woods, beams, and glass, is half a block from the beach. Shore pines on the property give upper-floor patios a treehouse feel, all rooms have decks, and two have skylights. A nearby café serves breakfast and you can walk to restaurants. In winter, the inn is a great place for storm-watching. | 13 rooms in 4 buildings. No air-conditioning in some rooms, some kitchenettes, some microwaves, refrigerators, in-room hot tubs, cable TV, some room phones, no smoking. | 67 Laneda Ave., Box 243 | 503/368–6754 | fax 503/368–5941 | dromano@nehalemtel.net | www.neahkahnie.net | $105–$150, 2-night minimum on weekends | MC, V.

MCKENZIE BRIDGE

MAP 3, E5

(Nearby town also listed: Eugene)

Located on the beautiful McKenzie River, the town of McKenzie Bridge is surrounded by lakes, waterfalls, covered bridges, and wilderness trails in the Cascades. Fishing, skiing, backpacking, and rafting are among the most popular activities in the area.

Attractions

Blue River Dam and Lake. This 1,240-acre reservoir in the Willamette National Forest has miles of forested shoreline. From May through September, boats are launched from ramps at Saddle Dam and Lookout Creek. Recreational activities include fishing, swimming, water skiing, and camping at Mona Campground. | Forest Rd. 15 in Willamette National Forest | 541/822–3317 | Free | Daily.

Cougar Dam and Lake. Four mi outside of McKenzie Bridge is Cougar Dam, the highest embankment dam ever built by the Army Corps of Engineers—452 ft above the stream bed. The resulting reservoir on the South Fork McKenzie River covers 1,280 acres. The public recreation areas are in the Willamette National Forest. A fish hatchery is located here. You can visit the dam year-round, but the campgrounds are only open from May to September. | Forest Rd. 19 in Willamette National Forest | 541/822–3317 | Free | May–Sept., daily; most areas closed rest of year, inquire.

High Country Expeditions. This friendly family business provides guided white-water rafting and fishing trips on the McKenzie and Willamette Rivers, lasting from half a day to several days, for everyone from beginners to experts. In spring, High Country leads 5–

10-day white-water trips on the Owyhee River. | 56341 Delta Dr. | 541/822–8288 or 888/461–7238 | fax 541/822–8003 | www.highcountryexpeditions.com.

ON THE CALENDAR

SEPT.: ***Walterville Community Fair.*** You park in the cow pasture behind Millican Grange Hall in Walterville, a mile from town, where this half-century-old annual three-day fair is held. There are bake-offs, and local craftsmen and gardeners bring their wares and produce to sell. The whole town, including everybody's pet dog, participates in the parade. 541/896–3330.

Dining

Log Cabin Inn. Contemporary. This restaurant, which has log cabin walls in the saloon, is housed in a 1906 stagecoach station. There is a wraparound deck and tables set in the landscaped garden, which has views of the river. Try the Mesquite prime-rib and salmon, as well as the marion-berry cobbler. Kids' menu. Sun. brunch. | 56483 McKenzie Hwy. | 541/822–3432 | $15–$24 | D, MC, V.

Lodging

Holiday Farm Resort. American. Heavy and hearty cooking is what you'll get in this 1876 former stagecoach stop across the street from the river. Corned-beef hash, biscuits, and steak and eggs dominate the morning menu. Barbecued beef brisket is roasted in a pit outside all day for the evening crowd. You can also order fresh salmon, halibut, or stuffed pork chops. | 54455 McKenzie River Dr., Blue River | 541/822–3715 | $10–$25 | AE, MC, V.

Osprey Inn. All the rooms here have a view of the McKenzie River and there's white-water rafting on this stretch of it. There are two gazebos on the 1½-acre grounds, plus lots of Douglas firs and red cedars in this heavily wooded region. The large guest rooms, each done in unique eclectic styles, have sitting areas. Osprey Inn is near restaurants and 3 mi from Tokatee Golf Course. | 4 rooms. Complimentary breakfast, some refrigerators, no TV in some rooms, no kids under 16, no smoking. | 56532 North Bank Rd. | 541/822–8186 | fax 541/822–8186 | ospreyinn@aol.com | www.osprey-inn.com | $120–$155 | Closed Nov.–Apr. | No credit cards.

MCMINNVILLE

MAP 3, D3

(Nearby towns also listed: Newberg, Oregon City, Salem)

The Yamhill County seat, McMinnville lies at the center of Oregon's burgeoning wine industry. There is a larger concentration of wineries in Yamhill County than in any other area of the state, and the vineyards here also produce the most award-winning wines. Among the varieties are Chardonnay, Pinot Noir, and Pinot Gris. Most of the wineries in the area offer tours and tastings.

McMinnville is also home to Linfield College, and it is the headquarters of Evergreen International Aviation, which provides helicopters and fixed-wing service for humanitarian missions as well as fire fighting, agriculture, and industry. Of popular interest, Howard Hughes's famous Spruce Goose airplane is stored at the facility, where a future air museum is planned.

Information: Greater McMinnville Chamber of Commerce | 417 N.W. Adams St., McMinnville 97128 | 503/472–6196 | www.mcminnville.org.

Attractions

Lafayette Schoolhouse Antique Mall. This restored 1913 schoolhouse 5 mi north of McMinnville contains Oregon's largest permanent antiques show. This is a good place to look for pottery items and Depression glass. | 748 Hwy. 99 W | 503/864–2720 | www.myantique-mall.com | Free | Daily 10–5.

Linfield College. Founded in 1849, this oasis of brick and ivory is the second-oldest college in Oregon. The International Pinot Noir Celebration is held on the small campus every July | 900 S.W. Baker St. | 503/434–2200 | www.linfield.edu | Free | Daily.

Spirit Mountain Casino and Lodge. Its location on Highway 18, one of the main routes from Portland to the ocean, makes this casino which is owned and operated by the Confederated Tribes of the Grand Ronde Community of Oregon a popular destination or stop en route to the coast. Only 90 minutes from Portland and 45 minutes from Salem, this is the biggest casino resort in Oregon. The 183,000-square-ft casino has 1,100 slots, 15 poker tables, 35 blackjack tables, roulette, craps, Pai Gow poker, keno, bingo, and off-track betting. Big-name entertainers perform here, and there's an arcade for the kids. Patrons can take advantage of complimentary shuttle service from Portland and Salem. There are restaurants and a hotel. | 27100 S.W. Rte. 18, Grand Ronde | 503/879–2350 or 800/760–7977 | Free | Daily, 24 hrs.

Spruce Goose Museum. Officially known as the Capt. Michael King Smith Evergreen Aviation Education Center and Museum, this attractions claim to fame is the *Spruce Goose*, which will eventually be on permanent display. Also known as the Hughes Flying Boat, the famous plane, which eccentric billionaire Howard Hughes flew only once—on Nov. 2, 1947—has been disassembled since it was moved here in 1992 from Long Beach, California. There are also about a dozen military planes on display. Several aircraft from the museum collection are housed within the temporary museum. | 3850 Three Mile La. | 503/472–9361 | www.sprucegoose.org | $5 | Daily 9–4.

Yamhill Valley Vineyards. The Pinot Noir, Pinot Blanc, and Pinot Gris wines produced on this 300-acre estate 5 mi from McMinnville have won prestigious awards. There's a tasting room and a picnic area overlooking the vineyards. | 16250 S.W. Oldsville Rd. | 503/843–3100 or 800/825–4845 | fax 503/843–2450 | www.yamhill.com | Free | Mid-Mar.–Memorial Day, weekends 11–5; Memorial Day–Thanksgiving, daily 11–5.

ON THE CALENDAR

JULY: *Turkey Rama/Oregon Hazelnut Festival.* McMinnville, the "turkey capital of the world," celebrates its status every year with this nutty festival—nutty because it also highlights the fact that Oregon produces 95% of America's domestic hazelnut crop. The event, held on 3rd Street, includes a turkey barbecue and a carnival with live entertainment, starring, who else, turkeys. | 503/472–6196.

JULY–AUG.: *Yamhill County Fair.* This is a yearly event that features agricultural exhibits and competitions, food, and entertainment. | 2070 Lafayette Ave. | 503/434–7524.

Dining

Coty's Restaurant. Contemporary. Anthony Danna is chef at this 1895 former railroad depot. His specialties include salmon with pear chutney, demi-glazed pork with apples, and Asian duck. On Thursday try the barbecue special. | 729 N.E. 3rd St. | 503/474–1888 | Closed Sun. No lunch | $11–$20 | AE, MC, V.

Golden Valley Brew Pub. American/Casual. All the beers served here are brewed on-site in this former warehouse with high ceilings, wood paneling, and many booths in the dining room. Try the breaded (not battered) halibut fish and chips, made with large filet pieces, or the Tuscan chicken prepared in the house marinade. | 980 N.E. 4th St. | 503/472–2759 | $9–$20 | AE, D, MC, V.

★ **Nick's Italian Cafe.** Italian. Modestly furnished, but with a voluminous wine cellar, Nick's is a favorite of area wine makers. The food is spirited and simple, reflecting the owner's northern Italian heritage. The five-course prix-fixe menu changes nightly. A la carte options are also available. | 521 E. 3rd St. | 503/434–4471 | Reservations essential | Closed Mon. No lunch | $20–$35 | AE, DC, MC, V.

Lodging

★ **Flying M Ranch.** Decorated in a style best described as Daniel Boone eclectic, the log lodge is the centerpiece of the 625-acre Flying M Ranch, perched above the steelhead-filled Yamhill River. Choose between somewhat austere cabins (the cozy Honeymoon Cabin is the nicest) or riverside hotel units. | 28 rooms in lodge; 8 cabins. Bar with entertainment, dining room, picnic area, some kitchenettes, some in-room hot tubs, some room phones, no TV in some rooms, TV in common area, pond, tennis, hiking, horseback riding, fishing, cross-country skiing, snowmobiling, laundry facilities, business services, pets allowed. | 23029 N.W. Flying M Rd., Yamhill | 503/662–3222 | fax 503/662–3202 | $60, $85–$200 cabins | AE, D, DC, MC, V.

Paragon. This motel is located near the Spruce Goose Museum and a golf course. | 55 rooms. Complimentary Continental breakfast, refrigerators, cable TV, pool, laundry facilities, business services, pets allowed (fee), no smoking. | 2065 S. Rte. 99 W | 503/472–9493 or 800/525–5469 | fax 503/472–8470 | $45–$57 | AE, D, DC, MC, V.

Safari Motor Inn. More functional than fancy, this motel on McMinnville's main drag has modest rates and clean accommodations with up-to-date furnishings. | 90 rooms. Restaurant, hot tub, business services. | 345 N. Rte. 99 W | 503/472–5187 or 800/321–5543 | fax 503/434–6380 | $49–$58 | AE, D, DC, MC, V.

Steiger Haus. Stained-glass windows accentuate this small Northern European country-style B&B situated in a park-like setting. The rooms are plush and cozy. | 5 rooms. Picnic area, complimentary breakfast, no air-conditioning, no kids under 10, no smoking. | 360 Wilson St. | 503/472–0238 | fax 503/472–0100 | stay@steigerhaus.com | www.steigerhaus.com | $70–$130 | D, MC, V.

A' Tuscan Estate. Columns frame the entryway of this white, gabled two-story 1928 inn five blocks from downtown. An original red-oak floor, Honduras-mahogany doors and cabinets, wrought-iron canopy beds, and hand-painted faux Tuscan walls make this place worthy of its title. | 3 rooms, 1 suite. Complimentary Continental breakfast, cable TV. No air-conditioning. No in-room phones. No kids under 12. No pets. | 809 N.E. Evans St. | 503/434–9016, 800/441–2214 | $125, suite $195 | MC, V.

Youngberg Hill Vineyard. This huge replica of a classic American farmhouse commands breathtaking views over mountain and valley from atop a steep hill. The 700-acre estate has 10 acres of Pinot Noir vines. The spacious common areas of the house are filled with deep sofas and armchairs, and there's a wood-burning stove. The guest rooms are small to medium in size and cozy with golden oak and Victorian Cottage reproductions. There's a reasonably priced wine cellar, plus wedding facilities, if you're so inclined. | 4 rooms, 3 suites. Picnic area, complimentary breakfast. Some in-room hot tubs, no room phones, no TV, hiking, no kids under 12, no smoking. | 10660 Youngberg Hill Rd. | 503/472–2727 or 888/657–8668 | fax 503/472–1313 | youngberghill@netscape.net | $130–$150 | MC, V.

MEDFORD

MAP 3, D8

(Nearby towns also listed: Ashland, Grants Pass, Jacksonville)

Although Medford has only about 60,000 residents, the community is the professional, retail trade, and service center for eight counties in southern Oregon and northern California. As such, it offers more professional and cultural opportunities than might be expected for a city of its size. Four major shopping centers and the fruit marketers Harry and David are located in Medford.

Near two major rivers and more than 30 lakes and streams, Medford is an outdoor recreational paradise and an easy starting place for tours of two of Oregon's natural treasures. Crater Lake, the state's only national park, is 80 mi to the northeast, and the Oregon Caves, a series of limestone rooms and galleries, is 80 mi to the southwest.

Information: **Greater Medford Visitors Bureau** | 101 E. 8th, Medford 97501 | 541/779–4847 | www.visitmedford.org.

Attractions

Butte Creek Mill. This 1872 water-powered flour grist mill is listed in the National Historic Register and still produces whole grain food products, which you can buy at the country store here. | 402 Royal Ave. N, Eagle Point | 541/826–3531 | www.buttecreekmill.com | Free | Mon.–Sat. 9–5 | Closed all holidays.

Craterian Ginger Rogers Theater. The late Hollywood star retired to this area. This restored vaudeville house, named for her, presents concerts, ballets, theatrical works, and touring shows like the Vienna Boys Choir and Brazil Night. | 23 S. Central Ave., | 541/779–8195 | fax 541/779–8175 | www.craterian.org.

Crater Rock Museum. Jackson County's natural history and collections of the Roxy Ann Gem and Mineral Society are on display. | 2002 Scenic Ave., Central Point | 541/664–6081 | Free | Tues.–Sat. 10–4.

Joseph H. Stewart State Park. The campground, 34 mi from Medford, overlooks Lost Creek Reservoir where you can rent canoes. There are 8 mi of hiking trails. The campground has 151 electrical and 50 tent sites. | Hwy 62 | 541/560–3334 or 800/551–6949 | Free | Mar.–Nov., daily.

Rogue River National Forest. This forest covers 630,000 acres. Recreational activities include fishing, swimming, hiking, and skiing. Motorized vehicles and equipment—even bicycles—are prohibited in the 113,000-acre Sky Lakes Wilderness, which is located south of Crater Lake National Park. Its highest point is the 9,495-ft Mt. McLoughlin. Summers here are warm and dry, while winters are bitterly cold with lots of snow. | I–5 to exit 39, Hwy. 62 to Rte. 140 | 541/858–2200 | www.fs.fed.us/r6/rogue | Free for most of the forest; some of the trailheads have fees. Call for details | Daily.

Southern Oregon History Center. The focus here is the Rogue Valley's past. | 106 N. Central Ave. | 541/773–6536 | www.sohs.org | Free | Weekdays 9–5, Sat. 1–5.

Tou Velle State Park. This is a popular spot for weddings and picnics. There are beautiful hiking trails in this day use park that wind through a wildlife viewing area. | Off I–5 to Table Rock Road | 541/582–1118 or 800/551–6949 | www.prd.state.or.us | $3 per vehicle day-use fee | Daily.

ON THE CALENDAR

JUNE: *Medford Cruise.* On Father's Day weekend, the streets of Medford are filled with 500 or more vintage cars. From 8–4 on Saturday, there's a Show and Shine, with the cars parked on and around Main Street, and from 6–10 PM they cruise the streets. | 541/772–5222.

JULY: *Jackson County Fair.* This is primarily an agricultural fair with livestock exhibits and an auction held on the Jackson County Fairgrounds. A carnival, musical entertainment, a technology pavilion, food booths, and Smokey's playland for children round out the festivities. | 541/776–7237.

Dining

Chevy's. Mexican. This popular chain serves good Mexican dishes, including burritos, tamales, nachos, and fajitas, at reasonable prices. It's a kid-friendly place, but you can dine sans kids in the lounge, best known for its margaritas. The chips and salsa are made fresh daily. | 3125 Crater Lake Hwy. | 541/774–8844 | $13–$20 | AE, MC, V.

C.K. Tiffins. American/Casual. This downtown place focuses on health-conscious food—it serves poached eggs at breakfast, along with waffles, pancakes, and a variety of baked goods made fresh every morning on site. Try the popular chicken sesame salad or vegetarian lasagna at lunch. Red meat is not served. The restaurant is on the site of a former early 20th-century men's clothier and displays the work of local artists. | 226 E. Main St. | 541/779–0480 | No dinner | $4–$9 | AE, D, MC, V.

Mon Desir Dining Inn. Continental. This restaurant in a converted mansion is filled with antiques. The fireplace creates a warm mood on cool evenings. Try a Bavarian specialty of the house—baked rolled beef with carrots and pickles. There is seating on the patio. | 4615 Hamrick Rd., Central Point | 541/664–7558 | Closed Sun.–Mon. No lunch Sat. | $14–$26 | D, MC, V.

Samovar Restaurant. Russian. Vintage Russian advertisements from the early 20th century line the walls of this candlelit downtown place next to a bank. The restaurant serves vegetarian borscht, stuffed cabbage, *pelmeni* (Russian ravioli), and other traditional Russian specialties. | 101 E. Main St. | 541/733–4967 | Closed Sun. and Mon. | $13–$17 | MC, V.

Tasty Thai. Thai. Food is served family-style to lunching businesspeople and families who share the small, booth-filled dining room with two non-fruit-bearing banana trees. Try yellow chicken curry, or the classic pad thai. | 725 S. Central Ave. | 541/779–1348 | Closed Sun. | $7–$11 | MC, V.

Vinny's Italian Kitchen. Italian. You watch Vinny cook his family's Ischia Island recipes in the open kitchen of this place where the walls are covered with family photos. Try the La Vigna pasta with artichokes, broccoli, chicken, and olives. | 970 N. Phoenix Rd. | 541/618–8669 | Closed Sun. | $8–$10 | AE, MC, V.

Lodging

Best Inn. This no-frills hotel is less than ½ mi from Highway 5 and has two meeting rooms. | 112 rooms. Complimentary Continental breakfast, coin laundry, exercise equipment, outdoor pool, cable TV, air-conditioning. | 1015 S. Riverside Dr. | 541/773–8266 | $75–$102 | AE, D, DC, MC, V.

Best Western Horizon Inn. This reliable chain outlet with many amenities on the outskirts of town is next door to a restaurant and less than a mile from Highway 5. | 115 rooms, 8 suites. Restaurant, cable TV, air-conditioning, data ports, hot tub, outdoor pool, sauna, exercise equipment, business services. Some microwaves, refrigerators. | 1154 Barnett Rd. | 541/779–5085, 800/452–2255 | fax 541/772–6878 | $75–$105 | AE, D, DC, MC, V.

Best Western Pony Soldier. Rooms at this motel face the pool. | 74 rooms. Complimentary Continental breakfast, in-room data ports, microwaves, refrigerators, cable TV, pool, hot tub, cross-country and downhill skiing, laundry facilities, airport shuttle, some pets allowed. | 2340 Crater Lake Hwy. | 541/779–2011 or 800/634–7669 | fax 541/779–7304 | $85–$95 | AE, D, DC, MC, V.

Cedar Lodge Motor Inn. This centrally located motor inn is two blocks from the movie theater and within walking distance of restaurants. | 79 rooms. Bar, complimentary Continental breakfast, some microwaves, refrigerators, cable TV, pool, cross-country and downhill skiing, some pets allowed. | 518 N. Riverside Ave. | 541/773–7361 or 800/282–3419 | fax 541/776–1033 | www.oregonfishing.com | $40–$45 | AE, D, DC, MC, V.

Horizon Motor Inn. This large motel is close to shopping as well as downhill and cross-country skiing. | 129 rooms. Restaurant, bar, some microwaves, cable TV, pool, hot tub, airport shuttle, pets allowed (fee). | 1154 E.Barnett Rd. | 541/779–5085 or 800/452–2255 | www.horizoninns.com | $79–$145 | AE, DC, MC, V.

Motel 6. It's clean, cheap, and close to the Shakespeare Festival, the Mount Ashland ski area, and Crater Lake. | 101 rooms. Pool. | 950 Alba Dr. | 541/773–4290 or 800/466–8356 (central reservations) | fax 541/857–9574 | $42 | AE, D, DC, MC, V.

Red Lion Inn. Right in downtown Medford, this popular chain hotel is close to local entertainment and 1 mi from the closest shopping mall. | 186 rooms. Restaurant, bar with entertainment, dining room, in-room data ports, room service, cable TV, 2 pools, cross-country and downhill skiing, laundry facilities, business services, airport shuttle, pets allowed (fee). | 200 N. Riverside Ave. | 541/779–5811 | fax 541/779–7961 | $79–$89. | AE, D, DC, MC, V.

Reston Hotel. This is a business hotel with 10,000 square ft of meeting, exhibit, and banquet space. The rooms are comfortable and spacious. It is only ½ mi to local shopping and restaurants. | 164 rooms. Restaurant, bar, cable TV, indoor pool, business services, airport shuttle, some pets allowed (fee). | 2300 Crater Lake Hwy | 541/779–3141 or 800/779–7829 | fax 541/779–2623 | sales@restonhotel.com | www.restonhotel.com | $72 | AE, D, DC, MC, V.

Rogue Regency Inn. You are only 1 mi from the airport and close to area shopping and restaurants. | 123 rooms. Restaurant, bar, microwaves, refrigerators, room service, cable TV, pool, hot tub, airport shuttle. | 2345 Crater Lake Hwy. | 541/770–1234 or 800/535–5805 | fax 541/770–2466 | regency@rogueregency.com | www.rogueregency.com | $85–$250 | AE, D, DC, MC, V.

Rogue River Guest House. The wide front porch of the 1890s farmhouse 12 mi north of town looks out to fir, catalpa, and holly trees. This is one of the few bed and breakfasts that welcome children, and business travelers will find a small office at their disposal. | 3 rooms. Complimentary breakfast, cable TV in some rooms, business services. No in-room phones. Pets allowed. | 41 Rogue River Hwy., Gold Hill | 541/855–4485, 877/764–8322 | $100–$150.

Shilo Inn. This three-story chain hotel across from a pancake house has standard, clean rooms. Complimentary Continental breakfast, microwaves, refrigerators, sauna, exercise equipment, cable TV, hot tub, free airport shuttle. | 2111 Biddle Rd. | 541/770–5151, 800/222–2244 | fax 541/776–0417 | 48 rooms | $99–$109 | AE, D, DC, MC, V.

★ **Under the Greenwood Tree.** This intimate inn in a 130-year-old farmhouse has luxurious and romantic rooms. The 10-acre gardens have gigantic old oaks hung with hammocks. The complimentary breakfasts are cooked by the owner, a Cordon Bleu–trained chef. The interior is decorated in Renaissance style. Afternoon tea is served. | 5 rooms. Complimentary breakfast. | 3045 Bellinger La. | 541/776–0000 | $125 | MC, V.

Windmill Inn. Rooms at this pleasant inn are plush and comfortable. Complimentary hot beverage, juice, muffin, and newspaper are delivered to your door in the morning. | 123 rooms. Complimentary Continental breakfast, cable TV, pool, hot tub, bicycles, library, business services, airport shuttle, pets allowed. | 1950 Biddle Rd. | 541/779–0050 or 800/547–4747 | www.windmillinns.com | $84 | AE, D, DC, MC, V.

MOUNT HOOD NATIONAL FOREST

MAP 3, E4

(Nearby towns also listed: Hood River, The Dalles)

Majestic, snowcapped Mount Hood, the highest point in Oregon at more than 11,000 ft, is the focal point of the 1.1-million-acre Mount Hood National Forest. Attracting more than seven million visitors annually, the forest is an all-season playground for outdoor enthusiasts. Ninety-five campgrounds and 50 lakes, as well as an extensive system of trails, make these woods a mecca for hikers, horseback riders, mountain climbers, and cyclists, among others.

Attractions

★ **Mt. Hood National Forest.** This forest, 20 mi southeast of Portland, extends south from the Columbia River Gorge for more than 60 mi and includes 189,200 acres of designated wilderness. Mt. Hood is the fourth-highest peak in the Cascades—behind 14,000-ft giants Mt. Rainier and Mt. Shasta and 12,300-ft Mt. Adams. Like Rainier it is a stratovolcano. It has erupted twice in the past 200 years, in 1859 and 1865. There are numerous fumaroles emitting steam and other gases on the upper southwestern sides. A hiking trail encircles the volcano, much of which is protected within the Mt. Hood Wilderness Area in the Mt.

Hood National Forest. There are 86 campgrounds in the forest. | U.S. 26 and Rte. 224 | 503/622–4822 or 888/622–4822 | www.fs.fed.us/r6/mthood | $3 per vehicle day-use fee | Daily.

Mt. Hood Meadows. This ski area has a base elevation of 4,523 ft and a vertical rise of 2,777 ft. Parking requires a Sno-Park permit. | North of Government Camp on Rte. 35 | 503/337–2222 or 503/227–7669 (snow conditions) | Nov.–Apr., daily.

Timberline Lodge. Built at an elevation of 6,000 ft during the Great Depression, the 60-room lodge is all handmade and built with huge wooden beams. It is 1/4 mi past Government Camp. There is a fine restaurant, a bar, and a café. With snow lasting into summer, Timberline Ski Area has one of the longest ski seasons in North America. Parking requires a Sno-Park permit. | U.S. 26 | 503/272–3311 or 541/231–7979 | Daily | www.timberlinelodge.com.

ON THE CALENDAR

SEPT.: ***Labor Day Wine, Art and Crafts Fair.*** Wy'east Day Lodge, just across the parking lot from Timberline Lodge, normally provides services for skiers, but for the three-day holiday weekend it's home to crafts people who work in wood, pottery, textiles, and jewelry; eight or nine wineries offer samples; and folk musicians provide entertainment. 503/272–3311

Dining

Cascade Dining Room. Contemporary. Inside the Cascades Dining Room at Timberline Lodge, you'll find a huge stone fireplace and handcrafted furniture. Outside is a spectacular view of the Cascades and as many as five mountain peaks. For dinner, you might choose Angus beef tenderloin, salmon, or rack of lamb; make a selection from the great wine list; and finish up with Chocolate Decadence cake or marion-berry cobbler. | Timberline Rd., Timberline 97028 | 503/622–0700 or 800/547–1406 | fax 503/727–3710 | $16.95–$35. | AE, D, MC, V.

Falcon's Crest Inn. Contemporary. A nightly six-course prix-fixe dinner, open to nonguests at the inn, might include entrées such as French '95 chicken (stuffed with shrimp in a sauce of champagne and Pernod), Cornish game hen, or individual beef Wellington. For dessert, try the peach and huckleberry pie. The small room seats only 12 people. | 87287 Government Camp Loop Hwy., Government Camp | 503/272–3403 or 800/624–7384 | fax 503/272–3454 | Reservations essential | No lunch | $39.95 | AE, D, DC, MC, V.

Highlands. Contemporary. Enjoy a view of the gardens and pool from your table in this elegant dining room. The cuisine is Pacific Northwest featuring salmon, seafood, chicken, lamb, and steak. Try the fresh sea scallops, prawns, wild mushrooms, and three-olive fettucine tossed in a Gorgonzola cream sauce and garnished with roasted red peppers and olives. There are tables in the garden and the porch. Pianist plays on Friday and Saturday. Kids' menu. Sun. brunch, no smoking. | 68010 E. Fairway Ave., Welches | 503/622–3101 | Breakfast also available | $25–$40 | AE, D, DC, MC, V.

Lodging

Brightwood Guest House. This guest house has Oriental furnishings nestled in a Japanese garden with a footbridge and miniature koi pond, all surrounded by tall firs. There's a cozy sitting area and the kitchenette is stocked with exotic teas and microwave popcorn. The featherbed in the sleeping loft has a view of the water garden and you will be given kimonos and slippers, too. | 1 guest house with sleeping loft. Picnic area, complimentary breakfast, no air-conditioning, microwaves, refrigerators, pond, laundry facilities, no kids under 13, no smoking. | 64725 E. Barlow Trail Rd., Brightwood | 503/622–5783 or 888/503–5783 | fax 503/622–5783 | brightwoodbnb@hotmail.com | www.mounthoodbnb.com | $135 | AE, MC, V.

Falcon's Crest Inn. At 4,000 ft on the south flank of Mt. Hood, this 1983 cedar-and-glass chalet has broad mountain views from the floor-to-ceiling glass walls of the second and third floors. The theme-oriented guest rooms run the gamut from safari to French provincial. Best of all, the hosts will bring you tea or coffee in bed before breakfast. | 5 rooms. Restaurant, bar, complimentary breakfast, no air-conditioning, some in-room hot tubs, room phones, no TV, no kids under 6, no smoking. | 87287 Government Camp Loop Hwy., Box 185, Government Camp 97028 | 503/272–3403 or 800/624–7384 | fax 503/272–3454 | $105–$179 | AE, D, MC, V.

Mt. Hood Inn. The Mount Hood National Forest is right outside the east windows of this comfortable contemporary inn. Rooms facing the southwest have a remarkable view of the Ski Bowl, which is just across the street. Accommodations come in various sizes, from spacious standards to king-size suites. Among the amenities are complimentary ski lockers and a ski tuning room. | 56 rooms, 4 suites. Picnic area, complimentary Continental breakfast, some refrigerators, some in-room hot tubs, cable TV, hot tub, cross-country and downhill skiing, laundry facilities, business services, pets allowed (fee). | Box 400, Government Camp Loop, Government Camp | 503/272–3205 or 800/443–7777 | fax 503/272–3307 | $129–$159, $154–$164 suites | AE, D, DC, MC, V.

Old Welches Inn. This simple white clapboard house and the 8-ft-high stone fireplace on the covered patio are all that remain of the bustling 1890 Welches Hotel, the first structure and oldest hotel on Mt. Hood. The largest of the guest rooms overlooks Resort at the Mountain's 27-hole golf course and has views of Hunchback Mountain and the Salem River. The cabin, which dates from 1901, overlooks the first hole of the golf course and has a fireplace and kitchen. The rate for the cabin does not include breakfast. | 4 rooms, 1 2-bedroom housekeeping cabin. Picnic area, complimentary breakfast, some microwaves, some refrigerators, no room phones, no TV in some rooms, TV in common area, no kids under 10, no smoking. | 26401 E. Welches Rd., Welches 97067 | 503/622–3754 | fax 503/622–5370 | innmthood@cs.com | www.lodging-mthood.com | $75–$175 2–night minimum on holiday weekends | AE, D, DC, MC, V.

Resort at the Mountain. This sprawling golf and ski resort on 300 acres in the Cascade foothills is the Mount Hood area's most complete resort. Outdoor activities are plentiful, including fly fishing on the Salmon River, white-water rafting, and croquet. Accommodations run from double rooms to two-bedroom condos. The rooms are tastefully decorated; each has a deck or patio overlooking the forest, courtyard, or a fairway. | 160 rooms. Restaurant, bar with entertainment, picnic area, in-room data ports, some kitchenettes, room service, pool, hot tub, 27-hole golf courses, putting green, tennis, exercise equipment, hiking, horseback riding, boating, fishing, bicycles, cross-country and downhill skiing, laundry facilities, business services. | 68010 E. Fairway Ave., Welches | 503/622–3101 or 800/669–7666 | fax 503/622–5677 | $99–$139 | AE, D, DC, MC, V.

★ **Timberline Lodge.** This National Historic Landmark has withstood howling winter storms on an exposed flank of Mt. Hood for more than 50 years. The structure has a handcrafted, rustic feel, from the wrought-iron chairs with rawhide seats to the massive hand-hewn beams. The expert cuisine at the Cascade Dining Room incorporates the freshest Oregon products. | 70 rooms in two buildings. Bar, dining room, snack bar, many in-room data ports, no TV in some rooms, pool, hot tub, downhill skiing, children's programs (ages 4–12), business services. | Timberline | 503/272–3311 or 800/547–1406 | fax 503/272–3710 | www.timberlinelodge.com | $100–$180 | AE, D, MC, V.

NEWBERG

MAP 3, D3

(Nearby towns also listed: Beaverton, Hillsboro, McMinnville, Oregon City, Portland, Salem)

Fertile fields of the Willamette Valley surround the community of Newberg, named by the first postmaster for his Bavarian hometown, Newburgh. Many of its early settlers were Quakers from the Midwest who founded the school that has become George Fox University, an accredited four-year institution. Newberg's most famous resident, likewise a Quaker, was Herbert Hoover, the 31st President of the United States. For about five years during his adolescence, he lived with an aunt and uncle at the Hoover-Minthorn House, now a museum listed on the National Register of Historic Places.

In addition to numerous well-reputed wineries, the Newberg area also offers slightly more out-of-the-ordinary entertainment with tours of nine llama ranches and the Pacific Northwest's largest hot air balloon company.

Information: **Newberg Area Chamber of Commerce** | 115 N. Washington, Newberg 97132 | 503/538–2014 | nacc@teleport.com | www.newberg.or.us.

Attractions

Champoeg State Park. This area on the south bank of the scenic Willamette River was once occupied by ancient Native Americans. The 615 acre park has 10 mi of hiking and cycle trails. A campground has 48 electrical and 58 tent sites and 6 yurts. | Champoeg Rd. | 503/678–1251 or 800/551–6949 | www.prd.state.or.us | $3 per vehicle day-use fee | Daily.

Newell House Museum. A replica of Robert Newell's 1844 home was rebuilt inside the Champoeg State Park grounds in 1959 and paid for by the Oregon State Society Daughters of the American Revolution. The first floor is furnished with 1860s antiques. Pioneer quilts and a collection of gowns worn by the wives of Oregon governors at inaugurations are displayed on the second floor. There's also a pioneer jail and school house. | 8089 Champoeg Rd., NE | 503/678–5537 | $2; $1 for children | Mar.–Oct., Fri.–Sun. 1–5, Wed. and Thurs. by appointment.

Pioneer Mother's Memorial Log Cabin contains pioneer artifacts from the Oregon Trail era. | 8035 Champoeg Rd., NE | 503/633–2237 | $2 | Feb.–Nov., Mon.–Sat. noon–5.

George Fox College. Named by *U.S. News and World Report* as one of America's Best Colleges, this small college founded by the Quakers in 1884 is on a 75-acre shady campus in a residential neighborhood. Centennial Tower is surrounded by a campus quad and academic buildings, the library, and the student commons. Hess Creek Canyon cuts through the campus. | 414 N. Meridian | 503/538–8383, ext 222 | www.georgefox.edu | Free | Daily.

Hoover-Minthorn House Museum. This is the boyhood home of President Herbert Hoover, where he lived with his uncle and aunt. It is filled with memorabilia from his life in Newberg. | 115 S. River St. | 503/538–6629 | $2 | Mar.–Nov., Wed.–Sun. 1–4; Dec., Feb., weekends 1–4.

Rex Hill Vineyards. Rex Hill produces Pinot Noir, Pinot Gris, and Chardonnay wines. You can visit the tasting room and gift shop, and, if you bring your own lunch (there's no food available), you can eat at the picnic tables and tents provided. Tours are offered on summer weekends only at 2 PM. | 30835 N. Hwy. 99 W | 503/538–0666 or 800/739–4455 | fax 503/538–1409 | www.rexhill.com | Daily 11–5.

ON THE CALENDAR

JULY: *Newberg Old-Fashioned Festival.* This community party begins on the Thursday before the last full weekend in July at Memorial Park. Visit arts and crafts booths, enjoy the food, and take the kids to the carnival. | 503/538–9455.

Dining

Joel Palmer House. Contemporary. Joel Palmer was an Oregon pioneer and his 1857 home in Dayton is now on the National Register of Historic Places. There are three small dining rooms, each seating about 15 people, and you'll probably have a view of the flower garden. The chef here specializes in wild mushroom dishes and a popular starter is Heidi's three-mushroom tart. Entrées include rib-eye au poivre, rack of lamb, breast of duckling, and coq au vin, and desserts include apricot-walnut bread pudding and crème brûlée. | 600 Ferry St., Dayton | 503/864–2995 | fax 503/864–3246 | Closed Sun.–Mon. No lunch Sat. | $17.50–$22.50 | AE, D, DC, MC, V.

VACATION COUNTDOWN Your checklist for a perfect journey

Way Ahead

- ❑ Devise a trip budget.
- ❑ Write down the five things you want most from this trip. Keep this list handy before and during your trip.
- ❑ Book lodging and transportation.
- ❑ Arrange for pet care.
- ❑ Photocopy any important documentation (passport, driver's license, vehicle registration, and so on) you'll carry with you on your trip. Store the copies in a safe place at home.
- ❑ Review health and home-owners insurance policies to find out what they cover when you're away from home.

A Month Before

- ❑ Make restaurant reservations and buy theater and concert tickets. Visit fodors.com for links to local events and news.
- ❑ Familiarize yourself with the local language or lingo.
- ❑ Schedule a tune-up for your car.

Two Weeks Before

- ❑ Create your itinerary.
- ❑ Enjoy a book or movie set in your destination to get you in the mood.
- ❑ Prepare a packing list.
- ❑ Shop for missing essentials.
- ❑ Repair, launder, or dry-clean the clothes you will take with you.
- ❑ Replenish your supply of prescription drugs and contact lenses if necessary.

A Week Before

- ❑ Stop newspaper and mail deliveries.
- ❑ Pay bills.
- ❑ Stock up on film and batteries.
- ❑ Label your luggage.
- ❑ Finalize your packing list—always take less than you think you need.
- ❑ Pack a toiletries kit filled with travel-size essentials.
- ❑ Check tire treads.
- ❑ Write down your insurance agent's number and any other emergency numbers and take them with you.
- ❑ Get lots of sleep. You want to be well-rested and healthy for your impending trip.

A Day Before

- ❑ Collect passport, driver's license, insurance card, vehicle registration, and other documents.
- ❑ Check travel documents.
- ❑ Give a copy of your itinerary to a family member or friend.
- ❑ Check your car's fluids, lights, tire inflation, and wiper blades.
- ❑ Get packing!

During Your Trip

- ❑ Keep a journal/scrapbook as a personal souvenir.
- ❑ Spend time with locals.
- ❑ Take time to explore. Don't plan too much. Let yourself get lost and use your Fodor's guide to get back on track.

Lodging

Shilo Inn. In the heart of the wine country, this all-minisuites property looks out into the commercial neighborhood from the front, while the rooms in back overlook a quiet residential neighborhood. | 60 rooms. Complimentary Continental breakfast, microwaves, refrigerators, pool, hot tub, exercise equipment, laundry facilities, business services, airport shuttle, pets allowed (fee). | 501 Sitka Ave. | 503/537–0303 | fax 503/537–0442 | $69–$79 | AE, D, DC, MC, V.

Travelodge Suites. This reliable and inexpensive chain hotel was built in 1997. It's the closest to Portland of the hotels in Newberg and you can walk to restaurants. The large rooms have a sitting areas and desks, and guests have complimentary admission to a gym in the same block. | 41 rooms. Complimentary Continental breakfast, in-room data ports, microwaves, refrigerators, some in-room hot tubs, cable TV, room phones, pool, hot tub, laundry facilities, business services. | 2816 Portland Rd. | 503/537–5000 or 800/578–7878 | fax 503/537–9099 | www.travelodge.com | $50–$63 | AE, D, DC, MC, V.

NEWPORT

MAP 3, C4

(Nearby towns also listed: Depoe Bay, Lincoln City, Yachats)

One of the largest commercial fishing fleets on the Oregon Coast operates out of the historic bayfront of Newport. Charter boats, too, set out from Yaquina Bay for fishing, whale watching, and sailing. The area's abundance of seafood, most notably Dungeness crab, has been famous since the mid-1800s, when the Yaquina Bay oyster beds were first discovered. Shops, galleries and restaurants skirt the bay for those who prefer to watch the harbor's goings-on. Lighthouses, which you can tour along with neighboring tidepools, dot the coastal area along Hwy. 101 and at Yaquina Head.

Information: **Greater Newport Chamber of Commerce** | 555 S.W. Coast Hwy., Newport 97365 | 541/265–8801 or 800/262–7844 | chamber@newportnet.com | www.newportnet.com.

Attractions

Bayfront. With its tall-masted fishing fleet, well-worn buildings, seafood markets, and art galleries and shops, Newport's old Bayfront is an ideal place for an afternoon stroll. So many male sea lions in Yaquina Bay loiter near crab pots and bark from the piers that local people call the area the Bachelor Club. | Free.

Beverly Beach State Park. This beachfront park, 7 mi north of Newport, extends from Yaquina Head to the headlands of Otter Rock. It has a campground with 53 full hookups, 76 electrical and 136 tent sites, and 14 yurts. | Hwy. 101 | 541/265–9278 or 800/551–6949 | www.prd.state.or.us | Free | Daily.

Devil's Punch Bowl State Natural Area. A rocky shoreline separates this day-use park from the surf. It's a popular whale-watching site just 9 mi north of Newport and has excellent tidepools. | U.S. 101 | 541/265–9278 | Free | Daily.

Hatfield Marine Science Center of Oregon State University. The interactive and interpretive exhibits at this Oregon State University research center help explain marine research from all perspectives. The star of the show is a large octopus in a touch tank near the entrance. Guided by a staff volunteer, you can sometimes reach in to stroke her suction-tipped tentacles. The center is connected by a trail to the Oregon Coast Aquarium. | Marine Science Dr. | 541/867–0100 | www.hmsc.orst.edu. | $4 (suggested) | Memorial Day–Labor Day, daily 10–6; Labor Day–Memorial Day, Thurs.–Mon. 10–4.

Lincoln County Historical Society Museums. These museums include a log cabin and an 1895 Victorian house. Exhibits focus on Native American, maritime, and coastal settlement history. | 579 S.W. 9th St. | 541/265–7509 | Donations accepted | June–Sept., Tues.–Sun. 10–5; Oct.–May, Tues.–Sun. 11–4.

Marine Discovery Tours. This outfit offers two-hour narrated sealife tours on Yaquina Bay in the 65-ft excursion boat *Discovery.* Most of the tours spot one or more whales. You can also ride a 27-ft (Coast Guard–inspected) inflatable called the "Oregon Rocket." This one, the company says, is "all about speed." | 345 S.W. Bay Blvd. | 541/265–6200 or 800/903–2628 | fax 541/265–6894 | www.marinediscovery.com | $19.95 | Closed Nov.–Jan.

Ona Beach State Park. This day-use park is a popular beachcombing and picnic spot, 5 mi south of Newport. | U.S. 101 S | 541/867–7451 | Free | Daily.

★ **Oregon Coast Aquarium.** One of the most popular attractions in the state, this complex contains re-creations of offshore and near-shore Pacific marine habitats, all teeming with life: playful sea otters, comical puffins, fragile jellyfish, and a 60-pound octopus. There's a hands-on interactive area for children, and North America's largest seabird aviary. For a few years the biggest attraction was Keiko, the 4-ton killer whale and star of the movie *Free Willy.* He was moved to Iceland in 1998, and the aquarium has developed some new attractions in the space he occupied. There is a new 35,000-gallon saltwater salmon and sturgeon exhibit. You should plan to spend at least three hours on your visit. | 2820 S.E. Ferry Slip Rd. | 541/867–3474 | www.aquarium.org | $8.75 | July–Labor Day, daily 9–8; Labor Day–Memorial Day, daily 10–5; Memorial Day–June, daily 9–6.

Ripley's—Believe It or Not. Part of Mariner Square, which includes Wax Works and Undersea Gardens, this attraction features strange but true exhibits. | 250 S.W. Bay Blvd. | 541/265–2206 | Call for prices | Mid-June–mid-Sept., daily 9–9; mid-Sept.–Oct., mid-Feb.–mid-June, daily 10–5; Nov.–mid-Feb. daily 11–4.

Sea Gulch. Ray Kowalski invented the art of chain-saw sculpture. For years, he displayed 300 of his sculptures of cowboys, Indians, trolls, gnomes, and other figures at a park here called Sea Gulch, 10 mi south of Newport. The park is gone now, fallen victim to flashier tourist attractions, but Ray still presides over the busy workshop where his sons turn out new figures, mostly of bears. You're welcome to come by, take a look at the workshop, and buy small wooden sculptures in a small shop. You'd do best to call ahead. | Hwy. 101 | 541/563–2727 | Free.

South Beach State Park. Fishing, crabbing, boating, windsurfing, hiking, and beachcombing are popular here. A campground has 238 electrical and 6 primitive sites, and 16 yurts. | U.S. 101 S | 541/867–4715 or 541/867–7451 | Free | Daily.

Undersea Gardens. This is part of Mariner Square on Yaquina Bay which also includes Wax Works and Ripley's Believe-It-or-Not. This attraction has scuba diving shows, marine plants, and animal exhibits. | 250 S.W. Bay Blvd. | 541/265–2206 | Call for prices | Mid-June–mid-Sept., daily 9–9; mid-Sept.–Oct., mid-Feb.–mid-June, daily 10–5; Nov.–mid-Feb. daily 11–4.

Wax Works. Part of Mariner Square, this attraction features wax figure exhibits of famous people. | 250 S.W. Bay Blvd. | 541/265–2206 | Call for prices | Mid-June–mid-Sept., daily 9–9; mid-Sept.–Oct., mid-Feb.–mid-June, daily 10–5; Nov.–mid-Feb., daily 11–4.

Yaquina Bay State Park. Located at the north end of Yaquina Bay near its outlet to the Pacific, this park is home to a historic lighthouse that in more recent years was used as a Coast Guard Lifeboat Station. It's been restored and is now open to the public. | U.S. 101 S | 541/867–7451 | Free | Daily.
The tallest lighthouse on the Oregon Coast is the 93 foot **Yaquina Head Lighthouse,** which is on a rocky peninsula. Guided morning tours are limited to 15 people. | 4 mi north of bridge in Newport | 541/574–3100 | Call for prices | Mid-June–mid-Sept., daily noon–4. In winter, call ahead.

ON THE CALENDAR

FEB.: *Seafood and Wine Festival.* Pacific Northwest fish, shellfish, and wines plus local arts and crafts are displayed and on sale in more than 120 booths at this annual street event, which takes place the last full weekend in February at the Newport Marina. | 541/265–8801.

MAY: *Loyalty Days and Sea Fair Festival.* This patriotic festival began after World War II and is held the 1st weekend in May. The focus is a marching parade that starts at Highway 101 and 21st Street. There is also a procession of navy ships. | 541/265–8801.

JULY: *Ernest Bloch Music Festival.* Composer and teacher Ernest Bloch, famed for his compositions employing Hebrew folk themes, was a resident of Agate Beach from 1940 to 1959. This music festival in the third week of July presents three or four concerts of music composed by Bloch along with other chamber and symphonic programs, plus a showcase for new composers. Performances are at the Newport Performing Arts Center. | 541/265–2787 or 800/262–7844.

Dining

Canyon Way Restaurant and Bookstore. Seafood. Cod, Dungeness crab cakes, bouillabaisse, and Yaquina Bay oysters are among the popular dishes at this Newport dining spot which is up the hill from the center of the Bayfront. There's also a deli counter for take-out. The restaurant has patio tables set up only for lunch, which give a great view of the bay. The patio is to one side of a well-stocked bookstore. | 1216 S.W. Canyon Way | 541/265–8319 | Closed Sun.–Mon. | $15–$30 | AE, MC, V.

Italian Food Co. Italian. The Italian Food Co. (formerly Don Petrie's) is a block from the beach in the increasingly trendy Nye Beach area. In a building that was once an electrical machine shop, it now has the look of a funky trattoria. You come here for such basics as spaghetti and meatballs or pasta with a wide choice of sauces, and if you come early, before 5:30, you'll get 15% off the price of your dinner entrée. | 613 N.W. 3rd St. | 541/265–3663 | Closed Tues. No lunch | $9–$16.50 | D, MC, V.

Nye Beach Cafe. Contemporary. This roomy café, with a full bar, grand piano, fireplace, and a deck that stretches out over the beach, is in the Nye Beach Hotel. It serves breakfast, lunch, and dinner, and specializes in spicy seafood dishes. The clam chowder is popular and so is the seafood Cioppino, an Italian fish stew, and desserts include homemade flan and chocolate carrot cake. | 219 N.W. Cliff St. | 541/265–3334 | fax 541/265–3622 | $6.75–$9.50 | AE, D, MC, V.

Tables of Content. Contemporary. In this restaurant at the literary-theme Sylvia Beach Hotel, the setting is unadorned, with family-size tables; the main plot is a prix-fixe menu that changes nightly; the central character might be local seafood, like grilled salmon fillet in a sauce Dijonnaise (but you can choose among four entrées, one of them vegetarian); and the conclusion will certainly be a decadent dessert, such as Chocolate Oblivion Torte. | 267 N.W. Cliff St. | 541/265–5428 | Reservations essential | No lunch | $17.95 | AE, MC, V.

Whale's Tale. Seafood. This bay-front restaurant is casual and family-oriented. Fresh local seafood, thick clam chowder, fish-and-chips, burgers, and sandwiches make this a popular spot. Kids' menu. | 452 S.W. Bay Blvd. | 541/265–8660 | Breakfast also available. Closed Jan.–Feb. and Wed. until June | $15–$27 | AE, D, DC, MC, V.

Lodging

The Embarcadero. This resort of vacation rental condos at the east end of Bay Boulevard has great views of Yaquina Bay and its graceful bridge. The public areas have a casual air and the grounds are nicely landscaped. All rooms have sitting areas and private balconies and the Townhouse suites have two bedrooms. The resort has a private crabbing dock and marina. | 45 rooms, 40 suites. Restaurant, no air-conditioning, some kitchenettes, some microwaves, some refrigerators, cable TV, room phones, pool, outdoor hot tub, sauna, gym, dock, fishing, laundry facilities, business services. | 1000 S.E. Bay Blvd. | 541/265–8521 or 800/547–4779 | fax 541/265–7844 | donna@actionnet.net | www.embarcadero-resort.com | $119–$129 | AE, D, DC, MC, V.

Little Creek Cove. The units at this condominium property have access to the beach as well as ocean and beach views from private decks. All the units are individually furnished and have fireplaces. Agate Beach Golf Course is across the street. | 29 rooms. Kitchenettes, microwaves, cable TV, in-room VCRs, business services. | 3641 N.W. Ocean View Dr. | 541/265-8587 or 800/294-8025 | fax 541/265-4576 | lcc@newportnet.com | www.newportnet.com/lcc | $109–$169 | AE, D, DC, MC, V.

Nye Beach Hotel. Despite its century-old appearance, suitable to the historic Nye Beach district, the Nye Beach Hotel was built in 1992. It stands on a cliff above the beach and all the guest rooms have balconies with ocean views, private baths, and fireplaces. The pastel colors and potted tropical plants in the lobby remind some guests of Key West. Keep an eye out for the macaw and the African love birds. | 18 rooms. Restaurant, some in-room hot tubs, cable TV. | 219 N.W. Cliff St. | 541/265-3334 | fax 541/265-3622 | nyebeach@teleport.com | www.nyebeach.com | $60–$125 | AE, D, MC, V.

Shilo Inn Ocean Front Resort. On a bluff overlooking the beach, this resort is 2 mi from the center of downtown Newport. | 179 rooms. Restaurant, bar with entertainment, some kitchenettes, microwaves, refrigerators, in-room VCRs, room service, 2 pools (1 indoor), beach, laundry facilities, business services, airport shuttle, some pets allowed (fee). | 536 S.W. Elizabeth St. | 541/265-7701 | fax 541/265-5687 | $145–$199 | AE, D, DC, MC, V.

★ **Sylvia Beach Hotel.** This 1913-vintage beachfront hotel has antiques-filled rooms named for famous writers. A pendulum swings over the bed in the Poe room. The Christie, Twain, and Colette rooms are the most luxurious; all have fireplaces, decks, and great ocean views. A well-stocked split-level upstairs library has decks, a fireplace, slumbering cats, and too-comfortable chairs. Every night at 10 mulled wine is served. | 20 rooms. Complimentary Continental breakfast, restaurant, no room phones, no TV in rooms, library. | 267 N.W. Cliff St. | 541/265-5428 | $68–$150 | AE, MC, V.

Tyee Lodge. Tyee means "chinook salmon" in the Indian trading language. This 1940s house in Agate Beach is on a bluff and a nearby trail leads down to the beach. The guest rooms all have pine furniture and views of the ocean through towering Sitka spruce trees. Breakfast is served family-style in a bay-windowed room facing the ocean. Composer Ernest Bloch lived nearby. | 5 rooms. Complimentary breakfast, no air-conditioning, no room phones, no TV, no kids under 16, no smoking. | 4925 N.W. Woody Way | 541/265-8953 or 888/553-8933 | mcconn@teleport.net | www.tyeelodge.com | $110–$130 | AE, D, MC, V.

Whaler. All rooms at this motel have ocean views; some have fireplaces. Set in a residential area across from the city park and the beach, it's a short walk to the Yaquina Bay Lighthouse. | 73 rooms. Complimentary Continental breakfast, some microwaves, some refrigerators, cable TV, laundry facilities, airport shuttle, some pets allowed. | 155 S.W. Elizabeth St. | 541/265-9261 or 800/433-9444 | fax 541/265-9515 | $95–$105 | AE, D, DC, MC, V.

NORTH BEND

MAP 3, C6

(Nearby towns also listed: Bandon, Coos Bay, Reedsport)

Named by the town's founder, sea captain and shipbuilder Asa Simpson, for its location on the north bend of Coos Bay, this town continues a decades-long tradition by making its livelihood from forest products, fishing, agriculture, and tourism. North Bend and its neighbors Coos Bay and Charleston make up the Bay Area, the largest urban area on the Oregon coast.

North Bend sits at the south end of the 41-mi-long Oregon Dunes National Recreation Area. With 32,000 acres of open dunes, grasslands, marshes, and forest land, Oregon

Dunes offers visitors opportunities for fishing, crabbing, clamming, and hiking. Dune buggies and all-terrain vehicles are permitted in some areas as well.

Information: Bay Area Chamber of Commerce | 1380 Sherman Ave., North Bend 97459 | 541/756–4613 | bacc@ucinet.com | www.ucinet.com/~bacc.

Attractions

Coos County Historical Society Museum. The highlight here is a 1922 steam locomotive used in Coos County logging. On display are a formal 1900 parlor, a pioneer kitchen, and exhibits on Native American history, agriculture, and industry such as logging, shipping, and mining. | 1220 Sherman St. | 541/756–6320 or 541/756–4847 | $2 | Tues.–Sat. 10–4.

The Mill Casino-Hotel. This complex has a casino with 350 slots, blackjack, poker, and bingo. There's a waterfront restaurant and a showroom that features big-name entertainers. | 3201 Tremont Ave. | 541/756–8800 or 800/953–4800 | fax 541/756–0431 | www.themill-casino.com | Free | Daily 24 hrs.

Oregon Dunes National Recreation Area. The Oregon Dunes stretch along the Oregon coast from Florence to North Bend. The NRA has fine beaches, campgrounds, boat launch ramps, and picnic areas. Hiking trails pass through green areas that are home to many species of wildlife. All-terrain vehicles are permitted in some areas. | The office is located at 855 Hwy. 101, Reedsport | 541/750–7241 | $3 day-use fee | Daily dawn–dusk.

ON THE CALENDAR

AUG.: *Farwest Gem Craft Show.* This two-day show at North Bend Junior High School is held on the first full weekend in August. Ten or more dealers display specimens of gems and other stones for both collectors and crafts people, and there are demonstrations of lapping, faceting, and other skills. | 541/269–5085.

Dining

Hilltop House. Seafood. Enjoy a view of the bay, harbor, and sand dunes from your table while dining on seafood, steak, or pasta. | 166 N. Bay Dr. | 541/756–4160 | $13–$30 | AE, MC, V.

Plank House. Contemporary. The Plank House, at the Mill Casino-Hotel, satisfies a wide range of tastes with everything from meatloaf, chicken pot pie, and chicken-fried steak to fresh salmon and halibut and a large selection of steaks. All the baking, including chocolate decadence tortes and cheesecakes, is done right here. The restaurant serves breakfast, lunch, and dinner and the outside deck, though not for eating, has a nice view of Coos Bay. | 3201 Tremont Ave. | 541/756–8800 or 800/953–4800 | fax 541/756–0431 | $8.95–$19.95 | AE, D, MC, V.

Lodging

Bay Bridge. This small motel is on Pacific Bay with views of the bay. The rooms are simple and basic. | 16 rooms. Some kitchenettes, some refrigerators, cable TV, some pets allowed (fee). | 33 U.S. 101 | 541/756–3151 or 800/557–3156 | $39–$65 | AE, D, DC, MC, V.

Mill Casino-Hotel. The grounds here are landscaped with native plants and each has signage that explains the traditional use of the plant by the Coquille Indians, who own the resort. The hotel and room designs follow through with a Northwest flavor; the lobby has open beams and a stone fireplace and guest rooms have rustic hickory beds. About half the rooms have a view of Coos Bay. | 112 rooms, 3 suites. 2 restaurants, 2 bars, complimentary Continental breakfast, room service, in-room data ports, some refrigerators, some in-room hot tubs, cable TV, room phones, shops, video games, laundry service, business services. | 3201 Tremont Ave. | 541/756–8800 or 800/953–4800 | fax 541/756–0431 | themill@themillcasino.com | www.themillcasino.com | $99.50 | AE, D, MC, V.

ONTARIO

MAP 3, L5

(Nearby town also listed: Baker City)

Situated at the far eastern edge of Oregon, less than 5 miles from the Idaho border, Ontario is the largest town in the state's second-largest county, Malheur. Its 10,000 residents make up more than one-third of the county's population. For the adventurous visitor, the Ontario area offers an abundance of outdoor recreation, most notably hunting and fishing.

Information: **Ontario Chamber of Commerce, Visitor Bureau** | 676 S.W. 5th Ave., Ontario 97914 | 541/889–8012 or 888/889–8012.

Attractions

Farewell Bend State Park. This desert park on the Snake River's Brownlee Reservoir includes historic markers and displays concerning Farewell Bend's role on the Oregon Trail. Recreational activities on the lake include fishing, waterskiing, swimming, and boating. A campground has 93 electrical and 45 primitive sites, 4 tepees, and 2 cabins. | Exit 353 off I–84 | 541/869–2365 or 800/551–6949 | www.prd.state.or.us | $3 per vehicle day-use | Daily.

Four Rivers Cultural Center and Museum. The museum highlights Ontario's multi-ethnic heritage and its population of Northern Paiute Indians, Japanese-Americans, Mexican-Americans, and people from the Basque country. Most interesting and moving is a reconstructed barracks from a Japanese-American WWII internment camp. A 645-seat theatre presents music, drama, and other events, from local productions to the Oregon Symphony. | 676 S.W. 5th Ave. | 541/889–8191 or 888/211–1222 | fax 541/889–7628 | www.4rcc.com | $4 (Museum) | Mon.–Sat. 10–5.

Lake Owyhee State Park. This park is 28 mi from Ontario and has picture-perfect views of the surrounding mountains. It is next to a 53-mi-long reservoir formed by the Owyhee Dam. The area is home to bighorn sheep, pronghorn antelope, golden eagles, coyotes, mule deer, wild horses, and a few cougars. A campground has 30 electrical and 10 tent sites, and 2 teepees. | Off Rte. 201 | 800/551–6949 | www.prd.state.or.us | $3 per vehicle day-use fee | Mar.–Nov., daily.

Ontario State Recreation Area. Boat, fish, swim, or picnic at this park on the west bank of the Snake River. | Exit 371 off I–84 | 541/869–2365 | Free | Daily.

Owyhee Recreation Area. This area of Malheur County is rich in geological formations, including an impressive canyon. | 1298 Owyhee Dam Rd., Adrian | 541/869–2365 | Free | Daily.

ON THE CALENDAR

JULY: *Japan Nite Obon Festivities.* This Japanese cultural festival has been held in Ontario since 1946. You can see displays of ikebana (flower arranging), kimonos and samurai swords from local personal collections, and demonstrations of Japanese drumming and dancing. Booths sell Japanese food, and it all takes place on the grounds of the Idaho-Oregon Buddhist Temple | 541/889–8691.

AUG.: *Malheur County Fair.* This is an annual event featuring agricultural exhibits and competitions, food, and entertainment. | 795 N.W. 9th St. | 541/889–3431.

Dining

DJ's. American. Chicken-fried steak is served for breakfast, lunch, and dinner at this place, which provides room service for the Holiday Motel next door. You can order a burger, steak, chicken pot pie, or one of the popular breakfast cinnamon rolls at a table or at the coffee bar. | 625 E. Idaho Ave. | 541/889–4386 | fax 541/889–4303 | $7–$12 | D, MC, V.

Fiesta Guadalajara. Mexican. Tuck into all the traditional favorites—burritos, enchiladas, quesadillas, and chalupas—from a high-backed, lacquered wooden chair amid the brightly colored murals and south-of-the-border artifacts that fill this downtown eatery. | 336 S. Oregon St. | 541/889–8064 | $7–$9 | D, MC, V.

Mongolian Express. Pan-Asian. You choose the size of your bowl and the ingredients that go in it, watch the cooks stir-fry your meal, and take it to your table at this local favorite. | 1182 S.W. 4th Ave. | 541/889–0448 | Closed Sun. | $7–$10 | MC, V.

Nichols Steak House. Steak. Paintings by local artists and antiques cover the walls of this steak house decorated in Western style. It is known for prime rib and 22-oz T-bone steak suppers. There is a salad bar. Kids' menu. | 411 S.W. 3rd St., Fruitland | 208/452–3030 | Closed Mon. No lunch Sat. | $12–$26 | D, MC, V.

Lodging

Best Western Inn and Suites. This inn is right on the freeway, near the Snake River and close to area shopping. The rooms are typical of Best Western style—they are comfortable and spacious. | 61 rooms, 12 suites. Complimentary Continental breakfast, some minibars, refrigerators (in suites), cable TV, indoor pool, hot tub, exercise equipment, laundry facilities, some pets allowed (fee). | 251 Goodfellow St. | 541/889–2600 | fax 541/889–2259 | www.bestwestern.com | $56–$76, $95–$165 suites | AE, D, DC, MC, V.

Carlile Motel. Most of the rooms in this mom-and-pop motor lodge five blocks from downtown have kitchenettes, and some have full kitchens with stoves. | 18 rooms. Cable TV, air-conditioning, in-room phones. Some microwaves, refrigerators. No smoking. | 589 N. Oregon St. | 541/889–8658 | $38–$63 | AE, D, DC, MC, V.

Colonial Motor Inn. This motel overlooking the Necanicum River is just 1 mi from Ontario Center and within walking distance of the mall. | 84 rooms. In-room data ports, cable TV, indoor pool, hot tub, business services, no smoking. | 1395 Tapadera Ave. | 541/889–9615 or 800/727–5014 | $29–$50 | AE, D, MC, V.

Holiday Inn. You will be right off I–84 and ¼ mi from the Snake River when you stay at this hotel. | 100 rooms. Restaurant, room service, cable TV, pool, airport shuttle. | 1249 Tapadera Ave. | 541/889–8621 or 800/525–5333 | fax 541/889–8023 | $69–$79 | AE, D, DC, MC, V.

Holiday Motel. The basic budget accommodations here are convenient to restaurants and fishing. It is five blocks from the Snake River. | 72 rooms. Restaurant, cable TV, pool, business services, pets allowed. | 615 E. Idaho Ave. | 541/889–9188 | fax 541/889–4303 | $38–$59 | AE, D, DC, MC, V.

Motel 6. The rooms here are standard, but they are close to area restaurants and the whole motel has been updated and upgraded. | 102 rooms. Cable TV, pool. | 275 N.E. 12th St. | 541/889–6617 | fax 541/889–8232 | $30–$36 | AE, D, DC, MC, V.

Sears & Roebuck Bed & Breakfast. This 1900 Sears & Roebuck mail-order Victorian is the closest B&B to Ontario, 17 mi west of town in nearby Vale. The two-story inn has a wide front porch with a bird-cleaning room, dog kennels, and horse stables and hosts many pheasant hunters. The rooms are ornately furnished in period pieces, including brass and four-poster beds. | 4 rooms. Complimentary Continental breakfast, cable TV, air-conditioning. No in-room phones. | 484 N. 10th St., Vale | 541/889–9009 | www.moriah.com/sears | $65–$85.

Sleep Inn. This three-story no-frills motor lodge was built in 1997 off Highway 84 next to a movie theater and a bowling alley. | 65 rooms. Complimentary Continental breakfast, indoor pool, cable TV, air-conditioning, in-room phones. | 1221 S.E. 1st Ct. | 541/881–0007 | $50–$84 | AE, D, DC, MC, V.

Super 8. This is a centrally located chain with typically basic but functional rooms. | 63 rooms. Complimentary Continental breakfast, cable TV, indoor pool, laundry facilities. | 266 Goodfellow St. | 541/889–8282 | fax 541/881–1400 | www.super8.com | $49–$59 | AE, D, DC, MC, V.

OREGON CITY

MAP 3, E3

(Nearby towns also listed: Beaverton, Forest Grove, Newberg, Portland, Salem)

Oregon City is a treasure chest of Western U.S. history. It was the first incorporated city west of the Rocky Mountains, the first capital of the Territorial Government in 1848, site of the first Oregon legislative session, and site of the only federal and district court west of the Rockies in 1849, when the city of San Francisco was platted. (The plat, filed in 1850, is still in Oregon City.)

Oregon City was the destination for thousands of pioneer families, who traveled the Oregon Trail from St. Louis, Missouri, to the promised land on the western frontier. Several of Oregon's prominent early residents built homes in Oregon City on the Willamette River's east bank, where the river plunges 40 feet over a basaltic ridge at Willamette Falls. The official End of the Oregon Trail Interpretive Center in Oregon City debuted in 1993 to commemorate the 150-year anniversary of the Oregon Trail. Dozens of historic homes, churches, and other buildings have been restored and now offer tours into times past.

Today, more than 20,000 people live in multilevel Oregon City, the seat of Clackamas County, one of three counties that make up the Portland metropolitan area.

Information: Oregon City Chamber of Commerce | Box 226, Oregon City 97045 | 503/656–1619.

Attractions

End of the Oregon Trail Interpretive Center. Exhibits on the history of the 2,000-mi Oregon Trail journey are featured at this 8½-acre site. Living history interpreters in costume tell the story. The Oregon Trail Pageant, an outdoor music drama, is performed during July and August in the amphitheater. Heritage Gardens contains plants grown by settlers in the mid-19th century. There's also a gallery, a trades and craft workshop, and a general store. | 1726 Washington St. | 503/657–9336 | www.endoftheoregontrail.org | $5.50 | Mon–Sat. 9–5, Sun. 10–5.

John Inskeep Environmental Learning Center. Waterfowl are part-time residents at this ½-acre site on the Clackamas Community College campus, which has a trail that circles two ponds at the headwaters of Newell Creek. | 19600 S. Molalla | 503/657–6958, ext. 2351 | fax 503–650–6669 | www.clackamas.cc.or.us/elc | $2 donations accepted | Daily dawn to dusk.

McLoughlin House National Historic Site. Dr. John McLoughlin, who crossed the Rockies in 1824 and established Ft. Vancouver in 1825, moved his family into this mansion in 1846. He died here in 1857. His key role in Oregon's history led the Legislature to name him the "Father of Oregon." | 713 Center St. | 503/656–5146 | $4 | Feb.–Dec., Tues.–Sat. 10–4, Sun. 1–4.

Milo McIver State Park. Along the Clackamas River and only 45 minutes from Portland, this is a popular rafting, canoeing, and kayaking area. An annual civil war reenactment is staged here in April in which 300 actors participate. A campground has 44 electrical and 9 primitive sites. | Rte. 213 N to Rte. 212 and Rte. 211 SE | 503/630–7150 or 800/551–6949 | www.prd.state.or.us | $3 per vehicle day-use | Daily; some areas open Mar.–Nov., daily.

Wasson Brothers Winery. Best known for its fruit and berry wine, this small winery in the rolling hills outside Sandy, 21 mi northeast of Oregon City, enjoys a growing reputation for its grapes. You can visit the shop, but check ahead for tours. | 41901 Hwy. 26, Sandy | 503/668–3124 | fax 503/668–3124 | Daily 9–5.

Willamette Falls Locks. The Willamette Falls are created when the Willamette River at Oregon City spills 40 ft over a basaltic ridge. The locks were built in the early 1870s to move river traffic around the falls. | On Willamette River, in West Linn | 503/656–3381 | Daily; Information Center Apr.–Oct., daily 9:30–8; Nov.–Mar., daily 7:30–6.

ON THE CALENDAR

AUG.: ***Oregon City Open Air Antique Fair.*** On the last Sunday of August, 8 blocks of Main Street and some of the side streets are lined with a hundred or more booths of dealers in antiques and collectibles. Most items for sale are, understandably, portable, but this happens to be a good fair for finding furniture. Also here for the day is a fresh fruit, vegetable, and flower market, all from local growers. | 8–5 | 503/656–1619.

Dining

McMenamin's Pub. American/Casual. You can order a Communication Break-down Burger among other sandwiches, and creative ales like chocolaty Black Rabbit Porter or raspberry Ruby Ale at this bustling family favorite, which becomes a bar after 10 PM. | 102 9th St. | 503/655–8032 | $5–$8 | AE, D, MC, V.

Lodging

Brookside Bed and Breakfast. The grounds of this hillside country home in Sandy are populated by chickens, ducks, geese, peacocks, goats, and llamas. There's a koi pond and perennial flower beds on the seven acres of wooded property. The owner is an antiques dealer and the guest rooms are furnished in different and eclectic styles. A hearty breakfast is served family-style in the dining area. | 5 rooms. Picnic area, complimentary breakfast, no air-conditioning, no room phones, no TV in some rooms, laundry facilities, no smoking. | 45232 S.E. Paha Loop, Box 1112, Sandy | 503/668–4766 | brooksidesandy@hotmail.com | www.brooksidebandb.com | $50–$65 | No credit cards.

Rivershore Hotel. All rooms overlook the Willamette River and have decks with patio furniture. It is close to shopping and restaurants. | 120 rooms. Restaurant, bar, room service, cable TV, pool, hot tub, some pets allowed (fee). | 1900 Clackamette Dr. | 503/655–7141 or 800/443–7777 | fax 503/655–1927 | $54–$142 | AE, D, DC, MC, V.

PACIFIC CITY

MAP 3, D6

(Nearby town also listed: Lincoln City)

This quiet oceanfront town has fallen victim to the coastal development trend, but the result is some good places to eat and stay. The town is the home of the dory "fleet", a group of locally owned small rounded fishing boats. They launch and dock in the surf from the beach. If you see one coming, watch out. The heavy surf washes the boats ashore quickly. Pacific City is 18 mi north of Lincoln City, about 2 hrs from Portland.

Information: **Pacific City Chamber of Commerce** | Box 331, Pacific City 97135 | 503/965–6161 or 888/kiwanda | www.pacificcity.net.

Attractions

Cape Lookout State Park/Cape Kiwanda State Natural Area. The coastal bluffs make this a popular hang-gliding and kite-flying area. This park, 1 mi north of Pacific City has great views of the ocean and easy access to the beach. A campground has 54 full hookups, 1 electrical and 191 tent sites; 4 yurts. The Cape Lookout Trail, 10 mi north of Pacific City, follows the headland for more than 2 mi. | Whiskey Creek Rd. | 800/551–6949 | www.prd.state.or.us | Day use $3, camping $16.

Mugg Estuarine Park. This small 350-ft stretch on the Nestucca River is an ideal bird-watching vantage point. | 2 blocks from center of town. Across the bridge | 503/965–6161.

Three Capes Scenic Route. The coastal drive begins in Tillamook and winds for about 25 mi through Oceanside and south to Pacific City. Highlights are Cape Lookout State Park (above) and the Cape Meares Lighthouse. | West of U.S. 101.

ON THE CALENDAR

AUG.: *Cape Kiwanda Long Board Classic.* Held on the beach at Cape Kiwanda on the first weekend in August, the competition involves the locally famous dory fishing boats. | 503/965–7500 | fax 503/972–1056.

Dining

Pelican Pub and Brewery. American. Breakfast, lunch, and dinner are served daily at this oceanfront restaurant. The large windows provide a majestic view of Cape Kiwanda to Cascade Head. Dine outdoors on a patio right on the beach. The menu includes steaks, fresh fish, pizza, burgers, and beer brewed in-house. | 33180 Cape Kiwanda Drive | 503/965–7007 | $6–$16 | AE, D, DC, MC, V.

Riverhouse. American. Fresh seafood, sandwiches, and home-baked desserts are the specialties at this casual dining spot overlooking the Nestucca River. | 34450 Brooten Road | 503/965–6722 | $7–$20 | MC, V.

Tidewater Restaurant and Lounge. Seafood. The menu features steaks, fresh fish, and salads. Breakfast is served all day. The full bar opens daily at noon. | 34455 Brooten Road | 503/965–6960 | $8–$18 | AE, D, MC, V.

Lodging

Eagles View Bed and Breakfast. This small inn with clapboards was built in 1995 and is set amidst tall trees overlooking the Nestucca Bay and River about 1 mi from town. All rooms have a view of either the forest or the bay. Children and pets are not permitted. | 5 rooms. Outdoor hot tub, 3 rooms have whirlpool tubs, no kids allowed, no pets allowed, no smoking. | 37975 Brooten Rd. | 503/965–7600 or 888/846–3292 | moriah.com/eaglesview | $95–$115 | Full breakfast | D, MC, V.

Inn at Cape Kiwanda. All the rooms at this three-story inn built in 1998 on the Three Capes Scenic Loop have gas fireplaces, minibars, and a view of the ocean. | 35 rooms. Exercise room, coin laundry, data ports, pets allowed, no smoking. | 33105 Cape Kiwanda Dr. | 503/965–7001 | fax 503/965–7002 | www.innatcapekiwanda.com | $99–$219, suites $199–$279 | AE, D, DC, MC, V.

Inn at Pacific City. Walk to the beach and restaurants from this ground-level inn on the Nestucca River. | 16 rooms. Kitchettes with microwaves, refrigerators, no-smoking rooms, pets allowed (fee). | 35215 Brooten Rd., Box 1000, | 503/965–6366 or 888/722–2489 | fax 503/965–6812 | $37–$69, suites $59–$95 | AE, D, DC, MC, V.

PENDLETON

MAP 3, J2

(Nearby towns also listed: Hermiston, La Grande, Umatilla)

At the end of the summer of 1910, a group of eastern Oregon farmers and ranchers gathered to celebrate the harvest and launched the now-world-famous Pendleton Round-Up, the fastest-moving rodeo in America. To many people outside of northeast Oregon, the name Pendleton *is* the Round-Up.

Pendleton also attracts visitors during the other 11 months of the year. The Pendleton Woolen Mills offers a close-up look at the production of the robes and shawls for which it earned its reputation. Another side of Pendleton comes to light on underground tours through the Old Town area with highlights of the Shamrock Card Room, Hop Sing's Chinese Laundry, a 1930s Prohibition card room, and the Cozy Room bordello.

Information: **Pendleton Chamber of Commerce/Visitors Bureau** | 501 S. Main, Pendleton 97801 | 541/276–7411 or 800/547–8911 | pendleton@pendleton-oregon.org | www.pendleton-oregon.org.

Attractions

Emigrant Springs State Heritage Area. Near the summit of the Blue Mountains, this park in an old-growth forest is the site of a popular pioneer stopover along the Oregon Trail. A campground has 18 full hookups, 33 tent sites, and 7 cabins. | Off I–84 | 541/983–2277 or 800/551–6949 | www.prd.state.or.us | Free | Mar.–Nov., daily.

Hamley's Western Store. This shop stocks authentic cowboy and cowgirl clothes and leather products. The craftspeople here make hand-tooled saddles that are considered among the best in the world. | 30 S.E. Court St. | 541/276–2321 | Free | Open only during the Pendelton Round-Up .

Pendleton Underground Tours. In the first half of this 90-minute tour, you'll visit the subterranean tunnels that hid Pendleton's secrets a century ago: gambling rooms, an opium den, the chilly rooms of Chinese laborers, and more; in the second half, the bordello run by the town's most famous madame. There is no fixed schedule for this tour, so you'll have to call ahead to see what's available. The same organization operates the Working Girls Hotel. | 37 S.W. Emigrant Ave. | 541/276–0730 or 800/226–6398 | www.pendletonundergroundtours.org | $10 | Daily.

Pendleton Woolen Mills. Native American blankets and Pendleton shirts and sportswear are produced here. A free 20-minute tour describes the weaving process. The mill's retail store sells blankets and clothing and has bargains on factory seconds. | 1307 S.E. Court Pl. | 541/276–6911 | www.pendleton-usa.com | Free | Tours: weekdays 9, 11, 1:30, 3:00.

Round-Up Hall of Fame Museum. The collection here spans the rodeo's history since 1910 with photographs, saddles, guns, and costumes. The most popular items are an exhibition of Native American beadwork and basketware, a stuffed championship bronco named War Paint, and photographs of all the Round-Up Rodeo queens since 1910. | Round-Up Grounds, 1205 S.W. Court Ave. | 541/278–0815 | Free | May–Oct., daily 10–5. Closed Sun.

Spout Springs. This ski area in the Umatilla National Forest has an elevation of 4,950 ft at the base, 5,550 ft at the top, and a vertical drop of 550 ft. There are 11 runs, and 21 km of Nordic trails. | Summit of Hwy. 204 at Tollgate, Milepost 22 | 541/566–0327 | Jan.–mid-Mar., Wed.–Thurs. 5–10 and Fri.–Sun. 9–4.

Tamastslikt Cultural Institute. This museum at the Wildhorse Casino Resort, operated by the Confederated Tribes of the Umatilla Indian Reservation, has exhibits depicting history from the perspective of the Cayuse, Umatilla, and Walla Walla tribes. An art gallery showcases the work of tribal artists, and there's a theatre with lectures and occasional Indian dance and music performances. | 72789 Hwy. 331 | 541/966–9748 | fax 541/966–9927 | $6 | Daily 9–5.

Ukiah-Dale Forest State Scenic Corridor. The North Fork of the John Day River and Camas Creek, which flow through this area, offer excellent trout, steelhead, and salmon fishing. A campground has 27 primitive sites. | U.S. 395 | 541/983–2277 or 800/551–6949 | www.prd.state.or.us | Free | Mid-Apr.–Nov., daily.

Umatilla Indian Reservation. The Wildhorse Casino Resort, which includes a casino, a hotel, an RV park, and a golf course, is located on this 172,000-acre reservation 6 mi east of Pendleton. The Tamastslikt Cultural Institute has archives, artifacts, and a photo collection. | Mission Hwy. (U.S. 30) | 541/276–3873 | Cultural Institute: $6 | Daily 9–5.

Umatilla National Forest. This 1.4-million-acre forest contains three wilderness areas, Spout Springs Ski Area, the Blue Mountain Scenic Byway, and 22 campgrounds. It's in the Blue Mountains of northeastern Oregon and southeastern Washington and is northeast and south of Pendleton. Because of its acreage it can be reached by a number of routes including I–84, U.S. 395, or Routes 11, 204, 82, 244, 207 and WA U.S. 12. | 541/276–3811 | $3 per vehicle day-use fee | June–Nov., daily.

ON THE CALENDAR

AUG.: ***Jammin' for Salmon.*** This Native American music festival, held on the first weekend in August, features all-Native American musicians and bands and you might hear jazz, blues, or reggae music. There are also activities for kids, arts and crafts vendors, and a program of speakers and symposia on the subject of salmon. | 541/278–2274 or 800/654–9453.

SEPT.: ***Pendelton Round-Up.*** More than 50,000 people roll into town for this highly anticipated annual event. Held the second full week of September, it attracts rodeo performers and fans for four days of rodeo events, wild-horse races, barbecues, parades, and milking contests. Vendors line the length of Court Ave. and Main St., selling beadwork and western-style curios while country bands twang in the background. Make your reservations far in advance. | 800/457–6336.

Dining

Cimmiyotti's. Italian. Eat here just to enjoy the Old West feeling which permeates this restaurant, complete with chandeliers and flocked wallpaper. Well-prepared steaks and Italian food are the main fare. Kids' menu. | 137 S. Main St. | 541/276–4314 | Closed Mon. No lunch | $10–$21 | AE, D, MC, V.

Great Pacific Wine and Coffee Company. Café. This downtown 1887 Masonic temple with a restored facade is now a café that closes at 8 PM. Coffee, bagels, muffins, and deli sandwiches, plus dozens of exotic beers and wines, are menu mainstays. Among the most popular dishes are the Greek salad, nachos with fresh veggies, and the turkey, avocado, and Monterey Jack sandwich. It is just around the corner from Pendleton Underground Tours. | 403 S. Main St. | 541/276–1350 | fax 541/966–8362 | Closed Sun. | $5.95–$7.95 | AE, MC, V.

Raphael's. Contemporary. Raphael's is in a restored 1876 Queen Anne house and has three dining rooms. Besides offering traditional steaks and seafood, all with a Northwest accent, the menu includes seasonal fare such as venison, elk, and rattlesnake. Local people come for the prime rib, hickory-smoked on the premises. There's also a unique huckleberry daiquiri and you can dine in a garden out back. | 233 S.E. 4th St. | 541/276–8500 or 888/944–2433 | fax 541/276–8333 | Closed Sun.–Mon. No lunch | $11–$35 | AE, D, DC, MC, V.

Lodging

Chaparral. Affordable accommodations 1 mi from downtown, this lodging is visible from the highway and in front of the Pendleton Forest Service. | 51 rooms. Some kitchenettes, cable TV, pets allowed (fee). | S.W. 620 Tutuilla Rd. | 541/276–8654 | fax 541/276–5808 | $36–$57 | AE, D, DC, MC, V.

Parker House. This pink stucco home, a blend of French neoclassical and Italianate styles, is virtually unchanged since it was built in the North Hill area in 1917. It still has its original Chinese wallpaper, custom fittings, and woodwork. The comfortable rooms have eclectic furniture and beautiful rugs, and three of them have French doors and balconies. The three-story house also has an elevator. | 4 rooms, 1 suite. Picnic area, complimentary breakfast, some in-room safes, room phones, no TV, library, no kids under 12, no smoking. | 311 N. Main St. | 541/276–8581 or 800/700–8581 | www.parkerhousebnb.com | $75–$95 | AE, MC, V.

Tapadera Inn. This centrally located inn, convenient to shopping and restaurants, has basic, affordable rooms. | 47 rooms. Restaurant, bar, room service, cable TV, indoor pool, hot tub, business services, pets allowed (fee). | 105 S.E. Court Ave. | 541/276–3231 or 800/722–8277 | fax 541/276–0754 | $41–$63 | AE, D, DC, MC, V.

Wildhorse Casino Resort. The casino, standing amid wheat fields at the base of the Blue Mountains 6 mi east of Pendleton, has 400 slot machines, poker, blackjack, keno, bingo, and off-track betting. The rooms are simple but comfortable. There's also a 100-space RV park. | 100 rooms. 3 restaurants, complimentary Continental breakfast, some in-room hot tubs, cable TV, room phones, pool, hot tub, sauna, driving range, 18-hole golf course, putting green, laundry facilities. | 72789 Hwy. 331 | 541/278–2274 or 800/654–9453 | fax 541/276–0297 | info@wildhorseresort.com | www.wildhorseresort.com | $65–$70 | AE, D, DC, MC, V.

Working Girls Hotel. This 1890 building, the only hotel in downtown Pendleton, was a bordello and a boardinghouse in the past and is now on the National Register of Historic Places. The lobby has Victorian furniture and a fireplace, and the rooms have 18-ft ceilings and furnishings from the early 1900s. And, yes, gentlemen are welcome to stay here. | 4 rooms, 1 suite. Some in-room data ports, cable TV, no room phones, laundry facilities, no kids under 16, no smoking. | 17 S.W. Emigrant Ave. | 541/276–0730 or 800/226–6398 | fax 541/276–0665. | $50 | Closed Dec.–Feb. | D, MC, V.

KODAK'S TIPS FOR PHOTOGRAPHING THE CITY

Streets
- Take a bus or walking tour to get acclimated
- Explore markets, streets, and parks
- Travel light so you can shoot quickly

City Vistas
- Find high vantage points to reveal city views
- Shoot early or late in the day, for best light
- At twilight, use fast films and bracket exposures

Formal Gardens
- Exploit high angles to show garden design
- Use wide-angle lenses to exaggerate depth and distance
- Arrive early to beat crowds

Landmarks and Monuments
- Review postcard racks for traditional views
- Seek out distant or unusual views
- Look for interesting vignettes or details

Museums
- Call in advance regarding photo restrictions
- Match film to light source when color is critical
- Bring several lenses or a zoom

Houses of Worship
- Shoot exteriors from nearby with a wide-angle lens
- Move away and include surroundings
- Switch to a very fast film indoors

Stained-Glass Windows
- Bright indirect sunlight yields saturated colors
- Expose for the glass not the surroundings
- Switch off flash to avoid glare

Architectural Details
- Move close to isolate details
- For distant vignettes, use a telephoto lens
- Use side light to accent form and texture

In the Marketplace
- Get up early to catch peak activity
- Search out colorful displays and colorful characters
- Don't scrimp on film

Stage Shows and Events
- Never use flash
- Shoot with fast (ISO 400 to 1000) film
- Use telephoto lenses
- Focus manually if necessary

PORTLAND

MAP 3, E2

(Nearby towns also listed: Beaverton, Gresham, Lake Oswego, Oregon City, Troutdale)

Three well-known sagas have long been associated with the Portland of the West: the Lewis and Clark Expedition, the arrival of the Hudson Bay Trading Company, and the Oregon Trail migration. Another story, however, is actually more telling about the founding of the "Rose City" itself. In 1843, Tennessee drifter William Overton and Massachusetts lawyer Asa Lovejoy beached their canoe on the banks of the Willamette River. Overton saw great potential for the timber-rich land encircled by mountains, and he borrowed 25 cents from Lovejoy to file a claim to the 640-acre site he called "The Clearing." Soon bored with clearing trees and building roads, however, Overton sold his half to Francis Pettygrove and moved on. Then Lovejoy and Pettygrove began debating what to name their new township, with Lovejoy advocating for his native Boston and Pettygrove determined to name it for his hometown. Two coin tosses out of three declared Pettygrove the winner, and it became the namesake of his hometown, Portland, Maine.

Situated just 78 mi east of the Pacific Ocean and 65 mi west of Mount Hood, Portland is Oregon's largest city. Well over 500,000 people live within its borders, while the metropolitan area includes almost 2 million residents. Historically, Portland's economy has been based on timber and wood products. The past several years, however, have seen the emergence and proliferation of technology, athletic apparel, tourism, and manufacturing sectors.

The first art museum in the Pacific Northwest opened in Portland in 1892, and ever since, the city has been recognized as a regional cultural center. The Portland Art Museum, designed by renowned architect Pietro Belluschi, houses collections that span 35 centuries and several continents and has become a primary West Coast showcase for traveling exhibitions. A couple of blocks away, the Portland Center for the Performing Arts encompasses four theatres in three buildings. The Oregon Symphony, the oldest major orchestra west of the Mississippi, performs at the Arlene Schnitzer Concert Hall, formerly a grand movie palace. Galleries, auditoriums, and church and school buildings, old and new, public and private, provide venues throughout the city for fine folk and ethnic art and for performances by the Portland Opera, the Portland Baroque Orchestra, the Northwest Afrikan American Ballet, the Oregon Ballet Theatre, and many more. Jazz, rock, and blues musicians gather in Portland for world-class festivals every summer, while creativity is celebrated in a community that is known for its authors, animators, photographers, and filmmakers. Robert Redford acknowledged the city's cultural appetite by selecting Portland for one of his first Sundance Cinemas, highlighting the works of independent, documentary, and foreign filmmakers.

In addition to the richness of its indoor treasures, Portland is also at the center of some of the continent's best outdoor recreational opportunities. Just to the east, Mount Hood and the Cascades provide a fine venue for summer and winter sports, from skiing and snowboarding to hiking and mountain climbing. For those more inclined to water sports, there are the white waters of the nearby Clackamas, Sandy, White Salmon and Klickitat Rivers for rafters; the broader, quieter waters of the Willamette and Columbia Rivers attract boaters, skiers, swimmers, sailors, wake boarders, and jet skiers. Anglers visit all of them. Golf courses are plentiful in the Rose City, and golf publications rank some of them among the nation's best, while Portland's fame as a running and cycling capital is known coast to coast.

Portland is 100 mi inland from the mouth of the Columbia River, but water plays as central a role in Portland as it does in coastal cities. The Columbia skirts the city to the north, forming the boundary between Oregon and Washington. The Willamette River flows through Portland's center and is spanned through the metro area by 17 bridges, including the world's only telescoping double-deck vertical lift bridge (Steel), the world's oldest lift bridge (Hawthorne) and the nation's longest tied-arch bridge (Fremont). Parks along the urban riverbanks of the Willamette invite pedestrians, cyclists, runners, boaters, skiers, and event-goers to enjoy the river up close. On a small scale, Portland's numerous fountains include the Benson Bubblers, elegant freshwater drinking fountains commissioned in 1912 by a lumber baron who wanted to offer his workers something besides alcohol to drink, and the Skidmore Fountain (1888), the city's oldest piece of public art. Water on a larger scale makes possible the Port of Portland's floating dry dock, which is one of the world's largest and is able to handle ships nearly three football fields in length.

Portland residents have long committed themselves to maintaining a high quality of life and respect for the natural resources of their environment in the face of population growth throughout the region. The city's 37,000 acres of park space include prime downtown real estate as well as the 5,000-acre Forest Park, the nation's largest forested urban wilderness. Surrounding countryside is usually only a 20-minute drive from the city's core, and an extensive network of light-rail trains and buses moves commuters and visitors around the area. Portland is pedestrian-friendly, too. Parks, fountains, benches, statues, coffee carts, and flower stands dot the city blocks. Based on a European model, the blocks are just half as long as those in most other cities in the U.S.

NEIGHBORHOODS

Pearl District. The Pearl District is a 50-city-block area just east of I–405 in the northwest quadrant of Portland. Remnants of its days as a bustling industrial warehouse district now mingle with upscale lofts, art galleries, one-of-a-kind shops and salons, furniture and accessories boutiques, nationally known micro-brewpubs, restaurants, and bookstores, as well as art, media, and advertising studios. An active nightlife gets even livelier the first Thursday of every month, when art galleries open their doors for special showings, music, and receptions.

Old Town. Old Town, in the northwest section, stretches east from Northwest Broadway to Tom McCall Waterfront Park on the Willamette River, including the Chinatown area at Northwest Fourth Avenue and Burnside Street. Restored buildings in this historic section house specialty shops and restaurants. An elaborate ceremonial gate, given to Portland by its Chinese sister city, Kaohsiung, Taiwan and the People's Republic of China, marks the entrance to Chinatown. Traditional red facades, ornate lampposts, and cherry trees define the area. The largest continuously operating open-air market for handcrafted goods, Saturday Market, offers 250-plus craft booths as well as live entertainment and international foods on weekends from March through Christmas. At the north end of Waterfront Park, the Japanese-American Historical Plaza is a sculpture garden, replete with 100 cherry trees, dedicated to Japanese Americans detained in Oregon during World War II.

Nob Hill. No doubt foretelling the future, a California transplant opened the Nob Hill grocery store in the late 1800s in an affluent Portland neighborhood and unwittingly named what has become one of the city's most vibrant communities. The elegant homes that line these Northwest streets between Burnside and Thurman and from 21st Avenue west evoke images of San Francisco. Many of the Victorian and Georgian mansions along 21st and 23rd have been refurbished with hundreds of shops, acclaimed micro-brewpubs, and restaurants, bakeries, music and bookstores, coffee shops, and galleries. A myriad of shoppers, strollers, and sightseers makes it one of the best people-watching spots in the Rose City.

Hawthorne Boulevard and Sellwood. Two neighborhoods in the southeast quadrant of the city, which were popular as residential areas during earlier parts of the 20th century, have recently been revitalized. The Hawthorne Boulevard district is accessible from downtown Portland via the Hawthorne Bridge and mixes upscale retail stores with an earthy, eclectic blend of specialty shops, alternative boutiques, bookstores, and restaurants. One of the first neighborhoods to enjoy a resurrection of more dynamic times, Sellwood is

© Artville

MICROBREWS OF THE PACIFIC NORTHWEST

Freshly poured ale sparkles a rich amber in the light of a sun-dappled May afternoon on the loading-dock beer garden of the Bridgeport Brewpub in Portland, Oregon. To the south rise the office towers of downtown Portland, which supply not a few of Bridgeport's customers. To the north is the graceful span of the Fremont Bridge, the bridge from which the tiny brewery takes its name.

The customer tips back his glass and takes a long, thirsty swallow. The ale cascades along his tongue, tweaking taste buds that for years have known only pale, flavorless industrial lagers. A blast of sweet malt explodes at the back of his mouth, counterpointing the citrusy sting of the hops. *This* is flavor, something missing from American beer for far too long.

There's something inherently noble about a well-crafted pint, something ancient and universal. Anthropologists theorize that agriculture and brewing may have provided the stimulus for the very foundation of human civilization. Certainly there is nothing new in the idea of a city or region being served by a number of small, distinctive breweries. More than 5,000 years ago, in Egypt, the many breweries of ancient Pelusium were as famous as the city's university. (Even then, books, beer, and scholarly contemplation went hand in hand.) The ancient Greeks and Romans, though more partial to wine than grain beverages, drank beer; evidence shows that there were more than 900 public houses in Herculaneum before Mount Vesuvius sounded its fateful "last call" in AD 79.

It may be a coincidence that during the 1970s Britain's Campaign for Real Ale movement—credited with single-handedly restoring fine ale to United Kingdom pubs—paralleled the resurgence in the British economy and national pride. It may also be a coincidence that the return of the microbrewery ale to the Northwest signaled the end of a bitter recession here, and the beginning of a rapid climb into prosperity.

The best place to sample the Northwest's handcrafted ale is a well-run brewpub, which stimulates the human spirit with conviviality, pleasant warmth, intelligent conversation, the scent of malt, and hearty food. Combatting the region's chilly, damp climate, brewpubs become places of refuge where you can shake the tears of a hostile world from your umbrella, order a pint of cask-conditioned bitter, and savor a complex substance that caresses the senses.

Microbreweries (companies producing fewer than 20,000 kegs per year) can be found from Minneapolis to Maui, but it all started in the Pacific Northwest. On any given evening, several dozen locally brewed beers and ales are available for tasting in pubs in Portland and Seattle. Most East Coast entries in the microbrewing sweepstakes produce German-style lagers—the most familiar brewing style to American palates—but the microbrewers of the Pacific Northwest go for wildly adventuresome bitters, stouts, and porters.

With all these beers to choose from, where do you begin? What should you look for in a microbrewery ale? First and foremost, variety. At any given time in Portland and Seattle, there are several dozen fresh, locally made brews on tap. They range in strength from a standard 3½ percent alcohol to an ominous 8½ percent.

And the flavor? Well, you'll just have to taste for yourself. There is the rich sweetness of malt, counterbalanced by good bitter hops. There are the mocha java overtones of roasted barley, used in stouts and porters, and the spiciness of malted wheat. There are sweet ales and tart ales, mild inconsequential ales, and ales so charged with flavor they linger on the palate like a fine Bordeaux.

Above all else, you should look for an ale you can savor, an ale you can taste without wanting to swallow too quickly. The dearest emotion to a brewer's heart is the beer drinker's feeling of regret that the last swig is gone.

—By Jeff Kuechle

a blend of carefully restored homes and dozens of antique shops. The Sellwood Bridge crosses the Willamette River to join the Sellwood neighborhood near Tacoma and Southeast 13th Avenue to the John's Landing area in the city's southwest quadrant.

Hayden and Tomahawk Islands. Hundreds of Portland-area residents make their homes on the water at Hayden and Tomahawk Islands, at the north end of Portland on the Columbia River near Jantzen Beach. Living quarters range from live-aboard boats and "combis" (apartment and boathouse combinations) to elaborate homes with multiple stories, decks, and docks. The common denominator is a foundation that floats. Since most of the homes aren't mobile for recreational purposes, many homeowners tie sail- and motorboats to the sides of their homes. Like neighborhoods on terra firma, the community has its own restaurants and service businesses.

Information: Portland Oregon Visitors Association | 26 S.W. Salmon | 503/222–2223 or 877/678–5263 | tori@pova.com | www.pova.com.

TRANSPORTATION INFORMATION

Airports: The Portland area is served by the award-winning **Portland International Airport.** Just 20 minutes from downtown, the airport offers service by 19 passenger airlines to more than 120 cities worldwide. 7000 N.E. Airport Way, north of I–84 and west of I–205, 503/460–4234.

Airport Transportation: Raz Tranz (503/684–3322) operates buses from the airport to some downtown hotels, as well as the Amtrak and Greyhound depots. Departures are every 30 minutes between 5 AM and midnight. The fare is $8.50 one-way and $15.50 round-trip. Alternatively, you can catch the **Tri-Met** Bus 12, which runs to and from the airport every 15 minutes. The fare is $1.15. A taxi from the airport to downtown Portland will take approximately 30 minutes and cost around $30.

Amtrak serves the city from Union Station (800 N.W. 6th Ave.). Call 800/872–7245 for schedules and fares.

Bus Lines: Greyhound serves Portland from its terminal at 550 N.W. 6th Ave. Call 503/243–2317 or 800/231–2222 for schedules and fares.

Intra-city Transit: Once in the city, transportation options include **Tri-Met** bus service (503/238–7433) throughout the greater Portland area; the **MAX** light rail (503/228–7246), which links the eastern and western Portland suburbs to downtown; and taxis.

DRIVING AROUND PORTLAND

Finding a parking space in downtown Portland can be a challenge. If you can, take MAX light rail or the bus.

Parking is extremely limited in the Nob Hill neighborhood in Northwest Portland and in the Hawthorne District. Parking at meters on the street costs $1 an hour.

Meters are free after 6 PM and on Sundays and major holidays (New Year's Day, Martin Luther King Day, Presidents Day, Memorial Day, Fourth of July, Labor Day, Veterans Day, Thanksgiving, and Christmas). In the Lloyd District from Weidler to Lloyd Boulevard and from Grand Avenue to the river, meters are enforced until 10 PM and cost 50¢ an hour. Some meters have 90-minute or 3-hour limits. The city also operates several Smart-Park garages in the downtown area, which charge 95¢ an hour. If you park here, you won't have to keep feeding the meter. Several neighborhoods also have restricted parking for residents with permits.

Attractions

ART AND ARCHITECTURE

City Hall. The four-story, granite-faced City Hall is an 1895 example of the Renaissance Revival style. Italian influences can be seen in the porch, the pink scagliola columns, the cornice embellishments, and other details. | 1221 S.W. 4th Ave. | 503/823–4000 | Weekdays 8–5.

Justice Center. Besides courts, this modern building houses the Police Museum (16th floor), which has uniforms, guns, and badges of the Portland Police Department. The center's hallways are lined with travertine sculptures, ceiling mosaics, stained-glass windows, and photographic murals. Visitors are welcome. | 1111 S.W. 2nd Ave. | 503/823–0019 | Free | Mon.-Thurs. 10-3.

KOIN Center. This tapering 1984 tower recalls the style of Art Deco skyscrapers. Made of brick with limestone trim and a blue metal roof, it houses offices (including those of KOIN, a local TV and radio station), a multiplex cinema, and, on its top floors, some of the priciest condominiums in town. | 222 SW Columbia St.

Mark O. Hatfield U. S. Courthouse. This 1997 skyscraper has an exterior of Indiana limestone, and the courtroom lobbies have expansive glass walls. Public rooftop terraces yield great views of the city. | S.W. 2nd Ave. between Main and Salmon Sts.

Pettygrove House. In 1845, Francis Pettygrove bought most of what is now downtown Portland for $50. He and Asa Lovejoy, his partner, flipped a coin for the right to name the town. Pettygrove won and called it Portland after the town in his native Maine. His 1892 Victorian gingerbread house has been beautifully restored, but is not open for tours. | 2287 N.W. Pettygrove St.

★ **Pittock Mansion.** The publisher of the *Oregonian* newspaper built this mansion, which combines French Renaissance and Victorian styles. The opulent manor, erected in 1914, is filled with art and antiques of the 1880s. The grounds, north of Washington Park and 1,000 ft above the city, have superb views of the skyline, rivers, and Cascade Range. | 3229 N.W. Pittock Dr. | 503/823–3624 | $4.50 | Feb.–Dec., daily noon–4.

Portland Building. One of the first postmodern buildings in the United States, the Portland Building is buff-colored with brown and blue trim and dark interior spaces. Portlandia, the second-largest hammered-copper statue in the world (after the Statue of Liberty), kneels on the second-story balcony. The Metropolitan Center for Public Art, a permanent exhibit of public art and original works by local artists, is also there. | 1120 S.W. 5th Ave. | 503/823–4000 | Free | Weekdays 8-6.

BEACHES, PARKS, AND NATURAL SIGHTS

Chapman and Lownsdale Squares. In the 1920s, these parks were segregated by sex. Chapman, between Madison and Main Streets, was for men, while Lownsdale, between Main and Salmon Streets, was for women. The elk statue between them, on Main Street, supposedly honors an elk that grazed here in the 1850s. | Free | Daily.

Crystal Springs Rhododendron Garden. For much of the year this 7-acre retreat near Reed College is used by bird-watchers. In April thousands of rhododendron bushes and azaleas burst into flower. The peak blooming season is May; by late June the show is over. | S.E. 28th Ave. | 503/823–2223 | $3 | Daily.

Forest Park. The nation's largest (5,000 acres) urban wilderness, this city-owned oasis, home to more than 100 species of birds and 50 species of mammals, contains more than 50 mi of trails. | At the end of N.W. Upshur St. | 503/823–2223 or 503/228–8733 | Free | Daily.

Hoyt Arboretum. Ten miles of trails wind through this nature park, which has more than 800 species of plants and one of the nation's largest collections of coniferous trees; pick up trail maps at the visitors center. Also here are the Winter Garden and a memorial to veterans of the Vietnam War. | 4000 S.W. Fairview Blvd. | 503/228–8733 | Free | Daily dawn to dusk.

Laurelhurst Park. Manicured lawns, stately trees, and a wildfowl pond make this 25-acre, southeast Portland park a favorite urban hangout. Laurelhurst, one of the city's most beautiful neighborhoods, surrounds the park. | S.E. 39th Ave. and Start St. | Daily dawn–dusk.

Governor Tom McCall Waterfront Park. This broad and grassy park stretches for a mile along the Willamette River and offers probably the best ground-level view of Portland's bridges and skyline. In summer, bikers, joggers, and skaters cool off at the Salmon Street Fountain. The park hosts the Rose Festival, the Oregon Brewers' Festival, and classical and blues concerts. | Across from S.W. Naito Pkwy. from S.W. Clay St. to Glisan St. | Free | Daily.

Mill Ends Park. Sitting in the middle of a traffic island on Naito Parkway, this patch of urban tranquillity, all of 24 inches in diameter, has been recognized by the Guinness Book of Records as the world's smallest official city park. | S.W. Naito Pkwy. at Taylor St.

Mt. Tabor Park. Dirt trails and an asphalt road wind through forested hillsides and past good picnic areas to the top of Mt. Tabor, which looks out toward Portland's West Hills to the west and Mt. Hood to the east. Mt. Tabor is an extinct volcano. | S.E. 60th Ave. and Salmon St. | 503/823–2223 | Free | Daily.

Multnomah Falls. The second-highest year-round waterfall in the U.S. plunges 620 ft down the side of a cliff in the Columbia Gorge. A trail leads to an arch bridge, where you can get a close-up view of the cascading water. There's also a lodge with a restaurant that serves breakfast, lunch, and dinner, and a snack bar. | Exit 31 off I–84 | 503/695–2376 | Free | Daily.

Terry Schrunk Plaza. A terraced amphitheater of green lawn and brick, shaded by flowering cherry trees, the plaza is a popular lunch spot for the office crowd. | Between S.W. 3rd and 4th Aves. and S.W. Madison and Jefferson Sts.

Skidmore Fountain. This graceful 1888 fountain is the centerpiece of Ankeny Square, site of many community activities. Two nymphs hold the brimming basin on top; horses once drank from the granite troughs at the base. | Between 1st and Naito Pkwy.

State Parks. The Portland area has a variety of state parks, where city dwellers and visitors can go hiking, fishing, boating, and swimming.

The small lake at **Benson State Park,** 30 mi from Portland, is perfect for rafting, canoeing, swimming, and fishing. It's stocked with thousands of rainbow trout. | Exit 30 off I–84 | 503/695–2261 or 800/551–6949 | www.prd.state.or.us | $3 per vehicle day-use.

Enjoy spectacular views of the Columbia River Gorge from **Crown Point State Park,** which is located on a high bluff. Vista House, a two-tier octagonal structure built in 1916, houses a museum and an interpretive display of Gorge history and geology. | On the U.S. 30 Scenic Rte | 503/695–2261 or 800/551–6949 | www.prd.state.or.us | Free | Mar.–Oct., daily.

The secluded location of **Guy W. Talbot State Park** keeps it uncrowded even on the best days. A trail underneath the Historic Columbia River Highway leads to Latourell Falls. There are picnic tables and a shelter. | On the U.S. 30 Scenic Rte | 800/551–6949 | www.prd.state.or.us | Free | Daily.

★ **International Rose Test Garden.** Set on 4 acres and displayed in three terraced gardens, the area has 10,000 bushes and 400 different types of roses growing. The best time to see the flowers is in June, July, September and October. On clear days you can see a wonderful view of Mt. Hood. Concerts are held here occasionally in a large outdoor amphitheater. | 400 S.W. Kingston in Washington Park | 503/823–2223 | Free | Daily.

★ **Japanese Garden.** An authentic Japanese garden is on 5½ acres in Washington Park above the International Rose Test Garden. Designed by a Japanese landscape master, it opened to the public in 1967. Five separate garden styles are represented: Strolling Pond Garden, Tea Garden, Natural Garden, Sand and Stone Garden, and Flat Garden. The Tea House was built in Japan and reconstructed here. The west side of the Pavilion has a majestic view of Portland and Mt. Hood. | 611 S.W. Kingston Ave. in Washington Park | 503/223–1321 | $6 | Apr.–Sept., daily 10–7; Oct.–Mar., daily 10–4.

Lewis and Clark State Park. A trail leads to Broughton's Bluff, the geologic boundary between the Cascades foothills and the Willamette Valley. The park's location in the Columbia Gorge near the mouth of the Sandy River offers swimming and boating. | Exit 18 off I–84E | 503/695–2261 | Free | Daily.

Rooster Rock State Park. Located along the Columbia River, this park has 3 mi of sandy beaches. At the far east end is a nude sunbathing and swimming area. It's not visible from the clothing-required area. This area is also popular with windsurfers. | Exit 25 from I–84E | 503/695–2261 or 800/551–6949 | www.prd.state.or.us | $3 per vehicle day use | Daily.

Washington Park. Set in the forested West Hills, Washington Park is home to the Japanese Garden, International Rose Test Garden, and the ever-expanding Oregon Zoo. It can be reached via W. Burnside St., Southwest Park Place, or Canyon Rd. | 503/823–2223 (weekdays) | Free | Daily.

World Forestry Center. The center, across from the Oregon Zoo in Washington Park, takes its arboreal interests seriously—its spokesperson is a 70-ft-tall talking tree. Outside, a 1909 locomotive and antique logging equipment are displayed, and inside are two floors of exhibits, a multi-image "Forests of the World," a collection of 100-year-old wood, and a gift shop. | 4033 S.W. Canyon Rd. | 503/228–1367 | $4.50 | Late May–early Sept., daily 9–5; early Sept.–late May, daily 10–5.

CULTURE, EDUCATION, AND HISTORY

Chinatown Gate. Recognizable by its five roofs, 64 dragons, and two huge lions, the Chinatown Gate is the official entrance to the Chinatown District. During the 1890s, Portland had the second-largest Chinese community in the United States. Today's Chinatown is compressed into several blocks with restaurants, shops, and grocery stores. | N.W. 4th Ave. and Burnside St.

Civic Auditorium. Part of the Portland Center for the Performing Arts, the home of the Portland Opera and Oregon Ballet Theater also hosts traveling musicals and other theatrical events. Facing the entrance is the Ira Keller Fountain, a series of 18-ft-high waterfalls. | S.W. 3rd Ave. and Clay St. | 503/274–6560 | Call for prices.

Glazed Terra-Cotta National Historic District. Terra-cotta was popular a century ago for its use in decorating buildings. The rooflines of this district's turn-of-the-20th-century structures are embellished with elaborate lions' heads, griffins, floral displays, and other classical motifs. Sculptures on 5th Avenue include one that reflects light and colors, a nude woman in bronze, a copper and redwood tribute to the Norse god Thor, and a large limestone cat. Sixth Avenue has a steel-and-concrete matrix, a granite-and-brick fountain, and an abstract depiction of an ancient Greek defending Crete. | S.W. 5th and S.W. 6th Aves. between S.W. Oak and S.W. Yamhill Sts.

Japanese-American Historical Plaza. Flowering cherry trees, bronze columns depicting Japanese-American daily life, and simple granite blocks carved with haiku poems fill a park commemorating the more than 110,000 Japanese-Americans who were interned during the war. | North End of Tom McCall Waterfront Park near the Steel Bridge.

Lewis & Clark College. The college was founded by Presbyterian pioneers as Albany Collegiate Institute in 1867. The school moved to the former Lloyd Frank estate in Portland's southwest hills in 1942 and took the name Lewis & Clark College. The campus is situated in a wooded residential area 6 mi from downtown Portland | S.W. Palatine Hill Rd. | 503/768–7000 | www.lclark.edu | Free | Weekdays.

★ **Pioneer Courthouse Square.** This brick piazza echoes the central plazas of European cities as a premier site for people-watching and special events. Best time is noon, when a goofy weather machine confirms the day's weather with fanfare: either a shining sun, a stormy dragon, or a blue heron rising out of a misty cloud appear. Across the street is the sedate 1869 Pioneer Courthouse, the oldest public building in the Northwest. | 701 S.W. 6th Ave. | 503/223–1613.

Portland Center for the Performing Arts. The Arlene Schnitzer Concert Hall hosts the Oregon Symphony, other musical events, and lectures. Across Main Street, but also part of the center, is the 292-seat Delores Winningstad Theater, whose stage design and size are based on those of an Elizabethan theater. The 916-seat Intermediate Theater houses Portland Center Stage, a resident theater company. The street between the buildings is often closed for food fairs, art shows, and other events. | S.W. Broadway and S.W. Main St. | 503/796–9293.

Portland State University. This urban university is located on a beautiful shady campus along the South Park Blocks downtown. It's a great place to take a walk on a spring or fall day. There's a farmers' market on weekend mornings. | Visitors information center at S.W. Broadway and College St. | 503/725–3000 | www.pdx.edu | Free | Daily.

Reed College. A small college that has become one of the nation's preeminent institutions of the liberal arts and sciences. The campus is located in a residential area about 2 to 3 mi from downtown Portland. | 3203 S.E. Woodstock Blvd. | 503/771–1112 | fax 503/777–7769 | web.reed.edu | Free | Daily.

Yamhill National Historic District. Many examples of 19th-century cast-iron architecture are preserved within this district's six square blocks. North and west of the district, along 2nd Avenue, galleries exhibit fine art, ceramics, photography, and posters. On the first Thursday of each month, new shows are unveiled and most galleries stay open until 9 PM. | Between S.W. Naito Pkwy. and S.W. 3rd Ave. and S.W. Morrison and S.W. Taylor Sts.

MUSEUMS

American Advertising Museum. This museum is devoted to advertising. Exhibits celebrate memorable campaigns, print advertisements, radio and TV commercials, and novelty and specialty products. | 5035 S.E. 24th Ave. | 503/226–0000 | $3 | Weekdays by appointment, Sat. noon–5.

Children's Museum. Hands-on play is the order of the day at this museum with exhibits, a clay shop, and a child-size grocery store. By July 2001 the museum will be moving into a new home in Washington Park across from the Oregon Zoo. | 3037 S.W. 2nd Ave. | 503/823–2227 | $4 | Tues.–Sun. 9–5.

Jeff Morris Memorial Fire Museum. Horse-drawn pumps and other fire-fighting equipment are visible through large windows of this museum, on the north side of the Central Fire Station. Cast-iron medallions, capitals, and grillwork from other buildings decorate the wall; cast-iron columns mark the border of Ankeny Square beside the museum. | 111 S.W. Naito Pkwy.

Oregon History Center. The museum's collection includes books, photographs, film, manuscripts, maps, and artifacts documenting Oregon's diverse past. | 1200 S.W. Park Ave. | 503/222–1741 | www.ohs.org | $6 | Tues., Wed., Fri., Sat. 10–5, Thurs. 10–8, Sun. noon–5.

Oregon Maritime Center and Museum. Most of the models of ships that plied the Columbia River were created by local model makers. Prime examples of cast-iron architecture grace the building's exterior. Admission includes entrance aboard the last operating stern-wheel steam tug in the United States, docked across the street. | 113 S.W. Naito Pkwy. | 503/224–7724 | $4 | Memorial Day–Labor Day, Fri.–Sun. 11–4; Labor Day–Memorial Day, Thurs.–Sun. 11–4.

★ **Oregon Museum of Science and Industry.** An Omnimax theater and planetarium are among the main attractions at the Northwest's largest astronomy educational facility, which also has a hands-on computer center, a space wing with a mission-control center, and many permanent and touring scientific exhibits. A 240-ft submarine is moored in the Willamette River as part of the museum. | 1945 S.E. Water Ave. | 503/797–4000 | www.omsi.org | $6.50 | Memorial Day–Labor Day, daily 9:30–7 (until 8 on Thurs.); Labor Day–Memorial Day, Tues.–Sun. 9:30–5:30.

Portland Art Museum. The treasures at the Northwest's oldest visual- and media-arts facility span 35 centuries of Asian, European, and American art, with collections of Native American, regional, and contemporary art. The film center presents the annual Portland International Film Festival in February and March and the Northwest Film Festival in early November. | 1219 S.W. Park Ave. | 503/226–2811 | www.pam.org | $7.50 | Tues.–Sat. 10–5, Sun. noon–5.

State of Oregon Sports Hall of Fame. This museum houses memorabilia of such prominent Oregon athletes as Heisman Trophy winner Terry Baker, the Portland Trail Blazers basketball team, and Mickey Lolich, who pitched for the Detroit Tigers in three World Series. | 321 S.W. Salmon St. | 503/227–7466 | $3 | Mon.–Sat., 10–6.

RELIGION AND SPIRITUALITY

Grotto—The National Sanctuary of Our Sorrowful Mother. Owned by the Catholic Church, the Sanctuary of Our Sorrowful Mother, as it's officially known, displays more than 100 statues and shrines in 62 acres of woods. The grotto was carved into the base of a 110-ft cliff and features a replica of Michelangelo's *Pieta*. From this vantage point you'll get a fantastic view of the Columbia River and the Cascades. There is a dazzling Festival of Lights at Christmastime (late Nov. through Dec.) with 250,000 lights, and holiday concerts in the 600-seat chapel. Sun. Masses are held here, too. | 8840 N.E. 85th Ave. | 503/254–7371 | fax 503/254–7948 | www.thegrotto.org | $2 | Daily 9–4.

Old Church. This prime 1882 example of Carpenter Gothic architecture has tall spires, original stained-glass windows, and an exterior of rough-cut lumber. The acoustically resonant church has one of the few operating Hook and Hastings tracker pipe organs and hosts free classical concerts at noon on Wednesdays. | 1422 S.W. 11th Ave. | 503/222–2031 | Free | Weekdays 11–3, Sat. by appointment.

SHOPPING

Lloyd Center. This shopping center near the Rose Quarter contains more than 170 shops, including Nordstrom and Meier and Frank, a large food court, a multi-screen cinema, and an ice-skating pavilion. It's on the MAX light rail. | N.E. Multnomah St. | 503/282–2511 | Free | Mon.–Sat. 10–9, Sun. 11–6.

NikeTown. This futuristic building is the showplace for the international sportswear giant, Nike, based in nearby Beaverton. The store mixes merchandise with video monitors, sports memorabilia, and statuary, including a life-size plaster cast of Michael Jordan in mid-jump. Prices are full retail, so don't expect bargains. | 930 S.W. 6th Ave. | 503/221–6453 | Mon.–Thurs. and Sat. 10–7, Fri. 10–8, Sun. 11:30–6:30.

★ **Northwest 23rd Avenue.** Shops and restaurants fill both new structures and century-old homes. North of Lovejoy Street, the avenue is quieter. Between Overton and Pettygrove streets, a block of open-porch frame houses, now shops, satisfies the New Age side of Portland. Clear Creek Distillery is near Quimby Street.

★ **Portland Saturday Market.** On Saturday and Sunday from March to Christmas, this is North America's largest open-air handicraft market. Crystals, yard goods, beaded hats, stained glass, bird houses, jewelry, flags, wood and rubber stamps, custom footwear, and decorative boots are all available, as well as entertainers, food, and produce booths. | Under west end of Burnside Bridge, from S.W. Naito Pkwy. to Ankeny Sq | 503/222–6072 | Mar.–Dec., Sat. 10–5, Sun. 11–4:30.

Powell's City of Books. This is the largest used and new retail bookstore in the world (more than 1.5 million volumes); it covers an entire city block. Powell's also carries rare and hard-to-find editions. | 1005 W. Burnside St. | 503/228–4651.

Sellwood. This charming neighborhood just east of the Sellwood Bridge was annexed by Portland in the 1890s. On weekends the antiques stores along 13th Avenue do a brisk business. Each store has a plaque with the year it was built and its original purpose. | S.E. 13th Ave. between Malden and Clatsop Sts.

Southeast Hawthorne Boulevard. Though it's becoming more upscale, this neighborhood of bookstores, coffeehouses, taverns, restaurants, antiques stores, and boutiques still has a countercultural feel. | S.E. Hawthorne Blvd. between 30th and 42nd Aves.

Water Tower in Johns Landing. South of downtown along the Willamette River in the John's Landing neighborhood is this pleasant smaller mall with 35 specialty shops and six restaurants. | 5331 S.W. Macadam Ave. | 503/274–2786 | Free | Daily.

SPORTS AND RECREATION

NBA (Portland Trail Blazers). Portland's only major sports team plays at the Rose Garden Arena from October to June. | 1 Center Court | 503/234–9291 | Prices vary | Call for schedule.

SIGHTSEEING TOURS/TOUR COMPANIES

Gray Line Tours. This company operates tours of area attractions and scheduled service to Chinook Winds Casino in Lincoln City; call for departure times. | 4320 North Suttle Rd. | 503/285–9845 or 800/422–7042 | fax 503/285–5202 | www.grayline.com | $24–$54 | Call for schedule.

OTHER POINTS OF INTEREST

Oregon Zoo. In the West Hills area, this animal park has been a successful breeding ground for Asian elephants. Major exhibits include an African section with rhinos, hippos, giraffes, and zebras, as well as an aviary with 15 species of birds, and meerkats. Other popular attractions include an Alaskan tundra exhibit, with wolves, musk ox, and grizzly bears; a penguinarium; and habitats for beavers, elk, birds, and reptiles native to the west side of the Cascade Range. In summer a 4-mi-round-trip narrow-gauge train operates from the zoo through the woods to a station at the International Rose Test Garden and the Japanese Garden. True native habitats for bald eagles, black bears, and cougars are among the projects scheduled for the new millennium. These species actually lived in the Washington Park woods before the encroachment of civilization. Take the MAX light rail to the Washington Park station. | 4001 S.W. Canyon Ct. | 503/226–1561 | www.oregonzoo.org | $6.50. Apr.–Sept., daily 9–6; Oct.–Mar., daily 9–4

Oaks Amusement Park. It may not be Disneyland, but there's a small-town charm to this park with thrill rides and miniature golf in summer and roller-skating year-round. In summer 1999 Oaks Park opened Acorn Acres, complete with a 360°-loop roller coaster. The skating rink, built in 1905, is the oldest continuously operating one in the United States. | S.E. Oaks Park Way | 503/233–5777 | www.oakspark.com | Entry is free; prices of activities vary | May–June, weekends noon–5; July–Oct., Tues.–Sat. noon–10, Sun. noon–7.

ON THE CALENDAR

APR.–OCT.: ***Greyhound Racing.*** Even when the dogs aren't running at Multnomah Greyhound Park, you can still bet on greyhound races around the country and watch the results on satellite TV. | 503/667–7700.

MAY: ***Cinco de Mayo Festival.*** Portland's Cinco de Mayo Festival is one of the largest this side of Guadalajara. | 503/222–9807.

LATE MAY–LATE JUNE: ***Portland Rose Festival.*** This is one of the largest events on the West Coast, lasting for almost one month with some 2 million participants. The festivities begin with the naming and coronation of the Rose Queen followed by a fireworks spectacular that explodes over the Willamette River on opening night. On the first Saturday about 350,000 people turn out to see the dozens of illuminated floats in the Starlight Parade. The highlight of the 25 days of events and festivities is the Grand Floral Parade on the second Saturday in June, when around half a million people jam downtown streets to watch dozens of all-floral floats, marching bands, and equestrian performers. The parade is the second-largest all-floral parade in North America, second only to the Tournament of Roses Parade. The Rose Festival coincides with Fleet Week, which usually gets under way around June 10. Thousands of sailors and marines cruise into town on dozens of military ships that dock downtown, along the seawall on the west side of the Willamette River. | 503/227–2681.

JUNE: ***Budweiser Indy Car World Series.*** This 200-mi race, held at the Portland Speedway, lures the top names on the Indy Car circuit. | 503/285–2883.

JUNE–JULY: ***Chamber Music Northwest.*** Internationally acclaimed musicians from around the U.S. perform in concerts at Reed College and the Catlin Gable School during this five-week event that began in 1971 as a series of summer concerts. | For information: 522 S.W. Fifth Ave., Suite 725 | 503/223–3202.
JULY: ***Oregon Brewers' Festival.*** This beer lover's delight is held in Governor Tom McCall Waterfront Park. | 503/778–5917.
JULY: ***Portland Scottish Highland Games.*** This event at Mt. Hood Community College includes bagpipe music and drumming; athletic competition with hammer and stone throwing, caber tossing, and tug of war; and dancing. Genealogical information is available. | 503/293–8501 or 503/241–1124.
JULY: ***Waterfront Blues Festival.*** This music festival features Oregon's finest blues artists along with national recording stars. | 503/973–3378.
OCT.–APR.: ***Horse Racing.*** You can bet on live races or on simulcast races from around the nation at Portland Meadows. | 1001 N. Schmeer Rd. | Thurs.–Sat. evenings at 5:35 | 503/285–9144.
OCT.: ***Portland Marathon.*** One of the top 10 events of its kind in the U.S. includes 5-mi and 26.2-mi races. The main race starts at City Hall (S.W. 4th Ave. and S.W. Madison Ave.) and ends at the Justice Center (S.W. 3rd Ave. and S.W. Madison Ave.) 503/226–1111
DEC.: ***Holiday Parade of Christmas Ships.*** About 60 boats decorated with lights cruise the Willamette and Columbia Rivers. Boat owners design and build their lighted Christmas displays and pay their own operating costs. It continues nightly for two weeks leading up to Christmas. 503/225–5555

PORTLAND WALKS

Portland is not one of those cities where they roll in the sidewalks at 5:30 after every one heads home from work. The downtown area is vibrant, pleasant, and very walkable. Begin your tour at **Pioneer Courthouse Square** at Morrison and Broadway, the heart of the city. East of the square is the old courthouse, which is now a post office.

From the square walk west one block to Park Avenue and head south along the shady South Park Blocks. At Jefferson Street on the east side of the parks blocks is a mural depicting Lewis and Clark's trek along the Oregon Trail; on the west side is the Portland Art Museum.

Continue south along Park Avenue to **Portland State University.** From the campus head east down Market Street about three blocks to Southwest 4th Avenue and turn left. About four blocks north are **Lownsdale and Chapman Squares,** which are surrounded by government buildings. Salmon Street runs east and west on the north side of the squares. Walk east down Salmon to Southwest 2nd Avenue and pick up some tourist brochures at the **Portland/Oregon Visitors Association Center.**

From the visitors center head east one more block to **Tom McCall Waterfront Park** on the bank of the Willamette River. If it's a nice day, pick a bench and watch the boats. Stroll along the river under the Morrison Bridge to the next span—the Burnside Bridge. Just before this bridge is **Skidmore Fountain,** at the corner of Ankeny and Naito Parkway. Walk west under the bridge to Southwest 1st Avenue and visit the **Portland Saturday Market** and its many arts and crafts booths, food vendors, and restaurants. The market is open both Saturday and Sunday, but many shops and restaurants are open daily.

If you want to extend your tour, continue walking north on 1st Avenue under the Burnside Bridge to the **Old Town/Chinatown District,** home of several Chinese restaurants and gift shops. If you want to skip this area, from the market walk south on 1st Avenue along the MAX light-rail tracks to Washington Street. Turn right and continue to Southwest 5th Avenue. Head south and see some of the buildings in the **Glazed Terra-Cotta National Historic District.** Many have classical motifs on their roofs.

This tour takes about half a day. If you plan to tour the Portland Art Museum, add a few more hours.

Dining

INEXPENSIVE

★ **Assaggio.** Italian. Everything about this Sellwood trattoria (food, decor, price) is extremely pleasant. The Italian dishes are authentic, many are available as family-style samplers, and the pastas are all properly al dente. Try the salad sampler or any of the *bruschette* (grilled garlic bread with various toppings). An excellent wine cellar favors Italian vintages. The interior, burnt sienna with classical architectural motifs, lovingly evokes Italy. | 7742 S.E. 13th Ave. | 503/232–6151 | Reservations accepted for parties of 6 or more | Closed Sun.–Mon. No lunch. | $10–$14 | MC, V.

Bastas. Italian. This former Tastee Freeze is now a stylish restaurant serving pasta, fish, and meat dishes from all over Italy. The walls are painted with Italian earth shades and Etruscan decorative motifs and there's a small side garden for al fresco dining in good weather. | 410 N.W. 21st Ave. | 503/274–1572 | $8–$18 | AE, MC, V.

Bridgeport Brew Pub. Pizza. Thick, hand-thrown pizza on sourdough beer-wort crust and frothing pints of Bridgeport's English-style ale, brewed on the premises, are served to boisterous crowds inside a cool, ivy-covered, century-old industrial building. In summer, the flower-festooned loading dock is transformed into a beer garden. | 1313 N.W. Marshall St. | 503/241–3612 | $10–$19.75 | MC, V.

Dan and Louis Oyster Bar. Seafood. A collection of steins, plates, and marine art covers the walls of this restaurant that opened in 1907. Oysters come deep fried, stewed, broiled, or on the half shell. Crab stew—virtually impossible to find elsewhere in town—is also popular. Kids' menu. | 208 S.W. Ankeny St. | 503/227–5906 | $8–$20 | AE, D, DC, MC, V.

Esparza's Tex Mex Cafe. Tex-Mex. South-of-the-border craziness rules at this popular local eatery. Wild West kitsch festoons the walls. Look for offerings like lean smoked-sirloin tacos—Esparza's is renowned for its smoked meats—and, if you are an adventurous eater, ostrich enchiladas. Try the stuffed pork loin with ground buffalo meat mixed with cactus and spices or the carne asada rib-eye steak. Kids' menu. No smoking. | 2725 S.E. Ankeny St. | 503/234–7909 | Closed Sun.–Mon. | $10–$20 | AE, MC, V.

Kornblatt's. Delicatessen. This kosher deli, reminiscent of a 1950s diner, serves the best bagels in Portland. The fresh-cooked pastrami, corned beef, and tongue are lean and tender, and the home-smoked salmon and sablefish are simply the best. For breakfast, try the poached eggs with spicy corned-beef hash. | 628 N.W. 23rd Ave. | 503/242–0055 | Reservations not accepted | $5.75–$9.95 | MC, V.

Mandarin Cove. Chinese. One of Portland's best Chinese restaurants features Hunan- and Szechwan-style beef, chicken, pork, seafood, and vegetarian dishes. There are almost two dozen seafood choices. Try the sautéed scallops simmered in spicy tomato sauce. | 111 S.W. Columbia St. | 503/222–0006 | No lunch Sun. | $11–$25 | AE, DC, MC, V.

Mayas Taqueria. Mexican. This downtown outpost of a popular local chain is right on the MAX light rail and within walking distance of many downtown hotels. It serves up good Mexican food at very reasonable prices. The generous taco is one of the best deals in town. | 1000 S.W. Morrison St., | 503/226–1946 | $5–$12 | MC, V.

Montage. Cajun. This sassy bistro under the Morrison Bridge on Portland's east side is loud, crowded and casually hip. Spicy Cajun fare reigns from the jambalayas and blackened pork and catfish to the hoppin' John and rabbit tenders; these plus old-fashioned macaroni dishes, are served up from about noon till the wee hours. | 301 S.E. Morrison St. | 503/234–1324 | Reservations not accepted | No lunch on weekends | $4–$16 | No credit cards.

Old Spaghetti Factory. Italian. Dine in an old trolley car with a view of the Willamette River at this chain eatery that's filled with antiques. The place is casual and can hold up to 500 diners. Try the "Manager's Favorite": pasta with a blend of two sauces chosen from a choice of four. Kids' menu. | 0715 S.W. Bancroft St. | 503/222–5375 | Reservations not accepted | $10–$15 | AE, D, DC, MC, V.

Original Pancake House. American/Casual. Not a chain imitation, this is a real pancake house. Antique plates cover the walls in the Colonial, cabin-like setting. Known for waffles, crêpes, omelettes, and 20 varieties of pancakes. Try the Dutch Baby Pancake which is a huge sourdough version of the original. | 8601 S.W. 24th Ave. | 503/246–9007 | Closed Mon.–Tues. | $7–$10 | No credit cards.

Pizzacato. Pizza. This local chain serves pizzas topped by inventive combinations such as red potato and prosciutto. The restaurant is clean, bright, and modern. Beer and wine are available. | 705 S.W. Alder St., 503/226–1007 or 505 N.W. 23rd Ave., 503/242–0023 | $7.75–$18.75 | AE, MC, V.

Poor Richard's. American. The cooking is American home style served in a Colonial-style dining room. There are homemade soups, pot pies, hand-cut steaks, fish and chips, chicken-fried steak, and whipped potatoes. Check out the "two-fer" menu—buy one, get one free—and the inexpensive (under $10) nightly specials. Kids' menu. | 3907 N.E. Broadway | 503/288–5285 | No lunch Sat. | $10–$22 | AE, D, MC, V.

Rock Bottom Brewing Co. American/Casual. This is one of the ritzier examples of that authentically Portland experience, the brew pub. Have a pint of ale—brewed on the premises, of course—and sample the fine pub foods such as burgers, pasta, and salads. Snacks, too. | 210 S.W. Morrison St. | 503/796–2739 | $8.50–$18.95.

Saigon Kitchen. Vietnamese. The decor is no-nonsense diner, but don't let that deter you. Consistently good Vietnamese stir-fry dishes and Thai noodles and soups have made Saigon Kitchen a neighborhood favorite. Fried salted calamari and fiery chili noodles with prawns or chicken are delectable standouts. | 835 N.E. Broadway | 503/281–3669 | $9–$15 | AE, D, MC, V.

Torrefazione Italia. Café. The coffee is hot, hot, hot on Northwest 23rd. The best of the smaller cafés is Torrefazione Italia, which exudes a bright Italian charm and serves delicious coffee (none of it flavored) in Deruta ceramic cups. | 838 N.W. 23rd Ave. | 503/228–1255 | $5–$9.

Widmer Gasthaus. German. Enjoy traditional German food with a slight upscale flair at this casual pub located next to the Widmer brewery. The sandwiches are thick and the desserts are sinfully delicious. You can see into the brewery from your booth seat. Try the schnitzel, sauerbraten, or sausages with your Hefeweizen. There are sidewalk tables to complete the European feeling. No smoking. | 955 N. Russell St. | 503/281–3333 | No lunch Sun. | $8–$15 | AE, D, MC, V.

MODERATE

Al-Amir. Middle Eastern. Dishes at this downtown restaurant that features Middle Eastern cuisine include broiled kebabs, falafel, hummus, tabbouleh, and baba ghanoush. Kids' menu. No smoking. | 223 S.W. Stark St. | 503/274–0010 | Reservations essential (Fri., Sat.) | No lunch weekends | $15–$20 | AE, D, DC, MC, V.

Alexis. Greek. In addition to all the traditional Greek favorites that focus on lamb, favorite entrées include deep fried squid, and Garithes souvlaki, shrimp marinated and charbroiled on a skewer. There is music and a belly dancer Fri. and Sat. | 215 W. Burnside St., | 503/224–8577 | Closed Sun. No lunch Sat. | $16–$25 | AE, D, MC, V.

Brewhouse Taproom. Contemporary. The copper beer-making equipment at the door tips you off to the specialty of the house—beer. The restaurant is part of a 27,000-square-ft brewery complex. Try the MacTarnahan's fish and chips: The batter is made with the Brewhouse's signature ale. The haystack back ribs with garlic rosemary fries are popular. Asparagus artichoke lasagne served with salad is a good vegetarian option. Eat it all on the patio overlooking the landscaped garden. Kids' menu. No smoking. | 2730 N.W. 31st Ave. | 503/228–5269 | $16–$24 | AE, MC, V.

Bush Garden. Japanese. This authentic Japanese restaurant, which opened in 1960, is known for its sashimi and sukiyaki but also offers traditional favorites such as udon noodles, bento, tempura, and teriyaki. There is karaoke singing Mon.–Sat. | 900 S.W. Morrison St. | 503/226–7181 | No lunch weekends | $13–$25 | AE, D, DC, MC, V.

Café Azul. Mexican. Café Azul moved from McMinnville to the early 20th-century Graphic Arts Building in Portland's Pearl district. The small dining room with an open kitchen is warm with gold and pumpkin colors beneath a high ceiling and huge beams. The chef here, formerly at Chez Panisse in Berkeley, California, prepares regional Mexican cuisine, emphasizing fresh vegetables, handmade corn tortillas, wild herbs, salted fish, and salads. Specialties include various Mexican sauces and spicy marinated pork wrapped in banana leaves and braised in the juice of Seville oranges. | 112 N.W. 9th Ave. | 503/525–4422 | Closed Sun.–Mon. No lunch | $16.50–$26.50 | D, DC, MC, V.

Chart House. Contemporary. Located on a hill high above the Willamette River, the Chart House offers a panoramic view of the city and the surrounding mountains. Known for prime rib, but try the coconut-crunchy shrimp covered in tempura batter and deep-fried, available as an entrée or appetizer. Kids' menu. No smoking. | 5700 S.W. Terwilliger Blvd. | 503/246–6963 | No lunch weekends | $20–$30 | AE, D, DC, MC, V.

Huber's. American. Turkey supper with all the fresh-made trimmings and Spanish coffee is Huber's claim to fame. But they also serve steaks and other home style meals. | 411 S.W. 3rd Ave. | 503/228–5686 | Reservations not accepted (for lunch or Mon.–Thurs., Sat.) | Closed Sun. | $14–$26 | AE, D, DC, MC, V.

Il Fornaio. Italian. This outpost of the San Francisco–based trattoria and bakery serves handmade pastas, pizzas, and sandwiches. A cuisine from a different region of Italy is featured every month. Many dishes are cooked in a wood-burning pizza oven and rotisserie. Try the pizza con la luganega, the pollo toscano, or the grigliata di vitello. Kids' menu. Sun. brunch. No smoking. | 115 N.W. 22nd Ave. | 503/248–9400 | $16–$36 | AE, D, MC, V.

Ivy House. Continental. This restaurant offers upscale dining in a kid-friendly environment. The Pacific Northwest cuisine includes wild mushroom risotto with Asiago cheese and grilled steelhead trout with smoked tomato-and-cucumber salsa. Try the Ivy House salmon with a toasted hazelnut crust bathed in a cider and Reisling sauce. There are two play areas for kids and seating outside on the patio in the center of a blooming rose garden. Weekend brunch. Beer and wine only. | 1605 S.E. Bybee Blvd. | 503/231–9528 | $18–$26 | MC, V.

Jake's Grill. American. Home-style cooking rules at this casual restaurant in the Governor Hotel. Grilled steaks, salmon, chicken breast, burgers, and garlic mashed potatoes are popular selections. Dine at street level in intimate wooden booths set in front of windows with curtains or have a drink at the massive mahogany bar. On clear days dine at tables set out on the sidewalk. Kids' menu. | 611 S.W. 10th Ave. | 503/220–1850 | Breakfast also available | $14–$28 | AE, D, MC, V.

L'Auberge. French. Fresh Pacific Northwest ingredients are used in the entrées at this elegant tri-level French dining room with two fireplaces. A bistro menu is available at the bar. Try the marinated quail crêpe with vegetables or the potato-crusted halibut with curried sauce. Dine outside on the backyard deck surrounded by flowers and trees. | 2601 N.W. Vaughn St. | 503/223–3302 | No lunch weekends | $21–$39 | AE, D, DC, MC, V.

Mazzi's Italian-Sicilian Food. Italian. Enjoy fresh calzone, pastas, and seafood at this cozy dining room with fireplaces and a Mediterranean-style interior. Salad bar (lunch). No smoking. | 5833 S.W. Macadam Ave., | 503/227–3382 | No lunch weekends | $15–$20 | AE, MC, V.

Newport Bay at RiverPlace. Seafood. The circular glass room, literally floating on the Willamette River, provides city-skyline views along with your meal. Newport Bay serves whatever seafood is in season worldwide: Oregon spring salmon, Maine lobster, Australian lobster tail, Alaskan halibut, New Zealand roughy, as well as swordfish, marlin, and shark. | 0425 S.W. Montgomery St. | 503/227–3474 | $14.95–$22.95 | AE, D, DC, MC, V.

Papa Haydn. Continental. Many patrons come here just for the luscious European pastries and desserts, but this corner restaurant also makes a convenient lunch or supper stop. For lunch, try the mesquite-grilled chicken breast sandwich on a roll with bacon, avocado, basil, and tomato. Favorite supper entrées are the Bresola filet mignon and the pan-seared pork medallions with a pear tarragon demi-glace. There are sidewalk tables for people-watching in the Nob Hill neighborhood. Sun. brunch. Beer and wine only. | 5829 S.E. Milwaukee | 503/232–9440 | Reservations essential (for Sun. brunch) | $22–$35 | AE, MC, V.

Pazzo Ristorante. Italian. The aromas of roasted garlic and wood smoke greet patrons at this bustling street-level dining room. Pazzo's frequently changing menu relies on simple Italian cuisine—pastas, risottos, grilled meats, seafood, and poultry. The decor is a mix of dark wood, Italian marble floors, and dangling Parma hams. There's a mahogany bar and dining in the wine cellar and tables set up for sidewalk dining. | 624 S.W. Washington St. | 503/228–1515 | Breakfast also available | $23–$36 | AE, D, DC, MC, V.

Perry's on Fremont. Contemporary. This diner, still famous for burgers, chicken pot pies, and fish and chips, recently went a bit more upscale with the addition of pricier menu items such as steak and salmon. Eat outside on the large patio among the flowers. Kids' menu. No smoking. | 2401 N.E. Fremont St. | 503/287–3655 | Closed Sun.–Mon. No lunch Tues.–Fri. | $12–$22 | AE, D, MC, V.

Plainfield's Mayur. Indian. Portland's finest Indian cuisine is served in a Victorian mansion amid quietly elegant surroundings or on the secluded patio surrounded by trees, flower beds and gazebo. The dining room surrounds an Indian clay oven. The tomato-curry soup and *dahi wadi* (crispy fried lentil croquettes) are popular. Try the lobster in brown onion sauce and Tandoori chicken. | 852 S.W. 21st Ave. | 503/223–2995 | www.plainfields.com | No lunch | $20–$35 | AE, D, DC, MC, V.

Red Star Tavern and Roast House. Contemporary. Entrées are cooked in the wood-roasting oven or on the wood grill in the contemporary dining room to prepare what this restaurant calls regional American cuisine. Try the Chilean spiced marinated spit-roast chicken with southwestern blue potato hash. | 503 S.W. Alder St. | 503/222–0005 | Breakfast also available | $19–$35 | AE, D, DC, MC, V.

Rheinlander. German. A strolling accordionist and singing servers entertain as patrons dine on authentic traditional German food including sauerbraten, hasenpfeffer, schnitzel, sausage, and rotisserie chicken. Kids' menu. Early-bird suppers. | 5035 N.E. Sandy Blvd. | 503/288–5503 | $15–$27 | AE, MC, V.

Salty's on the Columbia. Contemporary. Pacific Northwest salmon (choose blackened or grilled, a half or full pound) is what this comfortable restaurant overlooking the Columbia River is known for. Try the seafood pesto fettuccine with prawns, scallops, halibut, salmon, grape tomatoes, pine nuts, and pesto. The menu includes chicken and steak offerings. There is a heated, covered deck and an uncovered deck for open-air dining. Kids' menu. Sun. brunch buffet. | 3839 N.E. Marine Dr. | 503/288–4444 | $28–$54 | AE, D, DC, MC, V.

Sayler's Old Country Kitchen. Steak. Home of the massive 72-ounce steak, Sayler's is less trendy and more family style. They serve all types of locally raised beef with one of the most extensive steak menus around. Kids' menu. | 10519 S.E. Stark St. | 503/252–4171 | No lunch | $15–$25 | AE, D, MC, V.

Sylvia's Class Act. Italian. This combo restaurant–dinner theater offers multiple dining options: Dine in a private candlelit booth, family style, in a banquet room setting, in the lounge away from the kids, or in the theater. The food is classic southern Italian. Try the spinach lasagne or fettucine Ricardo with strips of boneless chicken breast, zucchini, and onions tossed in an Alfredo sauce. Kids' menu, early-bird suppers. | 5115 N.E. Sandy Blvd. | 503/288–6828 | Reservations essential (for theater) | No lunch | $18–$32 | AE, D, MC, V.

Typhoon! Thai. A Buddha with burning incense watches over diners at this trendy restaurant in the Imperial Hotel. Come here for excellent Thai food at reasonable prices in a cozy but lively atmosphere. The spicy chicken or shrimp with crispy basil, the curry and noodle dishes, and the vegetarian spring rolls are standouts. It's packed for lunch but never feels uncomfortably crowded. Jazz performances on weekend evenings. Beer and wine only. | 400 S.W. Broadway | 503/224–8285 | Closed Sun. No lunch Sat. | $15–$30 | AE, D, DC, MC, V.

EXPENSIVE

Alessandro's. Italian. This cozy eatery turns out Roman-style Italian pastas and entrées made with seafood, poultry, and veal. Try the cioppino, or filetti Rossini, two filet medallions with portabello mushrooms and pancetta bacon, laced with a red wine sauce. No smoking. | 301 S.W. Morrison St. | 503/222–3900 | Reservations essential | No lunch Sun. | $20–$30 | AE, DC, MC, V.

Cafe Des Amis. French. Entrée selections at this intimate restaurant include filet of beef with garlic in a port sauce, salmon, duck, and grilled pork loin. No smoking. | 1987 N.W. Kearney St. | 503/295–6487 | Closed Sun. No lunch | $23–$38 | AE, MC, V.

Caprial's. Eclectic. This small bistro and wine bar uses fresh Pacific Northwest ingredients. The supper menu offers only a few choices including chicken, salmon, steak, and a Portobello mushroom dish. At lunch choose from pasta, sandwiches, crab, and fish and chips. No smoking. | 7015 S.E. Milwaukee Ave. | 503/236–6457 | Reservations essential | Closed Sun.–Mon. | $30–$35 | MC, V.

Couch Street Seafood and Fine Steaks. Seafood. This famous fish house added an expanded selection of steaks to its menu and amended its name. It is known for Chinook salmon, live Maine lobster and Dungeness crab. Try the fillet tenderloin served with a shiitake mushroom demi-glaze. Early bird supper. No smoking. | 105 N.W. 3rd Ave. | 503/223–6173 | No lunch | $30–$50 | AE, D, MC, V.

★ **Couvron.** French. This is Portland's finest restaurant for contemporary French cuisine. Signature dishes include a honey-glazed Oregon duck breast with curry and anise, a pan-roasted foie gras with summer truffles and diced organic root vegetables in a red wine sauce, rack of lamb, and sautéed salmon mignon on a chiffonade potato cake with stewed leeks. No smoking. | 1126 S.W. 18th Ave. | 503/225–1844 | Reservations essential | Closed Sun.–Mon. No lunch | $25–$50 | AE, D, MC, V.

Esplanade at Riverplace. Continental. You'll find both fine cuisine and a good view in this split-level dining room. Large windows look out over the Willamette River. Fresh Pacific Northwest ingredients are used in the country French dishes and inventive Northwestern regional cuisine. Try the risotto made with halibut and peas. There is dining on the terrace, the bar-deck, and a patio all overlooking a landscaped garden and the water. Kids' menu. Sun. brunch. No smoking. | 1510 S.W. Harbor Way | 503/228–3233 | Breakfast also available | $22–$35 | AE, D, MC, V.

★ **Heathman.** Contemporary. Fresh fish, game, wild mushrooms, and other ingredients of the Northwest are featured. The menu changes with the season and may include seared ahi tuna, roasted pesto salmon, and lamb. The 1927 Heathman Hotel's formal dining room, scented with wood smoke and adorned with Andy Warhol prints, is a favorite for special occasions. Sit on the sidewalk at one of the six tables shaded by umbrellas. Entertainment. | 1001 S.W. Broadway | 503/790–7752 | Breakfast also available | $20–$50 | AE, D, DC, MC, V.

Jake's Famous Crawfish. Seafood. Diners have been enjoying fresh Northwest seafood in Jake's warren of wood-paneled dining rooms for more than a century—the back bar came around Cape Horn during the 1880s, and the chandeliers hanging from the high ceilings date from 1881. But it wasn't until 1920, when crawfish was added to the menu, that the restaurant began to get a national reputation. Try to come during crawfish season, from May to September, when you can sample the tasty crustacean in pie, cooked Creole style, or in a Cajun-style stew over rice. | 401 S.W. 12th Ave. | 503/226–1419 | No lunch weekends | $30–$40 | AE, D, DC, MC, V.

London Grill. Continental. The plush dining room in the historic Benson Hotel serves classic dishes made with fresh, seasonal local ingredients with an Asian influence. Try the salmon glazed with sake and ginger. There is a harpist Wed.–Sat. Kids' menu. Sun. brunch. | 309 S.W. Broadway | 503/295–4110 | Jacket required (supper) | Breakfast also available | $30–$50 | AE, D, DC, MC, V.

Lucy's Table. Mediterranean. A quiet casual yet romantic setting. All the dishes are made with locally grown produce. Try the grilled beef tenderloin in a carmelized smoked tomato sauce or the Troll King salmon in roasted green grapes and almonds with a barley risotto. No smoking. | 704 N.W. 21st St. | 503/226–6126 | Closed Sun. No lunch | $25–$40 | AE, MC, V.

Paley's Place. French. This charming bistro in the trendy Northwest neighborhood features Pacific Northwest-style French cuisine. Paley's entrées include sweetbreads, duck, New York steak, chicken, pork tenderloin, and halibut. A vegetarian dish is also available. Kids' menu. No smoking. | 1204 N.W. 21st Ave. | 503/243–2403 | No lunch | $29–$48 | AE, MC, V.

Ringside. Steak. Red meat and onion rings are legendary at this popular restaurant. The atmosphere is macho with dark woods, red booths, and low light. The beef is 28-day-aged prime and choice Angus corn-fed from the Midwest. There's also a large selection of seafood including lobster, sandwiches, and a few chicken entrées. | 2165 W. Burnside St. | 503/223–1513 | No lunch | $20–$45 | AE, D, DC, MC, V.

Ringside East. Steak. This outpost has the same menu as the downtown Ringside (see below), but the atmosphere is more like a country club. | 14021 N.E. Glisan St. | 503/255–0750 | No lunch weekends | $23–$26 | AE, D, DC, MC, V.

Southpark. Seafood. One of Portland's newest fine restaurants, Southpark features wood-fired Mediterranean seafood. The art deco–tinged room is comfortable. There's a wide selection of fresh Pacific Northwest oysters and fine regional wines available by the glass. It's near the Arlene Schnitzer Concert Hall and the Portland Art Museum. Try the grilled grape leaf–wrapped salmon with pomegranate and sherry glaze, and tuna au poivre with mashed potatoes and red wine demi-glace. No smoking. | 901 S.W. Salmon St. | 503/326–1300 | $23–$40 | AE, D, DC, MC, V.

★ **Wildwood.** Contemporary. Blond wood chairs and a stainless steel open kitchen set the tone at this trendy Northwest neighborhood eatery. The entrée choices are plentiful, including dishes made with quail, lamb, pork loin, chicken, steak, and fish. There's also patio dining. Sun. brunch. | 1221 N.W. 21st Ave. | 503/248–9663 | $20–$50 | AE, MC, V.

Winterborne. French. The chef calls the seafood cuisine "Northwest with a French flavor." The atmosphere is intimate and relaxing with soft lighting. Splurge with the Bouillabaisse Royale, made with lobster tail, whitefish, mussels, and clams in a fish broth with saffron. All entrées come with soup, salad, and bread. Kids' menu. No smoking. | 3520 N.E. 42nd Ave. | 503/249–8486 | Closed Sun.–Tues. No lunch | $27–$35 | AE, D, MC, V.

VERY EXPENSIVE

Atwater's. Contemporary. Atwater's has an outstanding view of the Willamette River, the Cascade Range, and the city's skyline. The cuisine relies almost exclusively on ingredients indigenous to the Northwest—depending on the season, everything from fresh salmon to chicken, duck, and game. Dansk linens, silver cutlery, crystal glasses, and an orchid on every table lend a touch of elegance. Entertainment Wed.–Sat. Kids' menu. No smoking. | 111 S.W. 5th Ave. | 503/275–3622 | No lunch Sun. | $35–$60 | AE, D, DC, MC, V.

★ **Genoa.** Italian. This ten-table restaurant is widely regarded as the finest Italian restaurant in Portland. A seven-course, prix fixe menu is served on Friday and Saturday evenings while four courses are served weekdays. The menu changes every two weeks and focuses on genuine Italian cuisine. Poultry, meat, and fish main courses are offered. | 2832 S.E. Belmont St. | 503/238–1464 | Reservations essential | Closed Sun. No lunch | $50 | AE, D, DC, MC, V.

Higgins. Contemporary. Pacific Northwest ingredients are used in the traditional French dishes that incorporate other international influences. A lighter bistro menu is also available. Try the country-style terrine of venison, chicken, and pork with dried sour cherries and a roasted-garlic mustard, or the Alaskan spot prawns, Totten Inlet mussels, and halibut simmered in a tomato-saffron broth and served with spring vegetables. Kids' menu. No smoking. | 1239 S.W. Broadway | 503/222–9070 | No lunch weekends | $35–$45 | AE, D, DC, MC, V.

Lodging

INEXPENSIVE

Best Western Fortniter Motel. Rooms here near the airport have a lived-in, put-your-feet-up feel. The motel provides a shuttle to a nearby restaurant. Public transportation to downtown Portland is close by. | 52 rooms. Complimentary Continental breakfast. kitchenettes, refrigerators, pool, laundry facilities, laundry service, airport shuttle, parking (fee in summer). | 4911 N.E. 82nd Ave. | 503/255–9771 | fax 503/255–9774 | www.bestwestern.com | $60–$72 | AE, D, DC, MC, V.

Best Western Inn at the Convention Center. Rooms are done in pleasing creams and rusts, and those with king-size beds usually have wet bars. The hotel is four blocks west of Lloyd Center, directly across the street from the Portland Convention Center, and on the MAX line. | 97 rooms. Coffee shop, laundry facilities, free parking. | 420 N.E. Holladay St. | 503/233–6331 | fax 503/233–2677 | www.bestwestern.com | $70–$119 | AE, D, DC, MC, V.

Best Western—Rose Garden Hotel. The Rose Garden Arena and Lloyd Center are in walking distance of this motel on the east side of the river. It's near the MAX light rail. | 181 rooms. Restaurant, bar, in-room data ports, room service, cable TV, indoor pool, business services. | 10 N. Weidler | 503/287–9900 | fax 503/287–3500 | $79–$99 | AE, D, DC, MC, V.

Chestnut Tree Inn. An inexpensive option near Portland Airport. This inn is close to the mall and area restaurants. | 58 rooms. Refrigerators, cable TV, business services. | 9699 S.E. Stark St. | 503/255–4444 | $45–$56 | AE, DC, MC, V.

Clinkerbrick House. This gabled 1908 Dutch Colonial, surrounded by gardens and stately chestnut trees, is in northeast Portland's Irvington neighborhood. Pine cabinets, a corner bench, brickwork, and leaded-glass cabinetry create the atmosphere, and there's a quiet back patio for breakfast on fine mornings. Guest rooms have their own entrance. The largest, the Garden Room, has a private balcony and windows on three sides. A kitchen, phone, and TV are in the common room. | 1 double room with shower, 2 doubles share bath. Complimentary breakfast, no smoking. | 2311 N.E. Schuyler St. | 503/281–2533 | fax 503/281–1281 | clinker@teleport.com | $55–$70 | MC, V.

Courtyard by Marriott—Airport. Only 8 mi from downtown Portland, this medium-sized hotel has a trail on the property that runs along the Columbia River. | 140 rooms, 10 suites. Restaurant, bar, refrigerators (in suites), room service, cable TV, some in-room VCRs, pool, hot tub, exercise equipment, laundry facilities, business services, airport shuttle. | 11550 N.E. Airport Way | 503/252–3200 | fax 503/252–8921 | $69–$102, $118 suites | AE, D, DC, MC, V.

Days Inn—North. Set in a commercial neighborhood, this inn is convenient to the Expo Center and the Portland International Raceway. Many rooms have views of Mt. Hood. | 213 rooms. Complimentary Continental breakfast, in-room data ports, cable TV, laundry facilities, business services, airport shuttle, pets allowed (fee). | 9930 N. Whitaker Rd. | 503/289–1800 or 800/833–1800 | fax 503/289–3778 | $65–$85 | AE, D, DC, MC, V.

Days Inn—South. Although the setting is residential, this Days Inn is within walking distance of many restaurants. It's a 25-minute drive to downtown Portland. | 110 rooms. Complimentary Continental breakfast, some refrigerators, cable TV, pool, hot tub, business services, airport shuttle. | 9717 S.E. Sunnyside Rd., Clackamas | 503/654–1699 | fax 503/659–2702 | $64–$95 | AE, D, DC, MC, V.

Fairfield Inn by Marriott—Airport. Fifteen mi from downtown Portland, this hotel is great for those traveling on business. | 106 rooms. Complimentary Continental breakfast, cable TV, pool, hot tub, exercise equipment, business services, airport shuttle. | 11929 N.E. Airport Way | 503/253–1400 | fax 503/253–3889 | $69–$73 | AE, D, DC, MC, V.

General Hooker's. Rooms at this small bed and breakfast in an 1888 Victorian house are bright and decorated with quilts, antiques, and rattan. It's within walking distance of Portland's Saturday Market. The roof-top deck provides views of the city. | 4 rooms (2 with shared bath, 1 with shower only). Complimentary Continental breakfast, cable TV, in-room VCRs (movies), no kids under 10. | 125 S.W. Hooker St. | 503/222–4435 or 800/745–4135 | fax 503/295–6410 | www.generalhookers.com | $75–$150 | AE, MC, V.

Georgian House. This red brick Georgian Colonial–style house with neoclassical columns is on a quiet, tree-lined street in the Irvington neighborhood. The gardens in back can be enjoyed from a solarium and from a vine-canopied deck and gazebo. The largest and sunniest of the guest rooms is the Lovejoy Suite, with a tile fireplace and brass canopy bed. | 1 double room with bath, 2 doubles share 1½ baths, 1 suite. Complimentary breakfast, air-conditioning, 2 rooms have TVs, 1 room has gas fireplace, no room phones, TV in common area, no smoking. | 1828 N.E. Siskiyou St. | 503/281–2250 or 888/282–2250 | fax 503/281–3301 | www.thegeorgianhouse.com | $65–$100 | MC, V.

Hawthorne Inn and Suites This hotel is close to the airport and restaurants. | 71 rooms, 23 suites. Complimentary Continental breakfast, in-room data ports, some refrigerators, cable TV, indoor pool, hot tub, exercise equipment, some pets allowed, laundry facilities, business services. | 2323 N.E. 181st Ave. Gresham | 503/492–4000 | fax 503/492–3271 | $73–$83, $90–$130 suites | AE, D, DC, MC, V.

Howard Johnson Express Inn. This motel is located in a quiet, park-like setting in suburban Tigard, away from the noise of the freeway. Downtown Portland is 5 mi away. | 117 rooms. Complimentary Continental breakfast, cable TV, pool, business services. | 11460 S.W. Pacific Hwy., Tigard | 503/245–6421 or 800/547–8828 | fax 503/245–6425 | $62–$86 | AE, D, DC, MC, V.

Mallory Hotel. The years have been kind to this 1920s-vintage hotel eight blocks from the downtown core. Its gilt-ceiling lobby has fresh white paint and floral carpeting; crystal chandeliers and a leaded-glass skylight hark back to a more genteel era. The rooms are old-fashioned but clean and cheerful and have been refurbished; corner suites and rooms on the east side of the building have impressive skyline views. The staff is friendly and knowledgeable. | 131 rooms, 10 suites. Restaurant, bar, some refrigerators, cable TV, business services, pets allowed (fee). | 729 S.W. 15th Ave. | 503/223–6311 or 800/228–8657 | fax 503/223–0522 | $75–$140, $140 suites | AE, D, DC, MC, V.

Mark Spencer. Located near Portland's gay bar district and Powell's City of Books, the world's largest bookstore, the Mark Spencer offers one of the best values in town. The rooms are clean and comfortable. It's also near the MAX light rail and Jake's seafood restaurant. There is a rooftop garden. | 101 rooms. Complimentary Continental breakfast, kitchenettes, cable TV, laundry facilities, business services, pets allowed (fee). | 409 S.W. 11th Ave. | 503/224–3293 or 800/548–3934 | fax 503/223–7848 | mspencer@ipinc.net | www.markspencer.com | $79–$129 | AE, D, DC, MC, V.

Radisson Hotel. This modern Radisson on the east side of the river has bright rooms. It's near the Rose Garden Arena and Lloyd Center. | 240 rooms. Restaurant, bar, cable TV, pool, exercise equipment, business services, airport shuttle. | 1441 N.E. 2nd Ave. | 503/233–2401 | fax 503/238–7016 | $89–$149 | AE, D, DC, MC, V.

Ramada Inn—Airport. Rooms at this Ramada 2 mi from the airport have comfortable and perfect for short stays. | 202 rooms. Restaurant, bar, room service, cable TV, pool, hot tub, exercise equipment, laundry facilities, business services, airport shuttle. | 6221 N.E. 82nd Ave. | 503/255–6511 | fax 503/255–8417 | $70–$89 | AE, D, DC, MC, V.

Red Lion Inn Coliseum. The restaurant and many of the rooms here overlook both the Willamette River and a railroad line, so courtside rooms are quieter. The rooms, done in pinks, whites, mauve, and sea-foam green, have queen-size beds and modern oak furnishings. | 211 rooms. Restaurant, bar, room service, pool, laundry service, airport shuttle, free parking. | 1225 N. Thunderbird Way | 503/235–8311 | fax 503/232–2670 | $79–$89 | AE, D, DC, MC, V.

Sheraton—Portland Airport. Prices at this chain hotel near the airport are a bit lower than at other hotels in the area. It has clean, comfortable, standard rooms. | 213 rooms. Restaurant, bars, minibars, room service, cable TV, indoor pool, hot tub, exercise equipment, business services, airport shuttle. | 8235 N.E. Airport Way | 503/281–2500 | fax 503/249–7602 | $89–$149 | AE, D, DC, MC, V.

Shilo Inn. The rooms and suites are plush and cozy at this hotel, which is ten minutes from downtown. There's a courtyard with a gazebo and fountains. | 136 rooms, 6 suites. Restaurant, bar with entertainment, complimentary Continental breakfast, refrigerators, room service, cable TV, pool, pond, exercise equipment, business services, airport shuttle. | 9900 S.W. Canyon Rd. | 503/297–2551 or 800/222–2244 | fax 503/297–7708 | $69–$79, $99–$175 suites | AE, D, DC, MC, V.

Shilo Inn—Washington Square. This motel just south of Portland is next to Washington Square Mall. The rooms are modern and have in-room first-run movies. | 77 rooms. Complimentary Continental breakfast, some kitchenettes, cable TV, exercise equipment, laundry facilities, business services, pets allowed (fee). | 10830 S.W. Greenburg Rd., Tigard | 503/620–4320 | fax 503/620–8277 | $69–$89 | AE, D, DC, MC, V.

Super 8. An inexpensive option if you need to stay on the far south side of the metropolitan area. | 72 rooms. Cable TV, laundry facilities, business services, pets allowed (fee). | 25438 S.W. Parkway Ave., Wilsonville | 503/682–2088 | fax 503/682–0453 | $43–$61 | AE, D, DC, MC, V.

Sweetbrier Inn. This inn is approximately 10 mi south of Portland. The large rooms feature traditional-style furniture and have views of a garden with tall firs. | 100 rooms, 32 suites. Restaurant, bar with entertainment, picnic area, in-room data ports, refrigerators (in suites), room service, cable TV, pool, playground, business services, pets allowed (fee). | 7125 S.W. Nyberg, Tualatin | 503/692–5800 or 800/551–9167 | fax 503/691–2894 | www.sweetbrierinn.com | $75–$115, $120 suites | AE, D, DC, MC, V.

Travelodge. The Rose Garden arena, Memorial Coliseum, and Oregon Convention Center are all only three blocks away, and several restaurants are within easy walking distance. | 44 rooms. Complimentary Continental breakfast, sauna, laundry facilities, airport shuttle, free parking. | 1506 N.E. 2nd Ave., 97232 | 503/231–7665 | fax 503/236–6040 | $59–$99 | AE, D, DC, MC, V.

Travelodge. This small downtown motel is about 1 mi from Portland State University and right next to Portland's sports venues. | 40 rooms, 2 suites. Restaurant, bar, some refrigerators, cable TV, pool, business services. | 2401 S.W. 4th Ave. | 503/226–1121 or 800/248–0506 | fax 503/274–2681 | $50–$70, $65–$85 suites | AE, D, DC, MC, V.

Tudor House. This 5,400-square-ft house, set on extensive grounds edged with laurel bushes, hawthorn trees, and azaleas, resembles a Tudor manor. Antiques crowd the house, the guest rooms, and the dining room where breakfast is served. | 1 double room with bath, 2 doubles share bath, 1 suite. Complimentary breakfast, cable TV, in-room VCRs, room phones, no smoking. | 2321 N.E. 28th Ave. | 503/287–9476 | fax 503/288–8363 | www.moriah.com/tudor | $75–$100 | AE, D, MC, V.

MODERATE

Best Western Pony Soldier—Airport. This property is a good choice if you want to stay near the airport. The building surrounds a pleasant courtyard with pool. Only 8 mi to downtown Portland. | 103 rooms, 15 suites. Complimentary Continental breakfast. Some in-room hot tubs, cable TV, pool, hot tub, exercise equipment, laundry facilities, business services,

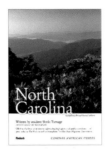

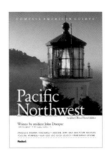

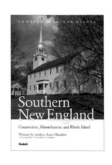

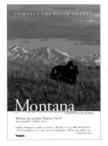

airport shuttle. | 9901 N.E. Sandy Blvd. | 503/256–1504 or 800/634–7669 | fax 503/256–5928 | www.bestwestern.com | $98–$118, $123 suites | AE, D, DC, MC, V.

Days Inn–City Center. Free parking is a premium at this downtown motel only blocks from entertainment, restaurants, and Portland State University. It's near the MAX light rail. The rooms are bright and comfortable. | 173 rooms. Restaurant, bar, in-room data ports, room service, cable TV, pool, business services. | 1414 S.W. 6th Ave., | 503/221–1611 or 800/899–0248 | fax 503/226–0447 | $109–$129 | AE, D, DC, MC, V.

Doubletree—Columbia River. On Hayden Island between Portland and Vancouver, Wash., this Doubletree is convenient to downtown and the airport. Rooms are decorated in earth tones and many have riverfront views. | 351 rooms. Restaurants, bars with entertainment, in-room data ports, some refrigerators, room service, some in-room hot tubs, cable TV, pool, beauty salon, putting green, business services, airport shuttle, pets allowed (fee). | 1401 N. Hayden Island Dr. | 503/283–2111 | fax 503/283–4718 | $109–$139 | AE, D, DC, MC, V.

Doubletree—Jantzen Beach. On the banks of the Columbia River, there is a beautiful rose garden around the pool. | 320 rooms. Restaurant, bar with entertainment, room service, some in-room hot tubs, cable TV, pool, hot tub, tennis, exercise equipment, dock, business services, airport shuttle, pets allowed (fee). | 909 N. Hayden Island Dr. | 503/283–4466 | fax 503/283–4743 | $119–$129 | AE, D, DC, MC, V.

★ **Doubletree—Lloyd Center.** This busy, well-appointed, business-oriented hotel maintains a huge traffic in meetings and special events. The public areas are a tasteful mix of marble, rose-and-green carpet, and antique-style furnishings. The large rooms have views of the mountains or the city center. Lloyd Center and the MAX light rail are across the street; the Oregon Convention Center is a five-minute walk away. | 382 rooms, 17 suites. Restaurant, bar with entertainment, refrigerators, some in-room hot tubs, cable TV, pool, exercise equipment, business services, airport shuttle, pets allowed. | 1000 N.E. Multnomah St. | 503/281–6111 | fax 503/284–8553 | $139–$149, $269–$575 suites | AE, D, DC, MC, V.

Heron Haus. This lovely bed-and-breakfast is inside a stately, three-story 90-year-old Tudor mansion near Forest Park. Special features include a tulip-shape bathtub in one room and a tiled, seven-headed antique shower in another. All rooms have work desks and fireplaces. | 6 rooms. Complimentary Continental breakfast, in-room data ports, cable TV, movies, pool, business services, no smoking. | 2545 N.W. Westover Rd. | 503/274–1846 | fax 503/248–4055 | www.europa.com/~hhaus | $135–$185 | MC, V.

Hilton Portland. The Hilton is located within walking distance of the Performing Arts Center, Pioneer Courthouse Square, the Portland Art Museum, and the MAX light rail. Alexander's restaurant, specializing in Pacific Northwest cuisine, offers a panoramic view of the Portland metro area from the 23rd floor. More than 60 restaurants are within three blocks. | 455 rooms. Restaurant, bar with entertainment, in-room data ports, cable TV, indoor pool, beauty salon, exercise equipment, business services, parking (fee). | 921 S.W. 6th Ave. | 503/226–1611 | fax 503/220–2565 | $99–$195 | AE, D, DC, MC, V.

Holiday Inn—Airport. The somewhat plainly decorated rooms here are 2 mi from the airport. | 286 rooms. Restaurant, bar, room service, cable TV, indoor pool, hot tub, exercise equipment, video games, laundry facilities, business services, airport shuttle. | 8439 N.E. Columbia Blvd. | 503/256–5000 | fax 503/257–4742 | $89–$118 | AE, D, DC, MC, V.

Imperial Hotel. This restored downtown hotel preserves its historic charm with a lobby that has the original columns and moldings dating from 1908. There is some antique furniture in the lobby; however, the rooms are standard. It's conveniently located near restaurants, entertainment, and the MAX light rail. The Typhoon! Thai restaurant is off the lobby. | 136 rooms. Restaurant, in-room data ports, cable TV, pets allowed (fee). | 400 S.W. Broadway | 503/228–7221 or 800/452–2323 | fax 503/223–4551 | $85–$125 | AE, D, DC, MC, V.

Lion and the Rose. This 1906 Queen Anne–style mansion, built for a brewing magnate, is one of Portland's premier B&Bs. Oak and mahogany floors, original light fixtures, antique silver, and the coffered dining room ceiling set a tone of formal elegance. Guest rooms and the three-course breakfast are equally opulent, and afternoon tea is available. The inn is just a block from Northeast Broadway in an area filled with fine restaurants and shopping. | 4 double rooms with baths, 2 doubles share bath. Air-conditioning, in-room data ports, television, no smoking. | 1810 N.E. 15th Ave. | 503/287–9245 or 800/955–1647 | fax 503/287–9247 | www.lionrose.com | $99–$140 | AE, MC, V.

★ **MacMaster House.** This comfortable 1886 Colonial Revival mansion is on King's Hill, less than 10 minutes by foot from fashionable Northwest 23rd Avenue. A mixture of Victorian furniture and antiques fills the parlors. The spacious Artist's Studio, tucked garretlike under the dormers, has a high brass bed and fireplace. | 5 double rooms share 2 ½ baths, 2 suites. Air-conditioning, cable TV, free parking, no smoking. | 1041 S.W. Vista Ave. | 503/223–7362 or 800/774–9523 | fax 503/224–8808 | www.macmaster.com | $80–$120 | AE, D, DC, MC, V.

Marriott. The large rooms here are decorated in off-whites; the best ones look east to the Willamette and the Cascades. Champions Lounge, filled with sports memorabilia, is a singles' hot spot on weekends. It's near the MAX light rail. | 503 rooms. Restaurant, bar with entertainment, some, refrigerators, cable TV, indoor pool, hot tub, exercise equipment, laundry facilities, business services, pets allowed. | 1401 S.W. Naito Pkwy. | 503/226–7600 | fax 503/221–1789 | www.marriott.com | $114–$159 | AE, D, DC, MC, V.

Portland's White House. Hardwood floors with oriental rugs, chandeliers, antiques, and fountains create a warm and romantic mood at this elegant bed and breakfast inn in a Greek Revival mansion in the historic Irvington district. The mansion, built in 1911, is on the National Register of Historic Landmarks. Rooms have mahogany canopy or four-poster queen- and king-size beds. | 9 rooms. Complimentary breakfast, in-room data ports, video game room, business services, no smoking. | 1914 N.E. 22nd Ave. | 503/287–7131 | fax 503/249–1641 | www.portlandswhitehouse.com | $98–$159 | AE, MC, V.

Sheraton Four Points. This hotel is decorated in a classic European style and is conveniently located downtown, close to shopping and restaurants. Guests receive complimentary access to a nearby health club. | 139 rooms, 1 suite. Restaurant, bar, room service, business services, parking (fee), some pets allowed (fee). | 50 S.W. Morrison St. | 503/221–0711 or 800/899–0247 | fax 503/274–0312 | $90–$170, $200–$250 suite | AE, D, DC, MC, V.

Silver Cloud Inn. Comfortable rooms, conveniently located in downtown Portland, are within walking distance of a major shopping area, restaurants, and Forest Park, which offers 50 mi of hiking and walking trails. | 81 rooms. Complimentary Continental breakfast, in-room data ports, some refrigerators, cable TV, hot tub, exercise equipment, laundry facilities, business services. | 2426 N.W. Vaughn St. | 503/242–2400 or 800/551–7207 | fax 503/242–1770 | $99–$139 | AE, D, DC, MC, V.

EXPENSIVE

The Benson. Portland's grandest hotel was built in 1912. The hand-carved Russian Circassian walnut paneling and the Italian white-marble staircase are among the noteworthy design touches in the public areas. In the guest rooms expect to find small crystal chandeliers, inlaid mahogany doors, and the original ceilings. | 286 rooms, 44 suites. Restaurant, bar with entertainment, in-room data ports, minibars, room service, cable TV, exercise equipment, business services, airport shuttle, pets allowed (fee), parking (fee). | 309 S.W. Broadway | 503/471–3920 | fax 503/226–4603 | $140–$225, $199–$275 suites | AE, D, DC, MC, V.

5th Avenue Suites. The 1912 Lipman Wolfe Department Store building reopened as a boutique hotel in 1997. It is designed to look like a turn-of-the-20th-century, American country home. A tall vestibule with a marble mosaic floor leads to the art-filled lobby. Curtained sliding doors divide the 10-story property's 550-square-ft suites. The large bathrooms are stocked with every amenity. | 221 rooms, 139 suites. Restaurant, bar, complimentary Continental breakfast, in-room data ports, refrigerators, cable TV, in-room VCRs (movies), exercise equipment, business services, some pets allowed. | 506 S.W. Washington | 503/222–0001 or 800/711–2971 | fax 503/222–0004 | $160–$180, $180–$275 suites | AE, D, DC, MC, V.

★ **The Governor.** With its mahogany walls and mural of Northwest Indians fishing in Celilo Falls, the clubby lobby of the distinctive Governor sets the overall tone for the hotel's 1920s Arts and Crafts style. Painted in soothing earth tones, the guest rooms have large windows; some have fireplaces. Jake's Grill is located off the lobby. | 100 rooms, 32 suites. Restaurant, bar, minibars, refrigerators, room service, some in-room hot tubs, cable TV, indoor pool, barbershop, beauty salon, hot tub, gym, business services. | 611 S.W. 10th | 503/224–3400 or 800/554–3456 | fax 503/241–2122 | $155–$175, $200–$240 suites | AE, D, DC, MC, V.

★ **Heathman.** Superior service, an award-winning restaurant, a central downtown location (adjoining the Performing Arts Center), and swank public areas have earned the Heathman its reputation for quality. From the teak-panel lobby hung with Warhol prints to the rosewood elevators and marble fireplaces, this hotel exudes refinement. The guest rooms are luxuriously comfortable, if not overly spacious. | 115 rooms, 35 suites. Restaurant, 3 bars with entertainment, in-room data ports, minibars, room service, cable TV, exercise equipment, business services. | 1001 S.W. Broadway | 503/241–4100 or 800/551–0011 | fax 503/790–7110 | $135–$200, $180–$220 suites, $650 for master suite | AE, D, DC, MC, V.

Riverplace. This luxury resort is right on the Portland waterfront. The hotel, which has a decidedly European feel, overlooks the marina and the surrounding Riverplace neighborhood. All the rooms have beautiful wood paneling and some have fireplaces. | 84 rooms, 16 suites. Restaurant, bar with entertainment, complimentary Continental breakfast, in-room data ports, minibars, some refrigerators, room service, cable TV, hot tub, shops, business services, some pets allowed (fee), parking (fee). | 1510 S.W. Harbor Way | 503/228–3233 or 800/227–1333 | fax 503/295–6161 | www.riverplacehotel.com | $219, $219–$499 suites | AE, D, DC, MC, V.

Shilo Inn Suites—Airport. This all-suites property is modern and comfortable. Some of the rooms face a grove of fir trees and a small lake. | 200 suites. Restaurant, bar with entertainment, complimentary buffet breakfast, in-room data ports, microwaves, refrigerators, room service, cable TV, indoor pool, hot tub, exercise equipment, laundry facilities, business services, airport shuttle. | 11707 N.E. Airport Way | 503/252–7500 | fax 503/254–0794 | $149–$159 suites | AE, D, DC, MC, V.

Vintage Plaza. This historic building's dramatic decor was inspired by Oregon's wine industry and a vineyards motif is carried on throughout the European-style hotel. | 107 rooms, 23 suites. Restaurant, bar, in-room data ports, minibars, room service, cable TV, exercise equipment, business services. | 422 S.W. Broadway | 503/228–1212 or 800/243–0555 | fax 503/228–3598 | $150–$190, $325–$400 suites | AE, D, DC, MC, V.

PORT ORFORD

MAP 3, B7

(Nearby towns also listed: Bandon, Gold Beach)

The most westerly incorporated city in the contiguous United States, Port Orford is surrounded by forests, rivers, lakes, and, of course, beaches of the Pacific Ocean. The jetty at Port Orford offers little protection from storms, so every night the fishing boats are lifted out and stored on the docks. Commercial fishing boats search for crab, tuna, snapper, and salmon in the waters out of Port Orford, and diving boats gather sea urchins for Japanese markets. The area is a favorite spot for sport divers because of the near-shore, protected reef and for whale watchers in fall and early spring. Humbug Mountain State Park is especially popular with campers.

Information: Port Orford Chamber of Commerce | Box 637, Port Orford 97465 | 541/332–8055 | pochamb@harborside.com | www.portorfordoregon.com.

Attractions

Cape Blanco State Park. Oregon's most westerly point—jutting out more than a mile to sea—makes this park, which is 5 mi north of Port Orford, a good place to watch gray whales. There are 8 mi of trails through woodlands and wetlands with spectacular ocean vistas. An extra-large, private, wind-protected campground has 58 electrical sites and 4 cabins. | Off U.S. 101 on Cape Blanco Rd. | 541/332–6774 or 800/551–6949 | www.prd.state.or.us | $3 per vehicle day-use fee | Daily.

Humbug Mountain State Park. This campground, 6 mi south of Port Orford, usually has warm weather, thanks to the nearby mountains which block the ocean breezes. Windsurfing and scuba diving are popular here. Hiking trails lead to the top of Humbug Mountain. The campground has 30 electrical and 78 tent sites. | U.S. 101 | 541/332–6774 or 800/551–6949 | www.prd.state.or.us | $3 per vehicle day-use fee | Daily.

Lodging

Floras Lake House by the Sea. This 1991 cedar home is on freshwater Floras Lake, which is spring-fed and separated from the ocean by only a sand spit. The owners run a windsurfing school on the lake. The interior of the house is light, airy, and comfortable with picture windows, exposed beams, contemporary couches, and a wood stove. Two rooms have fireplaces and all have private deck entrances. Outside, there's a garden, with a sauna beside the lake. | 4 rooms. Complimentary breakfast, no room phones, no TV, lake, sauna, no smoking. | 92870 Boice Cope Rd., Langlois | 541/348–2573 | fax 541/348–9912 | floraslk@harborside.com | www.floraslake.com | $100–$130 | Closed mid-Nov.–mid-Feb. | D, MC, V.

Home by the Sea. This 1985 three-story shingle house is on a headland jutting into the Pacific. A nearby path leads down to the beach. Both guest rooms have views of the ocean, as does the lower-level solarium and breakfast room, a great spot for watching whales (Oct.–May is the best time) and winter storms. One room has a myrtlewood bed. | 2 rooms. Complimentary breakfast, no air-conditioning, in-room data ports, refrigerators, cable TV, room phones, laundry facilities, no smoking. | 444 Jackson St. | 541/332–2855 | alan@homebythesea.com | www.homebythesea.com | $95–$105 | MC, V.

PRINEVILLE

MAP 3, G5

(Nearby towns also listed: Bend, Madras, Redmond)

Prineville is the only incorporated city in Crook County. In its colorful past, Prineville has seen Indian raids, range wars between sheepmen and cattlemen, and vigilante justice. Home to tire magnate Les Schwab, the Prineville area attracts thousands of hunters, anglers, boaters, sightseers, and rock hounds to its nearby streams, reservoirs, and mountains. Rimrocks nearly encircle Prineville, and rock hounds dig for free agates, limb casts, jasper, and thunder eggs on mining claims provided by the local chamber of commerce.

Information: Prineville-Crook County Chamber of Commerce | 390 N. Fairview, Prineville 97754 | 541/447–6304.

Attractions

Ochoco National Forest. Covering almost 1,500 square mi in central Oregon, this forest is part of the old Blue Mountain Forest Reserve, which was established in 1906 by President Theodore Roosevelt. It is 26 mi east of Prineville and has three wilderness areas—Mill Creek, Black Canyon, and Bridge Creek—plus 28 campgrounds. | U.S. 26 E | 541/416–6500 | www.fs.fed.us/r6/ochoco | Free | Daily.

Prineville Reservoir State Park. Mountain streams flow out of the Ochoco Mountains and join together to create the Crooked River. Bowman Dam on the river forms Prineville Reservoir. Recreational activities include boating, swimming, fishing, and hiking. A campground has 22 full hookups, 23 electrical and 25 tent sites, and 5 cabins. | Juniper Canyon Rd. | 541/447–4363 or 800/551–6949 | www.prd.state.or.us | $3 per vehicle day-use fee | Daily.

Dining

Crooked River Railroad Company Dinner Train. American. This excursion train winds through the rimrock-lined Crooked River valley between Prineville and Redmond. The draw is not really the four-course dinner, but the 2½–3-hour ride and the show. On Saturday nights year-round and Friday nights June–September, a murder mystery is staged. A Jesse James–style train robbery enlivens the ride and meal. | 4075 O'Neil Rd., Redmond | 541/548–8630 | fax 541/548–8702 | Reservations essential | $71 Fri.–Sat., $59 Sun. | AE, D, MC, V.

Dad's Place. American. Dad's is a typical American diner, serving up breakfast and lunch from a low-fuss, high-cholesterol menu at this downtown location. | 229 N. Main St. | 541/447–7059 | Closed Sun. No dinner | $5–$7 | MC, V.

Lodging

Best Western Prineville Inn. This chain property is near fishing and a golf course. It's 23 mi from the Redmond airport. The rooms have a Southwestern flavor. | 67 rooms. Cable TV, indoor pool, hot tub, laundry facilities. | 1475 E. 3rd St. | 541/447–8080 or 800/528–1234 | fax 541/447–1011 | $55–$85 | AE, D, DC, MC, V.

Elliott House. With its wraparound porch, Tuscan columns, bay windows, and manicured lawn, this 1908 Queen Anne house is a standout in an otherwise unremarkable neighborhood. Suitable antiques fill the interior, including a working 1916 Wurlitzer nickelodeon in the parlor and an Edison cylinder phonograph in the breakfast room. The rooms have down comforters and quilts and one has an antique iron bed. | 2 rooms. Complimentary breakfast, no air-conditioning, no room phones, no TV, TV in common area, bicycles, no kids under 12, no smoking. | 305 W. 1st St. | 541/416–0423 | fax 541/416–9368 | andybet@bendnet.com | www.empnet.com/elliotthouse | $70 | No credit cards.

Rustler's Inn. With some nicely tooled woodwork and brass doorknobs, the Rustler's Inn has a western look. The rooms have an eclectic mix of antiques and reproductions. There's a Mexican restaurant called Ranchero on the premises. | 20 rooms. Restaurant, complimentary Continental breakfast, some kitchenettes, some microwaves, some refrigerators, cable TV, room phones. | 960 N.W. 3rd St. (Hwy. 26) | 541/447–4185 | fax 541/447–4185 | www.majesty-hotels.com | $50.95–$55.95 | AE, D, DC, MC, V.

REDMOND

MAP 3, G5

(Nearby towns also listed: Bend, Madras, Prineville)

Redmond sits at the western end of Oregon's High Desert, just four miles from the Deschutes River and within minutes of several lakes. As with Deschutes County, Redmond has experienced some of the most rapid growth in the state during the past 10 years, largely owing to a dry and mild climate and year-round recreational opportunities for downhill and cross-country skiing, fishing, hunting, hiking, mountain biking, and searching for rocks. Smith Rock State Park, just north of Redmond, attracts rock climbers from around the world for its hundreds of climbing routes and hiking trails. Wildlife is abundant in the park, which is a nesting area for birds of prey.

Information: Redmond Chamber of Commerce | 446 S.W. 7th, Redmond 97756 | 541/548–5191 | rcc@empnet.com | www.empnet.com/redmond/.

Attractions

Cline Falls State Park. Picnicking and fishing are popular at this rest area on the Deschutes River 5 mi west of Redmond. | Rte. 126 | 800/551–6949 | www.prd.state.or.us | Free | Daily.

Firemen's Pond. During trout season this small lake is jumping with fish. Only children and disabled adults are permitted to fish in the lake. | Lake Rd. and Sisters Ave. | 541/548–6068 | Free | Daily.

Operation Santa Claus. Just 2 mi west of Redmond, you can observe a herd of more than 100 reindeer on this 10-acre property. The gift shop is open all year, selling Christmas tree ornaments and collectibles, many with old-fashioned designs. Special events are scheduled at Christmastime. | 4355 W. Hwy. 26 | 541/548–1330 | www.oscreindeer.com | Daily, daylight hours.

Petersen's Rock Gardens. A local farmer created this 4-acre rock garden near Bend. All of the petrified wood, agate, jasper, lava, and obsidian came from within an 85-mi radius of the garden and was used to make miniature buildings and bridges, terraces and towers. Among the structures is the Statue of Liberty. The castle near the parking lot is 6" tall with hundreds of windows. The attraction includes a small museum, and picnic tables where you can have lunch. | 7930 S.W. 77th St. | 541/382–5574 | $3 (suggested) | Daily 9–5.

Peter Skene Ogden Wayside. This small scenic viewpoint is set at the top of a river canyon 10 mi north of Redmond. | U.S. 97 N | 541/548–7501 | Free | Daily.

Smith Rock State Park. This park, 8 mi north of Redmond, is known for rock climbing. Wildlife like golden eagles, prairie falcons, mule deer, river otters, and beavers can be seen. Due to the environmental sensitivity of the region, the animal leash law is strongly enforced. | Off U.S. 97 | 541/548–7501 or 800/551–6949 | www.prd.state.or.us | $3 per vehicle day-use | Daily.

ON THE CALENDAR

JULY: ***Central Oregon Draft Horse Show.*** Friday and Saturday of the second weekend in July bring the big horses to the Deschutes County Fairground in Redmond. You can see giant Clydesdales, Shires, Belgians, and the jet black Frisians with arching necks that were preferred by medieval knights. For contrast, there are some miniature horses, too. | 541/923–2453 or 800/682–4786.

JULY–AUG.: ***Deschutes County Fair and Rodeo.*** This annual summer event, 17 mi north of Bend, features livestock and agricultural exhibits and competitions, food, and entertainment. | 541/548–2711.

Lodging

Best Western Rama Inn. This property is close to the Expo Center and the fairgrounds. Fishing and a golf course are also nearby. | 49 rooms. Complimentary Continental breakfast, in-room data ports, microwaves, refrigerators, cable TV, cross-country and downhill skiing, indoor pool, hot tub, exercise equipment, laundry facilities, business services, airport shuttle. | 2630 S.W. 17th Place | 541/548–8080 | $62–$170 | AE, D, DC, MC, V.

Eagle Crest Resort. Eagle Crest is 5 mi west of Redmond, above the canyon of the Deschutes River. In this high desert area, the grounds are covered with juniper and sagebrush. The hotel rooms are in a single building on the landscaped grounds, and some of the suites have gas fireplaces. The resort is on nearly 1,700 acres. There are 10 mi of bike trails and a 2-mi hiking trail where you can fish in the river. | 100 rooms, 38 suites, 300 town houses. Bar, dining room, picnic area, some kitchenettes, microwaves (in suites), cable TV, cross-country and downhill skiing, pool, beauty salon, hot tub, driving range, 18-hole golf courses, putting green, tennis court, gym, hiking, horseback riding, bicycles, children's program (ages 6–12), playground, laundry facilities, business services, airport shuttle. | 1522 Cline Falls Rd.

| 541/923–2453 or 800/682–4786 | fax 541/923–1720 | www.eagle-crest.com | $93–$105 rooms, $127–$139 suites, $212–$299 town houses | AE, D, MC, V.

Motel 6. This in town chain motel opened in 1999. It's on the main road between Bend and Madras, and there are restaurants within walking distance. | 83 rooms. In room data ports, cable TV, room phones, hot tub, spa, laundry facilities. | 2247 S. Hwy. 97 | 541/923–2100 or 800/466–8356 | fax 541/548–2122 | $61.99 | AE, D, DC, MC, V.

Redmond Inn. Nearby outdoor activities include horseback riding, skiing, fishing, swimming, and golf or if you prefer to stay closer to home there is a patio by the pool. Just three blocks from the center of town, this inn is convenient to both restaurants and sights. | 46 rooms. Complimentary Continental breakfast, kitchenettes, microwaves, refrigerators, cable TV, pool, some pets allowed (fee). | 1545 U.S. 97 S | 541/548–1091 or 800/833–3259 | $40–$57 | AE, D, DC, MC, V.

Travel Lodge. Built in 1927, this inn has a grand lobby with a fireplace, wood beam ceiling, and grandfather clock. | 48 rooms. Restaurant, bar, complimentary Continental breakfast, cable TV, spa, exercise equipment, airport shuttle. | 521 S. Sixth St. | 541/923–7378 | fax 541/923–3949 | $49–$70 | AE, D, DC, MC, V.

REEDSPORT

MAP 3, C6

(Nearby towns also listed: Coos Bay, Florence, North Bend)

Reedsport is located at the center of the more than 40 miles of Oregon Dunes National Recreation Area. The area offers numerous recreational opportunities, from open sand and riding trails for off-road vehicles to camping, horseback riding, crabbing, clamming, hiking, and whale watching. There is chinook, steelhead, shad, sturgeon, and striped bass fishing in the Umpqua River. Visitors are welcome at the functioning Umpqua River Lighthouse and the Dean Creek Elk Viewing Area, and jet boats cruise up and downstream for guided observations. Nearby Winchester Bay is home to one of Oregon's largest marinas, Salmon Harbor, with year-round amenities for sport and pleasure boats alike.

Information: Reedsport/Winchester Bay Chamber of Commerce | Box 11, Reedsport 97467 | 541/271–3495 or 800/247–2155 | www.coos.or.us/~reewbycc.

Attractions

Dean Creek Elk Viewing Area. A large herd of Roosevelt elk can be seen at this 1,000-acre site with pasture, woodlands, and wetlands. | Rte. 38 E | 541/756–0100 | Free | Daily.

Oregon Dunes National Recreation Area. The Oregon Dunes stretch along the Oregon coast from Florence to North Bend. The NRA has fine beaches, campgrounds, boat launch ramps, and picnic areas. Hiking trails pass through green areas that are home to many species of wildlife. All-terrain vehicles are permitted in some areas. | The Vistors Center, at U.S. 101 and OR 38 | 541/271–3611 | $3 day-use fee | Daily.

Salmon Harbor. Located 2 mi south of Reedsport at the mouth of the Umpqua River, this is one of the largest marinas on the Oregon Coast. An RV park is near the county-operated facility. | U.S. 101 | 541/271–3407 | Free | May–Sept., daily; Oct.–Apr., weekdays.

Umpqua Discovery Center. This educational and cultural center on the coast has exhibits about early settlers to the area. A new exhibit focuses on the history of Native Americans and early explorers. | 409 Riverfront Way | 541/271–4816 | $3 | Daily, 10–4.

Umpqua Lighthouse State Park. This 65-ft lighthouse and museum is at the entrance to Winchester Bay in the Oregon Dunes. Just 4 mi from Reedsport, the campground has 20 full hookups, 42 tent sites, 2 yurts, and 2 cabins, and surrounds Lake Marie. Recreational activities include non-motorized boating and swimming. There is also a small beach. | Off U.S. 101 | 541/271–4118 or 800/551–6949 | www.prd.state.or.us | $3 per vehicle day-use fee | Daily.

William M. Tugman State Park. On Eel Lake near the town of Lakeside, this little-known park is surrounded by a dense forest of spruce, cedar, fir, and alder. Recreational activities include fishing, swimming, canoeing, and sailing. A campground has 115 electrical sites and 3 yurts. | U.S. 101 S | 541/888–4902 or 800/551–6949 | www.prd.state.or.us | $3 per vehicle day-use fee | Daily.

ON THE CALENDAR

JULY: ***Ocean Fest.*** On the third or fourth weekend of July, this little seaside town throws a three-day weekend party on Beach Boulevard, parallel to the marina. There's a free concert on Friday evening, an hour-long parade on Saturday at 1 PM, plus additional music by local bands, crafts booths, and a salmon barbecue by local restaurants. The local quilting guild sponsors a display of heirloom and family quilts, and sometimes there are quilts for sale. | 541/271–3495.

Lodging

Anchor Bay Inn. Right in the center of Reedsport, this motel has easy access to the dunes. Elk viewing is only 4 mi away. | 21 rooms. Complimentary Continental breakfast, some kitchenettes, some microwaves, some refrigerators, cable TV, pool, laundry facilities, business services, some pets allowed (fee). | 1821 Winchester Ave. | 541/271–2149 or 800/767–1821 | fax 541/271–1802 | anchorbay@presys.com | $55–$69 | AE, D, MC, V.

Best Budget Inn. This centrally located, small inn is clean and inexpensive. The Continental breakfast is limited to coffee and rolls, but it's there and it's free. | 23 rooms. Complimentary breakfast, no air-conditioning, some kitchenettes, some microwaves, some refrigerators, cable TV, room phones. | 1894 Winchester Ave. (Hwy 101) | 541/271–3686 | fax 541/271–4019 | $45 | AE, D, DC, MC, V.

Best Western Salbasgeon Inn. This chain property is a few feet away from the tranquil Schoelfield River, yet close to area shopping and dining. Some of the immaculately kept rooms have river views and fireplaces. | 56 rooms, 9 suites. Complimentary Continental breakfast, some kitchenettes, minibars, refrigerators, cable TV, indoor pool, hot tub, exercise equipment, laundry facilities, business services, pets allowed (fee). | 1400 Highway Ave. | 541/271–4831 | fax 541/271–4832 | $79–$88, $75–$125 suites | AE, D, DC, MC, V.

Economy Inn. This inexpensive inn is in the middle of town, close to restaurants and a large shopping center. | 39 rooms, 2 suites. Complimentary Continental breakfast, no air-conditioning in some rooms, in-room data ports, some kitchenettes, some microwaves, some refrigerators, cable TV, room phones, pool. | 1593 Hwy. 101 | 541/271–3671 or 800/799–9970 | $35–$75 | AE, D, DC, MC, V.

Salbasgeon Inn of the Umpqua. In the heart of fishing country, this inn takes its name from salmon, striped bass, and sturgeon. It overlooks the Umpqua River and all rooms have river views. | 12 rooms. Picnic area, some kitchenettes, cable TV, putting green, some pets allowed (fee). | 45209 Rte. 38 | 541/271–2025 | Redel@salbasgeon.com | www.inn-net.com/umpqua.htm | $68–$98 | AE, D, DC, MC, V.

ROCKAWAY BEACH

MAP 3, C2

(Nearby towns also listed: Cannon Beach, Manzanita, Seaside, Tillamook)

Rockaway Beach, a small community of just over 1,000 residents, sits between Nehalem Bay and the Manzanita area to the north and Tillamook Bay and Tillamook dairy-farming country to the south. Rockaway originated in the early 1900s as a summer vacation destination for Portlanders, a role it now fills for visitors from elsewhere in the state and country

Information: Rockaway Beach Chamber of Commerce | 276 S. Miller St., Rockaway Beach 97136 | 503/355–8108.

Attractions

ON THE CALENDAR

AUG.: ***Arts and Crafts Festival.*** On the third weekend in August, Rockaway Beach holds a two-day crafts fair in an open area near the beach that local people call the "wayside." Booths feature jewelry, quilting, wooden items, and some paintings. Local food vendors provide sustenance and prices are moderate. Just look near the beach for the red caboose, home of the Chamber of Commerce. | 503/355–8108.

Dining

Beach Pancake and Dinner House. American. This cozy restaurant's specialty is homemade chicken and dumplings; it has a children's menu, offers senior discounts, is wheelchair accessible, and serves breakfast all day. A popular item here is liver and onions, but don't be surprised by the homemade Mexican dishes; the owners have a Mexican son-in-law and now they insist on the real thing. Kid's menu. Senior discounts. | 202 N. Hwy. 101 | 503/355–2411 | Breakfast served.

Lodging

Silver Sands. Each room in this beach-front motel has a balcony and view of the ocean. It's central to local shopping and restaurants and is right in the middle of town. | 64 rooms. No air-conditioning, many kitchenettes, refrigerators, cable TV, indoor pool, hot tub. | 215 S. Pacific | 503/355–2206 or 800/457–8972 | fax 503/355–9690 | $98–$136 | AE, D, DC, MC, V.

ROSEBURG

MAP 3, D6

(Nearby town also listed: Grants Pass)

Roseburg is the seat of Douglas County, which contains almost 3 million acres of commercial forest lands and the largest stand of old-growth timber in the world. About 25 to 30 percent of the county's labor force works in the forest products industry.

The north and south branches of the Umpqua River meet up just north of Roseburg. The roads that run parallel to this river give spectacular views of the falls, and the North Umpqua route also provides access to trails, a hot springs, and the Winchester fish ladder. White-water rafting, riverside hiking, horseback riding, mountain biking, steelhead and salmon fishing, snowmobiling, and skiing are some of the sports available in the area.

Located 60 miles due west of the northern gateway to Crater Lake National Park and in the Hundred Valleys of the Umpqua, Roseburg's mild climate produces world-class wines. Six wineries are located in and around Roseburg, producing such varieties as Gewürztraminer, Riesling, Pinot Noir, and Cabernet.

Information: Roseburg Visitors Information Center | 410 S.E. Spruce, Roseburg 97470 | 541/672–9731 | www.oregonnews.com/visitroseburg.

Attractions

Callahan Ridge Winery. Wines are produced here in a restored 1878 barn, which also houses the tasting room. Merlot is a specialty. | 340 Busenbark La. | 541/673–7901 | www.callahanridge.com | Free | Daily 11–5.

Douglas County Museum of History and Natural History. This small museum has a large collection focusing on 8,000 years of activity in the Umpqua Valley. | 123 Museum Dr. | 541/957–7007 | www.co.douglas.or.us/museum | $3.50 | Daily, Call for hours.

Henry Estate Winery. Pinot Noir, Pinot Gris, and Chardonnay are all produced at this family-owned winery 16 mi from Roseburg near Umpqua. The original vineyard was planted in the early 1970s. | 66 Hubbard Creek Rd., Umpqua | 541/459–5120 | www.henryestate.com | Free | Daily 11–5.

Hillcrest Vineyard. This winery near Roseburg is known for its Rieslings and Cabernet Sauvignon. | 240 Vineyard La. | 541/673–3709 or 800/736–3709 | Free | Daily 11–5.

La Garza Cellars and Gourmet Kitchen. This winery, known best for its Cabernet Sauvignon, also produces Merlot, dry Riesling, Pinot Gris, and a dry Cabernet blush. The restaurant here serves lunch only, with an eclectic menu that might include spinach-hazelnut-feta ravioli or pork loin enchiladas, plus vegetarian dishes, using homegrown vegetables and herbs. The bread is homemade, too. | 491 S.W. Winery La. | 541/679–9654 | fax 541/679–3888 | www.winesnw.com/lagarzacellars.htm | June–Sept., daily 11–5; Oct.–mid-Dec. and Feb.–May, Wed.–Sun. noon–4.

Seven Feathers Hotel and Casino Resort. Located just south of Roseburg, about halfway between Medford and Eugene, is a hotel and a casino owned by the Cow Creek Tribe. It features 500 slots, blackjack, roulette, poker, craps, keno, and bingo. Big-name entertainers perform in the showroom, and, for the kids, there's an arcade and an ice cream parlor. Guests of the hotel receive a complimentary Continental breakfast. There's also a 32-space RV park. | 146 Chief Miwaleta Lane, Canyonville; off I–5 | 800/548–8461 | Free | Daily.

Umpqua National Forest. This forest covers nearly 1 million acres on the western slopes of the Oregon Cascades. Mt. Bailey has downhill skiing. There are 38 campgrounds. You can get there by taking Route 118 along the North Umpqua River. | Forest Service, 2900 N.W. Stewart Parkway | 541/672–6601 | www.fs.fed.us/r6/umpqua | Free | Daily.

★ **Wildlife Safari.** You can drive through this 600-acre wildlife park, which is 6 mi from Roseberg, and see free-roaming animals such as cheetahs, lions, tigers, and bears. Animals indigenous to Africa, Asia, and America are all represented. There is also a petting zoo, a miniature train, and elephant rides. The admission price includes two drive-thrus in the same day. | Safari Road, Winston | 541/679–6761 or 800/355–4848 | fax 541/679–9210 or 800/355–4848 | www.wildlifesafari.org | $12.95 | Daily; call for specific hours.

ON THE CALENDAR

AUG.: ***Douglas County Fair.*** Livestock and agricultural exhibits and competitions, food, and entertainment take center stage at the Douglas County Fairgrounds for this annual event. 541/957–7010

JUNE: ***Umpqua Valley Roundup.*** Southern Oregon's only summertime pro rodeo takes place on the Douglas County Fairgrounds and lasts for three days. There is also a downtown parade and a dance. 541/957–7010

JULY: ***Roseburg Graffiti Week.*** This five-day event focuses on classic automobiles. There are car displays and shows, and races. Events are held downtown, at the Douglas County Fairgrounds, and at the Seven Feathers Casino. 541/672–1071

JULY: ***Wine and Music Festival.*** The Callahan Ridge Winery, which has won prizes for its Zinfandel and late-harvest Rieslings, hosts this festival of music, wine, beer, food, and crafts. For a modest fee, you can relax from 2 until 8 PM on the grass in a shady grove behind the winery (bring a blanket or lawn chairs), and enjoy the food, beverages, and crafts booths, plus the music of several blues performers. 541/673–7901 or 888/946–3487

SEPT.: ***Umpqua Valley Wine, Art and Jazz Festival.*** Sponsored by the Umpqua Valley Winegrowers, the festival includes wine tasting and an arts and crafts street fair. 800/782-2686

Dining

Seven Feathers Hotel and Casino Resort. Contemporary. The Camas Room (named for a local lily) at this casino resort prides itself on top-level service in a handsome room accented with mahogany and marble. Local people come here for the Oregon-grown lamb, but you can also have other seafood, pastas, steaks, and nightly specials. Just leave room for the most popular dessert, apple pie with caramel sauce. Coffee is elegantly served in French presses at the table, producing a superior flavor. | 146 Chief Miwaleta La., Canyonville | 541/839–1111 or 800/548–8461 | $16–$24 | AE, MC, V.

Steamboat Inn. Contemporary. The restaurant at Steamboat Inn is famous for its nightly Fisherman's Dinner, a multi-course meal served around a 20-ft-long sugar-pine dinner table that's been here since the inn opened in 1931. The prix-fixe dinner begins with wine in the library, but continues casually in a room with a rock floor and paneled and rock walls. A single entrée might be salmon, halibut, lamb, or duck (vegetarians can be accommodated), while dessert might be Swedish crème brûlée, ginger custard, or lemon-raspberry crêpes. | 42705 N. Umpqua Hwy., Steamboat | 541/498–2230 | fax 541/498–2411 | Reservations essential | Closed Jan.–Feb. | $37 | MC, V.

Tolly's. Contemporary. Tolly's serves breakfast, lunch, and dinner (except as noted) in a 1903 building in the center of little Oakland, 18 mi north of Roseburg. There are several distinct dining rooms, one of which is decorated with antiques, while another is reserved exclusively for couples. The dinner menu might offer pan-seared filet of salmon, spring lamb, or artichoke-glazed pork chops, and you can end your meal with the heavenly chocolate of French silk. | 115 Locust St., Oakland | 541/459–3796 | fax 541/459–1819 | No dinner Mon.–Tues. | $17–$25 | AE, D, MC, V.

Lodging

Best Inn and Suites. Just off the highway, 2 mi from downtown Roseberg, this renovated hotel has simple, modern rooms. | 70 rooms. Complimentary Continental breakfast, some microwaves, cable TV, pool, exercise equipment, business services. | 427 N.W. Garden Valley Blvd. | 541/673–5561 or 800/626–1900 | fax 541/957–0318 | $45–$70 | AE, D, DC, MC, V.

Best Western Douglas Inn. This motel in downtown Roseburg is close to a variety of restaurants, shops, art galleries, and museums. | 52 rooms. Complimentary Continental breakfast, in-room data ports, cable TV, hot tub, exercise equipment, business services. | 511 S.E. Stephens St. | 541/673–6625 | fax 541/667–9610 | $50–$70 | AE, D, DC, MC, V.

Best Western Garden Villa. Roseburg's other Best Western is next to Garden Valley Shopping Center and 6 mi from Wildlife Safari. There is a walking trail just across the street. | 122 rooms. Complimentary Continental breakfast, cable TV, pool, exercise equipment, laundry facilities, some pets allowed. | 760 N.W. Garden Valley Blvd. | 541/672–1601 | fax 541/672–1316 | $69–$89 | AE, D, DC, MC, V.

House of Hunter. This 1900 Italianate Victorian house overlooks downtown Roseburg, while the back patio looks out on a flower garden. Inside is a very formal dining room, filled with massive cabinets of china and cut glass, and a more inviting living room. Guest rooms run to lace, ruffles, fringes, and frills. | 2 rooms, 2 2-bedroom suites. Complimentary breakfast, no room phones, TV in common area, laundry facilities, no smoking. | 813 S.E. Kane St. | 541/672–2335 or 800/540–7704 | www.wizzards.net/hunter | $70 | D, MC, V.

Seven Feathers Hotel and Casino Resort. The casino, located 25 mi south of Roseburg on I–5, has 500 slots, blackjack, roulette, poker, craps, keno, and bingo. Guest rooms are upscale and elegant, and each has a sitting area. The top restaurant here is the Camas Room. | 150 rooms. 3 restaurants, 1 bar, complimentary Continental breakfast, room service, cable TV, room phones, pool, hot tub, sauna, gym, video games, laundry service. | 146 Chief Miwaleta

La., Canyonville | 541/839–1111 or 800/548–8461 | information@sevenfeathers.com | www.sevenfeathers.com | $99–$109 | AE, MC, V.

★ **Steamboat Inn.** In the 1930s, western writer Zane Grey wrote about the Steamboat Inn, helping to make it the world's most famous fishing lodge. Every fall, the world's top fly fishermen gather here, high in the Cascades, in search of 20-pound steelhead in the North Umpqua River. The riverside guest cabins have broad decks, while the larger cottages are set among trees. Some units have Japanese soaking tubs. Gardens enhance the wooded mountain setting. Guide services are available, as are fishing equipment rentals and sales. The lodge is 38 mi east of Roseburg on Hwy. 138. | 2 suites, 8 cabins, 5 cottages, 4 3-bedroom houses. Restaurant, no air-conditioning in some rooms, some kitchenettes, some refrigerators, some room phones, no TV, library, baby-sitting, laundry facilities, no smoking. | 42705 N. Umpqua Hwy., Steamboat | 541/498–2230 or 800/840–8825 | fax 541/498–2411 | stmbtinn@rosenet.net | www.thesteamboatinn.com | $135 | Closed Jan.–Feb. | MC, V.

Travelodge. This city center motel is in a landscaped private park and picnic area. Some room have river views and balconies. | 40 rooms. Picnic area, cable TV, pool. | 315 W. Harvard Blvd. | 541/672–4836 | $55–$80 | AE, D, DC, MC, V.

Windmill Inn. Rooms at this pleasant inn are plush and comfortable. Complimentary hot beverage, juice, muffin, and newspaper are delivered to your door in the morning. | 128 rooms. Restaurant, bar, complimentary Continental breakfast, in-room data ports, cable TV, pool, hot tub, exercise equipment, laundry facilities, business services, airport shuttle, free parking, some pets allowed. | 1450 Mulholland Dr. | 541/673–0901 or 800/547–4747 | www.windmillinns.com | $70–$90 | AE, D, DC, MC, V.

SALEM

MAP 3, D3

(Nearby towns also listed: Albany, McMinnville, Newberg, Oregon City, Portland, Silverton)

Originally referred to as Chemeketa, a Calapooya Indian name meaning "place of rest," Salem is said to have been renamed by missionaries. According to one story, the name is an anglicized form of the Hebrew "shalom," or peace, while another story suggests it was named specifically for Salem, Massachusetts. Although trappers and farmers preceded them in the Willamette Valley, the Methodist missionaries had come in 1834 to minister to Native Americans, and they are credited with the founding of Salem. They also established the first academic institution west of the Rockies in 1842, now known as Willamette University.

Salem became the official capital when Oregon achieved statehood in 1859, replacing Oregon City as the capital of the Oregon Territory. Today, with a population of over 120,000, Salem is the third largest city in Oregon and serves as the seat to Marion County as well as the home of the state fairgrounds. As the state capital and county seat, government ranks as a major industry in the community, while the city's placement in the heart of the fertile Willamette Valley stimulates rich agricultural and food-processing industries. Extensive nearby farmlands are devoted to the cultivation of vegetables, berries, hops, and flowers, and at least 15 wineries are located in and near Salem.

Numerous gardens around the city are likewise indicative of the moderate climate and lush growing conditions. Among them are the Bush House Gardens, one of the oldest greenhouses in the West, dating from 1882, and the Mission Mill Village Flower Gardens, including herbs, wildflowers, and varieties thought to have been brought west by pioneers.

Information: Salem Convention & Visitors Association | 1313 Mill St. SE, 97301 | 503/581–4325 or 800/874–7012 | www.scva.org.

TRANSPORTATION INFORMATION

Airports: Though Salem is not served by major commercial airlines, it does have an airport for private planes. The Salem airport is at McNary Field, 2960 25th St. SE. For information, call 503/588–6314.

Bus Lines: Greyhound serves Salem from its terminal at 450 Church St. For fares and schedules, call 503/362–2428 or 800/231–2222.

Intra-city Transit: Cherriots is the local bus service. For information, call 503/588–2877.

DRIVING AROUND SALEM

The city of Salem has more than 5,000 free customer parking spaces downtown. In areas with parking meters, the rate is 65¢ an hour. Meters at the library cost 25¢ an hour. Parking is free after 6 PM, on Sunday, and on major holidays. In many neighborhoods on-street parking is reserved for residents with permits.

Attractions

ART AND ARCHITECTURE

Bush House. A museum is housed in this 1878 Italianate mansion that was built by the founder of the *Salem Statesman* newspaper. The house and gardens are on the National Register of Historic Places. It's on 90 acres filled with trees and gardens. | Bush's Pasture Park, 600 Mission St. SE | 503/363–4714 | $3 | Oct.–Apr., Tues.–Sun. 2–5; May–Sept., Tues.–Sun. noon–4:30.

SALEM

INTRO
ATTRACTIONS
DINING
LODGING

Bush Barn Art Center. This small community art gallery is behind the Bush House and showcases the work of Northwest artists. | 600 Mission St. SE | 503/581–2228 | Free | Tues.–Fri. 10–5, weekends noon–5.

Capitol. A brightly gilded bronze statue of the Oregon Pioneer stands atop the 140-ft-high Capitol dome, looking north across the Capitol Mall. Built in 1939 with blocks of gray Vermont marble, Oregon's Capitol has an elegant yet austere neoclassical feel. New east and west wings were added in 1978. Relief sculptures and deft historical murals soften the interior. Tours of the rotunda, the house and senate chambers, and the governor's office leave from the information center under the dome. | 900 Court St. | 503/986–1388 | Free | Daily.

Elsinore Theatre. This flamboyant Tudor Gothic vaudeville house opened on May 28, 1926 with Edgar Bergen in attendance. Clark Gable (who lived in Silverton) and Gregory Peck performed on the stage. The theatre was designed to look like a castle, with a false stone front, chandeliers, ironwork, and stained glass windows. It's now a lively performing arts center with a busy schedule of bookings ranging from Rita Rudner to the Glenn Miller Orchestra, and there are concerts on its Wurlitzer pipe organ. | 170 High St. SE | 503/375–3574 | fax 503/375–0284 | www.elsinoretheatre.com.

Historic Deepwood Estate. This 1894 Queen Anne–style mansion in Bush's Pasture Park overlooks six acres of formal English gardens. | 1116 Mission St. SE | 503/363–1825 | www.oregonlink.com/deepwood | $4 | May–Sept., Sun.–Fri. noon–5; Oct.–Apr., Tues.–Sat. noon–5; gardens daily dawn–dusk.

CULTURE, EDUCATION, AND HISTORY

Willamette University. Behind the Capitol, across State Street but half a world away, are the brick buildings and grounds of Willamette University, the oldest college in the West. Founded in 1842, Willamette has long been a mecca for aspiring politicians (former Oregon Senators Mark O. Hatfield and Robert Packwood are alumni). Hatfield Library, built in 1986 on the banks of Mill Stream, is a handsome brick and glass building with a striking campanile; tall, prim Waller Hall, built in 1841, is one of the oldest buildings in the Pacific Northwest. | 900 State St. | 503/370–6300 | Free | Daily.

MUSEUMS

Gilbert House Children's Museum. The museum in a Victorian house celebrates the inventions of A. C. Gilbert, including Erector sets and American Flyer trains. | 116 Marion St. | 503/371–3631 | $4 | Tues.–Sat. 10–5, Sun. noon–5.

Mission Mill Village. The Thomas Kay Woolen Mill Museum complex (circa 1889), complete with working waterwheels and millstream, looks as if the work stopped just minutes ago. All the original machinery is on display. The Jason Lee House, the John D. Boon Home, and the Methodist Parsonage are also part of the village and they reveal a great deal about domestic life in the 1840s. | 1313 Mill St. SE. | 503/585–7012 | www.missionmill.org | Free for grounds. For mill or museum tour $4 ($6 for both) | Tues.–Sat. 10–4:30.

SPORTS AND RECREATION

Enchanted Forest. This is the closest thing Oregon has to a theme park. The park, 7 mi south of Salem, has several attractions in a forest setting, including the Big Timber Log Ride where you ride logs through flumes that pass through a lumber mill and the woods. The ride—the biggest log ride in the Northwest—features a 25-ft roller-coaster dip and a 40-ft drop at the end. Other attractions include the Ice Mountain Bobsled roller coaster, the Haunted House, English Village, Storybook Lane, the Fantasy Fountains Water Light Show, Fort Fearless, and the western town of Tofteville. | 8462 Enchanted Way SE | 503/363–3060 or 503/371–4242 | www.enchantedforest.com | $6.95 | Mid-Mar.–Labor Day, daily 9:30–6; Sept. weekends 9:30–6.

OTHER POINTS OF INTEREST

Honeywood Winery. The oldest producing winery in the state is in downtown Salem. Pinot Noir, Riesling, and Chardonnay are specialties. | 1350 Hines St. SE | 503/362–4111 | Free | Weekdays 9–5, Sat. 10–5, Sun. 1–5.

Mount Angel Abbey. This peaceful Benedictine monastery, founded in 1882, sits atop a 300-ft-high butte 18 mi northeast of Salem. Mass is said every morning, there's a retreat house, and a walking path has the Stations of the Cross. The 1970 library is one of only two American buildings designed by famed Finnish architect Alvar Aalto. There's a Bach Festival in July, using the organ in the chapel. | 1 Abbey Dr., St. Benedict | 503/845–3030 | fax 503/845–3594 | www.mtangel.edu | Free.

ON THE CALENDAR

FEB.: *Oregon Wine and Food Festival.* For a three-day weekend in mid–February, as many as 20 of Oregon's top wineries bring their current releases to the Oregon State Fair and Exposition Center, where wine lovers can taste them for a modest fee. A dozen or so local restaurants set up booths, and some arts and crafts are also for sale. | 503/378–3247.

JULY: *Salem Art Fair and Festival.* More than 200 artists display their work at Bush's Pasture Park during this three-day event that also includes food booths and live performances. | 503/581–2228.

AUG.–SEPT.: *Oregon State Fair.* The focus of this 12-day event held at the Oregon State Fairgrounds is on farming—livestock competition and a horse show. An artisans' village features pottery, glass blowing, and blacksmithing. Big-name musicians perform. Also included are Familyville for younger people, a carnival, food booths, the Oregon State Fair Professional Wine Competition, and visual arts exhibits. Stroll through the fair's permanent floral gardens. | 503/378–3247.

SALEM WALKING TOUR

Salem's pleasant downtown is centered around the Capitol and the tree-lined Capitol Mall. The pace here is laid-back compared to the hustle and bustle of Portland. The Capitol complex is located between Court and State streets west of 12th Street. A walking tour of the Capitol and following attractions takes about three hours. If you want to explore inside, add additional time.

The first stop is the **Capitol** built in 1939 with a Greek design and expanded in the late 1970s. Tours of the rotunda and legislative chambers leave from the rotunda daily on the hour between Memorial Day and Labor Day and by appointment the rest of the year.

South of the Capitol complex, across State Street, is the campus of **Willamette University,** the oldest college in the western United States. Prominent buildings and structures on the campus include 63,000-square-ft Hatfield Library with its campanile; Walker Hall; the Putman University Center, which has a cafe; and Smith Fine Arts Center with its 1,250-seat auditorium.

East of Willamette University and across the Amtrak railroad tracks is **Mission Mill Village,** a reconstructed woolen mill built in 1889 that now serves as the Marion County Museum of History. Tours are led by guides in period costumes. The village is set on a 5-acre park that also is home to the Bush Conservatory greenhouse and rose gardens.

South of Mission Mill Village is the newly restored **Amtrak train station** (13th Street and Oak Street), a neoclassical revival building originally built in 1918.

Walk south on 12th Street three blocks to the historic **Deepwood Estate,** an 1894 Queen Anne mansion on 6 acres of English gardens. West of Deepwood Estate also on Mission Street is **Bush's Pasture Park,** 105 acres of English gardens and open space. The park's focal point is Bush House, an 1878 Italianate mansion filled with furnishings from the period. The park and its structures are listed on the National Register of Historic Places.

If you want to include a view of the Willamette River in your walk, head west on State Street and cross Front Street to **Riverfront Park.**

Dining

INEXPENSIVE

Gerry Frank's Konditorei. Café. Furnished in red, black, and white, and with windows all around, this small café is Salem's source for rich desserts. You can have sandwiches, salads, and soup, but most people head for the display cases to check out the homemade tortes, cheesecake, and other goodies. Gerry Frank's is famous locally for everything from quiche to chocolate blackout cake and carrot cake. You might have to wait on line, but the café stays open till 11 during the week and midnight on weekends. | 310 Kearney St. SE | 503/585–7070 | fax 503/585–7070 | $5–$6.95 | D, MC, V.

Thompson Brewery & Public House. American/Casual. This intimate pub mixes 1960s rock 'n' roll memorabilia with hand-painted woodwork and serves hearty sandwiches, salads, and pasta dishes. The house specialty is linguine in a sauce flavored with garlic, spinach, and hazelnuts. Hammerhead and Poleaxe Pale Ale are produced in a tiny brewery. Families and children are welcome. | 3575 Liberty Rd. S | 503/363–7286 | fax 503/363–7827 | $4.50–$7.75 | AE, D, MC, V.

MODERATE

Alessandro's Park Plaza. Italian. This restaurant in downtown Salem overlooks a park with waterfall and cooks up dishes that are definitely Roman in flavor. The pepper steak and shrimp scampi are highly recommended. There is also an exclusive martini bar. Kids' menu. | 325 High St. SE | 503/370–9951 | Closed Sun. | $15–$28 | AE, D, MC, V.

EXPENSIVE

DaVinci. Italian. Salem politicos flock to this two-story restaurant for Italian-inspired seafood and pasta dishes cooked in a wood-burning oven. The staff is courteous and extremely professional. | 180 High St. | 503/399–1413 | No lunch Sun. | $20–$25 | AE, DC, MC, V.

Lodging

INEXPENSIVE

Best Western New Kings Inn. Set on six landscaped acres, this inn is only 3 mi from downtown Salem. | 101 rooms. Refrigerators, cable TV, indoor pool, hot tub, tennis, exercise equipment, playground, laundry facilities, business services, airport shuttle. | 1600 Motor Court | 503/581–1559 | fax 503/364–4272 | www.bestwestern.com | $55–$65 | AE, D, DC, MC, V.

Tiki Lodge. This inexpensive motel has simple rooms and is located near a golf course. | 50 rooms (20 with shower only). Cable TV, pool, playground, business services, pets allowed. | 3705 Market St. | 503/581–4441 | fax 503/581–4442 | $33–$49 | AE, D, DC, MC, V.

MODERATE

A Creekside Inn, the Marquee House. The guest rooms in this 1938 Mt. Vernon Colonial-style house are decorated with movie themes—*Topper, Auntie Mame, Blazing Saddles,* and others—and there are movies and popcorn in the evening. Only nine blocks from the center of town, the house is on half an acre of flower gardens bordering Mill Creek, a view that you can enjoy from the large porch out back. | 5 rooms. Picnic area, complimentary breakfast, some in-room data ports, some room phones, TV in common area, no smoking. | 333 Wyatt Ct. NE | 503/391–0837 or 800/949–0837 | fax 503/391–1713 | rickiemh@open.org | www.marqueehouse.com | $65–$90. 2-night minimum during holidays and university events | D, DC, MC, V.

Phoenix Inn. This quiet all-suites hotel is just 5 mi from downtown Salem. | 89 suites. Complimentary Continental breakfast, refrigerators, some in-room hot tubs, cable TV, indoor pool, hot tub, exercise equipment, laundry facilities, business services, some pets allowed (fee). | 4370 Commercial St. SE | 503/588–9220 or 800/445–4498 | fax 503/585–3616 | $69–$79 suites | AE, D, DC, MC, V.

Red Lion Inn—Salem. The chief virtue of this clean, functional hotel is its location, about five minutes from the Capitol. | 150 rooms. Restaurant, bar with entertainment, room service, cable TV, indoor pool, hot tub, exercise equipment, laundry facilities, business services, free parking, pets allowed (fee). | 3301 Market St. | 503/370–7888 | fax 503/370–6305 | $72–$89 | AE, D, DC, MC, V.

EXPENSIVE

Ramada Inn. This full-service hotel in downtown Salem is within walking distance of the Capitol. The rooms and suites are comfortable and bright. | 99 rooms, 15 suites. Restaurant, complimentary Continental breakfast, in-room data ports, no-smoking rooms, pool, hot tub, gym, laundry facilities. | 200 Commercial St. SE | 503/363–4123 or 800/272–6232 | fax 503/363–8993 | $105, $115–$185 suites | AE, D, DC, MC, V.

Shilo Inn. This all-suites inn near the Capitol is on the fringe of the business district, so it is quiet. | 89 suites. Complimentary Continental breakfast, in-room data ports, microwaves, refrigerators, pool, hot tub, exercise equipment, business services, airport shuttle. | 3304 Market St. | 503/581–4001 | fax 503/399–9385 | $85–$95 suites | AE, D, DC, MC, V.

SEASIDE

MAP 3, C2

(Nearby towns also listed: Astoria, Cannon Beach)

The now-busy resort town of Seaside has grown up around the spot where the Lewis and Clark Expedition finally reached the Pacific Ocean. A bronze statue of the two explorers commemorates the end of their trail and faces the ocean at the center of Seaside's historic Promenade. The Prom was originally built in 1908 as a wooden walkway, and in 1920 it was extended to its current length, 1½ mi, with concrete sidewalks.

Seaside is split by a series of waterways, including Necanicum River and Neawanna Creek, where residents and visitors enjoy kayaking and canoeing, fishing, crabbing, and bird-watching for the numerous waterfowl and bald eagles that make their home near the river. The downtown area provides a variety of entertainment especially popular with kids and teens: candy shops, arcades, amusement rides, an aquarium, a carousel, and a skate park. Just south of town, world-class waves draw surfers to the Cove, a spot jealously guarded by locals.

Information: Seaside Chamber of Commerce | 7 N. Roosevelt, Seaside 97138 | 503/738–6391 or 800/444–6740 | seaside@aone.com | www.seasideor.com.

OR

SEASIDE

INTRO
ATTRACTIONS
DINING
LODGING

Attractions

Ecola State Park. Ecola State Park, 5 mi south of Seaside, is a playground of sea sculpted rocks, sandy shoreline, green headlands, and panoramic views. The main beach can be crowded in summer, but Indian Beach has an often deserted cove and explorable tide pools. | Hwy. 101 | 800/551–6949 | www.prd.state.or.us | $3 per vehicle | Daily dawn–dusk.

Saddle Mountain State Park. It's a 2.5-mi hike from the parking lot to the summit of Saddle Mountain. It's much cooler at that elevation. The campground, which is 14 mi north of Seaside, has 10 primitive sites. | Off U.S. 26 | 503/861–1671 or 503/436–2844 | $3 per vehicle day-use fee | Mar.–Nov., daily.

Seaside Aquarium. Jellyfish, giant king crab, octopus, moray eels, wolf eels, and other sea life are swimming in 35 tanks at this attraction on the 2-mi-long beachfront Promenade. You can feed the harbor seals. | 200 N. Promenade | 503/738–6211 | $6 | Wed.–Sun., 9–5.

Tillamook Head. Follow signs on Hwy. 101 south of Seaside. From a parking area, a 2-mi hike will bring you to the 1,100-ft-high viewing point atop Tillamook Head. From here, you can see the Tillamook Rock Light Station, a mile or so out to sea. The lonely beacon, built in 1881 on a straight-sided rock, towers 41 ft above the ocean. Decommissioned in 1957, it is now a columbarium, used to bury human remains. | Hwy. 101 | 800/551–6949 | www.prd.state.or.us.

ON THE CALENDAR

SEPT.: *Bite of Seaside.* Seafood booths, live bands, trampolines, and a petting zoo are the features at this festival which takes place on First Avenue. 503/738–8585 or 800/394–3303

Dining

Breakers Restaurant and Lounge. Contemporary. The Breakers in the Best Western is a very high-quality family restaurant, serving steaks, chicken, seafood, and pastas. You can choose Oregon crab cakes or be a rebel and have Alaskan salmon and halibut. Local people often come for the prime rib and the western steak (rib-eye coated in Creole seasoning). Plan on having the Oregon blueberry white chocolate cheesecake for dessert. | 414 N. Promenade | 503/738–3334 or 800/234–8439 | fax 503/738–5959 | No lunch | $9.95–$23.95 | AE, D, DC, MC, V.

Dooger's Seafood and Grill. Seafood. This Dooger's (the original is in Cannon Beach) serves the same superb seafood and steaks in a casual, contemporary setting. Don't pass up the famous clam chowder. Kids' menu. No smoking. | 505 Broadway | 503/738–3773 | Closed first 2 weeks in Dec. | $18–$25 | MC, V.

Premier Pasta Italian Dining Room. Italian. Dishes at this restaurant on the Necanicum River focus on pasta—it's owned by a pasta maker. There are several varieties of fettucine, linguine, and rotelle plus homemade sauces, which you can buy. Try the three-layered lasagna filled with sweet Italian sausage, red sauce, three cheeses, and black olives. | 1530 S. Holladay Dr. | 503/738–3692 | Closed Sun.–Mon. No lunch | $15–$21 | D, MC, V.

Sam's Seaside Café. American/Casual. This quiet, casual place half a block from the boardwalk and beach is the spot for inexpensive burgers, salads, seafood dishes, and homemade cakes and pies at lunch and dinner. Sam's stays open late, too. | 104 Broadway | 503/717–1725 | $8–$10 | AE, MC, V.

Shilo Restaurant and Lounge. Contemporary. Sixteen windows give you a view of the ocean outside, while inside candlelight glints off brass rails in this two-level dining room. A familiar entrée list is enhanced by beautiful plate presentation and such specialties as razor clams, grilled herb-crusted salmon, and a wide selection of steaks. The lounge has nightly entertainment. | 30 N. Promenade | 503/738–8481 | $13.95–$26.95 | AE, D, DC, MC, V.

Stephanie Inn. Contemporary. The cozy dining room at this three-story oceanfront hotel serves four-course prix-fixe suppers of innovative Pacific Northwest cuisine. The menu changes daily but might include fresh Dungeness crab cakes, artichoke and pine nuts salad, salmon or lamb chops, and dessert. | 2740 S. Pacific St. | 503/436–2221 or 800/633–3466 | Reservations essential | $37 | AE, D, DC, MC, V.

Lodging

Best Western Ocean View Resort. Many rooms at this motel on the beach have oceanview rooms. | 104 rooms, 20 suites. Restaurant, bar, no air-conditioning, in-room data ports, some kitchenettes, some refrigerators, room service, indoor pool, hot tub, laundry facilities, business services, some pets allowed (fee). | 414 N. Promenade | 503/738–3334 | fax 503/738–3264 | $70–$99, $160–$325 suites | AE, D, DC, MC, V.

Coast River Inn. This inn has comfortable rooms and is located four blocks from the beach and downtown and ½ mi from an outlet mall. | 26 rooms. No air-conditioning, some kitchenettes, refrigerators, many room phones, cable TV. | 800 S. Holladay Dr. | 503/738–8474 | $69–$90 | D, MC, V.

Comfort Inn Boardwalk. This comfortable chain hotel is three blocks from the ocean, but some of its balconies and patios overlook the Necanicum River. Management prides itself on good service and the Continental breakfast reaches the level of deluxe. | 65 rooms. Complimentary Continental breakfast, some in-room data ports, some kitchenettes, some microwaves, some refrigerators, some in-room hot tubs, cable TV, room phones, pool, hot tub, sauna, laundry facilities. | 545 Broadway | 503/738–3011 or 800/226–9815 | fax 503/738–4397 | www.comfortinn.com | $96–$129 | AE, D, DC, MC, V.

Convention Center Inn. Two-bedroom suites are available at this motel on the Necanicum River a few blocks from the Promenade. | 48 rooms. Complimentary Continental breakfast, some kitchenettes, some refrigerators, cable TV, indoor pool, hot tub, laundry facilities, business services, pets allowed (fee). | 441 2nd Ave. | 503/738–9581 or 800/699–5070 | fax 503/738–3212 | $99–$149 | AE, D, DC, MC, V.

Ebb Tide. Right on the beach, this motel has some rooms with ocean views. | 99 rooms. In-room data ports, some kitchenettes, refrigerators, cable TV, indoor pool, hot tub, gym, business services. | 300 N. Promenade | 503/738–8371 or 800/468–6232 | fax 503/738–0938 | $90–$160 | AE, D, DC, MC, V.

Gearhart by the Sea. Units have ocean views and fireplaces at this large beachfront condominium development, which is 3 mi from Seaside. One- or two-bedroom floor plans are available. | 80 apartments. Restaurant, bar, no air-conditioning, kitchenettes, cable TV, indoor pool, 18-hole golf course, laundry facilities. | 1157 N Marion Ave., Gearhart | 503/738–8331 or 800/547–0115 | fax 503/738–0881 | $119–$184 apartments | D, MC, V.

Gilbert Inn Bed and Breakfast. The common area in this 1892 Queen Anne Victorian inn one block from the ocean has country French print furniture and antiques. | 10 rooms, 2 suites. Complimentary breakfast, no air-conditioning, cable TV, airport shuttle, no smoking. | 341 Beach Dr. | 503/738–9770 or 800/410–9770 | fax 503/717–1070 | gilbertinn@theoregonshore.com | www.gilbertinn.com | $99–$115, $105 suites | Closed Jan. | AE, D, MC, V.

Hillcrest Inn. The Hillcrest is only one block from both the beach and the Convention Center, and little more than that to the downtown area and a selection of restaurants and shops. The inn has been owned by the same family for more than two decades, and friendliness, cleanliness, and convenience are bywords here. You're welcome to use the picnic tables, lawn chairs, and even the barbecue on the grounds. | 21 rooms, 5 suites, 3 2-bedroom cottages. Picnic area, no air-conditioning in some rooms, some kitchenettes, microwaves, refrigerators, some in room hot tubs, cable TV, room phones, sauna, laundry facilities. | 118 N. Columbia St. | 503/738–6273 or 800/270–7659 | fax 503/717–0266 | $59–$98 | AE, MC, V.

Hi-Tide. Some rooms at this small beach-front motel have fireplaces and most rooms have ocean views. It's close to shopping and restaurants. | 64 rooms. No air-conditioning, kitchenettes, cable TV, indoor pool, hot tub, business services. | 30 Avenue G | 503/738–8414 or 800/621–9876 | fax 503/738–0875 | $85–$115 | AE, D, DC, MC, V.

Royale. This small motel right in the center of downtown is close to shopping and restaurants. It's 3½ blocks from the beach and some rooms have river views. | 26 rooms. No air-conditioning. | 531 Ave. A | 503/738–9541 | $57–$60 | D, DC, MC, V.

Seashore Resort Motel. If you want a convenient motel directly on the beach, the Seashore Resort is the place. Some rooms have a view of the ocean. | 54 rooms. Complimentary Continental breakfast, no air-conditioning, some kitchenettes, some microwaves, some refrigerators, cable TV, room phones, pool, hot tub. | 60 N. Promenade | 503/738–6368 or 888/738–6368 | fax 503/738–8314 | www.seashoreresortmotel.com | $95–$145 | AE, D, DC, MC, V.

Shilo Inn. Located right on the beach at Seaside's circle, this mid-rise hotel provides spectacular views of the Pacific. Many of the rooms have balconies so the soothing views can be enjoyed in the privacy of your room. | 112 rooms. Restaurant, bar, no air-conditioning, many kitchenettes, room service, cable TV, indoor pool, hot tub, exercise equipment, laundry facilities, business services. | 30 N. Promenade | 503/738–9571 | fax 503/738–0674 | $109–$269 | AE, D, DC, MC, V.

Shilo Inn—Seaside East. This modernized Shilo has rooms and minisuites that are 5½ blocks from shopping, restaurants and the beach. | 58 rooms, 46 suites. Complimentary Continental breakfast, some microwaves, some refrigerators, cable TV, indoor pool, hot tub, laundry facilities, business services, airport shuttle. | 900 S. Holladay Dr. | 503/738–0549 | fax 503/738–0532 | $89–$129, $99–$145 suites | AE, D, MC, V.

SILVERTON

MAP 3, E3

(Nearby towns also listed: Newberg, Oregon City, Salem)

Near the foothills of the Cascade Mountains, south of Portland and east of Salem, Silverton takes pride in the fact that it stands apart from the fast pace of urban life. Silverton remains an agricultural center, much as it was when it was established in the mid-1800s. The town is the largest producer in the world of the bearded iris.

Silverton is the gateway to Silver Falls State Park, the largest state park in Oregon with 10 waterfalls, miles of hiking, biking, and horse trails, and picnicking and camping facilities. Also notable in Silverton, is the Oregon Garden, a 240-acre world-class exhibition garden and botanical complex.

Information: Silverton Area Chamber of Commerce | 306 S. Water, Silverton 97381 | 503/873–5615.

Attractions

Cooley's Gardens. View up to 1 million irises in bloom from mid-May until early June. This is the largest producer of bearded irises in the world. | 11553 Silverton Rd. NE | 503/873–5463 | fax 503/873–5812 | www.cooleysgardens.com | Free | mid-May–early June, daily 8–7.

Country Museum/Restored Train Station. Photos and artifacts related to farming and logging in the Silverton area are displayed in a 1908 house. | 428 S Water St. | 503/873–4766 | $1 | Mar.–Dec., Thurs., Sun. 1–4.

The Oregon Gardens. Once the site of an Arabian horse ranch, this 60-acre botanical garden opened in April 2000. Among its features are a water garden with a waterfall, showcasing Oregon flora; a wetlands area that is home to birds, deer, and other wildlife; an oak forest more than two centuries old; and an interactive children's garden. Summer concerts by the Oregon Symphony and pop acts are held in an amphitheatre. | 879 W. Main St. | 503/874–8100 | fax 503/874–8200 | www.oregongardens.org | $7 | April–Sept., daily 10–6.

Silver Falls State Park. Set in a temperate rain forest 14 mi south of Silverton along the banks of the north and south forks of Silver Creek, this park has a nationally recognized trail system. The Trail of Ten Falls takes you to 10 majestic waterfalls. A campground has 54 electrical and 51 tent sites. | Rte. 214 | 503/873–8681, ext. 31 or 800/551–6949 | www.prd.state.or.us | $3 per vehicle day-use | Daily.

ON THE CALENDAR

AUG.: ***Homer Davenport Days.*** Homer Davenport, a native son of Silverton, was a political cartoonist for the Hearst newspapers at the turn of the last century, and was also the first to import Arabian horses into the U.S. Now he lends his name to a three-day festival on the first weekend in August, featuring food, crafts, contests, and a barbecue at Coolidge-McLean Park. On Saturday morning, antiques and collectibles dealers set up booths on Main Street. The highlight of the weekend is the "davenport races." Yes, sofas on wheels. | 503/873–5615.

Lodging

Nordic Motel and Apartments. The inexpensive Nordic is the only motel in town. Built in 1963, it has large rooms. It's within walking distance of the center of town, and the Rose of Sharon Restaurant is across the street. The Oregon Gardens are a little over a mile away. | 8 rooms, 2 suites. Room phones. | 310 N. Water St. | 503/873–5058 | $39 | MC, V.

SISTERS

MAP 3, F5

(Nearby town also listed: Redmond)

Sisters derived its name from a group of three Cascade peaks (Faith, Hope, and Charity) that rise to the southwest. If you enter the Central Oregon high desert area from Santiam Pass or the McKenzie River Highway, Sisters appears to be a town out of the Old West. Rustic cabins border a llama ranch on the edge of town. Western storefronts give way to galleries. A bakery occupies the former general store, and the town blacksmith's home now houses a flower shop. Although its population remains under 1,000, Sisters increasingly attracts visitors as well as urban refugees who appreciate its tranquility and charm.

Throughout central Oregon, recreational opportunities abound on the many lakes and rivers, in the forests and on the mountains. The Metolius River in the Riverside area near Sisters is a special find for wildflower lovers, with an extensive variety of blooms from early spring to late summer.

Information: Sisters Area Chamber of Commerce | 164 N. Elm Street, Sisters 97759 | 541/549–0251 | chamber@outlawnet.com.

Attractions

Hinterland Ranch. Hinterland Ranch, 3½ mi east of Sisters, has been breeding llamas and Polish Arabian horses since 1965 and has one of the largest (250) and oldest llama herds in North America. This is a working ranch where you can observe the llamas and a small number of horses. | 67750 Hwy. 20 W, Box 1839 | 541/549–1215 | fax 541/549–5262 | Mon.–Sat. 7:30 AM–5 PM.

ON THE CALENDAR

JUNE: *Sisters Rodeo and Parade.* Started in 1941 and held on the second weekend in June at the KOA Rodeo Grounds, the Sisters Rodeo is billed as the "Biggest Little Show in the World." The four performances, with a purse that can reach six figures and sanctioned by the Professional Rodeo Cowboy Association, are enhanced by a Saturday morning parade and a Sunday pancake breakfast. Get information at www.sistersrodeo.com. | 541/549–0121 (for information) or 800/827–7522 (for tickets).

Dining

Hotel Sisters Restaurant. American. The most popular restaurant in town opened as a hotel in 1912. The western-style dining room has swinging doors and the large menu emphasizes broiled steaks, barbecued chicken and ribs, and Mexican dishes. In summer, you can eat outside on the deck. | 190 W. Cascade St. | 541/549–7427 | Closed Nov.–March. No lunch weekdays | $9.95–$21.95 | MC, V.

Lodging

Conklin's Guest House. You'll get a great view of the snowcapped Sisters from poolside or while having breakfast in the conservatory. The house is in a country setting on five acres with flower gardens and ponds (for catch-and-release fishing), but you can walk to downtown. The large rooms are decorated in classic country style and there's an old telephone booth in the entry hall. The owners like to think of this as a romantic getaway spot. | 5 rooms with bath. Picnic area, complimentary breakfast, some refrigerators, no room phones, no TV, pool, pond, massage, laundry facilities, no kids under 11, no smoking. | 69013 Camp Polk Rd. | 541/549–0123 or 800/549–4262 | fax 541/549–4481 | www.conklinsguesthouse.com | $90–$140 | No credit cards.

Metolius River Resort. The wood-shake cabins in this upscale resort in the Deschutes National Reserve, 14 mi from Sisters, have fully equipped kitchens, knotty pine interiors, river-rock fireplaces, log beds, and large riverside decks. All are set up for at least four guests. From late spring to fall, you can eat at the adjacent Kokanee Cafe. | 11 cabins. No air-conditioning, in-room data ports, kitchenettes, microwaves, refrigerators, no TV in some rooms, fishing, no smoking. | 2551 S.W. Forest Service Rd. 1419, Camp Sherman | 541/595–6281 or 800/818–7688 | fax 541/595–6281 | reservations@metolius-river-resort.com | www.metolius-river-resort.com | $160 | MC, V.

SWEET HOME

MAP 3, E4

(Nearby town also listed: Albany)

Situated on the south fork of the Santiam River near the foothills of the Cascades, Sweet Home has heritage as a timber town, but that has given way to thriving recreational activities afforded by the middle and south forks of the river. Sweet Home is also in the midst of the fertile Willamette Valley, where the mild climate and ample rain and sun produce one of the state's most diversified farming areas, leading the nation in the production of common and perennial ryegrass. There are also many dairy and berry farms.

Information: **Sweet Home Chamber of Commerce** | 1575 Main St., Sweet Home 97386 | 541/367–6186.

Attractions

East Linn Museum. The trials and joys of pioneer life are graphically displayed with artifacts, pictures, and documents from the years 1850–1940. | 746 Long St. | 541/367–4580 | Donations accepted | Memorial Day–Labor Day, Tues.–Sat. 11–4, Sun. 1–4; Labor Day–Memorial Day, Thurs.–Sat. 11–4, Sun. 1–4; or by appointment.

ON THE CALENDAR

AUG.: ***Oregon Jamboree in Sweet Home.*** Sweet Home's Jamboree, held on the first weekend in August, is a major festival of country and western music, with two acts appearing on each of three days, and local bands adding to the music. Past headliners have included Dwight Yoakam, Charlie Daniels, Sawyer Brown, Reba McIntyre, and Faith Hill. The concerts are on the grounds of Sweet Home High School and in adjoining Sankey Park, which are linked by a reproduction covered bridge. 541/367–8800 or 888/613–6812

Dining

Mountain House Country Restaurant. American. This 1876 lodge, filled with knotty pine, log beams, and a stone fireplace, is in the Willamette National Forest. You can choose among Black Angus steak, organic hamburgers, Cajun catfish, jambalaya, and other dishes, and then finish up with marion-berry cobbler. | 52855 Santiam Hwy. (Hwy. 20) | 541/367–3074 | Closed Jan.–March | $9.95–$17.95 | AE, MC, V.

Lodging

Sweet Home Inn. This is a centrally located inn with a contemporary feel. Some rooms overlook a wooded creek, while others have balconies. | 31 rooms. Some in-room hot tubs, microwaves, refrigerators, cable TV, hot tub, gym, laundry facilities. | 805 Long St. | 541/367–5137 | fax 541/367–8859 | $49–$89 | AE, MC, V.

THE DALLES

MAP 3, G2

(Nearby town also listed: Hood River)

The Dalles lies on a crescent bend of the Columbia River where the river narrows and once spilled over a series of rapids, creating a flagstone effect. French voyagers christened it "dalle," or flagstone. The Dalles is the seat of Wasco County and the trading hub of north central Oregon. It gained fame early in the region's history as the town where the Oregon Trail branched, with some departing to travel over Mount Hood on Barlow Road and the others continuing down the Columbia River. This may account for the small-town Old West feeling that still permeates the area.

The Dalles area has its share of more intellectually oriented venues as well. In addition to numerous historic buildings and museums, there is Crate's Point Interpretive Complex, which portrays the historical, geological, and cultural aspects of the Columbia River Gorge National Scenic Area. Celilo Falls, one of the important fisheries in North America, is a reminder of the rich Native American history in the area.

Information: **The Dalles Chamber of Commerce** | 404 W. 2nd St., The Dalles 97058 | 541/296–2231 or 800/255–3385 | www.thedalleschamber.com.

Attractions

Celilo Converter Station. On a hill overlooking the Columbia Gorge, this Bonneville Dam hydroelectric station transmits enough power for the entire Los Angeles–Hollywood area.

You can view the control room and also look at a variety of exhibits. | U.S. 197 | 541/296–4694 or 541/296–3615 | www.bpa.gov/corporate/kcc/celilo/celilox.shtml | Free | Daily.

Celilo Park. A favorite of windsurfers, this park also has swimming, sailboarding, and fishing. It's 7 mi east of The Dalles. | Exit 99 off I–84 | 541/296–1181 | Free | Daily.

Columbia Gorge Discovery Center—Wasco County Historical Museum. Exhibits highlight the geological history of the Columbia Gorge, back 40 million years when volcanoes, landslides, and floods carved out the area. Also here is the Wasco County Historical Museum, which focuses on 10,000 years of Native American life and exploration of the region by white settlers. | 5000 Discovery Dr. | 541/296–8600 | www.gorgediscovery.org | $6.50 | Daily 10–6.

The Dalles Dam and Reservoir. At this hydroelectric dam just east of the Bonneville Dam you can ride the free Dalles Dam Tour Train to the fish ladder and powerhouse. There's also a sturgeon pond at the visitors center. | Exit 87 (in summer) or exit 88 other times off I–84 | 541/296–1181 | Free | Daily; tour train departs: second weekend in April–Sept., Wed.–Sun. 8–4; Labor Day–Memorial Day, daily 8–5.

Ft. Dalles Museum. This 1856 doctor's office, a museum since 1905, illustrates pioneer and 19th-century life through personal effects such as clothing, guns, and an early hand washing machine. In addition, there's a collection of early automobiles, including a 1904 Electric Studebaker and a 1908 Knox, and there are some old hearses, too. The entrance fee also gains you admission to the Anderson House museum across the street, which has more pioneer artifacts. | 500 W. 15th St. | 541/296–4547 | fax 541/296–4547 | $3 | Apr.–Sept., daily 10–5; Oct.–Mar., weekends 10–5.

Maryhill Museum of Art. This castlelike mansion, high on a cliff on the Washington side of the Columbia River, has a collection of Rodin sculptures, plasters, and watercolors, prehistoric Native American tools and artifacts, and a miniature post–World War II French fashion mannikins. The house was dedicated as a museum in 1926 by Queen Marie of Romania, whose coronation gown and personal artifacts are also on display. Three mi east of the museum, just off Washington State Highway 14, is a replica of Stonehenge, built by the original owner of Maryhill. | 35 Maryhill Museum Dr., Goldendale, WA | 509/773–3733 | fax 509/773–6138 | www.maryhillmuseum.org | $6.50 | Open mid-Mar.–mid-Nov., daily 9–5.

Mayer State Park. View the lower part of the park from the top of Rowena Crest. Recreational activities include swimming, boating, fishing, and picnicking. | Exit 77 off I–84 | 800/551–6949 | www.prd.state.or.us | $3 per vehicle day-use | Daily.

Wasco County Courthouse. The museum in this 1859 courthouse, the oldest between the Cascades and Omaha, illustrates the life of pioneers on the Oregon Trail through pictures and old court records. You can visit the jail cells and, if you like, arrange to get married in the courtroom. | 410 W. 2nd Pl. | 541/296–4798 | Free (donation suggested) | May–Sept., Thurs.–Mon. 11–3; June–Aug., Thurs.–Mon. 10–4. Closed Oct.–Apr.

ON THE CALENDAR

APR.: ***Northwest Cherry Festival.*** This 9-day event, downtown in The Dalles, celebrates the return of the Hood River Valley's cherry blossoms. It includes a parade, live entertainment, a food court, arts and crafts booths, and a 5K walk and run. | 800/255–3385.

JULY: ***Fort Dalles Rodeo.*** In addition to the usual rodeo events, activities include dancing, a parade, and a 5K walk and run. It takes place at the Milt Tumilson Arena. | 800/255–3385.

JULY: ***Rough and Wild Parade.*** This parade through the streets of town is part of the Rough and Wild Pro Rodeo and takes place on the Saturday of the third weekend in July. There are floats, police officers, motorcycles, horses, and rodeo queens, and it all begins at the Armory. | 800/255–3385.

Dining

Bailey's Place. Contemporary. Bailey's opened in 1999 in an 1865 house on the National Register of Historic Places. Inside are 10-ft ceilings and period chandeliers. Prime rib is the specialty here, but do think about the chicken Ole style, in a brandy, cream, and mushroom sauce. Desserts include a huckleberry sundae, chocolate orange cheesecake, and black bottom cappuccino chocolate mousse cake. | 515 Liberty St. | 541/296–6708 | Closed Sun.–Mon. | $10–$28 | AE, D, MC, V.

Cousins'. American. Home cooking rules at this family restaurant decorated in a frontier motif. Try the pot roast or turkey supper with all the trimmings. Kids' menu. | 2114 W. 6th St. | 541/298–2771 | Breakfast also available | $7–$11 | AE, D, DC, MC, V.

Lodging

Inn at the Dalles. Views of the Columbia River, Mt. Hood, and the Dalles Dam await you in this inn's rooms. | 45 rooms. Some kitchenettes, cable TV, indoor pool, business services, airport shuttle. | 3550 S.E. Frontage Rd. | 541/296–1167 or 800/982–3496 | fax 541/296–3920 | $45–$55 | AE, D, DC, MC, V.

Lone Pine Village. This property on the Columbia River has simple, comfortable rooms and is right on the Eastern edge of town, next to I–84. Many rooms have views of the river. | 57 rooms. Bar, complimentary Continental breakfast, microwaves, refrigerators, some in-room hot tubs, pool, hot tub, driving range, exercise equipment, laundry facilities, business services, airport shuttle, some pets allowed (fee). | 351 Lone Pine Dr. | 541/298–2800 or 800/955–9626 | fax 541/298–8282 | $67–$78 | AE, D, DC, MC, V.

Quality Inn. This chain motel is close to shopping and 2 mi from downtown. The rooms are standard but comfortable and placed in three buildings. Cousin's Restaurant is located here. | 85 rooms. Restaurant, in-room data ports, some kitchenettes, cable TV, pool, hot tub, laundry facilities, business services, pets allowed (fee). | 2114 W. 6th St. | 541/298–5161 | fax 541/298–6411 | $60–$73 | AE, D, DC, MC, V.

Shaniko Hotel. When this brick hotel opened in 1901, Shaniko's population was in the thousands, but it's been a ghost town since the 1940s, complete with buildings leaning and shutters flapping in the high plains winds. The old firehouse has horse-drawn wagons and the blacksmith shop makes reproduction carriages. The restored hotel has a player piano and part of the original counter in the lobby, and the main staircase is wide enough for hoop skirts. There's a bridal suite, and you can see Mt. Hood from some of the rooms. Next door, a new building has an ice cream parlor and photo studio. | 18 rooms, 1 suite. Complimentary breakfast, restaurant, no smoking. | 4th and E Sts., Shaniko | 541/489–3441 or 800/483–3441 | fax 541/489–3444 | dholbrook@palmain.com | www.shaniko.com | $56–$96 | MC, V.

TILLAMOOK

MAP 3, C3

(Nearby towns also listed: Lincoln City, Rockaway)

More than 100 inches of annual rainfall and the confluence of three rivers contribute to the lush green pastures around Tillamook, probably best known for its thriving dairy industry and cheese factory. The Tillamook County Cheese Factory ships about 40 million pounds of cheese around the world every year. Both Tillamook and the Blue Heron French Cheese Factory offer visitors a look at their cheese-making processes.

Just south of town is the largest wooden structure in the world, one of two gigantic buildings constructed in 1942 by the U.S. Navy to house blimps that patrolled the Pacific Coast during World War II. Hangar A was destroyed by fire in 1992 and Hangar B was subsequently converted to the Tillamook Naval Air Station Museum.

The Three Capes Scenic Route over Cape Meares, Cape Lookout, and Cape Kiwanda offers spectacular views of the ocean and coastline. A lighthouse and an old Indian burial Sitka spruce, Octopus Tree, are worth the trip to Cape Meares, while Cape Lookout is one of the Northwest's best whale-watching viewpoints. Along the route from Tillamook's small resort area of Oceanside, take a look at Three Arch Rocks, a National Wildlife Refuge home to hundreds of sea lions and seals and nesting habitat for as many as 200,000 birds.

Information: Tillamook Chamber of Commerce | 3705 Hwy. 101 N, Tillamook 97141 | 503/842–7525 | tillchamber@wcn.net.

OR

Attractions

Blue Heron French Cheese Company. In business since 1979, Blue Heron specializes in Camembert, Brie, and other French-style cheeses. There's a petting zoo, a deli with seating, and a gift shop that carries Oregon wines, jams, mustards, and other products, and you can eat outside at picnic tables. A popular addition is a tasting room where you can sample the products of Oregon wineries. | 2001 Blue Heron Dr. | 503/842–8281 or 800/275–0639 | fax 503/842–8530 | www.blueheronoregon.com | Free | Memorial Day–Labor Day, daily 8–8; Labor Day–Memorial Day, daily 9–5.

Pioneer Museum. The displays in Tillamook's 1905 county courthouse include Native American, pioneer, logging, and natural history exhibits, plus antique vehicles and military artifacts. Most popular are the collections of dolls, quilts, and guns. | 2106 2nd St. | 503/842–4553 | fax 503/842–4553 | $2 | Mon.–Sat. 8–5, Sun. 11–5.

Tillamook County Creamery. The largest cheese-making plant on the West Coast, 2 mi north of Tillamook, draws more than 750,000 visitors each year. Here the milk from local Holstein and brown Swiss cows becomes ice cream, butter, and cheddar and Monterey Jack cheeses. You can see exhibits and get free samples. | 4175 Hwy. 101 N | 503/842–4481 | fax 503/842–6039 | www.tillamookcheese.com | Free | June–mid-Sept., daily 8–8; Mid-Sept.–May, daily 8–6.

Tillamook Naval Air Station Museum. During World War II blimps based here in massive hangars patrolled the coast to watch for enemy submarines. Today the remaining hangar is home to a museum that displays vintage aircraft. | 6030 Hangar Rd. | 503/842–1130 | www.tillamookair.com | $8.00 | Daily, 10–5, except Thanksgiving and Christmas Day.

ON THE CALENDAR

JUNE: *June Dairy Festival and Parade.* On the third weekend in June, the fun begins with a kids' parade on Friday evening. On Saturday morning, there's a parade through town, and the rodeo begins at the Tillamook County Fairgrounds in the afternoon and continues on Sunday. On Saturday evening, there's a big country and western dance in the streets. | 503/842–7525.

JUNE: *Tillamook Dairy Festival and Parade.* Tillamook County's famous dairy industry is highlighted at this annual event which takes place on Main Street the 4th weekend in June. | 503/842–7525.

AUG.: *Tillamook County Fair.* The Tillamook Fairgrounds hosts this summer event featuring agricultural exhibits and competitions, food, and entertainment. | 503/842–7525.

Dining

Artspace. Eclectic. Everything is homemade at Artspace in Bay City, 6 mi north of Tillamook, and you can enjoy it surrounded by artwork in a very casual and comfortable setting. The menu may include garlic-grilled oysters, vegetarian dishes, and other specials, all beautifully presented, often with edible flowers. And if you reserve in advance, you'll get a complimentary appetizer for your thoughtfulness. | 9120 5th St., Bay City | 503/377–2782 | fax 503/377–2010 | Closed Sun.–Wed. | $13.50–$16.75 | No credit cards.

Cedar Bay. Steak. This casual restaurant downtown is known for its steaks, prime rib, and seafood. Kids' menu. | 2015 1st St. | 503/842–8288 | $12–$18 | MC, V.

Roseanna's. Seafood. Roseanna's is 9 mi west of Tillamook in Oceanside, in a rustic 1915 building on the beach opposite Three Arch Rock, so you might be able to watch sea lions and puffins while you eat. Amid a casual beach atmosphere, enhanced in the evening with candlelight and fresh flowers, you can have fresh halibut or salmon in half a dozen preparations, poached baked oysters, or Gorgonzola seafood pasta. | 1490 Pacific Ave., Oceanside | 503/842–7351 | Reservations not accepted | $12–$22 | MC, V.

Lodging

Hudson House. The son of the original owner of this 1906 farmhouse was a photographer who pictured the area's rough beauty on postcards. The larger suite is downstairs, with a parlor and private porch overlooking the Nestucca Valley. The more popular upstairs suite has a bedroom in the house's turret. The two guest rooms are under the high gabled roof. The house has a wraparound porch from which you can enjoy a view of the surrounding woods. | 2 rooms, 2 suites. Picnic area, complimentary breakfast, no air-conditioning, some in-room data ports, no room phones, TV in common area, hot tub, library, no kids under 12, no smoking. | 37700 Hwy. 101 S, Cloverdale | 503/392–3533 or 888/835–3533 | www.hudsonhouse.com | $110 | MC, V.

Marclair Inn. This family-owned hotel is set on a landscaped garden abloom with flowers. It is located 2½ miles from the Air Museum and within walking distance of restaurants. | 47 rooms. Restaurant, some kitchenettes, hot tub, pool, pets allowed. | 11 Main Ave. | 503/842–7571 or 800/331–6857 | $60–$103 | AE, D, MC, V.

Sandlake Country Inn. Tucked into a bower of old roses on 2 acres, this intimate bed and breakfast is in a farmhouse built of timbers that washed ashore from a ship wreck in 1890. It is listed on the Oregon Historic Registry and filled with antiques. | 4 rooms, 1 suite. Complimentary breakfast, no air-conditioning, some kitchenettes, cable TV, in-room VCRs, some room phones, hot tub, no smoking. | 8505 Galloway Rd., Sandlake | 503/965–6745 | fax 503/965–7425 | $90–$135 | AE, D, MC, V.

Shilo Inn. Shilo's Tillamook outpost is less than 1 mi from the Tillamook Cheese Factory and close to shopping. The rooms are standard for this chain. One suite is a full-size apartment. | 101 rooms. Complimentary full breakfast, some kitchenettes, restaurant, refrigerators, cable TV, indoor pool, hot tub, exercise equipment, laundry facilities, business services, some pets allowed (fee). | 2515 N. Main St. | 503/842–7971 | fax 503/842–7960 | $89–$129 | AE, D, DC, MC, V.

Whiskey Creek Bed and Breakfast. The builder of this 1900 cedar-shingle house owned a sawmill where he made spruce oars, using the leftovers to panel the interior. Surrounded by forest, the house is unfussy and comfortable and filled with the artist owner's oil and watercolor landscapes. The two small rooms upstairs have terraces overlooking Netarts Bay. The apartment downstairs has one bedroom, plus bathroom and kitchen. In winter, the inn is a retreat, with yoga and shiatsu massage on site. | 2 rooms, 1 apartment. Picnic area, complimentary breakfast, no air-conditioning in some rooms, some kitchenettes, some microwaves, some refrigerators, cable TV, no TV in some rooms, library, baby-sitting, no smoking. | 7500 Whiskey Creek Rd. | 503/842–2408 | whiskeycreek@oregoncoast.com | $65–$90 | Closed Dec. | MC, V.

TROUTDALE

MAP 3, E2

(Nearby towns also listed: Gresham, Lake Oswego, Portland)

An eastern suburb of Portland on the Columbia River, Troutdale was named by its founder for the fish ponds he built and stocked. The Historical Old Columbia River Gorge Highway extends into the gorge from Troutdale, offering some of the most photographed and expansive vistas in the area. Along the way, Dabney State Park provides access to the Sandy River.

Information: Troutdale Chamber of Commerce | 338 East Historic Columbia River Hwy., Troutdale 97060 | 503/669–7473.

Attractions

Dabney State Park. This park, 4 mi east of Troutdale, is just south of Lewis and Clark State Park on the Crown Point Highway in Troutdale. It is also on the Sandy River. Recreational activities include boating, hiking, and fishing. It's also a popular summer swimming hole. There's an 18-hole golf course. A boat ramp is open from October through May—when no one is swimming. | Rte. 30 | 800/551–6949 | www.prd.state.or.us. | $3 per vehicle day-use | Daily.

Dining

Black Rabbit. Contemporary. Located at McMenamins Edgefield, a historic 25-acre bed and breakfast estate, this restaurant in the main lodge features fresh Northwestern cuisine and traditional favorites such as New York steak. There is open air dining. Kids' menu, no smoking. | 2126 S.W. Halsey St. | 503/492–3086 | Breakfast also available | $25 | AE, D, MC, V.

Multnomah Falls Lodge. Contemporary. This 1925 lodge near the base of 620-ft Multnomah Falls, listed on the National Register of Historic Places, has vaulted ceilings and stone fireplaces. Specialties include prime rib, freshwater trout, salmon, a platter of prawns, halibut, and scallops, and the lodge's famed wild-huckleberry daiquiris and desserts. | 50000 Historic Columbia River Hwy. | 503/695–2376 | $16–$20 | AE, D, MC, V.

Lodging

McMenamins Edgefield Bed and Breakfast. At the mouth of the Columbia River Gorge, this 25-acre estate was built in 1911 as a county poor farm. It was renovated in the style of a European village complete with theater, winery, and brewery. The rooms are beautiful, bright, and comfortable. Shared baths for men or women are centrally located in each wing. | 114 rooms (100 with shared baths). Restaurant, bar, complimentary breakfast, no room

KODAK'S TIPS FOR PHOTOGRAPHING WEATHER

Rainbows
- Find rainbows by facing away from the sun after a storm
- Use your auto-exposure mode
- With an SLR, use a polarizing filter to deepen colors

Fog and Mist
- Use bold shapes as focal points
- Add extra exposure manually or use exposure compensation
- Choose long lenses to heighten fog and mist effects

In the Rain
- Look for abstract designs in puddles and wet pavement
- Control rain-streaking with shutter speed
- Protect cameras with plastic bags or waterproof housings

Lightning
- Photograph from a safe location
- In daylight, expose for existing light
- At night, leave the shutter open during several flashes

phones, no TV in rooms, business services, no smoking. | 2126 S.W. Halsey St. | 503/669–8610 or 800/669–8610 | fax 503/492–7750 | edge@mcmenamins.com | www.mcmenamins.com | $85–105 | AE, D, MC, V.

Phoenix Inn—Troutdale. This all-minisuites motel near the mouth of the Columbia River Gorge has rooms with pretty views of the garden. | 73 rooms. Bar, complimentary Continental breakfast, cable TV, indoor pool, hot tub, exercise equipment, business services, airport shuttle, pets allowed (fee). | 477 N.W. Phoenix Dr. | 503/669–6500 or 800/824–6824 | fax 503/669–3500 | $61–$75 | AE, D, DC, MC, V.

UMATILLA

MAP 3, I2

(Nearby towns also listed: Hermiston, Pendleton)

Umatilla is located at the confluence of the Umatilla and Columbia rivers. It was founded in the mid-1800s as a trade and shipping center during the gold rush, and today it is a center for fishing activities. Just east of Umatilla, Hat Rock State Park contains the unusual geological formation from which it gets its name. Further upstream, McNary Dam generates extensive hydroelectric power and impounds a lake that extends from Umatilla to Richland, Washington, some 70 miles away.

Information: Umatilla Chamber of Commerce | 1530 6th St., Umatilla 97882 | 541/922–4825.

Attractions

Hat Rock State Park. On the south shore of Lake Wallula, 9 mi east of Umatilla, Hat Rock was the first major landmark that Lewis and Clark passed on their expedition down the Columbia. It's one of the few sites not underwater. The lake is noted for walleye and sturgeon. Waterskiing, jet skiing, swimming, and boating are popular. | U.S. 730 | 800/551–6949 | www.prd.state.or.us | Free | Mid-Mar.–Oct., daily.

McNary Lock and Dam. This Columbia River hydroelectric dam impounds a lake that extends 70 miles upstream from Umatilla to Richland, Washington. Below the dam are McNary Wildlife Nature Area and two picnic areas. Above the dam, McNary Beach Park's picnic area overlooks a large swim beach, while Hat Rock Scenic Corridor leads to Hat Rock State Park. | U.S. 730 | 541/922–4388 | Free | Daily; marinas June–Sept., daily.

Umatilla Marina Park. The campground has 26 sites with full hookups. There's a marina and boat launch. | 3rd Ave. on the Columbia River | 541/922–3939 | Free for day use | Marina, daily 7–7; Park, daily.

ON THE CALENDAR

JUNE–AUG.: *Music in the Parks.* Irrigon and Boardman, two neighboring towns of Umatilla, sponsor a series of 12 concerts every summer. In each town, events take place in the marina park along the river, and you might hear an a capella quartet, a family of singers, or someone who plays the hammer dulcimer. 541/922–3386

Dining

Desert River Inn. Contemporary. Tablecloths would obscure the beautiful wood tables here that combine with the cream and brown colors to create a relaxing atmosphere. Prime rib is the main item on the menu but there's plenty of fresh seafood plus pasta and vegetarian dishes, too. Desserts, including chocolate temptation cake, are homemade. | 705 Willamette Ave. | 541/992–1000 or 877/922–1500 | $9.95–$25 | AE, D, DC, MC, V.

Lodging

Desert River Inn. This 1977 inn is 1 mi from the Columbia River and 3 mi from downtown Umatilla. It is next to an 18-hole golf resort. The rooms are plush with large comfortable beds. | 68 rooms. Restaurant, bar, room service, in-room data ports, some kitchenettes, some mircrowaves, some refrigerators, cable TV, room phones, pool, outdoor hot tub | 705 Willamette Ave. | 541/922–1000 or 800/447–7529 | fax 541/922–4773 | $59–$80 | AE, D, DC, MC, V.

Tillicum Inn. This motel is near shopping and a golf course. The rooms are cozy and housed in a relaxed setting within walking distance of restaurants and antique shops. | 79 rooms. Kitchenettes, playground. | 1481 6th St. | 541/922–3236 | fax 541/922–5889 | $39–$62 | AE, D, DC, MC, V.

WARM SPRINGS

MAP 3, F4

(Nearby towns also listed: Madras, Prineville, Redmond)

WARM SPRINGS
INTRO
ATTRACTIONS
DINING
LODGING

Home to about 3,000 people, Warm Springs is the seat of government for the 1,000-square-mi Warm Springs Indian Reservation. The Warm Springs Tribal Council is responsible for governing the town and the reservation, which is recognized as a sovereign nation by the U.S. government. Numerous cultural and recreational activities are extended to visitors all over the reservation and throughout the year.

Information: Confederated Tribes of the Warm Springs Reservation | 541/553–1112.

Attractions

Museum at Warm Springs. The Confederated Tribes of the Warm Springs Reservation operate this museum to preserve their history and traditions. On display are tribal heirlooms, beaded artifacts, baskets, ceramics, traditional dwellings, and historic photographs. | 2189 Hwy. 26 | 541/553–3331 | fax 541/553–3338 | $6 | Daily 9–5.

ON THE CALENDAR

JUNE: *Pi-Ume-Sha.* Pi-Ume-Sha means "social gathering," and that's just what this is for the Warm Springs, Wasco, and Paiute tribes who share the Warm Springs Reservation, where it takes place on the third or fourth weekend of June. You can watch dance contests, an Indian stick-game tournament, an endurance horse race, and an all-Indian rodeo. You'll also find some crafts booths and a little carnival for the kids. | 541/553–1196.

Dining

Kah-Nee-Tah Resort and Casino. Contemporary. Juniper Dining Room at the Kah-Nee-Tah resort has two walls of windows and candlelight in the evening. The biggest seller here is prime rib, but the menu also offers buffalo steak, venison, and Northwest chinook salmon. The house specialty is bird-in-clay, a cornish game hen with a bread and fruit stuffing, encased in clay (of flour, eggs, water, and salt), and baked for three hours. It's presented in a basket, and you can crack it open with a mallet. | 6823 Hwy. 8 | 541/553–6123 or 800/831–0100 | fax 541/553–6119 | $14.95–$22.95 | AE, D, DC, MC, V.

Lodging

Kah-Nee Tah. Located in a remote desert spot in the middle of the Warm Springs Reservation, Kah-Nee Tah is perfect for a quick getaway from Portland. In addition to the hotel and casino, which has 300 slots, blackjack, and poker, there's also an RV park and Spa Wanapine, which offers aromatherapy, massage, reflexology, facials, and manicures. Mineral hot springs bubbling up from the desert floor fill baths and pools. If you like to rough it, check into one of the wood-frame, canvas-covered, unfurnished tepees. Kayak float trips can be arranged. | 139 rooms in lodge, 31 apartments, 20 tepees. Bars, dining room, some in-room hot tubs, cable TV, 2 pools, hot tubs, spa, driving range, 18-hole golf course, putting green, tennis, gym, hiking, boating, bicycles, video game room, pets allowed. | 100 Main St. | 541/553–1112 or 800/554–4786 | fax 541/553–1071 | $129–$219, $229–$259 apartments, $70 tepees | AE, D, DC, MC, V.

YACHATS

MAP 3, C5

(Nearby towns also listed: Florence, Newport)

Pronounced "YAH-hotz," Yachats is a Native American term meaning "dark waters at the foot of the mountain." The small town is at the mouth of the Yachats River, and from its rocky shoreline, which includes the highest point on the Oregon Coast, trails lead to beaches and dozens of tide pools. The Cape Perpetua Viewpoint just south of town offers visual perspectives that stretch for miles up and down the coast and out to sea. Hundreds of feet below "at the foot of the mountain," Devil's Churn stirs up foaming white water and thunderous waves, while north of Yachats, the historic 804 Trail provides dramatic views along the ocean's edge.

Information: Yachats Area Chamber of Commerce | 441 Hwy. 101, Yachats 97498 | 541/547–3530.

Attractions

Cape Perpetua Campground. Just 3 mi south of Yachats, a group site here can accommodate 100 campers. There are 37 sites for RVs, tents, or trailers; picnic tables; fire grills; flush toilets; potable water; and a dump station. | U.S. 101 | 541/547–3289 | Call for prices | Mid-May–late Sept., weekends.

★ **Cape Perpetua Visitors Center.** The Interpretive Center is inside the Siuslaw National Forest and provides information about the cultural and natural history of the central Oregon Coast. But the big attraction here is the panoramic view. The 2,700-acre Cape Perpetua Scenic Area was created to protect the area's Sitka spruce rain forest. | U.S. 101 | 541/547–3289 | Free | May, Wed.–Sun. 10–4; June–Labor Day, daily 9–5; Labor Day–Apr., weekends 10–4.

Neptune State Park. You can look for animals, watch the surf, or reflect on the view over Cumming Creek from the benches set on the cliff above the beach. It's also a great spot for whale watching. Low tide provides access to a natural cave and tidepools. | U.S. 101 S | 800/551–6949 | www.prd.state.or.us | Free | Daily.

Sea Rose. Sea Rose, 6 mi south of Yachats, sells seashells from Oregon and around the world, plus gift items and souvenirs, and serves both casual visitors and serious shell collectors. A free museum displays shells and sealife. There's an exhibit of glass fishing floats, but everybody's favorite item is the giant clam. | 95478 Hwy. 101 | 541/547–3005 | fax 541/547–5197 | Memorial Day–Labor Day, daily 9:30–6; Labor Day–Memorial Day, daily 10–5.

Strawberry Hill. Strawberry Hill, just south of Yachats, is one of the best spots on the Oregon coast to view harbor seals resting on rocky islets just offshore, and to see the starfish, anemones, and sea urchins exposed at low tide. | Hwy. 101.

Tillicum Beach Campground. This oceanside campground 3½ mi north of Yachats is so popular there is a 10-day stay limit. Stairs provide access to the beach. Open year-round, there are 61 sites. | U.S. 101 | 541/563–3211 | Free for day-use | Daily.

Yachats Ocean Road State Recreation Area. The Yachats River meets the Pacific Ocean here just 1 mi from Yachats. Whale watching is a popular activity. | U.S. 101 to Yachats Ocean Rd. | 541/997–3851 or 800/551–6949 | www.prd.state.or.us | Free | Daily.

TOP TIPS FOR TRAVELERS

Smart Sightseeings

Don't plan your visit in your hotel room. Don't wait until you pull into town to decide how to spend your days. It's inevitable that there will be much more to see and do than you'll have time for: choose sights in advance.

Organize your touring. Note the places that most interest you on a map, and visit places that are near each other during the same morning or afternoon.

Start the day well equipped. Leave your hotel in the morning with everything you need for the day—maps, medicines, extra film, your guidebook, rain gear, and another layer of clothing in case the weather turns cooler.

Tour museums early. If you're there when the doors open you'll have an intimate experience of the collection.

Easy does it. See museums in the mornings, when you're fresh, and visit sit-down attractions later on. Take breaks before you need them.

Strike up a conversation. Only curmudgeons don't respond to a smile and a polite request for information. Most people appreciate your interest in their home town. And your conversations may end up being your most vivid memories.

Get lost. When you do, you never know what you'll find—but you can count on it being memorable. Use your guidebook to help you get back on track. Build wandering-around time into every day.

Quit before you're tired. There's no point in seeing that one extra sight if you're too exhausted to enjoy it.

Take your mother's advice. Go to the bathroom when you have the chance. You never know what lies ahead.

Hotel How-Tos

How to get a deal. After you've chosen a likely candidate or two, phone them directly and price a room for your travel dates. Then call the hotel's toll-free number and ask the same questions. Also try consolidators and hotel-room discounters. You won't hear the same rates twice. On the spot, make a reservation as soon as you are quoted a price you want to pay.

Promises, promises. If you have special requests, make them when you reserve. Get written confirmation of any promises.

Settle in. Upon arriving, make sure everything works—lights and lamps, TV and radio, sink, tub, shower, and anything else that matters. Report any problems immediately. And don't wait until you need extra pillows or blankets or an ironing board to call housekeeping. Also check out the fire emergency instructions. Know where to find the fire exits, and make sure your companions do, too.

If you need to complain. Be polite but firm. Explain the problem to the person in charge. Suggest a course of action. If you aren't satisfied, repeat your requests to the manager. Document everything: Take pictures and keep a written record of who you've spoken with, when, and what was said. Contact your travel agent, if he made the reservations.

Know the score. When you go out, take your hotel's business cards (one for everyone in your party). If you have extras, you can give them out to new acquaintances who want to call you.

Tip up front. For special services, a tip or partial tip in advance can work wonders.

Use all the hotel resources A concierge can make difficult things easy. But a desk clerk, bellhop, or other hotel employee who's friendly, smart, and ambitious can often steer you straight as well. A gratuity is in order if the advice is helpful.

ON THE CALENDAR

DEC. AND MAR.: *Whale Watch Week.* Run by volunteers from the Hatfield Marine Science Center and Oregon State University, these whale watches on Cape Perpetua last 4 to 5 hours and are held the end of December and again during spring break week. 541/547–3289

Dining

Adobe Restaurant. Seafood. The dining room of the Adobe Hotel has an extraordinary ocean view. Try the baked crab pot, a rich, bubbling casserole filled with Dungeness crab and cheese in a shallot cream sauce, or the captain's seafood platter, heaped with prawns, scallops, grilled oysters, and razor clams. | 1555 U.S. 101 | 541/547–3141 | $18–$30 | AE, D, DC, MC, V.

La Serre. Seafood. Don't be dismayed by the vaguely steak-and-salad-bar ambience at this skylit, plant-filled restaurant—the chef's deft touch with fresh seafood attracts knowledgeable diners from as far away as Florence and Newport. Mouthwatering desserts complete the package. Try the tender geoduck clam, breaded with Parmesan cheese and flash-fried in lemon-garlic butter. Sun. brunch. | 160 Beach St. | 541/547–3420 | Closed Jan. and Tuesdays. No lunch | $17–$37 | AE, MC, V.

Traveler's Cove. Beneath umbrellas on the deck, or in the upstairs room with skylights and an ocean view, you can choose from black bean and chicken chili in a sourdough bread bowl, Caesar salad with salmon, hot crab on toast, various seafood chowders, and other delights, and there's always hot apple dumpling for dessert. Even breakfast is special here; homemade beer bread is used for the French toast. | 373 N. Hwy. 101 | 541/547–3801 | No dinner | $4.95–$10.95 | MC, V.

Lodging

Adobe Motel. The knotty-pine rooms in this unassuming resort motel on the ocean are on the small side, but are warm and inviting. High-beam ceilings and picture windows frame majestic views. Many of the rooms have wood-burning fireplaces. | 84 rooms, 10 suites. Restaurant, bar, some kitchenettes, refrigerators, in-room hot tubs (in suites), cable TV, in-room VCRs, hot tub, exercise equipment, business services, some pets allowed (fee). | 1555 U.S. 101 | 541/547–3141 or 800/522–3623 (western U.S.) | fax 541/547–4234 | $58–$75, $150–$175 suites | AE, D, DC, MC, V.

Fireside Motel. The west building faces the ocean and every room has a spectacular view. Some units have gas fireplaces. | 43 rooms; 3 cottages. Refrigerators, some in-room hot tubs, cable TV, some pets allowed (fee). | 1881 U.S. 101 N | 541/547–3636 or 800/336–3573 | fax 541/547–3152 | $50–$95, $115 cottages | D, MC, V.

Kittiwake. This modern ocean-front home 7 mi south of Yachats was designed to include comfortable guest rooms with large bathrooms and scenic views. Two rooms have window seats and the decks overlook the pounding surf. The 2½-acre grounds attract deer, birds, and butterflies, and there are tide pools to explore below the bluff. Both beach and rain gear are provided, along with a big German breakfast. | 3 rooms. Complimentary breakfast, no air-conditioning, some in-room hot tubs, cable TV, no room phones, no TV in some rooms, no kids under 18, no smoking. | 95368 Hwy. 101 | 541/547–4470 | fax 541/547–4415 | holidays@kittiwakebandb.com | www.kittiwakebandb.com | $125–$140 | AE, D, MC, V.

Sea Quest. This bed-and-breakfast is 8 mi south of Yachats and right on the ocean. There is a massive fireplace in the main sitting area, where breakfast is served. All rooms have queen-size beds and views of the ocean, where you might see a migrating whale pass by. | 5 rooms. Complimentary breakfast, in-room hot tubs, no room phones, no TV, TV in common area, beach, no kids under 14, no smoking. | 95354 U.S. 101 | 541/547–3782 or 800/341–4878 (for reservations) | fax 541/547–3719 | www.seaq.com | $140–$160 | MC, V.

Serenity. This inn, which has many genuine Bavarian touches because of the family's origins, sits on 10 peaceful acres in a wooded area above the Yachats River, 6 mi inland from the town of Yachats. One of the accommodations is a detached second-floor suite with a canopy bed and windows overlooking rolling lawns where deer often congregate. All the rooms have stereos. | 3 suites. Picnic area, complimentary breakfast, refrigerators, in-room hot tubs, some in-room VCRs, no room phones, no smoking. | 5985 Yachats River Rd. | 541/547–3813 | $110–$150 | MC, V.

Shamrock Lodgettes. This property is on the beach. The quarters here are mostly individual log cabins, although there are some buildings with more than one unit. The grounds are beautifully and elaborately landscaped; some people come just to walk through the gardens. All rooms have ocean or Yachats River views. | 19 rooms, 11 cottages. Kitchenettes (in cottages), refrigerators, some in-room hot tubs, cable TV, some pets allowed (fee). | 105 Highway 101 | 541/547–3312 or 800/845–5028 | fax 541/547–3843 | www.beachesbeaches.com | $75–$100, $99–$118 cottages | AE, D, DC, MC, V.

Ziggurat. This four-story cedar-and-glass pyramid built in 1987 is 6½ mi south of Yachats. It's filled with odd angles, furniture by famous modern designers, and original works of art. The two first-floor suites open on a grassy stretch to a short bluff above the beach. Both have slate floors with carpets and one has a private sauna. | 2 suites. Complimentary breakfast, no air-conditioning, in-room data ports, no room phones, no TV, no kids under 14, no smoking. | 95330 Hwy. 101 | 541/547–3925 | www.newportnet.com/ziggurat | $165 | No credit cards.

WA

Washington

Washington, the most northwesterly state of the contiguous United States, is full of contrasts. Even its nickname, the Evergreen State, has been a bone of contention ever since it was coined. For one thing, it is not true. Very little of Washington is evergreen. Much of the land is covered by tall mountains, and while the dense forests of the Olympic Peninsula get as much as 140 inches of rain (or more) per year, a large section of the state gets as little as 6 inches.

Even western Washington has its dry spots, of course—on the northeastern Olympic Peninsula, in the rain shadow of the mountains, and from central Whidbey Island north through the San Juans. Here exposed rocks are often bare, instead of sporting a furry cover of lichens, mosses, and ferns.

And the dry east side has its wet spots, in the northeastern mountains, in the Palouse Hills, along the eastern edge of the state, and in the Blue Mountains. That's because rainfall increases the further the clouds travel beyond the rain shadow of the Cascade Mountains.

Washingtonians often claim they live in two different states, one west and one east of the Cascade Mountain Crest. But that's not exactly true, either. Washington is really made up of four different regions, not two.

The western lowlands run from the Cascade foothills to the ocean and include the coast range, the Olympic Mountains, the Salish Sea (Puget Sound, Hood Canal, Admiralty Inlet, Juan de Fuca Strait, the San Juan Islands, and the southernmost part of Georgia Strait), and Pugetopolis, the metropolitan area that sprawls from Seattle north to Arlington, west to the Kitsap Peninsula, east to Snoqualmie Falls, and south to the state capital of Olympia.

The Cascade Mountains are a world unto themselves, with few roads and even fewer towns or other settlements.

CAPITAL: OLYMPIA	POPULATION: 4,866,692	AREA: 68,192 SQUARE MI
BORDERS: ID, OR, CANADA, PACIFIC OCEAN	TIME ZONE: PACIFIC	POSTAL ABBREVIATION: WA
WEB SITE: WWW.TOURISM.WA.GOV		

East of the mountains matters get more complicated, but it's easiest to grasp this vast region by dividing it into two blocks, a moist northern, and dry southern one. Much of the center is taken up by the Columbia Plateau, which stretches from the edge of the Cascade foothills east to Spokane and south to Oregon. It is bordered by the Palouse Hills and the Blue Mountains to the east, by the Rocky Mountains to the north.

A western spur of the Rocky Mountains, which reaches from Idaho west to the Okanogan Valley, forms the second distinct region of eastern Washington. It is a land of granite uplands, deeply glaciated valleys, and green forests.

The steppes of the Columbia Plateau are, by contrast, mostly covered by dry grasses and sagebrush (except for the settled region, where irrigated fields and orchards dominate). The Columbia River enters the regions from the north, cutting south through the Rocky Mountains. It skirts the Columbia Plateau, squeezes through a deep canyon between the plateau and the Cascades before turning east across the Columbia Basin (a low-lying section of the plateau) and breaking through the Horse Heaven Hills at the Wallula gap and turning west toward the ocean by way of the Columbia Gorge, a deep (almost sea-level) canyon the big river has cut through the mountains.

The Columbia and its tributaries—the Snake, Yakima, Wenatchee, Methow, and Okanogan—carry snow-melt water from the high mountains to the dry steppe, making irrigated agriculture possible. Without the water of these life-giving rivers, there would be little agriculture in eastern Washington apart from dryland wheat, cattle range, and perhaps a few vineyards. Because of this water, more than 85 percent of Washington's agricultural products are produced in this dry region.

It seems a bit of an anomaly that Washington's biggest rivers are in the dry part of the state, but so are the biggest lakes, and most of the wetlands. Interior Washington also has more waterfowl and shorebirds than the coastal section of the state, and a lot more wildflowers.

History

Washington's history is closely tied to its geography. Prehistoric settlement patterns weren't all that different from modern ones. The shores, rivers, and native prairies of the western lowlands were mostly occupied by Indians speaking languages of the Coast Salish group, while a few tribes—the Makah, Quileute, and Chinook—belonged to other linguistic groups but shared the same culture. The Cascade Mountains, then as now, were mostly unoccupied and exploited seasonally for game and berries. The lands east of the Cascades were split into two major language groups: the Interior Salish (Wenatchi, Okanogan, Spokane, Kalispel, among others) to the north, and Sahaptin speakers (Yakama, Palus, Cayuse, and Nez Perce) to the south.

Timeline

11,000–9,000 years ago
Hunters of the Clovis culture occupy Wenatchee area (as judged by artifacts found in a local orchard).

c.4,200 years ago
Early Northwest Coast culture settlements on the Olympic Peninsula (radiocarbon dating).

c. 1100 AD
Oldest house foundations in Ozette Village, Olympic Peninsula (radiocarbon dating).

1579
Sir Francis Drake claims New Albion for England. (Note: the naming of America's West Coast as New England precedes the naming of the North Atlantic region now known by that name.)

Coastal natives had perfected making canoes carved from cedar logs, creating some of the most beautiful, swift, and seaworthy watercraft the world has ever seen. The horse was introduced to plateau natives by the Utes to the southeast early in the 18th century, thus creating an equestrian culture that rivaled and even surpassed that of the Great Plains.

Buffalo were once native to eastern Washington and Oregon but, as the herds were decimated, they were pushed east, first to southern Idaho, then across the Rocky Mountains. By the late 18th century native hunters on horseback traveled east across the mountain passes, hunted buffalo on the Great Plains, and returned with loads of dried buffalo meat. Trade, and occasional warfare, with Plains tribes were a part of these expeditions.

But the plateau tribes, like those of the coast, also benefited from salmon, the great staple food of the Pacific Northwest. Salmon ascended the rivers in great numbers in spring and autumn to spawn in the streams of their birth and die. Native fishermen intercepted the fish wherever currents, river rapids, or waterfalls slowed the migration. Almost every lowland river had fish weirs and traps; the plateau fishermen speared salmon or caught them in dip nets at the cascades of the Columbia and at rapids on the Snake, Yakima, and Spokane Rivers. Major fishing stations were at Celilo, Wanapum, Priests Rapids, and Spokane Falls. Kettle Falls on the Columbia, near Lyle on the Klickitat is the only one still in use today. Native fishing at these sites continued until dams built on the Columbia and Snake in the 1930s and '40s drowned the rapids.

The Pacific Northwest was also rich in game and furbearers. After British explorer James Cook discovered the Northwest Coast in 1778, fur traders arrived by sea, bartering valuable sea otter hides which they then sold at high profits in China. This profitable trade attracted the attention of the Spanish, who controlled the West Coast from northern California south to Cape Horn and who claimed the Northwest as part of their territories. After a few expeditions to the Northwest Coast, Juan de Fuca Strait, and the San Juan Islands, the Spanish withdrew and ceded the region to the British. While the quarrel lasted, the Spanish did build a short-lived fort at Neah Bay in 1792, the first European settlement in what is now Washington State.

While British explorer George Vancouver haggled with the Spanish over possession of Vancouver Island and Puget Sound, American trader Robert Gray discovered Grays Harbor and the Columbia River. After Gray mentioned his discovery, Vancouver sent a brig upriver and claimed the territory for Britain.

Americans refused to accept that claim, because Gray, and not Vancouver, had discovered the river, entered it first, and had named it after his ship. This dispute was one reason why Thomas Jefferson sent the Lewis and Clark Expedition to the Northwest.

Until Lewis and Clark crossed the Rockies in 1804–05 and proved that an overland route to the Pacific Northwest existed, contact with the East Coast had mostly been

1592
A Greek navigator, sailing for Spain and using the name Juan de Fuca, claims to have discovered a vast strait. Two centuries later Bruno Heceta and Juan Francisco Bodega claim the Washington coast for Spain.

c. 1750
The Indians of the Columbia Plateau obtain, and master, horses and soon create a unique Plateau culture which precedes the horse culture of the Great Plains.

1778
In search of the fabled Northwest Passage, British explorer Captain James Cook sights and names Cape Flattery at the tip of the Olympic Peninsula. One of Cook's crew members is the first American to visit the Northwest Coast.

1792
British explorer George Vancouver charts and names Puget Sound; American fur trader Robert Gray discovers Grays Harbor and the Columbia River.

1805
American explorers Lewis and Clark enter Washington from the east and follow the Columbia downriver to the Pacific Ocean at Cape Flattery.

by sea. The Indians, of course, had their own, long-established trade routes reaching west to the Great Plains and as far south as the pueblos of Arizona and New Mexico.

The first American settlement in the Northwest was established in 1811 by John Jacob Astor's fur traders near the mouth of the Columbia as a joint sea-and-land effort. But the ship on which the traders arrived was captured by natives on Clayoquot Sound on Vancouver Island and blown to bits by the fatally injured purser, and the overland party encountered unexpected problems. After the outbreak of the War of 1812, Astor sold his fort to the British Northwest Company, one step ahead of its imminent capture by a British man-of-war.

At the time, the Northwest Company was engaged in a surprisingly bloody war with the Hudson's Bay Company over fur trapping territories in the west. The war was forcibly settled by the British government; the two companies were merged and took on the name of the older one, the Hudson's Bay Company. Almost overnight, the HBC found itself in control of vast territories in the Northwest. In 1825 the company built a new fort and trading depot further up on the Columbia, at present-day Vancouver, across from the mouth of the Willamette, near the head of tidewater.

The fort proved to be an exceptionally profitable trading depot, but those pesky Americans wouldn't stay away, arriving by land and sea in a small but continuous trickle. The fur trappers were followed by missionaries who established missions in eastern Washington, and by farmers who began to settle in the fertile Willamette Valley in the 1830s.

By 1845 American settlers had moved north of the Columbia, as far as southern Puget Sound. After Britain and the U.S. agreed to split the Oregon Territory along the 49th Parallel, more American immigrants arrived, and in 1853 Washington Territory was separated from Oregon. But while Oregon became a state in 1859, Washington had to wait until 1889 to achieve statehood.

By then Washington had not only become a major producer of lumber, salmon, wheat, and cattle, but had also established the first irrigated fields and orchards east of the Cascades. Major fires devastated Seattle, Ellensburg, and Spokane, but the cities soon rose from the ashes, built of brick and stone instead of wood. Shipbuilding became a major Puget Sound industry in the late 19th century. In 1916, Bill Boeing built his first airplane, an act from which the Seattle region has benefited ever since. In the 1930s and '40s irrigation and hydroelectric dams were built on the Columbia and Snake. The biggest, Grand Coulee, was finished just in time to supply the new Hanford Atomic Works with energy for producing an atom bomb which helped defeat Japan in the Second World War.

In the 1980s Microsoft took off, and other high-tech industries began to change the nature of Washington's industries. As logging and fishing were phased out, due to declining resources, Washington began to market its natural beauty, and in the 1990s tourism became a major growth industry.

1811
John Jacob Astor's Pacific Fur Company establishes Astoria trading post near mouth of the Columbia (soon sold to the British and renamed Fort George).

1824–25
British doctor John McLoughlin establishes Hudson's Bay Company's Fort Vancouver on the Columbia River near its confluence with the Willamette.

1836
The Beaver, the first steamship on the Northwest Coast, arrives in Puget Sound.

1837
Marcus and Narcissa Whitman establish mission at Waiilatpu, near present Walla Walla. The Whitmans were killed and the mission destroyed in an 1847 attack by Cayuse Indians.

1845
Michael T. Simmons's party, the first American settlers in Puget Sound region, arrive at Tumwater.

The Regions

1. PUGETOPOLIS

Seattle, its suburbs, and the other cities of the Puget Sound region form a metropolis some 100 mi long, from Arlington in the north to Olympia in the south, and some 30 to 40 mi wide, from the Snoqualmie Falls to the east to the far reaches of the Kitsap Peninsula to the west. What makes this metropolis unique is the fact that it is split in half along a north/south axis by Puget Sound, a saltwater inlet that is crossed by a single bridge, the Tacoma Narrows Bridge. Commuters to the north and south of the bridge have to cross by automobile and passenger ferry. Other inlets and several lakes further subdivide the region. The largest of these, Lake Washington, which divides Seattle from Kirkland and Bellevue, is crossed by two floating bridges. A third floating bridge crosses the Hood Canal to connect the Kitsap to the Olympic Peninsula.

There are a few floating bridges elsewhere in the region, but only in Seattle do floating bridges carry multilane freeways across water (and only in western Washington can car drivers become seasick while crossing a bridge during a storm).

Many of western Washington's industries, as well as its social and cultural life, are centered in Pugetopolis. Yet Pugetopolis is not one giant, homogenous amoeba of urban sprawl. As outlying cities became engulfed, they managed to preserve their own unique personalities. Washingtonians do not think of Seattle as one giant super city that stands as a paradigm for an entire region, the way Californians look at Los Angeles. Washingtonians still consider Seattle, Bellevue, Edmonds, Everett, Marysville, Bainbridge Island, Tacoma, and Olympia as separate entities, even as freeways, bridges, and the subdivisions of urban sprawl tie them ever closer together.

Despite the urban sprawl, the islands in the sound south of Tacoma are still mainly unspoiled and wooded, though some of them have waterfront homes and weekend cabins. Seals, sea lions, and an occasional gray whale still patrol the waters of the Salish Sea; seabirds congregate on the shores of sound and lake, wild ducks and geese invade waterfront parks; deer and an occasional black bear or cougar wander through the woods; and bald eagles soar above urban lakes. Pods of orcas cause traffic jams when they swim past the Seattle waterfront, which happens several times a year.

Towns listed: Arlington, Bainbridge Island, Bellevue, Bremerton, Edmonds, Enumclaw, Everett, Issaquah, Marysville, North Bend, Olympia, Puyallup, Renton, Seattle, Seattle-Tacoma International Airport Area, Snohomish, Tacoma

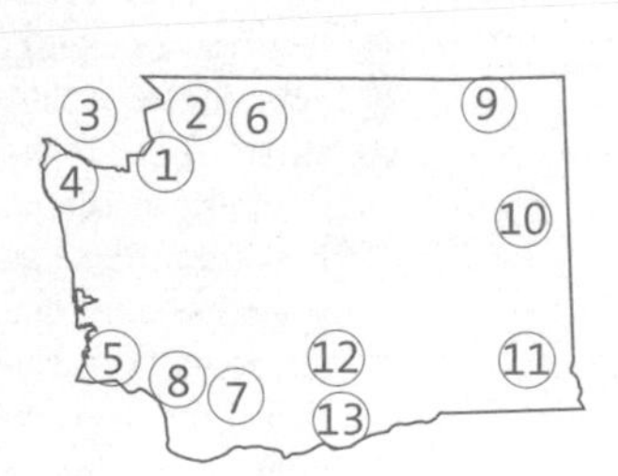

2. NORTHWESTERN LOWLANDS

In the lowlands between the Snohomish River and the Canadian border, you are never far from saltwater or from the mountains. Besides the Snohomish, the valleys of three other rivers form the

1851
Seattle founded by the Denny party at Alki Point, but the town is soon moved to deeper waters in present waterfront.

1853
Washington Territory created out of Oregon region north of Columbia.

1889
On November 11, Washington is admitted to the Union. Fires devastate Seattle, Spokane, and Ellensburg.

1916
Bill Boeing, Sr., builds the first Boeing aircraft.

1980
Mt. St. Helens erupts.

lowlands with their spreading alluvial fans: the Stillaguamish, the Skagit, and the Nooksack. Like all of the Salish Sea region, these lowlands were heavily glaciated by a continental glacier pushing south from Canada during the last Ice Age, covering the land to a depth of 3,500 to 4,500 ft. Alpine glaciers pushing west from the high Cascades Peaks added to the ice mass. Because the hardness of the underlying rocks varied, the glaciers cut unevenly, carving isolated outcroppings of hard rock separated by channels. The largest of these rocks are now known as the San Juan Islands. Other rocky isles stood closer to shore and were eventually joined to the land by river-borne silt. Such former islands rise as hills above Burlington, La Conner, and Mount Vernon. As the glaciers receded, they also left behind glacial moraines, some of which became islands. Whitbey and Camano Islands are the largest such moraines. A few of the rocky islands still rise offshore, though their proximity to the land almost makes them Peninsulas: Camano and Fidalgo Islands are separated from the mainland by river sloughs only; Lummi Island by a narrow passage. Samish Island is now a peninsula.

All of this makes for a varied and very beautiful landscape, especially since the flats are a patchwork of green pastures and vegetable fields highlighted in spring by acres of colorful tulip fields, and the moraine uplands and rocky outcroppings are covered with evergreen forest. White-water creeks gush from the mountains, and placid streams meander through the lowlands, providing havens for ducks, geese, and blue herons. In winter the low-lying flats are white with snow geese and swans.

Most of the towns and villages of this region are built along saltwater bays or on the banks of navigable rivers, because the land was swampy and overgrown by tall trees when the first settlers arrived, and travel was feasible only by water. This is why towns as far up the narrow rivers as Snohomish, Mount Vernon, and Lynden were once served by steamboats.

Today, with logging in a decline, dairy and berry farming are the mainstay of the local economy, though Bellingham and Mount Vernon also have some light industry. But increasingly the small towns and villages of this region have begun to market their real asset: the natural beauty of their setting.

Towns listed: Bellingham, La Conner, Mount Vernon, Sedro Woolley, Whitbey Island

3. SAN JUAN ISLANDS

It is not an exaggeration to say that the San Juan Islands, which lie between the Washington mainland and Vancouver Island, are one of the most beautiful places on earth. Sheer rock faces rising straight from the water make them look about as dramatic as islands get. Some are bare or covered with just a few grasses and wildflowers; others have shorelines of gnarled shore pines or red-trunked madrona trees; yet others are densely covered with Douglas firs. Since the islands lie in the rain shadow of the Olympic Mountains and Insular Range, they receive only half as much rain as other Salish Sea lowlands; those with poor, rocky soils may have stands of prickly pear cacti or junipers (plants otherwise unknown in western Washington).

Several of the islands are quite flat, though these too have steep, rocky shores interrupted by sandy or marshy coves (Lopez, Shaw, and Waldron, among the larger islands). Others are mountainous, with some peaks reaching more than a thousand feet, and one, Mt. Constitution on Orcas Island, more than two thousand feet. Island peaks look taller than they are, since they rise straight from saltwater and not from some elevated plain or plateau.

The great thing about the San Juans is that you can relax without having to do anything. But you can walk beaches, hike mountains, kayak, watch birds or whales, wander through fields of wildflowers, visit galleries, dine on local delicacies, or sip coffee in a sidewalk café.

Islands listed: Lopez Island, Orcas Island, San Juan Islands

4. OLYMPIC PENINSULA AND RAIN FOREST

The Olympic Peninsula is surrounded by saltwater on three sides and bordered by the Chehalis River and its tributaries to the south. It rises from the waters like a giant, tree-covered shield, with Mt. Olympus as its buckle and other tall peaks as subsidiary bosses. In summer, the slopes below the snow-covered peaks glow with wildflowers, and hundreds of lakes sparkle like diamonds in the sun. Because of the peninsula's shape, river valleys, many of them deeply glaciated, radiate out in all directions.

The western river valleys are filled with a temperate rain forest of giant trees covered by humps of mosses so thick and fuzzy with thin, curly leaves and capsuled spore stalks that they look like damp, green fur coating the forest floor, engulfing rocks, clinging to the trunks and branches of trees. These clusters, humps, and mounds seem alive with arrested motion, hunched up to spring forth, vibrating in the slightest breeze, animated by the passing footsteps of bear, elk, or man.

Major differences between this temperate rain forest and the tropical rain forests of the world are the scarcity of mosquitoes and other noxious insects, the total absence of poisonous snakes, and the size of the trees, which are about twice as tall as they grow in the tropics.

While the peninsula's west coast is very wet, much of the north coast lies in the rain shadow of the mountains and may receive as little as 16 inches of rain. (The western slopes, by contrast, may receive as much as 16 ft.)

The heart of the mountains is protected by Olympic National Park and is approached by few roads and crossed by none, making this a great area for backpacking. But many people come here just to take a walk in the woods, watch storm-tossed surf, or relax by a mountain stream.

Towns listed: Aberdeen, Copalis Beach, Hoquiam, Moclips, Neah Bay, Olympic National Park, Port Angeles, Sequim, Shelton

5. SOUTHERN COAST AND MOUTH OF THE COLUMBIA

Along much of Washington's southern coast, the mountains are separated from the ocean by wide sandy beaches and broad inlets, which in turn are protected by sandy spits. The great exception is Cape Disappointment at the mouth of the Columbia.

There are depressions in the sand that hold bogs, many of which are planted with commercial cranberries. The mainland margins of the inlets and the banks of the lower Columbia are swampy and cut by many channels into marshy islands. These are as close to Louisiana bayou country as the Northwest comes. A few even have their own breed of swamp dwellers, fishermen or oyster growers, who live on house barges tied to the shore. This part of the coast is also very wet, and several of the lowland rivers are bordered by rain forest.

But the area is also beautiful, and alive with shorebirds and waterfowl. Even bald eagles are common. Willapa Bay, the southernmost estuary on the Washington coast, is the most productive coastal ecosystem in the United States. One of every six U.S. oysters is grown here. It also helps, of course, that Willapa Bay is the cleanest body of tidewater in the country. When you add the oysters grown in Grays Harbor, the Hood Canal, Samish Bay, and southern Puget Sound, you'll understand why Washington is the Number One oyster-producing state in the Union.

Towns listed: Ilwaco, Long Beach, South Bend, Westport

6. NORTH CASCADES

The North Cascades look like a different world, and they are. Some geologists believe that they once were a Pacific Ocean island that drifted eastward and bumped into the North American continent, or, as geologists like to say, docked, since the experts don't consider these attachments permanent.

Rising from valley floors only a few hundred feet above sea level, 4,000-, 6,000-, even 7,000-ft peaks crowd out the sky. Further east the peaks top 9,000 ft. Some, like Mt. Shuksan, glow with blue glacial ice, others are marked by white streaks of cascading creeks. In summer the hanging valleys are densely covered with wildflowers; in autumn they glow red and yellow with the fall foliage of huckleberry, mountain ash, and aspen. In winter, these mountains have the greatest measured snowfall on earth—more than 80 ft in the high places of the western slopes. Because of the depth of the glaciated valleys, these mountains are uncommonly accessible by roads and short, albeit steep, hiking trails. Passes are low, in the 3,000- to 5,000-ft range, making crossing feasible even at the height of winter.

While the Cascade Range in general is of volcanic origin, the North Cascades have only two prominent volcanic peaks, both more than 10,000 ft tall. Glacier Peak is almost hidden amid tall nonvolcanic mountains, but Mt. Baker, to the north, stands west of the main range and can be seen far out to sea.

The North Cascades run north into British Columbia, and south to Snoqualmie Pass. This region is the ultimate hiking and backpacking country, but it also has good fishing, quiet streams and lakes for boating, and shady trails for taking refreshing strolls.

Towns listed: Cashmere, North Cascades National Park, Skykomish, Twisp, Winthrop

7. SOUTH CASCADES

The Cascade Mountains south of Snoqualmie Pass are more heavily eroded than those to the north and thus not as high (though a few peaks do top 7,000 ft), but two of its volcanic peaks are taller than any of the northern Washington mountains: Mt. Adams reaches a height of more than 12,000 ft, and Mt. Rainier more than 14,000 ft. The third of the southern peaks, Mt. St. Helens, blew its top in 1980, and is now little more than 8,000 ft tall. Once called the Mt. Fuji of Washington and worshiped by admirers of natural beauty, it now has a following of disaster freaks. Valleys in the southern Cascades are not as heavily glaciated as those to the north, but V-shaped river canyons penetrate deep into the mountains.

West of the Cascade crest, trees face only one timberline; east of the crest they are subjected to two: an upper timberline in the alpine zone like that of western Washington mountains, and a lower timberline, where the land becomes too dry to support trees and grasses or steppe scrub take over.

The southern Cascades run from Snoqualmie Pass south to the Columbia River Gorge. This is a great area for exploring volcanoes, mountain trails, waterfalls, and wildflower meadows, and for picking huckleberries in fall.

Towns listed: Cle Elum, Mt. Rainier National Park, Wenachee

8. SOUTHERN LOWLANDS

The southern lowlands are part of a long trough that runs from the Georgia Strait in southern British Columbia to Oregon's southern Willamette Valley. The area is bordered in the west by the low hills of the coast ranges, to the east by the foothills of the Cascades, to the north by Puget Sound, and to the south by the Columbia. It is bisected by two rivers: the Chehalis in the north, and the Cowlitz River, which flows west from the southern slopes of Mt. Rainier, then turns south to the Columbia.

The landscape of these lowlands is pretty and pleasingly pastoral but rarely dramatic, except where it crosses ash flows from the 1980 Mt. St. Helens eruption.

The cities of this region are in many ways closer to Oregon than to Washington and look to Portland, rather than Seattle, for cultural guidance.

Towns listed: Ashford, Centralia, Chehalis, Vancouver

9. NORTHEASTERN MOUNTAINS

The northeastern mountains from the Okanogan to the Pend Oreille Valley are a truly beautiful landscape of granite mountains, glaciated cliffs, grassy uplands, and sunlit forests. Few Washingtonians seem to know about the attractions of this region, however. Even at the height of the summer vacation season, its roads and trails are rarely crowded, while Lake Roosevelt, to the south, is crowded with houseboats and fishing skiffs.

The hidden jewel of these mountains is the Sanpoil River Valley, which is a miniature Yosemite Valley, with vertical rock walls rising some 2,000–3,000 ft straight from the river, the steepness heightened by the narrowness of the canyon. The valley has no amenities and is still in the possession of its original owners, the Indians of the Colville Reservation, who have preserved its beauty. These wild highlands have few visitor facilities, but the old gold mining town of Republic provides food and lodging, as do Kettle Falls, Colville, and Newport. The Okanogan Valley and the regional metropolis of Spokane, on the fringes of the region, offer a more varied selection of services.

Towns listed: Colville, Newport, Republic

10. COLUMBIA PLATEAU

The Columbia Plateau was created by a series of lava flows that were later deeply cut by glacial floods. Because its soil is mostly made up of alluvial deposits and windblown silt (known to geologists as loess), it is very fertile. Since it receives little annual rainfall, however, its vast central section (of more than 30,000 square mi) stretching from the foothills of the Cascades and the northeastern mountains east to Idaho and south to Oregon, has no forests. In fact, except for a few scattered pine trees in the north, oaks in the southwest, and willows and cottonwoods along creeks and rivers, it has no trees.

This treeless expanse is part of an even larger steppe and desert region that runs north into Canada and south through eastern and southern California all the way to Mexico and the the Sea of Cortez. But, due to a quirk of nature, there is water and because of it large parts of the low-lying areas are very green today. The water is carried from the mountains by the great rivers—the Columbia and the Snake—and by their tributaries and is diverted to irrigation channels. Thus this region's cities are verdant with shrubs, trees, and flowers, and its fields bear a great variety of crops—asparagus and potatoes, apples and peaches, alfalfa and zucchini, grapes and sweet corn, wheat and lentils, and much more. Because agriculture prospers, villages and cities prosper and are able to provide their residents with the amenities of modern civilization. In other words, the Columbia Plateau is no cultural backwater, but a highly civilized countryside, with symphony and opera houses, theaters, art museums, universities, and great restaurants. Because its agriculture lives in harmony with nature, it is also beautiful, rich in wildlife, with more animals and species than it had before civilization began to encroach.

Towns listed: Cheney, Coulee Dam, Ellensburg, Ephrata, Moses Lake, Pullman, Spokane

11. PALOUSE, WALLA WALLA, AND BLUE MOUNTAINS

To the southeast of the Columbia Plateau lies a pleasant region of rolling hills that supports fields of wheat, lentils, and peas. Unlike the farmers of the Plateau, those of the Palouse and of the foothills of the Blue Mountains need no irrigation waters to make their fields bear fruit, as they get enough rain to produce record crops from their fertile soils. It is a blessed landscape, flowing green and golden under the sun in waves of loam.

Not only is the region fertile, it is historically significant as well. The Lewis and Clark expedition passed through the Palouse in 1805, and Walla Walla was one of the earliest settlements in the inland Northwest. Museums in the area document this early history.

Towns listed: Walla Walla

12. YAKIMA VALLEY AND HORSE HEAVEN HILLS

This is a region of great contrasts, a natural grass steppe turned green by irrigation waters, and snow-capped volcanic peaks towering over golden hills. It is a curious fact that Washington's tallest mountain stands west of the Cascade Crest but is seen most often by those living east of the mountains, where the air is clear and the clouds are few. To the south looms broad-shouldered Mt. Adams, at more than 12,000 feet in height even more of a presence than Rainier because it is closer. It is the sacred mountain of the Yakama and borders their reservation, where wild horses still run free. It is a land of eagles and curlews, of deer and elk, and of some of the most productive agriculture land in the nation. But while the valley is well known for its fruits and vegetables, its beef and lamb, its real fame rests on its wines, which rival the best produced anywhere in the world.

Towns listed: Kennewick, Pasco, Richland, Sunnyside, Toppenish, Yakima

13. COLUMBIA RIVER GORGE

Cut thousands of feet deep by the Columbia River, this chasm through the basalt ridges of the Cascade Mountains has often been compared to the scenery of Europe's Rhine River. But that is not a fair comparison, since the Columbia is by far the fairer of the two, as well as the more dramatic.

The rushing waters of the untamed, wild river encountered by American and British explorers gave their name to the bordering mountains. The Native Americans of the Pacific Northwest knew the wild river and its cascades well and came here, in season, to harvest its bounty of salmon, to trade, and to socialize. But the river has been hobbled by dams, and the salmon (as well as the Indians) are all but extinct. But even in this captive state, the river is still exceptionally beautiful, and one of the wonders of the natural world. Fortunately, its cliffs and their tall, cascading waterfalls, its forest and wildflower meadows have been preserved from further development.

The drive up the Washington side of the river is more scenic than that on the Oregon side. For one thing, Rte. 14 is a narrow, twisting, two-lane highway that winds around headlands and skirts tall cliffs; for another, there are full views of the spectacular waterfalls, most of which are on the Oregon side and can be seen in their full glory only from a distance. The road passes through villages and towns that have stood here for more than a hundred years.

Towns listed: Goldendale, Stevenson

When to Visit

For a state that's as far north on the globe as Labrador, Washington weather is surprisingly mild in all seasons. Even in the hottest summers temperatures rarely soar above ninety (and then only in a few places) and in the coldest winters they rarely drop below zero°F. The record high, recorded in eastern Washington at Wahluke Slope (July 24, 1928) and Ice Harbor Dam (August 5, 1961) is 118°F; the record low, recorded during the arctic winter of 1968/69 at Mazama and Winthrop in the Methow Valley (December 30, 1968) stands at -48. Extremes like that are rare, however.

Washington's weather does have great climatic divergences between the wet coastal lowlands west of the Cascade Mountains (which divide the state from north to south) and the dry uplands and plateaus east of the Cascades. In the west, skies can be gray for days, even weeks on end. In the east, the heavens seem eternally blue.

In autumn, winds often turn into tempests, which may reach hurricane force on the coast. In the dry inland region, now dotted with fallow wheat fields, sudden dust storms make driving exceedingly dangerous, especially on I–90, I–82, and U.S. 395, where cars and trucks travel at freeway speeds.

But storms are rare and the weather is usually quite balmy, even in winter. Snow falls mostly in the mountains. What little snow falls in the lowlands does not linger for more than a few days. West of the Cascades, it quickly melts or is washed away by rains; east of the mountains, it usually blows away. But whenever it falls in the cities, it causes major traffic jams. In the Cascades, which have the highest amounts of snowfall on earth, mountain passes may be closed for days.

Chances are that the weather, at all seasons, is mild and sunny, rather than windy or rainy. In fact, it can be so calm and even bland that you won't notice it at all. Best of all, smog, that bane of most American metropolitan areas, rarely occurs, even in the densely settled Puget Sound region. But there often is some haze in the air, and Seattleites bless those days (and mention them on the daily news) when Mt. Rainier can be seen from the city. It is known as "when the mountain is out."

CLIMATE CHART

Average High/Low Temperatures (°F) and Monthly Precipitation (in inches)

	JAN.	FEB.	MAR.	APR.	MAY	JUNE
ABERDEEN	46/35	50/36	53/37	57/40	62/45	66/49
	5	4	3.8	2.8	2	1.5
	JULY	AUG.	SEPT.	OCT.	NOV.	DEC.
	69/52	70/52	69/49	62/44	52/39	47/36
	1	1.3	1.6	3.4	5.6	6
	JAN.	FEB.	MAR.	APR.	MAY	JUNE
SEATTLE	47/37	50/38	54/40	59/44	65/49	70/53
	5	3.9	3.8	2.8	2	1.5
	JULY	AUG.	SEPT.	OCT.	NOV.	DEC.
	74/57	75/57	70/53	60/50	51/40	47/37
	1	1.3	1.5	3.4	5.6	6
	JAN.	FEB.	MAR.	APR.	MAY	JUNE
SPOKANE	33/21	39/25	48/31	58/37	67/44	74/50
	2	1.6	1.9	1.1	1.4	1.2
	JULY	AUG.	SEPT.	OCT.	NOV.	DEC.
	84/56	83/55	72/47	59/38	43/30	35/24
	.6	.6	.8	1.1	2	2.1

FESTIVALS AND SEASONAL EVENTS

SPRING

May **Viking Fest.** The Norwegian community of Poulsbo celebrates its proud heritage. | 360/779–3378.

May **Northwest Folklife Festival.** This gathering in Seattle is one of the nation's largest folk-music festivals. | Memorial Day weekend | 206/684–7200

SUMMER

July	**Pacific Northwest Arts and Crafts Fair.** This juried show held in Bellevue presents the works of several hundred artists. | 425/454–3322.
Late Aug.	**International Kite Festival.** Participants send kites of all shapes and sizes flying above Long Beach the third week in August. | 800/451–2542.
Early–mid-Sept.	**Western Washington Fair.** The fair brings top entertainment, animals, food, exhibits, and rides to the town of Puyallup. | 253/841–5045.

State's Greats

Snow-capped peaks rising above saltwater inlets and inland lakes, lush forests and dry steppes, rocky coulees and moist canyons carved by waterfalls—Washington is a state of many natural wonders.

The Columbia River Gorge, the wildflower meadows of Mt. Rainier, the blasted volcanic landscape of Mt. St. Helens, the jagged peaks of the North Cascades, the islands of the Salish Sea, and the dense coniferous rain forests and rocky shores of the Olympic Peninsula are among the state's best known scenic wonders. Eastern Washington's vast coulee country of steep-walled rocky canyons is unique among the geologic features of the world.

While much of Washington consists of lowlands and gently rolling uplands and plateaus, the landscape is dominated by mountains. The tall volcanic peaks of **Mt. Baker** (10,775 ft), **Glacier Peak** (10,541 ft), **Mt. Rainier** (14,411 ft), **Mt. St. Helens** (8,388 ft), and **Mt. Adams** (12,276 ft) tower over the low ridges of the Cascades; **Bonanza Peak** (9,511 ft), the state's tallest nonvolcanic mountain, rises above the shores of Lake Chelan; the **Olympic Peninsula** rises from saltwater to 7,995-ft high Mt. Olympus. These mountains have always been popular with climbers, hikers, sightseers, and folks looking for solitude. Even now, they are scarcely settled.

The **Salish Sea,** a large body of saltwater dotted with islands, stretches from Juan de Fuca Strait south into Puget Sound and north to Canada's Georgia Strait and the Inland Passage. Most of the state's large cities including Olympia are found along its shores. Its waters are immensely popular with boaters.

Curiously, the "dry" eastern half of the state has more rivers and lakes than the "wet" western half, and thus attracts more boaters. The Columbia River bisects the state, before swinging west and gliding to the sea between Washington and Oregon. It's a gorge augmented by steep-walled canyons and coulees. The latter, carved by floodwaters at the end of the last ice age, were almost forgotten in recent history but are now visited by ever increasing numbers of boaters, hikers, campers, and wildlife watchers.

Beaches, Forests, Mountains, and National Parks

Washington has several different types of beaches:

The long, sandy, surf-tossed ocean beaches of the southwestern coast are popular with hikers, kite flyers, bird-watchers, surfers (the surf is very rough and the water is cold: only experienced surfers in wet suits should attempt surfing), and, in season, clam diggers who flock here in the thousands to dig for tasty razor clams. The beaches of the rugged Olympic coast are often rocky, but a few sandy coves are tucked between the headlands.

The beaches of the Salish Sea are often muddy, but they are popular with **clamdiggers** probing for the clammer's hard-shelled mollusks. Sandy beaches are scarce, even in the San Juan Islands. More often than not, the glacier-cut rocks drop straight down into the water. But the tide pools of rocky shores, which teem with sea slugs, crabs, sea anemones, and tiny fish, hold a fascination all their own and are very popular with children of all ages. **Bird watching** is great along all of these shores. **California gray whales** migrate close to the beaches of the outer shore and frequently visit the sheltered waters of the Salish Sea. The safest time for **boating** is from May to September, though storms can surprise boaters even in mid-summer. **Sea kayaking** has become very popular in the last two decades; most of the Salish Sea harbors have kayak rentals.

Forests in western Washington are commonly dense and overgrown with ferns, mosses, and other vegetation. This is not only true for the rain forests of the southwest coast and the Olympic Peninsula, but for the forests on the western slopes of the Cascades as well. From the San Juan Islands south, and on the mainland from Tacoma south, open prairies of Oregon white oak break up the evergreens. Trees in the alpine areas of the mountains are often gnarled and bent by snow and wind into fascinating shapes; forests east of the Cascades are sunny and contain open stands of ponderosa pine. In spring the forest floor is covered with wildflowers, as are the steppes of the Columbia Plateau.

Hiking trails in the forests are exceedingly popular. Plan to visit during the off-season to avoid getting trampled. The best times are in May to June or mid-October to mid-November. These popular attractions can get even more crowded than the other parks; it is not uncommon to wait in long traffic lines en route to Mt. Rainier. Relax and plan for extra time. The wait is well worth it.

The **lakes and coulees** of eastern Washington are best visited between April and mid-October, when the weather is at its best. These, too, are very popular during the height of the travel season, but the scenic and very beautiful Okanogan highlands and northeastern mountains are uncrowded at all times of the year, as are the Blue Mountains in southeastern Washington. Washington's turbulent mountain streams and rivers are very popular with rafters and white-water kayakers.

Culture, History, and the Arts

Several wooden blockhouses (Centralia, Tacoma, Whidbey Island) survive from the Indian wars of the turbulent mid-19th-century settlement period. Remnants of **old U.S. army forts** survive at White Swan near Yakima and Fort Spokane on Lake Roosevelt, as well as at Port Townsend and on Marrowstone and Whidbey Islands. Almost every town has a museum of local history. Seattle and Spokane also have excellent **art museums.** (Spokane's collection of Indian art and Seattle's collection of Asian art are world-renowned.) Seattle and Spokane also have first-rate symphonies and opera companies. Even some of the smaller towns have well-respected theaters. Performances are very popular with the locals; reservations for the **Seattle Symphony, Seattle Opera,** and the **Pacific Northwest Ballet** should be made long ahead of time (several months at a minimum). Many towns and cities host annual art shows and competitions, concerts, and other cultural events. (Contact the local visitors bureau or chamber of commerce for details.)

Sports

Seattle is the Northwest's sports capital, with major-league professional baseball, football, basketball, and ice hockey teams. The **Seattle Mariners** play at the new **Safeco Field,** and the **Seahawks** are also building a brand-new stadium. Home games of the **Supersonics** are very popular as well. Several smaller cities, most notably **Everett, Tacoma, Yakima,** and **Spokane,** have minor-league professional teams, but the hearts of local fans belong to local softball and high school football teams.

Rules of the Road

License Requirements: Washington drivers must be at least 16 years old, possess a valid driver's license, and carry proof of insurance. (Uninsured cars may be impounded.)

Right Turn on Red: Permitted throughout the state unless posted signs state otherwise.

Seat belt and Helmet Laws: Seat belts are mandatory for the driver and for all passengers. Children under 40 pounds of weight must be strapped into approved safety seats. Motorcyclists must wear helmets.

Speed Limit: Speed limits on highways and interstates vary from 60 to 70 mph. Follow posted signs.

For more information: call 360/753–6197.

A Volcano and Wine Tour

THE SEATTLE LOOP

Distance: approximately 530 miles Time: 4–7 days (18 hours driving time)
Breaks: Longmire or Paradise, Yakima

This is a fun tour that will take you to the two tallest volcanic peaks in Washington, Mt. Rainier and Mt. Adams, and to the most violent, Mt. St. Helens, which blew its top in 1980 and still rumbles occasionally.

1. Begin your tour in **Seattle.**

2. From Seattle, head south on I–5/705 to Rte. 7 and continue south on Rte. 7 to **Longmire,** the main southern gateway to Mt. Rainier National Park. Be sure to fill up your car before you enter the mountains; the few gas stations in the back country charge a premium for gasoline. NOTE: If you're coming from Portland, you should probably head north on I–5 to Rte. 504 west into Mt. St. Helens National Volcanic Monument Park before heading to Mt. Rainier.

   But let's assume you've departed Seattle and are well on your way with Mt. Rainier looming on the horizon. Turn on your car radio and check the weather forecast (KIRO radio, AM 710, or KOMO radio, AM 1000). You might also want to tune in AM 1610, the radio frequency on which the state broadcasts warnings (if you hear only static that's good news: nothing bad is happening).

3. **Mt. Rainier National Park** is celebrating its 100th anniversary, amid fears that it is being trampled to death because too many visitors walk its trails and crush its wildflower meadows. (If you're worried about summer crowds, you might want to approach the mountain from the northeast, via Rte. 410 from Enumclaw. This winding road takes you past the Sunrise entrance of the park, and over Cayuse and Chinook Passes down the Naches Valley—an ancient route over the Cascades used by Indians and American immigrants—to Yakima. It also has a picnic area with wildflowers and some great views of the mountain if you don't have time to stop and hike.)

   The advantage of having taken the southern route, of course, is that you can stay at either Longmire or Paradise, in the shadow of the mountain. (Remember: reservations are essential!) Curiously, even though Mt. Rainier is a volcano and slightly taller than California's Mt. Shasta, it appears to have none of the spiritual significance new-age philosophers claim for the latter peak.

4. After you've had your fill of the mountain head east, cross the Cascade Crest on U.S. 12 through White Pass, and descend the Tieton River Valley to the Naches River and head south on I–82 into **Yakima.**

   The drive from Mt. Rainier to Yakima is about 100 miles and, because of winding roads, may take as much as three hours. Give yourself plenty of time to stop and look around, since either of the pass roads winds through spectacular scenery. The tall mountain looming to the south is Mt. Adams, at 12,276 ft Washington's second tallest mountain. Yakima is a large city and a perfect place for a stop-over.

5. When you're finished exploring Yakima, head south on I–82 for about 5 mi to **Union Gap** and the first winery, **Staton Hills.** At Staton Hills you can pick up the most recent Washington Wine Commission booklet for reference in selecting wineries you wish to visit. Among the wineries you don't want to miss are **Kiona, Hogue, Chinook, Hinzerling** (Washington's oldest family-owned winery—still housed in a converted garage),

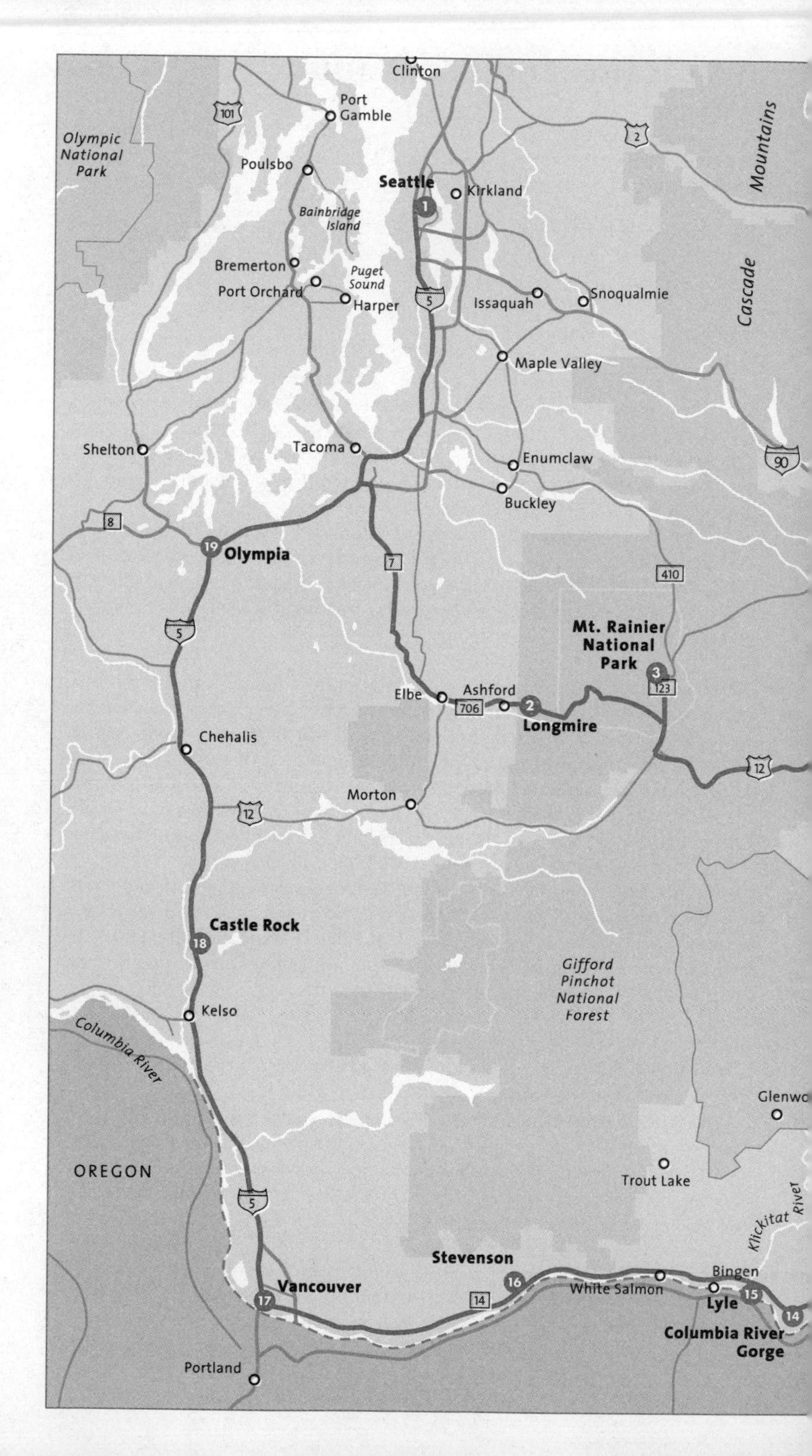
Clinton
Port Gamble
101
Olympic National Park
Poulsbo
Seattle
1
Kirkland
2
Mountains
Bainbridge Island
Bremerton
Puget Sound
Port Orchard
Harper
5
Issaquah
Snoqualmie
Cascade
Maple Valley
Shelton
Tacoma
Enumclaw
90
Buckley
8
19
Olympia
7
410
5
Mt. Rainier National Park
3
123
Elbe
Ashford
706
2
Longmire
Chehalis
12
Morton
12
Castle Rock
18
Gifford Pinchot National Forest
Kelso
Columbia River
Glenwo
OREGON
Trout Lake
Klickitat River
5
Stevenson
16
Vancouver
17
14
White Salmon
Bingen
Lyle
15
14
Columbia River Gorge
Portland

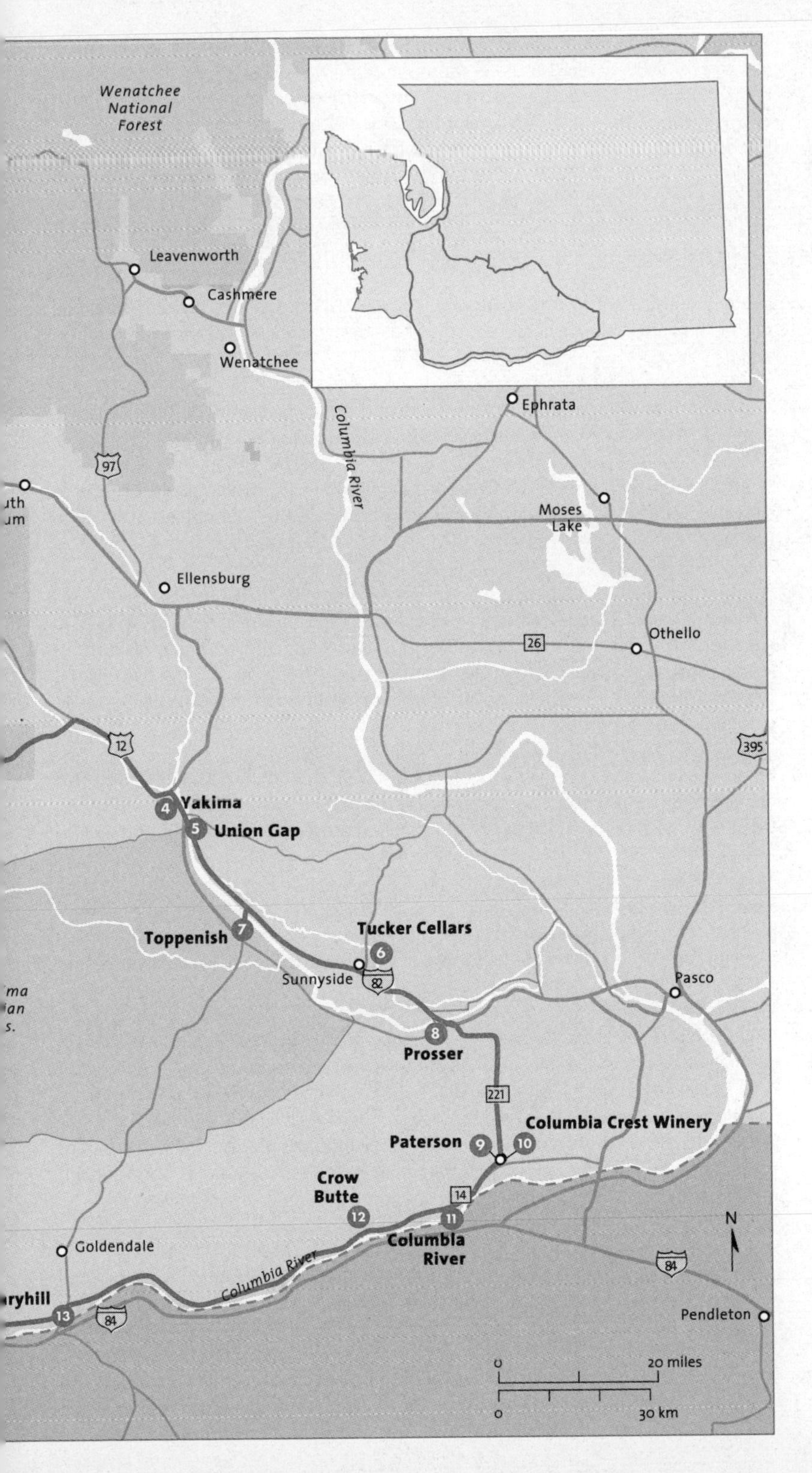

INTRODUCTION
HISTORY
REGIONS
WHEN TO VISIT
STATE'S GREATS
RULES OF THE ROAD
DRIVING TOURS

Portteus, and **Covey Run.** The latter sits high up on a slope north of **Zillah,** with great views of the valley (which should, in spring, be white with apple, cherry, or apricot blossoms or pink with blooming peach trees), the green Horse Heaven Hills, and the snow-capped peak of Mt. Adams. It's a great place for a picnic. Listen for the cry of curlews over the hills and watch the sky for hawks (with luck, you may even spot a golden eagle).

NOTE: If you don't plan on visiting any wineries, you can shorten your trip by heading south to the Columbia Gorge by taking U.S. 97 for approximately 25 mi from Union Gap to Toppenish, another 60 mi across the Horse Heaven Hills via Satus Pass to Goldendale and Maryhill. Pick up the itinerary at Maryhill and continue west through the gorge.

6. You might also want to stop at **Tucker Cellars,** off U.S. 12 just east of **Sunnyside,** and buy fresh Yakima Valley asparagus (some of the best in the West) at this winery's farm stand.

7. And don't miss the excellent tribal museum at the **Yakama Nation Cultural Center** in **Toppenish** (you can't miss it; follow signs directing you to the casino).

8. The Yakima Valley is level and only some 50 miles long, giving you plenty of time to slow down and explore. From Toppenish, head south on Rte. 22 for about 35 miles to **Prosser.**

9. From Prosser, take Rte. 221 south across the **Horse Heaven Hills** to **Paterson** on the Columbia River (about 26 mi, 40 minutes). Be sure to fill up your car here; there will be no gas station for more than a hundred miles. This road winds steeply up the hillside from Prosser. Stop at turnouts for great views of the Yakima Valley. Once you've reached the top, you'll find yourself on a rolling plain of wheat. A century ago, these hills were covered with bunch grass and wild horses ran free.

10. Before you descend to the river, you might want to stop at **Columbia Crest winery.** This winery looks like a French country château and is particularly known for its red wines. Don't look for a "town" at Paterson. All you'll find are a couple of houses and a highway junction.

11. From Paterson, turn right/east (downriver) on Rte. 14 and you'll run into the **Columbia River.** At this point the river runs through a steep-walled rock-sided canyon which is green for only a short time in spring, except for irrigated fields, vineyards, and orchards.

12. At 671-ft-high **Crow Butte** (14 miles west of Paterson), in the Umatilla National Wildlife Refuge, take a trail to the top (370 ft above the river) and see some great views of the river (here backed up by John Day Dam and known as Lake Wallula) and of local wildlife. You can look all the way to Mt. Hood (south of the river in Oregon) and, if you're lucky, watch hawks and golden eagles soar in the updrafts of the cliffs. At the foot of the butte are dunes and a sandy beach. Best of all, in summer the water is warm enough for swimming.

13. From Crow Butte, Rte. 14 runs west to **Maryhill** (Paterson to Maryhill is 65 miles; 2 hours' driving time if you don't stop at Crow Butte). Take the short detour on U.S. 97 up the hill to the Flemish château at the **Maryhill Museum of Art.** It has a spectacular view of river and mountains and an equally spectacular collection of Rodin sculptures.

14. Return to Rte. 14 and enter the **Columbia Gorge.** The Gorge is some 80 mi long and has some truly beautiful scenery. As you drive down the Washington side of the river,

you'll get a good view of the tall waterfalls dropping from the cliffs of the Oregon side. The Washington side has fewer falls, because here the rock tilted and caused massive landslides. This has led to white-water rivers raging down from the mountains.

⑮ One such river, the **Klickitat,** still has Indian fishing scaffolds near **Lyle** (30 mi, 40 minutes west of Maryhill on Rte. 14). In season (usually fall) you can watch Native Americans dip-netting salmon here in the traditional fashion.

⑯ From Lyle continue downriver on Rte. 14, through Bingen (which has a winery), to **Stevenson** (which has an excellent interpretative center; Bonneville Dam has a fish ladder). That 28-mi drive should take about 40 minutes. West of Skamania, 834-ft-tall Beacon Rock has a trail to the top with great views of the gorge. From Beacon Rock, continue downriver to **Vancouver, WA** (Stevenson to Vancouver, 50 miles; 1½ hours' driving time without stops).

⑰ **Vancouver** was founded in 1825 by the Hudson's Bay Company as Fort Vancouver, a fur-trading depot. Today it is a bedroom community for Portland, OR, which is 8 miles to the south. The reconstructed **Fort Vancouver** is well worth a visit. Vancouver has comfortable lodgings and good restaurants and is a good stopover place before continuing to Mt. St. Helens, the most active volcano in the contiguous United States.

⑱ After you've rested and enjoyed Vancouver, take I–5 north to **Castle Rock** (48 mi north of Vancouver; about 50 minutes' driving time each way), then drive east on Rte. 504 to the Coldwater Ridge Visitor Center (43 mi; about an hour's driving time) on the eastern edge of **Mt. St. Helens National Volcanic Monument.**

⑲ Return to I–5 and drive north to Seattle via I–5 (116 mi, about 2 hours' driving time). You might want to take some extra time to visit the state capital of **Olympia** with its beautiful State Capitol campus, situated high on the hill, overlooking Capital Lake (you'll see it from I–5 as you drive north; follow signs from the freeway), and you might want to explore Olympia's old and friendly downtown. Even if you decide to have dinner in Olympia, you can easily drive back to Seattle that evening (it's about an hour's drive from Olympia to Seattle, depending on traffic).

NOTE: Before setting out on a winery tour, obtain the most recent free edition of the Washington Wine Commission's guide booklet, *Touring the Washington Wine Country,* by calling the Commission at 206/667–9463, or e-mail: wawinectr@aol.com or www.washingtonwine.org

The Washington Waterfront Driving Tour

ISLAND HOPPING BY CAR AND FERRY

Distance: approximately 175 miles — Time: 4 hrs. actual driving time, but allow 1 to 2 days with stops

Breaks: Port Townsend, with its cafés and Victorian mansions, makes a nice place to stop for dinner or spend the night.

This trip starts in Seattle and will you take to two peninsulas and three islands, and help you explore several different waterfront towns. You'll start at Seattle's downtown waterfront.

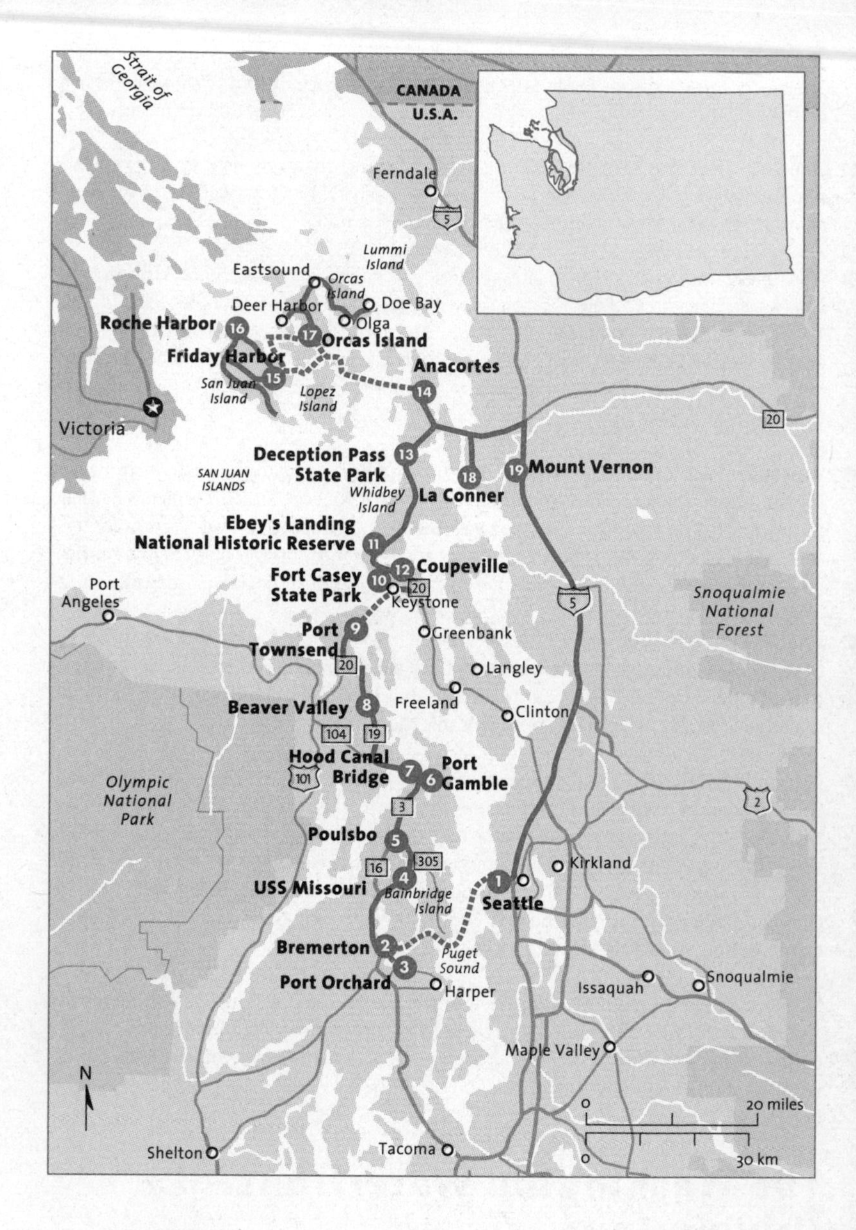

❶ Today **Seattle** has a busy port, but it has moved south, beyond Pioneer Square, to the shores of the lower Duwamish and to Harbor Island. The wharves of the downtown waterfront now house shops, restaurants, a waterfront park on Pier 57 (a great place for a picnic), **Odyssey,** the Maritime Discovery Center on Pier 66, and the **Seattle Aquarium** on Pier 59. Almost all ship traffic is gone, except for the harbor tours leaving from Pier 55 and Pier 57, the Victoria Clipper passenger ferry leaving from Pier 69 at the northern end of the downtown waterfront, and the Washington State Ferry terminal at Colman Dock on Pier 52. The latter dock has been busy since the days when the small steamers of the **Mosquito Fleet** (*see* box) docked here and puttered their way to small and large towns up and down the Sound.

2. Early in the morning, drive to the **Colman Dock on Pier 52** to board the ferry for **Bremerton.** The crossing should take about an hour, but give yourself an extra half hour to buy your ticket and get in line. Once you're on the ferry you can lock and leave your car and go upstairs for a grand view of saltwater and the mountains. If you haven't had breakfast yet, this is a good time to get it. You won't find a better window seat at any restaurant in the city.

   After leaving the Colman Dock, the ferry crosses **Elliott Bay** and rounds **Duwamish Head,** turns southwest across **Puget Sound,** and heads west into **Rich Passage,** which separates Bainbridge Island from the Kitsap Peninsula. If you look closely at the headlands to either side of the inlet, you'll notice the gun emplacements of turn-of-the-20th-century forts that once guarded the entrance to the Bremerton Navy Base.

3. The Naval Shipyard and Navy docks loom up ahead of you after the ferry turns into **Port Orchard,** which is the name both of an inlet and of the county seat on its southern shore. (If you had a boat and were to turn right, up the inlet, you'd come to Liberty Bay, and your next stop, Poulsbo.) The town of Port Orchard is an interesting old town with the usual gaggle of galleries, shops, and restaurants.

4. After returning from Port Orchard to Bremerton by ferry, you can turn left and drive along the waterfront of one of the largest navy bases in the country. Until she was moved to Pearl Harbor in 1998, the USS *Missouri,* on whose deck the Japanese surrendered in World War II, was docked here. (Look for signs telling which navy ship has open house and allows visitors.) Continue driving west until you get to Rte. 3; turn right (north). Take Rte. 3 north. Shortly after this road ceases to be a freeway, you should see Liberty Bay to your right (east). To the west, out of sight on the east shore of the Hood Canal is Bangor with its Trident submarine base. Since these huge subs are the modern replacements for battleships like the *Missouri,* they are named after states (as ships-of-the-line were in the days before battleships).

5. Take Rte. 305 north for about 17 mi into **Poulsbo** and follow signs to the waterfront. Poulsbo was founded in the 19th century by Norwegian immigrants as a fishing port, and still has an old-country bakery and some other Scandinavian touches. But yachts have taken over the fishing boat slips, and modern-day Poulsbo looks a lot more like a marina city than a grungy fishing port where cod was once dried on racks.

   You can have lunch in Poulsbo or buy the fixings for a picnic and eat at **Kitsap Memorial State Park** north of Lofall (which has a ferry terminal used, when the Hood Canal Bridge was destroyed in a storm, for a ferry run crossing the Hood Canal to South Point on the Olympic Peninsula).

6. After your lunch or picnic drive north on Rte. 3 to its junction with Rte. 104 and continue north for about 8 mi to **Port Gamble,** a pleasant (and well-restored) New England–style village that gives little indication that only a hundred years ago it had one of the largest lumber mills in the world, as well as several shipyards. Today, it's a great place for taking a relaxed stroll.

7. After you've finished your visit to Port Gamble, return on Rte. 104 to the junction with Rte. 3 and turn right across the **Hood Canal Bridge.** The predecessor of this floating bridge was sunk by a storm gusting up to 150 mph. Today the bridge's draw-span is opened during high winds (to relieve pressure). The draw-span is also opened for the huge Trident submarines, but chances are you'll be able to cross without impediment.

❽ West of the bridge turn north on Rte. 19 toward Port Townsend. If you haven't had lunch (or a picnic) yet, you might want to take a short detour to Port Ludlow, a sister town of Port Gamble (they were owned by the same company) that's now a retirement community.

As you continue north on Rte. 19, you'll pass through **Beaver Valley,** where Betty MacDonald lived in the 1920s and wrote the best-seller *The Egg and I.* The locals claim they were unhappy with the way she wrote about the region, but there is an Egg and I Road, named after the book. (Look for the street sign on Rte. 19 north of Beaver Valley.)

❾ Shortly after you pass through small and rustic Chimakum, you'll get to Rte. 20. Turn right to **Port Townsend.** Port Townsend is a well-preserved holdover from the Victorian age. It's a great place for strolling through watertown, the mostly brick-built port quarter, with its shops, cafés, and taverns, or through uptown, reached by steps climbing the bluff, where the former mansions of local merchants have been turned into comfortable inns.

❿ Port Townsend is a great place for spending the night and having dinner, but if you're running early, you could take the ferry across Admiralty Inlet to **Keystone** on **Whidbey Island.** (Crossing time: 30 minutes.) Keystone is another one of those places that's merely a name on a map. Look to the left as you approach the ferry landing. The grassy bluffs hide the gun emplacements of former Fort Casey. The lighthouse towering above the fort was built in 1899; it is now part of **Fort Casey State Park.**

When you land at Keystone and look around, it seems hard to believe that a city named "Chicago" stood here a hundred years ago with aspirations of outdoing its "rival" in the Midwest. Today, not even the foundations remain.

⓫ When leaving the ferry at Keystone, ignore the direction signs and turn LEFT, not right (Rte. 20). Drive past the fort (or turn left into the grounds and take a walk through the old batteries and on the grassy bluffs) and continue north on Fort Casey Road to Hill/Ebey's Landing Road. Turn left. After passing a pretty bluff topped by pines (that looks like part of the California Coast), the road drops to the beach at **Ebey's Landing National Historic Reserve.** This is the place where a Tlinkit raiding party landed its canoes on August 11, 1857, and attacked the cabin of Colonel Isaac Ebey which stood on the embankment south of Ebey Road, where it leaves the beach. The Alaska natives shot Ebey and took his head, in retaliation for the death of a Tlinkit chief killed by gunfire from the USS *Massachusetts.* You can take a walk up the peaceful beach or hike a narrow trail up the bluff with is bedecked with wildflowers in spring. Both walks will take you to a vantage point from which you can look straight down Juan de Fuca Strait.

To leave the beach take Ebey Road to Rte. 20 and proceed south about 4 mi; turn right, and then left at Main Street (the next traffic light). This will take you to Coupeville's waterfront on Penn Cove.

⓬ **Coupeville,** founded in 1853, has more historic buildings than any other town in Washington and enjoys an incredible scenic setting. The shops on the cove side of narrow Front Street stand above the sandy beach on pilings and are lapped by waves at high tide. Streets rise from the waterfront to the residential district which has great views of the water and, on clear days, of Mt. Baker and the North Cascades. Coupeville is a very comfortable town just made for strolling. If you spend the night here, you might want to do as the locals do and drop in at **Toby's Tavern** on the waterfront to drink beer and play pool (and perhaps have a hamburger).

Leave Coupeville via Coveland Street to Madrona Way, which winds along the southern shore of Penn Cove past the historic Captain Whidbey Inn to Rte. 20. The road takes its name from the gnarled, red-trunked madrona trees that line the bluff on the waterside.

Turn right on Rte. 20 and drive north for 10 mi through Oak Harbor to **Deception Pass,** a narrow rock-bound inlet separating Whidbey Island from Fidalgo Island to the north. The rocks you see are the only bedrock on Whidbey Island which is a glacial moraine almost 40 mi long. Deception Pass has Washington's most popular and perhaps most scenic state park.

⑬ If you're planning to camp in **Deception Pass State Park,** you need to make a reservation well ahead of time.

⑭ Rte. 20 takes you north to Rte. 20. The roads are a bit confusing here, because the state highway running north from Keystone and the highway running east from Anacortes have the same number. After the merger, the road continues east to I–5 and eventually becomes the North Cascades Highway. But you want to turn left at the merger and drive to **Anacortes,** a pleasant waterfront town that has the ferry landing for the San Juan Islands.

⑮ Take the ferry to **San Juan Island.** Crossing time is about an hour and a half to two hours, depending on how many stops the ferry makes. (Consult the schedule.) Park your car in **Friday Harbor** and walk around. Friday Harbor is the county seat and a pleasant small town, perfect for strolling. If you plan to stay here, you can leave your car in Anacortes (fee lot); but you'll want it to explore the island. You can stay in Friday Harbor or drive to Roche Harbor at the island's northern tip (stop at **Westcott Bay Oyster Farm** on the way up for some of Washington's best oysters). The harbor, protected by an island, is very picturesque.

⑯ Head north on San Juan Island Road for 5.4 mi to **Roche Harbor,** a former industrial town, though it doesn't look it. The limestone mined here helped build towns throughout the Salish Sea region. You can still see the old lime kilns, but all other traces of the village's industrial past are gone. Roche Harbor today is a pleasant waterfront community with a 19th-century hotel and modern condominiums. It is very popular with visiting yachtsmen and in summer the docks are quite lively. The road along the island's western shore is very scenic and not only has great views but gives you the chance of watching whales and orcas swim by.

⑰ Leave San Juan Island by taking the ferry from Friday Harbor to **Orcas Island.** You'll arrive at the tiny harbor of Orcas, its streets lined with shops in the shadows of big trees and an old clapboard hotel. Orcas is the biggest of the San Juans and you'll need a car to get around. You'll want to drive north on the main road to **Eastsound,** a pleasant waterfront village with a sandy beach at the head of East Sound, the inlet that almost cuts the island in two. Eastsound is the flattest of all the towns we have visited so far. It has some interesting shops and Orcas Islands' best restaurant (**Christina's**), where you'll want to eat if you stay at one of the island's comfortable inns. It also has the islands' tallest mountain with a road to the top and great views of all the islands.

From Orcas, take the ferry back to Anacortes. Drive east on Rte. 20 for about 14 mi and look for signs directing you to La Conner, a pleasant waterfront town on the Swinomish Slough, a saltwater channel that separates Fidalgo Island from the mainland.

⑱ **La Conner** occupies a rocky outcropping on the landward side of the slough, which separates it from an Indian village on the west side of the channel. The town's business district sits partly on pilings out over the channel; both the waterfront and the residential hill have several nice inns. This is another good place for spending a night.

(19) Leave La Conner on the Whitney/La Conner Road, through fields that are golden, red, and purple in spring with myriad tulips. Turn left (north) on McLean Road and continue for about 11 mi; this will take you to **Mount Vernon,** a pleasant riverfront city on the Skagit River. Turn right onto Main Street just after you cross the Skagit River, park your car, and walk through downtown Mount Vernon with its well-aged business buildings. You can explore its streets and shops, or sit on the bulkhead where steamboats once landed and just watch the river flow by. Mount Vernon also has several very good restaurants.

From Mount Vernon, take I–5 south for about 60 mi back to Seattle.

NOTE: For up-to-date ferry information, call the following numbers for schedule information, (in WA) 888/808–7977 or 800/84–FERRY (206/464–6400 outside WA); for fares, 888/808–7977 (the rates are listed in a separate *Passenger and Vehicle Fares* brochure). For schedule information on the Internet: www.wsdot.wa.gov/ferries/. Please note that the schedule changes with the seasons; fewer ferries run in fall, winter, and spring.

ABERDEEN

MAP 8, B5

(Nearby towns also listed: Hoquiam, Ocean Shores, Westport)

A Chehalis River town, Aberdeen got its start back in 1867 when George Benn settled here. It saw its first growth in 1878, when Scotsman George R. Hume started the Aberdeen Fish Packing Company to process locally caught salmon, but it did not really get going until the first sawmill was built in 1884. Soon tall ships crowded the narrow harbor to load lumber, and waterfront bars were busy with sailors fresh from the sea and "timberbeasts" fresh from the woods. The timber stood so thick at the time that travel could only be managed by water or by skid road. It was only later that roads and logging railroads were built. Homesteaders tried to farm the cleared woods but, because of the heavy and almost constant rains on this very wet coast, the ground proved too soggy for most crops. Farming did not really become successful until cranberries were planted in the bogs and oysters were raised in the shallow bays of Grays Harbor, the protected inlet into which the Chehalis River flows.

The reason a former lumber town like Aberdeen has so many buildings of stone and brick is simple: back in 1903 when the town was built of wood and the streets were paved with sawdust, the whole town burned down during a dry spell—in record time.

Today, when the seemingly limitless salmon and timber resources have become exhausted, Aberdeen, like other coastal communities, is marketing the scenic beauty of the bay and woods. Aberdeen is the home of the *Lady Washington*, the replica of a sloop that accompanied Robert Gray's ship *Columbia* to the Northwest Coast back in 1792, when Gray discovered the harbor now bearing his name and the river he named after his ship.

Information: Grays Harbor Chamber of Commerce | 506 Duffy St., Aberdeen 98520 | 360/532–1924 | chamber@graysharbor.org | graysharbor.org.

Attractions

Aberdeen Museum of History. A pleasant small museum with a collection of canoes from local tribes, as well as a good collection of historical photographs from Aberdeen's logging/shipping history. | 111 E. 3rd St. | 360/533–1976 | Donations accepted | June–Labor Day, Wed.–Sun. 11–4; Labor Day–May, weekends noon–4.

Compass Rose and River Walkway. A 40-ft-in-diameter compass laid in brick indicates both magnetic north and true north. The walkway follows the Wishkah river to the Chehallis and then follows the Chehallis River. There are beautiful views from the walkway which stretches about 1½ mi east from Heron St. | Heron St. | free | Daily.

Grays Harbor Historical Seaport. The main element of this boatyard and historical park (still under development, as money becomes available) is a replica of Robert Gray's sloop *Lady Washington* (which has been rerigged from a one-masted sloop as a two-masted brig, because the one-master was too hard to handle under sail). | 712 Hagara St., Junction City | 360/532–8611 | fax 360/533–9384 | www.ladywashington.org | $3 | Daily.

Lake Sylvia State Park. A state park on a small lake with a boat launch, campsites, and picnic tables. | U.S. 12E to unnumbered road | 360/249–3621 | www.parks.wa.gov | $12–$17 | Daily.

Samuel Benn Park. A pleasant city park with a rose and rhododendron garden, playground, tennis court, and picnic tables. | East 9th and North I Sts. | 360/537–3230 | fax 360/537–3350 | Free | Daily.

Schafer State Park. A riverfront park on the Satsop River with campsites; the boat ramp is a good place for launching a canoe or kayak. | U.S. 12 E to unnumbered road | 360/482–3852 | www.parks.wa.gov | $11–$16 | daily, camping: in Apr.–mid-Dec, daily; mid-Dec.–Mar., weekends.

ON THE CALENDAR

MAY: *Discovery Days.* A festival celebrating Robert Gray's discovery of Grays Harbor on the tall-masted sailing ship *Columbia* in 1792. | 800/200–5239.

YEAR-ROUND: *Voyages of Discovery.* Short trips aboard the sailing ship *Lady Washington,* one of the ships used in Robert Gray's expedition to the Northwest Coast in 1792. | 800/200–5239.

Dining

Billy's. American/Casual. This place has an interesting collection of sporting prints recalling Aberdeen's bawdy past (the most popular brothel in town used to be right across the street). The restaurant takes its name from a notorious local bad man who shanghaied sailors. They serve burgers, salads, and even yak. Kids' menu. | 322 E. Heron | 360/533–7144 | $10–$16 | AE, DC, MC, V.

Bridges. American. This café takes its name not from the bridges spanning the Wishkah and Chehalis Rivers, but from owner Sonny Bridges, who's been running local restaurants for more than 30 years. Bridges is a classy, pastel-hued place with some of the best seafood in town. But, as everywhere on the coast, steaks are also big. Kids' menu. | 112 N. G St. | 360/532–6563 | No lunch weekends | $12–$25 | AE, D, DC, MC, V.

Duffy's Restaurant. American. The interior of this local favorite has a vaguely Irish theme, evoked by small trinkets and memorabilia. The menu includes such standards as burgers, steaks, chops, and fish and chips; but some of the most popular dishes are the Swedish pancakes, the prime rib, and the wild blackberry pie. | 1605 Simpson Ave. | 360/532–3842 | Breakfast also available | $10–$15 | AE, D, DC, MC, V.

Parma. Italian. This downtown storefront restaurant serves the best Italian food on the coast. Everything is good here. Try the spinach gnocchi, the wild boar with polenta, or the seafood dishes. The pasta is made on the premises, and a grill bestows the right flavor on steaks, chops, and sausages. | 116 W. Heron St. | 360/532–3166 | Closed Sun.–Mon. | $15–$25 | AE, D, MC, V.

Lodging

Aberdeen Mansion. This 1905 mansion was originally the home of Edward Hulbert who made a fortune in the lumber industry. It is set on 1 acre of landscaped grounds with flower beds of azaleas and rhododendrons. | 5 rooms. Complimentary breakfast, no air-conditioning, cable TV, VCRs, no room phones, off-street parking, no kids under 12, no smoking. | 807 N. M St. | 360/533–7079 | fax 360/537–9607 | $80–$135 | AE, D, MC, V.

Cooney Mansion Bed and Breakfast Inn. Comfortable B&B in a 1908 timber tycoons mansion. | 8 rooms, 3 with shared bath. No-smoking rooms, spa, gym. | 1705 Fifth St., Cosmopolis | 800/9–SPRUCE or 360/533–0602 | fax 360/533–0602 | cooney@techline.com | www.cooneymansion.com | $80–$175 | D, MC, V.

Guest House International Suites and Inn. The hotel overlooks the Wishkah River and is directly adjacent to the Wishkah mall and the city center. | 60 rooms. Complimentary Continental breakfast, in-room data ports, microwaves, refrigerators, cable TV, in-room VCRs, pool, hot tub, gym, laundry facilities, business services, pets allowed. | 701 E. Heron St. | 360/537–7460 or 800/21–GUEST | fax 360/537–7462 | ghao8@aol.com | www.guesthouse.net | $78–$140 | AE, D, MC, V.

Harbor View Bed and Breakfast. You can see the harbor from every room in this 1905 Victorian. The house contains parlors, sunrooms, three fireplaces, hand-stenciled walls, and a ballroom staircase. Rooms are furnished with period antiques from the local area. | 4 rooms. Complimentary breakfast, no air-conditioning, cable TV, no room phones, no pets, no kids under 8, no smoking. | 11 W. 11th St. | 360/533–7996, 360/533–0433, or 877/533–7996 | fax 360/533–0433 | harborview@olynet.com | www.olynet.com/users/harborview | $75–$95 | AE, MC, V.

Red Lion Inn. This hotel is right in the heart of downtown. | 67 rooms. Complimentary Continental breakfast, cable TV, pets allowed. | 521 W. Wishkah | 360/532–5210 | fax 360/533–8483 | $55–$109 | AE, D, DC, MC, V.

ANACORTES

MAP 8, D2

(Nearby towns also listed: Coupeville, La Conner, Mount Vernon, Oak Harbor, San Juan Islands, Sedro Woolley)

Anacortes is the only town on rock-bound Fidalgo Island, which is separated from the mainland to the east by narrow, swampy Swinomish Slough, and sliced off from Whidbey Island to the south by the steep-walled tidal canyon of Deception Pass. Access to the island is by highway bridges only. Guemes Island to the north, and Burrows and Allen Islands to the southwest protect the town's moorage basins from storms. Rocks abound everywhere: Anacortes has a city park on a rocky headland at either end of town, Cape Sante to the east, and Washington Park (on Fidalgo Head) to the west, plus another park atop Mt. Erie, whose 270-ft-high rocky summit has deep striations left by continental glaciers during the last Ice Age. A road leads to the top of this mountain, whose southern face drops almost straight down to Lake Campbell. This cliff is a popular hangout for eagles and hang gliders. The view from the mountaintop is great: You can look down onto Deception Pass and on the Salish Sea or look east to the snow-capped peaks of the Cascades and south to those of the Olympic Mountains.

Anacortes is a pleasant community with many old houses and a greater than usual assortment of hotels, restaurants, and shops, because it is also the eastern terminal for the automobile ferry to the San Juan Islands.

Information: Anacortes Visitor Information Center | 819 Commercial Ave., Ste. G, Anacortes, 98221 | 360/293–3832 | www.anacortes-chamber.com.

Attractions

Anacortes Historical Museum. The changing exhibits of this museum focus on the history and culture of Fidalgo and nearby Guemes Island. Past exhibits include installations on the history of boat building and on the history of Commercial Avenue in Anacortes. | 1305 8th St. | 360/293–1915 | www.anacorteshistoricalmuseum.org | $2 suggested donation | Mon., Thurs.–Sun. 1–5.

Deception Pass State Park. A beautiful park on the southern tip of Fidalgo and the northern tip of Whidbey Island, with a rocky chasm in the center separating the two sections. Canoe Island in the center of the pass can be reached by the Rte. 20 highway bridge, which crosses the gorge. There are campsites, picnic areas, sandy beaches (although the water is too cold and turbulent for swimming), shaded trails in the woods, and sunny trails on the headlands. Watch for the wildflowers in spring. | Rte. 20S | 360/675–2417 | fax 360/675–3288 | www.prd.state.or.us | $12–$17 | Daily.

Washington Park. This beautiful park has dense forests and sunny meadows and is west of Anacortes, near the ferry landing, with boat launch and trails. Overlooks with views of islands and saltwater can be reached by a narrow loop road which winds through woods and over cliffs. | 12th St. (Oakes Ave.) | 360/293–1927 | fax 360/293–1928 | free, camping $12–$15 | Daily.

ON THE CALENDAR

MAY: *Anacortes Waterfront Festival and Boat Show.* A popular event which includes, besides the boat show, educational exhibits relating to boats and the marine environment, a model ship regatta, a number of different events for children, a marine swap meet, and a street fair. | 360/293–7911.

AUG: *Salmon Barbecue.* The Eagles Restaurant has a three-day salmon barbecue with salmon, chicken, and ribs. All the cooking is done right out in front of the restaurant. | 901 7th St. | 360/293–3012.

Dining

Bella Isola. Italian. This restaurant, in a turn-of-the-20th-century structure, has three intimate dining rooms, two of which overlook the downtown area. The menu includes a large number of Italian specialties, including pizzas, pastas, lasagnas, grilled fish, and chicken entrées. Daily specials are usually fresh fish and seafood such as halibut, salmon, or langostino. | 619 Commercial Ave. | 360/299–8398 | No lunch Sun. | $8–$21 | AE, D, MC, V.

La Petite. French. This small restaurant has a very short menu—only six dishes are offered at a time, but the quality is high. Everything is good, from chops to desserts. | 3401 Commercial Ave. | 360/293–4644 | No lunch, no dinner Mon. | $17–$30 | AE, D, DC, MC, V.

Randy's Pier 61. Seafood. The only waterfront restaurant in Anacortes, with generic nautical decor and nice views across the Guemes Channel to Guemes and the San Juan Islands. Known for steak, lobster, fresh seafood. There is a patio for dining outside. Kids' menu. | 209 T Ave. | 360/293–5108 | $12–$30 | AE, D, MC, V.

KODAK'S TIPS FOR USING LIGHTING

Daylight
- Use the changing color of daylight to establish mood
- Use light direction to enhance subjects' properties
- Match light quality to specific subjects

Dramatic Lighting
- Anticipate dramatic lighting events
- Explore before and after storms

Sunrise, Sunset, and Afterglow
- Include a simple foreground
- Exclude the sun when setting your exposure
- After sunset, wait for the afterglow to color the sky

From *Kodak Guide to Shooting Great Travel Pictures* © 2000 by Fodor's Travel Publications

Lodging

Albatross. This 1927 Cape Cod–style house sits across the street from the marina and only two blocks away from Washington Park. The rooms each have their own character. The Scarlett O'Hara Room has lace curtains and genuine plantation furnishings, while Monet's Garden is named for the views it affords of the backyard garden. | 4 rooms. Complimentary breakfast, no room phones, TV in common area, pets allowed, no kids under 5, no smoking. | 5708 Kingsway W | 360/293–0677 or 800/622–8864 | fax 360/299–2262 | albatros@cnw.com | www.cnw.com/~albatros | $85–$95 | AE, D, MC, V.

Anacortes Inn. This small motel is 2 mi from the city center and next door to a pretty park with old trees. The rooms have views of the water. | 44 rooms. Some kitchenettes, microwaves, refrigerators, cable TV, pool, business services, pets allowed (fee). | 3006 Commercial Ave. | 360/293–3153 or 800/327–7976 | fax 360/293–0209 | $50–$100 | AE, D, DC, MC, V.

Channel House. Very comfortable B&B, this 1902 Craftsman has wonderful views of the ferry landing. The rooms are individually styled, but all have high ceilings, Oriental rugs and hardwood floors. | 6 rooms. Complimentary breakfast and afternoon tea, no room phones, hot tub, local airport and ferry shuttles, no kids under 12, no smoking. | 2902 Oakes Ave. | 360/293–9382 or 800/238–4353 | fax 360/299–9208 | beds@sos.net | www.channelhouse.com | $85–$109 | AE, D, MC, V.

Hasty Pudding House. The collection of antique china and silver that graces the cupboards, together with the handmade quilts and pillows, contributes to this inn's special charm. Rooms are thoughtfully appointed with walnut or oak antiques. An outdoor garden is replete with lilacs, tulips, and azaleas. | 4 rooms. Complimentary breakfast, no air-conditioning, some in-room VCRs, no room phones, no TV in some rooms, hot tub, no pets, no kids under 10, no smoking. | 1312 8th St. | 360/293–5773 or 800/368–5588 | fax 360/293–5773 | hasty@halcyon.com | www.hastypudding.net/hasty | $75–$95 | AE, D, MC, V.

★ **Majestic Hotel.** Magnificently restored 1889 hotel occupying a rather dull street corner in downtown Anacortes. The top of the hotel has a cupola with 360-degree views of Mt. Baker and the North Cascades, several bays and inlets of the Salish Sea, the San Juan Islands, and the distant Olympic Mountains. | 23 rooms. Restaurant, bar, complimentary Continental breakfast, no-smoking rooms, business services. | 419 Commercial Ave. | 360/293–3355800/588–4780 | fax 360/293–5214 | $98–$225 | AE, D, MC, V.

Ship Harbor Inn. This is a comfortable family motel with great views. It is on 6½ wooded acres, overlooking the ferry terminal. | 16 rooms, 10 cottages. Bar, picnic area, complimentary Continental breakfast, no air-conditioning, refrigerators, microwaves, cable TV, playground, laundry facilities. | 5316 Ferry Terminal Rd. | 360/293–5177 or 800/852–8568 (US), 800/235–8568 (Canada) | fax 360/299–2412 | shi@shipharborinn.com | www.shipharborinn.com | $65–$100 | AE, D, DC, MC, V.

ARLINGTON

MAP 8, E3

(Nearby town also listed: Marysville)

Arlington sprawls across the rich farmlands of the Stillaguamish River plain and is surrounded by pastures and woods. The local airfield is very popular with builders of experimental planes, and on sunny days you can watch all sorts of odd-looking aircraft take to the skies. In early spring the woods are white with trillium and the pastures bordering it have some splendid stands of the big yellow candles of skunk cabbage.

Information: The Greater Arlington Chamber of Commerce | 120 N. Olympic Ave., Arlington, 98223 | 360/435–3708 | www.arlington-chamber.com.

Attractions

Air Station Flying Museum. Sitting in a World War II hangar, this is an all-volunteer air museum that houses planes from the eras of this country's major wars. Among the seven planes on display are a Fiesler Storch, a German observation plane. | 18008 59th Dr. NE | 360/403–9352 | Donation | Sat. 10–4.

ON THE CALENDAR

AUG.: ***Festival of the River.*** Native American activities provide the fun at this summer festival. | 360/435–2755.

Dining

Bistro. Contemporary. One of the most romantic spots in town, this restaurant sometimes hosts a harpist who sets the mood amid candlelit tables. The staff serve only organic food which includes seafood, steaks, and pastas. Try the sesame-encrusted oysters with a hoisin-chili sauce. | 231 North Olympic | 360/403–9341 | Closed Sun.– Mon. | $12–$35 | AE, MC, V.

Lodging

Mt. Higgins House. Seventeen mi east of Arlington, in the Stillaguamish River Valley, this cedar A-frame is part of a 70-acre horse farm. Both bedrooms have views of the towering mountains behind the house, while the living room's wall of windows overlooks a pond. A smattering of antiques adds a rustic color to the simple rooms. You can hunt trout in the pond or hike through the woods to the river for fly-fishing. | 2 rooms. Complimentary breakfast, no air-conditioning, no room phones, TV in common area, pond, hiking, fishing, no pets, no kids under 15, no smoking. | 29805 State Rte. 530 NE | 360/435–9757 or 888/296–3777 | fax 360/435–9757 | mthigginshouse@juno.com | www.snohomish.org/accom/MtHigginsHouse.htm | $95–$115 | AE, MC, V.

ASHFORD

MAP 8, E6

(Nearby towns also listed: Crystal Mountain, Mount Rainier, National Park)

Ashford sits astride an ancient trans-Cascades trail used by the Yakama Indians to trade with the natives of western Washington. The mountain village began as a logging railway terminal; today, the village provides access to Longmire-Paradise entrance, the only year-round access to Mt. Rainier National Park, and caters to visitors with lodges, restaurants, groceries, and gift shops.

Information: Mt. Rainier Business Association | Box 214, Ashford, 98304 | 360/569–0910 | www.mt-rainier.com/ashford.shtml.

Attractions

Mount Rainier Scenic Railroad. Beginning at Elbe, 11 mi west of Ashford, the train will take you through lush forests and across scenic bridges. In all it covers 14 mi of incomparable beauty. | Hwy. 7, Elbe | 888/STEAM–11 | $11.50 | June–Sept., weekends and holidays; trains leave at 11, 1:15, and 3:30.

ON THE CALENDAR

OCT.: ***Lark at the Mountain Music Festival.*** Folk, jazz, and bluegrass are all apart of this three-day celebration, held on the first weekend in October. The festival is free and encourages family attendance. | 877/886–4662.

Dining

Alexander's Country Inn. Contemporary. This is a classic, woodsy Northwest country inn which dates from the early 1900s. The trout is caught fresh from the pond on the premises.

The steak and homemade blueberry pie are favorite dishes. Dine outside on a patio overlooking the trout pond and a waterfall. Kids' menu. | 37515 State Rd. 706 E. | 360/569–2300 | Breakfast also available. Closed Nov.–Mar. Mon.–Thurs. | $11–$25 | MC, V.

Scaleburgers. Fast Food. What started out as a state weigh station in 1939 has been converted into a popular restaurant serving hamburgers, fries, milkshakes, and ice cream made from only the finest of ingredients. You eat outside on tables overlooking the hills and scenic railroad. The restaurant is located 7 mi west of Ashford. | 54109 Mountain Hwy. E, Elbe | 360/569–2247 | $2.75–$4.05 | No credit cards.

Lodging

Alexander's Country Inn. Rustic and comfortable old lodge dating from 1912 that's been thoroughly updated to meet modern creature-comfort standards. It's 1 mi from the southwest Nisqually entrance to Mt. Rainier National Park. In summer fish for trout in the stocked pond and then eat your catch on the outside deck. | 12 rooms; 2 cottages. Restaurant, complimentary breakfast and afternoon wine, no air-conditioning, no room phones, no TVs in rooms, no smoking. | 37515 State Rd., 706 E | 360/569–2300 or 800/654–7615 | fax 360/569–2323 | $85–$200, $240 cottages | MC, V.

The Bunkhouse. Nestled among the trees 4 mi east of Ashford toward Mt. Rainier, this is "the place to stop on the way to the top." Originally built as a house for loggers in 1908, the furnishing are simple. You can stay in a bunk in a large dormitory-style room or have your own private suite. | 18 rooms, 1 bunk room. No air-conditioning, no room phones, no TVs in rooms, no pets, no smoking. | 30205 Hwy. 706 E | 360/569–2439 | fax 360/569–2436 | $25–$90 | MC, V.

Mountain Meadows Inn Bed and Breakfast at Mt. Rainier. Antiques, Native American baskets, and a collection of John Muir memorabilia adorn the living room of this homey inn, 6 mi southwest from Mt. Rainier National Park. The modern cottage has three units, each with its own private entrance and kitchen. | 6 rooms, 3 efficiencies. Complimentary breakfast, no air-conditioning, no room phones, no TV, pond, hot tub, no pets, no smoking. | 28912 State Rte. 706 E | 360/569–2788 | mtmeadow@mashell.com | www.mt-rainier.net | $85–$140 | MC, V.

Nisqually Lodge. This hotel-lodge is a few miles west of Mt. Rainier National Park between Ashford and the park. There is a grand stone fireplace in the lobby. The rooms are comfortable, but nothing special, and they suffer from thin walls which is a common plague of older establishments in WA. | 24 rooms. Complimentary Continental breakfast, cable TV, air-conditioning, hot tub, playground, laundry facilities, business services, no smoking. | 31609 State Rd., 706 E | 360/569–8804 | fax 360/569–2435 | $76–$80 | AE, DC, MC, V.

Wellspring. Nestled in the woodlands outside Ashford, the accommodations here include log cabins, a tree house, and a room in a greenhouse. The furnishings also vary but are all appealing; for instance, the Nest Room has a queen-size feather bed suspended by ropes beneath a skylight. Also available at the facility are a variety of spa-like amenities. | 5 rooms, 6 cabins, 1 cottage. Some kitchenettes, some microwaves, some refrigerators, no room phones, no TV, pond, hot tub, massage, spa, outdoor hot tub, sauna, hiking, no pets, no smoking. | 54922 Kernehan Rd. | 360/569–2514 | $79–$129 | MC, V.

BAINBRIDGE ISLAND

MAP 7, B2

(Nearby town also listed: Seattle)

This residential island, which has incorporated itself as a city to keep outsiders at bay, is a scenic half-hour ferry ride from Seattle. The island began its "civilized" life as one of Puget Sound's major logging centers, with big mills at Port Blakely and Port Madison. The former is said to have had the largest lumber mill in the world. Some of the local lumber was used to build ships at island shipyards. Today few traces remain of the island's industrial past, and even the berry farms that followed, and made Bainbridge famous for its strawberries, are now mostly gone.

Information: Bainbridge Island Chamber of Commerce | 590 Winslow Way E, Bainbridge Island, 98110 | 206/842–3700 | www.bainbridgechamber.org.

Attractions

Brainbridge Island Vineyard and Winery. Come taste the wines or go for a tour at the only winery in Puget Sound to produce estate bottled wines. | 682 Hwy. 305 | 206/842–9463 | $1 | Wed.–Sun. noon–5.

ON THE CALENDAR

FEB., MAY, AUG., NOV.: *Arts Walk.* The arts walk is held through downtown Winslow four times a year on the first Sunday of the month. Galleries and other businesses host artists, poets, performers, and musicians. | 206/842–8388.

MAR.: *St. Patrick's Day Parade.* A fun children's parade winds through town. | 509/662–0059.

JULY: *Bainbridge in Bloom.* Tours of six local gardens are sponsored by the Bainbridge Arts and Humanities Council. | 206/219–3182.

Dining

Bistro Pleasant Beach. Mediterranean. The former owners of the white-linen Pleasant Beach Grill reopened at this new location with a simpler, informal bistro-style restaurant. Try the seafood chowder, the linguine with crisp prawns, kalamata olives, fresh spinach and feta, or the roasted lamb with cabernet glaze. | 241 Winslow Way W | 206/842–4347 | Closed Mon. | $15–$23 | AE, MC, V.

Cafe Nola. American. This stylish restaurant is where islanders gather to socialize during the week and to enjoy dinner on weekends. In warm weather, there's outdoor seating. Known for pan-seared scallops and filet mignon. | 101 Winslow Way E | 206/842–3822 | Closed Mon. Weekend brunch | $12–$18 | MC, V.

Moonfish. Contemporary. Part of a century-old manor, this restaurant overlooking the Puget Sound has gorgeous views and scrumptious food. The dining room's mango walls and subdued lighting are the perfect environment for enjoying dishes like phyllo-wrapped Pacific salmon served with a soy-ginger beurre blanc. A garden patio in the backyard permits outdoor dining in the summer. | 4738 Lynwood Center Rd. | 206/780–3473 | Reservations essential on weekends | $14–$20 | AE, MC, V.

Lodging

Agate Pass Waterfront Bed and Breakfast. Originally a nursery, this B&B has spectacular gardens that overlook Port Orchard Narrows and Agate Passage. Rooms, which have views of the water or gardens, are appointed with antiques and comfortable contemporary furnishings. Located just beyond Brainbridge Island, the lodging is only 50 ft away from the beach, making a stroll on the beach almost compulsory. If coming from Bainbridge Island, take a left at the first light immediately after the bridge; if from Poulsbo, a right at the light just before the bridge. | 3 rooms. Complimentary breakfast, kitchenettes, microwaves, refrigerators, cable TV, in-room VCRs, beach, no pets, no smoking. | 16045 Hwy. 305, Poulsbo | 206/842–1632 or 800/869–1632 | beds@agatepass.com | www.agatepass.com | $75–$125 | AE, D, DC, MC, V.

BELLEVUE

MAP 8, E4

(Nearby towns also listed: Issaquah, Seattle)

Bellevue is one of those nondescript suburban cities that have been trying their hardest—for decades—to be more than bedroom communities centered around a mall. But Bellevue *is* a pleasant bedroom community, with interesting shops and restaurants, an art museum, and a charming Old Town, with many buildings dating from the early 20th century.

Information: **East King County Convention & Visitors Bureau** | 520 112th Ave. NE, Bellevue, 98004-5503 | 425/455–1926, 800/252–1926 | eastkingcounty.org.

Attractions

Bellevue Art Museum. The museum hosts a different exhibit every two months, concentrating on the art of contemporary Northwest artists. | 510 Bellevue Way | 425/454–3322 | www.bellevueart.org | $3 | Tues. and Sat. noon–8; Wed, Thurs., Fri. 10–5; Sun. noon–5.

Bellevue Botanical Garden. A beautiful 36-acre public garden best known for its alpine and rock garden, spectacular perennial borders, and rhododendrons. | 12001 Main St. | 425/451–3755 | www.bellevuebotanial.org | Free | Daily, 7–dusk.

Château Ste. Michelle. Washington's mega winery is set in a faux French château. With the Columbia winery across the road, it makes up Woodinville's wineland, with an almost theme park–like bustle on major holiday weekends. | 14111 N.E. 145th St., Woodinville | 425/488–1133 | fax 425/415–3657 | www.ste-michelle.com | Free | Daily 10–4:30.

Rosalie Whyel Museum of Doll Art. This museum, known for its wide and varied collection of dolls, has been called the "Best Doll Museum in the World." | 1116 108th Ave. NE | 425/455–1116 | fax 425/455–4793 | www.dollart.com/dollart | $6 | Mon.–Sat. 10–5, Sun. 1–5.

On the Calendar

JULY: *Bellevue Art Museum Fair.* The third weekend in July, over 300 artists from around the country display their fine art on the west side of Bellevue Sq. There is also an art demonstration and performance stage. | 425/454–3322, ext. 125.

Dining

Bis on Main. Continental. The intimate, romantic dining room is given special flair from the rotating exhibits of modern art that adorn the walls. The most popular of the many scrumptious entrées are the crabcakes and the crispy garlic chicken, a free-range chicken de-boned and marinated then pan-seared and roasted, served with horseradish mashed potatoes. | 10213 Main St. | 425/455–2033 | $12–$24 | AE, D, DC, MC, V.

Burgermaster. American/Casual. Since 1952, carhops at this drive-in have been serving people from their car windows. The specialty, of course, is hamburgers, but the drive-in also serves a variety of fish sandwiches, all of which are fresh and savory. | 10606 Northup Way | 425/827–9566 | $7–$10 | AE, D, DC, MC, V.

Coco's Bakery Restaurant. American/Casual. All the family is welcome at this local eatery that serves everything from salads to seafood. The restaurant is particularly known for its pies, muffins, and cookies baked on the premises. | 530 112th Ave. NE | 425/453–8138 | Breakfast also available | $7–$14 | AE, D, DC, MC, V.

Crab Pot Restaurant. Seafood. Sitting on Lake Washington, with spectacular views of Seattle, the restaurant is famous for its *seafeasts*: seafood poured over butcher paper. A mallet is all that stands between you and your meal. The menu also includes steak and chicken entrées. | 2 Lake Bellevue Dr. | 425/455–2244 | $10–$12 | AE, D, DC, MC, V.

Daniel's Broiler. Steak. Occupying the entire 21st floor of the Bank of America building, this restaurant has unbeatable views of Mt. Rainier, Seattle, the Cascades, and Lake Washington. Known primarily for its high quality steaks, the restaurant also serves an assortment of seafood, including cold water lobster tail. | 10500 N.E. 8th St., 21st floor | 425/462–4662 | $22–$27 | AE, D, DC, MC, V.

Factoria Red Robin. American/Casual. Over 22 varieties of hamburgers are served at this fun family eatery. The menu also includes sandwiches, salads, and soups. Festive music plays while the kids can enjoy the video games. | 3909 Factoria Mall | 425/641–3989 | $7–$10 | AE, D, DC, MC, V.

Jake O'Shaughnessey's. American. Once you step through the doors of this clubby restaurant you'll immediately forget that you're actually in one of the northwest's biggest shopping malls. The interior makes you feel like you're close to water, though you're not; the open kitchen adds a note of comfort. Serving steaks and seafood. There is open-air dining on the patio, in the mall courtyard. Kids' menu. Smoking in bar only. | 401 Bellevue Sq. | 425/455–5559 | $13–$25 | AE, D, DC, MC, V.

Polaris. Contemporary. A pleasant modern restaurant with a rather generic contemporary look, serving Northwest cuisine. Try the oven-roasted king salmon, or the niçoise shrimp pasta. There is open-air dining on the patio. Kids' menu. No smoking. | 11200 S.E. 6th St. | 425/455–1616 425/637–4608 | No lunch weekends, breakfast only | $18–$25 | AE, MC, V.

Sans Souci. Mediterranean. White tablecloths and candlelight give the dining room a romantic, though casual, air. The menu changes daily but regularly includes a pasta and seafood dish. The restaurant is particularly known for its veal entrées, which are also frequently showcased on the menu. | Winter Garden at Bellevue Place | 425/467–9490 | $10.25–$24.75 | AE, D, DC, MC, V.

Spazzo Mediterranean Grill. Mediterranean. A very pleasant, friendly, and vivacious upstairs restaurant with close-up views of Bellevue high-rise office buildings and distant views of Lake Washington and Seattle office towers. Serving a variety of Greek and Italian dishes, including "tapas" (appetizers) and a variety of pastas and fresh fish. Kids' menu. | 10655 N.E. Fourth St. | 425/454–8255 | No lunch weekends | $10–$30 | AE, D, DC, MC, V.

Lodging

Bellevue Bed and Breakfast. One of Bellevue's only bed and breakfasts, this homey lodging has large picture windows that overlook the downtown area. It is only a block from Lake Washington. | 2 rooms. Complimentary breakfast, no air-conditioning, no room phones, TV in common area, no pets, no kids under 10, no smoking. | 830 100th Ave. SE | 425/453–1048 or 888/453–1048 | fax 425/452–9086 | innkeepers@bellevuebandb.com | www.bellevuebandb.com | $87–$150 | No credit cards.

Bellevue Club. A very comfortable and luxurious hotel away from the noise of downtown and the I–405 freeway. The rooms are beautifully appointed. | 67 rooms (2 with shower only). Restaurant, bar with entertainment, in-room data ports, minibars, room service, cable TV, indoor pool, hot tub, massage, tennis, gym, children's programs (ages 1–12), business services. | 11200 S.E. 6th | 425/454–4424 or 800/579–1110 | fax 425/688–3101 | www.bellevueclub.com | $235–$295 | AE, DC, MC, V.

Best Western Bellevue Inn. Set among landscaped gardens planted with rhododendrons and azaleas, this modern hotel in downtown Bellevue is 9 mi west of Seattle and 1 mi east of the mall. | 181 rooms. Restaurant, bar with entertainment, in-room data ports, refrigerators, room service, cable TV, in-room video games, pool, exercise equipment, business services, free parking. | 11211 Main St. | 425/455–5240 | fax 425/455–0654 | $129–$159 | AE, D, DC, MC, V.

Candlewood Suites. Although this is primarily an extended-stay hotel, you might find its location—less than a mile from exit 11 off I–90—convenient. | 126 rooms. Kitchenettes, microwaves, refrigerators, cable TV, in-room VCRs, gym, laundry service, pets allowed (fee).

| 15805 S.E. 37th St. | 425/373–1212 | fax 425/373–1500 | www.candlewoodsuites.com | $115–$135 | AE, D, DC, MC, V.

Courtyard Bellevue. Just a block from exit 148 off Rte. 520, this hotel is also conveniently close to the Over Lake shopping mall. | 152 rooms, 8 suites. Restaurant, bar, room service, in-room data ports, cable TV, pool, hot tub, gym, laundry facilities, business services, no pets, no smoking. | 14615 N.E. 29th Place | 425/869–5300 | fax 425/883–9122 | www.courtyard.com | $109–$154 | AE, D, MC, V.

Doubletree Inn. A glassed-in seven-story atrium is the centerpiece of this large high-rise hotel. Rooms facing the freeway can be noisy. | 353 rooms. Restaurant, in-room data ports, cable TV, pool, hot tub, barbershop, beauty salon, exercise equipment, business services. | 300 112th Ave. SE | 425/455–1300 | fax 425/450–4119 | $109–$200 | AE, D, DC, MC, V.

Hilton. Upscale and comfortable hotel with a modern lobby. | 180 rooms. Two restaurants, bar, in-room data ports, cable TV, indoor pool, hot tub, sauna, gym, business services. | 100 112th Ave. NE | 425/455–3330 | fax 425/451–2473 | $79–$174 | AE, D, DC, MC, V.

Hyatt Regency Bellevue. This high-rise hotel in the center of Bellevue is across the street from a large shopping mall. There is a glass-enclosed garden atrium inside, as well as several shops. | 382 rooms, 29 suites. Restaurant, bar, in-room data ports, some refrigerators, cable TV, barbershop, beauty salon, business services. | 900 Bellevue Way NE | 425/462–1234 or 800/233–1234 | fax 425/646–7567 | $119–$270, $375–$1300 suites | AE, D, DC, MC, V.

Residence Inn by Marriott. This residential-style hotel is designed for longer stays and is also perfect for entertaining clients. | 120 suites. Picnic area, complimentary Continental breakfast, in-room data ports, microwaves, refrigerators, cable TV, pool, laundry facilities, business services. van shuttle service, free parking, pets allowed (fee). | 14455 N.E. 29th Place | 425/882–1222 or 800/331–3131 | fax 425/885–9260 | $125–$170 suites | AE, D, DC, MC, V.

Silver Cloud Inn. This business travelers' hotel is in a convenient downtown location. | 97 rooms (12 with shower only). Complimentary Continental breakfast, in-room data ports, refrigerators, microwaves, cable TV, pool, hot tub, exercise equipment, laundry facilities, business services. | 10621 N.E. 12th | 425/637–7000 or 800/205–6937 | fax 425/455–0531 | $104–$164 | AE, D, DC, MC, V.

Westcoast Bellevue Hotel. This modernized hotel in the heart of Bellevue is minutes from the Meydenbauer Convention Center. Newly remodelled business travelers' and family hotel. | 176 rooms. Restaurant, bar, in-room data ports, room service, cable TV, pool, exercise equipment, business services. | 625 116th Ave. NE | 425/455–9444 or 800/426–0670 | fax 425/455–2154 | $99–$140 | AE, D, DC, MC, V.

BELLINGHAM

MAP 8, D2

(Nearby towns also listed: Blaine, Sedro Woolley)

Much of Bellingham's waterfront is marred by one of Puget Sound's few remaining pulp mills and by rock breakwaters protecting a large marina. But South Bellingham, once the independent city of Fairhaven, has a very pretty and accessible waterfront.

Downtown has a few old buildings, most notably the old turreted city hall (1892), which now serves as the Whatcom Museum of History and Art, and several good restaurants. On a bluff near the bay stands a small house built in the late 1850s by Captain George E. Pickett, who was stationed at nearby Fort Bellingham before riding off to fame and eventual death in the Civil War.

There's a waterfall on Whatcom Creek behind the downtown post office, where visitors can watch salmon leap upstream in autumn. Whatcom Falls Park, several miles upstream, has several more falls and trails along the creek leading to a park, with sandy beach, at the north end of Lake Whatcom. The trail passes Scudder Pond, near the outflow of the creek, and a marsh where beavers are active at dawn and dusk. Otters and great blue herons can also be spotted here at times. Cornwall Park and Fairhaven Park also have tree-shaded lawns and salmon streams. Boulevard Park allows access to the bay shore, where harlequin ducks frolic in winter.

Information: Bellingham/Whatcom County Convention and Visitors Bureau | 904 Potter St., Bellingham, 98226 | 800/487–2032 | bellingham.org.

Attractions

Bellingham Antique Radio Museum. Over 1,000 radios fill this small museum whose operator has been collecting them for over half a century. | 1315 Railroad Ave. | 360/671–4663 | Wed.–Sat., noon–5 or by appointment.

Chuckanut Drive. This 7 mi stretch of highway runs from the Skagit Valley flats (in winter, look for tundra and trumpeter swans in the meadows) north to Fairhaven in South Bellingham. En route it winds and twists its way along the sheer sandstone face of Chuckanut mountain and crosses creeks with waterfalls. Pullouts along the cliff side are framed by gnarled madrona trees and pines and offer great views of the San Juan Islands (the best views you can get from any mainland shore). Bald eagles cruise along the cliffs or hang out on top of tall firs. Drive carefully: the cliffs are so steep in places that rock slides are common (the road washes out about once or twice each winter). | Fairhaven Park along Rte. 11 to Larrabee State Park | 360/676–2093 | Free | Daily.

Arroyo Park. This is an undeveloped woodland park south of town, off Chuckanut Park. A trail leads north into Bellingham and south to Chuckanut Drive and to Teddy Bear Cove, Whatcom County's only nude beach. To find the park, turn east into Samish Way at the Chuckanut Gallery. | Old Samish Rd. | 360/676–6985 | fax 360/647–6367 | www.cob.org | Free | Daily.

Bloedel Donovan Park. This is a grassy, tree-shaded meadow at the north end of Lake Whatcom which provides the only public access to this 14-mi-long lake. Locals swim in the sheltered waters of a cove, but visitors tend to find the water too cold. You might spot beavers, river otters, ducks, great blue herons, and yellow pond lilies at Scudder Pond which is another 100 ft west (reached by trail from a parking area at Northshore and Alabama). | 2214 Electric Ave. | 360/676–6985 | fax 360/647–6367 | www.cob.org | $3 summer parking fee (out-of-county cars) | Daily.

Boulevard Park. Bellingham has little public access to saltwater, but you can walk the beach at Marine Park in Fairhaven, or the lawns of Boulevard Park just to the north (a trail is being built to connect the two). Call the phone number below to ask for a Greenways map, which shows all public trails. There is also some water access at John Glenn Spit and Squalicum Harbor at the northern end of the waterfront. The central part of the waterfront is occupied by a very ugly pulp mill and its settling lagoon. | S. State St. and Bayview Dr. | 360/676–6985 | fax 360/647–6367 | www.cob.org | Free | Daily.

Civic Field Athletic Complex. There are playing fields and an indoor swimming pool. | Lakeway Dr. and Orleans St. | 360/676–6985 | fax 360/647–6367 | www.cob.org | Call for prices | Event dependent; call for schedule.

Cornwall Park. A wooded park with some very big trees on the north side of town. | 2800 Cornwall Ave. | 360/676–6985 | fax 360/647–6367 | www.cob.org | Free | Daily.

Fairhaven Park. A beautiful park along both shores of Padden Creek that has unfortunately just lost its rose garden (which once was famous throughout the state) to civic neglect. Chum salmon run and spawn in Padden Creek in November. | 107 Chuckanut Dr. | 360/676–6985 | fax 360/647–6367 | www.cob.org | Free | Daily.

Lake Padden Park. This park is at the far southern edge of town with a boat ramp, a golf course, and the usual playing fields. In spring the lake is stocked with trout. Trails from the western shore lead into wilder woods. | 4882 Samish Way | 360/676–6985 | fax 360/647–6367 | www.cob.org | Free | Daily.

Sehome Hill Arboretum. A hilltop arboretum above Western Washington University with good views of Bellingham Bay and Lummi Island. | 25th St. and McDonald Pkwy. | 360/676–6985 | fax 360/647–6367 | www.cob.org | Free | Daily.

Whatcom Falls Park. A pleasant park on upper Whatcom Creek that's increasingly encroached upon by housing developments (the ruffed grouse living here 20 years ago are now gone). The creek has a number of pretty waterfalls; one has the local high school kids' swimming hole, although the water is VERY cold. Trails lead down creek and up the creek to Scudder Pond and Bloedel Donovan Park. | 1401 Electric Ave. | 360/676–6985 | fax 360/647–6367 | www.cob.org | Free | Daily.

Fairhaven District. Bellingham's best preserved district was an independent town until its merger with New Whatcom to the north created the city of Bellingham back in 1903. Fairhaven suffered an economic setback in the merger, which has helped preserve its historic buildings, which now house shops, galleries, and restaurants. Harris Street runs downhill to Padden Lagoon where you'll find geese, ducks and herons at the mouth of Padden Creek, the Alaska Ferry Terminal, and Marine Park. | 12th St. and Harris Ave. | 360/676–6985 | fax 360/647–6367 | www.cob.org | Free | Daily.

Ferndale. A pleasant farm town, with many dairy farms, that has burst its seams in recent years as urban sprawl arrived. It has the best views of Mt. Baker in the county. Be sure to visit Houander Park while you are here. | Exit 262 off I–5 | 360/384–3444 | Free | Daily.

Larrabee State Park. A very scenic 2,000-acre hillside park shaded by trees, with two rock-bound coves on Samish Bay, 7 mi south of Bellingham. | Rte. 11 | 360/676–2093 | Free | Daily.

Maritime Heritage Center. A small park on Whatcom Creek, below the old city hall/Whatcom Museum of History and Art, and upstream from the pulp mill. Salmon return to a hatchery to spawn. This park is still under development. | 1600 C St. | 360/676–6806 | www.cob.org | Free | Daily.

Mount Baker Theatre. The theatre, which opened in 1927, hosts a variety of plays, concerts, and dances throughout the year in one of Bellingham's architectural jewels. But, be on your guard! A ghost named Judy is said to lurk in the corridors and on the grounds. | 104 N. Commercial St. | 360/733–5793 or 360/734–6080 | fax 360/671–0114 | www.mtbakertheatre.com | Open year round.

Mt. Baker–Snoqualmie National Forest. A vast area including much of the mountain and forest land encircling North Cascades National Park. The region has many hiking trails, but because the snowline is quite low in Washington State, the upper part of the ridges and mountains is covered by snow for much of the year, making for a short hiking season, usually running from mid-July to mid-September or October. (For this reason, the wildflower season is also short but spectacular; expect fall color by late August and early September.) | Hwy. 542 | 360/599–2714 | www.fs.fed.us | Free | Daily.

Mt. Baker Ski Area. This ski area has the most snow and the longest season in North America. The vertical drop is 1,500 ft. It is very popular with snowboarders and is the starting point for the Memorial Day weekend Ski to Sea Race. | Rte. 542 | 360/734–6771 or 360/671–0211 (snow conditions) | fax 360/734–5332 | www.mountbakerskiarea.com | Nov.–Mar., daily; Apr., Fri.–Sun.

Squalicum Harbor Marina. There are beautiful views of the bay from this marina where you can sometimes see whales. Lounging, picnicking, walking, jogging, and biking are also possibilities. | Roeder Ave. and Coho Way.

Western Washington University. Located on the side of Sehome Hill, facing the bay, this may well be the most scenic campus in Washington. There's an outdoor sculpture collection of mostly rusty metal pieces. | 516 High St. | 360/650–3000 | fax 350/650–6817 | www.wwu.edu | Free | Daily.

Whatcom Museum of History and Art. Set in the former Gothic city hall, this museum has a good collection of historic photos. There's a totem pole carved by a Lummi carver outside. | 121 Prospect St. | 360/676–6981 | fax 360/738–7409 | www.cob.org | Free; $2 children's museum | Tues.–Sun., noon–5.

Victoria/San Juan Cruises. Sail to Victoria, British Columbia, and the San Juan Islands on a day trip or for an overnight visit. The views of whales and sunsets cannot be beat. | 355 Harris Ave., inside the Bellingham Cruise Terminal | 360/738–8099 or 800/443–4552 | Mid-May–first weekend in Oct.

ON THE CALENDAR

JUNE: *Bellingham Highland Games.* Held on the first Saturday of June at the Hovander Homestead Park in the Ferndale, the Highland Games include bagpipe competitions, Scottish dance competitions, and other traditional forms of Highland amusement. | $7 | 360/647–8500; 360/479–3579.

MAY: *Ski to Sea Festival.* A downhill, cross-country ski, foot, bicycle, and canoe relay race, as well as a sea kayak sprint from the slopes of Mt. Baker to the Fairhaven waterfront, is held on Memorial Day weekend. | 360/734–1330.

JUNE: *Deming Logging Show.* Loggers challenge each other in traditional skill contests and proceeds go to help loggers injured or maimed while working in the woods, and to the families of loggers killed in logging accidents. | 360/592–3051.

JUNE: *Lummi Stommish.* You'll find canoe races and a salmon barbecue at the Lummi Reservation, but the dates depend on the tides; there needs to be enough water in shallow Hale Passage to allow the canoes to race near shore. | 360/384–2304.

Dining

Boundary Bay Brewery Bistro. Contemporary. This is a bright, pleasant downtown brew pub with some of the best food in Bellingham. The decor isn't much, but the beer and food more than make up for it. The hearty dishes match the complex flavors of the beers. In warm weather, the front opens up to let in the sunshine. It is known for vegetarian dishes and lamb burgers. | 1107 Railroad Ave. | 360/647–5593 | $7–15 | MC, V.

Chuckanut Manor. American/Casual. The glassed-in dining room and bar have views of the Samish River, the adjacent mudflats, the bay, and a few of the easterly San Juan Islands. Steak and seafood are the specialties here. Especially popular is the seafood sauté. | 302 Chuckanut Dr. | 360/766–6191 | $10–$25 | AE, MC, V.

Colophon Cafe. American. Sharing space with Village Books in Fairhaven, this comfortable cafe is very popular with the locals and tourists. Known for soups, sandwiches and pies. | 1208 11th St. | 360/647–0092 | Reservations not accepted for parties of fewer than 5 | Breakfast also available | $4–$10 | AE, D, MC, V.

Marina Restaurant. Seafood. This is a very generic waterfront restaurant that serves Northwest cuisine, including seafood and steaks. There is open-air dining on the patio. Kids' menu. | 985 Bellwether Way | 360/733–8292 | $14–$30 | AE, MC, V.

Orchard Street Brewery. American/Casual. A very pleasant brew pub in a rather nondescript office park near the north end of town. Beers are brewed on the premises. Try the pizza baked in a wood-fired oven. | 709 W. Orchard Drive, No. 1 | 360/647–1614 | Closed Sun. | $10–$20 | AE, MC, V.

Oyster Bar. Seafood. Famous for its spectacular view of the sound below, this intimate restaurant sits above the shore on a steep, wooded bluff. Sunsets here are unbeatable. The menu often changes but great seafood can always be found. The restaurant serves a variety of fresh, raw oysters according to what's in season. | 2578 Chuckanut Dr., Bow | 360/766–6185 | $22–$28 | AE, MC, V.

Oyster Creek Inn. Seafood. Window tables overlook the purling creek below where you might spy an otter fishing for its dinner. Oysters prepared in traditional and imaginative ways are the restaurant's specialty, although the other seafood dishes are also superb. The wine list includes the Northwest's best selection of regional wines. | 2190 Chuckanut Dr., Bow | 360/766–6179 | $14–$28 | AE, MC, V.

Pacific Café. Pan-Asian. White walls, rice-paper screens, and wood shutters set the stage for the Asian-inspired cuisine dished-up here. Try the Alaska spot prawns in a garlicky black-bean sauce. Large portions are the rule, so be advised. The homemade, European-style desserts are wickedly delicious. The wine list is extensive. | 100 N. Commercial St. | 360/647–0800 | $15–$19 | Closed Sun. No lunch Sat. | AE, DC, MC, V.

Stanello's Restaurant. Mediterranean. This Fairhaven restaurant sits high up on the hill, with distant views of the waterfront, Bellingham Bay, and the Lummi Peninsula. The food is simple but tasty, ranging from a superbly flavorful minestrone to pastas, pizzas, chicken dishes, and steak. Try the spinach salad, the Greek *salata kota* (chicken salad), and the vegetarian lasagna. | 1514 12th St. | 360/676–1304 | No lunch Mon.–Thurs. | $12–$20 | AE, D, DC, MC, V.

Wild Garlic. American. This small, elegant restaurant is tucked into a tiny space across the street from the Whatcom Museum of History and Art. It has a narrow dining room with booths on one side and seems almost too sophisticated for fussy downtown Bellingham, but it has a very loyal local clientele. Garlic reigns supreme in the kitchen, but it is handled with finesse, especially in the dish called "swimming garlic," an appetizer that is a delicate version of an Italian bagna cauda. The service is friendly and very professional. Try the stuffed scampi with roasted garlic, asiago, and herbs. | 114 Prospect St. | 360/671–1955 | Closed Sun. No lunch Sat. | $14–$25 | MC, V.

Lodging

Anderson Creek Lodge. Eight miles northeast of downtown, the 65 acres of this property are split between woods and pastures filled with llamas. The rooms have hand-carved furniture, exposed beams, and stained-glass windows. Each overlooks the garden and landscaped grounds that surround the lodge. Hikes are conducted on a regular basis throughout the year. Although the property's seclusion is suitable for romantic getaways, the lodge can also accommodate families. | 3 rooms. Complimentary breakfast, no air-conditioning, cable TV, in-room VCRs, no room phones, outdoor hot tub, hiking, business services, pets allowed, no smoking. | 5602 Mission Rd. | 360/966–0598 | AndersonCreek@compuserve.com | www.andersoncreek.com | $85 | MC, V.

Best Western Heritage Inn. This is an elegantly furnished Victorian-style family hotel across the street from a major shopping mall. | 90 rooms. Complimentary Continental breakfast, some refrigerators, microwaves, cable TV, pool, hot tub, business services, airport shuttle, free parking. | 151 E McLeod Rd. | 360/647–1912 | fax 360/671–3878 | $70–$100 | AE, D, DC, MC, V.

Best Western Lakeway Inn. This chain hotel is 3 mi from the Alaska Ferry Terminal and historic Fairhaven. | 132 rooms. Restaurant, bar with entertainment, room service, cable TV, indoor pool, beauty salon, hot tub, gym, laundry facilities, business services, airport shuttle, free parking, some pets allowed (fee). | 714 Lakeway Dr. | 360/671–1011 | fax 360/676–8519 | $79–$99 | AE, D, DC, MC, V.

Big Trees Bed and Breakfast. Appropriately named, this 1907 Craftsman stands in the shade of towering old-growth cedars and firs near Lake Whatcom. The inn's corbeled ceiling, stone fireplace, and fir woodwork preserve the inn's homey charm. The rooms each have a different character; the Cedar room is home to a king-size feather bed, while the Rhodie Room has a decoupage floor. | 3 rooms share 2 baths. Complimentary breakfast, no air-conditioning, cable TV, in-room VCRs, no pets, no smoking. | 4840 Fremont St. | 360/647–2850 or 800/647–2850 | bigtrees@nas.com | www.bigtrees-bedandbreakfast.com | $95–$115 | MC, V.

Days Inn. This hotel is centrally located and caters to business travelers and families. | 70 rooms. Complimentary Continental breakfast, some refrigerators, cable TV, pool, hot tub, laundry facilities, pets allowed (fee). | 125 E. Kellogg Rd. | 360/671–6200 | fax 360/671–9491 | $45–$125 | AE, D, DC, MC, V.

DeCann House Bed-and-Breakfast. This Victorian house sits in a residential neighborhood 1 mi north of downtown. The antique pool table is the main attraction in the common area which also contains walls lined with hardwood shelves. Quilts, heirlooms, and antiques give character to both rooms. | 2 rooms. Complimentary breakfast, no air-conditioning, some room phones, TV in common area, no pets, no smoking. | 2610 Eldridge Ave. | 360/734–9172 | hudson@pacificrim.net | www.decannhouse.com | $70–$85 | No credit cards.

Fairhaven Bed and Breakfast. This Victorian mansion is filled with antiques and is great for a romantic getaway. There are stained glass windows, a dining room, and a large deck. Walking trails are on the grounds. | 2 rooms. Complimentary breakfast. | 1714 12th St. | 360/734–7243 | $85–$105 | D, MC, V.

Hampton Inn. This four-story hotel is minutes from the Canadian border. Cookies and milk or coffee are served each evening. | 132 rooms. Complimentary Continental breakfast, in-room data ports, cable TV, pool, in-room video games, exercise equipment, business services, airport and ferry shuttles. | 3985 Bennett Dr. | 360/676–7700 | fax 360/671–7557 | www.hampton-inn-bellingham.com | $59–$89 | AE, D, DC, MC, V.

North Garden Inn. Comfortable downtown B&B in a historic Queen Anne Victorian house dating from the late 1800s. It is near Western Washington University. There is a grand piano in the lobby. | 10 rooms (2 with shared bath). Complimentary breakfast. | 1014 N. Garden St. | 360/671–7828 or 800/922–6414 | $50–$125 | AE, D, MC, V.

Quality Inn Baron Suites. You will be very close to area shopping malls when you stay at this suite hotel which is just 3 mi from the airport. City center is 6 mi northeast. | 86 suites. Complimentary Continental breakfast, in-room data ports, some refrigerators, cable TV, pool, hot tub, exercise equipment, laundry facilities, business services, airport shuttle. | 100 E. Kellogg Rd. | 360/647–8000 | fax 360/647–8094 | $60–$100 suites | AE, DC, MC, V.

Ramada Inn. This chain hotel is minutes from downtown and easily accessible to I–5. If you are continuing your trip north, it is just 20 minutes to the Canadian border. | 66 rooms. Complimentary Continental breakfast, some refrigerators, cable TV, room phones with voice mail, pool, business services. | 215 Samish Way | 360/734–8830 | fax 360/647–8956 | $75–$85 | AE, D, DC, MC, V.

Schnauzer Crossing. This luxury B&B overlooks Lake Whatcom, on 1½ acres of gardens, including a Japanese Garden and tea house, a meditation garden, and a koi pond. Its wonderful library and Northwest art make it popular with local authors and artists. | 2 rooms, 1 suite, 1 cottage. Complimentary breakfast, hot tub. | 4421 Lakeway Drive | 360/733–0055 | fax 360/734–2808. | www.schnauzercrossing.com | $125–$215 | AE, D, MC, V.

Stratford Manor Bed-and-Breakfast. Once a private school, this large and sumptuously furnished B&B sits on 30 landscaped acres 7 mi east of Bellingham. Among the common areas are a solarium, a living room with fireplace, a library, and two decks. Each of the three spacious rooms has oak furnishings, a gas fireplace, and a sitting area. A fourth room is available during the summer. | 3 rooms. Complimentary breakfast, in-room hot tubs, some in-room VCRs, no TV, no room phones, outdoor hot tub, putting green, gym, library, no pets, no kids under 15, no smoking. | 4566 Andersen Way | 360/715–8441 or 800/240–6779 | fax 360/671–0840 | lohse@aol.com | www.stratfordmanor.com | $125–$175 | MC, V.

Travelers Inn. This motel is near the Belli-Fair Mall and caters to families. | 124 rooms. Some refrigerators, microwaves, cable TV, pool, hot tub, laundry facilities, business services, some pets allowed. | 3750 Meridian St. | 360/671–4600 | fax 360/671–6487 | $45–$75 | AE, D, DC, MC, V.

Val-U-Inn. This family motel, just off I–5, is close to downtown and only 25 mi south of the Canadian border. | 82 rooms. Complimentary Continental breakfast, some refrigerators, cable TV, hot tub, laundry facilities, business services. Airport and ferry terminal shuttles, free parking, pets allowed (fee). | 805 Lakeway Dr. | 360/671–9600, 800/443–7777 | fax 360/671–8323 | $47–$75 | AE, D, DC, MC, V.

BLAINE

MAP 8, D1

(Nearby town also listed: Bellingham)

This small town has a busy fishing port and yacht moorage in Drayton Harbor, a bay protected from the storm waters of Georgia Strait by sandy Semiahmoo Spit. Blaine also has Washington's two busiest border crossings into Canada: one, on I–5, becomes BC 99 north of the border; the other, a couple of miles further east, is known as the "truck crossing," because here is where big semis have to go through customs. Travelers in passenger sedans cross here, too, especially since border lineups tend to be shorter. On a busy summer weekend, it can take as much as two hours or longer to cross at the I–5 crossing.

A white "Peace Arch" stands right above the border, in the middle of the I–5/BC 99 crossing, in border-straddling Peace Park. It was built in 1921 to celebrate the peaceful nature of this undefended border. On September 6, 1921, the *Bellingham Herald* proclaimed: "The Anglo-Saxon peoples clasped hands at Blaine today through the open doors of the world's first peace arch."

Information: Blaine Visitor Information Center | 215 Marine Dr., Blaine, 98231 | 360/332–4544. | www.ci.blaine.

Attractions

Birch Bay State Park. This is saltwater park with northwest Washington's only warm sandy beach. Swimming, fishing, crabbing, and clamming are all popular activities here. | Helwig Rd. | 360/371–2800 or 800/233–0321 | www.parks.wa.gov | Free. Camping $12–$17 | Daily, 6:30–dusk, Memorial Day–Labor Day, reservations advised.

International Peace Arch. This large white concrete arch straddles the center of the border crossing, with large bronze doors permanently standing open to symbolize the open border between the U.S. and Canada. The arch incorporates fragments both of the *Mayflower* of Pilgrim fame, and of the Hudson's Bay Company ship *Beaver*, the first steamer on the Northwest Coast. (You'll learn how "open" this border really is when you try to cross.) | North at point where I–5 reaches Canadian border | 360/332–6484 | Free | Daily.

Lighthouse Point, Point Roberts. Take the easy ½- to 1-mi trail along the shore to the Lighthouse Marine Park. The park has a view tower from which you look across Georgia Strait to the Gulf and San Juan Islands, with Vancouver Island looming on the horizon. At times gray whales and orcas pass close to this point. Undeveloped Monument Park, just south of the Canadian border, has a rough and steep trail down to the beach. Lily Point, at the southeast corner of Point Roberts, has eroding 200-ft-high bluffs. Nearby stands a grove of old-growth big-leaf maples. | 1611 Riverside Ave. | 360/945–4911 (for camping information) | Free | Daily.

Lynden Pioneer Museum. This small museum has a very eclectic collection of old artifacts. | 217 Front St., Lynden | 360/354–3675 | www.lyndenpioneermuseum.com | $3 | Mon.–Sat. 10–4 except from June–August, 10–5.

ON THE CALENDAR

JAN.: *Polar Bear Swim.* January 1 plunge into the cold waters of Birch Bay. Hot chile, hot chocolate, and other warming refreshments as well as prizes are the reward. | 360/371–7800.

APR.–MAY: *Holland Days.* Lynden farmers celebrate their Dutch heritage with a parade, street music, klompen (wooden shoe) dancing, and booths selling Dutch-style treats at Lynden which is east of Blaine. | 360/354–5995.

JUNE: *Peace Arch Celebration.* This celebration of peace and brotherhood between the United States and Canada is held the second Sunday in June in Peace Arch Park, which sits on the U.S. and Canadian border. Veteran and scout groups gather with others under the Peace Arch monument. There are also parades and military bands. | 360/332–4544.

Dining

Harbor Café. American/Casual. The dining room of this pleasant portside tavern and family restaurant overlooks the fishing fleet moored in Drayton Harbor. Locals flock here for the fish and chips, which are the best being served anywhere in the county and have held pride of place for at least two decades. | 295 Marine Drive | 360/332–5176 | Breakfast also available | $8–$15 | AE, D, DC, MC, V.

Stars. Contemporary. From this quiet and romantic dining room at the SemiAhMoo Resort, you can enjoy inspiring sunsets across the bay. Among the entrées are a charbroiled filet of beef with roasted garlic and hazelnut crust and chianti glaze and a pan-seared salmon with pepper and ginger and Grand-Marnier reduction. | 9565 Semiahmoo Pkwy. | 360/371–2000 | Breakfast also available. No lunch | $17–$32 | AE, D, DC, MC, V.

Lodging

Driftwood Inn Motel. This early '60s motel sits across the street from the beach. If swimming in the ocean is not your cup of tea, the motel also has a large outdoor pool. The rooms have simple, modern furnishings. The cottages have patios that overlook the Terrell Creek. | 3 rooms, 4 suites, 1 condo, 4 cottages. No air-conditioning, some kitchenettes, refrigerators, cable TV, no room phones, pool, volleyball, no pets. | 7394 Birch Bay Dr. | 360/371–2620 or 800/833–2666 | fax 360/371–5926 | www.birchbaywa.com | $49.50–$150 | D, MC, V.

Inn at SemiAhMoo. A sprawling country resort on a sandy peninsula, 15 minutes from downtown Blaine. | 198 rooms, 14 suites. Bar with entertainment, dining rooms, snack bar, in-room data ports, room service, cable TV, indoor-outdoor pool, beauty salon, hot tub, spa, driving range, 18-hole golf course, putting green, tennis, gym, marina, water sports, boating, bicycles, video games and pool table, laundry facilities, business services, pets allowed (fee). | 9565 Semiahmoo Pkwy. | 360/371–2000 | fax 360/371–5490 | www.semiahmoo.com | $179–$219 rooms, $239–$279 suites | AE, D, DC, MC, V.

BREMERTON

MAP 8, D4

(Nearby town also listed: Seattle)

Considering that Bremerton has one of the largest navy bases and shipyards on the West Coast, it is a surprisingly green city. Some of the trees looming on hillsides above the port are large enough to dwarf the tall radio masts of the warships moored on the Sinclair Inlet waterfront. The city has recently made some major efforts to restore its business waterfront along the Port Washington Narrows. The best way to experience the might of the naval presence and the beauty of the natural surroundings is to take a harbor tour; a small, privately operated passenger ferry crosses the water to the county seat of Port Orchard. Built in 1817, the MV *Carlisle II* is the oldest continuously operating ferry in Puget Sound, and one of the last survivors of the region's famed Mosquito Fleet. Nearby Illahee State Park is very popular with weekend campers.

Information: Bremerton Area Chamber of Commerce | 301 Pacific Ave., Bremerton, 98337 | 360/479–3579 | www.bremertonchamber.org.

Attractions

Belfair State Park. This small park, 3 mi from Belfair, occupies a sheltered waterfront on the lower part of the Hood Canal, where the canal hooks north for a few miles. It's great for canoeing and kayaking and, in very warm summers, the water may even be warm enough for swimming. | Hwy. 300 | 360/275–0668 or 800/452–5687 | fax 360/275–8734 | Free, Camping $12–$17 | Daily.

Bremerton Marina. You can walk or picnic here while watching the boats and ferries come and go. Right on the water, you will also see a host of birds and wildlife. | Off Washington Ave.

Bremerton Naval Museum. A small museum, in the ferry terminal, with a few ship models, historic displays, and American and Japanese war artifacts. | 130 Washington Ave. | 360/479–SHIP | fax 360/377–4186 | Free | Tues.–Sat 10–5, Sun. 1–5; Summer open Mon. 10–5 also.

Illahee State Park. On the shore of Port Orchard (with 25 campsites), this park is mainly for day use, providing beach access for nearby urban areas. | Rte. 306 | 360/478–6460 or 800.223–0321 | fax 360/792–6067 | www.parks.wa.gov | Free | Daily, 8–dusk.

Kitsap County Historical Society Museum. A small, local museum with pioneers' artifacts, nautical items of local historical interest, and a collection of old photographs. | 280 4th St. | 360/479–6226 | www.waynes.net/kchsm | Donations accepted | Tues.–Sat. 9–5.

Naval Undersea Museum. The museum houses the country's largest collection of undersea artifacts, including submarines, torpedoes, diving equipment, and undersea mines. Exhibits also treat the ocean environment and undersea naval technology. The museum is located in Key Port, approximately 10 mi north of Bremerton. | Downtown Key Port | 360/396–4148 | num.kpt.nuwc.navy.mil | Free | Oct.–May, Daily 10–4; closed Tues.

Scenic Beach State Park. This small park, on the eastern shore of the Hood Canal, has campsites, oyster beds, and great views of the Olympic Mountains mirrored in the waters of the "canal." | Rte. 3 to Newberry Hill exit, 1½ mi to Seabeck Hwy. | 360/830–5079 or 800/233–0321 | www.parks.wa.gov | Free, Camping $12–$18 | Daily.

USS *Turner Joy*. Now that the USS *Missouri* has been towed to Pearl Harbor, this Navy destroyer is currently the only vessel open for regular visiting. Check for roadside sandwich boards announcing other ships open for visits. | 300 Washington Beach Ave. | 360/792–2457 | $7 | May–Sept., daily 10–4; Oct.–Apr., daily 10–4.

ON THE CALENDAR

APR.: ***Sea Gull Calling Contest.*** A wacky contest with prizes awarded for the best seagull imitation, most seagulls called, and the best costume. It takes place in Port Orchard, and can be reached by passenger ferry from the downtown waterfront. | 800/982–8139.

MAY: ***Armed Forces Festival and Parade.*** Bremerton goes all out for the boys in navy blue on Armed Forces Day, with a big parade, a golf tournament, concerts, and exhibits. | 360/479–3579.

SEPT.: ***Blackberry Festival.*** Blackberry specials and kids' events are the focus of this two-day festival held at the Bremerton Boardwalk on the waterfront. | 360/377–3041.

MAY–JUNE: ***Mountaineers' Forest Theater.*** Mountaineer's Club members present a play every year in an outdoor amphitheater in the middle of the woods. | 206/284–6310.

Dining

Boat Shed. Contemporary. This rough-sided, deliberately Northwest rustic, waterfront restaurant serves the best seafood in Bremerton. In warm weather, there's outside seating on the deck. The atmosphere is casual and clam chowder, steamed clams, and mussels are among the highlights. There is boat moorage available. No smoking. Sunday brunch. | 101 Shore Dr. | 360/377–2600 | $15–$25 | AE, MC, V.

Illahee Manor Restaurant. Contemporary. When you dine here on a clear night, the moon shimmers off Port Orchard Bay and, together with the candlelight, many plants, and purling fountain, creates an inimitable dining environment. The prix-fixe dinner consists of five to six courses, with entrées like salmon, crab cakes, or stuffed cornish game hen. | 6680 Illahee Rd. NE | 360/698–7555 or 800/693–6680 | fax 360/698–0688 | innkeeper@illaheemanor.com | www.illaheemanor.com | No lunch | $25 prix fixe | AE, D, MC, V.

THE RETURN OF THE MOSQUITO FLEET

There once was a steamer named the *Eliza Anderson*, a plain sidewheeler with a tall stovepipe stack, that plied the waters of the Salish Sea. She faithfully carried cargo, cattle, and passengers up and down the inland water ways. Built in Portland, Oregon, in 1858 for the Columbia River trade, she soon moved to Puget Sound. She wasn't much to look at, but she was reliable and made regular runs from Seattle to Olympia, Bellingham Bay, and Victoria for almost 40 years. (She was wrecked at Unalaska during the Klondike gold rush.)

The *Eliza Anderson* was not alone. A fleet of launches, boats, and small ships, dubbed the "mosquito fleet" because of the small size of the vessels and because of the way they buzzed from port to port, catered to the needs of travelers on the inland waters until they were driven out of business by improved roads, automobiles, and trucks. But until well into the 1920s, transportation in western Washington was easier and quicker by water than by land, even though railroads had arrived in the 1880s.

As Lelah Jackson Edson wrote in *The Fourth Corner*, "Thirty years after the first settlement on Bellingham Bay there were as yet no passable roads into the back country. Staples could be landed by water from the Atlantic more cheaply than by packhorse from the Whatcom hinterland." Sternwheelers, some of them so shallow-drafted they were said to float on "a heavy dew," ascended rivers that today seem scarcely navigable for canoes, to carry away the farmers' produce. Towns and villages established along waterways thrived. Those that weren't failed.

The first ship of the mosquito fleet was the 80-foot Bellingham-built schooner *General Harney*, launched in 1859. But it quickly became clear that winds on the inland waters were rather unpredictable, and steamboats were introduced.

The tidal channels of the Salish Sea are often narrow and dangerous—currents can race around rocky headlands at 8 knots or more, making navigation difficult and often risky even for steamboats. The weather usually did not cooperate either. What might be a pleasant excursion on a sunny day at slack tide could quickly turn into a harrowing adventure for novice skippers on a foggy or rainy and windy day. But the captains of the mosquito fleet knew their business, even when they couldn't see from bow to headland. There were few wrecks, even though the vessels had no radar, echo sounders, GPS, or other modern navigational aids. As David Richardson wrote in Magic Islands, piloting a boat through the San Juan Islands "became an art unmatched, probably, in any corner of the world." Skippers "perfected the science of navigating through narrow, twisting channels that would make a conventional four-striper blanch." Richardson adds that, until the introduction of radar, inter-island vessels were navigated during heavy fogs "on the horn," with the skipper "listening to the echo of the boat's whistle, noting the direction of the returning sound, and the time it takes to come back." Other skippers steered by "familiar sounds, like a dog barking or a rooster crowing." Yet others could "read" the odor of kelp.

After the original mosquito fleet went into decline, only a few of the original boats survived, most notably the *Carlisle*, which carries passengers between Bremerton and Port Orchard, and the *Virginia V*, now an excursion boat. But as more and more people began to visit the islands, a need was felt for boats smaller and more flexible than the big bulky Washington State ferries. By the late 1990s, privately operated passenger ferries were making daily runs between Bellingham, San Juan Island, and Victoria, B.C., with "whistle" stops in between. "Crew boats," fast and comfortable launches, served ships anchored in bay or strait, waiting for a berth, supplying them with food, taking crew members ashore, and bringing them back to the ship. In 1998, a "commuter" ferry ran for the first time in decades to remote islands like Matia, Sucia, and Patos, which could previously only be reached by private boat. The Mosquito Fleet had returned.

Oyster Bay Inn Restaurant. Contemporary. The large picture windows of this restaurant offer tremendous panoramic views of the bay and the tree-lined coast. Chandeliers add an extra flair. The menu emphasizes seafood, but there is a variety of choices, including steaks and pasta dishes. | 4412 Kitsap Way | 360/377–5510 | kangmail@email.msn.com | www.oysterbaymotel.com | $6.50–$29 | AE, D, DC, MC, V.

Yacht Club Broiler. Contemporary. This simple but elegant restaurant 10 mi north of Bremerton overlooks Dyes Inlet. The seafood dishes are uncommonly fresh and prepared with flair. This restaurant is also known for Nebraska corn-fed prime steak. There is open-air dining on the deck, and on a grassy knoll. Kids' menu. Sun. brunch. | 9226 Bayshore Dr., Silverdale | 360/698–1601 | $15–$25 | AE, D, MC, V.

Lodging

Flagship Inn. Rooms here have private balconies which overlook Oyster Bay and the Olympic Mountains. Complimentary tea, coffee, fruit, and cookies are available all day. | 29 rooms. Complimentary Continental breakfast, in-room data ports, kitchenettes, refrigerators, cable TV, in-room VCRs (movies), pool, business services. | 4320 Kitsap Way | 360/479–6566 or 800/447–9396 | fax 360/479–6745 | $60–$85 | AE, D, DC, MC, V.

Howard Johnson Plaza Hotel. Built in 1981 and recently modernized, this hotel is close to Puget Sound Naval Base. Most of the rooms have glorious views of the water and mountains. | 143 rooms. Restaurant, no-smoking rooms, pool, hot tub. | 5640 Kitsap Way | 360/373–9900 | fax 360/377–8529 | $57–$172 | AE, D, DC, MC, V.

Illahee Manor Bed and Breakfast. This 1920s manor sits directly on the bay and has its own private beach. The 6 acres of woods, orchards, and gardens on which the manor sits are also home to miniature deer and llamas. The bedrooms are all large; some have fireplaces and balconies, those in the manor's turret have wraparound windows. | 5 rooms, 2 cabins. Restaurant, complimentary breakfast, room service, some microwaves, refrigerators, some in-room hot tubs, cable TV, in-room VCRs, pond, pets allowed. | 6680 Illahee Rd. NE | 360/698–7555 or 800/693–6680 | fax 360/698–0688 | innkeeper@illaheemanor.com | www.illaheemanor.com | $115–$195 rooms, $175–$225 cabins | AE, D, MC, V.

Mid Way Inn. This inn is in a quiet area with large comfortable rooms. It is within walking distance of area restaurants. | 60 rooms. Complimentary Continental breakfast, some kitchenettes, refrigerators, cable TV, in-room VCRs (movies), laundry facilities, business services. | 2909 Wheaton Way | 360/479–2909 or 800/231–0575 | fax 360/479–1576 | $55–$60 | AE, D, DC, MC, V.

Oyster Bay Inn. Most rooms at this inn have beautiful panoramic views of the bay. Stroll down the back lawn to see the bay up close. The rooms are well maintained and appointed with many modern amenities. | 76 rooms. Restaurant, bar (with entertainment), complimentary Continental breakfast, some kitchenettes, microwaves, refrigerators, cable TV, pets allowed (fee). | 4412 Kitsap Way | 360/377–5510 or 800/393–3862 | kangmail@email.msn.com | www.oysterbaymotel.com | $68 | AE, D, DC, MC, V.

Silverdale on the Bay-West Coast. This resort hotel is on a saltwater inlet with a large brick sun deck, close to the shopping mall. | 142 rooms, 8 suites. Restaurant, bar with entertainment, refrigerators (in suites), room service, cable TV, indoor pool, hot tub, sauna, tennis, exercise equipment, game room (pinball machines), business services, free parking. | 3073 N.W. Bucklin Hill Rd., Silverdale | 360/698–1000 or 800/544–9799 | fax 360/692–0932 | $70–$115, $150–$295 suites | AE, D, DC, MC, V.

CASHMERE

MAP 8, G4

(Nearby towns also listed: Leavenworth, Wenatchee)

Surrounded by snow capped mountain peaks, Cashmere is one of eastern Washington's oldest towns, founded by Oblate Missionaries back in 1853, when the Wenatchi and their vast herds of horses still roamed free over the bunch grass lands of the region. Some of the great Wenatchi leaders are buried in the mission cemetery. Today, Cashmere is the apple, apricot, and pear capital of the Wenatchee valley. Its orchards produce not only great peaches but incredibly luscious and deeply flavorful apricots as well.

Information: Cashmere Chamber of Commerce | 101 Cottage Ave., Cashmere, 98815 | 509/782–7404.

Attractions

Aplets and Cotlets/Liberty Orchards Co., Inc. This company was founded by two Armenian brothers who escaped the massacres of Armenians by Turks early in the 20th century, settled in this peaceful valley, and became orchardists. When a marketing crisis hit the orchards in the 1920s, they remembered a dried-fruit confection from their homeland, recreated it, and named it aplets (made from apples) and cotlets (made from apricots). Sales took off almost immediately, and today aplets and cotlets are known as the combination that made Cashmere famous. Get free samples when you tour the plant. | 117 Mission St. | 509/782–2191 | fax 509/782–1487 | www.libertyorchards.com | Free | May–Dec., daily; Jan.–Apr., weekdays.

Chelan County Historical Society's Museum and Pioneer Village. This is one of the state's best historical museums, with an excellent collection of Indian artifacts, as well as 18 pre-1900 Chelan County buildings that were reassembled here and furnished with period furniture and other historic objects. | 600 Cotlets Way | 509/782–3230 | $4 | Mar. 1–Dec. 15, daily 9:30–5.

Riverside Park. Walk along the Wenatchee river or picnic under a tree. There are magnificent views of the hills and mountains across the river from the park. | Aplets Way.

ON THE CALENDAR

MAY: *Apple Blossom Weekend.* Square and round dancing take place amongst the apple blossoms in nearby Wenatchee. Other events are held at various locations around town. | 509/782–2123.

JUNE: *Founders' Day.* A grand parade, crafts and food booths, kids' games, more than 2,000 prize-filled Ping-Pong balls dropped from a helicopter, and other entertainment take place at the Chelan County Historical Museum. | 509/782–7404.

Dining

Pioneer House. American/Casual. The menu of this family eatery offers a wide assortment of steaks, chops, and chicken dishes, in addition to many pastas, burgers, and sandwiches. Friday nights you can eat all that you want at the seafood buffet, which includes lobster, crab, clams, prawns, fish, and champagne. On weekends the lounge has live entertainment. | 128 Cottage Ave. | 509/782–3003 | No lunch | $5.50–$16 | D, MC, V.

Lodging

Grandview Orchard Inn. This hillside home is part of a working orchard overlooking the town of Cashmere. An antique cast-iron bed and pine and mahogany antique furniture complement the inn's homey environment. The common area has a piano and organ. You are welcome to stroll among the many apple, pear, and cherry trees. | 3 rooms (1 with private bath). Complimentary breakfast, some in-room hot tub, no room phones, no TV in some rooms. | 5105 Moody Rd. | 509/782–2340 | $60–$70 | No credit cards.

Village Inn Motel. This small motel fits in perfectly with the very small town of Cashmere. It is downtown and near a candy factory. | 21 rooms. Cable TV, business services. | 229 Cottage Ave. | 509/782–3522 | fax 509/782–8190 | $40–$57 | AE, D, MC, V.

Wedge Mountain Inn. All the brightly colored rooms at this quiet inn have private decks with views of the surrounding scenery. It is 7 mi west of Cashmere and close to area skiing. | 28 rooms. Cable TV, laundry facilities. | 7335 U.S. 2 | 509/548–6694 or 800/666–9664 | $69–$74 | AE, D, MC, V.

CATHLAMET

MAP 8, C7

(Nearby towns also listed: Kelso, Longview)

The houses of Cathlamet, the county seat of tiny Wahkiakum County, rise on a hillside above the Cathlamet Channel of the Columbia River. The town started back in 1846 as the trading post of James Birnie, a retired Hudson's Bay Company trader, just above a Chinook Indian village in Elochoman Slough, west of town. The first salmon cannery on the lower Columbia opened in 1866; a cannery on the Cathlamet waterfront followed in 1869. The huge riverfront sheds survive and serve as net and boat storage. Cathlamet has several houses from this early period, including one built by James Birdie in 1857. Until the last logging camp in Wahkiakum County was closed in 1859, logging also served as a mainstay of the local economy. Today Cathlamet serves as a shopping center for nearby farmers, as well as road and river travelers.

Information: **Lower Columbia Economic Development Council** | Box 98, Steam Flough Rd., Skamakowa, 98647 | 360/795–3996.

Attractions

Julia Butler Hansen National Wildlife Refuge. Occupying close to 5,000 acres of meadows and woodlands, this refuge is home to endangered white-tailed deer. Elk and water birds are numerous and easy to spot. Entry to the refuge is found on Steamboat Slough Road, 2 mi west of Cathlamet. | Steamboat Slough Rd. | 360/795–3915 | Free | Daily, dawn–dusk.

ON THE CALENDAR

JULY: ***Bald Eagle Festival.*** Parade, street fair, fireworks, and food booths, celebrate the noble bird which lives here year-round. | 360/795–3545.

JULY: ***Wooden Boat Festival.*** Floating festival of wooden boats on the Columbia River, with a variety of wooden craft. Barbecue and family fun. | 360/795–3420.

AUG.: ***Wahkiakum County Fair.*** This three-day event features amusement rides, horse and animal shows, commercial vendors, dances, free entertainment, food, and, like so many other festivals, a salmon barbecue. | 360/795–3480.

Lodging

Bradley House/Country Keeper. It's not in the country, but in "downtown" Cathlamet which is, admittedly, a bit rustic. This B&B was born as a mansion, and later served as the town library. But it has preserved its charm as well as its 1907 hardwood floors and light fixtures. Today it is a comfortable inn with lots of books to keep the library's memory alive and a porch which, weather permitting, offers a glimpse of the Columbia. | 4 rooms. Dining room, complimentary breakfast, no-smoking rooms. | 61 Main St. | 360/795–3030 | $65–$100 | MC, V.

Nassa Point Motel. Three mi east of Cathlamet, at the base of a evergreen-covered hill, this small roadside motel is a favorite with fishers who choose the lodging for its proximity to the Columbia River across the street. Wind surfing and swimming are also possible 2 mi east. The rooms are appointed with simple, basic furnishings and amenities. |

6 rooms. No air-conditioning, kitchenettes, refrigerators, no room phones, pets allowed. | 851 E State Rte. 4 | 360/795–3941 | $40 | MC, V.

Redfern Farm Bed and Breakfast. This farm B&B on Puget Island is separated from Cathlamet by a slough and connected by bridge, and separated from Oregon by the Columbia River and connected by ferry. | 2. Complimentary breakfast, no-smoking rooms, hot tub. | 277 Cross Dike Rd. | 360/849–4108 | $55–$65 | No credit cards.

Riverview Restaurant. American. Although it serves a variety of dishes, including breakfast all day, the eatery is known for its seafood, especially the Halibut Basket: batter-fried halibut and fries. On Wednesday nights the restaurant serves Mexican food, and on Thursdays it focuses on Chinese cuisine. The river is visible from the restaurant's bar which also serves food. The dining room is large and welcoming. | 88 Main St. | 360/795–8033 | Breakfast also available | $4–$15 | MC, V.

WA

CENTRALIA

MAP 8, C6

(Nearby town also listed: Chehalis)

Centralia was founded by George Washington, a freed slave from Virginia, who faced serious discrimination in several other states and territories before settling here in 1852. Centralia has a well-maintained historic business district. In a park just off I–5 stand the historic Borst Blockhouse (built during the 1855–56 Indian Wars) and the elegant Borst farmhouse from 1857.

Information: **Tourism Lewis County** | 500 N.W. Chamber of Commerce Way, Chehalis, 98532 | 800/525–3323 | chamberway.com.

Attractions

Fort Borst/Joseph Borst Home. Originally constructed as a fort during the Indian Wars, Fort Borst was later used for grain storage. Standing within a 100-acre park, the Borst Home is a Greek Revival Mansion, built in 1857. | Borst Park, 2500 Bryden Ave. W | 360/330–7688 | $2 | Thanksgiving–Christmas and Memorial Day–Labor Day, weekends 1–4.

ON THE CALENDAR

NOV.: *Dickens of a Christmas.* A celebration of old-fashioned Christmas spirit, with costumes, decorations, and music, takes place Thanksgiving weekend. | 360/525–3323.

Dining

Olympic Club. American/Casual. When it opened in 1908, the Olympic Club was an exclusive gentlemen's resort. Now, it houses a restaurant, a bar, and a pool hall. The Tiffany chandeliers, card room, and signs remain almost as they were when the club began. The menu includes burgers, sandwiches, pastas, steak, and fish. The club bottles its own wine, brews its own beer, and distills its own liquors. | 112 N. Tower Ave. | 360/736–5164 | $5.75–$11.75 | AE, D, MC, V.

Winter Kitchen. American. This small restaurant is surprisingly pleasant despite its somewhat kitschy year-round Christmas decor. The lunch menu is short and inexpensive, running to sandwiches, salads, and soups. Alcohol is not served. | 827 Marsh St. | 360/736–2916 | Closed Sun. No supper | $6–$15 | No credit cards.

Lodging

Ferryman's Inn. Just off I–5 at exit 82, this two-story motel is located between the Riverside Park, behind which the Skookumchuk River flows, and Borst Park, adjacent to the Chehalis River. Try for an upstairs room. | 84 rooms. Complimentary Continental breakfast, no smoking rooms, pool, spa, pets allowed. | 1003 Eckerson Rd. | 360/330-2094 | $48-$55 | AE, D, DC, MC, V.

Inn of Centralia. Only steps away from factory outlet stores and the antique malls, this hotel sits conveniently close to I-5, less than two blocks from exit 82. The rooms are modern and well-maintained. | 88 rooms. Complimentary Continental breakfast, picnic area, some refrigerators, some in-room hot tubs, cable TV, pool, pets allowed (fee). | 702 Harrison Ave. | 360/736-2875 | fax 360/736-2651 | $59-$64 | AE, D, DC, MC, V.

CHEHALIS

MAP 8, C6

(Nearby town also listed: Centralia)

Chehalis (pronounced "che-hay-liss") did not come into its own until the railroad came through in 1873—and bypassed the county seat of Claquato. Local merchants transferred their business to the railroad, and the county seat to a new town along the Northern Pacific Railroad tracks. Downtown has a log home from 1859, as well as several buildings from the late 1800s and early 1900s, a museum, vintage homes, and steam train rides.

Information: Tourism Lewis County | 500 NW Chamber of Commerce Way, Chehalis, 98532 | 800/525-3323 | chamberway.com.

Attractions

Chehalis-Centralia Steam Train Ride. Through scenic landscapes and over covered bridges, the authentic steam engines will carry you from Chehalis to Centralia and back again on rails originally laid for logging. | 1945 S. Market Blvd. | 360/748-9593 | $8-$11 | Memorial Day-Labor Day, weekends.

Historic Claquato Church. A pretty but austere white clapboard church, built in 1858, stands 3 mi west on Claquato Hill. The bell was cast in Boston in 1857, and the tower is capped with a "crown of thorns" steeple. | Claquato Hill | 360/360/740-1135 | Free | By appointment only.

Lewis County Historical Museum. A small museum with regional pioneer memorabilia, some Chehalis Indian art, and a collection of children's dolls and toys. | 599 N.W. Front Way | 360/748-0831 | $2 | Tues.-Sat. 9-5, Sun. 1-5; closed Mon.

Rainbow Falls State Park. Set on 125 acres, this wooded park is on the road to the coast, with several shallow waterfalls cascading down shelves of rock. | Rte. 6 | 360/291-3767 or 800/233-0321 | www.parks.wa.gov | Free | Daily.

ON THE CALENDAR

AUG.: *Southwest Washington Fair.* A demolition derby, carnival, and country & western entertainment are highlights of this five-day event off exit 79 from I-5. | 360/736-6072.

Dining

Kit Carson. American. The whole family will feel at home at this casual eatery. You can order from a range of options like steak, seafood, pastas, and salads. The restaurant is famous for its giant cinnamon rolls and grilled Dungeness crab sandwiches. | 107 S.E. Interstate Ave. | 360/740-1084 | $6-$16 | AE, D, DC, MC, V.

Mary McCrank's Dinner House. American. The atmosphere of this farmhouse restaurant is cozy, but definitely elegant, with arm chairs in the waiting parlor, and fireplaces in some of the dining rooms. This restaurant has survived the Great Depression, a World War, and ownership changes—but the chicken and dumplings are as good as ever, the dessert pies sublime. Kids' menu. No smoking. | 2923 Jackson Hwy. | 360/748-3662 | Closed Mon. | $10-$20 | D, MC, V.

Lodging

Howard Johnson. This standard chain hotel is located 1 mi from the Lewis County Historical Museum and within walking distance of restaurants. | 71 rooms. Complimentary Continental breakfast, no-smoking rooms, pool, hot tub. | 122 Interstate Ave. | 360/748–0101 | $70–$90 | AE, D, DC, MC, V.

Parkplace Inn and Suites. Just off I–5 at exit 76, this chain has rooms with views of Mt. Rainier. Three blocks away is a park with a playground for kids. | 61 rooms. Complimentary Continental breakfast, in-room data ports, refrigerators, microwaves, cable TV, pool, hot tub, gym, laundry services, business services, pets allowed (fee). | 201 S.W. Interstate Ave. | 360/748–4040 or 877/748–0008 | www.bestwester.com | $64–$118 | AE, D, DC, MC, V.

CHELAN

MAP 8, H3

(Nearby town also listed: Wenatchee)

Long before the first American settlers arrived at the lake, Chelan was the site of a Chelan Indian winter village. The Indians would range far and wide on their horses during spring and summer, following the newly sprouting grass from the river bottoms into the mountains; in winter they converged in permanent villages to feast, perform sacred rituals, and wait out the cold weather and snow. During the winter of 1879–80, Chelan served briefly as an army post, but the troops were soon transferred to Fort Spokane. American settlers arrived in the 1880s. Today, Chelan serves as the favorite beach resort of western Washingtonians, who flock here during damp west-side summers to soak up the heat and lie in the sun. The mountains surrounding the fjordlike lake rise from a height of about 4,000 ft near Chelan to 8,000 and 9,000 ft near the head of the lake. Bonanza Peak, south of the lake, is, at 9,511 ft, the tallest nonvolcanic peak in Washington.

Information: Lake Chelan Chamber of Commerce | Box 216, 102 E. Johnson, Chelan, 98816 | 800/4–CHELAN | lakechelan.com.

Attractions

Alta Lake State Park. Alta Lake is in a coulee above the Columbia and Methow; as with other coulees in the region, it was carved during an Ice Age flood but is unique in not having any visible inlet or outlet. Since it tends to be warmer than surrounding lakes because there is no influx of chilly glacier-fed streams, it is a popular local swimming hole. The fishing is good, as is the camping under the old-growth Douglas firs. | U.S. 97N to Rte. 153 | 509/923–2473 or 800/233–0321 | fax 509/923–2980 | www.parks.wa.gov | Free | Apr.–Sept., daily dawn–dusk; closed Nov.–Mar.

Banjo Creek Farms. This family-run working farm, 11½ mi northwest of Chelan, is home to shops including a soap store, a country store, and an antique furniture shop. You can ride on wagons and horse-drawn carriages or you can pan for gold. The petting zoo has llamas, sheep, miniature horses, pygmy goats, chickens, and ducks. | Green Ave., Manson | 509/687–0708 | www.banjocreekfarms.com | Free | Daily 9–5.

Lake Chelan. This 55-mi-long fjord, which is the deepest lake in the state, is surrounded by mountains that appear to get taller as your boat penetrates deeper into them. There is no road that runs the length of the lake, so a boat is the only way. Several resorts line the eastern (and warmer) shore of the lake. The western end, at Stehekin, just reaches North Cascades National Park. | 800/4–CHELAN | Free | Daily.

Lake Cruises. The *Lady of the Lake* carries passengers and their gear between Chelan and other lakefront communities, all the way to Stehekin. She also stops to let off passengers for the trailhead of the lakeshore trail (and picks them up again at a prearranged time).

| 1418 Woodin Ave. | 509/682–4584 or 509/682–2224 | fax 509/682–8026 | www.ladyofthelake.com | $23 | Daily; call for schedule.

Lake Chelan State Park. Right on the lake, 9 mi west of Chelan on the opposite (less crowded) shore, this is a favorite hangout for folks from the cool west side of the Cascades who want to soak up some sun. In summer, Lake Chelan is one of the hottest places in Washington, with temperatures often soaring above 100°F. There is a boat ramp for launching boats, and there are docks for tying them up, plus RV sites with full hookups (so you can run your motorhome air-conditioner if things get too hot), as well as lots of campsites for a more civilized approach to camping. | U.S. 97 W to South Shore Dr. or Navarre Coulee Rd. | 800/452–5687 | www.parks.wa.gov | Free | Apr.–Oct., daily; Nov.–Mar., weekends.

Twenty-Five Mile Creek State Park. This state park further up the same side of the lake has many of the same facilities, plus it has a swimming pool, and is less crowded because it's more remote. | South Shore Dr. | 509/687–3610 or 800/452–5687 | fax 509/687–3163 | www.parks.wa.gov | Free | Apr.–Sept., daily dawn–dusk.

ON THE CALENDAR

JAN.: ***Winterfest.*** Join in the Polar Bear Splash (after a hole is hacked in the ice), the snow sculpture contest, fireworks, and a chili cook-off at City Park on Manson Hwy. on January 2. | 800/424–3526.

MAY: ***Apple Blossom Festival.*** The beautifully blue lake and hillsides covered with pinkish-white clouds of blooming apple trees make for a soul-warming experience on Mother's Day weekend in Manson. | 800/424–3526.

MAY: ***Salmon Derby.*** Fishermen compete to catch the biggest lake salmon and win prizes on Lake Chelan. | 509/682–2802.

JULY: ***WPRA Rodeo.*** In addition to rodeo events, make sure you don't miss the cowboy breakfast and evening dances. There are also a beer garden and plenty of food booths at the Rodeo Grounds. | 71 Union Valley Rd. | 509/682–5526.

Dining

Campbell House Café. American/Casual. Old hardwood walls give this dining room at the Campbell's Resort a nautical feel. Popular among local residents, the café serves a selection of seafood, steak, chicken, and pasta dishes. | 104 W. Woodin Ave. | 509/682–4250 | Reservations essential | No lunch weekends | $9.25–$23 | AE, MC, V.

Lodging

Campbell's Resort. This lakefront resort in Chelan has been receiving guests since the turn of the last century. | 172 rooms; 2 cottages. Restaurant, bar, in-room data ports, some kitchenettes, some minibars, refrigerators, cable TV, 2 Pools, hot tubs, beach, cross-country skiing, dock, business services. | 104 W. Woodin Ave. | 509/682–2561 or 800/553–8225 (WA) | fax 509/682–2177 | $146–$166 | AE, MC, V.

Caravel Resort. All the rooms at this large resort one-half block from downtown Chelan have terraces that overlook the lake. | 93 rooms. Some kitchenettes, some refrigerators, cable TV, some in-room hot tubs, pool, business services, boating. | 322 W. Woodin Ave. | 509/682–2582 or 800/962–8723 | fax 509/682–3551 | www.caravelresort.com | $99–$260 | AE, D, DC, MC, V.

Quail's Roost Inn. This Queen Anne Victorian from 1902 perches on North Hill overlooking the city, lake, and mountains. Rooms have a handsome collection of period antiques and collectibles. The Sewing Room, for instance, has antique oak furniture, an antique sewing machine, and wedding dress. From the wraparound veranda and landscaped yard you can sit and enjoy the wonderful views of the lake. | 3 rooms. Complimentary breakfast, no room phones, TV in common area, no pets, no kids under 12, no smoking. | 121 East Highland Ave. | 509/682–2892 or 800/681–2892 | www.aquailsroostinn.com | $115–$185 | MC, V.

CHENEY

MAP 8, K4

(Nearby town also listed: Spokane)

As you walk the tree-shaded streets of this small, quiet college town, it's hard to believe that Cheney once competed with Spokane for regional dominance. Most of the buildings on the Eastern Washington University campus date from the post–World War II education boom, but a few older buildings have aged gracefully.

Information: West Plains Chamber of Commerce, | 201 1st St., Cheney, 99004 | 509/235–8480 | fax 509/235–9338 | westplainschamber.org.

Attractions

Cheney Historical Museum. There is a collection of artifacts of local and regional historic importance, including a 1935 fire truck at this museum. | 614 3rd St. | 509/235–4343 or 509/235–4466 | Free | Mar.–Oct., Tues. and Sat. 1–3; Nov.–Mar., call for appointment.

Eastern Washington University. This tree-shaded campus has a couple of older buildings, but most of the campus dates from the post–World War II education boom, with the usual assortment of concrete-and-glass structures. | 526 5th St. | 509/359–2397 | fax 509/359–6692 | www.ewu.edu | Free | Daily.

Gallery of Art. This college gallery has changing exhibits throughout the school year. | 526 5th St. | 509/359–2493 | fax 509/359–4841 | www.visual.arts.ewu.edu | Free | Weekdays 8–4:30.

Turnbull National Wildlife Refuge. This 17,000-acre preserve of rolling hills, pine woods, lakes, and marshes 6 mi south of Cheney is an ideal wildlife habitat. Look for ducks and geese, hawks, falcons, and songbirds. This preserve is the exception among wildlife "refuges" because it is not open for hunting in season. It has the only known nesting site of the endangered trumpeter swan in Washington. | Cheney–Plaza Rd. | 509/235–4723 | fax 509/235–4703 | www.r1.fws.gov/turnbull/turnbull | $3 | Daily.

ON THE CALENDAR

JULY: *Cheney Rodeo Days.* Rodeo events are in the evening, but be sure to check out the parades, quilt shows, and street vendors during the day on the second weekend in July. | 509/235–8480.

Dining

Willow Springs Station. American. Sitting behind the Willow Springs Motel, this restaurant occupies an old railroad station, the original details of which—such as a tin ceiling—have been retained. Memorabilia and railroad equipment adorn the walls. Some of the popular dishes include liver and onions, meatloaf, and biscuits and gravy. | 809 1st St. | 509/235–4420. | Breakfast also available | $7.50–$15.00 | AE, D, MC, V.

Lodging

Rosebrook Inn. Visiting parents tend to stay at this motel, which is just seven blocks from Eastern Washington University. The rooms are given a country touch with lace curtains and flowery wallpaper. | 12 rooms. Picnic area, microwaves, refrigerators, cable TV, pets allowed. | 304 W. 1st St. | 509/235–6538 or 888/848–9853 | fax 509/235–9229 | rosebinn@worldnet.att.net | $64 | AE, D, DC, MC, V.

Willow Springs Motel. This small motel is in a quiet neighborhood close to Eastern Washington University and 12 mi from Spokane. | 44 rooms. Complimentary Continental breakfast on weekends, some kitchenettes, air-conditioning, cable TV, laundry facilities, pets allowed (fee). | 5 B St. | 509/235–5138 | fax 509/235–4528 | $39–$54 | AE, D, DC, MC, V.

CLARKSTON

MAP 8, L7

(Nearby town also listed: Pullman)

This former ferry town was founded in 1862 as a way station for travelers heading to the Idaho goldfields. It is the twin city of Lewiston, Idaho, across the river. Clarkston is surrounded by grass-covered hills, which are green in spring and turn golden in summer. But it stays green along the river, where a pleasant walkway, called the Greenbelt and Swallows Park, invites visitors to explore. (You can walk all the way downriver to Asotin.) Nearby Swallow Rock is dotted with the jug-shaped mud nests of cliff swallows. Clarkston has all the amenities of a civilized life, including a symphony orchestra, a civic theater, and art galleries.

Information: Clarkston Chamber of Commerce | 502 Bridge St., Clarkston, 99403 | 800/933–2128 | clarkstonchamber.org.

Attractions

Asotin County Museum. This small museum in the county seat of Asotin preserves a few old buildings moved here from nearby communities, including a blacksmith's forge set up in a log cabin. There's a very good collection of local branding irons (a rustler's dream) and old carriages. | 215 Filmore St., Asotin | 509/243–4659 | Free, donations accepted | Tues.–Sat. 1–5.

Chief Timothy State Park. This park, 8 mi west of Clarkston, sits on an island in the middle of the Snake River. Swimming and boating are the two primary activities at this spot. | 13766 Hwy. 12 | 509/758–9580 | Daily, dawn–dusk.

Fields Spring State Park. This is a butte 30 mi south of Clarkston located near the lower tree line of the Blue Mountains where the grass ends and the trees begin. You will have great views and there is wonderfully rewarding year-round bird watching. In spring there are spectacular displays of wildflowers. Camping is allowed, but the sites are primitive. | Rte. 129 | 509/256–3332 | fax 509/256–3332 | www.parks.wa.gov | Free | Daily dawn–dusk.

Petroglyphs. The petroglyphs (ancient writings on the cliffs) are more than 500 years old, difficult to find, and difficult to get to. They can be found near the town of Asotin at Buffalo Rock, a short distance above Buffalo Rapids near water level; so don't search for them during spring floods. Check with the Clarkston Chamber of Commerce for directions. | 800/933–2128 | fax 509/751–8767 | www.clarkstonchamber.org | Free | Daily.

Umatilla National Forest. The open woods of this forest of pines and firs reach north from Oregon's Blue Mountains into Washington State. Deer, elk, cougars, and other wildlife abound. Meadows are covered with wildflowers in spring. | U.S. 12, near Pomeroy | 800/933–2128 | Free | Daily.

Valley Art Center. This art center has rotating exhibits and special shows. | 842 6th St. | 509/758–8331 | www.valleyarts.qpg.com | Free | Weekdays 9–4.

ON THE CALENDAR

APR.: ***Asotin County Fair.*** Held on the last full weekend in April, 5 mi south of Clarkston in Asotin, the fair includes rodeos, arts and crafts exhibits, vendors, and animal husbandry competitions. | 509/243–4101.

APR.: ***Dogwood Festival.*** A celebration of blooming dogwood trees, which put on a spectacular local display. | 509/758–7712.

Dining

South Shore Landing. American/Casual. Sitting within the Quality Inn, the dining room overlooks the lawns of the putting course and the Snake River. Large picture windows and floral arrangements render the room bright and airy. The menu concentrates on steak and seafood dishes; also popular are the prime rib and salmon entrées. | 700 Port Dr. | 509/758–9500 | $13–$19 | AE, D, DC, MC, V.

Lodging

Best Western Rivertree Inn. Comfortable two-story highway motel in town, away from the river. | 61 rooms. Picnic area, complimentary Continental breakfast, some kitchenettes, refrigerators, cable TV, pool, hot tub, gym, business services. | 1257 Bridge St. | 509/758–9551 | fax 509/758–9551 | $69–$110 | AE, D, DC, MC, V.

Cliff House Bed and Breakfast. Perched on a bluff 500 ft above a bend in the Snake River (7 mi west of Clarkston), this B&B has views up and down the valley. On the three decks that surround the house you can sit in a hammock and watch barges and ships pass. A Native American motif dominates one room, while an imposing river view gives character to the other. | 2 rooms. Complimentary breakfast, no air-conditioning, no room phones, TV in common area, hot tub, exercise equipment, no pets, no smoking. | 1227 Westlake Dr. | 509/758–1267 | www.northwestmedia.net/cliffhouse | $80–$85 | No credit cards.

Quality Inn. Riverfront hotel with a great view of the river and the grass-covered hills of the southern Palouse. It is next to the convention center. | 75 rooms, 22 suites. Restaurant, bar, room service, cable TV, pool, laundry facilities, business services, free parking. | 700 Port Dr. | 509/758–9500 | fax 509/758–5580 | $55–$85 | AE, D, DC, MC, V.

CLE ELUM

MAP 8, F5

(Nearby town also listed: Ellensburg)

A former railroad, coal, and logging town, Cle Elum now caters mostly to travelers stopping for a breath of air before tackling Snoqualmie Pass. The Cle Elum Bakery, first opened in 1906, still operates at the original location (502 E. First). The bread is great, and the bakery sells pastries as well as the makings for a first-rate picnic. What you can't get at the bakery you can pick up at the sausage shop across the street. (Note: there's a notorious speed trap on wide open I–90, east of town; the freeway is patrolled by aircraft.)

Information: Cle Elum/Roslyn Chamber of Commerce | Box 43, Cle Elum, 98922 | 509/674–5958 | cityguides/washington/cleelum.html.

Attractions

Cle Elum Telephone Museum. Cle Elum was the last municipality to change from switchboard to rotary dialing in the United States, in 1966. On display are the old switchboards and the related equipment. | 221 E. 1st St. | 509/674–5702 | $2 | Memorial Day–Labor Day, weekends noon–4.

ON THE CALENDAR

JULY: *Pioneer Days Celebration.* A parade, fireworks show, street fair, softball tournament, and hula hoop contest are all a part of this Cle Elum celebration that takes place at 1st St. on the Independence Day weekend. | 509/674–5958.

Dining

Brick Tavern. American/Casual. The oldest operating bar in Washington dates from 1889, the year of statehood, and is built of stone not brick. It has a water-fed spittoon which runs the length of the bar (at foot level), where annual spittoon-boat races are held. Past winners are displayed in the tavern. Besides some good local and regional microbrews, this tavern serves standard bar food, but is known for good hamburgers, salads, and fish and chips. | 100 Pennsylvania Ave., Roslyn | 509/649–2643 | Breakfast also available | $5–$12 | MC, V.

Mama Vallone's. Italian. This restaurant in an old 1906 boarding house seems like quite a surprise find in a small mountain town like Cle Elum, until you recall that miners from all over the world once worked here. Mama Vallone's represents the Italian contingent—and with flair. There's a splendid *bagna cauda,* a hot dipping sauce of olive oil, anchovies, and lots of garlic. Plus such Italian standards as veal scallopine, ravioli, tortellini, and, of course, steak. Sun. brunch. | 302 W. 1st St. | 509/674–5174 | No lunch | $15–$25 | AE, D, MC, V.

Roslyn Cafe. American. Lots of TV viewers are familiar with the facade of this cafe, which appeared in the TV series *Northern Exposure* (as did the Brick Tavern, above). The high-ceilinged dining room has walls of stone, and there's an old jukebox and a neon sign to add nostalgia. The kitchen serves up such favorites as pot roast stew, chicken and dumplings, and 18 kinds of ⅓-pound hamburgers. No alcohol. | 201 West Pennsylvania Ave., Roslyn | 509/649–2763 | Breakfast also available | $7–$12 | MC, V.

Sunset Café and Quetzal Room. Italian. Since 1936, this restaurant has been serving such favorites as its homemade ravioli to the Cle Elum community. Today the Italian dishes are complemented by some traditional American favorites such as hamburgers. The dining room is large and accommodating. | 318 E. 1st St. | 509/674–2241 | Breakfast also available | $7–$17 | AE, D, DC, MC, V.

Lodging

Cascade Mountain Inn. This affordable lodging is located in the downtown area, near exit 84 off I–90. The rooms are all spacious and, with the many amenities, give a home-away-from-home comfort. | 43 rooms. Complimentary Continental breakfast, kitchenettes, microwaves, refrigerators, some in-room hot tubs, cable TV, pets allowed. | 906 E. 1st St. | 509/674–2380 or 888/674–3975 | fax 509/674–7099 | $50–$60 | AE, D, DC, MC, V.

Hidden Valley Guest Ranch. A motley collection of cabins on an old ranch surrounded by incredibly beautiful scenery, especially in spring, when the wildflowers bloom. | 8 rooms, 5 cabins. Dining room, complimentary breakfast, complimentary lunch and dinner in summer, pool, hot tub, massage, hiking, horseback riding. | 3942 Hidden Valley Rd. | 509/857–2344 | $110 | MC, V.

Iron Horse Inn Bed and Breakfast. This old railroad boarding house on the Iron Horse Trail (formerly railroad tracks across the Cascades) has been turned into a very comfortable country inn. | 11 rooms. Dining room, complimentary breakfast, hot tub. | 526 Marie Ave. | 509/674–5939 | maryp@cleelum.com | www.ironhorseinbb.com | $60–$135 | MC, V.

COLVILLE

MAP 8, K2

(Nearby town also listed: Spokane)

This small town, the county seat of Stevens County, sits in a beautiful rustic valley, surrounded by lakes, forests, and mountains teeming with wildlife. The town has many well-maintained old houses and a pleasant, well-to-do atmosphere. Colville became regionally famous in 1983 when Mike Hale opened Hale's Microbrewery in Colville. But he has since transferred operations to a brewery at Moss Bay, near the Kirkland waterfront.

Information: **Colville Chamber of Commerce** | 121 E. Astor, Colville, 99114-0267 | 509/684–5973 | cityguides/washington/colville.html | chamberofcommerce@plix.com.

Attractions

Colville National Forest. A vast region encompassing much of the mountain forests and meadows north of Rte. 20, between the Sanpoil Kettle River valleys and the Pend Oreille River Valley. It is a beautiful, wild area, where only the river bottoms are dotted with widely spaced settlements and where the mountains (whose average height is 4,000 to

5,000 ft) are largely pristine. The streams abound with trout, and the forests with deer and black bear. This is perfect backpacking country, with many trails to remote mountain lakes. | 765 South Main St. | 509/684–7000 | fax 509/684–7280 | Free | Daily.

Lake Gillette Recreation Area. This 87-ft-deep lake on the little Pend Oreille River east of Colville has camping, boating, and fishing. It is only open in summer. | Tiger Hwy., Rte. 20 | 509/684–5657 | Free | Daily.

Keller Heritage Center. See a farmstead, lookout tower, trappers' cabins, blacksmith shop, sawmill, and museum. The museum's exhibits and displays tell the history of the area. | 700 N. Wynne St. | 509/684–5968 | May 1–Sept. 30, 10–4.

ON THE CALENDAR

AUG.: *Rendezvous.* Held on the first weekend of each August, this family-oriented festival draws as many as 12,000 people each year who come to compete in the numerous tournaments, browse the craft booths, and enjoy the free, live entertainment at City Park (Elm and Hawthorne Sts.). | 509/684–5973.

SEPT.: *Northeast Washington Fair.* Food, carnivals, and animal shows are featured at this fair held on the Stevens County Fairgrounds. | 509/684–2585.

Dining

Café Italiano. Continental. Specializing in French and northern Italian cuisine, the chef embellishes the menu with Greek, Arabic, and Indian dishes, resulting in a menu with at least 125 items. When you enter the dining room, it is like entering an Italian villa. The ceiling is painted the color of a bright blue sky with passing clouds. A rose garden with water fountain provides outdoor dining during the warmer months. | 153 W. 2nd Ave. | 509/684–5957 | No lunch on Sat. and Sun. | Reservations essential | $7–$15 | MC, V.

Lodging

Benny's Colville Inn. This is a comfortable family motel nestled in a pristine valley between the Kettle and Selkirk Mountain ranges. | 105 rooms. Restaurant, no-smoking rooms, pool, hot tub, gym, pets allowed. | 915 S. Main | 509/684–2517 or 800/680–2517 | fax 509/684–2546 | www.colvilleinn.com | $40–$125 | AE, D, MC, V.

Comfort Inn. Majestic mountains look down on this chain hotel. You cannot forget you are near the forest with the enormous amount of wildlife around the hotel. | 53 rooms. Complimentary Continental breakfast, in-room data ports, cable TV, pool, hot tub, laundry service, pets allowed. | 166 N.E. Canning Dr. | 509/684–2010 or 800/228–5150 | fax 509/684–1918 | comfortinn@coville.com | www.comfortinn.colville.com | $56–$125 | AE, D, DC, MC, V.

My Parents' Estate. This classy country inn, 7 mi north of Colville, was once a convent. The building sits on 49 acres bordering the Colville River, and its landscape is perfect for meditations of a religious or temporal nature. Rooms are quite large and spacious. | 4 rooms, 1 suite, 1 cottage. Complimentary breakfast, no kids allowed, no smoking. | Box 724, Kettle Falls; 395 N | 509/738–6220 | $75–$110 | Closed Oct.–Apr. | MC, V.

COPALIS BEACH

MAP 8, A5

(Nearby towns also listed: Aberdeen, Hoquiam, Ocean Shores)

This coastal village, at the mouth of the Copalis River, was a Native American village for several thousands of years, before American settlers moved here in the 19th century. Once famous for its razor-clam digging and fishing, it is still popular for beachcombing (especially after winter storms) and has more recently became a favorite surfing spot. The beach is one of the places on the Washington coast where it is still legal to drive on the sand, which may be one reason why razor clams have become scarce in recent years. From about 1870 to 1903 watchtowers lined the beach, from which observers signaled to hunters who stalked and then shot sea otters. Today, any sea otters remaining on this coast are fully protected. (Not every otter swimming in saltwater is a sea otter: In Washington, river otters commonly take to saltwater.) The first oil well in Washington State was dug on the beach in 1901; fortunately for the local ecology it proved to be unproductive, but geologists claim that the continental shelf off the Olympic Peninsula holds major oil reserves.

Information: Washington Coast Chamber of Commerce | 2615 State Rte. 109,Box 562, Ocean City | 360/289–4552 | ohwy.com/wa/c/copalisb.htm.

Attractions

Griffiths-Priday Ocean State Park. You can hike or ride horses at this park. The park is a protected area for the Snowy Plover, so there are plenty of fowl to watch. | 3119 Rte. 109 | 800/233–0321 | Daily, dawn–dusk.

ON THE CALENDAR

AUG.: ***Copalis Heritage Days.*** Held on the first weekend of August each year, this small community celebrates its history with live music and food. From booths on Hwy. 109 local vendors sell antiques, historical knickknacks, and crafts. | 360/289–4552.

Dining

Green Lantern Tavern. American. You can sit at your table at this 21-and-over tavern and gaze at the small river flowing beneath. The dinner menu includes traditional pub dishes such as BLTs, grilled cheese sandwiches, and fish sandwiches, although the specialty is burgers. | 3119 Rte. 109 | 360/289–2297 | Breakfast also available | $5–$8 | No credit cards.

Lodging

Echoes of the Sea. Sitting on 8 acres of wooded land just north of Copalis, this motel is only a short walk to the beach. A recreation room provides space to relax and play billiards or Ping-Pong. The property also contains a number of campsites. | 8 rooms. Picnic area, no air-conditioning, cable TV, hiking, gift shop, pets allowed (fee), no smoking. | 3208 Rte. 109 | 360/289–3358 or 800/578–ECHO | $55–$90 | AE, D, MC, V.

Iron Springs Resort. This long-established resort with a loyal following is right on the beach. | 28 rooms. Pool, pets allowed (fee). | 3707 Rte. 109 | 360/276–4230 | fax 360/276–4365 | $66–$104 | AE, D, MC, V.

COULEE DAM

MAP 8, I3

(Nearby town also listed: Spokane)

At 550 ft tall and 5,225 ft long, Coulee Dam is the world's biggest all-concrete structure. During construction, it spawned a town straddling both sides of the Columbia River, with the western half known as "Engineers City," and the eastern one as "Mason City." The former had individual family homes; the latter provided communal housing. The dam has been beneficial for both, while concerned Washingtonians have recently begun a campaign to breach it and the other dams on the Columbia and Snake Rivers to allow the waters to flow freely once again, and thus to encourage the return of the almost extinct salmon runs. There are free dam tours. Native tribes operate the Coulee Dam Casino.

Information: Grand Coulee Dam Area Chamber of Commerce/VIC | Box 760, 306 Midway, Grand Coulee, 99133-0760 | 800/COULEE–2 or 509/268–5332 | www.grandcouleedam.org.

Attractions

Colville Confederated Tribes Museum and Gift Shop. A small museum with an excellent collection of baskets, fishing gear, and historical photographs. | 512 Mead Way | 509/633–0751 | fax 509/633–2320 | Free | Mon.–Sat. 10–6.

Fort Spokane. Don't expect any turreted walls at this fort: The 1880–98 army post looks more like a college campus than a military establishment. Meadows make for pleasant strolling and picnicking. | 44150 District Office Lane N | 509/725–2715 | fax 509/633–3834 | Free | Daily dawn–dusk.

Grand Coulee Dam. The largest concrete structure in the world. There is a nightly laser light show from Memorial Day to the end of September. | Near Jct. Rte. 155 | 509/633–3074 or 509/633–3838 | fax 509/633–2320 | www.grandcouleedam.org | Free | Daily.

Historical Walking Tour. Beginning at the Visitor Arrival Center at the base of the dam in Mason City Park, this self-guided tour will take you through the historical part of town, across the bridge, and to the old engineers' town. | Mason City Park | 800/COULEE–2 | Free.

Lake Roosevelt National Recreation Area. A 150-mi-long lake created by the Columbia River when it was backed up by Grand Coulee Dam. Several native villages, historic sites, and towns lie beneath the waters. | 1008 Crest Dr. | 509/633–9441 | fax 509/633–9332 | Free | Daily dawn–dusk.

Steamboat Rock State Park. This 2,200-ft-high flat-topped lava butte rises 1,000 ft above Banks Lake, the 31-mi-long irrigation reservoir filled with water from Lake Roosevelt by giant pumps and siphons. Water is distributed from the south end of the lake throughout the Columbia Basin. The state park has campsites and is popular with boaters and fishermen. | Rte. 155 | 509/633–1304 or 800/452–5687 | www.parks.wa.gov | Free | Daily.

ON THE CALENDAR

MAY: *Colorama Festival and PWRA Rodeo.* Professional rodeo and fair with parades, a carnival, live music, and family fun night, which takes place at the Grand Coulee Dam. | 800/268–5332.

MAY: *Laser Light Festival.* A 35-minute laser light show on the history of the Grand Coulee Dam projected across the spillway. | 800/268–5332.

MAY: *Memorial Day Celebration.* This holiday is commemorated with the season's first laser light show, together with numerous food booths and arts and crafts vendors. All this takes place at Mason City Park, directly beneath the dam. | 800/COULEE–2.

Dining

Flo's Cafe. American. This diner, 1 mi south of the dam, dishes up local color as well as logger's and cowboy food: biscuits and gravy, corned beef hash, hamburgers, chicken-fried steak, and chef's salad. | 316 Spokane Way, Grand Coulee | 509/633–3216 | Breakfast also available. No supper | $4–$7 | No credit cards.

Hollywood Steakhouse. Steak. As you might guess from the name, posters and pictures of Hollywood's greats adorn the walls of the four dining rooms, each of which has its own character. The menu emphasizes steak, although it includes other options like pastas, chicken and seafood dishes, and salads. | 113 Midway Ave. | 509/633–6693 | Closed Mon. | $8–$18 | AE, D, DC, MC, V.

Melody Restaurant. Contemporary. A casual, family-friendly cafe with great views of Grand Coulee Dam. Known for sandwiches, steaks, seafood dishes, pastas. | 512 River Drive, Coulee Dam | 509/633–1151 | Breakfast also available | $8–$15 | AE, D, MC, V.

Siam Palace. Thai. Locals love this small, informal restaurant that dishes up tasty Chinese, Thai, and American food. | 213 Main St., Grand Coulee | 509/633–2921 | Sept.–Apr., closed Mon. | $10–$15 | D, MC, V.

Lodging

Columbia River Inn. The spacious brightly colored rooms all have private decks at this inn across the street from Grand Coulee Dam, with easy access to hiking trails and fishing. | 35 rooms. Some refrigerators, some microwaves, in-room data ports, cable TV, pool, in-room hot tubs, business services, airport shuttle. | 10 Lincoln St. | 509/633–2100 or 800/633–6421 | fax 509/633–2633 | $49–$95 | AE, D, MC, V.

Coulee House. This is a great spot for viewing the laser light show at the Grand Coulee Dam. The casino is across the street. | 61 rooms. Some kitchenettes, some refrigerators, cable TV, pool, hot tub, laundry facilities, business services, pets allowed. | 110 Roosevelt Way | 509/633–1101 or 800/715–7767 | fax 509/633–1416 | $64–$120 | AE, D, DC, MC, V.

Gold House Inn. Breathtaking views of the dam and lake await you at this up-to-date B&B situated atop a hill. Each of the seven spacious rooms has its own personality. The Artist's Room, for instance, showcases a series of paintings done by the owner's son. | 7 rooms. Complimentary breakfast, no room phones, no TV in some rooms, TV in common area, no pets, no smoking. | 411 Partello Park, Grand Coulee | 509/633–3276 or 800/835–9369 | members.aol.com/coug89/gold.htm | $50–$75 | AE, D, MC, V.

USEFUL EXTRAS YOU MAY WANT TO PACK

- ❏ Adapters, converter
- ❏ Alarm clock
- ❏ Batteries
- ❏ Binoculars
- ❏ Blankets, pillows, sleeping bags
- ❏ Books and magazines
- ❏ Bottled water, soda
- ❏ Calculator
- ❏ Camera, lenses, film
- ❏ Can/bottle opener
- ❏ Cassette tapes, CDs, and players
- ❏ Cell phone
- ❏ Change purse with $10 in quarters, dimes, and nickels for tollbooths and parking meters
- ❏ Citronella candle
- ❏ Compass
- ❏ Earplugs
- ❏ Flashlight
- ❏ Folding chairs
- ❏ Guidebooks
- ❏ Luggage tags and locks
- ❏ Maps
- ❏ Matches
- ❏ Money belt
- ❏ Pens, pencils
- ❏ Plastic trash bags
- ❏ Portable TV
- ❏ Radio
- ❏ Self-seal plastic bags
- ❏ Snack foods
- ❏ Spare set of keys, not carried by driver
- ❏ Travel iron
- ❏ Travel journal
- ❏ Video recorder, blank tapes
- ❏ Water bottle
- ❏ Water-purification tablets

*Excerpted from *Fodor's: How to Pack: Experts Share Their Secrets*

COUPEVILLE

MAP 8, D3

(Nearby towns also listed: Oak Harbor, Port Townsend)

Washington's second oldest town and the county seat of Island County, Coupeville has narrow waterfront streets and the greatest number of historic structures of any Washington town. It rises rather picturesquely from Penn Cove, a protected inlet that almost cuts Whidbey Island in half. The beauty of this part of the island was first praised by members of the Vancouver expedition in 1792. But the explorers also noted that the local Indians, a tribe of the Skagit, had to protect themselves against raiding parties of northern Indians from British Columbia and Alaska by surrounding their village with a tall stockade. Several blockhouses built by white settlers during the 1855 Indian War survive, including the Alexander blockhouse, near the Coupeville waterfront, next to the historical museum.

Today, Coupeville is a pleasant waterfront town, which seems so authentically New England that it has served as a stage setting for New England scenes in several movies.

Madrona trees growing west of town, at the edge of the cove, are most dramatic, with gnarled reddish trunks and dark green foliage. In spring wildflowers dot the meadows, wild rhododendrons bloom in the woods, and wild strawberries reward the hiker.

Information: Central Whidbey Chamber of Commerce | Box 152, 302 N. Main St., Coupeville, 98239 | 360/678–5434 | islandweb.org/tourism.html.

Attractions

Alexander Blockhouse. Built in 1855, the blockhouse now stands near the waterfront, next to the historical museum. Note the squared logs and dove-tailed joints of the corners—no overlapping log ends. Several native canoes are exhibited in an open, roofed shelter. | 902 N.W. Alexander St. | 360/678–3310 | $2 | Oct.–Apr., Fri.–Mon. 10–4; May–Sept., daily 10–5.

Ft. Casey State Park. Four mi outside Coupeville above the Keystone ferry landing is a turn-of-the-20th-century army fort with concrete gun emplacement and a couple of 8" "disappearing" guns. The Admiralty Head Lighthouse Interpretive Center is north of the gunnery emplacements. | Hwy. 20 | 360/678–4519 or 800/233–0321 | www.parks.wa.gov | Free | Daily 8 AM–dusk.

Ft. Ebey State Park. West of Coupeville on Point Partridge, this park has campsites in the woods, trails to the headlands, World War II gun emplacements, wildflower meadows, spectacular views down Juan de Fuca Strait, several miles of sand and shingle beach, a boggy pond, and large stands of native rhododendrons, which bloom about Memorial Day. | Whidbey Island | 360/678–4636 or 800/233–0321 | www.parks.wa.gov | Free | Daily.

ON THE CALENDAR

OCT.: *Uniquely Whidbey Showcase.* A trade fair and show highlight local products, foods, and services of Whidbey Island. | 360/678–5434.

Dining

Christopher's. Mediterranean. The ambience is warm and casual at this eclectically furnished restaurant whose tables are set with linens, fresh flowers, and candles. Known for seafood and pasta dishes, as well as salads and soups. | 23 Front St. | 360/678–5480 | $15–$20 | AE, D, DC, MC, V.

Rosi's. Italian. Inside a Victorian home, this restaurant has three candlelit dining rooms serving a combination of Italian and Pacific Northwest cuisine. Among the entrées on the menu are chicken mascarpone, osso buco, lamb chops, and Penn Cove mussels. | 602 N. Main St. | 360/678–3989 | No lunch | $17–$22 | AE, MC, V.

Lodging

Anchorage Inn. The exterior of this reproduction Victorian has fanciful details such as gables, dormer windows, and a tower. Inside, hardwood floors, reproduction furniture, and antiques harmonize with the Victorian theme. There are splendid views of the harbor from each of the bedrooms. | 6 rooms, 1 suite. Complimentary breakfast, cable TV, in-room VCRs, no room phones, bicycles, no pets, no kids under 5, no smoking. | 807 N. Main St. | 360/678–5581 or 877/230–1313 | archorag@whidbey.net | www.anchorage-inn.com | Dec. 20–Feb. 7 | $75–$125 | D, MC, V.

Captain Whidbey Inn. Built from madrona logs, a notoriously hard (and difficult-to-work) wood, this sturdy inn sits on landscaped bluff-top grounds overlooking Penn Cove. It is surrounded by madrona and fir trees. In spring, wild rhododendrons bloom in nearby woods, wild strawberries grow along the roadside, and wild irises and other wildflowers grow in the meadows. | 32 rooms (12 with shared bath), 3 cottages. Bar, complimentary breakfast, no air-conditioning, some kitchenettes, beach, dock, boating, library, business services. | 2072 Captain Whidbey Inn Rd. | 360/678–4097 or 800/366–4097 | fax 360/678–4110 | captain@whidbey.net | www.captainwhidbey.com | $85–$160, $185–$225 cottages | AE, D, DC, MC, V.

Colonel Crockett Farm. The farmhouse,standing amid 3 acres of lawn and flower gardens, was built by Davy Crockett's relative in 1855. Among the architectural details of the interior are the stained- and leaded-glass windows, red oak paneling, and a slate fireplace. A variety of antiques fill the five bedrooms some of which have views of the harbor and meadows. | 5 rooms. Complimentary breakfast, no air-conditioning, no room phones, no TV, library, no pets, no kids under 14, no smoking. | 1012 S. Fort Casey Rd. | 360/678–3711 | fax 360/678–3707 | bnbwhitlow@aol.com | www.crockettfarm.com | $75–$105 | MC, V.

Compass Rose Bed and Breakfast. Inside this 1890 Queen Anne Victorian a veritable museum of art, artifacts, and antiques awaits you. The proprietor's navy employment carried him and his wife to all corners of the globe from which they have collected the inn's many unique adornments. The innkeepers' friendliness will make your stay all the more enjoyable and interesting. | 2 rooms. Complimentary breakfast, cable TV, no smoking. | 508 S. Main St. | 360/678–5318 or 800/237–3881 | www.compassrosebandb.com | $85 | No credit cards.

Fort Casey Inn. Built in 1909 as housing for army officers, the nine Georgian revival duplexes overlook a former parade ground. Tin ceilings, old quilts, rag rugs, hand-painted furniture, and sundry collectibles ornament the interior. Each duplex has a kitchen, fireplace, living room, and two bedrooms. | 9 units. Complimentary Continental breakfast, no TV, no pets, no smoking. | 1124 S. Engle Rd. | 360/678–8792. | www.fortcaseyinn.com | $135 | AE, MC, V.

Inn at Penn Cove. This single inn is composed of two stately Victorian homes standing side-by-side in the center of Coupeville's historic district. Fir floors, reproduction Victorian wallpaper, an antique pump organ, and a Victorian music box give special charm to Kineth House's parlor. The bedrooms of Coupe-Gillespie House, though less ornate than those of Kineth House, are equally comfortable and have stenciled wall trim and Victorian bedsteads. | 6 rooms (4 with private bath). Complimentary breakfast, no air-conditioning in some rooms, no room phones, TV in common area, no pets. | 702 N. Main St. | 360/678–8000 or 800/688–2683 | penncove@whidbey.net | www.whidbey.net/penncove | $60–$125 | AE, D, MC, V.

CRYSTAL MOUNTAIN

(See Mt. Rainier National Park)

DAYTON (COLUMBIA COUNTY)

MAP 8, K7

(Nearby town also listed: Walla Walla)

The tree-shaded county seat of Columbia County is the kind of Currier & Ives place many people conjure up when they imagine the best qualities of rural America. This tidy town has some 83 buildings listed on the National Register of Historic Places, including the state's oldest railroad depot and courthouse.

Information: Dayton Chamber of Commerce | Box 22, 166 E. Main St., Dayton, 99328 | 509/382–4825 | historicdayton.com.

Attractions

Dayton Historical Depot Society. Visit Washington's oldest standing depot which also houses a museum with exhibits illustrating the history of Dayton and surrounding communities. | 222 Commercial | 509/382–2026 | $2 | Tues.–Sat. 11–4.

Lewis and Clark Trail State Park. This park on the Touchet River has campsites under trees and a trout-filled river. | U.S. 12 | 509/337–6457 or 800/233–0321 | www.parks.wa.gov | Free | Daily.

Ski Bluewood. The Blue Mountain Ski Area is 22 mi south of Dayton, in the Umatilla National Forest. | 4th St. (N. Touchet Rd.), in Umatilla National Forest | 509/382–4725 | fax 509/382–4726 | www.bluewood.com | mid-Nov.–Apr.

ON THE CALENDAR

APR.: *Junior Livestock Show.* Livestock showing and judging by young ranchers, who often do a marvelous job and exhibit and compete with infectious enthusiasm in Waitsburg on U.S. 12. | 509/337–6207.

MAY: *Days of Real Sports.* Macho cattle country event with horse racing, pari-mutuel betting, parade, red meat, and beer, held at Waitsburg, on U.S. 12. | 509/337–6621.

SEPT.: *Columbia County Fair.* This annual event has a demolition derby, off-road motorcycle races, barbecues, exhibits and children's games all held on the Dayton Fairgrounds. | 800/882–6299.

OCT.: *Historical Home Tours.* Historical private homes welcome the public with guided tours as do the oldest Courthouse and train depot in Washington. | 509/382–2026.

Dining

Patit Creek Restaurant. Contemporary. This small café has been southeastern Washington's best restaurant for some 20 years. The service is excellent and the food can be truly sublime. Meat dishes are the specialty of the house and the beef, lamb, and pork that the chef turns out are inspired. The wine list is short, but lists some rare vintages from Walla Walla Valley wineries. | 725 E. Dayton Ave. | 509/382–2625 | Closed Sun–Tues. No lunch Sat. | $20–$30 | MC, V.

Weinhard Café. Contemporary. Sitting adjacent to the Weinhard Hotel, this restaurant, which was originally a pharmacy, has the air of a past era. Try a panini sandwich for lunch and for dinner the homemade ravioli with parmesan and potato stuffing, served with wilted greens and smoked bacon. The scrumptious pastries and huge chocolate chip cookies are homemade. | 229 E. Main St. | 509/382–1681 | Closed Mon.–Tues. | $16–$22 | MC, V.

Lodging

Purple House Bed and Breakfast. This Queen Anne Italianate–style house was built in 1882 by a pioneer physician. Today a mixture of European art and Chinese collectibles adorn the interior. The bedrooms are individually appointed with a tasteful selection of Victorian antiques. Afternoon pastries and tea are presented in the parlor. | 4 rooms. Complimentary breakfast, TV in common area, pool, pets allowed, no kids under 16, no smoking. | 415 Clay St. | 509/382–3159 or 800/486–2474 | fax 509/382–3159 | $85–$125 | MC, V.

Weinhard Hotel. Built in the late 1800s as a saloon and lodge by the nephew of beer baron Henry Weinhard, this hotel was lovingly restored (with modern amenities added) a few years ago. The rooms are furnished with period antiques, and there's a pleasant roof garden for catching the breezes. The dining room is open from mid-morning through dinner, Thursday–Monday. | 15. Dining room, complimentary Continental breakfast, no-smoking rooms, pets allowed. | 235 E. Main St. | 509/382–4032 | fax 509/382–2640 | $75–$125 | AE, MC, V.

EDMONDS

MAP 8, D4

(Nearby towns also listed: Bellevue, Seattle)

A charming waterfront town described by Seattle writer Bill Speidel as "a pocket of civilized living amongst urban sprawl," a comment as accurate today as it was 20 years ago. Edmonds has waterfront restaurants, a small but lively downtown, and the eastern landing for the ferry to Kingston on the Kitsap Peninsula.

Information: Edmonds Chamber of Commerce | Box 146, 125 5th Ave. N, Edmonds, 98020 | 425/776–6711 | edmondswa.com.

Attractions

Olympic Beach. The sunsets are spectacular from this beach, which honors the area's many Olympic athletes and champions. | Waterfront | 425/776–6711 | Free | Daily dawn–dusk.

ON THE CALENDAR

MAY: *Waterfront Festival.* The crown jewel of similar festivals along the Puget Sound waterfront, with an arts and crafts fair, food and beer garden, and various waterfront activities. | 425/771–1744.

Dining

Arnie's in Edmonds. Seafood. Sitting directly across from the sound, the dining room has views of the water. The restaurant's specialty, seafood, means that the menu is constantly changing according to what's in season. One especially popular dish is "Prawns Undecided": prawns prepared in three different ways—crab-stuffed, garlic roasted, and beer battered. | 300 Admiral Way | 425/771–5688 | $17–$25 | AE, MC, V.

Lodging

Edmonds Harbor Inn. A "country inn" in the city with luxurious rooms, but, alas, no water views. It is near the Kingston ferry terminal and the marina. | 60. Dining room, complimentary Continental breakfast, no-smoking rooms, pets allowed (fee). | 130 W. Dayton | 425/771–5021 or 800/441–8033 | fax 425/672–2880 | www.nwcountryinns.com/harbor | $79–$135 | MC, V.

Maple Tree Bed and Breakfast. This 1923 home sits amid flowers and lawns overlooking the harbor to the east and the Olympic Mountains to the west. The wooden walls, floor, and ceiling of the single room give it a cozy charm. A backyard patio provides lounging space during the warm months. | 1 room. Complimentary breakfast, no air-conditioning, no room phones, no TV, no pets, no smoking. | 18313 Olympic View Dr. | 425/774–8420 | briansea@gte.net | home1.gte.net/briansea | $70 | No credit cards.

ELLENSBURG

MAP 8, G5

(Nearby town also listed: Yakima)

This university and college town is one of the friendliest and most easy-going places east of the Cascades. Downtown has many well-preserved buildings from the early 20th century, as well as interesting shops and comfortable cafés. Central Washington University has an appealing mix of old and new buildings, and there are whimsical public artworks, a famous bull sculpture, the Kittitas County Historical Museum, a Japanese garden, and a primate research institute to round things out. On Labor Day weekend, the Old West invades the town with the famed Ellensburg Rodeo.

Information: Ellensburg Chamber of Commerce | 801 S Ruby, Ellensburg, 98926 | 509/925–3137 or 888/925–2204 | chamber@kvalley.com | ellensburg-wa.com.

Attractions

Central Washington University. The university has a pleasant, tree-shaded campus, with several old, but mostly late 1900s, buildings. | 400 E. 8th Ave. | 509/963–1111 | www.cwu.edu | Free | Weekdays 10–2.

Chimpanzee and Human Communication Institute. A world-famous primate research center, where chimpanzees have learned to communicate with humans through sign language. | 14th and D Blvd. | 509/963–2244 | fax 509/963–2234 | www.cwu.edu/cwu.chci | $10, $7 students | Tours: Sat. 9:15 and 10:45, Sun. 12:30 and 2:00.

Sarah Spurgeon Art Gallery. This college gallery in Randall Hall on the Central Washington University campus has rotating exhibits of local and visiting artists. | 509/963–2665 | fax 509/963–1918 | Free | Sept.–June, weekdays 8:30–4:30.

Clymer Museum of Art. Here a permanent collection of works by the artist John Clymer is on display. | 416 N. Pearl | 509/962–6416 | fax 509/962–6424 | www.ellensburg.com/~clymer | Free | Weekdays 10–5, weekends noon–5.

Gallery I. This gallery in the Stewart Building on the University campus features rotating shows by visiting and regional artists. | 408 ½ N. Pearl St. | 509/925–2670 | Free | Mon.–Sat. 11–5.

Ginkgo and Wanapum State Parks. These two state parks 28 mi east of Ellensburg on the Columbia River are separated by the I–90 freeway. Wanapum State Park, 3 miles south, has camping and river access for boaters. Ginkgo State Park preserves a petrified forest of ginkgos and other trees. There is an Interpretive Center. | I–90 E to exit 136 in Vantage | 509/856–2700 | fax 509/856–2294 | www.parks.wa.gov | Free, Camping $17 | Daily.

Kittitas County Farmer's Market. This market offers a great selection of seasonal regional produce. | Fifth and Anderson Sts. | 509/962–2723 | Free | May–Oct., Sat.

Olmstead Place State Park-Heritage Site. This original Kittitas Valley pioneer farm has 8 buildings and an interpretive trail. | N. Ferguson Rd. | 509/925–1943 or 509/856–2700 | fax 509/925–1955 | www.parks.wa.gov | Free | Daily.

Wanapum Dam Heritage Center. Local Indian and pioneer artifacts are exhibited, along with displays on modern hydroelectric power and a fish viewing. | Rte. 243 S | 509/754–3541 ext. 2571 | Free | Weekdays 8:30–4:30, weekends 9–5.

ON THE CALENDAR

MAY: *National Western Art Show and Auction.* Ellensburg is the Northwest's Western Art capital, and this is *the* big annual show. There are nationally known artists, quick draws, demonstrations, and auction of original art work. | 509/962–2934.

SEPT.: *Antique Equipment Show and Threshing Bee.* A tractor-lovers' dream! This weekend festival of antique farm equipment such as tractors, trucks, threshers, and engines takes place at the Olmstead Place State Park. Don't miss the tractor pull, parade of antique tractors, and flea market. | 509/925–1943.

SEPT.: ***Ellensburg Rodeo.*** This four-day event held every Labor Day weekend since 1923 showcases some of America's finest roping, riding, wrestling, and racing. The rodeo is held in conjunction with the county fair at the Kittitas County Fairgrounds. | 509/962–7831.
SEPT.: ***Kittitas County Fair.*** Concerts, food, and a rodeo with cattle roping and draft horse pulling take place on Labor Day weekend. | 800/426–5340.

Dining

Casa De Blanca. Mexican. This plain café serves up some very delectable Mexican and American fare, but its main attraction for the locals who flock here is the steaks. Even in cattle country good beef cookery can be hard to find. Known for prime rib, steak. Kids' menu. | 1318 S. Canyon Rd. | 509/925–1693 | $10–$20 | AE, D, MC, V.

Pub Minglewood. American/Casual. This comfortable college town eatery in a historic downtown building is enlivened with local artwork, and has dancing and two cocktail bars. Known for pasta and burgers. Kids' menu. | 402 N. Pearl St. | 509/962–2260 | Closed Sun. No lunch | $7–$13 | AE, D, MC, V.

Valley Cafe. Contemporary. Some folks drive all the way from Seattle to Ellensburg just to eat at this art deco–style restaurant. Selections run the gamut, from the popular peniolo lamb to a variety of vegetarian dishes. | 105 W. 3rd Ave. | 509/925–3050 | $20–$30 | AE, D, DC, MC, V.

Yellow Church Café. American/Casual. Originally built in the 1920s as a Lutheran church, seating is available in the nave or choir loft. A range of soups, salads, sandwiches, and pastas are available for dinner, in addition to a special dish which varies according to the whim of the chef. | 111 S. Pearl St. | 509/933–2233 | Breakfast available on weekends | $6–$15 | AE, MC, V.

Lodging

Best Western Ellensburg Inn. A comfortable freeway motel that's a favorite with traveling salesmen, families, and visiting college professors. | 105 rooms. Restaurant, bar with entertainment, room service, cable TV, indoor pool, wading pool, hot tub, exercise equipment, business services, free parking, pets allowed (fee). | 1700 Canyon Rd. | 509/925–9801 | fax 509/925–2093 | $54–$77 | AE, D, DC, MC, V.

Inn at Goose Creek. Each room of this modern house has its own theme. The Homespun/Shaker Room contains an assortment of black Shaker-style furniture, plain walls, and—like all the other rooms—a special handmade rug. The inn sits conveniently at exit 109 off I–90. | 10 rooms. Complimentary Continental breakfast, in-room data ports, refrigerators, in-room hot tubs, cable TV, in-room VCRs, no pets, no smoking. | 1720 Canyon Rd. | 509/962–8030 or 800/533–0822 | fax 509/962–8031 | goosecrk@ellensburg.com | www.innatgoosecreek.com | $89–$109 | AE, MC, V.

ENUMCLAW

MAP 8, E5

(Nearby towns also listed: Puyallup, Tacoma)

Today Enumclaw serves as a residential community with easy commuter access to Seattle and Tacoma, but the town began life in the 1850s as one of Washington's earliest pioneer settlements. Later it became a railroad, lumber, and dairy town. Enumclaw takes its name from a nearby mountain which, curiously, signifies "Abode of Evil Spirits," in the native Salish language.

Information: **Enumclaw Area Chamber of Commerce and Visitor Information Center** | 1421 Cole St., Enumclaw, 98022 | 360/825–7666 | enumclawchamber.com.

Attractions

Federation Forest State Park. The park preserves 619 acres of virgin forest, plus parts of the Naches Trail, a Native American and pioneer trail over the Cascades. There is a hiking trail, picnic tables, and interpretive displays. | Rte. 410 SE | 360/663–2207 | fax 360/663–0172 | www.parks.wa.gov | Free | May–Labor Day 8–dusk; the rest of the year by appointment.

Green River Gorge Conservation Area. This 12-mi-long gorge has caves in sheer rock walls 130 to 300 ft high. Wildflowers bloom in spring and early summer at this conservation area 12 mi north of Enumclaw. | Rte. 169 | 253/931–3930 | Free | Daily.

Flaming Geyser State Park. There are no "flaming geysers" in this pleasant riverside park although two geysers did exist for testing coal some years ago. | 23700 Southeast Flaming Geyser Rd. | 253/931–3930 | fax 253/931–6379 | Free | Daily.

King County Fairgrounds. These fairgrounds are constantly abuzz with activity including car shows, Highland Games, the county fair, and dog shows to name just a few. | 45224 284th Ave. SE | 360/825–7777 or 800/325–6165.

Mud Mountain Dam. One of the highest earthen dams in the world, this flood control structure has picnic tables, a nature trail, playground, and views across the White River Valley. | Rte. 410 SE | 360/825–3211 | fax 206/764–3307 | Free | Daily.

ON THE CALENDAR

JULY: ***King County Fair.*** Held for five days the third week of each July, the fair is the locus for animal and livestock shows, arts and crafts exhibitions, as well as food booths. | 360/825–7777 or 800/325–6165.

JULY: ***Pacific Northwest Scottish Highland Games.*** This Scottish games and culture festival, featuring traditional Highland field events, plus dancers, drummers and pipers, with plenty of food available, is held at the King County Fairgrounds. | 206/522–2541.

JULY: ***King County Fair.*** Children's carnival, entertainment exhibits and plenty of rides are held at the fairgrounds. | 206/296–8888.

Dining

Pony Express Café. American/Casual. This restaurant, which occupies what was once an old soda shop, serves a variety of dishes including burgers, salads, halibut, and salmon, but it is famous for its prime rib. Homemade soups and desserts complement the menu. Old photographs of the establishment's former incarnation adorn the walls. | 1239 Griffin | 360/825–2055 | Reservations not accepted | Breakfast also available | $5–$13.30 | AE, MC, V.

Lodging

Best Western Park Center Hotel. This is a comfortable motel only 7 mi away from a recreation area, including Mud Mountain Dam, which also makes it ideal for families. | 40 rooms. Restaurant, bar picnic area, in-room data ports, microwaves, some refrigerators, room service, cable TV, hot tub, business services, pets allowed (fee). | 1000 Griffin Ave. | 360/825–4490 | fax 360/825–3686 | $69–$78 | AE, D, DC, MC, V.

White Rose Inn. The rooms of this Colonial-style mansion built in 1922 showcase beautiful period antiques and original features like 10-ft ceilings, crown moldings, and hardwood floors. The deck overlooks the backyard's 100 rose bushes. | 4 rooms. Complimentary breakfast, no air-conditioning, no room phones, TV in common area, no pets, no smoking. | 1610 Griffin Ave. | 360/825–7194 or 800/404–7194 | innkeepr@whiteroseinnbb.com | www.whiteroseinnbb.com | $85–$95 | AE, MC, V.

EPHRATA

MAP 8, H5

(Nearby towns also listed: Moses Lake, Quincy, Soap Lake)

Ephrata is a pleasant small farm town and the Grant County seat, situated in the exact center of Washington. It was settled quite early because its abundant natural springs made it an oasis in the very dry steppe country of the Columbia basin. Wandering tribes of Native Americans visited the local springs, as did cattle drovers after American ranchers stocked the open range. Ephrata began to grow as a town after the Great Northern Railroad established a terminal here in 1892. At the time thousands of wild horses roamed the range.

Cattlemen took advantage of the railroad to round up and ship out thousands of wild horses. The last great roundup was held in 1906, when the last 2,400 horses of a herd that once numbered some 25,000 were corralled and shipped out by rail.

Information: Ephrata Chamber of Commerce | Box 275, Ephrata, 98823 | 509/754–4656.

Attractions

Grant County Courthouse. Built in the 1920s, this redbrick structure has a facade framed by white columns and a majestic set of stairs. Although it may seem antique from the exterior, the building has actually embraced alternative energy sources and is heated by thermal springs. | 30 C St. NW | 800/COULEE–2.

Grant County Historical Village and Museum. This museum consists of the 18 buildings of a pioneer village brought here from other parts of Grant County. They include a blacksmith forge, saloon, barbershop, and printing office. | 742 Basin St. N | 509/754–3334 | $3 | May–Sept., Mon.–Tues., Thurs.–Sat. 10–5; Sun. 1–4.

Oasis Park. This park, 1½ mi southwest, occupies the site of ancient Indian encampments, which later became an important watering place for cattle drovers. | On WA 28 | 509/754–5102 | fax 509/754–1355 | Free | Daily.

ON THE CALENDAR

APR.: *Anniversary Celebration.* Square dance and round dancing take place at the Wheatland Whirlers Square Dance Hall. | 509/754–3025.

JUNE: *Sage and Sun Festival.* Start of the summer festival takes place throughout downtown with vendors' booths on the streets. Parades, live bands, talent shows, and a carnival. | 509/754–4656.

SEPT.: *Pioneer Day.* Demonstrations of pioneer crafts of daily living, such as wool spinning, rope making, knot tying, wood branding, and butter churning, bring history to life at Grant County Historical Village and Museum. You can also ramble through 30 preserved buildings to get a feel for Grant County's history. | 509/754–3334.

Dining

Country Deli. American/Casual. Located in the center of town, this popular eatery serves burgers, salads, and pastas in a comfortable, low-key dining room. A gazebo sits in the front of the restaurant, providing outdoor dining in the warmer months. | 245 Basin St. NW | 509/754–3143 | Breakfast also available. No dinner Sun.–Mon. | $7–$12 | AE, MC, V.

Lodging

Ivy Chapel Inn Bed and Breakfast. Occupying a brick church from the '40s, this B&B has a unique structure. The chapel, with its cathedral ceilings and large stained-glass windows, has been preserved as a chapel for weddings and meetings. The B&B's residential location is only two blocks from downtown, close to shops and restaurants. | 6 rooms. Complimentary breakfast, cable TV, no room phones, hot tub, no pets, no smoking. | 164 D St. SW | 509/754–0629 | fax 509/754–0791 | ivychapel@hotmail.com | www.ivychapelinn.com | $80 | AE, D, DC, MC, V.

Sharlyn Motel. Business travelers' and family motel. | 19 rooms. Cable TV. | 848 Basin St. SW | 509/754–3575 | $40–$95 | MC, V.

EVERETT

MAP 8, E3

(Nearby towns also listed: Marysville, Seattle)

Everett is the county seat of Snohomish County. Much of this industrial town sits high on a bluff above Port Gardner Bay and the Snohomish River. The waterfront was once lined by so many lumber, pulp, and shingle mills that Everett proudly called itself "the city of smokestacks." Downtown Everett has many elegant old commercial buildings, dating from the period when John D. Rockefeller heavily invested in the then fledging town, hoping to profit from the nearby Monte Cristo mines which, however, turned out to be a flop. Then another scheme failed when James J. Hill made Everett the western terminal of the Great Northern Railroad, hoping to turn it into the major port on Puget Sound. Today, Everett is best known for the Boeing Aircraft plant south of town where the giant Boeing 747 is built, and for its naval station, which is home to an aircraft carrier and a support flotilla.

Information: Everett Area Convention and Visitor Bureau | Box 1086, 909 S.E. Everett Mall Way, Suite C30, Everett, 98206 | 425/438–1487 | snobiz.org. **Snohomish County Tourism Bureau/VIC** | 101 128th St. SE,Suite 5000 Everett, 98208 | 888/338–0976 | www.snohomish.org.

Attractions

Aquasox Baseball Club. This affiliate of the Seattle Mariners plays its games in an open ballpark and is a favorite of aficionados of old-fashioned baseball. | 3802 Broadway | 425/258–3673 | fax 425/258–3675 | www.aquasox.com | $5–$10 | June–Aug; call for schedule.

Captain Cook Cruises. Tours of the Everett waterfront and the navy's home port. | 404 14th St. | 425/259–5010 | fax 425/339–4175 | www.captaincookcrusies.com | $34–$50 | Call for schedules.

Boeing Everett Facility. Boeing 747s are built here in the world's largest building under one roof. | State Hwy. 526 W | 206/544–1264 | www.boeing.com | $5; special rates (and height requirements) for children | Weekdays 9–3.

Forest Park This park has a heated indoor pool, a children's zoo, a huge Floral Hall built with stone and peeled logs, and, in summer, live music performances. | 802 Mukilteo Blvd. | 425/257–8300 | fax 425/257–8325 | www.ci.everett.wa.us/everett/parks/eprd/index.htm | Free | Daily 6–10.

Mukilteo. This pleasant waterfront town southwest of Everett has a ferry landing for the Clinton (South Whidbey Island) ferry, an old lighthouse, and waterfront park. An important Indian Treaty was signed in 1855 at nearby Point Elliott. | Visitors Information Center: 909 S.E. Everett Mall Way | 888/338–0976 | fax 425/348–5701 | Free | Daily.

Snohomish County Historic Museum. Local Indian artifacts and a collection of historic photos are the highlights of this museum. | 2817 Rockefeller Ave. | 425/259–2022 | fax 425/258–5402 | www.snownet.org/snocomuseum/ | Donations accepted | Wed.–Sat. 1–4.

ON THE CALENDAR

APR.–SEPT.: ***Auto Racing.*** Check out NASCAR racing at the Evergreen Speedway, one of the super speedways of the Northwest. | 360/805–6100.

JUNE: ***Salty Sea Days.*** Festival with parades, street vendors, and live blues music throughout the fair. | 425/339–1113.

JULY: ***Fourth of July Parade.*** Floats, bands, drill teams, classic cars, and Navy vehicles parade down Colby Avenue during Everett's Independence Day parade, part of a day-long festival that includes a fireworks show and musical performances at the nearby Navy base. | 425/438–1487.

Dining

Alligator Soul. Cajun/Creole. People rave about this casual hot spot of Louisiana cooking. From the exposed brick walls and Mardi Gras beads to the hot barbecue sauce, spicy corn relish, and fried catfish served up by the kitchen, this is the real deal. | 2013½ Hewitt Ave. | 425/259–6311 | $10–$17 | MC, V.

Anthony's Homeport. Seafood. Large windows, overlooking Port Gardner Bay, afford wonderful sunset vistas at this restaurant known for its fresh Dungeness crab and wild Chinook salmon. In summer don't miss trying one of the fabulous desserts made from the best of Washington's produce. | 1726 W. Marine View Dr. | 425/252–3333 | $14–$25 | AE, MC, V.

The Sisters. American. This funky breakfast and lunch café with eclectic cooking is as popular now as it was a decade ago. Perhaps that's because the blueberry or pecan hot cakes, the soups, and the sandwiches are as good as ever. No alcohol. | 2804 Grand St. | 425/252–0480 | Breakfast also available. No dinner | $6–$8 | MC, V.

Lodging

Best Western Cascadia Inn. This hotel is 1 mi from the Amtrak station and 3 mi from the marina, naval station, and waterfront dining. | 134 rooms. Complimentary Continental breakfast, some refrigerators, cable TV, pool, hot tub, laundry facilities, business services. | 2800 Pacific Ave. | 425/258–4141 | fax 425/258–4755 | $79–$149 | AE, D, DC, MC, V.

Gaylord House. The front porch and back deck of this turn-of-the-20th-century craftsman home allow you to enjoy the surrounding natural beauty in the fresh air. The friendly and accommodating owners have filled the rooms with antiques and original art. Some rooms have views of the Cascade Mountains. | 5 rooms. Complimentary breakfast, in-room data ports, some in-room hot tubs, cable TV, in-room VCRs (movies), library, no pets, no smoking. | 3301 Grand Ave. | 425/339–9153 or 888/507–7177 | fax 425/303–9713 | gaylord_house@msn.com | www.gaylordhouse.com | $85–$175 | AE, D, MC, V.

Harbor Hill Inn. The inn, formerly the Blackman Mansion, was built in 1910 in view of Puget Sound and the Olympic Mountains. Antique furnishings and quilts complement original details such as exposed beams and fir paneling. | 5 rooms. Complimentary breakfast, no room phones, TV in common area, pool, outdoor hot tub, no pets, no smoking. | 2208 Rucker Ave. | 425/259–3925 or 888/572–3925 | fax 425/259–6265 | www.harborhillinn.com | $75–$105 | MC, V.

Holiday Inn Hotel and Conference Center. Upscale business travelers' hotel convenient to all area activities. | 249 rooms. Restaurant, no-smoking rooms, pool, gym, pets allowed (fee). | 101 128th St. SE | 425/337–2900 | fax 425/337–0707 | $95–$129 | AE, D, DC, MC, V.

Howard Johnson Plaza. This is a big hotel that has undergone several ownership and stylistic changes and may finally have found a formula that works. | 247 rooms. Restaurant, bar with entertainment, some refrigerators, room service, indoor pool, hot tub, exercise equipment, business services. | 3105 Pine St. | 425/339–3333 or 800/IGO–HOJO | fax 425/259–1547 | $79–$139 | AE, D, DC, MC, V.

Marina Village Inn. This is a comfortable inn with great views of Port Gardener Bay and Olympic Mountain. | 26 rooms, 16 suites. Complimentary Continental breakfast, many in-room hot tubs, refrigerators, mini bars, business services, free parking. | 1728 W. Marine View Dr. | 425/259–4040 or 800/281–7037 | fax 425/252–8419 | $95–145, $168–$229 suites | AE, D, DC, MC, V.

Welcome Motor Inn. This budget motel is close to the Boeing Facility and the navy base. | 42 rooms. Complimentary Continental breakfast, cable TV, refrigerators, microwaves. | 1205 Broadway | 425/252–8828 or 800/252–5512 | fax 425/252–8880 | $43–$62 | AE, D, DC, MC, V.

FORKS

MAP 8, A3

(Nearby town also listed: Port Angeles)

Forks is a friendly, former logging town that takes its name from its proximity to the junction of the Bogachiel and Calawah Rivers; together with the Soleduck, they form the Quillayute, which empties into the Pacific at the Indian village of La Push. Since the decline of logging, due to a shortage of trees, Forks has been marketing the beauty of the neighboring rain forests and rivers. The countryside surrounding Forks is exceptionally green, since the town receives more than 100 inches of rain in an average year.

Information: Forks Chamber of Commerce | 1411 S. Forks Ave., Forks, 98331 | 800/443–6757 | www.forkswa.com.

Attractions

Hoh River Rain Forest. South of Forks, an 18 mi spur road leads from U.S. 101 to the Hoh River Rain Forest, with spruce and hemlock trees soaring to heights of more than 200 ft. Alders and big-leaf maples are so densely covered with moss that they look more like shaggy prehistoric animals than trees. A visitor center explains how the forest functions and has short trails leading among the trees. Look for elk browsing in shaded glens. | Upper Hoh Rd. to Hoh Rain Forest Visitor Center | 360/374–6925 | $10 | Daily; the Visitor Center is often unstaffed Sept.–May.

ON THE CALENDAR

APR.: ***Rainfest.*** A celebration of arts and crafts inspired by the huge annual rainfall of 100+ inches takes place mid-April right in downtown Forks. | 800/443–6757.

JULY: ***Fourth of July Celebration.*** A salmon bake, a parade, a demolition derby, and an arts and crafts exhibits are some of the events at Forks's four-day-long Independence Day festival. | 800/443–6757.

Dining

Kalaloch Lodge. American. The restaurant is one of the best features at this old-fashioned lodge. Enjoy unobstructed ocean views while sampling the specialties, salmon and halibut. | 157151 U.S. 101, Forks-Kalaloch | 360/962–2271 | fax 360/962–3391 | Breakfast also available | $15–$30 | AE, MC, V.

Smoke House Restaurant. Steak. Since 1975, this restaurant has operated as a smokehouse, serving such popular items as its own smoked salmon. Steak is also a specialty here; the prime rib is especially delicious. The rough panel walls and pictures of the local area give the dining room a rustic appeal that is not out of keeping with the surrounding country. | 193161 Hwy. 101 | 360/374–6258 | No lunch on weekends | $10–$20 | D, MC, V.

Lodging

Eagle Point Inn. About 10 mi north of Forks, this comfortable, spacious B&B is a log lodge on the Soleduck River and bordered by timberlands. There are mushroom hunting and a rain forest nearby. | 3 rooms. Dining room, complimentary breakfast, hot tub, fishing. | MP 202 Stormin' Norman Road, Beaver | 360/327–3236 | $85 | No credit cards.

Forks Motel. Forks's largest motel has guest rooms, small suites, larger suites with two bedrooms and full kitchens and a single suite with a hot tub. Each year a portion of the motel is renovated. | 73 rooms. No air-conditioning in some rooms, some kitchenettes, cable TV, pool, wading pool, laundry facilities, business services, pets allowed. | 351 S. Forks Ave. | 360/374–6243 or 800/544–3416 | fax 360/374–6760 | www.forksmotel.com | $54–$135 | AE, D, DC, MC, V.

Hoh Humm Ranch Bed and Breakfast. This B&B sits on a 200-acre ranch 20 mi south of Forks. The simple, comfortable rooms overlook the valley and river below. Kids love the llamas, deer, and goats that are raised on the ranch. | 4 rooms. Complimentary breakfast, no air-conditioning, no room phones, TV in common area, pets allowed, no smoking. | 171763 Hwy. 101 | 360/374–5337 | fax 360/374–5344 | hohhumm@olypen.com | www.olypen.com/hohhumm | $35–$55 | No credit cards.

Kalaloch Lodge. This venerable, weather-beaten lodge is on the wild outer coast of the National Park, with rustically simple, no-frills accommodations. But the isolated beach is worth the lack of amenities. There is a convenience store on the property, with a gas station. | 10 rooms, 4 suites; 4 cabins; 10 rooms, 2 suites in lodge. Restaurant (*see* Kalaloch Lodge), bar, no air-conditioning, some kitchenettes, some refrigerators, no room phones, pets allowed (fee). | 157151 U.S. 101 | 360/962–2271 | fax 360/962–3391 | www.visitkalaloch.com | $122–$140, $120–$225 suites, $135–$225 cabins | AE, MC, V.

Manitou Lodge. This secluded cedar lodge B&B is set amidst 10 acres of coastal rain forest, near Rialto Beach. The main room has a huge vaulted ceiling and a towering stone fireplace. Just a short drive from Lake Cresent and the Sol Duc Hot Springs, and Cape Flattery. | 5 rooms in main house, 2 rooms in cottage, 1 cabin (2 campsites also available). Picnic area, complimentary breakfast, no air-conditioning, no room phones, no kids under 5, no smoking. | Kilmer Rd. | 360/374–6295 | fax 360/374–7495 | manitou@olypen.com | www.manitoulodge.com | $90–$120 | AE, D, DC, MC, V.

Miller Tree Inn Bed and Breakfast. Originally a farmhouse, this B&B is bordered on two sides by pasture land. The inn's many windows make the rooms bright, cheerful places to relax amid the assortment of antiques, knick-knacks, and quilts. A porch and back deck allow for summer lounging. | 7 rooms. Complimentary breakfast, no air-conditioning, no room phones, no TV in some rooms, TV in common area, hot tub, pets allowed, no smoking. | 654 E. Division St. | 360/374–6806 or 800/943–6563 | fax 360/374–6807 | info@millertreeinn.com | www.millertreeinn.com | $75–$135 | MC, V.

Pacific Inn Motel. This 2-story exterior corridor motel, built in 1990, sits in the center of town, close to restaurants and shops. | 34 rooms. Cable TV, microwaves, refrigerators, air-conditioning, laundry facilities, business services. | 352 Forks Ave. (U.S. 101) | 360/374–9400 or 800/235–7344 | fax 360/374–9402 | $47–$65 | AE, D, DC, MC, V.

GOLDENDALE

MAP 8, F8

(Nearby town also listed: The Dalles, OR)

The county seat of Klickitat County and the commercial center for ranchers and farmers, Goldendale is a pretty town with many old clapboard houses. First settled in 1872, Goldendale still projects a down-to-earth atmosphere. Goldendale Observatory State Park, 1½ miles north of town via Columbus Avenue, has the nation's largest public telescope.

Information: Greater Goldendale Area Chamber of Commerce | 131 W. Court St., Goldendale, 98620 | 509/773–3400 | klickitatcounty.org.

Attractions

Brooks Memorial State Park. A shaded park on the upper Klickitat River 12 mi north of Goldendale where campsites and picnic tables are available. | U.S. 97 N | 509/773–4611 or 800/233–0321 | www.parks.wa.gov | Free | Daily dawn–dusk.

Goldendale Observatory. The nation's largest public observatory, with a 24½-inch reflecting telescope. | 1602 Observatory Dr. | 509/773–3141 | fax 509/773–6929 | www.perr.com/gosp | Free | Apr.–Sept., Wed.–Sun. 2–5 and 8–midnight; Oct.–Mar., call for schedule.

Horsethief Lake State Park. You can fish, hike, windsurf, and rock climb at this park, located approximately 20 mi southwest of Goldendale. The park is famous for its petroglyphs; tours are given of the glyphs from April to October, Fridays and Saturdays at 10 o'clock. You must call ahead to make reservations. | Hwy. 14 | 509/767–1159 | Free | Daily 6:30–dusk.

Klickitat County Historical Museum. A small but delightful museum with local Indian and pioneer artifacts. | 127 W. Broadway | 509/773–4303 | $3 | Apr.–Oct., daily 9–5; Nov.–Mar., by appointment.

Maryhill Museum of Art. An oddity in the wilds of the Columbia River canyon: a first-rate Flemish château-style museum built in the 1920s by railroad magnate Sam Hill. It houses, among other objects, an excellent collection of Rodin sculptures. | 35 Maryhill Museum Dr. | 509/773–3733 | fax 509/773–6138 | www.maryhillmuseum.org | $6.50 | mid-Mar.–mid-Nov., daily 9–5.

Mt. Adams Recreation Area. This 12,276-ft-tall mountain, northwest of Goldendale, is enclosed by a wilderness area and by the Yakama Indian Reservation. Camping and hiking is permitted in the latter only by permission of the tribe. (Call 509/865–5121, ext. 657, the Tribe's Forestry Development Program for information, or the Mt. Adams Ranger Station phone number below.) | Between Yakima Valley and Columbia Gorge | 509/395–2501 | fax 509/395–3424 | $5 | July–Sept. dawn–dusk.

ON THE CALENDAR

JULY: ***Goldendale Community Days.*** Usually held on the first weekend after July 4th, this celebration includes a hot-air balloon race, quilt show, car show, and parade. There is also a bull riding contest at the fairgrounds. | 509/773–3400.

AUG.: ***Klickitat County Fair and Rodeo.*** Riding, roping, a carnival, a parade, and entertainment take place on the fairgrounds. | 509/773–3900.

Dining

Ranch House. American. Horse shoes and western pictures adorn the walls of this eatery which specializes in home-cooking. The menu includes a full range of American classics. All the pastries are baked on the premises; the cinnamon rolls are especially popular. Prime rib is served on Friday and Saturday night. | 100 E. Main St. | 509/773–6855 | Breakfast also available | $8–$13 | MC, V.

Lodging

Farvue Motel. Family motel with great views of Mt. Hood and Mt. Adam. | 48 rooms. Restaurant, bar, refrigerators, cable TV, pool, business services. | 808 E. Simcoe Dr. | 509/773–5881 or 800/358–5881 | fax 509/773–5881 | $49–$121 | AE, D, DC, MC, V.

Ponderosa Motel. This 2-story motel in the heart of the city sits just a ¼ mi north of Highway 97 at exit 142. Restaurants and shops are all within easy walking distance. | 28 rooms. Some kitchenettes, cable TV, business services, pets allowed (fee). | 775 E. Broadway St. | 509/773–5842 | fax 509/773–4049 | $40–$65 | AE, D, DC, MC, V.

Victorian House Bed and Breakfast. Built in 1910 by a doctor, this cozy Victorian lodging is within walking distance of many shops and restaurants, and only ¾ mi from Highway 97. You have the option of choosing simply coffee and tea for breakfast, a Continental meal, or a full breakfast. Weather permitting, you can sit on the porch swing and watch the world go by. | 4 rooms (all shared bath). Complimentary breakfast, no room phones, no TV in some rooms, TV in common area, no pets, no smoking. | 415 E. Broadway St. | 509/773–5338 | $47.50–$65.50 | MC, V.

HOQUIAM

MAP 8, B5

(Nearby towns also listed: Aberdeen, Ocean Shores, Westport)

Hoquiam (pronounced "hoh-quee-am") is a historic lumber town on the Hoquiam River, where it joins Grays Harbor. A deep-water port 16 mi from the Pacific Ocean, Hoquiam docks cargo and fishing vessels, cans the harvest of the sea, and manufactures wood products and machine tools.

Bordering Hoquiam, Grays Harbor, discovered by Robert Gray in 1792, is the second largest estuary in Washington, one of the largest estuaries on the U.S. Pacific coast, and one of only eight natural harbors between Mexico and Canada.

Information: Grays Harbor Chamber of Commerce | 506 Duffy St., Aberdeen, 98520 | 360/532–1924 | chamber@graysharbor.org | graysharbor.org.

Attractions

Grays Harbor National Wildlife Refuge. A stopover point for migrating fowl, this is a perfect place for bird watching. You can stroll leisurely on the 1,800 ft boardwalk. To reach the refuge, drive west on Highway 109 to Pawlson Road where you will take a left. Drive until you come to Airport Way where you should turn right. | Airport Way | 360/753–9467 | Free | Daily dawn–dusk.

Polson Park and Museum. Artifacts from Grays Harbor's historic past and from its logging industry are on display; the park has a rose garden and exotic trees. | 1611 Riverside Ave. | 360/533–5862 | www.polsonmuseum.org | $2 | June–Aug., Wed.–Sun. 11–4; Sept.–May, weekends noon–4.

ON THE CALENDAR

SEPT.: *Loggers' Playday.* People come from far and wide to enjoy and participate in this festival honoring the city's logging roots on the first Saturday after Labor Day. School bands, logging trucks, and Scottish pipe bands parade through downtown Hoquiam. Then, at Grizzly Stadium you can see such old-time competitions as ax-throwing, log rolling, and tree topping. | 360/532–9479.

Dining

Duffy's Number Three. American. The traditional favorites are well represented on the menu here—steaks, chops, burgers, and fried fish; the locals favor the Swedish pancakes, the salmon, the prime rib, and the wild blackberry pie. The vaguely Irish decor seems half-hearted. | 825 Simpson Ave. | 360/532–1519 | Breakfast also available | $10–$15 | AE, D, DC, MC, V.

Lodging

Hoquiam's Castle Bed and Breakfast. This spectacular Victorian mansion, registered as a state and national historic site, has 28 rooms and three floors filled with cut crystal chandeliers, Tiffany-style lamps, and exquisite period antiques. Stained-glass windows and wood paneling add further charm to the interior. The bedrooms overlook the town and harbor. | 5 rooms. Complimentary breakfast, no air-conditioning, no room phones, TV in common area, no pets, no kids under 12, no smoking. | 515 Chenault Ave. | 360/533–2005 | info@hoquiamscastle.com | www.hoquiamscastle.com | $110–$140 | AE, D, MC, V.

Lytle House. A historic, Queen Anne Victorian mansion, this comfortable B&B retains all the original woodwork, and is filled with antiques. | 8 rooms (2 with shared bath, 1 with shower only). Complimentary breakfast and afternoon tea and snacks, no air-conditioning, cable TV, no room phones, hot tub, business services. | 509 Chenault Ave. | 360/533–2320 or 800/677–2320 | fax 360/533–4025 | $75–$135 | AE, DC, MC, V.

ILWACO

MAP 8, B7

(Nearby towns also listed: Long Beach, Astoria, OR)

Ilwaco (pronounced "Ill-wahco") has been a fishing port for thousands of years, first as a village of the native Chinook tribe and, since about 1840, as an American settlement. Ilwaco has a colorful port where fishermen gather in the early morning, a picturesque downtown of well-preserved old buildings some of which are decorated with murals, an old coastal battery, a lifesaving station, and two lighthouses atop rocky headlands. There are also forests where deer roam, surf-washed coves, breakwaters where seabirds hang out, and sandy beaches. Lewis and Clark slept here before deciding to winter on the Oregon Coast.

U.S. 101 N from Chinook, along the rocky shores of Willapa Bay, is one of the most scenic drives in Washington.

Information: Long Beach Peninsula Visitor's Bureau | Box 562, Long Beach, 98631 | 800/451–2542 | funbeach.com.

Attractions

Cape Disappointment. More than 250 ships have sunk on this rocky cape since it was named in 1788 by Captain John Mearles. The Cape Disappointment Lighthouse, built in 1856, is the oldest lighthouse on the West Coast still in use. | Fort Canby State Park | 360/642–3078.

Fort Canby State Park. Once a military installation, this 1,700-acre park still contains many of the emplacements for canons that once guarded the mouth of the Columbia. Deer are easily spotted on the trails and eagles perch on the cliffs overhead. The park is also home to the Lewis and Clark Interpretive Center which tells the tale of the famous duo's 8,000 mi trek across the continent with artwork, photographs, and journal entries. | 100 Loop Rd. | 360/642–3029 or 360/642–3078 | Park and interpretive center free | Park daily dawn–dusk; interpretive center daily 10–5.

Fort Columbia State Park and Interpretive Center. The site of a former coastal artillery corps post, the park is set on 580 acres. | U.S. 101 | 360/992–1821 or 800/233–0321 | Free | Memorial Day–Sept., Wed.–Sun 10–5.

Ilwaco Heritage Museum. Dioramas and miniatures of Long Beach towns tell the history of this region, beginning with the Native American habitation, moving on to the influx of traders, missionaries, and settlers, and concluding with contemporary workers, fishers, and farmers. | 115 S.E. Lake St. | 360/642–3446 | $3 | May–Aug., Mon.–Sat. 9–5, Sun. noon–4; Sept.–Apr., Mon.–Sat. 10–4.

North Head Lighthouse. From Cape Disappointment follow the Spur 100 road 2 miles to find this lighthouse built in 1899 to warn sailers of the treacherous sands. Superb views of the Long Beach Peninsula are provided on a bluff above the pounding surf. | Fort Canby State Park | 360/642–3078 | $1 | Apr.–Sept., daily 10–5; Oct.–Mar., weekends only.

ON THE CALENDAR

OCT.: *Cranberrian Fair.* Cranberry vendors show off all kinds of cranberry products and a tour bus will take you to visit the cranberry bogs of the Long Beach Peninsula where you can watch the cranberry harvest. | 800/451–2542.

Dining

Joan's Portside Café. American. Just two blocks from the dock and boat launch, this place is a favorite among locals who come to enjoy the homemade biscuits and gravy, homemade soups, and especially the homemade pies. | 303 Main St. | 360/642–3477 | Breakfast also available. No dinner | $5–$8 | MC, V.

Sanctuary Restaurant. Contemporary. The dining room is set in the nave of a former turn-of-the-20th-century church. The old pews have been rearranged to serve as dining booths, while soft light filters through the stained-glass windows and reflects off the high ceiling. The fare runs from local seafood and well-aged beef to Scandinavian specialties such as Swedish meatballs, pork loin stuffed with prunes, and "Scandi-Sushi," which is smoked lox wrapped in *lefse* (very thin bread). Kids' menu. | 794 Rte. 101, Chinook | 360/777–8380 | Reservations essential | Closed Mon.–Tues. No lunch | $20–$30 | AE, D, MC, V.

Lodging

China Beach Retreat. This secluded B&B, sitting between the port of Ilwaco and Fort Canby State Park, is surrounded by wetlands and has wonderful views of Baker's Bay and the mouth of the Colombia River. Each of the three rooms is adorned with antiques and original art. | 3 rooms. Complimentary breakfast, no air-conditioning, in-room hot tubs, no room phones, no TV, no pets, no kids under 16, no smoking. | 222 Robert Gray Dr. | 360/642–5660 | innkeeper@chinabeachretreat.com | www.chinabeachretreat.com | $189–$229 | AE, MC, V.

Eagle's Nest Resort. Just ½mi east of Ilwaco, this resort sits on 94 acres of wooded land. The accommodations vary from cedar cottages to parked trailers. The cottages have full kitchens, though the cabins and trailers are simpler. | 5 cottages, 3 cabins. Restaurant, no air-conditioning, some kitchenettes, some microwaves, some refrigerators, some in-room hot tubs, cable TV, pool, hot tub, miniature golf, basketball, volleyball, shops, video games, playground, pets allowed. | 700 W. North Head Rd. | 360/642–8351 | fax 360/642–8402 | eaglenr@pacifier.com | www.eaglesnestresort.com | $100–$125 | D, MC, V.

Inn at Ilwaco. This B&B is in a renovated church building on quiet, dead-end street. | 9 rooms. Complimentary breakfast and afternoon snacks, no air-conditioning, no room phones, business services, no smoking. | 120 Williams St. N.E. | 360/642–8686 | fax 360/642–8642 | $89–$149 | MC, V.

INDEX

MAP 8, E4

(Nearby towns also listed: Skykomish, Snohomish)

Index illustrates one of the anomalies of western Washington geography; the village lies only 500 ft above sea level yet looks like a remote alpine settlement. That's because river valleys in western Washington are deeply glaciated and crowded by jagged ridges and tall peaks as you drive deeper into the mountains. Rising above Index are 5,979-ft-tall Mt. Index, and 6,125-ft-tall Mt. Baring. Besides logging, granite quarrying was once a major local industry. The nearby Cascades Tunnel was built to protect trains from the mountains' devastating avalanches.

Information: Sultan Chamber of Commerce | Box 46, Sultan, 98294 | 360/793–2565 | skyvalley.net.

Attractions

The Wall. The mammoth rock face that towers over this tiny community goes by the simple name "The Wall." You can climb the face, if you are so inclined, or you can take a dirt path to the top.

ON THE CALENDAR

JULY: ***Fourth of July Parade and Celebration.*** The Independence Day festival hosted by this quaint village is pure Americana. The parade and street fair are only two blocks long, but the enthusiasm and energy exerted are unmatched anywhere. | 360/793–2565.

Dining

Bush House Country Inn. American. Prime rib and pot pie are two of the favorites at this small inn, nestled between the trees and rocks. The 1898 inn has a back patio and garden in which to enjoy your dinner. Don't miss the blackberry cobbler. Sunday brunch is famous. | 300 5th St. | 360/793–2312 | No lunch | $12–$19 | D, DC, MC, V.

Lodging

Bush House Country Inn. Originally built as an inn in 1898, this structure abuts Town Wall, a rock face that towers over the village. The inn's many idiosyncracies, like the buckled wooden floors and its nooks and crannies, lend the rooms a rustic charm, something augmented by the selection of antiques that fill the rooms. | 11 rooms. Restaurant, bar, complimentary Continental breakfast, no room phones, no TV, no pets, no smoking. | 300 5th St. | 360/793–2312 | $80–$90 | D, DC, MC, V.

WA

ISSAQUAH

MAP 8, E4

(Nearby towns also listed: Bellevue, North Bend, Seattle)

ISSAQUAH

INTRO
ATTRACTIONS
DINING
LODGING

Once known mostly for the gliders (sailplanes) at its airport and for Boehm's Chocolates, Issaquah is now a generic suburban bedroom community at the southern end of Lake Sammamish. The airport is gone as the property was too valuable not to be developed into more lucrative real estate, but the candy store is still there, near the eastern edge of town, all but overwhelmed by suburban sprawl. Even so, salmon are still running seasonally in local streams. Note: There is a notorious WA State Patrol speed trap east of town on I–90.

Information:Issaquah Chamber of Commerce | 155 N.W. Gilman Blvd., Issaquah, 98027 | 425/392–7024 | ci.issaquah.wa.us/.

Attractions

Boehm's Chocolate Factory. You can tour the factory and see how the candy is made. | 255 N.E. Gilman Blvd. | 425/392–6652 | fax 425/557–0560 | www.chocoholic.com | Free | Tours: May–Sept., weekends 1 PM, by reservation.

Issaquah Salmon Hatchery. Depending on what time of the year you come, at the hatchery you can see adult salmon, their eggs, or juveniles waiting to be released into the ocean. | 125 W. Sunset Way | 425/391–9094 | Free | Daily 8–4:30.

Lake Sammamish State Park. This urban waterfront park 2 mi west of Issaquah has a swimming beach and a boat ramp, but no camping. | Off I–90W | 425/455–7010 or 800/233–0321 | www.parks.wa.gov | Free | Daily dawn–dusk.

ON THE CALENDAR

OCT.: ***Issaquah Salmon Days.*** Held on the first full weekend each October, this arts, crafts, and music festival celebrates the return of the spawning salmon. A Saturday parade on Front Street kicks off this family-oriented event. | 425/392–0661.

Dining

JaK's Grill. Steak. The specialty of this popular local restaurant is steak; people come from as far as Bellevue for it. The menu also includes seafood dishes and pastas. The large and open dining room is often loud and boisterous. | 14 Front St. | 425/837–8834 | No lunch | $12–$27 | DC, MC, V.

Lodging

Holiday Inn. Just north of I–90 at exit 15, this 2-story chain hotel sits on the north end of Issaquah, not even a mile south of Lake Sammamish State Park, and a little over a mile south of the Salmon Hatchery. To relax you might take a swim in the pool shaped like a giant salmon. | 100 rooms. Restaurant, bar, in-room data ports, room service, cable TV, pool, wading pool, laundry facilities, business services. | 1801 12th Ave. NW | 425/392–6421 | fax 425/391–4650 | $105–$119 | AE, D, DC, MC, V.

Water's Edge Guest House. The guest house, sitting directly on Lake Pine, is surrounded by well-manicured lawns. The rooms of the house are appointed with a mixture of elegant antiques and plush furniture. A covered patio overlooks the lake and private beach. Nature is not the only thing to distract you here; there are two TVs and two VCRs. | 1 room. No air-conditioning, kitchenettes, microwaves, refrigerators, cable TV, in-room VCRs, beach, boating, fishing, no pets, no kids under 12, no smoking. | 2736 222nd Ave. SE, Sammamish | 425/392–7727 | pinelakebb@aol.com | www.watersedgeonpinelake.com | $90–$110 | No credit cards.

KELSO

MAP 8, C7

(Nearby town also listed: Longview)

Kelso is the county seat of Cowlitz County, in a pleasant green valley above the Columbia River, at the confluence of the Cowlitz and Coweeman. Downtown Kelso has several interesting turn-of-the-20th-century buildings. The town's river levees are great for relaxed walking. Right off I–5 is a major shopping area with chain motels, restaurants, and all the usual amenities to serve Interstate travelers.

Information: Kelso Visitor and Volcanic Information Center | 105 Minor Rd., Kelso, 98626 | 360/577–8058 | www.rivercitieschamber.com.

Attractions

Castle Rock. The site takes its name from a tree-covered knob that once stood on the banks of the Cowlitz River and served as a navigational landmark for Hudson's Bay Company trappers and traders. The landscape changed dramatically when the 1980 Mt. St. Helens eruption filled the Toutle and Cowlitz Rivers with hot volcanic mush. Castle Rock's location on I–5 at the Spirit Lake Highway makes it a major point of entry for the Mt. St. Helens National Monument. A local visitor center has an exhibit hall portraying the history of Castle Rock and Mt. St. Helens. | Visitors Center: Hwy 504 | 360/274–2100.

Cowlitz County Historical Museum. On display is a good collection of Chinook and Cowlitz Indian, as well as Oregon Trail, artifacts. | 405 Allen St. | 360/577–3119 | www.cowlitz-county.org/museum | Donations accepted ($2 suggested) | Tues.–Sat. 9–5, Sun. 1–5.

Seaquest State Park. This 300-acre park offers campsites and a bass-fishing hole en route to Mt. St. Helens Coldridge Visitor Center. | Rte. 504 E | 360/274–8633 or 800/233–0321 | www.parks.wa.gov | Free, camping $12–$17 | Daily 8–dusk.

Volcano Information Center. Stop here for directions to Mt. St. Helens and its sights and amenities. | 105 Minor Rd. | 360/577–8058 | fax 360/578–2660 | Free | May–Oct., daily 8–6; Nov.–Apr., Wed.–Sun. 9–5.

ON THE CALENDAR

FEB.: *Quilt Show.* See an impressive display of locally made quilts at Castle Rock, north of Kelso on I–5 at the turn-off to Mt. St. Helens, exits 48 and 49. | 360/274–6603.

Dining

Kelso Theater Pub. Pizza. A mixture of a pub and theater; you can sit down and watch a feature while being served a beer or item from the somewhat limited menu. Pizzas, sandwiches, and salads are available. The movies are only shown at night. | 214 S. Pacific Ave., Longview | 360/414–9451 | No lunch | $3–$15 | MC, V.

Lodging

Blue Heron Inn Bed and Breakfast. This contemporary B&B, 10 mi north of Kelso, overlooks Silver Lake beyond which rises Mount St. Helens. Beautiful wood floors, exposed beams, and furnishings give the interior a clean, modern feel. For fresh air you can lounge on your private balcony overlooking the lake or you can relax on one of two verandas. The price of the room includes not only a breakfast but also a dinner. | 7 rooms. Complimentary breakfast, some in-room hot tubs, cable TV, no room phones, no pets, no kids under 5, no smoking. | 2846 Spirit Lake Hwy., Castle Rock | 360/274–9595 or 800/959–4049 | www.blueheroninn.com | $165–$215 | D, MC, V.

Comfort Inn. Comfortable business travelers' and family motel. | 57 rooms. Complimentary Continental breakfast, in-room data ports, cable TV, in-room VCRs, indoor pool, hot tub, gym, game room, business services, free parking. | 440 Three Rivers Dr. | 360/425–4600 | fax 360/423–0762 | $69–$84 | AE, D, DC, MC, V.

KENNEWICK

MAP 8, I7

(Nearby towns also listed: Pasco, Richland)

In its 100-year history, Kennewick has undergone many changes, from railroad town, to farm-supply center, to bedroom community for Hanford workers from nearby Richland, to food-processing capital of the Columbia Basin. The climate is much more mild here than in other parts of eastern Washington. The name Kennewick translates as "grassy place," and Native Americans had winter villages here, at the confluence of the Columbia and the Yakima, long before the first white explorers, Lewis and Clark, visited the region. Proof that this river flat was settled long ago comes not only from arrowheads and other artifacts found here, but from a most unusual discovery: the 9,000-year-old skeleton of Kennewick Man, which is currently being studied by scientists at the University of Washington, to determine if its features are Indian or, as some claim, Caucasian.

Beautiful, 3-mi-long Columbia Park runs along the west bank of the Columbia River. The Kennewick Man skeleton was discovered here. In summer, hydroplane races are held here.

Information: Tri-Cities Visitor and Convention Bureau | 6951 W. Grandridge Blvd., Tri-Cities, 99302 | 800/254–5824 | visittri-cities.com.

Attractions

Columbia Park. The 3-mi-long riverfront park is one of Washington State's great parks, with boat ramps, a golf course, picnic area, and tennis courts. | U.S. 12W to Lake Wallula | 509/783–3711 | Daily.

East Benton County Historical Museum. The entire entryway is made of petrified wood, a unique architectural feature that was part of the impetus for the museum's construction. Photographs, agricultural displays, and a large collection of arrowheads help to tell the history of the local area. | 205 Keewaydin Dr. | 509/582–7704 | www.owl.com/ebchs | $2 | Tues.–Sat. 12–4.

Two Rivers Park. You'll find this park on the west bank of the Columbia. Lake Wallula is across from the mouth of the Snake River, north of Wallula Gap. The park has a boat ramp, swimming beach, and picnic tables. | U.S. 397, left on Finley Rd. | 509/783–3118 | Free | Daily.

ON THE CALENDAR

JULY: ***Columbia Cup Hydroplane Races.*** Annual boat race down the Columbia River takes place on the last Sunday in July. | 509/547–2203.

AUG.: ***Benton Franklin County Fair.*** There's a Rodeo, entertainment, and a variety of food at the county fairgrounds. | 509/586–9211.

Dining

Blue Moon. Contemporary. A stone fireplace stands in the center of this intimate dining room where candles and fresh flowers set the tone. The prix-fixe menu changes every month but usually includes a rack of lamb and ostrich entrée such as sautéed ostrich with a wild mushroom demi-glace. | 20 W. Canal Dr. | 509/582–6598 | Reservations essential | No lunch. Closed Sun.–Thurs. | $30 | MC, V.

Casa Chapala. Mexican. At this delightful restaurant the dishes are as authentic as Mexican fare gets hereabouts. It is known for an extensive menu, including arroz con pollo and chile verde. Kids' menu. No smoking. | 107 E. Columbia Drive | 509/582–7848 | $6–$15 | AE, D, DC, MC, V.

Sundance Grill. Contemporary. Table candles and live piano music make this restaurant an intimate, romantic spot for dinner. Sandwiches, salads, and pasta dishes are served at lunch, while fresh seafood entrées such as seared salmon with garlic shrimp sherry sauce fill the dinner menu. The wine list proudly includes many Washington wines. | 413 N. Kellogg | 509/783–6505 | Reservations essential on weekends | $12–$30 | AE, D, MC, V.

Lodging

Best Western Kennewick Inn. One of Kennewick's newest lodgings, this chain is conveniently close to I–82, to the city's shopping, restaurants, and to an 18-hole golf course. | 87 rooms. In-room data ports, microwaves, refrigerators, some in-room hot tubs, cable TV, pool, hot tub, sauna, gym, laundry services, business services, pets allowed (fee). | 4001 W. 27th Ave. | 509/586–1332 | fax 509/586–0263 | www.bestwestern.com | $74 | AE, D, DC, MC, V.

Casablanca Bed and Breakfast. Orchards, vineyards, and pastures surround this quaint B&B in the middle of this burgeoning wine region. Each of the uniquely appointed rooms has French doors which lead to a garden terrace. The lodging is close to 10 golf courses and the Columbia River. | 3 rooms. Complimentary Continental breakfast, no room phones, TV in common area, horseback riding, no pets, no smoking. | 94806 E. Granada Ct. | 509/627–0676 or 888/627–0676 | fax 509/627–0768 | casab-b@oneworld.owt.com | www.owt.com/casablancabb | $65–$85.

Cavanaugh's at Columbia Center. This comfortable conference and convention hotel is next to a major regional shopping mall. | 161 rooms. Restaurant, bar with entertainment, room service, cable TV, pool, hot tub, gym, business services, airport shuttle, pets allowed (fee). | 1101 N. Columbia Center Blvd. | 509/783–0611 or 800/325–4000 | fax 509/735–3087 | $60–$125 | AE, D, DC, MC, V.

Nendels Inn. This is a two-story family motel in the center of town. | 106 rooms. Some kitchenettes, some refrigerators, cable TV, pool, business services, pets allowed (fee). | 2811 W. 2nd | 509/735–9511 or 800/547–0106 | fax 509/735–1944 | $43–$63 | AE, D, DC, MC, V.

Silver Cloud Inn. Comfortable business travelers' and family hotel. | 125 rooms, 30 suites. Complimentary Continental breakfast, refrigerators, cable TV, 2 pools (1 indoor), hot tub, gym, laundry facilities, business services. | 7901 W. Quinault Ave. | 509/735–6100 | fax 509/735–3084 | $52–$120, $110–$120 suites | AE, D, DC, MC, V.

Tapadera Inn. This budget motel, is within walking distance of movie theaters and restaurants. | 61 rooms. Restaurant, complimentary Continental breakfast, some refrigerators, cable TV, pool, pets allowed (fee). | 300 N. Ely | 509/783–6191 | fax 509/735–3854 | $38–$56 | AE, D, DC, MC, V.

KENT

MAP 8, D4

(Nearby town also listed: Renton)

A former truck gardening community once served by steamboats from Seattle, Kent has recently become an industrial suburb with its own Boeing plant space center.

Information: City of Kent | 220 4th Ave. S., Kent, 98032 | 253/859–3355 | www.ci.kent.wa.us.

Attractions

Kent Market. A 1902 barn is the center of the market which has over 75 vendors selling everything from yard art and crafts to fresh popcorn. Toys, jewelry, soaps, and flowers are among some of the other goods on sale. | 206 Railroad Ave. N | 253/813–6976 | Free | Tues.–Sat. 9–5; Sun. 11–4.

ON THE CALENDAR

JULY: *Cornucopia Days.* The Northwest's largest street fair with almost 600 vendors, this festival, held on the second weekend in July, occupies many of Kent's downtown streets. The festivities include a carnival, live entertainment, and a parade. | 253/852–5466.

Dining

Paolo's Italian Restaurant. Italian. Among the many wonderful dishes served at this hillside restaurant decorated with earth tones, are the filet of steak prepared in a red wine and gorgonzola sauce and the fettucine Paolo served with grilled chicken, artichokes, and sundried tomatoes. The sautéed calamari is a favorite appetizer. | 23810 104th Ave SE | 253/850–2233 | No lunch weekends | $8.50–$18 | AE, MC, V.

Lodging

Victorian Gardens 1888 Bed and Breakfast. This elegant Victorian sits on 2 acres amid sprawling lawns, gardens, and orchards. Wood paneling and antique furnishings complement the many other Victorian-era details. Each of the individually appointed rooms has its own covered balcony that overlooks the property and its grounds. | 3 rooms. Complimentary breakfast, in-room data ports, cable TV, in-room VCRs, no smoking. | 9621 S. 200th St. | 253/850–1776 or 888/850–1776 | fax 253/850–8590 | info@victoriangardensbandb.com | www.victoriangardensbandb.com | $125 | AE, MC, V.

KIRKLAND

MAP 7, E1

(Nearby town also listed: Bellevue)

Kirkland is a pleasant lakefront town on the eastern shore of 20-mi-long Lake Washington. Downtown Kirkland is officially centered on Moss Bay, an inlet that has not existed since the Seattle Ship Canal was completed in 1916, lowering the level of the lake by nine feet. Kirkland began in the late 1800s as a mill town for processing locally dug iron ore into steel. But neither the mine nor the mill ever materialized, and Kirkland soon became the quiet residential community it is today.

Kirkland's downtown is very pedestrian-friendly, with shops, galleries, and lakefront restaurants. It has more publicly owned waterfront than any other town on the lake.

Information: Greater Kirkland Chamber of Commerce | 401 Parkplace, Suite 102, Kirkland, 98033 | 425/822–7066 | kirklandchamber.org.

Attractions

Marina Park. Wide lawns, a long waterfront promenade, and a spacious pavilion make this a perfect place to relax, exercise, or picnic. The park is located downtown off Central and Kirkland Avenues. | 425/828–1217.

© Corbis

BALD EAGLES

Bald eagles are so ubiquitous in Washington State, to both sides of the Cascade Mountains (wherever there are large bodies of water), that they can lay claim to the title of "state bird" (rather than the goldfinch). Though their numbers plummeted during the notorious DDT era, the big birds were never endangered here.

You cannot mistake mature bald eagles for any other bird: their large size and white heads and tails are too distinctive. But immatures are more difficult to identify and have been confused with golden eagles, which are also quite common in parts of Washington. I have seen bald eagles gliding past me below the basalt cliffs of the lower Columbia River, watched them as they effortlessly kept pace with a San Juan Island's ferry, and spotted them from low-flying seaplanes, unperturbed by the presence of their noisy mechanical cousins. They congregate each fall in vast numbers on the upper Skagit River, to feed on spawned-out salmon, but I have also seen them soar above my backyard, eyeing the pigeons and crows assembled on my roof, and I have seen them flying low over backyards in Seattle. They do not seem to mind the presence of man.

About six pairs nest each year, within city limits; others nest in suburban Kent and on Chuckanut Island. On the Samish Bay flats, north of Burlington, they sometimes sit on power lines. They can also be spotted on snags along rocky Chuckanut Drive, as they scan the waters below, waiting for prey. Like the birds, the nests are big and bulky—some are more than twelve feet across. The eagles prefer to build their nests in tall trees, but in the treeless expanses of the Columbia Basin, they may settle for rocky crags and tors near lakes and rivers. They have even been known to build ground nests on islands.

At one nest, in Kent, a web cam has recorded that the young are fed mainly on fish and crows, but eagles are also scavengers. They will eat anything. One gentleman farmer near Sequim is trying to get them to take food from his hand by setting pieces of meat onto fence posts, but so far the eagles have played coy. But they swoop down to grab the meat as soon as he turns his back.

Bald eagles have also been known to follows fishing boats, begging for scraps in the manner of gulls. Look for bald eagles resting atop snags (tall dead trees), or flying along the shore looking for prey-dead or alive. But be prepared to encounter them almost anywhere there is water. And don't be afraid. Bald eagles do not attack humans; not even small children (as popular myths sometimes incorrectly claim).

ON THE CALENDAR

SEPT.: ***Taste! Kirkland Family Festival.*** Held on the third weekend in September at Marina Park, the festival is an introduction to the many wonderful restaurants in the Kirkland area. In addition to food booths, the festivities include a 10K run, a bike and dog parade, and many art booths from local galleries. | 425/822–7066.

Dining

Bistro Provençal. French. What has been bringing people back for decades to this popular French restaurant near the Kirkland waterfront, besides the food, is the old-country ambience. The food is superb, whether it's the simple onion soup, or the more ambitious preparation of duck or lamb. | 212 Central Way | 425/827–3300 | No lunch | $20–$30 | AE, DC, MC, V.

Cafe Juanita. Italian. The casual and comfortable dining room overlooks a park. The carefully prepared, country Italian food has been consistently good for more than 20 years. The proprietor Peter Dow made history in the mid-1980s when he became the first restaurateur to be allowed to make his own wine (it called for a change in state liquor law); today his Cavatappi winery, in the restaurant's basement, is so successful, the wines are rarely listed on the restaurant's wine list, since new vintages sell out almost immediately. But the winery's success has not affected the quality of the food and service in the restaurant. There's no printed menu, by the way; all of the night's dishes are listed on an oversized blackboard. Open-air dining. Kids' menu, no smoking. | 9702 120th Pl. N.E. | 425/823–6533 | No lunch | $15–$27 | AE, MC, V.

The Herbfarm. Contemporary. The sumptuous nine-course meals served here are the paradigm for Pacific Northwest cuisine. The delectables you will encounter include goat cheese biscuits, green pickled walnuts, and salmon with a sauce of fresh herbs. The restaurant moved to this location, approximately 10 mi northeast of Kirkland, from Issaquah at the beginning of 2001. | 14590 N.E. 145th, Woodinville | 206/784–2222 | Reservations essential | No lunch | $150 | AE, MC, V.

Mondo Shrimp. Seafood. This seafood-only restaurant has recently branched out from its original downtown Olympia location and opened a satellite restaurant on the Kirkland waterfront. Here, too, it serves nothing but shrimp in various, generally spicy preparations. | 166 Lake St. | 425/893–9458 | $10–$16 | AE, DC, MC, V.

Third Floor Fish Cafe. Seafood. This intimate, clubby restaurant, with boats moored near the shore, may well serve Kirkland's best seafood. It should, since it's also pricey, and Eastsiders like to get their money's worth. No smoking. | 205 Lake St. S | 425/822–3553 | Reservations accepted | No lunch | $21–$36 | AE, D, DC, MC, V.

Tommy Thai's. Thai. In the Rose Hill Shopping Mall, this is one of the most popular Thai restaurants in the region. The entrées, spiced with ingredients such as lemon grass, lime leaf, and basil, tend to run on the spicy side, so be warned. | 8516 122nd Ave. NE | 425/889–2447 | $6–$10 | MC, V.

Waters Lakeside Bistro. Contemporary. Panoramic views dominate this dining room which is located inside the Woodmark Hotel. The restaurant's "bistro cuisine" includes Dungeness crab cakes, tenderloin steaks, and pan-seared salmon. Outdoor seating under canvas umbrellas is available during the warmer months. | 1200 Carillon Point | 425/803–5595 | mail@watersbistro.com | www.watersbistro.com | Breakfast also available. No dinner on Sun. | $16.50–$29.50 | AE, DC, MC, V.

Yarrow Bay Grill and Beach Café. Seafood. Adjacent to the marina, the restaurant and café have large windows and outdoor decks overlooking the boats and Lake Washington. Upstairs at the grill, the gleaming hardwood details, tables, and booths create an elegant environment to enjoy such imaginative seafood dishes as braised halibut served wrapped in red chard with a fennel-vegetable broth. The downstairs café is more casual, serving fish and chips and pastas. | 1270 Carrillon Point | 425/889–0303 | $15–$27 | AE, D, MC, V.

Lodging

Best Western Kirkland Inn. Sitting conveniently at exit 20A off I–405, this chain hotel is only 1 mi from shopping, dining, and Lake Washington. | 110 rooms. Complimentary Continental breakfast, some microwaves, some refrigerators, some in-room hot tubs, cable TV, pool, hot tub, laundry facilities, pets allowed. | 12223 N.E. 116th St. | 425/822–2300 or 800/332–4200 | fax 425/889–9616 | www.bestwestern.com | AE, D, DC, MC, V.

Cottage Creek Inn. Five mi east of Kirkland, the 3½ acres of property includes a pond, gazebo, flower gardens, and woods. Each room of this Tudor-style house has its own distinctive features; the gabled windows and skylights of the Stephanotis Room, for instance, allow you to count stars at night, or watch the pond and creek for fowl. | 4 rooms. Complimentary breakfast, no air-conditioning, some in-room hot tubs, some in-room VCRs, pool, pond, hot tub, no pets, no smoking. | 12525 Avondale Rd. NE | 425/881–5606 | cotcreek@brigadoon.com | www.cottagecreekinn.com | $89–$125 | AE, MC, V.

Shumway Mansion. A very elegant and comfortable inn, two blocks from Juanita beach, and close to downtown Kirkland. It is near nature trails and parks. | 8 rooms. Complimentary breakfast and evening snacks, no air-conditioning, in-room data ports, business services, no kids under 12, no smoking. | 11410 99th Place NE | 425/823–2303 | fax 425/822–0421 | www.shumwaymansion.com | $70–$105 | AE, MC, V.

Silver Cloud Inn. Built in 1982, this two-story hotel is set among carefully manicured gardens and is close to most Kirkland attractions. | 99 rooms. Complimentary Continental breakfast, in-room data ports, refrigerators, room service, cable TV, pool, hot tub, exercise equipment, laundry facilities, business services. | 12202 N.E. 124th St. | 425/821–8300 or 800/205–6933 (reservations) | fax 425/823–1218 | www.scinns.com | $78–$175 | AE, D, DC, MC, V.

Woodmark Hotel on Lake Washington. Just 7 mi east of Seattle, this hotel is on the banks of Lake Washington. Every room has a view of either the lake, the marina, or the creek. | 100 rooms, 21 suites. 2 Restaurants, bar, complimentary evening snacks, room service, in-room data ports, minibars, refrigerators, cable TV, spa, marina, business services. | 1200 Carillon Point | 425/822–3700 or 800/822–3700 | fax 425/822–3699 | woodmarkhotel@compuserve.com | www.thewoodmark.com | $195–$250, $305–$1400 suites | AE, DC, MC, V.

LA CONNER

MAP 8, D2

(Nearby towns also listed: Anacortes, Mount Vernon)

This small waterfront town on the east bank of the Swinomish Channel, which separates Fidalgo Island from the mainland, has a well-preserved false-front business district along the waterfront and an attractive residential neighborhood of mostly 19th-century houses on the hill above. Newer houses spread across the flats, which were a waterlogged swamp and sloughs until they were drained early in the 20th century.

La Conner was founded as a trading post in 1867 along the important waterway that allowed steamers to pass from Seattle to Bellingham Bay without having to brave strong tidal currents and potentially devastating storms off Whidbey Island's western shore. By 1875, as the Skagit lowlands were diked and drained, La Conner served as a steamer port for carrying Skagit Valley hay, grain, and produce to Seattle.

Today vast tulip fields spread across the flats north of La Conner. With a number of comfortable B&Bs, waterfront restaurants, galleries, and shops, La Conner has become a mecca for weekend trippers from Pugetopolis.

Information:La Conner Chamber of Commerce | Box 1610, 41 A. Morris St., La Conner, 98257 | 888/642–9284 | laconnerchamber.com.

Attractions

Gaches Mansion. A collection of turn-of-the-20th-century furnishings are displayed on the first floor of this Victorian mansion, while the Quilt Museum exhibits its large collection of quilts on the second and third floors. | 703 S. 2nd St. | 360/466–4288 | $3 | Wed.–Sat. 11–4; Sun. 12–4.

Museum of Northwest Art. A collection of works by artists living or working in La Conner and the Skagit Valley are displayed. This is not to be confused with the art of Northwest Indians. | 121 S. 1st St. | 360/466–4446 | fax 360/466–7431 | $3 | Tues.–Sun. 10–5; closed Mon.

Roozengaarde. This is the largest cultivator of tulips, daffodils, and irises in the United States. There are over 200 varieties here to choose from. | 15867 Beaver Marsh Rd. | 360/424–8531 | Mar.–May, daily 9–5; June–Feb., Mon.–Sat. 9–5.

Skagit County Historical Museum. A great little museum on the very top of the hill with a lot of interesting artifacts including a moonshine still, still in working order. | 501 Fourth St. | 360/466–3365 | fax 360/466–1611 | www.home.skagit | $2 | Tues.–Sun. 11–5.

Volunteer Fireman's Museum. The turn-of-the-20th-century fire equipment at this museum is visible through the building's large windows. | 611 S. 1st St. | No phone.

ON THE CALENDAR

APR.: *Skagit Valley Tulip Festival.* Two-week festival with art shows, street fairs, and a salmon barbecue. The festival is centered in Mount Vernon, but most of the tulip fields are within a mile or so of La Conner. | 360/428–5959.

Dining

Calico Cupboard. Café. This storefront bakery/café turns out some of the best pastries in Skagit County. The place is very popular for breakfast and lunch and can become uncomfortably crowded on summer weekends (in which case you can buy the goodies at the take-out counter for a picnic in the park). | 720 S. 1st St. | 360/466–4451 | Breakfast also available. No dinner | $5–$15 | No credit cards.

Kerstin's. Contemporary. The small, intimate dining room is located on the restaurant's second floor overlooking the channel. The menu, which changes seasonally, includes fresh king salmon, pork tenderloin, tenderloin steak, halibut, and lamb shank. The oysters baked in a garlic-cilantro butter and finished with Parmesan are particularly popular. | 505 S. 1st St. | 360/466–9111 | Closed Tues. | $16–$28 | AE, DC, MC, V.

Palmer's Restaurant and Pub. American. Palmer's is La Conner's favorite restaurant. It's a comfortable place, on a hillside with the pub–the favorite local watering hole–downstairs, and the dining room above. The food preparations tend to be hearty and straightforward. Try the wilted spinach salad with smoked duck, or halibut Amontillado (which is hazelnut-crusted halibut with sherry). Open-air dining on the deck. | 205 E. Washington St. | 360/466–4261 | Lunch only on weekends | $22–$28 | AE, MC, V.

Lodging

Country Inn. This quaint and charming inn is just off the waterfront, and has cathedral ceilings and fireplaces. | 28 rooms. Dining room, complimentary Continental breakfast, no air-conditioning, room service, cable TV, business services. | 107 S. Second St. | 360/466–3101 or 888/466–4113 | fax 360/466–5902 | laconnerlodging.com | $93–$150 | AE, D, DC, MC, V.

Heron. This B&B, in a Victorian house, has a stone fireplace in the parlor. The rooms are spacious, and the homemade breads and muffins served with breakfast are scrumptious. | 9 rooms, 3 suites. Complimentary breakfast, no air-conditioning, hot tub, some pets allowed (fee). | 117 Maple Ave. | 360/466–4626 | fax 360/466–3254 | $100, $125–150 suites | AE, MC, V.

Hotel Planter. The oldest hotel in La Conner, this building is on the National Register of Historic Places. Handmade country-style furniture fills the homey rooms which have wonderful views of the courtyard or waterfront. | 12 rooms. Cable TV, hot tub, no pets, no kids under 10, no smoking. | 715 1st St. | 360/466–4710 or 800/488–5409 | fax 360/466–1320 | $79–$129 | AE, MC, V.

Katy's Inn. This B&B is in a comfortable, beautifully restored Victorian house. All the rooms have French doors, and there are two ponds and waterfalls, as well as a gazebo, on the grounds. It is within walking distance of galleries, shops, and restaurants. | 2 rooms, 2 suites. Picnic area, dining room, complimentary breakfast and evening snacks, no air-conditioning, some cable TV, no room phones, hot tub. | 503 S. Third | 360/466–3366 or 800/914–7767 (reservations) | www.home.ncia.com/katysinn | $90–$125 | D, MC, V.

La Conner Channel Lodge. This luxurious cedar lodge on the La Conner waterfront has great views. | 40 rooms. Complimentary Continental breakfast, some hot tubs in rooms, no-smoking rooms. | 205 N. 1st | 360/466–1500 | fax 360/466–1525 | laconnerlodging.com | $119–$254 | AE, D, DC, MC, V.

Rainbow. This B&B in a turn-of-the-20th-century farmhouse ½ mi east of town has a view of Mt. Baker and the North Cascade Mountains. There are lovely gardens and you can't stay much closer to the tulip fields of spring. | 8 rooms (3 with shared bath). Picnic area, complimentary breakfast, no room phones, hot tub, no smoking. | 12757 Chilberg Rd. | 360/466–4578 | $80–$115 | D, MC, V.

Ridgeway Farm Bed and Breakfast. Occupying a prime spot on Skagit Valley's justly famous Tulip Route, this 1928 brick Dutch Colonial sits among 100,000 tulips and daffodils. Early American antiques, lace curtains, and quilts harmonize nicely with each room's architectural details. | 6 rooms (4 with private bath), 1 suite. Complimentary breakfast, no air-conditioning, no room phones, TV in common area, no smoking. | 14914 McLean Rd. | 360/428–8068 or 800/428–8068 | fax 360/428–8880 | ridgeway@winstarmail.com | www.placestostay.com/LaCon-RidgewayFarm | $95–$115, $175 suite | AE, D, MC, V.

Wild Iris. Right next to the Heron, this B&B is also in a Victorian inn, and features a restaurant called Cafe Flats. | 7 rooms, 12 suites. Restaurant, complimentary breakfast, no air-conditioning. | 121 Maple Ave. | 360/466–1400 | $115–$180 | AE, MC, V.

LANGLEY

MAP 8, D3

(Nearby towns also listed: Everett, Marysville)

Langley is a very pleasant bluff-top village on south Whidbey Island; its business district spreads out on a low bluff above a shingle beach. A terrace below the bluff has been turned into a greensward and picnic area. Langley has galleries, a performing arts center, superb restaurants and inns, interesting shops, a regionally famous tavern, a microbrewery, and—nearby—a winery.

Information: Langley Chamber of Commerce | Box 403, Langley, 98260 | 360/221–5676 | www.whidbey.com¢langley.

Attractions

South Whidbey Historical Museum. In a former bunk house built at the turn of the 20th century, this museum displays old Victrolas, farm tools, kitchen utensils, and antique toys. | 312 2nd St. | 360/221–2101 | Donation | Weekends, 1–4.

ON THE CALENDAR

AUG.: ***Island County Fair.*** Live entertainment and food vendors. | 360/221–4677.

Dining

Country Kitchen. Contemporary. The dining room's focus at this restaurant at the Inn at Langley is the open kitchen where you can see the chef prepare and cook your meal. Relying primarily on local produce and meats, dinners may include such dishes as mussels in a black-bean sauce, breast of duck in a loganberry sauce, or Columbia River salmon. The five-course prix-fixe dinner is served only on Friday and Saturday (and Sunday from late May to September). | 400 1st St. | 360/221–3033 | Reservations essential | $75 | AE, MC, V.

Doghouse Backdoor Restaurant. American/Casual. Folks come all the way from Seattle to relax at this old-time waterfront tavern/family restaurant. The food is not fancy but it is tasty: hamburgers, fries, homemade chili, pizza, and low-salt vegetarian dishes. Local microbrews are on tap, and the back room has a fine view of Saratoga Passage and, on clear days, of distant Mt. Baker. Entertainment Fri.–Sat. | 230 1st St. | 360/221–9825 | $5–$12 | No credit cards.

Garibyan Brothers Cafe Langley. Mediterranean. A pleasant street-front café with terra-cotta tile floors, oak tables, hanging plants, and exotic aromas. The Garibyan brothers are Armenian, and the menu runs the gamut of dishes from the Levant to western America. Try the mixed grill, the Mediterranean seafood stew, or the Washington lamb. No smoking. | 113 First St. | 360/221–3090 | Closed Nov.–Apr., Tues. | $15–$25 | AE, MC, V.

Star Bistro. Contemporary. The Star Store has everything a specialty general store should have; the elegant little bistro upstairs turns some of these ingredients into sumptuous dishes with a Northwest flare and an emphasis on fresh seafood. Open-air dining on the deck, with nice views of the water. Kids' menu. No smoking. | 201½ 1st St. | 360/221–2627 | Closed Mon. | $10–$23 | AE, MC, V.

Trattoria Giuseppe. Italian. Everything is just right in this tiny café in a strip mall on the island's main highway—the pasta, the mussels, the ambience—once you step into the Tuscan interior. | 4141 E. Hwy. 525 | 360/341–3454 | No lunch weekends | $10–$20 | AE, D, DC, MC, V.

Lodging

Country Cottage of Langley. Standing on 2 landscaped acres that were once a farm, this 1927 farmhouse overlooks downtown Langley, the water, and the Cascade Mountains. Dormer windows and a gabled entrance are some of the charming architectural details, complemented by the interior's stone fireplace and white-washed wainscoting. Other distinctive features include the dining room's murals which depict the four seasons. Rooms are appointed according to their themes; some have fireplaces and views of the mountains or water. | 5 rooms, 1 cottage. Complimentary breakfast, refrigerators, some in-room hot tubs, cable TV, in-room VCRs, hot tub, no smoking. | 215 6th St. | 360/221–8709 or 800/713–3860 | www.acountrycottage.com | $129–$179 | AE, MC, V.

Drake's Landing. At the edge of town, across the street from the harbor, this is Langley's most affordable lodging. The room is humble but clean with a quilt on the bed. | 1 room. No air-conditioning, cable TV, no room phones, no smoking. | 203 Wharf St. | 360/221–3999 | $65 | MC, V.

Eagle's Nest. Views of the Saratoga Passage and Cascade Mountains abound at this hilltop inn. The octagonal shape of the contemporary building allows for maximum privacy in the rooms, each of which has a private balcony. The living room's 17-ft brick fireplace is flanked by elongated octagonal windows in clear and peach-color glass. | 4 rooms, 1 cottage. Complimentary breakfast, cable TV, in-room VCRs, no room phones, hot tub, hiking, no pets, no kids under 12, no smoking. | 4680 Saratoga Rd. | 360/221–5331 | eaglnest@whidbey.com | www.eaglesnestinn.com | $95–$235 | D, MC, V.

Inn at Langley. Very elegant and exceedingly comfortable waterfront inn at the north end of town. The meals served in the dining room are among Washington's great culinary experiences. | 24 rooms, 4 cottages. Complimentary Continental breakfast, no air-conditioning, in-room data ports, refrigerators, in-room hot tubs, cable TV, in-room VCRs (movies), business services, no kids under 12, no smoking. | 400 First St. | 360/221–3033 | fax 360/221–3033 | www.innatlangley.com | $199–$375, $495 cottages | AE, MC, V.

Lone Lake Cottage and Breakfast. Here, you can stay in a cottage, a lakeside suite, or a houseboat. The boat has a queen-size loft bed and tiny galley; the cottages have rattan and soap-stone-inlaid furniture, Oriental screens, and covered decks. | 1 houseboat, 1 suite, 2 cottages. Complimentary Continental breakfast, kitchenettes, microwaves, refrigerators, in-room hot tubs, cable TV, in-room VCRs, boating, fishing, bicycles, no smoking. | 5206 S. Bayview Rd. | 360/321–5325 | www.lonelake.com | $140 | No credit cards.

Saratoga Inn. This inn—formerly known as Harrison House—sits at the edge of Langley, within walking distance of the town's shops and restaurants. Wood shingle siding, gabled roofs, and wraparound porches lend the inn a Pacific Northwest authenticity. This theme extends to the interior which is adorned with wood floors and fireplaces. The carriage house offers more privacy. | 15 rooms, 1 carriage house. Complimentary breakfast, no air-conditioning, cable TV, business services, no pets, no smoking. | 201 Cascade Ave. | 360/221–5801 or 800/698–2910 | fax 360/221–5804 | www.foursisters.com | $110–$275 | AE, D, MC, V.

LEAVENWORTH

MAP 8, G4

(Nearby towns also listed: Cashmere, Wenatchee)

The best thing that can be said about this "Bavarian" village is that its architecture becomes more "authentic" with each tourist season. Architectural "theme" pieces started out as appliqué panels slapped onto the outside of generic, flat-roofed, slab-sided shop buildings, but they are becoming more integrated as new buildings go up. The facades appear to work, as this former railroad town is very popular with tourists. But what really works is the mountain scenery, which is truly spectacular in all seasons.

Information:Leavenworth Chamber of Commerce | Box 327, 894 Hwy. 2, Leavenworth, 98826 | 509/548–5807 | www.leavenworth.org.

Attractions

Icicle Junction. This is an amusement arcade in the wilderness replete with bumper car rides, miniature golf, and other activities. | U.S. 2 at Icicle Rd. | 509/548–2400 | Mon. noon–6, Sat. 10–9, Sun. 10–5.

Leavenworth Ski Hill. Not only can you enjoy great skiing here, thanks in part to a Nordic ski jump, but in summer the hill provides a wonderful place to enjoy the wildflowers or view the Leavenworth Summer Theatre's production of "The Sound of Music." The ski hill is located 1 mi north of downtown Leavenworth. | Ski Hill Dr. | 509/548–5807.

National Fish Hatchery. Salmon and trout hatched here are released into the river in the hope they will return someday to spawn and keep the species alive while still providing fish for fishermen to catch. | 12790 Fish Hatchery Rd. | 509/548–7641 | www.lvnwcmplx.org | Free | Daily 8–4.

Nutcracker Museum. A collection of thousands of nutcrackers made famous by ballet and literature is on display. | 735 Front St. | 509/548–4708 | fax 509/548–4760 | www.tannenbaumshoppe.com | $2.50 | May–Oct., daily 9–6; Nov.–Apr., weekends and by appointment.

ON THE CALENDAR

JAN.: ***Bavarian Ice Fest.*** This winter festival has dogsled rides, a NW Regional Dogsled Pulling Competition, sleigh rides, an ice cube hunt for kids, snow sculpturing, and fireworks. | 509/548–5807.

FEB.: ***Fasching.*** A Bavarian-style "Mardi Gras" celebration; live music, dancing in the streets, contest for best costume. | 509/548–5807.

MAY: ***Maifest.*** A spring bash with beautiful flowers, oompah music, a Grand March (parade), and Bavarian dances. | 509/548–5807.

DEC.: ***Christmas Lighting.*** Annual event to kick off the holiday season. | 509/548–5807.

Dining

Andreas Keller. German. The portions of hearty German fare like spaetzle, Wiener schnitzel, and red cabbage are large at this fun, kid-friendly eatery. From June to January there is music every night, and from January to May music is played four nights a week. If you're lucky, an accordion player will be on hand to play traditional German themes tableside. | 829 Front St. | 509/548–6000 | $8–$17 | MC, V.

Baran Haus. American. The spacious, noisy, and often crowded dining room evokes the beer halls of Austria and Germany. The servings are generous and the prices low for the basic American fare such as burgers, fries, and salads. | 208 9th St. | 509/548–4535 | $6–$16 | MC, V.

Danish Bakery. Café. This small shop specializes in tasty homemade pastries and strong espresso drinks. The cinnamon bread and pretzels are two of the favorites. | 731 Front St. | 509/548–7514 | $1.50 | No credit cards.

Home Fires Bakery. Café. This homey bakery, with a German wood-fired oven, turns out several absolutely delicious breads, as well as muffins, cinnamon rolls, and other baked goods. Take-out only, but on a sunny day you can sit outside at a picnic table and enjoy the view while sipping coffee and munching on goodies. | 13013 Bayne Rd. | 509/548–7362 | Closed Tues.–Wed. | $1–$15 | D, MC, V.

Lorraine's Edel House. Eclectic. The dining rooms are candlelit in this pleasant quiet restaurant that serves up international dishes. Known for Asian-accented pastas, game (grilled wild boar), fish, and braised oxtail. Try the portobello mushrooms with goat cheese, or the mussels in an orange cream sauce. | 320 Ninth St., Leavenworth | 509/548–4412 | No lunch | $15–$23 | D, MC, V.

Restaurant Oesterreich. Austrian. At this cellar restaurant, the chef dishes up truly sumptuous fare—food that ranks with the best Europe has to offer: crawfish strudel, marinated duck breast in a dumpling coating, or braised lamb shank. But keep in mind that the menu changes daily, depending on what foods are fresh and in season. Open-air dining on the patio with a view of the river from May–Oct. | Tyrolean Ritz Hotel, 633A Front St. | 509/548–4031 | Nov.–Apr., closed Mon.–Tues., lunch on weekends only; May–Oct., closed Mon. | $16–$30 | AE, D, DC, MC, V.

Visconti's. Italian. Adjacent to Leavenworth's only brewery, this eatery serves all the beers made next door. The menu includes pastas, pizzas, and other Italian favorites. Especially popular is the pasta with prawns. The upstairs has a more elegant feel with table cloths and jazz music, while the downstairs has coppertop tables and wooden chairs, more reminiscent of a pub. | 636 Front St. | 509/548–1213 | $11–$18 | AE, D, MC, V.

Lodging

Abendblume Pension. The carved wood walls and ceilings of this Austrian-style country chalet give it an authentic Alpine appearance. The B&B, 3/4 of a mile from downtown Leavenworth, overlooks the Leavenworth valley. Wonderful views of the mountains and valley are afforded from each room's private balcony. Rooms are individually decorated; four have wood-burning fireplaces. | 7 rooms. Complimentary breakfast, some in-room hot tubs, in-room VCRs, hot tub, spa, no pets, no kids under 12, no smoking. | 12570 Ranger Rd. | 509/548–4059 or 800/669–7634 | fax 509/548–4059 | abendblm@rightathome.com | www.abendblume.com | $85–$165 | AE, D, MC, V.

Best Western Icicle Inn. A "Bavarian"-style, somewhat noisy but comfortable motel. There is a "Fun Center" on the property, with video games, mini-golf, bumper boats, concessions, and a movie theater. | 93 rooms. Complimentary breakfast buffet, some refrigerators, cable TV, pool, hot tub, gym, business services. | 505 W. Hwy. 2 | 509/548–7000 or 800/558–2438 | fax 509/548–7050 | $109–$229 | AE, D, DC, MC, V.

Der Ritterhof Motor Inn. Deluxe motel with a vaguely "Bavarian" theme. All of the rooms enjoy views of the mountains. | 51 rooms. Picnic area, some kitchenettes, cable TV, pool, hot tub, putting green, business services, pets allowed (fee). | 190 U.S. 2 | 509/548–5845 or 800/255–5845 | fax 509/548–4098 | $76–$98 | AE, MC, V.

Enzian Motor Inn. This is a deluxe conference motel also with a "Bavarian" theme, including carvings by an "authentic" Bavarian. | 104 rooms. Complimentary breakfast, cable TV, 2 pools (1 indoor), 2 Hot tubs, gym, racquetball, business services. | 590 U.S. 2 | 509/548–5269 or 800/223–8511 | fax 509/548–9319 | $95–$105, suites 165–175 | AE, D, DC, MC, V.

Evergreen Inn. Built in the 1930s as a roadside inn, the lodging is popular for its proximity to downtown (only one block) and for its distance from the highway. A sun deck and balconies, some of which are private, have views of the surrounding Cascades. | 40 rooms. Complimentary Continental breakfast, in-room data ports, some minibars, some in-room hot tubs, cable TV, outdoor hot tub, pets allowed, no smoking. | 1117 Front St. | 509/548–5515 or 800/327–7212 | fax 509/548–6556 | info@evergreeninn.com | www.evergreeninn.com | $65–$135 | AE, D, DC, MC, V.

Haus Lorelei. This rambling lodge-style house, built in 1903 by the town's largest lumber company, sits just two blocks from Leavenworth's center, and yet perches above the Wenatchee River amid the seclusion of evergreens and lovely mountain views. All the rooms have antiques; some have four-poster canopy beds with lace hangings. Three rooms upstairs have more space and are appropriate for families. | 8 rooms, 1 guest house. Complimentary breakfast, no air-conditioning in some rooms, no room phones, TV in common area, hot tub, tennis courts, basketball, hiking, bicycles, no pets, no smoking. | 347 Division St. | 509/548–5726 or 800/514–8868 | fax 509/548–6548 | info@hauslorelei.com | www.hauslorelei.com | $95–$129 | No credit cards.

Haus Rohrbach Pension. This is the hotel that helped kick off the Bavarian theme park years ago, and is still one of the most comfortable places in town. It's very family-friendly, and offers spectacular views. | 5 rooms, 5 suites. Picnic area, complimentary breakfast, no room phones, pool, hot tub, cross-country skiing, no smoking. | 12882 Ranger Rd. | 509/548–7024 or 800/548–4477 | fax 509/548–5038 | www.hausrohrbach.com | $85–$110, $140–$175 suites | AE, D, MC, V.

Hotel-Pension Anna. Fresh flowers and authentic European pine furnishings fill the rooms of this Austrian-style pension, giving each an individual charm. Balconies—open to all—afford splendid views of the Cascade Mountains. Suites have dark wood antiques and fireplaces. Two rooms are in an adjacent, renovated chapel with 15 ft ceilings. | 12 rooms, 3 suites. Complimentary Continental breakfast, some refrigerators, some in-room hot tubs, cable TV, no pets, no smoking. | 926 Commercial St. | 509/548–6273 or 800/509–ANNA | fax 509/548–4656 | info@pensionanna.com | www.pensionanna.com | $89–$199 | AE, D, MC, V.

Mountain Home Lodge. This contemporary cedar and redwood inn sits in the middle of a 20-acre alpine meadow atop a mountain (3 mi south of Leavenworth), where breathtaking views of the Cascade Mountains abound. Handmade quilts, crafted peeled-pine and vine maple furniture fill the rooms, which also contain binoculars, robes, and port wine. The price of a room in the winter includes a complimentary breakfast, lunch, and dinner. | 10 rooms, 2 cabins. Complimentary breakfast, no room phones, no TV, pool, hot tub, tennis courts, cross-country skiing, no pets, no kids under 16, no smoking. | Mountain Home Rd. | 509/548–7077 or 800/414–2378 | fax 509/548–5008 | info@mthome.com | www.mthome.com | $100–$330 | D, MC, V.

Mrs. Anderson's Lodging House. Established in 1903, this is the oldest wood frame commercial building in Leavenworth. The quaint, rustic rooms, some of which share decks overlooking the Wenatchee River, are adorned with many antique quilts—a passion of the proprietors. | 10 rooms (8 with private bath). Complimentary Continental breakfast, cable TV, no room phones, no pets, no smoking. | 917 Commercial St. | 509/548–6173 or 800/253–8990 | info@quiltersheaven.com | www.quiltersheaven.com | $39–$70 | D, MC, V.

Oysterville Guest House. Nestled in the north end of Oysterville, this peaceful, private cottage has three bedrooms, a wood burning stove, and panoramic views of Willapa Bay. | 3 rooms. Kitchenettes, microwaves, refrigerators, cable TV, in-room VCRs, laundry facilities, pets allowed, no smoking. | Territory Rd., Oysterville | 206/726–8004 | ligre@willapabay.org | $125 | No credit cards.

Pine River Ranch. This secluded B&B sits 15 mi west of Leavenworth, encircled by the majestic peaks of the Cascade Mountains. The spacious rooms have attractive contemporary pine furnishings, fireplaces, plus a whole range of amenities. | 6 rooms. Complimentary breakfast, no air-conditioning in some rooms, minibars, microwaves, in-room hot tubs, cable TV, no pets, no kids under 16, no smoking. | 19668 Hwy. 207 | 509/763–3959 | fax 509/763–2073 | lodger@prranch.com | www.prranch.com | $165 | AE, D, MC, V.

Run of the River. This inn on the Icicle River is built from hand-hewn logs. The beds are hand-hewn, as well. It is surrounded by a bird refuge, and offers complimentary snow shoes and mountain bikes. | 6 rooms. Picnic area, complimentary breakfast, cable TV, no room phones, hot tub, business services, no kids allowed, no smoking. | 9308 E. Leavenworth | 509/548–7171 or 800/288–6491 | fax 509/548–7547 | $105–$160 | D, DC, MC, V.

Sleeping Lady. The accommodations of this inn are rather unique: Five cabin complexes, housing 10 rooms each, are spread across the property's 67 acres. The rooms have peeled-log furniture and wrought-iron fixtures made by local artisans. The price of the room includes complimentary breakfast, lunch, and dinner. | 58 rooms. Dining room, bar, complimentary breakfast, no TV, pool, hot tub, massage, sauna, library, business services, no pets, no smoking. | 7375 Icicle Rd. | 509/548–6344 or 800/574–2123 | fax 509/548–6312 | info@sleepinglady.com | www.sleepinglady.com | $250 | AE, D, MC, V.

LONG BEACH

MAP 8, A7

(Nearby towns also listed: Cathlamet, Ilwaco)

Long Beach defies the biblical rule of not building on sand. It occupies part of Washington's longest sandy spit and has prospered for more than a hundred years as a beach resort. Main Street of this elongated roadside village consists of the usual aggregate of shops, motels, and gas stations, but the side streets are lined with pretty cottages, some of them more than a century old. The sandy beach—at 28 mi the nation's longest continuous, natural sandy beach—is truly spectacular, despite the fact that it is open to automobile traffic. A ten-block boardwalk along the edge of the dunes allows you to enjoy its beauty without becoming a traffic fatality. For more than a hundred years, the beaches of the Long Beach peninsula and the dunes have kept growing, but after dams on the Columbia started cutting off the supply of sand, the beaches began

WHAT TO PACK IN THE TOY TOTE FOR KIDS

- ❑ Audiotapes
- ❑ Books
- ❑ Clipboard
- ❑ Coloring/activity books
- ❑ Doll with outfits
- ❑ Hand-held games
- ❑ Magnet games
- ❑ Notepad
- ❑ One-piece toys
- ❑ Pencils, colored pencils
- ❑ Portable stereo with earphones
- ❑ Sliding puzzles
- ❑ Travel toys

© Artville

*Excerpted from *Fodor's: How to Pack: Experts Share Their Secrets*

shrinking, a process that seems to be accelerating. To compete in one local sport, your car is raced as close to the surf as possible. The real losers hit soft patches and have to watch as the tide and sands gobble up their cars.

Information: Long Beach Peninsula Visitor's Bureau | Box 562, Long Beach, 98631 | 360/642–2400 or 800/451–2542 | fax 360/642–3900 | funbeach.com.

Attractions

Long Beach Boardwalk. The ½-mi-long boardwalk provides a place to stroll while watching the sunset or to picnic in sight of the waves. It is located just ¼ mi west of downtown. | 10th St. and Bolstead.

Oysterville. This 1850s town on the shores of Willapa Bay has buildings from the 1880s and later, an old church, and a one-room schoolhouse. Once the county seat and a bustling oyster port, it is now a sleepy village. | Sandridge Rd. | 360/642–2400 or 800/451–2542 | Free | Daily.

Seascape Scenic Drive. Follow the signs for a scenic drive around the peninsula, but don't confuse them with the Tsunami Evacuation signs, which look similar. | 800/451–2542 | Free | Daily.

ON THE CALENDAR

AUG.: *International Kite Festival.* Kite enthusiasts from all over the world flock to Long Beach to fly their colorful kites in this spectacular competition. | 800/451–2542.
MAY: *Loyalty Day Celebration.* A fun parade and "time to renew allegiance to our country." Also a great time for flying a kite on the windy beach. | 800/451–2542.
JUNE: *Northwest Stunt Kite Championships.* Annual competition of dynamic kite-flying displays. | 800/451–2542.

Dining

Ark Restaurant and Bakery. Contemporary. This rambling bay-front restaurant is the oldest restaurant on Long Beach peninsula, with views of the oyster beds and cord grass meadows lining the shore overlooking Willapa Bay. Casual and relaxed, the restaurant offers innovative northwestern cooking featuring seafood, vegetarian, and meat entrees. Baked goods and desserts are prepared on the premises, and there is a take-out bakery in the front. You can also have lighter fare and the great desserts in the Willapa Cafe/Pub while enjoying the view. Try the Scotch Salmon, which is lightly pan-fried and deglazed with scotch and orange juice. Kids' menu. Sun. brunch. | 273 Sandridge Rd., Nahcotta | 360/665–4133 | Closed Mon. No lunch in winter. Seasonal hours during winter; call for schedule | $20–$30 | AE, D, MC, V.

Dooger's. Contemporary. A simple restaurant that's a favorite local hangout, known for its seafood and clams. Kids' menu. | 900 S. Pacific Hwy. | 360/642–4224 | $10–$20 | AE, D, MC, V.

42nd Street Cafe. Contemporary. This small restaurant on the main highway is bright with fresh flowers and with the cheerful paintings of local artists. The kitchen has a flair for coaxing the best flavors from fish and shellfish, meat and fowl, vegetables and wild mushrooms. The sauces are silky smooth and full of flavor and the desserts are simply marvelous. Try the fried Willapa Bay oysters or razor clams, cedar-plank salmon, and sturgeon in port wine and cranberry sauce. | 4201 Pacific Way, Seaview | 360/642–2323 | Breakfast also available. Closed selected holidays | $9–$18 | MC, V.

Milton York Restaurant. American. Sitting adjacent to the beach, this historic establishment began making candy and chocolate in 1882 and has been a mainstay of the community ever since. The dinner menu includes seafood dishes, steaks, and chicken courses; on Friday nights prime rib is served. The ice cream is homemade, and you absolutely can't leave before trying some of the candy, the recipes for which date back in some cases over 100 years. | 107 S. Pacific St. | 360/642–2352 | www.miltonyork.com | Breakfast also available | $13.50–$17 | MC, V.

My Mom's Pie and Chowder House. American. This small café has reopened as a take-away restaurant with five favorites on the menu: meatloaf sandwiches, clam chowder, crab quiche, chicken almond potpie, and chicken curry salad. For dessert choose from 11 types of pie. There is some seating inside and six patio tables to enjoy the scenery and the food at the same time. | 1113 Pacific Ave. SW | 360/642–2342 | May 1–Oct. 31, 11–6 | Closed Sun.–Tues. | $10–$20 | No credit cards.

Shoalwater Restaurant. Contemporary. This restaurant, in the Shelburne Inn, has the most formal dining room on the peninsula. The food—fresh oysters and other local seafood—is great, but the breads and pastries are exceptional. They're by far the best found anywhere on this coast. The HERON AND BEAVER PUB (same owners), across the hallway from the front door, is cozy and serves lighter fare (but you can also order off the Shoalwater menu here). It is one of Washington's most comfortable pubs. Known for duck, lamb, crab-and-shrimp cakes, oysters, pasta, salmon. Homemade breads. Kids' menu. | 4415 Pacific Hwy., Seaview | 360/642–4142 | 11:30 AM–3 PM (at the pub), 5:30–9 PM (pub and dining room) | $25–$35 | AE, D, DC, MC, V.

Lodging

Anchorage Motor Court. This beachfront motel with fireplaces and free firewood in the rooms overlooks the dunes and the distant ocean. | 10 rooms. No air-conditioning, kitchenettes, cable TV, playground, some pets allowed (fee). | 2209 Boulevard N. | 360/642–2351 or 800/646–2351 | $60–$120 | AE, D, MC, V.

Boreas Bed and Breakfast. An artfully renovated 1920s vintage beach home, this B&B offers a private path through the dunes to the beach. There is a nice collection of books and music, and antiques are scattered throughout the house. The breakfasts are extravagant and they also offer full concierge service. | 5 suites, 3 with shower only. Complimentary breakfast and afternoon tea and snacks, no air-conditioning, no room phones, hot tub, no smoking. | 607 N. Ocean Beach Blvd. | 360/642–8069 | fax 360/642–5353 | www.boreasinn.com | $100–$103 | MC, V.

Breakers. Rather generic condominiums that look a bit like a public housing project, in a splendid location next to the dunes and beach, with great views of the surf and ocean. It is next to a public golf course. | 116 rooms. No air-conditioning, some kitchenettes, some refrigerators, cable TV, indoor pool, hot tub, business services, pets allowed (fee). | 210 26th St. N | 360/642–4414 or 800/219–9833 | fax 360/642–8772 | breakerslongbeach.com | $59–$200 | AE, D, MC, V.

Caswell's on the Bay Bed and Breakfast. A wraparound porch gives this 1995 house, which sits alone on three secluded acres, the appearance of a Victorian home. Large windows overlook Willapa Bay and Long Island Wildlife Sanctuary. Rooms are large with sitting areas, appointed with antique furniture. The inn is located approximately 9 mi north of Long Beach. | 5 rooms. Complimentary breakfast, no air-conditioning, cable TV, in-room VCRs, no room phones, no pets, no kids under 8, no smoking. | 25204 Sandridge Rd., Ocean Park | 360/665–6535 or 888/553–2319 | fax 360/665–6500 | bcaswell@willapabay.org | www.caswellsinn.com | $110–$160 | MC, V.

Chautauqua Lodge. Conference resort bordering the dunes. | 180 rooms. Restaurant, bar, no air-conditioning, some kitchenettes, refrigerators, indoor pool, hot tub, sauna, game room, laundry facilities, business services, pets allowed (fee). | 304 14th St. NW | 360/642–4401 or 800/869–8401 | fax 360/642–2340 | $55–$160 | AE, D, DC, MC, V.

Edgewater Inn. A very plain motel in a great spot on the beach with an ocean view. Boardwalk nearby, as well as bike and hiking trails, and horseback riding. | 84 rooms. Cable TV, some pets allowed (fee). | 409 10th St. SW | 360/642–2311 or 800/561–2456 | fax 360/642–8018 | $49–$104 | AE, D, DC, MC, V.

Historic Sou'wester Lodge. Built in 1892 as a summer retreat for a timber baron and U.S. Senator, this lodge sits directly adjacent to dunes that lead to the ocean. Rooms are eclectically appointed in what is described by the proprietor as "early Salvation Army beach decor." In the mornings you are invited to make your own breakfast in the lodge's kitchen. The parlor is frequently the setting for soirées, discussions, theater performances, and chamber music concerts. | 6 suites, 4 cabins, 10 trailers. No air-conditioning, no room phones, no TV in some rooms, pets allowed, no smoking. | Beach Access Rd. 38th place, Seaview | 360/642–2542 | info@souwesterlodge.com | www.souwesterlodge.com | $39–$129 | D, MC, V.

Our Place at the Beach. Comfortable dune-front hostelry within easy walking distance of the beach, and all the area restaurants and shops. | 25 rooms. Picnic area, some kitchenettes, refrigerators, 2 hot tubs, sauna, gym, business services, pets allowed (fee). | 1309 South Blvd. | 360/642–3793 or 800/538–5107 | fax 360/642–3896 | www.ohwy.com/wa/ourplace | $49–$63, cabins $80 | AE, D, DC, MC, V.

Scandinavian Gardens Inn. At this lovely inn, it is easy to see why its owners insist on bare feet: the floors are covered in white carpeting. The guest rooms, however, are warmly decorated, each according to a Scandinavian theme. | 4 rooms (1 with shower only), 1 suite. Complimentary breakfast, no air-conditioning, some refrigerators, no room phones, hot tub, sauna, game room with card table and puzzles, library, business services, no kids under 2, no smoking. | 1610 California St. | 360/642–8877 or 800/988–9277 | fax 360/642–8764 | www.longbeachwa.com | $105–$153, $145–$153 suite | D, MC, V.

Shaman. A plain but very comfortable motel off the beaten path near the dunes and beach. One of the better local low-budget choices. | 42 rooms. No air-conditioning, some kitchenettes, some refrigerators, cable TV, pool, business services, some pets allowed (fee). | 115 3rd St. SW | 360/642–3714 or 800/753–3750 | fax 360/642–8599 | www.shamanmotel.com | $79–$104 | AE, D, DC, MC, V.

Shelburne Inn. Enclosed within flower gardens and behind a white picket fence sits Washington's oldest continuously run hotel. Antiques, original art, and fresh flowers ornament the rooms of this 1896 Victorian home. Some rooms share private decks. | 15 rooms. Restaurant, bar, complimentary breakfast, no air-conditioning, no room phones, no TV, no pets, no smoking. | 4415 Pacific Way | 360/642–2442 or 800/INN–1896 | fax 360/642–8904 | innkeeper@theshelburneinn.com | www.theshelburneinn.com | $109–$179 | AE, MC, V.

Super 8. This is a comfortable chain motel with nicely appointed rooms and a very friendly and knowledgeable staff. It's within easy walking distance of the downtown Long Beach bookshops and restaurants and the boardwalk through the dunes starts a couple of blocks to the west. | 50 rooms. Complimentary Continental breakfast, no air-conditioning, laundry facilities, business services. | 500 Ocean Beach Blvd. | 360/642–8988 | fax 360/642–8986 | $99–$110 | AE, D, DC, MC, V.

LONGVIEW

MAP 8, C7

(Nearby towns also listed: Chehalis, Kelso)

Longview is the largest planned community in the United States after Washington, D.C., but it is so well put together that it looks anything but planned. For one thing, the city is not laid out on the familiar grid system, but has a roundabout where the civic center is located, surrounded by curving streets that are crossed by diagonal roads (which creates a somewhat out-of-kilter grid). To top it off, there's Lake Sacajawea, a former oxbow of the Cowlitz, that's now a city park encircling about one-third of downtown.

Downtown Longview, with its broad streets and beautiful parks, is cut off from the Columbia River by a rather grungy industrial district and port. A 1,200-ft-long, 195-ft-high bridge, built in 1950, crosses from here to the Oregon side of the river.

Information: Longview Area Chamber of Commerce | 1563 Olympia Way, Longview, 98632. | 360/423–8400 | www.rivercitieschamber.com.

Attractions

Lake Sacajawea Park. A 120-acre park which runs along a former oxbow of the Cowlitz River. | Bet. Kessler and Nichols Blvds. | 360/577–3345 | www.ci.longview.wa.us | Free | Daily.

Mt. St. Helens Visitor Center. (*See* Mt. St. Helens National Volcanic Monument.) | 5 miles E. Castle Rock in Silver Lake, I–5 to exit 49, Rte. 504 E, milepost 5 | 360/274–2100.

Nutty Narrows. Not a traditional bridge, this structure is only for squirrels and serves as a safe passage for the animals across Olympia Way, between the Public Library and Civic Center. | Olympia Way.

ON THE CALENDAR

MAY: *International Festival.* A multinational celebration with food and entertainment from around the world. | 360/636–2791.

AUG.: *Thunder Mountain Pro Rodeo/Cowlitz County Fair.* A traditional rodeo and carnival with live entertainment and children's activities takes place at the fairgrounds. | 360/577–3121.

Dining

Henri's. Contemporary. This large but comfortable restaurant is the local businessmen's lunch hangout, but dinner is also very popular for its hearty fare such as good seafood bisque, rack of lamb, and steaks. Kids' menu. | 4545 Ocean Beach Hwy. | 360/425–7970 | Closed Sun. No lunch Sat. | $15–$25 | AE, D, MC, V.

Rutherglen Mansion. Contemporary. Standing at the center of the dining room is an 8-ft stone fireplace flanked by a tile mural depicting a scene from the nearby forests. The menu includes a range of traditional Northwest favorites; especially popular are the champagne salmon and Jack Daniel's New York steak. Friday and Saturday night the restaurant serves prime rib. | 420 Rutherglen Rd. | 360/425–5816 | No lunch. Late May–early Sept. closed Mon.–Tues. | $12–$19 | AE, MC, V.

Lodging

Patrician Inn and Suites. The lobby's many antiques give this quiet hotel, located 3 mi from the highway, a comfortable homey feel. There are guest rooms, mini-suites, and one larger suite with a hot tub. | 50 rooms. Complimentary Continental breakfast, no-smoking rooms, pool, hot tub, pets allowed (fee). | 723 7th Ave. | 360/414–1000 | fax 360/414–1076 | $65–$79 | AE, D, DC, MC, V.

Rutherglen Mansion. Sitting on the crest of a hill in the middle of 30 wooded acres, this 1926 English Colonial mansion enjoys a stupendous view of the town. All the rooms have fireplaces and tile baths. | 4 rooms. Restaurant, complimentary breakfast, no air-conditioning, no TV, no pets, no smoking. | 420 Rutherglen Rd. | 360/425–5816 | fax 360/636–3655 | www.rutherglenmansion.com | $80 | AE, MC, V.

LOPEZ ISLAND

MAP 8, D2

(Nearby town also listed: San Juan Islands)

Lopez is the third largest of the San Juan Islands and one of four islands served by Washington State ferries on a regular schedule. It's also flat enough to make bicycle riding a favorite local sport. Lopez is famous throughout the Northwest for its friendliness and for the Lopez wave, a special kind of hand motion you'll learn about within minutes of leaving the ferry landing at Upright Head. It's a sort of, "Hi, there, I don't know you, and I don't have time to talk to you right now, but welcome to our island anyway" wave.

As you walk, drive, or ride down island roads, you'll see small farmhouses in pastures where animals graze contentedly. In spring, there are flowers everywhere.

Lopez has one large, protected harbor, Fisherman's Bay, and lots of small sandy or rocky coves luring boaters to bide awhile. There are B&Bs and campgrounds, even a few shops, a bakery, and restaurants. Lopez doesn't have many really old buildings, but there's one church which dates from 1881, and another from 1904, plus an old red schoolhouse. But after a few hours you're not going to miss the historical perspective. There are enough island people to meet, woods to wander through, and tide pools to explore to keep you busy for weeks.

SEA KAYAKING

Imagine yourself silently coasting along a rocky wooded shore. The only sounds you hear in the morning air, are the warbling of birds in the woods, the lapping of the waves on boulders, and the cries of sea gulls. A great blue heron emerges from the mist slowly flapping its wings as it scans the shallow waters for fish, or a bald eagle may glide past on stiff wings; or you may hear a sudden snort and smell the fishy breath of a whale emerging from the deep.

Since kayaks are slim and light boats, they are surprisingly easy to propel, but you may find yourself spending a lot of time drifting, to get a better look at the marine wildlife. Sitting low in the water, you pose no threat to wild animals, who may consider you with the same interest with which they examine a floating log. In a sea kayak, you can travel with seals and sea lions, look orcas and whales straight in the eye, and look up at bald eagles perching on rocks.

You can cruise through shallow bays and look down into tidepools and their beds of colorful sea anemones, kelp, and scallops; you can paddle past shorelines where wildflowers grow down to the high tide line, and where the branches of cedars may sweep the waters, the tips of their branches encrusted with tiny barnacles and mussels. A kayak allows you to enter a magic world inaccessible in other ways.

But kayaking is not limited to coastal waters. It is also a great way of exploring Washington's inland lakes and reedy sloughs, where ducks, grebes, avocets, sandpipers, and plovers mate and breed. You can watch the mad mating dance of Western Grebes from your kayak; you'll meet ducks and ducklings, and the odd, reddish chicks of coots. You can watch beavers at work, and minks on the hunt. Ospreys may cover you with spray as they plunge into the water to snatch fish.

Sea kayaking is the best way to experience Washington's coastal and inland waters. The boats are generally so stable and safe that even beginning paddlers can join one of the many tours offered throughout the state. Beginners should take a tour with an experienced guide before venturing out on their own, since some of Washington's coastal waters have strong tidal currents (a few even have tidal falls), and local knowledge is necessary to navigate them safely. Inland lakes are subject to sudden storms; here, too, local knowledge is essential.

Check with local park districts; many of them offer seasonal kayak tours. For guided tours of San Juan Island's west coast (where you are most likely to encounter orcas and whales), contact www.outdoorodyssey.com

Information: Lopez Island Chamber of Commerce | Box 102, Lopez Island, 98261 | 360/468–4664 | www.lopezisland.com.

Attractions

Lopez Island Historical Museum. The museum houses impressive models of ships and boats. There are also displays of Native American artifacts as well as pioneer tools and implements. | 28 Washburn Pl. | 360/468–2049 or 360/468–3447 | Donations | July–Aug., Wed.–Sun. noon–4; May, June, and Sept., Fri.–Sun. noon–4.

Lopez Island Vineyard. This is the San Juan Islands' oldest vineyard. Come to the tasting room and savor its wines or picnic on the grounds. | 724 Fisherman Bay Rd. | 360/468–3644 | $1 | Apr. 15–June, Fri.–Sat. noon–5; July–Labor Day, Wed.–Sun. noon–5; Labor Day–Dec., Fri.–Sat. noon–5.

Odlin County Park. One mi south of the ferry landing you will see a variety of marine wildlife including, but not limited to, sea anemones, yellow, pink, and white sea slugs, bright orange sea cucumbers, purple sea stars, and blue-green shore crabs. Eagles, seals, otters, and herons are also easily visible. | 148 Odlin Park | 360/468–2496 | Free | All the time.

Spencer Spit State Park. This park, 3 mi northeast of Lopez Village on the shore, has 130 acres on which you can clam, crab, kayak, and bike. The marsh is home to a wide variety of fowl and wildlife. | 521A Baker View Rd. | 360/468–2251 | Free | Daily, 8–dusk.

Dining

Bay Cafe. Seafood. This funky, casual restaurant is an island favorite and offers a full-water view with beautiful sunsets. A briny theme also pervades the dining room, from classical northwest cuisine to international dishes. Try the fresh Dungeness crab and shrimp cake or the wild Mexican prawns with a sweet chili citrus marmalade curry. There is a deck overlooking the waterfront for outdoor dining. | 9 Old Post Rd. | 360/468–3700 | Breakfast available weekends. Closed Mon.–Tues. Oct.–Feb. | $15–$30 | D, MC, V.

Lodging

Edenwild Inn. The inn's exterior with its wraparound porch might fool you into thinking it is a restored Victorian, but it was built in 1990. Custom-designed bedrooms contain floral arrangements, original art, books, and antiques. From four of the rooms you can see either Fisherman's Bay or San Juan Channel. Three rooms have fireplaces and antique soaking tubs. | 8 rooms. Complimentary breakfast, no air-conditioning, no room phones, no TV, no pets, no smoking. | Eades Lane at Lopez Village Rd. | 360/468–3238 or 800/606–0662 | fax 360/468–4080 | edenwildinn@msn.com | www.edenwildinn.com | $110–$165 | AE, MC, V.

Inn at Swifts Bay. This Tudor-style B&B is in quiet cedar grove 2 mi from the Lopez Island ferry landing. The rooms are individually decorated and the common room has a large videotape library and French doors which open onto the deck. | 5 rooms (2 with shared bath). Complimentary breakfast and afternoon snacks, some refrigerators, TV in common area, no room phones, hot tub, gym, business services, no kids allowed, no smoking. | 856 Port Stanley Rd. | 360/468–3636 | fax 360/468–3637 | www.swiftsbay.com | $95–$185 | AE, D, MC, V.

Islander Lopez Marina Resort. The place to go to if you DON'T want to get away from it all. It's a big, bustling resort on the east shore of Fisherman Bay, Lopez Island's only harbor. | 26 rooms, 2 suites. Restaurant, lounge, no-smoking rooms, pool, hot tub, marina. | 2864 Fisherman Bay Rd. | 800/736–3434 | fax 360/468–3382 | $80–$260 | AE, MC, V.

MacKaye Harbor Inn. Sitting on 3 acres, this 1920s Victorian sea captain's house faces the harbor's placid waters. Bedrooms are appointed with period antiques and have windows overlooking the bay and English gardens. One room, the Harbor Suite, has an Italian golden oak bedroom set, a fireplace, and French doors that lead to a private, covered deck. | 5 rooms. Complimentary breakfast, no air-conditioning, no room phones, no TV, bicycles, no pets, no kids under 9, no smoking. | 949 MacKaye Harbor Rd. | 360/468–2253 or 888/314–6140 | fax 360/468–2393 | mckay@pacificrim.net | www.san-juan.net/mackayeharbor | $99–$175 | MC, V.

MARYSVILLE

MAP 8, E3

(Nearby town also listed: Everett)

When you look at the green fields and light woods surrounding Marysville today, it's hard to believe that these forests were once so dense that overland travel was all but impossible and communications were mainly by boat along the shore and on the rivers. Marysville's first settler was an Indian agent who established a trading post here in 1877 to trade with the Snohomish Indians at the nearby Tulalip Reservation. The Tulalip originally occupied southeastern Whidbey Island and the lower Snohomish Valley, but by the last quarter of the 19th century they had been pushed onto a narrow coastal strip north of the Snohomish.

Other shops soon joined the trading post; a corduroy road (a road made of logs laid next to each other) was built through the swamps of the Snohomish delta; settlers drained and diked the lowlands, raised dairy cows, and planted upland fields with strawberries; loggers cut the trees; and in no time at all a thriving community had established itself. Marysville did not grow much for a century, until the I–5 freeway was built and the town became a bedroom community for Everett and the other cities of the Pugetopolis. Today Marysville still has close connections to the Tulalip Reservation and is the home of the popular Tulalip Casino.

Information: **Marysville/Tulalip Visitor Information Center** | Off I–5, Exit 199, Marysville, 98271 | 360/653–2634 | snohomish.org.

Attractions

Jennings Memorial Park and Jennings Nature Center. The two parks, comprising 51 acres, are the site of playgrounds, picnic facilities, hiking trails, and a petting zoo. A 17-acre wetland observatory sits adjacent to the parks. | 6915 Armar Rd. | 360/651–5085 | Free | Daily, dawn–dusk.

Tulalip Reservation. A waterfront reservation of the Snohomish Indians on Possession Sound, west of Marysville. Tulalip is a native expression meaning "almost land-locked bay," and is the name of a bay on the reservation shore. Explorer George Vancouver landed here on June 4, 1792, the birthday of British King George III, to take formal possession of the region for England. In 1988 the Tulalips carved a traditional cedar canoe (the first in more than a hundred years) from a big cedar trunk. It can hold 20 people and carry more than a ton of cargo. It is stored in the tribe's carving shed, next to the tribal museum, which has exhibits of tribal artifacts. | I–5, exit 199 | 360/651–4000 | fax 360/651–4032 | Free | Weekdays 8–4:30.

Wenberg State Park. This park off I–5 on Lake Goodwin has campsites, picnic tables, and excellent fishing. | E. Lake Goodwin Rd. | 360/652–7417 | fax 360/652–1785 | Free, camping $10–$15 | Daily 8–dusk.

ON THE CALENDAR

JUNE: ***Marysville Strawberry Festival.*** One of Washington's oldest festivals is held on the third weekend of June each year in downtown Marysville. The celebration encompasses a talent show, swing dance, outhouse race, car show, parade, and more. | 360/659–7664.

Dining

Fanny's Restaurant. American. Down-home dinners are the specialty here, fried chicken, breaded veal, and meatloaf, though the restaurant also serves prime rib and an assortment of pastas. Hanging plants and floral patterns create a comfortable environment in which to enjoy your meal. The restaurant is family friendly and offers a kids' menu. | 505 Cedar Ave. | 360/653–8164 | No reservations on Sun. | Closed on Mon. | $9–$14 | D, MC, V.

The Village. Contemporary. Popular family restaurant and steakhouse that also serves good seafood. Kids' menu. No smoking. | 220 Ash Ave. | 360/659–2305 | Breakfast also available | $12–15 | AE, D, DC, MC, V.

Lodging

Best Western Tulalip Inn. This chain sits across the road from the Tulalip Casino and Bingo, just off I-5 at exit 199. Restaurants and shops are nearby. | 69 rooms. Restaurant, complimentary Continental breakfast, room service, some microwaves, some refrigerators, some in-room hot tubs, cable TV, pool, spa, laundry services, business services, pets allowed. | 6128 33rd Ave. NE | 360/659–5688 or 800/481–4804 | fax 360/659–5688 | $69–$103 | AE, D, DC, MC, V.

Village Motor Inn. Small personal service is the hallmark of this comfortable 3-story motel in central Marysville. | 45 rooms, 6 suites. Complimentary Continental breakfast, in-room data ports, cable TV, business services, free parking, some pets allowed (fee). | 235 Beach Ave. | 360/659–0005 | fax 360/658–0866 | $52–$130, $95–$130 suites | AE, D, DC, MC, V.

MOCLIPS

MAP 8, B5

(Nearby town also listed: Copalis Beach)

Moclips (pronounced "mow-clips") is a small beach town at the edge of the Quinault Indian Nation. It is popular with storm watchers, beachcombers, clammers, and, in recent years, surfers. Please note that different rules and regulations apply in Quinault territory: Only tribal members are allowed to leave the main highway leading to the tribal capital of Taholah and to drive on the beach. Nontribal members need to contact the tribal office for permission to go on to tribal land. Littering is also seriously frowned upon. Check current rules as you cross the boundary.

Information: Washington Coast Chamber of Commerce | 2602 SR 109, Box 562, Ocean City, 98569 | 360/289–4552.

Attractions

Pacific Beach State Park. This state park with beachfront campsites, surf fishing (surfperch), beachcombing, and (if there's an open season) razor-clam digging is a few miles south of Moclips. There's also excellent fishing for sea-run cutthroat trout in the Moclips River but be careful not to trespass onto Indian land: The Quinault Reservation starts north of the river. | Rte. 109 S | 360/289–3553 | fax 360/289–9059 | Free | Daily dawn–dusk.

ON THE CALENDAR

SEPT.: ***Operation Shore Patrol Beach Cleanup.*** Bring gloves and join in at this ecologically correct event held on the Pacific Coast Beaches. There's free camping for participants. | 800/537–7845.

Dining

Restaurant at Ocean Crest Resort. American. Trees festooned with mosses frame the ocean view of this restaurant. The food served in the modern dining room is standard coastal fare: Dungeness crab and other seafood served with heavy sauces, as well as pasta, steak, and lamb. | 4651 Hwy. 109 | 360/276–4465 | Breakfast also served | $15–$25 | AE, D, MC, V.

Lodging

Hi-Tide Ocean Beach Resort. At this typical beach town resort all the rooms have great ocean views. | 25 suites. No air-conditioning, kitchenettes, cable TV, business services, pets allowed (fee). | 4890 Railroad Ave. | 360/276–4142 or 800/662–5477 (WA) | fax 360/276–0156 | $95–$169 suites | D, MC, V.

Moonstone Beach Motel. Each room of this small motel, which sits directly on the beach, has an unbeatable view of the ocean. Some rooms have full kitchens and open onto the beach itself. | 8 rooms. No air-conditioning, some kitchenettes, some microwaves, some refrigerators, cable TV, no room phones, pets allowed. | 4849 Pacific Ave. | 888/888–9063 | $65–$85 | AE, MC, V.

Ocean Crest Resort. This resort, in a grove of Sitka spruce, has some of the best views (and most comfortable rooms) on this coast. | 45 rooms. Restaurant, bar, no air-conditioning, some kitchenettes, cable TV, indoor pool, hot tub, sauna, gym, laundry facilities, business services. | 4651 Hwy. 109 | 360/276–4465 or 800/684–8439 | fax 360/276–4149 | $60–$130 | AE, D, MC, V.

Sandpiper Beach Resort. The resort sits 3 mi south of Moclips directly on a secluded beach. The clean, contemporary suites have fireplaces, exposed wood ceilings, and sliding glass doors that lead to a porch overlooking the beach and ocean. | 31 suites. No air-conditioning, kitchenettes, microwaves, refrigerators, no room phones, no TV, pets allowed (fee), no smoking. | 4159 Rte. 109, Pacific Beach | 360/276–4580 or 800/56–PIPER | esandpiper@hotmail.com | www.sandpiper-resort.com | $85–$130 | MC, V.

MONTESANO

MAP 8, B5

(Nearby towns also listed: Aberdeen, Hoquiam)

Montesano has a split personality. Down by U.S. 12 and the lumber mill, the county seat of Grays Harbor County is not at all appealing, but a few blocks up the hill, in the old part of town, it turns outright pretty. The Grays Harbor County courthouse (1912) is big for such a small town and has a soaring clock tower and a classical, pillared entrance. The lobby has a marble staircase flanked by murals depicting Robert Gray in 1792, discovering the harbor that bears his name, and Territorial Governor Isaac Stevens negotiating with the natives at Cosmopolis in 1855. Never mind that the natives wear feathered headdresses and mill about in front of tepees—neither one was used by the local Chehalis. By contrast City Hall (1914) is built in Mission Revival style and glows like a mirage of sunny southern California in rainy Grays Harbor County. The town has a number of other old buildings, many of them dating from the late 1800s and early 1900s.

Montesano (Spanish for "healthy mountain") was first settled back in 1852 and became a town in 1870. The town got a newspaper, the *Vidette,* in 1863, even before it existed officially as a municipality. The paper has been published continuously since then. It seems crazy when you look at the size of the Chehalis River at the bottom of the hill to envision steamboats churning their way upriver. But they did, from 1859 until railroad tracks arrived in 1885.

Information: **Montesano Chamber of Commerce** | 128 Brumfield Ave., Monte Square, Montesano, 98563 | 360/249–5522 or 888/294–0483 | montechamber@techline.com | www.montesano-wa.com.

Attractions

Schaefer State Park. A pleasant river front park in the southern foothills of the Olympic Mountains, where the east fork of the Satsop River meanders over Carstairs Prairie, with campsites and picnic tables. | Rte. 507 N | 360/482–3852 | fax 360/753–1594 | www.parks.wa.gov | Free | Daily 8–dusk.

ON THE CALENDAR

AUG.: *McCleary Bear Festival.* Decades-old event with a parade, regionally famous bear stew, craft and food vendors, and bear fun is held in the center of McCleary. | 360/495–4425.

Dining

Savory Fare. Café. In the French café–style dining room, the restaurant serves sandwiches, homemade soups, salads, and quiches. The eatery is known especially for its home-baked breads and desserts. The cinnamon rolls and amaretto bread pudding are both very popular. | 135 S. Main St. | 360/249–3701 | Breakfast also available. No dinner | $4–$6 | AE, D, MC, V.

Lodging

Abel House. A comfortable B&B in downtown Montesano, this old country manor house was built in 1908, and has a wonderful English garden. Relax in front of the fireplace in the sitting room or have some fun in the game room, which has a piano and a pool table. | 5 rooms. Complimentary breakfast, non-smoking rooms. | 117 Fleet Street S | 360/249–6002 or 800/235–ABEL | abelhouse@aol.com | $75–$95 | AE, D, MC, V.

MOSES LAKE

MAP 8, I5

(Nearby town also listed: Ephrata)

This sprawling town on the shores of a natural lake seems almost like an anomaly in the dry landscape of east-central Washington. But ever since the Columbia Basin Project took shape, there's been water everywhere. The I–90 freeway approaching Moses Lake from the west passes through lushly green irrigated fields; to the east lie vast stretches of wheat fields. Irrigation canals crisscross the countryside, and waterfowl and other birds are everywhere. Potholes Reservoir is an artificial lake to the south which supports as much wildlife as does the Columbia Wildlife Refuge. The lakes of this region have more shorebirds than Washington's ocean beaches. The Winchester Wasteway west of Moses Lake is a great waterway for paddling a kayak or canoe and watching birds as you glide along the reedy banks. The city of Moses Lake has motels, restaurants, and other amenities of civilized life. The airfield, north of town, was once a major air force base and now serves as a training facility for airline pilots.

Information: Moses Lake Area Chamber of Commerce | 324 S. Pioneer Way, Moses Lake, 98837 | 509/765–7888 or 800/992–6234 | information@moses-lake.com.

Attractions

Adam East Museum. Fossils collected all over North America, including prehistoric land and marine animals, are exhibited at this museum. | 3rd and Ash Sts. | 509/766–9395 | fax 509/766–9392 | Free | Tues.–Sat. 11–5.

Cascade Park. This beach park on Moses Lake has swimming (yes, here the water gets warm enough in summer), boating, and camping. The park is popular with water-skiers and can be quite noisy. | Valley Rd. and Cascade Valley | 509/766–9240 | fax 509/766–9243 | Free | Daily dawn–10.

Moses Lake. A claw-shaped 38-ft-deep, 18-mi-long, natural lake filled with the waters of Crab Creek (which originates in hills west of Spokane) with three side branches known as Parker Horn, Lewis Horn, and Pelican Horn. The city sprawls over the peninsulas formed by these "horns" and can therefore be a bit difficult to get around in. With Potholes Reservoir to the south, Moses Lake, the state's second largest lake, forms a vast wildlife habitat. | Rte. 17, off Rte. I–90 | 509/766–9240 | fax 509/766–9243 | Free | Daily.

Moses Lake State Park. On the west shore of the lake, across the water from the town of Moses Lake, this park offers picnicking and great fishing for trout, bluegill, crappie, and catfish. Day-use only. It's 5 mi west of downtown Moses Lake. | I–90 | 509/765–5852 | fax 509/766–9243 | Free | Daily dawn–10.

Potholes Reservoir. This is an artificial lake in a natural depression carved by the huge Spokane Floods. Its waters are contained by O'Sullivan Dam, one of the largest earth-filled dams

in the country. With Moses Lake to the north and The Columbia National Wildlife Refuge to the south, Potholes forms a vast wildlife area. | Rte. 17 to Rte. 170 | 509/346–2758 | Daily.
Potholes State Park. This state park is 20 mi southwest of Moses Lake on the west side of O'Sullivan Dam. Camping and boating, as well as fishing for trout, perch, and walleye, are popular diversions. | Rte. 17 to Rte. 170 | 509/346–2758 or 800/452–5687 (reservations) | www.parks.wa.gov | Call for camping prices | Daily, reservations required mid-May–Sept.
Winchester Wasteway. A slough west of Moses Lake, off I–90, carries excess irrigation waters south toward the Columbia. Reed-lined, it is a great place for watching waterfowl, rails, songbirds, muskrats, and beavers. | Dodson Rd. S | 509/765–7888 | Free | Daily.

Columbia Basin Farmers' Market. Vendors come each Saturday between mid-June and mid-October to Civic Center Park, behind the public library, to sell fresh produce and handmade arts and crafts. | Civic Center Park | 509/762–5500 | Sat. 7:30–1.

ON THE CALENDAR

FEB.: ***Presidents' Day.*** A BIG birthday cake for George Washington as well as children's events, games, entertainment and indoor food booths can all be found at Martha's Inn in George, west of Moses Lake on I–90. | 509/785–3831.
MAY: ***Spring Festival.*** Entertainment, a carnival, and bed and radio car races are some of the highlights held here on Memorial Day weekend. | 509/765–8248.

Dining

Cade's Lakefront Restaurant and Lounge. American. Part of the Best Western Hallmark Inn, this restaurant has large windows which overlook the lake. The menu includes a range of seafood, beef, chicken, pasta, and salad options, but the most popular dish is prime rib. | 3000 W. Marina Dr. | 509/765–9211 | Breakfast also available | $9–$18 | AE, D, DC, MC, V.

Michael's on the Lake. American/Casual. The golden rays of sunset will wash over the dining room and deck at this lakeside restaurant as you indulge in your meal. The menu ranges from soups and sandwiches to heartier fare like prime rib and lobster. | 910 W. Broadway Ave. | 509/765–1611 | $13–$16 | AE, D, DC, MC, V.

Porter House Restaurant and Lounge. Steak. Candlelight sets a subdued tone in the dining room of this family-friendly eatery, which is famous for its steaks. Complementing the beef entrées are a variety of chicken, seafood, and pasta dishes. | 217 N. Elder St. | 509/766–0308 | $12–$19 | AE, MC, V.

Lodging

Best Value El Rancho Motel. Commercial travelers' and family motel. | 20 rooms. Some kitchenettes, refrigerators, cable TV, pool, some pets allowed. | 1214 S. Pioneer Way | 509/765–9173 or 888/315–BEST (2378) | fax 509/765–1137 | www.bestvalueinn.com | $32–$60 | AE, D, DC, MC, V.

Best Western Hallmark Inn. This comfortable waterfront motel overlooks the lake and fields and hills to the west. | 161 rooms. Restaurant, bar with entertainment, refrigerators, room service, cable TV, pool, wading pool, hot tub, sauna, tennis, dock, laundry facilities, business services, airport shuttle, some pets allowed, free parking. | 3000 Marina Dr. | 509/765–9211 | fax 509/766–0493 | $64–$140 | AE, D, DC, MC, V.

Country Inn Bed and Breakfast. The five rooms of this Queen Anne Victorian are furnished according to each room's special theme. The Train Room, for instance, has custom built beds—made of oak and railroad rails—old lanterns made into lamps, and an armoire displaying train-related knickknacks. Landscaped grounds surround a gazebo and a deck from which can be seen the lake. | 5 rooms. Complimentary breakfast, some in-room hot tubs, cable TV, no room phones, no pets, no smoking. | 2801 W. Peninsula Dr. | 509/766–7466 or 800/761–7466 | fax 509/766–7529 | fun@countryinnbb.com | www.countryinnbb.com | $90–$130 | AE, D, MC, V.

Interstate Inn. Off I-90 at exit 176, this two-story motel sits just 1 mi east of Moses Lake State Park. | 30 rooms. Some refrigerators, cable TV, indoor pool, hot tub, sauna, business services, pets allowed. | 2801 W. Broadway | 509/765–1777 | fax 509/766–9452 | $45–$54 | AE, D, DC, MC, V.

Moses Lake Travelodge. This chain hotel, at the center of downtown, is close to restaurants and shopping. A park directly adjacent to the hotel allows room for outdoor relaxation. | 40 rooms. Microwaves, refrigerators, cable TV, pool, spa, pets allowed ($5 fee). | 316 S. Pioneer Way | 509/765–8631 or 800/578–7878 | fax 509/765–3685 | www.travelodge.com | $59–$75 | AE, D, DC, MC, V.

Motel 6. Right off the freeway, this motel offers very familiar basic accommodations with a minimum of frills. | 89 rooms. Cable TV, pool, laundry facilities. | 2822 Wapato Dr. | 509/766–0250 | fax 509/766–7762 | $30–$44 | AE, D, DC, MC, V.

Shilo Inn. The friendly staff at this motel lifts it above the average chain lodging. | 100 rooms. Some kitchenettes, refrigerators, microwaves, cable TV, indoor pool, hot tub, sauna, gym, laundry facilities, business services, free parking, airport shuttle. | 1819 E. Kittleson Rd. | 509/765–9317 | fax 509/765–5058 | $65–$99 | AE, D, DC, MC, V.

MT. RAINIER NATIONAL PARK

MAP 8, D2

(Nearby towns also listed: Crystal Mountain, Packwood)

Mt. Rainier National Park is unique in that it is a park dedicated to just one mountain, albeit a very special one. At 14,410 feet, Mt. Rainier is one of the tallest peaks in the contiguous United States, and the way it stands alone, towering far above the surrounding foothills and mountains, is truly majestic. Its glaciers can be seen from far away; closer up, its cliffs, wildflower meadows, waterfalls, and forests cannot help but impress. The mountain is so spectacular that beholding it in all its glory is an almost religious experience. The first attempt to climb it was in the 1830s, when a Hudson's Bay Company doctor stationed at Fort Nisqually on Puget Sound made it part way up, as the Native Americans looked on in horror. They knew the mountain, which they called Tahoma, that is, "breast of milk-white waters," was sacred and should not be violated, or it might become angry. It had expressed its anger in the past, when eruptions spewed ash high into the sky or mud flows raced down its flanks killing everything in the way. But that didn't deter the Americans. Since the first successful ascent in 1870, hundreds have climbed the mountain each year, though quite a few others have perished.

But the mountain is also accessible to those who aren't rugged outdoor types. The visitors' center is at Longmire, at an elevation of 2,761 ft; Paradise is at 5,400 ft, and the highest place reachable by road is Sunrise, at 6,400 ft (there's also a visitor center here). A great place to see the mountain from the north is Rte. 410, the Chinook Pass Highway, which is closed in winter.

Mt. Rainier National Park recently celebrated its 100th anniversary, amidst rising concerns that both the mountain and the park are being quite literally loved to death.

In winter, Mt. Rainier has some of the highest snowfalls in the world, exceeded only by Mt. Baker to the north.

Except for Longmire and Paradise, there are no lodging facilities in the park (except for campgrounds), but the surrounding towns and villages have inns with a wide range of prices.

The Mt. Rainier area includes the communities of Alder, Ashford, Crystal Mountain, Eatonville, Elbe, Glenoma, Greenwater, Morton, and Packwood.

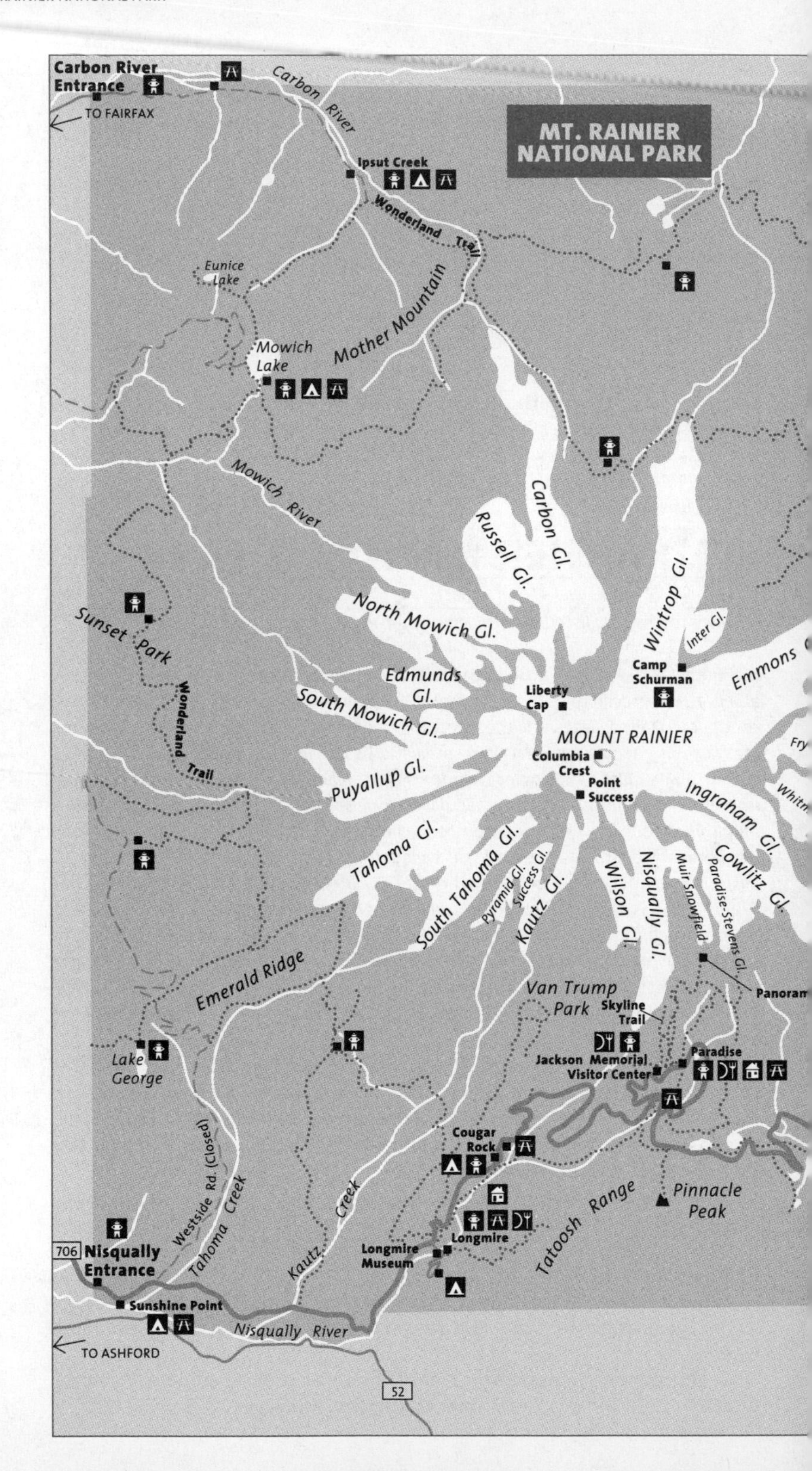
MT. RAINIER NATIONAL PARK
Carbon River Entrance
TO FAIRFAX
Carbon River
Ipsut Creek
Wonderland Trail
Eunice Lake
Mother Mountain
Mowich Lake
Mowich River
Carbon Gl.
Russell Gl.
Wintrop Gl.
Inter Gl.
North Mowich Gl.
Camp Schurman
Emmons
Sunset Park
Edmunds Gl.
Liberty Cap
South Mowich Gl.
Wonderland Trail
MOUNT RAINIER
Columbia Crest
Point Success
Puyallup Gl.
Ingraham Gl.
Tahoma Gl.
South Tahoma Gl.
Pyramid Gl.
Success Gl.
Kautz Gl.
Wilson Gl.
Nisqually Gl.
Muir Snowfield
Paradise-Stevens Gl.
Cowlitz Gl.
Emerald Ridge
Van Trump Park
Skyline Trail
Jackson Memorial Visitor Center
Paradise
Lake George
Westside Rd. (Closed)
Cougar Rock
Tahoma Creek
Kautz Creek
Pinnacle Peak
Tatoosh Range
Longmire
Longmire Museum
706
Nisqually Entrance
Sunshine Point
Nisqually River
TO ASHFORD
52

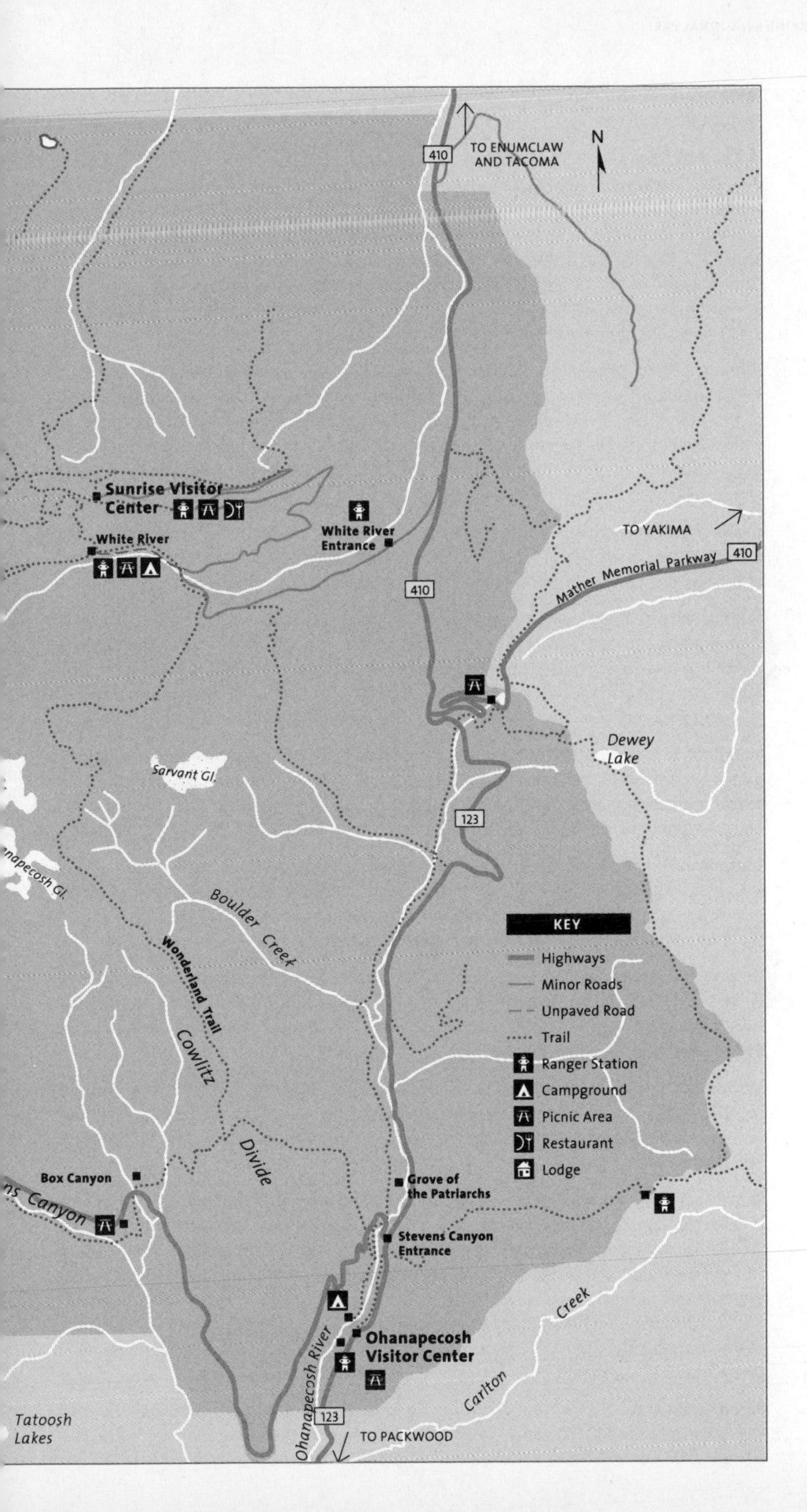
410
TO ENUMCLAW AND TACOMA
N
Sunrise Visitor Center
White River
White River Entrance
TO YAKIMA
410
Mather Memorial Parkway
410
Dewey Lake
Sarvant Gl.
123
napecosh Gl.
Boulder Creek
Wonderland Trail
Cowlitz
Divide
KEY
Highways
Minor Roads
Unpaved Road
Trail
Ranger Station
Campground
Picnic Area
Restaurant
Lodge
Box Canyon
ns Canyon
Grove of the Patriarchs
Stevens Canyon Entrance
Ohanapecosh Visitor Center
Ohanapecosh River
Carlton Creek
Tatoosh Lakes
123
TO PACKWOOD

Information: Mt. Rainier Business Association | Box 214, Ashford, 98304 | 360/569–0910 | mt-rainier.com.

Attractions

Camping. Mt. Rainier offers two types of camping experiences: campsites with running water and flush or pit toilets at Cougar Rock, Ipsut Creek, Ohanapecosh, Sunshine Point, and White River; and remote wilderness camps available to backpackers. Space is available on a first-come, first-served basis at most of the campsites; Cougar Rock and Ohanapecosh require reservations. Keep in mind that Mt. Rainier attracts almost two million visitors a year. | 360/569–2211 ext. 3301 or 800/365–2267 (reservations) | fax 360/569–2170 | www.nps.gov/mora | $12–$14 | Daily.

Fishing. Rainier is *not* one of Washington's great fishing areas. Wild mountain trout are wily and small. If you want to enjoy fishing during your trip, plan for a night or two at one of the many lakes south of the mountain. Check with a ranger to learn about closed waters and limits. No license is required on National Park lands, but you'll need a Washington State license for fishing outside the park. | 360/569–2211 | fax 360/569–2170 | www.nps.gov/mora | Free | Daily.

Grove of the Patriarchs. One of the park's gems, this small island in the Ohanapecosh River is home to 1,000-year-old Douglas firs, cedars, and hemlocks. A 2-mi trail begins just west of the Stevens Canyon entrance. | Hwy. 706 | 360/569–2211.

Hiking. Because the snowline is quite low in Washington State, the upper part of the park is covered by snow for much of the year, making for a short hiking season, usually running from mid-July to mid-September or October. (For this reason, the wildflower season is also short but spectacular; expect fall colors by late August and early September.) | 360/569–2211 | fax 360/569–2170 | www.nps.gov/mora | free | May.–Oct., daily dawn to dusk.

Interpretive Programs and Walks. The National Park Service presents regular slide programs and schedules nature walks and other activities from June through Labor Day. Programs are prominently posted at the visitor centers and campgrounds. | 360/569–2211 | fax 360/569–2170 | www.nps.gov/mora | Free | Daily.

Longmire. The entrance for the ranger station, visitor services, and lodging is at an elevation of 2,761 ft near the Nisqually entrance, in the southwest corner of the park. The visitor center has park information, displays, and seasonal programs. | 360/569–2211 ext. 3317 | fax 360/569–2170 | www.nps.gov/mora | Free | Daily.

Longmire Museum. The history of the park is illustrated here through photos and displays. Preserved plants and stuffed animals stand as examples of the park's flora and fauna. | Hwy. 706, Longmire | 360/569–2211, ext. 3314 | Free with park admission | July–Labor Day, daily 9–6; Labor Day–June, daily 9–4:15.

Mountain Climbing. A very popular activity at Mt. Rainier, attracting about 8,000+ climbers per year. Given the number of climbers, the park now issues plastic bags to pack out human waste. | 360/569–2211 | fax 360/569–2170 | www.nps.gov/mora | Free | Daily May–Oct. dawn–dusk.

Paradise. There's a ranger station, visitor services, and lodging at 5,400 ft. The visitor center has 360-degree views of the park, information, displays, and seasonal programs. The Stevens Canyon Road from Paradise to Ohanapecosh is truly spectacular, with close-up views of the mountain, wildflowers, and the red and yellow fall foliage of huckleberry, mountain ash, and alpine dwarf willow. It is accessible from the Nisqually entrance at the southwest corner of the park, and from Stevens Canyon entrance at the southeast corner of the park (summer only). | 360/569–2211 ext. 2357 | fax 360/569–2170 | www.nps.gov/mora | Free | May–mid-Oct., daily; mid-Oct.–Apr., weekends; closed weekdays.

Paradise Ski Area. Cross-country ski tours, inner tubes, and soft platters only can be used from December to April. Check with rangers for any restrictions that may apply. The Paradise Visitor Center offers snowshoe walks from late December through March. | Accessible from Nisqually entrance at southwest corner of park, and from Stevens Canyon entrance at southeast corner of park (summer only). | 360/569–2211 | fax 360/569–2170 | www.nps.gov/mora | May–mid-Oct., daily; mid-Oct.–Apr., weekends.

White Pass Village. This ski area has 54 privately owned condominiums and is about 10 mi east of the Stevens Canyon entrance to the park. | On U.S. 12 | 509/672-3101

Trail of Shadows. Commencing across the road from the National Park Inn, this ½-mi trail passes colorful soda springs, the cabin homestead of James Longmire, and the foundation of the Longmire Springs Hotel—destroyed near the turn of the 20th century. | Hwy. 706, Longmire | 360/569–2211.

Sunrise. The highest place reachable by road, at 6,400 feet, is on the northeast side of the mountain. The visitor center has park information, displays, and seasonal programs. | 360/569–2211 | fax 360/569–2170 | www.nps.gov/mora | Free | Late June–Sept.

Dining

National Park Inn. American. Large restaurant with the looks of a generic country inn. The fare here is simple American: For lunch you can order hamburgers, soups, sandwiches, and chili. For dinner, entrees include beef, chicken, and pasta. For breakfast, try the home-baked cinnamon rolls with cream-cheese frosting. The inn also has 25 rooms. | Rte. 706 near Nisqually entrance, Ashford | 360/569–2275 | Breakfast also available | $10–$20 | AE, D, DC, MC, V.

Paradise Inn. American. This full-service dining room which is part of a 75-yr-old inn serves leisurely Sunday brunches in summer, and standard American lunch and dinner fare including sandwiches, soups, steak, seafood, and pasta. | Rte. 706, Ashford | 360/569–2275 or 360/569–2413 | Breakfast also available. Closed Oct.–mid-May | $20–$30 | AE, D, DC, MC, V.

Lodging

National Park Inn. A large stone fireplace takes pride of place in the common room which otherwise has a generic country-inn feel at this lodging, one of only two in the park. Rooms have rustic details like wrought-iron lamps and antique bentwood headboards. The inn is located 6 mi east of the Nisqually entrance. | 25 rooms. Restaurant, no air-conditioning, no room phones, no TV, no pets, no smoking. | Mt. Rainier National Park, Longmire | 360/569–2275 | fax 360/569–2770 | $77–$107 | AE, D, DC, MC, V.

Paradise Inn. This inn is 19 mi into the park and has a sumptuous lobby with two fireplaces and Indian rugs. The views are wonderful. | 117 rooms (47 with shared bath). Restaurant (*see* Paradise Inn), bar, no air-conditioning, no room phones, business services, no smoking. | Rte. 706, Ashford | 360/569–2275 | fax 360/569–2770 | www.guestservices.com/rainier | $72–$108 | Closed early Oct.–Apr. | AE, D, DC, MC, V.

Randle Motel. There are basic accommodations at this motor inn which sits in the center of Randle, adjacent to restaurants and stores. The rooms are all furnished with double beds. | 10 rooms. No air-conditioning, no room phones, pets allowed. | 9780 Hwy. 12, Randle | 360/497–5346 | $35–$45 | MC, V.

MT. ST. HELENS NATIONAL VOLCANIC MONUMENT

MAP 8, D7

(Nearby towns also listed: Kelso, Packwood)

Since its eruption in 1980, Mt. St. Helens has become a popular destination. The 8,367-ft-high mountain, formerly 9,665-ft high, is part of the string of volcanic peaks in the Cascade Range that includes Mt. Rainier and Mt. Baker to the north and Mt. Hood (in Oregon) to the south. The mountain is most easily accessed by driving along the Spirit Lake Memorial Highway (Highway 504), whose predecessor was destroyed in a matter of minutes on May 18, 1980. The highway has unparalleled views of the mountains and the surrounding Toutle River.

Information: Mt. St. Helens Visitor Center | Hwy. 504, east of I–5, Silver Lake | 360/274–2100 | Sat.–Wed. 9–4.

Attractions

Ape Cave. At some 12,810 ft, this cave is the longest lava tube in the Americas, and one of the longest in the world. It gets its odd name from the supposed Sasquatch/Bigfoot sightings in the region. Ape Cave has a visitor center where you can obtain information and rent lanterns. Naturalists lead a walk through the cave every summer afternoon. | Forest Service Rd. 8303 | 360/750–3900 | Free | Daily.

Camping. Seaquest State Park on Rte. 504, across from the Silver Lake Visitor Center, has both RV and tent sites; more campsites can be found at the Lewis and Clark State Park off U.S. 12 to the north; Forest Service campgrounds on the mountain's south and southeast

© Corbis

MT. ST. HELENS

Until 1980, Mt. St. Helens was a serene-looking, 9,677-ft volcano, younger, slightly smaller, and easier to climb than the Cascades other landmark peaks. Visitors to nearby Spirit Lake enjoyed the reflection of the perfectly symmetrical cone in the lake's blue water, although folks had long noticed steam coming out of the mountain's vents. Then, geologists noticed some ominous rumblings and warned that St. Helens was about to erupt.

No one was really prepared for what happened. On the morning of May 18, 1980, the mountain exploded. More than 1,300 ft of its top simply disappeared. Instead of going straight up, the blast went north, destroying everything in its path. Old-growth forests were vaporized. Big trees a little farther from the blast were scattered across the hillsides like straw or simply killed where they stood. Soil was incinerated, too, and nearby slopes were scoured down to bedrock. Volcanic ash fell on 22,000 square mi of land, including much of eastern Washington. The sky in many eastern Washington communities darkened at midday, and ash piled up like drifted snow on the streets and sidewalks. Snow and glacial ice melted by the blast poured down the mountain, creating rivers of mud that swelled the Toutle River, which rose 66 ft above its normal level, sweeping away homes and bridges. Mud flowed down to the Cowlitz and Columbia, where millions of tons had to be dredged from the shipping channel. Fifty-seven people died. The devastation appeared complete.

But pocket gophers living underground survived the blast. Within a year fireweed and other plants started recolonizing some of the blast area. Soon herds of huge brown elk wandered comfortably across the mud and the ridges above. Much of the area remains a moonscape, but life is returning as it has after volcanic eruptions in the Cascades for millions of years. Weyerhaeuser, which owned most of the land in the path of the blast, traded some to the federal government, which included it in a new Mt. St. Helens National Volcanic Monument.

From a helicopter at the crater's rim, you can look into an amphitheater of sheer gray cliffs and see a lava dome steaming in the shadows.

side have rather basic facilities. | 360/274–2100 or 360/274–2131, 360/750–3900 (for National Forest Camping) | Call for prices.

Coldwater Ridge Visitor Center. This multimillion-dollar facility documents the great blast and its effects on the surrounding 150,000 acres, which were devastated but are in the process of a remarkable recovery. A ¼-mi trail leads from the visitor center to Coldwater Lake and its recreation area. | Hwy. 504 at milepost 43 | 360/274–2131 | Free | Daily 9–5.

Hiking. Inquire at the information centers about hiking trails open or re-opened (landslides, snow, and other natural obstacles can close them at any time of the year, since the ground in this region is still very unstable). | 360/274–2100 or 360/274–2131, 360/750–3900 (for National Forest Hiking).

Hoffstadt Bluffs Visitor Center. From this spot you can see the mountain, the decimated Toutle Valley, and the surrounding area. At the visitor center you can have a meal, browse through the unique items in the gift shop, or take a helicopter tour of the mountain. | Hwy. 504 | 360/274–7750 | Free | Summer Mon.–Thurs. 10–4; Fri.–Sun. 10–8. Call for hours at other times of the year.

Mt. St. Helens Visitor Center. Before making the long drive to the mountain along Rte. 504, stop at the National Park Service Visitor Center at Silver Lake, where you can walk through a giant model of the volcano and pick up maps and information for touring. It is also possible to hire guides to lead you into the volcano's blast zone for overnight camping. | Outside the monument, on Rte. 504, milepost 5 | 360/274–2100 or 360/274–2131 | Sat.–Wed. 9–5.

Summit Climb. You need a permit and you should hire a guide to take you to the summit. Call the phone number below to learn if you physically qualify for this strenuous hike. | 360/247–3961 or 360/247–3900.

ON THE CALENDAR

JUNE: ***Annual Fishing Clinic.*** This family-oriented event allows parents and kids to fish for free. Prizes, games, storytelling, and a costume parade add extra flair to this day. | 360/247–3900.

Dining

Hoffstadt Bluffs Visitor Center. American. Arresting views of the mountain and the Toutle Valley surround the restaurant inside the visitor center—the only full-service restaurant along Highway 504. The numerous dishes served here include favorites such as hamburgers, ribs, chicken sandwiches, and salads. | Hwy. 504 | 360/274–7750 | $3–$8 | AE, D, DC, MC, V.

MOUNT VERNON

MAP 8, D2

(Nearby towns also listed: Anacortes, La Conner, Sedro Woolley)

This attractive Skagit riverfront town is the county seat of Skagit County and was founded in 1870–71. After a giant log jam on the lower Skagit was cleared, steamers began churning up the river, and Mount Vernon soon became the major commercial center of the Skagit Valley, a position it has never relinquished. More recently, Mount Vernon was named Best Small City in the U.S. by *The New Rating Guide to Life in America's Small Cities.*

The city is surrounded by dairy pastures, vegetable fields, and bulb farms, and is famous for its annual Tulip Festival in April, when thousands of people visit to admire the floral exuberance. The 972-ft-high Little Mountain, rising above downtown and the river, is a city park with a view. It used to be an island until the mudflats were filled in by Skagit River silt. Glacial striations in rocks near the top of the mountain, dating from the last continental glaciation (10,000–20,000 years ago), were made when the mountain (and all of the Puget Sound region) was covered by some 3,500 feet of ice.

Information: Mount Vernon Chamber of Commerce | 117 N. 1st St. Mount Vernon, 98273 | 360/428–8547 | www.mvcofc.org.

Attractions

Bay View State Park. This is a bayfront park adjoining the small waterfront community of Bay View on Padilla Bay. There's a campground in the woods and picnic table on the low grassy bluff above the bay. Note: If you do any boating here (including canoeing and kayaking), watch the tides. Padilla Bay runs almost dry at low tide, when water is restricted to a few, creeklike tidal channels. It's no fun to sit on the mudflats for an hour or two until the water returns (and don't even think about wading through the soft mud). | 10905 Bay View-Edison Rd., 98273 | 360/757–0227 or 800/452–5687 | www.parks.wa.gov | Free | Daily 8–dusk.

Hillcrest Park. This pleasant park in the shadow of Little Mountain has a small Oriental garden, picnic tables, a playground, and tennis and basketball courts. There is also a small, grassy park on the left bank of the Skagit River just north of downtown reached by taking Freeway Drive north of Division St. | 13th St. and Blackburn Rd. | 360/336–6213 | fax 360/336–6290 | www.mvparks@ci.mount-vernon.wa.us | Free | Daily dawn–dusk.

Little Mountain A 490-acre city park atop the 927-ft Little Mountain at the southeastern edge of town. Great views of the Skagit Valley (especially in March and April, when the daffodils and tulips are in full bloom), of the river, the San Juan Islands, and the distant Olympic Mountains. | Blackburn Rd. W | 360/336–6213 | fax 360/336–6290 | www.mvparks@ci.mount-vernon.wa.us | Free | Daily.

Padilla Bay National Estuarine Reserve. Breazeale Interpretive Center has displays and trails into the woods and to a rocky beach (great bird watching). The Padilla Bay Trail starts at the south end of Bayview (look for signs directing you to the parking area, which is away from the water off east side of road). A great place for watching waterbirds, shorebirds, and songbirds, particularly black brant geese, raptors, peregrine falcons, and bald eagles. | 10441 Bayview-Edison Rd. | 360/428–1558 | fax 360/428–1491 | www.imletgeol.sc.edu/PDB/home.html | Free | Wed.–Sun. 10–5.

ON THE CALENDAR

APR.: ***Skagit Valley Tulip Festival.*** A truly spectacular display of not just acres, but miles of blooming tulips. Parking is tight, so you might want to call ahead for the shuttle bus schedule. There is a street fair in downtown Mount Vernon with food, crafts, and other fun events. | 360/428–5959.

JULY: ***Skagit Valley Highland Games and Scottish Faire.*** Celtic folk music, traditional athletic competitions, and sheepdog shows are some of the events of this festival, held on the second weekend in July at Edgewater Park. | $10 | 360/416–4934.

Dining

Calico Cupboard. American/Casual. All natural products, the majority of which are organic, are the inspiration for the wide variety of foods at this cozy eatery. Try the turkey pot pie or the roasted vegetable sandwich on homemade bread. There are two other locations, one in La Conner (720 S. 1st St.) and another in Anacortes (901 Commercial Ave.). | 121 Freeway Dr. #B | 360/336–3107 | Breakfast also available. No dinner Sun.–Wed. | $5–$9 | MC, V.

Skagit River Brewing Company. American/Casual. A former produce warehouse now houses one of western Washington's best microbreweries along with a pub that's serving better than average food. Hewn-wood tables and comfortable couches make lounging inviting. There's a barbecue grill right outside, where the chef will do your ribs or chicken wings, or try the wood-oven pizza. | 404 S. 3rd St. | 360/336–2884 | $6–$12 | AE, MC, V.

Wildflowers. Contemporary. This elegant restaurant, in a house from the 1920s, surrounded by mature gardens, has been serving up exemplary food for more than a decade. Chef David Day has a light touch with seafood and meats; owner Michele Kjosen runs the front of the house and has just the right touch with the guests. All in all it's a very successful combination. | 2001 E. College Way | 360/424–9724 | Closed Sun.–Mon. No lunch | 15–$27 | AE, MC, V.

Lodging

Best Western College Way Inn. Comfortable off freeway inn near the Skagit River. It's centrally located, with easy access to several restaurants. | 66 rooms. Complimentary Continental breakfast, no air-conditioning, in-room data ports, some kitchenettes, some refrigerators, cable TV, pool, hot tub, business services, pets allowed (fee). | 300 W. College Way | 360/424–4287 | fax 360/424–6036 | $73–$91 | AE, D, DC, MC, V.

Best Western Cotton Tree Inn. Plain but comfortable off-freeway motel that's not far from the casinos. | 120 rooms. Bar, complimentary Continental breakfast, in-room data ports, some refrigerators, cable TV, pool, laundry facilities, business services, free parking, pets allowed (fee). | 2300 Market St. | 360/428–5678 | fax 360/428–1844 | www.cottontree.net | $79–$89 | AE, D, DC, MC, V.

Colonial Manor Bed and Breakfast. Standing on 1½ acres of landscaped lawn, gardens, and fruit trees, this plantation-style mansion was built in 1907 by one of Skagit Valley's founding families. Beautiful oak antiques fill all the rooms and conceal modern amenities such as TVs and VCRs. | 5 rooms. Complimentary Continental breakfast, in-room data ports, cable TV, in-room VCRs, no pets, no smoking. | 17550 McLean Rd. | 360/424–3237 or 800/893–1022 | cmanor@fidalgo.net | www.colonialmanorbandb.com | $100–$150 | AE, MC, V.

Storyville. This 1904 house overlooking the Skagit Valley farmlands is surrounded by a series of gardens and flower beds—as many as a thousand tulips and daffodils. Rooms are appointed with a selection of antiques that evoke the Victorian era and contribute to the romantic aura of the interior. | 5 rooms (3 with private bath). Complimentary breakfast, cable TV, in-room VCRs, no pets, no kids under 12, no smoking. | 18772 Best Rd. | 360/466–3207 or 360/770–7901 | www.ncia.com/storyville/ | $80–$125 | MC, V.

White Swan Guest House. This B&B is in a Queen Anne farm house on Fir Island in the Skagit River delta (near the tulip fields). The house was built about 1890 but thoroughly updated. There are lovely English-style gardens. | 3 rooms (all with shared baths), 1 cottage. Complimentary Continental breakfast, no air-conditioning, kitchenette (in cottage), no room phones, no smoking. | 15872 Moore Rd. | 360/445–6805 | www.thewhiteswan.com | $75–$85, $135–$150 cottage | MC, V.

NEAH BAY

MAP 8, A2

(Nearby town also listed: Port Angeles)

Neah Bay (pronounced "nee-ah"), on the Makah Indian Reservation at the northwesternmost tip of the Olympic Peninsula, is one of the oldest villages in Washington, dating back at least several thousand years. The Makah tribe (pronounced "MA-kah") has lived here since "before time began." Neah Bay is surrounded by a beautiful, albeit wet, landscape of forests, rocky cliffs, and beautiful beaches.

Cape Flattery, to the west, is the westernmost point in the contiguous United States. It got its name in 1778 from master mariner and explorer James Cook, who thought it flattered him with the prospect of an inlet. Cook did not see Juan de Fuca Strait, which was hidden by fog and rain squalls. In 1792 Spanish mariners established a short-lived fort here, which was the first European settlement in what is now Washington State.

The local Makah tribe is more closely related to the Nootka of Vancouver Island than to any other Washington Indians. Like their ancestors, they hunt whales from canoes, so you might find both whales and protesters on a local beach during your visit.

Neah Bay has a first-rate history museum, with a reconstructed longhouse and artifacts from Ozette village at Cape Alava, which was buried by a landslide several hundred years ago.

Information: Makah Tribal Council | Box 115, Hwy. 112, Building 12, Neah Bay, 98357 | 360/645–2201 | makah.com.

Attractions

Makah Cultural and Research Center. A truly great museum with a display of artifacts found in Ozette Village, which was destroyed by a mud slide hundreds of years ago; Makah art; and a reconstructed cedar longhouse. | 1880 Bayview Ave. | 360/645–2711 | fax 360/645–2656 | www.makah.com | $3 | May–Sept., daily 10–5; Nov.–Apr., Wed.–Sun. 10–5.

Makah National Fish Hatchery. View salmon as they make their way over fish ladders to the hatchery's spawning area. The most exciting time to visit is in fall and winter, before the salmon are released on the first of February. To reach the hatchery, follow the signs out of Neah Bay south for 7 mi. | 1 Fish Hatchery Rd. | 360/645–2521 | Free | Daily 7–4.

ON THE CALENDAR

AUG.: *Makah Days.* Canoe races, Indian dances, vendors, Native American arts and crafts, salmon bake, parade, and fireworks. | 360/645–2201.

Dining

Makah Maiden Café. Seafood. Freshly caught fish and seafood, sautéed or fried, is the specialty of this popular waterfront café. Outdoor seating is available on picnic benches. The restaurant occasionally hosts salmon bakes on the weekends for which salmon is prepared in a fire pit on cedar sticks. | 1471 Bay View Ave. | 360/645–2924 | Breakfast also available | $10–$17 | MC, V.

Lodging

Silver Salmon Resort Motel. Sitting in the center of Neah Bay and across from the Marina, this motel is only a hop, skip, and a jump away from restaurants and shopping; the beach is a block from your door. Rooms are appointed with basic furnishings. | 11 rooms. Picnic area, no air-conditioning, some kitchenettes, some microwaves, some refrigerators, no room phones, no TV, shop, pets allowed. | 1280 Bayview Ave. | 360/645–2388 or 888/713–6477 | silvsalm@centurytell.net | www.silversalmonresort.com | $51.50–$62 | Dec.–Feb. | D, MC, V.

Tyee Motel. A plain motel in a rather plain Indian village on a gorgeous coastline. | 41 rooms. RV park, pets allowed. | Bayview Ave. | 360/645–2223 | $42–$108 | Labor Day–mid-Apr. | MC, V.

NEWPORT

MAP 8, L3

(Nearby town also listed: Spokane)

Newport is the county seat of Pend Oreille County, in the far northeastern corner of Washington. A former mining town, Newport today caters mostly to visitors coming to relax in the Pend Oreille River Valley, a pastoral Shangri La. The river meanders across the silted-in bed of a former glacial lake and has several colonies of ospreys. Other wildlife include deer and black bear, as well as a few grizzlies. Woodland caribou winter on Sullivan Mountain. Nearby Scotia Gorge was cut by glacial melt waters and has walls up to 1,400 ft high; Z Canyon is a narrow gorge 400 ft deep with rock walls only 20 ft apart in places. Just north of Newport is the Kalispel Indian reservation, where this Salish tribe raised buffalo for tradition and profit.

Information: **Newport/Oldtown Chamber of Commerce** | 325 W. 4th St., Newport, 99156 | 509/447–5812 | www.povn.com/~chamber.

Attractions

Historical Society Museum. A collection of Indian and pioneer artifacts is on display at this museum in Centennial Plaza. | 402 S. Washington St. | 509/447–5500 | Free, donations accepted | Mid-May–Sept., daily 10–4.

ON THE CALENDAR

JULY: ***Pend Oreille River Poker Paddle.*** Teams using canoes or other non-motorized boats on the Pend Oreille River stop at designated locations, draw a card, and proceed to the finish line. Best poker hands in each division win. It starts at the USK Bridge. | 509/447–5812.

Lodging

Golden Spur Motor Inn. This two-story motel sits just west of downtown on Highway 2. Renovated in 1999, the rooms are clean and well-maintained. | 24 rooms. Restaurant, bar, some kitchenettes, some microwaves, refrigerators, cable TV, pets allowed (fee). | 924 W. Hwy. 2 | 509/447–3823 | users.rightathome.com/~goldspur | $45–$68 | AE, D, MC, V.

Newport City Inn. Small-town motel within walking distance of restaurants, in downtown Newport. | 13 rooms. No-smoking rooms, some pets allowed (fee). | 220 N. Washington | 509/447–3463 | fax 509/447–2168 | $52–$58 | AE, MC, V.

NORTH BEND

MAP 8, E4

(Nearby town also listed: Seattle)

This truck stop gets its name from a bend in the Snoqualmie River, which here turns north. The surrounding scenery is beautiful, dominated by 4,167-ft Mt. Si (with many popular hiking trails), 4,420-ft Mt. Washington, and 4,788-ft Mt. Tenerife. But the mountains also translate into high rainfall: North Bend is one of the wettest places in western Washington, with an annual precipitation often in excess of 100 inches.

The TV show *Twin Peaks* was based in North Bend, and some of its scenes were shot here, though most of the work was done in studios in Seattle.

North Bend is the last town on I–90 for gassing up before driving through the mountain wilderness lying between the settled regions and Snoqualmie Pass.

Information: **East King County Convention and Visitors Bureau** | 520 112th Ave. NE, Bellevue, 98004-5503 | 425/455–1962 or 800/252–1926 | eastkingcounty.org.

Attractions

Alpental Ski Area. One of several major ski areas on Snoqualmie Pass, with a base height of about 3,000 ft, an average elevation of 5,500 ft, and a vertical drop of about 2,200 ft. | I–90 to Alpental Rd. | 425/434–6112 or 425/236–1600 (for snow conditions) | Fri.–Sun.

Hyak Ski Area. One of several ski areas on Snoqualmie Pass, with a base height of about 3,000 ft, an average elevation of 5,400 ft, and a vertical drop of 2,200 ft. | I–90, at Snoqualmie Pass | 425/434–7600 or 425/236–1600 (snow conditions) | call for hours.

Mount Si. Climb the 3,200 ft along the 4-mi trail to see breathtaking views of Seattle, Mt. Rainier, and other Cascade Mountains. Midway up, there is an old growth forest and interpretive area. Be warned: There are no facilities along the trail and climbing it could take as much as three hours. You are encouraged to bring your own water. | Mount Si Rd. | 360/825–1631 | Free | Daily.

Ski Acres. One of several major ski areas on Snoqualmie Pass, with a base height of about 3,000 ft, an average elevation of 5,400 ft, and a vertical drop of 2,200 ft. | I-90 at Snoqualmie Pass | 425/434-6671 or 425/236-1600 (snow conditions) | Fri.-Sun.

Snoqualmie Valley Historical Museum. Pleasant museum with Indian, pioneer, and logging industry artifacts. | 320 S. Bendego Blvd. | 425/888-3200 | $1 | Apr.-Oct., Thurs.-Sun. 1-5; rest of the year, tours available by appointment.

ON THE CALENDAR

AUG.: ***Alpine Days.*** A parade, live music, fireworks, and street dancing are part of North Bend's exciting Alpine Days, an event which has been held since 1970 in downtown North Bend at Gardiner Weeks Park during the second weekend in August. | 425/888-8535 | www.snovalley.org/alpinedays.

Dining

The Reef. Fast food. Serving quality fast food such as broiled fish and teriyaki chicken over rice, burgers, and fish sandwiches, the restaurant is most famous for its fish and chips. There are wonderful views of Mount Si from the patio. | 426 Main Ave. S | 425/888-2424 | Closed Sun. | $4.50-$9 | MC, V.

Lodging

Roaring River Bed and Breakfast. Tucked away on 2½ acres above the fork of the Snoqualmie River, this B&B has unbeatable views of the river, mountains, and surrounding wilderness. Rooms have such details as wood-paneled wainscoting, fireplaces, and private decks. It's difficult to find this secluded spot, so ask for directions when you make your reservation. | 4 rooms. Complimentary breakfast, no air-conditioning, some in-room hot tubs, cable TV, no room phones, no pets, no kids under 12, no smoking. | 46715 S.E. 129th St. | 425/888-4834 or 877/627-4647 | roaring@centurytell.net | www.azl.com/roaringriv | $95-$175 | AE, D, MC, V.

NORTH CASCADES NATIONAL PARK

MAP 8, F1

(Nearby town also listed: Sedro Woolley)

North Cascades National Park is a rugged jumble of tall peaks, jagged ridges, and deeply glaciated valleys. It is broken into two sections. The larger, north of the Trans Cascades Highway, Rte. 20, is further split by the Ross Lake Recreation area which has a water taxi to transport hikers to wilderness trailheads. The highway itself is surrounded by a national recreation area. The southern half of the park is most easily entered from Rte. 20 in the north or from Lake Chelan (Stehekin) in the south. Because it is closer to urban centers, the southern half of the park tends to be more overrun with hikers. As with Washington's other mountain parks, the North Cascades have wildflower meadows, and an abundance of wildlife, which here include not only pika, deer, and ptarmigan, but also grizzly bears, which are rare and not generally encountered.

There are no lodging facilities in the park (except for campgrounds), but the surrounding towns and villages have inns with a wide range of prices.

Information: Headquarters | North Cascades NPS Complex, 2105 State Rte. 20, Sedro Woolley 98284 | 360/856-5700 | www.nps.gov.

Attractions

North Cascades Scenic Highway. The park is divided in half by Rte. 20, the North Cascades Highway. The northern section is further divided into two halves by Ross Lake National

Recreation Area, which has campgrounds, trailheads, lodges, resorts, and boat launches. Adjacent National Forest lands also have campgrounds, albeit with somewhat basic facilities. East of Ross Lake, several pullouts offer great views of the lake and the snow-capped peaks surrounding it. The whitish rocks in the road cuts are limestone and marble. Meadows along this stretch of the highway are covered with wildflowers from June to September; nearby slopes are golden and red with fall foliage from late August to October. The high point of the highway is a 5,477-ft-high Washington Pass, east of which the road drops down to the Methow Valley. The pass is closed in winter, usually from October to April or May, depending on the snowfall. | Free | May–Sept.

Seattle City Light Skagit Hydroelectric Project. One of the nation's largest civic power projects with power plants on the Skagit River and on northeast Washington's Pend Oreille River. | 62 mi east of I–5/Mount Vernon on Rte. 20 (North Cascades Hwy) in Diablo, in Ross Lake National Recreation Area | 206/684–3030 | $25 | July–Labor Day, Thurs.–Mon.; call for tour times.

Gorge Powerhouse/Ladder Creek Falls and Rock Gardens. A powerhouse is a powerhouse, but the rock gardens overlooking Ladder Creek Falls, 7 mi west of Diablo, are beautiful and inspiring. Tours are available from mid-June through September. | Hwy. 20 | 206/684–3030 | Free | May–mid-Oct., daily.

Trail of the Cedars. A short walk through a grove of big cedar trees. | End of Main St., Newhalem | 206/684–3030 | Free | Daily, depending on weather.

ON THE CALENDAR

FEB.: ***Upper Skagit Bald Eagle Festival.*** Commemorating the national bird, this festival takes place during the prime eagle spotting season (Jan.–Feb.) and includes speeches, bluegrass workshops, concerts, an arts and crafts show, as well as a "get acquainted" session with several live birds. The celebration takes place primarily in the Concrete School Complex in Concrete, though there is also an Interpretive Center in Rockport on weekends. | 360/853–7009.

Dining

Buffalo Run Restaurant. American/Casual. This restaurant, located just west of the park, serves a wide variety of different meat and vegetarian dishes, but specializes in non-traditional meats such as buffalo, venison, elk, and ostrich. Buffalo heads and old west memorabilia hang from the dining room's walls; a patio provides seating next to a garden outside. | 60084 State Rte. 20, Marblemount | 360/873–2461 | $12–$15 | AE, D, MC, V.

Lodging

Salmonberry Way Bed and Breakfast. This Victorian road house from the early 1900s stands on 8 acres of wilderness, next to the Skagit River, just 4 mi west of the park. The hiking here is unbeatable. Rooms are appointed with antiques that evoke bygone days when gold miners would stay at this road house on their way prospecting. | 2 rooms. Complimentary breakfast, no room phones, no TV, pets allowed, no smoking. | 61008 S.R. 20, Marblemount | 360/873–4016 | $49–$59 | No credit cards.

OAK HARBOR

MAP 8, C3

(Nearby towns also listed: Anacortes, Coupeville, Everett, Port Townsend)

Oak Harbor is a hybrid city. Located on a beautiful, south-facing bay; its Pioneer Way along the waterfront still has the original business district. But most of the rest of the town has gone to strip malls and used-car sales lots due to rapid growth induced by the nearby Whidbey Island Naval Air Station. On an island of small towns and rustic villages, Oak Harbor is the only place where you might not want to walk around after dark.

Information: **Greater Oak Harbor Chamber of Commerce** | 32630 SR 20, Oak Harbor, 98277 | 360/675–3535 | www.oakharborchamber.org.

Attractions

Deception Pass State Park. Occupying the northernmost portion of Whidbey Island and the southernmost section of Fidalgo Island, this is the state's most popular park with 19 mi of rocky shore and beaches and 38 mi of forest and meadow trails. | Hwy. 20 | 360/675–2417 | Free | Apr.–Sept., daily 6:30–dusk; Oct.–May, daily 8–dusk.

Holland Gardens. Shrub and flower gardens surround a blue-and-white windmill in this popular spot. The tulips are on display in spring. | Corner of S.E. 6th Ave. and S.E. Ireland St. | 360/679–5551 | www.oakharbor.org | Free | Daily.

ON THE CALENDAR

JULY: *Whidbey Island Race Week.* Recognized as one of the top 20 regattas in the world; consisting of competition sailing by day and social events by night. | 360/679–6399.

Dining

Island Grill. Seafood. Sitting just south of the Deception Pass Bridge, this family-friendly restaurant serves steak and seafood, most with Mediterranean flair. The bouillabaisse is a house specialty. Local watercolors depicting Northwest scenes ornament the walls. You can also dine outdoors amid numerous plants. | 41020 S.R. 20 | 360/679–3194 | Closed Mon. | $12–$18 | MC, V.

Kasteel Franssen. Contemporary. Built to resemble a Dutch castle, there is a moat out front, and a waterwheel. Dutch paintings and knickknacks ornament the walls of the interior. The menu has seafood dishes such as the house-smoked salmon and more imaginative dishes such as the flaming duck or loin of ostrich. | 33575 S.R. 20 | 360/675–0724 | No lunch. Oct.–May, closed Sun. | $13–$20 | AE, D, DC, MC, V.

Lodging

Auld Holland Inn. Highway motel with a European-style exterior and an antique-filled interior. | 34 rooms; 24 mobile homes. Restaurant, bar, complimentary Continental breakfast, some kitchenettes, microwaves, refrigerators, cable TV, pool, hot tub, sauna, tennis, gym, playground, laundry facilities, business services, free parking. | 33575 Rte. 20 | 360/675–2288 or 800/228–0148 | fax 360/675–2817 | www.auldhollandinn.com | $55–$145 | AE, D, DC, MC, V.

Best Western Harbor Plaza. This three-story highway motel is 1 mi from the city beach and recreation area. | 80 rooms. Lounge, complimentary Continental breakfast, in-room data ports, microwaves, refrigerators, cable TV, pool, hot tub, gym, business services, free parking, some pets allowed (fee). | 33175 SR. 20 | 360/679–4567 | fax 360/675–2543 | $80–$129 | AE, D, DC, MC, V.

Coachman Inn. This motel caters to families and each room is individually decorated. | 100 rooms. Picnic area, complimentary Continental breakfast, some kitchenettes, refrigerators, cable TV, pool, hot tub, gym, playground, laundry facilities, business services. | 32959 Rte. 20 | 360/675–0727 or 800/635–0043 | fax 360/675–1419 | www.thecoachmaninn.com | $64–$175 | AE, D, DC, MC, V.

Inn at the Bay Bed and Breakfast. This one-suite B&B, sitting on a hillside overlooking the bay, has steep gabled roofs and a stained wood exterior that give it the appearance of an Alpine home. The suite has a sitting room, deck, and balcony. | 1 room. Complimentary breakfast, cable TV, in-room VCR, no pets, no smoking. | 5129 N. Alto Ln. | 360/679–8320 | www.moriah.com/bayinn | $80 | No credit cards.

North Whidbey Inn. You're only a short stroll to the beach when you stay at this motel, which sits in a quiet, residential neighborhood. The spacious rooms were remodelled in 1998; some have full kitchens. | 16 rooms. No air-conditioning, some kitchenettes, some microwaves, refrigerators, cable TV, no pets. | 461 S.E. Midway Blvd. | 360/675–5911 or 877/820–1700 | fax 360/679–3208 | nwimotel@whidbey.net | $60–$90 | AE, D, DC, MC, V.

OCEAN SHORES

MAP 8, A5

(Nearby towns also listed: Aberdeen, Hoquiam, Westport)

Ocean Shores differs from other communities along the sandy stretch of Grays Harbor County known as North Beach in that it was deliberately planned by developers. While the other communities along this coast more or less just "happened" over a period of time, here the developers took advantage of a time when sand carried by the ocean widened the spit at the north entrance to Grays Harbor. But the process has reversed itself in recent years, and residents are scrambling to save their homes and condominiums from the ocean's fury. While the beaches last, this seaside resort has flat sandy beaches, a golf course, canals providing boat moorage, and comfortable accommodations.

Information: Ocean Shores Chamber of Commerce | 120 Chance a la Mer, Ocean Shores, 98569 | 800/76–BEACH (23224) | www.oceanshores.org.

Attractions

Ocean Shores Interpretive Center. Exhibits at the center treat the seaside environment, local community history, and Native American history. | Discovery and Catala Aves | 360/289–4617 | Free | May–Sept., daily 11–4; Oct.–Apr., by appointment.

ON THE CALENDAR

MAR.: *Beachcomber's Fun Fair.* A show which displays the strange things you can find on beaches; seminars on the weather, environment, and local wildlife. | 800/874–6737.

Dining

Alec's by the Sea. American. Alec's is the best place on the coast to taste the famous razor clams (unless you're willing to dig and cook your own, season permitting). But the large menu has other items as well—something for everyone, in fact. The portions are big and the staff is friendly, making for a very pleasant dining experience at the beach. | 131 E. Chance a la Mer Blvd. | 360/289–4026 | $10–$25 | AE, D, DC, MC, V.

Mariah's Restaurant. American/Casual. Sitting behind the dunes, adjacent to the beach, this restaurant is part of the Polynesian Resort. The menu includes a variety of steak and seafood options, but the most popular is the prime rib. | 615 Ocean Shores Blvd. NW | 360/289–3315 | No lunch | $6–$35 | AE, D, DC, MC, V.

Lodging

Canterbury Inn. Luxury oceanfront resort condominiums, right on the beach, with pleasant views of the ocean. | 45 apartments. No air-conditioning, in-room data ports, kitchenettes, cable TV, VCRs, gym, indoor pool, hot tub, laundry facilities, business services. Local airport shuttle. | 643 Ocean Shores Blvd. | 360/289–3317 or 800/562–6678 | fax 360/289–3420 | $82–$180 apartments | AE, D, DC, MC, V.

Grey Gull. A post-modernist beach resort within walking distance of all of the restaurants and shops. Trails from the hotel lead right down to the beach. All rooms have ocean views and fireplaces. | 34 suites, 36 apartments. No air-conditioning, kitchenettes, refrigerators, cable TV, pool, hot tub, sauna, laundry facilities, business services, some pets allowed (fee). | 651 Ocean Shores Blvd. | 360/289–3381 or 800/562–9712 (WA) | www.thegreygull.com | $110–$125 studios, $120–$275 suites | AE, D, DC, MC, V.

Polynesian Resort. Only a short stroll through the dunes separates you from the beach when you stay at this resort, replete with modern amenities. The upper floors have views of the water and most rooms come with a fireplace and full kitchen. | 71 rooms. Restaurant, picnic area, kitchenettes, microwaves, refrigerators, cable TV, pool, spa, sauna, basketball, volleyball, beach, pets allowed. | 615 Ocean Shores | 360/289–3361 or 800/562–4836 | $79–$320 | AE, D, DC, MC, V.

Shilo Inn. Big glitzy oceanfront resort with all the bells and whistles as well as a friendly staff. | 113 rooms. Restaurant, bar, room service, in-room data ports, cable TV, video games, indoor pool, hot tub, sauna, gym, laundry facilities, business services. Local airport shuttle. | 707 Ocean Shores Blvd. NW | 360/289–4600 | fax 360/289–0355 | $99–$239 | AE, D, DC, MC, V.

Silver Waves Inn Bed and Breakfast. Opened in 1998, this inn sits directly on the Grand Canal. The individually appointed rooms each have their own charm; the Captains Room, for instance, has a private deck with views of the sunset and sunrise. A sumptuous breakfast is served in the sunroom, overlooking the water. | 4 rooms, 1 cottage. Complimentary breakfast, no air-conditioning, cable TV, no room phones, no pets, no smoking. | 982 Point Brown Ave. SE | 360/289–2490 or 888/257–0894 | fax 360/289–9291 | silverwave@techline.com | www.techline.com/~silverwave | $85–$130 | AE, MC, V.

OLYMPIA

MAP 8, C5

(Nearby towns also listed: Centralia, Tacoma)

Olympia has been state (and before that, territorial) capital of Washington since 1853, right from the beginning of city and state. It is small for the capital city of a major state, but that makes it all the more pleasant to visit. Downtown is compact and easy on the feet. You can walk almost anywhere within minutes—from the State Capitol campus to the shops and restaurants of the charming old downtown at the foot of the hill, to Capitol Lake, bordering downtown to the west, to the harbor at Budd Inlet to the north. You don't see much saltwater from downtown, unless you take the harborside boardwalk, because bluffs, trees, and buildings block the view.

The folks who planned the layout of the capitol grounds did a great job. The park surrounding the capitol and other government buildings is a very user-friendly grassy expanse much visited by walkers, joggers, and aerobic exercisers. In spring the grounds are fragrant with lilacs and white with cherry blossoms.

The very imposing state capitol, finished in 1928, seems almost too big for such a small town. Like a fortress, it occupies the crest of a hill. Its height is further emphasized by a skirt of magnificent granite steps. The monumental 287-ft-high dome is the fourth largest masonry dome in the world (only St. Peter's in Rome, St. Paul's in London, and the National Capitol in the other Washington are larger). The capitol is flanked by the colonnaded Temple of Justice and the state insurance building. To the west, between the capitol and Capitol Lake, rise the tree-shaded grounds of the Governor's Mansion, which is not open to the public.

Information: State Capitol Visitor Information Center | Box 41020, 14th St. and S. Capitol Way Olympia, 98504 | 360/586–3460 | www.ci.olympia.wa.us/.

NEIGHBORHOODS

Because, in the past, many residents lived here only during the legislative session, Olympia has failed to develop distinctive neighborhoods as have Seattle and Spokane. Olympia's most expensive residences border on (or overlook) Budd Inlet. Several clifftop residences have slid into the water in recent years, as bluffs have become unstable, due to excessive development. The adjoining cities of Lacey and Tumwater are, for all practical purposes, part of Olympia. But they are politically independent.

Capitol Campus. To get there, take the well-marked exit off I-5 and follow directions. Don't try to get there by way of downtown. It's easier to get to the downtown from the Capitol Campus than vice versa. You'll see signs for off-campus parking and a shuttle, but there is always ample on-street parking.

Downtown. Olympia lies north (downhill) of the state capitol and the government office buildings. Sylvester Park, east of Capitol Avenue, was once the center of the state's political gravity, when the Old Thurston County courthouse (known as the "Old Capitol") was the seat of government.

Compared to the elegance of the capitol campus, downtown appeared grungy, almost a bit seedy, until about ten years ago, when young people (many associated with nearby Evergreen State College) moved in and revitalized the urban core. While many of the old downtown brick buildings still look a bit rundown, there's now a healthy sprinkling of ethnic cafés, used-book stores, record shops, and boutiques.

At night, there's a lively (and safe) bar scene. Part of downtown is on a peninsula, which reaches into Budd Inlet to the north, with its working waterfront. The southwestern part of downtown is bordered by Capitol Lake and its parkland shores to the west. Many of Olympia's early residential neighborhoods were established east and south of downtown, but the west bluffs, west of Budd Inlet, became the favored residential neighborhood in the period between the two World Wars.

West Bluffs (District west of Capitol Lake and Budd Inlet). Capitol Lake, southwest of downtown, is bordered by parks and by bike and walking paths. The Deschutes River enters Budd Inlet at the northern end of the lake.

The low ridge between Capitol Lake/Budd Inlet and Eld Inlet/Mud Bay has some of Olympia's most upscale residential neighborhoods, which blend into the Evergreen State College campus to the northwest. Evergreen is a modern concrete-building campus set into the woods above Eld Inlet (to reach it, follow signs from U.S. 101). To the southwest, near the U.S. 101 freeway, stretches a blight of suburban shopping malls. The Black Lake area, farther southwest, is another upscale residential area.

Tumwater and Lacey. These small towns blend into Olympia; Lacey to the east and Tumwater to the south are all but indistinguishable as independent communities. They have their own business districts and well-mannered residential neighborhoods.

Lacey started as a retirement community and has recently become "mall city," as the region's population began to boom. Tumwater is the oldest American settlement north of the Columbia River. The town was founded at the falls of the Tumwater River in 1845 ("tumwater" means "noisy water" in the Chinook jargon, which served as a 19th-century trade language in the Pacific Northwest).

PARKING IN OLYMPIA

Olympia's rush hour is nothing but a minuscule blip in I-5 traffic (which passes through town and is very busy 24 hours a day) and in the traffic heading west and north on U.S. 101. Parking is no problem, even when the legislature is in session. Parking lots are well marked.

Attractions

ART AND ARCHITECTURE

Capitol Group. Overlooking Capitol Lake from a high bluff, this is one of the most scenic state capitol complexes in the country. The grounds feature beautifully landscaped lawns dotted with trees, a sunken rose garden, and a conservatory. It is especially striking when the flowering cherry trees and rhododendrons bloom. | Between 11th and 14th Aves | 360/586–8687 or 360/586–3460 (tours) | www.walishome/wash.htm | Free | Daily 10–3.

Legislative Building. The soaring 287-ft dome of the State Capitol is the fourth largest stone dome in the world. | Between 11th and 14th Aves | 360/586–8687 | www.walishome/wash.htm | Free | Daily 10–3.

Washington State Library. A modern colonnaded building decorated with murals, mosaics, paintings, and sculptures by Northwest artists. Plus, of course, an excellent research library on topics relating to Washington state. | Capitol Way bet. 11th and 14th Aves | 360/586–8687 | www.walishome/wash.htm | Free | Weekdays 8–4.

Temple of Justice. A colonnaded building housing, among other offices, the State Supreme Court Room and the Law Library. | Capitol Way, between 11th and 14th Aves | 360/586–8687 | www.walishome/wash.htm | Free | Weekdays 10–4.

BEACHES, PARKS, AND NATURAL SIGHTS

Capitol Lake. Capitol Lake was formed in 1951, by damming the Deschutes River at the mouth. The former mud flats are now covered with some 30 ft of water; salmon can be seen ascending the fish ladders in autumn. The lake is surrounded by parks and serves as a magnificent reflecting pool for the state capitol. | Deschutes Pkwy. | Free | Daily.

Millersylvania State Park. This 335-acre park has a deep lake as well as camping, picnicking, and boating facilities. The site was first settled by Imperial Austrian general John Mueller, who married a daughter of Austrian Emperor Franz Josef I, without official permission. As a result of this misalliance, both he and his wife were exiled. | Exit 95 off I–5 | 360/753–1519 | www.parks.wa.gov | Free, camping $12–$17 | Daily 8–dusk.

Olympic National Forest. This forest surrounds Olympic National Park on the east, south, and northwest sides. Once inside there is lots to do, from the excellent trout fishing to hiking and even hunting. It can be reached from many roads which branch off U.S. 101. From Olympia the best is to take I–5 to U.S. 101 NE to exit 104 | 360/956–2400 | fax 360/956–2430 | www.fs.fed.uf/r6/olympic | Free | Headquarters: May–Sept., weekdays 8–4:30 hours of forest change with conditions, ranger stations closed in winter.

Priest Point Park. A 253-acre park with Budd Inlet waterfront, hiking trails, picnic tables. | E. Bay Dr. | 360/753–8380 | Free | Daily, dawn–dusk.

Tumwater Falls Park. This long and narrow park south of Olympia follows the rapids and cascades of the Tumwater River to Capitol Lake. It is particularly pretty in spring, when the rhododendrons bloom along the river and the cherry trees bloom on the shores of the lake. In fall, salmon ascend the rapids and fish ladders. | Deschutes Way and C St., Tumwater | 360/943–2550 | Free | Daily.

Tumwater Historical Park. In 1845 the first American settlement on Puget Sound was where this pleasant riverfront park sits today. It has a picnic area and a boat launch. | 777 Simmons Rd. SW | 360/754–4160 | fax 360/754–4166 | www.olywa.net/tumwater | Free | Daily, dawn–dusk.

MUSEUMS

Evergreen State College. Modern architecture mixes with tall evergreens on the campus of this nontraditional college where written evaluations replace grades and where students engage in interdisciplinary approaches to their fields of interest. This modern campus was designed for walking. It is encircled by a loop service road from which covered walkways run to the different buildings of the academic core (a map of the campus can be obtained at the library). Because as much of the pristine forest as possible was preserved during construction, a walk around this campus shows how modern buildings can be fitted into natural surroundings. | 2700 Evergreen Pkwy. NW | 360/866–6000 | Free.

State Capital Museum. Housed in the 1923–25 C. J. Lord Mansion, this museum has exhibits on pioneers, Washington's territorial period, and other items of historical interest. | 211 W. 21st Ave. | 360/753–2580 | fax 360/586–8322 | www.wshs.org | $2 | Tues.–Fri. 10–4, weekends noon–4.

ON THE CALENDAR

FEB.: *Ethnic Celebration.* Seventy-five agencies and community groups come together to participate in this celebration. Ethnic foods, crafts, informative displays, and live entertainment are all at the Olympia Center. | 360/753–8380.

MAY: *Capital City Marathon and Relay.* A marathon, a half-marathon, and kids' races take place in several locations, among them rural Tumwater, Lacey, and Olympia. | 360/786–1786 | www.capitalcitymarathon.org.

MAY: *Wooden Boat Fair.* Wooden boats, arts, crafts, children's boat building booth, musical entertainments, and booths selling international foods are all happening at Percival Landing on the waterfront in downtown Olympia. | 360/943–5404.

JULY–AUG.: *Thurston County Fair.* Carnival, games, and exhibits take place at the fairgrounds in Lacey. | 360/445–3413.

SEPT.: *Harbor Days.* This festival has tugboat races, arts and crafts, and food booths, and is held on Labor Day weekend at the harbor. | 800/788–8847.

WALKING TOUR

Capitol Campus and Downtown. The 8-acre Capitol campus overlooking **Capitol Lake** is a world of its own, with its broad lawns, groves of flowering cherry trees, government buildings, sculptures, and monuments. It is surrounded by even more office buildings housing various state agencies. The core of the campus consists of several buildings unified in style: the **Legislative Building** (State Capitol; 1927–28) with its tall dome; the **Temple of Justice** (1917–1920); and the **Insurance Building** (1921). The Governor's mansion to the west and a turn-of-the-20th-century conservatory predate the government buildings. You can spend all your time walking around the campus, or you can extend your walk by a block south to the **Washington State Capital Museum,** 211 W. 21st Avenue, which sits in a pretty old residential neighborhood, or you can walk a few blocks north to downtown with its cafés and shops, and continue north to Olympia's waterfront on Budd Inlet.

Dining

INEXPENSIVE

Ben Moore's Restaurant. American. An old-fashioned café serving homey South Sound fare such as oysters and razor clams, plus hamburgers and microbrews. Full bar offering beer, wine, and spirits. Sun. night DJ music at bar. | 112 W. Fourth Ave. | 360/357–7527 | No lunch or dinner Sun. | $8–$16 | AE, MC, V.

Fish Bowl Brew Pub. Tex-Mex. The Fish Bowl Brew Pub in downtown Olympia has great microwbrews and nibbles in a very "fishy" setting. | 515 Jefferson St. | 360/943–3650. | $6–$8 | D, MC, V.

Fourth Avenue Tavern. American/Casual. Up to 26 beers are on tap at this bar which contains many pool tables and assorted games. The pub menu includes homemade pizzas, burgers, pastas, fish and chips, and clam steamers. On weekends, rock bands perform here. | 210 E. 4th Ave. | 360/786–1444 | $5–$11 | AE, MC, V.

Mondo Shrimp. Seafood. Shrimp is the one characteristic universal to all the items on the menu: there are shrimp salad, shrimp tortilla, and shrimp cocktail. The quirky storefront attracts a hip, younger crowd. | 415 Water St. | 360/352–5759 | $7–$14 | AE, D, DC, MC, V.

Wagner's. Cafés. A long-established bakery and deli serving sumptuous pastries and delectable sandwiches. | 1013 Capitol Way | 360/357–7268 | Closed Sun. No dinner | $5–$10 | AE, MC, V.

MODERATE

Alice's Restaurant. Contemporary. This rural restaurant is housed in a Skookumchuck Valley farmhouse next to the Johnson Creek Winery, about 15 mi southeast of Olympia. The restaurant suggests calling for driving directions. The winery's offerings accompany elegant five-course meals that are sophisticated variations on classical American cuisine. Vegetable appetizers, Alice's famous peanut soup, a fish course, and home-baked bread precede robust entrées—anything from wild game to duck or from steak to pasta—and lastly, dessert. Despite its distance from Olympia, this restaurant is very popular with politicians and lobbyists, as well as wedding parties. | 19248 Johnson Creek Rd. SE, Tenino | 360/264–2887 | Reservations essential | Fri.–Sun. dinner only, other times by arrangement (groups) | $13–$27 | AE, D, DC, MC, V.

Falls Terrace. American. An elegant, multi-level restaurant with large windows offering an unobstructed view of the cascading Tumwater Falls. Steaks, burgers, and seafood are as fancy as the food gets. There is dining on the deck, but you have to be over 21. Kids' menu, early bird suppers (Mon.–Sat) | 106 S. Deschutes Way | 360/943–7830 | $15–$30 | AE, D, DC, MC, V.

EXPENSIVE

La Petite Maison. French. A converted 1890 farmhouse (which now stands almost in the middle of the expanding city) houses an intimate restaurant serving up great, French-inspired food made with local ingredients wherever possible. Highlights include fresh local oysters (including the hard-to-find tiny native Olympias), crab cakes, and rack of lamb marinated in rosemary, garlic, and Dijon mustard. But do make sure to leave room for the excellent desserts. | 101 Division NW | 360/943–8812 | Closed Sun. No lunch Sat.–Mon. | $25–$30 | MC, V.

Lodging

MODERATE

Best Western Aladdin Motor Inn. Comfortable, friendly downtown motel favored by politicians and lobbyists because it is within easy walking distance of the Capitol grounds and government offices. | 99 rooms. Restaurant, bar, in-room data ports, no-smoking rooms, cable TV, pool, hot tub, gym, laundry facilities. | 900 Capitol Way | 360/352–7200 or 800/367–7771 | fax 360/352–0846 | $75–$85 | AE, D, DC, MC, V.

Best Western Tumwater. This faux-brick, mission-style motel is next to golf and tennis and ½ mi from Tumwater Falls. It's also 1 mi from the Olympia and Miller Brewing Co. | 89 rooms. Complimentary Continental breakfast, in-room data ports, refrigerators, microwaves, cable TV, gym, hot tub, sauna, laundry facilities, business services, some pets allowed (fee). | 5188 Capitol Blvd. S., Tumwater | 360/956–1235 | fax 360/956–1235, ext. 277 | $70–$83 | AE, D, DC, MC, V.

Cavanaughs Motel. Business travelers' and lobbyists' motel with easy access to I–5. | 185 rooms, 10 suites. Restaurant, bar, in-room data ports, room service, cable TV, video games, pool, hot tub, gym, laundry facilities, business services, free parking. | 2300 Evergreen Park Dr. | 360/943–4000 | fax 360/357–6604 | $115, $175 suites | AE, D, DC, MC, V.

Harbinger Inn. The white pillars and wide balconies that grace the exterior of this 1910 mansion almost give it the appearance of a plantation house. The rooms, which are appointed with period antiques and adorned with original wall stencilings, have stupendous views of the bay and mountains. | 5 rooms, 1 cottage. Complimentary breakfast, some in-room VCRs, some room phones, no TV in some room, library, no kids under 12, no smoking. | 1136 E Bay Dr. | 360/754–0389 | fax 360/754–7499 | www.harbingerinn.uswestdex.com | $60–$125 | AE, MC, V.

Ramada Inn–Governor House. This hotel right in the center of town is a favorite with lobbyists. | 123 rooms. Restaurant, bar, in-room data ports, refrigerators, cable TV, pool, hot tub, exercise equipment, laundry facilities, business services. | 621 S. Capital Way | 360/352–7700 | fax 360/943–9349 | $59–$190 | AE, D, DC, MC, V.

Swantown Inn. Antiques and lace ornament every room of this stylish Victorian inn, originally built as a mansion in 1893, then used as a boarding house, and then, according to some, a brothel. Today gardens and landscaped lawns surround the inn. The rooms overlook these gardens and the capitol dome. | 4 rooms. Complimentary breakfast, no room phones, TV in common area, no pets, no kids under 9, no smoking. | 1431 11th Ave. SE | 360/753–9123 | swantown@olywa.net | www.olywa.net/swantown | $85–$125 | MC, V.

Tyee Hotel. Fat-cat lobbyists' and convention motel south of Olympia in wooded setting. | 146 rooms. Restaurant, bar with entertainment, picnic area, in-room data ports, room service, some in-room hot tubs, cable TV, pool, beauty salon, tennis, business services. | 500 Tyee Dr., Tumwater | 360/352–0511 or 800/386–8933 | fax 360/943–6448 | $69–$150 | AE, D, DC, MC, V.

OLYMPIC NATIONAL PARK

MAP 8, B3

(Nearby towns also listed: Forks, Port Angeles, Sequim)

Olympic National Park encompasses more than 1,300 square mi of wilderness in the heart of the Olympic Mountains and in a 57-mi-long coastal strip on the Pacific Coast. It is the most geographically diverse of our national parks. Mountains and valleys radiate outward from glacier-crowned, 7,965-ft Mt. Olympus into steep-sided, deeply cut glacier and river valleys. Besides Mt. Olympus, the park has several other high peaks in the 6,000- to 7,000-ft range; wildflower meadows; a rugged, rocky shoreline; sandy, windswept beaches; white-water rivers; and an abundance of wildlife.

No roads cross the park, which means that if you want to explore its more remote regions you will have to do some backpacking. Except for that, it almost seems like a neighborhood park, since you can see it from many places in western Washington. Its peaks loom up high against the horizon whether you live in Olympia or Seattle, Bellingham or Port Angeles.

The park can be approached from all directions, since it is encircled by highways. A popular but steep approach is from the Hood Canal, but roads and trails climb quickly into the mountains. Western approaches have more gentle slopes but are a lot wetter. An excellent road runs from Port Angeles south to a visitor center at Hurricane Ridge, which has some truly spectacular views of the heart of the mountains.

YOUR FIRST-AID TRAVEL KIT

- ❑ Allergy medication
- ❑ Antacid tablets
- ❑ Antibacterial soap
- ❑ Antiseptic cream
- ❑ Aspirin or acetaminophen
- ❑ Assorted adhesive bandages
- ❑ Athletic or elastic bandages for sprains
- ❑ Bug repellent
- ❑ Face cloth
- ❑ First-aid book
- ❑ Gauze pads and tape
- ❑ Needle and tweezers for splinters or removing ticks
- ❑ Petroleum jelly
- ❑ Prescription drugs
- ❑ Suntan lotion with an SPF rating of at least 15
- ❑ Thermometer

*Excerpted from *Fodor's: How to Pack: Experts Share Their Secrets*

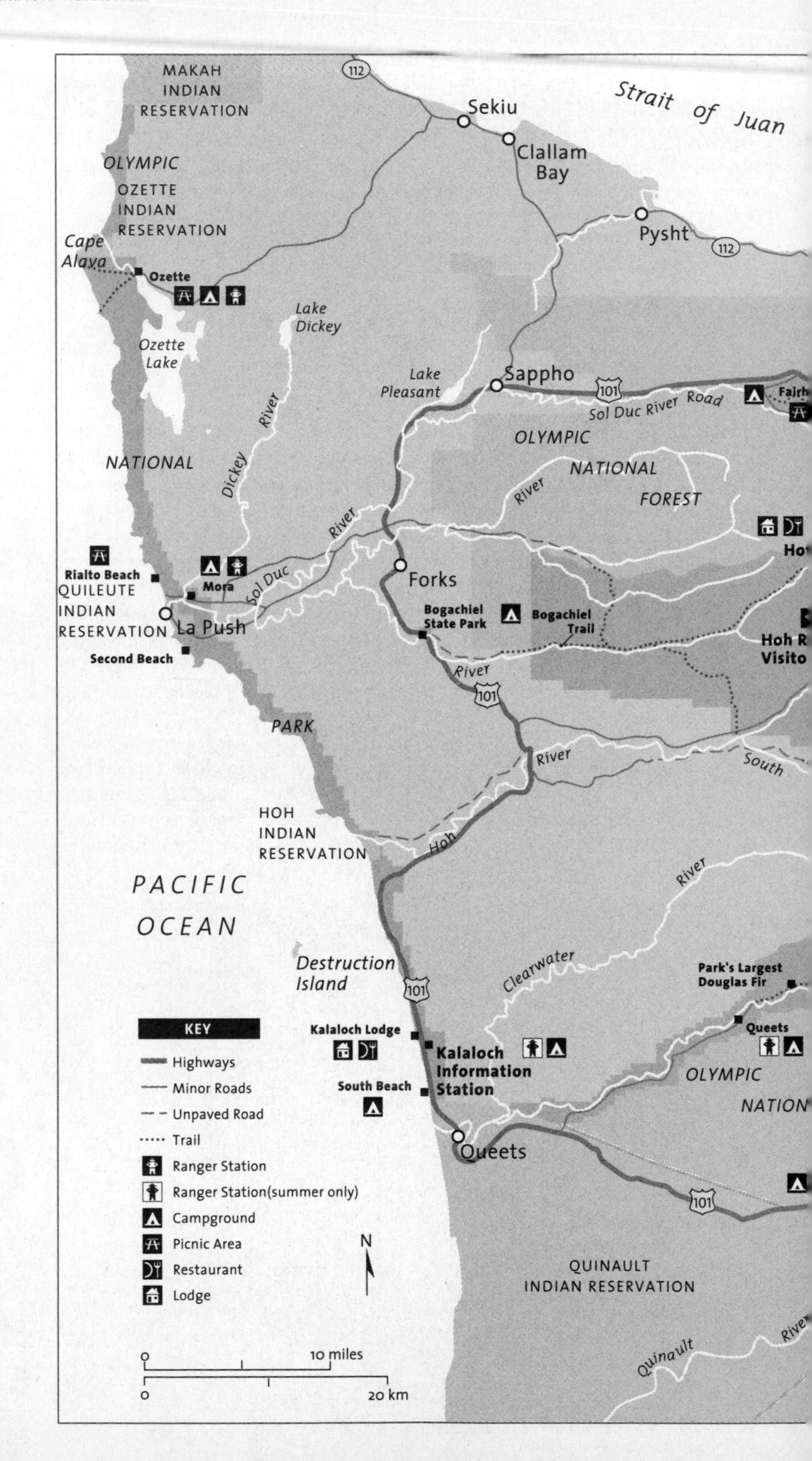
MAKAH
INDIAN
RESERVATION
Sekiu
Strait of Juan
Clallam
Bay
OLYMPIC
OZETTE
INDIAN
RESERVATION
Pysht
Cape
Alava
Ozette
Lake
Dickey
Ozette
Lake
Lake
Pleasant
Sappho
Sol Duc River Road
Dickey
River
OLYMPIC
NATIONAL
FOREST
NATIONAL
River
River
Forks
Rialto Beach
Mora
Sol Duc
QUILEUTE
INDIAN
RESERVATION
La Push
Second Beach
Bogachiel
State Park
Bogachiel
Trail
River
PARK
River
South
HOH
INDIAN
RESERVATION
Hoh
PACIFIC
OCEAN
River
Destruction
Island
Clearwater
Park's Largest
Douglas Fir
KEY
Highways
Minor Roads
Unpaved Road
Trail
Ranger Station
Ranger Station(summer only)
Campground
Picnic Area
Restaurant
Lodge
Kalaloch Lodge
Kalaloch
Information
Station
South Beach
Queets
Queets
OLYMPIC
N
QUINAULT
INDIAN RESERVATION
10 miles
20 km
Quinault

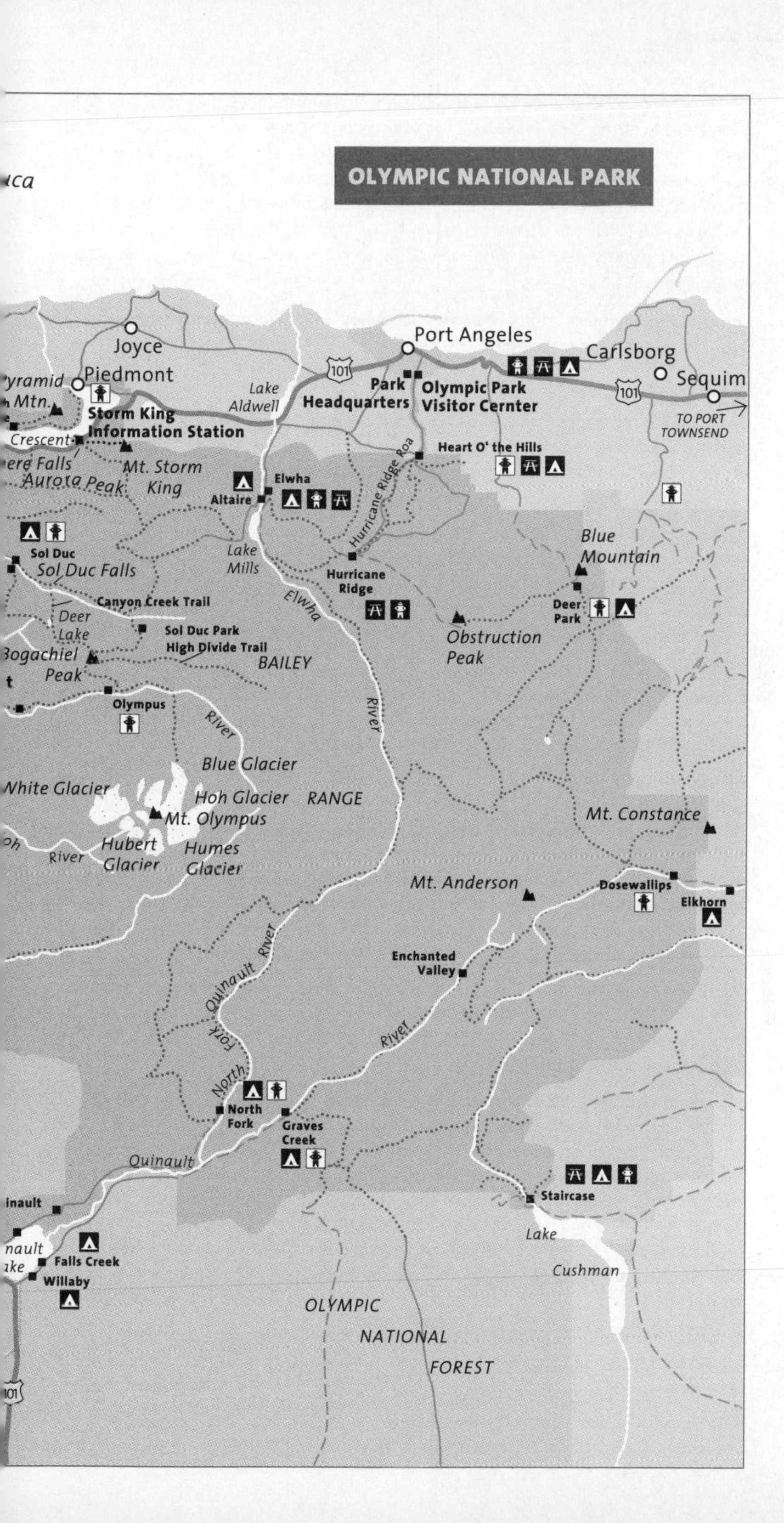
OLYMPIC NATIONAL PARK
Joyce
Piedmont
Port Angeles
Carlsborg
Sequim
Lake Aldwell
Park Headquarters
Olympic Park Visitor Cernter
Storm King Information Station
TO PORT TOWNSEND
Crescent
Heart O' the Hills
Mt. Storm King
Aurora Peak
Elwha
Altaire
Blue Mountain
Lake Mills
Sol Duc
Sol Duc Falls
Hurricane Ridge
Hurricane Ridge Roa
Canyon Creek Trail
Deer Lake
Deer Park
Sol Duc Park
High Divide Trail
Obstruction Peak
BAILEY
Elwha River
Olympus
Blue Glacier
White Glacier
Hoh Glacier
RANGE
Mt. Olympus
Mt. Constance
Hubert Glacier
Humes Glacier
River
Mt. Anderson
Dosewallips
Elkhorn
Enchanted Valley
Quinault River
North Fork
Graves Creek
Quinault
Staircase
Lake Cushman
Falls Creek
Willaby
OLYMPIC NATIONAL FOREST
101

One experienced Olympic Mountains backpacker commented that you have to hike a long way in other parts of the park to get the kinds of views you can drive to at Hurricane Ridge. Not only that, but Hurricane Ridge also has an uncommonly fine display of all variety of wildflowers in spring and summer, including columbines, monkey flowers, geum, lupine, larkspur, avalanche lily, glacier lily, fireweed, and wild sweet pea.

Except for Lakes Crescent and Quinault, there are no lodging facilities in the park outside of campgrounds, but the surrounding towns and villages have inns with a wide range of prices.

Information: **Olympic National Park Headquarters** | 600 E. Park Ave., Port Angeles 98362 | 360/452–4501 | www.nps.gov

Attractions

Beach. Along the park's 63 mi of wilderness shore you can spy whales, otters, and seals swimming beyond and between the rocky, rugged islands that dot the coast. Tide pools provide opportunities for observing sea stars, anemones, and other marine wildlife. | Hwy. 101 | 360/452–4501.

Camping. Campgrounds in Olympic National Park don't have some of the modern amenities many campers have gotten used to, such as hot water and showers. If that's too primitive for you, camp at one of the state parks nearby: Dosewallips, Sequim Bay, Bogachiel, or Pacific Beach. Availability is on a first-come, first-served basis. | Entrance: 600 Park Ave., Port Angeles | 360/452–0330 | fax 360/452–4501 ext. 207 | www.nps.gov/olym | $10–$12 | July–Labor Day, daily.

Fishing. Lake Crescent has good fishing (rent rowboats at the lodge), and you can fish the coastal strip; salmon have become scarce in the rivers. | In Olympic National Park | 360/452–0330 | fax 360/452–4501 ext. 207 | www.nps.gov/olym | $10 | Daily.

Hiking. Hiking trails enter the park from all directions; in fact, the only way to cross the park is by hiking (and backpacking), since no road crosses the mountains. You also need to hike to get to the most scenic beaches, since automobile access is very limited. Most trails on the ocean side of the mountains can be very wet, even in summer. If you like to walk in the sunshine, take a trail leading from the Hood Canal into the mountains, or one of the many alpine trails starting at Hurricane Ridge. The short (¼-mi) Marymere Falls Trail takes you from Lake Crescent Lodge to the 90-ft falls. | In Olympic National Park | 360/452–0330 | fax 360/452–4501 ext. 207 | www.nps.gov/olym | $10 | Daily.

Hurricane Ridge Winter Use Area. Hurricane Ridge offers weekend skiing only; the ski area may be closed during severe snowfall. When the ski area is open, the ridge is also great for snowshoeing. | In Olympic National Park | 360/452–0329 | fax 360/452–4501 ext. 207 | Daily, call for weather conditions.

Mountain Climbing. Mt. Olympus and other peaks in the park are very popular with climbers, perhaps because they are rugged but not overly high (Mt. Olympus, the tallest, tops out at 7,965 ft). But do get expert advice before setting out. The mountains are steep, the landscape is broken up by escarpments and ridges, and there are bridgeless creeks and rivers to cross. It's easy to take a fall or to get lost (which happens every year to inexperienced hikers and climbers). | In Olympic National Park through the rain forest | 360/452–0330 | fax 360/452–4501 ext. 207 | www.nps.gov/olym | A Wilderness Permit is needed. Cost is $5 per group, up to 12 people; $2 per person additional per night for people over 16 | Daily, weather permitting.

Pyramid Peak Trail. The 3½-mi trail climbs 2,600 feet from the north shore of the lake to the summit on which sits a WWII aircraft surveillance station. Views of the lake and the Strait of Juan de Fuca are found along the way. | Lake Crescent | 360/452–4501.

Rain Forests. The temperate rain forests are among the world's most spectacular, not only because they are bathed in a green gloom, but because the trees are more than 50 percent higher than trees of the tropical rain forests. The Pacific Coast from northern California to Alaska has the tallest trees in the world, and here you see them at their best. Be prepared for rain: the region receives 140 inches or more of rain a year (that's 12 ft and up). At times, you may feel as if you're drowning in the rain because you are. Rain forests are not limited to Olympic National Park but occur elsewhere in the Pacific Northwest (near Willapa Bay, on the Oregon Coast, and elsewhere), but here they come with trails and interpretive centers. The three most extensive rain forests in the park are in the valleys of the Hoh, the Bogachiel, and the Queets Rivers. | Hwy. 101, 20 mi off Upper Hoh Rd. | 360/452–0330 | fax 360/452–4501 ext. 207 | $10 per vehicle (7-day pass) | Daily.

Dining

Lake Crescent Lodge. American. As part of the original 1916 lodge (21 mi west of Port Angeles), the dining room overlooks the lake and there are spectacular views of the sunset. The classic American dishes served up here are complemented by a variety of seafood entrées. | 416 Lake Crescent Rd., Port Angeles | 360/928–3211 | Breakfast also available. Mid-Oct.–mid-Apr. | $15–$25 | AE, D, DC, MC, V.

Sol Duc Hot Springs Resort. Contemporary. The attractive dining room serves unpretentious meals (breakfast, lunch, and dinner) drawing on the best of the Northwest: salmon, crab, fresh vegetables, and fruit. | Soleduck Rd. and Hwy. 101 | 360/327–3583 | fax 360/327–3398 | Closed mid-Oct.–mid-May | $11–$17 | AE, D, MC, V.

Lodging

Lake Crescent Lodge. Sitting directly on the lake 21 mi west of Port Angeles and surrounded by tall firs and hemlocks, the main building hearkens back to 1916 when it served as a tavern. A stuffed elk head hangs above the huge stone fireplace in the antiques-filled lobby. The simple pine furniture of the cedar-paneled guest rooms gives them a spartan flavor. Making up for this, however, are the wonderful mountain and water views from the bedroom windows. | 52 rooms. Restaurant, no air-conditioning, no room phones, no TV, pets allowed, no smoking. | 416 Lake Crescent Rd., Port Angeles | 360/928–3211 | www.olypen.com/lakecrescentlodge | $66.50–$141.50 | AE, D, DC, MC, V.

Sol Duc Hot Springs. This rustic resort, 12 mi off Hwy. 101, has had some ups-and-downs, but is currently on the upswing again. Great location in the park and great hot springs. | 32 cottages. Dining room, picnic area, no air-conditioning, some kitchenettes, 4 pools, wading pool, massage, pets allowed. | Soleduck Rd. and Hwy. 101 | 360/327–3583 | fax 360/327–3593 | $98–$118 cottages | Closed Oct.–Mar. | AE, D, MC, V.

OMAK

MAP 8, H2

(Nearby town also listed: Winthrop)

Omak (pronounced "oh-mack"), a small town in the beautifully rustic Okanogan Valley of north-central Washington, has in recent years been criticized by animal lovers as making a business out of attempted suicide. The quarrel concerns the annual mid-August Omak Stampede and Suicide Race, a wild horse race down a steep bluff and across the Okanogan River in which horses have been killed and riders seriously injured. Most of the riders are from the Colville Reservation, and elders defend the race as being part of Indian culture. Despite the detractors, more and more spectators attend the event every year.

Omak is a small mill and orchard town that has outgrown the adjoining county seat of Okanogan. Lake Omak to the southeast, on the Colville Reservation, is part of an ancient channel of the Columbia River, which ran north prior to the last Ice Age before turning south at Omak in what is now the lower Okanogan Valley.

Information: Omak Visitor Information Center | 401 Omak Ave., Omak, 98841 | 509/826–4218 or 800/225–6625 | www.omakchronicle.com/ | omakvic@northcascades.net.

Attractions

Okanogan County Historical Museum. Historic items and displays of Okanogan pioneer life are exhibited here. | 1410 Second St., Okanogan | 509/422–4272 | Donations accepted ($2 suggested) | May–Sept., daily 10–4; by appointment rest of the year.

Okanogan National Forest. A beautiful region of open woods and meadows in the Okanogan highlands (a granite batholith), with pastoral river valleys, and lots of wildlife: deer, black bear, coyotes, badgers, bobcats, cougars, grouse, hawks, and golden eagles. Campgrounds are scattered throughout the region. Ski areas are at Loup, Loup Pass, and Sitzmark. There are also six snow parks for snowmobilers (groomed trails). Cross-country skiing is good wherever there's enough snow and the slopes aren't too steep. | 1240 2nd Ave. S | 509/826–3275 | www.fs.fed.us/r6/oka | Free | Weekdays 7:45–4:30.

ON THE CALENDAR

AUG.: ***Omak Stampede and World Famous Suicide Race.*** Held on the second weekend in August at the Omak Stampede Arena, the rodeo, which began in 1933, is famous throughout the northwest. In addition to a variety of cowboy competitions, the festivities also include a Western and Native art show, and numerous parades. The Suicide Race consists of cowboys riding their horses down a steep slope, then swimming across the Okanogan River. | $5–$12 | 800/933–6625.

Dining

Wauconda Cafe, General Store, and Post Office. American. A very pleasant store-café that looks as though it has sprung straight from a tale of the Old West. The food is fresh and simple; the hamburgers are famous throughout the region. | 2432 Rte. 20, Wauconda | 509/486–4010 | Breakfast also available. Closed Sun. Dec.–Apr. | $8–$14 | MC, V.

Whistler's Family Restaurant. American. Next to the Omak Inn, this restaurant opened in 1999. Its traditional range of American classics is complemented by a Thursday night Italian buffet and the Friday and Saturday night prime rib specials. | 914 Koala Dr. | 509/826–6375 | Breakfast also available | $9–$15 | AE, D, MC, V.

Lodging

Motel Nicholas. This family motel is close to the local shopping center. | 21 rooms. Refrigerators, microwaves, cable TV. | 527 E. Grape Ave. | 509/826–4611 | fax 509/826–4611 Ext. 38 | $42–$45 | AE, D, DC, MC, V.

Omak Inn. Located just off I–97, this motel—built in 1995—is close to restaurants and shopping. A small patio and expansive lawn behind the pool allow for relaxing in the summer heat. | 49 rooms. Complimentary breakfast, in-room data ports, some microwaves, some refrigerators, some in-room hot tubs, cable TV, pool, hot tub, gym, laundry facilities, business services, pets allowed (fee). | 912 Koala Dr. | 509/826–3822 or 800/204–4800 | fax 509/826–2980 | dlawver@northcascades.net | www.omakinn.com | $62 | AE, D, MC, V.

ORCAS ISLAND

MAP 8, C2

(Nearby town also listed: San Juan Islands)

The largest of the San Juan Islands, Orcas is also the most mountainous. The islands' highest mountain is the 2,409-ft-high Mt. Constitution. Orcas also has the islands' largest bays, including one, East Sound, which almost cuts the island in half. And, to add to this island's superlatives, it also has the largest state park.

WHERE THE COWBOYS WERE INDIANS

The mustang, a descendant of Spanish horses first obtained by Indians of the American Southwest through raid or trade, was adopted by the Indians of the Northwest's Columbia Plateau sometime before 1750. On the Great Plains, the mustang, which had Arab and Barb blood, soon deteriorated into horses that were "hammer-headed, ewe-necked, mutton-withered, roach-backed, cow-hocked and tied-in below the knee," as one British author pointedly states. But that was not true for the Northwest, where the native horsemen not only maintained the quality of their stock but improved it through selective breeding. The author quoted above sings a different tune when talking about the Appaloosa of the Nez Perce, the only modern horse breed developed by an Indian tribe. After talking about its unusual color (spotted hind quarters) and calling it an "all-round saddle horse," he says: "It is very agile, of exceptionally tractable disposition, and possesses both speed and stamina. It also jumps well."

The Nez Perce understood the horse better than any other native tribe, and even traveled to Sutter's Fort in California in the mid-1840s to obtain high-quality breeding stock to improve their herds. They also planted orchards and raised beef cattle, and by the 1840s, they were selling meat and produce to starving immigrants on the last leg of the Oregon Trail, where game was scarce.

Their neighbors, the Cayuse, also bred horses for special traits, mostly endurance. The Cayuse was the horse the Indians brought with them when they were driven off their lands by American immigrant ranchers and became cowboys.

Indians made great cowboys. They had stamina, rarely fell from the saddle, and almost instinctively knew how to handle cattle. In this their horses helped them. For more than a hundred years, Northwest Indians rode their horses across Rocky Mountain passes to hunt buffalo on the great plains. Their horses not only had to be sure footed on primitive trails and have strong backs to carry heavy loads of dried buffalo meat, but they also had to be fleet-footed and have the skill of cutting a swift, foul-tempered bison from the herd, since the Northwest Indians' hunting season on the Plains was very short. These horses' ability of going from a stop to a full run in seconds, and of being able to stop in a split second and turn on a dime, came in very handy when the Indians became cowboys and used their "cayuses" as cutting horses for handling cattle. We might say that the "Cow sense" possessed by a good cutting horse stems from the time when their ancestors helped their masters hunt bison.

When you watch a modern rodeo cowboy do his stuff, he's continuing a tradition begun by his Indian forebears more than 200 years ago. And take a good look at the horses used by today's rodeo stars. Many of them look a lot like the "cayuses" depicted by such artists as Frederic Remington.

Even today, the basic cowboy horse is still known in the Northwest as a "cayuse." That horse, incidentally, may constitute a separate breed, like the Appaloosa, and some horse breeders in the Northwest began, in the late 1990s, to bring it back and restore it to its full glory.

With horses and skills like that, it should come as no surprise that Indians also make excellent rodeo riders, as the annual mid-August Omak Stampede and Suicide Race attests.

There are several villages on Orcas Island. Deer Harbor, at the far west of the island has an eponymous harbor and is very popular with pleasure boaters because of its sheltered moorage and spectacular sunsets.

Doe Harbor, on the eastern half of the island, has an on-again/off-again resort with a somewhat checkered history. Right now, it's on again, and it's a favorite with Washington residents.

Eastsound, Orcas Island's main village, at the head of East Sound, almost covers the narrow neck of land separating the two halves of the island. The business district has a few 19th-century buildings, plus restaurants, shops, moorage, a hardware emporium, a grocery, and a pharmacy. By island standards it is practically a big city.

West Sound is a peaceful place today, with gardens stretching down to the high tide mark. But it wasn't always so. Massacre Bay at the head of the inlet, and Skull Island and Victim Island (both state parks), speak of a history of bloody tribal warfare in the 19th century between local Lummis and raiding British Columbian and Alaskan tribes.

Olga is a waterfront hamlet south of Moran State Park. The local store sells vegetarian food as well as arts and crafts created by local artists.

The hamlet of Orcas, at the southernmost tip of the western half of the island, has the Washington State ferry dock, a few shops, and a restored hotel dating from 1904.

Information: Orcas Island Chamber of Commerce | Box 252, Eastsound, 98245 | 360/376–2273 | fax 360/376–6972 | chamber@orcasisland.org | www.orcasisland.org.

Attractions

Emmanuel Church. Built in 1886 to resemble an English countryside church, this house of worship sits directly on the sound and is a favorite place for weddings. Concerts are held each summer Thursday at noon. | Main St., Eastsound Village.

Moran State Park. Wooded 5,000-acre Moran State Park is part of the former estate of Robert Moran (of Rosario fame). The mountainous park has lakes, trails, campsites, and 2,409-ft high Mt. Constitution, with a road leading to the top. There are great views across the islands and the Salish Sea. The park is *very* popular; you may have to make campsite reservations as much as a year ahead of time. | 3572 Olga Rd., Eastsound | 360/376–2326 or 800/452–5687 | fax 360/376–2360 | www.parks.wa.gov | Free, camping $12–$17 | Daily.

ON THE CALENDAR

JULY: *Fourth of July Celebration.* The whole town of Eastsound is closed off during the Independence Day festivities, which include a historical parade, pie-eating contests, a pancake feed, and barbecues. During the fireworks display, the chamber of commerce hands out free hot dogs. | 360/376–2273.

Dining

Bilbo's Festivo. Mexican. Weavings from New Mexico hang from the stucco walls of this eatery where wooden benches provide seating. Enchiladas, burritos, and other south-of-the-border favorites fill the menu; the specialties are fresh Northwest seafood and marinated meats cooked on a mesquite grill. The courtyard is a perfect place to enjoy a fresh-squeezed lime margarita in the summer. | N. Beach Rd., Eastsound | 360/376–4728 | No lunch Oct.–May | $6–$19 | MC, V.

★ **Christina's.** Contemporary. This is a beautiful restaurant filled with fresh flowers and with food that is even better than the setting or the view. The chef is a genius when it comes to handling fresh local seafood, but also has a deft touch with meats. Servings are generous and the wine list is ample. There is open-air dining on a rooftop deck overlooking Eastsound. Full bar. Kids' menu, no smoking. | 310 Main St. | 360/376–4904 | Closed Nov. 1 day before Thanksgiving. No lunch | $20–$29 | AE, D, DC, MC, V.

Inn at Ship Bay. Seafood. This comfortable farmhouse restaurant is the islanders' favorite local seafood house. Oysters—raw, baked, stewed, or pan fried—are the mainstay. But there are also fresh fish and the occasional meat dish. | 326 Olga Rd. | 360/376–5886 | Call for hours | $17–$27 | AE, D, MC, V.

Lodging

Chestnut Hill Inn. This turn-of-the-20th-century Victorian farmhouse sits atop a grassy knoll overlooking the valley's fields and forest and adjacent to a century-old pear orchard. The French country furniture, including four-poster and canopy beds, the polished hardwood floors, and the many fireplaces all contribute to making this an exquisite romantic retreat. | 5 rooms. Complimentary breakfast, no air-conditioning, some in-room VCRs, some room phones, no TV in some rooms, no pets, no kids under 16, no smoking. | John Jones Rd., Orcas | 360/376–5157 | fax 360/376–5283 | chestnut@pacificrim.net | www.chestnuthillinn.com | $165–$215 | MC, V.

Deer Harbor Inn. The original log lodge, which was built in 1915, no longer houses guests, but is now used as the inn's dining room. Today you can stay in a 1987 log lodge or in one of four cottages that stands in the center of an orchard. The lodge rooms have peeled-log furniture, quilts, and balconies from which to view the meadows, water, and inquisitive wildlife. | 8 rooms, 4 cottages. Restaurant, complimentary Continental breakfast, no air-conditioning, some kitchenettes, some microwaves, refrigerators, no room phones, no TV in some rooms, pets allowed, no smoking. | 33 Inn Ln., Deer Harbor | 360/376–4110 | fax 360/376–2237 | stay@deerharborinn.com | www.deerharborinn.com | $119–$299 | AE, MC, V.

Doe Bay Village Resort. Once an art colony, today this resort is a haven for neo-hippies and outdoorsy families who come to enjoy the property's 45 acres of woods and waterfront. An old general store, built in 1908, houses a small, mostly vegetarian restaurant. The patchwork of accommodations includes cabins, yurts, a hostel, and campsites. Clothing is optional. | 47 rooms. Restaurant, no air-conditioning, no room phones, no TV, hot tub, massage, sauna, no pets, no smoking. | 107 Doe Bay Rd., Olga | 360/376–2291 | fax 360/376–5809 | info@doebay.com | www.doebay.com | $16–$109 | AE, D, MC, V.

Orcas Hotel. This white, red-roofed clapboard hotel from the turn of the 20th century is surrounded by a covered porch and overlooks the island's ferry landing and the shops and boat slips making up the tiny port. | 12 rooms (7 with shared bath). Restaurant, bar, no room phones, business services, no smoking. | Orcas Landing | 360/376–4300 | fax 360/376–4399 | orcas@orcashotel.com | www.orcashotel.com | $79–$180 | AE, MC, V.

Resort at Deer Harbor. Originally constructed in the 1930s as housing for apple-pickers, these cottages clustered on a hillside overlook the marina. Each cottage has a fireplace, indoor hot tub, outdoor hot tub, and deck from which to view the serene sunsets across the water. | 26 cottages. Restaurant, complimentary Continental breakfast, no air-conditioning, in-room data ports, microwaves, refrigerators, in-room hot tubs, cable TV, in-room VCRs, pool, massage, no pets, no smoking. | Deer Harbor Rd., Deer Harbor | 360/376–4420 or 888/376–4480 | fax 360/376–5523 | info@deerharbor.com | www.deerharbor.com | $189–$389 | AE, MC, V.

Rosario Resort. This three-story waterfront mansion, surrounded by broad verandas, was built in 1906 by shipbuilding magnate Robert Moran from concrete, a material that is not congenial to the wet Northwest climate. As a result, the old mansion has taken on a somewhat musty odor over the years. In the old days, the mansion was surrounded by thousands of acres of Moran's estate (much of which he later gave to the state as Moran State Park). The resort includes only a tiny remnant of some 30 acres, much of which are taken up with rental condominiums. Washingtonians visiting the island usually prefer to stay at one of the smaller B&Bs but the place is very popular with casual visitors. The huge pipe organ installed in the mansion by Moran is still in playing order, and organists occasionally give concerts. | 98 rooms, 29 suites. Restaurant, bar, no air-conditioning, some kitchenettes, 3 pools (1 indoor), hot tub, spa, tennis, gym, marina, boating, laundry facilities, airport shuttle, no smoking. | 1400 Rosario Rd. | 360/376–2222 or 800/562–8820 | fax 360/376–3680 | info@rosarioresort.com | www.rosario-resort.com/ | $188–$348, $252–$615 suites | AE, D, DC, MC, V.

★ **Spring Bay Inn.** Secluded by the 137 acres that surround it, this B&B sits directly on the bay. In your room you can get cozy next to a wood-burning fire, or you can watch herons and eagles soar above the bay from your featherbed. Trails meander throughout the park and complimentary kayak tours are offered depending on the weather. The road on which the inn is located—Spring Bay Trail—is just off Trailhead Road. | 5 rooms. Complimentary breakfast, no air-conditioning, refrigerators, some in-room hot tubs, no room phones, no TV, spa, no pets, no smoking. | Spring Bay Trail | 360/376–5531 | fax 360/376–2193 | info@springbayinn.com | www.springbayinn.com | $195–$235 | AE, D, MC, V.

Turtleback Farm Inn. A very comfortable farm B&B nestled in a green valley, overlooking 80 acres of forest and farmland in the shadow of Turtleback Mountain. The house was built in the late 1800s, and features a pleasant blend of antiques and contemporary pieces. | 11 rooms, 4 in orchard house. Complimentary breakfast and afternoon snacks, some refrigerators, no air-conditioning, no smoking. | 1981 Crow Valley Rd., Eastsound | 360/376–4914 or 800/375–4914 (reservations) | fax 360/376–5329 | turtleback@interisland.net | turtlebackinn.com | $80–$210 | D, MC, V.

Windsong Bed and Breakfast. This is one of the areas most popular and comfortable B&B's. The turn-of-the-20th-century schoolhouse features large, spacious rooms, with high ceilings and beautiful paintings. Three of the rooms have fireplaces, and there are also a sun room and a deck. | 4 rooms (3 with shower only). Picnic area, complimentary breakfast, cable TV in common room, no room phones, hot tub, airport shuttle, no kids under 10, no smoking. | 213 Deer Harbor Rd. | 360/376–2500 or 800/669–3948 (reservations) | fax 360/376–4453 | windsong@pacificrim.net | www.windsonginn.com | $120–$150 | MC, V.

OTHELLO

MAP 8, I6

(Nearby town also listed: Moses Lake)

There's got to be something special about a farm town named after the main character from a Shakespearean tragedy, even if all you see at first glance are potato sheds, acres of farm machinery for sale, and the other accoutrements of well-to-do country living.

The landscape makes Othello unique. It sits right smack in the middle of some interesting scabland channels and ponds carved by the Spokane floods. That is why the Columbia National Wildlife Refuge is just north of here. The refuge doesn't just have lots of birds; it also has some rare ones seldom seen elsewhere in Washington, such as sandhill cranes, black-necked stilts, avocets, and American willets. But don't visit during hunting season. The locals and some visitors not only love to watch birds, they also love to eat them.

Information: Greater Othello Chamber of Commerce | 33 E. Larch, Othello, 99344 | 800/684–2556 | televar.com/chambers/othello.

Attractions

Columbia National Wildlife Refuge. The potholes, marshes, and grasslands south of Potholes Reservoir attract a great number of birds: from hawks, falcons, golden eagles, ducks, and geese to plovers, sandpipers, sandhill cranes, herons, American avocets, black-necked stilts, yellow-headed and red-winged blackbirds, and many songbirds, as well as beavers, muskrats, badgers, coyotes, and a few deer. | Refuge headquarters at 735 E. Main Street | 509/488–2668 | fax 509/488–0705 | www.r1.fws.gov | Free | Daily.

ON THE CALENDAR

MAR.: *Sandhill Crane Festival.* A celebration in honor of the sandhill cranes visiting nearby Columbia National Wildlife Refuge, with bus tours, guided bird watching trips, and hikes, as well as refreshments. | 800/684–2556.

JULY: ***Sun Fair.*** Othello celebrates Independence Day with a basketball tournament, a soccer tournament, food vendors, and live music. The festivities take place at Lions Park on Pine Street. | 800/684–2556.
SEPT.: ***Adams County Fair/PRCA Rodeo.*** Professional rodeo and carnival with live entertainment takes place at the fairgrounds. | 509/488–6130.

Dining

Mar Don Café. American. Located at the Mar Don Resort, this casual restaurant serves a traditional array of American classics such as hamburgers, steaks, and fish and chips. Some tables have views of the reservoir. | 8198 Hwy. 262 | 509/346–9688 | Closed Nov.–Feb. | $7–$17 | D, MC, V.

Lodging

Best Western Lincoln Inn. A basic motel that sufficiently caters to creature comforts so you are refreshed for bird watching in nearby Columbia Wildlife Refuge. | 50 rooms. Cable TV, pool, hot tub. | 1020 E. Cedar St. | 509/488–5671 | fax 509/488–5084 | $42–$62 | AE, DC, MC, V.

Cabana Motel. Remodelled in 1999, this one-story motor inn sits in the center of Othello, close to shops and restaurants. | 55 rooms. Some kitchenettes, some refrigerators, cable TV, pool, hot tub. | 665 Windsor St. | 509/488–2605 or 800/442–4581 | fax 509/488–0885 | $38–$80 | AE, D, DC, MC, V.

Mar Don Resort. Sitting along the shores of the Potholes Reservoir, the 25 rooms of this facility provide an escape from the modern world. There are lots of activities to pursue around the lake, including numerous water sports and hikes. The rooms have basic furnishings, 10 have cooking facilities and six overlook the reservoir. | 25 rooms. Restaurant, picnic area, some kitchenettes, some microwaves, some refrigerators, no room phones, no TV, hiking, volleyball, beach, dock, boating, fishing, pets allowed (fee). | 8198 Hwy. 262 SE | 509/346–2651 or 509/765–5061 or 800/416–2736 | www.mardonresort.com | $40–$75 | D, MC, V.

PACKWOOD

MAP 8, E6

(Nearby town also listed: Crystal Mountain)

Surrounded by Cascades' peaks, Packwood is a pretty mountain village on U.S. 12, below White Pass. Located between Mt. Rainier and Mt. St. Helens, it makes for a perfect jumping-off point for local wilderness areas. From Randle to the west, a road runs through National Forest land to the east side of Mt. St. Helens and the Windy Ridge Viewpoint, the best place from which to observe the destruction wrought by the 1980 eruption, and the dramatic renewal of the natural landscape.

Information: **Destination Packwood Association** | Box 64, Packwood, 98361 | 360/494–2223 | www.destinationpackwood.com.

Attractions

Goat Rocks Wilderness. The crags in Gifford Pinchot National Forest, south of Mt. Rainier are aptly named: You often see mountain goats, especially when you hike into the backcountry. Goat Lake is a particularly good spot for viewing these elusive beasts. You can see the goats without backpacking by taking Forest Roads 21, 2140 south from U.S. 12 near Packwood to Stonewall Ridge (ask for exact directions in Packwood, or ask a National Forest Ranger). The goats will be on Stonewall Ridge looming up ahead of you. | Forest Headquarters 10600 N.E. 51st St. Circle, Vancouver | 360/891–5000 | fax 360/891–5045 | www.fs.fed.us/gpnf | Free | Call for weather conditions.

Tatoosh Wilderness. This wilderness sits on the southern border of the Mt. Rainier National Park and is the terminus of the Tatoosh Range. The hiking trail that leads to the summit of the mountain can be done in two days, or part of it can be traversed in a single day. To reach the trail head, drive north from Packwood on Forest Road 52 for 4½ mi to 5270 Road and follow the latter until it ends. | 5270 Rd. | 360/494–0600.

ON THE CALENDAR

FEB.: *White Pass Winter Carnival.* A giant snow castle is the main attraction, with face painting and plenty of games for children held in White Pass, on the Cascade Crest on U.S. 2. | 509/672–3101.

Lodging

Cowlitz River Lodge. Comfortable two-story family motel off of the highway. | 32 rooms. Complimentary Continental breakfast, cable TV, hot tub. | 13069 U.S. 12 | 360/494–4444 | fax 360/494–2075 | $57–$73 | AE, MC, V.

Inn of Packwood. Mt. Rainier and the Cascade Mountains tower above this inn surrounded by lawns at the center of Packwood. Pine paneling and furniture lend the rooms a rustic, country charm. You can swim in an indoor heated pool beneath skylights, or picnic beneath a weeping willow. | 34 rooms. Picnic area, complimentary Continental breakfast, some kitchenettes, some microwaves, some refrigerators, cable TV, pool, spa, no pets. | 13032 Hwy. 12 | 360/494–5500 | reservations@innofpackwood.com | www.innofpackwood.com | $50–$145 | MC, V.

PASCO

MAP 8, I7

(Nearby towns also listed: Kennewick, Richland)

Tree-shaded Pasco, a college town and the county seat of Franklin County, is an oasis of green on the Columbia River, even though the Columbia Basin north of Pasco is the driest region in Washington, with an annual precipitation of only about 6 inches. This sub-region, known as the "Pasco Basin," has some of the state's most fertile land.

You can sample the bounty of local produce at the Pasco Farmers' Market, held downtown every Saturday during the growing season. The Pasco Basin, the nearby Snake River benchlands, and the Yakima Valley to the west have first-rate vineyards and wineries.

Downtown Pasco thrives to the beat of Latin music; the sidewalks are lively with shoppers, and street-corner taco wagons sell meaty tacos made with fresh, hand-patted tortillas. The neoclassic Franklin County Courthouse (1907) is worth a visit for its fine marble interior. Pasco, which started as a railroad switchyard, now has a busy container port.

Information: **Tri-Cities Visitor and Convention Bureau** | Box 2241, 6951 Grandridge Blvd., Tri-Cities, 99302 | 800/254–5824 | www.visittri-cities.com.

Attractions

Franklin County Historical Museum. Once the Pasco Carnegie Library, this museum is home to numerous items illustrating the history of the local area. Among them are artifacts from Native American Tribes. | 305 N. 4th Ave. | 509/547–3714 | Free | Tues.–Sat. noon–4.

Ice Harbor Lock and Dam. Single-lift locks 103 ft high are among the highest in the world. Cars can cross the dam on a narrow road. | 2339 Ice Harbor Dr., Burbank 99323 | 509/547–7781 | fax 509/543–3201 | Free | Apr.–Sept., daily 9–5.

Kahlotus. Kahlotus is a small farm and railroad town in Washtucna Coulee, north of the Snake River. Its three-block business district was refurbished in the 1970s and now has a covered sidewalk (a boon in the hot summer sun). Kahlotus Lake to the east is the local fishing and swimming hole. | U.S. 395 and Rte. 260 NE | 509/282–3372 | Free | Daily.

McNary Lock and Dam. Thirty mi south of Pasco, on the Columbia River at Umatilla, Oregon, this dam backs up the 61-mi Lake Wallula, which stretches through the Wallula Gap to the Tri-Cities (Kennewick, Pasco, Richland) and up the Snake River to Ice Harbor Dam. McNary National Wildlife Refuge, next to the dam and in patches up and down the lake, has large flocks of migrating waterfowl in fall, winter, and spring. Hawks, falcons, and bald and golden eagles can also be seen here. | Rte. 14, Umatilla, OR | 541/922–4388 | www.nww.usace.army.mill/ | Free | Daily 7:30–5. Guided tours in summer.

Preston Estate Vineyards. One of the Pasco Basin's oldest wineries. The tasting room is high up in the main building and has great views of surrounding fields. | 502 E. Vineyard Dr. | 509/545–1990 | fax 509/545–1098 | www.prestonwines.com | Free | Daily 10–5:30.

Sacajawea State Park. This park is 2 mi east of Pasco at the confluence of the Snake and Columbia rivers on the south side of the Snake River (Lake Wallula). There is a small archaeological museum, a boat ramp, and picnic sites, no camping. | Off U.S. 12 in Franklin County | 509/545–2361 or 800/233–0321 | www.parks.wa.gov | Free | Daily.

ON THE CALENDAR

MAR.: ***Quilt Show.*** An important show, featuring the works of local and national quilters, held at the Track Building in Pasco. | 509/582–3257.

APR.–MAY: ***Cinco De Mayo.*** A celebration of Mexican culture in conjunction with the annual opening of the farmers' market. | 509/545–9776.

APR.: ***Jazz Unlimited.*** A two-weekend music festival with jazz and concert bands and choir performances at the Columbia Basin Community College. | 509/547–0511.

Dining

Fran's Heidi Haus. German. This is the area's only restaurant that specializes in authentic German food, including sauerbraten and spätzle. It is located only a quarter mile from I–182 in a quiet neighborhood off exit 7. | 3214 Rd. 68 | 509/547–3993 | Closed Mon. | $8–$16 | AE, D, MC, V.

Vineyard Steak House at the Doubletree Inn. American. This formal dining room is where the locals like to come for a dress-up dinner and to dine on fresh seafood and well-aged beef. | 2525 N. 20th St. | 509/547–0701 | $15–$25 | AE, D, DC, MC, V.

Lodging

Doubletree Hotel. This large hotel has all the amenities, plus it is close to the airport. | 269 rooms, 10 suites. 2 Restaurants, bar with entertainment, in-room data ports, some refrigerators, room service, cable TV, 2 Pools, hot tub, gym, business services, airport shuttle, free parking, pets allowed. | 2525 N. 20th St. | 509/547–0701 | fax 509/547–4278 | $75–$115, $125–$200 suites | AE, D, DC, MC, V.

Tri-Cities Sleep Inn. Right off I–182 at exit 7, this hotel is only a short walk from the outlet mall. The hotel strives to add a personal touch to its many chain amenities. Thus, there is a cooler stocked with beverages for your convenience; lattes are available; and if you don't want to go out to eat, the staff will prepare a TV dinner or oven pizza for you. | 62 rooms. Complimentary Continental breakfast, in-room data ports, some microwaves, cable TVs, pool, spa, laundry services, business services, no pets. | 9930 Bedford St. | 509/545–9554 or 800/SLEEP–INN | $55–$115 | AE, D, DC, MC, V.

PORT ANGELES

MAP 8, B3

(Nearby towns also listed: Neah Bay, Sequim)

The county seat, Clallam County, was first settled in 1856, but it took a while before it became a town, even though some folks had high hopes for its bay, protected by sandy Ediz Hook as a major naval anchorage. On June 9, 1862, Abraham Lincoln signed a presidential decree creating the 5-square-mi townsite and proposed military reservation, with the street plan of Cincinnati as a guide. But nothing came of that. The military soon abandoned the site and Port Angeles became a mill town and fishing port. The mill is gone, and Port Angeles, the largest town on northern Olympic Peninsula, now serves as ferry port for both car and passenger ferries to Victoria and as a major gateway to Olympic National Park.

Information: Port Angeles Chamber of Commerce Visitor Information Center | 121 E. Railroad Ave., Port Angeles, 98362 | 360/452–2363 | portangeles.org.

Attractions

Clallam County Historical Museum. Housed in a 1927 Federal building, the museum's exhibits illustrate the history and lifestyles of the town's Native Americans and Anglo communities. | 138 W. 1st St. | 360/452–2662 | Free | Weekdays 8:30–4.

Ferry Service to Victoria, BC, Canada. Two ferries connect Port Angeles to Victoria, the capital of British Columbia, north of Juan de Fuca Strait. The *MV Coho* carries both passengers and cars; the *Victoria Express* carries passengers only. Schedules change with the seasons; call the numbers below for information and schedules before planning your trip. | 101 E. Railroad Ave. | 360/457–4491 or 360/452–8088 (Victoria Express) | fax 360/457–4493 | www.northolympic.com/coho | Call for ferry schedule | $7.

Hurricane Ridge. The panoramic view from this 5,200-ft-high ridge, 17 mi south of Port Angeles, encompasses the Olympic range, the Strait of Juan de Fuca, and Vancouver Island. Guided tours are given in the summer along the many paved and unpaved trails on which you will see wildflowers and wildlife such as deer, marmots, and mountain goats. Take Highway 101 to Race Street. Follow Race Street south until it becomes Mt. Angeles Road and after the Visitors Center bear right to Hurricane Ridge Road. | Top of Hurricane Ridge Rd. | 360/452–0330 | Daily 10–5.

Port Angeles Fine Arts Center. The former residence of artist and publisher Esther Barrows Webster is now home to a small, sophisticated museum exhibiting both emerging and well-established Pacific Northwest artists. From the center's sculpture park you'll have a magnificent panoramic view of the city and harbor from the center's sculpture park. | 1203 E. Lauridsen Blvd. | 360/457–3532 | Free | Tues.–Sun. 11–5.

Olympic Raft and Kayak. Summer raft trips on the Elwha River, which flows through a beautiful green canyon. | 123 Lake Aldwell Rd. | 360/452–1443 or 888/452–1443 | info@raftandkayak.com | www.northolympic.com/olmpicraft | $39–$69 | Apr.–Sept., daily 8–7; Oct.–Mar., by appointment.

Olympic Tours and Charters. This company offers guided eco tours into Olympic National Park or shuttle service for backpackers to all national park trail heads. | Box 2201 | 360/452–3858 or 888/457–3500 | fax 360/457–3545 | www.northolympic.com | $19–$52 (includes lunch) | Jun.–Oct.

ON THE CALENDAR

MAY: *Duck Derby.* This is a serious plastic duck race: the owner of the winning ducky receives a choice of car or truck, and there are prizes for runners-up as well. Held on the third weekend in May. | 360/683–3840.

Dining

Bella Italia. Italian. Since this restaurant is in the basement of a local health food store, it makes sense that the meals are wholesome, especially when fresh local products are in season. Try the flash-fried calamari with olives, artichokes, tomatoes, and roasted garlic on polenta. Kids' menu. Sun. brunch. No smoking. | 117-B E. First St. | 360/457–5442 | fax 360/457–6112 | No lunch | $15–$20 | AE, MC, V.

Bushwhacker. Contemporary. A warmly decorated Pacific Northwest steak and seafood house. Salad bar. Kids' menu. | 1527 E. First St. | 360/457–4113 | No lunch | $15–$25 | AE, D, MC, V.

C'est Si Bon. French. The Olympic Peninsula's most elegant dining room is a bit chichi with its blood-red walls and academic oil paintings but it's also romantic in an off-beat fashion. The food is ambitiously French, and sometimes uneven in quality. The wine list is superb. There is open-air dining on the glass-enclosed terrace. Kids' menu by request. | 23 Cedar Park Dr. | 360/452–8888 | Closed Mon. No lunch | $19–$25 | AE, D, DC, MC, V.

Crab House. Seafood. Part of the Red Lion Hotel, this restaurant looks directly onto the bay and the Strait of Juan de Fuca. You can enjoy such dishes as Dungeness crab bisque, fresh king salmon, or roasted halibut with sundried tomato. In addition, they have pastas, steaks, and chicken dishes. | 221 N. Lincoln | 360/452–9215 | No lunch | $11–$22 | AE, D, DC, MC, V.

First Street Haven. American. This small and informal storefront restaurant serves tasty breakfasts and lunches, plus good espresso drinks and desserts. The cinnamon rolls are a local favorite. No alcohol. Sun. brunch. | 107 E. 1st St. | 360/457–0352 | Breakfast also available. No supper | $5–$7 | No credit cards.

Landings. Contemporary. A modern restaurant serving mostly standard meat and seafood dishes. Popular favorites include the fish and chips and the clam chowder. There is outside dining on a deck overlooking the Coho ferry. | 115 E. Railroad Ave. | 360/457–6768 | Breakfast also available | $8–$20 | AE, MC, V.

Toga's International. Contemporary. This restaurant serves an eclectic collection of dishes, ranging in influence from German to Pacific Rim, featuring Dungeness crab cakes and prawns, aged prime rib, and New Zealand rack of lamb. Windows open to a view of the Olympic Mountains. There is open-air dining on the patio with wooden chairs and umbrellas. Kids' menu. No smoking. | 122 W. Lauridsen Blvd. | 360/452–1952 | Reservations essential | Closed Sept., Jan. Closed Sun.–Mon. | $16–$26 | MC, V.

Lodging

BJ's Garden Gate Bed and Breakfast. This waterfront Victorian-style home has five exquisitely appointed guest rooms, all of which have panoramic water views and fireplaces. The "Victoria's Rose" room, for example, has a finely carved half-tester English oak bed and a balcony overlooking the Strait of Juan de Fuca. Numerous flower gardens fill the 2½ acres on which the inn sits, making this an ideal romantic getaway. | 5 rooms. Complimentary breakfast, in-room hot tubs, cable TV, in-room VCRs, no pets, no smoking. | 397 Monterra Dr. | 800/880–1332 | bjgarden@olypen.com | www.bjgarden.com | $125–$175 | AE, MC, V.

Colette's Bed and Breakfast. This contemporary B&B sits on 10 acres of gorgeous waterfront property overlooking the Strait of Juan de Fuca, 10 mi east of Port Angeles. The rooms, which overlook the water, have contemporary luxury furnishings with a range of modern amenities. Eagles, fox, and deer are some of the animals you will meet while strolling through the expansive grounds with planted perennial gardens and over 200 rhododendrons. | 5 rooms. Complimentary breakfast, refrigerators, in-room hot tubs, cable TV, in-room VCRs, no pets, no kids under 15, no smoking. | 339 Finn Hall Rd. | 360/457–9197 | fax 360/452–0711 | colettes@olypen.com | www.colettes.com | $175–$235 | MC, V.

★ **Domaine Madeleine.** This delightfully comfortable B&B sits among bluff-top trees above the Strait of Juan de Fuca, and has some great views of the Vancouver Island mountains to the north and Mt. Baker to the far northeast. | 5 rooms (1 with shower only). Picnic area, complimentary breakfast and afternoon snacks, in-room data ports, some microwaves and refrigerators, cable TV, some in-room hot tubs, cable TV, in-room VCRs and movies, business services, local airport, ferry shuttles, no kids under 12, no smoking. | 146 Wildflower Ln. | 360/457–4174 | fax 360/457–3037 | romance@domainemadeleine.com | www.domainemadeleine.com | $174–$195 | AE, D, MC, V.

Flagstone Motel. Many of the small but well-maintained rooms of this motel have views of Mount Olympus and the surrounding Olympic Mountains. The motel is just off Highway 101 and is only a short way from the harbor. | 45 rooms. No air-conditioning, some microwaves, some refrigerators, cable TV, pool, sauna, pets allowed. | 415 E. 1st St. | 360/457–9494 | $65 | AE, D, DC, MC, V.

Port Angeles Inn. This is a comfortable modernized motel, with views of the water, overlooking Juan de Fuca Strait. | 24 rooms. Complimentary Continental breakfast, no air-conditioning, cable TV, business services. | 111 E. Second St. | 360/452–9285 or 800/421–0706 | fax 360/452–7935 | $70–$120 | D, MC, V.

Red Lion. This is a big resort hotel on the harbor, next to the Victoria ferry landing. | 187 rooms. Restaurant, no air-conditioning, cable TV, pool, hot tub, business services, pets allowed. | 221 N. Lincoln | 360/452–9215 | fax 360/452–4734 | $59–$155 | AE, D, DC, MC, V.

Sea Suns Bed and Breakfast. On the edge of town, this cozy inn offers water and mountain views, and is surrounded by extensive gardens. Built in 1926, the house features many period furnishings. | 5 rooms (all have private baths). Picnic area, complimentary breakfast and afternoon snacks, no air-conditioning, cable TV in common room, no room phones, local airport and ferry shuttle, no kids under 12, no smoking. | 1006 S. Lincoln | 360/452–8248 or 800/708–0777 | fax 360/417–0465 | www.seasuns.com | $85–$125 | MC, V, AE.

Tudor Inn. This comfortable inn was originally built in 1910, but has been wonderfully restored. High enough uphill from the ferry landing to avoid the bustle, this B&B is quiet and peaceful, and features well-maintained grounds. | 5 rooms. Complimentary breakfast and afternoon tea and snacks, no air-conditioning, no room phones, no TV in rooms, TV in common area, library, no kids under 12, no smoking. | 1108 S. Oak | 360/452–3138 | info@tudorinn.com | www.tudorinn.com | $85–$135 | AE, D, MC, V.

Uptown Inn. South of town, at the green edge of the Olympic Mountain foothills, this inn offers views of the mountains, as well as the harbor. | 51 rooms. Complimentary Continental breakfast, no air-conditioning, some kitchenettes and microwaves, refrigerators, cable TV, some pets allowed (fee). | 101 E. 2nd St. | 360/457–9434 or 800/858–3812 | fax 360/457–5915 | $69–$169, depending on views | AE, D, DC, MC, V.

PORT GAMBLE

MAP 8, D3

(Nearby towns also listed: Port Ludlow, Seattle)

Port Gamble is a 19th-century mill town that looks like it had been picked up in New England and plopped down, lock, stock, and barrel, on Puget Sound. Most employees came from Maine, and the new town was styled to look like East Machias. Port Gamble was founded in 1853 to exploit the Kitsap Peninsula's tall stands of timber. Today, the mill and much of the timber are gone and Port Gamble has settled in as a quiet, visitor-friendly village. Many of the original houses, plus the 1870 St. Paul's Episcopal Church (a copy of the East Machias Parish Church), have been carefully restored.

Information: Kitsap Peninsula Visitor and Convention Bureau | 2 Rainier Ave., Port Gamble, 98364 | 800/416–5615 | www.visitkitsap.com.

Attractions

Heronswood. This is not only one of the great gardens and nurseries of the Pacific Northwest but also of the country. Its gardens and unique plant collection attract visitors from around the world. Garden "Open Days" in late May, mid-July, and early September have docents on hand to explain the gardens which are not generally open to the public. | 7530 N.E. 288th St., Kingston | 360/297–4172 | fax 360/297–8321 | www.heronswood.com | $1 | mid-May–Jan., by appointment.

Kitsap Memorial State Park. A waterfront park 4 mi south of Port Gamble on the Hood Canal with boating, fishing, hiking, picnicking, and camping. You can also dig clams and gather oysters as long as you have a license. | Rte. 3 | 360/779–3205 | fax 360/779–3161 | Free | Daily dawn–dusk.

Of Sea and Shore Museum. An amazing array of shells are located in the General Store. The deli in the General Store is locally famous for its sandwiches. | 1 Rainier St. | 360/297–2426 | fax 360/297–2426 | www.ofseaandshore.com | Donations accepted | Daily 9–5.

Port Gamble Historic Museum. Exhibits from the heydays of the Pope and Talbot Timber Co. which built the town, plus period rooms from houses and hotels. | 1 Rainier Ave. | 360/297–8074 | fax 360/297–7455 | www.ptgamble.com | $2 | Daily May–Oct. 10:30–5; Mar., Apr., and Nov., weekdays by appointment only.

Dining

General Store. American. A turn-of-the-20th-century general store with a deli that dishes up some delectable sandwiches. Or you can buy the fixings for a picnic from the grocery section. | 1 Rainier Ave. | 360/297–7636 | No supper | $5–$7 | AE, D, DC, MC, V.

WA

PORT LUDLOW

MAP 8, D3

(Nearby towns also listed: Port Gamble, Seattle)

A former lumber mill town on a protected bay on the western shore of the Olympic Peninsula, Port Ludlow is now a resort and retirement community. The entrance to the Hood Canal is between Tala Point east of Port Ludlow and Foulweather Bluff on the Kitsap Peninsula.

Information: Olympic Peninsula Gateway Visitor Center | 93 Beaver Valley Rd., Port Ludlow, 98365 | 360/437–0120 | gatewayvcr@olympus.net | www.portludlow.com.

Attractions

Resort at Port Ludlow. The resort has a golf course and a marina with row boat and sailboat rentals. You don't have to be a guest at the resort to rent. | 200 Olympic Place | 360/437–2222 | fax 360/437–2482 | www.portludlowresort.com | Varies according to activity | Daily.

Dining

Dining Room at the Heron Beach Inn. Contemporary. This out-of-the-way restaurant is one of the finest on the shores of the Salish Sea. Fresh local seafood is dressed up with herbs grown in the kitchen garden—all enjoyed while looking at some pretty spectacular scenery. Kids' menu. No smoking. | 1 Heron Rd. | 360/437–0411 | No lunch. No dinner Mon.–Tues. | $12–$25 | AE, D, DC, MC, V.

Harbormaster Restaurant at Port Ludlow Resort. Seafood. Two large sails hang from the dining room's cathedral ceiling, suggestive of the restaurant's culinary inclination: fresh seafood. Chicken and steak entrées round out the menu. The restaurant, overlooking Ludlow Bay, also has a sundeck for outdoor dining. | 200 Olympic Pl | 360/437–2222 or 800/732–1239 | Breakfast also available | $12–$18 | AE, MC, V.

Lodging

Heron Beach Inn. Despite the fact that this is a comfortable luxurious inn with a great location, it has never quite attracted the following it deserves. Nor has its restaurant helped, though it has been called the best dining room along the inland waters. Hence several name changes, designed to attract a strangely reluctant clientele. Perhaps it's because urban folks in Western Washington still think of Port Ludlow as a grimy mill town, and don't recognize the changes the place has undergone. As it is, many zip by on their way to Port Townsend, leaving this area a quiet backwater. | 37 rooms, 3 suites. Restaurant (*see* Dining Room at the Heron Bay Inn), complimentary Continental breakfast, no air-conditioning, in-room data ports, refrigerators, in-room VCRs (movies), business services, some pets allowed (fee), no smoking. | 1 Heron Rd. | 360/437–0411 | fax 360/437–0310 | www.heronbeach.com | $165, $165–$450 suites | AE, D, DC, MC, V.

Old Church Inn. Built as a Methodist church in 1906, this one-unit inn has cathedral ceilings, beautiful hardwood floors, exposed beam ceilings, and tall windows. The inn can sleep as many as ten, but is appropriate for smaller families and even couples. The rooms are appointed with a mixture of antiques and overstuffed furniture, making the inn comfortable and elegant. Less than two blocks from the water, you can smell the tide from the open windows. Your stay begins with a complimentary homemade pie. | 1 room. No air-conditioning, kitchenette, microwave, refrigerator, cable TV, in-room VCR, volleyball, no pets, no smoking. | 130 Randolph, Port Hadlock | 360/732–7552 | www.olypen.com/inn | $95 | No credit cards.

Port Ludlow Resort and Convention Center. This modern resort on the Olympic Peninsula has not yet found its stride, perhaps because it is off the beaten path to Port Townsend. | 190 rooms. Bar with entertainment, dining room, picnic area, no air-conditioning, some kitchenettes, cable TV, pool, hot tub, driving range, 27-hole golf course, putting green, tennis, exercise equipment, marina, boating, bicycles, children's programs (ages 4–12), playground, laundry facilities, business services, airport shuttle. | 200 Olympic Pl. | 360/437–2222 or 800/732–1239 (WA) | fax 360/437–2482 | portludlowresort.com | $105–$475 | AE, D, MC, V.

PORT TOWNSEND

MAP 8, C3

(Nearby towns also listed: Coupeville, Everett, Oak Harbor)

Port Townsend gives you two towns in one, both Victorian: a lower "water town," where the port is, and a more stately upper town of elegant mansions atop the bluff. At one time these two "towns" were socially so segregated that they even had their own shopping districts. Port Townsend was founded by folks who just knew the transcontinental railroad would stop here, and weren't even crushed when the tracks stopped in Tacoma. Like Seattle, Port Townsend tried to build its own connecting railroad but had to give up because the Hood Canal cliffs to the south were just too formidable. As a result, the town became a sleeping beauty that did not wake from its Victorian dream until the latter part of the 20th century. This is why the town has been preserved so delightfully and remains so appealing to visitors, who stroll its streets, dine at its cafés, stay in its Victorian mansions (many of which have been converted into comfortable inns), or just hang out on the waterfront.

A scheduled Washington State ferry runs from Port Townsend to Keystone on Whidbey Island—unless the weather is stormy.

Information: Port Townsend Chamber of Commerce and Visitor Information Center, | 2437 Sims Way, Port Townsend, 98368 | 888/365–6978 | ptchamber@olympus.com | ptguide.com.

Attractions

Ft. Flagler State Park. This is the third in a group of batteries called the "Iron Triangle" designed to protect Admiralty Inlet from attack by enemy fleets. This fort, atop a headland at the northern tip of Marrowstone Island 20 mi southeast of Port Townsend, is also now a state park with campsites and picnic area. | North end of Marrowstone Island | 360/385–1259 | fax 360/379–1746 | www.parks.wa.gov | Free, camping $12–$17 | Daily dawn–dusk.

Ft. Worden State Park. This former army fort was designed to guard the approaches to Admiralty Inlet with disappearing guns. Now it is a pleasant, tree-shaded park. The turn-of-the-20th-century officers' quarters and barracks are now a conference center. The gun emplacements atop the bluff are like those at Fort Casey (*see* Whidbey Island), but have no guns. Point Wilson Lighthouse, at the tip of a sandy spit, still serves as an aid to navigation. There are campsites and picnic areas. | 200 Battery Way | 360/344–4400 or 800/233–0321 | fax 360/385–7248 | www.olympus.net/ftworden | Free | Daily.

Jefferson County Historical Museum. Housed in the 1898 City Hall building, the museum contains four floors of Native American artifacts, photos of the region, and exhibits illustrating the history of Port Townsend. | 210 Madison St. | 360/385–1003 | $2 | Mon.–Sat. 11–4, Sun. 1–4.

Old Ft. Townsend (Historical) State Park. Only a gazebo remains from the original fort, but the bluff-top meadows, picnic area, campground, and miles of hiking trails make this a very popular park. Built in 1856 to help suppress a possible Indian attack, the fort was built too late to be of any use in the Puget Sound Indian War (besides, the local natives remained friendly); nor did its soldiers fire a shot when they were sent to fight in the Pig War. | 1370 Old Fort Townsend Rd. | 360/385–3595 or 800/233–0321 | fax 360/385–7248 | www.olympus.net/ftworden | Free | Mid-Apr.–Sept. 6:30–dusk.

Rothschild House. Built in 1858 by D. C. H. Rothschild, a local merchant, this simple home is furnished with 19th-century household goods and surrounded by herb and flower gardens. | Jefferson and Taylor Sts. | 360/385–2722 | www.ptguide.com | $2 | Apr.–mid-Oct., Wed.–Sun. 10–5; mid-Oct.–Apr., weekends only 10–3.

ON THE CALENDAR

MAR.: ***Port Townsend Victorian Festival.*** One of the Pacific Northwest's great festivals devoted to Victoriana, with workshops relating to the preservation and restoration of 19th-century homes and antiques. Events portraying Victorian life-styles, including the importance of wine to Victorians are also included. | 360/385–7911.

SEPT.: ***Wooden Boat Festival.*** A wide variety of wooden boats are on display throughout town with boating-related activities, such as workshops, ship-building classes, and storytelling. | 888/365–6978.

Dining

Ajax Café. Seafood. Wonderful harbor views are afforded from all the tables at this unique eatery. You'll check in with a hostess at a 1965 Cadillac front desk. Then, if you so choose, try on a hat or tie from the collection of vintage accessories. The menu includes wild salmon, mahi-mahi, snapper, and halibut as well as a selection of pastas and steaks. Live music is hosted here Thursday through Sunday. | 271 Water St., Port Hadlock | 360/385–3450 | No lunch. Closed Mon. | $11–$17 | MC, V.

Bayview. American. Sitting on the harbor, right next to the ferry dock, the restaurant is a fun place to go for a true blue American meal. The award-winning staff is friendly and accommodating. | 1539 Water St. | 360/385–1461 | Breakfast also available | $6–$16.50 | AE, D, DC, MC, V.

The Belmont. American/Casual. Dine in this historical 1880s building and enjoy the serene view of ships sailing in and out of the harbor. The menu includes a variety of pasta, chicken, steak, and seafood dishes; most popular are the clam chowder, the Dungeness crab sandwich, and the clams and mussels with a pesto cream sauce. | 925 Water St. | 360/385–3007 | $6–$22 | AE, D, DC, MC, V.

Elevated Ice Cream Company. Café. The proprietors first served their homemade ice cream from an antique Victorian elevator cage in 1977. Since then, they have expanded into two storefronts: one serves candy, the other serves homemade ice cream, Italian ices, freshly baked desserts, and espresso drinks. | 627 and 631 Water St. | 360/385–1156 | $1–$5 | MC, V.

Fountain Cafe. Contemporary. This tiny storefront café always seems packed with locals and visitors, who come here to feast on vegetarian pasta with artichokes, olives and feta,

Oysters Dorado, or seafood pastas. The desserts, too, have long brought raves. | 920 Washington St. | 360/385–1364 | Reservations not accepted | Closed Thurs. | $10–$15 | MC, V.

Khu Larb Thai. Thai. A restaurant that stands out from the crowd with a pretty dining room with Thai accents. Try the prawns with Thai basil leaves. | 225 Adams St. | 360/385–5023 | Closed Mon. | $10–$20 | MC, V.

Lanza's Ristorante and Pizzeria. Italian. This local favorite in the historic Uptown District has been serving Lanza-family recipes since 1985. Grandma Gloria's meatballs, for instance, are made from a recipe that is a century old. Another specialty is the fettuccine with smoked salmon and a feta cream sauce. Pizza and fresh seafood are also served. Live piano music on the weekends. | 1020 Lawrence St. | 360/379–1900 | Closed Sun. No lunch | $10–$14.50 | MC, V.

Lonny's. Seafood. The food is eclectic but accomplished and the service is impeccably professional. Dishes change with the season, but rely heavily on fresh seafood cooked with Northwestern flair. The wine list is extensive. | 2330 Washington St. | 360/385–0700 | Open 4th July–Oct., daily; Nov.–July; closed Tues. No lunch | $12–$20 | AE, D, MC, V.

Manresa Castle. Contemporary. This huge stone pile, looking vaguely like a castle, is the one place in Port Townsend you *can't* miss—it sticks out like a sore thumb. The dining room is as opulent as the building. The food tends to be less impressive but fresh fish in season can be quite good. Try rack of lamb, King salmon, beef tournedos, osso buco, and vegetarian dishes. Sun. brunch. No smoking. | Seventh and Sheridan | 360/385–5750 | Sun. breakfast also available. No lunch. No dinner Sun.–Tues. from mid-Oct.–Apr. | $15–$18 | D, MC, V.

Salal Cafe. Contemporary. An informal and bright restaurant popular with locals for its healthful menu items, especially the breakfast omelets. Lunch tends to run to Mexican dishes; dinner entrees can be ambitious, with such dishes as tofu Stroganoff, mushroom risotto with oysters, or pan-seared sea scallops. Try for a table in the glassed-in back room which faces a plant-filled courtyard. | 634 Water St. | 360/385–6532 | Reservations not accepted | No supper Tues., Wed. | $10–$15 | MC, V.

Silverwater Cafe. Contemporary. This warm, comfortable restaurant on the first floor of the historic Elks' Club building dishes up great food on plates handmade by one of the owners. The lemon poppy seed cake has become a local legend. Try artichoke pâté, the sauteed fresh oysters, or the seafood pasta. Kids' menu. No smoking. | 237 Taylor St. | 360/385–6448 | $12–$18 | MC, V.

Lodging

Ann Starrett Mansion. This incredible, multigabled, turreted mansion is the sort of glorious excess only possible during the Victorian age. Today it is a comfortable inn, with views of the Salish Sea, Mt. Rainier, North Cascade Peaks, and the Olympic Mountains. It is beautifully furnished with American antiques, and features a frescoed ceiling, spiral staircase, and elaborate moldings. | 7 rooms, 4 suites. Complimentary breakfast, no air-conditioning, some cable TV, business services, no kids under 11, no smoking. | 744 Clay St. | 360/385–3205 or 800/321–0644 | fax 360/385–2976 | www.starrettmansion.com | $138–$199, $185–$225 suites | AE, D, MC, V.

The Belmont. Built in the 1880s as a restaurant and saloon, this waterfront hotel has high ceilings and beautiful views of the harbor. The guest rooms have exposed brick walls and floral, Victorian wallpaper; windows overlook the water. | 4 rooms, 3 suites. Restaurant, bar, no air-conditioning, TV in common area, no pets, no smoking. | 925 Water St. | 360/385–3007 | www.the-belmont.com | $69–$89, $99–$109 suites | AE, D, DC, MC, V.

Bishop Victorian Guest Suites. This English inn built in 1890 was an office and warehouse building. At the west end of town, near the boatyards, you would be hard pressed today to see even a passing resemblance to its former incarnation. Nor should you care; just enjoy it as it is today: comfortable, warm and inviting. | 14 suites (8 with shower only). Complimentary Continental breakfast, no air-conditioning, kitchenettes, in-room data ports, some microwaves, refrigerators, cable TV, business services, some pets allowed (fee), no kids under 12, no smoking. | 714 Washington St. | 360/385-6122 or 800/824-4738 (reservations) | fax 360/379-1840 | www.bishopvictorian.com | $99–$179 suites | AE, D, MC, V.

Blue Gull Inn. Each room of this 1868 Gothic Revival home is uniquely appointed: "Teddy's Room," for example, has pink walls and white wicker furniture, while "Grandma's Room" has hardwood antiques, a claw foot tub, and a small sun porch from which to gaze on the numerous flower gardens. | 5 rooms. Complimentary breakfast, no air-conditioning, some in-room hot tubs, no room phones, no TV, no pets, no kids under 12, no smoking. | 1310 Clay St. | 360/379-3241 or 888/700-0205 | bluegull@olypen.com | www.bluegullinn.com | $85–$165 | AE, D, MC, V.

Captain John Quincy Adams House Bed and Breakfast. Built in 1887 by the great, great grandson of John Quincy Adams, the Victorian details are given extra flair by the red accents on window frames and roofs. Floral patterned wallpaper, hand-carved antiques, and claw foot bath tubs are some of the features that evoke the Victorian era. Among the many common areas, a Victorian pool table provides turn-of-the-20th-century entertainment in the billiards room. | 3 rooms, 1 suite. Complimentary breakfast, no air-conditioning, no room phones, no TV, hot tub, no pets, no kids under 12, no smoking. | 1028 Tyler St. | 360/379-8832 | owner@capnjqadams.com | www.captnjqadams.com | $125 | MC, V.

Chanticleer Inn. Built in 1876, this Victorian farmhouse is filled with period furnishings. It has a small English garden and is within walking distance of a local park. | 4 rooms (3 with shower only), 1 cottage. Complimentary breakfast and afternoon snacks, some in-room hot tubs, no room phones, no kids under 14, no smoking. | 1208 Franklin St. | 360/385-6239 or 800/858-9421 | fax 360/385-3377 | www.northolympic.com/chanticleer | $95–$160, $160 cottage | MC, V.

English Inn. This inn is west of town and away from the action—and views—of watertown and uptown,and is furnished with antiques. | 4 rooms (1 with shower only). Complimentary breakfast and afternoon snacks, no air-conditioning, cable TV in sitting room, hot tub, no room phones, ferry shuttle, no kids under 14, no smoking. | 718 "F" St. | 360/385-5302 or 800/254-5302 | fax 360/385-5302 | nancy@englishinn | www.english-inn.com | $95–$105 | MC, V.

Hastings House/Old Consulate Inn. Exquisitely decorated and very comfortable, this house on the bluff has a large collection of antique dolls that adds a friendly touch. Relax inside or take advantage of the hot tub in the gazebo. | 8 rooms (5 with shower only), 3 suites. Complimentary breakfast and afternoon snacks and desserts, cable TV in common rooms, no room phones, hot tub, business services. Local airport shuttle, no kids under 12, no smoking. | 313 Walker St. | 360/385-6753 or 800/300-6753 | fax 360/385-2097 | www.oldconsulateinn.com | $106–$210 | AE, MC, V.

Holly Hill House. This bluff-top inn, an 1872 Victorian, offers great views and extensive gardens, with 185 rose bushes and a white picket fence. It's within walking distance of downtown. | 5 rooms, 1 suite. Complimentary breakfast and afternoon snacks, no air-conditioning, no room phones, no kids under 12, no smoking. | 611 Polk St. | 360/385-5619 or 800/435-1454 | hollyhill@olympus.net | www.hollyhillhouse.com | $78–$145 | MC, V.

James House. When it was first built in 1891, this large Queen Anne Victorian served as the home of a sea captain. It is now a comfortable inn furnished with antiques and blessed with a great seaside garden. Some of the rooms can get quite chilly when a nor'easter blows across the water, making you want to snuggle up near a parlor fireplace with a good book. | 12 rooms (2 with shared bath). Complimentary breakfast and afternoon snacks, in-room data ports, no air-conditioning, no smoking. | 1238 Washington St. | 360/385-1238 or 800/385-1238 | fax 360/379-5551 | jameshouse@olympus.net | www.jameshouse.com | $80–$185 | AE, D, MC, V.

Lizzie's. A wildly ornate place with great views of the Salish Sea and the North Cascades (enjoy the views from your bath tub!). Lizzie, a tugboat captain's wife, knew what she wanted. Built in 1889, this B&B features two parlors with fireplaces, and wonderful gardens. | 7 rooms. Complimentary breakfast and afternoon tea, no air-conditioning, no room phones, no kids under 10. | 731 Pierce St. | 360/385–4168 or 800/700-4168 | fax 360/385–9467 | www.kolke.com/lizzies | $70–$135 | D, MC, V.

Manresa Castle. This was the original creation of an immigrant baker. Today it has been turned into a comfortable inn. Many of the rooms have (distant) views of the bay and mountains. | 40 rooms. Restaurant, bar, complimentary Continental breakfast, no air-conditioning, cable TV, business services. | Seventh and Sheridan Sts. | 360/385–5750 or 800/732–1281 | fax 360/385–5883 | www.olympus.net/manresa | $68–$175 | D, MC, V.

Palace Hotel. This 1889 watertown inn in the heart of downtown Port Townsend occupies an old brick building that was once a sailors' bordello. | 17 rooms. Complimentary Continental breakfast, no air-conditioning, some refrigerators, cable TV, no room phones, laundry facilities, pets allowed (fee). | 1004 Water St. | 360/385–0773 or 800/962–0741 | fax 360/385–0780 | palace@olympus.net | www.olympus.net/palace | $65–$189 | AE, D, MC, V.

Quimper Inn. Also known as Harry G. Barthrop House, this square, 1888 Georgian-style inn has a broad walking porch overlooking Admiralty Inlet. Guest rooms are individually appointed with antiques and modern reproductions and each has its own special personality. | 5 rooms (3 with private bath). Complimentary breakfast, no air-conditioning, no room phones, no TV, no pets, no kids under 12, no smoking. | 1306 Franklin St. | 360/385–1060 or 800/557–1060 | fax 360/385–2688 | thequimps@olympus.net | www.olympus.net/quimper | $80–$140 | MC, V.

Ravenscroft Inn. Set in a Colonial Charleston home, this southern plantation–style inn is located on the bluff above the ferry landing. Most rooms have views of the Cascade Mountains and the seaport. | 6 rooms (some with shower only), 2 suites. Complimentary breakfast and afternoon snacks, no air-conditioning, cable TV in library, library, business services, no kids under 13, no smoking. | 533 Quincy St. | 360/385–2784 or 800/782–2691 | fax 360/385–6724 | ravenscroft@olympus.net | www.ravenscroftinn.com | $85–$155, $180–$190 suites | AE, D, MC, V.

Swan Hotel. Encircled by verandas and with a widow's walk on top, this comfortable inn has all the views you might possibly want. | 4 suites, 4 cottages, 1 penthouse loft. In-room data ports, kitchenettes (in suites, cottages), refrigerators, cable TV, business services, local airport shuttle, some pets allowed (fee), no smoking. | 222 Monroe St. | 360/385–1718 or 800/776–1718 (reservations) | fax 360/379–1010 | swan@waypt.com | www.theswanhotel.com | $105–155 suites, $105–$135 cottages, $175–$500 penthouse | AE, DC, MC, V.

Tides Inn. Sitting directly on the beach, this inn also has views of the surrounding Olympic and Cascade mountains. The rooms have contemporary furniture, which works with the pine walls and ceilings. Some rooms have decks that stretch over the water; the suites all have fireplaces, hot tubs, and views of the bay and mountains. The inn is close to the historic downtown area, restaurants, and shopping. | 21 rooms, 21 suites. Complimentary Continental breakfast, some kitchenettes, some microwaves, some refrigerators, some in-room hot tubs, cable TV, in-room VCRs, hot tub, pets allowed. | 1807 Water St. | 360/385–0595 or 800/822–8696 | fax 360/379–1115 | www.tides-inn.com | $85–$140 | AE, D, MC, V.

POULSBO

MAP 8, D4

(Nearby towns also listed: Bremerton, Port Gamble, Seattle)

Poulsbo was founded in the 1880s as a Norwegian village on Liberty Bay, just off Puget Sound on the Kitsap Peninsula. At one time, it not only had Norwegian shops and bakeries but also a cod-drying facility where cod was processed into that Norwegian delicacy (lutefisk). Today, lutefisk is still served at special communal holiday feasts, as it is in other Puget Sound communities with a strong Norwegian element (such as Bellingham), but it is no longer made here. Poulsbo has kept an interesting waterfront, main street, and its spirit, while being crowded by sprawling Pugetopolis.

Information: **Greater Poulsbo Chamber of Commerce** | 19168 Jenson Way, Box 1063, Poulsbo, 98370 | 360/779–4848 or 877/poulsbo | poulsbo@silverlink.net | www.poulsbo.net/gpcc.

Attractions

Poulsbo Marine Science Center. "Please touch the animals" could be the motto for this unique science museum which encourages you to "get personal" with over 100 species of marine life typical of the Puget Sound region such as sea stars, tube worms, and crabs. | 18743 Front St. NE | 360/779–5549 | www.poulsbomsc.org | $4 | Daily 11–5.

ON THE CALENDAR

MAY: *Viking Fest.* A celebration of Poulsbo's Norwegian heritage, with a parade, carnival, ethnic entertainment, a fun run, and food booths. | 360/779–3378.

Dining

Christopher's at the Inn. Contemporary. Part of the Manor Farm Inn, this dining room recalls the inn's clean, simple aesthetic: white walls, exposed beams, gleaming hard wood floors, and plenty of windows. The menu changes seasonally but may include such international dishes as Jamaican jerk chicken or Argentinian flank steaks. | 26069 Big Valley Rd. NE | 360/779–4628 | Breakfast also available. No lunch. No dinner Mon.–Tues. | $15–$25 | AE, MC, V.

Lodging

Manor Farm Inn. This classic 1886 white clapboard farmhouse sits at the heart of a 25-acre "gentleman's farm", populated with sheep, horses, donkeys, and other animals. White walls, rough-hewn beams, and wide sunny windows generate a pleasant, relaxing tranquility in the spacious guest rooms. The rooms are appointed with French country antiques. Two rooms have wood-burning fireplaces. | 7 rooms. Restaurant, complimentary breakfast, no room phones, no TV, bicycles, no pets, no smoking. | 26069 Big Valley Rd. NE | 360/779–4628 | fax 360/779–4876 | information@manorfarminn.com | www.manorfarminn.com | $120–$170 | AE, MC, V.

PULLMAN

MAP 8, L6

(Nearby town also listed: Clarkston)

This funky, liberal college town is home of Washington State University in the heart of the rather conservative Palouse wheat, pea, and lentil country. The town's free-wheeling style can perhaps be explained by the fact that most of the students come from Seattle and other parts of western Washington.

The Palouse River, whose upper course flows though the town, is an exception among Washington rivers: because of the high erosion of the light Palouse loess soils, it usually runs muddy, almost like a gruel during floods, while most Washington Rivers run clear, even after major storms. The 198-ft-high Palouse Falls further downstream, near Washtucna, dramatically drop as a thin sheet of water into a steep-sided box canyon.

Information: **Pullman Chamber of Commerce** | N. 415 Grand Ave., Pullman, 99163 | 509/334–3565 or 800/365–6948 | pullmancofc@completebbs.com | www.pullman-wa.com.

Attractions

Kamiak Butte County Park. The 3,360-ft-tall butte is part of a mountain chain that was here long before the lava flows of the Columbia basin erupted millions of years ago. There is a county park 10 mi north of Pullman, with campsites, picnic area, and a 1-mi trail to the top. Great views of the Palouse hills and of the snow-capped peaks of Idaho to the east. | U.S. 27 to road #5100 to road #6710 | 509/397–6238 | fax 509/397–6239 | Free | Daily dawn–dusk.

Steptoe Butte State Park. Steptoe Butte is named after an army officer who lost a battle in 1858 against the local Indians at nearby Rosalia. The lieutenant colonel and most of his troops survived the aftermath by secretly sneaking away at night (a retreat historians think was permitted by the Indians, whose method of warfare did not include annihilation). Almost two decades later, George Custer was not as fortunate at Montana's Little Bighorn. The state park has picnic table but no water; no camping. | East of town center | 509/459–3551 | www.parks.wa.gov | Free | Weekdays; closed weekends.

Washington State University. Opened in 1892 as Washington State's agriculture school, this university has long been a general purpose university. The sprawling campus stretches almost all the way to the Idaho state line, where it is met by the sprawling campus of the University of Idaho. To park on campus while visiting any of the attractions below, stop first at the campus Police Department in the Security Building (on Wilson Road) to pick up a parking pass and directions to a parking lot you may use. | 1 S.E. Stadium Way | 509/335–4527 | fax 509/335–9113 | www.wsu.edu | Free | Weekdays.

Ferdinand's. A soda fountain/cheese shop in Troy Hall on the Washington State University campus where one can count on being able to buy Aged Cougar Gold, a cheddar-type cheese that comes in cans for aging. | Fairway Lane | 509/335–2141 | fax 509/335–9113 | www.wsu.edu | Free | Weekdays; closed weekends.

Museum of Art. A small museum in the Fine Arts Building of Washington State University that has exhibitions and lectures. | WSU Fine Arts Center | 509/335–1910 or 509/335–6607 | fax 509/335–1908 | www.wsu.edu | Free | Sept.–May, Mon., Wed.–Fri. 10–4, Tues. 10–9, weekends 1–5.

The Charles R. Conner Museum of Zoology. The finest collection of (stuffed) birds and mammals and preserved invertebrates in the Pacific Northwest can be found on the campus of Washington State University. | Fine Arts Center | 509/335–3515 or 509/335–6607 | fax 509/335–1908 | www.wsu.edu | Free | Sept.–May, daily 8–5.

Pullman Summer Palace Theater. Theatrical performances are held in June through Sept. | Fine Arts Center | 509/335–7236 | fax 509/335–4255 | www.wsu.edu | Call for schedule.

ON THE CALENDAR

APR.: ***Palouse Duck Dash.*** Adopt a duck and race it down the concrete river channel. The first 40 ducks at this event held in the nearby county seat of Colfax win prizes. | 509/397–3712.

AUG.: ***National Lentil Festival.*** This event kicks off with a lentil chili feed and includes a lentil-pancake breakfast, a street dance, games for children, live music, and a skateboard competition. | 800/365–6948.

Dining

Basilio's Italian Café. Italian. Sitting in the heart of downtown, this affordable restaurant serves up such classics as pasta, lasagna, and chicken Parmesan, in addition to an assortment of sandwiches. The sidewalk seating gives you the chance to enjoy your meal gazing on the scenic downtown area. | 337 E. Main St. | 509/334–ROME | $3.75–$7 | MC, V.

Sella's Calzone and Pastas. Pizza. Starting from scratch daily, the calzones are always fresh at this cozy storefront. The most popular is The Coug (pepperoni, mushrooms, and black olives), or the Frugal Gourmet (artichoke hearts, sun-dried tomatoes, pesto sauce, and mozzarella). Pizzas, sandwiches, pastas, and salads are also served. | 1115 E. Main St. | 509/334–1895 | $4.50–$6.75 | AE, MC, V.

Lodging

American Travel Inn. Comfortable family motel with a sun deck. | 35 rooms. Restaurant, cable TV, pool. | 515 S. Grand Ave. | 509/334–3500 | fax 509/334–0549 | www.palouse.net/allamerican | $40–$75 | AE, D, DC, MC, V.

Churchyard Inn. Registered as a National and State historic site, this 1905 Flemish-style inn, sitting next to the St. Boniface Catholic Church in Uniontown, 15 mi southeast of Pullman, was once a parish house and then a convent before becoming a B&B in 1995. Ceiling fans whirr above the period antiques that adorn each room. A 1,200-square-ft suite has a full kitchen and fireplace. | 7 rooms. Complimentary breakfast, no air-conditioning, some in-room hot tubs, TV in common room, no pets, no kids under 14, no smoking. | 206 St. Boniface St., Uniontown | 509/229–3200 | fax 509/229–3213 | cyi@inlandnet.com | www.bedandbreakfast.com | $60–$150 | D, MC, V.

Country Bed and Breakfast. This 1893 farmhouse sits approximately 5½ mi south of Pullman, surrounded by junipers and flowering trees. Although the B&B's interior with cherry paneling might appear a bit suburban, the warm hospitality of its owners makes a visit here a thoroughly enjoyable experience. | 7 rooms (4 with private bath). Complimentary Continental breakfast, no air-conditioning in some rooms, no room phones, TV in common area, hot tub, outdoor hot tub, pets allowed, no smoking. | 2701 Staley Rd. | 509/334–4453 | fax 509/332–5163 | mtenwick@aol.com | $50–$100 | D, MC, V.

Holiday Inn Express. This motel caters to the business traveler and is close to the Washington State University campus. | 130 rooms. Restaurant, complimentary Continental breakfast, some no-smoking rooms, pool, hot tub, gym, pets allowed, local airport shuttle. | S.E. 1190 Bishop Blvd. | 509/334–4437 | fax 509/334–4447 | $79–$99 | AE, D, DC, MC, V.

Paradise Creek Quality Inn. This comfortable motel is within walking distance of the WSU campus, but far enough off the beaten path to make for quiet lodging. If you hear a creek purling through your dreams, you're not hallucinating: the motel is built above Paradise Creek. | 66 rooms, 15 suites. Restaurant, in-room data ports, some refrigerators (suites), cable TV, pool, hot tub, sauna, business services, local airport shuttle, free parking. | S.E. 1400 Bishop Blvd. | 509/332–0500 | fax 509/334–4271 | $62–$94, $130 suites | AE, D, DC, MC, V.

PUYALLUP

MAP 8, D5

(Nearby towns also listed: Enumclaw, Tacoma)

Puyallup (pronounced "pyoo-AL-lup") is one of western Washington's oldest towns. Ezra Meeker, the founder of Puyallup, had come west on the Oregon trail in 1806/07 when he decided, at the age of 76, to take an ox-drawn covered wagon back east to visit President Theodore Roosevelt and get him to prod Congress into marking the Oregon Trail before its route was forgotten. And that's exactly what Meeker did. But he caused quite a stir when he decided to take a detour to New York City and ride his ox-drawn covered wagon down Broadway. The New York City police told him he couldn't. But he did it anyway, before driving his wagon to the White House and getting the president's endorsement.

The 1890 Meeker mansion is still Puyallup's most important building. Mt. Rainier towers over the mansion and over the daffodil fields (and the new freeways and subdivisions) of the Puyallup Valley.

Information: The Chamber of East Pierce County | 322 Second St. SW, Puyallup, 98371 | 253/845–6755 | fax 253/848–6164 | www.puyallupchamber.com.

Attractions

Ezra Meeker Mansion. The house, which belonged to the man who preserved and remarked the Oregon Trail, is a 17-room Italianate Victorian mansion. Listed on the National Register of Historic Sites, the historical society is currently attempting to restore the mansion to its 1891 condition. | 312 Spring St. | 253/848–1770 | www.meekermansion.org | $4 | Mar.–mid-Dec., Wed.–Sun. 1–4.

Northwest Trek. A wildlife park devoted to animals native to the Pacific Northwest. The animals are kept in very natural surroundings—so natural that in 1998 a cougar entered the park and started snacking on the deer. It was finally trapped and relocated to a remote spot in the North Cascades. | from Seattle, I–5 to exit 154A, I–405 | 360/832–6117 | fax 360/832–6118 | www.nwtrek.org | $8.75 | Apr.–Oct., daily; Nov.–Mar., Fri.–Sun.

Pioneer Farm Museum. A museum devoted to educating people about what pioneer life was really like: grinding grain, milking a cow, churning butter. Guided tours take an hour and a half and leave every 20 minutes. | Hwy. 7, off Ohop Valley Rd. | 360/832–6300 | fax 360/832–4533 | $6.50 | Mid-Mar.–June, weekends; summer, daily.

Pioneer Park. A community park beside the library, with a wading pool, toy area, and summer concert series. | 324 S. Meridian St. | 253/841–5457 | fax 253/770–3369 | Free | Daily.

ON THE CALENDAR

JAN.: ***Kids and Critters Naturefest.*** Kids test their survival skills in activities galore in the predator-prey connection. Don't worry: it's only make-believe: they do not turn the cougars and wolves loose on the kids. | 253/832–6117.

JUNE–JULY: ***Ezra Meeker Community Festival.*** A week-long celebration in late June/early July, with barbecue and extended mansion hours at the Ezra Meeker Mansion, 312 Spring St. | 253/848–1770.

Dining

Powerhouse Brewery and Restaurant. American/Casual. Originally a railroad powerhouse, the interior is adorned with glass insulators and high-voltage signs. In all, 12 brews are served here, six that are brewed on the premises and six brewed at a sister brewery. The pub fare includes salads, pizzas, burgers, sandwiches, and pastas. | 454 E Main Ave. | 253/845–1370 | $7–$9 | MC, V.

Lodging

Best Western Park Plaza. Nicely appointed business travelers' and family motel. Reclining wingback chairs and traditional cherrywood furnishings adorn plushly carpeted rooms, some with four-poster canopy beds. | 100 rooms. Restaurant, complimentary Continental breakfast, no-smoking rooms, pool, hot tub, gym. | 620 S. Hill Park Drive | 253/848–1500 | fax 253/848–1511 | $84–$190 | AE, D, DC, MC, V.

Murphy's Corner Bed and Breakfast. Standing in the middle of Puyallup, this 1905 Victorian is only a short stroll from antique stores, restaurants, fairgrounds, and the Farmers'

PACKING IDEAS FOR COLD WEATHER

- ❑ Driving gloves
- ❑ Earmuffs
- ❑ Fanny pack
- ❑ Fleece neck gaiter
- ❑ Fleece parka
- ❑ Hats
- ❑ Lip balm
- ❑ Long underwear
- ❑ Scarf
- ❑ Shoes to wear indoors
- ❑ Ski gloves or mittens
- ❑ Ski hat
- ❑ Ski parka
- ❑ Snow boots
- ❑ Snow goggles
- ❑ Snow pants
- ❑ Sweaters
- ❑ Thermal socks
- ❑ Tissues, handkerchief
- ❑ Turtlenecks
- ❑ Wool or corduroy pants

*Excerpted from *Fodor's: How to Pack: Experts Share Their Secrets*

Market. Floral patterns dominate the two, sun-infused rooms which have heirlooms and wicker furniture. | 2 rooms. Complimentary breakfast, no air-conditioning, no room phones, TV in common area, no pets, no kids under 12, no smoking. | 601 4th Ave. SW | 253/841–1499 or 888/640–0404 | mcbbreakfast@uswest.com | www.bigboyproductions.com/murphy/index.htm | $65–$75 | AE, D, MC, V.

QUINAULT

MAP 8, B4

(Nearby town also listed: Olympic National Park)

Quinault is the main village on 4½-mi-long and 300-ft-deep Lake Quinault, the quintessential inland rain forest lake, surrounded by intensely green, moss-covered trees. A river runs down from the mountains towering above the forests and feeds the lake, as do numerous small streams. It seems almost hard to believe, but the scenery becomes even prettier as you ascend the river. Enchanted Valley, high up near the river's source, is a deeply glaciated valley that's closer to the Hood Canal than to the Pacific Ocean. If a road were to cross the Olympics (which it does NOT), this valley would probably be overrun by weekend visitors. Accessible only by trail, it has stayed remote and beautiful.

Information: Lake Quinault Visitor Information Center | 6084 Hwy. 101, Amanda Park, 98526 | 360/288–2644 | visitkalaloch.com. also called the **Quinault Rain Forest Visitor Information Center.**

Attractions

Quinault National Fish Hatchery. Over eight million salmon are raised and released from this hatchery, located 5 mi south of Quinault. The adult fish return in fall and early winter, making this time of year the best for visiting. An information center illustrates the hatchery's role on the reservation. | Moclips Hwy., 3 Sockeye Rd., Humptulits | 360/288–2508 | Free | Daily 9–3.

Dining

Lake Quinault Lodge. Contemporary. The restaurant here is uncommonly good for a resort. The old-fashioned bar is lively and pleasant. Try the baked salmon with capers and onions, or the halibut. Also serves a variety of pastas, and great montecristos. | S. Shore Road, Lake Quinault | 360/288–2900 | fax 360/288–2901 | Breakfast also available | $15–$23 | AE, MC, V.

Salmon House Restaurant. Seafood. Particularly known for its salmon which arrives fresh thanks to the Quinault tribe, this restaurant also serves steak and chicken dishes plus other seafood entrées. It is part of the Rain Forest Resort Village and sits directly on the lake, offering unbeatable views of the water and surrounding peaks. | 516 S. Shore Rd. | 360/288–2535 or 800/255–6936 | No lunch. Closed mid-Nov.–mid-Dec. | $15–$20 | AE, D, MC, V.

Lodging

Lake Quinault Lodge. This massive cedar lodge was built in the 1920s. The newer lakeside rooms cater more to the creature comforts of 21st-century man. | 92 rooms. Restaurant (*see* Lake Quinault Lodge), no air-conditioning, no room phones, indoor pool, sauna, beach, boating, game room with arcade and pool table, business services. | 345 South Shore Rd. | 360/288–2900 or 800/562–6672 | fax 360/288–2901 | $105–$165 | AE, MC, V.

Rain Forest Resort Village. Sitting directly on the lake, surrounded by tall, tree-covered peaks, this resort is an oasis in the rain forest. Guest rooms have wood paneling and modern furnishings; most have lake views. The cabins all have fireplaces and decks overlooking the lake; some have kitchens and jetted bath tubs. | 16 rooms, 10 cabins. Restaurant, no air-conditioning, some kitchenettes, some microwaves, some refrigerators, some in-room hot tubs, cable TV, hiking, beach, shops, no pets, no smoking. | 516 S. Shore Rd. | 360/288–2535 or 800/255–6936 | rfr@techline.com | rfrv.com | $90–$95, $125–$185 cabins | AE, D, MC, V.

QUINCY

MAP 8, H5

(Nearby towns also listed: Ellensburg, Ephrata, Wenatchee)

Quincy is a small, friendly farm town in the middle of the Quincy Basin, a region of rich, deep soil where temporary lakes formed during the Spokane Floods dropped silt before their waters spilled over the rocky rim to the west into the Columbia River or escaped by way of the Crab Creek drainage and the Drumheller Channels to the south.

Information: Quincy Valley Chamber of Commerce | Box 668, 119 F St. E, Quincy, 98848 | 509/787–2140 | fax 507/787–4500 | www.quinceyvalley.org.

Attractions

Crescent Bar Park. A waterfront park on Wanapum Reservoir (Columbia River) 8 mi west of Quincy has a swimming beach, boat ramp, playground, picnic area, campground, tennis courts, and a golf course. It is popular with fishermen and water-skiers. | Rte. 28 | 509/787–1511 | Free | Apr.–Oct., daily.

ON THE CALENDAR

SEPT.: ***Farmer-Consumer Awareness Day.*** Since 1980 on the second Saturday in September, this community has brought the public in touch with the farm community through an arts and crafts fair, food booths, live entertainment, and two parades. The festival takes place behind the local high school (16 6th Ave., SE), and the parades march through the downtown area (C Street, SW). | 509/787–2140.

Dining

Idle Hour Café and Steakhouse. American/Casual. Established in 1906, the restaurant still has its old storefront with crystal glass windows. The lunch menu includes sandwiches, burgers, and salads, while the dinner menu emphasizes heartier entrées such as steaks, chicken and seafood dishes. Especially popular are the fresh, pan-seared oysters. | 18 B St., SE | 509/787–3714 | Reservations essential on weekends | No lunch on weekends; no dinner Sun.–Tues. | $12–$20 | D, MC, V.

Lodging

Sun Downer Motel. Renovated in 1999, the motel has rooms which contain a full range of modern amenities conveniently close to local restaurants (only one block away). The motel is located on Highway 28. | 24 rooms. Refrigerators, microwaves, cable TV, pool, pets allowed. | 414 F St. SE | 509/787–3587 | fax 509/787–3485 | $55–$72 | AE, D, DC, MC, V.

Traditional Inns. This motel caters to families and is close to the concert series at the Gorge. | 24 rooms. Refrigerators, microwaves, cable TV, laundry facilities, pets allowed (fee). | 500 S.W. F Street, off of Rte. 28 | 509/787–3525 | fax 509/787–3528 | $66 | AE, D, DC, MC, V.

RENTON

MAP 8, D4

(Nearby towns also listed: Bellevue, Kent, Seattle)

The industrial city of Renton, at the southern end of Lake Washington, has an old, refurbished downtown and a public library dramatically built on a bridge across the Cedar

River. But the city has, according to Seattle writer Bill Speidel, always gotten the short end of the stick when it came to regional development: "You sort of hesitate to suggest that Renton is always the bridesmaid and never the bride, but the fact is that she's been used and re-used by some of the stars of the show for the last century or more." One of the incidents Speidel quotes is that Seattleites got Renton to agree to the ship canal connecting Lake Washington and Puget Sound by telling the Rentonites they'd get a seaport in return. Instead, the canal caused the lake's level to drop by 9 ft and all Renton got was mudflats. Maybe. Renton Airport and the Boeing 737 plant now stand on those mudflats and, over the years, have provided Renton with a lot more income than a port would have. But there is a curious postscript: The airstrip is so short that finished Boeing 737s can take off from it but not land, if there's any trouble during takeoff. Luckily that's never happened. A pleasant beach park runs along the shore north of the Boeing plant.

Information: Greater Renton Chamber of Commerce | 300 Rainier Ave. N, Renton, 98055 | 425/226–4560 | fax 425/226–4287 | ci.renton.wa.us/.

REPUBLIC

INTRO
ATTRACTIONS
DINING
LODGING

Attractions

Renton Historical Museum. The museum's exhibits illustrate the history of the city which began as a Duwamish Indian encampment, then became a coal-mining and logging town, and now is a center for manufacturing. | 235 Mill Ave., S | 425/255–2330 | Donation | Tues. 9–4; Wed.–Sun. 1–4.

ON THE CALENDAR

JULY: *Renton River Days.* The week-long festival, held each year during the last week of July, celebrates the city's history and culture. Family entertainment includes live music, arts and crafts booths, a parade, golf and soccer tournaments and a classic car show. The activities take place at different times and locations. The parade begins in the morning on Saturday and runs down 3rd St. | 425/430–6528.

Dining

Spirit of Washington Dinner Train. American/Casual. You can eat a delicious meal while enjoying splendid views of Lake Washington, Mercer Island, and Mount Rainier on this totally unique dining experience. The train stops for 45 minutes at the Columbia Winery in Woodinville for a wine tasting and tour. The entrées include prime rib, roasted salmon, stuffed chicken, crab crêpes, and vegetarian options. The entire trip takes 3¼ hours. | 625 S. 4th St. | 425/227–7245 | Reservations essential | No lunch weekdays | $60–$70 | AE, MC, V.

Lodging

Holiday Inn Select. The upscale lobby, which overlooks the pool, contains a large fireplace, cherry paneling, and marble details. The chain is located immediately off I–405 at exit 2B. | 226 rooms. Restaurant, bar, room service, in-room data ports, refrigerators, cable TV, pool, hot tub, gym, business services, airport shuttle, no pets. | 1 South Grady Way | 425/226–7700 or 800/521–1412 | fax 425/271–2315 | www.holiday-inn.com/rentonwa | $149 | AE, D, DC, MC, V.

REPUBLIC

MAP 8, I2

(Nearby town also listed: Colville)

Republic is a small mountain town and county seat of Ferry County with an authentic western-style, false-front downtown. It takes its name from the nearby Republic Mine. Gold is still the lifeblood of the town, with one gold mine still producing. In the 19th century, Republic gold made Spokane rich, and helped finance that city's ambitious building programs.

Information: Republic Area Chamber of Commerce | 979 S. Clark St., Republic, 99166 | 509/775–2704 | www.republic-wa.com.

Attractions

Stonerose Interpretive Center and Eocene Fossil Site. Plants and animals from almost 50 million years ago are preserved in shale deposits on view at this center. You can dig for fossils yourself and take them home with you (3 per day), provided you have not made a rare discovery. | 15-1 Kean St. | 509/775–2295 | $2.50 | May–Oct., Tues.–Sat. 10–5, Sun. 10–4.

ON THE CALENDAR

JAN.: ***Winterfest Carnival.*** Nordic skiing, snowmobiling, ice sculpture demonstrations, snowshoe softball, outdoor trade show (Brrr!! Bundle up for this one!), chili cook-off to warm up, and other events. | 509/775–2587.

JULY: ***Draft Horse Show.*** Single and Team Driving Events, farm working teams and a log-skidding-weight pull all take place at the Fairgrounds. | 509/634–4388.

Dining

Esther's. Mexican. The site of live music on the weekends, this eatery has an outdoor patio, in addition to the lively dining room, on which to enjoy the many south-of-the-border specialties. | 90 N. Clark Ave. | 509/775–2088 | $4–$7 | MC, V.

Lodging

K-Diamond-K Guest Ranch. This guest ranch, set on 1,400 acres, offers a great way of experiencing the Old West in beautiful surroundings. Join in the ranch activities or relax and enjoy the views. B&B also available. | 4 rooms. Dining room, complimentary breakfast, no-smoking rooms, pets allowed. | 15661 Hwy. 21 S. | 509/775–3536 or 888/345–5355 | fax 509/775–3536 | www.kdiamondk.com | $65–$115 | No credit cards.

Northern Inn. The motel's fort-like structure includes a tower and a covered walkway that provides access to each room. Fossils and historical pictures adorn the walls of the lobby where local crafts are sold and where there is an espresso coffee shop. Rooms are appointed with contemporary furnishings and many amenities. | 23 rooms. Complimentary Continental breakfast, in-room data ports, microwaves, refrigerators, cable TV, hot tub, sauna, pets allowed. | 852 S. Clark Ave. | 509/775–3371 or 888/801–1068 | fax 509/775–2089 | www.northern-inn.com | $53 | AE, D, DC, MC, V.

RICHLAND

MAP 8, I7

(Nearby towns also listed: Kennewick, Pasco)

Richland, founded in the 1880s, was a pleasant farming village until 1942, when the Federal government moved in, dispossessed the farmers and established the Hanford Nuclear Reservation to make atom bombs for the war with Japan. The locals are proud of their nuclear tradition: the local high school team calls itself "The Bombers" and uses a nuclear cloud as its emblem.

When the government moved in, it erected modular housing for its employees, graded by size and the importance of the occupants: the letters "A" and "B" designated two-story duplexes; "E" and "F" were single-family duplexes; "Q" and "R," larger homes near the river and its parks. Today, many of these distinctions have been blurred by remodeling and gardens, giving the residential areas a prosperous, well-lived-in look, which is a far cry from its appearance during the war years.

Information: Tri-Cities Visitor and Convention Bureau | Box 2241, 6951 W. Groundridge Blvd., Tri-Cities, 99302 | 800/254–5824 | www.visittri-cities.com.

Attractions

Columbia River Journeys. Cruises on Lake Wallula and the Columbia River. | 1229 Columbia Park Trail, Box 26, | 509/943–0231 | $42, $32 kids | May–mid-Oct.

CREHST Museum. CREHST stands for the Columbia River Exhibition of History, Science, and Technology. This is a hands-on museum where you can explore science and technology through educational exhibits. | 95 Lee Blvd. | 509/943–9000 | fax 509/943–1770 | www.crehst.org | $3.50 | Mon.–Sat. 10–5, Sun. noon–5.

ON THE CALENDAR

MAR.–APR.: ***Bacchus Wine and Food Festival.*** A fun fest highlighting local wines, food and music. | 509/946–1651.

Dining

Emerald of Siam. Thai. This small storefront restaurant has long had the best Asian food in eastern Washington. That's because owner chef (as well as poet and cookbook author) Ravadi Quinn has an uncommon understanding of food and its basic ingredients, and can coax the most of flavor from any dish. Try the pad Thai and curried dishes. Buffet lunch served weekdays. | 1314 Jadwin Ave. | 509/946–9328 | Closed Sun. No lunch Sat. | $7–$11 | AE, D, MC, V.

Mandarin House. Chinese. Among the favorite dishes at this popular downtown eatery are the Mongolian beef and garlic chicken. The interior is decorated in a familiar Chinese theme. | 1035 Lee Blvd. | 509/943–6843 | $6–$9 | MC, V.

O'Callahan's Restaurant and Lounge. American/Casual. This restaurant is part of the Shilo Inn; the lounge enjoys a view of the Columbia River, and outdoor dining on a deck overlooking the water is available in the warmer months. There are a lot of choices on the menu including seafoods, pastas, Angus steaks, and salads. Some popular items are the country fried steak and the southern fried catfish. | 50 Comstock St. | 509/946–9006 | Breakfast also available | $8–$18 | AE, D, DC, MC, V.

Rattlesnake Mountain Brewing Company. American/Casual. The spacious deck of this pub and family restaurant has wonderful views of the Columbia River. Serving a variety of different chicken, steak, pasta, and shrimp dishes, the eatery is famous for its buffalo wings and its seven home-brewed beers. There's also a kids' menu. | 2696 N. Columbia Center Blvd. | 509/783–5661 | $6–$14 | AE, D, DC, MC, V.

Lodging

Bali Hi Motel. Small hotel frequented by families. It is 1 mi from downtown and Columbia Park is nearby. | 44 rooms. Refrigerators, cable TV, pool, business services. | 1201 George Washington Way | 509/943–3101 | fax 509/943–6363 | $37–$47 | AE, D, DC, MC, V.

Best Western Tower Inn. Big corporate hotel in the heart of wine country. Many rooms overlook a tropical garden courtyard. | 195 rooms. Complimentary Continental breakfast, some refrigerators, cable TV, pool, wading pool, hot tub, sauna, laundry facilities, business services, airport shuttle. | 1515 George Washington Way | 509/946–4121 or 800/635–3980 | fax 509/946–2222 | $69–$119 | AE, D, DC, MC, V.

Hampton Inn Richland. This enormous chain hotel stretches along the west shore of the Columbia River adjacent to a park and a riverfront promenade. Many of the rooms have spectacular views of the river; some have balconies. | 130 rooms. Complimentary Continental breakfast, microwaves, refrigerators, some in-room hot tubs, cable TV, pool, gym, laundry service, business services, airport shuttle, pets allowed. | 486 Bradley Blvd. | 509/943–4400 or 800/HAMPTON | www.northwestinns.com/richland.html | $79–$89 | AE, D, DC, MC, V.

Palmer Farm. Ten mi west of Richland, this 1902 inn sits on 10 acres near many wineries and only a short walk to the Yakima River. Amid the shaded lawns stands a quaint gazebo in which you may, if you wish, enjoy your complimentary breakfast. Lace and floral patterned wallpaper complement the antiques and heirlooms of the guest rooms. The large windows and sloped ceilings add an extra charm. Although the rooms all have sinks, the B&B's four bathrooms are located outside the rooms. | 4 rooms (all shared baths). Complimentary breakfast, no room phones, no TV, library, no pets, no kids under 15, no smoking. | 42901 N. River Rd., Benton City | 509/588–4011 | palmerfarm@bentonrea.com | www.palmerfarm1902.hypermart.net | $70–$75 | No credit cards.

Red Lion Hotel. Hotel overlooking Columbia River at the southern end of Hanford Reach, the last free-flowing stretch of the river between Bonneville Dam and the Canadian border. Ask for a room with a river view. The hotel borders a greenbelt park on the river and has easy access to levee trails. | 149 rooms. Restaurant, bar, room service, gym, pool, local airport shuttle, free parking, pets allowed. | 802 George Washington Way | 509/946–7611 | fax 509/943–8564 | $74–$84 | AE, D, DC, MC, V.

Richland Day's Inn. This two-story motel is 1 mi north of I–182, and two blocks west of Howard Amon Park and the Columbia River. | 98 rooms. Complimentary Continental breakfast, refrigerators, microwaves, cable TV, pool, laundry facilities, business services. | 615 Jadwin Ave. | 509/943–4611 or 800/DAYSINN | fax 509/967–2271 | $58–$79 | AE, D, DC, MC, V.

Shilo Inn Rivershore. Hotel bordering Columbia River above the mouth of the Yakima. It has easy access to riverside trails with a park upriver and downriver. | 150 rooms, 13 suites. Restaurant, bar, some kitchenettes, refrigerators (in suites), cable TV, room service, pool, wading pool, hot tub, gym, laundry facilities, business services, airport shuttle, free parking, pets allowed (fee). | 50 Comstock St. | 509/946–4661 | fax 509/943–6741 | $59–$129, $109–$169 suites | AE, D, DC, MC, V.

RITZVILLE

MAP 8, J5

(Nearby town also listed: Moses Lake)

Straddling the junction of two major highways, I–90 and UC 395, the Adams county seat has long occupied a central position in eastern Washington, despite its small size. Its old downtown has several interesting buildings, most notably the eclectic house built by Dr. Frank R. Burroughs in 1889 (now the county historical society's museum). Ritzville is in the heart of the wheat country. The town made headline news in 1980, when it received more than its share of Mt. St. Helen's ash.

Information: Ritzville Area Chamber of Commerce | 201 W. Railroad, Box 122, Ritzville, 99169 | 509/659–1936 | chamber@ritzcom.net | www.ritzcom.net/chamber.

Attractions

Dr. Frank Burroughs House. An 1889–92 mansion furnished with period pieces and historic objects. | 408 Main St. | 509/659–1936 | www.ritzcom.net/ritzville | Free | By appointment.

ON THE CALENDAR

JULY: *Ritzville Blues Festival.* The small downtown area of Ritzville is blocked off during this day of "blues, brews, and barbecue". Local bars and restaurants sponsor live, mostly acoustic, performances, and an outdoor stage is the site of amplified concerts. The festival takes place usually in the middle of the month. | 509/659–1936 | www.ritzvilleblues.com.

SEPT.: *Wheatland Communities Fair.* A carnival with food and games over Labor Day weekend. | 509/659–1936.

Dining

Circle T Restaurant. Contemporary. This wheat country steak and seafood house is a favorite hangout of local farmers. Specialities include New York steak and grilled oysters. | 214 W. Main St. | 509/659–0922 | Breakfast also available. No dinner Mon. | $10–$20 | MC, V.

Jake's Café. American. This quintessential roadside diner—adjacent to a gas station off I-90—is open 24 hours a day, seven days a week. All the menu items are available at any time. The dinner menu has many favorites, including steaks, burgers, and sandwiches. | 1500 W. 1st Ave. | 509/659–1961 | Breakfast also available | $7–$12 | AE, D, MC, V.

Lodging

Best Inn and Suites Heritage Inn. Comfortable business travelers' and family motel. | 52 rooms, 2 suites. Complimentary Continental breakfast, cable TV, pool, hot tub, laundry facilities, business services, pets allowed. | 1513 Smitty's Blvd. | 509/659–1007 | fax 509/659–1025 | $69–$89, $129–$159 suites | AE, D, DC, MC, V.

The Portico. Built in 1902 in a variety of styles (Queen Anne, Classical Revival, and Craftsman), this B&B has been beautifully maintained and appointed by its owners. The parquet floor in the entrance hall with its pattern of light and dark oak, bordered with serpentine work in maple, is a perfect example. Rooms are furnished with antiques like a carved walnut canopy bed with a mermaid at its head and an angel at its foot. | 4 rooms. Complimentary breakfast, cable TV, no smoking. | 502 S Adams St. | 509/659–0800 | portico@porticobandb.com | www.porticobandb.com | $59–$74 | AE, D, MC, V.

SAN JUAN ISLANDS

MAP 8, D2

(Nearby town also listed: Anacortes)

The San Juan Islands are a cluster of large and small rocky outcroppings in the Salish Sea. Isolated from the mainland by saltwater channels and aided by the fact that many year-round residents are retirees, the island people have developed a very relaxed, easygoing lifestyle. Wildlife abounds, especially in nearby waters where you can see orcas, sea lions, seals, porpoises, and an occasional whale. Bald eagles can be seen near the shore. If you hear the sweet trill of an unfamiliar bird, it may be a skylark, a European bird introduced to Vancouver Island's Sanich Peninsula decades ago and now naturalized on many of the islands. A few of the small, isolated islands are bird sanctuaries where tufted puffins and other uncommon seabirds nest.

Four of the islands, Lopez, Shaw, Orcas, and San Juan, are served several times a day by the regularly scheduled Washington State Ferry. One daily ferry makes a daily return trip from Anacortes to the Islands and to Sidney, on Vancouver Island. A daily passenger ferry runs from Bellingham to San Juan Island and to Victoria, a "commuter" ferry goes daily from Bellingham to Friday Harbor and makes "whistle stops" at islands not served by Washington State Ferries, including those with state parks, like remote Matia, Sucia, and Patos Islands.

Information: San Juan Island Chamber of Commerce | Box 98, Friday Harbor 98250 | 360/378–5240 | chamber@sanjuanisland.org | www.sanjuanisland.org.

Attractions

Lime Kiln State Park. Come view whales rollicking in Haro Strait from this viewpoint 10 mi northwest of Friday Harbor. The prime whale-sighting months are from April through August. A local pod of orcas regularly passes by this rocky shore. | 1567 Westside Rd. | 360/378–2044 | Free | Daily 8–dusk.

San Juan Island National Historical Park. This park comes in three sections: a visitor center in downtown Friday Harbor, American Camp on a windswept bluff in the south end, and English Camp in a protected cove near the northwest end of the island. The camps were established in 1859, when the British challenged American claims to the San Juan Islands. No shots were fired, and Kaiser Wilhelm I of Germany settled the dispute in favor of the U.S. in 1872. Guidebooks like to make fun of the fact that the Americans chose such a windy side for their camp, while the British picked a warm, sheltered cove. But in case of war, guns placed at American Camp could effectively shut down not only the southern sea route to British Columbia's ports, but Victoria Harbor and the Esquimalt Navy Base as well. Both places are, incidentally, great birding spots. | Friday Harbor | 360/378–2240 | fax 360/378–2615 | www.nps.gov/sajh | Free | Daily.

The Whale Museum. A great little museum that puts you into a whale of a mood through intelligent displays and piped-in whale sounds. | 62 1st St. N, Friday Harbor | 360/378–4710 or 800/946–7227 | fax 360/378–5790 | www.whale-museum.org | $5 | Daily 10–5.

ON THE CALENDAR

MAY: ***Return of the Orcas.*** Celebration of the annual return of pods of killer whales to local waters at Roche Harbor, San Juan Island's northern end. | 800/451–8910.

Dining

Downrigger. Contemporary. A glitzy restaurant overlooking the harbor, good for watching the ferries and featuring fresh local seafood in dishes such as the twisted salmon and halibut with fried crab, and the fish and chips. Or try the chicken gorgonzola salad. Open-air dining on the deck. No smoking. | 10 Front St. | 360/378–2700 | Breakfast served weekends | $15–$25 | AE, MC, V.

Duck Soup Inn. Contemporary. San Juan Island's best restaurant has been consistent over the years. Everything served in the small dining room is made from scratch and is absolutely delicious. Try lightly smoked oysters from nearby Westcott Bay, pan-seared sea scallops, filet Béarnaise, or vindaloo curry seafood stew. Their carefully selected wine list includes California, Northwest, and French vintages, as well as Italian and Australian. | 50 Duck Soup Lane, Friday Harbor | 360/378–4878 | Reservations essential | Closed Nov.–Mar. and Mon.–Tues. No lunch | $18–$27 | D, MC, V.

Friday Harbor House Restaurant. Contemporary. Emphasizing local, fresh food, the menu often fluctuates according to season and weather, but it is always scrumptuous and well-presented. Soft lighting sets an intimate tone for the dining room, which overlooks the harbor and marina. | 130 West St., Friday Harbor | 360/378–8453 | No lunch. | $14–$23 | AE, MC, V.

Front Street Ale House. English. This English-style ale house serves sandwiches, salads, and traditional pub fare—lamb stew, meat pasties, steak and kidney pie, and the like. For vegetarians there's a vegetable patty lightly sauteed, then stacked with cheese, mushrooms, lettuce, tomato, and onions. On-tap brews from the San Juan Brewing Company carry such locally inspired names as Pig War Stout. | 1 Front St., Friday Harbor | 360/378–2337 | Reservations not accepted | $7–$15 | MC, V.

Springtree Café. Contemporary. Serving Pacific Northwest fare, the restaurant specializes in fresh seafood, pasta dishes, and hand-cut steaks. There are a lot of vegetarian options and an extensive wine list. Original local art hanging from the wall can be observed in the warm glow of candles. An outdoor patio overlooks a century-old elm tree. | 310 Spring St., Friday Harbor | 360/378–4848 | $16–$24 | D, MC, V.

Lodging

Argyle House. This country B&B, in an original 1910 Craftsman home, is surrounded by pleasant gardens. It's close to town, but remains a quiet and peaceful refuge. | 3 rooms (shower only), 1 cottage. Picnic area, complimentary breakfast, no air-conditioning, no TVs in rooms, cable TV in common area, no room phones, hot tub, airport shuttle, no kids under 10, no smoking. | 685 Argyle Ave., Friday Harbor | 360/378–4084 or 800/624–3459 (reservations) | www.argylehouse.net | $120–135, $135 cottage | MC, V.

Friday Harbor House. Standing on a bluff above the harbor, this contemporary lodging and its rooms have clear views of the marina, ferry landing, and San Juan Channel. The rooms each have fireplaces and sleek, modern wood wall units; most have hot tubs in the center of the room overlooking the harbor; some have balconies. | 20 rooms. Restaurant, complimentary Continental breakfast, no air-conditioning, in-room data ports, refrigerators, in-room hot tubs, cable TV, no pets, no smoking. | 130 West St., Friday Harbor | 360/378–8455 | fax 360/378–8453 | fhhouse@rockisland.com | www.fridayharborhouse.com | $200–$300 | AE, MC, V.

Friday's Historical Inn. This former bunkhouse, built in 1891, has been turned into a very comfortable inn. It has managed to meld the past with its many antique pieces and the present with its upgrading and modernization of its rooms. | 14 rooms (3 with shared bath). Complimentary Continental breakfast and afternoon snacks, no air-conditioning, refrigerators, some cable TV, no room phones, local airport shuttle, no smoking. | 35 First St. | 360/378–5848 or 800/352–2632 | fax 360/378–2881 | information@friday-harbor.com | www.friday-harbor.com | $90–$215 | MC, V.

Harrison House Suites. This beautifully restored 1905 Craftsman home sits atop a quiet hill overlooking the harbor. Just 1½ blocks from the ferry terminal, the rooms have pleasant views of the water, and the area is wonderfully landscaped. Many of the ingredients for breakfast come straight from their prize-winning gardens, and meals are served in the garden café. | 5 suites. Complimentary Continental breakfast, no air-conditioning, in-room data ports, microwaves, refrigerators, room service, many in-room hot tubs, cable TV, in-room VCRs (movies), stereos, pool, hot tub, massage, laundry facilities, business services, airport and ferry shuttles, no smoking. | 235 C St., Friday Harbor | 360/378–3587 or 800/407–7933 (reservations) | fax 360/378–2270 | hhsuites@rockisland.com | $100–$260 suites | AE, D, MC, V.

PIG WAR

At a time when the British had not yet become the friends they were in the 20th century (memories of the war of 1812 were only some 50 years old, and Britain was thought to be sympathetic to the Southern Cause in the Civil War), the British began to reexamine the Treaty of 1846. This treaty gave the land south of the 49th parallel to the U.S., with the exception of southern Vancouver Island and a few other odd islands, and it drew the water boundary through the "center of the main channel." That, everyone seemed to understand, meant Haro Strait, making the San Juan Islands American. But the Brits realized that if any of the recently developed long-range guns were placed on San Juan Island, they could effectively block the entrance to Victoria Harbor and the Esquimalt naval base.

While the British were suggesting that Rosario, not Haro, should be the border strait, American settlers moved in. So did the Hudson's Bay Company. Matters came to a head in 1859, when an American settler shot a British pig on San Juan Island. Tempers flared, and for a few months it looked like the incident might lead to war. The Brits even sent in the *Ganges,* a four-decker ship-of-the-line. But cooler heads prevailed and decided on joint occupation until a decision could be reached. The British established a camp, now called "English Camp," in a sheltered cove near the island's northern end; the Americans picked a site on a less comfortable windswept prairie near the southern end. It was a spot that would have made a splendid battery site for an attack on Victoria. But no shots were fired. In fact, the troops fraternized and celebrated holidays together. In 1872 Kaiser Wilhelm I of Germany was asked to arbitrate, and he made Haro Strait the boundary and awarded the islands to the U.S. That is why a picture of Emperor Billy has been hanging in the San Juan County court house ever since.

Highland Inn of San Juan Island. Perched on a hillside overlooking the Haro Strait, this B&B has splendid views of orcas and other wildlife from the rooms and its expansive, 88-ft-long deck. The two spacious rooms have wood-burning fireplaces and plush, contemporary furnishings such as sofas and reclining chairs. To protect the guests' privacy, the address is kept secret by the proprietress, but it is less than 1 mi south of the Lime Kiln Lighthouse. | 2 rooms. Complimentary breakfast, in-room data ports, in-room hot tubs, refrigerators, cable TV, hiking, no pets, no smoking. | Box 135, Friday Harbor | 360/378–9450 or 888/400–9850 | fax 360/378–1693 | helen@highlandinn.com | www.highlandinn.com | $250 | AE, D, MC, V.

Hillside House. A charming B&B overlooking Friday Harbor (on clear days you can see Mt. Baker in the far distance). The gardens feature a two-story atrium and several ponds. | 7 rooms (2 with shower only). Complimentary breakfast, no air-conditioning, some room phones, business services. | 365 Carter Ave., Friday Harbor | 360/378–4730 or 800/232–4730 | fax 360/378–4715 | info@hillsidehouse.com | www.hillsidehouse.com | $95–$225 | AE, D, MC, V.

Panacea. A comfortable B&B in a turn-of-the-20th-century Craftsman bungalow. Convenient walk from ferry landing. | 4 rooms, 2 with shower only. Picnic area, complimentary breakfast, no air-conditioning, some in-room hot tubs, cable TV, no room phones, local airport and ferry shuttle, no kids under 17, no smoking. | 595 Park St., Friday Harbor | 360/378–3757; res: 800/639–2762 | fax 360/378–8543 | www.friday-harbor.net/panacea | $140–$170 | MC, V.

Roche Harbor. Ten mi northwest on Roche Harbor Rd., on San Juan Island, this classic old resort dates back to the 19th century when this was a limestone quarry. The old (1886) Hotel de Haro (formerly the quarry's guest house) dating from 1886 has plain but comfortable rooms. More up-to-date accommodations are available in modern condominiums. | 20 suites (16 with shared bath), 9 cottages, 30 apartments. Some kitchens (cottages), restaurant, bar with entertainment, picnic area, snack bar, no air-conditioning, no TV in rooms, pool, tennis, marina, hiking, beach, boating, children's programs (ages 5–18), laundry facilities, business services, no smoking. | 4959 Tarte Memorial Dr. | 360/378–2155 or 800/451–8910 | fax 360/378–6809 | www.rocheharbor.com | $79–$150, $145–$195 cottages, $125–$280 apartments | AE, MC, V.

San Juan Inn. This delightful B&B is just a half block from the water on Friday Harbor's main street. Set in an updated 1873 Victorian home, the inn is carefully decorated with period furniture. | 11 rooms (5 with shared bath), 2 suites. Complimentary Continental breakfast, no air-conditioning, no kids under 5, no smoking. | 50 Spring St., Friday Harbor | 360/378–2070 or 800/742–8210 | fax 360/378–6437 | www.san-juan.net/sjinn | $95–$195 | AE, D, MC, V.

Trumpeter Inn Bed and Breakfast. Two mi from the ferry landing, in the San Juan Valley, this B&B sits on 10 acres, encompassed by ponds and meadows. Rooms are individually appointed and each has its own character. The "Yarrow", for instance, has a springtime feel, evoked through the room's lemon yellow color and wildflower-embroidered comforter. | 5 rooms. Complimentary breakfast, no room phones, TV in common area, pond, hot tub, fishing, no pets, no kids under 12, no smoking. | 318 Trumpeter Way, Friday Harbor | 360/378–3884 or 800/826–7926 | fax 360/378–8235 | swam@rockisland.com | www.trumpeterinn.com | $105–$140 | AE, D, MC, V.

Tucker House. A comfortable B&B in a turn-of-the-20th-century home, 2 blocks from the ferry terminal, and a park. | 6 rooms, 2 suites, 3 cottages. Picnic area, complimentary breakfast and afternoon snacks, no air-conditioning, some kitchenettes, microwaves, some refrigerators, cable TV, some in-room hot tubs, hot tub, some pets allowed (fee), no kids under 18 (except in cottages), no smoking. | 260 B St., Friday Harbor | 360/378–2783 or 800/965–0123 (reservations) | fax 360/378–6241 | www.tuckerhouse.com | $115–$175 rooms, $120–$165 cottages | MC, V.

SEATTLE

MAP 8, D4

(Nearby towns also listed: Bellevue, Bremerton, Edmonds, Everett, Poulso, Tacoma)

Seattle's waterfront had been occupied by Native Americans for thousands of years before white settlers arrived in the mid-1800s. The natives fished for salmon, dug clams, lived relatively happy lives, and rarely entered the deep forests of huge (200-ft) trees rising straight from the saltwater shore. The American settlers started cutting down those trees right after their arrival. A sawmill was followed by a waterfront business district, warehouses, canneries, and factories; shipyards soon followed. After the Klondike Gold Rush, the port grew; trade with Alaska has been one of the mainstays of Seattle's economy ever since. In 1916 William Boeing built his first airplane in a local barn—and the rest is history. The greater Seattle area has benefitted from the presence of Boeing plants for three-quarters of a century. More recently, Microsoft and other high-tech companies have had a major impact on the local economy and on the local lifestyle, turning a mainly blue-collar region into a white-color one.

Information: Seattle-King County Convention and Visitors Bureau | 800 Convention Place, Seattle, 98101 | 206/461–5800 | fax 206/461–3855 | www.seeseattle.org.

NEIGHBORHOODS

Downtown. Downtown is Seattle's business and shopping district, with some of the best views in town because, curiously, much of it is built on one of the city's steepest slopes. West–east streets (and sidewalks) rising from the waterfront can be very steep (several end at First Avenue in bluff-side steps); north–south streets, on the other hand, are almost level. North of the central business district in the area known as Belltown (or Denny Regrade), the streets are level above Second Avenue; to the south, in Pioneer Square and the International district almost all streets are level. As you walk along downtown sidewalks, look down at the manhole covers: many have Northwest Indian designs cast into the iron. Other whimsical touches include duck-foot prints changing from concrete to bronze as they emerge from a sidewalk, a walk-through fountain, and a tree-shaded park built right above the I–5 freeway. Almost every office building has a café where you may sample Seattle's famous lattes; many have a great view of Elliott Bay and the Olympic Mountains. Downtown has Seattle's major office buildings, shops, hotels, and restaurants. Even so, it tends to "die" at night, when the action shifts to neighborhood restaurants and pubs.

Pike Place Market. Perched on a bluff high above the Elliott Bay waterfront, the Pike Place Market began as a place for farmers to sell their fresh food produce directly to the consumer. Today, even though a few farmers still sell here, the market is better known for its restaurants, shops, street performers, and crafts vendors. But it is still immensely popular, and finding a parking space, especially during the height of the visitor season, can be an exercise in ingenuity.

Pioneer Square. This is where Seattle began but did not stay long. As business people moved north of Yesler, less savory folk moved in and, until urban rehabilitation cleaned up this area, it was known as Seattle's red light district. Today, it is clean (except for a gaggle of homeless people and panhandlers), and its shops and restaurants cater to a mostly upscale clientele, as well as to sports fans attending games at the nearby baseball stadium and football area. To the southeast, the Seattle Mariners' new (retractable-roof) baseball stadium has risen. Pioneer Square also has an active nightlife and is particularly well known for its comedy clubs.

International District. Southeast of Pioneer Square, this is Seattle's Asian Quarter, in an older part of town, mainly between the I–5 freeway and the sports stadiums, although parts have begun spilling uphill beyond the freeway overpass onto Beacon Hill. Here you will find the freshest geoduck (a delectable giant clam), exotic produce, properly aged Smithfield ham, and handmade noodles. Shops sell exotic imports, rice paper, antique Chinese art objects and furniture; restaurants serve first-rate Cambodian and Vietnamese food and good dim sum. For the best in Chinese, Japanese, and Thai food, you'll have to go uptown.

Belltown and the Denny Regrade. The area was once a mountain, Denny Hill, until the city quite literally washed it into the bay. This neighborhood lingered as a low-income housing and shopping area but in recent years it has experienced gentrification. Many of Seattle's hottest restaurants are now in Belltown, as well as an ever-increasing number of high-rise condominiums.

Lake Union. Below Queen Anne Hill, north of downtown, this urban lake has long served as a major mooring basin for fishing vessels, NOAA research ships, and yachts. The ship canal runs west from Lake Union to the Chittenden Locks and Puget Sound and east through the Montlake Cut to Lake Washington. It is deep enough to allow ocean-going vessels access to Lake Washington and it can be explored on a harbor tour.

Queen Anne Hill. This residential area northwest of and uphill from Seattle Center has great views of the sound, the city, and snow-capped peaks. Several streets are lined with very prolific chestnut trees bearing fruit in fall.

Fremont. This laid-back neighborhood is Seattle's "Left Bank," with odd shops, pubs, and very relaxed residents. It's separated from staid Queen Anne Hill by the ship canal. A concrete sculpture near the canal, called *Waiting for the Interurban,* portrays a group of commuters waiting for an electric tram. It is decorated, in season, with flowers, birthday greetings, and empty beer bottles. A bit up the hill and around the corner stands a bronze statue of Lenin rescued by a local artist from a now-defunct Eastern bloc country, and high up on the slope, below the eastern end of the Aurora Avenue Bridge, which soars high above the canal, squats a huge sculpture of the Fremont Troll, forever arrested in the act of eating a (real) VW beetle. It, too, is at times decorated with flowers.

Capitol Hill. Capitol Hill is an eclectic neighborhood high above the eastern shore of Lake Union. It's part old money and stately mansions, part apartment buildings and rather eclectic folk. It sports shops and restaurants along Broadway, a splendid Asian Art Museum in Volunteer Park (with great views of Puget Sound and the Olympic Mountains), a conservatory and, in Lake View Cemetery to the north, the graves of prominent Seattle pioneers as well as those of movie star Bruce Lee and his son, Brandon.

Ballard. Despite its reputation as a Scandinavian enclave, Ballard has some of Seattle's finest palm trees (near the Chittenden Locks at the Ship Canal). Ballard has its own downtown and an interesting working waterfront with ship moorage and boat yards. Waterfront restaurants on Shilshole Bay to the west have great views of Puget Sound and the Olympic Mountains. Ballard drivers are notorious throughout Seattle for their slow, meticulous driving habits.

Arboretum/Japanese Garden. South of the U District and the Ship Canal at the Montlake Cut, is this place of rest. Trails lead through a marsh and through different plantings of native and exotic trees. A small Japanese garden is a place of perfect repose, replete with a cat so inscrutable you'll swear she's a bodhisattva in disguise. An authentic teahouse is only open for authentic tea ceremonies and instruction. A lake has colorful koi carp, turtles, water lilies, and irises. The walls of the garden are lined with some truly splendid bamboos.

U District. This is the home of the University of Washington, better known for its athletic than for its academic successes. Centered on University Way (known locally as "The Ave") with its shops and restaurants, the U-District attracts not just students, but all sorts of colorful, even exotic, hangers-on.

Green Lake. Green Lake is a pleasant residential neighborhood where ducks and yuppies loll and exercise. East of the lake are a number of interesting restaurants, some with a view of the water.

Central District. Southeast of downtown and the International District, this is Seattle's most ethnic neighborhood, with a largely Black, Ethiopian, and southeast Asian population.

Madrona. Further west, Madrona is where ethnic meets Lake Washington. This upscale district is often only a couple of blocks wide—on one side of the streets shops may specialize in soul food, on the other, new American cuisine.

West Seattle. Separated from the rest of the city by the wharves and cranes of Harbor Island, this headland jutting out into Puget Sound is the "original" Seattle, founded here in 1851 on Alki Point. The point is a favorite hangout of storm- and whale watchers (a pod of orcas regularly cruises past). West Seattle has some of the city's finest beaches, a lively restaurant scene along California Avenue, and a Chinese Garden (under construction). The latter is a fitting symbol of the neighborhood's rapidly increasing Asian population. A ferry runs between Fauntleroy Cove, Vashon Island, and the Kitsap Peninsula.

Vashon Island. Formerly rural, now mostly residential, Vashon Island is part of King County and is connected to Seattle by ferry from Fauntleroy Cove in West Seattle. Despite encroaching urbanization, many of the island's farms, forests, and beaches are still largely unspoiled.

TRANSPORTATION INFORMATION

Airports: Seattle is served by the **Seattle-Tacoma International Airport** (206/433–5388), known as Sea-Tac, and about 15 mi south of downtown Seattle on I–5. Major commercial airlines offer regularly scheduled domestic and international flights.

KODAK'S TIPS FOR PHOTOGRAPHING PEOPLE

Friends' Faces
- Pose subjects informally to keep the mood relaxed
- Try to work in shady areas to avoid squints
- Let kids pick their own poses

Strangers' Faces
- In crowds, work from a distance with a telephoto lens
- Try posing cooperative subjects
- Stick with gentle lighting—it's most flattering to faces

Group Portraits
- Keep the mood informal
- Use soft, diffuse lighting
- Try using a panoramic camera

People at Work
- Capture destination-specific occupations
- Use tools for props
- Avoid flash if possible

Sports
- Fill the frame with action
- Include identifying background
- Use fast shutter speeds to stop action

Silly Pictures
- Look for or create light-hearted situations
- Don't be inhibited
- Try a funny prop

Parades and Ceremonies
- Stake out a shooting spot early
- Show distinctive costumes
- Isolate crowd reactions
- Be flexible: content first, technique second

Airport Transportation. A taxi from Sea-Tac to downtown Seattle costs about $30. **Gray Line Airport Express** (206/626–6088) service to downtown hotels costs $7.50. **Shuttle Express** (425/981–7000) has 24-hour door-to-door service costing from $16 to $30, depending on the location of pickup. **Metro Transit** (206/553–3000 or 800/542–7876) city buses (Express Tunnel Bus 194 and regular Buses 174 and 184) pick up passengers outside the baggage claim areas, and cost $1.25.

Amtrak (800/872–7245) trains serve downtown's King Street Station (303 S. Jackson St., 206/382–4125).

Bus Lines: Greyhound Lines (800/231–2222) serves Seattle at 8th Avenue and Stewart Street (206/628–5508).

Intracity Transit: Metropolitan Transit (821 2nd Ave., 206/553–3000) is convenient, inexpensive, and fairly comprehensive. For questions about specific destinations, call the Automated Schedule Line (206/287–8463). Most buses run until around midnight or 1 AM; some run all night. The visitor center at the Washington State Convention and Trade Center has maps and schedules.

DRIVING AROUND TOWN

Sorry, but you'll have to be prepared for the worst. Traffic and parking in Seattle are among the worst in the nation (on the West Coast only L.A. is worse for traffic, and San Francisco worse for parking). It's so bad, the local papers write periodic stories about the mess, telling residents something they already know. Seattle has only one rush hour, which usually runs from four in the morning till ten at night, but it can go on for 24 hours if there's road construction or if accidents block the freeways. After you make it off the freeways, expect congestion on downtown streets. Traffic in Bellevue and other communities east of Lake Washington is as bad or even worse than Seattle's, but parking is a lot easier and cheaper.

Finding a parking place in Seattle can be a nightmare, especially when there's a ball game or a convention. There is lots of on-street parking, but the meters gobble quarters like they're chicken feed, and you don't want to even think about letting your meter run out, or about meter feeding. The parking enforcers are fierce and merciless and fines are high. It's a lot cheaper to park in a garage.

Parking is prohibited in all alleys—though there are no signs to tell you so—and enforcement is swift and ruthless. (It's Seattle's equivalent of the Southern speed traps). Parking along many arterials is banned during rush hour (here commonly defined until nine or ten in the morning and after two or three in the afternoon). Move your car or you'll get towed. On-street parking rates are cheaper at the margins of downtown, but enforcement is as fierce.

The good news is that there are plenty of parking garages all over Seattle; the bad news is that many of them fill up early. Grab what you can, and be prepared to walk. Park your car for the day and walk, or take the free downtown bus. Fees are very high for short-term parking, but get better if the car is parked for the whole day. They also vary widely from one garage to the next, but don't indulge in comparison shopping: the garage of your final choice may have filled up while you cruised for a bargain. In other words, grab what you can and stay put.

Attractions

BEACHES, PARKS, AND NATURAL SIGHTS

Alki Beach. A point in West Seattle jutting far out into Puget Sound, this beach is where the Denny party founded Seattle in November of 1851. But they soon realized that they needed a port to survive and moved the fledgling settlement to Seattle's present waterfront. Alki Point has remained a residential backwater ever since. | Alki Ave. S.W. and 59th Ave. SW | 206/684–4081 | www.ci.seattle.wa.us/parks | Free | Daily, dawn–11:30.

Carkeek Park. A woodsy park north of Shilshole Bay with a picnic area, playground, and trails; a footbridge leads across Seattle's ubiquitous waterfront railroad tracks to a narrow sandy beach. Even though the air and water are COLD, locals sunbathe and swim here. | 950 N.W. Carkeek Park Rd. | 206/684–0877 | fax 206/364–4685 | www.ci.seattle.wa.us/parks | Free | Daily.

Columbia Winery. The oldest winery in the state, the vineyard sits at the same latitude as France's best wine producing regions. There are complimentary wine tastings, daily cellar tours, and a gift shop in which to purchase some of the wines themselves. To reach the winery from Seattle, drive east on I–90 to north I–405. Take exit 23 east (State Route 522) to the Woodinville exit and turn right. Turn right again on 175th Street and then left on Highway 202. | 14030 N.E. 145th St., Woodinville | 425/488–2776 or 800/488–2347 | Free | Daily 10–7.

Discovery Park. This is Seattle's largest park and, like other large urban parks, it acts as an island of "wilderness," attracting a lot of animals you would not normally see in an urban setting. Here it is mostly birds, with an occasional raccoon in the woods; seals, sea lions, orcas, and gray whales now and then swim past the shoreline. The visitor center at the east entrance to the park at West Government Way and 36th Avenue (8:30–5 daily) has a map and a bird checklist (half the bird species found in the state have been seen in this park at least once). The Wolf Tree Nature Trail (½ mi) is a self-guided nature trail; other trails lead to the beach and into the woods. | 3801 W. Government Way | 206/386–4236 | www.ci.seattle.wa.us/parks | Free | Daily 8:30–5.

Freeway Park. A pleasant urban park which is mostly concrete stairs and boxes; the latter filled with shrubs and trees built above the I–5 freeway, just south of the Convention Center. | 6th and Seneca | 206/684–4075 | www.ci.seattle.wa.us/parks | Free | Daily.

Gas Works Park. The former Seattle Gas Works are now a grassy park on a broad peninsula on Lake Union's North Shore. Some of the old pipes and boilers stand out on the lawn, others have been incorporated into a picnic shelter/community hall. There is a snack bar. This is a great place for watching boats, ducks and geese, and for flying a kite. | 2101 N. Northlake Way (at Meridian N) | 206/684–4081 | www.ci.seattle.wa.us/parks | Free | Daily.

Golden Gardens. A shoreline park backed by a wooded slope in northwest Seattle. | 8498 Seaview Place NW | 206/684–4081 | www.ci.seattle.wa.us/parks | Free | Daily.

Green Lake Park. An urban lake encircled by a green park with the city's most popular walking, jogging, and biking trail. It's so popular that it has lane lines painted on its surface to separate the traffic. Ducks and geese congest the lawns. | 7201 E. Green Lake Dr. | 206/684–4074 | www.ci.seattle.wa.us/parks | Free | Daily.

Japanese Garden. This small Japanese Garden is perfect for taking a time out from normally hectic life. There's an authentic tea house, a lake with colorful koi carp and a garden lined with some truly splendid bamboos. | 1502 Lake Washington Blvd. (in Washington Park Arboretum) | 206/684–4725 | www.ci.seattle.wa.us/parks | $2.50 | Daily dawn–dusk.

Lake Union. A thoroughly urbanized lake, connected to saltwater by the Lake Washington Ship Canal and to Lake Washington by the Montlake Cut. It once served as a major moorage basin for ocean-going ships, and still has a few boatyards. But condominiums, house boats, restaurants, and yacht slips are replacing the docks (though NOAA ships and fishing boats still dock here). The lake is also a floatplane base. Seaplanes take off from here for all parts of the maritime Northwest. Despite the urban environment beavers have been known to cut down thoroughly urbanized trees, and river otters and bald eagles have been spotted by diners. Many of the restaurants have outdoor terraces (with heaters for cold days). There's public access at Gasworks Park on the north shore and at Chandler's Cove on the south shore (lawns, shoreline path). It can be seen from the George Washington Memorial Bridge. | Gas Works Park, 2101 N. Northlake Way | 206/684–4075 | www.ci.seattle.wa.us | Free | Daily.

Lake Washington Ship Canal. This canal was built to allow oceangoing ships to travel inland from Shilshole Bay to Lake Washington. En route, the canal passes through the Ballard Locks, Salmon Bay with its fishing fleet, and Lake Union. The final stretch between Lake

Union and Lake Washington is known as the Montlake Cut. The canal and the lakes are freshwater, which is a boon to ships, because the freshwater kills encrustations of barnacles, mussels, and other saltwater critters that attach themselves to the outside of hulls and slow down the ships by their bulk and weight. | Can be seen from Seaview Ave. NW or NW 54th St. | 206/684–4075 | www.ci.seattle.wa.us | Free | Daily.

Lincoln Park. A waterfront park just north of the Fauntleroy ferry terminal (to Vashon Island and Southworth). | 8603 Fauntleroy Ave. | 206/684–7494 | www.ci.seattle.wa.us/parks | Free | June–Sept., daily.

Myrtle Edwards/Elliott Bay. A waterfront park north of Pier 70 on Elliott Bay. | 3130 Alaska Way W | 206/684–4075 | www.ci.seattle.wa.us/parks | Free | Daily.

Schmitz Park. A large urban park in West Seattle, with the usual facilities. | 5551 S.W. Admiral Way | 206/684–4075 | www.ci.seattle.wa.us/parks | Free | Daily dawn–11:30 PM.

Seward Park. This forested peninsula is pretty wild for an urban park. It has some old-growth Douglas firs six feet in diameter, red-trunked madrona trees, big-leaf maple woods, nature trails, a beach, and picnic tables. On a clear day, you can get a good view of Mt. Rainier from the park's southern shore. | Lake Washington Blvd. S and S. Orcas St. | 206/684–4081 | www.ci.seattle.wa.us/parks | Free | Daily.

Volunteer Park. A hilltop park with great views of Seattle—you look down at the Space Needle, from the terrace in front of the Seattle Asian Art Museum—an old stone water tower, and a conservatory. | 1247 15th Ave. E | 206/684–4075 | www.ci.seattle.wa.us/parks | Free | June–Sept., daily.

Warren G. Magnuson Park. A waterfront park with 1 mi shoreline on Lake Washington is on 200 acres. | N.E. 65th and Sand Point Way N.E | 206/684–4075 | www.ci.seattle.wa.us/parks | Free | Daily.

★ **Washington Park Arboretum.** South of the U District and the Ship Canal at the Montlake Cut, this is a spot for relaxing. Trails lead through a marsh and through different plantings of native and exotic trees. The Graham Visitor Center has maps of the garden and other information and sells garden books and art objects. At times, special plants are for sale. You might want to take a look at the tall palms growing at the southern end of the parking lot, outside the greenhouse. | 2300 Arboretum Dr. E (visitor center) | 206/543–8800 | www.ci.seattle.wa.us/parks | Free | Daily 7 AM–dusk.

CULTURE, EDUCATION, AND HISTORY

Benaroya Hall. Seattle's new concert hall, across 2nd Avenue from the art museum. | 200 University St. | 206/215–4747 | www.seattlesymphony.org | Tues.–Sun., call for performance times.

Lake View Cemetery. This hillside cemetery has the graves of Seattle's pioneers like the Dennys and Doc Maynard, as well as those of actor Bruce Lee and his son, Brandon. | 1554 15th Ave. E | 206/322–1582 | fax 206/322–0523 | Free | Daily.

Seattle University. A hilltop university between downtown and the Central District. | 900 Broadway | 206/296–6000 | fax 206/296–5656 | www.seattleu.edu | Free | Weekdays 8–4:30.

University of Washington. The University occupies a prominent site above the Montlake Cut and Lake Union's Portage Bay. With almost 35,000 enrolled students, the campus has over 120 buildings including a stadium. The main entrance is at 17th Ave. NE and N.E. 45th St. | Visitor Information Center, 4014 University Way NE | 206/543–9198 | fax 206/543–0786 | www.washington.edu | Free | Daily.

MUSEUMS

Burke Museum. The exhibits at this museum on the University of Washington campus explore the cultural and natural history of Washington State from the dinosaur era to today. | 17th Ave. NE and N.E. 45th | 206/543–5590 | www.washington.edu/burkemuseum | $5.50 (suggested) | Fri.–Wed. 10–5, Thurs. 10–8.

Center for Wooden Boats. Awaiting you here are many historic vessels, such as the 1897 schooner *Wawona.* You can watch the staff restore old ships, rent boats for sailing on Lake Union, or take a picnic next to the water. | 1010 Valley St. | 206/382–2628 | Free | Memorial Day–Labor Day, daily 11–6; Labor Day–Memorial Day, Wed.–Mon. 11–5.

Charles and Emma Frye Art Museum. A museum of traditional, occasionally kitschy art. | 704 Terry Ave. | 206/622–9250 | fax 206/223–1707 | www.fryeart.org | Free | Tues.–Sat. 10–5, Thurs. 10–9, Sun. 12–5.

Children's Museum. Climbing and camping in the Northwest is introduced to kids in a mountain wilderness area. There are also a giant maze of pipes and slides, arts and crafts games, special exhibits, and workshops. | 305 Harrison St. | 206/441–1768 | www.thechildrensmuseum.org | $5 | Weekdays 10–5, weekends 10–6.

Experience Music Project. Built in the shape of a gigantic guitar, this museum (opened in 2000) houses a large assortment of rock 'n' roll paraphernalia, including the world's largest collection of Jimi Hendrix artifacts. There is an interactive sound lab in which you can experiment with instruments and recording equipment. | 5th Ave. and Broad St. | 206/770–2700 | www.experience.org | $19.95 | Daily 9–11.

Henry Art Gallery. The Henry offers a compelling mix of international contemporary work of importance and a fresh examination of regional art from the first half of the 20th century. It is housed on the University of Washington campus. | 15th Ave NE and N.E. 41st | 206/543–2280 | fax 206/685–3123 | www.henryart.org | $5 | Tues.–Sun. 11–5, Thurs. 11–8.

Klondike Gold Rush National Historical Park-Seattle Unit. This hole-in-the wall museum in Seattle's Pioneer Square district, with some Klondike artifacts and historic information, is actually only the southernmost outpost of the southeastern Alaskan park. | 117 S. Main St. | 206/553–7220 | fax 206/553–0614 | www.nps.gov | Free | Daily 9–5.

★ **Museum of Flight.** This is one of the best aviation museums in the world. It has Bill Boeing's red barn, where the Seattle pioneer built his first airplane in 1916, which now houses an exhibit on the history of human flight. Other high-flying attractions include World War I planes, modern jets, and a lot of flying objects in between. Best of all, you can clamber around in many of them, including JFK's Air Force 1. | 9404 E. Marginal Way S | 206/764–5720 | fax 206/764–5707 | www.museumofflight.org | $8 | Fri.–Wed. 10–5, Thurs. 10–9.

Museum of History and Industry. Permanent and rotating exhibits on Seattle's history are inside. Outside the 1-mi loop Waterfront Trail runs from the east side of the museum through marshes (on a boardwalk) to the Washington Park Arboretum and back. This is a good place to see waterbirds, shorebirds, and songbirds. Despite the roar of the freeway overhead, where it crosses the marsh on stilts, this can be a relaxing place. | 2700 24th Ave. E | 206/324–1125 | www.seattlehistory.org | $5.50 | Daily 10–5.

Nordic Heritage Museum. A small museum highlighting the Scandinavian heritage of the Pacific northwest. | 3014 N.W. 67th St. | 206/789–5707 | www.artguidenw.com/Nordic | $4 | Tues.–Sat. 10–4, Sun. 12–4.

Seattle Art Museum. The collections of the Seattle Art Museum number approximately 23,000 objects, representing a wide range of art from ancient Egyptian reliefs to contemporary American installations using photography and video. The collections are particularly strong in five areas: Asian, African, Northwest Coast Native American, modern art and European painting, and decorative arts. Their range and depth are unmatched in the region. | 100 University St. | 206/654–3100 | www.seattleartmuseum.org | $7 (suggested) | Fri.–Sun. and Tues.–Wed. 10–5, Thurs. 10–9.

Seattle Asian Art Museum. This museum housed in the old Art Deco Seattle Art Museum building, has one of the country's best collections of Japanese art, including the famed Crow Screen. | 1400 E. Prospect St., Volunteer Park | 206/654–3100 | www.seattleartmuseum.org | $7 (suggested) | Fri.–Sun. and Tues.–Wed. 10–5, Thurs. 10–9.

Seattle Center. You can see the remnants of the 1962 World's Fair and a lot more on this 74-acre landmark, where there is always something going on (*see* below). The Seattle Opera, Pacific Northwest Ballet, Intiman Theater, and Seattle Repertory Theatre are based here, as well. | 305 Harrison St. | 206/684–7200 or 206/684–8582 (recording) | fax 206/684–7342 | www.seattlecenter.com | Free | Daily dawn–dusk.

Center House. A cavernous hall with a food court. | 305 Harrison St. | 206/684–7200 or 206/684–8582 (recording) | fax 206/684–7342 | www.seattlecenter.com | Free | Weekdays 10–8, weekends 10–11.

Fun Forest Amusement Park. The old midway from the world's fair. | 305 Harrison St. | 206/728–1585 | fax 206/684–7342 | www.funforest.com | June–Labor Day, daily; early Sept.–Nov., Mar.–June, Fri.–Sun.

International Fountain. A musical fountain that is dry more often than not. Many outdoor civic events are held here. | 305 Harrison St. | 206/684–7200 | fax 206/684–7342 | www.seattlecenter.com | Free | Daily.

Monorail. A survivor from the world's fair, and a Seattle favorite, this elevated train runs between Seattle Center and the Westlake mall downtown at Fifth and Pine. The city has been trying to tear it down for years, but the people like it so much, they passed a referendum in 1998 to extend it to Sea-Tac Airport. The city says it doesn't have the money; the voters are getting ready to pass another referendum. | 305 Harrison St. | 206/441–6038 | www.seattlemonorail.com | $1.25 | Daily.

Pacific Science Center. A science museum with 200 hands-on exhibits that are very popular with children. | 200 2nd Ave. N | 206/443–2001 or 206/443–2880 | fax 206/443–3631 | www.pacsci.org | $7.50 | Weekdays 10–5, weekends 10–6.

★ **Space Needle.** A 520-ft-tall tower that looks like a cocktail fork carrying a skewered oyster was built for the 1962 world's fair. It has a view deck and a revolving restaurant on top. | 305 Harrison St. | 206/443–2100 or 800/937–9582 | fax 206/684–7342 | www.spaceneedle.com | $8 | Sun.–Thurs. 9 AM–11 PM; Fri. and Sat. 9 AM–midnight.

Wing Luke Asian Museum. The well-organized exhibits of this small museum focus on the history and culture of Asian people who have settled in America. Costumes, fabrics, crafts, basketry, and photographs are some of the items that can be seen here. | 407 7th Ave. S | 206/623–5124 | $2.50 | Tues.–Fri. 11–4:30, weekends noon–4.

SHOPPING

Fremont Center. This strip of shops and cafés along Fremont Avenue, between the Ship Canal to N. 36th Street, is also home to a statue of Lenin and the Fremont Troll. | Fremont Ave.

International District. In Seattle's Chinatown, Vietnamese and Southeast Asian shops and restaurants augment the Chinese emporiums. Uwajimaya, a Japanese/Pan-Asian supermarket/department store, is one of the best of its kind in the country (even Japanese visitors shop here). | 4th Ave. to I–5 and Yesler to S. Dearborn Sts. | 206/389–7200 | www.ci.seattle.wa.us/html/visitor | Free | Daily.

★ **Pike Place Market.** One of the great public markets in the country, this bluff-top collection of shops and restaurants still has a few tables where local farmers sell their (often organic) produce. Most farmers come on set days; weekends are especially good but very crowded. The Hillclimb steps connect the market to the waterfront and the Seattle Aquarium. It is lined with shops and restaurants. | First Ave. and Pike St. | 206/682–7453 | www.ci.seattle.wa.us/html/visitor | Free | Daily.

Pike-Pine Corridor. The numerous restaurants, clubs, thrift shops, music stores, and galleries that line Pike and Pine Streets make this a lively, youthful area. | Pike and Pine Sts. between 6th Ave. and Broadway.

Westlake Center. A terminus for the Seattle Center Monorail, this three-story mall houses such shops as Made in Washington, which sells products manufactured in the state. | 1601 5th Ave. | 206/467–1600 | Free | Mon.–Sat. 9:30–8, Sun. 11–6.

SPORTS AND RECREATION

American League Baseball (Seattle Mariners). This team has been playing in brand new Safeco Field since July 1999. | Safeco Field, 1250 First Ave. S | 206/346–4000 | fax 206/346–4100 | www.mariners.org | Apr.–Oct., call for schedule.

NBA (Seattle Supersonics). The home games of this basketball team are very popular and cause traffic jams all over downtown. | Key Arena, at Seattle Center, 1st Ave. N between Thomas and Republican | 206/283–3865 | fax 206/281–5839 | www.supersonics.com | Oct.–Apr., call for schedule.

NFL (Seattle Seahawks). This football team finished the 1999 season at its home field in the Kingdome, but has temporarily moved to Husky Stadium at the University of Washington, while a new stadium is being built on the old site. The new stadium (201 S. King St.) is scheduled to open in 2002. | Husky Stadium 3800 Montlake | 888/635–4295 | www.seahawks.com | Sept.–Jan., call for schedule.

WA

SEATTLE

INTRO
ATTRACTIONS
DINING
LODGING

SIGHTSEEING TOURS/TOUR COMPANIES

Gray Line Bus Tours. Has sightseeing tours of Seattle, and one-day and longer tours from Seattle to Mt. Rainier and Olympic National Parks, Mt. St. Helens, the North Cascades, and the Washington Wine Country (Yakima Valley). | 4500 Marginal Way SW | 206/624–5077 or 800/426–7505 | fax 206/626–5209 | www.graylineofseattle.com | Call for prices and schedules.

Underground Tour. When Seattle was rebuilt after the big 1889 fire, the city fathers wisely decided to raise the level of the old downtown, since it was so close to tidewater that sewers flowed backward during spring tides. But the old storefronts were not torn down, new ones were simply added at the new street level. This left a ghostly underground city of abandoned shop fronts intact. The underground tour takes you to the surviving parts of that "lost city." | 608 1st Ave. | 206/682–4646 or 888/608–6337 | www.undergroundtour.com | $8 | Daily 11–4.

OTHER POINTS OF INTEREST

Boeing Field—King County Int'l Airport. A general aviation airport with charter flights and very few scheduled flights. | 7233 Perimeter Rd. | 206/296–7380 | fax 206/296–0190 | www.metrokc.gov/airport | Call for prices | Daily.

Evergreen Floating Bridge. This is one of two floating bridges connecting Seattle to the eastern shores of Lake Union. It carries Rte. 520 to Bellevue. The other, to the south, carries I–90, a multiple-lane freeway, to Mercer Island where it enters a tunnel and emerges at a regular bridge on the east side. Both bridges are becoming inadequate for carrying all the traffic, and the daily gridlock is getting longer and tempers are getting shorter. There has been talk of bringing back ferries, to relieve the strain. During storms, drivers crossing the bridges have been known to get seasick! | Rte. 520, near Montlake Pl | 206/386–1234 | www.ci.seattle.wa.us | Free | Daily.

Argosy Harbor Cruise. Harbor Cruises take you to the working harbor on Terminal Island and through the Lake Washington Ship Canal and Chittenden Locks to Lake Union. Other boats run between Lake Union and the Kirkland waterfront on Lake Washington. | Pier 55 at the bottom of Seneca St. | 206/623–1445 | fax 206/623–5474 | www.argosycruises.com | $13.50–$25.75 | Daily 8–5.

Ferry Trips. Washington State car ferries leave from Colman Dock, Pier 52, for Bainbridge Island and Bremerton (on the Kitsap Peninsula). Passenger-only ferries leave from Pier 50, to the south for Bremerton, and for Vashon Island. Car ferries also leave from Fauntleroy Cove in West Seattle for Vashon Island and for Southworth on the Kitsap Peninsula. | Seattle Ferry Terminal, Colman Dock at the foot of Madison St. | 206/464-6400 or 800/843-3779 | www.wsdot.wa.gov/ferries | $6.50–$24.75 | Daily 5–2 AM.

Lake Washington Floating Bridge. When it was built in 1939, this bridge, officially known as the Lacey V. Murrow Floating Bridge after the engineer who designed it, was the first of its kind in the world. It sank during a severe storm in 1990, and has since been replaced by a new multilane floating bridge that carries I–90 across Lake Union. | I–90 leads right into the bridge | 360/705–7075 | Free | Daily.

Odyssey: The Maritime Discovery Center. Further north along the waterfront at Pier 66, the discovery center has exhibits on Puget Sound, its fisheries, and its maritime trade. There's also a transient boat moorage, a conference center, a fish processor and market, and a restaurant. | Pier 66, 2205 Alaskan Way | 206/374–4000 | fax 206/374–4002 | www.ody.org | $6.50 | Daily 10–5.

The Seattle Aquarium. A waterfront aquarium which exhibits Northwest marine life. The domed walk-through aquarium is spectacular. Puget Sound habitats have been recreated and you can watch seals and sea otters dive and play in their pools. | 1483 Alaskan Way | 206/386–4300 (recording) | fax 206/386–4328 | www.seattleaquarium.org | $8.25 | Day after Labor Day–Memorial Day, 10–5; Memorial Day–Labor Day, 10–7.

Shilshole Bay Marina. This marina is on Puget Sound north of the Ship Canal. The shore to the south has several excellent waterfront restaurants. | 7001 Seaview Ave. NW | 206/728–3385 | Free | Office open weekdays 8–4:30, Sat. 8–1.

Smith Cove. A cove on the southern end of the Magnolia Bluffs, with a small marina, beach, and a restaurant. Most of the cove is taken up by grain and automobile shipping docks (this is where Japanese cars arrive). | Can be seen from Elliott Ave. and W. Garfield St. | 206/386–1234 | www.ci.seattle.wa.us | Free | Daily.

Tillicum Village. A ferry takes visitors to a reconstructed longhouse for dances and a salmon barbecue at Blake Island State Park. | Pier 56, foot of Seneca St. | 206/443–1244 or 800/426–1205 | fax 206/443–4723 | www.tillicumvillage.com | $55.25 | May–mid-Oct., daily; mid-Oct.–Apr., Sat., call for hours.

Waterfront Drive. To see Seattle's varied waterfront follow Alaskan Way south along Elliott Bay or walk north along the downtown waterfront from Colman Dock, where the ferries land, past the docks where the harbor tours start and over to Waterfront Park, the Seattle Aquarium, and old piers now converted to shops and restaurants | At the waterfront | 206/386–1234 | www.ci.seattle.wa.us | Free | Daily.

★ **Woodland Park Zoological Gardens.** A great zoo in a wooded park where animals are displayed in as natural a setting as possible (occasionally monkeys and other climbing critters get loose and prove hard to see in the foliage and difficult to catch in the tall trees). The tropical rain forest exhibit is spectacular. | 5500 Phinney Ave. N | 206/684–4800 (recording) | fax 206/615–1070 | www.zoo.org | $9 | Daily 9:30–6.

ON THE CALENDAR

FEB.: ***Northwest Flower and Garden Show.*** A truly spectacular event held downtown at the Convention Center; one of the largest such shows in North America, and a perfect respite from gray-weather winter blues. | 206/789–5333.

APR.: ***Japanese Cherry Blossom Festival.*** A Japanese cultural event centering around the viewing of the cherry blossoms which are truly spectacular in Seattle at this time of the year, plus Japanese dances and foods. | 206/684–7200.

MAY: ***Maritime Festival.*** Tugboat races and other waterfront events. | 206/461–5800.

MAY: ***University District Street Fair.*** Seattle's biggest and most popular street fair attracts visitors from all over Washington. There are more than 500 crafts booths, two ethnic food gardens, and live music and entertainment. | 206/632–9084.

MAY: ***Northwest Folklife Festival.*** The biggest and most exciting as well as most popular ethnic festival in the Pacific Northwest is held on Memorial Day weekend. Food and crafts booths, entertainment, music—the works. | 206/684–7200.

SEPT.: ***Bumbershoot.*** The Pacific Northwest's biggest arts festival is at Seattle Center on Labor Day weekend. | 206/684–7788.

WALKING TOUR

Pike Place Market, the Waterfront, Pioneer Square, Chinatown, and Downtown with a side trip to Seattle Center and Lake Union. Park your car in either the Bon Marché garage at 3rd and Stewart or in the Pike Place Market garage off Western (south of Virginia). Start your walk at the **Pike Place Market.** Get there early (by 9 AM), while the farmers and vendors set up; it's the most interesting time, and the crowds will not yet have arrived. After your market tour, take the Hillclimb steps down to the waterfront and **Seattle Aquarium.** Spend some time in the aquarium; it displays a fascinating slice of Puget Sound submarine life. From the aquarium, head south along the waterfront to Yesler Way and **Pioneer Square.** Here you'll find plenty of old buildings, plus art galleries, stores, a great bakery (Grand Central), and book shops.

Double back up 1st Avenue to the **Seattle Art Museum** (First and University) and have lunch in the café, or walk the few blocks up Jackson to the **International District** (also known as "Chinatown") and enjoy a meal of dim sum. Be sure to visit Uwajimaya, a Japanese supermarket/department store with a truly amazing selection of goods from fresh fruits, vegetables, and seafood, to porcelain elephants. After lunch, walk back along Fourth and Fifth to the downtown shopping district. Most of the exciting shops are within a few blocks of Westlake Mall. From Westlake Mall, you can take the monorail to **Seattle Center.** After exploring the Center and the new EMP monument to rock and roll (for the most up-to-date info, go to www.emplive.com), you can walk east to Lake Union to dine at a lakefront restaurant. You will not find the best food in town here, but the views and the atmosphere are great. Westlake will take you back south to Stewart and the parking garages.)

Capitol Hill. Take Denny Way uphill to Broadway and look for free parking on one of the side streets. **Broadway** is one of the livelier young-people hangouts in Seattle with great espresso, Thai food, shops, and boutiques. Look for the dance steps let into the sidewalk pavement. Capitol Hill northeast of Broadway has old mansions with large, beautiful gardens lining narrow streets shaded by large trees. Wander through this neighborhood to **Volunteer Park,** which has great views from the top of an old water tower, a Victorian conservatory, and Seattle's Asian Art Museum with its superb collections of Chinese and Japanese paintings, sculptures, and porcelain.

Dining

INEXPENSIVE

Assimba Ethiopian Cuisine. Ethiopian. Small, very casual, homey restaurant founded by Ethiopian immigrants to serve the local immigrant community, which makes the food extremely authentic. The dishes are vegetarian and can be very spicy. You eat by picking up morsels and soaking up the sauces with pieces of tortilla-like flat bread made with teff, an Ethiopian grain. | 2722 E. Cherry St., | 206/322–1019 | $6–$10 | No credit cards.

Athenian Inn. American. This casual Pike Place Market restaurant overlooks Elliott Bay and the Olympic Mountains. One of Seattle's longest established restaurant and featured in *Sleepless in Seattle*. Breakfast is served all day and the seafood is fresh. Known for omelets, hash browns, and clam chowder. | 1517 Pike Place Market (look for the sign in the main arcade), | 206/624–7166 | Closed Sun. and major holidays | $10–$22 | AE, DC, MC, V.

Bakeman's Restaurant. Delicatessen. This bright and untouristy lunch place near Pioneer Square serves its trademark turkey and meatloaf sandwiches to a steady stream of local business people. The homemade soups and salads are also very popular. Be prepared to order your soup or sandwich by the time you get to the counter. | 122 Cherry St. | 206/622–3375 | Reservations not accepted | No dinner | $1.50–$4 | No credit cards.

B&O Espresso. Café. Capitol Hill hipsters and solitary types frequent this local favorite that serves its own European pastries like chocolate raspberry torte and espresso mousse torte. On the weekends, brunch is served in the morning, while appetizers are available each evening. | 204 Belmont Ave. E | 206/322–5028 | No lunch | $4–$6 | MC, V.

Burrito Loco. Mexican. Bright Mexican restaurant serving homemade burritos and chile. Try the mole or the pipian chicken. Also serves seafood dishes. There is limited open-air dining in front of the restaurant. Kids' menu. No smoking. | 9211 Holman Rd. NW | 206/783–0719 | $5–$11 | AE, D, MC, V.

Carmelita. Vegetarian. An old-style vegetarian restaurant set in a cavernous dining room. Many of the dishes are Mediterranean-inspired, and the menu changes seasonally. Popular favorites include the portabello mushroom roulade and the antipasto platter. Vegan options are also available. Open-air dining. Kids' menu. No smoking. | 7314 Greenwood Ave. N | 206/706–7703 | Closed Mon. No lunch | $10–$15 | MC, V.

Chef Wang. Chinese. The aim here is a balance between Belltown trendiness and the more familiar style of American-Chinese restaurants, with clean lines, bold colors, and dim lighting. Quality ingredients and extra care produce better-than-average versions of familiar menu dishes, such as Peking duck and mu shu pork. You can also create your own combination from the numerous meats, vegetables, and sauces. | 2230 1st Ave. | 206/448–5407 | $6.25–$17 | MC, V.

Chutneys. Indian. A plain restaurant where the spice is in the food, not the decor. Specialties include the curried mussels, shrimp pasta, and the rack of lamb. | 519 First Ave. N | 206/284–6799 | No lunch Sun. | $9–$14 | AE, D, DC, MC, V.

Dragonfish. Pan-Asian. Pachinko machines and colorful origami and rattan fans brighten this cheerful place. There are seafood and noodle specialties, but the local favorites are the small plates from the grill, such as the Korean *bulgogi* (skirt steak marinated in a tangy sauce of soy, mirin, and ginger) or the chicken wings in a caramel-ginger sauce. Top them off with a lime leaf and lemongrass "limontini." | 722 Pine St. | 206/467–7777 | $7–$16 | AE, D, DC, MC, V.

Doong Kong Lau. Chinese. A simple dining room enlivened with tanks full of fish that are not merely decorative, but serve to keep dinner alive (and thus fresh) until you place your order. | 9710 Aurora Ave. N | 206/526–8828 | $8–$10 | AE, D, DC, MC, V.

Elysian Brewing Company. American/Casual. The large, open dining room is part of the brewery—formerly it was a furniture warehouse. The menu includes a range of sandwiches and pastas, as well as daily specials such as grilled salmon. There are at least 14 beers on tap here. | 1221 E. Pike St. | 206/860–1920 | $5–$10 | AE, MC, V.

Emmett Watson's Oyster Bar. Seafood. This small, hole-in-the-wall restaurant is tucked away in an impossible corner, with a secluded courtyard next door, where you can dine on sunny days. The food preparations are old-time Seattle: simple, honest, and straightforward. The oysters are always fresh (and you pay a lot less for them than you do at nearby establishments). Try the clam chowder, salmon soup, or the fish-and-chips, which are some of the best in town. | 1916 Pike Pl. | 206/448–7721 | $6–$10 | No credit cards.

Five Spot. Eclectic. Up the hill from Seattle Center, the unpretentious Five Spot changes its regional American menu—Texas, Miami, San Francisco, for example—every four months or so. Sunday brunch is popular here. The related Jitterbug in Wallingford and the Coastal Kitchen in Capitol Hill have the same rotating menu policy but with an international accent. | 1502 Queen Anne Ave. N; Jitterbug: 2114 N. 45th St.; Coastal Kitchen: 429 15th Ave. E | 206/285–7768 (Five Spot); 206/547–6313 (Jitterbug); 206/322–1145 (Coastal Kitchen) | $9.75–$17.75 | MC, V.

Gravity Bar. Vegetarian. The juices at this juice bar—from any number of fruits and vegetables, alone or in combination—sometimes overshadow the sprouty sandwiches and other healthful items on the menu such as roll-ups and vegetable and rice dishes. | 415 Broadway E | 206/325–7186 | Breakfast also available | $5–$9 | MC, V.

Las Margaritas. Mexican. One of a small local chain of bright, friendly Mexican restaurants specializing in well-prepared dishes of the more or less standard repertoire of what might be called "Mexican comfort food." (The other restaurants are in Kent, Kirkland, Woodinville, Marysville, Redmond, and Bellevue.) Known for regional cuisine like carnitas and fajitas. Kids' menu. | 1122 Post Ave. | 206/623–7203 | $9–$13 | AE, D, DC, MC, V.

McCormick's Fish House. Seafood. A clubby restaurant that seems better suited to the 1920s or '30s. Serves Northwest cuisine, and offers the largest selection of oysters in town. There is open-air dining in front of restaurant. Raw bar. | 722 Fourth Ave. | 206/682–3900 | No lunch weekends | $10–$20 | AE, D, DC, MC, V.

Noodle Ranch. Pan-Asian. This is the place for what Noodle Ranch calls "Pan-Asian vittles." The only thing fancy here is chef Nga Bui's inexpensive menu items like *cha ca*, marinated catfish grilled and served room temperature over vermicelli rice noodles with cilantro, herbs, and peanuts. Japanese eggplant in ginger and the hot and sour coconut soup are also popular. | 2228 2nd Ave. | 206/728–0463 | Closed Sun. | $6–$13 | AE, MC, V.

Portage Bay Cafe. American. This casual, contemporary café is a favorite hang-out with the University crowd. Try the pot roast, pork chops, duck, and crab cakes. Open-air dining on patio. Kids' menu. Weekend brunch. No smoking. | 4130 Roosevelt Ave. NE | 206/547–8230 | Breakfast also available | $10–$15 | AE, D, MC, V.

Pyramid Alehouse. American/Casual. Across from Safeco fields and the waterfront, this rather mainstream brewery serves from a pub menu, which includes pizzas, burgers, sandwiches, and salads, not to mention the daily specials such as island prawn salad. | 1201 1st Ave. | 206/682–3377 | $8–$15 | AE, DC, MC, V.

★ **Saigon Gourmet.** Vietnamese. This small café in the International District is plain and parking nearby can be difficult, but the food is inexpensive and delicious. Go for the Cambodian soup, the shrimp rolls, and the unusual papaya with beef jerky. | 502 S. King St. | 206/624–2611 | Reservations not accepted | Closed Sun. | $4.50–$7.25 | MC, V.

Septieme. American/Casual. In the cozy dining room the staff serves everything from oatmeal to prime rib. The bar is also worth visiting, as its walls are lined completely with mirrors, giving it the character of a fun-house. Behind the restaurant is an open patio on which you can sip cocktails beneath the flicker of tiki torches. | 214 Broadway E | 206/860–8858 | Breakfast also available | $11–$18 | AE, D, DC, MC, V.

Siam. Thai. Thai food is almost mainstream in Seattle. Start with a satay skewer or *tom kah gai* (a soup of coconut, lemongrass, chicken, and mushrooms). You determine for yourself how hot you want entrées such as curries, noodle dishes, and the many prawn, chicken, and fish variations that fill the menu. The original Capitol Hill restaurant on Broadway is lively, the Fairview Avenue location more relaxed. | 616 Broadway or 1880 Fairview Ave. E | 206/324–0892 (Broadway); 206/323–8101 | No lunch weekends | $8–$12 | AE, MC, V.

Sit and Spin. American/Casual. This café and restaurant is connected to a laundromat, so you can do your laundry while you eat. In the bright and cheerful dining room the staff serves a menu concentrating in Italian dishes such as pastas and pizzas, though there is a range of other options including burritos and garden burgers. There is live entertainment on Thursday, Friday, and Saturday night. | 2219 4th Ave. | 206/441–9484 | $2.50–$7.50 | D, MC, V.

Stars. Contemporary. Twenty-five-foot ceilings, towering windows, and an enormous center fireplace create a fun and dramatic dining room, unlike any other. Seasonal dishes emphasizing simple flavors dominate the menu; the grilled ahi tuna served with summer beans, roasted tomatoes, and mizuna is a scrumptious example. Other wood-oven dishes include upscale pizzas, portabello mushroom sandwiches, and roasted shrimp entrées. | 600 Pine St. | 206/264–1112 | $7.50–$19 | AE, DC, MC, V.

Trolleyman Pub. American/Casual. Associated with the Red Hook Brewery in Woodinville, this brew pub has at least six different Red Hook brews on tap. The menu's options include soups, salads, burritos, and sandwiches. A Red Hook retail shop inside the pub sells shirts, hats, and assorted paraphernalia. | 3400 Phinney Ave. N | 206/443–3241 | No lunch Mon. and Tues. | $4–$6 | AE, MC, V.

Wild Ginger. Pan-Asian. A truly delightful, elegant, clubby restaurant serving southeast Asian food. Dark wood panelling and high-backed booths help to create an intimate atmosphere, but there's also a popular bar, and an even more popular satay bar where the dishes are prepared right before your eyes and reach you piping hot from the grill. The flavors are sophisticated and just about all the dishes are marvelously savory. Known for fresh seafood and curry. At the Southwestern edge of the Pike Place Market. | 1400 Western Ave. | 206/623–4450 | $15–$25 | AE, D, DC, MC, V.

MODERATE

Anthony's Pier 66 and Bell Street Diner. American/Casual. There are wonderful views of Elliott Bay from both the upstairs restaurant, Anthony's, and the downstairs diner. The menu at Anthony's is upscale, containing such items as applewood grilled ahi tuna with ginger—a particular favorite among local patrons; the diner serves a more traditional range of American classics. The diner is open for lunch and dinner, while the restaurant is open only for dinner. Both places have decks with magnificent views. | 2201 Alaskan Way | 206/448–6688 | $8–$27 (Bell Street Diner); $18–$30 (Anthony's Pier 66) | AE, MC, V.

Assaggio Ristorante. Italian. Bustling downtown restaurant overflowing with Italian high-spirits specializing in Northern Italian fare and seafood. Try one of the fresh daily specials, or the popular pollo mattone. Open-air dining on patio. No smoking. | 2010 Fourth Ave. | 206/441–1399 | Closed Sun. No lunch Sat. | $15–$25 | AE, D, DC, MC, V.

Axis. Contemporary. The food is also the entertainment here where almost every table has a view of the kitchen and its wood-fire grill. The menu merits the show, with such appetizers as crispy eggplant wonton and a Northwest grown rotisserie chicken with grilled mushroom polenta. | 2214 1st Ave. | 206/441–9600 | No lunch | $12–$27 | AE, DC, MC, V.

Bandoleone. Latin. This small almost austere restaurant is an outpost of peppy Spanish culture in Seattle's cool Scandinavian clime. The dishes are all made from scratch, which may cause some delays. The food is worth waiting for, with such dishes as grilled lamb chops served with a fermented black bean-rice cake, pan-seared duck breast in a rice paper basket, hickory smoked guajillo pork tenderloin, and an assortment of tapas. There is a lively back porch for open-air dining. Latino music Sun. from 7–9. Kids' menu. Sun. brunch in summer. | 2241 Eastlake Ave. E | 206/329–7559 | No lunch | $15–$30 | MC, V.

Brooklyn Seafood, Steak, and Oyster House. Contemporary. A darkish, wood-paneled, restaurant in a modern high-rise that has kept the facade of an old business building as accent. Across the street from Benaroya Hall and the Seattle Art Museum. Open-air dining on patio. | 1212 Second Ave. | 206/224–7000 | No lunch weekends | $17–$36 | AE, D, DC, MC, V.

Cactus. Mexican. A congenial restaurant in the Madison Park neighborhood that mixes excellent Spanish, Navajo, Mexican and New Mexican food with the ambience of an upscale southwestern cantina. Open-air dining. Kids' menu. | 4220 E. Madison | 206/324–4140 | No lunch Sun. | $15–$25 | D, MC, V.

Café Campagne. French. A light-hearted bistro-style café that doesn't take itself too seriously next door to its more formal parent, Campagne. Sun. brunch. | 1600 Post Alley | 206/728–2233 | Breakfast also available | $9–$18 | AE, DC, MC, V.

Café Flora. Vegetarian. Seattle's first upscale vegetarian restaurant, has shown local diners that vegetarian fare can be elegant. Serving an international menu that includes a variety of pizzas, as well as great desserts. Vegan options also available. Kids' menu. Sat. and Sun. brunch. Beer and wine only. No smoking. | 2901 E. Madison | 206/325-9100 | Closed Mon. | $15–$25 | MC, V.

Café Lago. Italian. A fun, low-key family-run trattoria that dishes out very tasty food including a variety of pastas made fresh every morning. Try the homemade lasagna or the wood-fire oven pizzas. This one is off the beaten path south of the Montlake Cut. No smoking. | 2305 24th Ave. E | 206/329-8005 | No lunch | $13–$22 | D, DC, MC, V.

Chinook's. Seafood. A big, rather sterile family seafood house with large windows overlooking fishing boats moored in Salmon Bay, one of the home ports of the Alaska salmon fleet. It is popular for its king salmon. Open-air dining on the patio with particularly pretty views. Kids' menu. | 1900 W. Nickerson | 206/283-4665 | Breakfast also available weekends | $11–$26 | AE, MC, V.

Cucina! Cucina! Italian. A fun restaurant that appeals to large families as well as to singles, perhaps because the atmosphere is relaxed, the food is tasty and the portions are big. Big and boisterous and post-modernist, the dining room overlooks Lake Union. If you dine on the deck outside, you might be buzzed by a floatplane about to land, or see a bald eagle cruise by. Typical Italian fare is on the menu: pizzas, pastas, calzones, and salads. Specials change monthly. Open-air dining on patio. Kids' menu. | 901 Fairview Ave. N | 206/447-2782 | Reservations not accepted (for supper) | $15–$25 | AE, D, DC, MC, V.

Dulces Latin Bistro. Continental. The warm glow of the cinnamon colored walls of this low-ceilinged Madrona bistro provide a warming touch for cold Seattle nights. The food, too, has a warming Latin touch, but there's more to it than that. The dishes run the gamut of North American and European cuisines, from clam chowder to roast lamb, from chiles rellenos to pasta. There's a cigar room so completely separate, its fumes won't annoy you. | 1430 34th Ave. | 206/322-5453 | Closed Mon. No lunch | $15–$25 | AE, D, MC, V.

El Camino. Mexican. The loud and funky personality of this Fremont storefront reflects the irreverent Northwest treatment of its Mexican cuisine. Rock-shrimp quesadillas, fresh fish tacos, and mole chicken enchiladas with braised greens are typical menu items, as is a salad of crispy romaine with toasted pumpkin seeds and a cool dressing of garlic, cilantro, and lime juice. A tart margarita, served in a pint glass, outside on the deck is a real treat. | 607 N. 35th St. | 206/632-7303 | No lunch | $12–$17 | AE, DC, MC, V.

El Greco. Greek. There's lots of entertainment and shopping on the stretch of Broadway through Capitol Hill, but few good dining choices, so El Greco stands out. Go for the fresh, unadorned Mediterranean dishes, the Moroccan vegetable stew, and the grilled lamb with rosemary. It's a good bet for Sunday brunch, too. | 219 Broadway E | 206/328-4604 | Closed Mon., no dinner Sun. | $11–$16 | AE, MC, V.

Elliott's Oyster House. Seafood. This bright dining room on a former shipping pier serves some of the best, fresh and seasonal seafood in Seattle. Not only are the oysters great, but so is the salmon, the halibut, the rockfish, and the cod. Harbor tour boats are moored on the next dock, and there's a view of Elliott Bay. Known for Pacific salmon, fresh Dungeness crab, and fresh oysters. Open-air dining on a patio overlooking the ocean. Kids' menu. | 1203 Alaskan Way | 206/623-4340 | $15–$35 | AE, D, DC, MC, V.

Etta's Seafood. Contemporary. This bright, sleek restaurant at the north end of the Pike Place Market serves seafood and other local fare to a mostly young and upscale crowd. There's a view of Victor Steinbrueck Park across the street, and a sliver of Elliott Bay, but the real view is of the people milling about outside, on their way to and from the market. Serving Northwest seafood specialties, including salmon and crabcakes. Kids' menu. No smoking. | 2020 Western Ave. | 206/443-6000 | Breakfast also available on weekends | $10–$26 | AE, D, DC, MC, V.

Fare Start. Eclectic. Fare Start is a job-training program for the homeless men and women here who prepare the simple lunch buffet during the week. On Thursday nights, a guest chef from a restaurant like Ray's Boathouse or the Metropolitan Grill takes over to prepare a special menu. It's a great meal, a great cause, and a great sample of Seattle's community spirit. | 1902 2nd Ave. | 206/443–1233 | Reservations essential for Thurs. dinner | No lunch on weekends, no dinner Fri.–Wed. | $14.50 | D, MC, V.

Four Seas. Chinese. This is one of the more elegant Chinese restaurants in town. The food, too, is a cut above the common crowd, with Cantonese and Mandarin specialties. | 714 S. King St. | 206/682–4900 | $7–$15 | AE, D, DC, MC, V.

Franco's Hidden Harbor. Contemporary. A long-established, Seattle favorite overlooking the Lake Union waterfront and the yachts moored near the shore. Much of the menu is Scandinavian-inspired, but Northwest favorites are also served including seafood and steaks. Open-air dining is on the patio. Kids' menu. | 1500 Westlake Ave. N | 206/282–0501 | $15–$34 | AE, D, DC, MC, V.

F.X. McRory's Steak, Chop and Oyster House. Contemporary. A small entrance lobby that looks a bit like a 1920s speakeasy opens into a large, high-ceilinged bar and clubby dining rooms. The bar is a favorite pre- and post-game hangout for Seattle Mariners' fans since the stadium is four blocks away. Serving typical American food such as salads and burgers, and of course, steaks and oysters. Open-air dining is off the bar on the deck. Kids' menu. | 419 Occidental Ave. S | 206/623–4800 | Reservations essential for game days | No lunch Sun., except on game days | $10–$27 | AE, D, DC, MC, V.

Geneva's. Continental. A small room, set like a pavilion in a small garden, makes this a very special urban restaurant. The food is superb, and the service has continental flair. A mix of European dishes that incorporate Northwest touches is served inside or outside on the patio. No smoking. | 1106 Eighth Ave. | 206/624–2222 | Closed Sun.–Mon. No lunch | $16–$27 | AE, MC, V.

Il Terrazzo Carmine. Italian. This is perhaps the best decorated Pioneer Square restaurant, with its ceiling-to-floor draperies and air of understated dignity. Serving a wide variety of regional Italian dishes, including osso buco, and rabbit. Open-air dining is on the patio. No smoking. | 411 First Ave. S | 206/467–7797 | Closed Sun. No lunch Sat. | $12–$35 | AE, D, DC, MC, V.

Ivar's Acres of Clams. Contemporary. A big restaurant on an old waterfront shipping pier, with windows overlooking Elliott Bay, this old Seattle favorite has held its own against the influx of bright new restaurants throughout the years. Seasonal dinner are featured as well as local standbys such as fish and chips and Atlantic salmon. Kids' menu. | Pier 54 | 206/624–6852 | $11–$25 | AE, MC, V.

Ivar's Salmon House. Seafood. This long dining room facing Lake Union is decorated with original Northwest Indian art works collected by the former owner. Known for fish and chips, and alder-smoked salmon. Parking. Open-air dining on the deck. Kids' menu. Sun. brunch. | 401 N.E. Northlake Way | 206/632–0767 | $12–$26 | AE, MC, V.

Jitterbug. Contemporary. A casual storefront diner with an ever-changing menu featuring American favorites with a twist. Even the artwork on the walls changes seasonally. For breakfast, try the delicious gingerbread waffles. For dinner, the pork chops or the chicken sandwich is popular. Also features a full bar. Kids' menu. | 2114 N. 45th St. | 206/547–6313 | Breakfast also available | $10–$20 | MC, V.

Linyen. Chinese. If it weren't in Chinatown, you would consider this elegant restaurant an upscale American café. But don't let the decor distract you from the authenticity and quality of the food. This is the place where Chinese chefs come to eat late at night, after they close down their own kitchens. Favorites include the honey walnut prawns and the Peking duck. | 424 Seventh Ave. S | 206/622–8181 | $8–$12 | AE, MC, V.

Luigi's Grotto. Italian. An underground (literally) restaurant in Pioneer Square that feels like an Italian countryside trattoria. Try the raisin-sweetened calamari or the spinach salad. Kids' menu. | 102 Cherry St. | 206/343–9517 | No lunch weekends | $15–$30 | AE, D, DC, MC, V.

Madison Park Cafe. Continental. This comfortable café is set in a renovated 1927 home, complete with working fireplace. Located in a quiet neighborhood by the lake, the café has had the same owner in charge for more than 20 years. The addition of popular Seattle chef Marianne Zdobysz served to make this great restaurant even better. The fare is French bistro–style, and the menu changes seasonally. Favorites include the homemade gnocchi and the rack of lamb in lavender honey. Open-air dining in the private cobblestone courtyard, which features a lovely garden. Weekend brunch. No smoking. | 1807 42nd Ave. E | 206/324–2626 | No lunch Tues.–Sat. No dinner Sun. | $13–$23 | AE, MC, V.

Meridian. Contemporary. A modern, comfortable restaurant with a view of the bluff above Lake Union. Panoramic view of Gasworks Park, the lake, and the Seattle skyline. Known for steak and Northwest seafood. Early-bird suppers (Sun.–Fri.). Sun. brunch. | 1900 N. Northlake Way | 206/547–3242 | $12–$20 | AE, MC, V.

Nell's Restaurant. Contemporary. Tiered seating and numerous windows allow you to see the surrounding park and Green Lake from your table at this upscale restaurant. The chef attempts to mold the menu as much as possible around Northwest ingredients including wild mushrooms, berries, and fruit. The Pacific Northwest influence is also perceptible in the range of entrées such as wild salmon and razor clams. Try the Dungeness crab salad, made with apples, radishes, and a dash of parsley oil. | 6804 E. Green Lake Way N | 206/524–4044 | No lunch | $16–$25 | AE, MC, V.

Nishino. Japanese. This is a very popular, often crowded Madison Park restaurant renowned for its fresh and imaginatively served sushi and sashimi, as well as other Japanese dishes. The spicy tuna rolls come highly recommended. There is seating outside. No smoking. | 3130 E. Madison | 206/322–5800 | No lunch | $15–$25 | AE, MC, V.

Palace Kitchen. Contemporary. Upscale restaurant featuring a large U-shaped bar and an open kitchen, serving rustic bistro-style cuisine. The rotisserie chicken with scallion mashers and fresh green beans is popular, as are the king salmon and the homemade pastas. | 2030 Fifth Ave. | 206/448–2001 | $9–$19 | AE, D, DC, MC, V.

Palomino. Mediterranean. A bright, almost gaudy, upscale downtown restaurant catering to a young, well-to-do after-work crowd. In some ways, more of a bar than a restaurant. Favorite dishes include rotisserie garlic chicken and pork loin. Kids' menu. | 1420 Fifth Ave. | 206/623–1300 | $20–$30 | AE, D, DC, MC, V.

Paragon. Contemporary. A comfortable Queen Anne Hill neighborhood bistro with a classy bar out front and a dining room in back, serving rustic Northwest cuisine, such as skirt steak, lemon chicken, or pork chops. Also offers a variety of fresh fish. No smoking. | 2125 Queen Anne Ave. N | 206/283–4548 | $10–$18 | AE, MC, V.

Piatti Ristorante. Italian. The decor and the staff are casual, the food is good, the ambience friendly. There is also a fireside dining room. What more can you ask for? The rotisserie chicken is a favorite, as well as the chicken marsala. Or try the ravioli stuffed with arugula and ricotta. Open-air dining is available on two patios. Kids' menu. No smoking. | 2800 N.E. University Village | 206/524–9088 | $10–$17 | AE, DC, MC, V.

Pink Door. Italian. A pink door off the Pike Place Market's Post Alley opens into this hidden restaurant. The rooftop patio is one of the best places in Seattle for sitting outside on a warm day and enjoying a great view of Elliott Bay and the distant Olympic peaks while dining on some of the city's best Italian food. Entertainment. Kids' menu. | 1919 Post Alley | 206/443–3241 | Closed Sun.– Mon. | $13–$20 | AE, MC, V.

★ **Ray's Boathouse.** Seafood. This seafood restaurant is about as close to the water as you can get, since it's built on pilings above the water. Ray's has some of the best views of Puget Sound and the Olympic Mountains in Seattle. The views are even better in the café upstairs, where the food and service are as good as and prices are lower than they are in the main dining room. On sunny days, you can sit out on the deck and look straight down at gulls, sea ducks, and frolicking sea lions. The seaward entrance of the ship canal is just to the south, making for a continuous parade of boats and ships of all sizes. If you're in the mood for something a little different, try the Chattam Straits black cod in sake kasu. Kids' menu. | 6049 Seaview Ave. NW | 206/789–3770 | $16–$45 | AE, D, DC, MC, V.

Rock Salt Steakhouse. Steak. A bright, modern restaurant whose windows overlook Lake Union and the yachts moored near the shore. Known for steak (including the Rock Salt Slammer, an 18-oz. porterhouse), chicken, seafood, pasta. Open-air dining on the patio. Kids' menu. | 1232 Westlake N | 206/284–1047 | No lunch Sat., Sun. | $8–$22 | AE, D, DC, MC, V.

Serafina. Italian. A delightful little restaurant east of Lake Union, with friendly staff and tasty food. On sunny days you'll want to eat outside in the very secluded garden courtyard. The food is country Italian, and the menu features agnello ai porcini, which is grilled lamb in a wild mushroom sauce. Live in-house entertainment Thurs.–Sat. | 2043 Eastlake Ave. E | 206/323–0807 | No lunch Sat.– Sun. | $12–$22 | MC, V.

Shiro's. Japanese. A very casual restaurant where all of the attention is given to the quality of the food rather than to the tables or walls. Superb sushi bar (perhaps the best in Seattle). No smoking. | 2401 Second Ave. | 206/443–9844 | No lunch | $15–$25 | AE, MC, V.

Simpatico. Italian. Friendly restaurant featuring Italian fare that incorporates fresh Northwest ingredients. The seasonal menu includes a Napoleon of eggplant Parmesan, as well as the Bomb, a double cut pork chop with gorgonzola and garlic. Open-air dining on the patio. Kids' menu. | 4430 Wallingford Ave. | 206/632–1000 | No lunch | $10–$18 | D, MC, V.

Stella's Trattoria. Italian. A lively U-district all-night trattoria next to a movie theatre. The dark, cavernlike space of the three intimate dining rooms is lightened up with paintings by local artists. The food is standard Italian; huge and delicious breakfasts are served all night; pasta is the best dish on the menu. Try the melanzane parmigiana, which is eggplant browned in the pan and topped with marinara, mozzarella, and Parmesan, served with garlic pasta. Open-air dining is in front on the sidewalk. Kids' menu. No smoking. | 4500 Ninth Ave. | 206/633–1100 | Open 24 hours | $9–$16 | AE, D, MC, V.

Szmania's. Continental. A small, elegant, and surprisingly friendly restaurant off the beaten path in Seattle's Magnolia neighborhood. The food is exquisitely presented. Serving Pacific Northwest cuisine, but also known for German dishes. Try to get one of the seats at the kitchen counter where you can eat amidst the cooking. The menu is always changing, so check out the web site for current menus and directions. Kids' menu. No smoking. | 3321 W. McGraw, | 206/284–7305 | www.szmanias.com | Closed Mon. No lunch | $13–$24 | AE, MC, V.

Trattoria Mitchelli. Italian. A funky Pioneer Square trattoria has been around for decades and is still as simple and fun as ever. The food is best described as American-Italian, and the menu features a variety of pizzas and pastas. Open-air dining on the sidewalk. Kids' menu. | 84 Yesler Way | 206/623–3883 | Reservations not accepted (Fri., Sat.) | $9–$13 | AE, D, MC, V.

Tulio. Italian. An elegant hotel restaurant with a wood-burning pizza oven. True, the pizzas are great here, but so are the other rustic Italian dishes, and the service is very good. There's also a small but friendly bar. Open-air dining on the patio. | 1100 Fifth Ave., 98101 | 206/624–5500 | Breakfast also available | $13–$23 | AE, D, DC, MC, V.

Union Bay Cafe. Contemporary. An intimate, friendly neighborhood café, where locals drop in after work for a quick bite to eat, or come to celebrate special occasions. The dining rooms are nicely appointed with bottles displayed in wine racks, and vases full of flowers. Northwest cuisine with an Italian flare is on the menu and game is a specialty. Open-air dining in the courtyard. Kids' menu. No smoking. | 3515 N.E. 45th St. | 206/527–8364 | Closed Mon. No lunch | $13–$22 | AE, D, DC, MC, V.

Union Square Grill. Seafood. A big, sprawling underground complex of dining rooms serving the same sort of fare as Elliott's and the Met Grill (same owners) near the Convention Center. Featuring popular Northwest fare including Dungeness crab cakes, rack of lamb, and lobster tail. | 621 Union St. | 206/224–4321 | $18–$40 | AE, D, DC, MC, V.

Wolfgang Puck Café. Contemporary. This laid-back place across the street from the Seattle Art Museum provides postmodern comfort food, such as smoked salmon pizza and meatloaf made with veal, pork, lamb, eggplant and wrapped in applewood-smoked bacon. Kids can make dough into little pizzas that are baked and returned to them. | 1225 1st Ave. | 206/621–9653 | $13–$22 | AE, D, DC, MC, V.

EXPENSIVE

Adriatica. Mediterranean. Adriatica is Seattle's longest-established Mediterranean-style restaurant, and arguably the city's best. Occupying the top of an old house, the restaurant's view of Lake Union has been blocked by a high-rise, but now the focus is on a hillside garden, which makes for a more intimate dining experience. The cuisine is an interesting blend of southern European fare, Northwest seafood, and even a little Pacific Rim. Try the pork tenderloin in cranberry port wine sauce, the filet mignon with crab legs, and the fresh king salmon. There is limited open-air dining on a small lounge deck. | 1107 Dexter N | 206/285–5000 | No lunch | $22–$30 | AE, DC, MC, V.

Al Boccalino. Italian. Pleasant relaxed restaurant in an old, brick-walled Pioneer Square building. Try the saddle of lamb or the king salmon stuffed with spinach and shallots. The menu changes seasonally. | 1 Yesler Way | 206/622–7688 | $30–$50 | AE, DC, MC, V.

Andaluca. Mediterranean. This restaurant in the Mayflower Park Hotel serves food that is eclectic, and heavy on the Spanish influence. For dinner, try the "crab tower," featuring Dungeness crab with gazpacho salsa and served with grapefruit. For dessert, the warm liquid chocolate cake with espresso chip ice-cream is absolutely delicious. | 407 Olive Way | 206/382–6999 | Reservations essential | Breakfast also available. No lunch Sun. | $18–$33 | AE, D, DC, MC, V.

Buca Di Beppo. Italian. A small, very popular downtown restaurant that serves its family-style dishes with flair and a few lucky diners get to eat in the kitchen. It's almost like home. The portions are enormous. The food is straightforward, cooked with a lot of tomatoes, garlic, and olive oil. The spaghetti and meatballs is an old favorite, or try the chicken cacciatore. Open-air dining on the patio in back. No smoking. | 701 Ninth Ave. N | 206/244–2288 | No lunch | $25–$35 | AE, DC, MC, V.

Campagne. French. This understated elegant restaurant is the parent of Café Campagne, the more casual bistro-style café next door. The food here is so good, you might not even notice the splendid scenery outside. Featuring a seasonal menu of regional French country cuisine. Open-air dining is in a private courtyard. | 86 Pine St. | 206/728–2800 | No lunch | $24–$30 | AE, DC, MC, V.

Cutter's. Seafood. Cutter's adds good service and a harbor view to its fresh fish selections prepared on an apple-wood grill. You can have traditional fish and chips or something with a European, Latin American, or Asian accent, such as Penn Cove mussels in a coconut-curry broth. | 2001 Western Ave. | 206/448–4884 | $15–$43 | AE, D, DC, MC, V.

Dahlia Lounge. Contemporary. A comfortable restaurant that, according to one old-timer, looks a bit like a Seattle bordello from a previous age. Eclectic fresh Pacific Northwest dishes are the stars of this menu. Try the crab cakes or the duck. | 2001 4th Ave. | 206/682–4142 | No lunch weekends | $17–$28 | AE, D, DC, MC, V.

Flying Fish. Seafood. The restaurant describes the food as having an Asian flair. Try the fried snapper platters with a pineapple and anchovy dipping sauce, which comes with rice paper so you can make your own roll-ups. The salt and pepper Dungeness crab is very popular. Open-air dining on the sidewalk on warm summer days. No smoking. | 2234 First Ave. | 206/728–8595 | No lunch | $13–$17 | AE, DC, MC, V.

Il Bistro. Italian. This intimate, sub-street level Pike Place Market restaurant has a pleasant lunch atmosphere and is a nighttime hangout. For an appetizer, try the Caesar salad, sauteed calamari, or homemade gnocchi. For dinner, the rack of lamb or the cioppino is recommended. Open-air dining on the patio. | 93A Pike St. | 206/682–3049 | $17–$35 | AE, DC, MC, V.

Kaspar's. Contemporary. The dining room of this Queen Anne restaurant is understated which only heightens the beautiful presentation of the food. The chef has a light hand with seafood, and the perfect touch with vegetables. The menu changes daily, but always includes dishes made with fresh local seafood, as well as a variety of meats and also vegetarian fare, such as the lemon gnocchi. Kids' menu. No smoking. | 19 W. Harrison St. | 206/298–0123 | Closed Sun., Mon. No lunch | $15–24 | AE, MC, V.

Le Gourmand. French. A small but very popular restaurant in a residential area off the beaten path. Try the beef tenderloin with a Merlot wine pressings sauce or the poached king salmon. | 425 N.W. Market St. | 206/84–3463 | Closed Sun.–Tues. No lunch | $24–$42 prix fixe | AE, MC, V.

★ **Marco's Supper Club.** Continental. A popular, upbeat supper club has a range of dishes of New Continental Cuisine. Open-air dining on the patio. | 2510 First Ave. | 206/441–7801 | No lunch | $14–$20 | AE, MC, V.

Maximilien-in-the-Market. French. This small place overlooking Elliott Bay (and the distant Olympic Mountains) is about as authentic a French bistro as you'll find anywhere in Seattle. The food is classical French cuisine, but incorporates fresh Northwest ingredients, and features an extensive wine list. Examples from the menu include the sea halibut with mushrooms and lobster sauce and the tournedo rossini, a beef tenderloin. Sun. brunch. | 81A Pike Place | 206/682–7270 | Closed Mon. | $18–$26 | AE, DC, MC, V.

McCormick and Schmick's. Seafood. A clubby, wood-paneled restaurant with an ever-changing menu featuring a wide variety of fresh fish and shellfish. Any kind of seafood you want—they've got it. | 1103 First Ave. | 206/623–5500 | No lunch weekends | $15–$20 | AE, D, DC, MC, V.

Nikko. Japanese. The ultrachic sushi bar sits at the center of this sophisticated Japanese eatery, where experienced chefs prepare some of Seattle's best sushi and sashimi. On the regular menu, the teriyaki salmon and the cod marinated in Kasu sake are outstanding favorites. | Westin Hotel, 1900 5th Ave. | 206/322–4641 | Closed Sun. No lunch Sat. | $17–$30 | AE, DC, MC, V.

Painted Table. Contemporary. This large, high-ceilinged dining room in the Alexis Hotel is in a building which has been through several incarnations since it was built in 1901, including a stint as a parking garage. But now it houses one of Seattle's most elegant hotels and one of its finest restaurants. The coriander crest of ahi tuna is a popular appetizer; for dinner, the grilled lamb chops with herbed potato gnocchi is a favorite. Weekend brunch. No smoking. | 92 Madison St. | 206/624–3646 | $17–$30 | AE, D, DC, MC, V.

Palisade. Seafood. There's a great view across Elliott Bay to downtown Seattle from this restaurant at the Elliott Bay Marina. Notice the restaurant's gurgling indoor stream, but concentrate on simpler menu items, like the signature plank-broiled salmon. An informal café downstairs, called Maggie Bluffs, is a good spot for lunch on a breezy summer afternoon. To reach this spot, take Elliot Avenue from downtown Seattle to the Magnolia Bridge and turn off at the exit in the middle of the bridge. | 2601 W. Marina Pl | 206/285–1000 | $16–$45 | AE, D, DC, MC, V.

Place Pigalle. Contemporary. Place Pigalle has to be one of Seattle's most underrated restaurants, perhaps because it is tucked away in such a quiet corner of the Pike Place Market. But it has a great, casual ambience, beautifully prepared food, and splendid views across Elliott Bay to the distant peaks of the Olympic Mountains. It serves an eclectic mix of Northwest dishes, including many seafood entrees. | 81 Pike St. | 206/624–1756 | Closed Sun. | $17–$23 | AE, MC, V.

Prego. Italian. A modern restaurant in the Renaissance Hotel, with an intimate dining room and grand views of downtown Seattle's business district as well as Lake Union, Elliott Bay, and beyond. The fare is Northern Italian, and features a variety of pastas, seafood dishes, and specials, as well as a good selection of wines. | 515 Madison St. | 206/583–0300 | No lunch | $17–$25 | AE, D, DC, MC, V.

Queen City Grill. Contemporary. An old-town café near the Pike Place Market with aged brick walls. Serving a variety of grilled seafood, as well as New York steaks. | 2201 1st Ave. | 206/443–0975 | No lunch weekends | $17–$26 | AE, D, DC, MC, V.

Sazerac. Contemporary. A hotel dining room serving food with French/Louisiana-style. Not as good as the hype—it's more of a place to be seen than a place where you wax ecstatic over the food. Open-air dining on the patio. Kids' menu. No smoking. | 1101 Fourth Ave. | 206/621–1770 | Breakfast also available | $10–$24 | AE, D, DC, MC, V.

VERY EXPENSIVE

Canlis. Contemporary. Formerly Seattle's most stodgy restaurant, Canlis has in recent years tried to upgrade its image, with mixed results. The decor is warm and elegant. Serving Pacific Northwest cuisine, mostly steaks and seafood dishes. | 2576 Aurora Ave. N | 206/283–3313 | Closed Sun. No lunch | $25–$45 | AE, D, DC, MC, V.

Chez Shea. Contemporary. High above the Pike Place Market, this cozy restaurant makes you feel like you're the honored guest at a private dinner. Except, of course, that the food is so much better than what friends can dish up. Known for its popular seasonal daily four-course special, the menu usually favors Northwest regional cuisine with a Pacific-French influence. No smoking. | 94 Pike St. | 206/467–9990 | Reservations essential | Closed Mon. No lunch | $40–$50 | AE, MC, V.

★ **El Gaucho.** Steak. From the outside, this dark, elegant Belltown restaurant looks a bit plain. The formal, elegant, rather slick, dining room takes you to a different world (there are four private rooms). The food is everything you expect from a place like this. And, yes, the steaks are very good. The filet mignon is a popular favorite, as is the Australian lobster tail. | 2505 First Ave. | 206/728–1337 | No lunch | $65–$82 | AE, DC, MC, V.

Fullers. Contemporary. Private booths surround a fountain, and its serenity is enhanced by smoked glass by Dale Chihuly. As for the menu, it won a four-star rating from *Bon Appetit*. Try the pan-seared king salmon. Kids' menu. No smoking. | 1400 Sixth Ave. | 206/447–5544 | Reservations essential | Closed Sun. No lunch | $45–$55 | AE, D, DC, MC, V.

Georgian Room. Contemporary. Elegant, very comfortable dining room with large, tall windows that bathe the tables in light during the day, heightening the elegance of the chateau-like setting. The food has a definite French influence, and includes fresh Northwest ingredients. Signature dishes include the sea bass with caviar and the tenderloin with oxtail. Breakfast also available. | 411 University St. | 206/621–7889 | Jacket requested for dinner | No lunch, no supper Sun. | $25–$50 | AE, D, DC, MC, V.

Hunt Club. Contemporary. An intimate dining room paneled in dark wood. The seasonal menu has Pacific Rim and Mediterranean influences. The lamb chops are a favorite for many diners. Weekend brunch. | 900 Madison Ave. | 206/343–6156 | Breakfast also available | $22–$39 | AE, D, DC, MC, V.

★ **Lampreia.** Italian. Elegant bistro which some folks love and others love to hate. The fare is eclectic, and includes popular items such as the oven roasted veal chops and the loin of lamb. No smoking. | 2400 First Ave. | 206/443–3301 | Closed Sun.–Mon. No lunch | $20–$34 | AE, MC, V.

★ **Metropolitan Grill.** Steak. Steak and clubby surroundings seem to go together in Seattle, and the Met Grill is no exception. The quality and preparation of the meat is such that the Met has long been Seattle's favorite steakhouse. No wonder. Even the hamburger is great! Best of all, since the Met is owned by the folks who run Elliott's, the seafood is fresh and prepared with flair. Kids' menu. | 820 Second Ave. | 206/624–3287 | No lunch weekends | $35–$125 | AE, D, DC, MC, V.

Ponti Seafood Grill. Eclectic. Ponti's adds a splash of Mediterranean sunshine to the somber shores of the Lake Washington Ship Canal. The food, too, is sunny and beautifully prepared from the freshest ingredients. Service is friendly and attentive. If you catch the right table, you'll see ships go by on the canal and the Fremont drawbridge go up and down. In warm weather you can sit outside on a terrace overlooking the canal. Kids' menu, early bird suppers. | 3014 Third Ave. N | 206/284–3000 | $40–$50 | AE, DC, MC, V.

★ **Rover's.** Contemporary. This elegant, small restaurant tucked into a Madison Valley garden is a delight. It's about as perfect as a Seattle restaurant gets, from the setting to the understated elegance of the dining room, the courteous service, and the incredible food. Rover's is the kind of place where other chefs come to eat to *learn* about food. The food is updated Northwest cuisine with French influences. Offering two five-course dinners, one vegetarian, one standard, and an eight-course dinner. Open-air dining on the patio and courtyard. No smoking. | 2808 E. Madison St. | 206/325–7442 | Closed Sun.– Mon. No lunch | $60–$105 prix fixe menus | AE, DC, MC, V.

Ruth's Chris Steak House. Steak. A large rather sterile chain restaurant specializing in steak dripping with butter, which is tucked into the ground floor of a high-rise office tower. Specials include the Oscar steak, which is served with crab, and the prime rib. Everything is served a la carte. | 800 Fifth Ave. | 206/624–8524 | No lunch | $30–$40 | AE, DC, MC, V.

Space Needle. Contemporary. A restaurant that is high above the ground and revolves for a panoramic view. Unfortunately, the view is a lot better than the food. The observation deck is a floor higher, and the view is even better. Known for regional dishes. Kids' menu. Sat. and Sun. brunch. No smoking. | 219 Fourth Ave. N | 206/443–2100 | No breakfast weekdays mid-Sept.–Labor Day | $55–$65 | AE, D, DC, MC, V.

Lodging

INEXPENSIVE

Bacon Mansion. This 1909 Edwardian-style Tudor sits on a quiet tree-lined street in the Harvard-Belmont Historical District. Each of the 11 rooms has a distinct shape and character; the Capitol Suite, for example, has a pine four-poster bed, a carved oak fireplace, and a view of the Space Needle, while the Iris Room is dominated by a floral theme and has a view of Mt. Rainier. A carriage house behind the mansion provides good lodging for families. | 11 rooms (9 with private bath). Complimentary Continental breakfast, no air-conditioning, in-room data ports, some refrigerators, library, no pets, no smoking. | 959 Broadway E, | 206/329–1864 or 800/240–1864 | fax 206/860–9025 | info@baconmansion.com | www.baconmansion.com | $99–$169 | AE, D, MC, V.

Beech Tree Manor. This inn was built in 1902 and is well appointed in the manner of an English home. | 7 rooms (2 with shared bath). Complimentary breakfast, no air-conditioning, cable TV in sitting room, no room phones, business services, pets allowed. No smoking. | 1405 Queen Anne Ave. N | 206/281–7037 | fax 206/284–2350 | $89–$129 | MC, V.

Best Western Executive Inn. Renovated business travelers' motel with easy access to local attractions. Nearby is the Monorail to take you downtown. | 123 rooms. Restaurant, bar, in-room data ports, some refrigerators, room service, cable TV, hot tub, gym, business services, free parking. | 200 Taylor Ave. N | 206/448–9444 | fax 206/441–7929 | executive.inn@juno.com | www.exec/inn.com | $104–$147 | AE, D, DC, MC, V.

Best Western Loyal Inn. This motel is four blocks from the Space Needle in the heart of downtown. It is a 15-minute walk to Pike Place Market. | 91 rooms. Complimentary Continental breakfast, in-room data ports, some refrigerators, cable TV, hot tub, sauna, laundry facilities, business services. | 2301 Eighth Ave. | 206/682–0200 | fax 206/467–8984 | $110–$149; $200 suites | AE, D, DC, MC, V.

Best Western–Pioneer Square Hotel. Comfortable upscale hotel in the heart of Pioneer Square, close to the Underground Tour, and the waterfront. | 75 rooms. Complimentary Continental breakfast, in-room data ports, cable TV, business services, parking (fee). | 77 Yesler Way | 206/340–1234 | fax 206/467–0707 | www.pioneersquare.com | $129–$209 | AE, D, DC, MC, V.

Camlin. Old-fashioned sailor's hotel with rather small rooms. It's close to malls and the convention center. | 132 rooms. Restaurant, bar with entertainment, no air-conditioning in many rooms, TV, pool, business services. | 1619 Ninth Ave. | 206/682–0100 or 800/426–0670 (res) | fax 206/682–7415 | $119–$128 | AE, D, DC, MC, V.

Chambered Nautilus. A comfortable B&B in a 1915 Georgian colonial home, the inn is set on top of a quiet hill in the town's University district. Many rooms have views of the Cascades, and the living room has a cozy fireplace. | 6 rooms. Complimentary breakfast and afternoon snacks, in-room data ports, no air-conditioning, business services, no smoking. | 5005 22nd Ave. NE | 206/522–2536 or 800/545–8459 | fax 206/528–0898 | chambered-nautilus@msn.com | $99–$129 | AE, MC, V.

Chelsea Station on the Park. Set in two brick Federal Colonial–style buildings built in 1929, this comfortable B&B is close to the zoo, the rose gardens, and the park. Some rooms have views of the Cascade Mountains. | 3 rooms, 6 suites. Complimentary breakfast and afternoon snacks, no air-conditioning, in-room data ports, business services, no kids under 12, no smoking. | 4915 Linden Ave. N | 206/547–6077 or 800/400–6077 | fax 206/632–5107 | www.bandbseattle.com | $95–$110, $125–$175 suites | AE, D, DC, MC, V.

Doubletree Guest Suites. Upscale suburban business travelers' hotel with tall atrium lobby and other period touches. Close to the shopping mall. | 221 suites. Restaurant, bar, refrigerators, cable TV, indoor pool, hot tub, gym, racquetball, business services, airport shuttle. | 16500 Southcenter Pkwy. | 206/575–8220 | fax 206/575–4743 | www.doubletreehotels.com | $109–$169 suites | AE, D, DC, MC, V.

Edmond Meany Hotel. In the heart of the University district, this contemporary hotel has views of Seattle or the campus of the University of Washington. It's a favorite with academics and conventioneers. | 155 rooms. Restaurant, bar, in-room data ports, room service, cable TV, gym, game room with pool table, business services. | 4507 Brooklyn Ave. NE | 206/634–2000 or 800/899–0251 | fax 206/547–6029 | www.meany.com | $99–$169 | AE, DC, MC, V.

★ **Gaslight.** This B&B was built in 1906, and is decorated with a blend of Northwest art, contemporary pieces, and antiques. The gardens showcase a variety of interesting plants, and some rooms have private decks or gardens. Many rooms have views, and there is also a sun deck. | 16 rooms (4 with shower only, 3 with shared bath), 7 suites in 2 buildings. Picnic area, complimentary Continental breakfast and afternoon snacks, no air-conditioning, in-room data ports, some refrigerators, cable TV, some room phones, pool, business services. | 1727–1733 15th Ave. | 206/325–3654 | fax 206/328–4803 | www.gaslight-inn.com | $88–$148, $128–$178 suites | AE, MC, V.

Hawthorne Inn and Suites. This modern hotel is downtown, catering mainly to families and business travelers. | 54 rooms, 18 suites. Complimentary breakfast, in-room data ports, cable TV, some refrigerators (in suites), hot tub, sauna, gym, laundry facilities, business services, free parking, pets allowed. | 2224 8th Ave. | 206/624–6820 | fax 206/467–6926 | $89–$134, $175 suites | AE, D, MC, V.

Hill House Bed and Breakfast. Made up of two turn-of-the-20th-century Victorian homes on Historic Capitol Hill, this inn is decorated with original Northwest artwork and antiques. In the living room you will find a great collection of art books and CDs. Also offers ample off-street parking, a definite bonus on busy Capitol Hill. | 5 rooms (2 with shared bath), 2 suites. Complimentary breakfast, no air-conditioning, some in-room data ports, some cable TV and VCRs (in suites), some room phones, no kids under 12. | 1113 E. John St. | 206/720–7161 or 800/720–7161 (reservations) | fax 206/323–0772 | www.seattlebnb.com | $75–$130, $160 suites | AE, D, MC, V.

Hostelling International/Seattle. Near the Pike Place Market, you can sleep here in dormitory-style rooms. Guests have access to a kitchen and dining rooms. | 205 beds share baths. No air-conditioning, TV in common area, library, laundry facilities, no pets, no smoking. | 84 Union St. | 206/622–5443 | fax 206/682–2179 | www.hiseattle.org | $16–$18 | AE, MC, V.

Inn at Virginia Mason. This is very popular with families whose relatives have been hospitalized at the Virginia Mason Hospital. | 79 rooms. Restaurant, in-room data ports, cable TV, business services, no smoking. | 1006 Spring St. | 206/583–6453 or 800/283–6453 | fax 206/223–7545 | $100–$220 | AE, D, DC, MC, V.

Mayflower Park. A beautifully appointed little hotel with very comfortable rooms and with Seattle's most urbane bar. The only drawback is the parking, which is by valet in a garage several blocks away, meaning it can take forever for your car to arrive. Check-in during the rush hour (the hotel is on one of Seattle's busiest streets) can be almost life-threatening. | 172 rooms. Restaurant, bar, in-room data ports, room service, cable TV, gym, business services, parking (fee). | 405 Olive Way | 206/623–8700 or 800/426–5100 | fax 206/382–6997 | www.mayflowerpark.com | $155–$365 | AE, D, DC, MC, V.

M.V. Challenger. This Bed and Breakfast does not sit on Lake Union, it floats on Lake Union. The converted 1944 U.S. Army tugboat is 96 ft long, with a solarium, sun deck, and a main salon in addition to the tastefully appointed, though somewhat snug, guestrooms. Papered with nautical maps, most rooms have double or queen-size beds with views of the water. | 8 rooms. Complimentary breakfast, no air-conditioning, cable TV, some in-room VCRs (movies), no pets, no smoking. | 1001 Fairview Ave. N | 206/340–1201 | fax 206/332–0303 | ctugboat@uswest.net | www.seattlebedandbreakfast.com | $90–$185 | AE, MC, V.

Pacific Plaza. This European-style hotel is right in downtown Seattle, convenient to everything. It's seven blocks to Pioneer Square and five blocks to the waterfront. | 160 rooms. Complimentary Continental breakfast, cable TV, business services. | 400 Spring St. | 206/623–3900 or 800/426–1165 (res) | fax 206/623–2059 | www.pacificplazahotel.com | $106–$135 | AE, D, DC, MC, V.

Pensione Nichols. Only a block away from Pike Place Market, the downtown setting gives this B&B an authentic Seattle air. Enclosed balconies, full kitchens, private baths, and large living rooms are features of the second-story suites. Rooms on the third floor mostly have skylights rather than windows and have a mixture of antique and contemporary furnishings. | 10 rooms share 4 baths, 2 suites. Complimentary Continental breakfast, no air-conditioning in some rooms, some kitchenettes, some microwaves, some refrigerators, some room phones, no TV, pets allowed, no smoking. | 1923 1st Ave. | 206/441–7125 or 800/440–7125 | www.seattle-bed-breakfast.com | $105–$190 | AE, D, DC, MC, V.

Prince of Wales. This Capitol Hill inn has rooms with views of the city, Puget Sound and the Olympic Mountains. There is a fireplace in the common room. | 4 rooms (2 with shower only). Complimentary breakfast and afternoon snacks, business services, no kids under 3, no smoking. | 133 13th Ave. E | 206/325–9692 or 800/327–9692 | fax 206/322–6402 | cnorton949@aol.com | www.princebedandbreakfast.com | $90–$125 | D, MC, V.

Radisson. This comfortable motel, south of the city, has changed hands and updated its look. | 308 rooms. Restaurant, lounge, in-room data ports, cable TV, pool, gym, business services, airport shuttle. | 1701 International Blvd. | 206/246–7000 | fax 206/246–1715 | $129–$189 | AE, D, DC, MC, V.

Salisbury House. A nicely restored inn on a tree-lined street on Capitol Hill, this B&B was originally built in 1904. The library is cozy, and has a fireplace. | 4 rooms, 1 suite. Complimentary breakfast, no air-conditioning, in-room data ports, business services, no kids under 12, no smoking. | 750 16th Ave. E | 206/328–8682 | fax 206/720–1019 | sleep@salisburyhouse.com | www.salisburyhouse.com | $95–$149 | AE, DC, MC, V.

Silver Cloud Inn. Comfortable business travelers' hotel, close to the mall, and the University of Washington. | 180 rooms. Complimentary Continental breakfast, in-room data ports, refrigerators, cable TV, indoor pool, hot tub, gym, van shuttle, business services. | 5036 25th Ave. NE | 206/526–5200 or 800/205–6940 | fax 206/522–1450 | heather@scinns.com | www.scinns.com | $115–$154 | AE, D, DC, MC, V.

Sixth Avenue Inn. Basic but comfortable and centrally located business travelers' hotel. | 80 rooms. Restaurant, bar, in-room data ports, room service, cable TV, business services, free parking. | 2000 Sixth Ave. | 206/441–8300 or 800/648–6440 | fax 206/441–9903 | $72–$256 | AE, D, DC, MC, V.

University Inn. This motel is four blocks from the University of Washington and caters to business travelers and academics. | 102 rooms. Restaurant, complimentary Continental breakfast, in-room data ports, cable TV, pool, exercise equipment, laundry facilities, business services, free parking. | 4140 Roosevelt Way NE | 206/632–5055 or 800/733–3855 | fax 206/547–4937 | Univinn@aol.com | www.universityinnseattle.com | $112–$134 | AE, D, DC, MC, V.

University Plaza Hotel. Popular among families and business travelers, this motor hotel sits across I–5 from the University of Washington. The rooms are spacious and appointed with cheerful teak furniture; the quieter rooms are away from the freeway. The staff is cheerful and ready to accommodate. | 135 rooms. Restaurant, bar, room service, cable TV, pool, beauty salon, gym, no pets. | 400 N.E. 45th St. | 206/634–0100 or 800/343–7040 | fax 206/633–2743 | $109 | AE, D, DC, MC, V.

Villa Heidelberg. Surrounded by manicured lawns and flower-filled gardens, this 1909 Craftsman has a wide porch from which you can see Puget Sound. The charms of the interior include hardwood floors, heavily embossed wallpaper, and lace tablecloths. Rooms are appointed with comfortable Arts and Crafts furnishings and many have splendid views of the sound, garden, or mountains. | 4 rooms share 2 baths, 2 suites. Complimentary breakfast, cable TV, no pets, no kids under 6, no smoking. | 4845 45th Ave. SW | 206/938–3658 or 800/671–2942 | fax 206/935–7077 | info@villaheidelberg.com | www.villaheidelberg.com | $80–$150 | AE, MC, V.

Warwick. Modern but very comfortable hotel that's a favorite of visiting actors, musicians, and other show biz celebrities. Central to the Pike Place Market. | 225 rooms, 4 suites. Restaurant, bar with entertainment, in-room data ports, some refrigerators, room service, in-room hot tubs (in suites), cable TV, indoor pool, hot tub, gym, van shuttle, business services. | 401 Lenora St. | 206/443–4300 or 800/426–9280 | fax 206/448–1662 | $120–220, $295–$350 suites | AE, D, DC, MC, V.

WestCoast Roosevelt Hotel. The elegant lobby of this older hotel, which sits near the convention center and shopping district, has a grand piano, a fireplace, a Chinese lacquered screen, and walls of windows, making it a perfect place to watch the world outside. The rooms are furnished with period reproductions and have insulated windows for good night's sleep. | 138 rooms, 13 suites. Restaurant, bar, room service, in-room data ports, some in-room hot tubs, cable TV, gym, laundry services, no pets. | 1531 7th Ave. | 206/621–1200 or 800/426–0670 | fax 206/233–0335 | www.westcoasthotels.com | $165–$190 | AE, D, DC, MC, V.

MODERATE

Crowne Plaza. Stay at this downtown Seattle hotel and you will be able to walk to Pioneer Square, Pike Place Market and the Waterfront. | 412 rooms. Restaurant, bar, in-room data ports, cable TV, hot tub, gym, business services. | 1113 Sixth Ave. | 206/464–1980 | fax 206/340–1617 | cplaza@wolfenet.com | www.basshotels.com | $149–$239 | AE, D, DC, MC, V.

Hotel Vintage Park. Every room in this centrally located hotel is named for a Washington winery or vineyard. The staff will go all out to accommodate you, even serving complimentary wine each evening around the lobby fireplace. | 126 rooms. Restaurant, in-room data ports, minibars, room service, cable TV, gym, business services, valet parking (fee). | 1100 Fifth Ave. | 206/624–8000 or 800/624–4433 | fax 206/623–0568 | www.hotelvintagepark.com | $175–$270 | AE, D, DC, MC, V.

★ **Inn at Harbor Steps.** At the base of the Harbor Steps apartment building, this small inn is in the heart of downtown Seattle's Arts and Business District, and a short walk from Pike Place Market. Every room has a fireplace, and most have lovely garden views. | 20 rooms. Restaurant, complimentary breakfast and afternoon snacks, in-room data ports, refrigerators, cable TV, indoor pool, hot tub, exercise equipment, business services. | 1221 First Ave. | 888/728–8910 (reservations) | fax 206/748–0533 | www.foursisters.com | $160–$220 | AE, DC, MC, V.

★ **Inn at the Market.** A great little hotel right above the Pike Place Market, with easy access to its shops and restaurants. Some of the rooms have splendid views of Elliott Bay and the Olympic Mountains. | 70 rooms, 10 suites. Refrigerators, cable TV, business services. | 86 Pine St. | 206/443–3600 or 800/446–4484 | fax 206/448–0631 | www.innatthemarket.com | $170–$245, $290–$360 suites | AE, D, DC, MC, V.

Marqueen Hotel. Converted into a hotel in 1998, this 1918 brick building was originally filled with apartments. It now sits next to the Seattle Center, convenient for those attending operas, ballets, or theater performances. The rooms—appointed with antique replicas—all have full kitchens and most have sitting rooms. | 45 rooms, 8 suites. Room service, in-room data ports, kitchenettes, microwaves, refrigerators, cable TV, laundry service, no pets. | 600 Queen Anne Ave. N | 206/282–7407 or 888/445–3076 | fax 206/283–1499 | www.marqueen.com | $129–$369; suites range $175–275; $10 each additional person | AE, D, DC, MC, V.

Plaza Park Suites. Near Capitol Hill and the Space Needle, this large suite hotel has wide city views. | 193 suites. Picnic area, complimentary Continental breakfast, in-room data ports, microwaves, refrigerators, many in-room hot tubs, cable TV, pool, 2 hot tubs, sauna, gym, laundry facilities, van shuttle, business services, valet parking (fee). | 1011 Pike St. | 206/682–8282 or 800/833–4353 (res) | fax 206/682–5315 | $119–$129 rooms, $140–$150 junior suites, $155–$179 1–bedroom suites, $245–$355 2–bedroom suites | AE, D, DC, MC, V.

Sheraton. Another large hotel which is a popular spot for business travelers because it is close to the convention center. The rooms on the upper floors are more luxurious than those below. | 840 rooms. Restaurant, bar with entertainment, in-room data ports, some minibars, room service, cable TV, indoor pool, barbershop, hot tub, gym, business services. | 1400 6th Ave. | 206/621–9000 | fax 206/621–8441 | www.starwood.com | $165–$235 | AE, D, DC, MC, V.

The Westin. This big high-rise hotel with two towers has great views of Puget Sound, Lake Union and the Space Needle. | 865 rooms. 2 restaurants, bar with entertainment, in-room data ports, minibars, refrigerators, room service, cable TV, pool, hot tub, gym, business services. | 1900 5th Ave. | 206/728–1000 | fax 206/728–2259 | $165–$280 | AE, D, DC, MC, V.

Wall Street Inn. Built in the 1950s for the sailors of the Union Pacific, half of the rooms have their original Murphy beds while half have queen-size beds. All rooms contain sitting areas, refrigerators, and an attractive combination of odd furniture. The hotel is located in the Belltown district, close to the Pike Place Market. | 20 rooms. Complimentary Continental breakfast, in-room data ports, some kitchenettes, some microwaves, refrigerators, cable TV, no pets, no smoking. | 2507 1st Ave. | 206/448–0125 | fax 206/448–2406 | www.wallstreetinn.com | $135–$155 | AE, MC, V.

EXPENSIVE

Alexis Hotel. Hard to believe that this charming small hotel was once a parking garage. It's near Pioneer Square and the waterfront. Each room is individually decorated, and the hotel has permanent and rotating art collections. Complimentary wine tastings in the evenings. | 65 rooms, 44 suites. Restaurant (*see* Painted Table), bar, cafe, in-room data ports, minibars, some refrigerators, room service, in-room hot tubs (in suites), cable TV and movies, bookstore, massage, gym, sauna, business services, pets allowed (fee), valet parking (fee). | 1007 1st Ave. | 206/624–4844 or 800/264–8482 | fax 206/621–9009 | www.alexishotel.com | $225–$245, $365–$450 suites | AE, D, DC, MC, V.

★ **Four Seasons Olympic Hotel.** Reflecting a 1920's Renaissance Revival–style, this large downtown hotel manages to be at once elegant and homey. With so much to offer inside, it might be difficult to actually leave the premises, but when you do you will be right in the heart of bustling Seattle. | 450 rooms. Restaurants, bar, in-room data ports, minibars, some refrigerators, room service, cable TV, indoor pool, barbershop, beauty salon, hot tub, sauna, spa, massage, exercise equipment, business services. | 411 University St. | 206/621–1700 | fax 206/682–9633 | $225–$285, $345–$425 suites | AE, DC, MC, V.

Hotel Monaco. A modern, very comfortable downtown hotel with whimsical yet elegant decor. The rooms are surprisingly cozy for such a splashy place. Offers a special "goldfish service"—guests can request a pet goldfish in their room during their stay. | 144 rooms, 45 suites. Restaurant (*see* Sazerac), bar, in-room data ports, minibars, refrigerators, room service, some in-room hot tubs, cable TV, stereos, some VCRs, massage, gym, business services, valet parking (fee), pets allowed. | 1101 Fourth Ave. | 206/621–1770 or 800/945–2240 (reservations) | fax 206/621–7779 | www.monaco-seattle.com | $230–$240, $295–$890 suites | AE, D, DC, MC, V.

Madison Renaissance Hotel. Upscale business travelers' hotel in the heart of downtown Seattle. There is an Italian restaurant as well as a smaller café. | 553 rooms. 2 restaurants, 2 bars, in-room data ports, minibars, room service, cable TV, indoor pool, barbershop, beauty salon, hot tub, gym, business services. | 515 Madison St. | 206/583–0300 or 800/228–9290 (res) | fax 206/447–0992 | www.renaissancehotels.com | $240–$300 | AE, D, DC, MC, V.

Paramount Hotel. Opened in 1996, this chain hotel was conceived as a companion to the big-budget entertainment sites nearby: Nike Town, Game Works, and a multi-screen cinema. Thus, it does not have an authentic Seattle flavor. This aside, the rooms are comfortable (with work spaces, lounge chairs, and large bathrooms) and the lobby spacious. | 146 rooms, 2 suites. Restaurant, room service, in-room data ports, cable TV, gym, laundry service, no pets. | 724 Pine St. | 206/292–9500 or 800/426–0670 | fax 206/292–8610 | www.westcoasthotels.com | $220–$240; $425 suites | AE, D, DC, MC, V.

Residence Inn Seattle–Lake Union. This extended residence hotel sits directly on the splendid Lake Union. Perfect for families, all the rooms have a living room and full kitchen. The lobby is part of a seven-story atrium, complete with waterfall and many areas to relax. | 234 suites. Complimentary Continental breakfast, room service, in-room data ports, kitchenettes, microwaves, refrigerators, cable TV, pool, spa, sauna, gym, business services, pets allowed (fee). | 800 Fairview Ave. N, | 206/624–6000 or 800/331–3131 | fax 206/223–8106 | www.marriott.com | $200–$300 | AE, D, DC, MC, V.

Seattle Hilton. Upscale hotel, west of I–5 atop the Seattle Athletic Club parking garage with views of the Olympic Mountains. It is popular with conventioneers because an underground passage connects it to the convention center as well as the Rainier Square Shopping concourse. | 237 rooms. Restaurant, bar, minibars, refrigerators, room service, cable TV, gym, business services, parking (fee). | 1301 Sixth Ave. | 206/624–0500 | fax 206/682–9029 | $200–$250 | AE, D, DC, MC, V.

Sorrento. Comfortable old hotel built in 1909 to look as authentically Italian as possible. It is on First Hill and overlooks downtown and Elliott Bay. Offers wine tasting and coffee service in the evenings. | 34 rooms, 42 suites. Restaurant, bar, in-room data ports, minibars, many cable TVs, massage, gym, business services, pets allowed. | 900 Madison St. | 206/622–6400 or 800/426–1265 (outside WA) | fax 206/343–6155 | www.hotelsorrento.com | $230–$250, $270–$500 suites | AE, D, DC, MC, V.

VERY EXPENSIVE

Hotel Edgewater. On Elliott Bay, this hotel has views of the Olympic Mountains and passing ferries and barges. | 237 rooms, 4 suites. Restaurant, bar with entertainment, in-room data ports, minibars, room service, cable TV, exercise equipment, bicycles, business services, valet parking (fee). | 2411 Alaskan Way | 206/728–7000 or 800/624–0670 | fax 206/441–4119 | $205–$305, $450–$1250 suites | AE, D, DC, MC, V.

SEATTLE-TACOMA INTERNATIONAL AIRPORT AREA

MAP 8, D4

(Nearby towns also listed: Seattle, Tacoma)

It may seem a bit odd to visitors that the "Seattle-Tacoma" International Airport, called "Sea-Tac" for short, isn't in either city but in a community in-between which has recently incorporated itself as the City of Seatac. Seatac has the largest concentration of hotel accommodations in the state and looks more like a Southern California suburb than a Northwest city. Seattleites usually come here only to catch a plane out of town or to attend a convention. Seatac is becoming the heart and center of the Seattle area's Hispanic population, where you can buy fresh tortillas and pan dulce at neighborhood shops.

Information: Southwest King County Chamber of Commerce | 16400 Southcenter Pkwy, Suite 210, Box 58591, Tukwila, 98188 | 206/575–1633.

Attractions

Sea-Tac International Airport. The parking garage at SEAttle-TAComa International airport is considered a modern architectural masterpiece. It is particularly pleasing from the air, with its tightly curled, snail-shell on and off ramps. | 17801 Pacific Highway S | 206/431–4444 | fax 206/431–5912 | www.portseattle.org | Parking fee, $18/day | Daily.

ON THE CALENDAR

JUNE: *International Festival.* Held at Angle Lake on International Boulevard, just south of the airport, this street fair celebrates the many cultures which make up the Pacific Northwest. | 206/575–1633.

Dining

Anthony's Homeport. Seafood. Overlooking Des Moines Marina, this restaurant is only 15 minutes south of the airport and serves a wide range of seafood delights, including baked salmon and Dungeness crab. | 421 S. 227th St., Des Moines | 206/824–1947 | $15–$25 | AE, MC, V.

Courtyard Café. American/Casual. The windows overlook the lobby at this restaurant located in the Sea-Tac Area Courtyard. The menu includes pastas, salads, pork teriyaki, hamburgers, and steaks. | 16038 W Valley Hwy., Tukwila | 425/255–0300 | Breakfast also available. No lunch | $7–$15 | AE, D, DC, MC, V.

CAR RENTAL TIPS

- ❑ Review auto insurance policy to find out what it covers when you're away from home.
- ❑ Know the local traffic laws.
- ❑ Jot down make, model, color, and license plate number of rental car and carry the information with you.
- ❑ Locate gas tank—make sure gas cap is on and can be opened.
- ❑ Check trunk for spare and jack.
- ❑ Test the ignition—make sure you know how to remove the key.
- ❑ Test the horn, headlights, blinkers, and windshield wipers.

*Excerpted from *Fodor's: How to Pack: Experts Share Their Secrets*

Filiberto's. Italian. The best restaurant in the airport area is this Roman trattoria just south of Hwy. 518. The dishes, whether they're pastas with Roman-style sauces or pizzas from the wood-fired oven, are always good, and the selection of Italian wines is excellent. The mood is friendly and relaxed. A bocce court out back adds another note of authenticity (it is lit to allow playing after dinner). | 14401 Des Moines Way Memorial Way Dr. | 206/248–1944 | Closed Sun.–Mon. | $8–$19 | AE, MC, V.

Gregory's Bar and Grill. American/Casual. Monday through Friday night there is karaoke at this eatery in the Westcoast Sea-Tac Hotel. In addition to the traditional American favorites, the menu includes fish and chips, BBQ ribs, and pastas. | 18220 International Blvd. | 206/246–5535 | $7–$16 | AE, D, DC, MC, V.

Maxi's. Continental. Upscale restaurant in the Doubletree Hotel Seattle Airport. | 18740 Pacific Hwy. | 206/246–8600 | Closed Sun., Mon. No lunch | $20–$30 | AE, D, DC, MC, V.

13 Coins. American/Casual. Across from the airport in the Killroy Airport Center, this restaurant is always open. Your food is prepared in full sight—dishes such as filet mignon, baked halibut, manicotti, and eggs Benedict. Breakfast, lunch, and dinner are available around the clock. This is the sister restaurant to the 13 Coins located in Seattle. | 18000 Pacific Hwy. S | 206/243–9500 | $10–$22 | AE, D, DC, MC, V.

Top of the Inn Restaurant. American/Casual. Mt. Rainier, the Olympic Mountains, and the airport are all within your sight at this revolving restaurant on the 12th floor of the Holiday Inn Sea-Tac. Staff will serve you Northwestern classics such as baked salmon or steak and afterward may even serenade you. On weekends there is live piano music. | 17338 International Blvd. | 206/248–1000 | $9–$15 | AE, D, DC, MC, V.

Tuckwilly's Grill. Steaks. Despite the dining room's plain flavor, the entrées are tasty and presented with flare. The menu includes a range of seafood, steak, and chicken options; the most popular is the cedar plank salmon filet. There is also a sports bar with many TVs. | Embassy Suites Seatac, 15920 W Valley Hwy., Tukwila | 425/227–9406 | Breakfast also available on weekends | $12–$26 | AE, DC, MC, V.

Vic's Broiler. Steaks. At what is described as an "exhibition-cooking bar," chairs line a bar behind which chefs prepare your meals. There is also dining available in a more traditional dining room. The menu includes a range of classic Northwest dishes such as prime rib and salmon, as well as pasta, salad, and burger options. | Best Western Southcenter, 15901 W. Valley Hwy., Tukwila | 425/226–1812 | Breakfast also available | $6–$9 | AE, D, DC, MC, V.

Lodging

Best Western Airport Executel. Business travelers' hotel convenient to everything in the Greater Puget Sound area, shopping malls, and downtown Seattle. | 138 rooms. Restaurant, bar, complimentary Continental breakfast, in-room data ports, cable TV, indoor pool, hot tub, exercise equipment, business services, airport shuttle.Free parking. | 20717 International Blvd., Seattle | 206/878–3300 | fax 206/824–9000 | $69–$129 | AE, D, DC, MC, V.

Best Western Executel. Business travelers' hotel located about 10 mi from the airport and minutes away from area attractions and major corporations. | 116 rooms. Restaurant, bar, in-room data ports, room service, cable TV, pool, hot tub, business services, airport shuttle, free parking, pets allowed (fee). | 31611 20th Ave. S, Federal Way | 253/941–6000 | fax 253/941–9500 | executel@ricochet.net | $99–$179 | AE, D, DC, MC, V.

Best Western Southcenter. Located at exit 1 off I–405, the three-story hotel is less than a mile from the Southcenter Mall and only 15 mi from downtown Seattle. The staff is friendly and accommodating. | 146 rooms. Restaurant, bar, room service, in-room data ports, some minibars, some microwaves, some refrigerators, some in-room hot tubs, cable TV, pool, hot tub, sauna, gym, laundry facilities, business services, airport shuttle, no pets. | 15901 W. Valley Hwy., Tukwila | 425/226–1812 or 800/544–9863 | fax 425/255–7856 | www.bestwestern.com | $109–$125 | AE, D, DC, MC, V.

Clarion Hotel Seatac Airport. Airport hotel that is close to the Southcenter Mall, 15 minutes from downtown Seattle and in close proximity to many local restaurants. | 211 rooms. Restaurant, bar, in-room data ports, some microwaves, some refrigerators, room service, cable TV, indoor pool, hot tub, exercise equipment, gym, laundry facilities, business services, airport shuttle. | 3000 S. 176th, Seattle | 206/242–0200 | fax 206/242–1998 | $109–$119 | AE, D, DC, MC, V.

Comfort Inn. Comfortable travelers' hotel, about 1 mi from the airport. | 176 rooms, 60 suites. Complimentary Continental breakfast, in-room data ports, refrigerators (in suites), cable TV, hot tub, gym, airport shuttle. | 19333 International Blvd., Seattle | 206/878–1100 | fax 206/878–8678 | $65–$95, $79–$109 suites | AE, D, DC, MC, V.

Doubletree Hotel. Luxurious business travelers' and family hotel next to a major shopping mall and close to corporate company headquarters. | 198 rooms. Restaurant, bar, room service, cable TV, pool, playground, business services, free parking. | 205 Strander Blvd., Seattle | 206/246–8220 | fax 206/575–4749 | www.doubletreehotels.com | $79–$134 | AE, D, DC, MC, V.

Doubletree–Seattle Airport. On 28 acres, this large hotel near the airport has views of lakes and mountains. One way to take advantage of the view is to ride the outdoor glass-enclosed elevators. | 850 rooms. 3 restaurants, 2 bars with entertainment, in-room data ports, room service, cable TV, pool, barbershop, beauty salon, hot tub, gym, business services, airport shuttle, parking (fee). | 18740 Pacific Hwy S, Seattle | 206/246–8600 | fax 206/431–8687 | $129–$159 | AE, D, DC, MC, V.

Embassy Suites Seatac. Rooms encircle a large atrium in which you can enjoy your complimentary breakfast (cooked to your specifications) or partake of complimentary evening snacks. Each room has a separate living room and bedroom, with many amenities. The hotel, sitting two blocks south of I–405, is 1 mi from the Southcenter Mall and 4 mi from the airport. | 238 rooms. Restaurant, bar, complimentary breakfast, room service, in-room data ports, microwaves, refrigerators, cable TV, pool, hot tub, sauna, gym, shops, laundry service, business services, airport shuttle, no pets. | 15920 W. Valley Hwy., Tukwila | 425/227–8844 or 800/EMBASSY | www.embassyseatac.com | $139–$179 | AE, D, DC, MC, V.

Hampton Inn Seattle-Southcenter. One mi from the mall and 4 mi from the airport, this four-story hotel is conveniently close to Highway 405. For those desiring outdoor exercise, a jogging trail runs behind the hotel. | 154 rooms. Complimentary Continental breakfast, some microwaves, some refrigerators, cable TV, pool, hot tub, gym, laundry facilities, airport shuttle, no pets. | 7200 S. 156th St., Tukwila | 425/228–5800 or 800/HAMPTON | fax 425/228–6812 | www.hampton-inn.com | $88–$104 | AE, D, DC, MC, V.

Holiday Inn. This hotel offers every amenity and is just across the street from SeaTac Airport. It is fully accessible for the handicapped and disabled. | 260 rooms. Restaurant, 2 bars, in-room data ports, room service, cable TV, indoor pool, hot tub, exercise equipment, gym, laundry facilities, business services, airport shuttle. | 17338 International Blvd., Seattle | 206/248–1000 | fax 206/242–7089 | $79–$129 | AE, D, DC, MC, V.

La Quinta. This 6-story hotel is close to the airport and offers the personal service that is the hallmark of this chain. | 143 rooms. Complimentary Continental breakfast, in-room data ports, cable TV, pool, hot tub, exercise equipment, gym, laundry facilities, business services, airport shuttle, some pets allowed. | 2824 S 188th St., Seattle | 206/241–5211 | fax 206/246–5596 | $79–$129 | AE, D, DC, MC, V.

Marriott Sea-Tac. Big, splashy airport hotel with 21,000-square-ft atrium with trees, plants, totem poles, waterfall. | 459 rooms. Restaurant, bar, in-room data ports, room service, cable TV, indoor pool, hot tub, spa, gym, game room with video games, business services, airport shuttle, free parking, pets allowed (fee). | 3201 S. 176th St., Seattle | 206/241–2000 | fax 206/248–0789 | $79–$159 | AE, D, DC, MC, V.

Quality Inn. Just west of I–5 at exit 156, this hotel is only ½ mile from a golf course and 4 mi from the airport. | 119 rooms. Complimentary Continental breakfast, some microwaves, refrigerators, cable TV, pool, spa, laundry service, business services, airport shuttle, no pets. | 13050 48th Ave. S, Tukwila | 206/241–2200 or 800/205–6941 | fax 206/246–0222 | www.choicehotels.com | $83–$93 | AE, D, DC, MC, V.

Radisson Seattle Airport. A large 2-story hotel near the airport. It is 14 mi south of downtown Seattle. | 308 rooms. Restaurant, bar, in-room data ports, room service, cable TV, pool, exercise equipment, gym, business services, airport shuttle. | 17001 International Blvd., Seattle | 206/244–6000 | fax 206/246–6835 | $109–$159 | AE, D, DC, MC, V.

Sea-Tac Area Courtyard. Located just 1/4 mile from exit 1 off I–405, this hotel is not even a mile from the Southcenter Mall and only 5 mi from the airport. Opened in 1999, this is one of the newest hotels in the area. | 211 rooms, 7 suites. Restaurant, bar, room service, in-room data ports, some minibars, some microwaves, some refrigerators, cable TV, pool, spa, gym, laundry facilities, business services, no pets. | 16038 W. Valley Hwy., Tukwila | 425/255–0300 or 800/321–2211 | fax 425/204–4975 | www.marriott.com | $124–$169 | AE, D, DC, MC, V.

Seattle Airport Hilton. Prize-winning modern hotel in garden setting, with large ballroom and conference center. It's a 30-minute drive to downtown Seattle. | 398 rooms. Restaurant, bar, in-room data ports, room service, cable TV, pool, hot tub, exercise equipment, business services, pets allowed, laundry facilities, airport shuttle, parking (fee). | 17620 International Blvd., Seattle | 206/244–4800 | fax 206/248–4495 | debra_noonan@hilton.com | www.hilton.com | $119–$179 | AE, D, DC, MC, V.

Travelodge. Airport hotel. | 106 rooms. In-room data ports, cable TV, sauna, laundry facilities, business services, airport shuttle, free parking. | 2900 S. 192nd St., Seattle | 206/241–9292 | fax 206/242–0681 | $48–$78 | AE, D, DC, MC, V.

Westcoast Sea-Tac Hotel. This hotel usually has a special "park and fly" deal—if you spend a night or two (depending on how long you're planning to be gone), you can park your car for free while you're away, and take the hotel shuttle to the terminal and back. The hotel itself is convenient to shopping and restaurants and all rooms have Nintendo systems. | 146 rooms. Restaurant, bar, room service, cable TV, some refrigerators, pool, hot tub, gym, business services, airport shuttle, pets allowed, free parking. | 18220 International Blvd., Seattle | 206/246–5535 or 800/426–0670 | fax 206/246–9733 | $89–$130 | AE, D, DC, MC, V.

SEDRO WOOLLEY

MAP 8, D2

(Nearby towns also listed: Anacortes, Bellingham, Mount Vernon)

Sedro Woolley (pronounced "ceedro wooley"), a former logging and steel-mill town, is an anomaly among Washington's twin cites. Instead of carrying on a rivalry (which in other parts of Washington, among other pairs of cities, has lasted for more than a hundred years), the neighboring cities of Sedro and Woolley joined to form one city, which (unlike another Northwest merger, that among the neighboring towns of New Whatcom and Fairhaven to form Bellingham) has actually worked out well. Today it's difficult to tell which part of the town used be Sedro and which once was Woolley, and that's just how it should be. That said, there isn't much else to say about Sedro Woolley which, in all fairness, is rather nondescript. But there is a bit of an old downtown and a smattering of Tarheel culture.

Sedro Woolley is also the headquarters for the North Cascades National Park, but if you don't slow down to a crawl as you enter the town, you're liable to miss it. Besides, even though Sedro Woolley advertises itself as a gateway to the North Cascades, it'll take you a while to get to either the mountains or the park. But you get a bonus: the beautiful Skagit Valley. As the mountains grow taller and the valley narrows, the river gets wilder, the trees get taller, and soon you're in an alpine landscape so beautiful it rivals anything the European Alps have to offer.

Information: Sedro-Woolley Chamber of Commerce | 714-B Metcalf St., Sedro Woolley, 98284 | 360/835–1582 or 888/225–8365 | fax 360/855–1582 | sedro-woolley.com.

Attractions

Clear Lake. Popular activities at this lake are swimming, hiking, camping, boating, fishing, and windsurfing. | Rte. 9 S | Free | Daily.

Lake Whatcom Railway. Eleven mi north of Sedro Woolley, you can ride this short-ride steam railway through the woods. | Rte. 9, in Wickersham | 360/595–2218 | $10 | Call for hours.

Dining

Ferry Street Bar and Grill. American/Casual. This popular local eatery in the historic downtown area serves a variety of entrées such as steaks, ribs, and pastas, not to mention the hand-tossed pizzas and calzones. Everything is homemade here, including the bread. | 208 Ferry St. | 360/855–2210 | Closed Sun. | $7–$15 | AE, D, MC, V.

Greenside Grill. Contemporary. A two-level family dining room with windows offering panoramic views of a golf course. Known for steak and seafood. Kids' menu. Sun. brunch. No smoking. | 1965 Woodcock | 360/683–3331 | Breakfast also available | $11–$19 | MC, V.

THE TARHEELS

The Tarheels are definitely one of the upper Skagit Valley's natural assets. Mountaineers from North Carolina first moved to Skagit County shortly after the turn of the 20th century, and they kept coming, right through the Great Depression, to work in the woods. For a while they formed a subculture of their own, based on self-sufficiency, neighborliness, great cooking, and a distrust of outsiders. Their descendants still proudly call themselves "Tarheels." They're great people if you get on the right side of them, and a bit difficult if you don't. A group of them once became upset at a State Patrol trooper who set up a speed trap on the main road into the mountains. They bided their time till he fell asleep at the wheel, waiting for speeders; then they took the wheels off his cars and sped by, honking their horns. The trooper, rumor had it, asked for a transfer. And then there was the time a group of bikers invaded a favorite Tarheel tavern and picked a fight. A couple of locals got into their logging trucks and drove back and forth over the motorbikes parked outside. That caused a riot that took sheriff's deputies, state troopers, plus police officers from several cities to quell. But the bikers haven't been back.

The Tarheels have also been great at making moonshine. Great moonshine. The reason, a Skagit county commissioner once said apologetically, is that they can't drink that awful store-bought stuff. Their favorite hangout in Sedro Woolley is the Iron Skillet cafe (360/855–0080), which serves a darn good dish of biscuits and gravy.

Moon Palace. Chinese. Basic country Chinese restaurant with Asian decor. Known for Cantonese and Mandarin dishes. Lunch specials. Sunday buffet. | 323 E. Washington | 360/683–6898 | Closed Mon. | $5–$12 | AE, D, MC, V.

Paradise. Contemporary. Fern bars are alive and well in Sequim, perhaps because so many Californians retire here. This place is a model of the genre, with many plants and etched-glass booth dividers. Known for steak, seafood, pasta. | 703 N. Sequim Ave. | 360/683–1977 | Closed Mon. | $8–$25 | AE, D, MC, V.

Three Crabs. Contemporary. This is a pleasant waterfront restaurant. The food alone would not bring you back, but the great views and the friendly ambience might. Stick to the simple dishes, such as fresh Dungeness crab, and you'll do just fine. Kids' menu. | 11 Three Crabs Rd. | 360/683–4264 | $10–$20 | MC, V.

Lodging

Skagit Motel. Basic but comfortable family motel. | 46 rooms. Some kitchenettes, cable TV, no-smoking rooms, pets allowed. | 1977 Rte. 20 | 360/856–6001 | $45–$50 | AE, D, DC, MC, V.

South Bay Bed and Breakfast. Standing above Lake Whatcom, 20 mi north of Sedro Woolley and 20 mi southeast of Bellingham, this Craftsman-style house is part of a nature lover's paradise. Not only are there exquisite views of the lake and mountains, the surrounding undeveloped park reserves create a secluded environment that is bursting with wildlife. Of the five tastefully furnished rooms, four have fireplaces and hot tubs. All have lake views. | 5 rooms. Complimentary breakfast, no air-conditioning, some in-room hot tubs, no room phones, no TV, beach, boating, fishing, bicycles, no pets, no smoking. | 4095 S. Bay Dr. | 360/595–2086 or 877/595–2086 | fax 360/595–1043 | southbay@gte.net | www.southbaybb.com | $135–$150 | MC, V.

SEKIU

MAP 8, A2

(Nearby town also listed: Port Angeles)

Sekiu is a fishing village on a shore where Native Americans have fished for at least 3,000 years. The modern village got its start in 1870, with a salmon cannery. In the early 1900s, logging became a mainstay of the local economy. Both industries shut down when the resources became overexploited. Sekiu had a short-lived career as a party boat village but more recently, as with towns and villages in similar straits, it has begun to sell the natural beauty of its surroundings to visitors. While salmon have become scarce, the Sekiu River still has fall runs of cutthroat trout and steelhead. The Sekiu jetty is popular with sports divers.

Information: **Clallam Bay/Sekiu Chamber of Commerce,** | Box 355, Clallam Bay, 98326 | 360/963–2339. | sekiu.com/.

Attractions

Clallam Bay. There are two waterfront parks on the sites of Indian fishing villages: Clallam Bay Spit is 33 acres and has no camping. It is popular with fishermen, scuba divers, and beachcombers. Pillar Point Fishing Camp to the east is a 4-acre park with campsites and a boat ramp. Dress warmly: "Pysht" (as in Pysht Bay) is an S'Klallam term meaning "where the wind blows from all directions." | Juan de Fuca Strait, off Hwy. 112 at Clallum Bay and Pysht Bay | Daily.

ON THE CALENDAR

JULY: ***Clallam Bay/Sekiu Fun Days.*** Family festival with a variety of foods, crafts, races, music, and fireworks. | 360/963–2339.

Dining

Breakwater Restaurant. Seafood. Claiming to be the most northwesterly dining establishment in the continental United States, this restaurant overlooks the Strait of Juan de Fuca. Seafood is the specialty here, served by a friendly and accommodating staff. Chicken dishes, burgers, and steaks fill out the menu. | Hwy. 112, Clallam Bay | 360/963–2428 | Breakfast also available | $9–$22 | MC, V.

Lodging

Winter Summer Inn Bed and Breakfast. Pieces from local artists adorn many of the walls in this late 1800s home, the oldest in the community. Rooms are filled with American antiques; one room has a private deck, a fireplace, and a billiard table. The private deck and house deck overlook Clallam Bay and the Strait of Juan de Fuca. | 3 rooms. Complimentary breakfast, no air-conditioning, some kitchenettes, some microwaves, some refrigerators, some room phones, no TV in some rooms, TV in common area, library, no pets, no smoking. | 16651 Hwy. 112, Clallam Bay | 360/963–2264 | kcw@olypen.com | www.northolympic.com/winters | $65–$85 | No credit cards.

SEQUIM

MAP 8, C3

(Nearby towns also listed: Neah Bay, Port Angeles, Port Townsend)

Sequim (pronounced "skwim") is a pleasant retirement town upland from Juan de Fuca Strait. The town lies in the rain shadow of the Olympic Mountains and likes to gloat about the fact that it gets less rain—about 16 inches—than almost everyone else in western Washington. Lavender flourishes because of the warm weather and is raised commercially in local fields.

Information: **Sequim–Dungeness Chamber of Commerce** | 1192 E. Washington St., Box 907, Sequim, 98382 | 360/683–6197 or 800/737–8462 | fax 360/683–6349 | cityofsequim.com/.

Attractions

Dungeness Recreation Area. A county park on the Juan de Fuca Strait with campsites at the base of Dungeness Spit, which is a National Wildlife Refuge with more than 250 species of birds. The protected bay is a major stopover point for migrating birds in autumn and spring. | 554 Voice of America W | 360/683–5847 | www.wa.gov/clallam | Free | Daily.

Jamestown S'Klallam Village. This is an Indian village, not a reservation, on the beach north of Sequim, although the site has been occupied by S'Klallams for thousands of years. The S'Klallams had been driven out by early settlers and relocated to the Skokomish Reservation on the Hood Canal, but in 1874, tribal leader James Balch, followed by some 130 S'Klallam, regained the site by paying hard cash for it. The S'Klallam have lived here ever since. A gallery sells native arts and crafts. | Off U.S. 101 N | Free | Daily.

Olympic Game Farm. This is a retirement home for four-legged Hollywood stars, as well as a training facility for animals aspiring to be movie stars. | 1423 Ward Rd. | 360/683–4295 | fax 360/681–4443 or 800/778–4295 | www.olygamefarm.com | $8 | Daily 9–4.

Sequim Bay State Park. This is an inlet, 4 mi southwest of Sequim, on Sequim Bay, protected by a sand spit. The woodsy park has picnic tables, campsites, hiking trails, tennis courts, and a boat ramp. | Off U.S. 101 | 360/683–4235 | www.parks.wa.gov | Free, camping $12–$17 | Daily 8–dusk.

ON THE CALENDAR

MAY: ***Irrigation Festival.*** A more-than-a-century-old celebration of the lack of rain in this town lying in the rain shadow of the Olympic Mountains. Antique car show, logging demonstrations, arts and crafts, dancing, parade, live music, and more. | 360/683-6197.

JULY: ***Celebrate Lavender Festival.*** Held on the second weekend of July, Sequim's celebration of lavender includes open tours of lavender farms, a street fair where vendors sell lavender crafts and foods, and live entertainment. | 360/683-5774.

Dining

Marina Restaurant. American/Casual. With tremendous views of John Wayne Marina and Sequim Bay, this family restaurant is a fun place to watch the ships placidly bob by. The menu includes seafood, pasta, salads, and sandwiches, but the emphasis is on steak, especially prime rib, which is served on Saturday night. | 2577 W. Sequim Bay Rd. | 360/681-0577 | Winter closed Tues. | $11-$18 | AE, D, MC, V.

Oak Table Café. American/Casual. Focusing primarily on breakfast dishes, this restaurant gives an inventive flair to traditional items like pancakes, waffles, and eggs. "Eggs Nicole," for instance, is a medley of sautéed mushrooms, spinach, onions, and scrambled eggs served over an open face croissant and covered with Hollandaise sauce. Although breakfast is dished up all day, there is also a lunch menu including burgers, salads, and sandwiches. | 292 W. Bell St. | 360/683-2179 | Breakfast also available. No dinner | $5.75-$9 | AE, D, MC, V.

Petals Garden Café. Contemporary. This restaurant at Cedarbrook Herb farm, overlooking Sequim and the Strait of Juan de Fuca, draws much of its inspiration from local produce. Soups, salads, and sandwiches dominate the lunch menu, while entrées such as pan-seared duck breast with thyme infused honey fill out the dinner menu. | 1345 S. Sequim Ave. | 360/683-4541 | No dinner Sun.-Tues. | $16-$23 | MC, V.

Lodging

Dungeness Panorama Bed and Breakfast. As you would expect from its name, unbeatable views of the Olympic Mountains, the strait, and bay encircle this B&B. The furnishings are built around a French provincial theme, reflecting the background of the proprietors. The bay is only a short walk from the backyard. Each suite has its own fireplace and deck overlooking the water. | 2 suites. Complimentary breakfast, room service, kitchenettes, microwaves, refrigerators, in-room VCRs (and movies), no pets, no kids under 12, no smoking. | 630 Marine Dr. | 360/683-4503 | info@awaterview.com | www.awaterview.com | $95-$125 | No credit cards.

Econo Lodge. Plain but comfortable family motel that features a mini-golf course. | 43 rooms. Complimentary Continental breakfast, microwaves, refrigerators, cable TV, laundry facilities, business services. | 801 E. Washington St. | 360/683-7113 | fax 360/683-7343 | $79-$125 | AE, D, DC, MC, V.

Greywolf. Snug B&B in a Northwest farmhouse with theme-oriented rooms enhanced by antiques. Located on a 5-acre hilltop, with views of Dungeness Valley and Sequim Bay. | 5 rooms. Picnic area, complimentary breakfast and afternoon snacks, no air-conditioning, some room phones, cable TV, some VCRs, hot tub, exercise equipment, business services, no kids under 12, no smoking. | 395 Keeler Rd. | 360/683-5889 or 800/914-9653 | fax 360/683-1487 | grywolf@olypen.com | www.greywolfinn.com | $75-$125 | AE, D, MC, V.

Groveland Cottage. A country inn with a cozy library/sitting room. A Victorian farmhouse built in 1886, this B&B features stained glass windows, and a mix of period furnishings and modern pieces. | 4 rooms, 1 cottage. Picnic area, complimentary breakfast, no air-conditioning, cable TV, VCRs (movies), some in-room hot tubs, kitchen in cottage, library, business services, pets allowed, no kids under 12, no smoking. | 4861 Sequim-Dungeness Way, Dungeness | 360/683-3565 or 800/879-8859 (reservations) | fax 360/683-5181 | www.sequimvalley.com | $80-$110 | AE, D, MC, V.

Sequim Bay Lodge. Comfortable lodge just off of the highway, near a wooded area. | 54 rooms (1 with shower only). Picnic area, complimentary Continental breakfast, no air-conditioning in some rooms, refrigerators (in suites), cable TV, pool, putting green, business services, pets allowed (fee). | 268522 U.S. 101 | 360/683-0691 | fax 360/683-3748 | $79-$91 | AE, D, DC, MC, V.

Toad Hall Bed and Breakfast. Inspiring views of the Olympic Mountains can be seen from each of the bedrooms' windows. Encircling the B&B are over 150 lavender plants, plus many gardens and ponds. Murals depicting Kenneth Graham's tale "Wind in the Willows" ornament many walls. | 3 rooms. Complimentary breakfast, refrigerators, some in-room hot tubs, cable TV, in-room VCRs, no room phones, pond, no pets, no kids under 16, no smoking. | 12 Jesslyn Ln. | 360/681–2534 | toadhall@olympus.net | www.toadhallbandb.com | $95–$140 | MC, V.

SHELTON

MAP 8, C5

(Nearby town also listed: Olympia)

Shelton, the county seat of Mason County, is a lumber town with an interesting 1920s-style downtown. After decades of arguing with local oyster growers over the damage caused by the effluent from its pulp mill, Shelton is now, with the pulp mill shut down, turning into the regional oyster capital of southern Puget Sound. Shelton is one of the few places where you can taste the native Olympia oyster and the immigrant Pacific oyster side by side and compare their taste. Mason County, incidentally, has had the odd distinction of having no building codes, which is why you can see some truly odd structures rising from local beaches and waterfront bluffs.

Information: Shelton-Mason County Chamber of Commerce | 221 W. Railroad, Box 2389, Shelton, 98584 | 800/576–2021 | www.sheltonchamber.org.

Attractions

Lake Cushman State Park. A campground on a lake popular with landlocked kokanee salmon, cutthroat, and rainbow trout. There's also a landlocked king salmon run (the only one known to exist). | Rte. 106 to U.S. 101 N to Hoodsport, then northwest via Lake Cushman Rd. | 360/877–5491 | www.parks.wa.gov | Free | Apr.–Nov. daily.

Twanoh State Park. A popular spot on the south side of lower Hood Canal for boating and waterskiing. | Hwy. 106 E, off U.S. 101 | 360/275–2222 | www.parks.wa.gov | Free | Daily 8–dusk.

ON THE CALENDAR

APR.: *Shellfish Shindig.* A fun event held at Hood Canal north of Shelton where state park rangers teach novices how to dig clams. Also a campfire program and beach walks. | 360/796–4415.

MAY: *Old Timers' Historical Fair and Exhibition.* A celebration of the tiny Olympic Mountains community of Matlock's timber-cutting heritage, with draft horses, antique machines and motors, demonstrations of the blacksmith's art, plus crafts, antiques, and fun things to do for the kids. West of Shelton. | 800/576–2021.

MAY–JUNE: *Mason County Forest Festival.* Logging demonstrations, 10K run, carnival, parades, timberbeasts, entertainment, and hearty food. | 800/576–2021.

Dining

Nita's Restaurant and Gallery. American. Begun in 1962, this is a favorite spot among residents who enjoy the homemade soups, milkshakes, and pies. Try the wild blackberry pie, it's especially popular. In addition to being a great cook, Nita is a patron of the arts; photographs and paintings from local artists ornament the walls. | 325 Railroad Ave. | 360/426–6143 | Breakfast also available. No dinner | $4–$7 | No credit cards.

Xinh's Clam and Oyster House. Seafood. This small, popular seafood restaurant does a great job showing off the best of the Olympic Peninsula's shellfish and fish. Little wonder, since the place is backed by Taylor United Inc., a local shellfish company. The fish is enhanced by intriguing Asian flavors. | 221 W. Railroad Ave., Suite D | 360/427–8709 | Closed Sun.–Mon. No lunch Tue.–Sat. | $10–$20 | MC, V.

Lodging

Shelton Inn Motel. Six blocks west of Hwy. 3, this two-story motel is in the middle of town, surrounded by shops. | 30 rooms. Restaurant, cable TV, some no-smoking rooms, pool, pets allowed (fee). | 628 W. Railroad Ave. | 360/426–4468 | fax 360/426–7927 | $52–$54 | AE, MC, V.

Shelton's Super 8 Motel. Located on Shelton's upcoming eastern side, this motel stands near new restaurants and new shops. | 38 rooms. Refrigerators, cable TV, pets allowed (fee), no smoking. | 2943 Northview Circle | 360/426–1654 or 800/800–8000 | fax 360/426–1847 | $60–$70 | AE, D, DC, MC, V.

SILVERDALE

MAP 8, D4

(Nearby town also listed: Bremerton)

Silverdale is an unincorporated community in the heart of the Kitsap Peninsula that has seen major developments especially in the form of shopping malls since the U.S. Navy developed its Trident submarine base on nearby Hood Canal. Silverdale has a pretty waterfront on Dyes Inlet, with grand views of the Olympic and Cascade Mountains.

Information: **Silverdale Chamber of Commerce** | 3100 Bucklin Hill Rd., Suite 108, Box 1218, Silverdale, 98383 | 360/692–6800 | fax 360/692–1370 | silverdalechamber.com.

Attractions

Old Town Silverdale. This historic neighborhood adjacent to Waterfront Park is home to a covey of small shops and cafés. | Byron St.

ON THE CALENDAR

JULY: ***Whaling Days.*** Fireworks mark the finale of this weekend-long celebration that also includes a parade, musical performances, and food and craft vendors. The festivities are held at Waterfront Park in Old Town during the last full weekend in July. | 360/692–1109.

Dining

Silver City Brewing Company. American. Showcasing six house brews, two or three of which change seasonally, the brewery serves pub fare such as burgers, pizzas, pastas, and gumbo. The prime rib that is offered on weekends is a particular favorite. The wooden tables and painted chairs will make you forget the brewery's adjacent to a mall. | 2799 N.W. Myhre Rd. | 360/698–5879 | $7–$17 | AE, DC, MC, V.

Lodging

Silverdale on the Bay Hotel. Sitting directly on Dyes Inlet, the hotel has many rooms with views of the water, some of which also have private balconies and fireplaces. The numerous amenities of this 1986 hotel make it a perfect spot for getaways. | 150 rooms. Restaurant, bar, in-room data ports, some minibars, cable TV, pool, hot tub, sauna, tennis court, gym, business services, no pets. | 3073 Bucklin Hill Rd. | 360/698–1000 or 800/544–9799 | fax 360/692–0932 | www.westcoasthotels.com | $95–$115 | AE, D, DC, MC, V.

SKYKOMISH

MAP 8, F4

(Nearby town also listed: Index)

Skykomish is a mountain and railroad village at the western end of the Cascades Tunnel, in a very dramatic setting, with a river roaring by and jagged peaks rising to the south and north. It was born in 1888, when the Great Northern surveyed a route across the mountains and prospectors and miners rushed in. Skykomish has not changed much since the tunnel was completed in the 1920s. Today, Skykomish is a jumping-off place for the North Cascades and the National Forest's Alpine Lakes Wilderness region. U.S. 2 crosses the Cascade crest on Stevens Pass (4,061 feet) east of the village.

Information: **Skykomish Chamber of Commerce** | 333 River Drive E, Box 397, Skykomish, 98288 | 360/677–2261 | www.eskimo.com/~bobcast/sky.html.

Attractions

Stevens Pass Ski Area. A very snowy ski area (avalanche danger and periodic closures in winter) with elevations ranging from 3,800 to 5,800 feet;a vertical drop of 1,800 feet; and 10 chair lifts. Very popular; limited parking area; try to get there early on sunny winter weekends or you may be turned away. | U.S. 2 | 206/973–2441.

ON THE CALENDAR

JULY: ***Tunnel Days.*** When the railroad men return from their work on the trains, the town celebrates with a day-long festival (usually the last Saturday in July), including picnics and parades. | 360/677–2261.

Dining

Skykomish Hotel Restaurant. American. Sitting with a full view of the railroad tracks, you can muse over the possibility of spying a ghost. The most popular dish on the menu is the meatloaf. | 102 Railroad Ave. E | 360/677–0309 | Breakfast also available | $5–$9 | No credit cards.

Lodging

Skykomish Hotel. Once a hotel for railroad crews, this rustic lodging sits directly on the railroad tracks. As the fog rolls in, you might feel a slight chill; be warned the hotel is said to be the residence of a ghost, Mary, who was murdered in room 32 in 1920. | 22 rooms. Restaurant, no air-conditioning, cable TV, no room phones, pets allowed. | 102 Railroad Ave. E, | 360/677–0309 | $35 | No credit cards.

SNOHOMISH

MAP 8, E3

(Nearby towns also listed: Everett, Marysville)

Snohomish began life in 1859 in typical Northwest fashion, with a shack in the woods. It didn't really come alive until one E. C. Ferguson built a house in Steilacoom, took it apart, and had it sent by boat upsound and upriver, to be reassembled as a store and hotel on the townsite. Snohomish soon became the county seat and a major riverboat landing. In 1896, it lost the county seat to Everett and life began to slow down when the railroad made Everett the major local port and industrial center. But that's all for the better, because it made it easy for Snohomish to keep its old downtown and its charm. Today, Snohomish is a quiet town of tree-shaded streets, which bills itself as the "Antique Capital of the Northwest," and with good reason, for it has more than its share of antiques emporiums. Some of them are even listed on the National Register of Historic Buildings.

Information: **Snohomish Chamber of Commerce** | 127 Ave. A, Box 135, Snohomish, 98290 | 360/568–2526 | www.cityofsnohomish.com.

Attractions

Blackman Historic Museum. This 1878 Victorian era home is filled with period antiques. | 118 Ave. B | 360/568–5235 | $2 | Mar.–Dec., Fri.–Sun. noon–4.

Mt. Baker–Snoqualmie National Forest. A vast region covering much of the North Cascades. Hiking, backpacking, fishing, hunting, mountain climbing, picnicking, camping are popular activities. | 21905 64th Ave. W, Mountlake Terrace | 800/627–0062 | fax 425/744–3255 | www.fs.fed.us/r6/mbs | $3 | Daily.

Star Center Antique Mall. One of the best places in Washington to pick up true antiques. | 829 2nd St. | 360/568–2131 | fax 360/568–1191 | www.myantiquemall.com | Free | Daily.

ON THE CALENDAR

JULY: ***Kla Ha Ya Days Festival.*** Held on the third weekend in July at the Harvey Airfield and in downtown Snohomish, this festival includes a car show, carnival rides, fireworks display, food vendors, and numerous contests. | 360/568–4084.

Lodging

Hannah's Garden Inn. This turn-of-the-20th-century brick mansion, designed by Kirkland Cutter, sits overlooking the city on South Hill on ½ acre of landscaped lawns and gardens. The rooms, which are painted according to the Victorian theme, are filled with antique dressers, commodes, and overstuffed chairs. | 5 rooms. Complimentary breakfast, no room phones, TV in common area, no pets, no smoking. | 820 W. 7th Ave. | 509/747–6235 | fax 509/747–8511 | info@hannahsgardeninn.com | www.hannahsgardeninn.com | $85–$125 | AE, D, MC, V.

Snohomish Grand Valley Bed and Breakfast. This country Victorian home overlooks the Snohomish valley. The comfortable rooms are decorated with antiques. Outside are large gardens and inside there is a fireplace in the living room. | 2 rooms. Complimentary breakfast, cable TV, no-smoking rooms, some pets allowed. | 88816 E. Lowell Larimer Rd., Snohomish | 360/568–8854 | fax 360/568–1919 | $75–125 | MC, V.

Susan's Surrey House. Atop a hill overlooking the town, the Queen Anne Victorian is encircled by lavish gardens that lend it a romantic air, something complemented by the tasteful selection of antiques filling each room. In the gardens you can relax on chairs, benches, or swings under the umbrage of century-old apple trees. | 2 rooms. Complimentary breakfast, pool, no pets, no kids under 12, no smoking. | 425 9th St. | 360/568–7081 | www.surreyhouse.com | $110 | MC, V.

SNOQUALMIE

MAP 8, E4

(Nearby town also listed: Issaquah)

Snoqualmie is a former railroad town that caters to weekend trippers. The 270-ft Snoqualmie Falls are about a mile downriver and can be viewed from a roadside overlook. Snoqualmie was, with North Bend, one of the sites of the TV series *Twin Peaks.*

The word "Snoqualmie" comes from the name of the native people once occupying this beautiful valley. It translates as "people of the moon," and indeed, the valley, surrounded by snow-capped peaks, is especially beautiful in the light of a full moon.

Information: **Upper Snoqualmie Valley Chamber of Commerce** | Box 357, North Bend, 98065 | 425/888–4440 | www.snovalley.org. **East King County Convention and Visitors Bureau** | 520 112th Ave. NE, Bellevue, 98004-5503 | 425/455–1962 | eastkingcounty.org.

Attractions

★ **Snoqualmie Falls.** The 268-ft-high Snoqualmie Falls are about a mile downriver and can be viewed from a roadside overlook on the south side of Fall City/Snoqualmie Road (Rte. 202). | Rte. 202 | Free | Daily.

Snoqualmie Valley Railroad. Beginning at the landmark Snoqualmie Depot, which has a railway museum, vintage cars from the 1910s carry you through woods and pastureland on a

50-minute trip to North Bend and back to Snoqualmie. | Snoqualmie Depot. 38625 SE King St., at Hwy. 202 | 425/888–3030 | www.trainmuseum.org | $7 | May–Sept., weekends; Oct. Sun. only; on the hour 11–4 from Snoqualmie; on the ½ hour from North Bend 11:30–3:30.

ON THE CALENDAR

AUG.: ***Snoqualmie Days.*** The first weekend in August is when Snoqualmie celebrates its heritage with carnival rides, a parade, dances, and live music. | 425/888–0021.

Dining

Adair's on the Green. American/Casual. Sitting with views of the 9th and 18th holes of Mount Si golf course, and beautiful Mt. Si, this restaurant serves burgers, hot and cold sandwiches, soups, and salads. Try the clam chowder. | 9010 Boalch Ave. SE | 425/888–2150 | Breakfast also available | $4.75–$8.75 | AE, MC, V.

Salish Lodge and Spa Dining Room. American. The Salish now appears to cater mostly to out-of-state visitors and wedding parties. The five-course country breakfast is a popular favorite. For dinner, there is a large menu offering items such as lamb pot-au-feu, pan-seared striped bass, and grilled beef tenderloin. Window seats have views of the falls, or sit by the fireplace. Open-air dining. Kids' menu. | 6501 Railroad Ave. | 425/888–2556 | Breakfast also available | $26–$32 | AE, D, DC, MC, V.

Lodging

★ **Kimball Creek Inn.** Secluded on a quiet country road, the inn (formerly the Old Honey Farm Inn) sits on 4 acres of meadows through which Kimball Creek runs. The rooms of this contemporary, New England–style house are appointed with antiques and a variety of collectibles. The inn is near Snoqualmie Falls and has wonderful views of Mt. Si. | 10 rooms. Complimentary breakfast, no air-conditioning, some in-room hot tubs, cable TV no room phones, pets allowed, no smoking. | 9050 384th Ave. SE | 425/888–9399 | $79–$155 | MC, V.

Salish Lodge and Spa. It's the location that makes this lodge, which was used in filming the TV series *Twin Peaks,* at the crest of spectacular 268-ft Snoqualmie Falls, special. The lodge has the occasional antique; most rooms have a view of the Snoqualmie Valley, a few have views of the river, and even fewer have a view of the falls. | 87 rooms. 2 Restaurants (*see* Salish Lodge and Spa Dining Room), bar, in-room data ports, minibars, refrigerators, room service, in-room hot tubs, cable TV, in-room VCRs, spa, gym, cross-country and downhill skiing, library, business services, some pets allowed (fee). | 6501 Railroad Ave., | 425/888–2556 or 800/826–6124 | fax 425/888–2533 | www.salishlodge.com | $249–$999 | AE, D, DC, MC, V.

SOAP LAKE

MAP 8, H4

(Nearby towns also listed: Coulee Dam, Ephrata)

The lake, at the southern end of the Grand Coulee where it opens to the Quincy Basin, has water high in dissolved carbonates, sulfates, and chlorides. Even though the lake has long been famous for its mineral waters and therapeutic mud baths, this small town has never quite succeeded as a resort—perhaps because the miraculous waters have been heavily diluted by irrigation waters. But agriculture is so much more profitable anyway, and many other beautiful recreation areas are nearby.

Sun Lakes State Park, up the Grand Coulee from Soap Lake, has several lakes with numerous campsites and hiking trails. Barrow's Goldeneye ducks nest in the basalt cliffs above Lake Lenore, and the lava cast of an ancient rhino was found in the cliffs above Blue Lake.

Information: Soap Lake Chamber of Commerce | 300 N. Daisy, Box 433, Soap Lake, 98851 | 509/246–1821 | www.soaplakecoc.org.

ON THE CALENDAR

JULY: ***Great Canoe Race.*** Marathon and relay teams follow the chain of lakes for 17½ mi in the bottom of Grand Coulee and compete for trophies. | 509/246–1821.

Dining

Don's. Steak. Popular steak house (with some Greek specialties as well) with a dark, almost gloomy interior. | 14 Canna | 509/246–1217 | No lunch Sat. | $10–$35 | MC, V.

Lodging

Inn at Soap Lake. Built in 1905 as a stable and blacksmith shop, this beachside structure was converted to an inn in 1915. Each room contains a soaking tub in which to enjoy Soap Lake's natural mineral water. Floral patterns dominate most rooms which are appointed with contemporary furnishings and modern amenities. | 20 rooms, 8 cottages. Picnic area, kitchenettes, microwaves, refrigerators, some in-room hot tubs, cable TV, massage, beach, no pets, no smoking. | 226 Main Ave. E | 509/246–1132 or 800/557–8514 | fax 509/246–1132 | soaplkinn@qwksilver.com | www.innsoaplake.com | $55–$85 | AE, D, MC, V.

Notaras Lodge. The rooms at this well-known three-building lodge on the shores of Soap Lake are individually decorated. Water from the lake is piped into the bathrooms (bring lots of room freshener). | 14 rooms. Restaurant, picnic area, microwaves, refrigerators, some in-room hot tubs, cable TV, pets allowed (fee). | 231 Main St. | 509/246–0462 | fax 509/246–1054 | $65–$125 | MC, V.

SOUTH BEND

MAP 8, B6

(Nearby towns also listed: Aberdeen, Westport)

The word "funky" is often used to describe odd little towns and villages, but it fits the Willapa River town of South Bend perfectly. South Bend has an interesting, though rather eclectic, riverfront, with restaurants and other buildings on pilings above the banks, and with parks that allow access to the water. But what you may notice most are the piles and piles of oyster shells, for this is the self-styled "Oyster Capital of the World." You can buy oysters—in the shell, shucked, or smoked—everywhere, even at the local gas stations.

The downtown business district, crowded onto a narrow shelf between the river and a hill, has many false-front 19th- and early 20th-century shops; the steep slopes above the river are densely packed with homes and cottages. The stately Pacific County courthouse (1910–11) towers above all this with its colorful glass dome and murals depicting events from local history.

As many of the shuckers and workers in local oyster processing plants are recent Southeast Asian immigrants, South Bend has a lively ethnic subculture.

Watch your speed as you travel U.S. 101 in Pacific County: State patrol cars hide above road cuts and in other hard-to-detect places. The short stretch of highway between South Bend and Raymond is a locally notorious speed trap.

Information: Raymond Chamber of Commerce and Visitor Center | 524 N 3rd St., Raymond, 98577 | 360/942–5419. | kwol.com/cityguides/southbend.html.

Attractions

Pacific County Historical Society Museum. The history of the region, its logging and fishing industry, early communities, and Native American habitation are illustrated with artifacts and interpretive displays. The museum is located at mile post 54 on Highway 101. | 1008 W. Robert Bush Dr. | 360/875–5224 | Free | Daily 11–4.

ON THE CALENDAR

SEPT.: ***Come and Play on Labor Day.*** Family-oriented event with parade, kids' activities, fireworks, vendors, barbecue, duck race, pole walk, and arts and crafts. | 360/942–5419.

Dining

Gardner's Restaurant. American/Casual. From your table you can enjoy not only the variety of steaks, seafoods, and pastas served here, but also views of the Willapa River. Especially popular among the local patrons are the oysters and the seafood fettucine. | 702 W. Robert Bush Dr. (Hwy. 101) | 360/875–4150 | Breakfast also available | $8–$20 | AE, D, DC, MC, V.

Lodging

Maring's Courthouse Bed and Breakfast. Perched above Willapa River, just five blocks from Highway 101, this B&B was originally built as a Baptist church in 1892. The rooms are large and each has a beautiful view either of the river or of the gardens. Antique furnishings fill the rooms. | 3 rooms. Complimentary breakfast, cable TV, no pets, no smoking. | 602 W. 2nd St., | 360/875–6519 or 800/875–6519 | fax 360/875–5808 | maringbb@willapabay.org | willapabay.org/~maringbb | $65 | AE, MC, V.

SPOKANE

MAP 8, K4

(Nearby town also listed: Cheney)

Spokane (pronounced "spo-CAN," not "spo-cane"), Washington's second largest city, takes its name from the local Spokan tribe of Salish Indians. It translates as "Children of the Sun," a fitting name for this sunny city.

Spokane is a city of flowers and trees, of public gardens, parks, and museums. Known as the "Capital of the Inland Empire," Spokane is the cultural and financial center of the inland Northwest.

Spokane began in ancient times as a native village at the roaring falls, where each autumn salmon ascended in great numbers. American settlers built a sawmill at the falls in 1873; several railroads arrived after 1881; and Spokane soon became the transportation hub of eastern Washington. Until they were cleared away for the 1974 World's Fair, bridges and railroad trestles hid the falls from view. Today, they form the heart of downtown's Riverfront Park.

The city rises from the falls in a series of broad terraces to the rim of the valley, as an open bowl that allows maximum access to the sun.

In 1885 Spokane built the first hydroelectric plant west of the Mississippi; downtown boomed after the fire of 1889, as the city grew rich from mining ventures in northeastern Washington, northern Idaho, and western Montana, and from shipping the wheat grown on the Palouse hills to the south.

Urban parks, many of them designed by the Olmsted brothers, are among Spokane's special assets, reflecting the best aspects of the "City Beautiful" movement.

Information: Spokane Area Convention and Visitors Bureau | 201 W. Main, Spokane, 99201 | 509/624–1341 or 800/248–3230. | www.visitspokane.com.

NEIGHBORHOODS

City Center. Downtown Spokane has many brick-and-stone buildings from the late 19th century, several soaring bridges across the river, an opera house, a beautiful park spanning both sides of the falls and the river, an eclectic Italian-style campanile surviving from the 1902 Great Northern Depot, a much-turreted, castlelike county courthouse, as well as its share of modern concrete brutalities. A system of sky bridges allows business people and shoppers to wander about downtown with ease on even the snowiest days of winter.

Browne's Addition. This exclusive residential area of big, often opulent, mansions west of downtown sits dramatically on a bluff above the river. The neighborhood takes its name from J. J. Browne, who arrived in Spokane in 1878 and homesteaded 160 acres near the falls.

The Hill. This fashionable neighborhood on a river terrace rising a few blocks south of downtown, was mostly developed after the 1889 fire. Many large mansions remain. Others have been replaced by modern office and apartment buildings, hospitals, schools, and other institutions.

Rockwood and Manito Park. A beautiful park, a magnificent cathedral, and stately mansions are the highlights of these neighborhoods, which were developed after the Hill became too crowded.

DRIVING IN SPOKANE

Traffic can be heavy on I–90 and on other major arteries (U.S. 2 and U.S. 395) passing through Spokane, but it rarely approaches gridlock—not even during the rush hour. Parking in Spokane is surprisingly easy. There's lots of metered on-street parking (but you'll encounter none of the viciousness of Seattle's parking enforcers). A seven-block downtown shopping core is interconnected by sky bridges, allowing visitors to walk with ease from parking garages to department stores and office buildings (this comes in very handy during summer heat waves and winter snow storms).

Attractions

Cathedral of St. John the Evangelist. An architectural masterpiece built with sandstone from Tacoma and Boise and limestone from Indiana is in the Rockwood and Manito Park neighborhood. It is thought to be one of America's most important and beautiful Gothic cathedrals. | 127 E., 12th Ave. | 509/838–4277 | fax 509/747–4403 | www.stjohns/cathedral.org | Free | Tours Mon., Tues., Thurs., Sat. noon–3.

Cat Tales. Among the over 40 large cats living at this zoological park (15 mi north of I–90) are lions, tigers, ligers (a combination of lion and tiger), leopards, puma, and lynx. Guided tours are given that introduce the animals and explain why they are here. There is also a small animal petting zoo. | 17020 N. Newport Hwy., Mead | 509/238–4126 | $6 | May–Sept., Tues.–Sun. 10–6; Oct.–Apr., Wed.–Sun. 10–4.

Cheney Cowles Memorial Museum. This museum traces Spokane's history, using audiovisual displays and artifacts. The museum's Native American collection includes baskets and beadwork of the Plateau Indians. Currently undergoing expansion and is slated to reopen in fall of 2001. | 2316 W. 1st Ave. | 509/456–3931 | $4 | Tues., Thurs.–Sat. 10–5, Wed. 10–9, Sun. 1–5.

Children's Museum of Spokane. Hands-on exhibits focus on building and construction, art, and bubbles. A Greek village allows children to dress in costume and play in a market, cottage, and kitchen. | 110 N. Post St. | 509/624–5437 | www.childrensmuseum.net | $3.75 | Tues.–Sat. 10–5.

Cliff Park. Urban Park at the edge of town, with the cities highest point at Review Rock. | 13th Ave. and Ben Garnett Way | 509/625–6200 | fax 509/625–6690 | www.spokanecity.org/parks | Free | Daily.

Comstock Park. An urban park at the west end of town, overlooking Hangman (Latah) Creek. | 29th Ave. and Howard St. | 509/625–6655 | fax 509/625–6690 | www.spokanecity.org/parks | Free | Daily.

Finch Arboretum. This 60-acre hilltop arboretum overlooks the city and the Spokane River Valley. The extensive garden has 2,000 labeled trees, shrubs, and flowers. | 3404 W. Woodland Blvd. | 509/625–6657 | fax 509/625–6958 | Free | Daily.

Flour Mill. When the mill was built in 1895, it was a huge technical innovation. Renovated in 1974, today it is home to shops, restaurants and offices. The mill sits virtually atop the falls, north of the river. | 621 W. Mallon | www.spokanecity.org | Free | Daily.

Gonzaga University. A Catholic university with a Romanesque brick and granite administration building dating from 1903–05. | 502 E. Boone Ave. | 509/328–4220 ext. 2234 | fax 509/323–5718 | www.gonzaga.edu | Free | Daily.

Manito Park. An excellent example of the Olmsted brothers' City Beautiful planning, this is one of the most beautiful urban parks of the Northwest. Besides flowers, shrubs, lawns, and trees, it has a duck pond, a rose garden, a lilac garden, a Japanese garden, a conservatory, and playing fields. | Grand Blvd. at 17th Ave. | 509/625–6622 | fax 509/625–6690 | www.spokanecity.org/parks | Free | Daily dawn–dusk.

Mt. Spokane. In winter, alpine skiing is especially popular. There's a 2,000-ft drop (and a chairlift to take you back up); there are also cross-country skiing trails. Snowshoeing. | Rte. 206, Mt. Spokane State Park | www.parks.wa.gov | Dec.–mid-Apr., Wed.–Sun.

Mt. Spokane State Park. The state park, 30 mi northeast of Spokane includes two mountains: 5,878-ft-high Mt. Spokane and 5,306-ft-high Mt. Kit Carson. You can drive to the top of Mt. Spokane in summer, or take a ski lift in winter. Camping, hiking, huckleberry picking; skiing in winter. | U.S. 2 and SR 206 | www.parks.wa.gov | Free | Daily.

Riverfront Park. A great 100-acre park on the site of Spokane's Expo '74, sprawling across both sides of the Spokane River and an island in the river above the falls. The Italianate clock tower in the park is all that's left from the 1902 Great Northern Depot. A carefully restored early 20th-century carousel from Natatorium Park (1909–1968; demolished) still operates and gives rides for a fee. The carousel animals and decorations were carved by Charles I. D. Louff for his daughter and her husband, who owned the park. The Spokane Opera House (Spokane Riverpark Center) was built as the Washington State Pavilion for the 1974 fair. | Spokane Falls Blvd. and Washington | 509/625–6600 or 800/336–7275 | www.spokanecity.org/parks | Free | Daily.

Riverside State Park. This park has campsites, horse rentals, and an off-road vehicle area. | Junction of SR 291 and Rifle Club Road | 509/456–3964 | www.parks.wa.gov | Free | Daily.

Spokane Falls. Two sets of cascades on the Spokane River, in the heart of downtown Spokane. The upper falls are 60 ft high; the lower falls 70. This was the site of a Spokane Indian village, where they once fished for salmon at the falls. | Downtown Spokane in Riverfront Park | 800/248–3230 | Free | Daily.

Worden's Winery. One of Washington's oldest wineries, making some of its lesser wines. Good for people with a sweet tooth. | 99224 W. Westbow | 509/455–7835 | fax 509/838–4723 | Free | Daily 12–5.

ON THE CALENDAR

MAY: *Spokane Lilac Festival.* Spokane's big annual bash honoring service people of the year, topped off with an Armed Forces torchlight parade. | 509/326–3339.

MAY: *Spring Barrel Tasting.* Six Spokane wineries hold open house for this two-day event and pour samples of their most promising young wines straight from the barrel. | 509/926–0164.

WALKING TOUR

Spokane's prime walks are in **Riverfront Park,** a landscaped gorge in the heart of downtown, with waterfalls separated by an island. Before the 1974 World's Fair, it was a rundown maze of railway trestles, switchyards, warehouses, and service buildings. Of these only a very picturesque (1902) Italianate tower remains, which stands watch over 100 acres of lawns, shade trees, and walking paths. Ducks, geese, and swans hang out on the river banks, hoping for handouts; marmots live in the bluffs of the gorge. Pedestrian bridges cross both branches of the rapidly flowing Spokane River, which pours over rocky cascades near the western end of the park. Besides its natural attractions, the park also has an antique, 1909 hand-carved carousel (that works, and gets some 250,000 riders a year!). A "Sculpture Walk," takes visitors on a visual arts journey along the Spokane River. Several of the 1974 World's Fair buildings remain: an IMAX theater, the Opera House, and the Riverfront Park Gondola Skyride over the falls. If you get tired of walking, you can ride the Park Tour Train on a narrated journey through the park. (For information, call the Spokane Parks and Recreation Department at 509/625–6200.)

The 37-mi-long **Spokane River Centennial Trail,** a paved path running along the Spokane River from the Idaho State line east of Spokane to Nine Mile Falls (in Riverside State Park west of Spokane), passes through Riverfront Park, and allows you to explore the river far beyond the confines of this downtown oasis. It is open to all types of non-motorized pursuits: you can walk or run, bike or in-line skate, ride horseback in designated areas, or launch a canoe or kayak. Or you an simply sit on the river bank, in the shade of a tree, to enjoy the natural beauty and contemplate the rhythmic flow of the river, or enjoy a picnic on the river's edge. This trail has been carefully designed to be usable by people of all ages and physical capabilities, and it is accessible to wheelchairs. The downtown section of the trail, which passes through Riverfront Park, is known as the "Miracle Mile." It begins just north of the **Opera House** in Spokane's Riverfront Park and extends east across the Kardong footbridge to the Gonzaga University neighborhood. Parts of the trail wind through urban neighborhoods, skirt historic sites, and overlook spectacular cascades. Other sections pass through virtual wilderness and are a great place to watch beavers, great blue herons, ospreys, hawks, and an occasional bald eagle.

Dining

Annie Fannie's. Steak. Classic American steakhouse with rustic decor. Known for steak, but seafood and pasta dishes are also available. Entertainment. Kids' menu. | 3827 E. Boone Ave. | 509/534–1212 | Closed Sun. No lunch Sat. | $10–$16 | AE, MC, V.

Clinkerdagger. American. A big, friendly, family restaurant in the Flour Mill, a shopping/office complex. Known for prime rib and fish. Open-air dining on the patio overlooking the river. Kids' menu. | 621 W. Mallon | 509/328–5965 | No lunch Sun. | $17–$26 | AE, D, DC, MC, V.

Elk Public House. American/Casual. This eatery in the relaxed Browne's Addition neighborhood, west of downtown, serves upscale pub food such as lamb sandwiches, pastas, salads, and many vegetarian dishes, together with 19 micro-brews, mostly from the Northwest. A copper bar stands along one wall, in front of a mirror, giving the interior a saloon-like appearance. | 1931 W. Pacific Ave. | 509/363–1973 | $5–$9 | MC, V.

Europa Pizzeria and Bakery. Italian. The name might fool you; pizza occupies only one part of the menu which also includes an extensive range of homemade pastas, calzones, and salads. Candles on the tables, murals, exposed brick, and wood beams give a European flavor to the dining room and adjacent pub—the most popular place to have a meal. | 125 S. Wall | 509/455–4051 | $10–$14 | D, MC, V.

Frank's Diner. American. Right off the Maple St. Bridge, this is the state's oldest railroad car restaurant. Originally an observation car in 1906, it has its original light fixtures, stained glass windows, and mahogany details. Breakfast is the specialty here, and you better arrive hungry because the portions are large. The dinner menu includes such dishes as turkey and mashed potatoes. Everything is made from scratch here with the greatest of care. | 1516 W. 2nd Ave. | 509/747–8798 | No dinner on Sun. | $4–$10 | D, MC, V.

Fugazzi Restaurant. Eclectic. This is Spokane's most splendid post-nouvelle-cuisine eatery, with a variety of herb-scented breads fresh from the oven, and such dishes as braised lamb, pork loin roulade with organic spinach, grilled tenderloin, coconut-and citrus crested mahi mahi, and grilled portobello mushrooms. | 1 N. Post St. | 509/624–1133 | $16–$22 | AE, D, DC, MC, V.

Italian Kitchen. Italian. Opened in 1999, this restaurant sits in the historic Hotel St. Regis, which was built in 1904. Tin ceilings and memorabilia give the dining room the flavor of the early 20th century. The menu includes Italian sandwiches, spaghettis, and veal piccata. | 113 N. Bernard | 509/363–1210 | $8–$20 | AE, D, MC, V.

Luna. American/Casual. A neighborhood restaurant turning out delectable pizzas from its wood-fired ovens, as well as pasta and seafood dishes. The wine list has an impressive 400 listings. Open-air dining on the patio during warm weather. Sun. brunch. | 5620 S. Perry St. | 509/448–2383 | $12–$24 | AE, D, DC, MC, V.

Mary Lou's Milk Bottle. American. Dine in a historic milk bottle! Built in 1933, the restaurant is shaped like a gigantic milk bottle. The focus is on burgers, which are all homemade, though some Greek dishes are also served. Since 1978, the eatery has been selling its own homemade ice cream. | 802 W. Garland | 509/325–1772 | $3.50–$5.75 | No credit cards.

Milford's Fish House. Seafood. This brick and terra-cotta tile structure was built in 1925 and the terrazzo floor and tin ceiling are relics of this era. The interior's exposed brick and wood details, lit by candles, create an intimate, romantic environment in which to enjoy the wide array of seafood dishes and steaks. Everything is fresh here and it is hard to predict what the menu will include, but you might find such items as tuna, shark, cod, salmon, snapper, mahi mahi, clams, and prawns. | 719 N. Monroe | 509/326–7251 | No lunch | $15–$20 | D, MC, V.

Mizuna Restaurant. Vegetarian. Fresh flowers adorn the red-brick walls, adding color to this downtown eatery. Local produce is the inspiration for the scrumptious vegetarian fare such as grilled eggplant, layered with vegetable and ricotta cheese and covered with an arugula-walnut pesto. | 214 N. Howard St. | 509/747–2004 | No lunch weekends, no dinner Sun.–Mon. | $12–$15 | AE, D, MC, V.

Mustard Seed. Pan-Asian. The dining room's exposed brick and wood interior provides an elegant environment in which to enjoy the Asian-inspired fare such as sweet and sour teriyaki, noodle dishes, and stir-fries. Most popular is the shrimp or chicken osaka: shrimp or chicken sautéed in butter, garlic, and ginger. | 245 W. Spokane Falls Blvd. | 509/747–2689 | $7–$12 | AE, D, DC, MC, V.

Niko's Greek Restaurant and Wine Bar. Greek. Sunlight streaming through the large storefront windows renders this eatery's dining room bright and cheerful. Lamb is the specialty here, served in a variety of ways including curried, grilled with rosemary, and grilled on skewers in a marinade of lemon garlic and white wine. Vegetarian dishes are plentiful, as are the wines—there are over 700 choices on the wine list. | 725 W. Riverside | 509/624–7444 | $12–$20 | AE, DC, MC, V.

Onion. American/Casual. Sitting within what was once a 1904 drugstore and saloon, this restaurant evokes the past with a pressed tin ceiling, old photographs, and an ornate bar built in 1905. The restaurant has been serving pastas, salads, burgers, and steaks with enthusiasm and spirit since it opened in 1974. | 302 W. Riverside | 509/747–3852 | $12–$20 | AE, D, DC, MC, V.

Paprika. Contemporary. A formal, intimate restaurant in the pricey South Hill neighborhood. But the dishes, which are anything but stuffy, include such delectable items as the pepper-crusted ahi tuna with horseradish mashed potatoes and the grilled salmon salad. Seasonal menu. | 1228 S. Grand Blvd. | 509/455–7545 | Closed Sun.–Mon. No lunch | $10–$20 | AE, D, DC, MC, V.

Patsy Clark's. Continental. Spokane's most formal restaurant occupies an opulent 1898 mansion with Tiffany stained glass and handmade furniture. The menu changes seasonally. Known for wild game and steak. Sun. brunch. | W. 2208 2nd Ave. | 509/838–8300 | No lunch weekends | $18–$35 | AE, D, DC, MC, V.

Rock City Grill. American/Casual. This upbeat, friendly downtown café/bar close to Riverfront Park prepares excellent pastas and gourmet pizzas baked in wood-fired ovens. Also try the daily specials. | 505 W. Riverside Ave. | 509/455–4400 | $6–$19 | AE, D, DC, MC, V.

Rocky Rococo's Pizza Restaurant. Pizza. Housed in a Renaissance Revival–style building that was once a movie theater, this restaurant has extremely high ceilings with the theater's original fixtures. The primary focus here is on pizza, though there are also other items on the menu such as salads and pastas. | 520 W. Main St. | 509/747–1000 | $5–$8 | AE, MC, V.

Steam Plant Grill. American/Casual. Built in 1916 as a steam plant (it generated power for the downtown area for over 70 years), this restaurant has several distinct dining rooms. You can eat inside a boiler, inside a hot water tank, or on a balcony overlooking the entire complex. The menu options are equally broad; there is a coconut curry salad, a halibut fish taco, steak, and lamb chops. The most popular dish is the fish and chips, fried in a batter made from beer brewed on the premises. | 159 S. Lincoln | 509/777–3900 | $5.50–$17 | AE, D, MC, V.

Winged Lion. Continental. Murals, ceiling frescos, and tapestries adorn this intimate restaurant in the historic Kempis Hotel. The menu includes such dishes as roast duckling, pan-roasted loin of lamb, rabbit stew, and beef tenderloin. | 326 W. 6th Ave. | 509/747–7100 | No lunch on weekends, no dinner Sun. | $15–$27 | AE, DC, MC, V.

Lodging

Angelica's Bed and Breakfast. On a tree-lined residential street, this 1907 Kirkland Cutter brick mansion is a paradigm of Victorian elegance: polished wood floors, lace curtains, beautiful antique furniture, and period lighting. The individually appointed rooms each have their own charm; "Yvonne", for example, has a tile fireplace and a canopy bed flanked by windows overlooking trees. | 4 rooms. Complimentary breakfast, some in-room data ports, no room phones, no TV in some rooms, no pets, no kids under 12, no smoking. | 1321 W. 9th Ave. | 509/624–5598 or 800/987–0053 | info@angelicasbb.com | www.angelicasbb.com | $90–$110 | AE, MC, V.

Best Western Thunderbird Inn. This hotel is seven blocks from Riverfront Park, the Opera House, and the Convention Center. It is easily accessible to I–90. | 89 rooms. Complimentary Continental breakfast, in-room data ports, cable TV, pool, business services, pets allowed (fee). | W. 120 3rd Ave. | 509/747–2011 | fax 509/747–9170 | $59–$74 | AE, D, DC, MC, V.

Best Western Trade Winds North. Comfortable business travelers' and family hotel. Three mi from Riverfront Amusement Park, 2 mi from Expo '74 Site and Gonzaga University. | 63 rooms. Complimentary Continental breakfast, cable TV, indoor pool, laundry facilities, business services, some pets allowed (fee). | N. 3033 Division St. | 509/326–5500 | fax 509/328–1357 | $64–$70 | AE, D, DC, MC, V.

Budget Inn. Business travelers' hotel near hospitals. | 153 rooms, 15 suites. Minibar in suites, cable TV, pool, laundry facilities, business services, airport shuttle, pets allowed. | E. 110 4th Ave. | 509/838–6101 | fax 509/624–0733 | $59–$69, $79–$84 suites | AE, D, DC, MC, V.

Cavanaugh's River Inn. Luxurious hotel overlooking the Spokane River east of Riverfront Park, in the heart of downtown. | 245 rooms, 2 suites. Restaurant, bar with entertainment, room service, cable TV, 2 pools, wading pool, hot tub, sauna, tennis, business services, airport shuttle, free parking, some pets allowed. | N. 700 Division St. | 509/326–5577 or 800/843–4667 | fax 509/326–1120 | $99–$119, $190–$240 suites | AE, D, DC, MC, V.

Comfort Inn Spokane Valley. Comfortable business travelers' and family hotel, just off of the freeway. | 63 rooms, 13 suites. Complimentary Continental breakfast, some refrigerators, cable TV, pool, hot tub, laundry facilities, business services, free parking, some pets allowed (fee). | N. 905 Sullivan Rd. | 509/924–3838 | fax 509/921–6976 | $59–$99, $89–$150 suites | AE, D, DC, MC, V.

Courtyard by Marriott. Upscale business travelers' hotel close to the Centennial Trail and Riverfront Park. | 149 rooms, 12 suites. Restaurant, bar, some refrigerators, microwaves, cable TV, indoor pool, hot tub, gym, laundry facilities, business services, free parking. | N. 401 Riverpoint Blvd. | 509/456–7600 | fax 509/456–0969 | $89–$119, $124 suites | AE, D, DC, MC, V.

Doubletree Hotel–Spokane City Center. This lively hotel is near the Convention Center and the Opera House. | 373 rooms, 4 suites. 2 restaurants, bar with entertainment, in-room data ports, cable TV, room service, gym, pool, business services, airport shuttle, pets allowed (fee), valet parking (fee). | N. 322 Spokane Falls Ct. | 509/455–9600 | fax 509/455–6285 | $109–$155, $209–$500 suites | AE, D, DC, MC, V.

Doubletree Hotel–Spokane Valley. This hotel is 11 mi east of the downtown area. Across the freeway is the Spokane Valley Mall. | 236 rooms. 2 restaurants, bar with entertainment, some refrigerators, room service, cable TV, pool, barbershop, beauty salon, hot tub, gym, airport shuttle, free parking, some pets allowed. | N. 1100 Sullivan Rd. | 509/924–9000 | fax 509/922–4965 | $79–$118 | AE, D, DC, MC, V.

Fotheringham House. A comfortable B&B in historic Browne's Addition, this Queen Anne–style house was originally built in 1891 for the mayor of Spokane. It has been beautifully restored and preserved, and is filled with antiques. The gardens are immaculately kept, and include a fountain and a birdbath. There is also a lovely veranda with a porch swing, as well as a park across the street. | 4 rooms (1 with shower only, 3 with shared baths). Complimentary breakfast and evening tea and snacks, no room phones, no kids under 12, no smoking. | 2128 W. 2nd Ave. | 509/838–1891 | fax 509/838–1807 | www.fotheringham.net | $90–105 | AE, D, MC, V.

Hotel Lusso. Italian marble tile ornaments many of the floors, archways, and fountains that fill the elegant lobby at this hotel. Guest rooms are appointed with European furnishings and contain many modern amenities. Each evening the hotel hosts a complimentary wine and cheese social. | 48 rooms. Restaurant, bar, room service, complimentary Continental breakfast, in-room data ports, minibars, some in-room hot tubs, cable TV, pets allowed, no smoking. | 808 W. Sprague St. | 509/747–9750 | fax 509/747–9751 | www.fugazzi.com | $250–$460 | AE, D, DC, MC, V.

Kempis Hotel Suites. Two beautiful stained-wood staircases stand in the atrium of this 1906 building, leading to wooden balconies which lead to your room. Turn-of-the-20th-century furniture fills the rooms which are also equipped with full kitchens and many modern amenities. | 14 suites. Restaurant, bar, complimentary Continental breakfast, kitchenettes, microwaves, refrigerators, cable TV, in-room VCRs, no pets, no smoking. | 326 W. 6th Ave. | 509/747–4321 or 888/236–4321 | www.thekempis.com | $129–$199 | AE, DC, MC, V.

Love's Victorian Bed and Breakfast. Built in 1986, the turret, gabled roofs, and wraparound porch make this B&B a paradigm of Victorian architecture. The house sits 15 mi north of Spokane on 5 acres, surrounded by exquisitely maintained gardens and lawns. The guest rooms are appointed with antiques such as the "Turret Suite's" 1840s high oak bed which is accessed by a small stool. | 3 rooms. Complimentary breakfast, cable TV, in-room VCRs, pets allowed, no smoking. | 31317 Cedar Rd., Deer Park | 509/276–6939 | lovesbandb@juno.com | www.bbhost.com/lovesvictorian | $75–$125 | MC, V.

Marianna Stoltz House. The dark fir woodwork that frames the windows, doors, and rooms of this 1908 American Four-square meld nicely with the Rococo Revival and Renaissance Revival furniture that fills the rooms. The individually appointed rooms have brass or mahogany beds which are covered with quilts handed down from the proprietor's ancestors. Century-old trees are all around and add an extra charm to this inn that is close to I–90 and only five blocks from Gonzaga University. | 4 rooms. Complimentary breakfast, cable TV, no room phones, no pets, no smoking. | 427 E. Indiana Ave. | 509/483–4316 or 800/978–6587 | fax 509/483–6773 | mstoltz@aimcomm.com | mariannastoltzhouse.com | $69–$99 | AE, D, MC, V.

Motel 6. Comfortable budget hotel off of freeway, close to restaurants and shops. | 92 rooms. Cable TV, business services, some pets allowed. | 1919 Hutchinson Rd. | 509/926–5399 | fax 509/928–5974 | $45–$65 | AE, D, DC, MC, V.

Oslo's Bed and Breakfast. This single-story B&B sits in a quiet residential neighborhood. A Norwegian theme dominates this residence, from the furnishings and details to the breakfasts. A patio overlooking flower and vegetable gardens provides a comfortable place to sit and relax outdoors. | 2 rooms. Complimentary breakfast, TV in common area, no pets, no kids under 12, no smoking. | 1821 E. 39th Ave. | 509/838–3175 or 888/838–3175 | oslo@aimcomm.com | aimcomm.com/oslosb&b | $65–$85 | No credit cards.

Quality Inn Valley Suites. The lobby at this four-story hotel is decorated in Mediterranean style. South of I–90 at exit 287, it is 6 mi east of downtown Spokane. | 127 rooms, 52 suites. Bar, picnic area, complimentary buffet breakfast, refrigerators, in-room data ports, cable TV, indoor pool, barbershop, beauty salon, hot tub, exercise equipment, laundry facilities, business services, free parking. | 8923 E. Mission Ave. | 509/928–5218 or 800/777–7355 | fax 509–928–5211 | $79–$99, $190–$225 suites | AE, D, DC, MC, V.

Ramada Inn. Business travelers' hotel, right across from the airport. | 168 rooms. Restaurant, bar with entertainment, room service, cable TV, 2 pools (1 indoor), hot tub, gym, business services, airport shuttle, free parking, pets allowed. | 8909 Airport Rd. | 509/838–5211 | fax 509/838–1074 | $65–$95 | AE, D, DC, MC, V.

Shangri-La Motel. Business travelers' and family motel far enough off the highway to escape the noise of the traffic and trains. | 20 rooms, 8 apartments. Picnic area, complimentary Continental breakfast, some kitchens, some refrigerators, microwaves, cable TV, pool, playground, business services, airport shuttle, some pets allowed, free parking. | W. 2922 Government Way | 509/747–2066 or 800/234–4941 | fax 509/456–8696 | $47–$76 | AE, D, DC, MC, V.

Shilo Inn. Comfortable family and business travelers' motel with friendly staff. | 105 rooms. Restaurant, bar, complimentary breakfast, in-room data ports, refrigerators, microwaves, room service, cable TV, indoor pool, gym, business services, airport shuttle, pets allowed (fee). | 923 E. 3rd Ave. | 509/535–9000 or 800/222–2244 (res) | fax 509/535–5740 | $69–$99 | AE, D, DC, MC, V.

Waverly Place Bed and Breakfast. This turreted 1902 Queen Anne house, minutes from downtown, sits across from Corbin Park in a historical neighborhood famous for its Victorian architecture. The gleaming fir woodwork on the mantlepiece and Grecian columns are the perfect frame for the distinctive late Victorian furniture that fills the rooms. | 4 rooms. Complimentary breakfast, no room phones, no TV, pool, hot tub, no pets, no kids under 6, no smoking. | 709 W. Wavery Pl. | 509/328–1856 | fax 509/326–7059 | waverly@waverlyplace.com | www.waverlyplace.com | $85–$115 | AE, D, MC, V.

Westcoast Ridpath Hotel. The way things are going, Cavanaugh's may soon be running every major hotel, not only in Spokane, but in much of eastern Washington, but that's okay since the company does do a good job. And, we're sorry to say, the Ridpath does need help. It's a downtown hotel with great possibilities that has, so far, never quite lived up to its potential. Perhaps it will now. | 342 rooms, 21 suites. 2 restaurants, 2 bars with entertainment, in-room data ports, some in-room hot tubs (suites), cable TV, pool, gym, barbershop, beauty salon, laundry facilities, business services, airport shuttle, some pets allowed (fee). | 515 W. Sprague Ave. | 509/838–2711 or 800/426–0670 | fax 509/747–6970 | $115–$140, $180–$495 suites | AE, D, DC, MC, V.

STEVENSON

MAP 8, E8

(Nearby town also listed: Vancouver)

The Skamania County seat, Stevenson is a hillside village overlooking the Columbia Gorge; It was once a major fishing town. Its Columbia River Gorge Interpretive Center has interesting displays of native artifacts, as well the replica of a fish wheel, a mechanical contraption that automatically scooped salmon from the river (they were outlawed in 1935 because they were too efficient and took too many fish).

Information: Skamania County Chamber of Commerce | 167 N.W. 2nd St., Stevenson, 98648 | 800/989–9178 | www.skamania.org.

Attractions

Columbia Gorge Interpretive Center. Dwarfed by the dramatic basalt cliffs that rise behind it, this museum stands on the north bank of the Columbia River Gorge, 1 mi east of Bridge of the Gods on Highway 14. Exhibits illustrate the geology and history of the region. Among the many artifacts are a Native American pit house, a fish wheel, and dip nets used for hunting salmon. Other artifacts pertain to the missionaries, pioneers, and soldiers who have passed through the gorge. | 990 S.W. Rock Creek Dr. | 509/427–8211 | $6 | Daily 10–5.

ON THE CALENDAR

APR.: *Festival of the Rain.* Stevenson, at the wet western end of the Columbia Gorge, usually gets soaked at this time of the year. The festival has a "Biggest Drip" contest, a 5-mile fun run called the "Rock Creek Ramble," and an arts and crafts fair on the Columbia River waterfront. | 800/989–9178.

Dining

Dining Room at Skamania Lodge. American/Casual. The wood ceilings, booths, and floors of this cavernous dining room give it a warm glow. Two mi east of the Bridge of the Gods on Highway 14, the restaurant overlooks the Columbia River Gorge. Salmon, crab cakes, scrumptious rack of lamb, and prime rib are some of the dishes cooked in the wood-burning oven. On Friday night the Gorge Harvest Seafood Buffet draws visitors from miles around. | Skamania Lodge Way | 509/427–7700 | Reservations essential | Breakfast also available | $15–$25 | AE, D, DC, MC, V.

Lodging

Carson Mineral Hot Springs Resort. This resort stands in a secluded woodsy area 4 mi east of Stevenson. The mineral-laden waters have been an attraction since the early part of the 20th century when the bathhouses and cabins were built. The rooms are spartan and rustic; the cabins have a few more amenities. | 9 rooms (all with shared bath), 12 cabins. Restaurant, no air-conditioning, no room phones, no TV, massage, 18-hole golf course, hiking, pets allowed (fee), no smoking. | 372 St. Martin's Springs Rd., Carson | 509/427–8292 or 800/607–3678 | fax 509/427–7242 | www.ohwy.com/wa/c/carminhs.htm | $35–$60 rooms and cabins | MC, V.

Econo Lodge–Stevenson. Inexpensive lodging on a scenic stretch of the river. | 30 rooms. Complimentary Continental breakfast, some microwaves, refrigerators, cable TV, some no-smoking rooms. | 40 N.E. Second St. | 509/427–5628 | fax 509/427–4995 | $45–$95 | AE, D, DC, MC, V.

Skamania Lodge. Built in the 1990s, the lodge perches on a hill overlooking the Columbia River 2 mi east of the Bridge of the Gods. The Gorge Room's pine floors, fir walls, and stone fireplace are indicative of the lodge's rustic splendor. Framed rubbings of petroglyphs ornament rooms which are appointed with lodge-style furniture covered with handwoven fabrics. From the rooms you can gaze on the river and the surrounding landscape. | 195 rooms. Restaurant, bar, minibars, cable TV, pool, hot tub, massage, outdoor hot tub, sauna, 18-hole golf course, 2 tennis courts, gym, hiking, volleyball, bicycles, library, business services, no pets. | Skamania Lodge Way | 509/427–7700 or 800/221–7117 | fax 509/427–2548 | www.skamania.com | $159–$350 | AE, D, DC, MC, V.

SUNNYSIDE

MAP 8, H7

(Nearby towns also listed: Richland, Toppenish)

Sunnyside is the lower Yakima Valley's commercial center, with all the usual amenities. At one time, the town, known as "Holy City," was a community of church people. Local deeds contained a clause clearly stating that the pursuit of any vices such as dancing, horse racing, and gambling would cause the property to revert to the township company. Today, Sunnyside is surrounded by vineyards and has several wineries. Some of Washington's best asparagus is also raised in local fields. In the late 1900s, many Mexican families settled in Sunnyside, and the school district is now more than 50 percent Hispanic. The Hispanic touch has been very positive, creating a fascinating cultural mosaic.

Information: **Sunnyside Chamber of Commerce** | 520 S. 7th St., Box 329, Sunnyside, 98944 | 800/457–8089 | fax 509/839–7462 | geocities.com/capitolhill/9886/tourvisi.htm.

Attractions

Darigold Dairy Fair. (Formerly the independent Yakima Valley Cheese Co.) A dairy information center that lets you know about how good milk and cheese products are for you. Tours; deli; gift shop; ice cream; and free cheese samples. | 400 Alexander Rd. | 509/837–4321 | www.darigold.com | Free | Daily 8–8.

Sunnyside Museum. Artifacts and documents illustrate the history of the city and its inhabitants. | 704 S. 4th St. | 509/837–6010 | Free | Apr.–Dec., Fri.–Sun. 1:30–4:30.

Tucker Cellars Winery. A small family winery that also has one of the best fruit and vegetable stands in the Yakima Valley. Very laid-back and friendly. A great place for buying Yakima Valley asparagus in spring. | 70 Ray Rd. | 509/837–8701 | www.tuckercellars.com | Free | Daily 9–5.

Washington Hills Cellar. One of Washington's best and least known wineries, with one of the state's most respected winemakers. Brian Carter makes wines under three labels, Washington Hills (easily drinkable wines), W. B. Bridgman (special varieties), and Apex (top-of-the-line wines). Even the least of these wines are better than the top wines of some other Yakima Valley wineries, and they are more reasonably priced. | 111 E. Lincoln | 509/839–WINE | fax 509/839–6155 | www.washingtonhills.com | Free | Daily 10–5:30.

ON THE CALENDAR

FEB.: *Red Wine and Chocolate.* A pairing of chocolate desserts with local wines at Yakima Valley wineries. | 800/258–7270.

APR.: *Spring Barrel Tasting.* This is the one time of the year when Yakima Valley vintners pour tastes of their most promising wines straight from the barrel. Held at Yakima Valley wineries from Wapato to Benton City. | 800/258–7270.

APR.: *Washington State Asparagus Festival.* A must-attend event for gourmands, since this gives them a chance to sample the nation's best asparagus with some of the country's best wines at a winemakers' dinner. Other food events with samples; live jazz. | 800/814–7004.

MAY: *Cinco de Mayo Fiesta Days.* An unabashed celebration of Mexican culture, arts, food, and dance in the Hispanic capital of the Yakima Valley. | 800/457–8089.

Dining

Dykstra House. American. In a wine valley with, as yet, few restaurants, the Dykstra house in Grandview has held its own for more than a decade. The food served in this 1914 mansion is simple and flavorful. Breads are made from hand-ground wheat grown in the nearby Horse Heaven Hills, and other ingredients are also local, whenever possible. Friday night dinners are Italian; the grand Saturday night dinners revolve around chicken, beef, or fish. The wines come from nearby Yakima Valley vineyards. | 114 Birch Ave. | 509/882–2082 | Reservations essential (Fri. and Sat. supper) | Closed Sun.–Mon. No dinner Tues.–Thurs. | $15–$25 | AE, D, DC, MC, V.

El Conquistador. Mexican. A basic Mexican restaurant with a familiar menu, but with better than usual execution of the dishes, since Sunnyside is the Hispanic heart of the Yakima Valley. The flavorful fare includes such favorites as burritos, fajitas, and camarones (shrimp), all served with some especially tasty hot sauces. | 612 E. Edison Ave. | 509/839–2880 | $8–$11 | AE, D, DC, MC, V.

WA

SUNNYSIDE

INTRO
ATTRACTIONS
DINING
LODGING

Taco Wagons. Tex-Mex. These large vans usually position themselves at street corners at lunch and dinner times, or head for the fields and processing plants where farm workers are laboring. The fare they dish up is simple, tasty, and inexpensive: soft tacos, made from handmade tortillas (made as you order), filled with an assortment of different meats, from shredded beef, pork, and chicken to tongue and other organ meats. These soft tacos come accompanied by a freshly made, and usually absolutely delicious and very spicy, salsa fresca. It's difficult to find food that good and fresh at most area restaurants, especially since everything is made to order right on the spot.

Taqueria La Fogata. Mexican. A small, roadside Mexican taqueria that has mastered the art of serving simple food quickly and inexpensively. The menu is simple, but includes such dishes as pozole and menudo. | 1204 Yakima Valley Hwy. | 509/839–9019 | Breakfast also available | $3–$11 | AE, MC, V.

Tillicum Restaurant. American. A favorite spot among locals, this eatery has a traditional range of dishes including steaks, seafood, barbecued ribs, and pastas. But what Sunnyside residents prefer over everything else is the succulent prime rib. | 410 Yakima Valley Hwy. | 509/837–7222 | Breakfast also available | $9–$16 | AE, D, MC, V.

Lodging

Sun Valley Inn. Comfortable downtown family motel. | 40 rooms. No-smoking rooms, pool, pets allowed. | 724 Yakima Valley Hwy. | 509/837–4721 | $39–$60 | AE, D, MC, V.

Sunnyside Inn Bed and Breakfast. Floral arrangements, wood-framed beds, and soft colors give the guest rooms in this 1919 house, which sits on Sunnyside's main road, a country flavor. Restaurants are only a short stroll away from the inn. Families are welcome. | 13 rooms. Complimentary breakfast, some in-room hot tubs, cable TV, no pets, no smoking. | 804 E. Edison Ave. | 509/839–5557 or 800/221–4195 | fax 509/839–3520 | sunnyside@sunnysideinn.com | www.sunnysideinn.com | $89–$109 | AE, D, MC, V.

TACOMA

MAP 8, D5

(Nearby town also listed: Puyallup)

Washington's third largest city rises above the mudflats of the Puyallup River delta and the southern shores of Commencement Bay (one of Puget Sound's best harbors). Tacoma has a revitalized downtown, with many historic buildings, as well as some of the state's best parks.

Like other Washington cities, Tacoma occupies the site of several ancient Indian villages. American settlement started in 1852, with the harvesting of local timber. The railroad arrived in 1873, when Tacoma became the nominal western terminal of the Northern Pacific.

One outstanding building remaining from the railroad era is Union Station (1901–11), a domed, neo-Baroque structure that was recently renovated as part of a federal courthouse. Other renovations have been done at the Tacoma Art Museum, which occupies the former Classic Revival National Bank of Washington building, and the 1918 Pantages Theater.

Information: **Tacoma-Pierce County Visitor and Convention Bureau** | 1001 Pacific Ave., Suite 400, Tacoma, 98402 | 253/627–2836 or 800/272–2662 | fax 253/627–8783 | tpctourism.org or tourtacoma.org.

Attractions

Broadway Center for the Performing Arts. Comprising three theatres, this center is the heart of Tacoma's cultural activity. The Pantages at 901 Broadway is a 1918 Greco-Roman–

KODAK'S TIPS FOR PHOTOGRAPHING LANDSCAPES AND SCENERY

Landscape
- Tell a story
- Isolate the essence of a place
- Exploit mood, weather, and lighting

Panoramas
- Use panoramic cameras for sweeping vistas
- Don't restrict yourself to horizontal shots
- Keep the horizon level

Panorama Assemblage
- Use a wide-angle or normal lens
- Let edges of pictures overlap
- Keep exposure even
- Use a tripod

Placing the Horizon
- Use low horizon placement to accent sky or clouds
- Use high placement to emphasize distance and accent foreground elements
- Try eliminating the horizon

Mountain Scenery: Scale
- Include objects of known size
- Frame distant peaks with nearby objects
- Compress space with long lenses

Mountain Scenery: Lighting
- Shoot early or late; avoid midday
- Watch for dramatic color changes
- Use exposure compensation

Tropical Beaches
- Capture expansive views
- Don't let bright sand fool your meter
- Include people

Rocky Shorelines
- Vary shutter speeds to freeze or blur wave action
- Don't overlook sea life in tidal pools
- Protect your gear from sand and sea

In the Desert
- Look for shapes and textures
- Try visiting during peak bloom periods
- Don't forget safety

Canyons
- Research the natural and social history of a locale
- Focus on a theme or geologic feature
- Budget your shooting time

Rain Forests and the Tropics
- Go for mystique with close-ups and detail shots
- Battle low light with fast films and camera supports
- Protect cameras and film from moisture and humidity

Rivers and Waterfalls
- Use slow film and long shutter speeds to blur water
- When needed, use a neutral-density filter over the lens
- Shoot from water level to heighten drama

Autumn Colors
- Plan trips for peak foliage periods
- Mix wide and close views for visual variety
- Use lighting that accents colors or creates moods

Moonlit Landscapes
- Include the moon or use only its illumination
- Exaggerate the moon's relative size with long telephoto lenses
- Expose landscapes several seconds or longer

Close-Ups
- Look for interesting details
- Use macro lenses or close-up filters
- Minimize camera shake with fast films and high shutter speeds

Caves and Caverns
- Shoot with ISO 1000+ films
- Use existing light in tourist caves
- Paint with flash in wilderness caves

influenced structure designed by B. Marcus Pritica with ornate columns, arches, and reliefs. The Theatre on the Square (adjacent to the Pantages), a very contemporary structure, is home to the Tacoma Actors Guild. The Rialto Theater (at 301 S. 9th Street) was built in 1918 and once presented many vaudeville performances. Free tours of the theaters are offered by the center. | 901 Broadway | 253/591–5890.

Children's Museum of Tacoma. Cultural, historical, and scientific topics are presented in fun, interactive exhibits. In addition, there are odd artifacts on display from civilizations past and present. | 936 Broadway | 253/627–6031 | $3 | Tues.–Sat. 10–5.

Emerald Downs. Washington's newest horse racing track, replacing Longacres near Renton, which was bought by Boeing to be turned into an office complex. | 2300 Emerald Downs Dr., Auburn | 253/288–7000 or 888/931–8400 | fax 253/288–7733 | www.emdowns.com | $3 | Mid-Apr.–mid-Sept., Wed.–Fri. 6 PM post times; weekends 1 PM post times.

Enchanted Village. An amusement park for children just east of I–5. | 36201 Enchanted Pkwy. S | 253/661–8000 or 253/925–8000 | fax 253/661–8065 | www.wildwaves.com | $14.95 | Daily 10–7.

Wild Waves Water Park. The northwest's largest and most complete water park includes four giant water slides, three drop slides, a 24,000-square-ft wave pool, and a Kids Splash Central for younger children. | 36201 Enchanted Pkwy. S | 206/661–8000 or 253/925–8000 | fax 253/661–8065 | www.wildwaves.com | $24.95 | Apr.–mid-Sept., daily 10–8.

Ferry. A scheduled car ferry crosses from Point Defiance in Tacoma to Tahlequah on Vashon Island. Crossing time: 15 minutes. | 5810 North Pearl St. | 206/464–6400 or 800/84–FERRY | $9 | Daily 5 AM–midnight.

Lakewold Gardens. One of the Northwest's great gardens, begun in 1912 and devoted to preserving endangered plant species from around the world. | 12317 Gravelly Lake Dr. SW, Lakewood | 253/584–3360 or 888/858–4106 | fax 253/584–3021 | www.lakewold.org | $5 | April–Sept., Thurs.–Mon. 10–4, Fri. noon–8; Oct.–Mar., weekends.

McChord AFB. This air force base south of Tacoma but north of Ft. Lewis is the home of huge C–130 and C–140 transport planes. | Exit 125 Lakewood, off I–5 | 253/984–5637 | fax 253/984–5025 | www.mcchord.af.mil | Free | Call for hours and tour times.

Narrows Bridge. The strait west of Tacoma is crossed by the Tacoma Narrows Bridge, whose predecessor, known as "Galloping Gertie," twisted herself to death and broke in half during a storm in 1940, only 4 months after completion. News reels of the event are still occasionally shown on TV as parts of documentaries. | Part of Hwy. 16 | Daily.

Tacoma Nature Center at Snake Lake. Fifty-four acres of marshland and evergreen forest, and a shallow lake in the midst of Tacoma. Like Seattle's Discovery Park, it is a wilderness island in the city, with 25 species of mammals and more than 100 species of birds. The lake has nesting pairs of wood ducks, rare elsewhere in western Washington. | 1919 S. Tyler St. | 253/591–6439 | fax 253/593–4152 | www.tacomaparks.com | Free | Daily.

Pacific Lutheran University. A religious university south of Tacoma. | East on Hwy. 512 | 253/535–7430 | fax 253/535–8331 | www.plu.edu | Free | Daily.

Point Defiance Park. One of the country's great urban parks, Point Defiance was set aside in 1866 as a military reservation. In 1888 the point was turned over to the city and was laid out as a park in 1905. The 698-acre park is surrounded by Puget Sound on three sides and still has some trees of the virgin forest originally covering the region. | N. 54th and Pearl Sts. | 253/305–1000 | fax 253/305–1098 | www.tacomaparks.com | Free | Daily.

Boathouse Marina. Marina with permanent slips and visitor moorage. Boat rentals. | 5912 North Waterfront Drive, in Point Defiance Park | 253/591–5325 | www.tacomaparks.com | Daily.

Camp Six Logging Exhibit (Western Forest Industries Museum). Camp Six, a Washington Forest Industries Museum, has a collection of steam-powered logging equipment. | Five-Mile Dr. in Point Defiance Park | 253/752–0047 | www.tacomaparks.com | $2.50 | Apr.–Oct., Wed.–Sun. 10–4.

Five-Mile Drive. A scenic drive through old-growth forest in Point Defiance Park. Viewpoints and picnic tables en route. | 253/305–1000 | www.tacomaparks.com | Free | Daily dawn–dusk.

Fort Nisqually. A reconstruction of the Hudson's Bay Company's Fort Nisqually (the first European settlement on Puget Sound, 1833). The 1843 granary, part of a bastion, and the factor's house were moved here from the original site at the mouth of the Nisqually River. The rest is reconstruction. | Five-Mile Dr. in Point Defiance Park | 253/591–5339 | www.tacomaparks.com | $2 | June–Aug., daily 11–6, Sept.–May, Wed.–Sun., 11–5

Gardens. Point Defiance has a number of specialty gardens devoted to dahlias, herbs, irises, native plants, rhododendrons, and roses. | Point Defiance Park | 253/305–1000 | www.tacomaparks.com | Free | Daily dawn–dusk.

Never Never Land. Children's play area filled with kids' favorite nursery rhyme characters. | Point Defiance Park | 253/591–5845 or 253/591–6439 | www.tacomaparks.com | June–Sept., Wed.–Sun. 11–6.

★ **Point Defiance Zoo and Aquarium.** Among Washington's finest, they were in need of upgrading and threatened with closure but were rescued from potential demise by a multimillion-dollar bond issue. The exhibits are very realistic and represent different habitats of the Pacific Rim, from Arctic Tundra to South Pacific reefs. | Point Defiance Park | 253/591–5337 | www.tacomaparks.com | $7.25 | Memorial Day–Labor Day, daily 10–7, rest of year, call for hours.

Rhododendron Species Botanical Garden. A 22-acre garden with more than 10,000 plants of some 2,000 varieties of 450 species, which bloom in succession. This garden is considered one of the finest rhododendron collections in the world. | 2525 S. 336 St. | 253/927–6960 | fax 253/838–4686 | www.halcyon.com/rsf | $3.50, free Nov.–Feb. | Mar.–May, 10–4, closed on Thurs., June–Feb., 11–4, closed Thurs.–Fri.

Tacoma Art Museum. This museum features 20th-century American and French Impressionist paintings, Pilchuck glass, and rotating exhibits. | 1123 Pacific Ave. | 253/272–4258 | fax 253/627–1898 | www.tacomaartmuseum.org | $5 | Tues.–Wed., Fri.–Sun. 10–5, Thurs. 10–8.

Tacoma Totem Pole. Built in 1903 and restored in 1976, this totem pole was carved by Alaskan Indians. | 9th and A Sts. | Free | Daily.

University of Puget Sound. A well-respected private university with 3,000 undergraduates. | 1500 N. Warner St. | 253/879–3100 | fax 253/879–3500 | www.ups.edu | Free | Daily.

Washington State History Museum. In its upgraded version this is truly a great museum, with interactive exhibits and multimedia installations about the exploration and settlement of the state. Indian and Inuit (Eskimo) artifacts are on display. The museum also has vast historical archives. | 1911 Pacific Ave. | 888/BE–THERE | www.wshs.org | $7 | call for hours.

Union Station. This faux-Baroque (1901–11) copper-domed structure which seems to consist of nothing but huge arches now houses federal district court rooms. | 17 Pacific Ave. | 253/572–9310 | www.wshs.org | Free | Weekdays 8–5.

Wright Park. Landscaping of this pleasant park began in 1890 with the glass-domed W. W. Seymour Botanical Conservatory. | 6th Ave. and I St. | 253/591–5331 or 253/591–3690 | Free | Daily.

ON THE CALENDAR

APR.: ***Daffodil Festival.*** Parade, visits to daffodil fields near Puyallup. | 253/627–6176.

SEPT.: ***Commencement Bay Maritime Festival.*** Food booths, historical displays, and events (like the sea chantey sing-off) fill Dock Street during this celebration of Tacoma's maritime culture. During the festivities a sample of Tacoma's tugboats parade up and down the Foss Waterway. | 253/272–1005.

Dining

Altezzo. Italian. On the top floor of the Sheraton Tacoma Hotel, you can enjoy a fabulous views of Puget Sound, Commencement Bay and Mt. Rainier along with Italian specialties of the house which change daily. Popular dishes include fresh pumpkin ravioli and grilled salmon with roasted garlic mash. | 1320 Broadway Plaza | 253/572–3200 | No lunch | $15–$25 | AE, D, DC, MC, V.

Antique Sandwich Company. American/Casual. A deli-style café that has been serving meals for over 25 years. The fare includes hearty soups, such classic children's dishes as waffles and peanut butter and jelly sandwiches, and tasty espresso drinks. Homemade breakfast croissants and pastries available for eat-in and takeout. Old posters on the walls, plastic bears for serving honey, and a toy-covered children's play area help set a cheerful mood. Live performances of folk and classical music on weekends. Breakfast also available. | 5102 N. Pearl St. | 253/752–4069 | Breakfast available | $3–$7 | D, MC, V.

Cliff House. Eclectic. In the past, most people came here primarily for the view, which is most spectacular when there's a full moon in the sky. In recent years, however, the food has become a draw as well. Serving Northwest cuisine—steaks, seafood, and wild game. The seared ahi tuna in a coconut and molasses sauce is a favorite, as are the citrus-marinated prawns. There is also a more casual bistro-style restaurant on the first floor. | 6300 Marine View Dr. | 253/927–0400 | $15–$30 | AE, D, DC, MC, V.

Copperfield's. Contemporary. A fish and chop house where popular items include the shrimp scampi and the crusted romano chicken. Sun. brunch. | 8726 S. Hosmer St. | 253/531–1500 | Breakfast also available | $8–$19 | AE, D, DC, MC, V.

E.R. Rogers Restaurant. American. One of the best, and most liked, of the Tacoma area restaurants is 10 mi south in Steilacoom, the oldest incorporated town in Washington. Housed in an 1891 Queen Anne–style mansion with views of the Tacoma Narrows Bridge, the E. R. Rogers is decorated in Victorian style, with lace valances, brass fixtures, and antiques. Known for prime rib, seafood. Sun. brunch | 1702 Commercial St., Steilacoom | 253/582–0280 | No lunch | $18–$25 | MC, V.

Harbor Lights. Contemporary. This waterfront institution is decorated as a marine curio shop with glass floats, stuffed fish, life preservers and other nautical accoutrements. The food is a lot better than the decor, though both have not changed much since the 1950s. The steamed clams are good; so is the chowder and the fish and chips. No wonder the place is as popular as ever. Limited open-air dining on the deck. Kids' menu. | 2761 Ruston Way | 253/752–8600 | Reservations highly recommended | No lunch Sun. | $12–$39 | AE, D, DC, MC, V.

Johnny's Dock. American. This harbor restaurant is one of Tacoma's old-time favorites, especially popular for its seafood and desserts. Open-air dining on the deck. Kids' menu. No smoking. | 1900 East D St. | 253/627–3186 | $19–$20 | AE, D, DC, MC, V.

Katie Downs. American/Casual. This tavern is justly famous for its Philadelphia-style deep-dish pizza, its steamer clams, its many appetizers, and its microbrews. No kids. | 3211 Ruston Way | 253/756–0771 | $7–$15 | MC, V.

Lobster Shop South. Seafood. A modern, elegant restaurant (unlike the original Lobster Shop on Dash Point, which looks like a weather-beaten oyster shack) with an upscale seafood menu and a view of Commencement Bay. Known, of course, for the rock lobster, but also offers steak and pasta dishes. Open-air dining on the deck, overlooking the water. Kids' menu, early bird suppers (Sun.–Fri). Sun. brunch. | 4013 Ruston Way | 253/759–2165 | No lunch Sat., Sun. | $15–$45 | AE, D, DC, MC, V.

Luciano's Casino Waterfront Ristorante. Italian. This restaurant has a spectacular waterfront setting that fits its Neapolitan menu. Try sauteed veal or one of the specials, such as the charbroiled king salmon topped with horseradish, lemon, and dill sauce. | 3327 Ruston Way | 253/756–5611 | $14–$25 | AE, MC, V.

Old House Café. Contemporary. This pleasant restaurant in the heart of the Proctor District shopping district is an oasis for repose at lunch. Antique accents enliven the café's interior, including a stained-glass window from an old Yakima building, and turn-of-the-20th-century light fixtures from a Seattle bank. Try the warm scallop salad or New York steak. | 2717 N. Proctor St. | 253/759–7336 | Closed Sun., Mon. | $12–$27 | AE, DC, MC, V.

FERRIES AND OTHER SCENIC OBSTACLES

You're planning your first trip to Washington, and you're looking at a map, trying to figure out how to get out of Seatac airport to the Olympic Peninsula and the San Juan Islands, and you panic. Water, water everywhere, you think. How am ever going to get anywhere? I don't have a boat!

Don't worry. You don't need one. That's why Washington has car ferries to take cars across the water.

You'll find most ferries in the Seattle metropolitan area, crossing Puget Sound from Tacoma to Vashon Island, from Seattle to Vashon, Bremerton, and Bainbridge Islands, from Edmonds to Kingston on the Kitsap Peninsula, and from Mukilteo to Clinton on South Whidbey Island. Other Washington State Ferries cross Admiralty Inlet between Whidbey Island (Keystone, about halfway up the island) to Port Townsend on the Olympic Peninsula, and connect the San Juan Islands to Anacortes on the mainland and to Sidney (north of Victoria) on Vancouver Island. A private car ferry travels between Port Angeles on the Olympic Peninsula to Victoria, BC.

Passenger-only ferries connect Seattle to Vashon Island and Bremerton. Private passenger-only ferries run between Seattle and Victoria, Port Angeles and Victoria, Port Townsend and San Juan Island, Bellingham and San Juan Island (as well as to some of the islands not served by Washington State ferry), and Bellingham and Victoria.

Riding a ferry, even if it is just for a short, 20-minute trip, is like stepping back in time to the early days of transportation along the inland waters. Until the 1920s, travel by water was easier in western Washington (and faster) than by road (*see* "Mosquito Fleet" box). But as the roads improved and bridges were built over rivers, means had to be found to take cars over larger bodies of water. Ferries seemed the perfect solution. All ferries were private until 1951, when the state took over essential routes, and made them part of the state highway system. Think of them as toll roads over water.

Washington State car ferries are efficient and fast, unless there's a bottleneck because a ferry broke down or because of extra demand for space (which can cause long backups on weekends and during the vacation season, especially in the San Juans). A few times a year it can get so bad, you might have to wait a few sailings until you finally make it aboard a ferry. So always get there early and be patient. (Cutting in line at a ferry terminal is illegal and will not only cost you a fine but your place in the lineup as well.) And do keep your cool while you wait. Relax. Enjoy the scenery. You'll get there sooner or later. And don't worry about getting someplace late. Everybody on the peninsula or in the island is used to ferry delays. They will probably have watched you waiting in line on the evening news.

You will need a ferry schedule; study it carefully. Schedules are confusing even for regular ferry commuters, who always carry an updated ferry schedule with them in case they have to change plans. Here's some important information:

For fares, call 888/808–7977.

For schedule information, call 800/84–FERRY (WA only).

For schedule information on the Internet:

www.wsdot.wa.gov/ferries/.

Please note that the schedule changes with the seasons; there are fewer ferry runs in fall, winter, and spring.

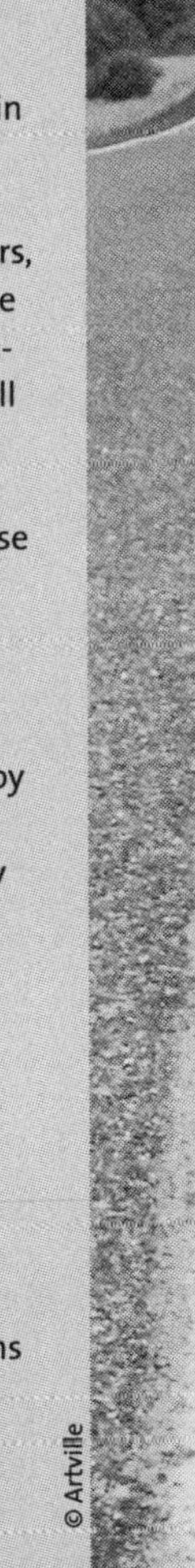

Shoreline Steak and Seafood Grill. Seafood. Mahogany tables fill this eatery that sits directly on the water, overlooking a marina. Not surprisingly, fresh seafood entrées monopolize the menu, although there are also steak, pasta, and salad options. The restaurant is located north of Tacoma in Gig Harbor. | 8827 N. Harborview Dr., Gig Harbor | 253/853–6353 | $16–$26 | AE, D, DC, MC, V.

The Swiss. American. A very popular Waterfront District eatery occupying the former Swiss Hall. A high, pressed-tin ceiling covers the main dining and bar area. The kitchen dishes up creative fare like sandwiches with artichoke hearts and pesto cream cheese. Rooms in back have pool tables and a soundstage. Live blues, jazz, and rock music on weekends. | 1904 S. Jefferson Ave. | 253/572–2821 | $9–12 | No credit cards.

Lodging

Austrian Bed and Breakfast Suites. Rustic Austrian antiques (some over 250 years old) fill each room of this 1891 home, hiding such modern amenities as TVs and telephones. Austrian folk art, paintings and pottery, hang from the walls and occupy the shelves. The house is located in a residential neighborhood 1 mi from the waterfront. | 4 suites. Complimentary breakfast, kitchenettes, microwaves, refrigerators, cable TV, no pets, no smoking. | 723 N Cushman | 253/383–2216 or 800/495–4293, pin 7097 | austrianbb@narrows.com | www.narrows.com/eb&b/ | $65–$105 | MC, V.

Best Western Executive Inn. This modern four-story hotel is 4 mi east of downtown Tacoma. | 138 rooms. Restaurant, bar, in-room data ports, some refrigerators, room service, cable TV, indoor pool, hot tub, business services, airport shuttle, some pets allowed (fee). | 5700 Pacific Hwy E, Fife | 253/922–0080 | fax 253/922–6439 | $85–$145 | AE, D, DC, MC, V.

Best Western Tacoma Inn. Comfortable business travelers' motel 5 minutes from the air force base. | 149 rooms. Restaurant, bar with entertainment, in-room data ports, some kitchenettes, some refrigerators and microwaves, room service, cable TV, pool, putting green, gym, playground, laundry facilities, business services, free parking, some pets allowed (fee). | 8726 S Hosmer St. | 253/535–2880 | fax 253/537–8379 | $79–$99 | AE, D, DC, MC, V.

Chinaberry Hill. The rooms of this 1889 mansion in Tacoma's historic Stadium District range from the luxurious to the sumptuous. | 3 rooms; 1 cottage. Complimentary breakfast and afternoon snacks, no air-conditioning, in-room data ports, many in-room hot tubs, cable TV, VCRs (movies), business services, no kids under 12 (except in cottage), no smoking. | 302 Tacoma Ave. N | 253/272–1282 | fax 253/272–1335 | chinaberry@wa.net | www.chinaberryhill.com | $95–$195, $225 cottage | AE, MC, V.

Commencement Bay Bed and Breakfast. Comfortable lodgings with views of Commencement Bay, Vashon Island, and a lighthouse. Set in a traditional colonial home, the inn offers mountain bikes for guests' use during their stay. | 3 rooms. Complimentary breakfast, cable TV, in-room VCRs (movies), hot tub, massage, exercise equipment, game room, business services, downtown shuttle, no kids under 12. | 3312 N. Union Ave. | 253/752–8175 | fax 253/759–4025 | greatviews@aol.com | www.bestinns.net/usa/wa/cb.html | $95–$125 | AE, D, MC, V.

Days Inn. Budget travelers' motel. | 123 rooms. In-room data ports, cable TV, pool, business services, free parking, pets allowed (fee). | 6802 Tacoma Mall Blvd. | 253/475–5900 | fax 253/475–3540 | $67–$129 | AE, D, DC, MC, V.

DeVoe Mansion Bed and Breakfast. Sitting on 1½ beautiful acres, this 1911 Colonial-style mansion is registered as a National and State Historic Site. The rooms, each named after a prominent women's suffragist, are appointed with antiques such as the queen-size oak sleigh bed with claw feet that occupies the Emma Smith DeVoe Room. | 4 rooms. Complimentary breakfast, in-room VCRs, no pets, no kids under 12, no smoking. | 208 E. 133rd St. | 253/539–3991 or 888/539–3991 | fax 253/539–8539 | innkeeper@devoemansion.com | devoemansion.com | $95–$125 | MC, V.

Green Cape Cod Bed and Breakfast. Built in 1929, this house stands in a residential neighborhood only blocks from University of Puget Sound campus and the historic Proctor shopping district. You're pampered here with bedside candies, robes, down comforters, and complimentary passes to the downtown YMCA. | 3 rooms. Complimentary breakfast, in-room data ports, cable TV, no room phones, no pets, no kids under 10, no smoking. | 2711 N. Warner | 253/752–1977 | fax 253/756–9886 | grncapecod@aol.com | www.greencapecod.com | $95–$115 | AE, MC, V.

Holiday Inn Express Hotels and Suites. The hotel, directly off an exit ramp of I–5, is within walking distance of restaurants; a shopping mall is only a five-minute drive away. | 78 rooms. Complimentary Continental breakfast, in-room data ports, some refrigerators, some in-room hot tubs, cable TV, pool, sauna, gym, business services, no pets. | 8601 S. Hosmer | 253/539–2020 | fax 253/620–6002 | info@holiday-inn.net | www.holiday-inn.net | $85–$95 | AE, D, DC, MC, V.

Keenan House. A pleasant B&B in two Victorian homes, one furnished with antiques, one in more country style. | 4 rooms (2 with shared bath). Picnic area, complimentary breakfast, no air-conditioning, no room phones, no smoking. | 2610 N. Warner St. | 253/752–0702 | fax 253/756–0822 | idvkeenan@aol.com | $60–$70 | MC, V.

King Oscar Motel. Six mi southeast of the downtown area, this chain motel sits just off I–5, next to several restaurants and close to many shops. | 135 rooms. Complimentary Continental breakfast, some kitchenettes, some microwaves, some refrigerators, cable TV, pool, hot tub, gym, laundry facilities, business services, no pets. | 8820 S. Hosmer | 253/539–1153 or 888/254–5464 | fax 253/539–1152 | kingoscartac@aol.com | www.kingoscarmotel.com | $60 | AE, D, DC, MC, V.

La Quinta. Freeway hotel, close to the Tacoma Dome, and about 10 minutes from downtown. | 157 rooms, 2 suites. Restaurant, bar, complimentary Continental breakfast, in-room data ports, room service, cable TV, pool, hot tub, gym, laundry facilities, business services, free parking, some pets allowed. | 1425 E. 27th St. | 253/383–0146 | fax 253/627–3280 | $72–$103 | AE, D, DC, MC, V.

Sheraton. This 26-story downtown hotel is convenient to restaurants and shopping. It has all the amenities you would expect to find at this type of upscale chain hotel. | 319 rooms, 20 suites. Restaurant (*see* Altezzo), bar with entertainment, in-room data ports, minibars, cable TV, pool privileges, barbershop, beauty salon, hot tub, sauna, business services. | 1320 Broadway Plaza | 253/572–3200 or 800/845–9466 | fax 253/591–4105 | $89–$170, $215–$400 suites | AE, D, DC, MC, V.

Shilo Inn. Comfortable family motel with friendly staff. Located near the Tacoma Dome, and many restaurants. | 132 rooms. Complimentary Continental breakfast, in-room data ports, some kitchenettes, microwaves, refrigerators, cable TV, indoor pool, hot tub, gym, laundry facilities, business services, free parking, pets allowed (fee). | 7414 S. Hosmer | 253/475–4020 | fax 253/475–1236 | $85–$109 | AE, D, DC, MC, V.

Thornewood Castle Inn and Gardens Bed and Breakfast. Sitting on 4 acres along American Lake, 12 mi south of Tacoma, this 1908 Gothic Tudor–style mansion has housed two American presidents: William Howard Taft and Theodore Roosevelt. Among the exquisite details found in the guestrooms are medieval stained-glass windows, gleaming wood floors, large mirrors, antiques, fireplaces, and hot tubs. From the lakeside patio you can meditate on the spectacular sunsets. | 6 rooms. Complimentary breakfast, some in-room hot tubs, cable TV, in-room VCRs, beach, library, no pets, no kids under 12, no smoking. | 8601 N. Thorne Ln. SW, Lakewood | 253/589–9052 | fax 253/584–4497 | thornewood@mindspring.com | www.thornewoodcastle.com | $175–$300 | AE, D, MC, V.

The Villa. This Italian Renaissance–style mansion, built in 1925, is on a peaceful residential street. The accommodations are among the most luxurious around. The inn is beautifully decorated with artwork and old photographs. Most rooms have large four-poster beds and private verandas, offering views of Puget sound. | 6 rooms. Complimentary breakfast, no air-conditioning, in-room data ports, cable TV, hot tub, business services, no kids under 12, no smoking. | 705 N. Fifth St. | 253/572–1157 or 888/572–1157 | fax 253/572–1805 | villabb@aol.com | www.villabb.com | $110–$200 | AE, MC, V.

TOPPENISH

MAP 8, G7

(Nearby towns also listed: Sunnyside, Yakima)

Toppenish is a real-life cowboy and Indian town, with a touch of Old Mexico thrown in. The Yakama Indian Cultural Center at the southern edge of town has a museum that is well worth a special visit. Downtown Toppenish is increasingly taking on the atmosphere of a small town in Mexico, due to a large influx of recent Mexican settlers.

Information: **Toppenish Chamber of Commerce** | Box 28, 5A Toppenish Avenue, Toppenish, 99848 | 509/865–3262 or 800/569–3982 | fax 509/865–3549 | www.toppenish.org.

Attractions

American Hop Museum. The United States' only hop museum, this center focuses on the history of the hop industry. Among the many items on display are antique tools and implements, photographs, and memorabilia. | 22 S. B St. | 509/865–HOPS | Donation | May–Sept., daily 11–4.

Ft. Simcoe Historical State Park. These residential quarters of an old army fort, erected in 1856, look more like a Victorian summer retreat than a military establishment. Exhibits focus on the history of local Yakama Indians and American settlers. | 5150 Ft. Simcoe Rd. | 509/874–2372 | www.parks.wa.gov | Free | Apr.–Sept., daily; Oct.–Mar., weekends.

Yakama Nation Cultural Center. This museum tells the story of the Yakama nation; a huge longhouse, shaped like a winter wigwam of old, serves as ceremonial center for dance performances, and social functions. | S on U.S. 97 | 509/865–2800 | fax 509/865–5749 | $4 | Daily 8–5.

ON THE CALENDAR

FEB.: *Cowboy Poetry Gathering.* Cowboy poetry is as big as western art east of the Cascades, and this is one of the most important gatherings of cowboy poets. Evening poetry readings. | 800/569–3982.

FEB.: *Washington Birthday Celebration and Powwow.* Traditional celebration to welcome the beginning of the root harvest. Supper every evening at 5 PM, followed by Native American dancers at 7 PM—a truly great show at the Yakama Nation Cultural Center which is south of town on U.S. 97. | 509/865–5121.

MAR.: *Speelyi-Mi Indian Arts and Crafts Fair.* Traditional, modern, and heirloom arts and crafts. A good place to find beautifully made modern objects as well as hard-to-find authentic older objects. | 509/865–7200.

MAY: *Longhouse Powwow.* Annual powwow of Native American dancers from the United States and Canada is held at Satus, southeast of Toppenish on Rte. 22. The non-tribal public is welcome to attend. | 509/865–5121.

AUG.: *Western Art Show.* Local and state artists come and exhibit their work at Railroad Park on Toppenish Avenue. The show is usually held on the second weekend in August in conjunction with a Rail and Transport Show. | 509/865–3262.

Dining

El Ranchito. Mexican. This authentic cafeteria-style restaurant is also home to a deli, and import shop. Try an enchilada; they are the most popular among the locals. | 1319 E. 1st St., Zillah | 509/829–5880 | Reservations not accepted | Breakfast also available | $5–$10 | MC, V.

Squeeze Inn. American. This family café on Zillah's main street carries its age well. It has served steak and prime rib, as well as hearty breakfasts, to the local farmers and ranchers since 1932, but there's also lighter fare, such as seafood, on the menu. | 611 E. First Ave., Zillah | 509/829–6226 | Breakfast also available on Sat. | $10–$36 | MC, V.

Lodging

Comfort Inn–Zillah. Business travelers' and family motel which serves complimentary cookies and milk in the evenings. | 40 rooms. Complimentary Continental breakfast, cable TV, some no-smoking rooms, pool, hot tub, pets allowed (fee). | 911 Vintage Valley Parkway, Zillah | 509/829–3399 | fax 509/829–3428 | $76 | AE, D, MC, V.

Ox Bow Motor Inn. This two-story indoor corridor motor inn sits at the junction of I–97 and Highway 22. There are restaurants and shopping within one block of the motel. | 44 rooms. Some kitchenettes, microwaves, refrigerators, cable TV, pets allowed (fee). | 511 S. Elm St. | 509/865–5800 or 888/865–5855 | fax 509/865–3623 | $32–$49 | AE, D, DC, MC, V.

Toppenish Inn Motel. Pleasant business traveler's and family motel. | 44 rooms. Complimentary Continental breakfast, some no-smoking rooms, pool, hot tub, gym. | 515 S Elm St. | 509/865–7444 | fax 509/865–7719 | $79–$89 | AE, D, MC, V.

TWISP

MAP 8, H2

(Nearby town also listed: Winthrop)

Twisp is a pretty, small farm town that has become very popular recently as a base for cross-country skiers and as a retirement place for well-off Seattleites (many of whom have built attractive homes on 5-acre "mini-ranches" throughout the valley). Despite the recent development, the town remains largely unspoiled and friendly. A town park at the confluence of the Methow and Twisp Rivers is just perfect for picnics.

Information: Twisp Visitor Information Center and Chamber of Commerce | 201 South Methow Valley Highway, Twisp, 98856 | 509/997–2926 | fax 509/997–2164 | www.twispinfo.com.

Attractions

Confluence Gallery. This art gallery exhibits regional and national artists and has a giftshop that sells the work of regional artisans. The gallery also conducts art classes and hosts events throughout the year. | 104 Glover St. | 509/997–2787 | Mon.–Sat. 10–3.

ON THE CALENDAR

JAN.: *Freeze Yer Buns Fest.* Celebrate the cold with a snowmobile drag race, a fun run, keg toss, and a snowman building contest. | 509/997–2926.

Dining

Methow Valley Brewing Company. American/Casual. Salmon, steak, and duck are some of the upscale items on the menu that also includes more standard fare like bratwurst and burgers. The brewery serves as many as seven to eight of its own beers plus a number of wines. Every Saturday night is open mike night at the brewery which also hosts other live performances. | 209 E. 2nd Ave. | 509/997–MVBC | $6–$15 | AE, D, DC, MC, V.

Lodging

Idle-A-While Motel. Comfortable family motel. | 25 rooms. Cable TV, some no-smoking rooms, hot tub, pets allowed (fee). | 505 N Rte. 20 | 509/997–3222 | fax 509/997–2105 | $55–$71 | AE, D, MC, V.

Methow Valley Inn. Guest rooms in this 1912 house are appointed with antiques and quilt-covered iron beds. Downstairs, the great room is home to a gigantic stone fireplace in front of a leather sofa. Fresh flowers in the rooms and complimentary seasonal fruits from an organic garden are some of the ways the proprietors will pamper you. | 7 rooms (4 with private bath). Complimentary breakfast, no air-conditioning, no room phones, TV in common area, no pets, no kids under 12, no smoking. | 234 E. 2nd Ave. | 509/997–2253 | mvinn@methow.com | www.methow.com/~mvinn | $89–$99 | MC, V.

VANCOUVER

MAP 8, D8

(Nearby town also listed: Portland, OR)

This sprawling river town started out as a Hudson's Bay Company fort and trading depot back in 1824 and soon became the frontier metropolis of the Pacific Northwest, dominating the fur trade for more than two decades. Chief factor John McLoughlin, a truly generous man, helped American settlers get a foothold in Oregon's Willamette Valley by providing equipment and supplies on credit. The U.S. Army built a fort on the bluff above the Hudson's Bay post when the Oregon Territory fell to the U.S. in 1846. Several buildings on "Officers' Row," built between 1867 and 1906, survive. Ulysses S. Grant served here as quartermaster from 1852–53. It is said that he tried to grow potatoes to raise enough money to bring his family out west. He failed as a farmer but succeeded as a Civil War general. The 1849 log cabin where Grant lived still stands. It was, however, remodeled in 1885. Downtown Vancouver has several buildings from the late 19th and early 20th centuries. The modern city sprawls over several river terraces, known locally as "plains," and has pleasant waterfront restaurants, hotels, and parks.

Information: Greater Vancouver Chamber of Commerce, | 404 E. 15th St., Suite 11, Vancouver, 98663 | 360/694–2588 | fax 360/693–8279 | www.vancouverusa.com.

Attractions

Clark County Historical Museum. Indian artifacts, the first piano north of the Columbia (built in 1836), an 1890 country store, a 1900 doctor's office, and more are on display. | 1511 Main St. | 360/695–4681 | www.fvhscc.org | Free | Tues.–Sat. 11–4.

Columbia River Waterfront Trail. Bike, skate, jog, or stroll the 4 mi promenade that follows the Columbia River. Visit the Old Apple Tree along the way and stop to enjoy the scenic vistas. | 100 Columbia or Wintler Park, 6400 Beach Tree | 360/696–8171.

Fort Vancouver National Historic Site. This splendidly reconstructed fort, with squared-log buildings, an encircling palisade, and corner bastions, was first established here by the Hudson's Bay Company in 1825. In summer, park rangers dress in period costume and demonstrate various pioneer skills. | 1501 E. Evergreen Blvd. | 360/696–7655 | www.nps.gov | Free | Daily.

Gifford Pinchot National Forest. A vast forest of evergreens stretching from Mt. St. Helens east to Mt. Adams, and north to Mt. Rainier. This is one of the oldest forests in Washington and is named for the first Chief of the Forest Service. | Forest Headquarters 10600 N.E. 51st Circle, accessible via Rte. 14, Rte. 25, or Rte. 503 | Free | Daily.

Officers' Row. The ten officers' houses and duplexes lining the former parade grounds were built between 1867 and 1906. Ulysses S. Grant lived in the 1849 log building now bearing his name when he was quartermaster of Vancouver Barracks from 1852 to 1853. | 750 Anderson St. | 360/693–3103 | fax 360/693–3192 | Free | Daily 9–5.

Pearson Air Museum. Vintage aircraft in working order are on display. | 1115 E. Fifth St. | 360/694–7026 | fax 360/694–0824 | www.pearsonairmuseum.org | $5 | Tues.–Sun. 10–5.

ON THE CALENDAR

JULY: *Fourth of July Celebration.* Among the events taking place at this festival held at the Vancouver National Historic Reserve are arts and crafts booths, food vendors, sky divers, an antique airplane show, a carnival, and the largest fireworks display west of the Mississippi. | 360/992–1840.

Dining

Beach's Restaurant. American/Casual. This restaurant, directly on the water, has gorgeous views up and down the river. The menu includes a range of pastas, fresh fish, steak, and salads. | 1919 S.E. Columbia River Dr. | 360/699–1592 or 503/222–9947 | $6–$23 | AE, D, DC, MC, V.

Bell Tower Brewhouse. American/Casual. In an old church, beneath a bell tower, this restaurant and brewery serves up a variety of steaks, ribs, burgers, and fish, not to mention six of its own beers. The cathedral ceilings, enormous windows, and two outdoor patios result in a unique dining experience, wherever you sit. Tuesday is prime rib night. | 707 S.E. 164th Ave. | 360/944–7800 | $6.85–$18.85 | AE, D, DC, MC, V.

The Crossing. American. You can dine in one of seven railroad cars including a sleeper and presidential car. The unique restaurant's menu contains such items as rotisserie chicken, seafood dishes, and sandwiches. Especially popular are the prime rib and king salmon. | 900 W. 7th Ave. | 360/693–9105 | Closed Sun. in summer | $10–$16 | AE, D, MC, V.

Sheldon's Cafe at the Grant House. American/Casual. Good grub in an old house built in the Civil War days where Ulysses S. Grant is supposed to have lived before gaining fame. Favorites include fresh smoked barbecue and roast pork loin. | 1101 Officer's Row | 360/699–1213 | Closed Sun.–Mon. | $12–$18 | MC, V.

Vancouver's Chart House. Seafood. Tier-dining guarantees that you'll have a wonderful view of the water from your table. The specialty is seafood (the lobster is particularly good), although the restaurant also serves steak and prime rib. Outdoor dining overlooking the river is very popular in the warmer seasons. | 101 E. Columbia Way | 360/693–9211 | Reservations essential weekends | No lunch weekends | $22–$30 | AE, D, DC, MC, V.

Who Song and Larry's Cantina Mexican Restaurant. Mexican. The fajitas—chicken, steak, or shrimp—come sizzling at this waterfront eatery. A deck that overlooks the river provides outdoor seating. | 111 E. Columbia Way | 360/695–1198 or 503/285–7395 | $9–$13 | AE, D, DC, MC, V.

Lodging

Best Inn and Suites. Budget travelers' motel located close to the Columbia Gorge and the Vancouver waterfront. Ask about their special "Evergreen Rooms," which feature extra-clean facilities, such as purified water, and air filters. | 118 rooms. Restaurant, complimentary Continental breakfast, cable TV, some no-smoking rooms, indoor pool, hot tub, business services, airport shuttle, free parking, pets allowed (fee). | 221 N.E. Chkalov Dr. | 360/256–7044 or 800/426–5110 | fax 360/256–1231 | $52–$139 | AE, D, DC, MC, V.

Comfort Inn. Business travelers' and family inn close to the fairgrounds, and about 15 minutes from the Portland Airport. | 58 rooms. Complimentary Continental breakfast, refrigerators, microwaves, cable TV, indoor pool, hot tub, exercise equipment, laundry facilities, business services. | 13207 N.E. 20th Ave. | 360/574–6000 | fax 360/573–3746 | $64–$125 | AE, D, DC, MC, V.

Comfort Suites. Business travelers' hotel, close to the Vancouver Mall. Offers a tanning room for guests. | 68 suites. Complimentary Continental breakfast, microwaves, refrigerators, cable TV, indoor pool, hot tub, gym, business services, free parking. | 4714 N.E. 94th Ave. | 360/253–3100 | fax 360/253–7998 | $83–$128 suites | AE, D, DC, MC, V.

Ferryman's Inn. Just west of I–5, at exit 4, this two-story blue with red-brick motel is 2 mi north of Vancouver. | 134 rooms. Complimentary Continental breakfast, some kitchenettes, cable TV, pool, laundry facilities, business services, pets allowed (fee). | 7901 N.E. 6th Ave. | 360/574–2151 | fax 360/574–9644 | $54–$68 | AE, D, DC, MC, V.

Heathman Lodge. Alpine-style lodge with massive hand-hewn logs in secluded urban setting. Just five minutes away from the Vancouver Mall. | 121 rooms, 22 suites. Restaurant, in-room data ports, microwaves, refrigerators, in-room hot tubs (in suites), cable TV, in-room VCRs, Nintendo, gym, indoor pool, hot tub, sauna. | 7801 N.W. Greenwood Dr. | 360/254–3100 or 888/475–3100 | fax 360/254–6100 | www.heathmanlodge.com | $89–$119, $159–$550 suites | AE, D, DC, MC, V.

Holiday Inn Express. This small two-story lodging is very popular with business travelers. | 56 rooms. Complimentary Continental breakfast, cable TV, indoor pool, hot tub. | 9107 N.E. Vancouver Mall Dr. | 360/253–5000 | fax 360/253–3137 | $65–$70 | AE, D, DC, MC, V.

Homewood Suites Portland-Vancouver. Near the banks of the Columbia River, this hotel sits close to Highway 14 and is especially well-suited to those staying longer than a single night. The outdoor barbecue grills and picnic area are a perfect place to relax. | 104 rooms. Picnic area, complimentary breakfast, in-room data ports, kitchenettes, microwaves, refrigerators, cable TV, pool, hot tub, tennis court, basketball, gym, shop, laundry services, business services, pets allowed. | 701 S.E. Columbia Shores Blvd. | 360/750–1100 or 800/CALL–HOME | fax 360/750–4899 | kimw@pacifier.com | www.homewood-suites.com | $129–$179 | AE, D, DC, MC, V.

Red Lion Inn at the Quay. This hotel overlooks the Columbia River and is close to Fort Vancouver. The Portland airport is only a 15-minute drive away. There is a 3K trail just outside the door. | 160 rooms. Restaurant, bar with entertainment, in-room data ports, room service, cable TV, pool, business services, airport shuttle, free parking. | 100 Columbia St. | 360/694–8341 | fax 360/694–2023 | $89–$120 | AE, D, DC, MC, V.

Shilo Inn–Downtown Vancouver. In the heart of downtown, this hotel is close to the Vancouver National Historic Site and is directly off I–5. There are several restaurants within walking distance. | 118 rooms. Complimentary Continental breakfast, some microwaves, some refrigerators, cable TV, pool, hot tub, sauna, steam room, gym, laundry service, business service, pets allowed (fee). | 401 E. 13th St. | 360/696–0411 or 800/222–2244 | fax 360/750–0933 | vancouver@shiloinns.com | www.shiloinns.com | $79–$95 | AE, D, DC, MC, V.

Shilo Inn–Hazel Dell. Comfortable motel. One of the early Shilo Inns that helped make this regional chain's reputation for comfort and friendly service throughout the Northwest. It is close to the Clark County Fairgrounds. | 66 rooms. Complimentary Continental breakfast, some kitchenettes, refrigerators, microwaves, cable TV, indoor pool, hot tub, sauna, steam room, laundry facilities, business services, airport shuttle, free parking, pets allowed (fee). | 13206 Hwy. 99 | 360/573–0511 | fax 360/573–0396 | $79–$109 | AE, D, DC, MC, V.

Sleep Inn. Only two blocks from I–205, this hotel sits across the street from the Vancouver Mall. Contemporary furnishings fill all the rooms. | 63 rooms. Complimentary Continental breakfast, in-room data ports, some microwaves, some refrigerators, cable TV, pool, hot tub, no pets, no smoking. | 9201 N.E. Vancouver Mall Dr. | 360/254–0900 | fax 360/254–9343 | www.sleepinn.com | $66–$100 | AE, D, DC, MC, V.

Vintage Inn. This 1903 Craftsman-style mansion sits in the heart of downtown, close to the Vancouver National Historic Reserve and many restaurants. Antiques fill all the rooms of the inn to the extent that some refer to it as a small museum. A working fireplace occupies one room while in another French doors lead to a sleeping porch overlooking an herb garden. | 4 rooms. Complimentary breakfast, no room phones, TV in common area, no pets, no smoking. | 310 W. 11th St. | 360/693–6635 or 888/693–6635 | info@vintage-inn.com | www.vintage-inn.com | $85 | MC, V.

WALLA WALLA

MAP 8, J7

(Nearby town also listed: Dayton)

This delightful town, founded in the 1850s on the site of a Nez Perce village, was Washington's first metropolis. As late as 1880s, its population was larger than that of Seattle. Walla Walla occupies a lush green valley below the rugged Blue Mountains. It has a beautifully maintained (and partly restored) downtown, with old residences, green parks, and the campus of Whitman College, Washington's oldest institution of higher learning. It is so pleasant a town that it is easy to forget that Walla Walla is also home to the state penitentiary. The surrounding countryside is famous for its sweet onions, asparagus, and wines.

Information: Walla Walla Area Chamber of Commerce | 29 E. Sumach, Box 644, Walla Walla, 99362 | 509/525–0850 or 877/998–4748 | info@wwchamber.com | wwchamber.com.

Attractions

Fort Walla Walla Park. This fort was in use from 1858 to 1910. The site now has picnic tables, a camp site, a museum, and an old military cemetery. | Dalles Military Rd. | 509/527–3770 | fax 509/525–0845 | www.ci.walla-walla.wa.us | Free | Daily.

Fort Walla Walla Museum. A collection of 14 original and re-created pioneer buildings, including an 1859 cabin and an 1880 railroad station. Five buildings are devoted to the age of horse-drawn engines, and include a 33-mule combine. | 755 Myra Rd. | 509/525–7703 | fax 509/525–7798 | www.bmi.net/fortw2 | $5 | Apr.–Oct., Tues.–Sun. 10–5.

Pioneer Park. A shady, square turn-of-the-20th-century park planted with native and exotic flowers and trees. | Division and Alder Sts. | 509/527–4527 | fax 509/525–0845 | www.ci.walla-walla.wa.us | Free | Daily.

Whitman College. Large, tree-lined lawns surround the many beautiful 19th-century brick structures of this campus. The school began as a Seminary in 1859 and became a college in 1883. | 345 Boyer Ave. | 509/527–5111.

Whitman Mission National Historic Site. This is a reconstruction of the mission founded by Marcus and Narcissa Whitman in 1837 and destroyed in 1847 by Cayuse Indians who were angry with the Whitmans because they thought the missionaries were encouraging white settlers to appropriate their lands. | 328 Whitman Mission Rd. | 509/522–6360 | fax 509/522–6355 | www.nps.gov/whmi | $2 | Daily.

ON THE CALENDAR

JUNE: *Lewis and Clark Festival.* Demonstrations and reenactments of 19th-century military activities. | 509/525–7703.

JULY: *Sweet Onion Festival.* A celebration of Walla Walla's favorite sweet fruit with onion games, entertainment, food booths, competitions, and arts and crafts. Come and taste the onion that makes Vidalias and Mauis taste like balls o' fire by comparison. Held at Fort Walla Walla Park. | 509/525–0850.

Dining

Merchants Ltd. Delicatessen. A comfortable, cluttered, very friendly deli and wine shop with a dining area in back and a glass-front bakery. In warm weather you can sit out front at sidewalk tables. The food is very good, from soups to sandwiches and salads. There's also an excellent and extremely popular Wednesday night spaghetti dinner. This is the one place in Walla Walla where you can reliably pick up caviar and champagne for that special picnic. Early bird dinner (Wed.). | 21 E. Main St. | 509/525–0900 | Breakfast also available. Closed Sun. No supper Mon.–Tues., Thurs.–Sat. | $4–$8 | AE, D, MC, V.

Paisano's. Italian. This Walla Walla mainstay sits in the center of the historic downtown area. Pastas, lasagnas, seafood, and steaks fill the menu; one of the most popular dishes is the smoked duck capellini. You can dine outside on Main Street among the many historic buildings. | 26 E. Main St., Suite 1 | 509/527–3511 | Sunday | $13–$20 | MC, V.

Red Apple. Contemporary. A comfortable, modern family restaurant where steak and seafood rule the day (and night). Entertainment Thurs.–Sun. | 57 E. Main St. | 509/525–5113 | Open 24 hours | $10–$20 | MC, V.

Lodging

Best Western Walla Walla Suites Inn. One mile from wineries and from Whitman College make this a very convenient place to stay while touring in the area. | 78 suites. Complimentary Continental breakfast, refrigerators, microwaves, coffee makers in each room, indoor pool, spa, business services, some pets allowed (fee). | 7 E. Oak St. | 509/525–4700 | fax 509/525–2457 | $59–$100 suites | AE, D, DC, MC, V.

Green Gables Inn. One block from the Whitman Campus, this 1909 Arts and Crafts–style mansion sits among flowering plants and shrubs on a quaint, tree-lined street. The names of rooms are derived from Lucy Maud Montgomery's novel *Anne of Green Gables.* Guest rooms, appointed with Victorian antiques, each have their individual charms. The "Idlewild" contains a fireplace, private deck, and a single-person in-room hot tub, while in "Dryad's Bubble" French doors lead to a small, private balcony. | 4 rooms, 2 suites. Complimentary breakfast, refrigerators, some in-room hot tubs, cable TV, in-room VCRs, no smoking. | 922 Bonsella St. | 509/525–5501 | greengables@wwics.com | www.greengablesinn.com | $95–$125 | AE, D, MC, V.

Hawthorne Inn and Suites. In downtown Walla Walla, next door to restaurants and shopping, this hotel sits right off Highway 12 at the 2nd Avenue exit. Hot baked cookies are served in the evenings. | 61 rooms. Complimentary Continental breakfast, some refrigerators, cable TV, indoor pool, business services, some pets allowed. | 520 N. 2nd Ave. | 509/525–2522 | fax 509/522–2565 | $69–$189 | AE, D, DC, MC, V.

Howard Johnson. This 2-floor 1960s chain hotel sitting on Main Street has quiet, well-maintained rooms, most of which open onto a courtyard with pool. | 85 rooms. Complimentary Continental breakfast, in-room data ports, some refrigerators, cable TV, pool, hot tub, sauna, exercise equipment, laundry facilities. | 325 E. Main St. | 509/529–4360 or 800/634–7669 ext. 25 | fax 509/529–7463 | $72–$90 | AE, D, DC, MC, V.

Marcus Whitman Hotel and Conference Center. Built in 1928 and undergoing renovation in 2000, this 12-story brick and marble luxury hotel has housed two U.S. presidents in its time: Dwight D. Eisenhower and Lyndon B. Johnson. The hotel will also be home to two art galleries and a motorcycle museum. | 75 rooms, 16 suites. Restaurant, bar, in-room data ports, cable TV, gym, shops, business services, airport shuttle, no pets. | 6 West Rose | 509/525–2200 | fax 509/529–9282 | www.marcuswhitmanhotel.com.

Walla Walla Travelodge. Across Main Street from Whitman College, this 2-story chain is only a short stroll away from shops and restaurants. | 39 rooms. Cable TV, pool, hot tub, business services. | 421 E. Main St. | 509/529–4940 | fax 509/529–4943 | $59–$79 | AE, D, DC, MC, V.

WENATCHEE

MAP 8, G4

(Nearby towns also listed: Cashmere, Leavenworth)

Wenatchee, the county seat of Chelan County, is an attractive city in a shallow valley at the confluence of the Wenatchee River and the Columbia. Surrounded by orchards, Wenatchee is known as the "Apple Capital of Washington." Downtown has many old business buildings, as well as apple-packing houses where visitors can buy locally grown apples by the case (at about half the price or less charged in supermarkets). Ohme Gardens, north of the river, is one of the great gardens of America.

Wenatchee was built on an ancient Wenatchi Indian village, which may have been occupied as long ago as 11,000 years, as recent archaeological finds of Clovis hunter artifacts suggest.

Information: Wenatchee Chamber of Commerce | 2 South Chelan Avenue, Wenatchee, 98801 | 509/663–2116 or 800/57–APPLE | fax 509/663–2022 | www.wenatchee.org.

Attractions

Mission Ridge Ski Area. Four lifts, 33 downhill runs, powder snow, and some 30 mi of marked cross-country trails make this one of Washington's most popular ski areas. There's a 2,100-ft vertical drop. | Squilchuck Rd. | 509/663–7631 or 800/374–1693 (snow conditions) | Oct.–Apr.

North Central Washington Museum. Displays of local Indian and pioneer artifacts, as well as a working antique apple sorter. | 127 S. Mission St. | 509/664–3340 | fax 509/664–3356 | $3 | Mon.–Sat. 10–4.

Ohme Gardens. A beautiful blend of native rock, waterfalls, rock gardens, and conifers makes this one of America's most acclaimed gardens. | 3327 Ohme Rd. | 509/662–5785 | www.ohmegardens.com | $6 | Mid-Apr.–mid-Oct., daily 9–7; Nov.–March, daily 9–6.

Rocky Reach Dam. This dam has picnic tables and elaborately landscaped grounds. The Gallery of the Columbia has the pilothouse of the late 1800s Columbia River steamer *Bridgeport*, as well as replicas of Indian dwellings, and Indian, logger, and railroad workers' tools. The Gallery of Electricity has exhibits explaining why dams and electricity are good for you. | U.S. 97A N | 509/663–7522 or 509/663–8121 | Free | mid-Feb.–Dec., daily.

Squilchuck State Park. A small downhill ski area with miles of cross-country trails. | Squilchuck Rd. | 509/664–6373 | www.parks.wa.gov | Mar.–Nov.

Wenatchee National Forest. A mostly pine forest on 2.2 million acres covering the eastern slopes of the Cascade Mountains, from the crest of the Wenatchee Mountains north to Lake Chelan. Camping, hiking, boating, fishing, hunting, and picnicking are popular activities. It can be reached from the north, south and west of town. | 509/662–4335 | fax 509/664–2731 | www.fs.fed.us/r6/wenatchee | Free | Weekdays 7:45–4:30.

ON THE CALENDAR

APR.–MAY: *Apple Blossom Festival.* Held on the last week in April and the first week in May, the celebration includes food vendors, arts and crafts booths, and musical entertainment, all of which occurs in Centennial Park below the Court House. A carnival takes place on the riverfront and at least two parades go through downtown. | 509/662–3616.

Dining

Carriage House of Prime Rib. Steak. Just behind the John Horan Steak and Seafood House is this slightly more casual eatery. The menu contains a variety of steak and seafood options prepared with less fanfare than the restaurant next door. You may dine on a patio overlooking the gardens and lawns. | 2 Horan Rd. | 509/663–0018 | No lunch | $7–$20 | D, DC, MC, V.

Wenatchee Roaster and Ale House. American/Casual. The top floor of the Westcoast Wenatchee Center Hotel houses a restaurant that overlooks downtown Wenatchee and the river. Specializing in house-smoked meats, the restaurant serves a variety of turkey, chicken, and steak dishes, not to mention a selection of salads and sandwiches. A reduced-fat menu is available if you're health-conscious. | 201 N. Wenatchee Ave. | 509/662–1234 | Breakfast also available | $8–$17 | AE, D, DC, MC, V.

The Windmill. Steak. This is eastern Washington's most venerable steakhouse, and people drive here all the way from Spokane, Yakima, Seattle, and beyond, to taste the meat, which is well-aged and cooked to perfection. Be sure to leave room for a piece of one of the glorious pies. | 1501 N. Wenatchee Ave. | 509/665–9529 | Closed Sun. from Labor Day–Memorial Day. No lunch | $12–$25 | AE, MC, V.

Lodging

Holiday Lodge. This motel is located between the shopping center and the convention center. | 59 rooms. Complimentary Continental breakfast, cable TV, pool, hot tub, exercise equipment, laundry facilities, business services. | 610 N. Wenatchee Ave. | 509/663–8167 or 800/722–0852 | fax 509/663–8167 | $38–$73 | AE, D, DC, MC, V.

Mickey O'Reilly's Inn at the River. Resort motel on the Columbia River with views of the Cascade and Wenatchee Mountains. Easy access to bike loop trails and close to Wenatchee Valley Mall. | 55 rooms. Restaurant, bar, complimentary Continental breakfast, cable TV, pool, hot tub, business services. | 580 Valley Mall Pkwy., East Wenatchee | 509/884–1474 or 800/922–3199 | fax 509/884–9179 | $62–$72 | AE, D, DC, MC, V.

Red Lion Hotel–Wenatchee. Right in the heart of Wenatchee, this Red Lion is a 15-minute drive from Pangborn Airport. | 149 rooms. Restaurant, bar with entertainment, in-room data ports, room service, cable TV, pool, business services, airport shuttle, pets allowed. | 1225 N. Wenatchee Ave. | 509/663–0711 | fax 509/662–8175 | $69–$89 | AE, D, DC, MC, V.

Rimrock Inn Bed and Breakfast. Three mi south of Wenatchee, this bed and breakfast draws its name from the boulders which sit on the canyon ridge. The 7 acres of land on which the house sits is frequently visited by a variety of wildlife including quail, deer, and coyote. Rooms have cedar and pine ceilings with exposed beams. The country furnishings accent these rustic charms. | 3 rooms. Complimentary breakfast, no room phones, TV in common area, no pets, no kids under 10, no smoking. | 1354 Pitcher Canyon Rd. | 509/664–5113 or 888/664–5113 | www.rimrockinn.com | $80 | MC, V.

Warm Springs Inn Bed and Breakfast. Roses, planted along the driveway, lead you to this 1917 mansion that sits amid gardens and trees on 10 acres. Individually appointed, the rooms are filled with a tasteful selection of art and antiques and overlook the gardens and lawns. | 5 rooms. Complimentary breakfast, cable TV, no room phones, hot tub, pets allowed, no smoking. | 1611 Love Ln. | 509/662–8365 or 800/543–3645 | fax 509/663–5997 | warmsi@warmspringsinn.com | www.warmspringsinn.com | $85–$110 | AE, D, MC, V.

Westcoast Wenatchee Center. Comfortable business travelers' and family vacation motel near the riverfront park and downtown. | 147 rooms. Restaurant, bar with entertainment, cable TV, indoor-outdoor pool, hot tub, exercise equipment, downhill skiing, business services, airport shuttle, pets allowed (fee). | 201 N. Wenatchee Ave. | 509/662–1234 | fax 509/662–0782 | $99–$200 | AE, D, DC, MC, V.

WESTPORT

MAP 8, A5

(Nearby towns also listed: Aberdeen, Hoquiam, Ocean Shores)

Westport is a pretty bayfront fishing village below the southern spit that protects the entrance to Grays Harbor from the fury of the Pacific Ocean. It is one of the best places on the coast to watch winter storms. In recent decades, Westport was Washington's favorite port for salmon-fishing charters, but since salmon stocks have declined dangerously, local party boats now offer lingcod, rockfish, and albacore fishing trips, as well as whale-watching tours. The beach at Westport is a great place for taking a walk or flying a kite. But, like other Washington beaches, it is too dangerous for swimming (though that does not appear to deter surfers) and too cold for sunbathing.

Information: Westport-Grayland Chamber of Commerce | 2985 S. Montesano, Westport, 98595 | 360/268–9422 or 800/345–6223 | fax 360/268–1990 | www.westportgrayland-chamber.org.

Attractions

Grays Harbor Lighthouse. At 107 ft (123 ft above the water), this 1898 brick lighthouse, off Hwy. 105, is the tallest on the Washington coast. It stands on Coast Guard–owned land, adjacent to Westport Light State Park, a day-use park with picnic tables and a beach. The interior of the lighthouse is not open to the public. | Ocean Ave. | 360/268–0078 | Free | Daily.

Harbor Walkway. Between the lighthouse and West Haven State Park, a [illegible] mi walkway winds along the sandy beach. The walkway is paved, so you can also skate or jog on it. | Ocean Ave.

Westport Maritime Museum. This museum, in a former coast guard station, has historical photos and a collection of sea mammal bones, as well as logging and cranberry industry artifacts. | 2201 Westhaven Dr. | 360/268–0078 | fax 360/438–3224 | www.westportwa.com/museum | $2 | Labor Day–Memorial Day, Thurs.–Mon. noon–4; Memorial Day–Labor Day, daily 10–4.

Twin Harbors State Park. An oceanfront park with campground, picnic areas, playground, sand dunes, nature trail, and about 3 mi of sandy beach. | Rte. 105S | 360/268–9717 | fax 360/268–0372 | www.parks.wa.gov | Free | Daily dawn–dusk.

Westport Aquarium. The aquarium's tanks hold such local marine life as sea anemones, bottomfish, octopi, and sharks. Entertainment is provided by performing sea lions. | 321 Harbor St. | 360/268–0471 | $3 | Feb.–Oct., daily; Nov., weekends.

ON THE CALENDAR

JAN.: ***Penguin Plunge.*** A communal dip in the chilly waters of the Pacific Ocean to greet the new year. Visitors welcome at Grayland and invited to plunge in on Jan. 2. Paramedics on stand-by. | 800/473–6018.

MAR.–MAY: ***Gray Whale Watching.*** As gray whales return north from their breeding grounds in Baja California to their summer feeding grounds in the Bering Sea, they pass close to Westport, and may even dig for clams on the beach (coming in as close as the water will bear them, which can be very close indeed). Observe from the coastline or walkways, or take one of the chartered cruises offered. | 800/473–6018.

MAR.: ***Beachcombers Annual Driftwood Show.*** Amateur and professional driftwood collectors exhibit their treasures and compete for prizes. Held at the Grayland Community Hall. | 509/248–3425.

APR.: ***World Class Crab Races and Crab Feed.*** A race in which prizes are awarded for the fastest crabs and for each crab *freed*—i.e., the competitors do not end up in the Crab Feed kettle. Held at marina across from float 12. | 800/345–6223.

Dining

The Diner. American. Only a few steps from the beach and lighthouse, this popular eatery complements the traditional variety of diner dishes with its home-baked pastries and fresh clam chowder. | 389 W. Ocean Ave. | 360/268–6097 | Breakfast also available | $7.50–$15 | D, MC, V.

Lodging

Chateau Westport Motel. Big, upscale family motel near the dunes and beach. | 108 rooms, 2 suites. Complimentary Continental breakfast, cable TV, indoor pool, hot tub, volleyball, playground. | 710 Hancock | 800/255–9101 | fax 360/268–1646 | www.ohwy.com/wa/c/chatwest/htm | $70–$73, $173–$229 suites | AE, D, DC, MC, V.

Harbor Resort. From the windows of your room, you might spy a whale. That's how close you are to the water. Rooms are all located on the second story and are appointed with contemporary furnishings. | 7 rooms, 7 cottages. Some kitchenettes, some microwaves, some refrigerators, cable TV, pets allowed (fee). | Float 20 | 360/268–0169 | fax 360/268–0338 | www.harborresort.com | $59–$65 rooms, $99–$120 cottages | AE, D, MC, V.

WA

WHIDBEY ISLAND

MAP 8, D3

(Nearby towns also listed: Coupeville, Langley, Oak Harbor)

Forty-mile-long Whidbey Island considers itself the longest island in the U.S, since a federal judge decided a few years back that New York's Long Island has so many bridges it has become a "peninsula"—which is a bit of a local joke, since Whidbey Island, too, has a bridge (across Deception Pass in the north) connecting the island to Fidalgo Island which in turn is connected to the mainland by two bridges.

Whidbey Island is largely residential now, with overflow from the Everett Section of Pugetopolis commuting via the Clinton Mukilteo ferry at the islands' southern tip, and with the navy town of Oak Harbor spreading far and wide. But it still has many unspoiled areas. Besides the famous Deception Pass, these include Fort Ebey State Park and Ebey's Landing National Historic Reserve.

Since Whidbey Island, with the exception of the rocky outcroppings of Deception Pass, consists of a long glacial moraine composed of gravels and silt, bluffs are very unstable and visitors should be careful when walking along the edge of steep seaward inclines.

Information: Greater Oak Harbor Chamber of Commerce | 32630 SR 20, Oak Harbor, 98277 | 360/675–3535 | fax 360/679–1624 | www.oakharborchamber.org.

Attractions

Deception Pass State Park. Rock-bound Deception Pass, 7 mi north of Oak Harbor, is a steep-walled tidal channel and Whidbey Island's most famous feature. The adjacent state park, with shady forest campsites, sunny cliff-top walks, sandy beaches, and a water lily pond, is Washington's most popular, hosting more than 4 million visitors a year. | Hwy. 20 | 360/675–2417 | Free | Apr.–Sept, daily 6:30 AM–dusk; Oct.–Mar., 8 AM–dusk.

Ebey's Landing National Historic Reserve. This 13,000-acre reserve encompasses two state parks and some privately held farmland. The first of its kind in the nation, the reserve preserves not only a site of major regional importance but its agricultural heritage as well. It was here that Colonel Isaac Ebey and his family homesteaded, and it was here that he lost his head to a party of raiding Tlinkit Indians. Today there are nearly 100 nationally registered historic structures on the reserve. A trail winding up a wildflower-strewn bluff offers great views of Juan de Fuca Strait. This is one of the few places on the Salish Sea where the storm watching is great.

Fort Casey State Park. Set on a bluff overlooking the Strait of Juan de Fuca, 3 mi south of Coupeville, this park was one of three forts built in 1890 to protect Puget Sound. There are an interpretive center, picnic areas, fishing spots, and a boat launch. | Off Hwy. 20 | 360/678–4519 | Free | Daily 8–dusk.

Fort Ebey State Park. This park, west of Penn Cove, is a lovely region of piney woods, wildflower-bedecked bluffs, log-strewn beaches, and native rhododendrons (which flower around Memorial Day). | Off Hwy. 20 | 360/678–4636 | Free | Daily 8–dusk.

Meerkerk Rhododendron Gardens. Thousands of rhododendrons line the numerous walking trails and ponds throughout the 53 acres of this garden. Flowers are in bloom throughout the year, but are most spectacular in April and May. The garden is located off Resort Road and Highway 525. | 3531 Meerkerk Ln | 360/678–1912 | www.whidbey.net/meerkerk/garden.html | $3 | Daily 9–4.

ON THE CALENDAR

JULY: ***Loganberry Festival.*** Sample jams and wines made from loganberries at this festival held at the Greenbank Farm Winery. There is an arts and crafts festival, as well as live entertainment. | 360/678–7700.

Dining

Teddy's on Whidbey. Contemporary. The restaurant is housed in a Victorian structure, complete with a turret, wraparound porch, a grand staircase, and lots of wood details. Sit in the deep comfortable booths and enjoy a fresh seafood dish, a steak, or an imaginative pasta entrée. The restaurant is known especially for its steaks. | 1804 E. Scott Rd., Freeland | 360/331–2882 | $11–$17 | AE, MC, V.

Lodging

Brierly Inn. Five acres of trees, lawns, gardens, and meadows surround this English Tudor manor. In the three rooms, antiques are mixed with more contemporary furnishings to provide the maximum of comfort and elegance—the featherbeds are especially popular. The large windows in the rooms make the interiors bright and cheerful. There is a two-night minimum. | 3 rooms. Complimentary breakfast, some in-room hot tubs, cable TV, some in-room VCRs, no room phones, hot tub, no pets, no kids under 12, no smoking. | 7510 Roseberry, Clinton | 360/579–1880 or 888/440–1880 | fax 360/579–1870 | brierly@whidbey.com | www.brierlyinn.com | $135–$175 | MC, V.

Guest House Log Cottages. This log house along with some cabins has views of Holmes Harbor and Saratoga Passage (Salish Sea), the North Cascades and Mt. Baker, but with the tall trees surrounding the cabins, they may be hard to spot. Spread out over 25 acres, the grounds feature a pond and many visiting birds. All of these comfortable rooms have fireplaces. Catering to couples looking for a romantic weekend. | 5 cabins, 1 suite, 1 luxury log house. Picnic area, complimentary breakfast, no air-conditioning in many rooms, kitchenettes (in cottages), microwaves, in-room hot tubs, cable TV, in-room VCRs (movies), no room phones, pool, exercise equipment, no kids, no smoking. | 24371 SR 525 Rte. 525, Greenbank | 360/678–3115 | fax 360/678–3115 | www.whidbey.net/logcottage | $125 suite, $310 lodge, call for cabin prices | AE, D, MC, V.

Harbour Inn. Twenty mi south of Coupeville in Freeland, this pleasant family motel has a convenient in-town location, but is set on 2 acres of land and is a short walk to the city beach. | 20 rooms. Complimentary Continental breakfast, no air-conditioning, refrigerators, cable TV, some pets allowed (fee). | 1606 E. Main | 360/331–6900 | fax 360/331–6900 | harborinn@whidbey.com | $64–$90 | AE, MC, V.

WINTHROP

MAP 8, G2

(Nearby town also listed: Omak)

A couple of decades ago, the small river town of Winthrop decided to adopt a false-front "Western" theme for its business district. That wasn't at all hard to do, since many old buildings survive from the 19th century, when cattle was king in this Methow Valley town. Among the most famous visitors of that period was writer Owen Wister, whose *Virginian* drew its literary portraits from some of the valley's local characters.

Before the cowboys came, the Methow Valley was a favorite gathering place for Indian tribes, who dug the plentiful and nutritious bulbs and hunted deer while their horses fattened on the tall native grasses. On hot summer days, the cool, glacier-fed river provides welcome relief; at night, its burbling lulls travelers to sleep.

"Methow," incidentally, translates from the native language as "land of sunflower seeds."

Information: Winthrop Chamber of Commerce | Box 39, Winthrop, 98862 | 888/4–METHOW | methownet.com.

Attractions

Okanogan National Forest. Numerous hiking trails, mountain bike trails, and scenic drives lace this forest that surrounds Winthrop on all sides. The forest's landscape varies from craggy mountains to soft, rolling meadows, to old growth forests. | 509/826–3275.

ON THE CALENDAR

JAN.: ***Methow Pursuit.*** Two-day 30K cross-country ski race and 1-day amateur race. | 509/996–3287.

JAN.: ***Rendezvous Mountain Tour.*** 35K cross-country ski tour/race over Rendezvous Pass, with food. | 509/996–3287.

Dining

Dining Room at Sun Mountain Lodge. Contemporary. The best thing here is that every table gets to enjoy the great scenery. The food is good but sometimes overly ambitious for the kitchen's capabilities. Serving several seafood dishes as well as a variety of meats, with an emphasis on fresh local ingredients. Also features an extensive wine list. Kids' menu. No smoking. | Patterson Lake Rd. | 509/996–2211 | Breakfast also available | $16–$30 | AE, DC, MC, V.

Duck Brand Cantina, Bakery and Hotel. American/Casual. This modern roadhouse was built to represent a frontier-style hotel—and it works. The Duck Brand takes its name from the cattle brand of the town's founder. It serves good, square meals at reasonable prices, ranging from burritos to sandwiches and pasta dishes. There is a restaurant and bakery (with rooms upstairs). The breakfast omelets and the breads baked on the premises are excellent. So are the cinnamon rolls and berry pies. | 248 Riverside Ave. | 509/996–2192 | Breakfast also available | $8–$17 | AE, D, DC, MC, V.

Virginian Resort. American. Part of the Virginian Resort, this restaurant has seating on a deck under umbrellas, or in the inside of the main building. The menu offers steaks, burgers, pastas, and salads. | 808 North Cascades Hwy. | 509/996–2535 or 800/854–2834 | Closed Oct.–Apr. | $11–$14 | D, MC, V.

Lodging

Chewuch Inn. This inn sits on 4 acres surrounded by the North Cascade Mountains just ⅓ mi south of Winthrop. The rooms are individually appointed with furnishings that reflect the rustic environment; murals ornament many of the walls. The cabins have TVs and VCRs, fireplaces, and kitchenettes. | 8 rooms, 6 cabins. Complimentary breakfast, some kitchenettes, no room phones, TV in common area, spa, hiking, horseback riding, no pets, no smoking. | 223 White Ave. | 509/996–3107 or 800/747–3107 | innkeeper@chewuchinn.com | www.chewuchinn.com | $70–$150 | AE, D, MC, V.

Duck Brand Cantina, Bakery and Hotel. Plainly furnished, inexpensive rooms (compared to the cost of other rooms locally) above the restaurant. | 6 rooms. Restaurant (*see* Duck Brand Cantina, Bakery and Hotel), no-smoking rooms. | 248 Riverside Avenue | 509/996–2192 | fax 509/996–2001 | $62–$70 | AE, D, DC, MC, V.

Freestone Inn. Over 2 million acres of forest surround this resort, 15 mi northwest of Winthrop. Rough hewn logs and rocks form the major building components of the inn and its cabins. The guestrooms have fireplaces and decks that overlook Freestone Lake. | 21 rooms, 15 cabins, 2 cottages. Restaurant, no air-conditioning in some rooms, some kitchenettes, some microwaves, some refrigerators, lake, hiking, fishing, bicycles, shops, no pets, no smoking. | 17798 Hwy. 20, Mazama | 509/996–3906 or 800/639–3809 | fax 509/996–3907 | info@freestoneinn.com | www.freestoneinn.com | $130–$255 | AE, D, DC, MC, V.

Sun Mountain Lodge. This hilltop lodge has great views of the surrounding Cascade Mountains and Methow Valley. Some guest rooms have views of Mt. Gardner or Mt. Robinson. The cabins are located 1½ mi below on the Patterson lakefront. | 102 rooms; 13 cottages. Restaurant (*see* The Dining Room at Sun Mountain Lodge), bar, picnic area, kitchenettes (in cottages), some refrigerators, room service, 2 pools, hot tub, tennis, exercise equipment, hiking, horseback riding, bicycles, cross-country skiing, children's programs (ages 4–10), playground, business services. | Patterson Lake Rd. | 509/996–2211 or 800/572–0493 | fax 509/996–3133 | smtnsale@methow.com | www.sunmountainlodge.com | $115–$255, $155–$340 cottages | AE, DC, MC, V.

Virginian Resort. Comfortable riverfront log lodge and restaurant. Though it is on the highway, at night you'll only hear the river purling over the rocks. | 37 rooms. Restaurant, no-smoking rooms, pool, hot tub, pets allowed. | 808 North Cascades Hwy. | 800/854–2834 | fax 509/996–2483 | $50–$95 | D, MC, V.

Winthrop Inn. Comfortable family motel with a large lawn and trees, far enough off the highway that it is quiet. On 4½ acres near the river edge. | 30 rooms. Picnic area, complimentary Continental breakfast, pool, hot tub, cable TV, microwaves, refrigerators, cross-country and downhill skiing, playground, business services, some pets allowed (fee). | 950 Hwy. 20 | 509/996–2217 or 800/444–1972 | fax 509/996–3923 | $55–$100 | AE, D, DC, MC, V.

YAKIMA

MAP 8, G6

(Nearby towns also listed: Ellensburg, Toppenish)

Yakima, the county seat of Yakima County, is south-central Washington's regional metropolis. Because of its size, Yakima has all the amenities you expect from a city. But it also has a very pleasant and well-maintained downtown, beautiful parks, as well as an arboretum and riverfront walk along the Yakima River. It also has a lot more sunshine than western Washington cities and bills itself as the "Palms Springs of Washington." Unlike Seattle, it has no palm trees.

The local economy is solidly based on agriculture, with a bit of lumber processing (with trees from nearby mountains) thrown in for extra profit. Yakima occupies the site of several villages of the Yakama Nation, whose reservation to the south—the state's largest—stretches from the Yakima Valley to the slopes of Mt. Adams.

Yakima is surrounded by mountain ridges, some of which rise to more than 2,000 or even 3,000 ft on three sides. Curiously, Yakima is legally not in the Yakima Valley, but in the Ahtanum Valley. The Yakima Valley wine appellation, eastern Washington's most important, begins at Union Gap, south of the city.

Information: Yakima Valley Visitor and Convention Bureau | 10 N. 8th St., Yakima, 98901 | 509/575–3010 or 800/221–0751 | fax 509/575–6252 | visityakima.com.

Attractions

Ahtanum Mission. This Catholic mission was first established in 1847 by Oblate priest Jean Charles Pandosy; it was burned by soldiers under Major J. J. Rains in November 1855, because the U.S. Army suspected the Catholic missionaries of materially aiding the Indians (a powder keg was found buried in the yard). The mission was temporarily abandoned in 1859 and the current chapel was built in 1867. You can visit the chapel and the surrounding grounds which are about 10 mi southwest of Yakima on unnumbered roads. | 509/966–0865 | $.50 | May–Sept., daily 9–7.

Central Washington Agricultural Museum. Antique farm machinery is displayed in 20 large buildings; there are also a collection of hand tools, a log cabin, and a windmill. | 4508 Main Street, Union Gap | 509/457–8735 | Free | Daily 9–dusk; call beforehand for guided tour of interior room.

Historic North Front Street. Yakima's old Northern Pacific Depot (1910) looks a bit like a California mission that got lost on a trip north. Today it houses America's oldest brew pub. Other old business buildings line Front Street which is across from the depot. Nearby downtown buildings of historic interest include the 1915 Miller Building (E. Yakima Ave. and N.

Second St.), the U.S. Post Office (S. Third and Chestnut St.), the 1915 Masonic Temple (321 E. Yakima Ave.), St. Michael's Episcopal Church of 1889 (E. Yakima and S. Naches Ave.), and the Capital Theater (Yakima Ave. and North Front St.). Built in 1920 and restored in 1978, the former movie theater is now a public performing arts center. | 509/248–2021 | fax 509/248–0601 | Free | Daily.

Painted Rocks. Here, 7 mi northwest of Yakima, you'll see remnants of Indian pictographs, some of which were destroyed by a 19th-century irrigation project; enough remain to give you a notion of how the local Indians marked important sites. | U.S. 12 | 509/248–2021.

White Pass Village. A full-service ski area southeast of Mt. Rainier with condominiums, snack bar, grocery store, and gas station. It has a base elevation of 4,500 ft, a summit elevation of 6,000 ft, and a vertical drop of 1,500 ft. Open woods of eastern slopes are popular with cross-country skiers. | U.S. 12 crosses the Cascade Crest | 509/672–3101 | fax 509/7672–3123 | www.skiwhitepass.com.

Yakima Area Arboretum The arboretum, south of the river, has a small Japanese garden. It is part of a series of parks connected by a paved path along the river. The river's riparian woodland has a dense overstory, which makes for shady walking or biking in the heat of summer. | 1401 Arboretum Dr. | 509/248–7337 | fax 509/248–8197 | www.ahtrees.org | Free | Daily dawn–dusk.

Yakima Sportsman State Park. North of the Yakima River, and 1 mi east of Yakima off Hwy. 82 on the road to Moxee, the park has campsites and a children's fishing pond stocked with trout. | Rte. 24 E. Keyes Rd. | 509/575–2774 | www.parks.wa.gov | Free | Daily dawn–dusk.

Yakima Valley Museum. In addition to Yakama Indian clothing and beadwork, the museum, in Franklin Park houses a comprehensive collection of horse-drawn vehicles, and a replica of Chief Justice William O. Douglas's office. | 2105 Tieton Dr. | 509/248–0747 | fax 509/453–4890 | www.yakimavalleymuseum.org | $3 | Weekdays 10–5, weekends noon–5.

ON THE CALENDAR

JAN.–FEB.: ***Art to Wear.*** Biannual juried exhibition that includes anything that adorns the body, including clothes. | 509/574–4875.
MAR.: ***Chocolate Fantasy.*** Sampling of chocolates made by Northwest and Canadian manufacturers held at Cavanagh's Hotel. | 509/966–6309.

Dining

★ **Birchfield Manor.** Contemporary. The Birchfield Manor, a 1910 Yakima Valley farmhouse, has the most elegant dining room in the eastern Washington wine country. Little has changed since it served as the mansion's private sitting and dining room, and the owners have a knack for making you feel like you're visiting a private home for dinner. The owner/chef also knows Yakima Valley wines like few others and not only has an exceptionally well-stocked cellar, but will gladly steer you to rare vintages from prime wineries. Known for seafood, veal, lamb. No smoking. | 2018 Birchfield Rd. | 509/452–1960 | Reservations essential | Open Sun.–Wed. for groups only and Thurs.–Sat. | $23–$35 | AE, DC, MC, V.

Deli De Pasta. Italian. Italian café that's very popular with the locals. The food is tasty, the service is friendly, and the atmosphere is very simpatico. Beer and wine only. No smoking. | 7 N. Front St. | 509/453–0571 | Closed Sun. | $15–$30 | AE, MC, V.

Gasperetti's. Contemporary. Yakima's favorite socialite hangout has a comfortable bar and an elegant dining room, dishing up such traditional fare as steak, as well as Italian and Northwest dishes featuring locally grown produce. The cellar has an excellent selection of wines, with some uncommon Italian varieties. | 1013 N. 1st St. | 509/248–0628 | Closed Sun., Mon. No lunch Sat. | $25–$29 | AE, DC, MC, V.

Grant's Brewery Restaurant/Pub. American/Casual. America's oldest brew pub is housed in a restored Mission-style railroad station. The bright dining room not only has windows to the outside, but to the gleaming copper kettles of the brew room as well. Enjoy bangers and Scottish eggs (hard-boiled eggs covered with seasoned sausage mixture, rolled in bread crumbs and then fried), served with English hot mustard. Live music on some weekends. Children allowed until 10 PM. | 32 N. Front St. | 509/575–2922 | $4–$8 | AE, MC, V.

Sub Link Internet Café. Café. Surf the web while you eat. Serving hamburgers, soups, salads, and a variety of sweets and coffees, staff here can answer any of your burning computer-related questions. | 913 S. 1st St. | 509/249–3035 | No dinner | $.79–$4.89 | AE, MC, V.

Lodging

Apple Country Bed and Breakfast. From the windows of this 1911 Victorian, which sits in the middle of a working ranch, you can spy quail, pheasants, gophers, and even coyotes. The rooms, with a mixture of antiques and contemporary furnishings, have spectacular views of the valley. | 3 rooms. Complimentary breakfast, cable TV, some in-room VCRs, laundry facilities, pets allowed, no smoking. | 4561 Old Naches Hwy. | 509/972–3409 or 877/788–9963 | fax 509/965–1591 | apple@yvn.com | $65–$90 | D, MC, V.

Best Western Oxford Inn. Riverfront motel off I–82 freeway; rooms have view of the river, which here is lined by cottonwood trees and meadows. | 96 rooms, 1 suite. In-room data ports, some kitchenettes, refrigerators, cable TV, pool, hot tub, laundry facilities, airport shuttle, free parking. | 1603 Terrace Heights Dr. | 509/457–4444 | fax 509/453–7593 | $65–$69 | AE, D, DC, MC, V.

Birchfield Manor. A comfortable 1910 farmhouse and restaurant has newly expanded quarters including a large guest cottage. The newer building has more amenities, but the original house has a lot more charm including a sunporch off one room. It is only 2 mi from town. | 11 rooms. Restaurant, complimentary breakfast, no TV in some rooms, some room phones, pool, many in-room hot tubs. | 2018 Birchfield Rd. | 509/452–1960 or 800/375–3420 | fax 509/452–2334 | reservations@birchfieldmanor.com | www.birchfieldmanor.com | $99–$199 | AE, D, MC, V.

Cavanaugh's. Freeway motel that can be noisy at times. | 171 rooms. Restaurant, bar, complimentary Continental breakfast, in-room data ports, some kitchenettes, some refrigerators, room service, cable TV, pool, laundry facilities, business services, pets allowed. | 9 N. 9th St. | 509/452–6511 | fax 509/457–4931 | $65–$95 | AE, D, DC, MC, V.

Cavanaugh's at Yakima Center. Convention hotel next to convention center and a few blocks from major shopping mall. The restaurant is not up to the quality of the lodging. | 153 rooms, 5 suites. Restaurant, bar with entertainment, some refrigerators, room service, cable TV, 2 pools, business services, airport shuttle, free parking, pets allowed (fee). | 607 E. Yakima Ave. | 509/248–5900 | fax 509/575–8975 | $87–$105, $150–200 suites | AE, D, DC, MC, V.

Doubletree Inn Hotel. Business travelers' and family vacation hotel (some westside families come here just to get out of the rain and to soak up some sun by the pool). | 208 rooms, 6 suites. Restaurant, bar with entertainment, in-room data ports, some refrigerators, room service, cable TV, 2 pools, hot tub, business services, free parking, pets allowed (fee). | 1507 N. 1st St. | 509/248–7850 | fax 509/575–1694 | $89–$135; $225 suites | AE, D, DC, MC, V.

Orchard Inn Bed and Breakfast. Just 7 mi northwest of downtown Yakima, the inn is secluded in a true cherry orchard in which you are invited to take strolls. The contemporary house is appointed with a refined country theme. The rooms each have a private entrance. Breakfast is served in an outdoor breakfast room in the orchard. | 3 rooms. Complimentary breakfast, in-room hot tubs, laundry facilities, no pets, no smoking. | 1207 Pecks Canyon Rd. | 509/966–1283 or 888/858–8284 | orchardinn@hotmail.com | www.1bbweb.com/orchardinn | $69–$89 | AE, D, MC, V.

Quality Inn. This 2-story motel is across from the Valley Mall. It's known for its reliable service to families and business travelers. | 85 rooms. Complimentary Continental breakfast, cable TV, pool, laundry facilities, business services, free parking, pets allowed. | 12 Valley Mall Blvd. | 509/248–6924 | fax 509/575–8470 | $59–$88 | AE, D, DC, MC, V.

Red Lion Inn. Stay eight blocks north of downtown Yakima at this spacious hotel. Mt. Rainier is a one-hour drive away. | 58 rooms. Cable TV, pool, business services, some pets allowed. | 818 N. 1st St. | 509/453–0391 | fax 509/453–8348 | $54–$99 | AE, D, DC, MC, V.

Touch of Europe Bed and Breakfast Inn. The many charms of this gracious 1889 Queen Anne Victorian, which stands on an acre of property among century-old trees, have been preserved like the box-beam ceiling, extensive mill-work, and stained-glass windows. Among the antiques that fill the guest rooms is a mid-1800s fainting couch. | 3 rooms. Complimentary breakfast, no pets, no kids under 17, no smoking. | 220 N. 16th Ave. | 509/454–9775 or 888/438–7073 | www.winesnw.com/toucheuropeb&b.htm | $75–$110 | AE, MC, V.

Index

A Creekside Inn, the Marquee House (Salem, OR), 166
A' Tuscan Estate (McMinnville, OR), 110
Abel House (Montesano, WA), 283
Abendblume Pension (Leavenworth, WA), 271
Aberdeen Mansion (Aberdeen, WA), 209
Aberdeen Museum of History (Aberdeen, WA), 208
Adair's on the Green (Snoqualmie, WA), 380
Adam East Museum (Moses Lake, WA), 283
Adobe Motel (Yachats, OR), 182
Adobe Restaurant (Yachats, OR), 182
Adriatica (Seattle, WA), 359
Agate Pass Waterfront B&B (Bainbridge Island, WA), 215
Ahtanum Mission (Yakima, WA), 413
Air Station Flying Museum (Arlington, WA), 213
Ajax Café (Port Townsend, WA), 323
Al Boccalino (Seattle, WA), 359
Al-Amir (Portland, OR), 143
Albatross (Anacortes, WA), 212
Alder House II (Lincoln City, OR), 101
Alec's by the Sea (Ocean Shores, WA), 299
Alessandro's (Portland, OR), 146
Alessandro's Park Plaza (Salem, OR), 165
Alexander Blockhouse (Coupeville, WA), 243
Alexander's Country Inn (Ashford, WA), 213, 214
Alexis (Portland, OR), 143
Alexis Hotel (Seattle, WA), 366
Alfred A. Loeb State Park (Brookings, OR), 41
Alice's Restaurant (Olympia, WA), 303
Alki Beach (Seattle, WA), 344
Alligator Soul (Everett, WA), 252
Alpental Ski Area (North Bend, WA), 295
Alta Lake State Park (Chelan, WA), 233
Altezzo (Tacoma, WA), 395
Alton Baker Park (Eugene, OR), 61
Always Welcome Inn (Baker City, OR), 31
Ambrosia (Eugene, OR), 63
American Advertising Museum (Portland, OR), 138
American Hop Museum (Toppenish, WA), 400
American Travel Inn (Pullman, WA), 328
Anacortes Historical Museum (Anacortes, WA), 210
Anacortes Inn (Anacortes, WA), 212
Anchor Bay Inn (Reedsport, OR), 158
Anchorage Inn (Coupeville, WA), 244
Anchorage Motor Court (Long Beach, WA), 275
Andaluca (Seattle, WA), 359
Anderson Creek Lodge (Bellingham, WA), 222
Andreas Keller (Leavenworth, WA), 271
Angelica's B&B (Spokane, WA), 387
Ann Starrett Mansion (Port Townsend, WA), 324
Annie Fannie's (Spokane, WA), 385
Anthony Lakes Ski Area (Baker City, OR), 29
Anthony's Homeport (Everett, WA), 252
Anthony's Homeport (Seattle-Tacoma International Airport Area, WA), 368
Anthony's Pier 66 and Bell Street Diner (Seattle, WA), 354
Antique Sandwich Company (Tacoma, WA), 396
Ape Cave (Mt. St. Helens National Volcanic Monument, WA), 290
Aplets and Cotlets/Liberty Orchards Co., Inc. (Cashmere, WA), 229
Apple Country B&B (Yakima, WA), 415
Apple Inn B&B (Cottage Grove, OR), 53
Applegate River Lodge (Jacksonville, OR), 87
Arbor House (Ashland, OR), 22
Arden Forest Inn (Ashland, OR), 23
Argosy Harbor Cruise (Seattle, WA), 349
Argyle House (San Juan Islands, WA), 338
Ark Restaurant and Bakery (Long Beach, WA), 274
Armitage County Park (Eugene, OR), 61
Arnie's in Edmonds (Edmonds, WA), 246
Artspace (Tillamook, OR), 175
Ashland Bakery and Café (Ashland, OR), 23
Ashland Main Street Inn (Ashland, OR), 24
Ashley Inn (Lincoln City, OR), 102
Asotin County Museum (Clarkston, WA), 236
Assaggio (Portland, OR), 142
Assaggio Ristorante (Seattle, WA), 354
Assimba Ethiopian Cuisine (Seattle, WA), 351
Astoria Column (Astoria, OR), 26
Astoria Dunes (Astoria, OR), 28
Astoria Inn (Astoria, OR), 28
Athenian Inn (Seattle, WA), 351
Atwater's (Portland, OR), 147
Auld Holland Inn (Oak Harbor, WA), 298
Austrian B&B Suites (Tacoma, WA), 398
Avery Park (Corvallis, OR), 49
Axis (Seattle, WA), 354
Azalea City Park (Brookings, OR), 41

B&O Espresso (Seattle, WA), 352
Bacon Mansion (Seattle, WA), 362
Bailey's Place (The Dalles, OR), 174
Bainbridge Island Vineyard and Winery (Bainbridge Island, WA), 215

Bakeman's Restaurant (Seattle, WA), 351
Baker City Cafe–Pizza à Fetta (Baker City, OR), 30
Bali Hi Motel (Richland, WA), 335
Bandoleone (Seattle, WA), 354
Bandon Beach State Park (Bandon, OR), 32
Bandon Bill's Steak and Seafood (Bandon, OR), 33
Bandon Boatworks (Bandon, OR), 33
Banjo Creek Farms (Chelan, WA), 233
Baran Haus (Leavenworth, WA), 271
Basilio's Italian Café (Pullman, WA), 328
Bastas (Portland, OR), 142
Bay Bridge (North Bend, OR), 122
Bay Cafe (Lopez Island, WA), 279
Bay House (Lincoln City, OR), 102
Bay View State Park (Mount Vernon, WA), 292
Bayberry Inn B&B (Ashland, OR), 24
Bayfront (Newport, OR), 118
Bayshore Motor Inn (Astoria, OR), 28
Bayview (Port Townsend, WA), 323
Beach (Olympic National Park, WA), 308
Beach Pancake and Dinner House (Rockaway Beach, OR), 159
Beach's Restaurant (Vancouver, WA), 403
Beachcombers Haven (Gleneden Beach, OR), 73
Beech Tree Manor (Seattle, WA), 362
Beekman House (Jacksonville, OR), 86
Belfair State Park (Bremerton, WA), 225
Bell Tower Brewhouse (Vancouver, WA), 403
Bella Isola (Anacortes, WA), 211
Bella Italia (Port Angeles, WA), 318
Bella Union (Jacksonville, OR), 87
Bellevue Art Museum (Bellevue, WA), 216
Bellevue B&B (Bellevue, WA), 217
Bellevue Botanical Garden (Bellevue, WA), 216
Bellevue Club (Bellevue, WA), 217
Bellingham Antique Radio Museum (Bellingham, WA), 219
The Belmont (Port Townsend, WA), 323
Ben Moore's Restaurant (Olympia, WA), 303
Benaroya Hall (Seattle, WA), 346
Bend Riverside Motel (Bend, OR), 38
Benjamin Young Inn (Astoria, OR), 28
Benny's Colville Inn (Colville, WA), 239
The Benson (Portland, OR), 152
Benson State Park (Portland, OR), 136
Benton County Historical Museum (Corvallis, OR), 49
Beryl House (Hood River, OR), 85
Best Budget Inn (Reedsport, OR), 158
Best Inn (Medford, OR), 112
Best Inn & Suites (Bend, OR), 38
Best Inn and Suites (Roseburg, OR), 161
Best Inn and Suites (Vancouver, WA), 403
Best Inn and Suites Heritage Inn (Ritzville, WA), 337
Best Value El Rancho Motel (Moses Lake, WA), 284
Best Western Airport Executel (Seattle-Tacoma International Airport Area, WA), 369
Best Western Aladdin Motor Inn (Olympia, WA), 304
Best Western Bard's Inn (Ashland, OR), 24
Best Western Beachfront Inn (Brookings, OR), 41
Best Western Bellevue Inn (Bellevue, WA), 217
Best Western Brookings Inn (Brookings, OR), 41
Best Western Cascadia Inn (Everett, WA), 252
Best Western Cavanaughs Hillsboro Hotel (Hillsboro, OR), 83
Best Western College Way Inn (Mount Vernon, WA), 293
Best Western Cotton Tree Inn (Mount Vernon, WA), 293
Best Western Douglas Inn (Roseburg, OR), 161
Best Western Ellensburg Inn (Ellensburg, WA), 248
Best Western Entrada Lodge (Bend, OR), 38
Best Western Executel (Seattle-Tacoma International Airport Area, WA), 369
Best Western Executive Inn (Seattle, WA), 362
Best Western Executive Inn (Tacoma, WA), 398
Best Western Fortniter Motel (Portland, OR), 148
Best Western Garden Villa (Roseburg, OR), 161
Best Western Grand Manor Inn (Corvallis, OR), 50
Best Western Grand Manor Inn (Eugene, OR), 65
Best Western Grants Pass Inn (Grants Pass, OR), 78
Best Western Hallmark Inn (Moses Lake, WA), 284
Best Western Harbor Plaza (Oak Harbor, WA), 298
Best Western Heritage Inn (Bellingham, WA), 222
Best Western Holiday (Coos Bay, OR), 48
Best Western Hood River Inn (Hood River, OR), 85
Best Western Horizon Inn (Medford, OR), 112
Best Western Icicle Inn (Leavenworth, WA), 271
Best Western Inn and Suites (Ontario, OR), 124
Best Western Inn at the Convention Center (Portland, OR), 148
Best Western Inn at the Rogue (Grants Pass, OR), 78
Best Western Inn of the Beachcomber (Gold Beach, OR), 75
Best Western Kennewick Inn (Kennewick, WA), 262
Best Western Kirkland Inn (Kirkland, WA), 266
Best Western Klamath Inn (Klamath Falls, OR), 95
Best Western Lakeway Inn (Bellingham, WA), 222
Best Western Lincoln Inn (Othello, WA), 315
Best Western Lincoln Sands Inn (Lincoln City, OR), 102
Best Western Loyal Inn (Seattle, WA), 362
Best Western New Kings Inn (Salem, OR), 166
Best Western New Oregon (Eugene, OR), 65
Best Western Ocean View Resort (Seaside, OR), 168
Best Western Olympic Inn (Klamath Falls, OR), 95
Best Western Oxford Inn (Yakima, WA), 415
Best Western Park Center Hotel (Enumclaw, WA), 249
Best Western Park Plaza (Puyallup, WA), 330
Best Western Pier Point Inn (Florence, OR), 69
Best Western–Pioneer Square Hotel (Seattle, WA), 362
Best Western Pony Soldier (Medford, OR), 112
Best Western Pony Soldier Motor Inn (Albany, OR), 21
Best Western Pony Soldier—Airport (Portland, OR), 150
Best Western Prineville Inn (Prineville, OR), 155
Best Western Rama Inn (Redmond, OR), 156
Best Western Rama Inn and Suites (La Grande, OR), 98
Best Western Rivertree Inn (Clarkston, WA), 237
Best Western—Rose Garden Hotel (Portland, OR), 148
Best Western Salbasgeon Inn (Reedsport, OR), 158
Best Western Skyline Motor Lodge (Lakeview, OR), 100
Best Western Southcenter (Seattle-Tacoma International Airport Area, WA), 369
Best Western Sunridge Inn (Baker City, OR), 31
Best Western Tacoma Inn (Tacoma, WA), 398
Best Western Thunderbird Inn (Spokane, WA), 387
Best Western Tower Inn (Richland, WA), 335
Best Western Trade Winds North (Spokane, WA), 387
Best Western Tulalip Inn (Marysville, WA), 281
Best Western Tumwater (Olympia, WA), 304

Best Western Village Green (Cottage Grove, OR), 53
Best Western Walla Walla Suites Inn (Walla Walla, WA), 406
Beverly Beach State Park (Newport, OR), 118
Big Daddy's (Grants Pass, OR), 77
Big K Guest Ranch (Drain, OR), 59
Big River (Corvallis, OR), 50
Big Trees B&B (Bellingham, WA), 222
Bilbo's Festivo (Orcas Island, WA), 312
Billy's (Aberdeen, WA), 209
Birch Bay State Park (Blaine, WA), 224
Birchfield Manor (Yakima, WA), 414, 415
Bis on Main (Bellevue, WA), 216
Bishop Victorian Guest Suites (Port Townsend, WA), 324
Bistro (Arlington, WA), 213
The Bistro (Cannon Beach, OR), 44
Bistro Pleasant Beach (Bainbridge Island, WA), 215
Bistro Provençal (Kirkland, WA), 265
BJ's Garden Gate B&B (Port Angeles, WA), 319
Black Butte Ranch (Bend, OR), 38
Black Rabbit (Troutdale, OR), 177
Black Sheep (Ashland, OR), 24
Blackman Historic Museum (Snohomish, WA), 378
Bloedel Donovan Park (Bellingham, WA), 219
Blue Gull Inn (Port Townsend, WA), 325
Blue Heron Bistro (Coos Bay, OR), 48
Blue Heron French Cheese Company (Tillamook, OR), 175
Blue Heron Inn B&B (Kelso, WA), 261
Blue Moon (Kennewick, WA), 262
Blue River Dam and Lake (McKenzie Bridge, OR), 107
Blue Sky Cafe (Manzanita, OR), 107
Boat Shed (Bremerton, WA), 226
Boathouse Marina (Tacoma, WA), 394
Boehm's Chocolate Factory (Issaquah, WA), 259
Boeing Everett Facility (Everett, WA), 251
Boeing Field—King County Int'l Airport (Seattle, WA), 349
Bonneville Lock and Dam (Hood River, OR), 84
Bontemps Hotel (Burns, OR), 43
Boreas B&B (Long Beach, WA), 275
Boulevard Park (Bellingham, WA), 219
Boundary Bay Brewery Bistro (Bellingham, WA), 221
Bradley House/Country Keeper (Cathlamet, WA), 230
Breakers (Long Beach, WA), 275
Breakers Restaurant and Lounge (Seaside, OR), 167
Breakwater Restaurant (Sekiu, WA), 374
Bremerton Marina (Bremerton, WA), 226
Bremerton Naval Museum (Bremerton, WA), 226
The Brewery (Grants Pass, OR), 77
Brewhouse Taproom (Portland, OR), 143
Brick Tavern (Cle Elum, WA), 237
Bridge Street Inn (Baker City, OR), 31
Bridgeport Brew Pub (Portland, OR), 142
Bridges (Aberdeen, WA), 209
Bridgewater Seafood Restaurant (Florence, OR), 69
Brier Rose Inn (Albany, OR), 21
Brierly Inn (Whidbey Island, WA), 411
Brightwood Guest House (Mount Hood National Forest, OR), 114
Broadway Center for the Performing Arts (Tacoma, WA), 392
Brooklyn Seafood, Steak, and Oyster House (Seattle, WA), 354
Brooks Memorial State Park (Goldendale, WA), 254
Brookside B&B (Oregon City, OR), 126
Buca Di Beppo (Seattle, WA), 359
Buckaroo Room (Frenchglen, OR), 72
Budget Inn (Albany, OR), 21
Budget Inn (Spokane, WA), 387
Buffalo Run Restaurant (North Cascades National Park, WA), 297
Bullards Beach State Park (Bandon, OR), 32
The Bunkhouse (Ashford, WA), 214
Burgermaster (Bellevue, WA), 216
Burke Museum (Seattle, WA), 346
Burrito Loco (Seattle, WA), 352
Bush Barn Art Center (Salem, OR), 163
Bush Garden (Portland, OR), 144
Bush House (Salem, OR), 163
Bush House Country Inn (Index, WA), 259
Bushwhacker (Port Angeles, WA), 318
Butte Creek Mill (Medford, OR), 111
Buzz Saw (Albany, OR), 21

C and M Stables (Florence, OR), 67
C.K. Tiffins (Medford, OR), 111
C'est Si Bon (Port Angeles, WA), 319
Cabana Motel (Othello, WA), 315
Cactus (Seattle, WA), 354
Cade's Lakefront Restaurant and Lounge (Moses Lake, WA), 284
Café Azul (Portland, OR), 144
Café Campagne (Seattle, WA), 354
Cafe Des Amis (Portland, OR), 146
Café Flora (Seattle, WA), 354
Café Italiano (Colville, WA), 239
Cafe Juanita (Kirkland, WA), 265
Café Lago (Seattle, WA), 355
Cafe Navarro (Eugene, OR), 64
Cafe Nola (Bainbridge Island, WA), 215
Cafe Zenon (Eugene, OR), 64
Calico Cupboard (La Conner, WA), 267
Calico Cupboard (Mount Vernon, WA), 292
Callahan Ridge Winery (Roseburg, OR), 160
Camlin (Seattle, WA), 363
Camp Six Logging Exhibit (Western Forest Industries Museum) (Tacoma, WA), 394
Campagne (Seattle, WA), 359
Campbell House (Eugene, OR), 66
Campbell House Café (Chelan, WA), 234
Campbell's Resort (Chelan, WA), 234
Camping (Mt. Rainier National Park, WA), 288
Camping (Mt. St. Helens National Volcanic Monument, WA), 290
Camping (Olympic National Park, WA), 308
Campus Cottage B&B (Eugene, OR), 66
Campus Inn (Eugene, OR), 65
Candlewood Suites (Bellevue, WA), 217
Canlis (Seattle, WA), 361
Cannon Beach Hotel (Cannon Beach, OR), 44
Canterbury Inn (Ocean Shores, WA), 299
Canyon Way Restaurant and Bookstore (Newport, OR), 120
Cape Arago Lighthouse (Coos Bay, OR), 47
Cape Arago State Park (Coos Bay, OR), 47
Cape Blanco State Park (Port Orford, OR), 154
Cape Disappointment (Ilwaco, WA), 257
Cape Lookout State Park/Cape Kiwanda State Natural Area (Pacific City, OR), 126
Cape Perpetua Campground (Yachats, OR), 180
Cape Perpetua Visitors Center (Yachats, OR), 180
Cape Sebastian State Park (Gold Beach, OR), 74
Capitol (Salem, OR), 163
Capitol Group (Olympia, WA), 301
Capitol Lake (Olympia, WA), 302
Caprial's (Portland, OR), 146
Capriccio (Albany, OR), 21
Captain Cook Cruises (Everett, WA), 251
Captain John Quincy Adams House B&B (Port Townsend, WA), 325
Captain Whidbey Inn (Coupeville, WA), 244
Captain's Table (Gold Beach, OR), 75
Caravel Resort (Chelan, WA), 234
Carkeek Park (Seattle, WA), 345
Carl G. Washburne Memorial (Florence, OR), 69
Carlile Motel (Ontario, OR), 124
Carmelita (Seattle, WA), 352
Carriage House of Prime Rib (Wenatchee, WA), 407
Carson Mineral Hot Springs Resort (Spokane, WA), 390
Casa Chapala (Kennewick, WA), 262
Casa De Blanca (Ellensburg, WA), 248
Casablanca B&B (Kennewick, WA), 262
Cascade Dining Room (Mount Hood National Forest, OR), 114
Cascade Mountain Inn (Cle Elum, WA), 238

Cascade Park (Moses Lake, WA), 283
Castle Rock (Kelso, WA), 260
Caswell's on the Bay B&B (Long Beach, WA), 275
Cat Tales (Spokane, WA), 383
Cathedral of St. John the Evangelist (Spokane, WA), 383
Catherine Creek State Park (La Grande, OR), 96
Cavalier Beachfront Condominiums (Gleneden Beach, OR), 74
Cavanaugh's (Yakima, WA), 415
Cavanaugh's at Columbia Center (Kennewick, WA), 262
Cavanaugh's at Yakima Center (Yakima, WA), 415
Cavanaugh's River Inn (Spokane, WA), 387
Cavanaughs Motel (Olympia, WA), 304
Cedar Bay (Tillamook, OR), 176
Cedar Bend Golf Course (Gold Beach, OR), 74
Cedar Lodge Motor Inn (Medford, OR), 112
Cedarwood Inn (Ashland, OR), 24
Celilo Converter Station (The Dalles, OR), 172
Celilo Park (The Dalles, OR), 173
Center for Wooden Boats (Seattle, WA), 347
Center House (Seattle, WA), 348
Central Washington Agricultural Museum (Yakima, WA), 413
Central Washington University (Ellensburg, WA), 247
Century Drive (Bend, OR), 36
Chambered Nautilus (Seattle, WA), 363
Champoeg State Park (Newberg, OR), 116
Chandler's Bed, Bread and Trail (Joseph, OR), 92
Channel House (Anacortes, WA), 212
Channel House Inn (Depoe Bay, OR), 56
Chanterelle (Eugene, OR), 64
Chanticleer Inn (Ashland, OR), 24
Chanticleer Inn (Port Townsend, WA), 325
Chaparral (Pendleton, OR), 129
Chapman and Lownsdale Squares (Portland, OR), 135
Charles and Emma Frye Art Museum (Seattle, WA), 347
The Charles R. Conner Museum of Zoology (Pullman, WA), 328
Charleston Marina Complex (Coos Bay, OR), 47
Chart House (Portland, OR), 144
Chata (Ashland, OR), 23
Chateau Lorane Winery (Cottage Grove, OR), 51
Château Ste. Michelle (Bellevue, WA), 216
Chateau Westport Motel (Westport, WA), 409
Chateaulin (Ashland, OR), 23
Chautauqua Lodge (Long Beach, WA), 275
Chef Wang (Seattle, WA), 352
Chehalis–Centralia Steam Train Ride (Chehalis, WA), 232
Chelan County Historical Society's Museum and Pioneer Village (Cashmere, WA), 229
Chelsea Station on the Park (Seattle, WA), 363
Cheney Cowles Memorial Museum (Spokane, WA), 383
Cheney Historical Museum (Cheney, WA), 235
Chestnut Hill Inn (Orcas Island, WA), 313
Chestnut Tree Inn (Portland, OR), 148
Chetco River Inn (Brookings, OR), 42
Chetco Valley Historical Museum (Brookings, OR), 41
Chevy's (Medford, OR), 111
Chewuch Inn (Winthrop, WA), 412
Chez Jeannette (Gleneden Beach, OR), 73
Chez Nous (Klamath Falls, OR), 94
Chez Shea (Seattle, WA), 361
Chief Timothy State Park (Clarkston, WA), 236
Children's Museum (Jacksonville, OR), 86
Children's Museum (Portland, OR), 138
Children's Museum (Seattle, WA), 347
Children's Museum of Spokane (Spokane, WA), 383
Children's Museum of Tacoma (Tacoma, WA), 394
Chimpanzee and Human Communication Institute (Ellensburg, WA), 247
China Beach Retreat (Ilwaco, WA), 258
Chinaberry Hill (Tacoma, WA), 398
Chinatown Gate (Portland, OR), 137
Chinook Winds (Lincoln City, OR), 101
Chinook's (Seattle, WA), 355
Christina's (Orcas Island, WA), 312
Christopher's (Coupeville, WA), 243
Christopher's at the Inn (Poulsbo, WA), 327
Chuckanut Drive (Bellingham, WA), 219
Chuckanut Manor (Bellingham, WA), 221
Churchyard Inn (Pullman, WA), 328
Chutneys (Seattle, WA), 352
Cimarron Motor Inn (Klamath Falls, OR), 95
Cimarron Motor Inn—North (Bend, OR), 39
Cimmiyotti's (Pendleton, OR), 129
Circle T Restaurant (Ritzville, WA), 336
City Grill (Brookings, OR), 41
City Hall (Portland, OR), 134
City Parks Arroyo Park (Bellingham, WA), 219
Civic Auditorium (Portland, OR), 137
Civic Field Athletic Complex (Bellingham, WA), 219
CJ Lodge (Maupin, OR), 106
Clallam Bay (Sekiu, WA), 373
Clallam County Historical Museum (Port Angeles, WA), 318
Clarion Hotel Seatac Airport (Seattle-Tacoma International Airport Area, WA), 370
Clark County Historical Museum (Vancouver, WA), 402
Clarno Unit (John Day, OR), 89
Cle Elum Telephone Museum (Cle Elum, WA), 237
Clear Lake (Sedro Woolley, WA), 372
Cliff House (Tacoma, WA), 396
Cliff House B&B (Clarkston, WA), 237
Cliff Park (Spokane, WA), 383
Cline Falls State Park (Redmond, OR), 156
Clinkerbrick House (Portland, OR), 148
Clinkerdagger (Spokane, WA), 385
Clymer Museum of Art (Ellensburg, WA), 247
Coachman Inn (Oak Harbor, WA), 298
Coast River Inn (Seaside, OR), 168
Coco's Bakery Restaurant (Bellevue, WA), 216
Coho Grill (Bend, OR), 37
Coho Inn (Lincoln City, OR), 102
Coldwater Ridge Visitor Center (Mt. St. Helens National Volcanic Monument, WA), 291
Colette's B&B (Port Angeles, WA), 319
Collett's Cabins and Fine Arts (Joseph, OR), 92
Collier Memorial State Park and Logging Museum (Klamath Falls, OR), 93
Colonel Crockett Farm (Coupeville, WA), 244
Colonial Manor B&B (Mount Vernon, WA), 293
Colonial Motor Inn (Ontario, OR), 124
Colophon Cafe (Bellingham, WA), 221
Columbia Basin Farmers' Market (Moses Lake, WA), 284
Columbia Gorge Discovery Center—Wasco County Historical Museum (The Dalles, OR), 173
Columbia Gorge Hotel (Hood River, OR), 85
Columbia Gorge Interpretive Center (Spokane, WA), 390
Columbia Gorge Sailpark (Hood River, OR), 84
Columbia National Wildlife Refuge (Othello, WA), 314
Columbia Park (Kennewick, WA), 261
Columbia River Court Dining Room (Hood River, OR), 85
Columbia River Inn (Coulee Dam, WA), 242
Columbia River Inn B&B (Astoria, OR), 28
Columbia River Journeys (Richland, WA), 335
Columbia River Maritime Museum (Astoria, OR), 26
Columbia River Waterfront Trail (Vancouver, WA), 402
Columbia Winery (Seattle, WA), 345
Columbian Café (Astoria, OR), 27
Colville Confederated Tribes Museum and Gift Shop (Coulee Dam, WA), 241

Colville National Forest (Colville, WA), 238
Combest House (Jacksonville, OR), 87
Comfort Inn (Colville, WA), 239
Comfort Inn (Grants Pass, OR), 78
Comfort Inn (Kelso, WA), 261
Comfort Inn (Seattle-Tacoma International Airport Area, WA), 370
Comfort Inn (Vancouver, WA), 403
Comfort Inn Boardwalk (Seaside, OR), 168
Comfort Inn Spokane Valley (Spokane, WA), 387
Comfort Inn–Zillah (Toppenish, WA), 401
Comfort Suites (Albany, OR), 21
Comfort Suites (Vancouver, WA), 403
Commencement Bay B&B (Tacoma, WA), 398
Compass Rose and River Walkway (Aberdeen, WA), 208
Compass Rose B&B (Coupeville, WA), 244
Comstock Park (Spokane, WA), 383
Confluence Gallery (Twisp, WA), 401
Conklin's Guest House (Sisters, OR), 171
Convention Center Inn (Seaside, OR), 168
Cooley's Gardens (Silverton, OR), 169
Cooney Mansion B&B (Aberdeen, WA), 210
Coos Bay Manor (Coos Bay, OR), 48
Coos County Historical Society Museum (North Bend, OR), 122
Copperfield's (Tacoma, WA), 396
Coquille River Museum (Bandon, OR), 32
Cornwall Park (Bellingham, WA), 219
Cottage (Cottage Grove, OR), 52
Cottage Creek Inn (Kirkland, WA), 266
Cottage Grove Lake (Drain, OR), 58
Cottage Grove Museum (Cottage Grove, OR), 51
Coty's Restaurant (McMinnville, OR), 109
Couch Street Seafood and Fine Steaks (Portland, OR), 146
Cougar Dam and Lake (McKenzie Bridge, OR), 107
Coulee House (Coulee Dam, WA), 242
Country B&B (Pullman, WA), 329
Country Cottage of Langley (Langley, WA), 269
Country Deli (Ephrata, WA), 250
Country Hills Resort (Cave Junction, OR), 46
Country Inn (La Conner, WA), 267
Country Inn B&B (Eugene, OR), 65
Country Inn B&B (Moses Lake, WA), 284
Country Kitchen (Langley, WA), 268
Country Museum/Restored Train Station (Seaside, OR), 170
Country Willows B&B Inn (Ashland, OR), 24
Courtyard Bellevue (Bellevue, WA), 218
Courtyard by Marriott (Beaverton, OR), 35
Courtyard by Marriott (Spokane, WA), 387
Courtyard by Marriott—Airport (Portland, OR), 148
Courtyard Café (Seattle-Tacoma International Airport Area, WA), 368
Cousins' (The Dalles, OR), 174
Couvron (Portland, OR), 146
The Cove Palisades State Park (Madras, OR), 104
Covered Bridges (Cottage Grove, OR), 51
Cowlitz County Historical Museum (Kelso, WA), 260
Cowlitz River Lodge (Packwood, WA), 316
Cozy Cove Beach Front Resort (Lincoln City, OR), 103
Crab House (Port Angeles, WA), 319
Crab Pot Restaurant (Bellevue, WA), 216
Cranberry Sweets and More (Bandon, OR), 32
Crater Lake Lodge (Crater Lake National Park, OR), 55
Crater Lake Volcano Cruises (Crater Lake National Park, OR), 53
Crater Rock Museum (Medford, OR), 111
Craterian Ginger Rogers Theater (Medford, OR), 111
CREHST Museum (Richland, WA), 335
Crescent Bar Park (Quincy, WA), 332
Crest Motel (Astoria, OR), 28
Crest Motel (Grants Pass, OR), 78
Crooked River Railroad Company Dinner Train (Prineville, OR), 155
The Crossing (Vancouver, WA), 403
Crown Pacific Inn (Depoe Bay, OR), 56
Crown Point State Park (Portland, OR), 136
Crowne Plaza (Lake Oswego, OR), 99
Crowne Plaza (Seattle, WA), 365
Crystal Springs Rhododendron Garden (Portland, OR), 135
Cucina! Cucina! (Seattle, WA), 355
Curry County Historical Museum (Gold Beach, OR), 74
Cutter's (Seattle, WA), 359

"D" Sands (Lincoln City, OR), 103
Dabney State Park (Troutdale, OR), 177
Dad's Place (Prineville, OR), 155
Dahlia Lounge (Seattle, WA), 359
The Dalles Dam and Reservoir (The Dalles, OR), 173
Dan and Louis Oyster Bar (Portland, OR), 142
Daniel's Broiler (Bellevue, WA), 217
Danish Bakery (Leavenworth, WA), 271
Darigold Dairy Fair (Sunnyside, WA), 391
Darlingtonia (Florence, OR), 67
David and Lee Manuel Museum (Joseph, OR), 90
DaVinci (Salem, OR), 165
Days Inn (Bellingham, WA), 222
Days Inn (Burns, OR), 43
Days Inn (Tacoma, WA), 398
Days Inn–City Center (Portland, OR), 151
Days Inn—North (Portland, OR), 148
Days Inn—South (Portland, OR), 148
Dayton Historical Depot Society (Dayton [Columbia County], WA), 245
Dean Creek Elk Viewing Area (Reedsport, OR), 157
DeCann House B&B (Bellingham, WA), 223
Deception Pass State Park (Anacortes, WA), 211
Deception Pass State Park (Oak Harbor, WA), 298
Deception Pass State Park (Whidbey Island, WA), 410
Deer Harbor Inn (Orcas Island, WA), 313
Deli De Pasta (Yakima, WA), 414
Depoe Bay Park (Depoe Bay, OR), 55
Der Ritterhof Motor Inn (Leavenworth, WA), 271
Deschutes Brewery & Public House (Bend, OR), 37
Deschutes Historical Museum (Bend, OR), 36
Deschutes Motel (Maupin, OR), 106
Deschutes National Forest (Bend, OR), 36
Deschutes River Inn (Maupin, OR), 106
Desert River Inn (Umatilla, OR), 178, 179
Devil's Elbow/State Park (Florence, OR), 67
Devil's Lake State Park (Lincoln City, OR), 101
Devil's Punch Bowl State Natural Area (Newport, OR), 118
DeVoe Mansion B&B (Tacoma, WA), 398
The Diner (Westport, WA), 409
Dining Room at Crater Lake Lodge (Crater Lake National Park, OR), 55
Dining Room at Salishan (Gleneden Beach, OR), 73
Dining Room at Skamania Lodge (Spokane, WA), 390
Dining Room at Sun Mountain Lodge (Winthrop, WA), 412
Dining Room at the Heron Beach Inn (Port Ludlow, WA), 321
Discovery Park (Seattle, WA), 345
DJ's (Ontario, OR), 123
Dock of the Bay (Lincoln City, OR), 103
Doe Bay Village Resort (Orcas Island, WA), 313
Doghouse Backdoor Restaurant (Langley, WA), 269
Domaine Madeleine (Port Angeles, WA), 319
Don's (Soap Lake, WA), 381
Dooger's (Cannon Beach, OR), 44
Dooger's (Long Beach, WA), 274
Dooger's Seafood and Grill (Seaside, OR), 167
Doong Kong Lau (Seattle, WA), 352
Dorena Lake (Cottage Grove, OR), 51
Dory Cove (Lincoln City, OR), 102
Doubletree Guest Suites (Seattle, WA), 363
Doubletree Hotel (Pasco, WA), 317
Doubletree Hotel (Seattle-Tacoma International Airport Area, WA), 370

Doubletree Hotel–Spokane City Center (Spokane, WA), 388
Doubletree Hotel–Spokane Valley (Spokane, WA), 388
Doubletree Inn (Bellevue, WA), 218
Doubletree Inn Hotel (Yakima, WA), 415
Doubletree Ranch (Grants Pass, OR), 78
Doubletree—Columbia River (Portland, OR), 151
Doubletree—Jantzen Beach (Portland, OR), 151
Doubletree—Lloyd Center (Portland, OR), 151
Doubletree–Seattle Airport (Seattle-Tacoma International Airport Area, WA), 370
Douglas County Museum of History and Natural History (Roseburg, OR), 160
Downrigger (San Juan Islands, WA), 338
Dr. Frank Burroughs House (Ritzville, WA), 336
Dragonfish (Seattle, WA), 352
Drain Castle (Drain, OR), 58
Drake's Landing (Langley, WA), 269
Dreamers Lodge (John Day, OR), 90
Drews Reservoir (Lakeview, OR), 99
Driftwood Inn Motel (Blaine, WA), 225
Driftwood Shores Resort (Florence, OR), 69
Duck Brand Cantina, Bakery and Hotel (Winthrop, WA), 412
Duck Soup Inn (San Juan Islands, WA), 338
Duffy's Number Three (Hoquiam, WA), 256
Duffy's Restaurant (Aberdeen, WA), 209
Dulces Latin Bistro (Seattle, WA), 355
Dungeness Panorama B&B (Sequim, WA), 375
Dungeness Recreation Area (Sequim, WA), 374
Dykstra House (Sunnyside, WA), 391

E.R. Rogers Restaurant (Tacoma, WA), 396
Eagle Cap Chalets (Joseph, OR), 92
Eagle Crest Resort (Redmond, OR), 156
Eagle Point Inn (Forks, WA), 253
Eagle's Nest (Langley, WA), 269
Eagle's Nest Resort (Ilwaco, WA), 258
Eagles View B&B (Pacific City, OR), 127
East Benton County Historical Museum (Kennewick, WA), 261
East Linn Museum (Sweet Home, OR), 172
East Rim Viewpoint (Frenchglen, OR), 72
Eastern Oregon Museum (Baker City, OR), 29
Eastern Oregon University (La Grande, OR), 96
Eastern Washington University (Cheney, WA), 235
Ebb Tide (Seaside, OR), 168
Ebey's Landing National Historic Reserve (Whidbey Island, WA), 410
Echoes of the Sea (Copalis Beach, WA), 240
Ecola State Park (Cannon Beach, OR), 44
Ecola State Park (Seaside, OR), 167
Econo Lodge (Sequim, WA), 375
Econo Lodge–Stevenson (Spokane, WA), 390
Economy Inn (Reedsport, OR), 158
Economy Inn of Hermiston (Hermiston, OR), 81
Eddie Rickenbacker's (Hillsboro, OR), 82
Edenwild Inn (Lopez Island, WA), 279
Edgewater Inn (Long Beach, WA), 275
Edmond Meany Hotel (Seattle, WA), 363
Edmonds Harbor Inn (Edmonds, WA), 246
El Camino (Seattle, WA), 355
El Conquistador (Sunnyside, WA), 391
El Gaucho (Seattle, WA), 361
El Greco (Seattle, WA), 355
El Ranchito (Toppenish, WA), 400
El Toreo (Burns, OR), 43
Eldorado Inn (Baker City, OR), 31
Elevated Ice Cream Company (Port Townsend, WA), 323
Elk Public House (Spokane, WA), 385
Elkhorn Drive (Baker City, OR), 29
Elliott House (Prineville, OR), 155
Elliott's Oyster House (Seattle, WA), 355
Elsinore Theatre (Salem, OR), 163
Elysian Brewing Company (Seattle, WA), 352
The Embarcadero (Newport, OR), 120
Embassy Suites Seatac (Seattle-Tacoma International Airport Area, WA), 370
Emerald Downs (Tacoma, WA), 394
Emerald of Slam (Richland, WA), 335
Emigrant Springs State Heritage Area (Pendleton, OR), 128
Emmanuel Church (Orcas Island, WA), 312
Emmett Watson's Oyster Bar (Seattle, WA), 352
Enchanted Country Inn B&B (Eugene, OR), 65
Enchanted Forest (Salem, OR), 164
Enchanted Village (Tacoma, WA), 394
End of the Oregon Trail Interpretive Center (Oregon City, OR), 125
English Inn (Port Townsend, WA), 325
Enzian Motor Inn (Leavenworth, WA), 272
Ernesto's Italian Restaurant (Bend, OR), 37
Esparza's Tex Mex Cafe (Portland, OR), 142
Esplanade at Riverplace (Portland, OR), 146
Ester Lee Motel (Lincoln City, OR), 103
Esther's (Republic, WA), 334
Etta's Seafood (Seattle, WA), 355
Eugene Hilton (Eugene, OR), 66
Eugene Saturday Market (Eugene, OR), 61
Eugene Travelodge (Eugene, OR), 65
Euphoria Chocolate Company (Eugene, OR), 61
Europa Pizzeria and Bakery (Spokane, WA), 385
Evergreen Floating Bridge (Seattle, WA), 349
Evergreen Inn (Leavenworth, WA), 272
Evergreen State College (Olympia, WA), 302
Excelsior Cafe (Eugene, OR), 64
Excelsior Inn (Eugene, OR), 65
Exhibit Center (Ashland, OR), 22
Experience Music Project (Seattle, WA), 347
Ezra Meeker Mansion (Puyallup, WA), 329

F.X. McRory's Steak, Chop and Oyster House (Seattle, WA), 356
Face Rock Wayside (Bandon, OR), 32
Factoria Red Robin (Bellevue, WA), 217
Fairfield Inn by Marriott—Airport (Portland, OR), 149
Fairhaven B&B (Bellingham, WA), 223
Fairhaven District (Bellingham, WA), 220
Fairhaven Park (Bellingham, WA), 219
Falcon's Crest Inn (Mount Hood National Forest, OR), 114
Fall Creek Trail (Eugene, OR), 62
Falls Terrace (Olympia, WA), 304
Fanny's Restaurant (Marysville, WA), 280
Fare Start (Seattle, WA), 355
Farewell Bend State Park (Ontario, OR), 123
Farvue Motel (Goldendale, WA), 255
Fat Cat Diner (Drain, OR), 59
Fathoms Restaurant and Bar (Lincoln City, OR), 102
Favell Museum of Western Art and Native American Artifacts (Klamath Falls, OR), 93
Federation Forest State Park (Enumclaw, WA), 249
Ferdinand's (Pullman, WA), 328
Ferndale (Bellingham, WA), 220
Ferry (Tacoma, WA), 394
Ferry Service to Victoria, BC, Canada (Port Angeles, WA), 318
Ferry Street Bar and Grill (Sedro Woolley, WA), 372
Ferry Trips (Seattle, WA), 349
Ferryman's Inn (Centralia, WA), 231
Ferryman's Inn (Vancouver, WA), 403
Fields Spring State Park (Clarkston, WA), 236
Fiery Manor (Grants Pass, OR), 78
Fiesta Guadalajara (Ontario, OR), 123
5th Avenue Suites (Portland, OR), 152
5th Street Public Market (Eugene, OR), 61
Filiberto's (Seattle-Tacoma International Airport Area, WA), 369
Finch Arboretum (Spokane, WA), 383
Finley National Wildlife Refuge (Corvallis, OR), 49

Fiorella's (Klamath Falls, OR), 94
Firemen's Pond (Redmond, OR), 156
Fireside Motel (Yachats, OR), 182
First Street Haven (Port Angeles, WA), 319
Fish Bowl Brew Pub (Olympia, WA), 303
Fishing (Mt. Rainier National Park, WA), 288
Fishing (Olympic National Park, WA), 308
Five Spot (Seattle, WA), 352
Five-Mile Drive (Tacoma, WA), 395
Flagship Inn (Bremerton, WA), 228
Flagstone Motel (Port Angeles, WA), 319
Flaming Geyser State Park (Enumclaw, WA), 249
Flavel House (Astoria, OR), 26
Flo's Cafe (Coulee Dam, WA), 241
Floras Lake House by the Sea (Port Orford, OR), 154
Flour Mill (Spokane, WA), 384
Flying Arrow Resort (Joseph, OR), 92
Flying Fish (Seattle, WA), 359
Flying M Ranch (McMinnville, OR), 110
Fogarty Creek State Park (Depoe Bay, OR), 56
Fontaine's Restaurant (Hermiston, OR), 81
Forest Park (Everett, WA), 251
Forest Park (Portland, OR), 135
Forks Motel (Forks, WA), 253
Fort Borst/Joseph Borst Home (Centralia, WA), 231
Fort Canby State Park (Ilwaco, WA), 257
Fort Casey Inn (Coupeville, WA), 244
Fort Casey State Park (Whidbey Island, WA), 410
Fort Clatsop National Memorial (Astoria, OR), 27
Fort Columbia State Park and Interpretive Center (Ilwaco, WA), 257
Fort Ebey State Park (Whidbey Island, WA), 410
Fort Nisqually (Tacoma, WA), 395
Fort Spokane (Coulee Dam, WA), 241
Fort Stevens State Park (Astoria, OR), 27
Fort Vancouver National Historic Site (Vancouver, WA), 402
Fort Walla Walla Museum (Walla Walla, WA), 405
Fort Walla Walla Park (Walla Walla, WA), 405
42nd Street Cafe (Long Beach, WA), 274
Fotheringham House (Spokane, WA), 388
Fountain Cafe (Port Townsend, WA), 323
Four Rivers Cultural Center and Museum (Ontario, OR), 123
Four Seas (Seattle, WA), 356
Four Seasons Olympic Hotel (Seattle, WA), 366
Fourth Avenue Tavern (Olympia, WA), 303
Fran's Heidi Haus (Pasco, WA), 317
Franco's Hidden Harbor (Seattle, WA), 356
Frank's Diner (Spokane, WA), 385
Franklin County Historical Museum (Pasco, WA), 316
Franklin Street Station B&B (Astoria, OR), 28
Freestone Inn (Winthrop, WA), 412
Freeway Park (Seattle, WA), 345
Fremont Center (Seattle, WA), 348
Fremont National Forest (Lakeview, OR), 100
Frenchglen Hotel (Frenchglen, OR), 72
Friday Harbor House (San Juan Islands, WA), 338
Friday Harbor House Restaurant (San Juan Islands, WA), 338
Friday's Historical Inn (San Juan Islands, WA), 339
Front Street Ale House (San Juan Islands, WA), 338
Ft. Casey State Park (Coupeville, WA), 243
Ft. Dalles Museum (The Dalles, OR), 173
Ft. Ebey State Park (Coupeville, WA), 243
Ft. Flagler State Park (Port Townsend, WA), 322
Ft. Klamath Museum and Park (Klamath Falls, OR), 93
Ft. Simcoe Historical State Park (Toppenish, WA), 400
Ft. Worden State Park (Port Townsend, WA), 322
Fugazzi Restaurant (Spokane, WA), 385
Full Sail Tasting Room and Pub (Hood River, OR), 85
Fullers (Seattle, WA), 361
Fun Forest Amusement Park (Seattle, WA), 348

Gables, The (Corvallis, OR), 50
Gaches Mansion (La Conner, WA), 267
Gallery at Salishan (Gleneden Beach, OR), 73
Gallery I (Ellensburg, WA), 247
Gallery of Art (Cheney, WA), 235
Gardens (Tacoma, WA), 395
Gardner's Restaurant (South Bend, WA), 382
Garibyan Brothers Cafe Langley (Langley, WA), 269
Gas Works Park (Seattle, WA), 345
Gaslight (Seattle, WA), 363
Gasperetti's (Yakima, WA), 414
Gaylord House (Everett, WA), 252
Gearhart by the Sea (Seaside, OR), 168
Geiser Grand Hotel (Baker City, OR), 30, 31
General Hooker's (Portland, OR), 149
General Store (Port Gamble, WA), 321
Geneva's (Seattle, WA), 356
Genoa (Portland, OR), 147
George Fox College (Newberg, OR), 116
Georgian House (Portland, OR), 149
Georgian Room (Seattle, WA), 361
Gepetto's (Ashland, OR), 23
Gerry Frank's Konditorei (Salem, OR), 165
Gifford Pinchot National Forest (Vancouver, WA), 402
Gilbert House Children's Museum (Salem, OR), 164
Gilbert Inn B&B (Seaside, OR), 168
Ginkgo and Wanapum State Parks (Ellensburg, WA), 247
Giuseppe's Ristorante (Bend, OR), 38
Glazed Terra-Cotta National Historic District (Portland, OR), 137
Goat Rocks Wilderness (Packwood, WA), 315
Gogi's Restaurant (Jacksonville, OR), 87
Gold House Inn (Coulee Dam, WA), 242
Gold Skillet Diner (Baker City, OR), 30
Golden and Silver Falls State Park (Coos Bay, OR), 47
Golden Gardens (Seattle, WA), 345
Golden Spur Motor Inn (Newport, WA), 295
Golden Valley Brew Pub (McMinnville, OR), 109
Goldendale Observatory (Goldendale, WA), 255
Gonzaga University (Spokane, WA), 384
Gorge Powerhouse/Ladder Creek Falls and Rock Gardens (North Cascades National Park, WA), 297
The Governor (Portland, OR), 153
Governor Tom McCall Waterfront Park (Portland, OR), 136
Grand Coulee Dam (Coulee Dam, WA), 241
Grandma Hoffy's Restaurant (Madras, OR), 105
Grandview B&B (Astoria, OR), 29
Grandview Orchard Inn (Cashmere, WA), 229
Grant County Courthouse (Ephrata, WA), 250
Grant County Historical Museum (John Day, OR), 89
Grant County Historical Village and Museum (Ephrata, WA), 250
Grant's Brewery Restaurant/Pub (Yakima, WA), 414
Grants Pass Museum of Art (Grants Pass, OR), 76
Gravity Bar (Seattle, WA), 353
Gray Line Bus Tours (Seattle, WA), 349
Gray Line Tours (Portland, OR), 140
Grays Harbor Historical Seaport (Aberdeen, WA), 209
Grays Harbor Lighthouse (Westport, WA), 409
Grays Harbor National Wildlife Refuge (Hoquiam, WA), 256
Great Pacific Wine and Coffee Company (Pendleton, OR), 129
Green Cape Cod B&B (Tacoma, WA), 399
Green Gables Inn (Walla Walla, WA), 406
Green Lake Park (Seattle, WA), 345
Green Lantern Tavern (Copalis Beach, WA), 240
Green River Gorge Conservation Area (Enumclaw, WA), 249

Greenside Grill (Sedro Woolley, WA), 372
Greenwood Inn (Beaverton, OR), 35
Gregory's Bar and Grill (Seattle-Tacoma International Airport Area, WA), 369
Gresham Farmers' Market (Gresham, OR), 80
Grey Gull (Ocean Shores, WA), 299
Grey Whale Inn (Cannon Beach, OR), 45
Greywolf (Sequim, WA), 375
Griffiths-Priday Ocean State Park (Copalis Beach, WA), 240
Grotto—The National Sanctuary of Our Sorrowful Mother (Portland, OR), 139
Grove of the Patriarchs (Mt. Rainier National Park, WA), 288
Groveland Cottage (Sequim, WA), 375
Guest House International Suites and Inn (Aberdeen, WA), 210
Guest House Log Cottages (Whidbey Island, WA), 411
Gunderson's Cannery Cafe (Astoria, OR), 27
Guy W. Talbot State Park (Portland, OR), 136

Hallmark Resort (Cannon Beach, OR), 45
Hamilton River House (Grants Pass, OR), 77
Hamley's Western Store (Pendleton, OR), 128
Hampton Inn (Bellingham, WA), 223
Hampton Inn (Bend, OR), 39
Hampton Inn Richland (Richland, WA), 335
Hampton Inn Seattle-Southcenter (Seattle-Tacoma International Airport Area, WA), 370
Hannah House (Jacksonville, OR), 88
Hannah's Garden Inn (Snohomish, WA), 379
Hanson Country Inn (Corvallis, OR), 50
Harbinger Inn (Olympia, WA), 304
Harbor Café (Blaine, WA), 225
Harbor Hill Inn (Everett, WA), 252
Harbor Lights (Tacoma, WA), 396
Harbor Resort (Westport, WA), 409
Harbor View B&B (Aberdeen, WA), 210
Harbor View Motel (Bandon, OR), 33
Harbor Walkway (Westport, WA), 409
Harbormaster Restaurant at Port Ludlow Resort (Port Ludlow, WA), 321
Harbour Inn (Whidbey Island, WA), 411
Harney County Historical Museum (Burns, OR), 42
Harris Beach State Park (Brookings, OR), 41
Harrison House B&B (Corvallis, OR), 50
Harrison House Suites (San Juan Islands, WA), 339
Hastings House/Old Consulate Inn (Port Townsend, WA), 325
Hasty Pudding House (Anacortes, WA), 212
Hat Rock State Park (Umatilla, OR), 178
Hatfield Marine Science Center of Oregon State University (Newport, OR), 118
Haus Lorelei (Leavenworth, WA), 272
Haus Rohrbach Pension (Leavenworth, WA), 272
Hawthorne Inn & Suites (Grants Pass, OR), 79
Hawthorne Inn and Suites (Albany, OR), 22
Hawthorne Inn and Suites (Portland, OR), 149
Hawthorne Inn and Suites (Seattle, WA), 363
Hawthorne Inn and Suites (Walla Walla, WA), 406
Heathman (Portland, OR), 146, 153
Heathman Lodge (Vancouver, WA), 404
Hellgate Jetboat Excursions (Grants Pass, OR), 76
Hells Canyon National Recreation Area (Joseph, OR), 91
Hendricks Park Rhododendron Garden (Eugene, OR), 61
Henri's (Longview, WA), 277
Henry Art Gallery (Seattle, WA), 347
Henry Estate Winery (Roseburg, OR), 160
The Herbfarm (Kirkland, WA), 265
Heron (La Conner, WA), 267
Heron Beach Inn (Port Ludlow, WA), 321
Heron Haus (Portland, OR), 151
Heronswood (Port Gamble, WA), 320
Heryford Inn (Lakeview, OR), 100
Hi-Tide (Seaside, OR), 169
Hi-Tide Ocean Beach Resort (Moclips, WA), 281
Hidden Valley Guest Ranch (Cle Elum, WA), 238
Higgins (Portland, OR), 148
High Country Expeditions (McKenzie Bridge, OR), 107
High Desert Museum (Bend, OR), 36
Highland Inn of San Juan Island (San Juan Islands, WA), 340
Highlands (Mount Hood National Forest, OR), 114
Hiking (Mt. Rainier National Park, WA), 288
Hiking (Mt. St. Helens National Volcanic Monument, WA), 291
Hiking (Olympic National Park, WA), 308
Hilander Restaurant (Burns, OR), 43
Hilgard Junction State Recreation Area (La Grande, OR), 96
Hill House B&B (Seattle, WA), 363
Hillcrest Inn (Seaside, OR), 168
Hillcrest Park (Mount Vernon, WA), 292
Hillcrest Vineyard (Roseburg, OR), 160
Hillsboro Travelodge (Hillsboro, OR), 83
Hillside House (San Juan Islands, WA), 340
Hillside Inn (Ashland, OR), 24
Hilltop House (North Bend, OR), 122
Hilton (Bellevue, WA), 218
Hilton Garden Inn (Beaverton, OR), 35
Hilton Portland (Portland, OR), 151
Hinterland Ranch (Sisters, OR), 171
Historic Claquato Church (Chehalis, WA), 232
Historic Deepwood Estate (Salem, OR), 163
Historic North Front Street (Yakima, WA), 413
Historic Orth House B&B (Jacksonville, OR), 88
Historic Sou'wester Lodge (Long Beach, WA), 275
Historical Society Museum (Newport, WA), 295
Historical Walking Tour (Coulee Dam, WA), 241
Hoffstadt Bluffs Visitor Center (Mt. St. Helens National Volcanic Monument, WA), 291
Hoffy's Motel (Madras, OR), 105
Hoh Humm Ranch B&B (Forks, WA), 254
Hoh River Rain Forest (Forks, WA), 253
Holiday Farm Resort (McKenzie Bridge, OR), 108
Holiday Inn (Eugene, OR), 65
Holiday Inn (Issaquah, WA), 260
Holiday Inn (Ontario, OR), 124
Holiday Inn (Seattle-Tacoma International Airport Area, WA), 370
Holiday Inn Express (Cottage Grove, OR), 53
Holiday Inn Express (Florence, OR), 70
Holiday Inn Express (Grants Pass, OR), 79
Holiday Inn Express (Pullman, WA), 329
Holiday Inn Express (Vancouver, WA), 404
Holiday Inn Express Hotel and Suites (Klamath Falls, OR), 95
Holiday Inn Express Hotels and Suites (Tacoma, WA), 399
Holiday Inn Hotel and Conference Center (Everett, WA), 252
Holiday Inn Select (Renton, WA), 333
Holiday Inn—Airport (Portland, OR), 151
Holiday Lodge (Wenatchee, WA), 408
Holiday Motel (Ontario, OR), 124
Holland Gardens (Oak Harbor, WA), 298
Holly Hill House (Port Townsend, WA), 325
Hollywood Steakhouse (Coulee Dam, WA), 241
Home by the Sea (Port Orford, OR), 154
Home Fires Bakery (Leavenworth, WA), 271
Home Spirit Bakery Café (Astoria, OR), 27
Homewood Suites Portland-Vancouver (Vancouver, WA), 404
Honeywood Winery (Salem, OR), 164
Hood River Hotel (Hood River, OR), 85
Hood River Vineyards (Hood River, OR), 84
Hoover-Minthorn House Museum (Newberg, OR), 116
Hoquiam's Castle B&B (Hoquiam, WA), 256
Horizon Motor Inn (Medford, OR), 112

Horsethief Lake State Park (Goldendale, WA), 255
Hostelling International/Seattle (Seattle, WA), 363
Hotel Edgewater (Seattle, WA), 367
Hotel Lusso (Spokane, WA), 388
Hotel Monaco (Seattle, WA), 367
Hotel Planter (La Conner, WA), 267
Hotel Sisters Restaurant (Sisters, OR), 171
Hotel Vintage Park (Seattle, WA), 365
Hotel-Pension Anna (Leavenworth, WA), 272
House Cafe (Enterprise, OR), 60
House of Hunter (Roseburg, OR), 161
Howard Johnson (Chehalis, WA), 233
Howard Johnson (Walla Walla, WA), 406
Howard Johnson Express Inn (Portland, OR), 149
Howard Johnson Plaza (Everett, WA), 252
Howard Johnson Plaza Hotel (Bremerton, WA), 228
Hoyt Arboretum (Portland, OR), 135
Huber's (Portland, OR), 144
Hudson House (Tillamook, OR), 176
Hult Center for the Performing Arts (Eugene, OR), 62
Humbug Mountain State Park (Port Orford, OR), 154
Hunt Club (Seattle, WA), 361
Hunter's Hot Springs (Lakeview, OR), 100
Hurricane Ridge (Port Angeles, WA), 318
Hurricane Ridge Winter Use Area (Olympic National Park, WA), 308
Hyak Ski Area (North Bend, WA), 295
Hyatt Regency Bellevue (Bellevue, WA), 218

Ice Harbor Lock and Dam (Pasco, WA), 316
Icicle Junction (Leavenworth, WA), 270
Idle Hour Café and Steakhouse (Quincy, WA), 332
Idle-A-While Motel (Twisp, WA), 401
Il Bistro (Seattle, WA), 359
Il Fornaio (Portland, OR), 144
Il Giardino (Ashland, OR), 23
Il Terrazzo Carmine (Seattle, WA), 356
Illahee Manor B&B (Bremerton, WA), 228
Illahee Manor Restaurant (Bremerton, WA), 226
Illahee State Park (Bremerton, WA), 226
Ilwaco Heritage Museum (Ilwaco, WA), 257
Imperial Hotel (Portland, OR), 151
Incredible and Edible Oregon (Florence, OR), 68
Indian Lodge (Joseph, OR), 92
Indian Village (Lakeview, OR), 100
Inn at Arch Rock (Depoe Bay, OR), 56
Inn at Cape Kiwanda (Pacific City, OR), 127
Inn at Face Rock (Bandon, OR), 33
Inn at Goose Creek (Ellensburg, WA), 248
Inn at Harbor Steps (Seattle, WA), 365
Inn at Ilwaco (Ilwaco, WA), 258
Inn at Langley (Langley, WA), 269
Inn at Manzanita (Manzanita, OR), 107
Inn at Nesika Beach (Gold Beach, OR), 75
Inn at Otter Crest (Depoe Bay, OR), 58
Inn at Pacific City (Pacific City, OR), 127
Inn at Penn Cove (Coupeville, WA), 244
Inn at SemiAhMoo (Blaine, WA), 225
Inn at Ship Bay (Orcas Island, WA), 312
Inn at Soap Lake (Soap Lake, WA), 381
Inn at Spanish Head (Lincoln City, OR), 103
Inn at Swifts Bay (Lopez Island, WA), 279
Inn at the Bay B&B (Oak Harbor, WA), 298
Inn at the Dalles (The Dalles, OR), 174
Inn at the Market (Seattle, WA), 366
Inn at Virginia Mason (Seattle, WA), 364
Inn of Centralia (Centralia, WA), 232
Inn of Packwood (Packwood, WA), 316
Inn of the Seventh Mountain (Bend, OR), 39
Inn of the White Salmon (Hood River, OR), 86
International District (Seattle, WA), 348
International Fountain (Seattle, WA), 348
International Peace Arch (Blaine, WA), 224
International Rose Test Garden (Portland, OR), 136
Interpretive Programs and Walks (Mt. Rainier National Park, WA), 288
Interstate 8 Motel (Lakeview, OR), 101
Interstate Inn (Moses Lake, WA), 285
Ireland's Rustic Lodges (Gold Beach, OR), 75
Iron Horse Inn B&B (Cle Elum, WA), 238
Iron Springs Resort (Copalis Beach, WA), 240
Island Grill (Oak Harbor, WA), 298
Islander Lopez Marina Resort (Lopez Island, WA), 279
Issaquah Salmon Hatchery (Issaquah, WA), 259
Italian Food Co. (Newport, OR), 120
Italian Kitchen (Spokane, WA), 386
Ivar's Acres of Clams (Seattle, WA), 356
Ivar's Salmon House (Seattle, WA), 356
Ivy Chapel Inn B&B (Ephrata, WA), 250
Ivy House (Grants Pass, OR), 79
Ivy House (Portland, OR), 144

Jackson F. Kimball State Park (Klamath Falls, OR), 93
Jacksonville Inn (Jacksonville, OR), 88
Jacksonville Museum (Jacksonville, OR), 86
JaK's Grill (Issaquah, WA), 259
Jake O'Shaughnessey's (Bellevue, WA), 217
Jake's Café (Ritzville, WA), 337
Jake's Famous Crawfish (Portland, OR), 146
Jake's Grill (Portland, OR), 144
James House (Port Townsend, WA), 325
Jamestown S'Klallam Village (Sequim, WA), 374
Japanese Garden (Portland, OR), 136
Japanese Garden (Seattle, WA), 345
Japanese-American Historical Plaza (Portland, OR), 137
Jeff Morris Memorial Fire Museum (Portland, OR), 138
Jefferson County Historical Museum (Port Townsend, WA), 323
Jefferson County Museum (Madras, OR), 104
Jennings Memorial Park and Jennings Nature Center (Marysville, WA), 280
Jerry's Rogue River Jet Boat Trips (Gold Beach, OR), 74
Jessie M. Honeyman Memorial (Florence, OR), 67
Jitterbug (Seattle, WA), 356
Joan's Portside Café (Ilwaco, WA), 257
Joel Palmer House (Newberg, OR), 116
John Day Fossil Beds National Monument (John Day, OR), 89
John Day Sunset Inn (John Day, OR), 90
John Inskeep Environmental Learning Center (Oregon City, OR), 125
Johnny's Dock (Tacoma, WA), 396
Johnson House (Florence, OR), 70
Joseph H. Stewart State Park (Medford, OR), 111
Josephson's (Astoria, OR), 27
Julia Butler Hansen National Wildlife Refuge (Cathlamet, WA), 230
Juniper Room (Maupin, OR), 106
Justice Center (Portland, OR), 135

K-Diamond-K Guest Ranch (Republic, WA), 334
Kah-Nee Tah (Warm Springs, OR), 179
Kah-Nee-Tah Resort and Casino (Warm Springs, OR), 179
Kahlotus (Pasco, WA), 316
Kalaloch Lodge (Forks, WA), 253, 254
Kam Wah Chung and Co Museum (John Day, OR), 89
Kamiak Butte County Park (Pullman, WA), 327
Kaspar's (Seattle, WA), 360
Kasteel Franssen (Oak Harbor, WA), 298
Katie Downs (Tacoma, WA), 396
Katy's Inn (La Conner, WA), 268
Keenan House (Tacoma, WA), 399
Keller Heritage Center (Colville, WA), 239
Kelso Theater Pub (Kelso, WA), 261
Kempis Hotel Suites (Spokane, WA), 388
Kent Market (Kent, WA), 263
Kerbyville Museum (Cave Junction, OR), 45
Kerstin's (La Conner, WA), 267
Khu Larb Thai (Port Townsend, WA), 324
Kimball Creek Inn (Snoqualmie, WA), 380
King County Fairgrounds (Enumclaw, WA), 249

King Oscar Motel (Tacoma, WA), 399
Kit Carson (Chehalis, WA), 232
Kitsap County Historical Society Museum (Bremerton, WA), 226
Kitsap Memorial State Park (Port Gamble, WA), 320
Kittitas County Farmer's Market (Ellensburg, WA), 247
Kittiwake (Yachats, OR), 182
Kjaer's House in the Woods (Eugene, OR), 65
Kla-Mo-Ya Casino (Klamath Falls, OR), 94
Klamath Basin National Wildlife Refuge Complex (Klamath Falls, OR), 93
Klamath County Museum (Klamath Falls, OR), 93
Klickitat County Historical Museum (Goldendale, WA), 255
Klondike Gold Rush National Historical Park-Seattle Unit (Seattle, WA), 347
Knight Library (Eugene, OR), 62
Knights Inn (Ashland, OR), 24
KOIN Center (Portland, OR), 135
Koji Osakaya (Beaverton, OR), 34
Kornblatt's (Portland, OR), 142
Kum-Yon's (Coos Bay, OR), 48
Kyllo's (Lincoln City, OR), 102

L'Auberge (Portland, OR), 144
La Conner Channel Lodge (La Conner, WA), 268
La Garza Cellars and Gourmet Kitchen (Roseburg, OR), 160
La Grande Howard Johnson (La Grande, OR), 98
La Petite (Anacortes, WA), 211
La Petite Maison (Olympia, WA), 304
La Pine (Bend, OR), 37
La Quinta (Seattle-Tacoma International Airport Area, WA), 370
La Quinta (Tacoma, WA), 399
La Serre (Yachats, OR), 182
Lafayette Schoolhouse Antique Mall (McMinnville, OR), 108
Lake Chelan (Chelan, WA), 233
Lake Chelan State Park (Chelan, WA), 234
Lake Crescent Lodge (Olympic National Park, WA), 309
Lake Cruises (Chelan, WA), 233
Lake Cushman State Park (Shelton, WA), 376
Lake Gillette Recreation Area (Colville, WA), 239
Lake Owyhee State Park (Ontario, OR), 123
Lake Padden Park (Bellingham, WA), 219
Lake Quinault Lodge (Quinault, WA), 331
Lake Roosevelt National Recreation Area (Coulee Dam, WA), 241
Lake Sacajawea Park (Longview, WA), 277
Lake Sammamish State Park (Issaquah, WA), 259
Lake Simtustus RV Park (Madras, OR), 104
Lake Sylvia State Park (Aberdeen, WA), 209
Lake Union (Seattle, WA), 345
Lake View Cemetery (Seattle, WA), 346
Lake Washington Floating Bridge (Seattle, WA), 350
Lake Washington Ship Canal (Seattle, WA), 345
Lake Whatcom Railway (Sedro Woolley, WA), 372
Lakeview Lodge Motel (Lakeview, OR), 101
Lakewold Gardens (Tacoma, WA), 394
Lamplighter Inn (Beaverton, OR), 35
Lampreia (Seattle, WA), 361
Landings (Port Angeles, WA), 319
Landmark Inn (Florence, OR), 70
Lane County Historical Museum (Eugene, OR), 62
Lanza's Ristorante and Pizzeria (Port Townsend, WA), 324
Lara House B&B Inn (Bend, OR), 39
Larrabee State Park (Bellingham, WA), 220
Las Margaritas (Seattle, WA), 353
Laurelhurst Park (Portland, OR), 135
Laurelwood Manor (Jacksonville, OR), 88
Lava Butte and Lava River Cave (Bend, OR), 36
Lazy Susan Café (Cannon Beach, OR), 44
Le Gourmand (Seattle, WA), 360
Leavenworth Ski Hill (Leavenworth, WA), 270
Legislative Building (Olympia, WA), 302
Legrand's (Grants Pass, OR), 77
Lewis & Clark College (Portland, OR), 137
Lewis and Clark State Park (Portland, OR), 136
Lewis and Clark Trail State Park (Dayton (Columbia County), WA), 245
Lewis County Historical Museum (Chehalis, WA), 232
Liberty Inn (Lincoln City, OR), 103
The Lighthouse (Bandon, OR), 33
Lighthouse Point, Point Roberts (Blaine, WA), 224
Lime Kiln State Park (San Juan Islands, WA), 337
Lincoln County Historical Society Museums (Newport, OR), 119
Lincoln Park (Seattle, WA), 346
Lincoln Shores (Lincoln City, OR), 103
Linfield College (McMinnville, OR), 109
Linyen (Seattle, WA), 356
Lion and the Rose (Portland, OR), 151
Lithia Park (Ashland, OR), 22
Lithia Springs Inn (Ashland, OR), 24
Little Creek Cove (Newport, OR), 121
Little Mountain (Mount Vernon, WA), 292
Lizzie's (Port Townsend, WA), 325
Lloyd Center (Portland, OR), 139
Lobster Shop South (Tacoma, WA), 396
Log Cabin Inn (McKenzie Bridge, OR), 108
London Grill (Portland, OR), 147
Lone Lake Cottage and Breakfast (Langley, WA), 269
Lone Pine Village (The Dalles, OR), 174
Long Beach Boardwalk (Long Beach, WA), 274
Longmire (Mt. Rainier National Park, WA), 288
Longmire Museum (Mt. Rainier National Park, WA), 288
Lonny's (Port Townsend, WA), 324
Lookout Point and Dexter Reservoirs (Eugene, OR), 61
Lopez Island Historical Museum (Lopez Island, WA), 279
Lopez Island Vineyard (Lopez Island, WA), 279
Lord Bennett's (Bandon, OR), 33
Lorraine's Edel House (Leavenworth, WA), 271
Lost Lake (Hood River, OR), 84
Love's Victorian B&B (Spokane, WA), 388
Luciano's Casino Waterfront Ristorante (Tacoma, WA), 396
Lucy's Table (Portland, OR), 147
Luigi's Grotto (Seattle, WA), 356
Luna (Spokane, WA), 386
Lynden Pioneer Museum (Blaine, WA), 224
Lytle House (Hoquiam, WA), 256

M.V. Challenger (Seattle, WA), 364
Macaroni's (Ashland, OR), 23
MacKaye Harbor Inn (Lopez Island, WA), 279
MacMaster House (Portland, OR), 152
Madison Park Cafe (Seattle, WA), 357
Madison Renaissance Hotel (Seattle, WA), 367
Magnoni's Market Place (Joseph, OR), 91
Majestic Hotel (Anacortes, WA), 212
Makah Cultural and Research Center (Neah Bay, WA), 294
Makah Maiden Café (Neah Bay, WA), 294
Makah National Fish Hatchery (Neah Bay, WA), 294
Malheur National Forest (John Day, OR), 89
Malheur National Wildlife Refuge (Burns, OR), 42
Mallory Hotel (Portland, OR), 149
Mama Vallone's (Cle Elum, WA), 238
Mamacita's (La Grande, OR), 96
Mandarin Cove (Portland, OR), 142
Mandarin House (Richland, WA), 335
Manito Park (Spokane, WA), 384
Manitou Lodge (Forks, WA), 254
Manor Farm Inn (Poulsbo, WA), 327
Manresa Castle (Port Townsend, WA), 324, 326
Maple Tree B&B (Edmonds, WA), 246
Mar Don Café (Othello, WA), 315
Mar Don Resort (Othello, WA), 315
Marclair Inn (Tillamook, OR), 176

Marco's Supper Club (Seattle, WA), 360
Marcus Whitman Hotel and Conference Center (Walla Walla, WA), 406
Mariah's Restaurant (Ocean Shores, WA), 299
Marianna Stoltz House (Spokane, WA), 388
Marina Park (Kirkland, WA), 264
Marina Restaurant (Bellingham, WA), 221
Marina Restaurant (Sequim, WA), 375
Marina Village Inn (Everett, WA), 252
Marine Discovery Tours (Newport, OR), 119
Maring's Courthouse B&B (South Bend, WA), 382
Maritime Heritage Center (Bellingham, WA), 220
Mark O. Hatfield U. S. Courthouse (Portland, OR), 135
Mark Spencer (Portland, OR), 149
Marqueen Hotel (Seattle, WA), 366
Marriott (Portland, OR), 152
Marriott Sea-Tac (Seattle-Tacoma International Airport Area, WA), 370
Mary Lou's Milk Bottle (Spokane, WA), 386
Mary McCrank's Dinner House (Chehalis, WA), 232
Maryhill Museum of Art (Goldendale, WA), 255
Maryhill Museum of Art (The Dalles, OR), 173
Matsukaze (Grants Pass, OR), 77
Maude Kerns Art Center (Eugene, OR), 61
Maupin City Park/Deschutes River (Maupin, OR), 105
Maverick Motel (Klamath Falls, OR), 95
Maxi's (Seattle-Tacoma International Airport Area, WA), 369
Maximillen-in-the-Market (Seattle, WA), 360
Maxwell Siding Railroad Display (Hermiston, OR), 81
Mayas Taqueria (Portland, OR), 142
Mayer State Park (The Dalles, OR), 173
Mayflower Park (Seattle, WA), 364
Mazama Village Motor Inn (Crater Lake National Park, OR), 55
Mazzi's Italian-Sicilian Food (Portland, OR), 144
McCall House (Ashland, OR), 25
McChord AFB (Tacoma, WA), 394
McCormick and Schmick's (Seattle, WA), 360
McCormick's Fish House & Bar (Beaverton, OR), 34
McCormick's Fish House (Seattle, WA), 353
McCully House (Jacksonville, OR), 87
McCully House Inn (Jacksonville, OR), 88
McLoughlin House National Historic Site (Oregon City, OR), 125
McMenamin's Grand Lodge (Forest Grove, OR), 71
McMenamin's Lighthouse Brew Pub (Lincoln City, OR), 102
McMenamin's Pub (Oregon City, OR), 126
McMenamins Edgefield B&B (Troutdale, OR), 177
McNary Lock and Dam (Pasco, WA), 316
McNary Lock and Dam (Umatilla, OR), 178
Meadows (Bend, OR), 38
Mediterranean Restaurant (Jacksonville, OR), 87
Meerkerk Rhododendron Gardens (Whidbey Island, WA), 410
Mekala's (Eugene, OR), 63
Melody Restaurant (Coulee Dam, WA), 241
Merchants Ltd. (Walla Walla, WA), 405
Meridian (Seattle, WA), 357
Methow Valley Brewing Company (Twisp, WA), 401
Methow Valley Inn (Twisp, WA), 402
Metolius River Resort (Sisters, OR), 171
Metropolitan Grill (Seattle, WA), 361
Mia & Pia's Pizzaria and Brewhouse (Klamath Falls, OR), 94
Michael's Landing (Corvallis, OR), 50
Michael's on the Lake (Moses Lake, WA), 284
Mickey O'Reilly's Inn at the River (Wenatchee, WA), 408
Mid Way Inn (Bremerton, WA), 228
Milford's Fish House (Spokane, WA), 386
The Mill Casino-Hotel (North Bend, OR), 122
Mill Ends Park (Portland, OR), 136
Miller Tree Inn B&B (Forks, WA), 254
Miller's Homestead Restaurant (Hillsboro, OR), 82
Millersylvania State Park (Olympia, WA), 302
Milo McIver State Park (Oregon City, OR), 125
Milton York Restaurant (Long Beach, WA), 274
Mission Mill Village (Salem, OR), 164
Mission Ridge Ski Area (Wenatchee, WA), 407
Mizuna Restaurant (Spokane, WA), 386
Mo's (Florence, OR), 69
Mon Desir Dining Inn (Medford, OR), 112
Mondo Shrimp (Kirkland, WA), 265
Mondo Shrimp (Olympia, WA), 303
Money Saver (Florence, OR), 70
Mongolian Express (Ontario, OR), 124
Monorail (Seattle, WA), 348
Montage (Portland, OR), 142
Monteith House Museum (Albany, OR), 20
Montinore Vineyards (Forest Grove, OR), 70
Moon Palace (Sedro Woolley, WA), 373
Moonfish (Bainbridge Island, WA), 215
Moonstone Beach Motel (Moclips, WA), 282
Moran State Park (Orcas Island, WA), 312
Morical House (Ashland, OR), 25
Morrison's Rogue River Lodge (Grants Pass, OR), 78, 79
Moses Lake (Moses Lake, WA), 283
Moses Lake State Park (Moses Lake, WA), 283
Moses Lake Travelodge (Moses Lake, WA), 285
Motel 6 (Medford, OR), 112
Motel 6 (Moses Lake, WA), 285
Motel 6 (Ontario, OR), 124
Motel 6 (Redmond, OR), 157
Motel 6 (Spokane, WA), 388
Motel Del Rogue (Grants Pass, OR), 79
Motel Nicholas (Omak, WA), 310
Mount Angel Abbey (Salem, OR), 164
Mount Baker Theatre (Bellingham, WA), 220
Mount Rainier Scenic Railroad (Ashford, WA), 213
Mount Si (North Bend, WA), 295
Mountain Climbing (Mt. Rainier National Park, WA), 288
Mountain Climbing (Olympic National Park, WA), 308
Mountain Home Lodge (Leavenworth, WA), 272
Mountain House Country Restaurant (Sweet Home, OR), 172
Mountain Meadows Inn B&B at Mt. Rainier (Ashford, WA), 214
Mrs. Anderson's Lodging House (Leavenworth, WA), 272
Mt. Adams Recreation Area (Goldendale, WA), 255
Mt. Ashland Inn (Ashland, OR), 25
Mt. Ashland Ski Area (Ashland, OR), 22
Mt. Bachelor Ski Area (Bend, OR), 37
Mt. Bachelor Village Resort (Bend, OR), 39
Mt. Baker Ski Area (Bellingham, WA), 220
Mt. Baker–Snoqualmie National Forest (Bellingham, WA), 220
Mt. Baker–Snoqualmie National Forest (Snohomish, WA), 379
Mt. Higgins House (Arlington, WA), 213
Mt. Hood Inn (Mount Hood National Forest, OR), 115
Mt. Hood Meadows (Mount Hood National Forest, OR), 114
Mt. Hood National Forest (Mount Hood National Forest, OR), 113
Mt. Hood Scenic Railroad and Dinner Train (Hood River, OR), 84
Mt. Spokane (Spokane, WA), 384
Mt. Spokane State Park (Spokane, WA), 384
Mt. St. Helens Visitor Center (Longview, WA), 277
Mt. St. Helens Visitor Center (Mt. St. Helens National Volcanic Monument, WA), 291
Mt. Tabor Park (Portland, OR), 136
Mud Mountain Dam (Enumclaw, WA), 249

Mugg Estuarine Park (Pacific City, OR), 126
Mukilteo (Everett, WA), 251
Multnomah Falls (Portland, OR), 136
Multnomah Falls Lodge (Troutdale, OR), 177
Murphy's Corner B&B (Puyallup, WA), 330
Museum at Warm Springs (Warm Springs, OR), 179
Museum of Art (Pullman, WA), 328
Museum of Flight (Seattle, WA), 347
Museum of History and Industry (Seattle, WA), 347
Museum of Northwest Art (La Conner, WA), 267
Mustard Seed (Spokane, WA), 386
My Mom's Pie and Chowder House (Long Beach, WA), 275
My Parents' Estate (Colville, WA), 239
Myrtle Edwards/Elliott Bay (Seattle, WA), 346

Narrows Bridge (Tacoma, WA), 394
Nassa Point Motel (Cathlamet, WA), 230
National Fish Hatchery (Leavenworth, WA), 270
National Historic Oregon Trail Interpretive Center (Baker City, OR), 30
National Park Inn (Mt. Rainier National Park, WA), 289
Naval Undersea Museum (Bremerton, WA), 226
NBA (Portland Trail Blazers) (Portland, OR), 140
NBA (Seattle Supersonics) (Seattle, WA), 349
Neahkahmie Mountain (Cannon Beach, OR), 44
Nehalem Bay Winery (Manzanita, OR), 106
Nell's Restaurant (Seattle, WA), 357
Nendels Inn (Kennewick, WA), 262
Neptune State Park (Yachats, OR), 180
Never Never Land (Tacoma, WA), 395
Newberry National Volcanic Monument (Bend, OR), 37
Newell House Museum (Newberg, OR), 116
Newport Bay at RiverPlace (Portland, OR), 144
Newport City Inn (Newport, WA), 295
NFL (Seattle Seahawks) (Seattle, WA), 349
Nichols Steak House (Ontario, OR), 124
Nick's Italian Cafe (McMinnville, OR), 109
Nike Town (Portland, OR), 139
Nikko (Seattle, WA), 360
Niko's Greek Restaurant and Wine Bar (Spokane, WA), 386
Nishino (Seattle, WA), 357
Nisqually Lodge (Ashford, WA), 214
Nita's Restaurant and Gallery (Shelton, WA), 376
Noodle Ranch (Seattle, WA), 353
Nor'wester Seafood (Gold Beach, OR), 75
Nordic (Lincoln City, OR), 103
Nordic Heritage Museum (Seattle, WA), 347
Nordic Motel and Apartments (Seaside, OR), 170
North Bank (Eugene, OR), 64
North Cascades Scenic Highway (North Cascades National Park, WA), 296
North Central Washington Museum (Wenatchee, WA), 407
North Garden Inn (Bellingham, WA), 223
North Head Lighthouse (Ilwaco, WA), 257
North Whidbey Inn (Oak Harbor, WA), 298
Northern Inn (Republic, WA), 334
Northwest 23rd Avenue (Portland, OR), 139
Northwest Trek (Puyallup, WA), 329
Notaras Lodge (Soap Lake, WA), 381
Novak's Hungarian Paprikas (Albany, OR), 21
Nutcracker Museum (Leavenworth, WA), 270
Nutty Narrows (Longview, WA), 277
Nye Beach Cafe (Newport, OR), 120
Nye Beach Hotel (Newport, OR), 121

O'Callahan's Restaurant and Lounge (Richland, WA), 335
Oak Hill Country B&B (Ashland, OR), 25
Oak Table Café (Sequim, WA), 375
Oaks Amusement Park (Portland, OR), 140
Oasis Park (Ephrata, WA), 250
Oasis Resort (Maupin, OR), 106
Ocean Crest Resort (Moclips, WA), 282
Ocean Shores Interpretive Center (Ocean Shores, WA), 299
Ochoco National Forest (Prineville, OR), 154
Odlin County Park (Lopez Island, WA), 279
Odyssey: The Maritime Discovery Center (Seattle, WA), 350
Of Sea and Shore Museum (Port Gamble, WA), 321
Officers' Row (Vancouver, WA), 402
Official Rogue River Mail Boat Hydro-Jet Trips (Gold Beach, OR), 74
Ohme Gardens (Wenatchee, WA), 407
Okanogan County Historical Museum (Omak, WA), 310
Okanogan National Forest (Omak, WA), 310
Okanogan National Forest (Winthrop, WA), 412
Old Church (Portland, OR), 139
Old Church Inn (Port Ludlow, WA), 322
Old Ft. Townsend (Historical) State Park (Port Townsend, WA), 323
Old House Café (Tacoma, WA), 396
Old Perpetual (Lakeview, OR), 100
Old Spaghetti Factory (Portland, OR), 142
Old Town Silverdale (Silverdale, WA), 377
Old Welches Inn (Mount Hood National Forest, OR), 115
Ole Country Kitchen (Maupin, OR), 106
Olmstead Place State Park-Heritage Site (Ellensburg, WA), 247
Olympic Beach (Edmonds, WA), 246
Olympic Club (Centralia, WA), 231
Olympic Game Farm (Sequim, WA), 374
Olympic National Forest (Olympia, WA), 302
Olympic Raft and Kayak (Port Angeles, WA), 318
Olympic Tours and Charters (Port Angeles, WA), 318
Omak Inn (Omak, WA), 310
Ona Beach State Park (Newport, OR), 119
Onion (Spokane, WA), 386
Ontario State Recreation Area (Ontario, OR), 123
Operation Santa Claus (Redmond, OR), 156
Orcas Hotel (Orcas Island, WA), 313
Orchard Inn B&B (Yakima, WA), 415
Orchard Street Brewery (Bellingham, WA), 221
Oregon Caves Lodge (Cave Junction, OR), 46
Oregon Caves National Monument (Cave Junction, OR), 46
Oregon Coast Aquarium (Newport, OR), 119
The Oregon Connection (Coos Bay, OR), 47
Oregon Dunes National Recreation Area (North Bend, OR), 122
Oregon Dunes National Recreation Area (Reedsport, OR), 157
Oregon Electric Station (Eugene, OR), 64
The Oregon Gardens (Seaside, OR), 170
Oregon History Center (Portland, OR), 138
Oregon Maritime Center and Museum (Portland, OR), 138
Oregon Museum of Science and Industry (Portland, OR), 138
Oregon State University (Corvallis, OR), 49
Oregon Trail Motel & Restaurant (Baker City, OR), 31
Oregon Trail Regional Museum (Baker City, OR), 30
Oregon Vortex Location of the House of Mystery (Jacksonville, OR), 86
Oregon Zoo (Portland, OR), 140
Original Pancake House (Portland, OR), 143
Oslo's B&B (Spokane, WA), 388
Osprey Inn (McKenzie Bridge, OR), 108
Oswald West State Park (Cannon Beach, OR), 44
Our Place at the Beach (Long Beach, WA), 276
Out N' About (Cave Junction, OR), 46
Oval Door B&B (Eugene, OR), 66
Owen Municipal Rose Garden (Eugene, OR), 61

Owyhee Recreation Area (Ontario, OR), 123
Ox Bow Motor Inn (Toppenish, WA), 401
Oxford Inn (Hermiston, OR), 82
Oyster Bar (Bellingham, WA), 221
Oyster Bay Inn (Bremerton, WA), 228
Oyster Bay Inn Restaurant (Bremerton, WA), 228
Oyster Creek Inn (Bellingham, WA), 221
Oysterville (Long Beach, WA), 274
Oysterville Guest House (Leavenworth, WA), 272

Pacific 9 Motor Inn (Eugene, OR), 64
Pacific Beach State Park (Moclips, WA), 281
Pacific Café (Bellingham, WA), 222
Pacific County Historical Society Museum (South Bend, WA), 381
Pacific Inn Motel (Forks, WA), 254
Pacific Lutheran University (Tacoma, WA), 394
Pacific Plaza (Seattle, WA), 364
Pacific Science Center (Seattle, WA), 348
Pacific University (Forest Grove, OR), 70
Padilla Bay National Estuarine Reserve (Mount Vernon, WA), 292
Painted Hills (John Day, OR), 89
Painted Rocks (Yakima, WA), 414
Painted Table (Seattle, WA), 360
Paisano's (Walla Walla, WA), 406
Paisley (Lakeview, OR), 100
Palace Hotel (Port Townsend, WA), 326
Palace Kitchen (Seattle, WA), 357
Paley's Place (Portland, OR), 147
Palisade (Seattle, WA), 360
Palmer Farm (Richland, WA), 335
Palmer's Restaurant and Pub (La Conner, WA), 267
Palomino (Seattle, WA), 357
Panacea (San Juan Islands, WA), 340
Paolo's Italian Restaurant (Kent, WA), 263
Papa Haydn (Portland, OR), 145
Paprika (Spokane, WA), 386
Paradise (Mt. Rainier National Park, WA), 288
Paradise (Sedro Woolley, WA), 373
Paradise Creek Quality Inn (Pullman, WA), 329
Paradise Inn (Mt. Rainier National Park, WA), 289
Paradise Ski Area (Mt. Rainier National Park, WA), 288
Paragon (McMinnville, OR), 110
Paragon (Seattle, WA), 357
Paramount Hotel (Seattle, WA), 367
Park Dunes (Hillsboro, OR), 83
Parker House (Pendleton, OR), 129
Parkplace Inn and Suites (Chehalis, WA), 233
Parma (Aberdeen, WA), 209
Pass Creek Covered Bridge (Drain, OR), 58
Patit Creek Restaurant (Dayton (Columbia County), WA), 245
Patrician Inn and Suites (Longview, WA), 277
Patsy Clark's (Spokane, WA), 386
Pavillion Trattoria (Beaverton, OR), 34
Pazzo Ristorante (Portland, OR), 145
Pearson Air Museum (Vancouver, WA), 402
Pedigrift House (Ashland, OR), 25
Peerless Hotel (Ashland, OR), 25
Peerless Restaurant (Ashland, OR), 23
Peggy's Restaurant (Drain, OR), 59
Pelican Pub and Brewery (Pacific City, OR), 127
Pelican Shores Inn (Lincoln City, OR), 103
Pendleton Underground Tours (Pendleton, OR), 128
Pendleton Woolen Mills (Pendleton, OR), 128
Pensione Nichols (Seattle, WA), 364
Pepper Tree Motor Inn (Beaverton, OR), 35
Perry's on Fremont (Portland, OR), 145
Persimmon Grille (Gresham, OR), 80
Petals Garden Café (Sequim, WA), 375
Peter Skene Ogden Wayside (Redmond, OR), 156
Petersen's Rock Gardens (Redmond, OR), 156
Petroglyphs (Clarkston, WA), 236
Pettygrove House (Portland, OR), 135
Phoenix Inn (Beaverton, OR), 35
Phoenix Inn (Eugene, OR), 66
Phoenix Inn (Salem, OR), 166
Phoenix Inn—Lake Oswego (Lake Oswego, OR), 99
Phoenix Inn—Troutdale (Troutdale, OR), 178
Phone Company (Baker City, OR), 31
Piatti Ristorante (Seattle, WA), 357
Pier 11 Feed Store Restaurant (Astoria, OR), 27
Pike Place Market (Seattle, WA), 348
Pike-Pine Corridor (Seattle, WA), 348
Pilot Butte (Bend, OR), 37
Pine Meadow (Grants Pass, OR), 79
Pine Mountain Observatory (Bend, OR), 37
Pine River Ranch (Leavenworth, WA), 273
Pine Room Cafe (Burns, OR), 43
Pine Tavern (Bend, OR), 38
Pink Door (Seattle, WA), 357
Pioneer Courthouse Square (Portland, OR), 137
Pioneer Farm Museum (Puyallup, WA), 330
Pioneer House (Cashmere, WA), 229
Pioneer Mother's Memorial Log Cabin (Newberg, OR), 116
Pioneer Museum (Tillamook, OR), 175
Pioneer Park (Puyallup, WA), 330
Pioneer Park (Walla Walla, WA), 405
Pittock Mansion (Portland, OR), 135
Pizzacato (Portland, OR), 143
Place Pigalle (Seattle, WA), 360
Plainfield's Mayur (Portland, OR), 145
Plank House (North Bend, OR), 122
Plaza Park Suites (Seattle, WA), 366
Point Defiance Park (Tacoma, WA), 394
Point Defiance Zoo and Aquarium (Tacoma, WA), 395
Polaris (Bellevue, WA), 217
Polson Park and Museum (Hoquiam, WA), 256
Polynesian Resort (Ocean Shores, WA), 300
Ponderosa Motel (Goldendale, WA), 255
Ponderosa Pine Inn (Grants Pass, OR), 79
Ponti Seafood Grill (Seattle, WA), 361
Pony Express Café (Enumclaw, WA), 249
Poor Richard's (Portland, OR), 143
Poppi's Anatolia (Eugene, OR), 64
Port Angeles Fine Arts Center (Port Angeles, WA), 318
Port Angeles Inn (Port Angeles, WA), 320
Port Gamble Historic Museum (Port Gamble, WA), 321
Port Ludlow Resort and Convention Center (Port Ludlow, WA), 322
Portage Bay Cafe (Seattle, WA), 353
Porter House Restaurant and Lounge (Moses Lake, WA), 284
The Portico (Ritzville, WA), 337
Portland Art Museum (Portland, OR), 138
Portland Building (Portland, OR), 135
Portland Center for the Performing Arts (Portland, OR), 137
Portland Saturday Market (Portland, OR), 139
Portland State University (Portland, OR), 138
Portland's White House (Portland, OR), 152
Portside (Coos Bay, OR), 48
Potholes Reservoir (Moses Lake, WA), 283
Potholes State Park (Moses Lake, WA), 284
Potting Shed (Jacksonville, OR), 88
Poulsbo Marine Science Center (Poulsbo, WA), 327
Powell's City of Books (Portland, OR), 139
Powerhouse Brewery and Restaurant (Puyallup, WA), 330
Prego (Seattle, WA), 360
Prehistoric Gardens (Gold Beach, OR), 75
Premier Pasta Italian Dining Room (Seaside, OR), 167
Preston Estate Vineyards (Pasco, WA), 317
Priest Point Park (Olympia, WA), 302
Prince of Wales (Seattle, WA), 364
Prineville Reservoir State Park (Prineville, OR), 155
Pub at McMenamin's (Forest Grove, OR), 71
Pub Minglewood (Ellensburg, WA), 248
Pullman Summer Palace Theater (Pullman, WA), 328

Purple House B&B (Dayton [Columbia County], WA), 245
Pyramid Alehouse (Seattle, WA), 353
Pyramid Peak Trail (Olympic National Park, WA), 308

Quail's Roost Inn (Chelan, WA), 234
Quality Inn (Baker City, OR), 31
Quality Inn (Clarkston, WA), 237
Quality Inn (Klamath Falls, OR), 95
Quality Inn (Seattle-Tacoma International Airport Area, WA), 370
Quality Inn (The Dalles, OR), 174
Quality Inn (Yakima, WA), 415
Quality Inn Baron Suites (Bellingham, WA), 223
Quality Inn Valley Suites (Spokane, WA), 389
Queen City Grill (Seattle, WA), 361
Quimper Inn (Port Townsend, WA), 326
Quinault National Fish Hatchery (Quinault, WA), 331

Radisson (Seattle, WA), 364
Radisson Hotel (Portland, OR), 149
Radisson Seattle Airport (Seattle-Tacoma International Airport Area, WA), 371
Rain Forest Resort Village (Quinault, WA), 331
Rain Forests (Olympic National Park, WA), 308
Rainbow (La Conner, WA), 268
Rainbow Falls State Park (Chehalis, WA), 232
Ramada Inn (Beaverton, OR), 35
Ramada Inn (Bellingham, WA), 223
Ramada Inn (Corvallis, OR), 50
Ramada Inn (Salem, OR), 166
Ramada Inn (Spokane, WA), 389
Ramada Inn—Airport (Portland, OR), 149
Ramada Inn–Governor House (Olympia, WA), 304
Ranch House (Goldendale, WA), 255
Randle Motel (Mt. Rainier National Park, WA), 289
Randy's Pier 61 (Anacortes, WA), 211
Raphael's (Pendleton, OR), 129
Rattlesnake Mountain Brewing Company (Richland, WA), 335
Ravenscroft Inn (Port Townsend, WA), 326
Ray's Boathouse (Seattle, WA), 357
Red Apple (Walla Walla, WA), 406
Red Lion (Port Angeles, WA), 320
Red Lion Hotel (Richland, WA), 336
Red Lion Hotel–Wenatchee (Wenatchee, WA), 408
Red Lion Inn (Aberdeen, WA), 210
Red Lion Inn (Astoria, OR), 29
Red Lion Inn (Coos Bay, OR), 48
Red Lion Inn (Eugene, OR), 66
Red Lion Inn (Klamath Falls, OR), 95
Red Lion Inn (Medford, OR), 112
Red Lion Inn (Yakima, WA), 416
Red Lion Inn at the Quay (Vancouver, WA), 404
Red Lion Inn Coliseum (Portland, OR), 150
Red Lion Inn—North (Bend, OR), 39
Red Lion Inn—Salem (Salem, OR), 166
Red Star Tavern and Roast House (Portland, OR), 145
Redfern Farm B&B (Cathlamet, WA), 231
Redmond Inn (Redmond, OR), 157
Redwood Motel (Grants Pass, OR), 79
Reed College (Portland, OR), 138
The Reef (North Bend, WA), 296
Renton Historical Museum (Renton, WA), 333
Residence Inn by Marriott (Bellevue, WA), 218
Residence Inn by Marriott (Hillsboro, OR), 83
Residence Inn by Marriott—South (Lake Oswego, OR), 99
Residence Inn Seattle–Lake Union (Seattle, WA), 367
Resort at Deer Harbor (Orcas Island, WA), 313
Resort at Port Ludlow (Port Ludlow, WA), 321
Resort at the Mountain (Mount Hood National Forest, OR), 115
Restaurant at Ocean Crest Resort (Moclips, WA), 281
Restaurant Oesterreich (Leavenworth, WA), 271
Reston Hotel (Medford, OR), 113
Rex Hill Vineyards (Newberg, OR), 116
Rheinlander (Portland, OR), 145
Rhododendron Species Botanical Garden (Tacoma, WA), 395
Riccardo's Ristorante (Lake Oswego, OR), 99
Rice Northwest Museum of Rocks and Minerals (Hillsboro, OR), 82
Richardson's Recreational Ranch (Madras, OR), 104
Richland Day's Inn (Richland, WA), 336
Ridgeway Farm B&B (La Conner, WA), 268
Rimrock Inn B&B (Wenatchee, WA), 408
Ringside (Portland, OR), 147
Ringside East (Portland, OR), 147
Ripley's Believe It or Not (Newport, OR), 119
Riverfront Park (Spokane, WA), 384
Riverhouse (Florence, OR), 70
Riverhouse (Pacific City, OR), 127
Riverhouse Motor Inn (Bend, OR), 39
Riverplace (Portland, OR), 153
Rivershore Hotel (Oregon City, OR), 126
Riverside Inn Resort and Conference Center (Grants Pass, OR), 79
Riverside Park (Cashmere, WA), 229
Riverside State Park (Spokane, WA), 384
Riverview Restaurant (Cathlamet, WA), 231
Road Kill Grill (Drain, OR), 59
Roaring River B&B (North Bend, WA), 296
Roche Harbor (San Juan Islands, WA), 340
Rock Bottom Brewing Co. (Portland, OR), 143
Rock City Grill (Spokane, WA), 386
Rock Salt Steakhouse (Seattle, WA), 358
Rock Springs (Bend, OR), 40
Rockhounding (Burns, OR), 42
Rocky Reach Dam (Wenatchee, WA), 407
Rocky Rococo's Pizza Restaurant (Spokane, WA), 387
Rodeway Inn (Ashland, OR), 25
Rodeway Inn on the Bay (Lincoln City, OR), 104
Rogue Regency Inn (Medford, OR), 113
Rogue River Guest House (Medford, OR), 113
Rogue River National Forest (Medford, OR), 111
Rogue River Room (Lincoln City, OR), 102
Romeo Inn (Ashland, OR), 25
Rooster Rock State Park (Portland, OR), 137
Roozengaarde (La Conner, WA), 267
Rosalie Whyel Museum of Doll Art (Bellevue, WA), 216
Rosario Resort (Orcas Island, WA), 313
Roseanna's (Tillamook, OR), 176
Rosebriar Hotel (Astoria, OR), 29
Rosebrook Inn (Cheney, WA), 235
Rosi's (Coupeville, WA), 243
Roslyn Cafe (Cle Elum, WA), 238
Ross Ragland Theater (Klamath Falls, OR), 94
Roszak's Fish House (Bend, OR), 38
Rothschild House (Port Townsend, WA), 323
Round-Up Hall of Fame Museum (Pendleton, OR), 128
Rover's (Seattle, WA), 362
Row River Trail (Cottage Grove, OR), 51
Royal Barge Thai Cuisine (Grants Pass, OR), 78
Royal Motor Inn (La Grande, OR), 98
Royal Vue (Grants Pass, OR), 80
Royale (Seaside, OR), 169
Run of the River (Leavenworth, WA), 273
Running Y Ranch Resort (Klamath Falls, OR), 95
Rustler's Inn (Prineville, OR), 155
Ruth's Chris Steak House (Seattle, WA), 362
Rutherglen Mansion (Longview, WA), 277

Sacajawea State Park (Pasco, WA), 317
Saddle Mountain State Park (Seaside, OR), 167
Safari Motor Inn (McMinnville, OR), 110
Saigon Gourmet (Seattle, WA), 353
Saigon Kitchen (Portland, OR), 143
Salal Cafe (Port Townsend, WA), 324

Salbasgeon Inn of the Umpqua (Reedsport, OR), 158
Salisbury House (Seattle, WA), 364
Salish Lodge and Spa (Snoqualmie, WA), 380
Salish Lodge and Spa Dining Room (Snoqualmie, WA), 380
Salishan (Gleneden Beach, OR), 74
Salmon Harbor (Reedsport, OR), 157
Salmon House Restaurant (Quinault, WA), 331
Salmonberry Way B&B (North Cascades National Park, WA), 297
Salty's on the Columbia (Portland, OR), 145
Sam's Seaside Café (Seaside, OR), 167
Samovar Restaurant (Medford, OR), 112
Samuel Benn Park (Aberdeen, WA), 209
Samuel H. Boardman State Park (Brookings, OR), 41
San Juan Inn (San Juan Islands, WA), 340
San Juan Island National Historical Park (San Juan Islands, WA), 337
Sanctuary Restaurant (Ilwaco, WA), 258
Sandlake Country Inn (Tillamook, OR), 176
Sandland Adventures (Florence, OR), 68
Sandpiper Beach Resort (Moclips, WA), 282
Sans Souci (Bellevue, WA), 217
Sarah Spurgeon Art Gallery (Ellensburg, WA), 247
Saratoga Inn (Langley, WA), 270
Satellite Restaurant (Klamath Falls, OR), 94
Sather House B&B (Bend, OR), 40
Savory Fare (Montesano, WA), 283
Sayler's Old Country Kitchen (Beaverton, OR), 34
Sayler's Old Country Kitchen (Portland, OR), 145
Sazerac (Seattle, WA), 361
Scaleburgers (Ashford, WA), 214
Scandinavian Gardens Inn (Long Beach, WA), 276
Scenic Beach State Park (Bremerton, WA), 226
Schaefer State Park (Montesano, WA), 282
Schafer State Park (Aberdeen, WA), 209
Schatzie's on the Green (Klamath Falls, OR), 94
Schminck Memorial Museum (Lakeview, OR), 100
Schmitz Park (Seattle, WA), 346
Schnauzer Crossing (Bellingham, WA), 223
Scoggin Valley Park and Hagg Lake (Forest Grove, OR), 71
Sea Gulch (Newport, OR), 119
Sea Hag (Depoe Bay, OR), 56
Sea Lion Caves (Florence, OR), 69
Sea Quest (Yachats, OR), 182
Sea Rose (Yachats, OR), 180
Sea Suns B&B (Port Angeles, WA), 320
Sea-Tac Area Courtyard (Seattle-Tacoma International Airport Area, WA), 371
Sea-Tac International Airport (Seattle-Tacoma International Airport Area, WA), 368
Seaquest State Park (Kelso, WA), 260
Sears & Roebuck B&B (Ontario, OR), 124
Seascape Scenic Drive (Long Beach, WA), 274
Seashore Resort Motel (Seaside, OR), 169
Seaside Aquarium (Seaside, OR), 167
Seattle Airport Hilton (Seattle-Tacoma International Airport Area, WA), 371
The Seattle Aquarium (Seattle, WA), 350
Seattle Art Museum (Seattle, WA), 347
Seattle Asian Art Museum (Seattle, WA), 347
Seattle Center (Seattle, WA), 348
Seattle City Light Skagit Hydroelectric Project (North Cascades National Park, WA), 297
Seattle Hilton (Seattle, WA), 367
Seattle University (Seattle, WA), 346
Sehome Hill Arboretum (Bellingham, WA), 220
Sella's Calzone and Pastas (Pullman, WA), 328
Sellwood (Portland, OR), 139
Senator George Baldwin Hotel Museum (Klamath Falls, OR), 94
Septieme (Seattle, WA), 353
Sequim Bay Lodge (Sequim, WA), 375
Sequim Bay State Park (Sequim, WA), 374
Serafina (Seattle, WA), 358
Serenity (Yachats, OR), 182
Seven Feathers Hotel and Casino Resort (Roseburg, OR), 160, 161
Seward Park (Seattle, WA), 346
Shaman (Long Beach, WA), 276
Shamrock Lodgettes (Yachats, OR), 183
Shangri-La Motel (Spokane, WA), 389
Shanico Inn (Corvallis, OR), 51
Shaniko Hotel (The Dalles, OR), 174
Sharlyn Motel (Ephrata, WA), 251
Sheep Rock Unit (John Day, OR), 89
Shelburne Inn (Long Beach, WA), 276
Sheldon's Cafe at the Grant House (Vancouver, WA), 403
Shelton Inn Motel (Shelton, WA), 377
Shelton's Super 8 Motel (Shelton, WA), 377
Sheraton (Seattle, WA), 366
Sheraton (Tacoma, WA), 399
Sheraton Four Points (Portland, OR), 152
Sheraton—Portland Airport (Portland, OR), 150
Shilo Inn (Astoria, OR), 29
Shilo Inn (Eugene, OR), 66
Shilo Inn (Grants Pass, OR), 80
Shilo Inn (Medford, OR), 113
Shilo Inn (Moses Lake, WA), 285
Shilo Inn (Newberg, OR), 118
Shilo Inn (Ocean Shores, WA), 300
Shilo Inn (Portland, OR), 150
Shilo Inn (Salem, OR), 166
Shilo Inn (Seaside, OR), 169
Shilo Inn (Spokane, WA), 389
Shilo Inn (Tacoma, WA), 399
Shilo Inn (Tillamook, OR), 176
Shilo Inn Ocean Front Resort (Newport, OR), 121
Shilo Inn Rivershore (Richland, WA), 336
Shilo Inn Suites (Klamath Falls, OR), 95
Shilo Inn Suites Hotel (Bend, OR), 40
Shilo Inn Suites—Airport (Portland, OR), 153
Shilo Inn–Downtown Vancouver (Vancouver, WA), 404
Shilo Inn–Hazel Dell (Vancouver, WA), 404
Shilo Inn—Oceanfront Resort (Lincoln City, OR), 104
Shilo Inn—Seaside East (Seaside, OR), 169
Shilo Inn—Washington Square (Portland, OR), 150
Shilo Restaurant and Lounge (Seaside, OR), 168
Shilshole Bay Marina (Seattle, WA), 350
Ship Harbor Inn (Anacortes, WA), 212
Ship Inn (Astoria, OR), 28
Shiro's (Seattle, WA), 358
Shoalwater Restaurant (Long Beach, WA), 275
Shore Acres State Park and Botanical Gardens (Coos Bay, OR), 47
Shore Cliff Inn (Gold Beach, OR), 76
Shoreline Steak and Seafood Grill (Tacoma, WA), 398
Shumway Mansion (Kirkland, WA), 266
Siam (Seattle, WA), 353
Sidedoor Cafe (Gleneden Beach, OR), 73
Silver City Brewing Company (Silverdale, WA), 377
Silver Cloud Inn (Bellevue, WA), 218
Silver Cloud Inn (Kennewick, WA), 262
Silver Cloud Inn (Kirkland, WA), 266
Silver Cloud Inn (Portland, OR), 152
Silver Cloud Inn (Seattle, WA), 364
Silver Falls State Park (Seaside, OR), 170
Silver Salmon Resort Motel (Neah Bay, WA), 294
Silver Sands (Rockaway Beach, OR), 159
Silver Spur (Burns, OR), 43
Silver Waves Inn B&B (Ocean Shores, WA), 300
Silverdale on the Bay Hotel (Silverdale, WA), 377
Silverdale on the Bay–West Coast (Bremerton, WA), 228
Silverwater Cafe (Port Townsend, WA), 324
Simpatico (Seattle, WA), 358
Siskiyou National Forest (Grants Pass, OR), 76
The Sisters (Everett, WA), 252
Sit and Spin (Seattle, WA), 353

Siuslaw National Forests (Corvallis, OR), 49
Siuslaw Pioneer Museum (Florence, OR), 69
Sixth Avenue Inn (Seattle, WA), 365
6th Street Bistro and Loft (Hood River, OR), 85
Skagit County Historical Museum (La Conner, WA), 267
Skagit Motel (Sedro Woolley, WA), 373
Skagit River Brewing Company (Mount Vernon, WA), 292
Skamania Lodge (Spokane, WA), 390
Ski Acres (North Bend, WA), 296
Ski Bluewood (Dayton (Columbia County), WA), 245
Skidmore Fountain (Portland, OR), 136
Skinner Butte Park (Eugene, OR), 62
Skykomish Hotel (Skykomish, WA), 378
Skykomish Hotel Restaurant (Skykomish, WA), 378
Slam Palace (Coulee Dam, WA), 241
Sleep Inn (Gresham, OR), 81
Sleep Inn (Ontario, OR), 124
Sleep Inn (Vancouver, WA), 404
Sleeping Lady (Leavenworth, WA), 273
Smith Cove (Seattle, WA), 350
Smith Rock State Park (Redmond, OR), 156
Smoke House Restaurant (Forks, WA), 253
Smokehouse (La Grande, OR), 96
Smuggler's Cove (Brookings, OR), 41
Snohomish County Historic Museum (Everett, WA), 251
Snohomish Grand Valley B&B (Snohomish, WA), 379
Snoqualmie Falls (Snoqualmie, WA), 379
Snoqualmie Valley Historical Museum (North Bend, WA), 296
Snoqualmie Valley Railroad (Snoqualmie, WA), 379
Sol Duc Hot Springs (Olympic National Park, WA), 309
Sol Duc Hot Springs Resort (Olympic National Park, WA), 309
Sonny's (Madras, OR), 105
Sorrento (Seattle, WA), 367
South Bay B&B (Sedro Woolley, WA), 373
South Beach State Park (Newport, OR), 119
South Shore Landing (Clarkston, WA), 236
South Slough National Estuarine Research Reserve (Coos Bay, OR), 47
South Whidbey Historical Museum (Langley, WA), 268
Southeast Hawthorne Boulevard (Portland, OR), 139
Southern Oregon History Center (Medford, OR), 111
Southpark (Portland, OR), 147
Space Needle (Seattle, WA), 348, 362
Spazzo Mediterranean Grill (Bellevue, WA), 217
Spencer Spit State Park (Lopez Island, WA), 279
Spindrift Motor Inn (Brookings, OR), 42
Spirit Mountain Casino and Lodge (McMinnville, OR), 109
Spirit of Washington Dinner Train (Renton, WA), 333
Spokane Falls (Spokane, WA), 384
Spout Springs (Pendleton, OR), 128
Spring Bay Inn (Orcas Island, WA), 314
Springtree Café (San Juan Islands, WA), 338
Spruce Goose Museum (McMinnville, OR), 109
Squalicum Harbor Marina (Bellingham, WA), 220
Squeeze Inn (Toppenish, WA), 401
Squilchuck State Park (Wenatchee, WA), 407
Stacy's Covered Bridge Restaurant (Cottage Grove, OR), 53
Stage Lodge (Jacksonville, OR), 88
Stagecoach Steakhouse (John Day, OR), 90
Stanello's Restaurant (Bellingham, WA), 222
Stang Manor B&B (La Grande, OR), 98
Star Bistro (Langley, WA), 269
Star Center Antique Mall (Snohomish, WA), 379
Stars (Blaine, WA), 225
Stars (Seattle, WA), 353
State Capital Museum (Olympia, WA), 302
State of Oregon Sports Hall of Fame (Portland, OR), 139
State Parks (Portland, OR), 136
Steam Plant Grill (Spokane, WA), 387
Steamboat Inn (Roseburg, OR), 161, 162
Steamboat Rock State Park (Coulee Dam, WA), 241
Steens Loop Road (Frenchglen, OR), 72
Steens Mountain Inn (Frenchglen, OR), 73
Steiger Haus (McMinnville, OR), 110
Stella's Trattoria (Seattle, WA), 358
Stephanie Inn (Cannon Beach, OR), 44
Stephanie Inn (Seaside, OR), 168
Steptoe Butte State Park (Pullman, WA), 328
Sternwheeler *Columbia Gorge* (Hood River, OR), 84
Stevens Pass Ski Area (Skykomish, WA), 378
Stonebrook Suites (Hillsboro, OR), 83
Stonehedge Gardens (Hood River, OR), 85
Stonerose Interpretive Center and Eocene Fossil Site (Republic, WA), 334
Storyville (Mount Vernon, WA), 293
Stratford Inn (Ashland, OR), 25
Stratford Manor B&B (Bellingham, WA), 223
Strawberry Hill (Yachats, OR), 180
Sub Link Internet Café (Yakima, WA), 415
Summit Climb (Mt. St. Helens National Volcanic Monument, WA), 291
Summit Grill and Alpine Patio (Joseph, OR), 92
Sumpter Valley Railroad (Baker City, OR), 30
Sun Downer Motel (Quincy, WA), 332
Sun Mountain Lodge (Winthrop, WA), 412
Sun Valley Inn (Sunnyside, WA), 392
Sundance Grill (Kennewick, WA), 262
Sunnyside Inn B&B (Sunnyside, WA), 392
Sunnyside Museum (Sunnyside, WA), 391
Sunrise (Mt. Rainier National Park, WA), 289
Sunriver Resort (Bend, OR), 40
Sunset Bay State Park (Coos Bay, OR), 47
Sunset Café and Quetzal Room (Cle Elum, WA), 238
Sunset Motel (Bandon, OR), 33
Sunshine Natural Foods (Grants Pass, OR), 78
Super 8 (Baker City, OR), 31
Super 8 (Klamath Falls, OR), 96
Super 8 (La Grande, OR), 98
Super 8 (Long Beach, WA), 276
Super 8 (Ontario, OR), 124
Super 8 (Portland, OR), 150
Surfrider Oceanfront Resort (Depoe Bay, OR), 58
Surfsand Resort (Cannon Beach, OR), 45
Susan's Surrey House (Snohomish, WA), 379
Swan Hotel (Port Townsend, WA), 326
Swantown Inn (Olympia, WA), 304
Sweet Home Inn (Sweet Home, OR), 172
Sweetbrier Inn (Portland, OR), 150
Sweetwaters (Eugene, OR), 64
The Swiss (Tacoma, WA), 398
Sylvia Beach Hotel (Newport, OR), 121
Sylvia's Class Act (Portland, OR), 145
Szmania's (Seattle, WA), 358

Tables of Content (Newport, OR), 120
Taco Wagons (Sunnyside, WA), 392
Tacoma Art Museum (Tacoma, WA), 395
Tacoma Nature Center at Snake Lake (Tacoma, WA), 394
Tacoma Totem Pole (Tacoma, WA), 395
Tamastslikt Cultural Institute (Pendleton, OR), 128
Tapadera Inn (Kennewick, WA), 263
Tapadera Inn (Pendleton, OR), 129
Taqueria La Fogata (Sunnyside, WA), 392
Tasty Thai (Medford, OR), 112
Tatoosh Wilderness (Packwood, WA), 315
Teddy's on Whidbey (Whidbey Island, WA), 411
Temple of Justice (Olympia, WA), 302
Terry Schrunk Plaza (Portland, OR), 136
Thai Pepper (Ashland, OR), 23
Theatre West (Lincoln City, OR), 101
Third Floor Fish Cafe (Kirkland, WA), 265

13 Coins (Seattle-Tacoma International Airport Area, WA), 369
Thompson Brewery & Public House (Salem, OR), 165
Thornewood Castle Inn and Gardens B&B (Tacoma, WA), 399
Three Capes Scenic Route (Pacific City, OR), 127
Three Crabs (Sedro Woolley, WA), 373
Tidal Rave (Depoe Bay, OR), 56
Tides Inn (Port Townsend, WA), 326
Tidewater Restaurant and Lounge (Pacific City, OR), 127
Tiki Lodge (Salem, OR), 166
Tillamook County Creamery (Tillamook, OR), 175
Tillamook Head (Seaside, OR), 167
Tillamook Naval Air Station Museum (Tillamook, OR), 175
Tillicum Beach Campground (Yachats, OR), 180
Tillicum Inn (Umatilla, OR), 179
Tillicum Restaurant (Sunnyside, WA), 392
Tillicum Village (Seattle, WA), 350
Timberline Lodge (Mount Hood National Forest, OR), 114, 115
Timbers Motel (Ashland, OR), 26
Toad Hall B&B (Sequim, WA), 376
Toga's International (Port Angeles, WA), 319
Tolly's (Roseburg, OR), 161
Tommy Thai's (Kirkland, WA), 265
Tony's (Bend, OR), 38
Top of the Inn Restaurant (Seattle-Tacoma International Airport Area, WA), 369
Toppenish Inn Motel (Toppenish, WA), 401
Torrefazione Italia (Portland, OR), 143
Tou Velle State Park (Medford, OR), 111
Touch of Europe B&B Inn (Yakima, WA), 416
Touvelle House (Jacksonville, OR), 88
Tradewinds (Depoe Bay, OR), 56
Traditional Inns (Quincy, WA), 332
Trail of Shadows (Mt. Rainier National Park, WA), 289
Trail of the Cedars (North Cascades National Park, WA), 297
Trattoria Giuseppe (Langley, WA), 269
Trattoria Mitchelli (Seattle, WA), 358
Travel Lodge (Redmond, OR), 157
Traveler's Cove (Yachats, OR), 182
Travelers Inn (Bellingham, WA), 223
Travelodge (Portland, OR), 150
Travelodge (Roseburg, OR), 162
Travelodge (Seattle-Tacoma International Airport Area, WA), 371
Travelodge Suites (Forest Grove, OR), 71
Travelodge Suites (Newberg, OR), 118
Tri-Cities Sleep Inn (Pasco, WA), 317
Trolleyman Pub (Seattle, WA), 354
Trumpeter Inn B&B (San Juan Islands, WA), 340
Tu Tu'Tun Lodge (Gold Beach, OR), 75, 76
Tualatin Hills Nature Park (Beaverton, OR), 34
Tuckaway Farm Inn (Drain, OR), 59
Tucker Cellars Winery (Sunnyside, WA), 391
Tucker House (San Juan Islands, WA), 340
Tuckwilly's Grill (Seattle-Tacoma International Airport Area, WA), 369
Tudor House (Portland, OR), 150
Tudor Inn (Port Angeles, WA), 320
Tulalip Reservation (Marysville, WA), 280
Tulio (Seattle, WA), 358
Tumalo (Bend, OR), 37
Tumalo Falls (Bend, OR), 37
Tumwater Falls Park (Olympia, WA), 302
Tumwater Historical Park (Olympia, WA), 302
Turnbull National Wildlife Refuge (Cheney, WA), 235
Turtleback Farm Inn (Orcas Island, WA), 314
Twanoh State Park (Shelton, WA), 376
Twenty-Five Mile Creek State Park (Chelan, WA), 234
Twin Harbors State Park (Westport, WA), 409
Two Rivers Park (Kennewick, WA), 262
Tyee Lodge (Newport, OR), 121
Tyee Motel (Neah Bay, WA), 294
Tyee Wine Cellars (Corvallis, OR), 49
Typhoon! (Portland, OR), 145

U. S. Bank (Baker City, OR), 30
Ukiah-Dale Forest State Scenic Corridor (Pendleton, OR), 128
Umatilla Indian Reservation (Pendleton, OR), 128
Umatilla Marina Park (Umatilla, OR), 178
Umatilla National Forest (Clarkston, WA), 236
Umatilla National Forest (Pendleton, OR), 128
Umpqua Discovery Center (Reedsport, OR), 157
Umpqua Lighthouse State Park (Reedsport, OR), 157
Umpqua National Forest (Roseburg, OR), 160
Under the Greenwood Tree (Medford, OR), 113
Underground Tour (Seattle, WA), 349
Undersea Gardens (Newport, OR), 119
Union Bay Cafe (Seattle, WA), 358
Union Square Grill (Seattle, WA), 358
Union Station (Tacoma, WA), 395
Unity Lake State Park (Baker City, OR), 30
University Inn (Seattle, WA), 365
University of Oregon (Eugene, OR), 62
University of Oregon Museum of Art (Eugene, OR), 62
University of Oregon Museum of Natural History (Eugene, OR), 62
University of Puget Sound (Tacoma, WA), 395
University of Washington (Seattle, WA), 346
University Plaza Hotel (Seattle, WA), 365
Uptown Inn (Port Angeles, WA), 320
USS *Turner Joy* (Bremerton, WA), 226

Vagabond Lodge (Hood River, OR), 86
Val-U-Inn (Bellingham, WA), 223
Valley Art Center (Clarkston, WA), 236
Valley Bronze of Oregon (Joseph, OR), 91
Valley Cafe (Ellensburg, WA), 248
Valley of the Rogue State Park (Grants Pass, OR), 76
Valley River Inn (Eugene, OR), 67
Vancouver's Chart House (Vancouver, WA), 403
Vic's Broiler (Seattle-Tacoma International Airport Area, WA), 369
Victoria/San Juan Cruises (Bellingham, WA), 221
Victorian Gardens 1888 B&B (Kent, WA), 263
Victorian House B&B (Goldendale, WA), 255
The Villa (Tacoma, WA), 399
Villa Heidelberg (Seattle, WA), 365
The Village (Marysville, WA), 281
Village Inn Motel (Cashmere, WA), 230
Village Motor Inn (Marysville, WA), 281
Vineyard Steak House at the Doubletree Inn (Pasco, WA), 317
Vinny's Italian Kitchen (Medford, OR), 112
Vintage Inn (Vancouver, WA), 404
Vintage Plaza (Portland, OR), 153
Virginian Resort (Winthrop, WA), 412, 413
Visconti's (Leavenworth, WA), 271
Volcano Information Center (Kelso, WA), 260
Volunteer Fireman's Museum (La Conner, WA), 267
Volunteer Park (Seattle, WA), 346

Wagner's (Olympia, WA), 303
Waldo Lake (Eugene, OR), 62
The Wall (Index, WA), 258
Wall Street Inn (Seattle, WA), 366
Walla Walla Travelodge (Walla Walla, WA), 406
Wallowa County Museum (Joseph, OR), 91
Wallowa Lake Lodge (Joseph, OR), 92
Wallowa Lake State Recreation Park (Joseph, OR), 91
Wallowa Lake Tramway (Joseph, OR), 91
Wallowa Mountain Loop (Joseph, OR), 91
Wallowa Outdoors (Enterprise, OR), 60
Wallowa-Whitman National Forest (Baker City, OR), 30
Wanapum Dam Heritage Center (Ellensburg, WA), 247
Warm Springs Inn B&B (Wenatchee, WA), 408
Warren G. Magnuson Park (Seattle, WA), 346

Warwick (Seattle, WA), 365
Wasco County Courthouse (The Dalles, OR), 173
Washington Hills Cellar (Sunnyside, WA), 391
Washington Park (Anacortes, WA), 211
Washington Park (Portland, OR), 137
Washington Park Arboretum (Seattle, WA), 346
Washington State History Museum (Tacoma, WA), 395
Washington State Library (Olympia, WA), 302
Washington State University (Pullman, WA), 328
Wasson Brothers Winery (Oregon City, OR), 125
Watchman Restaurant (Crater Lake National Park, OR), 55
Water Tower in Johns Landing (Portland, OR), 140
Water's Edge Guest House (Issaquah, WA), 260
Waterfront Drive (Seattle, WA), 350
Waters Lakeside Bistro (Kirkland, WA), 265
Wauconda Cafe, General Store, and Post Office (Omak, WA), 310
Waverly Place B&B (Spokane, WA), 389
Wax Works (Newport, OR), 119
Weasku (Grants Pass, OR), 80
Webb's Scenic Surf (Cannon Beach, OR), 45
Wedge Mountain Inn (Cashmere, WA), 230
Weinhard Café (Dayton (Columbia County), WA), 245
Weinhard Hotel (Dayton (Columbia County), WA), 246
Welcome Motor Inn (Everett, WA), 253
Wellspring (Ashford, WA), 214
Wenatchee National Forest (Wenatchee, WA), 407
Wenatchee Roaster and Ale House (Wenatchee, WA), 407
Wenberg State Park (Marysville, WA), 280
West Coast Game Park (Bandon, OR), 32
Westcoast Bellevue Hotel (Bellevue, WA), 218
Westcoast Ridpath Hotel (Spokane, WA), 389
WestCoast Roosevelt Hotel (Seattle, WA), 365
Westcoast Sea-Tac Hotel (Seattle-Tacoma International Airport Area, WA), 371
Westcoast Wenatchee Center (Wenatchee, WA), 408
Western Motel (Baker City, OR), 31
Western Washington University (Bellingham, WA), 220
The Westin (Seattle, WA), 366
Westlake Center (Seattle, WA), 349
Westport Aquarium (Westport, WA), 409
Westport Maritime Museum (Westport, WA), 409
Westside Bakery and Café (Bend, OR), 38
***Westward Ho!* Sternwheeler** (Florence, OR), 69
The Whale Museum (San Juan Islands, WA), 338
Whale's Tale (Newport, OR), 120
Whaler (Newport, OR), 121
Whatcom Falls Park (Bellingham, WA), 220
Whatcom Museum of History and Art (Bellingham, WA), 220
Wheelhouse (Bandon, OR), 33
Whiskey Creek B&B (Tillamook, OR), 176
Whistler's Family Restaurant (Omak, WA), 310
White Pass Village (Mt. Rainier National Park, WA), 289
White Pass Village (Yakima, WA), 414
White River Falls State Park (Maupin, OR), 105
White Rose Inn (Enumclaw, WA), 249
White Swan Guest House (Mount Vernon, WA), 293
Whitewater Rafting—Sun Country Tours (Bend, OR), 37
Whitman College (Walla Walla, WA), 405
Whitman Mission National Historic Site (Walla Walla, WA), 405
Who Song and Larry's Cantina Mexican Restaurant (Vancouver, WA), 403
Widmer Gasthaus (Portland, OR), 143
Wild Garlic (Bellingham, WA), 222
Wild Ginger (Seattle, WA), 354
Wild Iris (La Conner, WA), 268
Wild River Pizza Company & Brewery (Cave Junction, OR), 46
Wild Waves Water Park (Tacoma, WA), 394
Wilderness Inn (Enterprise, OR), 60
Wildflowers (Mount Vernon, WA), 292
Wildhorse Casino Resort (Pendleton, OR), 129
Wildlife Safari (Roseburg, OR), 160
Wildwood (Portland, OR), 147
Willamette Falls Locks (Oregon City, OR), 125
Willamette National Forest (Eugene, OR), 62
Willamette Pass (Eugene, OR), 63
Willamette Science and Technology Center (WISTEC) (Eugene, OR), 62
Willamette Shore Trolley (Lake Oswego, OR), 98
Willamette University (Salem, OR), 163
William M. Tugman State Park (Reedsport, OR), 158
Willow Springs Motel (Cheney, WA), 235
Willow Springs Station (Cheney, WA), 235
Winchester Country Inn (Ashland, OR), 23
Winchester Inn (Ashland, OR), 26
Winchester Wasteway (Moses Lake, WA), 284
The Windmill (Wenatchee, WA), 407
Windmill Inn (Medford, OR), 113
Windmill Inn (Roseburg, OR), 162
Windmill Inn of Ashland (Ashland, OR), 26
Windsong B&B (Orcas Island, WA), 314
Windward Inn (Florence, OR), 69
Winema National Forest (Klamath Falls, OR), 94
Winery Tours. Flerchinger Vineyards (Hood River, OR), 84
Wing Luke Asian Museum (Seattle, WA), 348
Winged Lion (Spokane, WA), 387
Winter Kitchen (Centralia, WA), 231
Winter Summer Inn B&B (Sekiu, WA), 374
Winterborne (Portland, OR), 147
Winthrop Inn (Winthrop, WA), 413
Wolfgang Puck Café (Seattle, WA), 359
Woodland Park Zoological Gardens (Seattle, WA), 350
Woodmark Hotel on Lake Washington (Kirkland, WA), 266
Woods House (Ashland, OR), 26
Worden's Winery (Spokane, WA), 384
Working Girls Hotel (Pendleton, OR), 130
World Forestry Center (Portland, OR), 137
Wright Park (Tacoma, WA), 395

Xinh's Clam and Oyster House (Shelton, WA), 376

Yachats Ocean Road State Recreation Area (Yachats, OR), 180
Yacht Club Broiler (Bremerton, WA), 228
Yakama Nation Cultural Center (Toppenish, WA), 400
Yakima Area Arboretum (Yakima, WA), 414
Yakima Sportsman State Park (Yakima, WA), 414
Yakima Valley Museum (Yakima, WA), 414
Yamhill National Historic District (Portland, OR), 138
Yamhill Valley Vineyards (McMinnville, OR), 109
Yankee Pot Roast (Grants Pass, OR), 78
Yaquina Bay State Park (Newport, OR), 119
Yaquina Head Lighthouse (Newport, OR), 119
Yarrow Bay Grill and Beach Café (Kirkland, WA), 265
Yellow Church Café (Ellensburg, WA), 248
Youngberg Hill Vineyard (McMinnville, OR), 110
Yuzen Japanese Cuisine (Lincoln City, OR), 102

Ziggurat (Yachats, OR), 183

Notes

Notes

TALK TO US

Fill out this quick survey and receive a free *Fodor's How to Pack* (while supplies last)

1 Which Road Guide did you purchase? (Check all that apply.)
- ❒ AL/AR/LA/MS/TN
- ❒ AZ/CO/NM
- ❒ CA
- ❒ CT/MA/RI
- ❒ DE/DC/MD/PA/VA
- ❒ FL
- ❒ GA/NC/SC
- ❒ ID/MT/NV/UT/WY
- ❒ IL/IA/MO/WI
- ❒ IN/KY/MI/OH/WV
- ❒ KS/OK/TX
- ❒ ME/NH/VT
- ❒ MN/NE/ND/SD
- ❒ NJ/NY
- ❒ OR/WA

2 How did you learn about the Road Guides?
- ❒ TV ad
- ❒ Radio ad
- ❒ Newspaper or magazine ad
- ❒ Newspaper or magazine article
- ❒ TV or radio feature
- ❒ Bookstore display/clerk recommendation
- ❒ Recommended by family/friend
- ❒ Other:____________________

3 Did you use other guides for your trip?
- ❒ AAA
- ❒ Compass American Guide
- ❒ Fodor's
- ❒ Frommer's
- ❒ Insiders' Guide
- ❒ Mobil
- ❒ Moon Handbook
- ❒ Other:________

4 Did you use any of the following for planning?
❒ Tourism offices ❒ Internet ❒ Travel agent

5 Did you buy a Road Guide for (check one):
- ❒ Leisure trip
- ❒ Business trip
- ❒ Mix of business and leisure

6 Where did you buy your Road Guide?
- ❒ Bookstore
- ❒ Other store
- ❒ On-line
- ❒ Borrowed from a friend
- ❒ Borrowed from a library
- ❒ Other:____________________

7 Why did you buy a Road Guide? (Check all that apply.)
- ❒ Number of cities/towns listed
- ❒ Comprehensive coverage
- ❒ Number of lodgings
- ❒ Driving tours
- ❒ Number of restaurants
- ❒ Maps
- ❒ Number of attractions
- ❒ Fodor's brand name
- ❒ Other:____________________

8 Did you use this guide primarily:
- ❒ For pretrip planning
- ❒ While traveling
- ❒ For planning and while traveling

9 What was the duration of your trip?
- ❒ 2-3 days
- ❒ 4-6 days
- ❒ 7-10 days
- ❒ 11 or more days
- ❒ Taking more than 1 trip

10 Did you use the guide to select
- ❒ Hotels
- ❒ Restaurants

11 Did you stay primarily in a
- ❒ Hotel
- ❒ Motel
- ❒ Resort
- ❒ Bed-and-breakfast
- ❒ RV/camper
- ❒ Hostel
- ❒ Campground
- ❒ Dude ranch
- ❒ With family or friends
- ❒ Other:____________

12 What sights and activities did you most enjoy?
- ❒ Historical sights
- ❒ Sports
- ❒ National parks
- ❒ State parks
- ❒ Attractions off the beaten path
- ❒ Shopping
- ❒ Theaters
- ❒ Museums
- ❒ Major cities

13 How much did you spend per adult for this trip?
- ❒ Less than $500
- ❒ $501-$750
- ❒ $751-$1,000
- ❒ More than $1,000

14 How many traveled in your party?
___ Adults ___ Children ___ Pets

15 Did you
- ❒ Fly to destination
- ❒ Drive your own vehicle
- ❒ Rent a car
- ❒ Rent a van or RV
- ❒ Take a train
- ❒ Take a bus

16 How many miles did you travel round-trip?
- ❒ Less than 100
- ❒ 101-300
- ❒ 301-500
- ❒ 501-750
- ❒ 751-1,000
- ❒ More than 1,000

17 What items did you take on your vacation?
- ❒ Traveler's checks
- ❒ Credit card
- ❒ Gasoline card
- ❒ Phone card
- ❒ Camera
- ❒ Digital camera
- ❒ Cell phone
- ❒ Computer
- ❒ PDA
- ❒ Other

18 Would you use Fodor's Road Guides again?
- ❒ Yes
- ❒ No

19 How would you like to see Road Guides changed?

❐ More	❐ Less	Dining
❐ More	❐ Less	Lodging
❐ More	❐ Less	Sports
❐ More	❐ Less	Activities
❐ More	❐ Less	Attractions
❐ More	❐ Less	Shopping
❐ More	❐ Less	Driving tours
❐ More	❐ Less	Maps
❐ More	❐ Less	Historical information

❐ Other: ______________________

20 Tell us about yourself.

❐ Male ❐ Female

Age:

❐ 18-24	❐ 35-44	❐ 55-64
❐ 25-34	❐ 45-54	❐ Over 65

Income:

❐ Less than $25,000	❐ $50,001-$75,000
❐ $25,001-$50,000	❐ More than $75,0c

Name: ______________________ E-mail: ______________________

Address: ______________________ City: ____________ State: ____ Zip: ______

Fodor's Travel Publications
Attn: Road Guide Survey
280 Park Avenue
New York, NY 10017

The information herein will be treated in confidence. Names and addresses will not be released to mailing-list houses or other organizations.

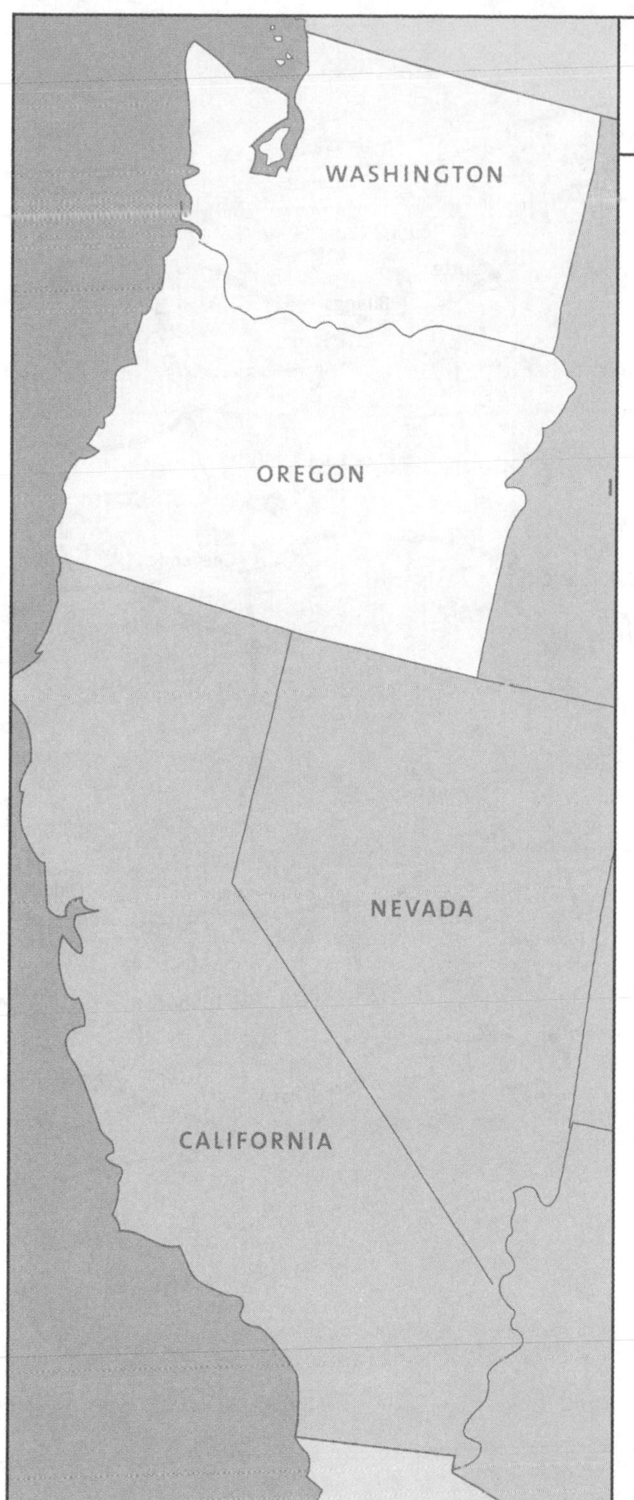

Atlas

MAP #

1 **U.S. HIGHWAYS**

2 **DISTANCES AND DRIVING TIMES**

3 **OREGON**

4 **PORTLAND, OR**

5 **SALEM, OR**

6 **EUGENE, OR**

7 **SEATTLE/ TACOMA AREA**

8 **WASHINGTON**

9 **SEATTLE, WA**

10 **SEATTLE AREA**

11 **OLYMPIA, WA**

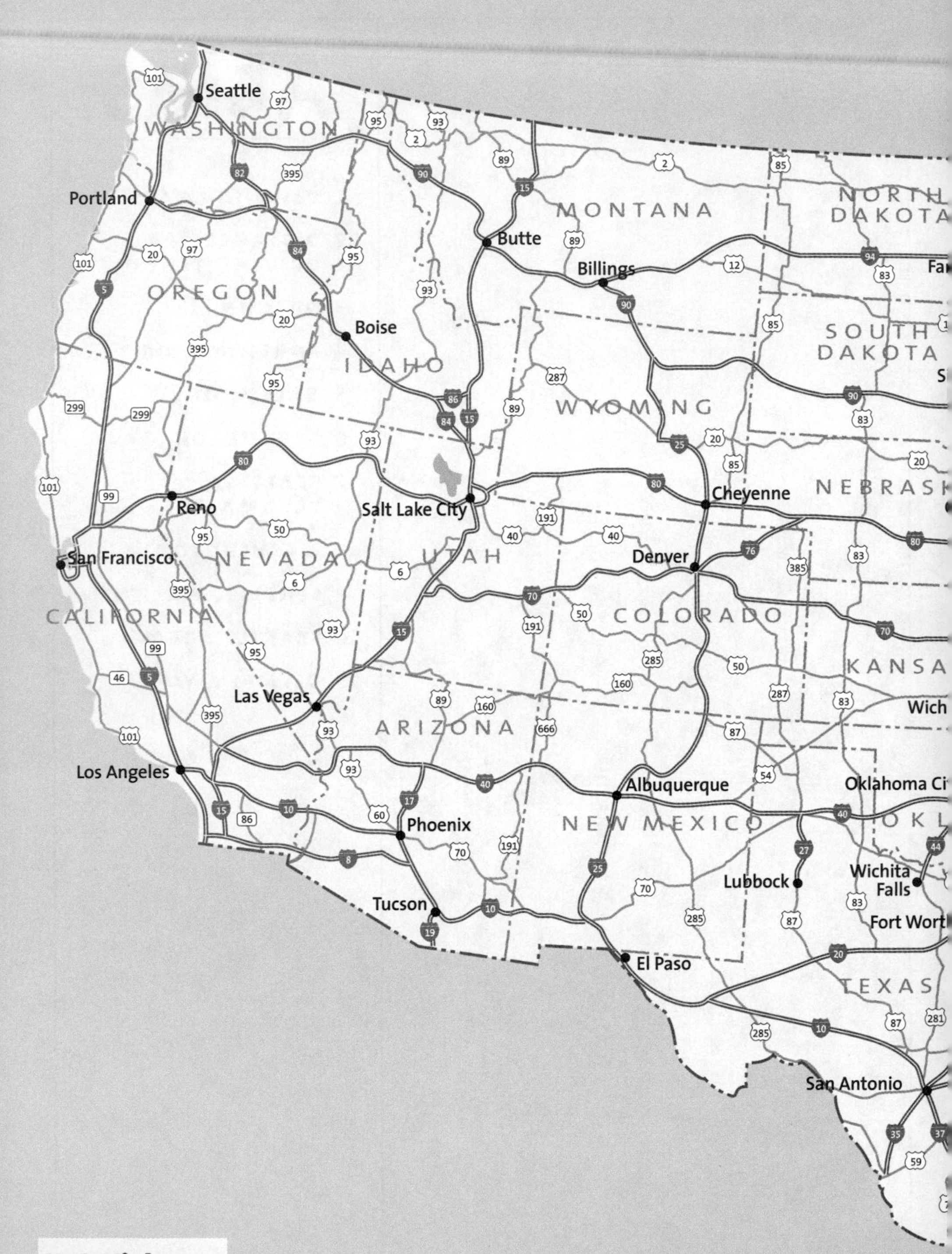
Seattle
WASHINGTON
Portland
OREGON
Boise
IDAHO
MONTANA
Butte
Billings
NORTH DAKOTA
SOUTH DAKOTA
WYOMING
Cheyenne
NEBRASKA
Reno
Salt Lake City
San Francisco
NEVADA
UTAH
Denver
COLORADO
CALIFORNIA
KANSAS
Las Vegas
ARIZONA
Los Angeles
Albuquerque
Oklahoma City
Phoenix
NEW MEXICO
Lubbock
Wichita Falls
Tucson
Fort Worth
El Paso
TEXAS
San Antonio

U. S. Highways

MAINE
Portland
Boston
MASS.
R.I.
CONN.
NEW YORK
New York
NEW JERSEY
DEL.
MD.
Washington, D.C.
PENNSYLVANIA
Pittsburgh
OHIO
Columbus
Cincinnati
WEST VIRGINIA
VIRGINIA
NORTH CAROLINA
Charlotte
SOUTH CAROLINA
Charleston
GEORGIA
Atlanta
Savannah
FLORIDA
Jacksonville
Orlando
Tampa
Miami
MICHIGAN
Detroit
INDIANA
Indianapolis
ILLINOIS
Chicago
WISCONSIN
Milwaukee
NNESOTA
eapolis
IOWA
Des Moines
MISSOURI
Kansas City
St. Louis
KENTUCKY
Louisville
TENNESSEE
Nashville
ARKANSAS
Little Rock
MISS
Jackson
ALABAMA
Birmingham
Montgomery
LOUISIANA
New Orleans
Houston

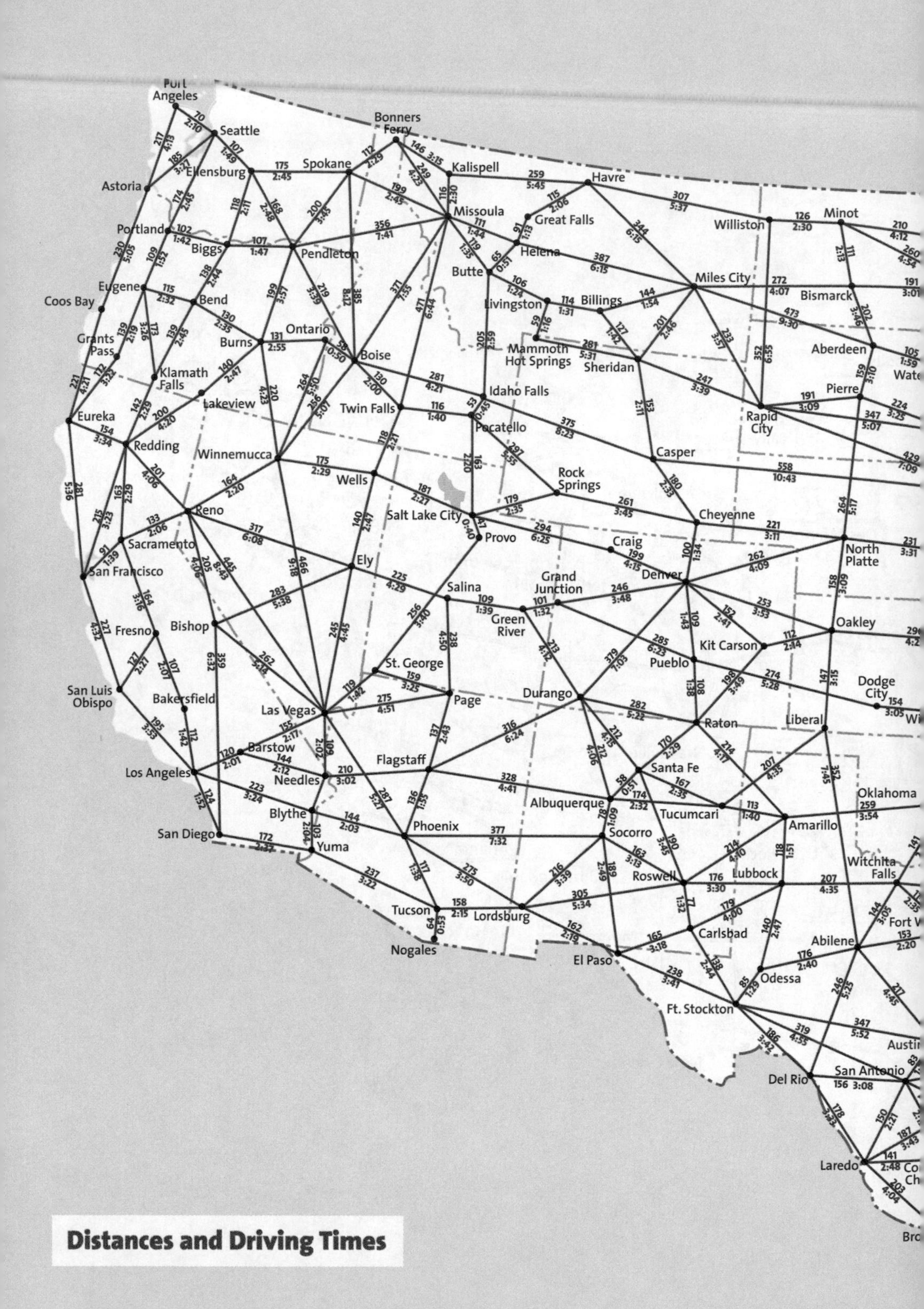

Distances and Driving Times

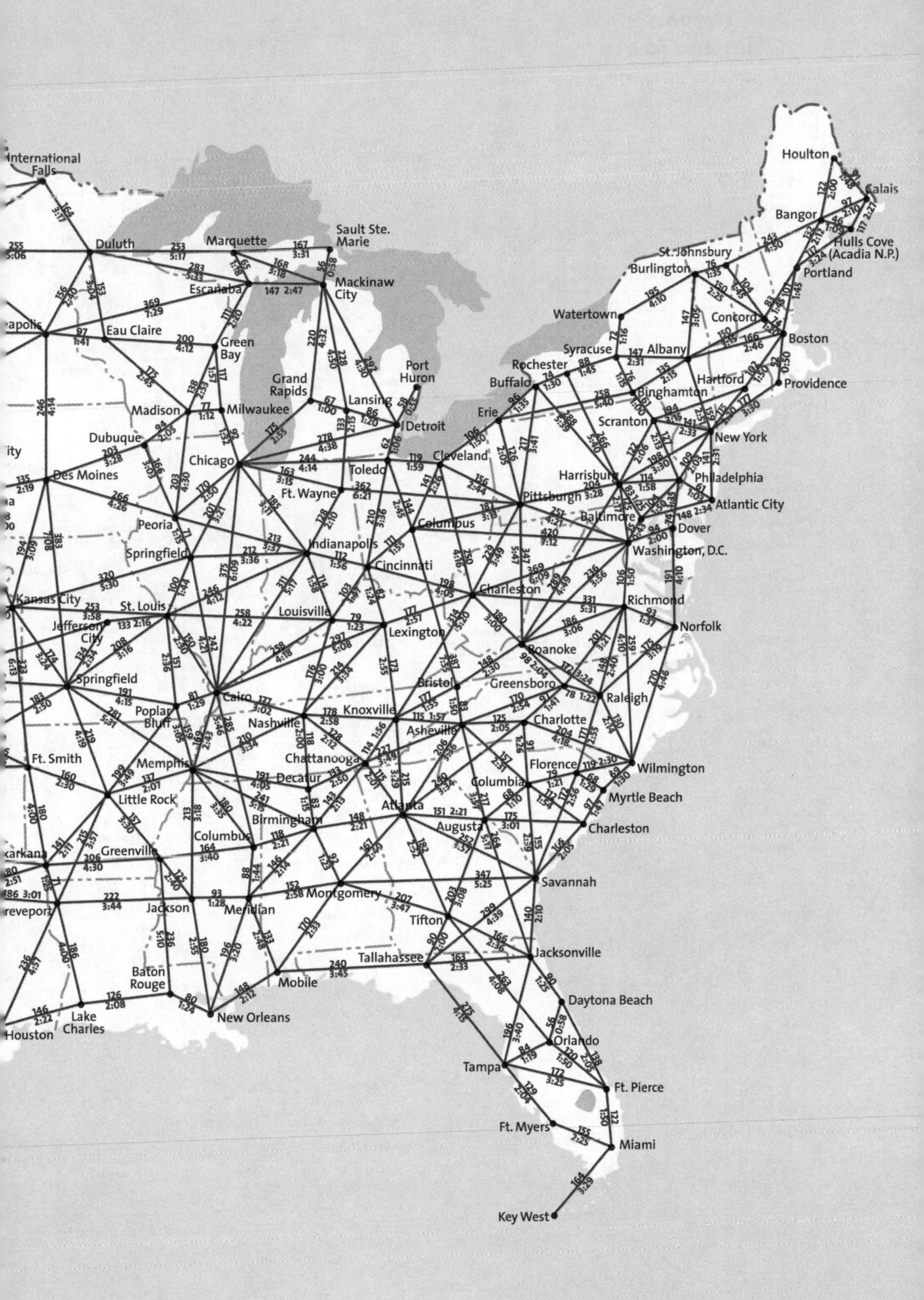
International Falls
Duluth
Marquette
Sault Ste. Marie
Escanaba
Mackinaw City
Eau Claire
Green Bay
Madison
Milwaukee
Grand Rapids
Lansing
Port Huron
Detroit
Dubuque
Chicago
Des Moines
Toledo
Cleveland
Erie
Buffalo
Rochester
Syracuse
Watertown
Burlington
St. Johnsbury
Concord
Albany
Boston
Hartford
Providence
Binghamton
Scranton
New York
Houlton
Calais
Bangor
Hulls Cove (Acadia N.P.)
Portland
Ft. Wayne
Peoria
Springfield
Indianapolis
Columbus
Pittsburgh
Harrisburg
Philadelphia
Atlantic City
Baltimore
Dover
Washington, D.C.
Cincinnati
Charleston
Kansas City
St. Louis
Jefferson City
Louisville
Lexington
Richmond
Norfolk
Springfield
Cairo
Roanoke
Greensboro
Raleigh
Bristol
Knoxville
Asheville
Charlotte
Poplar Bluff
Nashville
Ft. Smith
Memphis
Chattanooga
Florence
Wilmington
Little Rock
Decatur
Columbia
Myrtle Beach
Atlanta
Augusta
Charleston
Birmingham
Columbus
Greenville
Savannah
Montgomery
Jackson
Meridian
Tifton
Jacksonville
Tallahassee
Baton Rouge
Mobile
New Orleans
Lake Charles
Houston
Daytona Beach
Orlando
Tampa
Ft. Pierce
Ft. Myers
Miami
Key West

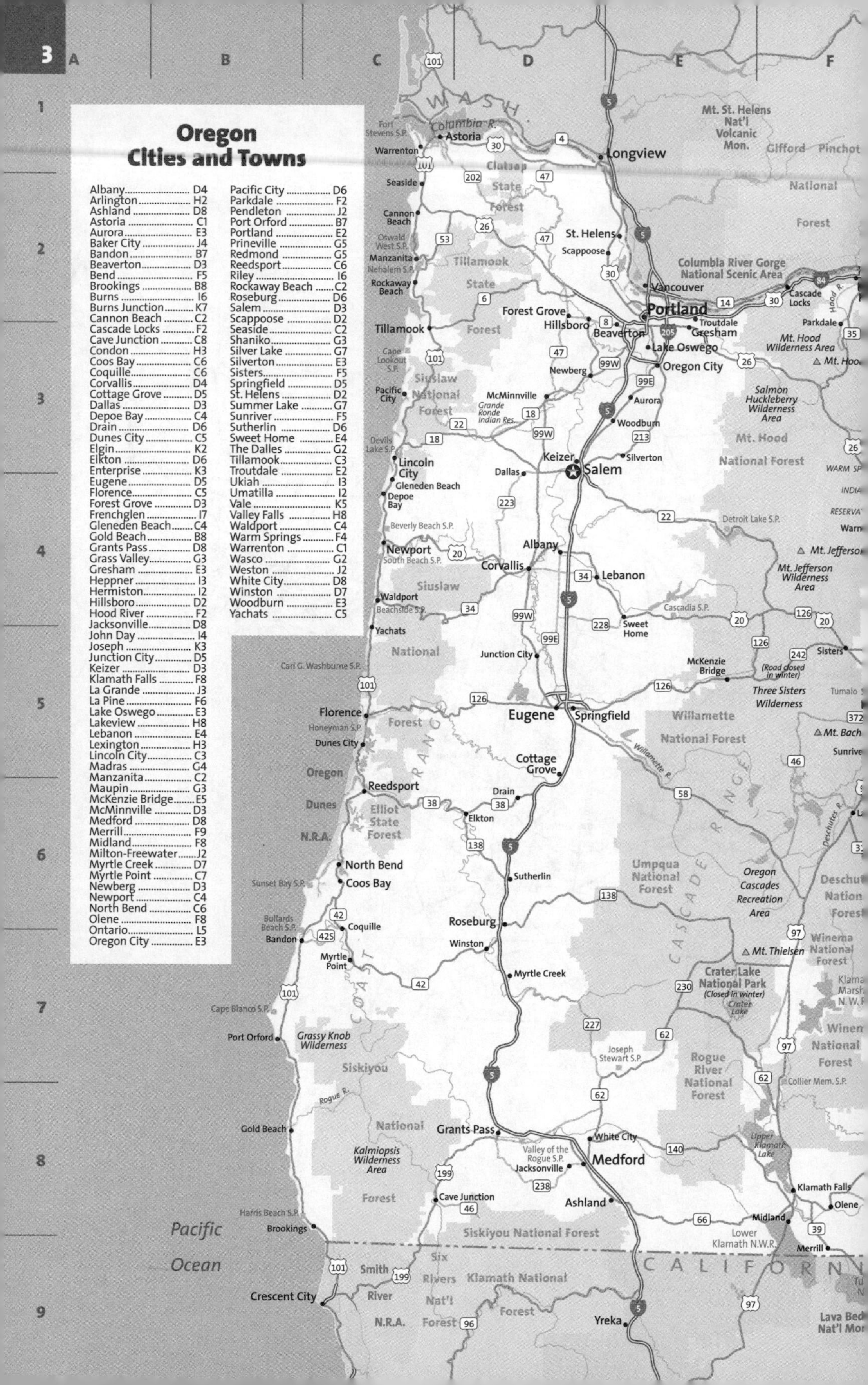
3
A
B
C
D
E
F
1
2
3
4
5
6
7
8
9
Oregon
Cities and Towns
Albany D4
Arlington H2
Ashland D8
Astoria C1
Aurora E3
Baker City J4
Bandon B7
Beaverton D3
Bend F5
Brookings B8
Burns I6
Burns Junction K7
Cannon Beach C2
Cascade Locks F2
Cave Junction C8
Condon H3
Coos Bay C6
Coquille C6
Corvallis D4
Cottage Grove D5
Dallas D3
Depoe Bay C4
Drain D6
Dunes City C5
Elgin K2
Elkton D6
Enterprise K3
Eugene D5
Florence C5
Forest Grove D3
Frenchglen I7
Gleneden Beach C4
Gold Beach B8
Grants Pass D8
Grass Valley G3
Gresham E3
Heppner I3
Hermiston I2
Hillsboro D2
Hood River F2
Jacksonville D8
John Day I4
Joseph K3
Junction City D5
Keizer D3
Klamath Falls F8
La Grande J3
La Pine F6
Lake Oswego E3
Lakeview H8
Lebanon E4
Lexington H3
Lincoln City C3
Madras G4
Manzanita C2
Maupin G3
McKenzie Bridge E5
McMinnville D3
Medford D8
Merrill F9
Midland F8
Milton-Freewater J2
Myrtle Creek D7
Myrtle Point C7
Newberg D3
Newport C4
North Bend C6
Olene F8
Ontario L5
Oregon City E3
Pacific City D6
Parkdale F2
Pendleton J2
Port Orford B7
Portland E2
Prineville G5
Redmond G5
Reedsport C6
Riley I6
Rockaway Beach C2
Roseburg D6
Salem D3
Scappoose D2
Seaside C2
Shaniko G3
Silver Lake G7
Silverton E3
Sisters F5
Springfield D5
St. Helens D2
Summer Lake G7
Sunriver F5
Sutherlin D6
Sweet Home E4
The Dalles G2
Tillamook C3
Troutdale E2
Ukiah I3
Umatilla I2
Vale K5
Valley Falls H8
Waldport C4
Warm Springs F4
Warrenton C1
Wasco G2
Weston J2
White City D8
Winston D7
Woodburn E3
Yachats C5
WASH
Columbia R.
Fort Stevens S.P.
Astoria
Warrenton
Longview
Clatsop State Forest
Seaside
Cannon Beach
Oswald West S.P.
Manzanita
Nehalem S.P.
Rockaway Beach
Tillamook State Forest
Tillamook
Cape Lookout S.P.
Pacific City
Siuslaw National Forest
St. Helens
Scappoose
Mt. St. Helens Nat'l Volcanic Mon.
Gifford Pinchot National Forest
Columbia River Gorge National Scenic Area
Vancouver
Portland
Cascade Locks
Troutdale
Gresham
Parkdale
Forest Grove
Hillsboro
Beaverton
Lake Oswego
Oregon City
Newberg
Mt. Hood Wilderness Area
Mt. Hood
McMinnville
Grande Ronde Indian Res.
Aurora
Woodburn
Salmon Huckleberry Wilderness Area
Mt. Hood National Forest
Devils Lake S.P.
Lincoln City
Gleneden Beach
Depoe Bay
Keizer
Salem
Silverton
Dallas
Warm Springs Indian Reservation
Detroit Lake S.P.
Beverly Beach S.P.
Newport
South Beach S.P.
Albany
Corvallis
Lebanon
Mt. Jefferson
Mt. Jefferson Wilderness Area
Siuslaw
Waldport
Beachside S.P.
Cascadia S.P.
Sweet Home
Yachats
National
Junction City
McKenzie Bridge
(Road closed in winter)
Sisters
Carl G. Washburne S.P.
Three Sisters Wilderness
Tumalo
Florence
Honeyman S.P.
Forest
Eugene
Springfield
Willamette National Forest
Mt. Bachelor
Sunriver
Dunes City
Oregon Dunes N.R.A.
Willamette R.
Cottage Grove
Reedsport
Drain
Elkton
Elliot State Forest
Cascade Range
Deschutes R.
North Bend
Coos Bay
Sunset Bay S.P.
Sutherlin
Umpqua National Forest
Oregon Cascades Recreation Area
Deschutes National Forest
Bullards Beach S.P.
Bandon
Coquille
Roseburg
Winston
Mt. Thielsen
Winema National Forest
Myrtle Point
Myrtle Creek
Crater Lake National Park
(Closed in winter)
Crater Lake
Coast Range
Cape Blanco S.P.
Port Orford
Grassy Knob Wilderness
Siskiyou
Joseph Stewart S.P.
Rogue River National Forest
Klamath Marsh N.W.R.
Collier Mem. S.P.
Rogue R.
Gold Beach
National
Grants Pass
White City
Kalmiopsis Wilderness Area
Valley of the Rogue S.P.
Jacksonville
Medford
Upper Klamath Lake
Klamath Falls
Olene
Forest
Cave Junction
Ashland
Midland
Harris Beach S.P.
Brookings
Siskiyou National Forest
Lower Klamath N.W.R.
Merrill
Pacific Ocean
CALIFORNIA
Smith River N.R.A.
Six Rivers Nat'l Forest
Klamath National Forest
Crescent City
Yreka
Lava Beds Nat'l Mon.

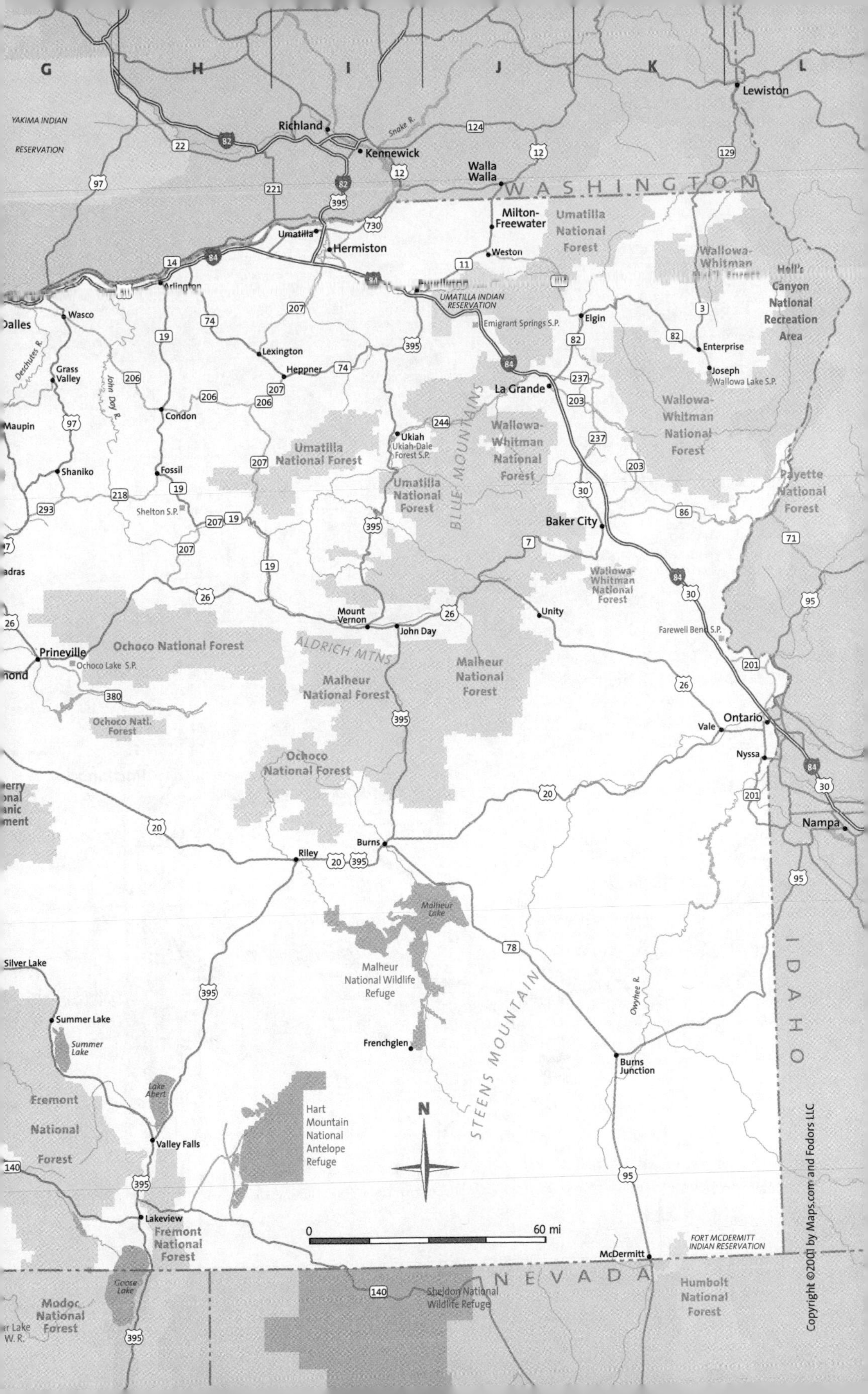

G
H
I
J
K
L
Lewiston
YAKIMA INDIAN RESERVATION
Richland
Kennewick
Snake R.
Walla Walla
WASHINGTON
Milton-Freewater
Umatilla National Forest
Umatilla
Hermiston
Weston
Wallowa-Whitman
Hell's Canyon National Recreation Area
Arlington
UMATILLA INDIAN RESERVATION
Emigrant Springs S.P.
Elgin
Dalles
Wasco
Deschutes R.
Lexington
Enterprise
Grass Valley
John Day R.
Heppner
Joseph
Wallowa Lake S.P.
La Grande
Maupin
Condon
Wallowa-Whitman National Forest
Ukiah
Ukiah-Dale Forest S.P.
Umatilla National Forest
BLUE MOUNTAINS
Shaniko
Fossil
Payette National Forest
Shelton S.P.
Baker City
Madras
Unity
Mount Vernon
John Day
Farewell Bend S.P.
Prineville
Ochoco National Forest
Ochoco Lake S.P.
ALDRICH MTNS
Malheur National Forest
Ochoco Natl. Forest
Ontario
Vale
Nyssa
Ochoco National Forest
Nampa
Burns
Riley
Malheur Lake
Silver Lake
Malheur National Wildlife Refuge
STEENS MOUNTAIN
IDAHO
Owyhee R.
Summer Lake
Frenchglen
Burns Junction
Lake Abert
Fremont National Forest
Hart Mountain National Antelope Refuge
N
Valley Falls
Lakeview
Fremont National Forest
0
60 mi
FORT MCDERMITT INDIAN RESERVATION
McDermitt
NEVADA
Goose Lake
Humbolt National Forest
Modoc National Forest
Sheldon National Wildlife Refuge
Copyright ©2001 by Maps.com and Fodors LLC

Portland, OR
WASHINGTON
OREGON
Vancouver
Ft. Vancouver N.H.S.
Hayden Island
Tomahawk Island
Bybee Lake
Smith Lake
Pier Park
West Delta Park
East Delta Park
Expo Center
Willamette R.
St. Johns Bridge
Univ. of Portland
Forest Park
Portland
Rose Garden
Lloyd Center
Pittock Mansion
Int'l Rose Test Gardens
Washington Park
Metro Washington Park Zoo
Portland Art Mus.
Portland State Univ.
Oregon Mus. of Science & Industry
Council Crest Park
Marquam Nature Park
West Slope
Raleigh Hills
Beaverton
Gabriel Park
Garden Home
Tigard
Oaks Bottom Wildlife Refuge
Willamette Park
Oaks Amusement Park
Lewis & Clark College
Tryon Creek S.P.
Milw
New Lower River Rd
Fruit Valley Rd
39th St
33rd St
Main St
Grand Blvd
Mill Plain Blvd
Evergreen
Sauvie Island Rd
Gillihan Loop Rd
Lombard St
Marine Dr
Newberry Rd
N. Burgard Rd
Columbia Blvd
North Portland Rd
Fessenden St
Smith St
Lombard St
Willamette Blvd
Willis Blvd
Germantown Rd
Springville Rd
Basin Ave
Denver Ave
Interstate Ave
Albina Ave
Vancouver Ave
Portland Blvd
Dekum St
Ainsworth St
Killingsworth
Alberta St
Prescott St
Going St
Front Ave
Yeon Ave
Skyline Blvd
Thompson Rd
Fremont St
Knott
29th Ave
Broadway
Cornell Rd
Leahy Rd
Miller Rd
Barnes Rd
SUNSET HWY
Burnside Rd
20th Ave
Hawthorne
Walker Rd
Jenkins Rd
Broadway Dr
Patton Rd
Dosch Rd
Canyon Rd
Powell Blvd
Beaverton Hillsdale Hwy
Sunset Blvd
Terwilliger Blvd
Holgat
Scholls Ferry Rd
Shattuck Rd
McLoughlin Blvd
Stee
Allen Blvd
Vermont St
30th Ave
45th Ave
Milwaukie Ave
13th Ave
Garden Home Rd
Taylors Ferry Rd
Macadam Ave
Hall Blvd
Sorrento Rd
Oleson Rd
80th Ave
125th Ave
17th Ave
32nd Ave
5
14
99E
30
BYP 30
405
84
26
8
10
217
210
99W
43

72nd Ave
112th Ave
49th St
137th Ave
162nd Ave
500
205
Plain
Blvd
39th
St
28th
Ave
St
Burton Rd
138th
18th
St
112th Ave
192nd Ave
Cascade Park
McArthur
Blvd
Liesser Rd
Mill Plain Blvd
1st
St
Lake Rd
N
Ellsworth Rd
14
164th Ave
LEWIS & CLARK HWY
Columbia R.
Evergreen Hwy
0
2 mi
Sand Island
WASHINGTON
OREGON
Lemon Island
Portland International Airport
Camas
14
6th Ave
Airport Way
Cornfoot Rd
Government Island
BYP 30
205
Cully Blvd
Ave
Marine Dr
Sandy Blvd
Blue Lake Park
185th Ave
72nd
Blvd
BYP 30
BUS 30
Sandy
30
84
213
San Rafael St
Halsey St
Halsey St
238th Dr
201st Ave
Ave
131st Ave
Glisan St
Glisan St
223rd Ave
Burnside St
Ave
Ave
Stark St
148th Ave
Mt. Tabor Park
76th Ave
Market St
Main St
Mill St
Ave
Burnside Rd
122nd
162nd
Ave
Ave
190th Ave
Birdsdale
Wallula
Division St
26
Powell
Blvd
Ave
174th
182nd
Roberts Ave
82nd Ave
205
Lents Park
Powell Butte Park
Hogan
Harold St
Rd
Woodstock Blvd
Jenne
Gresham
72nd Ave
Foster Rd
Towle Ave
Regner Rd
213
92nd Ave
Butler Rd
Flavel St
Flavel St
242nd Ave
Johnson
Clatsop St
172nd Ave
Creek Blvd
222nd Ave
Stanley Ave
132nd Ave

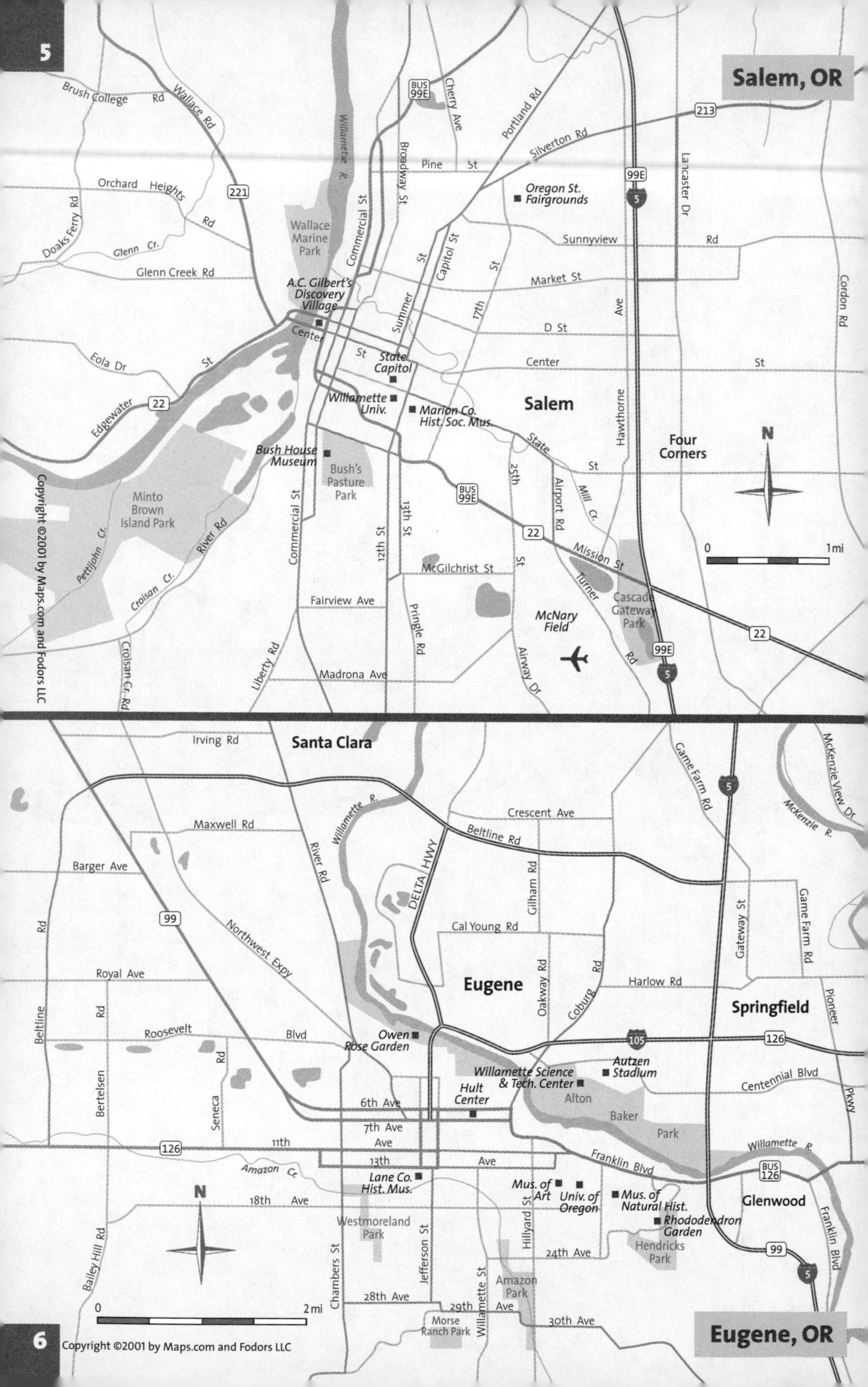
Salem, OR
Brush College Rd
Wallace Rd
Orchard Heights Rd
Doaks Ferry Rd
Glenn Cr.
Glenn Creek Rd
Willamette R.
Wallace Marine Park
Commercial St
Broadway St
Cherry Ave
Portland Rd
Silverton Rd
Pine St
Oregon St. Fairgrounds
Lancaster Dr
Sunnyview Rd
Capitol St
Summer St
17th St
Market St
A.C. Gilbert's Discovery Village
Center St
D St
Eola Dr
Edgewater St
State Capitol
Willamette Univ.
Marion Co. Hist. Soc. Mus.
Salem
Hawthorne Ave
Four Corners
State St
Bush House Museum
Bush's Pasture Park
Minto Brown Island Park
Pettijohn Cr.
River Rd
Croisan Cr.
Croisan Cr. Rd
12th St
13th St
25th St
Airport Rd
Mill Cr.
Mission St
McGilchrist St
Fairview Ave
Pringle Rd
Turner Rd
Cascade Gateway Park
McNary Field
Airway Dr
Liberty Rd
Madrona Ave
Cordon Rd
N
0
1mi
Copyright ©2001 by Maps.com and Fodors LLC
Eugene, OR
Irving Rd
Santa Clara
Willamette R.
Game Farm Rd
McKenzie View Dr
McKenzie R.
Crescent Ave
Beltline Rd
Maxwell Rd
River Rd
DELTA HWY
Gilham Rd
Barger Ave
Northwest Expy
Cal Young Rd
Gateway St
Oakway Rd
Coburg Rd
Harlow Rd
Eugene
Royal Ave
Springfield
Pioneer Pkwy
Beltline Rd
Roosevelt Blvd
Owen Rose Garden
Seneca Rd
Bertelsen Rd
Willamette Science & Tech. Center
Autzen Stadium
Alton Baker Park
Centennial Blvd
Hult Center
6th Ave
7th Ave
11th Ave
13th Ave
Franklin Blvd
Amazon Cr.
Lane Co. Hist. Mus.
Mus. of Art
Univ. of Oregon
Mus. of Natural Hist.
Glenwood
Rhododendron Garden
18th Ave
Westmoreland Park
Hillyard St
Hendricks Park
24th Ave
Bailey Hill Rd
Chambers St
Jefferson St
Willamette St
Amazon Park
28th Ave
29th Ave
30th Ave
Morse Ranch Park
N
0
2 mi

Seattle/Tacoma Area
Bainbridge Island........B2 Kirkland........................... E1
A
B
C
D
E
F
1
2
3
4
5
6
7
8
9
Fay Bainbridge State Park
Rollingbay
Bainbridge Island
Puget Sound
Illahee State Park
Bremerton
Manchester State Park
Manchester
Tilicum Village
Blake Island State Marine Park
Colby
Port Orchard
South Colby
Southworth
Vashon Heights
Bethel
Long L.
Banner Rd
Colvos Passage
Vashon Hwy
Vashon
Olalla
Ellisport
Vashon Island
Portage
Burton
Maury Island
Crescent Valley Dr
Dockton
Tahlequah
Gig Harbor
The Narrows
Pt. Defiance Zoo & Aquarium
Ruston
Wollochet
Tacoma
Fox Island
Bridgeport Way
Fircrest
Tacoma Dome
Pioneer Way
Dash Point State Park
Woodland Park Zoological Gardens
Discovery Park
15th Ave
Seattle
Seattle Center
Fauntleroy Ave
White Center
Burien
Normandy Park
Des Moines
Saltwater State Park
Federal Way
Univ. of Washington
Mus. of Hist. & Ind
Wash. Park Arboretum
Lake Washington
Boeing Field/ King Co. Int'l Airport
Museum of Flight
Seattle-Tacoma Int'l Airport
Juanita Dr
Kirkland
100th Ave
148th Ave
Bellevue
Mercer Island
Newcastle
Skyway
Renton
Tukwila
Petrovitsky Rd
140th Ave
Lake Youngs
132nd Ave
Kent
240th St
Auburn
Rhododendron Species Botanical Garden
West Valley Hwy
East Valley Hwy
Milton
Edgewood
Sumner
Lake Tapps
5
405
90
99
522
513
908
202
520
303
305
160
16
509
599
518
900
169
167
515
181
516
18
164
163
161
7
N
0
5 mi
Copyright ©2001 by Maps.com and Fodors LLC

8
A
B
C
D
E
F
1
2
3
4
5
6
7
8
9
Strait of Georgia
Point Roberts
Blaine
Abbotsford
99
1A
1
546
Ferndale
539
542
Mt. Baker-Snoqualmie Nat'l Forest
North
Rose Lake
Cowichan Lake
18
Bellingham
542
Mt. Baker
Cascades
Pacific Rim National Park
Sidney
Moran S.P.
Larrabee S.P.
Mt. Baker Nat'l Rec. Area
Baker Lake
1
Orcas I.
5
9
National
17
San Juan Islands
11
Lake Shannon
Skagit R.
San Juan I.
Anacortes
Sedro Woolley
20
Marblemount
14
Strait of Juan de Fuca
Lopez I.
20
Neah Bay
Victoria
Deception Pass S.P.
La Conner
Mount Vernon
MAKAH INDIAN RESERVATION
112
Whidbey I.
Flattery Rocks N.W.R.
Sekiu
Oak Harbor
9
530
Mt. Baker-
20
Coupeville
Olympic National Park
112
113
Lake Crescent
Port Angeles
Port Townsend
Arlington
101
Sequim
5
Ozette Lake
Olympic National Forest
20
525
TULALIP INDIAN RES.
92
Marysville
Snoqualmie
Fort Flagler S.P.
Langley
110
Forks
Sultan-Pilchuck S.P.
OLYMPIC MTS.
Olympic
Olympic
Everett
Wallace Falls S.P.
Quillayute Needles N.W.R.
104
Port Ludlow
Port Gamble
99
9
Snohomish
2
Index
National
National
National
405
Olympic Experimental State Forest
Edmonds
203
Forest
Poulsbo
Skykomish
SEE MAP 7
Silverdale
Park
Bellevue
202
4
3
Seattle
RANGE
101
90
Lake Quinault
Bremerton
Forest
Puget Sound
Issaquah
Snoqualmie
101
119
Renton
Tiger Mtn. S.F.
Quinalt
Tahuya S.F.
QUINAULT INDIAN RESERVATION
Olympic National Forest
North Bend
Pacific
SeaTac Int'l Airport
Kent
18
Snoqualmie Pass
90
106
3
Moclips
16
Auburn
Mt. Baker-
Ocean
Tacoma
169
Shelton
102
Snoqualmie
Puyallup
Enumclaw
101
Copalis Beach
410
Ocean City S.P.
108
5
National
410
Wenatchee Nat'l Forest
109
165
Olympia
(Closed in winter)
Hoquiam
8
Lacey
507
161
Montesano
Forest
Ocean Shores
12
Grays Harbor
Aberdeen
105
Chehalis R.
Capitol State Forest
510
Crystal Mountain
702
Westport
Millersylvania S.P.
Mt. Rainier National Park
12
507
Mt. Rainier
101
7
Ashford
(Closed in winter)
105
Centralia
706
123
Willapa Bay
Paradise Falls S.P.
Snoqualmie Nat'l Forest
Tahoma S.F.
South Bend
Willapa N.W.R.
Chehalis
12
508
Packwood
12
6
Ike Kinswa S.P.
12
Mayfield Lake
Riffe Lake
Cowlitz R.
Gifford Pinchot
103
5
505
101
CASCADE
Long Beach
Mt. St. Helens National Volcanic Mon.
Fort Canby S.P.
Ilwaco
401
4
504
504
National
Seaquest S.P.
Columbia R.
YAKAMA
Astoria
Cathlamet
Mt. St. Helens
(Closed in winter)
30
Longview
Kelso
Forest
101
Clatsop S.F.
26
Nehalem R.
202
Lake Merwin
Yale Lake
Swift Creek Res.
(Closed in winter)
Conboy Lake N.W.R.
N
47
503
26
141
142
503
Columbia River Gorge Nat'l Scenic Area
Tillamook State Forest
30
Yacolt-Burn S.F.
Beacon Rock S.P.
Stevenson
6
500
84
30
Vancouver
14
14
Camas
35
The Da
0
40 mi
Portland
101
Aberdeen B5
Anacortes D2
Arlington E3
Ashford E6
Auburn E5
Bainbridge Island See Map 7
Bellevue E4
Bellingham D2
Blaine D1
Bremerton D4
Camas D8
Cashmere G4
Cathlamet C7
Centralia C6
Chehalis C6
Chelan H3
Cheney K4
Clarkston L7
Cle Elum F5
Colfax K5
Colville K2
Copalis Beach A5
Coulee Dam I3
Coupeville D3
Crystal Mountain F5
Davenport J4
Dayton K7
Edmonds D4
Ellensburg G5
Enumclaw E5
Ephrata H5
Everett E3
Ferndale D1
Forks A3
Goldendale F8
Copyright ©2001 by Maps.com and Fodors LLC

G
H
I
J
K
L
CANADA
U.S.A.
Osoyoos
Trail
Okanogan
Loomis State Forest
Osoyoos Lake
Okanogan Nat'l Forest
Colville Nat'l Forest
Curlew Lake S.P.
Colville
National
Forest
Republic
Kettle River Range
Columbia R.
Colville Nat'l Forest
Pend Oreille R.
Kaniksu
Nat'l
Forest
Priest Lake
Colville
Little Pend Oreille N.W.R.
Colville Nat'l Forest
Kaniksu National Forest
Selkirk Mts.
National
Okanogan R.
Loup Loup S.P.
Omak
Okanogan
COLVILLE INDIAN RESERVATION
Franklin D. Roosevelt Lake
Ferry
Forest
Twisp
Newport
Lake Chelan
Columbia R.
Bridgeport S.P.
Coulee Dam
Ferry
Spokane R.
SPOKANE INDIAN RESERVATION
Mt. Spokane S.P.
Chelan
Banks Lake
Steamboat Rock S.P.
Lake Roosevelt N.R.A.
Davenport
Spokane
Couer d'Alene
Leavenworth
Wenatchee R.
Cashmere
Wenatchee
Sun Lakes S.P.
Cheney
Coeur d'Alene Lake
Soap Lake
Turnbull N.W.R.
COEUR D'ALENE INDIAN RESERVATION
Columbia R.
Ephrata
Quincy
Moses Lake
Ritzville
IDAHO
Ellensburg
Potholes Res.
Potholes S.P.
Columbia N.W.R.
Colfax
Wanapum S.P.
SADDLE MTS.
Othello
Moscow
Saddle Mtn. N.W.R.
Pullman
U.S. Military Res. Yakima Training Center
Palouse Falls S.P.
Yakima
U.S. Dept. of Energy Hanford Site
Chief Timothy S.P.
Lewiston
Clarkston
Snake R.
Toppenish
Sunnyside
Lake Sacajawea
Dayton
Richland
Pasco
Yakima R.
Kennewick
Umatilla National Forest
Fields Spring S.P.
Lake Wallula
Walla Walla
OREGON
Hells Canyon National Rec. Area
Crow Butte S.P.
Washington – Cities and Towns
oquiam B5
waco B7
dex E4
saquah E4
elso C7
ennewick I7
ent D4
rkland See Map 7
Conner D2
Lacey D5
Langley D3
Leavenworth G4
Long Beach A7
Longview C7
Marblemount F2
Marysville E3
Moclips B5
Montesano B5
Moses Lake I5
Mount Vernon D2
Neah Bay A2
Newport L3
North Bend E4
Oak Harbor D2
Ocean Shores A5
Okanogan H2
Olympia C5
Omak H2
Othello I6
Packwood E6
Pasco I7
Point Roberts C1
Port Angeles B3
Port Gamble D3
Port Ludlow D3
Port Townsend C3
Poulsbo D4
Pullman L6
Puyallup D5
Quinault B4
Quincy H5
Renton D4
Republic I2
Richland I7
Ritzville J5
Seattle D4
Sedro Woolley D2
Sekiu A2
Sequim C3
Shelton C5
Silverdale D4
Skykomish F4
Snohomish E3
Snoqualmie E4
Snoqualmie Pass F4
Soap Lake H4
South Bend B6
Spokane K4
Stevenson E8
Sunnyside H7
Tacoma D5
Toppenish G7
Twisp H2
Vancouver D8
Walla Walla J7
Wenatchee G4
Westport A5
Winthrop G2
Yakima G6

9
Warren Ave N.
2nd Ave N.
3rd Ave N.
4th Ave N.
5th Ave N.
Taylor Ave N.
6th Ave N.
Dexter Ave N.
8th Ave N.
Valley St
Roy St
Seattle Center Opera House
Mercer St
Broad St
Valley St
Fairview Ave
Aloha St
Valley St
Roy St
Belmont Ave E.
Boylston Ave E.
Harvard Ave E.
Broadway E.
10th Ave E.
Aloha St
E. Roy St
E. Mercer St
Tashkent Park
Key Arna
Seattle Center
Children's Museum
Pacific Science Center
Space Needle
W. Republican St
W. Harrison St
W. Thomas St
W. John St
Aurora Ave N.
Dexter Ave N.
6th Ave N.
8th Ave N.
9th Ave N.
Terry Ave N.
Boren Ave N.
Fairview Ave N.
Minor Ave N.
Pontius Ave N.
Yale Ave
Eastlake Ave
Melrose Ave E.
Bellevue Ave E.
Summit Ave E.
Belmont Ave E.
Boylston Ave E.
E. Republican St
E. Harrison St
E. Thomas St
John St
E. John St
10th Ave E.
Federal Ave E.
11th Ave E
Denny Park
Denny Way
Denny Way
E. Olive Way
E. Denny Way
Eagle St
Broad St
2nd Ave
Clay St
Cedar
Western Ave
Vine St
3rd Ave
4th Ave
Wall St
Elliott Ave
Battery St
Bell St
Blanchard St
7th Ave
6th Ave
5th Ave
Lenora St
Virginia St
Stewart St
Westlake Ave
8th Ave
9th Ave
Terry Ave
Boren Ave
Minor Ave
Howell St
E. Howell St
E. Olive St
E. Pine St
E. Pike St
E. Union St
Bellevue Ave
Boylston Ave
Harvard Ave
Broadway
Nagle Pl
11th Ave
10th Ave
99
Regrade Park
1st Ave
Pike Pl
Olive Way
Pine St
WA State Convention & Trade Center
Victor Steinbrueck Park
Pike St
Union St
University St
Seneca St
Spring St
Madison St
Marion St
Columbia St
Pike Market
Seattle Aquarium
Waterfront Park
Seattle Art Mus.
99
ALASKAN FWY
Western Ave
1st Ave
2nd Ave
3rd Ave
4th Ave
5th Ave
6th Ave
7th Ave
8th Ave
Minor Ave
Summit Ave
Boylston Ave E.
Seneca St
Spring St
Madison St
Marion St
Cherry St
James St
Jefferson St
Boren Ave
Terry Ave
9th Ave
Frye Art Mus.
Seattle University
Broadway
Cherry St
James Way
12th Ave
E. Jefferson St
Terrace St
Alder St
E. Spruce St
E. Fir St
S. Spruce St
9th Ave
Yesler Way
First Hill Park
Elliott Bay
Washington State Ferry Terminal
Pioneer Square Park
James St
Pioneer Square
Klondike Gold Rush Historic Park
S. Washington St
S. Main St
S. Jackson St
S. King St
Kobe Terrace
Hing Hay Park
S. Main St
S. Jackson St
S. King St
S. Weller St
S. Lane St
S. Dearborn St
S. Charles St
S. Plummer St
S. Weller St
Pier 48 Ferry Terminal
5th Ave S.
6th Ave S.
Maynard Ave S.
12th Ave S.
N
Alaskan Way S.
Kingdome
5
90
Golf Dr
0
0.5 mi
Ave S.
Ave S.
519
Dr. Rizal Park
S. Judkins St
Marginal Way S.
1st Ave S.
Occidental
3rd Ave S.
4th Ave S.
6th
S. Atlantic St
Airport Way S.
Ave S.
Ave S.
S. Atlantic St
12th
13th
Seattle, WA

Seattle Area
A
B
C
D
E
F
1
2
3
4
5
6
7
8
9
Northgate
Ballard
Magnolia Bluff
Seattle
Queen Anne Hill
Capitol Hill
University
Madrona Park
Harbor Island
West Seattle
Columbia
Tukwila
Puget Sound
Shilshole Bay
Salmon Bay
Elliott Bay
Green Lake
Lake Union
Union Bay
Lake Washington
Pontiac Bay
Wolf Bay
Andrews Bay
Golden Gardens Park
Discovery Park
Ft. Lawton Military Reservation
Magnolia Park
Mathews Beach Park
Warren G. Magnuson Park
Green Lake Park
Ravenna Park
Woodland Park Zoo
Woodland Park
University Village
Univ. of Washington
Husky Stadium
Webster Point
Gas Works Park
Washington Park Arboretum
Volunteer Park
Seattle Pacific Univ.
Seattle Center
Space Needle
Elliott Bay Park
Seattle Aquarium
Seattle Univ.
Madrona Park
Kingdome
Duwamish Head
Seattle's Birthplace Monument
Alki Point
Schmitz Park
Mt. Baker Park
Genesee Playground
Bailey Peninsula
Seward Park
Lincoln Park
Ferry Terminal
Westerest Park
King County Int'l Airport
Governor Albert D. Rosellini Bridge (Evergreen Point Floating Bridge)
Hadley & Murrow Mem. Bridge
95th St
85th St
80th St
75th St
70th St
65th St
55th St
50th St
45th St
Market St
Emerson St
Dravus St
McGraw St
Galer St
Mercer St
Denny Way
John St
Union St
Cherry St
Yesler Way
Dearborn St
Holgate St
Spokane St
Charlestown St
Alaska St
Genesee St
Orcas St
Graham St
Michigan St
Morgan St
Holden St
Myrtle Pl
Othello St
Cloverdale St
Henderson St
Barton St
Seaview Ave
32nd Ave
24th Ave
15th Ave
8th Ave
Phinney Ave
Greenwood Ave
Aurora Ave
Roosevelt Way
15th Way
Ravenna Ave
35th Ave
55th Ave
Banner Way
Lake City Way
Green Lake Dr
Green Lake Way
Ravenna Blvd
12th Ave
25th Ave
Sand Point Way
Leary Ave
Leary Way
Government Way
Gilman Ave
Nickerson St
Waterway
Stone Way
Pacific St
34th St
Montlake Blvd
Magnolia Blvd
34th Ave
Thorndyke Ave
28th Ave
3rd Ave
10th Ave
Olympic Pl
Queen Anne Ave
Westlake Ave
Eastlake Ave
Fairview Ave
Elliott Ave
Boyer Ave
23rd Ave
Lake Washington Blvd
Broad St
4th Ave
2nd Ave
Olive Way
Broadway
Madison St
Boren Ave
14th Ave
Alaskan Fwy
Rainier Ave
Martin Luther King Jr. Way
Lakeside Ave
Mercer Way
Alki Ave
California Ave
Harbor Ave
Admiral Way
1st Ave
Airport Way
Beacon Ave
15th Ave
23rd Ave
West Seattle Fwy
Beach Dr
Columbian Way
E. Marginal Way
W. Marginal Way SW
4th Ave
48th Ave
Fauntleroy Ave
Delridge Way
16th Ave
Sylvan Way
Dumar Way
Corson Ave
Swift Ave
Seward Park Ave
Wilson Ave
50th Ave
Lake Washington Blvd
9th Ave
Duwamish R.
5
99
90
509
520
522
513
N
0
2 mi

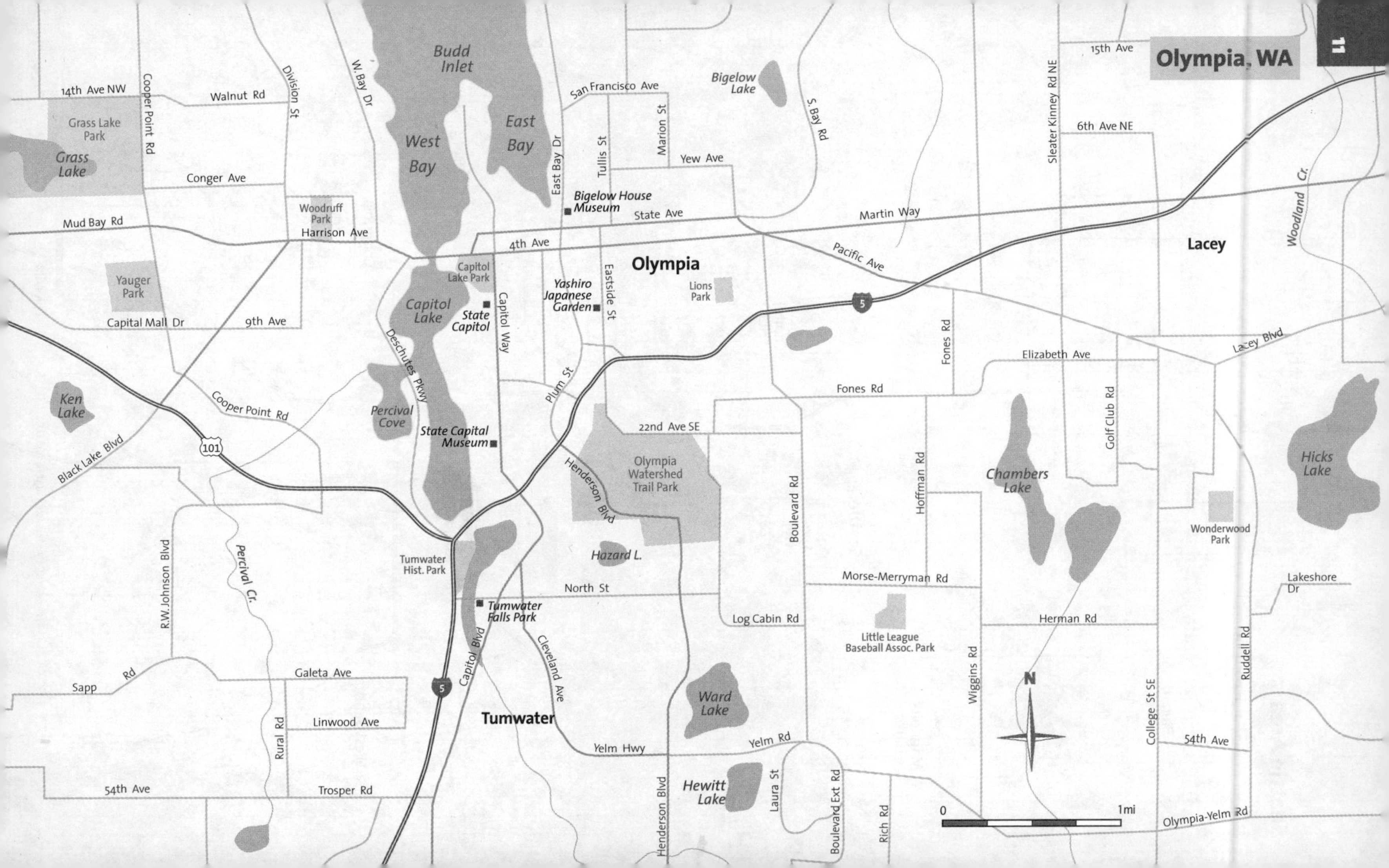

Olympia, WA
Olympia
Lacey
Tumwater
Budd Inlet
West Bay
East Bay
Capitol Lake
Capitol Lake Park
State Capitol
State Capital Museum
Percival Cove
Deschutes Pkwy
Bigelow House Museum
Yashiro Japanese Garden
Lions Park
Bigelow Lake
Grass Lake Park
Grass Lake
Woodruff Park
Yauger Park
Ken Lake
Olympia Watershed Trail Park
Hazard L.
Tumwater Hist. Park
Tumwater Falls Park
Ward Lake
Hewitt Lake
Chambers Lake
Hicks Lake
Wonderwood Park
Little League Baseball Assoc. Park
14th Ave NW
Walnut Rd
Division St
W. Bay Dr
San Francisco Ave
Marion St
Tullis St
East Bay Dr
Yew Ave
S. Bay Rd
15th Ave
6th Ave NE
Sleater Kinney Rd NE
Woodland Cr.
Cooper Point Rd
Conger Ave
Mud Bay Rd
Harrison Ave
State Ave
Martin Way
4th Ave
Pacific Ave
Eastside St
Capitol Way
Capital Mall Dr
9th Ave
Cooper Point Rd
Black Lake Blvd
101
5
Plum St
22nd Ave SE
Henderson Blvd
Fones Rd
Elizabeth Ave
Lacey Blvd
Golf Club Rd
Hoffman Rd
Boulevard Rd
Morse-Merryman Rd
Log Cabin Rd
North St
Herman Rd
Wiggins Rd
College St SE
Ruddell Rd
Lakeshore Dr
54th Ave
Olympia-Yelm Rd
R.W. Johnson Blvd
Percival Cr.
Sapp Rd
Galeta Ave
Linwood Ave
Rural Rd
54th Ave
Trosper Rd
Capitol Blvd
Cleveland Ave
Yelm Hwy
Yelm Rd
Henderson Blvd
Laura St
Boulevard Ext Rd
Rich Rd
N
0
1mi